EUROPEAN HUMAN RIGHTS LAW

TEXT AND MATERIALS

Third Edition

MARK W. JANIS

William F. Starr Professor of Law
University of Connecticut

Visiting Fellow in Law, formerly Reader in Law
University of Oxford

RICHARD S. KAY

Wallace Stevens Professor of Law
University of Connecticut

ANTHONY W. BRADLEY

Of the Inner Temple, Barrister
Emeritus Professor of Constitutional Law
University of Edinburgh

Research Fellow, Institute of European and Comparative Law
University of Oxford

WITH SPECIALIST CONTRIBUTIONS FROM

AILEEN McCOLGAN

Professor of Human Rights Law, King's College London

JIM MURDOCH

Professor of Public Law, University of Glasgow

OXFORD

UNIVERSITY PRESS

OXFORD

UNIVERSITY PRESS

Great Clarendon Street, Oxford OX2 6DP

Oxford University Press is a department of the University of Oxford.
It furthers the University's objective of excellence in research, scholarship,
and education by publishing worldwide in

Oxford New York

Auckland Cape Town Dar es Salaam Hong Kong Karachi
Kuala Lumpur Madrid Melbourne Mexico City Nairobi
New Delhi Shanghai Taipei Toronto

With offices in

Argentina Austria Brazil Chile Czech Republic France Greece
Guatemala Hungary Italy Japan Poland Portugal Singapore
South Korea Switzerland Thailand Turkey Ukraine Vietnam

Oxford is a registered trade mark of Oxford University Press
in the UK and in certain other countries

Published in the United States
by Oxford University Press Inc., New York

First published 1995
Second edition 2000
This edition 2008

British Library Cataloguing in Publication Data

Data available

Library of Congress Cataloging in Publication Data

Data available

Typeset by Newgen Imaging Systems (P) Ltd, Chennai, India
Printed in Great Britain
on acid-free paper by
Ashford Colour Press Ltd, Gosport, Hampshire

ISBN 978–0–19–927746–9

1 3 5 7 9 10 8 6 4 2

To Janet and our sons,
Matthew, Robert, Philip and Edward
M.W.J.

In memory of my parents,
Geraldine and Sidney Kay
R.S.K.

To my grandsons,
Jack, Adam, Larry and Joseph
A.W.B.

PREFACE

This book introduces European Human Rights Law. It explores the legal process and the substantive law developed over the last 50 years pursuant to the Council of Europe's Convention for the Protection of Human Rights and Fundamental Freedoms. When we embarked on these studies more than 20 years ago little serious attention had been given to what was already an extraordinary achievement. These days there is a professional and academic literature of great depth and variety. We hope that this book continues to provide a distinctive contribution.

Nowadays, the European Court of Human Rights in Strasbourg regularly finds nations in breach of their obligations under the international human rights law of the European Human Rights Convention. Remarkably, sovereign states have generally respected the adverse judgments of the Court. As of September 2007, there were 47 member states to the Convention. These states have, in response to the judgments of the Strasbourg Court, reformed police procedures, penal institutions, child welfare practices, administrative agencies, judicial processes, labour relations, morals legislation and many other important public matters. Moreover, these states have compensated individuals for their injuries. The willingness with which the decisions of the European Court of Human Rights have been accepted demonstrates the emergence of a crucial new fact in the Western legal tradition: an effective system of international law regulating some of the most sensitive areas of what had previously been thought to be within the exclusive domain of national sovereignty.

Obviously, European Human Rights Law is of critical importance within member states of the Council of Europe. Furthermore, there are at least three ways in which a study of European Human Rights Law ought to be helpful to judges, lawyers and law students outside Europe. First, the emergence of this law is an event of significance in its own right. No one should pretend to even a superficial knowledge of world legal systems without being acquainted with European Human Rights Law. Second, European Human Rights Law sheds light on the legal protection of the rights of individuals in general. It is a particular failing of North Americans, for example, too often to be reluctant to take notice of parallel experiences elsewhere. The Strasbourg Court and the European Human Rights Convention protect many of the same rights that have been interpreted and applied by the United States Supreme Court under the United States Constitution and, more recently, by the Supreme Court of Canada under the Canadian Charter of Rights and Freedoms. The way in which human rights law has been interpreted by the Strasbourg Court, insofar as it differs from courts in the United States and Canada or as it mirrors them, illuminates both the nature of these rights and the general process of constitutional adjudication. Finally, the development of European Human Rights Law engages some of the most basic issues of jurisprudence. In a remarkably short time we have witnessed the creation of a developed system of law. Analysis of this experience is bound to tell us something about what makes law and what law is. Incorporation of European Human Rights Law into the law of the United Kingdom with effect from October 2000 enabled that jurisprudence to engage directly with the historic traditions of the common law.

The materials that follow can be put to a number of different pedagogic uses. There is sufficient scope and depth here to support an independent course in a law school or in other undergraduate or graduate study. We have used the book in this way. Paired with materials on European Community Law, the book can help constitute a course in European Law. Similarly, the book can be used with other materials in a course on International or Comparative Human Rights Law. The book also may provide supplementary materials for courses in Public International Law, Comparative Law or Constitutional Law. Moreover, by bringing together the key extracts of the principal judgments of the Strasbourg Court, the book should prove a valuable professional resource to lawyers, judges, government officials and human rights advocates.

This third edition substantially enlarges the coverage of the book. Six new chapters have been added: new chapters on the rights associated with life, religion, discrimination, property and education, and a new chapter on the prospects for the system. Moreover, new sections on slavery and the equality of arms in legal proceedings have been added to existing chapters. We are delighted to have been able to collaborate in this edition with Aileen McColgan and Jim Murdoch, who have respectively prepared the new chapters on discrimination and property rights.

The first three chapters (principally prepared by Janis) focus on institutions and procedures. In describing and analysing the structure and process of European Human Rights Law, we have attempted to put them in the context of the development of international law and international dispute settlement generally. The next ten chapters (Chapters 4, 5, 6 and 8, principally prepared by Kay, Chapter 7 principally prepared by Janis, Chapter 9 principally prepared by McColgan, Chapter 10 principally prepared by Murdoch, Chapters 11 and 12 principally prepared by Bradley, and Chapter 13 jointly prepared by Janis, Kay and Bradley) cover selected substantive areas of adjudication. The technique here is both descriptive and comparative. In particular, we attempt to present parallel law on issues as they have arisen in the United States, Canada and the United Kingdom. Chapter 14 (principally prepared by Bradley) looks at the ways in which European Human Rights Law is applied in domestic law, particularly in the United Kingdom. Chapter 15 (principally prepared by Janis) previews prospects for Strasbourg law in the future. The three editors share responsibility for the complete book.

This book is not intended to provide a comprehensive treatment of European Human Rights Law. The range of topics and the specific illustrations are meant to furnish a solid foundation for understanding the major problems and features of the system. Certain important subjects have, as a concession to time and space, been omitted. Furthermore, we might point out that generally, except in Chapter 2, we have relied upon the judgments of the European Court of Human Rights rather than upon the extensive reports of the former European Commission of Human Rights.

A book of this kind always poses difficult choices both about the items presented and about their editing. While many of the selections have been rather drastically reduced in size, our preference has been to leave enough of the original language intact so that readers will be able to get a sense of the whole dispute and the character of the Court's approach. In our textual discussions, we draw on more limited quotations from court judgments to illustrate certain points. Readers should note that we have generally (although not invariably) omitted citations to other judgments and internal references to other parts of the same judgment. For practical reasons materials appearing after May 2007 have generally not been included.

An initial edition of this book (written by Janis and Kay) was published in 1990 by the University of Connecticut Law School Foundation Press. It was, at that time, something of a risky project. The decision by the Foundation to take that risk made the appearance of the subsequent OUP editions possible.

Though this volume's faults are ours alone, its virtues are largely due to the help and insights of many friends and colleagues. Our thanks are especially due to the judges, commissioners, and staff of the European Human Rights Law system, and especially to: Andràs Baka, Rudolf Bernhardt, Nicolas Bratza, Maud Buquicchio, Andrew Drzemczewski, Jochen Frowein, John Hedigan, Karel Jungwiert, Hans Christian Krüger, Gunnar Lagergren, Egils Levits, Ronald St. John Macdonald, Michael O'Boyle, Rolv Ryssdal, Henry Schermers, Viera Strážnická, Wilhelmina Thomasson, Riza Türmen, Brian Walsh, Gérard Wiarda, Luzius Wildhaber, Nina Vajić. Warm thanks are owed, too, to our academic and professional colleagues: John Bridge, Ian Brownlie, Thomas Buergenthal, Laura Dickinson, Sally Evans, Christine Gray, Jane Hanna, Hugh Macgill, Jeremy Paul, Dan Sarooshi, George Schatzki, David Seymour, Louis Sohn, Dennis Stone and Carol Weisbrod. We have benefited from the careful research assistance of Daniel Bender, Celia Byler, Shannon Bratt, Alice Carey, Sarah Cox, Jerrie Chiu, Jennifer Collins, Sanja Djajic, John Flynn, Jennifer Glaudemans, Betsy Golden, Sarah Hakimzadeh, Michael Hammond, Charles Hickey, Eric Hisey, Philip Janis, Brent Houston, Sarah Karwan, Rachel Kay, Hilary Kreitner, Peter Morgan, Gregory O'Neil, Marianne Reiner-Caputo, Scott Schaeffer, Kimberly Troland, Marc Ubaldi, Rebecca Ullman, Solange Wallace, Richard Wilde and Shelby Wilson. In particular, Alice Carey, Sarah Cox, Hilary Kreitner and Gregory O'Neil undertook most of the research and drafting of the note on prompt adjudication in Chapter 12. We are grateful, too, to Julia Dunlop, Mary Kate Cox and Bobette Reed Kahn of the University of Connecticut Law School Foundation, to Matthew Baldwin, Kristin Clayton, Matthew Cotton, Michaela Coulthard, Philippa Groom, Hussain Hadi, Richard Hart, Jasmine Naim, Helen Swann, John Whelan and Kate Whetter of Oxford University Press, and to our secretaries: Judy Bigelow, Janet Jendrzejewski, Margaret Kent, Sandy Michalik, Delia Roy and Joan Wood.

Mark W. Janis
Richard S. Kay
Anthony W. Bradley

Oxford & Hartford
October 2007

A NOTE ON CITATION

Changing formats adopted by different publishers of decisions of the European Court of Human Rights present a challenge to any attempt to employ a consistent, identifiable and accessible system of citation.

In this volume, we have provided the date of judgment and, where available, the citation to *European Human Rights Reports* published by Sweet and Maxwell. We have decided to forego any attempt at an 'official citation' in light of the various techniques with which the Court has experimented. We are not confident that it has yet settled on a permanent method.

Most importantly, only the case name and date of judgment are necessary to access the official full texts, usually in both English and French, through the Court's comprehensive and current website www.echr.coe.int.

With regard to citations to the *European Human Rights Reports*, it is important to note that we have followed the publishers in changing the citation format starting with cases in Volume 31. From that point on, the citation includes a reference not to the page number but to a case number assigned by the publishers. So 2 E.H.R.R. 20 refers to the judgment at page 20 of Volume 2 while 32 E.H.R.R. 20 refers to the twentieth judgment in Volume 32.

TABLE OF CONTENTS

PART III THE IMPACT OF THE STRASBOURG SYSTEM

14 THE EFFECT IN NATIONAL LAW OF THE EUROPEAN CONVENTION ON HUMAN RIGHTS

ACKNOWLEDGEMENTS

Extracts from the Decisions of the European Court of Human Rights are published on the official site www.echr.coe.int/ECHR and the official reports are published by Carl Heymanns Verlag KG, Luxemburger Str. 449, D-50939 Cologne, Germany.

We are grateful to all authors and publishers of copyright material used in this book and in particular to the following for permission to reprint from the sources indicated:

S. Greer: extracts from 'Improving Compliance' in *The European Convention on Human Rights: Achievements, Problems and Prospects* (Cambridge University Press, 2006), copyright © Steven Greer 2006, reprinted by permission of Cambridge University Press and the author.

H. C. Krüger: extract f.om 'Reflections Concerning Accession of the European Communities to the European Convention on Human Rights', 21 *Penn State International Law Review* 89 (2002), reprinted by permission of the Penn State International Law Review.

P. L. McKaskle: extracts from 'The European Court of Human Rights: What It Is, How It Works, and Its Future', 40 *University of San Francisco Law Review* 1 (2005), reprinted by permission of the University of San Francisco Law Review.

C. Ovey and R. C. A. White: extracts from *Jacobs and White: The European Convention on Human Rights* (4th edn., Oxford University Press, 2006), reprinted by permission of Oxford University Press.

L. Wildhaber: *The European Court of Human Rights 1998–2006: History, Achievements, Reform* (N. P. Engel, 2006), reprinted by permission of the publisher.

Every effort has been made to trace and contact copyright holders but this has not been possible in every case. If notified, the publisher will undertake to rectify any errors or omissions at the earliest opportunity.

TABLE OF CASES BEFORE
THE EUROPEAN COMMISSION
OF HUMAN RIGHTS

TABLE OF CASES BEFORE THE
EUROPEAN COURT OF HUMAN RIGHTS

(Page references in **bold** denote that substantial extracts from the case are reproduced in the text)

TABLE OF CASES FROM THE UNITED STATES

TABLE OF CASES FROM CANADA

TABLE OF CASES FROM THE UNITED KINGDOM

(Page references in **bold** denote that substantial extracts from the case are reproduced in the text)

TABLE OF OTHER CASES

TABLE OF STATUTES

TABLE OF INTERNATIONAL INSTRUMENTS

Page references in **bold** indicate that the text is reproduced in full.

PART I

THE CONVENTION AND THE COURT

1

THE EUROPEAN CONVENTION ON HUMAN RIGHTS

The European Convention for the Protection of Human Rights and Fundamental Freedoms[1] establishes not only the world's most successful system of international law for the protection of human rights, but one of the most advanced forms of any kind of international legal process. The European Human Rights Convention was drafted in the Council of Europe during 1949 and 1950 in the aftermath of World War II. The Convention was signed on 4 November 1950, and came into force on 3 September 1953, after its ratification by eight countries: Denmark, the Federal Republic of Germany, Iceland, Ireland, Luxembourg, Norway, Sweden and the United Kingdom. The number of members of the Convention has grown. As of September 2007, 47 states were bound by its terms: Albania, Andorra, Armenia, Austria, Azerbaijan, Belgium, Bosnia and Herzegovinia, Bulgaria, Croatia, Cyprus, Czech Republic, Denmark, Estonia, Finland, France, Georgia, Germany, Greece, Hungary, Iceland, Ireland, Italy, Latvia, Liechtenstein, Lithuania, Luxembourg, Malta, Moldova, Monaco, Montenegro, Netherlands, Norway, Poland, Portugal, Romania, Russia, San Marino, Serbia, Slovak Republic, Slovenia, Spain, Sweden, Switzerland, the former Yugoslav Republic of Macedonia, Turkey, Ukraine and the United Kingdom.[2]

This chapter introduces the European Human Rights Convention. It has three sections. First, there is a survey of some of the key documents elaborating the principle that governments ought to be limited by the rule of law: the Magna Carta (1215), John Locke's *Two Treatises of Government* (1689), the American Declaration of Independence (1776), the French Declaration of the Rights of Man and Citizen (1789), the U.S. Bill of Rights (1789), the Charter and Judgment of the Nuremberg Tribunal (1945–46) and the U.N. Universal Declaration of Human Rights (1948). These set the stage for the second section that reviews the negotiation of the European Human Rights Convention (1948–50). Finally, the third section explores the progress of the Convention over time (1950–2006).

---

[1] 213 U.N.T.S. 221, C.E.T.S. 5, U.K.T.S. 71 (1953), signed at Rome 4 Nov. 1950; entered into force 3 Sept. 1953, Council of Europe, www.conventions.coe.int (accessed 21 Sept. 2007) (hereinafter cited as 'Convention'). The Convention is set forth in Appendix A.

[2] Council of Europe, *Chart of Signatures and of Ratifications of the Convention for the Protection of Human Rights and Fundamental Freedoms*, www.echr.coe.int (accessed 21 Sept. 2007) (hereinafter cited as 'Signatures and Ratifications').

A. HUMAN RIGHTS LAW

The principle that the rule of law ought to protect the human rights of individuals against the abuses of government can be dated back at least as far as the Magna Carta, when, at Runnymede on 15 June 1215, British barons forced a reluctant King John to acknowledge a great many liberties, including some important rights respecting the rule of law and the courts:

John, by the grace of God King of England, Lord of Ireland, Duke of Normandy and Aquitaine, and Count of Anjou, to his archbishops, bishops, abbots, earls, barons, justices, foresters, sheriffs, stewards, servants, and to all his officials and loyal subjects, Greeting.

. . .

To all free men of our kingdom we have also granted, for us and our heirs for ever, all the liberties written out below, to have and to keep for them and their heirs, of us and our heirs:

. . .

(17) Ordinary lawsuits shall not follow the royal court around, but shall be held in a fixed place.

(18) Inquests of *novel disseisin, mort d'ancestor,* and *darrein presentment* shall be taken only in their proper county court. We ourselves, or in our absence abroad our chief justice, will send two justices to each county four times a year, and these justices, with four knights of the county elected by the county itself, shall hold the assizes in the county court, on the day and in the place where the court meets.

. . .

(20) For a trivial offence, a free man shall be fined only in proportion to the degree of his offence, and for a serious offence, correspondingly, but not so heavily as to deprive him of his livelihood. In the same way, a merchant shall be spared his merchandise, and a husbandman the implements of his husbandry, if they fall upon the mercy of a royal court. None of these fines shall be imposed except by the assessment on oath of reputable men of the neighborhood.

. . .

(38) In future no official shall place a man on trial upon his own unsupported statement, without producing credible witnesses to the truth of it.

(39) No free man shall be seized or imprisoned, or stripped of his rights or possessions, or outlawed or exiled, or deprived of his standing in any other way, nor will we proceed with force against him, or send others to do so, except by the lawful judgment of his equals or by the law of the land.

(40) To no one will we sell, to no one deny or delay right of justice.

. . .

(45) We will appoint as justices, constables, sheriffs, or other officials, only men that know the law of the realm and are minded to keep it well.[3]

[3] *British Library Treasures in Full: Magna Carta—English Translation,* www.bl.uk/treasures/magnacarta/translation.html (accessed 18 Dec. 2006).

Although John promptly withdrew from the Charter, claiming that his agreement had been exacted from him under duress, later monarchs were required by Parliament to re-issue and confirm the Charter, albeit with modifications. It is in the form of a 'Confirmation' that some provisions of Magna Carta remain in the statute-book today.

In *Two Treatises of Government*, published in 1690, John Locke argued that human rights, not governments, came first in the natural order of things:

If Man in the State of Nature be so free, as has been said; If he be absolute Lord of his own Person and Possessions, equal to the greatest, and subject to no Body, why will he part with his Freedom? Why will he give up this Empire, and subject himself to the Dominion and Controul of any other Power? To which 'tis obvious to Answer, that though in the state of Nature he hath such a right, yet the Enjoyment of it is very uncertain, and constantly exposed to the Invasion of others. For all being Kings as much as he, every Man his Equal, and the greater part no strict Observers of Equity and Justice, the enjoyment of the property he has in this state is very unsafe, very unsecure. This makes him willing to quit a Condition, which however free, is full of fears and continual dangers: And 'tis not without reason, that he seeks out, and is willing to join in Society with others who are already united, or have a mind to unite for the mutual *Preservation* of their Lives, Liberties and Estates, which I call by the general name, *Property*.[4]

Locke's prose celebrated the rights of the English under the limited government won by the Glorious Revolution of 1688–89. The particular advantages of England's unwritten constitution, especially the separation and balance of powers among the executive, legislative and judicial branches of government, were elaborated and popularized by the French political philosopher, Montesquieu, in the *Spirit of the Laws* in 1748.[5] In 1762, the revolutionary potential of human rights—'Man is born free; and everywhere he is in chains'—was proclaimed by Jean Jacques Rousseau.[6] Democratic revolutions were soon to follow in America and throughout Europe.

On 4 July 1776, the American Declaration of Independence issued from Philadelphia. The intellectual influences of the Magna Carta, Locke, Montesquieu and Rousseau on Thomas Jefferson's document were plain to see. In a ringing affirmation of human rights and the duty of governments to protect them, the delegates of the thirteen United States of America proclaimed:

We hold these truths to be self-evident, that all men are created equal, that they are endowed by their Creator with certain unalienable Rights, that among these are Life, Liberty and the pursuit of Happiness. That to secure these rights, Governments are instituted among Men, deriving their just powers from the consent of the governed. That whenever any Form of Government becomes destructive of these ends, it is the Right of the People to alter or to abolish it, and to institute new Government, laying its foundation on such principles and organizing its powers in such form, as to them shall seem most likely to effect their Safety and Happiness.

Politically, the last decades of the eighteenth century were a good time for affirmations of human rights. As the constitutions of the newly independent American

---

[4] J. Locke, *Two Treatises of Government* 368 (3rd edn. 1698) (Laslett 2nd edn. 1970).
[5] Montesquieu, 'L'esprit des lois', *Œuvres Complètes* 527 (Editions du Seuil 1964).
[6] J. J. Rousseau, *The Social Contract* 3 (Cole ed. 1950).

states were drafted in 1776, bills of rights enumerating specific rights were directly incorporated therein, even, as for Virginia, making up its first part.[7] The fashion of bills of rights spread to Europe. Jefferson wrote to James Madison from Paris on 12 January 1789: 'Everybody here is trying their hands at forming declarations of rights'.[8] Jefferson continued to play his part, reading and critiquing Lafayette's draft of what, on 27 August 1789, a few weeks after the fall of the Bastille, would become the French National Assembly's Declaration of the Rights of Man and Citizen.[9] Its indebtedness to Rousseau's philosophy and Philadelphia's practice was widely acknowledged.[10]

The French Declaration recognized and proclaimed 'in the presence and under the auspices of the Supreme Being, the following rights of man and citizen':

1. Men are born and remain free and equal in rights; social distinctions may be based only upon general usefulness.

2. The aim of every political association is the preservation of the natural and inalienable rights of man; these rights are liberty, property, security, and resistance to oppression.

3. The source of all sovereignty resides essentially in the nation; no group, no individual may exercise authority not emanating expressly therefrom.

4. Liberty consists of the power to do whatever is not injurious to others; thus the enjoyment of the natural rights of every man has for its limits only those that assure other members of society the enjoyment of those same rights; such limits may be determined only by law.

5. The law has the right to forbid only actions which are injurious to society. Whatever is not forbidden by law may not be prevented, and no one may be constrained to do what it does not prescribe.

6. Law is the expression of the general will; all citizens have the right to concur personally, or through their representatives, in its formation; it must be the same for all, whether it protects or punishes. All citizens, being equal before it, are equally admissible to all public offices, positions, and employments, according to their capacity, and without other distinction than that of virtues and talents.

7. No man may be accused, arrested, or detained except in the cases determined by law, and according to the forms prescribed thereby. Whoever solicits, expedites, or executes arbitrary orders, or has them executed, must be punished; but every citizen summoned or apprehended in pursuance of the law must obey immediately; he renders himself culpable by resistance.

8. The law is to establish only penalties that are absolutely and obviously necessary; and no one may be punished except by virtue of a law established and promulgated prior to the offence and legally applied.

---

[7] S. E. Morison, H. S. Commager & W. E. Leuchtenburg, 1 *The Growth of the American Republic* 210 (6th edn. 1969).

[8] T. Jefferson, Letter of 12 Jan. 1789, 14 *The Papers of Thomas Jefferson* 436, 437 (Boyd ed. 1958).

[9] T. Jefferson, Letter of 3 June 1789, to Rabaut de St. Etienne, 15 *The Papers of Thomas Jefferson* 166 (Boyd ed. 1958). One of Jefferson's biographers has commented that his influence on Lafayette's declaration of rights 'was probably greater than appears in any formal record'. D. Malone, *Jefferson and the Rights of Man* 223 (1951).

[10] L. Madelin, *La Révolution* 84–6 (1911).

9. Since every man is presumed innocent until declared guilty, if arrest be deemed indispensable, all unnecessary severity for securing the person of the accused must be severely repressed by law.

10. No one is to be disquieted because of his opinions, even religious, provided their manifestation does not disturb the public order established by law.

11. Free communication of ideas and opinions is one of the most precious of the rights of man. Consequently, every citizen may speak, write, and print freely, subject to responsibility for the abuse of such liberty in the cases determined by law.

12. The guarantee of the rights of man and citizen necessitates a public force; such a force, therefore, is instituted for the advantage of all and not for the particular benefit of those to whom it is entrusted.

13. For the maintenance of the public force and for the expenses of administration a common tax is indispensable; it must be assessed equally on all citizens in proportion to their means.

14. Citizens have the right to ascertain, by themselves or through their representatives, the necessity of the public tax, to consent to it freely, to supervise its use, and to determine its quota, assessment, payment, and duration.

15. Society has the right to require of every public agent an accounting of his administration.

16. Every society in which the guarantee of rights is not assured or the separation of powers not determined has no constitution at all.

17. Since property is a sacred and inviolable right, no one may be deprived thereof unless a legally established public necessity obviously requires it, and upon condition of a just and previous indemnity.

On 25 September 1789, less than a month after the promulgation of the French Declaration, the first Congress of the new Federal Government of the United States of America proposed the first ten amendments to the United States Constitution.[11] Coming into force following the tenth state ratification (Virginia's) on 15 December 1791, they make up the United States Bill of Rights:

1. Congress shall make no law respecting an establishment of religion, or prohibiting the free exercise thereof; or abridging the freedom of speech, or of the press; or the right of the people peaceably to assemble, and to petition the Government for a redress of grievances.

2. A well regulated Militia, being necessary to the security of a free State, the right of the people to keep and bear Arms, shall not be infringed.

3. No Soldier shall, in time of peace be quartered in any house, without the consent of the Owner, nor in time of war, but in a manner to be prescribed by law.

4. The right of the people to be secure in their persons, houses, papers, and effects, against unreasonable searches and seizures, shall not be violated, and no Warrants shall issue, but

---

[11] For the background to the drafting of the amendments, *see* B. Schwartz, *The Bill of Rights: A Documentary History* (1971).

upon probable cause, supported by Oath or affirmation, and particularly describing the place to be searched, and the persons or things to be seized.

5. No person shall be held to answer for a capital, or otherwise infamous crime, unless on a presentment or indictment of a Grand Jury, except in cases arising in the land or naval forces, or in the Militia, when in actual service in time of War or public danger; nor shall any person be subject for the same offence to be twice put in jeopardy of life or limb, nor shall be compelled in any criminal case to be a witness against himself, nor be deprived of life, liberty, or property, without due process of law; nor shall private property be taken for public use, without just compensation.

6. In all criminal prosecutions, the accused shall enjoy the right to a speedy and public trial, by an impartial jury of the State and district wherein the crime shall have been committed, which district shall have been previously ascertained by law, and to be informed of the nature and cause of the accusation; to be confronted with the witnesses against him; to have compulsory process for obtaining Witnesses in his favor, and to have the Assistance of Counsel for his defence.

7. In Suits at common law, where the value in controversy shall exceed twenty dollars, the right of trial by jury shall be preserved, and no fact tried by a jury, shall be otherwise re-examined in any Court of the United States, than according to the rules of the common law.

8. Excessive bail shall not be required, nor excessive fines imposed, nor cruel and unusual punishments inflicted.

9. The enumeration in the Constitution, of certain rights, shall not be construed to deny or disparage others retained by the people.

10. The powers not delegated to the United States by the Constitution, nor prohibited by it to the States, are reserved to the States respectively, or to the people.

Close in kinship and in substance, the American Declaration of Independence, the French Declaration of the Rights of Man and Citizen, and the United States Bill of Rights make up the eighteenth century's intellectual and documentary foundation on which two centuries of legal protection of human rights have come to be built. Constitutional guarantees of human rights are now widespread. One study showed that 82 per cent of the national constitutions drafted between 1788 and 1948, and 93 per cent of the constitutions drafted between 1949 and 1975, provided some sort of human rights and fundamental freedoms. Nowadays, more than 100 national constitutions explicitly protect human rights.[12]

Of course, the record of observing these guarantees has varied from country to country and from time to time. One important factor has been the reliance placed upon

[12] H. van Maarseveen & G. van der Tang, *Written Constitutions: A Computerized Comparative Study* 191–5 (1978). Some specific rights were more often guaranteed than others. For example, in constitutions drafted between 1949 and 1975, the right to a fair trial was protected in 91 per cent, the right to freedom of expression in 87 per cent, the right to liberty of person in 65 per cent, the right against torture or against cruel, inhuman or degrading treatment or punishment in 53 per cent, and the right to equal access to public service in 30 per cent. *Id.* at 195–8. *Constitutions of the Countries of the World* (Blaustein & Flanz eds. 20 vols. looseleaf). D. Weissbrodt, 'Globalization of Constitutional Law and Civil Rights', 43 *Journal of Legal Education* 261 (1993).

judicial review of executive and legislative action. In the United States, the tradition developed, beginning in 1803 in *Marbury v. Madison*,[13] that the courts should check the activities of the political branches of government when they violated constitutional standards. In England, France and generally on the Continent, notions of legislative supremacy dictated that the popularly elected parts of government were not to be restrained by appointed judges. It was not until 1920 that a European state, Austria, established a constitutional court that could invalidate acts of the legislature. After the Second World War, more European constitutional courts followed, e.g., in the Federal Republic of Germany in 1951, in Italy in 1953, in France in 1958 and in Spain in 1980.[14]

However, until relatively recently, there were no guarantees of human rights, much less methods of judicial review, at the level of international law comparable to those sometimes available at municipal law. The prevalent philosophy of international law in the nineteenth and early twentieth century, legal positivism, maintained that international law was a law for states alone. Hence, it was thought to be antithetical for there to be international legal rights which individuals could assert against states, especially their own states.[15] The traditional positivist doctrine appeared as late as Lauterpacht's 1955 edition of Oppenheim's classic international law treatise:

> Since the Law of Nations is primarily a law between States, States are, to that extent, the only subjects of the Law of Nations.... But what is the normal position of individuals in International Law, if they are not regularly subjects thereof? The answer can only be that, generally speaking, they are *objects* of the Law of Nations.[16]

The link of nationality did, according to traditional positivist doctrine, give a state the right to protect its nationals against abuses by other states. So, states might protest and remedy, for example, the uncompensated deprivation of a national's property by a foreign state. The Permanent Court of International Justice held in 1924 that '[i]t is an elementary principle of international law that a State is entitled to protect its subjects, when injured by acts contrary to international law committed by another State'; in so doing, a state was 'in reality asserting its own rights:.. [For] in the eyes of [an international tribunal] the State is sole claimant'.[17]

Nonetheless, the traditional positivist doctrine limited dramatically the access of private persons to international legal process. Whether or not an injury to an individual was to become the subject of an international claim depended ordinarily entirely on the discretionary decision of the individual's protecting state. Importantly, if the individual's own state inflicted an injury, no other state, usually, could protect the

---

[13] 1 Cranch (5 U.S.) 137 (1803).

[14] Kavass, 'The Emergence of Constitutional Courts in Europe: An Introduction', *Supranational and Constitutional Courts in Europe: Functions and Sources* 6–7 (I. Kavass ed. 1992).

[15] *See* M. W. Janis, *An Introduction to International Law* 239–53 (4th edn. 2003).

[16] L. Oppenheim, 1 *International Law* 636, 639 (Lauterpacht 8th edn. 1955). In the classical law of nations of the eighteenth century there was no such insistence that states were the only subjects of the discipline. Janis, 'Individuals as Subjects of International Law', 17 *Cornell International Law Journal* 61 (1984).

[17] *Mavrommatis Palestine Concessions Case*, 1924 P.C.I.J. Reports, ser. A, no. 2, at 12.

individual at international law. Moreover, states alone were given standing to bring contentious cases to the International Court at The Hague.[18]

This traditional nineteenth and early twentieth century positivist philosophy of international law foundered on the shoals of international practice in the 1940s when the Allies repudiated the human rights violations of the Axis powers. In their Moscow Declaration of German Atrocities of 30 October 1943, the United States, the United Kingdom, France and the Soviet Union declared that individual Germans would be held responsible for their violations of international law.[19] And in the 8 August 1945 Charter of the International Military Tribunal, the same four Allies established the Nuremberg Tribunal where individuals, not states, would be tried for:

(a) Crimes against peace: namely, planning, preparation, initiation or waging of a war of aggression, or a war in violation of international treaties, agreements or assurances, or participation in a common plan or conspiracy for the accomplishment of any of the foregoing;

(b) War crimes: namely, violations of the laws or customs of war. Such violations shall include, but not be limited to, murder, ill-treatment or deportation to slave labour or for any other purpose of civilian population of or in occupied territory, murder or ill-treatment of prisoners of war or persons on the seas, killing of hostages, plunder of public or private property, wanton destruction of cities, towns or villages, or devastation not justified by military necessity;

(c) Crimes against humanity: namely, murder, extermination, enslavement, deportation, and other inhumane acts committed against any civilian population, before or during the war, or persecutions on political, racial or religious grounds in execution of or in connexion with any crime within the jurisdiction of the Tribunal, whether or not in violation of the domestic law of the country where perpetrated.

Leaders, organizers, instigators and accomplices participating in the formulation or execution of a common plan or conspiracy to commit any of the foregoing crimes are responsible for all acts performed by any persons in execution of such plan.

The official position of defendants, whether as Heads of State or responsible officials in government departments, shall not be considered as freeing them from responsibility or mitigating punishment.

The fact that the defendant acted pursuant to order of his Government or of a superior shall not free him from responsibility, but may be considered in mitigation of punishment if the Tribunal determines that justice so requires.

The Tribunal shall have the right to impose upon a defendant, on conviction, death or such other punishment as shall be determined by it to be just.[20]

---

[18] 'Only States may be parties in cases before the Court', Statute of the International Court of Justice, Art. 34(1), 59 Stat. 1055, T.S. No. 993, 3 Bevans 1153 (signed at San Francisco 26 June 1945; entered into force 24 Oct. 1945). The P.C.I.J. Statute of 1920–1945 read the same. The International Court may render advisory opinions at the request of some international organizations (but not states).

[19] U.N. Doc. A/CN. 4/5 (3 March 1949), at 87–8.

[20] Agreement for the Prosecution and Punishment of the Major War Criminals, Arts. 6, 7, 8, 27, 59 Stat. 1544, 1547.

The 1946 judgment of the Nuremberg Tribunal confirmed the non-positivist norm that individuals, as well as states, were appropriate subjects of international law:

It was submitted that international law is concerned with the actions of sovereign states, and provides no punishment for individuals; and further, that where the act in question is an act of state, those who carry it out are not personally responsible, but are protected by the doctrine of the sovereignty of the State. In the opinion of the Tribunal, both these submissions must be rejected. That international law imposes duties and liabilities upon individuals as well as upon states has long been recognized. In the recent case of *Ex Parte Quirin* (1942, 317 U.S. 1, 63 S.Ct. 2, 87 L.Ed. 3), before the Supreme Court of the United States, persons were charged during the war with landing in the United States for purposes of spying and sabotage. The late Chief Justice Stone, speaking for the Court, said:

'From the very beginning of its history this Court has applied the law of war as including that part of the law of nations which prescribes for the conduct of war, the status, rights and duties of enemy nations as well as enemy individuals'.

He went on to give a list of cases tried by the Courts, where individual offenders were charged with offenses against the laws of nations, and particularly the laws of war. Many other authorities could be cited, but enough has been said to show that individuals can be punished for violations of international law. Crimes against international law are committed by men, not by abstract entities, and only by punishing individuals who commit such crimes can provisions of international law be enforced.[21]

The Nuremberg judgment has come to stand not only for the moral and political imperative that individuals be made legally responsible for violations of international law but also as evidence for the customary international legal rule that individual human rights ought to be protected at the level of international law. These moral, political and legal propositions are also to be found in the Preamble of the 1945 Charter of the United Nations. There the People of the United Nations reaffirm their 'faith in fundamental human rights'. Article 55 calls on the organization to promote 'universal respect for, and observance of, human rights and fundamental freedoms for all without distinction as to race, sex, language, or religion'.[22]

The transformation of the substantive norms of human rights law from national to international law was made complete in 1948 in the promulgation of the Universal Declaration of Human Rights, where the United Nations General Assembly followed in the footsteps of Jefferson, Lafayette and Madison.[23] The path in the United Nations had been laid by extensive debate in the Third Committee where there was a conscious sentiment among the delegates that the Declaration ought to reflect the great eighteenth century declarations of natural rights.[24] The large part of the Universal Declaration enumerated traditional human rights norms at the level of international law.

---

[21] The Nuremberg Trial 1946, 6 F.R.D. 69, 110 (1946).

[22] 59 Stat. 1031, T.S. No. 993, 3 Bevans 1153, signed at San Francisco 26 June 1945; entered into force 24 Oct. 1945.

[23] U.N.G.A. Resolution 217A (III), U.N. Doc. A/810, at 71 (1948). *See* Humphrey, 'The Universal Declaration of Human Rights: Its History, Impact and Juridicial Character', in *Human Rights: Thirty Years After the Universal Declaration* 21 (Ramcharan ed. 1979).

[24] J. Morsink, 'The Philosophy of the Universal Declaration', 6 *Human Rights Quarterly* 309 (1984).

The emergence of international human rights law in the Nuremberg Judgment and the Universal Declaration of Human Rights has been described as the most 'radical development in the whole history of international law' since it so rapidly established individuals as well as states as subjects of international law.[25] However, the Universal Declaration provided no legal machinery to enforce rules against recalcitrant states. Albeit subject to the norms of international human rights law, states in the United Nations system were left to their own devices in terms of fulfilling their obligations. Given the political disputes then and now dividing the United Nations, it has been slow work developing effective international human rights legal process on a universal basis.[26] So it made sense, especially in Europe, for there to be regional international human rights machinery which might provide realistic enforcement mechanisms.

B. THE NEGOTIATION OF THE CONVENTION

The proceedings at Nuremberg and the United Nations had special meaning for those who had witnessed the awful abuses of human rights in Nazi-occupied Europe. For the Europeans pressing for political union, human rights became an important priority. In May 1948, many of the organizations promoting European integration met at the Hague at the Conference of the International Committee of the Movements for European Unity.[27] There the delegates proclaimed:

We desire a Charter of Human Rights guaranteeing liberty of thought, assembly and expression as well as the right to form a political opposition; we desire a Court of Justice with adequate sanctions for the implementation of this Charter.[28]

Alongside the private pro-union movements, the European governments were preparing a treaty to establish a Council of Europe, with its own Assembly and Committee of Ministers, as a formal institutional step towards European unity. On 5 May 1949, the act creating the Council was signed by ten nations in London. It was widely expected that one of the early tasks of the Council would be to craft and implement a human rights convention for Europe.[29] Indeed, Article 3 of the Statute of the Council provided

---

[25] Humphrey, 'The Revolution in the International Law of Human Rights', 4 *Human Rights Law Journal* 205, 208–9 (1974–5).

[26] H. J. Steiner & P. Alston, *International Human Rights in Context* 557–778 (2nd edn. 2000); R. B. Lillich, H. Hannum, S. J. Anaya & D. L. Shelton, *International Human Rights: Problems of Law, Policy and Practice* 533–615 (4th edn. 2006).

[27] R. Beddard, *Human Rights and Europe* 19 (3rd edn. 1993).

[28] Council of Europe, 1 *Collected Edition of the Travaux Préparatoires* xxii (1975) (hereinafter cited as 'Travaux Préparatoires').

[29] A. H. Robertson, *The Council of Europe* 1–83 (1956).

that: 'Every Member of the Council of Europe must accept the principles of the rule of law and of the enjoyment by all persons within its jurisdiction of human rights and fundamental freedoms'.[30]

On 12 July 1949, a draft European Convention on Human Rights and a draft Statute for a European Court were prepared by Pierre-Henri Teitgen, Sir David Maxwell-Fyfe and Professor Fernand Dehousse and submitted to the Council's Committee of Ministers.[31] Nonetheless, at the first session of the Committee of Ministers on 9 August 1949, a seven to four vote with one abstention decided to eliminate the '[d]efinition, safeguarding and development of human rights and of fundamental liberties' as an agenda item for the forthcoming first meeting of the Council's Consultative Assembly. Delegates from Norway, France and Sweden opposed the human rights agenda item because the matter 'had already been extensively discussed' at the United Nations in the debates leading up to the Universal Declaration of Human Rights.[32]

Despite the decision of the Committee of Ministers, many of the delegates at the Consultative Assembly proved keen to draft a special human rights convention for Europe. Rasmussen, a representative from Denmark, on 13 August 1949, rejected the notion that work on human rights in Europe would merely duplicate the United Nations's efforts:

[A]lthough the question of human rights had been discussed at length by the United Nations, it had not yet been possible to draft a text which held good in International Law. The universal declaration lacked precision. It could not be otherwise in view of the differences in civilization and forms of Government existing in different Member States of the United Nations. It would be a very different matter if the question was reconsidered on a purely Western European basis, in which case a text might be elaborated which would be binding in the legal sense.[33]

In response to such criticism, the Committee of Ministers finally agreed, on 13 August 1949, to return human rights to the Consultative Assembly's agenda.[34] A new item read:

Measures for the fulfillment of the declared aim of the Council of Europe in accordance with Article I of the Statute in regard to the maintenance and further realisation of human rights and fundamental freedoms.[35]

On 19 August 1949, a motion was put to the Assembly by Teitgen of France, Maxwell-Fyfe of the United Kingdom and 45 others which read in part:

The Assembly recommends that the Member States of the Council of Europe should, in pursuance of the aim enunciated in Article I of the Statute, accept the principle of collective responsibility

---

[30] 1 *Travaux Préparatoires*, *supra* n. 28, at xxiv.
[31] *Id.* at xxiv; the full texts of the drafts are set forth in *id.* at 296–320.
[32] *Id.* at 10–12.
[33] *Id.* at 24.
[34] *Id.* at 26.
[35] *Id.* at 28.

for the maintenance of human rights and fundamental freedoms, and for this purpose should immediately conclude a convention by which each Member State would undertake:

(a) to maintain intact the human rights and fundamental freedoms assured by the constitution, laws and administrative practice actually existing in their respective countries at the date of the signature of the convention; and

(b) to set up a European Commission of Human Rights and a European Court of Human Rights for the purpose of assuring the observance of the above mentioned convention.[36]

In support of the motion, Teitgen linked the development of the new legal system to the human rights abuses of Nazi Europe:

Mr. President, while I was in the Gestapo prisons, while one of my brothers was at Dachau and one of my brothers-in-law was dying at Mauthausen, my father who was also a member of our French Parliament, was interned at Buchenwald. He told me that on the monumental gate of the camp was this outrageous inscription: 'Just or unjust, the Fatherland'.

I think that from our First Session we can unanimously proclaim that in Europe there will henceforth only be *just* fatherlands.

I think we can now unanimously confront 'reasons of State' with the only sovereignty worth dying for, worthy in all circumstances of being defended, respected and safeguarded—the sovereignty of justice and of law.[37]

Edberg of Sweden stressed the need to turn human rights theory into international legal practice:

Mankind to-day has had more than enough of high-sounding principles and beautiful declarations. Willingness and ability to make something real out of those declarations has too often been lacking. How many international organizations have undermined their authority by compromising their fundamental ideals, because it seemed for a moment to be the easiest way! When I cast my vote for concrete measures, to secure for the men and women of the European countries their human rights and fundamental freedoms, I shall do it with a fervent desire, first, that the definition of those fundamental freedoms will be so clearly formulated as to leave no room for doubts about their meaning, and secondly, that the Charter of Human Rights, which we are going to adopt, will be regarded as supreme and binding upon all Governments who adopt it. Only if we adhere strictly to those principles will this Council achieve the position in European life for which we all hope.[38]

The general debate on the motion closed on the day it had begun with a proposal for a European human rights convention being forwarded to the Consultative Assembly's Committee on Legal and Administrative Questions. Looking back decades later, Pierre-Henri Teitgen selected that day, 19 August 1949, as 'the date when the European Convention on Human Rights emerged into positive law'.[39] The Legal Committee met

---

[36] *Id.* at 36.

[37] *Id.* at 48–50.

[38] *Id.* at 78.

[39] Teitgen, 'Introduction to the European Convention on Human Rights', *The European System for the Protection of Human Rights* 3, 9 (Macdonald, Matscher & Petzold eds. 1993).

between 22 August and 5 September 1949; it decided at its first sitting, by eleven votes to five: '[t]hat it would be useful and opportune to recommend the Member States to organize a collective guarantee within the Council of Europe of all or some of the rights and liberties of man and of citizens'.[40] Unanimously, on 27 August 1949, the Legal Committee resolved that 'although each State is entitled to establish the rules by which human rights are protected within its territory, the object of the collective guarantee should be to ensure that such rules and their application are in accordance with the general principles of law recognized by civilized nations (Article 38 of the Statute of the Permanent Court of International Justice)'.[41]

On 5 September 1949, the Legal Committee reported to the Consultative Assembly.[42] The Legal Committee supported:

the establishment of a collective guarantee of essential freedoms and fundamental rights… [T]his guarantee would demonstrate clearly the common desire of the Member States to build a European Union in accordance with the principles of natural law, of humanism and of democracy; it would contribute to the development of their solidarity and would fulfill the longing for security among their peoples.[43]

'The Committee unanimously agreed that for the moment, only those essential rights and fundamental freedoms could be guaranteed which are, to-day, defined and accepted after long usage, by the democratic regimes'.[44] The rights were to be based 'as far as possible' on the rights enumerated in the Universal Declaration of Human Rights.[45] The Legal Committee's proposed draft convention listed twelve substantive rights, each explicitly referenced to articles of the Universal Declaration, called for the establishment of a European Court and Commission of Human Rights, and gave individuals as well as states the right of petition to the Commission; the Commission and states could refer cases to the Court.[46] Respecting the establishment of a Commission and a Court, the Legal Committee reported:

After a long debate, the Committee rejected as completely insufficient a proposal granting the victim of a violation of the Convention a simple right of petition, whether to the Committee of Ministers or to a Commission of Enquiry. It is in fact well known that any authority which, in such circumstances, receives a petition, may quite likely decide to ignore it.

After this the Committee decided that the guarantee should include a judicial ruling preceded by a preliminary investigation of the complaint, followed, if necessary, by an enquiry, and then an attempt at conciliation, to be carried out by a special Commission.

All persons or corporate bodies who are victims of a violation of the Convention, may petition the Commission, but the latter need not immediately refer it to the Court; the complaint will,

[40] 1 *Travaux Préparatoires*, *supra* n. 28, at 154.
[41] *Id.* at 166.
[42] *Id.* at 216–34.
[43] *Id.* at 216.
[44] *Id.* at 218.
[45] *Id.*
[46] *Id.* at 228–34.

if the Commission so decides, only be submitted to the Court for a judicial decision after a preliminary investigation of the case and after an attempt at conciliation has been made.[47]

The proposals for a Commission and a Court were not welcomed by all. Rolin of France
and Ungoed-Thomas of the United Kingdom proposed on 6 September 1949 that the
Legal Committee's recommendation of a Court be rejected.[48] Among other things,
Rolin and Ungoed-Thomas opposed letting private individuals 'bring one of the States
to trial even after examination and with the authority of a "sorting organization"'.[49]
Rejecting such arguments that supported the sanctity of state sovereignty and pleading in favour of the proposed Court, Teitgen of France returned to the theme of human
rights abuses in World War II with a speech on 7 September 1949:

Democracies do not become Nazi countries in one day. Evil progresses cunningly, with a minority operating, as it were, to remove the levers of control. One by one freedoms are suppressed,
in one sphere after another. Public opinion and the entire national conscience are asphyxiated.
And then, when everything is in order, the 'Führer' is installed and the evolution continues even
to the oven of the crematorium.

   It is necessary to intervene before it is too late. A conscience must exist somewhere which
will sound the alarm to the minds of a nation menaced by this progressive corruption, to warn
them of the peril and to show them that they are progressing down a long road which leads far,
sometimes even to Buchenwald or Dachau.

   An international Court, within the Council of Europe, and a system of supervision and guarantees, could be the conscience of which we all have need, and of which other countries have
perhaps a special need.[50]

Dominedo of Italy was equally plain in his support of a new European regional international court. He explained on 8 September 1949, why the International Court of
Justice at The Hague would not do:

I must observe that The Hague Court of International Justice is not a European court; it does
not fulfill the fundamental aim we have in mind, that is to say, the establishment of a European
legal organ. Appeal to a Court whose competence is extra-European does not contribute to the
progressive formation of European unity.

   But that is not good enough. Indeed, according to the Statute of the United Nations, the
International Court of Justice at the Hague only admits a complaint made by a State.

   We must tackle a delicate but very interesting question. We must decide whether we wish to
study the possibility of individual victims who claim that their fundamental human rights have
been violated, being able to submit a complaint or an appeal.[51]

Finally, after two full days of debate, on 8 September 1949, the proposed amendment
of Rolin and Ungoed-Thomas rejecting a European Court of Human Rights was itself
rejected; the idea of establishing a new Court would go ahead.[52]

---

[47] *Id.* at 224.
[48] *Id.* at 242.
[49] *Id.* at 244.
[50] *Id.* at 292.
[51] 2 *Travaux Préparatoires*, *supra* n. 28, at 156–8.
[52] *Id.* at 184.

Ungoed-Thomas then proposed that individuals not be allowed to petition the Commission.[53]

[P]ersonally I object to this right of individuals going to the Commission for this reason. I fore-see shoals of applications being made by individuals who imagine that they have a complaint of one kind or another against the country...In my opinion the objection to the Commission is as great as the objection to the Court.[54]

Sundt of Norway also opposed the right of individual petition:

I believe that the Commission will be of greater practical importance than the Court, because it is the Commission and its investigations which will form the basis for both public opinion, the decisions the Committee of Ministers will take, and likewise for the case which will eventually be carried to the Court. On the other hand, I also consider that the work of the Commission will be made practically impossible if thousands and thousands of individuals in the different Member States have the opportunity to send in their complaints.[55]

In rebutting such arguments, Maxwell-Fyfe said quite simply: '[W]e have to give the personal opportunity to the individual to establish the dignity of the individual human spirit and to prevent injustice'.[56] Ungoed-Thomas's proposal to delete the right of individuals to petition the Commission was rejected.[57]

On 8 September 1949, the Report of the Legal Committee with a few amendments but still recommending a Court, a Commission and the right of individual petition, was adopted by the Consultative Assembly with 64 votes in favour, one against, and 21 abstentions.[58] The Assembly's draft Convention then passed to the Committee of Ministers, which on 5 November 1949 invited the governments of the member states of the Council of Europe to appoint experts to a committee to draw up its own draft convention paying '[d]ue attention...to the progress which has been achieved in this matter by the competent organs of the United Nations'.[59] The Consultative Assembly, through its Standing Committee on 7–9 November 1949, expressed itself none too happy with the action of the Committee of Ministers:

The Standing Committee regrets that the Committee of Ministers did not think it desirable to give its approval in principle to the draft Convention for a collective guarantee of human rights, which the Assembly has adopted. It sees no objection to this question being remitted to a committee of lawyers for study, but it would like to point out that it would be regrettable if this committee was to be given a mandate to undertake the study of the question *ab initio*; the more so since the Assembly's draft was in fact based on work done by the United Nations. The Committee feared that to defer the matter until a decision is taken by the United Nations would mean that the proposal would merely be pigeon-holed.[60]

---

[53] *Id.* at 188.
[54] *Id.* at 188–90.
[55] *Id.* at 190.
[56] *Id.* at 200.
[57] *Id.* at 202.
[58] *Id.* at 274–86.
[59] *Id.* at 290.
[60] *Id.* at 302.

The Committee of Experts, composed of government lawyers, legislators, judges and law professors from the twelve nations then members of the Council of Europe, met between 2 February and 10 March 1950, at Strasbourg.[61] They had before them not only the draft Convention and Report prepared by Teitgen and the Consultative Assembly, but also Working Papers readied by the Secretariat of the Council of Europe.[62] And, despite or because of the worries of the Assembly, the Committee of Experts did not begin their work *ab initio*, but rather, from their very first sitting, used the Assembly's draft as their working document.[63]

The Committee of Experts reported to the Committee of Ministers on 16 March 1950.[64] The Committee included their own 'preliminary draft convention' which they noted was 'drawn up on the basis of the Consultative Assembly's draft'.[65] The Committee, however, pronounced itself unwilling to finally decide on the detail in which enumerated rights should be drawn or whether a Court should be included since these were fundamentally political decisions; it instead submitted alternative texts in both respects.[66] On receiving the Committee of Experts' Report, the Committee of Ministers decided on 1 April 1950 to convene a Conference of Senior Officials of the governments of the member states 'to prepare the ground for the political decisions to be taken by the Committee of Ministers'.[67]

The Conference of Senior Officials met between 8–17 June 1950.[68] In their Report to the Committee of Ministers,[69] the Conference noted that four countries (France, Ireland, Italy and Turkey) favoured simply enumerating rights as the Consultative Assembly had proposed and four countries (Greece, Norway, the Netherlands and the United Kingdom) favoured defining the rights in detail.[70] The Conference's proposed text was a compromise of the two positions ultimately acceptable to a majority of the Conference.[71]

With respect to a Court, seven countries (Denmark, Greece, Norway, the Netherlands, the United Kingdom, Sweden and Turkey) were opposed to its creation, while four (Belgium, France, Ireland and Italy) were in favour.[72] Sweden proposed the creation of an optional Court, a compromise supported by eight countries (Belgium, France, Greece, Ireland, Italy, Luxembourg, Sweden and Turkey), opposed by two (the Netherlands and the United Kingdom), and supported by two (Denmark and Norway) if supported by a majority of the governments.[73] Nine countries (Belgium, Denmark,

---

[61] 3 *Travaux Préparatoires, supra* n. 28, at 180–335.
[62] *Id.* at 2–178.
[63] *Id.* at 182–4. *See* the detailed discussion of proposed changes to the Assembly's draft, *id.* at 258–78.
[64] 4 *Travaux Préparatoires, supra* n. 28, at 2–82.
[65] *Id.* at 14.
[66] *Id.* at 16.
[67] *Id.* at 84.
[68] *Id.* at 100–240.
[69] *Id.* at 242–96.
[70] *Id.* at 246–8.
[71] *Id.* at 248.
[72] *Id.* at 248–50.
[73] *Id.* at 250–2.

France, Ireland, Italy, Luxembourg, Norway, Sweden and Turkey) supported the right of individual petition to the Commission, while three (Greece, the Netherlands and the United Kingdom), 'fearing that the right of petition might easily lead to abuse, particularly in the interests of subversive propaganda', reserved their position.[74]

With the enumerated rights agreed but disputes still raging about the role of the Court and the right of individual petition, the draft Convention returned to the hands of the Committee of Ministers. In August 1950, the Committee of Ministers decided to make both the jurisdiction of the Court and the right of individual petition optional.[75] This text then was substantially the same as that signed by the governments on 4 November 1950.[76] The European Convention for the Protection of Human Rights and Fundamental Freedoms came into force on 3 September 1953.[77]

C. THE PROGRESS OF THE CONVENTION

Merely as a European bill of rights, the Convention as drafted and adopted offered little that was exceptional on the international scene. What is extraordinary about the Convention is Strasbourg's enforcement machinery. The heart of its efficacy was for nearly 50 years provided by what were, until November 1998, two crucial 'optional' clauses: old Article 25 (now mandatory by new Article 34) giving individuals as well as states the right to petition the European Commission of Human Rights for relief and old Article 46 (now mandatory by new Article 32) that gave the European Court of Human Rights judicial jurisdiction to hear and try cases already reported upon by the Commission (the Commission's functions were merged into the Court in 1999).

What was crucial in the early days of the Convention was whether or not a European state would agree to accept individual petition and judicial jurisdiction. Historically, the Europeans were familiar with bills of rights but, unlike the Americans, they were generally unfamiliar with judicial enforcement of those rights. Domestically, they trusted the legislative and executive branches of government rather than the judicial branch to protect fundamental freedoms.[78] In the 1950s the question was whether Europeans would be willing to empower an international commission and a court to safeguard human rights.

At first, the European governments were reluctant to accept the optional clauses. Look, for example, at some of the parliamentary debates in Great Britain in 1958, several years before the government agreed to accept the two optional provisions:

Mr. Brockway asked the Secretary of State for Foreign Affairs whether Her Majesty's Government have accepted the compulsory jurisdiction of the European Court of Human Rights which is now being set up in accordance with the terms of the European Convention on Human Rights.

---

[74] *Id.* at 252.   [75] 1 *Travaux Préparatoires, supra* n. 28, at xxvi–xxviii.   [76] *Id.* at xxviii.

[77] Convention, *supra* n. 1; it is set forth in full in Appendix A.

[78] J. Frowein, 'European Integration Through Fundamental Rights', 18 *Journal of Law Reform* 5–7 (1984).

The Minister of State for Foreign Affairs (Mr. Ormsby-Gore): No, Sir. As my right Hon. and Learned Friend said on 29th July last year: 'The position which Her Majesty's Government have continuously taken up is that they do not recognize the right of individual petition, because they take the view that States are the proper subject of international law and if individuals are given rights under international treaties, effect should be given to those rights through the national law of the States concerned. The reason why we do not accept the idea of compulsory jurisdiction of a European court is because it would mean that British codes of common and statute law would be subject to review by an international court. For many years it has been the position of successive British Governments that we should not accept this status'. (Official Report, 29th July, 1957; vol. 574, c. 867–8).

Mr. Brockway: May I ask the right Hon. Gentleman what in the world is the good of ratifying a Convention theoretically if one does not accept the application of that Convention? Is it not the case that human rights involve personal individual rights and if we do not recognize that we are giving way to totalitarian conception?

Mr. Ormsby-Gore: As I understand it, if one subscribes to a Convention one then sees that the laws of one's country are in conformity with the convention, and the individual cases are then tried under the laws of one's own country.

Mr. S. Silverman: Would the Hon. Gentleman explain how he reconciles that view with the action the British Government—and in the opinion of most of us rightly—took in regard to the Nuremberg trials? Can one really maintain a view of international law, international rights, on the basis that a man may be individually subject to penalties for infractions of it, but not able to claim any rights under the same conception?

Mr. Ormsby-Gore: I quite agree that the procedure in the Nuremberg courts was entirely exceptional and was due to the actions that took place in the war. I agree that it does not square with all the other cases which we have in mind.

Mr. Brockway: In view of that unsatisfactory reply, I wish to ask your permission, Mr. Speaker, to raise the matter at the first opportunity on the Adjournment.[79]

Other sorts of governmental objections were raised elsewhere in Europe, for example in 1959, in the Netherlands, against recognizing the right of individual petition:

It was thought that such recognition was not necessary because there existed in this country effective guarantees in the municipal law; abuse was feared; it was feared that the European Commission, which would deal with the complaints, would have a political structure; it was thought that the procedure for individual petition was cumbersome and costly and, finally, it was pointed out that the right of individual petition would have far-reaching repercussions upon our legal system.[80]

---

[79] House of Commons, *Weekly Hansard*, No. 438, 26 Nov. 1958, col. 333–4, quoted in 2 *Yearbook of the European Convention on Human Rights* 546–8 (1958–1959). The relationship between the United Kingdom and the Strasbourg system has long been complex and controversial. *See* A. Lester, 'Fundamental Rights: The United Kingdom Isolated?', [1984] *Public Law* 46; A. Lester, 'U.K. Acceptance of the Strasbourg Jurisdiction: What Really went on in Whitehall in 1965', [1998] *Public Law* 237; and, for the most recent developments involving the incorporation of the Convention in British law, Chapter 14 *infra*.

[80] Second Chamber of the States General, Session 1959, *Preliminary Report of the Budget Committee for Foreign Affairs*, Document No. 5359, quoted in 2 *Yearbook for the European Convention on Human Rights* 560, 562 (1958–1959).

However, over time and one-by-one the members of the Council of Europe consented to what were, until November 1998, the two optional clauses. What had been originally conceived as real as well as legal options became perceived in Europe as politically non-optional. Indeed, by 1995, all 30 states then party to the Convention had accepted both Article 25's right of individual petition and Article 46's jurisdiction of the Court.[81] Looking at the progressive adoption of the optional clauses and the increasing case loads of the Commission and the Court, one sees distinctive tales for each of the six decades of the Convention.

The 1950s spoke of institutional development but had little actual case law about which to boast. The Convention was signed in 1950 and, ratified by eight states, came into force in 1953. In 1955 the Commission was granted the right to hear individual petitions against consenting states. The Court was constituted in 1958. Only on 2 June 1956 was an application declared admissible by the Commission (by Greece against the United Kingdom respecting Cyprus).[82] Altogether only five applications (two government, three individual) were deemed admissible in the 1950s. No case was heard by the Court.[83]

The 1960s saw both modest triumph and disquieting disobedience. There were some 54 applications admitted by the Commission (five government, 49 individual). The Court rendered its first ten judgments.[84] However, in 1969, following adverse reports by the Commission, Greece withdrew from the Council of Europe and denounced the European Convention on Human Rights.[85] This reduced the total membership in the system from 16 to 15 at the end of the decade. The number of states accepting the right of individual petition had grown to eleven. The same eleven states also accepted the jurisdiction of the Court.[86]

---

[81] As of 28 July 1994, the record showed that 21 countries chose to accept simultaneously Art. 25 and Art. 46: Ireland on 25 Feb. 1953; Denmark on 13 April 1953; Belgium on 5 July 1955; the Federal Republic of Germany on 5 July 1955; Luxembourg on 28 April 1958; Austria on 3 Sept. 1958; the United Kingdom on 14 Jan. 1966; Italy on 1 Aug. 1973; Switzerland on 28 Nov. 1974; Portugal on 9 Nov. 1978; Liechtenstein on 8 Sept. 1982; Malta on 1 May 1987; San Marino on 22 March 1989; Finland on 10 May 1990; the Czech Republic on 18 March 1992; the Slovak Republic on 18 March 1992; Hungary on 11 May 1992; Bulgaria on 7 Sept. 1992; Poland on 1 May 1993; Romania on 20 June 1994; and Slovenia on 28 June 1994; four nations first accepted Art. 25 individual petition and subsequently accepted Art. 46 jurisdiction of the Court: Sweden Art. 25 on 4 Feb. 1952 and Art. 46 on 13 May 1966; Iceland Art. 25 on 29 March 1955 and Art. 46 on 3 Sept. 1958; Norway Art. 25 on 10 Dec. 1955 and Art. 46 on 30 June 1964; and Turkey Art. 25 on 28 Jan. 1987, and Art. 46 on 22 Jan. 1990; five countries accepted Art. 46 first: the Netherlands Art. 46 on 31 Aug. 1954 and Art. 25 on 28 June 1960; France Art. 46 on 3 May 1974 and Art. 25 on 2 Oct. 1981; Greece Art. 46 on 30 Jan. 1979 and Art. 25 on 20 Nov. 1985; Spain Art. 46 on 15 Oct. 1979 and Art. 25 on 1 July 1981; and Cyprus, Art. 46 on 24 Jan. 1980 and Art. 25 on 1 Jan. 1989. The acceptances up to 2 Sept. 1993 are shown in Council of Europe, *Chart of Signatures and Ratifications of European Treaties: Updating as at 2 September 1993* (hereinafter cited as 'Chart') and updated by conversation with the Secretariat of the Commission 10 Mar. 1995.

[82] 1 *Yearbook of the European Convention on Human Rights* 128–30 (1955–1956–1957).

[83] 2 *Yearbook of the European Convention on Human Rights* (1958–1959).

[84] 'Alphabetical list of the 469 judgments delivered by the Eur Court HR (as of 23 June 1994)', 15 *Human Rights Law Journal* 116 (1994) (hereinafter cited as 'List of Judgments').

[85] 12 *Yearbook of the European Convention on Human Rights* 78–84 (1969).

[86] *Id.* at 88–9.

The 1970s showed a solid maturation of the system. Greece rejoined the Convention in 1974. By the end of the decade some 20 countries belonged, 14 accepting individual petition and 17 consenting to the jurisdiction of the Court.[87] 168 applications (five government, 163 individual) were deemed admissible by the Commission.[88] The Court began to develop a meaningful jurisprudence, as it delivered 26 judgments in the decade.[89]

The 1980s witnessed an explosion of activity under the Convention. By the end of the decade, 22 of the 23 nations in the Council of Europe (all except Finland) were parties to the Convention. All 22 ratifying states had also by the end of the decade accepted the right of individual petition and had consented to the jurisdiction of the Court.[90] In the 1980s some 455 applications were deemed admissible by the Commission.[91] And, most dramatically, 169 judgments were delivered by the Court, more than six times as many cases as had been decided by the Court in the previous decade.[92]

The 1990s exhibited the price of success. The system of European human rights law burst at the seams in terms of both its membership and its caseload. Finland, freed by the end of the Cold War from a rigidly 'neutral' foreign policy, adhered to the Convention in 1990, the twenty-third member state. Newly non-Communist Central and East European states joined soon thereafter: Czechoslovakia (later the Czech Republic and the Slovak Republic), Hungary and Bulgaria in 1992, Poland in 1993, Romania and Slovenia in 1994, Lithuania in 1995, Estonia and Albania along with Andorra in 1996, the former Yugoslav Republic of Macedonia, Ukraine, Latvia, Moldova and Croatia in 1997, Russia in 1998 and Georgia in 1999.[93] From 'only' 22 states parties in 1989, state participation almost doubled in a decade: 41 states were parties to the Convention in 1999. Looking at the caseload in the 1990s, there were 107,223 provisional files opened at the Commission, and after 1998, at the Court.[94] Of these, some 4,984 were deemed admissible, more than ten times as many as in the 1980s.[95] And, the Court delivered 809 judgments, five times as many as in the 1980s, and almost four times as many judgments as the Court had rendered altogether in the first forty years of the Convention.[96] The combined pressure of new members and burgeoning caseload persuaded the Council of Europe to reform Strasbourg's legal machinery, leading to the drafting and adoption of Protocol No. 11, and resulting in the merger of the Commission and the Court in 1999.

[87] 22 *Yearbook of the European Convention on Human Rights* 39–44 (1979).
[88] European Commission of Human Rights, *Stock-Taking on the European Convention on Human Rights: Supplement 1986* 105–7 (1988).
[89] List of Judgments, *supra* n. 84, at 116.
[90] Chart, *supra* n. 81.
[91] Council of Europe, European Commission of Human Rights, *Survey of Activities and Statistics 1992* 18 (1993).
[92] List of Judgments, *supra* n. 84, at 116.
[93] Signatures and Ratifications, *supra* n. 2.
[94] Council of Europe, European Court of Human Rights, *Survey of Activities 1999* 50, www.echr.coe.int (accessed 5 Jan. 2007).
[95] *Id.*
[96] *Id.*

The sixth decade of the Convention, beginning in 2000, is witnessing an international human rights legal system straining to keep up with its responsibilities. Six new states have ratified the Convention: Azerbaijan, Armenia, and Bosnia and Herzegovina 2002, Serbia in 2004, Monaco in 2005 and Montenegro in 2007.[97] There are now 47 member states; 22 were part of Communist central and eastern Europe before 1989. The Court's caseload, already beyond its capabilities in the 1990s, became a nightmare. In the first six years of the decade, 2000–05, the Court opened 220,254 provisional files, an average of 36,709 provisional files each year.[98] In the same six years, there were 5,022 applications declared admissible, an average of 837 admissible applications each year.[99] And, in the same six years, there were 4,954 judgments delivered by the Court, an average of 826 judgments each year.[100] Notwithstanding the explosion of case law in the 1980s and 1990s, these first six years of the first decade of the 2000s have recorded more than 80 per cent of all the judgments delivered by the European Court of Human Rights.

Debate about the reform of Strasbourg's legal machinery stretched from 1982 to 1998. Documentation and discussion about the then-ongoing debate occupied a chapter of the 1995 edition of this book.[101] The results of the reform figure significantly in the text in Chapters 2 and 3 below. It seems that the reforms instituted by Protocol No. 11 have proved inadequate in meeting the increased workload in Strasbourg. The pressures generated by Strasbourg's success continue unabated. The continuing controversy about the reform of the Convention are addressed in the final chapter of this book, 'Prospects'.

---

[97] Signatures and Ratifications, *supra* n. 2.

[98] Council of Europe, European Court of Human Rights, *Survey of Activities 2005* 33, www.echr.coe.int (accessed 8 January 2007).

[99] *Id.*

[100] *Id.*

[101] M. W. Janis, R. S. Kay & A. W. Bradley, 'Reform of the Commission and the Court', Chapter 4, *European Human Rights Law: Text and Materials* 88–118 (1st edn. 1995); commentary is to be found, *inter alia*, in A. Drzemczewski, 'Protocole no. 11 à la CEDH: préparation à l'entrée en vigueur', 8 *European Journal of International Law* 59 (1997); M. W. Janis, 'Russia and the "Legality" of Strasbourg Law', 8 *European Journal of International Law* 93 (1997); P. Leuprecht, 'Innovations in the European System of Human Rights Protection: Is Englargement Compatible with Reinforcement?', 8 *Transnational Law & Contemporary Problems* 313 (1998).

2

STRASBOURG'S LEGAL MACHINERY

What most sets European human rights law apart from other international human rights legal systems is its formal and remarkably effective legal machinery. More than any other international human rights legal system, Strasbourg's institutions work very much like an ordinary domestic legal system. European human rights law has become a legal system operated by lawyers, not simply dreamed of by idealists or mostly manipulated by politicians and diplomats. Not that idealists, politicians and diplomats do not play roles in Strasbourg—they do—but, by and large, Strasbourg's real legal machinery is in the hands of the lawyers who constitute Strasbourg's Court and Secretariat and who litigate at Strasbourg on behalf of individual claimants and defendant governments.

This chapter first introduces the European Commission of Human Rights; the Commission executed most of the system's pre-judgment functions from 1953 to 1998. Second, using *Earl Spencer's Case*, the *Icelandic Electoral System Case,* and the *Banković Case*, it explores the process and problems of admissibility, the whittling down each year of tens of thousands of submitted claims to several hundred processed cases. Third, examining the *Giama Case*, it looks at friendly settlement, how agreement is sometimes reached between the parties short of judicial settlement. Fourth, using the *Greek Case*, it explores some of the elements of fact-finding. The actual judgments of the Court and their implementation are topics reserved for Chapter 3.

A. THE EUROPEAN COMMISSION OF HUMAN RIGHTS: 1953–1999

As we have seen, during the negotiation of the Convention in the Council of Europe in 1949–50, delegates expressed the opinion that it would be advisable to establish not only a European Court but also a European Commission of Human Rights. The Commission's role was originally foreseen as being protective of the judicial function. A 'commission could form a kind of barrier—a practical necessity well known to all jurists—which would weed out frivolous or mischievous petitions'.[1] It was also intended that the Commission facilitate suits against states by private parties, perceived as a vital element in the system's efficacy:

If the Court is to carry out its work effectively in every case of a violation of human rights or fundamental freedoms, access to the Court must be available not only to the States, but also, after an opinion has been rendered by a Committee of the Council, to individuals and corporate bodies, thereby differing from the timid provisions of the Statute of The Hague Court.[2]

So, from its very beginnings, the Commission was blessed and cursed with an intermediate position in the system of European human rights law. On the one hand, the Commission was meant to shield the Court from a possible deluge of individual complaints, a function that also protected the traditional sovereignty of the member states. On the other hand, the Commission was meant to serve as an international institution directly accessible to individuals, a radical departure from traditional state-centred international legal process. Fashioned and acting in compromise, the Commission stood as an intermediary both between individuals and governments, and between individuals and the Strasbourg Court.

What was Article 19 of the European Convention on Human Rights set up the European Commission of Human Rights alongside the European Court of Human Rights, both explicitly required to 'ensure the observance of the engagements undertaken by the High Contracting Parties in the present Convention'.[3] The members of the Commission, equal in number to the number of parties to the Convention, were elected by the Council of Europe's Committee of Ministers from slates drawn up by the Consultative Assembly to serve six year renewable terms. The Commission met in Strasbourg ordinarily for periodic two-week sessions. For example, in 1992, with the press of considerable business, the Commission held eight sessions, meeting altogether for 16 weeks.[4] Though meant to be part-time, the Commission usually took up half or more of the time of an individual's employment. Many of the Commissioners were law professors whose universities released them for their work in Strasbourg (for which they were only partly compensated);[5] others were already retired from government, judicial or university employment. The Commission was assisted by a full-time and fully salaried Secretariat in Strasbourg, numbering in 1993, about 95 persons of whom about 40 were lawyers.[6]

---

[1] Council of Europe, 1 *Collected Edition of the Travaux Préparatoires* 48 (1975); speech by Teitgen to the Consultative Assembly, 19 Aug. 1949.

[2] *Id.* at 74; speech by Dominedo to the Consultative Assembly, 19 Aug. 1949.

[3] European Convention for the Protection of Human Rights and Fundamental Freedoms, 213 U.N.T.S. 221, E.T.S. 5, U.K.T.S. 71 (1953) signed at Rome 4 Nov. 1950; entered into force 3 Sept. 1953, Council of Europe print of Jan. 1994 (hereinafter cited as 'Old Convention'), Art. 19.

[4] European Commission of Human Rights, *Survey of Activities and Statistics: 1992* 1.

[5] S. Trechsel, 'Towards the Merger of the Supervisory Organs: Seeking a Way Out of the Deadlock', 8 *Human Rights Law Journal* 11, 16–17 (1987).

[6] P. van Dijk & G. J. H. van Hoof, *Theory and Practice of the European Convention on Human Rights* 23 (2nd edn. 1990); numbers up-dated in conversations with the Commission Secretariat, April 1993.

Complaints about violations of the human rights protected by the Convention were sent first to the Commission. Pursuant to old Article 24 of the Convention, states could refer to the Commission 'any alleged breach of the provisions of the Convention by another High Contracting Party'.[7] The Commission, which became competent to entertain Article 24 inter-state cases in 1953, heard its first such cases in 1955. These involved suits, brought by Greece against the United Kingdom, complaining about British administration of Cyprus, which were eventually settled in 1959.[8]

It should be noted that old Article 24 of the Convention was more generous to state suitors than is the comparable provision of the Statute of the International Court of Justice. Article 24 permitted any contracting state to complain about the conduct of any other contracting state, regardless of the nationality of the injured individual. Hence, there was no requirement, as imposed by the International Court that a private party only be protected by that person's own national state.[9] So, as proved important in practice, individuals were protected by foreign states even against their own government.

Furthermore and radically dissimilar from Article 34 of the ICJ Statute, which provides that '[o]nly States may be parties in cases before the Court', the European Convention provided that a state might agree to permit private parties themselves to petition the Commission for relief. This vital aspect of European human rights law was first to be found in old Article 25:

The Commission may receive petitions addressed to the Secretary General of the Council of Europe from any person, non-governmental organization or group of individuals claiming to be the victim of a violation by one of the High Contracting Parties of the rights set forth in this Convention, provided that the High Contracting Party against which the complaint has been lodged has declared that it recognizes the competence of the Commission to receive such petitions. Those of the High Contracting Parties who have made such a declaration undertake not to hinder in any way the effective exercise of this right.[10]

The Commission became legally competent to receive individual petitions pursuant to Article 25 in 1955.[11] By 28 July 1994, all 30 of the states then party to the Convention had agreed to recognize the admissibility of private petitions, ordinarily called 'applications' in the practice of the Commission.[12] The Commission's three principal functions—filtering complaints through admissibility proceedings, mediating disputes through the process called friendly settlement, and fact-finding and

---

[7] Old Convention, *supra* n. 3.

[8] 1 *Yearbook of the European Convention on Human Rights* 128–30 (1955–57); 2 *Yearbook of the European Convention on Human Rights* 178–86 (1958–59).

[9] The ICJ has so held both for individuals and for corporations. *See* the *Nottebohm Case*, 1955 I.C.J. Reports 4, 26, and the *Barcelona Traction Case*, 1970 I.C.J. Reports 4, 46.

[10] Old Convention, *supra* n. 3, Art. 25(1).

[11] European Commission of Human Rights, *Stock-Taking on the European Convention on Human Rights: The First Thirty Years: 1954 until 1984* 1 (1984) (hereinafter cited as 'Stock-Taking').

[12] 'European Convention on Human Rights and Additional Protocols: Chart of Signatures and Ratifications as of 28 July 1994', 15 *Human Rights Law Journal* 114–15 (1994); J. E. S. Fawcett, *The Application of the European Convention on Human Rights* 346 (2nd edn. 1987).

reporting on admitted but unsettled disputes—have all been absorbed since 1999 by the reformed European Court of Human Rights.

Until the merger of the Commission and the Court, a case already heard and reported upon by the Commission was referred by the Commission or a concerned state for the consideration of the European Court of Human Rights, which had and has the power to issue a binding legal decision; if a case was not referred to the Court within three months of referral of the Commission's report to the Committee of Ministers of the Council of Europe, then the Committee of Ministers had been entitled by a two-thirds vote to decide that there was a violation of the Convention.[13] If no such majority was forthcoming, the Committee of Ministers simply decided to take no action. Before the Court became particularly active, the Commission left important cases, such as the *Greek Case* discussed below, to the Committee of Ministers. Thereafter, the Commission usually only turned to the Committee of Ministers, a political body made up of the foreign ministers of the member states represented by permanent delegates in Strasbourg, when the majority of the Commission felt there had been no breach of the Convention or when it felt that the case needed the special political influence of the Committee of Ministers.[14]

B. ADMISSIBILITY

In 1960, noting that 710 of the first 713 individual applications submitted to the Commission had been declared inadmissible, one commentator remarked that cases 'denying the individual further hearing before an international tribunal, form by far the most significant part of the jurisprudence of the Commission'.[15] Moreover, many petitions never reached the members of the Commission for a formal decision on admissibility, but were screened out prior to registration by the lawyers in the Commission's Secretariat in Strasbourg.

Hans Christian Krüger, formerly the Secretary to the European Commission of Human Rights, has described the formal structure of the Secretariat's pre-Commission screening-out process:

[R]egistration may be refused, on the instructions of the President where the claim is wholly and totally outside the competence of the Commission, or where the applicant himself refuses to provide the information which is necessary for the adjudication of the matter under the Convention and which he is clearly able to provide.[16]

---

[13] Old Convention, *supra* n. 3, Arts. 32(1), 48, 52, 53.

[14] Beddard, *Human Rights and Europe* 57–9 (3rd edn. 1993); A. H. Robertson & J. G. Merrills, *Human Rights in Europe: A Study of the European Convention on Human Rights* 301 (3rd edn. 1993).

[15] Weil, 'Decisions on Inadmissible Applications by the European Commission of Human Rights', 54 *American Journal of International Law* 874 (1960).

[16] H. C. Krüger, 'The European Commission of Human Rights', 1 *Human Rights Law Journal* 66, 72 (1980).

Professor Michael Reisman has observed:

Nor should we be formalistic in identifying the role players. One cannot ignore, in bureaucracies such as those of the European rights system, the critical role of permanent clerks and administrative officials, those faceless bureaucrats who may sometimes play determinative roles by their characterization of claims, formulation of issues, and advice.[17]

The importance of the bureaucracy of the European human rights system is well illustrated by some statistics. In 1983, though the Commission opened some 3,150 provisional files, it formally registered only 499 applications, dismissed 407 applications and finally declared merely 29 applications admissible.[18] By 1989, the number of provisional files had grown to 4,900, while the number of registered applications reached 1,445; the cases declared inadmissible or struck off the list were 1,243 and those declared admissible were in total 95.[19] Between 1973 and 1985, about 80 per cent of all complaints were handled by the Secretariat without going to the Commission.[20]

In its first 43 years from 1955 to 1997, the Commission registered some 39,047 applications,[21] of which only 13 came from states,[22] the balance being submitted by individuals, and declared some 4,161 applications admissible.[23] From 1998, when the Court began to assume the functions of the Commission, to 2005, eight years altogether, there were some 261,035 applications registered, of which 6,515 were declared admissible.[24] Since more than 97 per cent of all applications are never declared admissible, admissibility remains one of the most important features of the system.

Since the implementation of Protocol No. 11 and the institution of the new European Court of Human Rights on 1 November 1998, admissibility proceedings have become the province of the Court itself.[25] Complaints are now sent in the first instance, not to the Commission, but directly to the Court. For inter-state cases, new Article 33 of the Convention replaces old Article 24 and reads: '[a]ny High Contracting Party may refer to the Court any alleged breach of the provisions of the Convention and the protocols thereto by another High Contracting Party'.[26] For individual applications, besides newly providing for direct reference to the Court, new Article 34 also makes jurisdiction over private suits, what was the province of old Article 25, mandatory for

---

[17] M. Reisman, 'Book Review', 77 *American Journal of International Law* 345, 346 (1983).

[18] Stock-Taking, *supra* n. 11, at 312.

[19] 1989 *Yearbook of the European Convention on Human Rights* 19 (1993).

[20] Fribergh, 'The Commission Secretariat's Handling of Provisional Files', *Protecting Human Rights: The European Dimension* 181 (eds. Matscher & Petzold 2nd edn. 1990).

[21] 1997 *Yearbook of the European Convention on Human Rights* 76 (1998).

[22] *Id.* at 79.

[23] *Id.* at 77.

[24] Council of Europe, European Court of Human Rights, *Survey of Activities 2005* 33, www.echr.coe.int (accessed 8 Jan. 2007).

[25] Council of Europe, Convention for Protection of Human Rights and Fundamental Freedoms (CETS No. 5), signed at Rome, 4 Nov. 1950, entered into force 3 Sept. 1953, as amended by Protocol No. 11 (ETS no. 155), signed at Strasbourg, 11 May 1994, entered into force 1 Nov. 1998, www.conventions.coe.int (accessed on 8 Jan. 2007) (hereinafter cited as 'Convention').

[26] *Id.* Art. 33.

all states parties to the Convention: '[t]he Court may receive applications from any person, non-governmental organisation or group of individuals claiming to be the victim of a violation by one of the High Contracting Parties of the rights set forth in the Convention or the Protocols thereto. The High Contracting Parties undertake not to hinder in any way the effective exercise of this right'.[27]

Respecting individual applications, Article 28 of the new Convention provides that a committee of three members of the Court[28] may, by a unanimous vote declare inadmissible an application or strike out of its list of cases an application submitted under Article 34 where such a decision can be taken without further examination. 'The decision shall be final'.[29] If no decision is made by a Committee that a private claim is inadmissible, for example, if a three-judge Committee either favours admission of an individual application or if there is a dissent on a vote of inadmissibility, then the decision on admissibility is made by a chamber of seven judges; this chamber may also decide on the merits of the individual claim, ordinarily in a subsequent decision.[30] Seven-judge chambers, not three-judge Committees, always decide on the admissibilty of state versus state cases.[31]

New Article 35 of the Convention deals with admissibility criteria in much the same language as old Article 27. The first admissibility provision sets out a criterion that applies to both inter-state and individual applications: '[t]he Court may only deal with the matter after all domestic remedies have been exhausted, according to the generally recognised rules of international law, and within a period of six months from the date on which the final decision was taken'.[32] Non-exhaustion of domestic remedies is the theme of the first case, *Spencer v. United Kingdom*, explored below. The second admissibility provision includes two criteria which apply only to individual applications: the claim must not be anonymous[33] nor can it be 'substantially the same as a matter that has already been examined by the Court or has already been submitted to another procedure of international investigation or settlement and contains no relevant new information'.[34] Finally, and most generally, the third admissibility provision gives the Court the power to 'declare inadmissible any individual application submitted under Article 34 which it considers incompatible with the provisions of the Convention or the protocols thereto, manifestly ill-founded, or an abuse of the right of application'.[35] The second case below, *X v. Iceland*, is an example of an inadmissibility decision based on the grounds that the application was 'manifestly ill-founded'.

Both *Earl Spencer's Case* and *X v. Iceland* were decided by the old Commission, the functions of which were merged, beginning in 1998, into the new Court. Our third

---

[27] *Id.* Art. 34.
[28] *Id.* Art. 27.
[29] *Id.* Art. 28.
[30] *Id.* Art. 29(1), (3).
[31] *Id.* Art. 29(2).
[32] *Id.* Art. 35(1).
[33] *Id.* Art. 35(2)(a).
[34] *Id.* Art. 35(2)(b).
[35] *Id.* Art. 35(3).

and final decision on admissibility, *Bankovic*, was decided in 2001, and hence by the Court itself. Because of its political importance—a claim against NATO member states for bombing Serbia—*Bankovic* ultimately reached Strasbourg's highest forum, a seventeen-judge Grand Chamber of the Court. The Grand Chamber decided that *Bankovic's* claims were extraterritorial and thus inadmissible.

1. EARL SPENCER'S CASE

Earl and Countess Spencer v. United Kingdom
Decision of the Commission of 16 January 1998 on the Admissibility of the Applicants
92–A Decisions and Reports of the European
Commission of Human Rights 56–75 (March 1998)
25 E.H.R.R. CD105

The facts

The application was introduced by the ninth Earl of Spencer (who is the brother of the late Diana Spencer, former Princess of Wales) and by his wife. The first applicant is a British citizen, born in 1964, and he has a permanent address in Northampton. The second applicant is a British citizen, was born in 1965 and has an address in South Africa. The applicants are represented before the Commission by Mr Simon Ekins, a solicitor practising in London.

A. Particular circumstances of the case

The facts of the case, as submitted by the parties, may be summarised as follows.

On 2 April 1995 the *News of the World,* a mass circulation newspaper, published an article entitled 'Di's sister-in-law in booze and bulimia clinic'. This article extended from the front page to the following two pages of that newspaper and reported the second applicant's admittance to a private clinic for treatment for an eating disorder and for alcoholism. It went into considerable detail on the applicants' personal and family problems and incidents (including the applicants' relationship, the second applicant's unhappiness about living on the large family estate inherited by the first applicant and the first applicant's alleged affair shortly after their marriage). Close friends of the applicants were referred to as sources. The article was accompanied by a photograph of the second applicant taken with a telephoto lens while she walked in the grounds of the private clinic, which photograph was captioned 'So thin: Victoria walks in the clinic grounds this week'.

On 2 April 1995 *The People,* also a mass circulation newspaper, published an article about the applicants in two parts. The first part was entitled 'Di's sister in therapy clinic ... exclusive' and also referred to the second applicant's admission to a private clinic for treatment for an eating disorder. The second part covered two pages, was entitled 'Dorm for Di's sister-in-law as she fights slimming disease' and detailed the state of the second applicant's health and the treatment regime at the clinic, and made reference to the amount of telephone calls made by the first applicant to the second applicant at the beginning of her stay at the clinic.

On the same day the *Sunday Mirror* (also a mass circulation newspaper) published an article entitled 'Althorp wife in clinic—Di's sister-in-law in addiction clinic'. This article announced that the 'long suffering' second applicant was being treated at a private clinic for a slimming disease and referred to the effect of the illness on the applicants' marriage and noted that it was also believed that the second applicant was receiving treatment for a drink problem.

Later on 2 April 1995 the first applicant issued a statement confirming the second applicant's admission to the clinic. He condemned the intrusion into the second applicant's personal affairs, asserted that the second applicant was a private individual and stated that he could see no justification for the publication of the story. He argued that if anybody needed privacy and freedom from harassment it was a person suffering from psychological disorders.

A response by the associate editor of the *News of the World* to that statement of the first applicant was reported in that newspaper on 14 May 1995. That editor argued that the first applicant was a public figure by birth, was no stranger to publicity, and had on many occasions encouraged media interest in his home and family in return for fees. As regards the second applicant's health, the associate editor referred to a report dated August 1993 in a magazine on the second applicant's attendance as a guest of honour at a charity evening in aid of the Eating Disorders Association where she had allegedly confirmed to the magazine journalist that she had suffered from such a disorder for many years. He also referred to an interview with the first applicant published in the *Daily Mail* on 5 August 1993 about the family estate, where the first applicant had revealed that the second applicant worked as a volunteer part-time at a hospital for young girls suffering from anorexia, which illness had plagued the second applicant's teenage years.

On 3 April 1995 the *Daily Mirror*, also a mass circulation newspaper, published a number of articles entitled 'Vicky's bravest battle'. The articles referred, *inter alia*, to the second applicant's admission to the clinic, to her illnesses, to the usual causes and symptoms of such illnesses, and to the alleged rift between the applicants which dated back, according to the article, to the first applicant's alleged affair shortly after their marriage. The applicants' friends were referred to as sources. A photograph of the second applicant, similar to that published by the *News of the World*, accompanied this article and was captioned 'Courageous Victoria strolls in the grounds of the clinic where she is trying to battle her way back to health'.

All of the articles were published and the photographs of the second applicant in the clinic were taken and published without the applicants' prior knowledge or consent.

On 3 April 1995 the first applicant complained about the *News of the World, The People* and the *Daily Mirror* to the Press Complaints Committee (PCC), claiming breaches of certain provisions of the Code of Practice relating to privacy (clause 4 of the Code of Practice), activities of journalists in hospitals and other similar institutions (clause 6) and harassment (clause 8).

Further to this complaint to the PCC, the *News of the World* printed an article entitled 'hypocrisy of the arrogant Earl Spencer' on 9 April 1995. The article alleged that the first applicant had seized every opportunity to put himself in the public eye. It claimed that the first applicant had received £250,000 in October 1992 from a magazine for an interview with the applicants at the family estate which resulted in a nineteen-page article. The article also stated that approximately two years later the same magazine was invited to a maternity hospital on the occasion of the birth of the applicants' fourth child. The article went on to point out that the first applicant had admitted having had an affair in interviews with journalists. The article contested the claim made by the first applicant before the PCC and stated that the relevant photograph was published after careful consideration, as the paper knew that it could be in breach of the Code of Practice.

The paper went on as follows:

'If it caused offence or distress to Lady Spencer, we apologise to her. But one reason we carried it was to prove our story was true. For Earl Spencer has a rather disturbing tendency to lie through the back of his teeth when the press he so loves to manipulate uncover less than complimentary stories against him'.

The PCC concluded that the *News of the World* had breached the Code of Practice. In the absence of a public interest justification, the PCC did not accept that the publication of a photograph 'taken with a telephoto lens of a indisputably unwell person walking in the private secluded grounds of an addiction clinic' could be anything other than a breach of the Code. The PCC considered that, while the first applicant's past relationship with the press may have affected the extent to which he was entitled to privacy in relation to particular aspects of his own life, this did not leave the press free to comment on any matter concerning the second applicant. The PCC did not accept that the second applicant had opened her illness to public scrutiny.

The *Daily Mirror* agreed to publish an apology prior to the determination of the PCC and therefore the PCC ruled that the complaint against that newspaper had been resolved. The apology of the *Daily Mirror* was published on 11 April 1995, was addressed to both applicants, and related to the publication of the photograph of the second applicant.

As regards the article in *The People*, the PCC considered that matters of health fell within the ambit of an individual's private life and that the intrusion into the second applicant's private life was not justified. The PCC considered that while the first applicant's past relationship with the press may have affected the extent to which he was entitled to privacy in relation to particular aspects of his own life, this did not leave the press free to report on any matter concerning the second applicant, particularly on the second applicant's health and psychological well-being. The PCC did not accept that the second applicant had opened her illness to public scrutiny and concluded that *The People* newspaper had breached the Code of Practice.

On 14 May 1995 the *News of the World* published the adjudication of the PCC against that newspaper together with an apology. That apology was addressed to the second applicant and related to both the article and the relevant photograph. *The People* newspaper also published the adjudication and an apology, which apology was addressed to both applicants.

On 17 May 1995 the applicants' solicitors wrote two separate letters to two former friends of the applicants, threatening breach of confidence proceedings for an injunction and the pursuit of a 'financial claim' and requesting an undertaking regarding further disclosures in order to avoid an injunction hearing. The applicants' solicitors noted that the 'grossest example' of their breach of confidence had resulted in the *News of the World* article of 2 April 1995—one of the friends had passed on a private letter from the second applicant to the press, which letter contained information about the state of her health, and both friends had also leaked related information.

...

[The applicants sued their former friends. This case was settled on 4 June 1995, the applicants obtaining an injunction restraining their former friends from disclosing information about the applicants' private life to the media.]

B. Relevant domestic law and practice

1. Relevant case-law

There is no law of privacy, as such, in England and Wales (*Kaye v. Robertson* [1991] FSR 62, Glidewell LJ at p. 66).

A remedy of breach of confidence exists. It is made up of three essential elements: the information itself must have 'the necessary quality of confidence about it', the information 'must have been imparted in circumstances importing an obligation of confidence' and there must have been an 'unauthorised use of that information to the detriment of the party communicating it' (*Coco v. A.N. Clark Engineers Ltd.* [1969] RPC 41, at 47).

...

[The relevant case law was reviewed by the Commission.]

2. The Press Complaints Committee (PCC)

This is a non-statutory body which was set up by the newspaper industry for the purposes of self-regulation. It commenced functioning in 1991. It is charged with the enforcement of a Code of Practice which was drafted by the newspaper industry's Committee and approved by the PCC in June 1993. The Code of Practice states that members of the press have a duty to maintain the highest professional and ethical standards and that in doing so they should have regard to the provisions of the Code of Practice. The Code of Practice includes provisions in relation to privacy (clause 4), activities of journalists at hospitals or similar institutions (clause 6), harassment and intimidation of subjects (clause 8) and in relation to certain public interest exceptions (clause 18).

If a newspaper has been found to be in breach of the Code of Practice, the newspaper is bound by the Code to print the adjudication by the PCC in full and with due prominence. However, the PCC has no legal power to prevent publication of material, to enforce its rulings, or to grant any legal remedy against the newspaper in favour of the victim.

...

The law

The applicants complain about a failure by the United Kingdom to fulfil its obligations under the Convention to protect their right to respect for their private lives in that it has failed to prohibit the publication and re-publication of information (photographs in the case of the second applicant) relating to their private affairs or to provide a legal remedy whereby they could have prevented such publication or claimed damages thereafter for the distress caused. They invoke Articles 8 and 13 of the Convention.

1. Article 8 of the Convention, in so far as relevant, reads as follows:

'1. Everyone has the right to respect for his private life.
2. There shall be no interference by a public authority with the exercise of this right except such as is in accordance with the law and is necessary in a democratic society for the protection of the rights and freedoms of others'.

...

The applicants essentially submit that the Government are under a positive obligation to provide effective protection for the rights guaranteed by the Convention. Given the terms of

Article 10 of the Convention, the absence of an effective domestic remedy as regards invasions of privacy by the press constitutes a failure effectively to respect their right to respect for their private lives as guaranteed by Article 8 of the Convention.

The Government argue that the domestic system as a whole (including remedies in breach of confidence and against trespass, nuisance, harassment and malicious falsehood, together with the Press Complaints Commission) provides adequate protection to individuals and an appropriate balance between the often competing rights guaranteed by Articles 8 and 10 of the Convention.

The Commission recalls that the obligation to secure the effective exercise of Convention rights imposed by Article 1 of the Convention may involve positive obligations on a State and that these obligations may involve the adoption of measures even in the sphere of relations between individuals.

On the facts as presented by the parties, the Commission would not exclude that the absence of an actionable remedy in relation to the publications of which the applicants complain could show a lack of respect for their private lives. It has regard in this respect to the duties and responsibilities that are carried with the right of freedom of expression guaranteed by Article 10 of the Convention and to Contracting States' obligation to provide a measure of protection to the right of privacy of an individual affected by others' exercise of their freedom of expression.

However, the Government's principal argument is that the failure of the applicants to pursue a breach of confidence action against, *inter alia*, the relevant newspapers amounts to non-exhaustion of domestic remedies within the meaning of Article 26 of the Convention. It is not disputed that the three essential elements of a breach of confidence action are those outlined by Megarry J in *Coco v. Clark Engineers* (*loc. cit.*).

. . .

The applicants submit that the breach of confidence action is in law and practice an ineffective remedy for the invasion of an individual's private life by the media.

. . .

The Commission recalls that Article 26 of the Convention reflects the position that States are dispensed from answering before an international body for their acts before they have had an opportunity to put matters right through their own legal system. In this regard, the provisions of Article 26 represent an important aspect of the principle that the machinery of protection established by the Convention is subsidiary to the national systems safeguarding human rights.

As to the requirements of Article 26 of the Convention, the Commission recalls that the applicants are only required to exhaust such remedies which relate to the breaches of the Convention alleged and which provide effective and sufficient redress. The applicants do not need to exercise a remedy which, although theoretically of a nature to constitute a remedy, does not in reality offer any chance of redressing the alleged breach. Accordingly, the Government must establish that the remedy in question was accessible, was one capable of providing redress in respect of the applicants' complaints and offered reasonable prospects of success. Once this burden has been discharged, it falls to the applicants to establish that the remedy advanced by the Government was, *inter alia*, for some reason inadequate and ineffective or that there were special circumstances absolving them from the requirement of exhaustion of domestic remedies. It has not been argued and the Commission does not consider that the applications give rise to any special circumstances which would absolve the applicants from exhausting domestic remedies.

Moreover, where there is doubt as to the prospects of success in a particular case it should be submitted to the domestic courts for resolution. This is particularly so in a common law system since, where the courts extend and develop principles through case-law, it is generally incumbent on an aggrieved individual to allow the domestic courts the opportunity to develop existing rights by way of interpretation.

...

The second main area of dispute between the parties relates to the remedies available on establishing a breach of confidence. The Commission accepts that the applicants have raised some doubt as to the availability of damages for breach of confidence where an injunction could not have been granted. Pursuant to Lord Cairns' Act 1858, it appears that damages are confined to a case where an injunction could have been granted but, for some reason, was not and that where publication has already taken place an injunction could not have been granted.

However, the Commission notes the judgment of Lord Goff in the *Spycatcher* case (a House of Lords judgment handed down more than ten years after the *Malone* case in the High Court). It considers that, at the very least, the extract quoted above (from p. 286 of that judgment) shows the developing state of the law relating to the award of damages. In any event, it is not disputed that an account of profits arises irrespective of the grant of an injunction. As regards the award of an account of profits where the publication has already taken place, the Commission notes that an account of profits was ordered against *The Sunday Times* in the Spycatcher case in relation to publications which had already taken place. Moreover, in light of Mr Justice Jacob's comments (albeit in the context of breach of copyright) in the Barrymore case (loc. cit.), the award of an account of profits in the Spycatcher case where the relevant articles were published along with numerous others and in view of the extensive nature of the coverage in the relevant newspapers on 2 April 1995, the Commission does not find the applicants' submissions as regards the difficulties in calculating the relevant profits sufficient to warrant a conclusion as to the ineffective nature in Convention terms of an order of an account of profits.

...

Finally, the Commission recalls the view expressed in the *Winer* case (No. 10871/84, Dec. 10.7.86, D.R. 48, pp. 154, 170) that the failure to take a breach of confidence action did not constitute a failure to exhaust domestic remedies in view of the uncertainty as to the precise scope and extent of that remedy. The Commission notes that, contrary to the position in the Winer case, the majority of the submissions in the present cases, both written and oral, focused on the scope and extent of that remedy. Based for the most part on judicial authorities dated after the Winer case (the more relevant of which are cited above and which include an important House of Lords judgment of 1990), the parties in the present cases were in a position to describe in detail the essential elements and application in practice of the breach of confidence remedy. Indeed, the Commission considers the extensive and detailed nature of the submissions, of itself, indicates that there has been significant clarification of the scope and extent of a breach of confidence action.

The Commission therefore considers that the parties' submissions in the present cases do not demonstrate the same level of uncertainty as to the remedy of breach of confidence which prevailed at the time of the Winer decision of the Commission, the domestic courts having extended and developed certain relevant principles through their case-law by interpretation.

Accordingly, the Commission considers that the parties' submissions indicate that the remedy of breach of confidence (against the newspapers and their sources) was available to the applicants and that the applicants have not demonstrated that it was insufficient or ineffective in the circumstances of their cases. It considers that, in so far as relevant doubts remain concerning the financial awards to be made following a finding of a breach of confidence, they are not such as to warrant a conclusion that the breach of confidence action is ineffective or insufficient but rather a conclusion that the matter should be put to the domestic courts for consideration in order to allow those courts, through the common law system in the United Kingdom, the opportunity to develop existing rights by way of interpretation.

In such circumstances, the Commission considers that the applicants' complaints under Article 8 of the Convention are inadmissible under Article 27 para. 3 of the Convention on the basis that the applicants have not exhausted domestic remedies within the meaning of Article 26 of the Convention.

...

For these reasons, the Commission, by a majority,

Declares the applications inadmissible.

2. EXHAUSTION OF DOMESTIC REMEDIES

Article 35(1) of the new Convention requires that '[t]he Court may only deal with the matter after all domestic remedies have been exhausted, according to the generally recognized rules of international law, and within a period of six months from the date on which the final decision was taken',[36] wording identical to that of Article 26 of the old Convention, except that there the Commission rather than the Court is mentioned.[37] This 'generally recognized rule of international law' is stated in many places; the ninth edition of Oppenheim's classic international law text (by Jennings and Watts in 1992), for example, reads: '[i]t is a recognized rule that, where a state has treated an alien in its territory inconsistently with its international obligations but could nevertheless by subsequent action still secure for the alien the treatment (or its equivalent) required by its obligations, an international tribunal will not entertain a claim put forward on behalf of that person unless he has exhausted the legal remedies available to him in the state concerned'.[38] The exhaustion of local remedies rule respects state sovereignty in that it gives a state itself an opportunity to redress an international wrong done to an individual before allowing the intervention of another state or of an international tribunal.[39]

As the Court itself put it:

The object of the rule on exhaustion of domestic remedies is to allow the national authorities (primarily the judicial authorities) to address the allegation made of violation of a Convention

---

[36] Convention, *supra* n. 25, Art. 35(1).
[37] Old Convention, *supra* n. 3, Art. 26.
[38] 1 *Oppenheim's International Law* 522–3 (Jennings & Watts 9th edn. 1992).
[39] G. Schwarzenberger, 1 *International Law* 602–4 (3rd edn. 1957).

right and, where appropriate, to afford redress before that allegation is submitted to the Court. In so far as there exists at national level a remedy enabling the national courts to address, at least in substance, the argument of violation of the Convention right, it is that remedy which should be used. If the complaint presented before the Court (for example, unjustified interference with the right of property) has not been put, either explicitly or in substance, to the national courts when it could have been raised in the exercise of a remedy available to the applicant, the national legal order has been denied the opportunity to address the Convention issue which the rule on exhaustion of domestic remedies is intended to give it. It is not suffi-cient that the applicant may have, unsuccessfully, exercised another remedy which could have overturned the impugned measure on other grounds not connected with the complaint of vio-lation of a Convention right. It is the Convention complaint which must have been aired at national level for there to have been exhaustion of 'effective remedies'. It would be contrary to the subsidiary character of the Convention machinery if an applicant, ignoring a possible Convention argument, could rely on some other ground before the national authorities for challenging an impugned measure, but then lodge an application before the Court on the basis of the Convention argument.[40]

Traditional international legal rules of exhaustion of local remedies, largely to be found in customary international law, focus on the rights of states to protect their nationals *vis-à-vis* foreign states. The exhaustion of local remedies rule in European human rights law differs, of course, from traditional rules in that it is set black-letter in a treaty. Moreover, the European human rights rule looks to individuals, as well as to states, as subjects of international law. As one commentator has noted: '[t]he individual is under the Convention protected *qua* individual, not as a national of any State but as a human being'.[41] Furthermore, the European rule has been subject to careful and continuous elaboration by the Strasbourg Commission and Court, yield-ing a complex and technical context in which to evaluate whether local remedies have been exhausted or not. Key to the Strasbourg jurisprudence is answering the question whether in any given case it is the individual applicant or the respondent state that has the burden of proof respecting the exhaustion of local remedies.[42] In *Earl Spencer's Case* is it the applicant or the state who is assigned this burden or is the burden really shared, the Court indulging, at the end of the day, with something of a weighing of the possibility of success for the applicant in the English legal system?

Earl Spencer's Case, like the *Sunday Times Case* that we explore in Chapter 3, had the advantage of broadly publicizing the Strasbourg human rights system. *Sunday Times* involved a judgment of the Court, but *Earl Spencer's Case* was 'merely' an admissibility decision by the Commission. Even so, the admissibility decision and an explanation of how the Strasbourg system works was widely reported in the United Kingdom,

[40] *Azinas v. Cyprus*, 28 April 2004, 40 E.H.R.R. 8, at para.38.
[41] A. Trindade, *The Application of the Rule of Exhaustion of Local Remedies in International Law: Its Rationale in the International Protection of Individual Rights* 15 (1983).
[42] C. Amersinghe, *Local Remedies in International Law* 291–6 (1990).

e.g., by *The Daily Telegraph*,[43] *The Guardian*,[44] *The Independent*,[45] *The Scotsman*,[46] and *The Times*.[47] As we discuss in Chapters 1 and 3, it is just this kind of publicity that helps cement the Strasbourg system into place as a 'legitimate' form of law and legal process.

3. THE ICELANDIC ELECTORAL SYSTEM CASE

X v. Iceland
Application No. 8941/80
Decision of the Commission of 8 December 1981
27 Decisions and Reports of the European
Commission of Human Rights 145–151 (Sept. 1982)

This application concerns the present Icelandic Electoral System . . .

Pursuant to this system the country is divided into 8 constituencies different in size and population, electing a total of 60 deputies to the Icelandic National Assembly (Althingi).

Forty nine of these deputies are chosen by direct elections in the 8 constituencies for proportional representation. The remaining 11 are allotted to the political parties which have seats in Parliament, in an endeavour to even out between the parties the number of deputies as compared to the total votes cast for each party . . .

[The Commission describes the Icelandic electoral system, making clear that the system favours the rural districts. This part of the Report concludes:]

If, however, the 60 deputies had been apportioned to the various constituencies on the basis of ordinary mathematical equality, the results would have been as follows:

	Votes	Deputies now	Deputies there ought to be
Reykjavik	56,402	15	24
Reykjanes	29,510	7	12
Vesturland	8,679	6	4
Vestfirdir	6,150	6	3
Nordurland West	6,560	6	3
Nordurland East	15,324	7	6
Austurland	7,683	6	3
Sudurland	11,765	7	5
	142,073	60	60

[43] 17 Jan. 1998, at 2.
[44] 17 Jan. 1998, at 2.
[45] 17 Jan. 1998, at 7.
[46] 17 Jan. 1998, at 2.
[47] 17 Jan. 1998, Home News.

The applicant believes majority rule to be the cornerstone of democracy and the principle of equal votes, one man/one vote, to be a condition without which the principle of majority rule would be meaningless.

But to rectify this injustice in the Icelandic Electoral System, it would be necessary to make yet another amendment to the constitution.

The machinery set up in the Constitution of 1944 for bringing about amendments calls for a majority vote in favour of an amendment by the Assembly in session, its subsequent dissolution and new election (held under the existing electoral laws), and then a majority vote in the new Assembly in favour of the amendments proposed in the old Assembly.

The applicant submits that it is thus evident that the injustices against which redress is sought tend to be self-perpetuating. The political party or parties who have in the past gained by the unequal votes are reluctant to propose and vote for the relative disenfranchisement of the voters who voted them into power.

In this context the applicant draws attention to the paradoxical fact that all the political parties have for many years had correction of this injustice in their platform, but nothing has been done.

Further, the applicant points out that the Constitutional Committee appointed as far back as 18 May 1972, appears to be able to do nothing. This is why he seeks the help of the Commission and believes that a modicum of outside and authoritative pressure and persuasion might be all it would take.

The applicant maintains that the only domestic remedy he could think of would be in the form of legal action against the Icelandic National Assembly—claiming that it change the constitution of the land—an action which he maintains the courts would be sure to dismiss.

The applicant submits that the Icelandic Electoral System, as described above—where each voter in the fourth constituency (Vestfirdir) is given 4.8 votes against the one vote given to each voter in the second constituency (Reykjanes)—is in breach of the basic assumptions of the Convention for the Protection of Human Rights and Fundamental Freedoms, cf. the reaffirmation in Clause 4 of the Preamble, that the Fundamental Freedoms 'are best maintained on the one hand by an effective political democracy ...', and the assumption in Clause 5 of the Preamble, that the High Contracting Parties consists of 'Governments of European countries which are like minded and have a common heritage of political traditions ...', cf. also numerous references in the articles of the Convention to 'democratic societies'.

The applicant furthermore submits that Article 3 of the First Additional Protocol would not make any sense except on the basis of an unconditional adherence by the High Contracting Parties to the principle of majority rule and equal votes: one man/one vote.

The applicant alleges that the Icelandic Government is in breach of Article 3 of Protocol No. 1 to the Convention, as they do not ensure the free expression of the opinion of the people in the choice of the legislature because of the great disparity of votes (as much as 1:4.8) behind each candidate in the different constituencies in Iceland.

It is true that Article 3 of Protocol No. 1 obliges the Government to hold free elections at reasonable intervals by secret ballots under conditions which ensure the free expression of the opinion of the people in the choice of the legislature.

It is not in dispute that elections to the Icelandic National Assembly (Althingi) are held at reasonable intervals by secret ballot. The examination of the application therefore relates to the words 'the free expression of the opinion of the people in the choice of the legislature'.

The applicant in effect contends that to ensure conformity with Article 3 of Protocol No. 1, there must be equal weight behind each vote in every constituency in Iceland, i.e. one man/one vote, as opposed to the present system which creates such disparity as 1 against 4.8.

The Commission considers that the words 'free expression of the opinion of the people' primarily signify that the elections cannot be made under any form of pressure in the choice of one or more candidates, and that in this choice the elector should not be unduly induced to vote for one party or another.

Furthermore, the word 'choice' signifies that the different political parties must be ensured a reasonable opportunity to present their candidates at elections.

However, there is here no contention that the present system of electing deputies to the Icelandic National Assembly fails to abide by the above conditions.

When applying Article 3 of the First Protocol, the Commission cannot disregard the wording and the background of the provisions concerned. Article 3 of the First Protocol gives an individual right to vote in the election provided for by this article. This is not the same as a protection of equal voting influence for all voters. The question whether or not equality exists in this respect is due to the electoral system being applied. Article 3 of the First Protocol is careful not to bind the States as to the electoral system and does not add any requirement of 'equality' to the 'secret ballot'.

The disparity of votes behind Members of Parliament from different constituencies has its origin in the migration that has taken place from the scarcely populated areas in Iceland to the densely populated areas. In spite of this fact, it is also clear that the Icelandic electoral system aims to guarantee the inhabitants in the scarcely populated areas a certain representation in Parliament at the expense of the weight of votes in the densely populated areas.

This cannot be considered to be in contravention of Article 3 of the First Protocol, which does not stipulate that the weight of votes behind each Member of Parliament shall be equal.

Full equality in the weight of votes would, as far as Iceland is concerned have the result that the majority of the Members of Parliament would be elected from a comparatively small part of the country, i.e. where it is densely populated (Reykjanes and Reykjavik constituencies). During this century changes have been made on the Icelandic electoral system and on the Icelandic constitution with the purpose of diminishing the difference between the weight of votes in the different constituencies in Iceland.

It is to be noted that the discrepancy between the weight of votes between different constituencies may have the side-effect that discrepancies also occur between political parties as to the number of votes behind Members of Parliament from different parties. Article 3 of the First Protocol to the Convention does not, however, oblige a Member State to establish an electoral system which secures that the number of deputies of each political party be proportionate to the votes cast for the parties.

The discrepancies created by the electoral system cannot be considered to be of such a degree as to be arbitrary or abusive. Furthermore, the system does not favour any particular political party at the expense of another, nor does it give any individual candidate an advantage in elections at the expense of another candidate ...

The Icelandic electoral system is a proportional representation system. It should further be noted that the Icelandic Constitution does contain provisions which aim specifically at avoiding the occurrence of discrepancies between political parties as to the number of deputies each party gets elected compared to the votes cast for it.

These provisions have in fact fairly well reached their aim, so that there is not a big difference in the number of votes behind each deputy from the different parties.

Consequently, on the basis of the above reasoning, the Commission cannot find that the Icelandic electoral system violates the provisions of Article 3 of the Convention's First Protocol.

It follows that the application is manifestly ill-founded within the meaning of Article 27, paragraph 2 of the Convention.

For these reasons, the Commission Declares this Application Inadmissible.

4. MANIFESTLY ILL-FOUNDED

The *Icelandic Electoral System Case* is an example of the broad discretionary power that the Commission and now the Court often exercise in deciding on the admissibility of individual petitions. Admissibility discretion now rests, after the implementation of Protocol No. 11 in November 1998, with the three-judge Committees of the Court. A unanimous Committee decision declaring an individual application inadmissible or striking it out of its list of cases is final and without appeal.[48] State complaints, relatively rare, always, however, require an admissibility decision by a seven-judge chamber of the Court.[49]

A great many applications have been deemed 'manifestly ill-founded' and declared inadmissible by the Commission and the Court on the grounds that they did not appear to have any realistic chance of being able to succeed on their merits. This procedure has allowed Strasbourg, at its discretion, to focus on what it decides at early stages of the proceedings to be the more important cases.[50] Will Strasbourg's discretion about inadmissibility only be exercised in cases clearly without merit?

Note in the *Icelandic Electoral System Case* that there is little in the Decision actually explaining why the dispute is inadmissible or even why the application is so without merit. Rather, the Commission rejects X's claim only after seriously, if in a preliminary way, weighing and evaluating Iceland's 'democratic' process: e.g., '[t]he discrepancies created by the electoral system cannot be considered to be of such a degree as to be arbitrary or abusive. Furthermore, the system does not favour any particular party at the expense of another, nor does it give any individual candidate an advantage in elections at the expense of another candidate'. These conclusions, it seems, could well be more fully and better tested after further evidence is provided both by X and by the government of Iceland. Why not admit the application, investigate the claim further, and then make a determination explicitly on the merits? Such a full hearing would also permit the case to be sent to the Court for its legally binding judgment.

[48] Convention, *supra* n. 25, Art. 28.
[49] *Id.* Art. 29(2).
[50] T. Zwart, *The Admissibility of Human Rights Petitions: The Case Law of the European Commission of Human Rights and the Human Rights Committee* 146–54 (1994).

Of course, there might have been very good, if unarticulated, political reasons for not admitting X's petition, investigating the claim, deciding on the merits, and sending it along to the Court for judgment. If Strasbourg were to choose to evaluate the legality under the Convention of the electoral system of Iceland, then why not test the legality of electoral schemes in more influential countries—the United Kingdom, France, Germany or Italy? Such evaluations of the merits of electoral systems of its member states by the Strasbourg legal machinery could be politically explosive. Enforcement of judgments about electoral reform might well be beyond the political capacity of the Council of Europe. In practice, the Commission has shielded the Court from having to settle a politically sensitive dispute. If that was the real reason for the Commission's decision in the *Icelandic Electoral System Case*, why not be more forthright and elaborate a 'political question' doctrine and say frankly that this is the kind of question that should be addressed politically and not judicially?

As it turned out, the Commission did not long shield the Court from having to decide whether Article 3 of Protocol No. 1 required equal treatment of all voters. The Court in *Mathieu-Mohin and Clerfayt v. Belgium*, ruling thirteen to five for Belgium, employed reasoning similar to that of the Commission in *X v. Iceland*:

It does not follow, however, that all votes must necessarily have equal weight as regards the outcome of the election or that all candidates must have equal chances of victory. Thus no electoral system can eliminate 'wasted votes'.

For the purposes of Article 3 of Protocol No. 1, any electoral system must be assessed in the light of the political evolution of the country concerned; features that would be unacceptable in the context of one system may accordingly be justified in the context of another, at least so long as the chosen system provides for conditions which will ensure the 'free expression of the opinion of the people in the choice of the legislature'.[51]

5. THE BANKOVIĆ CASE

Banković et al v. Belgium et al
Grand Chamber Decision of 12 December 2001
44 E.H.R.R. SE5

1. The applicants are all citizens of the Federal Republic of Yugoslavia ('FRY'). The first and second applicants, Vlastimir and Borka Banković, were born in 1942 and 1945, respectively and they apply to the Court on their own behalf and on behalf of their deceased daughter, Ksenija Banković. The third applicant, Živana Stojanović, was born in 1937 and she applies on her own behalf and on behalf of her deceased son, Nebojsa Stojanović. The fourth applicant, Mirjana Stoimenovski, applies on her own behalf and on behalf of her deceased son, Darko Stoimenovski. The fifth applicant, Dragana Joksimović, was born in 1956 and she applies on

---

[51] *Mathieu-Mohin and Clerfayt v. Belgium*, 2 March 1987, 10 E.H.R.R. 1, at para. 54.

her own behalf and on behalf of her deceased husband, Milan Joksimović. The sixth applicant, Dragan Suković, applies in his own right.

...

6. The conflict in Kosovo between Serbian and Kosovar Albanian forces during 1998 and 1999 is well documented. Against the background of the escalating conflict, together with the growing concerns and unsuccessful diplomatic initiatives of the international community, the six-nation Contact Group (established in 1992 by the London Conference) met and agreed to convene negotiations between the parties to the conflict.

7. On 30 January 1999, and following a decision of its North Atlantic Council ('NAC'), the North Atlantic Treaty Organisation ('NATO') announced air strikes on the territory of the FRY in the case of non-compliance with the demands of the international community. Negotiations consequently took place between the parties to the conflict from 6 to 23 February 1999 in Rambouillet and from 15 to 18 March 1999 in Paris. The resulting proposed peace agreement was signed by the Kosovar Albanian delegation but not by the Serbian delegation.

8. Considering that all efforts to achieve a negotiated, political solution to the Kosovo crisis had failed, the NAC decided on, and on 23 March 1999 the Secretary General of NATO announced, the beginning of air strikes (Operation Allied Force) against the FRY. The air strikes lasted from 24 March to 8 June 1999.

9. Three television channels and four radio stations operated from the RTS facilities in Belgrade. The main production facilities were housed in three buildings at Takovska Street. The master control room was housed on the first floor of one of the buildings and was staffed mainly by technical staff.

10. On 23 April 1999, just after 2.00 am approximately, one of the RTS buildings at Takovska Street was hit by a missile launched from a NATO forces' aircraft. Two of the four floors of the building collapsed and the master control room was destroyed.

11. The daughter of the first and second applicants, the sons of the third and fourth applicants and the husband of the fifth applicant were killed and the sixth applicant was injured. Sixteen persons were killed and another sixteen were seriously injured in the bombing of the RTS. Twenty-four targets were hit in the FRY that night, including three in Belgrade.

...

14. The Treaty of Washington came into force on 24 August 1949 ('the 1949 Treaty') and created an alliance called the North Atlantic Treaty Organisation ('NATO') of ten European states (Belgium, France, Luxembourg, the Netherlands, the United Kingdom, Denmark, Iceland, Italy, Norway, Portugal) with Canada and the United States. In 1952 Greece and Turkey acceded to the 1949 Treaty, the Federal Republic of Germany joined in 1955 and Spain also became a member in 1982. These countries were joined on 12 March 1999 by the Czech Republic, Hungary and Poland.

15. The essential purpose of NATO is to safeguard the freedom and security of all its members by political and military means in accordance with the principles of the UN Charter. Its fundamental operating principle is that of a common commitment to mutual co-operation among sovereign states based on the indivisibility of the security of its members.

...

28. The applicants complain about the bombing of the RTS building on 23 April 1999 by NATO forces and they invoke the following provisions of the Convention: Article 2 (the right to life), Article 10 (freedom of expression) and Article 13 (the right to an effective remedy).

29. The first to the fifth applicants rely on Articles 2, 10 and 13 on their own behalf and on behalf of their deceased close relatives. The sixth applicant, injured during the strike, relies on these Articles on his own behalf. With the consent of the Court, the parties' written and oral submissions were limited to the admissibility issues, the Governments' further accepting that they would not be arguing that the complaints were manifestly ill-founded.

30. As to the admissibility of the case, the applicants submit that the application is compatible ratione loci with the provisions of the Convention because the impugned acts of the respondent States, which were either in the FRY or on their own territories but producing effects in the FRY, brought them and their deceased relatives within the jurisdiction of those States. They also suggest that the respondent States are severally liable for the strike despite its having been carried out by NATO forces, and that they had no effective remedies to exhaust.

31. The Governments dispute the admissibility of the case. They mainly contend that the application is incompatible *ratione personae* with the provisions of the Convention because the applicants did not fall within the jurisdiction of the respondent States within the meaning of Article 1 of the Convention.

. . .

54. The Court notes that the real connection between the applicants and the respondent States is the impugned act which, wherever decided, was performed, or had effects, outside of the territory of those States ('the extra-territorial act'). It considers that the essential question to be examined therefore is whether the applicants and their deceased relatives were, as a result of that extra-territorial act, capable of falling within the jurisdiction of the respondent States.

55. The Court recalls that the Convention must be interpreted in the light of the rules set out in the Vienna Convention 1969 (Golder v. the United Kingdom judgment of 21 February 1975, Series A no. 18, § 29).

56. It will, therefore, seek to ascertain the ordinary meaning to be given to the phrase 'within their jurisdiction' in its context and in the light of the object and purpose of the Convention (Article 31 § 1 of the Vienna Convention 1969 and, amongst other authorities, Johnston and Others v. Ireland judgment of 18 December 1986, Series A no. 112, § 51). The Court will also consider 'any subsequent practice in the application of the treaty which establishes the agreement of the parties regarding its interpretation' (Article 31 § 3 (b) of the Vienna Convention 1969 and the above-cited Loizidou judgment (*preliminary objections*), at § 73).

57. Moreover, Article 31 § 3 (c) indicates that account is to be taken of 'any relevant rules of international law applicable in the relations between the parties'. More generally, the Court recalls that the principles underlying the Convention cannot be interpreted and applied in a vacuum. The Court must also take into account any relevant rules of international law when examining questions concerning its jurisdiction and, consequently, determine State responsibility in conformity with the governing principles of international law, although it must remain mindful of the Convention's special character as a human rights treaty (the above-cited Loizidou judgment (merits), at §§ 43 and 52). The Convention should be interpreted as far as possible in harmony with other principles of international law of which it forms part.

58. It is further recalled that the *travaux préparatoires* can also be consulted with a view to confirming any meaning resulting from the application of Article 31 of the Vienna Convention 1969 or to determining the meaning when the interpretation under Article 31 of the Vienna

Convention 1969 leaves the meaning 'ambiguous or obscure' or leads to a result which is 'manifestly absurd or unreasonable' (Article 32).

...

59. As to the 'ordinary meaning' of the relevant term in Article 1 of the Convention, the Court is satisfied that, from the standpoint of public international law, the jurisdictional competence of a State is primarily territorial. While international law does not exclude a State's exercise of jurisdiction extra-territorially, the suggested bases of such jurisdiction (including nationality, flag, diplomatic and consular relations, effect, protection, passive personality and universality) are, as a general rule, defined and limited by the sovereign territorial rights of the other relevant States.

60. Accordingly, for example, a State's competence to exercise jurisdiction over its own nationals abroad is subordinate to that State's and other States' territorial competence. In addition, a State may not actually exercise jurisdiction on the territory of another without the latter's consent, invitation or acquiescence, unless the former is an occupying State in which case it can be found to exercise jurisdiction in that territory, at least in certain respects.

61. The Court is of the view, therefore, that Article 1 of the Convention must be considered to reflect this ordinary and essentially territorial notion of jurisdiction, other bases of jurisdiction being exceptional and requiring special justification in the particular circumstances of each case.

62. The Court finds State practice in the application of the Convention since its ratification to be indicative of a lack of any apprehension on the part of the Contracting States of their extra-territorial responsibility in contexts similar to the present case. Although there have been a number of military missions involving Contracting States acting extra-territorially since their ratification of the Convention (inter alia, in the Gulf, in Bosnia and Herzegovina and in the FRY), no State has indicated a belief that its extra-territorial actions involved an exercise of jurisdiction within the meaning of Article 1 of the Convention by making a derogation pursuant to Article 15 of the Convention. The existing derogations were lodged by Turkey and the United Kingdom in respect of certain internal conflicts (in south-east Turkey and Northern Ireland, respectively) and the Court does not find any basis upon which to accept the applicants' suggestion that Article 15 covers all 'war' and 'public emergency' situations generally, whether obtaining inside or outside the territory of the Contracting State. Indeed, Article 15 itself is to be read subject to the 'jurisdiction' limitation enumerated in Article 1 of the Convention.

63. Finally, the Court finds clear confirmation of this essentially territorial notion of jurisdiction in the *travaux préparatoires* which demonstrate that the Expert Intergovernmental Committee replaced the words 'all persons residing within their territories' with a reference to persons 'within their jurisdiction' with a view to expanding the Convention's application to others who may not reside, in a legal sense, but who are, nevertheless, on the territory of the Contracting States.

64. It is true that the notion of the Convention being a living instrument to be interpreted in light of present-day conditions is firmly rooted in the Court's case-law.

...

65. However, the scope of Article 1, at issue in the present case, is determinative of the very scope of the Contracting Parties' positive obligations and, as such, of the scope and reach of the entire Convention system of human rights' protection as opposed to the question, under

discussion in the Loizidou case (*preliminary objections*), of the competence of the Convention organs to examine a case. In any event, the extracts from the *travaux préparatoires* detailed above constitute a clear indication of the intended meaning of Article 1 of the Convention which cannot be ignored. The Court would emphasise that it is not interpreting Article 1 'solely' in accordance with the *travaux préparatoires* or finding those *travaux* 'decisive'; rather this preparatory material constitutes clear confirmatory evidence of the ordinary meaning of Article 1 of the Convention as already identified by the Court (Article 32 of the Vienna Convention 1969).

66. Accordingly, and as the Court stated in the Soering case:

> Article 1 sets a limit, notably territorial, on the reach of the Convention. In particular, the engagement undertaken by a Contracting State is confined to 'securing' ('*reconnaître*' in the French text) the listed rights and freedoms to persons within its own 'jurisdiction'. Further, the Convention does not govern the actions of States not Parties to it, nor does it purport to be a means of requiring the Contracting States to impose Convention standards on other States.

67. In keeping with the essentially territorial notion of jurisdiction, the Court has accepted only in exceptional cases that acts of the Contracting States performed, or producing effects, outside their territories can constitute an exercise of jurisdiction by them within the meaning of Article 1 of the Convention.

...

71. In sum, the case-law of the Court demonstrates that its recognition of the exercise of extra-territorial jurisdiction by a Contracting State is exceptional: it has done so when the respondent State, through the effective control of the relevant territory and its inhabitants abroad as a consequence of military occupation or through the consent, invitation or acquiescence of the Government of that territory, exercises all or some of the public powers normally to be exercised by that Government.

...

74. The applicants maintain that the bombing of RTS by the respondent States constitutes yet a further example of an extra-territorial act which can be accommodated by the notion of 'jurisdiction' in Article 1 of the Convention, and are thereby proposing a further specification of the ordinary meaning of the term 'jurisdiction' in Article 1 of the Convention. The Court must be satisfied that equally exceptional circumstances exist in the present case which could amount to the extra-territorial exercise of jurisdiction by a Contracting State.

75. In the first place, the applicants suggest a specific application of the 'effective control' criteria developed in the northern Cyprus cases. They claim that the positive obligation under Article 1 extends to securing the Convention rights in a manner proportionate to the level of control exercised in any given extra-territorial situation. The Governments contend that this amounts to a 'cause-and-effect' notion of jurisdiction not contemplated by or appropriate to Article 1 of the Convention. The Court considers that the applicants' submission is tantamount to arguing that anyone adversely affected by an act imputable to a Contracting State, wherever in the world that act may have been committed or its consequences felt, is thereby brought within the jurisdiction of that State for the purpose of Article 1 of the Convention.

The Court is inclined to agree with the Governments' submission that the text of Article 1 does not accommodate such an approach to 'jurisdiction'. Admittedly, the applicants accept that jurisdiction, and any consequent State Convention responsibility, would be limited in the circumstances to the commission and consequences of that particular act. However, the Court is of the view that the wording of Article 1 does not provide any support for the applicants' suggestion that the positive obligation in Article 1 to secure 'the rights and freedoms defined in Section I of this Convention' can be divided and tailored in accordance with the particular circumstances of the extra-territorial act in question and, it considers its view in this respect supported by the text of Article 19 of the Convention. Indeed the applicants' approach does not explain the application of the words 'within their jurisdiction' in Article 1 and it even goes so far as to render those words superfluous and devoid of any purpose. Had the drafters of the Convention wished to ensure jurisdiction as extensive as that advocated by the applicants, they could have adopted a text the same as or similar to the contemporaneous Articles 1 of the four Geneva Conventions of 1949.

Furthermore, the applicants' notion of jurisdiction equates the determination of whether an individual falls within the jurisdiction of a Contracting State with the question of whether that person can be considered to be a victim of a violation of rights guaranteed by the Convention. These are separate and distinct admissibility conditions, each of which has to be satisfied in the afore-mentioned order, before an individual can invoke the Convention provisions against a Contracting State.

...

80. ...In short, the Convention is a multi-lateral treaty operating, subject to Article 56 of the Convention, in an essentially regional context and notably in the legal space (*espace juridique*) of the Contracting States. The FRY clearly does not fall within this legal space. The Convention was not designed to be applied throughout the world, even in respect of the conduct of Contracting States. Accordingly, the desirability of avoiding a gap or vacuum in human rights' protection has so far been relied on by the Court in favour of establishing jurisdiction only when the territory in question was one that, but for the specific circumstances, would normally be covered by the Convention.

...

82. The Court is not therefore persuaded that there was any jurisdictional link between the persons who were victims of the act complained of and the respondent States. Accordingly, it is not satisfied that the applicants and their deceased relatives were capable of coming within the jurisdiction of the respondent States on account of the extra-territorial act in question.

...

85. The application must therefore be declared incompatible with the provisions of the Convention and, as such, inadmissible pursuant to Article 35 §§ 3 and 4 of the Convention.

For these reasons, the Court unanimously

Declares the application inadmissible.

6. STRASBOURG'S JURISDICTION

What is the reach of European human rights law? As the Court noted in *Banković*, there have been exceptions to the presumed territorial application of the Convention. In the *Soering Case*,[52] the Strasbourg Court held that the United Kingdom should not

[52] 7 July 1989, 11 E.H.R.R. 439. See Chapter 5(C).

extradite a German national to Virginia to face the death penalty on a murder charge. The Court held that Soering possibly spending six to eight years on Virginia's 'death row' was a prospective violation of Article 3's prohibition on 'inhuman or degrading treatment or punishment'. After Virginia and the United States agreed not to seek the death sentence, Soering was extradited, tried, and, being found guilty, given two life terms.[53] Should the United Kingdom be legally responsible for prospective extraterritorial violations of the Convention?[54] Should non-parties to the Convention like Virginia and the United States be held to account by the Strasbourg Court? One commentator felt that *Soering* opened a Pandora's box.[55] Is *Banković* a step back from *Soering's* extraterritorial reach?

Another exception to the presumption of territorial jurisdiction of the European Convention on Human Rights seems to be when a member state has been deemed to be in 'effective occupation' of a territory otherwise extraterritorial to the state and to the Convention. In *Loizidou v. Turkey*, the applicant complained that she had been deprived of the right to use her property in Northern Cyprus because of Turkey's 1974 invasion and continuing occupation there.[56] When Turkey objected, *inter alia*, that this was an inadmissible extraterritorial claim, the Court responded:

Bearing in mind the object and purpose of the Convention, the responsibility of a Contracting Party may also arise when as a consequence of military action—whether lawful or unlawful—it exercises effective control of an area outside of its national territory. The obligation to secure, in such an area, the rights and freedoms set out in the Convention derives from the fact of such control whether it be exercised directly, through its armed forces or through a subordinate local administration.[57]

Commentators have attacked *Banković* for abandoning not only the wider extra-territorial jurisdiction approach of *Loizidou*, but also for promoting a narrow view of international human rights law:

Rather than using [*Banković*] to underscore the principle of the universality of human rights and to strengthen the idea that human rights inhere in all individuals (or, for that matter, simply declaring the claim unjusticiable), the Court took the exact opposite approach. It introduced the perverse idea that human rights can somehow be limited and parcelled out depending on membership in a particular class of persons.[58]

Is there an inconsistency between the hesitancy of the Court to protect the Serbian claimants in *Banković* from the readiness of the Court to protect the German claimant against Virginia in *Soering* and the Cypriot claimant in *Loizidou*?

[53] R. Lillich & H. Hannum, *International Human Rights* 768 (3rd edn. 1995).

[54] D. Seymour & J. Tooze, 'The *Soering Case*', in *International Law Stories* 115 (J. E. Noyes, L. A. Dickinson & M. W. Janis eds. 2007).

[55] C. Van den Wyngaert, 'Applying the European Convention on Human Rights to Extradition: Opening Pandora's Box', 39 *International and Comparative Law Quarterly* 757 (1990).

[56] *Loizidou v. Turkey (Preliminary Objections)*, 25 February 1995, 20 E.H.R.R. 99.

[57] *Id.* at para. 62.

[58] E. Roxstrom, M. Gibney & T. Einarsen, 'The NATO Bombing Case (*Bankovic et al. v. Belgium et al.*) and the Limits of Western Human Rights Protection', 23 *Boston University International Law Journal* 55, 62 (2005).

To what degree did special circumstances colour the Court's decision in *Banković*? Appearing on a panel, counsel for the applicants commented that because '*Banković* was argued six weeks after September 11[, there] can be no doubt that the "War on Terrorism" influenced the Court's decision'.[59] At the same panel, counsel for the defendant states countered that '[a] regional human rights tribunal cannot be the right forum in which to judge the legality of a targeting decision taken in the course of an armed conflict, especially where both the leading member of the alliance on one side and the state being targeted on the other were not parties to the human rights convention in question and were not able to take part in the proceedings'.[60]

In 2003, several countries, notably the United States and the United Kingdom, invaded and occupied Iraq. Does *Banković* limit the jurisdiction of the European Court of Human Rights to consider cases concerning, for example, Britain's attack on and occupation of Iraq? Answering 'no', one commentator distinguished *Banković* from the cases like *Loizidou* about Turkey's occupation of Northern Cyprus: 'the only restriction imposed by *Banković* was the refinement of the criteria for the exercise of "effective control" to exclude aerial bombardment'.[61] Another commentator has urged the Strasbourg Court, given the record of human rights violations in Iraq, 'to revise its stance concerning the applicability of the ECHR in military interventions'.[62] Is the extraterritorial limit in *Banković* inapplicable to the invasion and occupation of Iraq? If not, should *Banković* be reversed?

C. FRIENDLY SETTLEMENT

Once a case has been deemed admissible, it is still always possible for Strasbourg to decide to strike the case off its list if, as Article 37 of the new Convention provides, the Court determines that '(a) the applicant does not intend to pursue his application; or (b) the matter has been resolved; or (c) for any other reason established by the Court, it is no longer justified to continue the examination of the application'.[63] However, if the

[59] H. Hannum, Remarks, 'Bombing for Peace: Collateral Damage and Human Rights', 96 *American Society of International Law Proceedings* 95, 96, 99 (2002).

[60] C. Greenwood, Remarks, 'Bombing for Peace: Collateral Damage and Human Rights', 96 *American Society of International Law Proceedings* 95, 100, 104 (2002).

[61] J. Williams, '*Al Skeini*: A Flawed Interpretation of *Banković*', 23 *Wisconsin International Law Journal* 687, 688 (2003).

[62] K. Altiparmak, '*Banković*: An Obstacle to the Application of the European Convention on Human Rights in Iraq?', 9 *Journal of Conflict & Security Law* 213, 251 (2004). In 2007, the House of Lords applied *Bancović* when it dealt with claims under the Human Rights Act 1998, resulting from the death of Iraqi citizens during the conflict in Iraq. Five Iraqis who had been killed in the course of security operations conducted by British forces were held to have been outside the jurisdiction of the United Kingdom for the purposes of Convention Article 1; the sixth claimant, who had died after a period in which he had been in military custody and subjected to serious abuse and assaults, was held to have been within United Kingdom jurisdiction. *R (Al-Skeini) v. Secretary of State for Defence* [2007] U.K.H.L. 26, [2007] 3 All E.R. 482.

[63] Convention, *supra* n. 25, Art. 37(1).

case has been deemed admissible and so long as it has not been struck off, Article 38 of the Convention obliges the Court to 'pursue the examination of the case, together with the representatives of the parties, and if need be, undertake an investigation, for the effective conduct of which the States concerned shall furnish all necessary facilities'.[64] We explore the fact-finding function of the Court a little later.

While fact-finding is proceeding, Article 38 also obliges the Court to 'place itself at the disposal of the parties concerned with a view to securing a friendly settlement of the matter on the basis of the respect for human rights as defined in the Convention and the protocols thereto'.[65] Friendly settlement proceedings are confidential.[66] Article 39 provides that '[i]f a friendly settlement is effected, the Court shall strike the case out of its list by means of a decision which shall be confined to a brief statement of the facts and the solution reached'.[67] Similar provision was made for friendly settlement by the Commission until it was merged into the Court in 1999.[68]

Although a friendly settlement in law and in fact terminates a Strasbourg legal proceeding, a friendly settlement is not the same as a judgment. For one thing, friendly settlement involves 'neither a winner nor a loser'.[69] A friendly settlement is fundamentally a compromise not an adjudication and, as such, may be in many circumstances 'the most satisfactory termination of a legal dispute'.[70] A friendly settlement can result simply from bilateral negotiations between the parties, but oftentimes a friendly settlement emerges only after considerable mediation by the Strasbourg legal machinery, traditionally the Commission, nowadays the Court. The *Giama Case* that follows illustrates Strasbourg's friendly settlement process, showing not only a compromise agreed to by the parties but the active role played by the Strasbourg machinery.

1. THE GIAMA CASE

Application No. 7612/76
Report of the Commission of 17 July 1980
21 Decisions and Reports of the European
Commission of Human Rights 73, 84–94 (March 1981)
1980 Yearbook of the European Convention on
Human Rights 428

4. At its session on 17 July 1980, the Commission noted that the parties had arrived at a friendly settlement, and adopted this report which, in accordance with Article 30 of the Convention, is confined to a brief statement of the facts and of the solution reached...

---

[64] *Id.* Art. 38(1)(a).   [65] *Id.* Art. 38(1)(b).
[66] *Id.* Art. 38(2).
[67] *Id.* Art. 39.   [68] Old Convention, *supra* n. 3, Art. 28.
[69] H. C. Krüger & C. A. Norgaard, 'Reflections Concerning Friendly Settlement under the European Convention on Human Rights', *Protecting Human Rights: The European Dimension: Studies in Honour of Gerard J. Wiarda* 329 (F. Matscher & H. Petzold, 2nd edn. 1990) (hereinafter cited as 'Krüger & Norgaard').
[70] *Id.*

6. The applicant, who is of African origin and who, at the time when his application was submitted, possessed no papers indicating his identity or nationality, is represented by Maitre R. Cassiers, barrister at Antwerp.

7. The applicant was questioned by the police for the first time in Belgium on 5 July 1975, when a check was carried out in a café at Antwerp. He possessed no identity papers or money. He stated that his name was Manitu Giama, that he had been born in Durban (South Africa) on 26 November 1947 and that he was of South African nationality. He further stated that he was a sailor on the ship, 'White River', which had arrived at Amsterdam three days before, and that he had come to Antwerp by train on 4 July 1975 to visit friends.

8. On 5 July 1975, he was ordered to leave the country within 48 hours, on the grounds that he possessed neither means of subsistence nor identity papers.

9. On 15 July 1975, the Aliens Police found him in Antwerp once again without a passport. He was apprehended and a warrant issued for his arrest on 16 July 1975 for being unlawfully resident and for assaulting a representative of the forces of law and order. For these offences, the Antwerp police court sentenced him on 24 October 1975 to six months' imprisonment, including two months suspended for five years, and to a fine of 100 francs or one month in prison, suspended for five years.

10. The applicant's request for refugee status under Sections 2 (B) and 3 (2) of the Aliens Police Act was rejected on the grounds that the time limit had expired. In particular, his entry into Belgium on 4 July 1975 was considered irregular. The fact that the request had been made on 24 August 1975, more than a month after his arrival in the country, was also taken into consideration.

11. In response to a request for information lodged by the Belgian authorities on 10 September 1975, the Netherlands authorities stated that the 'White River' had not docked in Amsterdam since 1 January 1973. They added that the ship had arrived in Rotterdam on 17 July 1975 and left the following day, and that the applicant had not been a member of the crew.

12. In a telegram dated 26 September 1975, Interpol Pretoria (South Africa) stated that the applicant was not a South African citizen. Having visited the applicant on 2 October 1975, the representative in Belgium of the United Nations High Commissioner for Refugees confirmed that, in view of the applicant's refusal to co-operate, he could not recognize him as a refugee.

13. Since the applicant had claimed that he could persuade the Zambian diplomatic authorities to admit him to Zambia, the United Nations representative had referred the matter to the Zambian Ambassador. A letter dated 18 November 1975 showed, however, that immigration to Zambia was out of the question. This being so, the applicant was not released when his sentence expired on 12 November 1975, but was kept in custody at the disposal of the Aliens Police, since he lacked the travel documents and identity papers needed for lawful admission to another country or continued residence in Belgium.

14. Following a conversation with an official of the Aliens Police in the course of which the applicant stated that he did not wish to return to South Africa, the latter was released on 28 November 1975 and ordered to leave the country by midnight on 30 November 1975.

15. In December 1975, the Belgium authorities proceeded to make enquiries in a number of African countries, including Ghana, Niger, Nigeria, Uganda, Zaire and Zambia. On 13 January

1976, Interpol Lusaka (Zambia) replied that the applicant had no criminal record in Zambia. On 3 February 1976, Interpol Lagos (Nigeria) similarly replied that its records contained no mention of the applicant.

[The record continued: Giama was questioned in Antwerp on 1 February 1976, ordered to leave Belgium by 6 February, arrested on 9 February, released and ordered again to leave on 5 September, arrested again in Antwerp on 10 October, sentenced to jail on 4 January 1977, released again and crossed to the Netherlands on 18 October 1977, arrested again in Belgium on 6 October 1978, released again on 13 November 1978 and again ordered to leave the country.] ...

26. In his application to the Commission, submitted on 26 November 1975, the applicant essentially argued:

 a) that he had been obliged to leave South Africa for political reasons and had thus been unable to furnish fuller information for fear of compromising his comrades;

 b) that, despite the ministerial orders, his lack of travel documents had prevented him from leaving Belgium;

 c) that his periods of detention had left this situation unchanged, since he still lacked identity papers. In this connection, he referred to Article 5 (1) of the Convention;

 d) that he had no possibility whatsoever to challenge his detention before a court and considered himself the victim of discrimination, insofar as the authorities had refused to take into account his social position and the special circumstances of his case. In this connection, he referred to Articles 5 (4) and 14 of the Convention.

...

42. The hearing [before the Commission] was held on 11 December 1978. The parties were represented as follows:

 For the applicant:
 — Maitre Cassiers   Barrister at Antwerp
 For the Government:
 — Mr. J. C. Godfroid   Legal Adviser to the Aliens Office—Agent
 — Professor J. De Meyer   Counsel
 — Mr. A. Coppue   Assistant Legal Adviser to the Aliens Office.

The applicant attended the hearing, having been temporarily admitted to France for this purpose by the French authorities. Moreover, the applicant had received authorisation from the legal department of the Belgian Ministry of Justice to return to Belgium after the hearing...
 Finally, a friendly settlement was reached...

43. After the hearing on 11 December 1978, the Commission decided, in accordance with Article 28(b) of the Convention, to place itself at the parties' disposal for the purpose of reaching a friendly settlement. Its Secretary was instructed to resume contact with the parties at once and to ascertain any proposals which they might have.

On 12 December 1978, the respondent Government's counsel met the President and the Vice-President of the Commission. At this meeting, the Belgian authorities were asked to postpone expulsion of the applicant until the Commission's next session, which was due to begin on 26 February 1979. The applicant's counsel was immediately informed of this meeting and undertook to do everything possible to regularise the applicant's situation and facilitate his return to Africa. The respondent Government indicated that it would do everything in its power to assist the efforts made by the applicant's counsel.

By letter dated 20 December 1978, the respondent Government informed the Secretary to the Commission that, following the meeting of 12 December 1978, the applicant had been given a safe-conduct, valid until the end of February.

44. At its session in March 1979, the Commission noted that counsel's attempts to arrange for the applicant's departure to another African state had proved unsuccessful and that his position thus remained unchanged. It decided that these efforts should be continued, with a view to solving the problems raised by the application. For this purpose, the Commission, again acting in accordance with Article 28(b) of the Convention, asked the respondent Government to allow the applicant to remain on its territory until a solution had been found.

The President of the Commission also asked the applicant's counsel to contact various organizations and, in particular, the Organization of African Unity (OAU) and to ask their assistance in finding a country prepared to admit the applicant. The Secretary to the Commission was instructed to give counsel every possible assistance in this matter, provided that such assistance was compatible with the functions of the Commission, as laid down in the Convention and particularly Article 28(b).

In this connection, the Secretary informed counsel that the member-states of the OAU had adopted a convention on specific aspects of the problems of refugees in Africa in September 1969. He also suggested that counsel should approach religious organizations which might be prepared to help in finding a country to receive the applicant.

45. On 21 March 1979, counsel contacted OAU and requested its assistance referring in particular to the above convention. He sent copies of his letter to two religious organizations, asking them to support his request for help in finding a country to admit the applicant.

46. At its session in May 1979, the Commission decided to inform the respondent Government of all the action taken so far by the applicant's counsel.

47. By letter dated 6 June 1979, OAU informed the applicant's counsel, who had repeated his request of 21 March 1979 on 14 May 1979, that a reply had already been despatched on 9 April 1979. This letter, which counsel seemed never to have received, had stated that the applicant's lack of papers made it impossible to deal with his case.

48. On 10 July 1979, the Commission resumed its examination of the case in the light of the information supplied by counsel. It decided to fix the proceedings to be followed and, at the same time, to remain at the parties' disposal for the purpose of reaching a friendly settlement.

49. By letter dated 19 September 1979, the applicant's counsel submitted a new proposal to the Belgian authorities for the purpose of reaching a friendly settlement. He pointed out that, for the applicant to go to an African country, it was sufficient that he should be allowed to leave Belgium in a lawful and proper fashion. He further pointed out that the applicant's lack of papers had prevented OAU from dealing with his case. He referred to the Belgian authorities' view that the applicant should be regarded as being of indeterminate identity, and stressed that aliens in this category could be issued with the documents by the authorities and be authorised by the provincial Government to leave the country. He accordingly requested the authorities to issue the documents to the applicant.

Replying to this request, the Minister of Justice informed counsel that his department was prepared to issue the applicant—as a person lacking diplomatic protection—with a travel document for aliens who were not political refugees, on condition that a receiving country could be found with the help of OAU. Counsel was asked to indicate the States to which the applicant intended to go and his probable dates of departure. The Minister explained that this travel document would be issued merely for the purpose of arriving at a friendly settlement of the case, as envisaged by the Commission, and would in no way prejudice proceedings before the Council of State. The Minister argued that the applicant should still be regarded, provisionally, as being of indeterminate nationality and not as being stateless '*de jure*' under Article 1 of the Convention relating to the status of stateless persons, signed in New York on 28 September 1954 and approved by the Act of 12 May 1960.

50. At its session in October 1979, the Commission examined the applicant's situation in the light of these new developments.

The Commission informed the applicant's counsel that this travel document had been issued to meet the conditions laid down by OAU, which had stipulated that the case could only be dealt with if the applicant possessed papers. The applicant was accordingly asked to contact OAU again when he had received the document in question.

51. By letter dated 20 November 1979, the respondent Government's Agent informed the Secretary to the Commission that the Minister for Justice had authorised the issuing of a 'travel document for aliens who are not political refugees' to the applicant. This document would entitle the holder to go abroad and return to Belgium as long as the visa attached to it remained valid.

In the meantime, the applicant's counsel approached OAU. In his letter, he spoke of the applicant's wish to settle in Zaire or Tanzania. OAU's chief legal adviser replied that the applicant who, like other South Africans, had fled the agonies of 'apartheid', would be welcome in any other independent African State. He suggested that the applicant should apply to the authorities of the African state in which he had decided to reside as a refugee for an entry permit, enclosing his passport and a written account of his position.

In response to this communication, the applicant's counsel wrote to the embassy of the Republic of Zaire in Brussels on 22 January 1980. He repeated his request on 3 March 1980.

52. At its session in March 1980, the Commission examined the case in the light of these developments. It considered that the fact of the respondent Government's having issued the applicant with the said travel document for the purpose of reaching a friendly settlement might well be considered as constituting such a settlement. It thus declared its willingness to obtain the parties' agreement to such a settlement and to prepare a report in accordance with Article 30 of the Convention.

53. By letter dated 26 March 1980, the applicant's counsel informed the Secretary to the Commission that the applicant had approached various African embassies with photocopies of the travel document and that the Senegalese authorities had agreed to admit him, making vaccination the only condition.

By letter dated 17 April 1980, the applicant's counsel stated:

'Further to my letter of 26 March, I can only tell you that the applicant left Belgium for Senegal on Saturday, 12 April.
His travel expenses were paid by the Belgian Government.
In my view, this means that a final friendly settlement of the case has been arrived at'.

54. At its session on 17 July 1980, the Commission noted that the measure adopted by the Belgian Government and the declaration made by the applicant's counsel indicated that agreement had been reached between the parties on settlement of the case.

55. In view of this friendly settlement, based on respect for human rights within the meaning of Article 28(b) of the Convention, the Commission has adopted the present report.

56. With regard to its assessment of the general interest, to which it has regard according to its constant practice when a friendly settlement is reached, the Commission has the following observations to make:

It is true that, in principle, the authorities of a State cannot be held responsible for the fact that an alien who has not been authorised to reside in the country is unable to leave the country lawfully. In the present case the applicant was confronted with such a difficulty, which had serious repercussions on his personal situation.

The Commission also points out that Applications No. 7752/76 (*X v. Belgium*, struck off the list of cases on 15 December 1977) and No. 8108 (*X v. the Federal Republic of Germany*, declared inadmissible on 6 October 1978) were concerned with similar situations. Though particularly acute, the problems raised by the present application are thus neither exceptional nor restricted to Belgium.

In the light of these considerations, the Commission believes that the problems call for careful study by the High Contracting Parties who in a 'particularly liberal and humanitarian spirit'—the terms used in Resolution (67)14 on 'Asylum to persons in danger of persecution', adopted by the Ministers' Deputies on 29 June 1967—might consider it appropriate in arriving at a common solution to situations of this kind.

2. NEGOTIATIONS AT STRASBOURG

The decision whether or not to negotiate a friendly settlement of an admitted dispute is in the first place a matter at the discretion of the two parties. The decision to negotiate may be influenced, *inter alia*, by the anticipated length or cost of Strasbourg legal proceedings or by an intimation of the likely Strasbourg determination of the merits of the dispute.[71] However, once the decision to negotiate a settlement is reached, the Strasbourg machinery may, at the choice of the parties, be engaged.[72]

Giama is an excellent example of just how much work Strasbourg may do to reach a friendly settlement. Note how much networking the Commission did in the case. It reached out to at least the following: Belgium, The Netherlands, Interpol (South Africa), the United Nations High Commissioner for Refugees, Zambia, Ghana, Niger, Nigeria, Uganda, Zaire, Interpol (Zambia), the European Commission on Human Rights, the Council of Europe, France, the Organization of African Unity and Senegal. It is doubtful whether Giama or his lawyer could involve so many national and international organizations without the assistance of the Commission. Plainly,

[71] Krüger & Norgaard, *supra* n. 69, at 330.
[72] *Id.* at 331.

the Commission could not devote such time and energy to every refugee. It may well be that the Commission saw *Giama* as a useful precedent for other like cases or as an incentive for the fashioning of a more regular bureaucratic machinery for handling problems of stateless persons.[73]

It may be that an unintended consequence of the 1999 merger of the Commission into the Court is a lessened role for Strasbourg in friendly settlements. As one commentator puts it, nowadays the 'court's role in the friendly settlement procedure is usually little more than a post box', circulating settlement proposals made by the parties themselves.[74] Another commentary reports that 'most of the applications in which friendly settlements are reached, concern simple, repetitive cases, which do not raise substantive questions of human rights law and to which well established case law of the Court can be applied'.[75] Of course, as in *Giama*, the Court can always devote its own time and resources to a friendly settlement of a complex dispute, but, as we have seen, there is already more than enough to keep the new Court busy, and there is no longer a Commission.

Friendly settlements, as in *Giama*, though relatively common in cases brought by private parties, are unusual in inter-state cases. The first friendly settlement in an inter-state case came in 1985. The case involved five applications brought by France, Norway, Denmark, Sweden and the Netherlands in 1982, complaining that Turkey had violated six Articles of the Convention in its 1982 imposition of martial law.[76] In its Report of 7 December 1985, the Commission noted that the friendly settlement recognized the legislative changes and amendments made by Turkey to comply with its obligations under the Convention and imposed upon Turkey a periodic reporting requirement.[77] An 'indirect result' of the friendly settlement was Turkey's initial acceptance of the right of individual petition under Article 25, though the acceptance was limited by a number of controversial reservations.[78] The five applications against Turkey were 'apparently only the second set of inter-State cases which [were] not motivated by the applicants' self-interest, or political, religious or ethnic links with

---

[73] For a consideration of *Giama* in political and legal context, see H. Schermers, 'The Second Generation of Immigrants', 82 *Michigan Law Review* 1415, 1418–19 (1984). The problem of illegal immigration to Europe has only become more difficult over time; there is now a vast literature on the problems of immigration policy within Europe, including the response of European states to requests for political asylum, *see* G. Goodwin-Gill, *The Refugee in International Law* (2nd edn. 1996); S. Juss, 'Sovereignty, Culture, and Community: Refugee Policy and Human Rights in Europe', 3 *UCLA Journal of International Law & Foreign Affairs* 463 (1998–9).

[74] P. Leach, *Taking a Case to the European Court of Human Rights* 43 (2001).

[75] R. Ang & E. Berghman, 'Friendly Settlements and Striking Out of Applications', *Protocol 14 and the Reform of the European Court of Human Rights* 89, 92 (P. Lemmens & W. Vandenhold eds. 2005).

[76] Applications No. 9940–44/82 of 1 July 1982.

[77] European Commission of Human Rights, 'Report on the Applications of Denmark, France, Netherlands, Norway and Sweden against Turkey and the Conclusion of a Friendly Settlement', 25 *International Legal Materials* 308, 310, 314–16 (1986).

[78] Cameron, 'Turkey and Article 25 of the European Convention on Human Rights', 37 *International and Comparative Law Quarterly* 887 (1988).

the population of the State against which the application [was] lodged',[79] the other set being the *Greek Case* below.

D. FACT-FINDING

This section explores the role of fact-finding in European human rights law. We begin with one of the most important cases ever to come to Strasbourg, the violations of the Convention committed by the military government in Greece between 1967 and 1974. The suit brought against Greece by Denmark, Norway, Sweden and the Netherlands never reached the Court, the jurisdiction of which had not been accepted by Greece at the time. However, fact-finding by the Commission alone helped the Committee of Ministers to decide to expel Greece from the Council of Europe in 1970. This is the only example of a country losing its membership in the Council because of human rights violations. In the pages below there is an excerpt from the very extensive report of the Commission on Greece. Then we ask how much it was the Commission's fact-finding that led to the expulsion of Greece and whether expulsion from the Council of Europe contributed to the eventual toppling of the Greek military regime in 1974. There is more about fact-finding as a function of the Court in Chapter 4.

1. THE GREEK CASE

12 Yearbook of the European Convention on Human Rights: The Greek Case 196 (1969)

40. The applicant Governments of Denmark, Norway and Sweden, in their written applications of 20th September, 1967, and the applicant Government of the Netherlands, in its written application of 27th September, 1967, alleged that the respondent Government had, by a number of legislative and administrative measures, violated Articles 5, 6, 8, 9, 10, 11, 13 and 14 of the Convention. These allegations were further developed at the oral hearing before the Commission on 23rd and 24th January, 1968. In particular, the applicant Governments stated that:

— a state of siege had been declared and Articles 5, 6, 8, 10, 11, 12, 14, 20, 95 and 97 of the Greek Constitution of 1st January, 1952, had been suspended by Royal Decree No. 280 of 21st April, 1967;

— political parties and ordinary political activities had been prohibited and parliamentary elections scheduled for 28th May, 1967, had been cancelled;

[79] Drzemczewski, 'The European Convention on Human Rights', 2 *Yearbook of European Law* 327, 330 (1982).

— extraordinary courts martial had been established by Royal Decrees Nos. 280 and 281 of 21st April, 1967;

— thousands of persons had been imprisoned for a long period without being brought before a 'competent legal authority';

— the right to freedom of expression had been suppressed as was illustrated by an order of the Army Chief of Staff of 14th June, 1967;

— censorship had been applied to the press and private communications;

— many persons had been sentenced by extraordinary courts martial for their political opinions;

— the right to assemble freely or to associate freely with others had been abolished as was demonstrated by criminal charges and resultant harsh sentences in certain cases.

1. Article 3 of the Convention provides that: 'No one shall be subjected to torture or to inhuman or degrading treatment or punishment'.

. . .

9. At five hearings before the Sub-Commission or its delegates—from 25th to 28th November, in Strasbourg, from 18th to 20th December, 1968, in Strasbourg, from 10th to 20th March, 1969, in Athens, from 16th to 17th June, 1969, in Strasbourg, on 26th July, 1969, in Strasbourg—a total of 58 witnesses gave evidence with regard to Article 3 of the Convention.

Among these were:

16 alleged victims of physical ill-treatment or torture;

 7 persons who had been detained together with those alleged victims;

25 police officers and other Greek officials;

 2 political prisoners with regard to whom no torture allegations were made but who had been proposed by the respondent Government (Zervoulakos and Tambakis);

 8 other persons who had made observations concerning the treatment of political prisoners in Greece. . . .

10. 49 further witnesses whom the Sub-Commission decided to hear with regard to Article 3 were not heard for various reasons, among them 21 persons detained in Greece whom the respondent Government did not make available to the Sub-Commission for a hearing. . . .

13. The Sub-Commission also called medical experts who examined 8 alleged victims with their consent:

(a) Prof. J. Bernheim, Director of the Institute of Forensic Medicine at the University of Geneva, assisted by Dr. A. Rohner, Dr. P. Boggio and Dr. J. F. Moody, examined, and submitted opinions in the cases of the witnesses:

(i) Papagiannakis, Lendakis and Karaosman after having exchanged views in Athens with Prof. D. Ekonomos, Dr. J. Matsiotas and Dr. G. Adjutantis;

(ii) Vardikos, Korovessis, Meletis and Vlassis after having received the results of specialist or supplementary examinations from Dr. F. Borer, Geneva; Prof. Dr. M. Adloff, University of Strasbourg; Dr. R. Raber, Strasbourg; Prof. F. E. Camps, London Hospital Medical College; Prof. J. Lundevall, University of Oslo; Dr. R. Weyde, University of Oslo.

(b) Prof. J. Mehl and Prof. Dr. B. Keller of the University of Strasbourg examined the witness Mrs. Tsirka and submitted an opinion in her case.

14. During its investigation the Sub-Commission has received from the parties and from witnesses a great number of documents relating to Article 3, including statements from alleged victims of torture or ill-treatment, in particular also from witnesses whom the Sub-Commission decided to hear but who were prevented by the respondent Government from giving oral evidence.

The Sub-Commission had also requested the respondent Government to submit certain further medical records, reports of the International Committee of the Red Cross, and information on the results of certain administrative enquiries but the respondent Government did not comply with these requests.

15. The Sub-Commission has inspected the Security Police Headquarters of Athens and Piraeus, but was refused access to Averoff prison and the detention camps on the Island of Leros. The Sub-Commission had also envisaged inspecting the Dionysos military camp but, having regard to the refusal by the respondent Government to allow the hearing of the four witnesses allegedly tortured in this camp (Panagoulis, Maria Kallerghi, Petropoulos and Kiaos), did not carry out the visit to the camp. ...

Case of Vardikos

1. The applicant Governments proposed N. Vardikos as a witness in their letter of 7th February, 1969. In this letter they state that Vardikos, while detained as a political prisoner, had been severely tortured. The applicant Governments submitted an affidavit made by Vardikos in Liverpool on 16th November, 1968, in which he describes the torture in some detail.

2. The respondent Government has made no specific comments on the case of Vardikos and has not proposed any witnesses with regard to this case.

3. Nicolas Vardikos, foreman, aged 30, married, was heard by the Sub-Commission in Strasbourg on 16th June, 1969. He indicated that before 21st April, 1967, he had been Secretary General of a Trade Union, and that he had also been an active member of the Greek Democratic Youth and of the Centre Union Party. Since his escape from Greece and after having been granted political asylum in Great Britain, he works as a waiter in Liverpool. His wife and children are still living in Greece.

4. He stated that he was arrested by three plain clothes police officers on 23rd April, 1967, at 2 o'clock in the morning in his house in Lavrion while he was sleeping. He was not allowed to dress, and was handcuffed. He was taken to the Lavrion police station in an army car. After an hour a captain of the Military Police took him to the Athens Security Headquarters in Bouboulinas Street, where he was locked up in a cell in the basement. Being handcuffed, he hit his head on the stone wall when thrown into the cell. As a result of this he sustained a deep bleeding wound in his head.

5. After some hours two policemen led him to Mr. Lambrou's office on the second floor. Lambrou then started interrogating him:

'When I entered he asked me: "Are you Vardikos?" "Yes, I am Vardikos". "We have a few things to ask you about, and if you love your children and your wife and your relations, it is better to answer us, and you will be set free. Tell us first of all who opened the Greek

Democratic Youth offices and if it was you who opened them, what have you done with the documents?" My answer: "I opened the offices, I took the Greek Democratic Youth documents and burnt them". "Why did you burn them?" "They contained nothing against the State. I burnt them only because they contained names of members." "Tell us, at the time of the Valpex Company strike, why did you communicate personally with the Interior Minister, Tsirimokos, and ask for the withdrawal of the eight police cars which had come for the protection of the Valpex Company?" I answered to this that all this was past. Why did they ask me? Lambrou answered me: "You will answer what I am asking you"'.

6. Lambrou then asked him to sign a declaration in favour of the Government. He refused. Lambrou had him taken to another room where there was a wooden bench. As he still refused to make the declaration, the policemen knocked him against the bench and he lost two teeth. Police Inspector Georgiou struck him with a wire rope on his left arm and as a result he has a permanent scar. He was beaten all over his body, especially on his belly and on his genitals. The witness described the ill-treatment as follows:

'He (Inspector Georgiou) struck me lower down on my arm where my veins opened and I have got the stitches. After that they put me on the bench and they kept on beating me in the belly and the testicles. I lost my senses and after that I couldn't tell either the day or the hour of the day. I was moved to a camp, in a Deutz car. I thought it was a camp because I heard some orders being given. There in the camp they threw me in a cell, pulling off my pyjamas, so that I was left almost naked. After a lapse of two hours they called me in the office where they beat me again very badly. They did not offer me any medical help. The only thing that they offered me was a red medicine for my wounds which were in a terrible condition. All in blisters. How they moved me there I don't know, I was in a coma'.

7. When he recovered his senses, he found himself locked up alone in a wooden hut on the island of Yaros. As he continued to refuse to sign the declaration of loyalty, he was kept in detention.

8. Three months and two days later, on 27th July, 1967, he was released in Athens. He remained in Lavrion under police supervision and was re-arrested on 13th December, 1967, after the King's counter-coup. He was kept in isolation at the Lavrion police station for 17 days without food and drink 'at least from the official police'. As a result he lost a considerable amount of weight.

9. In order to leave Greece, he took up work as a sailor on a Greek merchant ship. But on instructions from the government he was locked in a cabin during the journey from Spain to England and only due to a British Customs check was he able to leave the ship at Liverpool and apply for political asylum.

10. In his detailed affidavit, mentioned above and dated 26th November, 1968, Vardikos mentions also having been tortured with an iron clamp that was placed on his head and screwed into both sides of his temples in a military camp in the presence of police officer Georgiou. He had already noticed in the office, where he was taken after his first interrogation by Lambrou, that there was a 'metal clamp-like instrument with a wooden screw'.

Except for this detail, his written statement coincides essentially with his testimony before the Sub-Commission.

11. As regards the localities described, Lambrou's office is actually on the second floor of the Asphalia building in Bouboulinas Street (office numbered 39 on the plan).

12. The examination carried out by the Sub-Commission's medical experts gave the following results:

'The patient has on the front of his head, near the edge of his scalp in the left paramedian region, an old linear scar probably resulting from an injury sustained when he was flung against a wall at the time of his arrest on 23rd April, 1967. This causal relation cannot, however, be established with certainty.

On his left shoulder, in the deltoid region, there is a broad scar, the size of the palm of one's hand with irregular contours, which is discoloured, particularly round the edge, and may also be a few years old at most.

In the fold of his left elbow is a linear transverse and slightly discoloured scar probably dating from the same period. These two scars were probably left by wounds which were caused by whipping with a metallic cable and subsequently turned septic.

An examination of the mouth shows that the two top left premolars are intact, but these may well be artificial teeth. This might bear out the patient's allegation that two of his teeth were broken when his head was seized by the hair and banged against the edge of a table.

There is no trace of any further injury.

Mr. Vardikos alleges that his skull was squeezed by a kind of metal crown which was placed around his head at the level of his temples and could be tightened by screws. There is at present no mark bearing evidence of such treatment.

The patient tells us that he suffered from severe headaches for a long time afterwards. It is not possible to express a medical opinion on the possible causal relation between the compression of the skull and the headaches from which the patient subsequently suffered. Such consequences can neither be confirmed nor ruled out medically.

We do not consider specialised hospital examinations to be necessary in Mr. Vardikos's case. It would, however, be helpful if we could study the medical reports of the doctors who treated Mr. Vardikos for his dental lesions, his shoulder and elbow wounds and his persistent headaches. The patient preferred, however, not to divulge the names of his doctors'.

13. The applicant Governments submitted that Vardikos's statements contain conclusive evidence as to the fact that he had been subjected to torture.

Analysis of evidence

14. With regard to the allegations of torture made by Vardikos, the respondent Government has submitted no observations, proposed no witnesses, filed no documents in relation to this case.

15. As regards possible motives for the witness to tell a false story:

(i) it is possible to suppose that Vardikos fabricated these allegations of ill-treatment for anti-Government purposes. Though he strongly denied being a Communist and followed the Centre Union party and its leader, G. Papandreou, he made a public statement about his treatment in an interview with the *Sunday Times* newspaper; and it appears that, as a consequence, his wife was called by the police to sign certain declarations and that difficulties of making contact with his family arose;

(ii) another possible motive for Vardikos to give a false story might be to cover up the fact that he had betrayed his friends during an interrogation by the police. He was never tried or summoned as a witness in a trial, and his case ended in deportation to the island of Yaros. No reason appears why he should have to justify himself by fabricating stories of ill-treatment. But, according to his statements, he had burnt documents containing names of his associates and he refused to sign a declaration of loyalty. Further, there is no evidence that he revealed information under interrogation.

16. A possible motive for the police to put Vardikos under pressure might have been to obtain information about the Greek Democratic Youth and its members, as indicated by himself. The police officers might well have doubted his affirmation that he had burnt the archives of the organization and they would naturally have been interested in finding these archives if they still existed.

Further, according to his own statement, Vardikos was a trade union official and had already interfered against the police in strike situations (like the Valpex incident, reported by him). Thus he was known to the police inspectors of the Security Service and it would be understandable that in view of this past a certain animosity existed towards him.

17. From the medical examination of the witness it results that:

— he bears scars on his forehead, left shoulder and left elbow which could correspond to blows received in 1967;

— his two upper teeth which are in perfect condition are possibly replacements. His account cannot be medically excluded;

— his descriptions of the application of an iron clamp screwed on his head can medically not be excluded or confirmed.

18. The Sub-Commission has no evidence before it from the respondent Government or other sources, contradicting the statements of Vardikos. As regards the possibility of fabrication referred to in paragraph 15(i) above, the Sub-Commission notes that his account of his ill-treatment is comparatively limited: for example, it is confined to one occasion and no suggestion is made of the familiar falanga, and the statement about food and drink at Lavrion is limited to its lack of provision by the prison authorities. Such restraint would not, in the view of the Sub-Commission, characterise a story invented for propaganda purposes. Further, the fact that allegations are repeated for propaganda purposes does not in itself make them untrue.

Certain positive evidence in the medical report of scars tends to confirm his statements. The Sub-Commission then accepts his account of his ill-treatment as substantially true.

[About 300 pages of additional evidence respecting other victims follows.]

Opinion of the commission

. . .

17. The Sub-Commission has investigated 30 cases to a substantial degree and expressed some conclusion with regard to 28 of them. With regard to these cases the Commission finds it established that:

(i)   torture or ill-treatment has been inflicted in 11 individual cases, namely:

— Vardikos, Vlassis, Leloudas, Miss Arseni, Mrs. Tsirka, Lendakis, Korovessis (by the Athens Security Police)

— Veryvakis (at the headquarters of the Athens Suburban Gendarmerie in Patissia)

— Meletis, Miss Pangopoulou (by the Security Police of Salonica)

— Livanos (at the 521 Marines Brigade camp near Aghia Paraskevi);

(ii) there has since April 1967 been a practice of torture and ill-treatment by the Athens Security Police, Bouboulinas Street, of persons arrested for political reasons, and that:

(a) this torture and ill-treatment has most often consisted in the application of 'falanga' or severe beatings of all parts of the body;

(b) its purpose has been the extraction of information including confessions concerning the political activities and associations of the victims and other persons considered to be subversive;

(iii) the evidence before the Commission of torture or ill-treatment having been inflicted on 17 other individuals demands further investigation, since it ranges from indications:

— Ambaticlos (by the Piraeus Security Police)

— Karaosman (at the Interrogation Centre of the Central Intelligence Service in Aghia Paraskevi)

and the establishment of *prima facie* cases:

— Miss Kallerghi, Petropoulos, Kiaos, Tsiloglou, Dakos (by the Athens Security Police)

— Notaras (by the Athens Security Police and on board the ship 'Elli')

to strong indications:

— Xintavelonis, Mrs. Papanicola (at the Athens Security Police)

— Panagoulis (at the 505 Marine Brigade camp near Dionysos)

— Papagiannakis and Yotopoulos (by the Piraeus Security Police)

— Nestor, Sipitanos and Pyrzas (in a military camp near the Sedes airfield in Salonica—Central Intelligence Service).

The Sub-Commission was in effect prevented, directly or indirectly, by the respondent Government from completing its investigation of these cases;

(iv) the competent Greek authorities, confronted with numerous and substantial complaints and allegations of torture and ill-treatment, having failed to take any effective steps to investigate them or to ensure remedies for any such complaints or allegations found to be true.[80]

18. The Commission also finds that:

(i) the conditions of detention in the cells in the basement of the Security Police building in Bouboulinas Street, in which persons arrested for political reasons have been held, are contrary to Article 3;

---

[80] Sub-sections (i) and (ii) were adopted by a majority of 12 members. Sub-sections (iii)—except the findings on 4 cases—and (iv) were adopted by a majority of 13 members. The findings on the cases of Ambaticlos, Karaosman, Papagiannakis and Yotopoulos were adopted by a majority of 10 members.

(ii) the combination of conditions described in Part VI above, in which political offenders
      are held in the Averoff Prison, and the extreme manner of the separation of detainees
      from their families and the conditions of gross overcrowding in the camps on Leros,
      also constitute breaches of Article 3.[81]

Resolution of the Committee of Ministers
of the Council of Europe

Resolution DH (70) 1
(Adopted by the Committee of Ministers on 15 April 1970)
The Greek Case
Applications No. 3321/67, Denmark v. Greece;
No. 3322/67, Norway v. Greece; No. 3323/67, Sweden v. Greece;
No. 3344/67, Netherlands v. Greece

The Committee of Ministers,

1. Having regard to Article 32 of the European Convention for the Protection of Human
Rights and Fundamental Freedoms (hereinafter called 'the Convention');

2. Having regard to the report drawn up by the European Commission of Human Rights
(hereinafter called 'the Commission') in accordance with Article 31 of the Convention and
relating to the Applications lodged on 20 September 1967 by the Governments of Denmark,
Norway and Sweden against the Government of Greece (Nos. 3321/67, 3322/67, 3323/67)
and on 27 September 1967 by the Government of the Netherlands against the Government of
Greece (No. 3344/67); ...

8. Considering that the Government of Greece has denounced on 12 December 1969, the
European Convention on Human Rights and the First Protocol and that, in accordance with
Article 65, paragraph 1 of the Convention, this denunciation will become effective on 13 June
1970;

9. Considering paragraph 2 of Article 65 of the Convention which provides that the denunciation 'shall not have the effect of releasing the High Contracting Party concerned from its
obligations under this Convention in respect of any act which, being capable of constituting
a violation of such obligations, may have been performed by it before the date at which the
denunciation became effective';

10. Voting in accordance with the provisions of Article 32, paragraph 1 of the
Convention;

11. Agreeing with the opinion of the Commission;

12. Decides:

(a) that the Government of Greece has violated Articles 3, 5, 6, 8, 9, 10, 11, 13 and 14 of
     the Convention and Article 3 of the First Protocol;

(b) that the Government of Greece has not violated Article 7 of the Convention and Article 1
     of the First Protocol;

---

[81] Sub-section (i) was adopted by a majority of 13 members. Sub-section (ii) was adopted by a majority
of 11 members.

13. Having regard to the denunciation of the Statute of the Council of Europe by the Government of Greece on 12 December 1969;

14. Having regard to the denunciation on the same date by the same Government of the European Convention on Human Rights and of its First Protocol, mentioned above;

15. Having regard to Resolution (69) 51 of 12 December 1969;

16. Having considered the proposals made by the Commission in accordance with paragraph 3 of Article 31 of the Convention;

17. Considering that the Greek Government has declared on 7 December 1969 that it considers the report of the Commission as 'null and void' and that it 'does not consider itself legally bound by the conclusions of the said report';

18. Considering that the Greek Government was given an opportunity to take part in the discussions of the Committee of Ministers when it was examining the report of the Commission, but in a letter of 19 February 1970 the Government stated that it had no intention whatsoever of doing so and that such a participation would be 'inconsistent with Greece's formal denunciation of both the Commission's report and the European Convention';

19. Considering that these circumstances and communications clearly established that the Greek Government is not prepared to comply with its continuing obligations under the Convention and thus with the system of collective protection of human rights established thereby, and that accordingly the Committee of Ministers is called upon to deal with the case in conditions which are not precisely those envisaged in the Convention;

20. Concludes that in the present case there is no basis for further action under paragraph 2 of Article 32 of the Convention;

21. Concludes that it must take a decision, in accordance with paragraph 3 of Article 32 of the Convention, about the publication of the report of the Commission;

22. Decides to make public forthwith the report drawn up by the Commission on the above-mentioned Applications;

23. Urges the Government of Greece to restore, without delay, human rights and fundamental freedoms in Greece, in accordance with the Convention and the First Protocol, taking into account, *inter alia*, the proposals made by the Commission which are attached hereto;

24. Also urges the Government of Greece, in particular, to abolish immediately torture and other ill-treatment of prisoners and to release immediately persons detained under administrative order;

25. And accordingly resolves to follow developments in Greece in this respect.

2. SHAME AT STRASBOURG

On-the-spot fact-finding has been less common for the European Commission and Court of Human Rights than for some other international institutions, such as the Inter-American Commission of Human Rights, probably because Strasbourg fact-finding is always related to a complaint brought pursuant to the Convention.[82] Indeed, on-the-spot investigations like that in the *Greek Case* have been characterized as 'rare'.[83]

However, it is worthwhile reviewing the *Greek Case* because it is the only example in a half century of a state being shamed by Strasbourg's fact-finding to a degree that it chose to leave the Council of Europe, albeit just before it was excluded by the other members of the institution. Expulsion is the only forcible sanction available to the Council when a state ignores findings of human rights violations. Is it enough? Was it enough in the *Greek Case*? Ultimately the military regime in Greece did collapse. Were the actions at Strasbourg in any way a contribution to the military regime's downfall? Let us look at the *Greek Case* in its political context.

The Greek military's coup d'état on 21 April 1967, was quickly followed on 24 April 1967, by a debate in the Consultative Assembly of the Council of Europe protesting infringements by the new Greek government of the European Human Rights Convention.[84] The four state complaints leading to the proceedings against Greece were lodged in response to a resolution of the Standing Committee of the Consultative Assembly of the Council of Europe on 23 June 1967:

[T]he Governments of the Contracting Parties to the European Convention on Human Rights [should] refer the Greek case, either separately or jointly, to the European Commission of Human Rights in accordance with Article 24 of the Convention.[85]

Before then, states bringing suit against other states before the Commission had had some sort of ethnic or religious link with the injured individuals, i.e., Greece with Greek Cypriots against the United Kingdom, Austria with ethnic Germans against Italy, and Ireland with Roman Catholics in Northern Ireland against the United Kingdom. Denmark, Norway, Sweden and the Netherlands had no such ethnic or religious ties to the Greek population. Rather, it seems that the four countries complained to the Commission because they felt they had a moral duty to do so. There was a sentiment, especially in the legal departments of the four Foreign Ministries, that if European human rights law was not employed against the Greek Colonels' military regime, the whole Strasbourg system would be endangered and the experiment in international human rights machinery defeated.[86]

Besides excluding Greece, the Council of Europe had little power to enforce an adverse decision of the Committee of Ministers. That exclusion was the Council's chief

---

[82] H. C. Krüger, 'The Experience of the European Commission of Human Rights', *International Law and Fact-Finding in the Field of Human Rights* 151 (B. G. Ramcharan ed. 1982).

[83] P. Leach, *Taking a Case to the European Court of Human Rights* 40 (2001).

[84] Coleman, 'Greece and the Council of Europe: the International Legal Protection of Human Rights by the Political Process', 2 *Israel Yearbook on Human Rights* 121–4 (1992).

[85] Buergenthal, 'Proceedings Against Greece Under the European Convention of Human Rights', 62 *American Journal of International Law* 441 (1968) (hereinafter cited as 'Buergenthal').

[86] Becket, 'The Greek Case Before the European Human Rights Commission', 1 *Human Rights Law Journal* 91, 94–6 (1970) (hereinafter cited as 'Becket').

'punishment' has been viewed by a disappointed Greek commentator as evidence of 'a total lack of effectiveness of the Convention, whether direct or indirect'.[87] However, Thomas Buergenthal, later President of the Inter-American Court of Human Rights, was more positive:

Had they [the four states] not referred this case ... [it] would have [been] unmistakably demonstrated that even as advanced a system for the international protection of human rights as the European Convention on Human Rights is doomed to fail whenever it must depend for its enforcement on disinterested governments.[88]

As the situation developed, were the Strasbourg human rights proceedings at all efficacious? Though Greece denounced the Convention on 12 December 1969, another commentator believed that the Commission's fact-finding, its Report and the Council's Resolution nonetheless constituted a significant restraint on the behaviour of the Greek authorities. Though it is difficult to demonstrate, it is most probable that fewer Greeks were tortured than otherwise might have been. The negotiations over a friendly settlement pushed the government to sign an agreement with the International Red Cross that imposed further restraints. Because of the Commission and international pressure the Greek government did not carry out serious reprisals against witnesses who testified before the Commission in Greece, and because these people testified, the truth was known abroad. The *Greek Case* cannot be considered a success in terms of protecting the human rights of Greeks, but it probably had something of a positive effect.[89]

A similar conclusion was reached by another observer:

Although invocation of the inter-state complaint procedure against it may have prompted Greece's decision to denounce the Council of Europe and the ECHR, the implementation of the complaint procedure arguably did more good than harm. The political motives so commonly associated with inter-state complaints were largely absent in the Greek cases. Greece returned to democracy several years later and the human rights situation improved drastically. While invocation of the inter-state complaint procedure was probably not the only cause of the eventual change in the Greek government, the in-depth and public consideration of the situation of human rights in Greece was a necessary adjunct to redemocratization, which might not have occurred as quickly without it. However, the political pressure exercised by the Consultative Assembly's Recommendation probably contributed to some degree to the resolution of the situation.[90]

---

[87] Bechlivanou, 'Greece', *The European Convention for the Protection of Human Rights: International Protection Versus National Restrictions* 151, 156 (Delmas-Marty ed. Chodkiewicz trans. 1992).

[88] Buergenthal, *supra* n. 85, at 450.

[89] Becket, *supra* n. 86, at 112–13.

[90] Leckie, 'The Inter-State Complaint Procedure in International Human Rights Law: Hopeful Prospects or Wishful Thinking?', 10 *Human Rights Quarterly* 249, 292 (1988).

It may well be that the increasing diplomatic isolation of Greece to which the *Greek Case* contributed made it difficult for the Colonels' regime to govern effectively. When Turkey invaded Cyprus in July 1974, the Greek military government was unable to respond meaningfully. The Colonels' regime then collapsed precipitously.[91]

[91] *See* R. Clogg, *A Short History of Modern Greece* 192–9 (1979).

3

THE EUROPEAN COURT OF HUMAN RIGHTS

The idea of using a regional international court to help protect human rights in Europe surfaced in the earliest debates leading to the European Human Rights Convention. Speaking as a representative of the United Kingdom, Winston Churchill declared at the first session of the Consultative Assembly of the Council of Europe on 17 August 1949:

[O]nce the foundation of human rights is agreed on the lines of the decisions of the United Nations at Geneva [the 1948 Universal Declaration of Human Rights]—but I trust in much shorter form—we hope that a European Court might be set up, before which cases of the violation of these rights in our own body of 12 nations might be brought to the judgment of the civilised world. Such a Court, of course, would have no sanctions and would depend for the enforcement of their judgment on the individual decisions of the States now banded together in this Council of Europe. But these States would have subscribed beforehand to the process, and I have no doubt that the great body of public opinion in all these countries would press for action in accordance with the freely given decision.[1]

Its jurisdiction made optional for many years by Article 46 of the European Human Rights Convention, the European Court of Human Rights was not constituted until 1958. Rarely used until the 1970s, the Court's caseload increased dramatically in the 1980s and 1990s. Nowadays, the European Court of Human Rights in Strasbourg ranks alongside the International Court of Justice in The Hague and the European Court of Justice in Luxembourg as one of the three premier courts of international adjudication.

This chapter begins in Section A by looking at the formal structure—the constitution—of the Court. Section B then explains the way in which the Court functions in practice by reviewing a case, *Sunday Times*, both as a sample Court judgment and to try to explain why the Court's judgments have, by and large, been accepted by the member states. Section C looks more thoroughly at Strasbourg remedies, using the *Barthold Case* to introduce the remedies available to the Court. Finally, Section D addresses three thorny question about efficacy: How does one measure the efficacy of the Strasbourg system? What is the relationship between the efficacy and the

---

[1] Council of Europe, 1 *Collected Edition of the Travaux Préparatoires* 34 (1975) (hereinafter cited as 'Travaux Préparatoires').

legitimacy of the Court? What does the efficacy of Strasbourg tell us about the efficacy of international law in general?

A. THE CONSTITUTION OF THE COURT

As with any public international institution, the European Court of Human Rights is created and defined by an international agreement. In this case, the European Convention on Human Rights serves as the constitution of the Court. Until 1999, the Court existed alongside the Commission both set up by Article 19 of the old Convention, to 'ensure the observation of the engagements undertaken by the High Contracting Parties in the present Convention'.[2]

Pursuant to old Article 46, '[a]ny of the High Contracting Parties may at any time declare that it recognises as compulsory *ipso facto* and without special agreement the jurisdiction of the Court in all matters concerning the interpretation and application of the present Convention'.[3] Eight state ratifications were needed to create the Court and in 1950 'it was generally doubted that this would ever happen'.[4] However, by 1958, eight states had consented to the jurisdiction of the Court, which became officially competent to hear cases on 3 September of that year.[5] As of 7 September 1994, all 30 states then party to the Convention had submitted to Article 46's compulsory jurisdiction.[6]

Since November 1998, the Court has been significantly refashioned under the terms of Protocol No. 11. As we have already seen, Protocol No. 11 merged, as of November 1999, the Commission into the Court and otherwise transformed the enforcement machinery of the Convention.[7] Section II of the new Convention is devoted to the new European Court of Human Rights.[8] New Article 19 constitutes the Court: '[to] ensure the observance of the engagements undertaken by the High Contracting Parties in the Convention and the Protocols thereto, there shall be set up a European Court of Human Rights, hereinafter referred to as "the Court". It shall function on a permanent basis'.[9]

---

[2] European Convention for the Protection of Human Rights and Fundamental Freedoms, 213 U.N.T.S. 221, E.T.S. 5, U.K.T.S. 71 (1953), signed at Rome 4 Nov. 1950; entered into force 3 Sept. 1953, Council of Europe print of Jan. 1994 (hereinafter cited as 'Old Convention'). For the creation of international institutions in general, *see* M. W. Janis, *An Introduction to International Law* 199–203 (4th edn. 2003) (hereinafter cited as 'Janis').   [3] Old Convention, *supra* n. 2, Art. 46(1).

[4] Sohn, 'Book Review', 57 *American Journal of International Law* 168, 169 (1963).

[5] European Commission of Human Rights, *Stock-Taking on the European Convention on Human Rights: The First Thirty Years: 1954 until 1984* 1.

[6] Council of Europe, *Chart of Signatures and Ratifications, as of 9 Sept. 1994* (hereinafter cited as 'Chart').

[7] Council of Europe, Convention for Protection of Human Rights and Fundamental Freedoms (ETS No. 5), signed at Rome 4 Nov 1950, entered into force 3 Sept 1953, as amended by Protocol No. 11 (ETS no. 155), signed at Strasbourg, 11 May 1994, entered into force 1 Nov. 1998, www.conventions.coe.int (accessed 14 Dec. 2006) (hereinafter cited as 'Convention'). The Convention is set forth in Appendix A.

[8] *Id.* Arts. 19–51.   [9] *Id.* Art. 19.

The number of judges is set at the number of High Contracting Parties,[10] presently 47; judges are to be of 'high moral character' and 'either possess the qualifications required for appointment to high judicial office or be jurisconsults of recognised competence'.[11] The judges 'sit on the Court in their individual capacity',[12] i.e., not as a representative of a state. Judges are elected by the Council of Europe's Parliamentary Assembly for renewable six-year terms, but they must retire at age 70.[13] The Court has a registry and 'shall be assisted by legal secretaries',[14] i.e., court clerks.

The Court as a whole is referred to as the 'Plenary Court', which elects its own President, two Vice-Presidents, Registrar and one or more Deputy Registrars.[15] As we have already examined in Chapter 2, the Court sits in three-judge Committees to determine the admissibility of applications submitted by individuals.[16] It also sits in seven-judge Chambers, the ordinary judicial panel, and in 17-judge Grand Chambers, special judicial panels for more important cases.[17] Article 30 provides that a Chamber is to relinquish jurisdiction to a Grand Chamber when a pending case 'raises a serious question affecting the interpretation of the Convention or the protocols thereto, or where the resolution of a question before the Chamber might have a result inconsistent with a judgment previously delivered by the Court'.[18]

In Chapter 2, we have already reviewed the pre-judgment functions of the Court.[19] If a case is deemed admissible and is not terminated by a friendly settlement and after fact-finding, the Court proceeds to a public hearing which is ordinarily open to the public.[20] 'If the Court finds that there has been a violation of the Convention or the protocols thereto, and if the internal law of the High Contracting Party concerned allows only partial reparation to be made, the Court shall, if necessary, afford just satisfaction to the injured party'.[21] Judgments of Chambers of the Court are final unless a case has been referred and accepted by a Grand Chamber, a decision made by a five-judge panel of a Grand Chamber; judgments of a Grand Chamber are final.[22] Final judgments of the Court are binding on states who are parties to a case.[23] 'The final judgment of the Court shall be transmitted to the Committee of Ministers, which shall supervise its execution'.[24]

Until October 1994, only the states party to the Convention and the Commission had standing to bring cases to the Court.[25] Most cases, however, were brought to the Court by the Commission. Though cases not referred to the Court were, by old Article 32, put within the 'adjudicatory' jurisdiction of the Council of Europe's Committee of Ministers, the Commission normally preferred to rely on the Court rather than the Committee of Ministers when the Commission sought a legally binding judgment,

---

[10] *Id.* Art. 20.
[11] *Id.* Art. 21(1).
[12] *Id.* Art. 21(2).
[13] *Id.* Arts. 22, 23.
[14] *Id.* Art. 25.
[15] *Id.* Art. 26.
[16] *Id.* Arts. 27–8.
[17] *Id.* Arts. 27, 30–1.
[18] *Id.* Art. 30.
[19] *Id.* Arts. 28, 29, 32–9.
[20] *Id.* Art. 40.
[21] *Id.* Art. 41.
[22] *Id.* Arts. 42–4.
[23] *Id.* Art. 46(1).
[24] *Id.* Art. 46(2).
[25] Old Convention, *supra* n. 2, Art. 44.

either to enforce its opinion against a recalcitrant government or when the Commission itself was closely divided.[26]

Although individuals did not for 40 years have standing to bring cases to the Court, private parties were almost always the initiators of the suits before the Commission which eventually reached the Court. It has long been recognized that in practice and in principle it was the individual, not the Commission, who was the true 'party' before the Court. As Sir Humphrey Waldock argued in 1960, appearing for the Commission before the Court in its first case, *Lawless*:

[T]he Commission, although not a Party to the case, participates in the proceedings and stands in a position intermediate between the Government and the individual. Moreover, if the Commission considers the rights of the individual to have been violated, it is the Commission's duty to say so in its report, and to present that opinion to the Court.... The function of the Commission before the Court, as we understand it, is not litigious: it is ministerial. It is not our function to defend before the Court, either the case of the individual as such or our own opinion simply as such. Our function, we believe, is to place before you all the elements of the case relevant for the determination of the case by the Court.[27]

Such a principle was fitting. One of the reasons the Strasbourg Court was fashioned in the first place was that the International Court of Justice at The Hague was and is still permitted to hear only complaints brought by states.[28] In *Lawless*, the Court rejected Ireland's arguments that the precedent of the International Court be followed and lawyers representing individuals be not allowed to argue before it:

[T]he Court must bear in mind its duty to safeguard the interests of the individual, who may not be a Party to any court proceedings [but] nevertheless the whole of the proceedings in the Court, as laid down by the Convention and the Rules of Court, are upon issues which concern the Applicant [and] accordingly, it is in the interests of the proper administration of justice that the Court should have knowledge of and, if need be, take into consideration, the Applicant's point of view.[29]

Originally, lawyers for individual petitioners could only appear before the Court at the discretion of the Commission and in the guise of rendering 'assistance' to the delegates of the Commission. With the adoption of new Rules of Court on 24 November 1982, effective January 1983, the initiation of proceedings before the Court was transmitted to the applicant, who was also invited to be individually represented. 'These provisions should avoid a recurrence of what happened in the *Golder Case*, when the applicant was apparently unaware of the fact that his case had come before the Court until he read newspaper reports about the proceedings'.[30]

---

[26] Nowak, Rosenmayr & Schwaighofer, 'Sixth International Colloquy about the European Convention on Human Rights', 7 *Human Rights Law Journal* 117, 120–1 (1986).

[27] Mahoney, 'Developments in the Procedure of the European Court of Human Rights: The Revised Rules of Court', 3 *Yearbook of European Law* 127, 128 (1983).

[28] *See* 1 *Travaux Preparatoires, supra* n. 1, at 226.

[29] 14 Nov. 1960, 1 E.H.R.R. 1, para. 15.

[30] Drzemczewski, 'The European Convention on Human Rights', 2 *Yearbook of European Law* 327, 328 (1982).

On 1 October 1994, the standing of individuals before the Court improved dramatically as Protocol No. 9 to the Convention came into force for 13 then consenting states.[31] Protocol No. 9, which was prepared and ready for signature in 1990, amended four articles of the old Convention, most importantly Articles 44 and 48, to include persons, non-governmental organizations and groups of individuals who have complained to the Commission among those who can refer a case to the Court. As we have already seen in Chapter 2, since 1 November 1998, persons, non-governmental organizations and groups of individuals are now entitled by the reforms wrought by Protocol No. 11 to bring cases against states party to the Convention to the Court, albeit in the first instance to three-judge admissibility committees.[32] Individuals are now, formally as well as practically, the real complainants before the Court.

We treat remedies more thoroughly in section C below, but, briefly here, the Court may not only decide whether the Convention has been violated; it may also award damages, the Convention's term being 'just satisfaction'. Article 50 of the old Convention provided that:

> If the Court finds that a decision or a measure taken by a legal authority or any other authority of a High Contracting Party is completely or partially in conflict with the obligations arising from the present Convention, and if the internal law of the said Party allows only partial reparation to be made for the consequences of this decision or measure, the decision of the Court shall, if necessary, afford just satisfaction to the injured party.[33]

Though it could be that the drafters of Article 50 meant it to be a last resort to be employed only when a national legal system failed to provide redress for a Court-decided violation of the Convention, in practice the Court has interpreted the just satisfaction article in a more activist fashion.[34] Looking to Article 52, 'the judgment of the Court shall be final',[35] the Court in *Ringeisen* in 1972 rejected Austria's assertion that applicants had to bring a new case after a judgment finding a violation of the Convention if applicants were to seek Article 50 redress:

> [Article 52's] sole object is to make the Court's judgment not subject to any appeal to another authority. It would be a formalistic attitude alien to international law to maintain that the Court may not apply Article 50 save on condition that it either rules on the matter by the same judgment which found a violation or that this judgment has expressly kept the case open.[36]

---

[31] Austria, the Czech Republic, Finland, Hungary, Ireland, Italy, Luxembourg, the Netherlands, Norway, Romania, Slovakia and Slovenia, Council of Europe, *Human Rights Information Sheet No. 34: January–June 1994* 2 (1995). [32] Convention, *supra* n. 7, Art. 34.

[33] Old Convention, *supra* n. 2, Art. 50.

[34] Gray, 'Remedies for Individuals Under the European Convention on Human Rights', 6 *Human Rights Law Review* 153, 156 (1986) (hereinafter cited as 'Gray'). [35] Old Convention, *supra* n. 2, Art. 52.

[36] 22 June 1972 (Article 50), 1 E.H.R.R. 524, paras. 17–18.

The Court's Article 50 judgments in *Ringeisen* and subsequent decisions 'removed a number of potential obstacles to victims of violations, thereby creating a possibility of both redress and development of the substantive law'.[37]

After making its judgment on the merits, the Court has sometimes postponed ruling on just satisfaction, permitting the state involved to settle on compensation or other redress with a private claimant. At other times, no such out-of-court settlement is possible and the parties have returned to the Court for an Article 50 ruling. In general, 'the Court has shown itself committed to the provision of swift reparation for individuals injured by violation of the Convention'.[38]

Article 50 has been replaced by the more succinct language of Article 41 of the new Convention, but with the same import:

If the Court finds that there has been a violation of the Convention or the Protocols thereto, and if the internal law of the High Contracting Party concerned allows only partial reparation to be made, the Court shall, if necessary, afford just satisfaction to the injured party.[39]

The 'High Contracting Parties undertake to abide by the final judgment of the Court in any case to which they are parties'; execution of the Court's decisions is entrusted to the supervision of the Committee of Ministers.[40] States have, generally, voluntarily complied with the Court's judgments.[41] Such compliance may involve payments to the injured party, as well as amendment of national law. Between 1959 and 1989, for example, the Court awarded 'just satisfaction' in 85 instances. These ranged from 100 Dutch guilders in *Engel* (about $40) to 1,150,000 Swedish Crowns (about $160,000) in *Spörrong and Lonnroth v. Sweden*.[42] We return to remedies in Section C, 'Remedies', and to questions of actual compliance in Section D, 'The Efficacy of the Court'.

B. THE ROLE OF THE COURT

The European Court of Human Rights did not become an effective legal instrument easily or rapidly. Although the Convention was signed in 1950, and entered into force in 1953, for 20 years it was, in the words of Jochen Frowein, a Vice President of the Commission, 'a sleeping beauty, frequently referred to but without much impact'.[43] It seems that the right of access of private suitors has been crucial to bringing the system

---

[37] J. G. Merrills, *The Development of International Law by the European Court of Human Rights* 63–6 (1993) (hereinafter cited as 'Merrills').   [38] Gray, *supra* n. 34, at 171.

[39] Convention, *supra* n. 7, Art. 41.   [40] Convention, *supra* n. 7, Art. 46.

[41] *See* Ganshof van der Meersch, 'European Court of Human Rights', 8 *Encyclopedia of Public International Law* 192, 205 (1985); Merrills, *supra* n. 37, at 2.

[42] 23 Sept. 1982, 5 E.H.R.R. 35.

[43] Frowein, 'European Integration Through Fundamental Rights', 18 *Journal of Law Reform* 5, 8 (1984).

of European human rights law alive. Between 1955 and 1997, there were only 13 state petitions filed with the Commission, but there were 39,034 private claims.[44]

Comparing the business of the European Court of Human Rights to that of the International Court of Justice, one is struck by how much it is the access of private claimants to the European human rights system that explains the difference in case-load. Unlike the work of the International Court which has remained more or less static for more than 80 years,[45] the activity of the European Court of Human Rights has been rapidly growing. While there were only ten judgments delivered by the European Court in the 1960s, there were 26 judgments in the 1970s, 169 in the 1980s, 809 in the 1990s and, in the first six years of the 2000s, already 4,954, an annual average more than 100 times that of the ICJ.

If the Court finds that the internal law of a state violates the Convention, then the state is obliged at international law to alter that law. The Court, however, neither has the authority to alter municipal law nor will it instruct the state on how a change in municipal law ought to be made. As the Court ruled in *Marckx* in 1979: 'It is for the respondent State, and the respondent State alone, to take the measures it considers appropriate to assure that its domestic law is coherent and consistent'.[46] This latitude may mean that there will be lingering doubts about whether the measures taken by the respondent government bring the state fully into compliance with the Convention and the Court's judgment.[47]

The Court has been increasingly willing to find states in violation of the Convention. In its early decisions, the Court seemed anxious to reassure its member states that it would be sensitive to their concerns and traditions. For example, in 1961, in its first substantive decision, *Lawless*, the Court decided that although Ireland would have otherwise violated Articles 5 and 6 of the Convention by detaining an IRA suspect for five months without trial, the state was permitted to deviate from the strict rules of the Convention because it was justified under the Convention's Article 15 in declaring a 'public emergency threatening the life of the nation' and taking extraordinary measures.[48] While decisions such as *Lawless* might have reassured states, they did little to encourage individual petitions. It was only in 1968, 18 years after the signing of the European Convention on Human Rights and almost 10 years after the Court became competent to hear cases, that a decision, *Neumeister*, was rendered against a member state, the Court holding that Austria's detention without trial for 26 months

---

[44] 1997 *Yearbook of the European Convention on Human Rights* 76–9 (1998).

[45] Between 1921 and 1945, the Permanent Court of International Justice issued roughly three or four decisions a year; the record of the International Court of Justice between 1946 and 1990 has been roughly the same. Janis, *supra* n. 2, at 126.

[46] 13 June 1979, 2 E.H.R.R. 330, para. 20. And *see* Chapter 14(B).

[47] *See*, e.g., Van Dijk, 'The Benthem Case and Its Aftermath in the Netherlands', 34 *Netherlands International Law Review* 5, 9–24 (1987). Article 52 of the Convention obliges member states upon request by the Secretary General of the Council of Europe to 'furnish an explanation of the manner in which its internal law ensures the effective implementation of any of the provisions of the Convention' (and *see* Chapter 14 below).

[48] 1 July 1961, 1 E.H.R.R. 15, paras. 54–63 (and *see* Chapter 12(H)).

of a businessman accused of tax fraud violated Article 5's guarantees to a trial within a reasonable time or to a release pending trial.[49] Even more encouraging to private litigants, beginning in the late 1970s, the Strasbourg judges were increasingly ready to upset member states with decisions that stretch the language of the Convention.[50]

However, this readiness to upset states was a risky business. States did not need to accept either the jurisdiction of the Court or the right of individual petition. Both were optional clauses, part of the compromise reached in the process of drafting the Convention.[51] If the Court was perceived by a state as going 'too far', then that state could have decided not to renew its acceptance of the optional clauses. Just such a perception might have arisen as a result of the *Sunday Times Case*. Why it did not may tell us something important not only about the development of the Court but also about its efficacy.

1. THE SUNDAY TIMES V. UNITED KINGDOM

Judgment of 26 April 1979
2 E.H.R.R. 245

8. Between 1958 and 1961 Distillers Company (Biochemicals) Limited ('Distillers') manufactured and marketed under license in the United Kingdom drugs containing an ingredient initially developed in the Federal Republic of Germany and known as thalidomide. The drugs were prescribed as sedatives for, in particular, expectant mothers. In 1961 a number of women who had taken the drugs during pregnancy gave birth to children suffering from severe deformities; in the course of time there were some 250 such births in all. Distillers withdrew all drugs containing thalidomide from the British market in November of the same year. . . .

10. . . . [B]y 1971, three hundred and eighty-nine claims in all were pending against Distillers. Apart from a statement of claim in one case and a defence delivered in 1969, no further steps were taken in those actions where writs had been issued. Distillers had announced in February 1968 that they would provide a substantial sum for the benefit of the remaining three hundred and eighty-nine claimants and both sides were anxious to arrive at a settlement out of court. The case in fact raised legal issues of considerable difficulty under English law. Had any of the actions come on for trial, they would have been heard by a professional judge sitting without a jury.

In 1971 negotiations began on a proposal by Distillers to establish a charitable trust fund for all the deformed children other than those covered by the 1968 settlement. The proposal was made subject to the condition that all the parents accepted but five refused, one, at least, because payments out of the fund would have been based on need. An application, on behalf of the parents who would have accepted, to replace those five by the Official Solicitor as next

---

[49] 27 June 1968, 1 E.H.R.R. 91; *see* Beddard, *Human Rights and Europe* 11 (1980) (hereinafter cited as 'Beddard').

[50] C. C. Morrisson, *The Dynamics of Development in the European Human Rights System* 19 (1981).

[51] *See* the legislative history in Chapter 1.

friend was refused by the Court of Appeal in April 1972. During subsequent negotiations, the original condition was replaced by a requirement that 'a substantial majority' of the parents consented. By September 1972 a settlement involving the setting-up of a £3,250,000 trust fund had been worked out and was expected to be submitted in October to the court for approval.

11. Reports concerning the deformed children had appeared regularly in *The Sunday Times* since 1967 and in 1968 it had ventured some criticism of the settlement concluded in that year. There had also been comment on the children's circumstances in other newspapers and on television. In particular, in December 1971, the *Daily Mail* published an article which prompted complaints from parents that it might jeopardise the settlement negotiations in hand; the *Daily Mail* was 'warned off' by the Attorney-General in a formal letter threatening sanctions under the law of contempt of court but contempt proceedings were not actually instituted. On 24 September 1972, *The Sunday Times* carried an article entitled 'Our Thalidomide Children: A Cause for National Shame': this examined the settlement proposals then under consideration, describing them as 'grotesquely out of proportion to the injuries suffered', criticised various aspects of English law on the recovery and assessment of damages in personal injury cases, complained of the delay that had elapsed since the births and appealed to Distillers to make a more generous offer. The article contained the following passage:

'...the thalidomide children shame Distillers...there are times when to insist on the letter of the law is as exposed to criticism as infringement of another's legal rights. The figure in the proposed settlement is to be £3.25 million spread over 10 years. This does not shine as a beacon against pre-tax profits last year of £64.8 million and company assets worth £421 million. Without in any way surrendering on negligence, Distillers could and should think again'.

A footnote in the article announced that 'in a future article *The Sunday Times* [would] trace how the tragedy occurred'. On 17 November 1972, the Divisional Court of the Queen's Bench Division granted the Attorney-General's application for an injunction restraining publication of this future article on the ground that it would constitute contempt of court...

17. The unpublished article which was the subject of the injunction opened with a suggestion that the manner of marketing thalidomide in Britain left a lot to be desired. It stated that Distillers:

'— relied heavily on the German tests and had not completed full trials of its own *before* marketing the drug;

— failed to uncover in its research into medical and scientific literature the fact that a drug related to thalidomide could cause monster births;

— before marketing the drug did no animal tests to determine the drug's effect on the foetus;

— accelerated the marketing of the drug for commercial reasons. Were not deflected by a warning from one of its own staff that thalidomide was far more dangerous than had been supposed;

— were not deflected by the discovery that thalidomide could damage the nervous system, in itself a hint that it might damage the foetus;

— continued to advertise the drug as safe for pregnant women up to a month from when it was withdrawn'.

The body of the article described how, after their apparently disappointing initial ventures into pharmaceutics, Distillers learned in 1956 that the German firm of *Chemie Gruenenthal* had developed a sedative considered harmless and unique—thalidomide. The very large market existing at the time for sedatives was becoming overcrowded and Distillers thought it necessary to act quickly. Their decision to market the drug was taken before they had seen technical information, other than the transcript of a German symposium, and before carrying out independent tests. Indeed, they seemed to believe that thalidomide would not need elaborate tests. Distillers put in hand a search of scientific literature but failed to discover the results of research in 1950 by a Dr. Thiersch showing that a chemical related to thalidomide could cause monster births; opinions differed as to whether his work should have been found.

Sales of thalidomide began in Germany in October 1957 and Distillers were committed under their licensing agreement to commence marketing in April 1958. They put the programme for the drug's launch in hand even though clinical trials were behind. Results of the first British trials were published in January 1958: it had been found that thalidomide suppressed the work of the thyroid gland and that its method of action was unknown; the researcher warned that more tests were needed. Distillers did not rely on this advice, basing their decision on 'flimsy' evidence, namely other trials in the United Kingdom and assurances concerning the results of research in Germany. The warning about anti-thyroid effects was particularly relevant since it was known that drugs affecting the thyroid could affect unborn children; it was reasonable to argue that Distillers should have delayed launching the drug pending further tests.

On 14 April 1958, continued the article, thalidomide went on sale in Britain, advertised as 'completely safe'. At the end of 1959, Distillers' pharmacologist discovered that thalidomide in liquid form was highly poisonous and that an overdose might be lethal, but his report was never published and the liquid product went on sale in July 1961. In December 1960, it was reported that patients who had taken thalidomide in the tablet form in which it had firstly been on sale showed symptoms of peripheral neuritis; this news had the result of holding up an application to market thalidomide in the United States of America where it was, in fact, never sold. Further cases of peripheral neuritis were reported in 1961 but Distillers' advertising continued to stress the drug's safety.

Early in 1961 children were born in the United Kingdom with deformities but there was at the time nothing to connect them with thalidomide. However, between May and October, a doctor in Australia discovered that the common factor in a number of monster births was that the mothers had taken thalidomide during pregnancy. This was reported to *Chemie Gruenenthal* on 24 November who withdrew the drug two days later following newspaper disclosures. Distillers ended the public sale of thalidomide immediately afterwards. Tests on animals, published in April 1962, confirmed that thalidomide caused deformities but sales to hospitals were not ended until December 1962.

The draft article concluded as follows:

'So the burden of making certain that thalidomide was safe fell squarely on [Distillers]. How did the company measure up to this heavy responsibility? It can be argued that:

1. [Distillers] should have found all the scientific literature about drugs related to thalidomide. It did not.

2. It should have read Thiersch's work on the effects on the nervous system of drugs related to thalidomide, have suspected the possible action on unborn babies and therefore have done tests on animals for teratogenic effect. It did not.

3. It should have done further tests when it discovered that the drug had antithyroid activity and unsuspected toxicity. It did not.

4. It should have had proof before advertising the drug as safe for pregnant women that this was in fact so. It did not.

For [Distillers] it could be argued that it sincerely believed that thalidomide was free from any toxicity at the time it was first put on the market in Britain; that peripheral neuritis did not emerge as a side effect until the drug had been on sale in Britain for two years; that testing for teratogenic effects was not general in 1958; that if tests had been done on the usual laboratory animals nothing would have shown because it is only in the New Zealand white rabbit that thalidomide produces the same effects as in human beings; and, finally, that in the one clinical report of thalidomide being given to pregnant women no serious results followed (because thalidomide is dangerous only during the first 12 weeks of pregnancy)...

There appears to be no neat set of answers...'.

21. Distillers made a formal complaint to the Attorney-General that *The Sunday Times* article of 24 September 1972 constituted contempt of court in view of the litigation still outstanding and, on 27 September, the Solicitor-General, in the absence of the Attorney-General, wrote to the editor of *The Sunday Times* to ask him for his observations. The editor, in his reply, justified that article and also submitted the draft of the proposed future article for which he claimed complete factual accuracy. The Solicitor-General enquired whether the draft had been seen by any of the parties to the litigation, as a consequence of which a copy of the draft was sent by *The Sunday Times* to Distillers on 10 October. On the previous day, *The Sunday Times* had been advised that the Attorney-General had decided to take no action in respect of the matter already published in September and October; Distillers also took no action. On 11 October, the Attorney-General's Office informed *The Sunday Times* that, following representations by Distillers, the Attorney-General had decided to apply to the High Court in order to obtain a judicial decision on the legality of the publication of the proposed article. On the following day, he issued a writ against Times Newspapers Ltd. in which he claimed an injunction 'to restrain the defendants... by themselves, their servants or agents or otherwise, from publishing or causing or authorising to be published or printed an article in draft dealing, *inter alia*, with the development, distribution and use of the drug thalidomide, a copy of which article had been supplied to the Attorney-General by the defendants'.

22. The Attorney-General's application was heard by three judges of the Queen's Bench Division from 7 to 9 November 1972; on 17 November the court granted the injunction.

In its judgment the court remarked:

'the article does not purport to express any views as to the legal responsibility of Distillers... but... is in many respects critical of Distillers and charges them with neglect in regard to their own failure to test the product, or their failure to react sufficiently sharply to warning signs obtained from the tests by others. No one reading the article could... fail to gain the impression that the case against Distillers on the footing of negligence was a substantial one'.

The editor of *The Sunday Times* had indicated that any libel proceedings following publication would be defended by a plea that the contents of the article were true and the court approached the article on the footing that it was factually accurate.

23. The reasoning in the court's judgment may be summarised as follows. The objection to unilateral comment, prior to conclusion of the court hearing, was that it might prevent the due and impartial administration of justice by affecting and prejudicing the mind of the tribunal itself, by affecting witnesses who were to be called or by prejudicing the free choice and conduct of a party to the litigation. It was the third form of prejudice that was relevant to the present case...

24. An appeal by Times Newspapers Ltd. against the Divisional Court's decision was heard by the Court of Appeal from 30 January to 2 February 1973. The court had before it an affidavit by the editor of *The Sunday Times* setting out developments in the intervening period both in the case itself and in public discussion thereof. With the leave of the court, counsel for Distillers made submissions on the contents of the proposed article, pointing to errors he said it contained. On 16 February, the Court of Appeal discharged the injunction....

25. Lord Denning said that the proposed article:

> '...contains a detailed analysis of the evidence against Distillers. It marshals forcibly the arguments for saying that Distillers did not measure up to their responsibility. Though, to be fair, it does summarise the arguments which could be made for Distillers'....

'Trial by newspaper', continued Lord Denning, must not be allowed. However, the public interest in a matter of national concern had to be balanced against the interest of the parties in a fair trial or settlement; in the present case the public interest in discussion outweighed the potential prejudice to a party. The law did not prevent comment when litigation was dormant and not being actively pursued....

28. Following the Court of Appeal's decision, *The Sunday Times* refrained from publishing the proposed article so as to enable the Attorney-General to appeal. The Court of Appeal refused him leave to appeal but this was granted by the House of Lords on 1 March 1973. The hearing before the House of Lords was held in May 1973. On 18 July 1973, the House gave judgment unanimously allowing the appeal and subsequently directed the Divisional Court to grant an injunction in the terms set out in paragraph 34 below....

29. Lord Reid said that the House must try to remove the uncertainty which was the main objection to the present law. The law of contempt had to be founded entirely on public policy; it was not there to protect the rights of parties to a litigation but to prevent interference with the administration of justice and should be limited to what was reasonably necessary for the purpose. Freedom of speech should not be limited more than was necessary but it could not be allowed where there would be real prejudice to the administration of justice....

The Court of Appeal had wrongly described the actions as 'dormant' since settlement negotiations were in hand and improper pressure on a litigant to settle could constitute contempt. As for the Court of Appeal's balancing of competing interests, Lord Reid said:

> '...contempt of court has nothing to do with the private interests of litigants. I have already indicated the way in which I think that a balance must be struck between the public interest in freedom of speech and the public interest in protecting the administration of justice from interference. I do not see why there should be any difference in principle between a case which is thought to have news value and one which is not. Protection of the administration of justice is equally important whether or not the case involves important general issues'.

Lord Reid concluded that publication of the article should be postponed for the time being in the light of the circumstances then prevailing; however, if things dragged on indefinitely, there would have to be a reassessment of the public interest in a unique situation.

[Summary of the concurring opinion of Lord Morris of Borth-y-Gest in the House of Lords omitted.]...

31. Lord Diplock said that contempt of court was punishable because it undermined the confidence of the parties and of the public in the due administration of justice. The due administration of justice required that all citizens should have unhindered access to the courts; that they should be able to rely on an unbiased decision based only on facts proved in accordance with the rules of evidence; that, once a case was submitted to a court, they should be able to rely upon there being no usurpation by any other person, for example in the form of 'trial by newspaper', of the function of the court. Conduct calculated to prejudice any of these requirements or to undermine public confidence that they would be observed was contempt of court...

[Summaries of concurring opinions of Lord Simon of Glaisdale and Lord Cross of Chelsea in the House of Lords omitted.]...

34. On 25 July 1973, the House of Lords ordered that the cause be remitted to the Divisional Court with a direction to grant the following injunction:

'That...Times Newspapers Ltd., by themselves, their servants, agents or otherwise, be restrained from publishing, or causing or authorizing or procuring to be published or printed, any article or matter which prejudges the issues of negligence, breach of contract or breach of duty, or deals with the evidence relating to any of the said issues arising in any actions pending or imminent against Distillers...in respect of the development, distribution or use of the drug "thalidomide"'.

The defendants were granted liberty to apply to the Divisional Court for discharge of the injunction.

The Divisional Court implemented the above direction on 24 August 1973.

35. On 23 June 1976, the Divisional Court heard an application by the Attorney-General for the discharge of the injunction. It was said on behalf of the Attorney-General that the need for the injunction no longer arose; most of the claims against Distillers had been settled and there were only four extant actions which could by then have been brought before the courts if they had been pursued diligently. As there was a conflicting public interest in *The Sunday Times* being allowed to publish 'at the earliest possible date', the Attorney-General submitted the matter to the court as one where the public interest no longer required the restraint. The court, considering that the possibility of pressure on Distillers had completely evaporated, granted the application...

[A discussion of the Phillimore Report on the Law of Contempt issued in December 1974 omitted.]...

38. In their application, lodged with the Commission on 19 January 1974, the applicants claimed that the injunction, issued by the High Court and upheld by the House of Lords, to restrain them from publishing an article in *The Sunday Times* dealing with thalidomide children and the settlement of their compensation claims in the United Kingdom constituted a breach of Article 10 of the Convention. They further alleged that the principles upon which the

decision of the House of Lords was founded amounted to a violation of Article 10 and asked the Commission to direct or, alternatively, to request the Government to introduce legislation overruling the decision of the House of Lords and bringing the law of contempt of court into line with the Convention.

39. In its decision of 21 March 1975, the Commission, after describing the question before it as 'whether the rules of contempt of court as applied in the decision of the House of Lords granting the injunction are a ground justifying the restriction under Article 10 §2', declared admissible and accepted the application...

[Additional allegations were made by the applicant under Articles 14 and 18 of the Convention; though considered by the Commission and by the Court, neither additional allegation was held by either body to have demonstrated a violation of the Convention.]...

41. In its report of 18 May 1977, the Commission...expressed the opinion:

— by eight votes to five, that the restriction imposed on the applicant's right to freedom of expression was in breach of Article 10 of the Convention; ...

42. The applicants claim to be the victims of a violation of Article 10 of the Convention which provides:

'1. Everyone has the right to freedom of expression. This right shall include freedom to hold opinions and to receive and impart information and ideas without interference by public authority and regardless of frontiers. This Article shall not prevent States from requiring the licensing of broadcasting, television or cinema enterprises.

2. The exercise of these freedoms, since it carries with it duties and responsibilities, may be subject to such formalities, conditions, restrictions or penalties as are prescribed by law and are necessary in a democratic society, in the interests of national security, territorial integrity or public safety, for the prevention of disorder or crime, for the protection of health or morals, for the protection of the reputation or rights of others, for preventing the disclosure of information received in confidence, or for maintaining the authority and impartiality of the judiciary'....

45. It is clear that there was an 'interference by public authority' in the exercise of the applicants' freedom of expression which is guaranteed by paragraph 1 of Article 10. Such an interference entails a 'violation' of Article 10 if it does not fall within one of the exceptions provided for in paragraph 2...The Court therefore has to examine in turn whether the interference in the present case was 'prescribed by law', whether it had an aim or aims that is or are legitimate under Article 10 §2 and whether it was 'necessary in a democratic society' for the aforesaid aim or aims.

...

[In parts of the Court's opinion omitted here, it was held that there had been an 'interference with the applicants' freedom of expression' but that 'the interference with the applicants' freedom of expression had an aim that is legitimate under Article 10 §2'. The crucial part of the judgment then followed: 'Was the interference "necessary in a democratic society" for maintaining the authority of the judiciary?']

65. As the Court remarked in its *Handyside* judgment, freedom of expression constitutes one of the essential foundations of a democratic society; subject to paragraph 2 of Article 10,

it is applicable not only to information or ideas that are favourably received or regarded as inoffensive or as a matter of indifference, but also to those that offend, shock or disturb the State or any sector of the population.

These principles are of particular importance as far as the press is concerned. They are equally applicable to the field of the administration of justice, which serves the interests of the community at large and requires the co-operation of an enlightened public. There is general recognition of the fact that the courts cannot operate in a vacuum. Whilst they are the forum for the settlement of disputes, this does not mean that there can be no prior discussion of disputes elsewhere, be it in specialised journals, in the general press or amongst the public at large. Furthermore, whilst the mass media must not overstep the bounds imposed in the interests of the proper administration of justice, it is incumbent on them to impart information and ideas concerning matters that come before the courts just as in other areas of public interest. Not only do the media have the task of imparting such information and ideas: the public also has a right to receive them.

To assess whether the interference complained of was based on 'sufficient' reasons which rendered it 'necessary in a democratic society', account must thus be taken of any public interest aspect of the case. The Court observes in this connection that, following a balancing of the conflicting interests involved, an absolute rule was formulated by certain of the Law Lords to the effect that it was not permissible to prejudge issues in pending cases: it was considered that the law would be too uncertain if the balance were to be struck anew in each case. Whilst emphasizing that it is not its function to pronounce itself on an interpretation of English law adopted in the House of Lords, the Court points out that it has to take a different approach. The Court is faced not with a choice between two conflicting principles but with a principle of freedom of expression that is subject to a number of exceptions which must be narrowly interpreted. In the second place, the Court's supervision under Article 10 covers not only the basic legislation but also the decision applying it. It is not sufficient that the interference involved belongs to that class of the exceptions listed in Article 10 §2 which has been invoked; neither is it sufficient that the interference was imposed because its subject-matter fell within a particular category or was caught by a legal rule formulated in general or absolute terms: the Court has to be satisfied that the interference was necessary having regard to the facts and circumstances prevailing in the specific case before it.

66. The thalidomide disaster was a matter of undisputed public concern. It posed the question whether the powerful company which had marketed the drug bore legal or moral responsibility towards hundreds of individuals experiencing an appalling personal tragedy or whether the victims could demand or hope for indemnification only from the community as a whole; fundamental issues concerning protection against and compensation for injuries resulting from scientific developments were raised and many facets of the existing law on these subjects were called in question.

As the Court has already observed, Article 10 guarantees not only the freedom of the press to inform the public but also the right of the public to be properly informed.

In the present case, the families of numerous victims of the tragedy, who were unaware of the legal difficulties involved, had a vital interest in knowing all the underlying facts and the various possible solutions. They could be deprived of this information, which was crucially important for them, only if it appeared absolutely certain that its diffusion would have presented a threat to the 'authority of the judiciary'.

Being called upon to weigh the interests involved and assess their respective force, the Court makes the following observations:

In September 1972, the case had, in the words of the applicants, been in a 'legal cocoon' for several years and it was, at the very least, far from certain that the parents' actions would have come on for trial. There had also been no public enquiry.

The Government and the minority of the Commission point out that there was no prohibition on discussion of the 'wider issues', such as the principles of the English law of negligence, and indeed it is true that there had been extensive discussion in various circles especially after, but also before, the Divisional Court's initial decision. However, the Court considers it rather artificial to attempt to divide the 'wider issues' and the negligence issue. The question of where responsibility for a tragedy of this kind actually lies is also a matter of public interest.

It is true that, if the *Sunday Times* article had appeared at the intended time, Distillers might have felt obliged to develop in public, and in advance of any trial, their arguments on the facts of the case; however, those facts did not cease to be a matter of public interest merely because they formed the background to pending litigation. By bringing to light certain facts, the article might have served as a brake on speculative and unenlightened discussion.

67. Having regard to all the circumstances of the case on the basis of the approach described in paragraph 65 above, the Court concludes that the interference complained of did not correspond to a social need sufficiently pressing to outweigh the public interest in freedom of expression within the meaning of the Convention. The Court therefore finds the reasons for the restraint imposed on the applicants not to be sufficient under Article 10 §2. That restraint proves not to be proportionate to the legitimate aim pursued; it was not necessary in a democratic society for maintaining the authority of the judiciary.

68. There has accordingly been a violation of Article 10...

[The European Court then rejected applicants' arguments that the United Kingdom had violated Articles 14 and 18 of the Convention protecting against discrimination and against the use of restrictions in the Convention for improper purposes.]...

For These Reasons, The Court

1. *holds* by eleven votes to nine that there has been a breach of Article 10 of the Convention;

2. *holds* unanimously that there has been no breach of Article 14 taken together with Article 10;

3. *holds* unanimously that it is not necessary to examine the question of a breach of Article 18;

4. *holds* unanimously that the question of the application of Article 50 is not ready for decision.

2. ACCEPTANCE OF THE COURT

For more background on the thalidomide drug, see H. Sjostrom & R. Nilsson, *Thalidomide and the Power of the Drug Companies* (1972); M. L. Kellmer Pringle & D. O. Fiddes, *The Challenge of Thalidomide* (1970). In the United States, Dr. Francis

Kelley of the Food and Drug Administration resisted considerable pressure and prevented thalidomide from being sold. She was awarded the Distinguished Federal Civilian Service Award in 1962 by President Kennedy. R. A. Fine, *The Great Drug Deception* 167–81 (1972).

The *Sunday Times* was not just being critical of Distillers. It had a complaint about English law, i.e., that it was unclear as a matter of law that Distillers would actually be liable, as well as a grievance against the English legal system, i.e., that the lawyers and the courts were taking too long getting reasonable compensation to the thalidomide children. Several years after the English litigation was concluded, but before the judgment of the Strasbourg Court, the editor of the *Sunday Times*, Harold Evans, wrote about the motivation of the newspaper in pursuing the matter:

When the thalidomide children were born, many without arms and legs, around 1960, they were left to seek remedy through private litigation. No government inquiry was set up. No government settlement was offered. Some 60 parents in Britain issued writs against the Distillers Company.... From that moment on the press had to be silent...

[When] the *Sunday Times* became aware that the children were being offered sums so grossly inadequate to their real needs on any proper actuarial basis... it was decided to mount a campaign. The dilemma was that the very first article of the campaign would have provided a citation for contempt and made it stillborn... Thanks to the ingenious advice of James Evans, a lawyer with the *Sunday Times,* we found a way forward. We began a campaign on the moral issue of the low compensation, deliberately saying that the legal issue of negligence was outside our area and that the company denied negligence. But we also announced that in a future issue of the paper we would publish some documentary evidence on the manufacture of the drug.

Evans, 'British Law of Contempt Thwarts Speech and Justice', *Florida Bar Journal,* vol. 52, no. 6 (June 1978), at 462, 464–6. In a case like *Sunday Times* where a municipal legal system is itself under attack, there is an especially good reason to seek adjudication in an international court.

Just satisfaction was decreed by the Court in its Judgment of 6 November 1980, 3 E.H.R.R. 317. There, by a thirteen to three vote, the Court decided to award the *Sunday Times* the costs and expenses of its legal proceedings in Strasbourg before the Commission and the Court, a total of £22, 626.78. We look more at available remedies in Section C below.

Decisions such as the *Sunday Times Case* certainly had the potential for discouraging governments from accepting or maintaining the then optional provisions of the European Human Rights Convention. In the *Sunday Times Case,* there was no doubt that the legal issue—balancing the public's right to know and the *Sunday Times'* right to freedom of expression against Distiller's right to a trial by the courts, not by the media, and the interest of the British government in the integrity of the judicial process—was a very close one. Eight British judges (three at the trial level and five in the House of Lords), five European Human Rights Commissioners, and nine European Human Rights judges felt that the scales tilted towards granting an injunction against the *Sunday Times.* Three British judges (in the Court of Appeal), eight

European Human Rights Commissioners, and 11 European Human Rights judges felt that the balance went for permitting the *Sunday Times* to publish the thalidomide article. Of 44 judges and commissioners who considered the case, half went one way and half the other. Reasonable men and women could and did differ.

Should the Strasbourg Court have been permitted to rule as it did? A distinguished British international lawyer, F. A. Mann, for one, felt that the European Court of Human Rights had gone too far:

However uncertain its definition and scope may be in some respects, contempt of court is undoubtedly one of the great contributions the common law has made to the civilised behaviour of a large part of the world beyond the continent of Europe where the institution is unknown.... Yet it is that very branch of the law which the European Court of Human Rights has seriously undermined by, in effect, overturning the unanimous decision of the House of Lords in the *Sunday Times Case*—a unique event in the history of English law. In fact, it is probably no exaggeration to say that the gravest blow to the fabric of English law has been dealt by the majority of 11 judges coming from Cyprus, Denmark, Eire, France, Germany, Italy, Portugal, Spain, Sweden and Turkey, who over the dissent of nine judges from Austria, Belgium, Holland, Iceland, Luxembourg, Malta, Norway, Switzerland and the United Kingdom, decided in favour of the *Sunday Times*... The reader will have to make up his or her own mind... whether the Strasbourg Court arrogated to itself powers of factual appreciation which it cannot possibly exercise convincingly... and ask whether according to the standards and traditions of English law and English public life it is the decision of the House of Lords or that of the European Court of Human Rights which more correctly assesses the 'social need' and 'the legitimate aim' of a civilized society... and whether the level of judicial reasoning is higher in London or Strasbourg?[52]

One can understand Mann's discomfort with the 'overturning' of the House of Lords by the Strasbourg Court, but did the *Sunday Times Case* really raise the question of which court's 'judicial reasoning' was 'higher'? As another observer remarked about another judgment against the United Kingdom, the *Golder* case:[53]

Membership of a European institution, and submission to the jurisdiction of its organs, means the acceptance of a European way of thinking. The European Commission and Court of Human Rights are likely to construe texts in the 'continental', not the common law manner.[54]

In any event, the United Kingdom was and is not obliged to forever accept 'a European way of thinking'. For his part Mann strongly suggested that the proper reaction to the *Sunday Times Case* was for Britain to withdraw its acceptance of the optional clauses:

In a potentially wide variety of cases the European Court may assume a revising function and impose continental standards or, perhaps one should say, abuses upon this country which, in the name of freedom of the press and discussion, are likely to lower English usages by the substitution

---

[52] Mann, 'Contempt of Court in the House of Lords and the European Court of Human Rights', 95 *Law Quarterly Review* 348, 348–9, 352 (1979) (hereinafter cited as 'Mann').

[53] 21 February 1975, 1 E.H.R.R. 524.

[54] Dale, 'Human Rights in the United Kingdom—International Standards', 25 *International and Comparative Law Quarterly* (1976) 292, 302.

of trial by media for trial by courts. It is a matter for legislative concern whether this country is prepared to assume the risk to which it is now exposed. If the answer is in the negative a change of English law so as to comply with the standards of the Strasbourg judgment, yet to avoid trial by newspaper is unlikely to prove workable. Rather there will be no alternative but to do what the majority of countries have done, which have supplied the judges of the European Court of Human Rights, that is to say, to refuse to make or confirm the declaration under Article 25 of the Convention submitting this country to *individual* applications and thus to the jurisdiction of the European Court. It would be a regrettable and sad course to take, but it may be a necessary one, particularly if it is remembered how poor some of the other judgments of the Court have been [criticizing specifically the Court's decisions in *Northern Ireland* and *Tyrer*].[55]

Mann's view of the seriousness of the challenge posed to the United Kingdom by the *Sunday Times Case* was not shared by all English commentators. Christine Gray, for example, writing in the same year as Mann, felt that:

The European Court [in *Sunday Times*] did not in fact give much general guidance as to the appropriate future development of the law of contempt of court in England, for it is careful (perhaps over-careful if uniform standards are to be established in States Parties to the European Convention on Human Rights) not to substitute its own assessment of what might be the best policy in restricting the exercise of rights under the Convention for the assessment of the national authorities.[56]

Gray felt that the more important lesson of the *Sunday Times Case* was for the English judge: 'Perhaps this case will remind English courts of the potentially embarrassing consequences of ignoring the existence of the European Convention on Human Rights and encourage in them a more constructive approach to its application'.[57] We return to this lesson in Chapter 14.

As it turned out, Mann was right at least about the general significance of the case. The *Sunday Times Case* did have an impact both on the development of English law respecting contempt of court[58] and on the development of European human rights law respecting the margin of appreciation allowed governments in restricting freedom of expression.[59] Ronald St. John Macdonald, then a judge on the European Court, wrote that the *Sunday Times Case*, was a 'landmark case in the development of the margin of appreciation', which showed the Court ready to reach its own objective evaluation of

---

[55] Mann, *supra* n. 52, at 352–3.

[56] Gray, 'European Convention on Human Rights—Freedom of Expression and the Thalidomide Case', [1979] *Cambridge Law Journal* 242.

[57] *Id.* at 245.

[58] *See* Boyle, 'The Contempt of Court Act 1981', 6 *Human Rights Review* 148 (1981); Lowe, 'Contempt of Court Act of 1981', [1982] *Public Law* 20; Bailey, 'The Contempt of Court Act 1981', 45 *Modern Law Review* 301 (1982); Wong, 'The Sunday Times Case: Freedom of Expression Versus English Contempt-of-Court Law in the European Court of Human Rights', *Journal of International Law and Politics* 35, 67–75 (1984).

[59] *See infra* Chapter 6; *see also* Nathanson, 'The Sunday Times Case: Freedom of the Press and Contempt of Court Under English Law and the European Human Rights Convention', 68 *Kentucky Law Journal* 971, 1015–25 (1979–80); Wagner, 'Human Rights: Government Interference with the Press—The Sunday Times Case', 21 *Harvard International Law Journal* 260, 265–8 (1980); Duffy, 'The Sunday Times Case: Freedom of Expression, Contempt of Court and the European Convention on Human Rights', 5 *Human Rights Review* 17 (1980).

the balance of interests rather than test merely whether the state had balanced rights and derogations reasonably and in good faith.[60]

However, whatever his foresight in predicting the importance of the *Sunday Times Case*, Mann proved quite wrong about the effect of the case on the readiness of governments to subscribe to the optional provisions of the European Convention. Mann, as we saw, suggested that Britain might have 'no alternative but to do what the majority of countries have done, which have supplied the judges of the European Court of Human Rights, that is to say, to refuse to make or confirm the declaration under Article 25 of the Convention submitting this country to individual applications and thus to the jurisdiction of the European Court',[61] an observation riddled with errors. First of all, Mann's argument mistakenly intertwined the two optional clauses: Article 25 provided for private petitions and Article 46 provided for the Court's jurisdiction. Countries did, over time, opt for one and not the other. Second, Mann was also quite mistaken about the position of the majority of states in 1979. At the time of the *Sunday Times Case*, 14 of the 21 Council of Europe states had already accepted Article 25 individual petition and 16 had consented to Article 46 jurisdiction of the Court.[62] Third and most important, Mann's 'no alternative but' did not prove true. Not only did the United Kingdom continue to renew its pledges to both Article 25 and Article 46, but so did the other then consenting states. By 1995, 16 more states acceded to Article 25 and 14 more to Article 46.[63] Far from discouraging governments, the *Sunday Times* judgment and cases like it did not slow the accession of states to the legal machinery of European human rights law. Indeed, as we have seen, since 1998, the Convention has been amended to make these vital aspects of that machinery mandatory for all states and no longer optional.

How far can the Court and the Commission go without upsetting the applecart of state consent? Writing just after *Sunday Times*, Ralph Beddard remarked on the caution exercised by the system's institutions up to that time:

> It is, and always has been, obvious that winning the confidence of the parties and the public was a first step in any attempt to establish judicial determination of the protection of human rights. The last 27 years have not been free of difficulties, however, and the confidence of the parties was won, particularly in the early days, by very careful treading on the part of the Commission. There are cases which, if presented to the Commission today, would probably make greater progress than they did at the time of application. However, a Commission leaning heavily in favor of governments would have lost the confidence of the public.[64]

Such caution apparently paid off. Even in 1980, Sir Humphrey Waldock, then President of the International Court of Justice but previously President of both the European Commission and later the European Court of Human Rights, could conclude that 'whether the system set up by the European Convention on Human Rights

---

[60] Macdonald, 'The Margin of Appreciation in the Jurisprudence of the European Court of Human Rights', *International Law at the Time of Its Codification: Essays in Honour of Roberto Ago* 187, 197 (1987).

[61] Mann, *supra* n. 52, at 352–3.   [62] Chart, *supra* n. 6.   [63] *Id.*

[64] Beddard, *supra* n. 49, at 4.

is, in general, effective is not, I believe, today open to serious question'.[65] We test this proposition below in Section D.

C. REMEDIES

It is important to remember the many differences that exist between the limited remedies available to the European Court of Human Rights and those more plentifully at hand to an ordinary domestic court. As one observer summarized it, the 'European Court of Human Rights has no power to reopen domestic proceedings, annul a wrongful conviction, or ensure that the reforms instituted benefit the individual that brought the case in the first place'.[66] An American commentator marvelled at how good compliance has been with such weak remedies: '[T]he court has no means to itself bring about the attachment of assets or the use of other means of execution of judgment, much less the contempt power that American courts have available to bring about compliance with their orders'.[67] In this section, we use a freedom of expression case, *Barthold*, to introduce a brief analysis of what the Court can and can not do to remedy violations of the Convention.

1. BARTHOLD V. GERMANY

Judgment of 25 March 1985
7 E.H.R.R. 383

10. Dr. Barthold, who was born in 1926, is a veterinary surgeon practising in Hamburg-Fuhlsbüttel. In 1978 and until March 1980, his practice operated as a 'veterinary clinic', of which there were eight in Hamburg at the time. He closed down this clinic on 5 March 1980 but subsequently re-opened it on 1 January 1983.

11. By virtue of the Hamburg Veterinary Surgeons' Council Act of 26 June 1964 (Tierärztekammergesetz—'the 1964 Act'), the applicant is a member of the Hamburg Veterinary Surgeons' Council, whose task, among other things, is to ensure that its members comply with their professional obligations. These obligations are laid down principally in the Rules of Professional Conduct of Hamburg Veterinary Surgeons (Berufsordnung der Hamburger Tierärzteschaft—'the Rules of Professional Conduct'), which were promulgated

---

[65] Waldock, 'The Effectiveness of the System Set Up by the European Convention on Human Rights', 1 *Human Rights Law Journal* 1 (1980).

[66] D. Shelton, 'The Boundaries of Human Rights Jurisprudence in Europe', 13 *Duke Journal of Comparative and International Law* 147, 148 (2003).

[67] J. C. Sims, 'Compliance Without Remands: The Experience Under the European Convention on Human Rights', 36 *Arizona State Law Journal* 639, 645–6 (2004).

on 16 January 1970 by the Council in pursuance of section 8 sub-section 1 no. 1 of the 1964 Act and approved on 10 February 1970 by the Government (Senat) of the Land of Hamburg.

12. As the director and proprietor of a clinic, Dr. Barthold provided a round-the-clock emergency service. This was not necessarily the case as far as other veterinary surgeons were concerned.

From 1974 onwards, the applicant—who was one of the authors of the above-mentioned Regulations and who had insisted on the provision of a round-the-clock service by clinics— advocated within the Council that a regular night service involving the participation, by rota, of all veterinary surgeons should be organised. However, the majority of his colleagues voted on two occasions, on 19 December 1974 and 7 December 1979, against such a proposal.

13. On 24 August 1978, there appeared in the daily newspaper Hamburger Abendblatt an article signed by Mrs. B, a journalist, and entitled 'Tierärzte ab 20 Uhr schwer erreichbar— Warum "Shalen" die Nacht doch noch überlebte' ('Veterinary surgeons hard to reach after 8 p.m.—why "Shalen" managed to survive the night after all').

The article, 146 lines and 4 columns long, comprised an introductory paragraph and in brackets, in bolder type, the three following sub-heads: 'Auf eine spätere Zeit vertröstet' ('Put off until later'), 'Unfreundliche Absage' ('Unfriendly refusal') and 'Zur Not hilft die Polizei' ('Police to the rescue').

The introductory paragraph, in bold type, read as follows:

'When the owner of a domestic pet needs help at night for his beloved animal, he may often become desperate: not one veterinary surgeon can be contacted. This state of affairs ought now to improve. There are plans to bring in a new Act on veterinary surgeons, along the lines of the Hamburg legislation governing doctors. According to Dr. Jürgen Arndt, veterinary surgeon and Chairman of the Hamburg Land Association which is part of the Federal Association of Veterinary Surgeons (Bundesverband praktischer Tierärzte e.V.), "it will also regulate the emergency night service". At present, it is true, a few clinics voluntarily provide an emergency service from time to time, and [other] veterinary surgeons also help, but this is not on a regular basis and does not give pet-owners security. They only do it voluntarily'.

The journalist writing the article began by recounting the efforts made by the owners of the cat 'Shalen' to find a veterinary surgeon prepared to help them one evening between 7.30 and 10.00 p.m. After telephoning in vain to two veterinary practices and to the emergency service, apparently they at last struck lucky: 'Dr. Barthold, director of the Fuhlsbüttel veterinary clinic, intervened'. The journalist then quoted the applicant as saying: 'It was high time; ... [the cat] would not have survived the night'.

According to the author, Mrs. B, the particular case disclosed a problem, namely the inadequacy of the emergency service, at least on weekdays between 8 p.m. and 8 a.m. There followed a passage which read:

'"I think that in a big city such as Hamburg there ought to be a regular service for attending to animals", Dr. Sigurd Barthold emphasised.

Hamburg's animal lovers—added the journalist, summarising her interview with Dr. Barthold—"would then no longer have to get sore fingers trying to ring up veterinary surgeons, looking for one who is prepared to help. In that case it would not only be the clinics which would voluntarily be on emergency duty round the clock; each of the 53 practising veterinary surgeons would be on night duty once a month if arrangements were made for two of them to be on duty each night".

The fact that there is a demand for an emergency service at night-time is illustrated by Dr. Barthold by reference to the number of calls received by his practice between 8 p.m. and 8 a.m.: "Our telephone rings between two and twelve times each night. Of course these are not all emergency cases. Sometimes advice over the telephone is all that is needed."'

The author concluded the article by presenting under the third sub-head comments of Dr. Jürgen Arndt, 'Vice-Chairman of the Hamburg Veterinary Surgeons' Council and himself director of a clinic in Hamburg'. Believing that an emergency service organised on a rota basis 'would not release clinics from dispensing their voluntary service but would lessen the strain on them', Dr. Arndt said that he was actively trying to promote such a service. He added that the appropriate Hamburg authorities envisaged drafting the Act on veterinary surgeons during the fourth quarter of the year. Until it came into force, owners of animals would have to call one veterinary surgeon after another—or else the police, who would normally be prepared to help them.

The article was illustrated by two photographs. The larger, centrally placed, showed a cat and had the caption: 'Um das Leben der kleinen "Shalen" wurde gekämpft—erfolgreich' ('They fought for the life of little "Shalen"—and won'). The second one was an identity photo- graph which appeared alongside the title and introductory paragraph of the article; it was a photograph of the applicant, though its caption erroneously gave the name of Dr. Arndt.

Below the photograph of the cat and outside the space occupied by the article, there was a short text under the heading 'Hamburg—Stadt der Tiere' ('Hamburg—city of animals'), giving the number of domestic pets, veterinary surgeons and veterinary clinics in Hamburg and the telephone number of the emergency service available at weekends and on public holidays.

14. On 25 August 1978, the Hamburger Abendblatt once again published the applicant's photograph under the heading 'Unter dem Foto ein falscher Name' ('Wrong name under photo'), together with the following explanation: 'An error crept into our report yesterday on the emergency veterinary service. Unfortunately, the wrong name appeared under the photograph. The person in question is in fact Dr. Sigurd Barthold, director of the Fuhlsbüttel veterinary clinic'.

15. A number of Dr. Barthold's fellow practitioners, who regarded the article in question as publicity conflicting with the Rules of Professional Conduct, referred the matter to the asso- ciation 'PRO HONORE—Verein für Treu und Glauben im Geschäftsleben e.V'. ('Pro Honore Association for fairness and trustworthiness in business'—'Pro Honore'). This association was founded in 1925 by the businessmen of Hamburg and exists in order to 'ensure honesty and good faith in all spheres of business life' and 'in particular to combat unfair competition, fraud in connection with moneylending and corruption'.

Between 1978 and 30 September 1980, Pro Honore was operating simultaneously as a branch organisation of the Zentrale zur Bekämpfung unlauteren Wettbewerbs e.V. Frankfurt- am-Main (the Frankfurt-am-Main Central Agency for Combatting Unfair Competition—'the Central Agency'). The latter has been active for decades in curbing unfair competition, and counts among its members all the chambers of industry, trade and crafts and some 400 other associations, including the Federal Association of Veterinary Surgeons. The Hamburg Veterinary Surgeons' Council and the Deutsche Tierärzteschaft e.V, which is the umbrella organisation of the councils and private associations of veterinary surgeons, are not members of the Agency.

Under section 13 of the Unfair Competition Act of 7 June 1909 (Gesetz gegen den unlauteren Wettbewerb—'the 1909 Act'), Pro Honore and the Central Agency are empowered to bring against anyone engaged in business proceedings to restrain that person from breaking certain rules set forth in the Act.

16. On 4 September 1978, Pro Honore wrote to the applicant to say that it had been informed by certain veterinary surgeons that he had 'instigated or tolerated, in the Hamburger Abendblatt of 24 August 1978, publicity on [his] own behalf'. The letter went on to quote extracts from the article in question. The applicant was said to have thereby infringed section 1 of the 1909 Act in conjunction with Rule 7 of the Rules of Professional Conduct.

Section 1 of the 1909 Act stipulates that: 'Any person who in the course of business commits, for purposes of competition, acts contrary to honest practices (gute Sitten) may be enjoined from further engaging in those acts (Unterlassung) and held liable in damages'.

Rule 7 of the Rules of Professional Conduct deals with advertising and publicity (Werbung und Anpreisung) and reads as follows:

'It is contrary to the ethics of the profession (standeswidrig):

(a) to advertise publicly one's veterinary practice,

(b) to instigate or tolerate publicity or public acknowledgements on television, radio or in the press or other publications,

(c) to disclose case histories or methods of operation or of treatment elsewhere than in specialised journals (Fachzeitschriften),

(d) to co-operate with non-veterinarians for the purpose of publicising one's own practice'.

Pro Honore asserted its right to bring proceedings against the applicant for unfair competition and called on him, for the purposes of a friendly settlement of the matter, to sign an enclosed declaration. Under the terms of this declaration, he would undertake not to make publicity on his own behalf by instigating or tolerating press articles such as that which had appeared in the Hamburger Abendblatt, to pay the Central Agency 1000 DM for each infringement and to pay Pro Honore 120 DM by way of costs incurred in asserting its right (Rechtsverfolgung).

17. A lawyer replied two days later on behalf of the applicant. The request made to Dr. Barthold was, he wrote, very close to blackmail. It was presumptuous (Zumutung) to speak of unlawful publicity. The reproaches directed against his client, who had not instigated the article complained of, had done considerable damage to his personal and professional reputation.

The applicant's lawyer asked Pro Honore to confirm in writing that it would be dropping its claim against his client, withdrawing its accusations and expressing regret. He also asked for reimbursement of his costs and announced that he would sue Pro Honore if it failed to meet his demands within three days.

18. The Central Agency then applied to the Hamburg Regional Court (Landgericht) for an interim injunction.

An interim injunction was issued on 15 September 1978 by the presiding judge of the 15th Civil Chamber. This decision forbade the applicant

'to report in the press (except in professional journals), giving his full name, a photograph of himself and an indication of his occupation as director of the Fuhlsbüttel veterinary clinic, that at least on working days between 8 p.m. and 8 a.m., animal lovers in Hamburg would get sore fingers from trying to telephone veterinary surgeons ready to help them, in conjunction with (in Verbindung mit)

(a) the statement that only veterinary clinics were on voluntary emergency duty round the clock, and/or

(b) the statement that in his practice the telephone rang between two and twelve times between 8 p.m. and 8 a.m., though not all these calls were emergency cases and advice over the telephone would sometimes be sufficient, and/or

(c) the description of a case in which the owner of an animal had tried in vain one ordinary weekday between 7.30 p.m. and 10 p.m. to find a veterinary surgeon to treat his cat, until finally he was lucky enough to contact Dr. Barthold, who acted when it was more than "high time", and/or to contribute to such reports by giving journalists information'.

For each and every breach of the injunction, he was liable to a maximum fine (Ordnungsgeld) of 500,000 DM or non-criminal imprisonment (Ordnungshaft) of up to six months, the precise penalty to be fixed by the court.

[When the case was tried in the Regional Court, Dr. Barthold prevailed. The Central Agency then appealed.]

22. On 24 January 1980, the Hanseatic Court of Appeal, after declaring admissible the appeal brought by the Central Agency, upheld the Agency's grounds of appeal, which reiterated the terms of the injunction granted on 15 September 1978.

The Court of Appeal held in the first place that the applicant had infringed Rule 7, paragraph (a), of the Rules of Professional Conduct, a legally valid (formell rechtmässig) provision that was in conformity with the Basic Law as well as other superior rules of law. That Rule did not unreasonably limit Dr. Barthold's right to freedom of expression as guaranteed by Article 5 of the Basic Law, for there was nothing to prevent him from freely stating his opinion and in particular from criticising deplorable situations, even if this had the inevitable effect of producing publicity favourable to himself. The Agency was not seeking to restrain Dr. Barthold from making public pronouncements about veterinary assistance. Its application was concerned solely with a given form of conduct comprising—'cumulatively!'—several aspects: the giving of Dr. Barthold's full name, the reproduction of his photograph, the mention of his being director of the Fuhlsbüttel veterinary clinic and the statement that, at least between 8 p.m. and 8 a.m. on working days, animal lovers in Hamburg would get sore fingers trying to telephone a veterinary surgeon willing to help them...

Objectively, the article complained of entailed publicity for Dr. Barthold: compared to other veterinary surgeons, it presented him as an exemplary practitioner, thereby being particularly likely to incite the owners of sick animals to turn to his clinic. Such publicity exceeded the bounds of objective comment on matters of justified concern for the applicant. If in the future he were to supply the press with information necessary for the writing of an article, he should, in order to avoid any infringement of Rule 7, paragraph (a), of the Rules of Professional Conduct, ensure beforehand that the text to be published did not involve any unlawful publicity or advertising, by reserving a right of correction or by agreeing on the form of the article with the journalist.

...

23. Dr. Barthold challenged the judgment of 24 January 1980 before the Federal Constitutional Court. He repeated various arguments on which he had based his constitutional application in the interim proceedings, namely non-observance of equality before the law, of freedom of expression and of freedom to practise a profession, as safeguarded by Articles 3,

5 and 12 of the Basic Law, and incompatibility of the obligation to belong to the Veterinary Surgeons' Council with freedom of association, as guaranteed by Article 9 of the Basic Law. In addition, he alleged violation of his right to be heard, in particular by a legally competent court (gesetzlicher Richter). On this latter point, he claimed that it was not within the province of the civil courts to apply the Rules of Professional Conduct.

The Constitutional Court, sitting as a bench of three judges, dismissed the constitutional application on 6 October 1980, on the ground that it lacked sufficient prospects of success.

[Dr. Barthold then complained to the European Commission on Human Rights. The Commission unanimously found that Germany had violated Dr. Barthold's freedom of expression under Article 10.]

. . .

36. Article 10 of the Convention provides:

'1. Everyone has the right to freedom of expression. This right shall include freedom to hold opinions and to receive and impart information and ideas without interference by public authority and regardless of frontiers. This Article (art. 10) shall not prevent States from requiring the licensing of broadcasting, television or cinema enterprises.

2. The exercise of these freedoms, since it carries with it duties and responsibilities, may be subject to such formalities, conditions, restrictions or penalties as are prescribed by law and are necessary in a democratic society, in the interests of national security, territorial integrity or public safety, for the prevention of disorder or crime, for the protection of health or morals, for the protection of the reputation or rights of others, for preventing the disclosure of information received in confidence, or for maintaining the authority and impartiality of the judiciary'.

. . .

[The Court held that Article 10 applied to the case, that the interference was 'prescribed by law', and that it had a legitimate aim. However, Article 10(2) also requires that the interference was 'necessary in a democratic society'.]

58. ... As the Court has already had the occasion to point out, freedom of expression holds a prominent place in a democratic society. Freedom of expression constitutes one of the essential foundations of a democratic society and one of the basic conditions for its progress and for the development of every man and woman. The necessity for restricting that freedom for one of the purposes listed in Article 10 para. 2 must be convincingly established. When considered from this viewpoint, the interference complained of went further than the requirements of the legitimate aim pursued.

It is true, as was stated in the judgment of the Hanseatic Court of Appeal, that the applicant retained the right to express his opinion on the problem of a night service for veterinary surgeons in Hamburg and even, in so doing, to divulge his name, have a photograph of himself published and disclose that he was the director of the Fuhlsbüttel veterinary clinic. He was, however, directed not to supplement his opinion, when accompanied by such indications, with certain factual examples drawn from his own experience and illustrating the difficulties encountered by animal owners in obtaining the assistance of a veterinary surgeon during the night.

It may well be that these illustrations had the effect of giving publicity to Dr. Barthold's own clinic, thereby providing a source of complaint for his fellow veterinary surgeons, but in the particular circumstances this effect proved to be altogether secondary having regard to the principal content of the article and to the nature of the issue being put to the public at large. The injunction issued on 24 January 1980 does not achieve a fair balance between the two interests at stake. According to the Hanseatic Court of Appeal, there remains an intent to act for the purposes of commercial competition, within the meaning of section 1 of the 1909 Act, as long as that intent has not been entirely overridden by other motives ('nicht völlig hinter sonstigen Beweggründen verschwindet'). A criterion as strict as this in approaching the matter of advertising and publicity in the liberal professions is not consonant with freedom of expression. Its application risks discouraging members of the liberal professions from contributing to public debate on topics affecting the life of the community if ever there is the slightest likelihood of their utterances being treated as entailing, to some degree, an advertising effect. By the same token, application of a criterion such as this is liable to hamper the press in the performance of its task of purveyor of information and public watchdog.

59. In conclusion, the injunctions complained of are not proportionate to the legitimate aim pursued and, accordingly, are not 'necessary in a democratic society' 'for the protection of the rights of others', with the result that they give rise to a violation of Article 10 of the Convention.

...

III. Application of Article 50

62. In his memorial of 21 February 1984, Dr. Barthold made several comments as to the application of Article 50 in the present case, but at the hearings on 23 October 1984 his lawyer asked the Court to reserve the question.

The Government replied that they did not propose to make any statement on the subject in the absence of specific claims put forward by the Commission.

63. The question is therefore not yet ready for decision. Accordingly, it is necessary to reserve the matter and to fix the further procedure, taking due account of the possibility of an agreement between the respondent State and the applicant.

For These Reasons, the Court

1. Holds by five votes to two that there is breach of Article 10;

...

3. Holds unanimously that the question of the application of Article 50 is not ready for decision; accordingly,

    (a) reserves the whole of the said question;

    (b) invites the applicant to submit, within the forthcoming two months, his written comments on the said question and, in particular, to notify the Court of any agreement reached between himself and the Government;

    (c) reserves the further procedure and delegates to the President of the Chamber power to fix the same if need be.

BARTHOLD V. GERMANY (ARTICLE 50)

Judgment of 31 January 1986
13 E.H.R.R. 431

1. The case was referred to the Court by the European Commission of Human Rights ('the Commission') on 12 October 1983. The case originated in an application against the Federal Republic of Germany lodged with the Commission on 13 July 1979 by a national of that State, Dr. Sigurd Barthold, a veterinary surgeon.

2. By its judgment of 25 March 1985, the Court found that a court order restraining the applicant from repeating certain statements in the general press gave rise to a violation of Article 10 of the Convention.

The only outstanding matter to be settled is the question of the application of Article 50 in the present case. Accordingly, as regards the facts, the Court will confine itself here to giving pertinent details.

3. In his memorial of 21 February 1984, Dr. Barthold had made several comments as to an award of just satisfaction, but at the hearings on 23 October 1984 his lawyer had asked the Court to reserve the question. The respondent Government ('the Government') had stated that they did not intend to make any statement on the subject in the absence of specific claims put forward by the Commission.

In its judgment of 25 March 1985, the Court reserved the whole of the question. It invited the applicant to submit his written observations on the subject within two months and, in particular, to notify it of any agreement which he might reach with the Government.

4. After several extensions of time granted by the President of the Chamber, the registry received

— on 25 July 1985, the applicant's claims and then on 28 August and 7 October supplementary observations of his lawyer;

— on 16 December, the Government's comments;

— on 10 January 1986, a letter from the Secretary to the Commission acting on behalf of the Delegate.

5. On 16 December 1985, the applicant's counsel lodged in the registry the text of a 'partial settlement' (Teilvergleich) which reads as follows (translation from German):

'Partial Settlement in Barthold v. Federal Republic of Germany (10/1983/66/101) between the Government of the Federal Republic of Germany, represented by its Agent, Mrs. Irene Maier, Ministerialdirigentin, and Dr. Sigurd Barthold, Farnstrasse 41, 2000 Hamburg 63, represented by Dr. Eberhard Eyl, Richard-Wagner Strasse 109, 7640 Kehl.

Introduction

The European Court of Human Rights found in its judgment of 25 March 1985 (10/1983/66/101) that the rights guaranteed to the applicant by Article 10 (art. 10) of the European Convention on Human Rights had been violated. The Court reserved its decision on the application of Article 50 (art. 50) of the Convention and called on the applicant to inform it of any agreement reached between himself and the Federal Government. Through

Dr. Eyl, the applicant has informed the Court of his compensation claims in his memorials of 25 July, 26 August and 1 October 1985.

The Federal Government and the applicant have reached the following partial settlement as regards compensation:

Article 1

The Government of the Federal Republic of Germany will ensure that the Free Hanseatic City of Hamburg, represented by its Ministry of Justice, pays Dr. Sigurd Barthold, the applicant, 28,000 DM (twenty-eight thousand Marks) by way of compensation. Payment of this compensation shall not be interpreted as a recognition of a legal obligation. The date for payment is fixed as 31 January 1986.

Article 2

The present partial settlement satisfies all possible claims submitted in the instant case by Dr. Barthold in Dr. Eyls memorial of 25 July 1985.

The present settlement does not cover the claims for compensation which the applicant made through Dr. Eyl in his memorials of 26 August and 1 October 1985. The European Court of Human Rights will determine these claims in the light of the parties' submissions.

Article 3

Dr. Barthold undertakes to inform the Registrar of the European Court of European Rights of this partial agreement without delay and in due course to confirm to him receipt of the payment.

Article 4

The applicant also declares that—subject to final payment of the sum of 28,000 DM agreed in Article 1—he will not bring before a German court or an international institution against the Federal Republic of Germany or the Free Hanseatic City of Hamburg any claims the subject of the present proceedings in the European Commission or Court of Human Rights.

Article 5

The above-written partial settlement shall be deemed retrospectively null if the European Court of Human Rights should refuse to endorse it in whole or in part'.

6. Having regard to the respective attitudes of the Government, the applicant and the Commission, the Court decided on 24 January 1986 not to hold a hearing.

7. Under Article 50 of the Convention,

'If the Court finds that a decision or a measure taken by a legal authority or any other authority of a High Contracting Party is completely or partially in conflict with the obligations arising from the ... Convention, and if the internal law of the said Party allows only partial reparation to be made for the consequences of this decision or measure, the decision of the Court shall, if necessary, afford just satisfaction to the injured party'.

8. Since delivering its judgment of 25 March 1985 on the merits of the case, the Court has been informed of a partial friendly settlement concluded between the Government and the

applicant. This settlement concerns the claims for fees and expenses and for loss of earnings which the applicant had put forward in his memorial of 25 July 1985 and which totalled DM 27,491.96, plus interest. Having regard to the terms of the settlement and to the absence of any objection on the part of the Delegate, the Court finds that the agreement is of an 'equitable nature', within the meaning of Rule 53 para. 4 of the Rules of Court. Accordingly, the Court takes note of the agreement and considers it appropriate to strike the case out of the list as far as those claims are concerned.

9. The applicant also sought compensation for the non-pecuniary damage which he alleged he had suffered as a result of the proceedings taken against him before the domestic courts, the public discussion of those proceedings, a heart attack brought about by these circumstances as a whole and the manner in which the proceedings were conducted before the Convention institutions. On 28 August, he stated that he left the amount of the compensation to the discretion of the Court, but added that it should not be less than DM 1. On 7 October, he specified that he was nevertheless not seeking purely token satisfaction; he evaluated the damage he had suffered at about DM 50,000.

The Government, whilst contending that these claims should be rejected as ill-founded, first raised the issue of their admissibility: Mr. Barthold had put forward these claims after 25 July 1985, the time-limit set by the President; and, furthermore, he had neither sought an extension of this time-limit nor reserved the right to supplement his pleadings on this point.

The Delegate of the Commission did not express any opinion.

10. The Court does not deem it necessary to rule on the admissibility of the applicant's claims: in any event, there is no evidence that his heart attack was attributable to the breach of Article 10 found by the judgment of 25 March 1985; whilst the proceedings conducted before the national courts and subsequently before the Commission and the Court may have caused Mr. Barthold a certain degree of non-material damage, in the particular circumstances of the case the above-mentioned judgment has already afforded him sufficient just satisfaction under this head for the purposes of Article 50.

For These Reasons, the Court Unanimously

1. Decides to strike the case out of the list as far as the claims filed by the applicant on 25 July 1985 are concerned;

2. Holds that, as regards the remainder of the applicant's claims, the judgment of 25 March 1985 constitutes of itself sufficient just satisfaction for the purposes of Article 50.

2. REMEDIES AT STRASBOURG

Barthold provides a good example of the Court's two ordinary remedies: declaratory relief and an award of monetary damages. That the Court's principal remedy is declaratory relief follows from Article 46 of the Convention. Article 46(1) obliges the parties to abide by the final judgment of the Court in any case to which they are parties.[68]

---

[68] Convention, *supra* n. 7, Art. 46(1).

Article 46(2) requires the Court to transmit its final judgment to the 'Committee of Ministers, which shall supervise its execution'.[69]

The first holding by the *Barthold* Court in its 25 March 1985 judgment is, of course, Barthold's declaratory relief: 'the Court... [h]olds by five votes to two that there is a breach of Article 10'. As we read in the *Barthold (Article 50)* judgment of 31 January 1986, Germany acted to comply with its Article 46(1) obligation to abide by the Court's final judgment. The German authorities negotiated with Barthold and his lawyer the 'partial settlement' for 28,000 DM that was lodged with the Court on 16 December 1985. As for Barthold's other financial claims, including that for non-pecuniary damages for his heart attack, we see that the Court held in its 31 January 1986 judgment that 'as regards the remainder of the applicant's claims, the judgment of 25 March 1985 constitutes of itself sufficient just satisfaction, for the purposes of Article 50'.

Respecting monetary damages, old Article 50 employed in *Barthold*, was replaced in 1998 by Article 41 of the new Convention:

If the Court finds that there has been a violation of the Convention or the Protocols thereto, and if the internal law of the High Contracting Party allows only partial reparation to be made, the Court shall, if necessary, afford just satisfaction to the injured party.[70]

Ordinarily, Article 41 monetary damages awards are very low, again highlighting the declaration as the Court's primary remedy.[71] There are, of course, exceptions to the rule. For example, in 2003 in *Sigurdsson v. Iceland*, the Court awarded the plaintiff unusually high non-pecuniary damages—€25,000—for a violation of the Article 61(1) right to fair trial.[72] Judge Ress explained:

In this case it may appear that the amount of just satisfaction for non-pecuniary damage is rather high. I have nevertheless voted with the majority in favour of awarding this amount of just satisfaction for reasons which should be explained.

Normally in such a case, where the decision of the national court was taken by a three-to-two majority and it appears that there was a violation of Article 6 § 1 because of a lack of impartiality—at least, according to appearances—on the part of one of the judges, the reopening of the national proceedings would seem to be the appropriate, if not logical, outcome of such a judgment. The Committee of Ministers has urged all Contracting States to introduce into their national legislation the possibility of reopening proceedings in cases where a judgment of the European Court of Human Rights establishes a violation of Article 6 § 1, especially where 'the violation found is based on procedural errors or shortcomings of such gravity that a serious doubt is cast on the outcome of the domestic proceedings complained of' (see Recommendation Rec (2000) 2 of the Committee of Ministers to member States on the re-examination or

---

[69] *Id.*, Art. 46(2). *See* T. Barkhuysen & M. L. van Emmerik, 'A Comparative View on the Execution of Judgments of the European Court of Human Rights', *European Court of Human Rights: Remedies and Execution of Judgments* 1, 3–4 (T. A. Christou & J. P. Raymond eds. 2005) (hereinafter cited as 'Barkhuysen & van Emmerik'); P. McKaskle, 'The European Court of Human Rights: What It Is, How It Works, and Its Future', 40 *University of San Francisco Law Review* 1, 31–2 (2005).

[70] Convention, *supra* n. 7, Art. 41.

[71] P. Leach, *Taking a Case to the European Court of Human Rights* 195–6 (2001).

[72] 10 July 2003, 40 E.H.R.R. 15, at paras. 49–51.

reopening of certain cases at domestic level following judgments of the European Court of Human Rights, adopted 19 January 2000). I think that that is true of this case. The applicant has already asked for the reopening of the proceedings and has failed, and Icelandic law does not apparently provide for any further possibility of reopening the proceedings. If there is a new ground for reopening the national proceedings after a judgment of the European Court, there should always be an appropriate procedure available.

Since this avenue is apparently blocked under Icelandic law, and there may be a long way to go until Iceland has changed its national legislation, there is undoubtedly not only quite a long period to take into account but also the possibility that in this case the applicant will never obtain the reopening of the proceedings.

It is of course a matter of speculation how the Supreme Court would have decided if the violation had not occurred, but a slight element of loss of real opportunities may also be observed in this regard. Therefore I think that a higher amount of just satisfaction for non-pecuniary damage in this case was justified.[73]

Cases like *Sigurdsson* are, however, the exception. Small or nominal damages are the rule. In practice, besides a declaration of a violation, the most typical remedy is an award of some of the legal costs and expenses of litigating the case.[74]

Hesitatingly, the Court has begun to issue remedies beyond declaratory relief and just satisfaction in the form of monetary compensation. In a few exceptional cases, 'the Court has been prepared to order the state to take steps other than to compensate the victim'.[75] So, for example, in *Papamichalopoulos v. Greece*,[76] the Court ordered Greece to restitute expropriated property or to pay the applicants the property's current market value:

PAPAMICHALOPOULOS V. GREECE (ARTICLE 50)

European Court of Human Rights
Judgment of 31 October 1995
40 E.H.R.R. 439

34. The Court points out that by Article 53 of the Convention the High Contracting Parties undertook to abide by the decision of the Court in any case to which they were parties; furthermore, Article 54 provides that the judgment of the Court shall be transmitted to the Committee of Ministers which shall supervise its execution. It follows that a judgment in which the Court finds a breach imposes on the respondent State a legal obligation to put an end to the breach and make reparation for its consequences in such a way as to restore as far as possible the situation existing before the breach.

---

[73] *Id.*, Concurring Opinion of Judge Ress.
[74] C. Oveny & P. White, *Jacobs & White, The European Convention on Human Rights* 492 (4th edn. 2006).
[75] P. Leach, 'Beyond the Bug River—A New Dawn for Redress Before the European Court of Human Rights', 2005(2) *European Human Rights Law Review* 148, 151.
[76] 31 October 1995, 40 E.H.R.R. 439.

The Contracting States that are parties to a case are in principle free to choose the means whereby they will comply with a judgment in which the Court has found a breach. This discretion as to the manner of execution of a judgment reflects the freedom of choice attaching to the primary obligation of the Contracting States under the Convention to secure the rights and freedoms guaranteed (Article 1). If the nature of the breach allows of restitutio in integrum, it is for the respondent State to effect it, the Court having neither the power nor the practical possibility of doing so itself. If, on the other hand, national law does not allow—or allows only partial—reparation to be made for the consequences of the breach, Article 50 empowers the Court to afford the injured party such satisfaction as appears to it to be appropriate.

35. In the principal judgment the Court held that 'the loss of all ability to dispose of the land in issue, taken together with the failure of the attempts made [up to then] to remedy the situation complained of, [had] entailed sufficiently serious consequences for the applicants de facto to have been expropriated in a manner incompatible with their right to the peaceful enjoyment of their possessions'.

36. The act of the Greek Government which the Court held to be contrary to the Convention was not an expropriation that would have been legitimate but for the failure to pay fair compensation; it was a taking by the State of land belonging to private individuals, which has lasted twenty-eight years, the authorities ignoring the decisions of national courts and their own promises to the applicants to redress the injustice committed in 1967 by the dictatorial regime.

The unlawfulness of such a dispossession inevitably affects the criteria to be used for determining the reparation owed by the respondent State, since the pecuniary consequences of a lawful expropriation cannot be assimilated to those of an unlawful dispossession. In this connection, international case-law, of courts or arbitration tribunals, affords the Court a precious source of inspiration; although that case-law concerns more particularly the expropriation of industrial and commercial undertakings, the principles identified in that field are valid for situations such as the one in the instant case.

In particular, the Permanent Court of International Justice held as follows in its judgment of 13 September 1928 in the case concerning the factory at Chorzów:

'...reparation must, as far as possible, wipe out all the consequences of the illegal act and reestablish the situation which would, in all probability, have existed if that act had not been committed. Restitution in kind, or, if this is not possible, payment of a sum corresponding to the value which a restitution in kind would bear; the award, if need be, of damages for loss sustained which would not be covered by restitution in kind or payment in place of it—such are the principles which should serve to determine the amount of compensation due for an act contrary to international law'. (Collection of Judgments, Series A no. 17, p. 47)

37. In the present case the compensation to be awarded to the applicants is not limited to the value of their properties at the date on which the Navy occupied them. In the principal judgment the Court took as its basis for assessing the impugned interference the length of the occupation and the authorities' inability for years on end to allot the applicants the land promised in exchange. For that reason it requested the experts to estimate also the current value of the land in issue; that value does not depend on hypothetical conditions, as it would if the land was in the same state today as in 1967. It is clear from the expert report that since then the land and its immediate vicinity—which by virtue of its situation had potential for

development for tourism—has undergone development in the form of buildings which serve as a leisure centre for naval officers and related infrastructure works. Nor does the Court overlook that the applicants themselves at the time had a scheme for the economic development of their properties, on which work had already begun.

38. Consequently, the Court considers that the return of the land in issue, an area of 104,018 sq. m—as defined in 1983 by the Athens second Expropriation Board—would put the applicants as far as possible in a situation equivalent to the one in which they would have been if there had not been a breach of Article 1 of Protocol No. 1; the award of the existing buildings would then fully compensate them for the consequences of the alleged loss of enjoyment....

Admittedly, as far back as 1980 the Government invoked reasons of national defence that prevented restitution, asserting that even if in peacetime the naval base was a holiday resort for officers and their families, it was ready for integration into the country's military structure in wartime.

39. If the respondent State does not make such restitution within six months from the delivery of this judgment, the Court holds that it is to pay the applicants, for damage and loss of enjoyment since the authorities took possession of the land in 1967, the current value of the land, increased by the appreciation brought about by the existence of the buildings, and the construction costs of the latter.

...

For These Reasons, the Court Unanimously

...

2. Holds that the respondent State is to return to the applicants, within six months, the land in issue of an area of 104,018 sq. m, including the buildings on it;

3. Holds that, failing such restitution, the respondent State is to pay the applicants, within six months, 5,551,000,000 (five thousand five hundred and fifty-one million) drachmas in respect of pecuniary damage, plus non-capitalisable interest at 6% from the expiry of the six-month period until payment.

In another example of an exceptional remedy, in 2005, in *Mamatkulov and Askarov v. Turkey*, the Court, acting in a Grand Chamber, held that Turkey had violated Article 34 of the Convention when it extradited two Uzbek nationals to Uzbekistan to stand trial for a terrorist attack on the Uzbeki President in disregard of the Court's interim order.[77] Article 34 of the Convention obliges a state party to comply with 'interim measures [which] have been indicated in order to avoid irreparable harm being caused to the victim of an alleged violation'.[78] Noting that *Mamatkulov and Askarov* 'is a dramatic departure' for the Court since theretofore the Court 'had not held [interim] measures to be legally binding'.[79] Professor Mowbray, however, questions the wisdom of the judgment:

[T]he contentious question is whether the Grand Chamber's judgment in Mamatkulov and Askarov exceeded the legitimate powers of interpretation given to the Court and strayed into

---

[77] 4 February 2005.

[78] Convention, *supra* n. 7, Art. 34.

[79] A. Mowbray, 'A New Strasbourg Approach to the Legal Consequences of Interim Measures', 5 *Human Rights Law Review* 377, 385–6 (2005).

the forbidden territory of international law making. There is much cogency in the dissentients' opinion that, given the persistent refusal of Member States to include an Article in the Convention making interim measures legally binding, the majority were legislating in defiance of the clear intention of these States. Whilst the majority could assert that they were seeking to protect vulnerable applicants, it may be concluded that a very desirable procedural reform has been achieved by judicial creativity that extends beyond the permissible limits of Convention interpretation.[80]

Has the Court gone too far in assuming legislative powers more appropriately left to the member states?

However, for now at least, remedies like those in *Papamichopoulos* and *Mamatkulov and Askarov* are the exceptions.[81] Generally, given the weaknesses of the remedies available, two commentators remark 'that many applicants who "win" their case in Strasbourg will nevertheless feel that they have been left empty-handed by the Court'.[82] They, accordingly, suggest that some typical domestic remedies be given the Court: (i) the power to revise or revoke national administrative orders, (ii) the power to pardon or acquit or reduce sentences in criminal cases, (iii) the power to reopen proceedings that have been closed as *res judicata*, and (iv) the power to sue a state in tort.[83] Should the Convention be amended to provide one or some such new remedial powers? If member states do not choose to so amend the Convention, should the Court claim such remedial powers in a quasi-legislative act?

D. THE EFFICACY OF THE COURT

1. MEASURING EFFICACY [84]

What do we really know and what might it be useful to know about the efficacy of Strasbourg? How does one define 'efficacy'? Although one might search out a definition that would distinguish 'efficacy' from other terms like 'compliance' and 'obedience', it

---

[80] *Id.* at 385–6.

[81] In another important remedial departure, in 2004, in *Broniowski v. Poland*, the Court identified a systemic problem in compensating almost 80,000 individuals for lost property rights pursuant to Article 1, Protocol 1. 22 June 2004, E.H.R.R. Poland complied with the Court's suggestion and instituted a friendly settlement that the Court accepted in 2005. *Broniowski v. Poland (Friendly Settlement)*, 28 September 2005, 43 E.H.R.R. 1. *See* J. L. Jackson, Note, '*Broniowski v. Poland*: A Recipe for Increased Legitimacy of the European Court of Human Rights as a Supranational Constitutional Court', 39 *Connecticut Law Review* 759 (2006).

[82] Barkhuysen & van Emmerik, *supra* n. 69, at 5.

[83] *Id.* at 5–7.

[84] This section is based on M. W. Janis, 'The Efficacy of Strasbourg Law', 15 *Connecticut Journal of International Law* 39 (2000).

makes little sense to do so. It seems that virtually all studies about how Strasbourg law 'works' do not bother to do so. Discussion about Strasbourg law 'working' or not, of it being 'efficacious', 'effective', or 'successful' or not, of there being 'compliance' with its norms or judgments or not, of its rules being 'respected' or 'put into practice' or not, makes all these terms more or less interchangeable.[85] Though one could also analyse Strasbourg law using a break-down of levels of compliance,[86] it appears more fruitful to break up the Strasbourg efficacy studies into three categories depending upon the kind of 'law' they explore: (1) judgments (and decisions), (2) legal rules, and (3) the legal system itself. This yields some interesting comparisons.[87]

Studies of the efficacy of Strasbourg judgments and decisons are the most numerous. There are a great many reports and examinations of the effects of individual judgments of the European Court of Human Rights, and the decisions of the European Commission of Human Rights and the Committee of Ministers of the Council of Europe.[88] Almost all of these reports or commentaries are interesting and informative. However, by their very nature, they fail to provide a general picture. The individual case studies must be read together and compared to yield some sort of overall conclusion about compliance or not with Strasbourg judgments and decisions.

It is just this sort of general study that is most lacking. Some of the work asserts to be comprehensive, but is frankly disappointing, being largely uninformative.[89]

[85] There is no harm in this. Much excellent discussion of compliance questions in international law proceeds similarly. *See*, for example, H. Koh, 'Why Do Nations Obey International Law?', 106 *Yale Law Journal* 2599 (1997).

[86] Harold Koh helpfully distinguishes coincidence, conformity, compliance, and obedience in norms and practice. *Id.* at 2600–1, n. 3. Looking at the motivation of those who appear to obey judgments, we can distinguish behavioural explanations based on 'prudential calculation' from those grounded on 'law following'. R. S. Kay, 'The European Human Rights System as a System of Law', 6 *Columbia Journal of European Law* 55 (2000) (hereinafter cited as 'Kay').

[87] Benedict Kingsbury has provided a persuasive account of how definitions of compliance with international law vary depending on the theory of law that one adopts. Kingsbury, 'The Concept of Compliance as a Function of Competing Conceptions of International Law', 19 *Michigan Journal of International Law* 345 (1998).

[88] There are both official and unofficial reports and commentary. For example, the Council of Europe has a website, reporting, usually in a sentence or two, responses of states to judgments of the Strasbourg Court, http://www.dhcour.coe.fr/eng/effects.htm. In an entry on *Jersild v. Denmark*, 23 Sept. 1994, 19 E.H.R.R. 1, the Council of Europe's website reports: 'On 24 January 1995 the Special Court of Review gave leave for the case against Mr Jersild and Others to be reopened'. *Id.* at 5.

[89] For example, in 1993, Peter Leuprecht, then the Director of Human Rights of the Council of Europe, promised a book chapter the purpose of which was 'to show that judgments of the European Court of Human Rights and decisions of the Committee of Ministers under Article 32 of the European Convention on Human Rights are not only legally binding, but actually executed'. Leuprecht, 'The Execution of Judgments and Decisions', *The European System for the Protection of Human Rights* 791 (Macdonald, Matscher & Petzold eds. 1993). However, the chapter refers in substance only to the formal language of the Convention itself and in no way substantiates the conclusion that '[o]n the whole, the record of execution of judgments of the Court and decisions of the Committee of Ministers is remarkably good'. *Id.* at 800. Probably, the real goal of the chapter is hortatory; Leuprecht concludes: 'It is to be hoped that the States concerned will continue to take *bona fide* all the measures necessary to execute the Court's judgments and the Committee of Ministers' decisions, and that the Committee itself will confirm and develop its now well-established practice to use its powers fully and responsibly, without being impeded by considerations of political expediency'. *Id.*

Other work provides more evidence,[90] but is still rather impressionistic.[91] The most impressive study of compliance with Strasbourg judgments and decisions covers only the compliance record of one country, the United Kingdom,[92] although the 29 cases reviewed do constitute about 31 per cent of all violations decided in the period.[93] This nuanced study of the U.K. shows how difficult it can be to really tell if Strasbourg judgments and decisions have in practice been properly executed.[94] Moreover, the study concludes that though in many cases it seems that the United Kingdom has complied with adverse judgments and decisions,[95] in other cases there had been doubtful compliance[96] or by some assessments even non-compliance.[97] It may well be that the record of executing Strasbourg judgments is no worse than the record of many

[90] For example, in 1996, the then President of the Strasbourg Court, Rolv Ryssdal, reviewed the compliance record of the Court, giving about 10 examples of cases either where he noted good compliance, e.g., Germany changing its rules about the cost of translators in criminal proceedings as a result of *Luedicke, Belkacem & Koc v. Germany*, 28 Nov. 1978, (No. 29), or where compliance was long-delayed, e.g., Belgium taking 8 years to implement the amendments to its family law called for by *Marckx v. Belgium*, 13 June 1979, 2 E.H.R.R. 330. Ryssdal, 'The Enforcement System Set Up Under the European Convention on Human Rights', *Compliance with Judgments of International Courts* 49, 54 (Bulterman & Kuijer eds. 1996).

[91] Ryssdal concludes that 'to date judgments of the European Court of Human Rights have, I would say, not only generally but always been complied with by the Contracting States concerned'. *Id.* at 67. However, in the same volume, another Strasbourg Court judge, S. K. Martens, in a commentary on Judge Ryssdal's contribution, reaches a slightly more pessimistic conclusion: 'For my part, I also have the impression that as a rule respondent States, after a judgment finding a violation, do modify their legislation sooner or later. There are, however, exceptions'. Martens, 'Commentary', *Compliance with Judgments of International Courts* 71, 73 (Bulterman & Kuijer eds. 1996). Martens cited three examples of probable non-compliance including the absence of adequate remedial legislation by Ireland in *Norris v. Ireland*, 26 Oct. 1988, 13 E.H.R.R. 186, and by the Netherlands in *Benthem v. Netherlands*, 23 Oct. 1985, 6 E.H.R.R. 283. *Id.*

[92] Churchill & Young, 'Compliance with Judgments of the European Court of Human Rights and Decisions of the Committee of Ministers: The Experience of the United Kingdom, 1975–1987', 62 *British Yearbook of International Law* 283 (1991) (hereinafter cited as 'Churchill & Young').

[93] *Id.* at 284.

[94] 'This paper also demonstrates some of the problems involved in carrying out a study of compliance with judgments of the Court and decisions of the Committee of Ministers…The relevant law is not always very accessible (e.g. in relation to prisoners), nor is it always easy to ascertain how the law applies in practice (e.g. in relation to the treatment of detainees in Northern Ireland)'. *Id.* at 346.

[95] These cases include *Campbell & Cosans v. United Kingdom*, 25 Feb. 1982, 4 E.H.R.R. 293, concerning corporal punishment; *Gillow v. United Kingdom*, 24 Nov. 1986, 11 E.H.R.R. 335 concerning housing laws in Guernsey; and *Young, James & Webster v. United Kingdom*, 13 Aug. 1981, 4 E.H.R.R. 38, concerning labour unions and the closed shop.

[96] Churchill & Young conclude that as a result of *Sunday Times v. United Kingdom*, 26 Apr. 1979, 2 E.H.R.R. 245, 'there was no sign of any attempt to review the reform of the law of contempt against the touchstone of the European Convention, with the result that the extent of compliance remains uncertain'. Churchill & Young, *supra* n. 92, at 346. The Contempt of Court Act 1981 was intended to bring law in the United Kingdom into line with the Convention.

[97] There was no reform of the law authorizing corporal punishment in the Isle of Man after *Tyrer v. United Kingdom*, 25 Apr. 1978, 2 E.H.R.R. 1, although the authors could find no example of corporal punishment being imposed in subsequent practice. *Id.* at 286–7.

domestic courts,[98] but one must be careful not to go too far in asserting a nearly perfect record for compliance with Strasbourg judgments and decisions.[99]

The second category of efficacy, compliance with Strasbourg's legal rules, ought in a way to be even more important than the first. After all, given the large number of alleged violations of European human rights law and the small number of cases that ultimately reach the Strasbourg Court, most meaningful enforcement of Strasbourg's substantive law must take place before national courts. There are a number of studies that discuss the ways in which the substantive legal rules of the Convention figure or not as rules of decision in the domestic legal systems of the member states.[100] There is also work available that discusses the effect of Strasbourg institutional case law on municipal judicial proceedings.[101] What is missing are general studies about how Strasbourg legal rules, whether in the form of the Convention's substantive provisions or in the precedent-like norms created by the Strasbourg institutions, have or have not influenced the actual practice of states or governments.[102]

The third category of efficacy, the efficacy of the legal system of Strasbourg itself, is both the most difficult to gauge and, probably, the most important. International law is sometimes accused of being irrelevant, but increasingly it seems that even ordinary critics of the function of law in international relations have come to acknowledge that international law and international legal institutions are playing increasingly

[98] One need go no further than the difficulties of enforcing school desegregation following the U.S. Supreme Court's landmark decision in *Brown v. Board of Education*, 347 U.S. 483 (1954), to see how much the practice of domestic law can vary from its judgments. That we tend to worry rather more about the efficacy of international law than about the efficacy of domestic law is probably due to the lingering doubt many share about international law being 'law' at all, a doubt that goes back to the very origins of the discipline. See M. W. Janis, 'Jeremy Bentham and the Fashioning of "International Law"', 78 *American Journal of International Law* 405 (1984).

[99] For example, '[t]he [European] Convention's reputation as a bulwark against arbitrary government interference stems at least in part from the fact that the decisions of its judicial enforcement organs, the European Court of Human Rights and the European Commission of Human Rights, are almost universally respected and implemented by the twenty-four European nations that have ratified the Convention'. L. R. Helfer, 'Consensus, Coherence and the European Convention on Human Rights', 26 *Cornell International Law Journal* 133–4 (1993).

[100] One of the most comprehensive, though now somewhat dated, general surveys is A. Drzemczewski, *The European Human Rights Convention in Domestic Law* (1983). Reviews of individual countries can more easily be kept up-to-date: see for example, U. Bernitz, 'The Incorporation of the European Human Rights Convention into Swedish Law—A Half Measure', 38 *German Yearbook of International Law* 178 (1995); I. Cameron, 'The Swedish Experience of the European Convention on Human Rights Since Incorporation', 48 *International and Comparative Law Quarterly* 20 (1999); M. Hunt, *Using Human Rights in English Courts* (1997).

[101] J. Polakiewicz & V. Jacob-Foltzer, 'The European Human Rights Convention in Domestic Law: The Impact of Strasbourg Case-Law in States where Direct Effect is Given to the Convention', 12 *Human Rights Law Journal* 65, 121 (1991). R. Blackburn & J. Polakiewicz, *Fundamental Rights in Europe: The European Convention on Human Rights and its Member States, 1950–2000* (2001).

[102] There is some anecdotal evidence, though, available both in some of the records of the enforcement or not of individual Strasbourg judgments, e.g., Churchill & Young, *supra* n. 92, and in some of the reviews of the respect paid to Strasbourg legal rules.

important roles in international society.[103] How, though, to determine the real impact of international law on international society? In particular, are the many assertions about the overall efficacy of the Strasbourg legal system at the end of the day merely impressionistic?[104]

Understanding how deeply a legal system permeates and regulates a society, especially an international society like Europe, may always be more a study in theory than of practice. This is not to say that the theoretical aspects of the question of the deep-rootedness or not of an international legal system will not be illuminating. For example, when explaining to others the nature and efficacy of the Strasbourg legal system, it may be useful to employ some of the ideas from the theoretical paradigm for legal systems in general devised by H. L. A. Hart.[105] Hart grounds much of his theory of a legal system upon a distinction between primary and secondary rules: primary rules being rules of obligation and secondary rules being rules that have to do with the functioning of the system, including rules about making and changing primary rules, as well as a rule of recognition that calls upon actors within the system to agree upon what is and what is not a legitimate legal rule.[106]

It is convenient to describe the Strasbourg system in this way: there are primary rules, especially the substantive human rights norms in the Convention, and secondary rules, including those in the Convention establishing the international enforcement machinery of the Strasbourg Court, which are tasked with the application, interpretation, and adjudication of the primary rules *vis-à-vis* the member states. What makes the Strasbourg legal system a more thorough-going international legal system than, say, United Nations human rights law, is that Strasbourg displays a much more settled and accepted system of secondary rules and institutions. Moreover, the actors within the system, both governments and individual litigants, as well as their lawyers, recognize the Strasbourg rules *and* the Strasbourg institutions as legitimate.

This last aspect, recognition of legitimacy,[107] may be the most crucial 'practical' test for the third sort of efficacy analysis, i.e., the efficacy of the Strasbourg legal system. Yet, testing recognition of the legitimacy of the Strasbourg system is very difficult and largely untried. It is much more usual to simply make positive assertions about the

---

[103] For the mutual respect between international political scientists and international lawyers, see R. O. Keohane, 'International Relations and International Law: Two Optics', 38 *Harvard International Law Journal* 487 (1997); and A. M. Slaughter Burley, 'International Law and International Relations Theory: A Dual Agenda', 87 *American Journal of International Law* 205 (1993).

[104] One of the present authors is as guilty as anyone in making grand claims about the efficacy of the Strasbourg legal system: 'What makes European human rights law special is not only its increasing case load, but also its effectiveness', Janis, *supra* n. 2, at 270.

[105] H. L. A. Hart, *The Concept of Law* (2nd edn. 1994). *See* Kay, *supra* n. 86, at 59–71.

[106] Although Hart's theory can be illuminating for understanding the role of international law in international society, Hart's own treatment of international law is disappointing. *Id.* at 213–37. This is probably due to his uncharacteristic reliance on rather simplistic positivist notions of the nature of international law, notions criticized elsewhere. M. W. Janis, 'Individuals as Subjects of International Law', 17 *Cornell International Law Journal* 61 (1984).

[107] Legitimacy in international law has been most persuasively explored by Thomas Franck. T. Franck, *The Power of Legitimacy Among Nations* (1990).

efficacy of the Strasbourg legal system.[108] Are there more quantifiable ways of testing the system's efficacy?

There are at least four possible tests: (1) case load in the European Court of Human Rights, (2) acceptance of what were before November 1998 the two optional clauses of the European Convention, (3) growth in the number of states joining the Council of Europe and ratifying the Convention, and (4) an increasing recognition of the legitimacy of the system. The first three tests are easily quantifiable and satisfied impressively. To some extent, of course, the fourth test, recognition of the legitimacy of Strasbourg law, can be gleaned from the other three tests. The burgeoning case load of the Commission and the Court, the now universal acceptance of the former optional clauses, and the doubled membership of European states in the Strasbourg legal system all point to individuals, governments, and lawyers in Europe taking the system more seriously, and perhaps to the conclusion that the players increasingly recognize the system's legitimacy.

Yet, 'increasing' recognition of Strasbourg's legitimacy is only relative; there is 'increased' legitimacy at least compared to what went before. Does that make it 'enough recognition' to say the system is properly 'legitimate'? This second question is also relative: 'enough recognition' calls for a comparison of the levels of recognition between the Strasbourg system and other legal systems, e.g., *vis-à-vis* both domestic legal systems where legitimacies will vary from country to country, say from an older Western democracy to a newer democratic entrant such as Russia,[109] and other international legal systems where legitimacies will vary too, say from international economic law to the international law regulating the use of force.[110] There are no such comparisons of legitimacy in the literature. This may be because tests of recognition of legitimacy do not easily form part of either legal or, even, political analysis. Gauging recognition of legitimacy of legal systems may be more a psychological, rather than a legal or political, exercise and in any case difficult to ascertain in any sort of definite way.[111] This may well be true for most any legal system, domestic or international.

---

[108] Such assertions are legion. As early as 1980, when the Strasbourg Court had rendered only about 40 judgments, the then president of the Court, Sir Humphrey Waldock, wrote that whether 'the system set up by the European Convention on Human Rights is, in general, effective is not, I believe, today open to serious question'. H. Waldock, 'The Effectiveness of the System Set Up by the European Convention on Human Rights', 1 *Human Rights Law Journal* 1 (1980). Hundreds of judgments later, Strasbourg Judge Juan Antonio Carrillo Salcedo remarked similarly: 'The European Convention constitutes, therefore, the first effective regional enforcement mechanism for human rights'. Salcedo, 'The Place of the European Convention in International Law', *The European System for the Protection of Human Rights* 15, 17 (Macdonald, Matscher & Petzold eds. 1993).

[109] *See infra.*

[110] Different international legal systems may be said to vary along a 'structural spectrum', some forms of international law being more 'law'-like than others. M. W. Janis, 'Do "Laws" Regulate Nuclear Weapons?', *Nuclear Weapons and International Law* 53, 60–1 (Pogany ed. 1987).

[111] It may be that anecdotal evidence from the media speaks of psychological acceptance rather well. For example, it seems meaningful when cartoons are printed assuming something of a knowledge of the Strasbourg system, for example, the one showing a student preparing himself to be caned in class with the caption, 'Your complete ignorance on every other subject is only matched by your detailed knowledge of each provision on corporal punishment by the European Court of Human Rights'. *Punch*, 10 Mar. 1982. Or when the main headline of a daily paper reads: '£40,000 Present for IRA Families: Britain Pays Terrorist Court Costs Early', *Daily Mail*, 27 Dec. 1995, at 1.

2. EFFICACY AND LEGITIMACY

As we have explored above, there can be little doubt that the efficacy of the European Court of Human Rights depends in good measure on its perception as a 'legitimate' institution, accepted as a rule enforcer across Europe. However, it seems in practice that perceptions of the legitimacy of the Court vary from member state to member state, that the Court's judgments are more efficacious in one place than another. Turkey, for example, announced on 4 June 1999 that it would refuse to comply with the judgment of the European Court of Human Rights in the *Loizidou Case*.[112] Such a blunt rejection of the Court is unprecedented in Strasbourg annals. Even the Greek Colonels in 1969 did not reject a judgment of the Court.[113] Moreover, Turkey has had numerous unsettling judgments against it concerning its treatment of its Kurdish population.[114] Turkey's record respecting European Human Rights has had negative implications for its attempts to become a full partner in European integration.[115]

Another test for the legitimacy of the Court is the accession of the newly democratic states of central and Eastern Europe. The excerpt below goes to the question of whether or not there can be a two-tier Strasbourg system with lower expectations of efficacy and legitimacy *vis-à-vis* some states than others.

MARK JANIS
'RUSSIA AND THE "LEGALITY" OF STRASBOURG LAW'
8 *EUROPEAN JOURNAL OF INTERNATIONAL LAW* 93 (1997)

On 28 February 1996, Russia acceded to the Statute of the Council of Europe, becoming the Council's thirty-ninth member.[116] Russia has been allotted eighteen seats in Strasbourg's Parliamentary Assembly, giving it, alongside France, Germany, Italy and the United Kingdom, one of the five largest national delegations.[117] Russia's accession followed an extensive debate within the Council of Europe about the suitability of the applicant for membership, and occurred despite an unfavourable Eminent Lawyers Report prepared at the request of the Bureau of the Parliamentary Assembly.[118] The Report concluded 'that the legal order of the Russian Federation does not, at the present moment, meet the Council of Europe standards as enshrined in the statute of the Council and developed by the organs of the European Convention

---

[112] M2 Communications Ltd, M2 Presswire, 4 June 1999: *Loizidou v. Turkey*, 23 Mar. 1995 (No. 310), 20 E.H.R.R. 99. For more on Turkey and Cyprus, *see* D. Wippman, 'International Law and Ethnic Conflict on Cyprus', 31 *Texas International Law Journal* 141 (1996).

[113] Albeit Greece had not accepted the Court's jurisdiction and was ultimately forced to withdraw from the Council of Europe altogether, *see supra* Chapter 2.

[114] *See infra* Chapters 4 and 5.

[115] M. Muftuler-Bac, 'The Never-Ending Story: Turkey and the European Union', 34 *Middle East Studies* 240 (1998); 'Turkey can be part of Europe', *The Economist*, 1 Apr. 1995, at 13.

[116] 'The 39 Member States of the Council of Europe (CoE) according to their date of membership (as at 31 July 1996)', 17 *Human Rights Law Journal* 234 (1996). [117] *Id.*

[118] Council of Europe, Parliamentary Assembly, Bureau of the Assembly, *Report on the Conformity of the Legal Order of the Russian Federation with Council of Europe Standards Prepared by Rudolf Bernhardt, Stefan Trechsel, Albert Weitzel, and Felix Ermacora,* 7 Oct. 1994, AS/Bur/Russia (1994) 7.

on Human Rights'.[119] As a condition of joining the Council of Europe, Russia has promised to ratify the European Convention for the Protection of Human Rights and Fundamental Freedoms[120] within one year of its accession to the Statute of the Council.[121]

···

The accession of Russia and of the other Central and Eastern European states to the Council of Europe and the European Convention on Human Rights may also be seen as a price of success. The promotion of human rights in the Soviet bloc via the 'Helsinki Process' was long a foreign policy goal of both the United States and Western Europe. At least as early as April 1991, a political decision had been made that there was a political and moral requirement to open up the Council of Europe to the new post-Communist governments in the East.[122] In October 1993, the Summit of the Council of Europe reiterated its commitment to pluralist and parliamentary democracy, the indivisibility and universality of human rights, the rule of law and a common heritage enriched by diversity'.[123] Moreover, the Summit proclaimed that it would welcome new Council members from 'the democracies of Europe freed from communist oppression', so long as an applicant had 'brought its institutions and legal system into line with the basic principles of democracy, the rule of law and respect for human rights'.[124] To test whether an applicant's legal system meets these standards, the Council of Europe commissioned Eminent Lawyers Reports, such as that which Russia failed.[125] The decision in February 1996 to admit Russia to the Council of Europe is commonly viewed as a result of giving greater weight to political factors than to legal criteria, a realistic judgment given the importance of integrating post-Communist Russia into the more democratic liberal realm of Western Europe.[126]

No matter how politically rational the decision to admit Russia to the Council of Europe, it must be recognized that Russia's accession will result in two important and probably negative consequences for the 'legality' of the Strasbourg human rights law system. First, the participation of Russia increases the possibility that European human rights law will both be disobeyed and be seen to be flouted. This has, of course, occurred before, notably by the Colonels' regime in Greece between 1967 and 1974. That situation led to the condemnation of Greece by the European Commission of Human Rights and the Committee of Ministers of the Council of Europe, as well as to the denunciation of the Convention by Greece in December 1969. Moreover, doubt has been expressed about the actual efficacy of the system, even with regard to the traditional liberal democracies.

[119] *Id.* at 85.

[120] 213 UNTS 221, ETS 5, UKTS 71 (1953), signed at Rome 4 Nov. 1950, entered into force 3 Sept. 1953, Council of Europe, Human Rights Information Centre (ed. 1995).

[121] Reuters News Service, 'Yeltsin Approves Russia Entry to Council of Europe', *Reuter Textline*, 23 Feb. 1996.

[122] Council of Europe, Committee of Ministers, 88th Session, 25 Apr. 1991, 12 *Human Rights Law Journal* 216 (1991).

[123] Council of Europe, Vienna Declaration of 8/9 Oct. 1993, 14 *Human Rights Law Journal* 373 (1993).

[124] *Id.* at 374.

[125] Council of Europe, *Report on the Conformity of the Legal Order of the Russian Federation with Council of Europe Standards* (1994). Other Eminent Lawyers Reports have been reprinted in the *Human Rights Law Journal*, including those on Slovenia, 14 *Human Rights Law Journal* 437 (1993); the Czech Republic, 14 *Human Rights Law Journal* 442 (1993); and Albania, 15 *Human Rights Law Journal* 242 (1995).

[126] Reuter News Service, 'Russia: Council Vote Pleases Yeltsin, Shocks Rights Monitors', 26 Jan. 1996; Reuter News Service, 'Czech Republic: Havel Gives Qualified Welcome to Russia in Council', 26 Jan. 1996; Reuter News Service, 'Russia: Human Rights Commission Says "Political Expediency" Prevailing Over Human Rights', 7 Feb. 1996; Gazzini, 'Considerations on the Conflict in Chechnya', 17 *Human Rights Law Journal* 93 (1996).

However, three aspects of Russia's accession are particularly troubling for the future of compliance with Strasbourg law. First, at the present time, as the Eminent Lawyers Report makes clear, Russia falls short of the usual European standard of the rule of law and the protection of human rights. Second, given Russia's lack of experience in protecting human rights at the level of municipal law, it is likely that a great many violations of European human rights law will be committed there, and that they will not be remedied domestically. Third, the same political importance of Russia that has prompted the Council of Europe to accept its admittance will make it especially difficult for Strasbourg to force the Russian government to comply with adverse findings.

The other significant consequence for the system of European human rights law posed by Russia's accession is likely to be a new challenge to what, along with Hart, we can call Strasbourg's 'internal point-of-view'. Given the difficulties of Russia effectively complying with European human rights law in its municipal legal order and of Strasbourg imposing its decisions upon the Russian government, there will be a strong temptation for the Strasbourg institutions to fashion a two-tier legal order, which would allow lower than normal expectations for Russia. This will have the likely benefit of enabling Russia's continued participation in the system, but it will threaten the perception of Hart's 'officials, lawyers or private persons' that Strasbourg law 'in one situation after another [is a guide] to the conduct of social life, as the basis for claims, demands, admissions, criticism or punishment, viz., in all the familiar transactions of life according to rules'.[127]

These probable challenges resulting from Russia's accession come at an awkward moment for Strasbourg. Not only is the ambit of European human rights law being widened to reach out to the former Soviet bloc, but the potency of Strasbourg law is being deepened by ever bolder Court judgments against national governments. This deepening, a welcome advance on international legal control, is proceeding just when the basic tenets of European unity are under increasing assault by nationalistic sentiments across Europe. This is true not least in the United Kingdom where both European human rights law and European economic law are perceived more and more, not as solutions to European-wide problems, but as foreign threats to national political and economic objectives. Hence, there is a danger that the failure of Russia to comply with European human rights law domestically and to obey the decisions of the Strasbourg institutions and the creation of a two-tier human rights system to accommodate Russia will give the governments of the existing member states all the more latitude in weakening their own commitment to the Strasbourg system. This all serves as a reminder that the 'breakthrough' of Strasbourg law to genuine legal obligation may not be forever.

3. STRASBOURG AND THE EFFICACY OF
INTERNATIONAL LAW

Quand je vais dans un pays, je n'examine pas s'il y a des bonnes lois, mais si on exécute celles qui y sont, car il y a des bonnes lois partout.[128]

When I go to a country, I do not look to see whether there are good laws, but whether those there are enforced, for good laws are everywhere.

---

[127] H. L. A. Hart, *The Concept of Law* 90 (2nd edn. 1994).
[128] Montesquieu, 'Notes sur l'Angleterre', in *Œuvres Complètes* 331, 332 (Editions du Seuil 1964).

Any difficulty in making good international law pales beside the problem of making good international law effective. The history of the international legal discipline is replete with examples of carefully crafted norms disregarded in practice. One need only mention the Kellogg-Briand Pact of 1928 and the Charter of the United Nations and their vain attempts to abolish war to evoke the commonplace that international law does not 'work'.

Yet, international law plainly does 'work' in its most frequent usage, the application of international law by national legal systems. When a treaty provision or a customary international law or any other international law norm is used as a rule of decision by a municipal court or administrative agency, international law has all the efficacy that a municipal legal system can muster.[129] For most international lawyers, this efficacy is enough because most international lawyers, especially those practising some sort of international economic law, such as international commercial, corporate, tax or trade law, rely upon national legal systems, not upon any international legal system, to get their job done. 'Piggy-backing' on national law-applying and law-enforcing institutions is quite an ordinary way in which international law is made effective. Indeed, one of the most helpful contributions which international law makes to international relations is to provide common rules which are applicable and effective simultaneously in two or more municipal legal systems.

When we think of the problem of international law being ineffective, we are not contemplating international law as it comes to be incorporated and enforced in municipal law. Rather, the particular ineffectiveness of international law arises in its application within whatever we have for an international legal system. It is not the body of rules of international law, so much as the process of international law, which is really at issue. The better question might be formulated: how are the rules of international law effective in international legal process?

A focus on the efficacy of international law in international legal process is reflected in the usual critiques of international law as not being real 'law'. In the nineteenth century, the leading English legal positivist, John Austin, concerned especially about the link between rules and rule-enforcement, argued that real 'law' required a sovereign to enforce it and that, therefore, with no international sovereign, international law was by definition not 'law' but a form of morality.[130] In 1961, H. L. A. Hart, in his modern construction of positivism, while accepting that linguistically and because of usage it was right to call international law 'law', wrote that international law, as he then observed it, resembled not a municipal legal system but a primitive legal system where there are primary rules of obligation but no secondary rules efficiently to make, recognize or enforce primary rules.[131]

---

[129] In the U.S., for example, Art. VI(2) of the Constitution makes 'all Treaties made, or which shall be made, under the Authority of the United States…the Supreme Law of the Land'. U.S. Const. Art. VI, cl. 2. Moreover, the Supreme Court has held that customary international law is part of the common law of the U.S. *The Paquete Habana*, 175 U.S. 677, 700 (1900). *See* Janis, *supra* n. 2, at 87–97. *See* Chapter 14(C).

[130] J. Austin, *The Province of Jurisprudence Determined* 208 (1st edn. 1832).

[131] H. L. A. Hart, *The Concept of Law* 209, 226 (1961) (hereinafter cited as 'Hart').

Whatever their differences, however, neither Austin's nor Hart's nor most other general jurisprudential characterizations of international law pay particular attention to the diversity of international legal process. That is, most discussions of the problem of the efficacy or the law-like quality of international law assume that there is *a* system—ineffective though it may be—of international law and suppose that there is something like a single, general, integrated, if not hierarchical, international legal process. Reality is otherwise. Although there is some international law and process which may purport to be universal, such as the United Nations and its law or some customary international law or perhaps natural law or *jus cogens*, most international law and process is pertinent only to a number of consenting states. This is true even for widely popular treaty frameworks, such as the General Agreement on Tariffs and Trade and the International Monetary Fund. It is no more accurate to say that there is *a* system of international law than to say that there is a system of municipal law. As there are many systems of municipal law, so there are many systems of international law.

Given the diversity of international legal process, the efficacy question might again be reformulated, and its answer tell us more, if we ask: what forms of international legal process are effective? The reformulated question assumes properly that there are different systems of international law and hints that some systems will be more effective than others. In analysing the relationship between law and society, Max Weber, at the turn of the twentieth century, defined 'law' as 'an order system endowed with certain specific guarantees of the probability of its empirical validity'.[132] Weber's necessary 'guarantees' for law were more sophisticated than Austin's necessary 'sovereigns' for law. Weber wrote of a 'coercive apparatus, i.e., that there are one or more persons whose special task it is to hold themselves ready to apply specially provided means of coercion (legal coercion) for the purpose of norm enforcement'. The 'coercive apparatus' may use psychological as well as physical means of coercion and may operate directly or indirectly against the participants in the system.[133]

Somewhat surprisingly, given the problem of efficacy in international law, there is relatively little academic attention paid to it. Most international legal studies are concerned with rules rather than process. Some of the scholarly reluctance is due probably to the division between international lawyers and political scientists; the lawyers feeling comfortable with rules but uncomfortable with international relations, and the political scientists vice versa.

The best known international legal tribunal, the International Court of Justice at the Hague, has been all too often part of a relatively ineffective international legal system, that of the United Nations. This does not make the United Nations system unimportant; politically it is very important indeed. It is only to say that the International Court and United Nations law might at present be relatively uninteresting to legal theorists because they usually are such ineffective legal instruments.

---

[132] M. Weber, *Law in Economy and Society* 13 (Rheinstein & Shils trans. 1954).

[133] *Id.* at 13. Hart describes the same kind of characteristics in his discussion of the 'internal' point of view essential to any mature legal system. *See* Hart, *supra* n. 131, at 111–14.

Much more interesting in theory (and perhaps as a harbinger) is the international legal system fashioned by the European Convention on Human Rights where formal legal structures, i.e., the European Court of Human Rights and, until its merger into the Court in 1999, the European Commission of Human Rights at Strasbourg, have exercised actual authority. Their demonstrated effectiveness has been unrivalled on the international plane, save perhaps by those other European international legal institutions, the European Union's Court of Justice and Court of First Instance at Luxembourg.

The discussion and materials in this book can, to some degree, illuminate the potential for the efficacy of international legal process. European human rights law provides, therefore, not only the most important body of case law about the substance of international human rights law, but one of the most refreshing and interesting examples of an effective international legal process. Of course, the European human rights law system is neither 'sovereign' in Europe nor are its institutions part of any sort of supranational sovereign authority system satisfying a narrow, Austinian positivist definition of 'law'. In some ways, this makes European human rights law a good model. Generally speaking, there are no Austinian supranational authorities operating in the world today, nor are there likely to be any soon emerging. It could be said that international institutions such as those involved in European human rights law evidence the existence of what Hart would call secondary rules. If so, these schemes would seem less like a primitive legal system and more like a familiar municipal legal system. In Weber's terms, an international legal system like European human rights law can very aptly be described as a structure for legal coercion, using psychological as well as physical means and operating indirectly as well as directly on the participants, specifically states, in the system.

At first blush it may seem surprising that such a phenomenon should emerge in a field like human rights. The kinds of politically sensitive problems with which such a system must deal may appear particularly poor candidates for engendering a supranational psychological consensus. Perhaps the explanation lies in an essential dichotomy between, on the one hand, agreement on the general character of the proposed rules of law and mechanisms for enforcement and, on the other, the actual application of the rules and operation of those mechanisms. That distinction is striking in the materials in this book. It was relatively easy in the wake of the brutal experience of the war against fascism for the European survivors to agree both on the importance of protecting human rights and on the inadequacy of relying solely on national enforcement systems. Moreover, while the debates which accompanied the drafting of the European Convention on Human Rights and Fundamental Freedoms reveal many disparate viewpoints and significant contention, these divisive forces were limited by the fact that the object of the enterprise was, all along, the production of highly general standards of public conduct. The more or less unprecedented machinery for enforcement was made more palatable by providing for phased options for national participation.

The real wonder has been the ever increasing acceptance of the system even after the appearance of highly controversial judgments of the European Court of Human Rights, many of which are reproduced in these materials. As will be seen, the nations adhering to the Convention have submitted to these decisions with a willingness that can only be called startling. The reasons are, no doubt, multiple and complex, but one feature is surely relevant to this discussion. That is the mystique of the forms of law. We cannot know for sure, but it is at least doubtful, that a national state would abandon its sodomy laws or reform its welfare procedures merely on the directive of some nonjudicial board composed almost completely of foreigners. But these same orders, when cast in the form of a judgment of law, have been harder to resist. Resistance would evince not merely a (justifiable) disagreement on matters of policy but a defiance of the commitment to human dignity and the rule of law made by the state when it adhered to the European human rights system in the first place. Such defiance in modern Europe has not usually seemed a politically viable alternative.

Of course, such a view of things is only logical if the Strasbourg Court's judgments are, in fact, nothing more than translations of the general standards of conduct which were agreed upon in the European Convention from its very beginning. Indeed, the Court's form of legal judgment seems to depend on that assumption. A general rule of law is cited and the Court engages in what appears to be a neutral process of reasoning from that rule to a challenged action. The invariable reality of such a direct causal connection has long ago been debunked in adjudication generally.[134] The gap between the promulgation of abstract standards and the controvertible application of those standards to particular cases is a persistent theme in constitutional adjudication. It was clearly foreseen in the deliberations accompanying the drafting of the Convention. One delegate from the United Kingdom cited the fluid construction of the due process clauses of the United States Constitution as a warning. He urged his colleagues to 'define clearly, and in such terms that there be no reasonable latitude for misrepresentation, the purpose we have in mind'. Another British delegate argued against terms with 'a thousand and one interpretations'.[135]

As the judgments reproduced below in the chapters on substantive law make plain, these warnings were both prophetic and unavailing. The language in which the rights were defined was usually broad and unspecific. The Strasbourg Court has exploited that breadth to create novel and, no doubt, little anticipated results. The Court has been explicit in embracing such creative interpretation as a proper part of its judicial duty. Its job, it has noted, is to 'develop the rules instituted by the Convention', which must be regarded as a living instrument.[136]

---

[134] A well-known example focusing on American constitutional law is T. R. Powell, 'The Logic and Rhetoric of Constitutional Law', 15 *Journal of Philosophy* 645 (1918).

[135] 1 *Travaux Préparatoires*, *supra* n. 1, at 80, 148 (remarks of Mr. Ungoed-Thomas and Mr. Nally). *See also id.* at 88 (remarks of M. Fayet of Belgium).

[136] *Ireland v. United Kingdom*, 18 Jan. 1978, 2 E.H.R.R. 25, para. 154; *Tyrer Case*, 25 Apr. 1978, 2 E.H.R.R. 1, para. 31.

We have thus come upon a paradox, but one present in every successful system of law. The existence of a legal system depends on a widely shared psychological attitude towards the rule-making and rule-applying institutions, but that attitude may, itself, be the product of an assumption that such institutions are themselves creatures of pre-existing law. This is a problem of chicken and egg; it is equally pointless here to seek to find which assumption takes priority. We can only say that sometimes a happy (or unhappy) confluence of political decisions, social attitudes and individual actors and actions makes possible the kind of breakthrough that converts ad hoc decision-making bodies into legal tribunals and turns acquiescence into legal obligation. It is that extraordinary phenomenon which we may now be observing in the European human rights system.

If so, it is a curious kind of legal system, one which crosses the boundaries of national jurisdictions and which lacks plenary authority over its subjects.[137] But, for the reasons suggested, that does not seem an adequate reason to deny it the title of 'law'. Whether European human rights law will maintain that position in the long term remains to be seen. There may be a critical moment in the development of any system of law when each exercise of authority ceases to be a risk but instead comes to reinforce the essential perception that the institutions involved are merely the executors of a pre-existing and binding law. When we consider the varied character of the decisions of the European Court of Human Rights, their controversial content, and even the flaws and weaknesses in the Court's arguments, together with the almost uniform respect and obedience rendered to the judgments, we may conclude that such a critical moment may well have been passed.

---

[137] Perhaps not all that curious. Much the same can be said of the 'central' legal systems of federal states.

PART II

SUBSTANTIVE ADJUDICATION IN THE COURT

4

THE RIGHT TO LIFE

ARTICLE 2

1. Everyone's right to life shall be protected by law. No one shall be deprived of his life intentionally save in the execution of a sentence of a court following his conviction of a crime for which this penalty is provided by law.

2. Deprivation of life shall not be regarded as inflicted in contravention of this article when it results from the use of force which is no more than absolutely necessary:

(a) in defence of any person from unlawful violence;

(b) in order to effect a lawful arrest or to prevent escape of a person lawfully detained;

(c) in action lawfully taken for the purpose of quelling a riot or insurrection.

Of all the substantive rights protected by the European Convention the right to life seems most 'self-evident'. A violation of this right makes meaningless the recognition of any other rights. The Universal Declaration of Human Rights included it in a terse composite right in Article 3 to 'life, liberty and security of the person'. Its importance is underscored by the fact that it is protected absolutely, one of the very few rights that may not be abridged even 'in time of war or other public emergency threatening the life of the nation'.[1] The exceptions written into section 2 of Article 2, moreover, are to be available only when the taking of life is 'absolutely necessary' for one of the purposes listed. This formulation contrasts with the more usual requirements for limiting rights—that the infringement be merely 'necessary'.[2] This is a distinction to which the Court itself regularly refers.[3]

This chapter will survey the European Court's jurisprudence on the right to life, noting particularly how the Court has extended a state's obligation far beyond limitations on the official taking of human life. Before dealing with those cases, however, it is necessary to ask: what constitutes human life? This question has been most pronounced in debates over the permissibility of abortion and the status of the unborn foetus. That issue is discussed more fully in Chapter 8 below. But the court has also dealt with the question of when life begins in a somewhat different context.

---

[1] Article 15(2). The single exception is with respect to 'deaths resulting from lawful acts of war'.

[2] E.g. Article 10(2).

[3] E.g. *Andronicou and Constantinou v. Cyprus*, 9 Oct. 1997, 25 E.H.R.R. 491.

A. WHEN DOES 'LIFE' BEGIN?

1. VO V. FRANCE

Judgment of 8 July 2004
40 E.H.R.R. 12.

...

10. On 27 November 1991 the applicant, Mrs Thi-Nho Vo, who is of Vietnamese origin, attended the Lyons General Hospital for a medical examination scheduled during the sixth month of pregnancy.

11. On the same day another woman, Mrs Thi Thanh Van Vo, was due to have a coil removed at the same hospital. When the doctor who was to remove the coil called out the name 'Mrs Vo' in the waiting room, it was the applicant who answered.

After a brief interview, the doctor noted that the applicant had difficulty in understanding French. Having consulted the medical file he sought to remove the coil without examining her beforehand. In so doing, he pierced the amniotic sac causing the loss of a substantial amount of amniotic fluid.

After finding on clinical examination that the uterus was enlarged, the doctor ordered a scan. He then discovered that one had just been performed and realised that there had been a mistake of identity. The applicant was immediately admitted to hospital.

Dr G. then attempted to remove the coil from Mrs Thi Thanh Van Vo, but was unsuccessful and so prescribed an operation under general anaesthetic for the following morning. A further error was then made when the applicant was taken to the operating theatre instead of Mrs Thi Thanh Van Vo, and only escaped the surgery intended for her namesake after she protested and was recognised by an anaesthetist.

12. The applicant left the hospital on 29 November 1991. She returned on 4 December 1991 for further tests. The doctors found that the amniotic fluid had not been replaced and that the pregnancy could not continue further. The pregnancy was terminated on health grounds on 5 December 1991.

13. On 11 December 1991 the applicant and her partner lodged a criminal complaint and applied to be joined as civil parties to the proceedings in which they alleged unintentional injury to the applicant entailing total unfitness for work for a period not exceeding three months and unintentional homicide of her child.

[Dr. G was acquitted partly based on a finding that a 20 to 21 week foetus was not yet viable and thus not a 'human person' within the meaning of the criminal code. This holding was overturned by the Lyons Court of Appeal but then reinstated by the Court of Cassation.]

...

11. In the majority of the member States of the Council of Europe, the offence of unintentional homicide does not apply to the foetus. However, three countries have chosen to create specific offences. In Italy a person negligently causing a pregnancy to terminate is liable to a prison sentence of between three months and two years under section 17 of the Abortion Act of 22 May 1978. In Spain Article 157 of the Criminal Code makes it a criminal offence to cause damage to the foetus and Article 146 an offence to cause an abortion through gross negligence. In Turkey Article 456 of the Criminal Code lays down that a person who causes damage to another shall be liable to a prison sentence of between six months and one year; if the victim is a pregnant woman and the damage results in premature birth, the Criminal Code prescribes a sentence of between two and five years' imprisonment.

...

74. The applicant complained that she had been unable to secure the conviction of the doctor whose medical negligence had caused her to have to undergo a therapeutic abortion. It has not been disputed that she intended to carry her pregnancy to full term and that her child was in good health. ... The central question raised by the application is whether the absence of a criminal remedy within the French legal system to punish the unintentional destruction of a foetus constituted a failure on the part of the State to protect by law the right to life within the meaning of Article 2 of the Convention.

75. Unlike Article 4 of the American Convention on Human Rights, which provides that the right to life must be protected 'in general, from the moment of conception', Article 2 of the Convention is silent as to the temporal limitations of the right to life and, in particular, does not define 'everyone' ('*toute personne*') whose 'life' is protected by the Convention. The Court has yet to determine the issue of the 'beginning' of 'everyone's right to life' within the meaning of this provision and whether the unborn child has such a right.

To date it has been raised solely in connection with laws on abortion. Abortion does not constitute one of the exceptions expressly listed in paragraph 2 of Article 2 but the Commission has expressed the opinion that it is compatible with the first sentence of Article 2 § 1 in the interests of protecting the mother's life and health because 'if one assumes that this provision applies at the initial stage of the pregnancy, the abortion is covered by an implied limitation, protecting the life and health of the woman at that stage, of the 'right to life' of the foetus'. ...

77. In ... *X v. the United Kingdom* ...the Commission considered an application by a man complaining that his wife had been allowed to have an abortion on health grounds. While it accepted that the potential father could be regarded as the 'victim' of a violation of the right to life, it considered that the term 'everyone' in several Articles of the Convention could not apply prenatally, but observed that 'such application in a rare case—e.g. under Article 6, paragraph 1—cannot be excluded'. The Commission added that the general usage of the term 'everyone' ('*toute personne*') and the context in which it was used in Article 2 of the Convention did not include the unborn. As to the term 'life' and, in particular, the beginning of life, the Commission noted a 'divergence of thinking on the question of where life begins' and added: 'While some believe that it starts already with conception, others tend to focus upon the moment of nidation, upon the point that the foetus becomes 'viable', or upon live birth'.

The Commission went on to examine whether Article 2 was 'to be interpreted: as not covering the foetus at all; as recognising a 'right to life' of the foetus with certain implied limitations;
or as recognising an absolute 'right to life' of the foetus'. Although it did not express an opinion
on the first two options, it categorically ruled out the third interpretation, having regard to
the need to protect the mother's life, which was indissociable from that of the unborn child:
'The 'life' of the foetus is intimately connected with, and it cannot be regarded in isolation of,
the life of the pregnant woman. If Article 2 were held to cover the foetus and its protection
under this Article were, in the absence of any express limitation, seen as absolute, an abortion
would have to be considered as prohibited even where the continuance of the pregnancy would
involve a serious risk to the life of the pregnant woman. This would mean that the 'unborn life'
of the foetus would be regarded as being of a higher value than the life of the pregnant woman'.
The Commission adopted that solution, noting that by 1950 practically all the Contracting
Parties had 'permitted abortion when necessary to save the life of the mother' and that in
the meantime the national law on termination of pregnancy had 'shown a tendency towards
further liberalisation'.

...

79. The Court has only rarely had occasion to consider the application of Article 2 to
the foetus. In the case of *Open Door and Dublin Well Woman* [(Judgment of 29 October
1992, Series A no. 246-A)] the Irish Government relied on the protection of the life of the
unborn child to justify their legislation prohibiting the provision of information concerning
abortion facilities abroad. The only issue that was resolved was whether the restrictions on the
freedom to receive and impart the information in question had been necessary in a democratic
society, within the meaning of paragraph 2 of Article 10 of the Convention, to pursue the
'legitimate aim of the protection of morals of which the protection in Ireland of the right
to life of the unborn is one aspect', since the Court did not consider it relevant to determine
'whether a right to abortion is guaranteed under the Convention or whether the foetus is
encompassed by the right to life as contained in Article 2'. Recently, where a woman had
decided to terminate her pregnancy against the father's wishes, the Court held that it was not
required to determine 'whether the foetus may qualify for protection under the first sentence of
Article 2 as interpreted [in the case-law relating to the positive obligation to protect life]', and
continued: 'Even supposing that, in certain circumstances, the foetus might be considered to
have rights protected by Article 2 of the Convention, ... in the instant case ... [the] pregnancy
was terminated in conformity with section 5 of Law no. 194 of 1978'—a law which struck a fair
balance between the woman's interests and the need to ensure protection of the foetus [See
Boso v. Italy, 5 Sept. 2002, (admissibility decision)].

...

82. As is apparent from the above recapitulation of the case-law, the interpretation of
Article 2 in this connection has been informed by a clear desire to strike a balance, and the
Convention institutions' position in relation to the legal, medical, philosophical, ethical
or religious dimensions of defining the human being has taken into account the various
approaches to the matter at national level. This has been reflected in the consideration given
to the diversity of views on the point at which life begins, of legal cultures and of national

standards of protection, and the State has been left with considerable discretion in the matter, as the opinion of the European Group on Ethics at Community level appositely puts it: 'the... Community authorities have to address these ethical questions taking into account the moral and philosophical differences, reflected by the extreme diversity of legal rules applicable to human embryo research... It is not only legally difficult to seek harmonisation of national laws at Community level, but because of lack of consensus, it would be inappropriate to impose one exclusive moral code'.

It follows that the issue of when the right to life begins comes within the margin of appreciation which the Court generally considers that States should enjoy in this sphere, notwithstanding an evolutive interpretation of the Convention, a 'living instrument which must be interpreted in the light of present-day conditions'. The reasons for that conclusion are, firstly, that the issue of such protection has not been resolved within the majority of the Contracting States themselves, in France in particular, where it is the subject of debate and, secondly, that there is no European consensus on the scientific and legal definition of the beginning of life.

83. The Court observes that the French Court of Cassation, in three successive judgments delivered in 1999, 2001 and 2002, considered that the rule that offences and punishment must be defined by law, which required criminal statutes to be construed strictly, excluded acts causing a fatal injury to a foetus from the scope of Article 221-6 of the Criminal Code, under which unintentional homicide of 'another' is an offence. However, if, as a result of unintentional negligence, the mother gives birth to a live child who dies shortly after being born, the person responsible may be convicted of the unintentional homicide of the child. The first-mentioned approach, which conflicts with that of several courts of appeal, was interpreted as an invitation to the legislature to fill a legal vacuum. That was also the position of the Criminal Court in the instant case: 'The court...cannot create law on an issue which [the legislature has] not yet succeeded in defining.' The French parliament attempted such a definition in proposing to create the offence of involuntary termination of pregnancy, but the Bill containing that proposal was lost, on account of the fears and uncertainties that the creation of the offence might arouse as to the determination of when life began, and the disadvantages of the proposal, which were thought to outweigh its advantages. The Court further notes that alongside the Court of Cassation's repeated rulings that Article 221-6 of the Criminal Code does not apply to foetuses, the French parliament is currently revising the 1994 bioethics laws, which added provisions to the Criminal Code on the protection of the human embryo and required re-examination in the light of scientific and technological progress. It is clear from this overview that in France, the nature and legal status of the embryo and/or the foetus are currently not defined and that the manner in which it is to be protected will be determined by very varied forces within French society.

84. At European level, the Court observes that there is no consensus on the nature and status of the embryo and/or foetus, although they are beginning to receive some protection in the light of scientific progress and the potential consequences of research into genetic engineering, medically assisted procreation or embryo experimentation. At best, it may be regarded as common ground between States that the embryo/foetus belongs to the human race. The potentiality of that being and its capacity to become a person—enjoying protection under the civil law, moreover, in many States, such as France, in the context of inheritance and gifts, and also in the United Kingdom—require protection in the name of human dignity, without making it a 'person' with the 'right to life' for the purposes of Article 2. The Oviedo Convention on Human Rights and Biomedicine, indeed, is careful not to give a definition of

the term 'everyone' and its explanatory report indicates that, in the absence of a unanimous agreement on the definition, the member States decided to allow domestic law to provide clarifications for the purposes of the application of that Convention. The same is true of the Additional Protocol on the Prohibition of Cloning Human Beings and the draft Additional Protocol on Biomedical Research, which do not define the concept of 'human being'. It is worth noting that the Court may be requested under Article 29 of the Oviedo Convention to give advisory opinions on the interpretation of that instrument.

85. Having regard to the foregoing, the Court is convinced that it is neither desirable, nor even possible as matters stand, to answer in the abstract the question whether the unborn child is a person for the purposes of Article 2 of the Convention ('*personne*' in the French text). As to the instant case, it considers it unnecessary to examine whether the abrupt end to the applicant's pregnancy falls within the scope of Article 2, seeing that, even assuming that that provision was applicable, there was no failure on the part of the respondent State to comply with the requirements relating to the preservation of life in the public-health sphere. With regard to that issue, the Court has considered whether the legal protection afforded the applicant by France in respect of the loss of the unborn child she was carrying satisfied the procedural requirements inherent in Article 2 of the Convention.

86. In that connection, it observes that the unborn child's lack of a clear legal status does not necessarily deprive it of all protection under French law. However, in the circumstances of the present case, the life of the foetus was intimately connected with that of the mother and could be protected through her, especially as there was no conflict between the rights of the mother and the father or of the unborn child and the parents, the loss of the foetus having been caused by the unintentional negligence of a third party.

87. In the aforementioned *Boso v. Italy* decision, the Court said that even supposing that the foetus might be considered to have rights protected by Article 2 of the Convention, Italian law on the voluntary termination of pregnancy struck a fair balance between the woman's interests and the need to ensure protection of the unborn child. In the present case, the dispute concerns the involuntary killing of an unborn child against the mother's wishes, causing her particular suffering. The interests of the mother and the child clearly coincided. The Court must therefore examine, from the standpoint of the effectiveness of existing remedies, the protection which the applicant was afforded in seeking to establish the liability of the doctor concerned for the loss of her child *in utero* and to obtain compensation for the abortion she had to undergo. The applicant argued that only a criminal remedy would have been capable of satisfying the requirements of Article 2 of the Convention. The Court does not share that view, for the following reasons. . . .

89. Those principles [deriving from the first sentence of Article 2] apply in the public-health sphere too. The positive obligations require States to make regulations compelling hospitals, whether private or public, to adopt appropriate measures for the protection of patients' lives. They also require an effective independent judicial system to be set up so that the cause of death of patients in the care of the medical profession, whether in the public or the private sector, can be determined and those responsible made accountable.

90. Although the right to have third parties prosecuted or sentenced for a criminal offence cannot be asserted independently, the Court has stated on a number of occasions that an effective judicial system, as required by Article 2, may, and under certain circumstances must, include recourse to the criminal law. However, if the infringement of the right to life or to physical integrity is not caused intentionally, the positive obligation imposed by Article 2 to

set up an effective judicial system does not necessarily require the provision of a criminal-law remedy in every case. In the specific sphere of medical negligence, 'the obligation may for instance also be satisfied if the legal system affords victims a remedy in the civil courts, either alone or in conjunction with a remedy in the criminal courts, enabling any liability of the doctors concerned to be established and any appropriate civil redress, such as an order for damages and for the publication of the decision, to be obtained. Disciplinary measures may also be envisaged'.

91. In the instant case, in addition to the criminal proceedings which the applicant instituted against the doctor for unintentionally causing her injury—she had the possibility of bringing an action for damages against the authorities on account of the doctor's alleged negligence. Had she done so, the applicant would have been entitled to have an adversarial hearing on her allegations of negligence and to obtain redress for any damage sustained. A claim for compensation in the administrative courts would have had fair prospects of success and the applicant could have obtained damages from the hospital. . . .

95. The Court accordingly concludes that, even assuming that Article 2 was applicable in the instant case, there has been no violation of Article 2 of the Convention.

[The Court held 14–3 that there had been no violation of Article 2.]

Separate Opinion of Judge Costa

3. I voted in favour of finding no violation of Article 2, but would have preferred the Court to hold that Article 2 was applicable, even if such a conclusion is not self-evident. Such a decision would perhaps have been clearer with only minimal inconvenience as regards the scope of the judgment. . . .

12. To my mind, this judgment of the highest French administrative court demonstrates that a decision by the European Court of Human Rights in which it is plainly stated that the 'end of life' of an unborn child is within the scope of Article 2 of the Convention would not threaten—at least not in essence—the domestic legislation of a large number of European countries that makes the voluntary termination of pregnancy lawful, subject, of course, to compliance with certain conditions. In a number of European States, such legislation has been held to be consistent with the domestic Constitution and even with Article 2 of the Convention. The Norwegian Supreme Court so found in 1983. The German Federal Constitutional Court and the Spanish Constitutional Court have also accepted that the right to life, as protected by Article 2 of the Convention, can apply to the embryo or the foetus (the question whether that right is *absolute* being a separate issue). These are examples of decisions in which the highest courts of individual countries have recognised that the right to life, whether set out in Article 2 of the European Convention on Human Rights or enshrined in domestic constitutional principles of like content and scope, *applies* to the foetus, without being absolute. Is there any reason why the Court, which aspires to the role of a constitutional court within the European human-rights order, should be less bold? . . .

14. Similarly, it might be contended that, since Article 15 of the Convention states that no derogation may be made from Article 2, it would be preposterous for the Court to find that Article 2 is not absolute, or is subject to implied exceptions other than those exhaustively set out in the second paragraph thereof. This would militate in favour of holding that Article 2 does not apply to the unborn child (as the unborn child is not one of the exceptions set out in

the second paragraph). However, I am not persuaded by either of these two arguments. The non-derogation rule only prohibits States parties that derogate from the Convention in time of war or other public emergency, as they are entitled to do by Article 15, from infringing Article 2. However, quite clearly situations and exceptional circumstances of this kind are quite unrelated to the killing of an unborn child. More disconcerting from a logical perspective is an argument based on the actual wording of Article 2. However, not only has the Court already decided the point (as it indisputably did in *Boso*), Article 2 cannot be conclusively construed as clearly prohibiting all voluntary terminations of pregnancy, if only because a number of Contracting States have ratified the Convention without any apparent problem, despite already possessing legislation permitting voluntary termination in certain circumstances. Even more persuasive when it comes to an evolutive interpretation of Article 2 is the fact that a large number of European countries passed legislation in the 1970s permitting the voluntary termination of pregnancy within a strict framework....

17. In sum, I see no good legal reason or decisive policy consideration for not applying Article 2 in the present case. On a general level, I believe (in company with many senior judicial bodies in Europe) that there is life before birth, within the meaning of Article 2, that the law must therefore protect such life, and that if a national legislature considers that such protection cannot be absolute, then it should only derogate from it, particularly as regards the voluntary termination of pregnancy, within a regulated framework that limits the scope of the derogation.

Separate Opinion of Judge Rozakis, joined by Judges Caflisch, Fishbach, Lorenzen and Thomassen

Even if one accepts that life begins before birth, that does not automatically and unconditionally confer on this form of human life a right to life equivalent to the corresponding right of a child after its birth. This does not mean that the unborn child does not enjoy any protection by human society, since—as the relevant legislation of European States, and European agreements and relevant documents show—the unborn life is already considered to be worthy of protection. But as I read the relevant legal instruments, this protection, though afforded to a being considered worthy of it, is, as stated above, distinct from that given to a child after birth, and far narrower in scope. It consequently transpires from the present stage of development of the law and morals in Europe that the life of the unborn child, although protected in some of its attributes, cannot be equated to post-natal life, and, therefore, does not enjoy a right in the sense of 'a right to life', as protected by Article 2 of the Convention. Hence, there is a problem of applicability of Article 2 in the circumstances of the case.

... By using the 'even assuming' formula as to the applicability of Article 2, and by linking the life of the foetus to the life of the mother ('the life of the foetus was intimately connected with that of the mother and could be protected through her...')—the majority has surreptitiously brought Article 2 of the Convention to the fore of the case. Yet, it is obvious from the case-law that reliance on the procedural guarantees of Article 2 to determine whether or not there has been a violation presupposes the prima facie applicability of that Article (and using the 'even assuming' formula does not alter the position if, in the end, the only real ground for the Court's findings is the hypothesis referred to in the formula); and in the circumstances of the case there was not even the remotest threat to the mother's right of life such as would justify bringing the procedural guarantees of Article 2 of the Convention into play.

For the reasons explained above, I am unable to agree with the reasoning of the majority and conclude that, as matters presently stand, Article 2 is inapplicable in this case.

Dissenting opinion of Judge Ress

3. In order to reach that conclusion, it seems necessary to find out whether Article 2 applies to the unborn child. I am prepared to accept that there may be differences in the level of protection afforded to an embryo and to a child after birth. Nevertheless, that does not justify the conclusion that it is not possible to answer in the abstract the question whether the unborn child is a person for the purposes of Article 2 of the Convention. All the Court's case-law and the Commission's decisions are based on the 'assuming that' argument (*in eventu*). Yet the failure to give a clear answer can no longer be justified by reasons of procedural economy. Nor can the problem of protecting the embryo through the Convention be solved solely through the protection of the mother's life. As this case illustrates, the embryo and the mother, as two separate 'human beings', need separate protection.

Even if it is assumed that the ordinary meaning of human life in Article 2 of the Convention is not entirely clear and can be interpreted in different ways, the obligation to protect human life requires more extensive protection, particularly in view of the techniques available for genetic manipulation and the unlimited production of embryos for various purposes. The manner in which Article 2 is interpreted must evolve in accordance with these developments and constraints and confront the real dangers now facing human life. Any restriction on such a dynamic interpretation must take into account the relationship between the life of a person who has been born and the unborn life, which means that protecting the foetus to the mother's detriment would be unacceptable.

...

6. The fact that various provisions of the Convention contain guarantees which by their nature cannot extend to the unborn cannot alter that position. If, by their very nature, the scope of such provisions can only extend to natural persons or legal entities, or to persons who have been born or are adults, that does not preclude the conclusion that other provisions such as the first sentence of Article 2 incorporate protection for the lives of human beings in the initial stage of their development.

7. It should be noted that the present case is wholly unrelated to laws on the voluntary termination of pregnancy. That is a separate issue which is fundamentally different from interference, against the mother's wishes, in the life and welfare of her child. The present case concerns wrongdoing by a third party resulting in the loss of a foetus, if not the death of the mother, whereas voluntary abortion is solely concerned with the relationship between the mother and the child and the question of their protection by the State. Although holding that Article 2 applies to human life before birth may have repercussions on the laws regulating the voluntary termination of pregnancy, that is not a reason for saying that Article 2 is not applicable. Quite the opposite.

8. There can be no margin of appreciation on the issue of the applicability of Article 2. A margin of appreciation may, in my opinion, exist to determine the measures that should

be taken to discharge the positive obligation that arises because Article 2 is applicable, but it is not possible to restrict the applicability of Article 2 by reference to a margin of appreciation....

9. Since I consider that Article 2 applies to human beings even before they are born, an interpretation which seems to me to be consistent with the approach of the Charter of Fundamental Rights of the European Union, and since France does not afford sufficient protection to the foetus against the negligent acts of third parties, I find that there has been a violation of Article 2 of the Convention. As regards the specific measures necessary to discharge that positive obligation, that is a matter for the respondent State, which should either take strict disciplinary measures or afford the protection of the criminal law (against unintentional homicide).

Dissenting Opinion of Judge Mularoni joined by Judge Straznicka

... I consider that one should not overlook the fact that the foetus in the instant case was almost as old as foetuses that have survived and that scientific advances now make it possible to know virtually everything about a foetus of that age: its weight, sex, exact measurements, and whether it has any deformities or problems. Although it does not yet have any independent existence from that of its mother (though having said that, in the first years of its life, a child cannot survive alone without someone to look after it either) I believe that it is a being separate from its mother.

Although legal personality is only acquired at birth, this does not to my mind mean that there must be no recognition or protection of 'everyone's right to life' before birth. Indeed, this seems to me to be a principle that is shared by all the member States of the Council of Europe, as domestic legislation permitting the voluntary termination of pregnancy would not have been necessary if the foetus was not regarded as having a life that should be protected. Abortion therefore constitutes an exception to the rule that the right to life should be protected, even before birth.

In any event, this case is wholly unconcerned with the States' domestic abortion laws, which have long been the subject matter of applications to the Convention institutions and have been found to be consistent with the Convention.

I consider that, as with other Convention provisions, Article 2 must be interpreted in an evolutive manner so that the great dangers currently facing human life can be confronted. This is made necessary by the potential that exists for genetic manipulation and the risk that scientific results will be used for a purpose that undermines the dignity and identity of the human being. The Court has, moreover, often stated that the Convention is a living instrument, to be interpreted in the light of present-day conditions....

2. THE EXTENT OF ARTICLE 2

The Court has held that a violation of Article 2 is possible even when no person (however defined) actually dies. In *Ilhan v. Turkey*[4] the applicant's brother had been arrested

---

[4] 27 June 2000, 34 E.H.R.R. 36.

by gendarmes and beaten severely, causing serious head injuries. He was kept under arrest and received no medical treatment for 36 hours. He survived but sustained an apparently permanent loss of function on his left side. The court, citing three prior cases, held it was proper to consider the case notwithstanding the victim's survival. The Court noted that this case and all prior cases where there had been no actual death involved a state's 'positive obligation' to protect life (see Section C, below). The Court then provided this cryptic explanation:

[I]t is only in exceptional circumstances that physical ill-treatment by State officials which does not result in death may disclose a breach of Article 2 of the Convention. It is correct that the criminal responsibility of those concerned in the use of force is not an issue in the proceedings under the Convention. Nonetheless the degree and type of force used and the unequivocal intention or aim behind the use of force may, among other factors, be relevant in assessing whether in a particular case the States' agents actions in inflicting injury short of death must be regarded as incompatible with the object and purpose of Article 2 of the Convention.[5]

In *Acar and Others v. Turkey* two applicants had been wounded but had survived a 'sustained and lethal' attack that killed eight people. The Court held they were 'victims of conduct which … put their lives at grave risk'. They were allowed to argue violations of Article 2.[6] The receipt of mere threats to kill, however, has been held not to engage Article 2.[7]

The Court rejected a different kind of extension of the right to life in *Pretty v. United Kingdom*.[8] The applicant was a woman suffering the advanced stages of motor neurone disease, an untreatable and progressively debilitating condition, leaving her paralysed from the neck down without the power of speech and fed through a tube. She wished to end her life, which was impossible without assistance, and English law made assisting suicide a crime. She claimed that Article 2 gave her a right 'to choose whether or not to go on living'. The Court rejected the idea that Article 2 included a 'negative aspect'. It distinguished its holding in Article 11 cases that the right of association implied a right not to associate. The right protected in Article 11 was a 'freedom' right protecting individual choice:

Article 2 of the Convention is phrased in different terms. It is unconcerned with issues to do with the quality of living or what a person chooses to do with his or her life. To the extent that these aspects are recognised as so fundamental to the human condition that they require protection from State interference, they may be reflected in the rights guaranteed by other Articles of the Convention, or in other international human rights instruments. Article 2 cannot, without a distortion of language, be interpreted as conferring the diametrically opposite right, namely

---

[5] *Id.* at para. 76.
[6] 24 May 2005.
[7] *Dizman v. Turkey*, 20 Sept. 2005, 44 E.H.R.R. 25.
[8] 29 April 2002, 35 E.H.R.R. 1.

a right to die; nor can it create a right to self-determination in the sense of conferring on an individual the entitlement to choose death rather than life.[9]

B. STATE OBLIGATIONS UNDER ARTICLE 2

An examination of the text of Article 2 gives little indication of the areas to which it has been applied. On its face it appears to require the state 1) to establish legal rules to prevent the taking of human life by anyone and 2) to refrain from taking life itself except when necessary to achieve one of the defined purposes in section 2. These exceptions recognize the inevitable risk to life involved in certain essential functions of the state. These are the state's obligation to protect citizens from private violence (2(a)), to enforce its criminal law by forcible detention (2(b)) and to maintain public order (2(c)). Moreover, while Article 15 generally excludes derogations from Article 2 even in times of 'war or other public emergency threatening the life of the nation', it permits such emergency derogations 'in respect of deaths resulting from lawful acts of war'.

The Court has inferred from the exceptions in section 2 that even the use of force that unintentionally results in taking a life is subject to scrutiny under Article 2. Indeed, as will be seen, the bulk of the Court's case law involves exactly that kind of situation—where the complaint is not that the state itself deliberately took a life but that it conducted itself in such a way as to contribute to the death of the applicants' decedent. The Court has summed up its approach to such cases in language that appears in roughly the same form in most of its Article 2 cases:

The text of Article 2 read as a whole, demonstrates that it covers not only intentional killing but also situations where it is permitted to 'use force' which may result, as an unintended outcome, in the deprivation of life. The deliberate or intended use of lethal force is, however, only one factor to be taken into account in assessing its necessity. Any use of force must be no more than is 'absolutely necessary' for the achievement of one or more of the purposes set out in sub-paragraphs (a) to (c). This term indicates that a stricter and more compelling test of necessity must be employed from that normally applicable when determining whether State action is 'necessary in a democratic society' under paragraphs 2 of Articles 8 to 11 of the Convention. Consequently the use of force must be strictly proportionate to the achievement of the permitted aims.[10]

The court's jurisprudence may be categorized as recognizing three kinds of state duties: 1) the use of excessive force in police and military functions; 2) inadequate planning and preparation in connection with those functions; and 3)

---

[9] *Id.* at para. 39.
[10] *McKerr v. United Kingdom*, 4 May 2001, 34 E.H.R.R. 20, para. 110.

failure adequately to investigate causes of death. All three duties were raised in the following case.

1. GÜL V. TURKEY

Judgment of 14 December 2000
34 E.H.R.R. 28

10. The facts of the case, particularly concerning events on 8 March 1993 when Mehmet Gül, the applicant's son, was shot dead by police officers firing through the door of his apartment during a search operation in Bozova, were disputed by the parties. The Commission, pursuant to former Article 28 § 1(a) of the Convention, conducted an investigation with the assistance of the parties....

13. Bozova was a small town, of about 15–16,000 people, located about 36 km from Şanliurfa in the south-east region of Turkey. It was close to the Atatürk dam which was perceived as a possible target for the PKK (the Kurdish Workers' Party). A company of commandos was stationed there. There was no evidence that PKK activity was particularly prevalent in Bozova itself or that there were any significant security problems.

14. The applicant, a business-man and an official in the local branch of the True Path Party, was well-known in Bozova and a respected citizen, unsuspected of any illicit activities. His son Mehmet Gül was less well-known, running a petrol station for him. There was no evidence prior to the events of 7–8 March 1993 that he was suspected of involvement with the PKK.

15. On 7 March 1993, Major Güder, the provincial gendarme commander, received a telephone call from an informant, naming three to four terrorists and indicating the addresses in Bozova where they could be found.

16. ... As a large number of addresses were searched during the night, the search was wider than the addresses originally mentioned by the informant. The basis on which those addresses were chosen was not established. Mehmet Gül had not been named as one of the terrorists by the informant and the reason why his apartment was to be searched was not provided in any of the written or oral evidence. ...

18. Shortly before 01.00 hours, the special operations team arrived at the applicant's apartment block with the intention of carrying out a search of Mehmet Gül's flat....

23. On the basis of its assessment of the evidence, the Commission found that there was no prolonged knocking on the door or any verbal warning given to those inside the flat. Mehmet Gül came to the door in answer to a light knocking. It was highly probable that the officers outside started firing through the door, as Mehmet Gül was in the process of opening the lock. It was possible that the click of the key turning sounded like a gun being cocked and that this triggered their reaction. The intensity of the firing destroyed fingers on Mehmet Gül's right hand and inflicted numerous wounds. As he turned away from the door, a bullet struck him in the back inflicting a fatal injury. He staggered back up the corridor, leaving blood stains against the wall. His wife, Filiz Gül, collided with him in the doorway of the bedroom and he collapsed on a sofa bed in that room. Meanwhile, in the flat next door, Mustafa Gül had heard

the shooting and after opening his door briefly, he realised that it was the police and came out. He was forced onto the ground with a gun to his head. When the applicant came downstairs, he saw Mustafa on the ground held at gunpoint by a security officer. He also saw that the lights were out and switched the mains switch back on. The applicant and Mustafa participated in the efforts to open the door by physical force as the lock had jammed under the force of the bullets and Filiz Gül had been unable to open it from the inside. When the door was kicked open, the applicant and Mustafa entered the flat to find his injured son at the same time as, or shortly after, police officers entered.

24. The applicant and other members of the family carried the severely injured Mehmet Gül downstairs and carried him to the local health centre in the applicant's car. There, he was transferred to an ambulance which took him to Şanliurfa hospital. He died however prior to his arrival. His body was taken to the morgue.

25. Meanwhile, a search was carried out at Mehmet Gül's flat. An incident report, and numerous statements of police officers, recorded that two guns were found in the flat—a Browning cocked with a bullet in the barrel and a French 10 rounder—and that a 9 mm empty cartridge was found in the corridor near the front door. These documents did not identify which of the signatories in fact witnessed the finding of these objects. The oral testimonies of the officers were confused and contradictory. No one was able to say who had found the French 10 rounder as alleged in a wardrobe. While Telçi claimed to have found the Browning, he was unable to recall whether it was bloodstained or not. There was no evidence that any precautions were taken in handling the guns with a view to preserving any forensic evidence. The finding of the guns was not properly recorded. They were not delivered to the public prosecutor until 12 March, three days later. The photograph taken of the guns shows them sitting on a desk, either at the police station or the prosecutor's office. The Commission did not find it established that the guns were found in the flat as alleged by the officers.

26. The special operations team returned to Şanliurfa after the search. They were not required to hand in their guns for examination or to account for the bullets expended during the operation....

36. On 26 February 1996, the [domestic] court appointed a gendarme lieutenant Güven Sağban as expert. He submitted a report dated 28 February 1996. This stated that from the file it was understood that the officers had called out warnings at the house, that the deceased had come out, fired one shot and shut the door again and that the officers fired at the lock to open it. The deceased, in the line of fire, was wounded and died. A subsequent search revealed the gun which had been fired and another, both unlicensed. It was noted that the complainants and other witnesses essentially disputed the statements of the security officers. It concluded that the defendants were members of a special operations team and had received serious and strict security training. During the incident and operation, conducted on the basis of intelligence information, the deceased fired a shot and the defendants were therefore 'precon-ditioned'. They were primarily concerned to open the door and also to protect themselves and their colleagues. For those reasons, they fired at the lock. The photographs indicated that the defendants' firing was concentrated round the lock to break it. Also the deceased's firing was intended to attack more than to defend. This indicated that although the defendants showed the care and attention expected from them, the incident occurred. No fault or ill-intention could be attributed to them....

39. None of the experts visited the scene or requested any further information or evidence but based themselves on the statements in the file.

40. On 9 December 1996, the court referring to the expert report of 16 July 1996 concluded that the defendants were not at fault and acquitted the three officers. The Commission noted that there was no indication that in any of the proceedings consideration had been given as to whether the accounts of the family were in any respect accurate or on what basis the version of events given by the security forces was to be preferred. It is not apparent that the applicant was informed of the criminal proceedings or afforded the opportunity to join as a party....

63. The Court reiterates its settled case-law that under the Convention system prior to 1 November 1998 the establishment and verification of the facts was primarily a matter for the Commission. While the Court is not bound by the Commission's findings of fact and remains free to make its own assessment in the light of all the material before it, it is however only in exceptional circumstances that it will exercise its powers in this area.

...

76. Article 2, which safeguards the right to life and sets out the circumstances when deprivation of life may be justified, ranks as one of the most fundamental provisions in the Convention, to which no derogation is permitted. Together with Article 3, it also enshrines one of the basic values of the democratic societies making up the Council of Europe. The circumstances in which deprivation of life may be justified must therefore be strictly construed. The object and purpose of the Convention as an instrument for the protection of individual human beings also requires that Article 2 be interpreted and applied so as to make its safeguards practical and effective.

77. The text of Article 2, read as a whole, demonstrates that it covers not only intentional killing but also the situations where it is permitted to 'use force' which may result, as an unintended outcome, in the deprivation of life. The deliberate or intended use of lethal force is only one factor however to be taken into account in assessing its necessity. Any use of force must be no more than 'absolutely necessary' for the achievement of one or more of the purposes set out in sub-paragraphs (a) to (c). This term indicates that a stricter and more compelling test of necessity must be employed from that normally applicable when determining whether State action is 'necessary in a democratic society' under paragraphs 2 of Articles 8 to 11 of the Convention. Consequently, the force used must be strictly proportionate to the achievement of the permitted aims.

78. In the light of the importance of the protection afforded by Article 2, the Court must subject deprivations of life to the most careful scrutiny, taking into consideration not only the actions of State agents but also all the surrounding circumstances. Use of force by State agents in pursuit of one of the aims delineated in paragraph 2 of Article 2 may be justified where it is based on an honest belief which is perceived for good reasons to be valid at the time but which subsequently turns out to be mistaken.

79. In the present case, it is undisputed that Mehmet Gül died as the result of bullet wounds inflicted when three police officers of a special operations team opened fire on the door behind which he stood. The Court has accepted the Commission's finding that there was insufficient evidence concerning the planning of the operation to establish that they

were under instructions to use lethal force or that this was the predetermined purpose of the operation. The applicant argued however that the facts surrounding the shooting clearly disclosed that the police officers themselves deliberately intended to kill the person who was behind the door.

80. The Court does not find it necessary to determine whether the police officers had formulated the intention of killing or acted with reckless disregard for the life of the person behind the door. It does not fulfil the functions of a criminal court as regards the allocation of degree of individual fault. It is satisfied that the police officers used a disproportionate degree of force in the circumstances for the reasons set out below.

81. It recalls the findings of the Commission that Mehmet Gül, who lived in his flat with his wife and children, came to answer the door at about 01.00 hours. While he was unlocking the door, the three police officers opened fire in one long, continuous burst. He was fatally injured by the gunfire which caused him multiple injuries. The intensity of the firing destroyed the fingers of his right hand. The assertion of the police officers that Mehmet Gül had fired one pistol shot at them was found to lack credibility and was unsupported by any other satisfactory evidence. The lack of proper recording of the alleged finding of two guns and a spent cartridge in the flat after the events removed the credibility of the police evidence in that regard.

82. In those circumstances, the firing of at least 50–55 shots at the door was not justified by any reasonable belief of the officers that their lives were at risk from the occupants of the flat. Nor could the firing be justified by any consideration of the need to secure entry to the flat as it placed in danger the lives of anyone in close proximity to the door. The Court recalls that the Commission, based on the assessment of its Delegates who heard the officers concerned, considered that the officers possibly opened fire in reaction to the sound of the door bolt being drawn back in the mistaken view that they were about to come under fire by terrorists. The reaction however of opening fire with automatic weapons on an unseen target in a residential block inhabited by innocent civilians, women and children was as the Commission found, grossly disproportionate. This case is therefore to be distinguished from Andronicou and Constantinou v. Cyprus[11] where the police officers fired on, and killed, a hostage taker, who was in known possession of a gun which he had fired twice, injuring a police officer and the hostage.

83. The Court concludes that the use of force by the police officers cannot be regarded as 'absolutely necessary' for the purpose of defending life. It follows that there has been a violation of Article 2 in that respect.

84. The Court's case-law establishes that in determining whether the use of lethal force was compatible with Article 2 the Court must subject deprivations of life to the most careful scrutiny, taking into consideration not only the actions of the individual agents of the State who actually administer the force, but also all the surrounding circumstances, including the planning and control of the actions under consideration. Anti-terrorist operations should be planned and controlled by the authorities so as to minimise to the greatest extent possible recourse to lethal force.

85. The applicant has pointed to a number of features about this operation as disclosing a lack of the requisite care and control e.g. the short, undetailed briefing given to the special

---

[11] Discussed *infra*.

team, and the lack of strategic or tactical planning with reference to alternative methods if entry to the flat was resisted.

86. The Court recalls however that the Commission was unable to make many findings of fact as to the planning of the operation as there was no contemporaneous notes of that planning or the briefings which took place and the recollections of the witnesses available many years after the event were imprecise and uncertain. It is not persuaded that any separate issue concerning this aspect of the operation can usefully be identified. If the officers had been more fully briefed or prepared, it may be speculated that they might have been more cautious. In any event however, the essence of the violation consisted in their disproportionate reaction to events at the door of the flat. The Court makes no separate finding of violation as regards this aspect of the case.

87. As regards the applicant's allegations that the failure of the police to give assistance at the scene of the incident disclosed a separate violation of the right to life, the Court notes that the assertion that Mehmet Gül might have survived if the police had helped is unsubstantiated by any medical evidence and is largely speculative. Though the callousness of the police attitude in leaving it to the family to take Mehmet Gül to the hospital may be deplored, the Court considers it inappropriate, on the facts of this case, to reach any separate finding of a violation.

88. The Court reiterates that the obligation to protect the right to life under Article 2 of the Convention, read in conjunction with the State's general duty under Article 1 of the Convention to 'secure to everyone within [its] jurisdiction the rights and freedoms defined in [the] Convention', requires by implication that there should be some form of effective official investigation when individuals have been killed as a result of the use of force.

89. In that connection, the Court notes that an investigation into the incident was carried out by the public prosecutor. Notwithstanding the seriousness of the incident however and the necessity to gather and record the evidence which would establish what had happened, there were a number of significant omissions. There was no attempt to find the bullet allegedly fired by Mehmet Gül at the police officers, which was their primary justification for shooting him. There was no proper recording of the alleged finding of two guns and a spent cartridge inside the flat, which was also relied on by the police in justifying their actions. The references in the police statements on this point were vague and inconsistent, rendering it impossible to identify which officer had found each weapon. No photograph was taken of the weapons at the alleged location. While a test was carried out on the Browning weapon to show that it had been recently fired, there was no testing of Mehmet Gül's hands for traces that would link him with the gun. Nor was the gun tested for prints. The failure of the autopsy examination to record fully the injuries on Mehmet Gül's body hampered an assessment of the extent to which he was caught in the gunfire, and his position and distance relative to the door, which could have cast further light on the circumstances in which he was killed. The Government submitted that further examination was not necessary since the cause of death was clear. The purpose of a *post mortem* examination however is also to elucidate the circumstances surrounding the death, including a complete and accurate record of possible signs of ill-treatment and injury and an objective analysis of clinical findings (see in that respect the Model Autopsy Protocol annexed to The Manual on the Effective Prevention and Investigation of Extra-legal, Arbitrary and Summary Executions adopted by the United Nations in 1991, which emphasises the necessity in potentially controversial cases for a systematic and comprehensive examination and report to prevent the omission or loss of important details, . . .).

90. Further, although the actions of the officers involved in an operation which resulted in a death required careful and prompt scrutiny by the responsible authorities, the public prosecutor did not take any statements from those involved. The lack of accountability of the officers for the use of their weapons and ammunition is an additional shortcoming in the procedures adopted after the incident. It was neither required by the officers' superiors or the public prosecutor that their guns be checked and a record made of the amount of ammunition expended.

91. Statements were only taken from the officers two months later by the inspector appointed by the administrative council. The Court has already found that the investigations undertaken by administrative councils into killings by security forces fail to satisfy the requirements of an independent investigation, in particular since the council and the officers under investigation were both hierarchically subordinate to the governor. While the inspector appointed by the council took statements from many relevant witnesses, it is not apparent that he took any steps to clarify the background of the operation, in particular as to the information on which the operation was based and conducted, which might have cast light on why Mehmet Gül's flat was included in the operation in the first place and the extent to which the special team officers were justified in expecting an armed resistance. In particular, no statements were taken from the gendarmes involved in setting up the operation and choosing the targets....

94. The Court observes that the [Supreme Administrative Court's] decision to acquit the three officers was based entirely on [an expert] opinion that there was no fault. There was no reasoning as to why the police officers' account was preferred to that of the family. The Court does not dispute that courts may rely in their assessment of fault or findings of fact on the opinions of competent experts. It is not apparent however that the experts in this case were relying on any technical expertise. In basing itself without any additional explanation on the experts' legal classification of the officers' actions, the court in this case effectively deprived itself of its jurisdiction to decide the factual and legal issues of the case.

95. The Court accordingly finds that the authorities failed to conduct an adequate and effective investigation into the circumstances of Mehmet Gül's death. In the circumstances, this rendered recourse to criminal and civil remedies equally ineffective in the circumstances.

...

[The Court held unanimously that there was a violation of Article 2 and by 6–1 that there had been a violation of Article 13.]

2. EXCESSIVE USE OF FORCE

Notice (para. 80) that the Court finds it unnecessary to make a decision as to whether or not the state forces in this case had the actual intention of killing the decedent or had acted with 'reckless disregard' for his life, since it is able to base a violation on the finding that death resulted from 'a disproportionate degree of force'. The Court states in paragraph 77 that the text of Article 2 'read as a whole, demonstrates that it covers not only intentional killing but also the situations where it is permitted to "use force" which may result as an unintended outcome, in the deprivation of life'. Paragraph (1) of Article 2 states that intentional killing is only permitted as the 'execution of a sentence of a court'. (As we will see below, official capital punishment is itself now barred under subsequent protocols.) It follows that the situations excluded from the effect of Article 2 in paragraph (2) must refer to unintentional actions. In those cases the Court will employ the very strict requirements inferable from the use of the term 'absolutely necessary'. In *Gül* the operation that resulted in the loss of Gül's life was arguably justified under the provisions for defending a person from unlawful violence, ((2)(a)), or to effect a lawful arrest, ((2)(b)), but was not found to be 'absolutely necessary' for either purpose.

The determination of whether or not excessive force was used must, in the nature of things, be an individualized decision turning critically on findings of fact. (On fact-finding see Section E, below.) In *Andronicou and Constantinou v. Cyprus*,[12] which the Court distinguishes in *Gül*, police were dealing with a disturbed man in possession of a shotgun who was holding his fiancée hostage in their flat. He had already beaten his captive and she was heard screaming that her captor was going to kill her. After a siege of more than 12 hours, police attempted a rescue and entered the flat. Weapons were fired and the occupants were killed. Among other things the applicants claimed that the officers used excessive force on this occasion by 'directing machine gun fire in ... a sustained manner in a badly lit and confined space'. The Court stated:

8. The Court accepts ... [the officers] honestly believed in the circumstances that it was necessary to kill him in order to save the life of Elsie Constantinou and their own lives and to fire at him repeatedly in order to remove any risk that he might reach for a weapon. It notes in this respect that the use of force by agents of the State in pursuit of one of the aims delineated in paragraph 2 of Article 2 of the Convention may be justified under this provision where it is based on an honest belief which is perceived, for good reasons, to be valid at the time but subsequently turns out to be mistaken. To hold otherwise would be to impose an unrealistic burden on the State and its law-enforcement personnel in the execution of their duty, perhaps to the detriment of their lives and the lives of others.

It is clearly regrettable that so much firepower was used in the circumstances to neutralise any risk presented by Lefteris Andronicou. However, the Court cannot with detached reflection substitute its own assessment of the situation for that of the officers who were required to react in the heat of the moment in what was for them a unique and unprecedented operation to save life. The officers were entitled to open fire for this purpose and to take all measures which they honestly and reasonably believed were necessary to eliminate any risk either to the young woman's life or to their own lives .... [O]nly two of the officers' bullets actually struck her. While tragically they proved to be fatal, it must be acknowledged that the accuracy of the officers' fire was impaired through Lefteris Andronicou's action in clinging on to her thereby exposing her to risk.

9. The Court considers therefore that the use of lethal force in the circumstances, however regrettable it may have been, did not exceed what was 'absolutely necessary' for the purposes

---

[12] 9 Oct. 1997, 25 E.H.R.R. 491.

of defending the lives of Elsie Constantinou and of the officers and did not amount to a breach by the respondent State of their obligations under Article 2 § 2(a) of the Convention.

These principles were applied in a subsequent case where a police officer fatally shot a man thought to be aiming a gun at him even though the gun turned out to be only a replica.[13]

In *Kakoulli v. Turkey*,[14] on the other hand, a soldier was held not justified in shooting a man who had crossed the ceasefire line into Turkish occupied Northern Cyprus and who had refused an instruction to stop when he attempted to escape back to the other side. The Court acknowledged that the border had been troubled by violent incidents occasioned by intruders and that weapons had been found on the body of the victim. But since there had been nothing to indicate an immediate 'risk of death or serious harm to [the soldier]' or others, lethal force could not be shown to be absolutely necessary.[15]

3. DEFECTS IN PLANNING AND CONTROL

In paragraphs 84–86 of the *Gül* case the Court declined to consider the applicants' separate claim that the lack of an adequate plan and lack of information provided to the officers led to the death of Mehmet Gül. The Court decided that it lacked sufficient facts to make an adequate evaluation of the planning of the operation and that, in any event, the 'essence' of the case was the use of excessive force on the scene.

The claim raises one of the most common inquiries undertaken by the Court in Article 2 cases. The Court has reasoned that an inadequately planned and executed military or police action that results in a death cannot, by definition, be a use of force 'absolutely necessary' for one of the purposes listed in Article 2(2).

A. MCCANN AND OTHERS V. UNITED KINGDOM

Judgment of 27 September 1995
21 E.H.R.R. 97

[The applicants were relatives of three IRA members shot and killed by British military personnel in Gibraltar in 1988. Before the incident, United Kingdom, Spanish and Gibraltar authorities suspected an imminent terrorist attack. An advisory group of military, police and Special Air and Security Service officers was formed. United Kingdom military personnel were present to assist Gibraltar police in arresting the suspected terrorists.

At midnight between 5 and 6 March 1988, the Gibraltar Police Commissioner held a briefing to explain the rules of engagement and firearms procedures and provide an assessment of the

---

[13] *Bubbins v. United Kingdom*, 17 March 2005, 41 E.H.R.R. 24.
[14] 22 Nov. 2005, 45 E.H.R.R. 12.
[15] *Id*. at para. 79.

expected attack, including the identities of the three suspects and the operational aspects of the attack which would likely be carried out by a remote controlled car bomb. The plan was for an arrest to be carried out once all the IRA members were present and identified and they had parked a car that they intended to leave.

On March 6, 1988 one of the suspects, Savage, was identified fiddling with something inside his parked car. The other two suspects, McCann and Farrell, entered Gibraltar on foot. Some time later the three were seen looking at the car. After confirming the identities of the suspects, and conducting an exterior examination of the car, it was determined to be a 'suspect car bomb'. After receiving this report and, in view of the fact that the three suspects were leaving the car behind, the Commissioner decided that the three suspects should be arrested on suspicion of conspiracy to murder.

After walking together for some distance, Savage left McCann and Farrell. Soldiers A and B followed McCann and Farrell, and Soldiers D and C followed Savage. When Soldier A was approximately ten metres from McCann, McCann looked back over his left shoulder and appeared to look directly at A and to realize who he was. McCann's hand moved suddenly and aggressively across the front of his body. Believing that McCann was reaching for the button to detonate the bomb, A opened fire. Out of the corner of his eye, A saw Farrell make a half turn to the right towards McCann, grabbing for her handbag, which was under her left arm. A thought that she was also reaching for a button and shot one round into her back. B had also opened fire on Farrell upon observing the same actions.

As D closed within three metres of Savage he heard gunfire. At the same time, C shouted, 'Stop'. Savage spun round and his arm went down towards his right hand hip area. C and D believed that Savage was reaching for a detonator. They opened fire from about two to three metres away. After the shooting, the bodies of the three suspects and Farrell's handbag were searched and no weapons or detonating devices were discovered. No explosives were found in the car.

The Court held that there was insufficient evidence to conclude that the killings were planned either by the soldiers or in response to indications from superior officers.]

186. [The applicants] submitted that the killings came about as a result of incompetence and negligence in the planning and conduct of the anti-terrorist operation to arrest the suspects as well as a failure to maintain a proper balance between the need to meet the threat posed and the right to life of the suspects.

187. The Government submitted that the actions of the soldiers were absolutely necessary in defence of persons from unlawful violence within the meaning of Article 2 para. 2(a)...of the Convention. Each of them had to make a split-second decision which could have affected a large number of lives. They believed that the movements which they saw the suspects make at the moment they were intercepted gave the impression that the terrorists were about to detonate a bomb. This evidence was confirmed by other witnesses who saw the movements in question. If it is accepted that the soldiers honestly and reasonably believed that the terrorists upon whom they opened fire might have been about to detonate a bomb by pressing a button, then they had no alternative but to open fire.

188. [The government] also pointed out that much of the information available to the authorities and many of the judgments made by them proved to be accurate. The three deceased were an IRA active service unit which was planning an operation in Gibraltar; they did have in their control a large quantity of explosives which were subsequently found in Spain;

and the nature of the operation was a car bomb. The risk to the lives of those in Gibraltar was, therefore, both real and extremely serious.

189. The Government further submitted that in examining the planning of the anti-terrorist operation it should be borne in mind that intelligence assessments are necessarily based on incomplete information since only fragments of the true picture will be known. Moreover, experience showed that the IRA were exceptionally ruthless and skilled in counter-surveillance techniques and that they did their best to conceal their intentions from the authorities. In addition, experience in Northern Ireland showed that the IRA is constantly and rapidly devel- oping new technology. They thus had to take into account the possibility that the terrorists might be equipped with more sophisticated or more easily concealable radio-controlled devices than the IRA had previously been known to use. Finally, the consequences of underestimating the threat posed by the active service unit could have been catastrophic. If they had succeeded in detonating a bomb of the type and size found in Spain, everyone in the car-park would have been killed or badly maimed and grievous injuries would have been caused to those in adjacent buildings, which included a school and an old-people's home.

190. The intelligence assessments made in the course of the operation were reasonable ones to make in the light of the inevitably limited amount of information available to the authorities and the potentially devastating consequences of underestimating the terrorists' abilities and resources. In this regard the Government made the following observations:

— It was believed that a remote-controlled device would be used because it would give the terrorists a better chance of escape and would increase their ability to maximise the proportion of military rather than civilian casualties. Moreover, the IRA had used such a device in Brussels only six weeks before.

— It was assumed that any remote-control such as that produced to the Court would be small enough to be readily concealed about the person. The soldiers themselves success- fully concealed radios of a similar size about their persons.

— As testified by Captain Edwards at the inquest, tests carried out demonstrated that a bomb in the car-park could have been detonated from the spot where the terrorists were shot.

— Past experience strongly suggested that the terrorists' detonation device might have been operated by pressing a single button. ...

— It would have been reckless for the authorities to assume that the terrorists might not have detonated their bomb if challenged. ...

191. The Commission considered that, given the soldiers' perception of the risk to the lives of the people of Gibraltar, the shooting of the three suspects could be regarded as abso- lutely necessary for the legitimate aim of the defence of others from unlawful violence. It also concluded that, having regard to the possibility that the suspects had brought in a car bomb which, if detonated, would have occasioned the loss of many lives and the possibility that the suspects could have been able to detonate it when confronted by the soldiers, the planning and execution of the operation by the authorities did not disclose any deliberate design or lack of proper care which might have rendered the use of lethal force disproportionate to the aim of saving lives....

197. As regards the shooting of Mr Savage, the evidence revealed that there was only a matter of seconds between the shooting at the Shell garage (McCann and Farrell) and the

shooting at Landport tunnel (Savage). The Commission found that it was unlikely that Soldiers C and D witnessed the first shooting before pursuing Mr Savage who had turned around after being alerted by either the police siren or the shooting...

Soldier C opened fire because Mr Savage moved his right arm to the area of his jacket pocket, thereby giving rise to the fear that he was about to detonate the bomb. In addition, Soldier C had seen something bulky in his pocket which he believed to be a detonating transmitter. Soldier D also opened fire believing that the suspect was trying to detonate the supposed bomb. The soldiers' version of events was corroborated in some respects by Witnesses H and J, who saw Mr Savage spin round to face the soldiers in apparent response to the police siren or the first shooting...

...

199. All four soldiers admitted that they shot to kill. They considered that it was necessary to continue to fire at the suspects until they were rendered physically incapable of detonating a device.... According to the pathologists' evidence Ms Farrell was hit by eight bullets, Mr McCann by five and Mr Savage by sixteen....

200. The Court accepts that the soldiers honestly believed, in the light of the information that they had been given, as set out above, that it was necessary to shoot the suspects in order to prevent them from detonating a bomb and causing serious loss of life. The actions which they took, in obedience to superior orders, were thus perceived by them as absolutely necessary in order to safeguard innocent lives.

It considers that the use of force by agents of the State in pursuit of one of the aims delineated in paragraph 2 of Article 2... of the Convention may be justified under this provision... where it is based on an honest belief which is perceived, for good reasons, to be valid at the time but which subsequently turns out to be mistaken. To hold otherwise would be to impose an unrealistic burden on the State and its law-enforcement personnel in the execution of their duty, perhaps to the detriment of their lives and those of others.

It follows that, having regard to the dilemma confronting the authorities in the circumstances of the case, the actions of the soldiers do not, in themselves, give rise to a violation of this provision....

201. The question arises, however, whether the anti-terrorist operation as a whole was controlled and organised in a manner which respected the requirements of Article 2... and whether the information and instructions given to the soldiers which, in effect, rendered inevitable the use of lethal force, took adequately into consideration the right to life of the three suspects.

202. The Court first observes that, as appears from the operational order of the Commissioner, it had been the intention of the authorities to arrest the suspects at an appropriate stage. Indeed, evidence was given at the inquest that arrest procedures had been practised by the soldiers before 6 March and that efforts had been made to find a suitable place in Gibraltar to detain the suspects after their arrest...

203. It may be questioned why the three suspects were not arrested at the border immediately on their arrival in Gibraltar and why, as emerged from the evidence given by Inspector Ullger, the decision was taken not to prevent them from entering Gibraltar if they were believed to be on a bombing mission. Having had advance warning of the terrorists' intentions it would

certainly have been possible for the authorities to have mounted an arrest operation. Although surprised at the early arrival of the three suspects, they had a surveillance team at the border and an arrest group nearby . . . In addition, the Security Services and the Spanish authorities had photographs of the three suspects, knew their names as well as their aliases and would have known what passports to look for . . .

204. On this issue, the Government submitted that at that moment there might not have been sufficient evidence to warrant the detention and trial of the suspects. Moreover, to release them, having alerted them to the authorities' state of awareness but leaving them or others free to try again, would obviously increase the risks. Nor could the authorities be sure that those three were the only terrorists they had to deal with or of the manner in which it was proposed to carry out the bombing.

205. The Court confines itself to observing in this respect that the danger to the population of Gibraltar—which is at the heart of the Government's submissions in this case—in not preventing their entry must be considered to outweigh the possible consequences of having insufficient evidence to warrant their detention and trial. In its view, either the authorities knew that there was no bomb in the car—which the Court has already discounted . . . —or there was a serious miscalculation by those responsible for controlling the operation. As a result, the scene was set in which the fatal shooting, given the intelligence assessments which had been made, was a foreseeable possibility if not a likelihood.

The decision not to stop the three terrorists from entering Gibraltar is thus a relevant factor to take into account under this head.

206. The Court notes that at the briefing on 5 March attended by Soldiers A, B, C, and D it was considered likely that the attack would be by way of a large car bomb. A number of key assessments were made. In particular, it was thought that the terrorists would not use a blocking car; that the bomb would be detonated by a radio-control device; that the detonation could be effected by the pressing of a button; that it was likely that the suspects would detonate the bomb if challenged; that they would be armed and would be likely to use their arms if confronted . . .

207. In the event, all of these crucial assumptions, apart from the terrorists' intentions to carry out an attack, turned out to be erroneous. Nevertheless, as has been demonstrated by the Government, on the basis of their experience in dealing with the IRA, they were all possible hypotheses in a situation where the true facts were unknown and where the authorities operated on the basis of limited intelligence information.

208. In fact, insufficient allowances appear to have been made for other assumptions. For example, since the bombing was not expected until 8 March when [a] changing of the guard ceremony was to take place, there was equally the possibility that the three terrorists were on a reconnaissance mission. While this was a factor which was briefly considered, it does not appear to have been regarded as a serious possibility . . .

In addition, at the briefings or after the suspects had been spotted, it might have been thought unlikely that they would have been prepared to explode the bomb, thereby killing many civilians, as Mr McCann and Ms Farrell strolled towards the border area since this would have increased the risk of detection and capture . . . It might also have been thought improbable that at that point they would have set up the transmitter in anticipation to enable them to detonate the supposed bomb immediately if confronted . . .

Moreover, even if allowances are made for the technological skills of the IRA, the description of the detonation device as a 'button job' without the qualifications subsequently described by the experts at the inquest..., of which the competent authorities must have been aware, over-simplifies the true nature of these devices.

209. It is further disquieting in this context that the assessment made by Soldier G, after a cursory external examination of the car, that there was a 'suspect car bomb' was conveyed to the soldiers, according to their own testimony, as a definite identification that there was such a bomb... It is recalled that while Soldier G had experience in car bombs, it transpired that he was not an expert in radio communications or explosives; and that his assessment that there was a suspect car bomb, based on his observation that the car aerial was out of place, was more in the nature of a report that a bomb could not be ruled out...

210. In the absence of sufficient allowances being made for alternative possibilities, and the definite reporting of the existence of a car bomb which, according to the assessments that had been made, could be detonated at the press of a button, a series of working hypotheses were conveyed to Soldiers A, B, C and D as certainties, thereby making the use of lethal force almost unavoidable.

211. However, the failure to make provision for a margin of error must also be considered in combination with the training of the soldiers to continue shooting once they opened fire until the suspect was dead. As noted by the Coroner in his summing-up to the jury at the inquest, all four soldiers shot to kill the suspects... Soldier E testified that it had been discussed with the soldiers that there was an increased chance that they would have to shoot to kill since there would be less time where there was a 'button' device... Against this background, the authorities were bound by their obligation to respect the right to life of the suspects to exercise the greatest of care in evaluating the information at their disposal before transmitting it to soldiers whose use of firearms automatically involved shooting to kill....

213. In sum, having regard to the decision not to prevent the suspects from travelling into Gibraltar, to the failure of the authorities to make sufficient allowances for the possibility that their intelligence assessments might, in some respects at least, be erroneous and to the automatic recourse to lethal force when the soldiers opened fire, the Court is not persuaded that the killing of the three terrorists constituted the use of force which was no more than abso-lutely necessary in defence of persons from unlawful violence within the meaning of Article 2 para. 2(a)... of the Convention.

[The Court held 10–9 that there had been a breach of Article 2(2).]

Joint Dissenting Opinion of Judges Ryssdal, Bernhardt, Thór Vilhjálmsson, Gölcüklü, Palm, Pekkanen, Sir John Freeland, Baka and Jambrek

8. Before turning to the various aspects of the operation which are criticised in the judgment, we would underline three points of a general nature.

First, in undertaking any evaluation of the way in which the operation was organised and controlled, the Court should studiously resist the temptations offered by the benefit of hindsight. The authorities had at the time to plan and make decisions on the basis of incom-plete information. Only the suspects knew at all precisely what they intended; and it was part of their purpose, as it had no doubt been part of their training, to ensure that as little as possible of their intentions was revealed. It would be wrong to conclude in retrospect that a particular course would, as things later transpired, have been better than one adopted at the time under the pressures of an ongoing anti-terrorist operation and that the latter course must therefore be regarded as culpably mistaken. It should not be so regarded unless it is established that in the circumstances as they were known at the time another course should have been preferred.

9. Secondly, the need for the authorities to act within the constraints of the law, while the suspects were operating in a state of mind in which members of the security forces were regarded as legitimate targets and incidental death or injury to civilians as of little conse-quence, would inevitably give the suspects a tactical advantage which should not be allowed to prevail. The consequences of the explosion of a large bomb in the centre of Gibraltar might well be so devastating that the authorities could not responsibly risk giving the suspects the opportunity to set in train the detonation of such a bomb. Of course the obligation of the United Kingdom under Article 2 para. 1 . . . of the Convention extended to the lives of the suspects as well as to the lives of all the many others, civilian and military, who were present in Gibraltar at the time. But, quite unlike those others, the purpose of the presence of the suspects in Gibraltar was the furtherance of a criminal enterprise which could be expected to have resulted in the loss of many innocent lives if it had been successful. They had chosen to place themselves in a situation where there was a grave danger that an irreconcilable conflict between the two duties might arise.

10. Thirdly, the Court's evaluation of the conduct of the authorities should throughout take full account of (a) the information which had been received earlier about IRA intentions to mount a major terrorist attack in Gibraltar by an active service unit of three individuals; and (b) the discovery which . . . had been made in Brussels on 21 January 1988 of a car containing a large amount of Semtex explosive and four detonators, with a radio-controlled system— equipment which, taken together, constituted a device familiar in Northern Ireland.

11. . . . The judgment does not, however, go on to say that it would have been practicable for the authorities to have arrested and detained the suspects . . . [before entering Gibraltar]. Rightly so, in our view, because at that stage there might not be sufficient evidence to warrant their detention and trial. To release them, after having alerted them to the state of readiness of the authorities, would be to increase the risk that they or other IRA members could suc-cessfully mount a renewed terrorist attack on Gibraltar. In the circumstances as then known, it was accordingly not 'a serious miscalculation' for the authorities to defer the arrest rather than merely stop the suspects at the border and turn them back into Spain.

12. Paragraph 206 of the judgment then lists certain 'key assessments' made by the authorities which, in paragraph 207, are said to have turned out, in the event, to be erroneous, although they are accepted as all being possible hypotheses in a situation where the true facts were unknown and where the authorities were operating on the basis of limited intelligence information. Paragraph 208 goes on to make the criticism that 'insufficient allowances appear to have been made for other assumptions'.

13. As a first example to substantiate this criticism, the paragraph then states that since the bombing was not expected until 8 March 'there was equally the possibility that the . . . terrorists were on a reconnaissance mission'.

There was, however, nothing unreasonable in the assessment at the operational briefing on 5 March that the car which would be brought into Gibraltar was unlikely, on the grounds then stated, to be a 'blocking' car . . . So, when the car had been parked in the assembly area by one of the suspects and all three had been found to be present in Gibraltar, the authorities could quite properly operate on the working assumption that it contained a bomb and that, as the suspects were unlikely to risk two visits, it was not 'equally' possible that they were on a reconnaissance mission.

In addition, ... [a] senior military adviser to the Gibraltar Commissioner of Police, gave evidence to the inquest that, according to intelligence information, reconnaissance missions had been undertaken many times before: reconnaissance was, he had been told, complete and the operation was ready to be run. In these circumstances, for the authorities to have proceeded otherwise than on the basis of a worst-case scenario that the car contained a bomb which was capable of being detonated by the suspects during their presence in the territory would have been to show a reckless failure of concern for public safety.

14. Secondly, it is suggested in the second sub-paragraph of paragraph 208 that, at the briefings or after the suspects had been spotted, 'it might have been thought unlikely that they would have been prepared to explode the bomb, thereby killing many civilians, as Mr McCann and Ms Farrell strolled towards the border area since this would have increased the risk of detection and capture'.

Surely, however, the question is rather whether the authorities could safely have operated on the assumption that the suspects would be unlikely to be prepared to explode the bomb when, even if for the time being moving in the direction of the border, they became aware that they had been detected and were faced with the prospect of arrest. In our view, the answer is clear: certainly, previous experience of IRA activities would have afforded no reliable basis for concluding that the killing of many civilians would itself be a sufficient deterrent or that the suspects, when confronted, would have preferred no explosion at all to an explosion causing civilian casualties....

17. Paragraph 209 of the judgment expresses disquiet that the assessment made by... [a superior officer] that there was a 'suspect car bomb' was conveyed to the soldiers on the ground in such a way as to give them the impression that the presence of a bomb had been definitely identified. But, given the assessments which had been made of the likelihood of a remote control being used, and given the various indicators that the car should indeed be suspected of containing a bomb, the actions which the soldiers must be expected to have taken would be the same whether their understanding of the message was as it apparently was or whether it was in the sense which the officer apparently intended. In either case, the existence of the risk to the people of Gibraltar would have been enough, given the nature of that risk, justifiably to prompt the response which followed.

We question the conclusion that the use of lethal force was made 'almost unavoidable' by failings of the authorities in these respects. Quite apart from any other consideration, this conclusion takes insufficient account of the part played by chance in the eventual outcome. Had it not been for the movements which were made by McCann and Farrell as [s]oldiers...closed on them and which may have been prompted by the completely coincidental sounding of a police car siren, there is every possibility that they would have been seized and arrested without a shot being fired; and had it not been for Savage's actions as [s]oldiers...closed on him, which may have been prompted by the sound of gunfire from the McCann and Farrell incident, there is every possibility that he, too, would have been seized and arrested without resort to shooting....

24. We are far from persuaded that the Court has any sufficient basis for concluding, in the face of the evidence at the inquest and the extent of experience in dealing with terrorist

activities which the relevant training reflects, that some different and preferable form of training should have been given and that the action of the soldiers in this case 'lacks the degree of caution in the use of firearms to be expected of law-enforcement personnel in a democratic society'. (We also question, in the light of the evidence, the fairness of the reference to 'reflex action in this vital respect'. To be trained to react rapidly and to do so, when the needs of the situation require, is not to take reflex action.)

...

We consider that the use of lethal force in this case, however regrettable the need to resort to such force may be, did not exceed what was, in the circumstances as known at the time, 'absolutely necessary' for that purpose and did not amount to a breach by the United Kingdom of its obligations under the Convention.

B. JUDICIAL REVIEW OF PUBLIC SAFETY DECISIONS

The *McCann* judgment was greeted with outrage in Britain. The Prime Minister, John Major, was reported as 'deeply angered' and 'an official' was quoted as calling the decision 'madness'. The most heated reaction came from the Deputy Prime Minister, Michael Hesseltine. He called the judgment 'ludicrous' and said that it would give 'succour to terrorists'. When an opposition MP called for observance of the Court's decision, Hesseltine attacked him for 'encouraging the terrorist mentality'. The government was said to be considering withdrawal from the European Human Rights system. Hessletine hinted that the government would refuse to comply with the Court's order to compensate the applicants for £40,000 in legal costs. But, just before the deadline set, the payment was made.[16]

Under the holding of *McCann* a state may violate Article 2 by launching an operation using life-threatening force without adequate planning or control if that operation results in a death. The application of this test not only raises difficult questions of fact-finding (see Section E below), it also requires the Court to make difficult evaluations of military and police strategy. In *Ergi v. Turkey*,[17] the Court reviewed the facts of a clash between security forces and suspected terrorists. The security forces planned an ambush operation but they established their position on one side of a village when the terrorists were expected to approach from the other. This resulted in the villagers being caught in a foreseeable crossfire. Since '[t]here was no information to indicate any steps or precautions had been taken to protect the villagers from being caught up in the conflict', the Court found a violation of Article 2.

In *Andronicou v. Cyprus*,[18] the hostage case described above, the applicants complained that the authorities had employed officers of a special trained police unit, the

[16] The *Times* (London) 28 September 1995, 27 December 1995.
[17] 28 July 1998, 32 E.H.R.R. 18.
[18] 9 Oct. 1997, 25 E.H.R.R. 491.

MMAD. These officers were trained to deal with terror and wartime situations and to shoot to kill if fired on. In this case, moreover, they were armed with machine guns. The applicants argued that this level of force was inappropriate in dealing with what was, at bottom, a domestic incident. The European Court noted that events had come to a desperate stage and the MMAD were highly trained professionals. They had been given explicit orders to use only proportionate force and not to fire unless the hostages' lives were in danger. The use of machine guns was held appropriate, given the uncertainty of the situation inside the apartment. The machine guns also had the advantage of being equipped with flashlights which helped identify the location of the hostage. In sum, the Court found the rescue operation was planned in such a way as to minimize risk to life to the greatest extent possible.

4. THE DUTY TO INVESTIGATE

In the *Gül* case the Court found that, in light of gaps and omissions, none of the several state inquiries into the incident were sufficient to discharge the state's duty to investigate. The rationale for inferring such a 'procedural' obligation is stated in the judgment (para. 88). It is based on the state's positive obligation to protect life stated in the first sentence of Article 2. Of course with respect to the individual decedent involved in a particular application, the quality of the subsequent investigation can do nothing. But, as we will see, the state appears to be obliged to provide a system of law that protects life, in general. An effective system to detect and punish those culpable for wrongful deaths seems to be an essential part of any such system. The same requirement of an investigation has been found implicit in Article 3's prohibition of torture or inhuman and degrading treatment dealt with in the next chapter.[19]

A. R. (AMIN) V. SECRETARY OF STATE FOR THE HOME DEPARTMENT

[2003] U.K.H.L. 51, [2004] 1 AC 653 (H.L.)

LORD BINGHAM OF CORNHILL:

1. My Lords, in March 2000 Zahid Mubarek, a 19-year-old prisoner serving a sentence in Feltham Young Offender Institution, was wantonly murdered by Robert Stewart, with whom he shared a cell. The issue in this appeal is whether the United Kingdom has complied with its duty under article 2 of the European Convention on Human Rights to investigate the circumstances in which this crime came to be committed.

---

[19] E.g. *Assenov and Others v. Bulgaria*, 28 Oct. 1998, 28 E.H.R.R. 653.

2. Zahid Mubarek ('the deceased') was born on 23 October 1980. He lived in East London. His criminal record was a short one. On 16 January 1997, for an offence of possessing an imitation firearm with intent to cause fear of violence, he was the subject of an attendance centre order. It appears the offence may have been committed in response to provocation and racist abuse. In March 1999 he was cautioned for handling stolen goods. On 17 January 2000 he was sentenced to a total of 90 days' detention in a young offender institution for offences of theft, going equipped for theft and interfering with a motor vehicle. These were offences which he committed, as it seems, to fund a growing heroin addiction. But it seems he had not complied with bail conditions imposed to address his drug problem. He was sent to Feltham, spent his first night there in the induction wing, and on 22 January 2000 was transferred to Swallow Unit where he was accommodated in cell 38, a double cell which he occupied on his own until the arrival of Stewart on 8 February. The evidence suggests that the deceased was a model prisoner who caused no trouble and appeared to have no enemies.

3. Robert Stewart was born on 4 August 1980 and lived at Hyde in Greater Manchester. Beginning with a conviction of arson when aged 13, he was convicted of 21 further offences before being sentenced for the first time to detention in a young offender institution in August 1995. Further such sentences followed in January 1996, February 1997 (after the making of community service and supervision orders), November 1997, October 1998 and January 2000. Only two of Stewart's convictions were of offences of personal violence (assault occasioning actual bodily harm and common assault). At the end of 1999 he faced charges under the Protection from Harassment Act 1997 which were due to be heard in London. It appears that these offences, or some of them, may have been thought to be racially motivated. His personal security file suggested that while in custody he had been implicated in violence, damage to prison property, escape attempts, hostage holding, the stabbing of other inmates (one of whom had lost his eye), suspected (but unproved) involvement in the murder of another prisoner, arson, the threatening of other inmates with a metal bar and a wooden table or chair leg and threats of violence against prison staff whose addresses he had ascertained. An intercepted letter suggested that he was in possession of a gun and knew the address of a prison governor. It appears that from about January 1999 his behaviour in custody improved, although he was later diagnosed to be suffering from 'a long-standing deep-seated personality disorder' and 'an untreatable mental condition'.

4. Stewart's first visit to Feltham was on 10 January 2000 for purposes of a court hearing in London. It was judged that he needed to be watched and he was put in a single cell. An intercepted letter written by him was found to contain a reference to 'Niggers'. An officer who read Stewart's security file at this time formed the opinion that Stewart was 'very dangerous and a threat to both staff and other inmates'. He made a note in Stewart's wing file: 'Staff are advised to see the security file on this inmate (held in security). Very dangerous individual. Be careful.' Having made his court appearance, Stewart returned to Hindley Young Offender Institution (from which he had come) on 12 January. ...

6. Stewart was transferred to Feltham on a longer-term basis on 7 February 2000. He spent his first night on a wing where he had not been before. On the following day, 8 February 2000, he was placed in cell 38 on Swallow Wing, with the deceased. It is said that the wing had a maximum capacity of 60 prisoners, that there were already 59 before the arrival of Stewart and that the vacant place in cell 38 was the only place available. The allocation decision was made by an officer who had, according to one source, been warned to 'watch

[Stewart] as he was dangerous'. The officer himself does not, it appears, recollect such a warning, and did not consult Stewart's security file, or his wing file which did not reach Feltham until later.

7. Stewart shared cell 38 with the deceased from 8 February to 21 March 2000. During that time he wrote and sent a letter, not intercepted, couched in violent and racist terms. On 19 March Stewart's sentence expired and he was thereafter held on remand pending trial of the outstanding charges, but he was not moved. There is no evidence of hostility or discord between the deceased and Stewart during the time they were sharing cell 38, although the deceased may have expressed a wish to share with someone else. There is evidence that other prisoners regarded Stewart as 'strange' and 'weird' and 'aggressive', partly because of his manner and behaviour, partly because of a cross, with the letters RIP, tattooed on his forehead.

8. On 21 March 2000 at about 3.35 am Stewart battered the deceased into a coma with a wooden table leg. The deceased was due to be released that day. He never recovered, dying in hospital of brain damage a week later. After the attack Stewart pressed the cell alarm button and, when an officer responded, said that his cellmate had had an accident. When moved to a nearby cell he drew a large swastika on the wall with the heel of his rubber shoe; above it he wrote 'Just killed me padmate' and below it 'RIP'. The Director General of HM Prison Service met the parents of the deceased at the hospital on the day of the attack and, on learning of the death, wrote a letter apologising unreservedly for the failure of the Prison Service to look after the deceased and accepting responsibility for his death. He told them of an internal inquiry he had set up under the leadership of Mr Ted Butt, a serving governor and senior investigating officer of the Prison Service.

9. Stewart was charged with murder, and his trial started on 24 October 2000. He admitted the killing. The issue was whether he was guilty of murder or of manslaughter by reason of diminished responsibility. He was convicted of murder. Although the court heard evidence of the circumstances immediately surrounding the killing, including the actions of prison officers at that time, there was no exploration at the trial of cell allocation procedures or other events before the murder. [An inquest into Mubarek's death was adjourned when the criminal proceedings were started. In addition to the prison services' own inquiry the police undertook an investigation to decide whether or not to prosecute the prison service or its employees. There was also an inquiry by the Commission for Racial Equality [CRE]. In all of these processes, the family of Mubarek sought and was denied a formal role. They declined to participate in a less direct way.]...

14. Very shortly after the death of the deceased, on 3 April 2000, solicitors for his family wrote to the responsible minister of state, asking for an independent public inquiry into the death. On 7 and 12 April the minister replied that it was too early to make a decision about a public inquiry pending the police investigation and the Butt inquiry. At a meeting on 2 November 2000 the minister did not agree to establish a public inquiry. On 31 July 2001 he was asked to reconsider this decision, but he replied that he saw no reason to reverse his earlier decision not to hold such an inquiry.

15. The appellant, an uncle of the deceased, sought judicial review of (a) the decision of the CRE not to allow the family to participate in the proceedings in any meaningful manner or to hold any significant part of its investigation in public, (b) the decision of the coroner not to resume the inquest and (c) the decision of the Home Secretary not to hold an inquiry in public.

Hooper J, before whom these applications came, adjourned the applications against the CRE and the coroner but granted permission to pursue the claim against the Home Secretary. This claim he upheld, ruling that the refusal to hold a public inquiry was a breach of article 2 of the Convention. He declared that

> 'an independent public investigation with the family legally represented, provided with the relevant material and able to cross-examine the principal witnesses, must be held to satisfy the obligations imposed by article 2 of the European Convention on Human Rights.'

[The Home Secretary's appeal was allowed by the Court of Appeal.]...

17. Section 8(1)(c) of the Coroners Act 1988, applicable in England and Wales, requires a coroner to hold an inquest on being informed that a person has died in prison. The inquest must be held in public. The family may attend and be legally represented. They or their representative may question witnesses at the hearing. The coroner is however ordinarily required by section 16(1)(a)(i) to adjourn the inquest on being informed that a person has been charged with the murder or manslaughter of the deceased and on the conclusion of the criminal proceedings has a discretionary power to resume the adjourned inquest 'if in his opinion there is sufficient cause to do so'....

24. In approaching the present case Hooper J had the benefit of a recent judgment of Jackson J in *R (Wright) v Secretary of State for the Home Department* [2001] UKHRR 1399. That case concerned a serving prisoner who suffered a severe asthmatic attack in his cell and died. An inquest was held at which the family of the deceased were present, but unrepresented for want of legal aid. There was no inquiry into the quality of the medical treatment the deceased had received in prison. It later emerged that the responsible medical officer had been suspended from duty and had previously been found guilty of serious professional misconduct. In a civil action against the Home Secretary liability was admitted, thus precluding forensic investigation of the case. The family sought judicial review on the grounds, among others, of a failure to protect the life of the deceased and a failure of the procedural obligation arising under article 2 of the Convention to investigate the circumstances of the death.

25. In a succinct and accurate judgment Jackson J reviewed the domestic and Strasbourg case law, deriving from *Jordan v United Kingdom* 37 EHRR 52 the requirement that an investigation, to satisfy article 2, must have certain features (para 41). (1) The investigation must be independent. (2) The investigation must be effective. (3) The investigation must be reasonably prompt. (4) There must be a sufficient element of public scrutiny. (5) The next-of-kin must be involved to an appropriate extent. From the recent case law Jackson J derived five propositions of which the fourth was: 'Where the victim has died and it is arguable that there has been a breach of article 2, the investigation should have the general features identified by the court in *Jordan v United Kingdom*, at paras 106–109.' The judge concluded on the facts that there had not been an effective official investigation into the death of the deceased and held that there should be an independent investigation, to be held in public, at which the family should be represented.

26. [Hooper, J concluded that in the Mubarek case] the inquiries and investigations which had been conducted did not, singly or cumulatively, satisfy the investigative duty of the United Kingdom under article 2.

...

31. The state's duty to investigate is secondary to the duties not to take life unlawfully and to protect life, in the sense that it only arises where a death has occurred or life-threatening injuries have occurred: *Menson v United Kingdom* (Application No 47916/99) (unreported) 6 May 2003, p 13. It can fairly be described as procedural. But in any case where a death has occurred in custody it is not a minor or unimportant duty. In this country, as noted above, effect has been given to that duty for centuries by requiring such deaths to be publicly investigated before an independent judicial tribunal with an opportunity for relatives of the deceased to participate. The purposes of such an investigation are clear: to ensure so far as possible that the full facts are brought to light; that culpable and discreditable conduct is exposed and brought to public notice; that suspicion of deliberate wrongdoing (if unjustified) is allayed; that dangerous practices and procedures are rectified; and that those who have lost their relative may at least have the satisfaction of knowing that lessons learned from his death may save the lives of others....

33. There was in this case no inquest. The coroner's decision not to resume the inquest is not the subject of review, and may well have been justified for the reasons she has given. But it is very unfortunate that there was no inquest, since a properly conducted inquest can discharge the state's investigative obligation, as established by *McCann v United Kingdom* 21 EHRR 97....

34. The police investigations into the criminal culpability of Stewart and the Prison Service were, very properly, conducted in private and without participation by the family. The Advice Report on which counsel based his advice not to prosecute the Prison Service or any of its members was produced in evidence during these proceedings but not before. It is written in an objective and independent spirit, but it raises many unanswered questions and cannot discharge the state's investigative duty.

35. The trial of Stewart for murder was directed solely to establishing his mental responsibility for the killing which he had admittedly carried out. It involved little exploration, such as would occur in some murder trials, of wider issues concerning the death.

36. There is no reason to doubt that Mr Butt set about his task in a conscientious and professional way. He explored the facts, exposed weaknesses in the Feltham regime and recommended changes which, it is understood, have been and are being implemented. It is however plain that as a serving official in the Prison Service he did not enjoy institutional or hierarchical independence. His investigation was conducted in private. His report was not published. The family were not able to play any effective part in his investigation and would not have been able to do so even if they had accepted the limited offer made to them.

37. The CRE report, which was not before the judge or the Court of Appeal, brings additional facts to light (although some of these, such as the discovery of a handmade wooden dagger under Stewart's pillow after the murder, raise many further questions). The report has been published. But the CRE inquiry, conducted under the Race Relations Act 1976, was necessarily confined to race-related issues and this case raises other issues. Save for a single day devoted to policy issues, the inquiry was conducted in private. The family were not able to play any effective part in it and would not have been able to do so even if they had taken advantage of the limited opportunity they were offered....

LORD SLYNN OF HADLEY

44. Even though there may be room for flexibility in the procedures adopted by different member states, the European Court of Human Rights has insisted on a minimum threshold. In my opinion, even if the United Kingdom courts are only to take account of the Strasbourg Court decisions and are not strictly bound by them where the Court has laid down principles and, as here a minimum threshold requirement, United Kingdom courts should follow what the Court has said. If they do not do so without good reason the dissatisfied litigant has a right to go to Strasbourg where existing jurisprudence is likely to be followed.

45. It seems to me that in the present case the judge did, but the Court of Appeal did not, give sufficient effect to the judgments of the Strasbourg Court.

46. There were here a number of inquiries of different kinds which went some way to fulfil the minimum threshold duty but for the reasons given by Lord Bingham there were features of each stage of the inquiry which did not achieve the minimum threshold....

The Court of Appeal plainly thought that in the case of acts by state agents causing death in custody there is a more exacting and rigorous duty to investigate than in cases of negligent omissions leading to death in custody. That cases in the former category may be a greater affront to the public conscience than cases in the latter category can readily be accepted. But the investigation of cases of negligence resulting in the death of prisoners may often be more complex and may require more elaborate investigation. Systemic failures also affect more prisoners. The European Court of Human Rights has interpreted article 2 of the European Convention on Human Rights as imposing minimum standards which must be met in all cases....

B. THE NEED FOR AN INVESTIGATION

In the *Amin* case Lord Bingham summarized the relevant question as being whether the legal system provides an investigatory process that is adequate to vindicate the substantive Convention rights. There is no particular set of procedures that must be observed in every case. In this case, English law provided three opportunities for the state to discharge this duty but none, according to this judgment, was satisfactory: The inquest was discontinued. The police investigation was conducted in private and excluded the participation of the family. Finally, the criminal trial of Stewart was directed at his guilt or innocence and not the responsibility of the prison and other officials.

The European Court, as the House of Lords noted in *Amin*, has suggested the basic requirements of an effective investigation. Rather clearly, the inquiry must be conducted by an authority independent of the individuals and agencies that are its subject. So when an applicant alleged that his brother's death had been the result of torture by the gendarmerie, an investigation by officers of the gendarmerie, some of whom were actually attached to the unit involved, could not be an effective investigation for the purposes of Article 2.[20] The investigation must also be reasonably complete given the circumstances of the death. In one case the government claimed that the applicant's husband had died of a heart attack while in police custody and that evidence of a broken sternum was explained by efforts to apply cardiac massage.

---

[20] *Aktaş v. Turkey*, 24 April 2003, 38 E.H.R.R. 18.

No photographs were taken of the body and the post-mortem examination omitted any dissection or medical analysis of the marks or injuries on it. The investigation was, therefore, insufficient.[21]

In *In re McKerr*[22] the House of Lords determined that the duty to investigate violent deaths caused by state agents did not apply to deaths occurring before the effective date of the Human Rights Act. It had already been determined that the Human Rights Act itself was not retroactive. Therefore, the House had to ask whether the duty to investigate under Article 2 was a continuing one which would have been breached with the coming into force of the Act. In his speech, Lord Rodger emphasized the connection between the challenged death and the duty to investigate: 'It would be curious to give a right under the Act, to the investigation of a killing to which the Act did not apply'.[23] This conclusion is in tension with the rationale for the duty to investigate mentioned earlier. That was that the procedural right was associated not with an individual violation (to the immediate victim to whom it would be of no use) but with the state's obligation to maintain an effective system to protect life.

C. POSITIVE OBLIGATIONS TO PROTECT LIFE

As will become clear in subsequent chapters, a state's obligations under the Convention may have both negative and positive aspects. That is, to observe a particular right, a state may be obliged either to refrain from some act or undertake some act. While, historically, constitutional rights tended to be predominantly of the former kind, more recent constitutions have often expressly guaranteed such rights as education, housing and health care. The European Convention for the Protection of Human Rights and Fundamental Freedoms was drafted at a time when rights were mainly conceived of in negative terms. Nevertheless, the European Court has found several apparent prohibitions on the state to entail certain positive duties. The dimensions of and problems with this doctrine are examined in connection with the right to private and family life in Chapter 8.

With respect to the right to life, however, no such interpretive issues arise. The first sentence of the Article explicitly enjoins states-party to protect everyone's right to life 'by law'. The obligation is thus to have a certain kind of legal regime, one that by its rules of conduct, and by its machinery of enforcement, enhances everyone's prospect of staying alive. Of course no legal system by itself can prevent death, even violent death or intentional killing. The question is what kind of legal system, both in design and operation, is enough to satisfy the state's duty.

---

[21] *Salman v. Turkey*, 27 June 2000, 34 E.H.R.R. 17.
[22] [2004] U.K.H.L. 12, [2004] 2 All E.R. 409.
[23] *Id*. at para. 83.

1. EDWARDS V. UNITED KINGDOM

Judgment of 14 March 2002
35 E.H.R.R. 19

. . .

9. Prior to his death, Christopher Edwards had shown signs of developing a serious mental illness. In 1991 a psychiatric assessment expressed the tentative diagnosis of schizophrenia. In July 1994 he stopped living at home with the applicants, his parents. At this time he stopped taking his medication.

10. On 27 November 1994 Christopher Edwards, then 30 years old, was arrested in Colchester by the police and taken to Colchester police station. He had been approaching young women in the street and making inappropriate suggestions. His behaviour before arrest, and at the police station where he attempted to assault a policewoman, led police officers to suspect that he might be mentally ill. He was assessed at the police station by an approved social worker, who discussed the matter on the telephone with a consultant psychiatrist. They agreed that, while there was some evidence of possible developing schizophrenia, he did not need urgent medical attention and that he was fit to be detained at the police station. Any psychiatric assessment could take place as part of a pre-sentencing exercise. Christopher Edwards was held in a cell on his own. The police officer responsible did not fill in a CID2 form identifying Christopher Edwards as an exceptional risk on ground of mental illness due to the opinion expressed by the social worker. The police officer did, however, note in the confidential information form (MG6A) her belief that if Christopher Edwards was not treated or seen by the mental health team he might seriously harm a female. She was not aware that her own suspicion of his mental state was sufficient to warrant categorising Christopher Edwards as an exceptional risk.

11. On 28 November 1994 Christopher Edwards was brought to Colchester Magistrates' Court. Immediately his handcuffs were removed, he pushed through the other prisoners and confronted a female prison officer. He was restrained, but struggled and tried to approach her again. He was placed in a cell on his own. During the morning, he continually banged on the cell door and shouted: 'I want a woman.' He shouted obscenities about women. The applicants met the duty solicitor at about 9.45 a.m. and explained that their son was mentally unwell and that they wanted him to receive medical care and not to be remanded in custody. When the duty solicitor attempted to talk to Christopher Edwards in his cell, he received no assistance from his client who continued to make obscene suggestions about women. The duty solicitor discussed the problem with the Clerk to the Justices.

12. On his way to court and in the courtroom, Christopher Edwards repeated his earlier comments about women. The prosecutor had in her possession the MG6A form and had been requested by the police to obtain his remand in custody as there was a risk that he would reoffend and there was a real question mark about his mental state....

13. The magistrates decided to remand Christopher Edwards in custody for three days, which was a shorter period than usual, bringing forward the date to 1 December so that instructions could be taken and legal aid forms completed.... Neither [the senior medical

officer] nor the probation officer passed on any...[information about Edwards' psychiatric condition] to the reception staff. [They did however, receive information about his behaviour from officers at the Magistrates' Court.]...

15. In the late afternoon, Christopher Edwards was taken to Chelmsford Prison.... No medical officer was on duty at the centre at this time, or was present in the prison. Christopher Edwards was admitted to the main prison and placed in cell D1-6.

16. He was detained in a cell on his own during this period.

17. Meanwhile, Richard Linford was arrested in Maldon on 26 November 1994 for assaulting his friend and her neighbour. At Maldon police station, he was seen by a police surgeon as it was suspected that he was mentally ill. The police surgeon certified that Richard Linford was not fit to be detained. Richard Linford was assessed by a psychiatric registrar who consulted on the telephone with a consultant psychiatrist, who decided that he did not need to be admitted to hospital and that he was fit to be detained. Richard Linford was transferred to Chelmsford police station, where the police surgeon also found him fit to be detained. While his conduct before and after arrest was bizarre, it was attributed by the doctors to the effects of alcohol abuse, amphetamine withdrawal and to a deliberate attempt to manipulate the criminal justice system. The registrar, who had previously treated Richard Linford, knew that he had been diagnosed at various times as suffering from schizophrenia or as having a personality disorder, but also knew him as someone who became ill when abusing alcohol and drugs. Over the weekend, Richard Linford showed further bizarre behaviour and was violent towards police officers. He was not reassessed by a doctor... Richard Linford arrived at Chelmsford Prison shortly after Christopher Edwards, where he was screened by the same member of the prison health care service who had seen Christopher Edwards and who saw no reason to admit him to the health care centre. Richard Linford did not behave in a bizarre fashion during the screening. Mr N. did not have knowledge of Richard Linford's previous convictions, which would have alerted him to his admittance to hospital in 1988.

18. Initially, Richard Linford was placed in cell D1-11 on his own. He was then moved into cell D1-6 with Christopher Edwards. This was due to shortage of space, as all the other cells on the landing were doubly occupied.

19. ...At 9 p.m., either Christopher Edwards or Richard Linford pressed the call button. A prison officer saw the green light outside the cell and was told that they wished one of the cell lights, operated from the exterior, to be switched off. He agreed to do so. He saw that the two men appeared to be 'getting on all right'. He noticed that while the green light had gone on the buzzer which should have been sounding continuously had not done so. He did not report the apparent defect.

20. Shortly before 1 a.m. on 29 November 1994, a prison officer heard a buzzer sound. He saw no red light on the D-landing control panel and saw a prison officer go to check the other landings. Some time later, he heard continuous banging on a cell door on his landing. On going to investigate he saw the green light on outside cell D1-6. Looking through the spy hole, he saw Richard Linford holding a bloodstained plastic fork and noticed blood on the floor and on Linford's feet. There was a delay of five minutes while officers donned protective clothing. They entered the cell to find that Christopher Edwards had been stamped and kicked to death. Richard Linford was making continual reference to being possessed by evil spirits and devils. D-landing had previously been patrolled at 12.43 a.m., which indicated that up to seventeen minutes could have elapsed since the pressing of the cell's call button.

21. At the time of the attack, Richard Linford was acutely mentally ill. He was transferred later on 29 November 1994 to Rampton Special Hospital.

22. On 21 April 1995 Richard Linford pleaded guilty at Chelmsford Crown Court to the manslaughter of Christopher Edwards by reason of diminished responsibility. The trial was therefore brief. The judge imposed a hospital order under section 37 of the Mental Health Act 1983 ('the 1983 Act'), together with a restriction order under section 41. Richard Linford is currently still at Rampton Special Hospital, diagnosed as suffering from paranoid schizophrenia....

25. In July 1995 a private, non-statutory inquiry was commissioned by three State agencies with statutory responsibilities towards Christopher Edwards—the Prison Service, Essex County Council and North Essex Health Authority.

...

32. The inquiry report was published on 15 June 1998. It concluded that ideally Christopher Edwards and Richard Linford should not have been in prison and in practice they should not have been sharing the same cell. It found 'a systemic collapse of the protective mechanisms that ought to have operated to protect this vulnerable prisoner'. It identified a series of shortcomings, including poor record-keeping, inadequate communication and limited inter-agency cooperation, and a number of missed opportunities to prevent the death of Christopher Edwards....

46. The applicants complain that the authorities failed to protect the life of their son and were responsible for his death. They also complain that the investigation into their son's death was not adequate or effective as required by the procedural obligation imposed by Article 2 of the Convention....

54. The Court reiterates that the first sentence of Article 2 § 1 enjoins the State not only to refrain from the intentional and unlawful taking of life, but also to take appropriate steps to safeguard the lives of those within its jurisdiction. This involves a primary duty on the State to secure the right to life by putting in place effective criminal-law provisions to deter the commission of offences against the person backed up by a law-enforcement machinery for the prevention, suppression and punishment of breaches of such provisions. It also extends in appropriate circumstances to a positive obligation on the authorities to take preventive operational measures to protect an individual whose life is at risk from the criminal acts of another individual.

55. Bearing in mind the difficulties in policing modern societies, the unpredictability of human conduct and the operational choices which must be made in terms of priorities and resources, the scope of the positive obligation must be interpreted in a way which does not impose an impossible or disproportionate burden on the authorities. Not every claimed risk to life, therefore, can entail for the authorities a Convention requirement to take operational measures to prevent that risk from materialising. For a positive obligation to arise, it must be established that the authorities knew or ought to have known at the time of the existence of a real and immediate risk to the life of an identified individual from the criminal acts of a third party and that they failed to take measures within the scope of their powers which, judged reasonably, might have been expected to avoid that risk.

56. In the context of prisoners, the Court has had previous occasion to emphasise that persons in custody are in a vulnerable position and that the authorities are under a duty to protect them. It is incumbent on the State to account for any injuries suffered in custody, which obligation is particularly stringent where that individual dies. It may be noted that this need for scrutiny is acknowledged in the domestic law of England and Wales, where inquests are automatically held concerning the deaths of persons in prison and where the domestic courts have imposed a duty of care on prison authorities in respect of detainees in their custody.

57. Christopher Edwards was killed while detained on remand by a dangerous, mentally ill prisoner, Richard Linford, who was placed in his cell. As a prisoner he fell under the responsibility of the authorities who were under a domestic-law and Convention obligation to protect his life. The Court has examined, firstly, whether the authorities knew or ought to have known of the existence of a real and immediate risk to the life of Christopher Edwards from the acts of Richard Linford and, secondly, whether they failed to take measures within the scope of their powers which, judged reasonably, might have been expected to avoid that risk.

58. As regards the state of knowledge of the authorities, the Court notes that it was considered in the inquiry report that any prisoner sharing a cell with Richard Linford that night would have been at risk to his life. It seems therefore to the Court that the essential question is whether the prison authorities knew or ought to have known of his extreme dangerousness at the time the decision was taken to place him in the same cell as Christopher Edwards.

59. That Richard Linford was mentally ill was known to the doctors who were treating him—he had been admitted to hospital in 1988 and been diagnosed as suffering from schizophrenia. He also had a history of violent outbursts and assaults. However, some weeks prior to his arrest on 26 November 1994, while fears had arisen that he was capable of serious violence, the consultant psychiatrist considered that one more effort to manage his behaviour through depot medication was required before steps were taken to detain him under the Mental Health Act 1983. At the police station, after his arrest, his bizarre behaviour led the police to suspect that he was mentally ill and the police surgeon considered that his mental state was such that he was not fit to be detained. This view was overruled, somewhat to the surprise of the police, by the psychiatric registrar who examined him and concluded that his behaviour could be a result of substance abuse and a deliberate attempt at manipulation. The registrar did not consult Richard Linford's notes which would have shown him that he was under consideration for compulsory committal. While in the police station, Richard Linford's behaviour continued to fluctuate with violent and bizarre episodes. When he arrived at the prison after being remanded in custody by the court, he bore visible signs of injury and was known to the screening health worker to have been 'difficult'. The screening health worker was not, however, made aware of his prison record or his previous committal to hospital and the police, prosecution and court did not pass on any detailed information relating to his conduct and his known history of mental disturbance.

60. The Court is satisfied that information was available which identified Richard Linford as suffering from a mental illness with a record of violence which was serious enough to merit proposals for compulsory detention and that this, in combination with his bizarre and violent behaviour on and following arrest, demonstrated that he was a real and serious risk to others and, in the circumstances of this case, to Christopher Edwards, when placed in his cell.

61. As regards the measures which they might reasonably have been expected to take to avoid that risk, the Court observes that the information concerning Richard Linford's medical

history and perceived dangerousness ought to have been brought to the attention of the prison authorities, and in particular those responsible for deciding whether to place him in the health care centre or in ordinary location with other prisoners. It was not. There was a series of shortcomings in the transmission of information, from the failure of the registrar to consult Richard Linford's notes in order to obtain the full picture, the failure of the police to fill in a CID2 form (exceptional risk) and the failure of the police, prosecution or Magistrates' Court to take steps to inform the prison authorities in any other way of Richard Linford's suspected dangerousness and instability.

62. The Government have pointed out that even if a CID2 form had been filled in by the police, this would not have conclusively led the prison to place Richard Linford in the health care centre rather than a cell with another prisoner. They submit that the screening process concentrated on the behaviour of the prisoner on admission and was not expected to be a full medical or psychiatric examination, a doctor generally visiting each prisoner within a day of arrival. However, the inquiry report considered that if the screening health worker had been properly informed of Richard Linford's background, he would have perhaps paid closer attention, noticing that Linford had lied in his answers in the questionnaire and he might in those circumstances have erred on the side of caution and not placed him on ordinary location. It is true that this is speculation to some extent. However, the Court considers that it is self-evident that the screening process of the new arrivals in a prison should serve to identify effectively those prisoners who require for their own welfare or the welfare of other prisoners to be placed under medical supervision. The defects in the information provided to the prison admissions staff were combined in this case with the brief and cursory nature of the examination carried out by a screening health worker who was found by the inquiry to be inadequately trained and acting in the absence of a doctor to whom recourse could be had in case of difficulty or doubt.

63. It is apparent from the inquiry report that in addition there were numerous failings in the way in which Christopher Edwards was treated from his arrest to his allocation to a shared cell. In particular, despite his disturbed mental state, no doctor was called to examine him in the police station, no CID2 form was filled in by the police and there was a failure to pass on to the prison screening officer information provided informally by the applicants, the probation service at the court and an individual police officer. However, although it would obviously have been desirable for Christopher Edwards to be detained either in a hospital or the health care centre of the prison, his life was placed at risk by the introduction into his cell of a dangerously unstable prisoner and it is the shortcomings in that regard which are most relevant to the issues in this case. On the same basis, while the Court deplores the fact that the cell's call button, which should have been a safeguard, was defective, it considers that on the information available to the authorities, Richard Linford should not have been placed in Christopher Edwards's cell in the first place.

64. The Court concludes that the failure of the agencies involved in this case (medical profession, police, prosecution and court) to pass information about Richard Linford on to the prison authorities and the inadequate nature of the screening process on Richard Linford's arrival in prison disclose a breach of the State's obligation to protect the life of Christopher Edwards. There has therefore been a breach of Article 2 of the Convention in this regard....

[The Court also found a violation of Article 13 based on the absence of a procedure in British law allowing the applicants to establish the responsibility of public officials for Edwards' death or to recover non-pecuniary damages resulting from that death.]

...

[The Court held unanimously that there had been violations of Article 2 and 13.]

2. THE EXTENT OF THE OBLIGATIONS

The judgment in *Edwards* deals with the right to life in the special context of persons confined by the state. In that situation, the positive obligations of the state may take on a special character. In *Keenan v. United Kingdom*[24] the applicant argued that the government had violated Article 2 by failing to prevent the suicide of her mentally ill son who was serving a four month prison term at the time of his death. The deceased had recently had his sentence extended by 28 days and had served a seven day disciplinary segregation because of an assault on two prison officers. The Court agreed that prison officials had an obligation under Article 2 to safeguard the lives of prisoners. In each case the question was whether the authorities knew or ought to have known that the applicant's son was subject to 'an immediate risk of suicide and, if so whether they did all that reasonably could have been expected of them'. In the particular circumstances of that case the Court concluded that while the suicide risk was known, the authorities acted reasonably in light of the decedent's behaviour in the period preceding his suicide. There was, therefore, no violation of Article 2.

The duty to protect detained persons has also been recognized by American courts as an interpretation of the Eighth Amendment to the Constitution (more fully discussed in the next chapter) prohibiting the infliction of cruel and unusual punishment. In *Farmer v. Brennan*[25] the Supreme Court noted:

[P]rison officials have a duty to protect prisoners from violence at the hands of other prisoners. Having incarcerated persons with demonstrated proclivities for antisocial criminal and often violent conduct, having stripped them of virtually every means of self-protection and foreclosed their access to outside aid, the government and its officials are not free to let the state of nature take its course.[26]

The Court went on to hold that this duty extended only to 'substantial risk[s] of serious harm' and that the relevant officials must have shown 'deliberate indifference' to those risks. The latter requirement engaged a subjective inquiry requiring evidence that the

---

[24] 3 April 2001, 33 E.H.R.R. 38.
[25] 511 U.S. 825 (1994).
[26] *Id* at 833 (quotation marks, citations and some punctuation removed).

officials 'knowingly and unreasonably disregard[ed] an objectively intolerable risk of harm'.[27] This standard was applied by a lower court in finding a violation of the Eighth Amendment when a detainee, who was being sexually assaulted by his cell-mate, pressed the emergency call button but the officer in charge failed to investigate.[28]

In addition to persons in state custody, the European Court of Human Rights has held that the general public is entitled to positive action by the state to protect life. Usually that requirement can be met by operation of an ordinary system of criminal law and prosecution. But the Court has gone on to indicate that the operation of that system must be reasonably competent in practice. In *Osman v. United Kingdom*[29] the applicants claimed that the police had failed to respond adequately to the apparent risk to the applicant and his family arising from the attention of a disturbed teacher who seemed obsessed with the applicant. The result was a shooting in which the applicant was wounded and his father killed:

It is common ground that the State's obligation in this respect extends beyond its primary duty to secure the right to life by putting in place effective criminal-law provisions to deter the commission of offences against the person backed up by law-enforcement machinery for the prevention, suppression and sanctioning of breaches of such provisions. It is thus accepted by those appearing before the Court that Article 2 of the Convention may also imply in certain well-defined circumstances a positive obligation on the authorities to take preventive operational measures to protect an individual whose life is at risk from the criminal acts of another individual. Another relevant consideration is the need to ensure that the police exercise their powers to control and prevent crime in a manner which fully respects the due process and other guarantees which legitimately place restraints on the scope of their action to investigate crime and bring offenders to justice, including the guarantees contained in Articles 5 and 8 of the Convention.... In the opinion of the Court where there is an allegation that the authorities have violated their positive obligation to protect the right to life in the context of their above-mentioned duty to prevent and suppress offences against the person, it must be established to its satisfaction that the authorities knew or ought to have known at the time of the existence of a real and immediate risk to the life of an identified individual or individuals from the criminal acts of a third party and that they failed to take measures within the scope of their powers which, judged reasonably, might have been expected to avoid that risk. The Court does not accept the Government's view that the failure to perceive the risk to life in the circumstances known at the time or to take preventive measures to avoid that risk must be tantamount to gross negligence or wilful disregard of the duty to protect life ...[I]t is sufficient for an applicant to show that the authorities did not do all that could be reasonably expected of them to avoid a real and immediate risk to life of which they have or ought to have knowledge. This is a question which can only be answered in the light of all the circumstances of any particular case.[30]

---

[27] *Id* at 834, 837–40, 846.

[28] *Velez v. Johnson*, 395 F.3d 732 (7th Cir. 2005). Because the victim was being held before trial, the Eighth Amendment's bar on cruel and unusual punishment was inapplicable. See Chapter 5(A) *infra*. The decision was based on the due process clause of the Fourteenth Amendment. The Court said there was 'little practical difference between the two standards'.

[29] 28 Oct. 1998, 29 E.H.R.R. 245.

[30] *Id*. at paras. 115–16.

In the case at issue the Court decided that the police had acted reasonably and, consequently, there had been no violation of Article 2.[31]

In *Akkoç v. Turkey*[32] the Court engaged in an examination of the adequacy of the Turkish legal system in southeast Turkey with respect to its capacity to investigate and deal with threats to the lives of political dissidents. The applicant's husband was shot and killed. She claimed that the killing was carried out by security forces because of her husband's activities in a Kurdish trade union. The government denied this, suggesting that the decedent may have been a victim of Kurdish terrorism and claiming that it was impossible to prevent every violent death given the unstable situation in that part of the country. '[B]earing in mind the difficulties in policing modern societies, the unpredictability of human conduct, any operational choices which must be made in terms of priorities and resources, the scope of the positive obligation must be interpreted in a way which does not impose an impossible or disproportionate burden on the authorities'. The Court determined that the government should have been aware of the special risk to the applicant's husband. In this case, notwithstanding the existence of the criminal code and prosecuting and adjudicatory institutions, the actual practice in the region displayed several defects. Offences charged against state officials were dealt with by special councils that were unduly influenced by security forces. Non-investigation and non-prosecution in response to complaints about security forces were common. By labelling incidents as related to terrorism the state was able to remit jurisdiction to national security courts whose impartiality had been questioned in earlier cases before the European Court. '[T]hese defects removed the protection which [the deceased] should have received by law'.[33] In a later case, the Turkish government was held to have failed in its obligations under Article 2 when it had been informed of the disappearance of the decedent, a Kurdish activist, but took no serious measures to locate him for months.[34]

D. THE DEATH PENALTY

The text of Article 2 provides an exception to the right to life in the case of judicially administered capital punishment. This provision seems to preclude any interpretation of *Article 3* that would prohibit the death penalty as 'inhuman or degrading punishment', although aspects of its imposition have been held to be in violation of

---

[31] Compare *DeShaney v. Winnebago County*, 489 U.S. 189 (1989) holding that the failure of child welfare officials to prevent abuse of a child in the light of known instances of prior abuse was not a constitutional violation. The Supreme Court held that the constitutional provision relied on did not guarantee 'minimal levels of safety and security'. *Id*. at 195.

[32] 10 Oct. 2000, 34 E.H.R.R. 51.

[33] *Id*. at paras. 81–93.

[34] *Koku v. Turkey*, 31 May 2005.

that article.[35] In 2005, however, the Grand Chamber of the Court endorsed a section judgment suggesting a contrary position. In a case involving the death sentence imposed on Abdullah Öcalan, the leader of the Kurdish Workers Party, the Court expressed the view that the death penalty itself may be inhuman and degrading treatment contrary to Article 3. (The Court considered the question notwithstanding the fact that Öcalan's sentence had been commuted in connection with Turkey's ratification of Protocol 6 discussed below.) The Court considered that the *de jure* and *de facto* abolition of capital punishment in all of the member states of the Council of Europe (also discussed below) 'signall[ed] the agreement of the Contracting States to abrogate, or at the very least to modify, the second sentence of Article 2 § 1'.[36]

In *Öcalan*, however, the Court went on to hold that, '[e]ven if the death penalty were still permissible under Article 2', its imposition in the particular circumstances of that case was incompatible with the Convention. In another part of the judgment the Court had held that Ocalan's trial did not conform to the requirements of Article 6 of the Convention on fair adjudication. This conclusion followed from the opening sentence of the article requiring life to be protected 'by law'. 'An arbitrary act cannot be lawful under the Convention ....' It was also implied by Article 2(2) which referred to a sentence imposed by 'a court'. Only an impartial and independent tribunal could properly be referred to as a court. The same reasoning was applied to Article 2's requirement that the sentence be 'provided by law'.[37] More generally

[t]he fear and uncertainty as to the future generated by a sentence of death, in circumstances where there exists a real possibility that the sentence will be enforced, must give rise to a significant degree of human anguish. Such anguish cannot be dissociated from the unfairness of the proceedings underlying the sentence which, given that human life is at stake, becomes unlawful under the Convention.[38]

In subsequent cases, the Court has continued to decline to hold definitively that Article 3 extended to capital punishment. It has, in fact, re-iterated the limits on Article 3 implied in Article 2(2).[39]

Questions concerning the death penalty under the Convention are becoming largely academic. Two subsequent protocols to the Convention have dealt explicitly with capital punishment. Protocol 6 agreed to in 1983 prohibits the death penalty unless provided for in a law directed at crimes committed 'in time of war or imminent war'. This Protocol has been ratified by and has entered into force in all of the members of the

---

[35] *Soering v. United Kingdom*, 7 July 1989, 11 E.H.R.R. 439. The death penalty cases under Article 3 are dealt with in Chapter 5(D), *infra*.

[36] *Öcalan v. Turkey*, 12 May 2005, 41 E.H.R.R. 45, para. 163 (quoting and approving the Chamber judgment).

[37] *Id.* at paras. 166–9.

[38] *Id.* at para. 168.

[39] *Shamayev and Others v. Georgia and Russia*, 12 April 2005, para. 333; *Bader and Others v. Sweden*, 8 Feb. 2005, paras. 41–2.

Council of Europe except Russia.[40] Russia signed the Protocol in 1997 and undertook to ratify it within three years of its accession to the Convention, but, as of July 2007, had not yet done so in light of serious domestic opposition. It has, however, maintained a moratorium on executions since 1996.[41] In 2002, Protocol 13 was ratified by a sufficient number of members to enter into force. It eliminates the exception for wartime, thus abolishing the death penalty in all circumstances. It has been signed by every member of the Council of Europe except Azerbaijan and Russia. Thirty-eight of the forty-three countries who signed the Protocol had ratified it as of July 2007.[42]

Notwithstanding the practical abolition of capital punishment in Europe, the Strasbourg Court will continue to deal with death penalty issues in connection with the possible deportation or expulsion of people to countries where it is still applied.[43]

E. FACT-FINDING IN THE EUROPEAN COURT OF HUMAN RIGHTS

As will become clear in subsequent chapters, cases coming before the European Court of Human Rights predominantly concern issues of law. These include, as we have seen with respect to the right to life, the definition and application of the words and concepts in the Convention. Even more prominently, the Court is regularly engaged in evaluating whether an admitted infringement of a protected right is justifiable as a proportionate response to an important social objective. This examination arising mainly, but not exclusively, under the second paragraphs of Articles 8–11, will be considered in some detail in Chapters 6–8.

The decisions of the Court, however, sometimes turn on the resolution of disputed questions of fact. Fact questions are particularly common in cases brought under Article 2 and Article 3 (the right not to be subjected to torture or inhuman or degrading treatment or punishment). The Court's jurisdiction, under Article 32, over 'all cases concerning the interpretation and application' of the Convention reserves to it the final resolution of all disputed fact issues. In cases that arose before the effective date of Protocol 11 in November, 1998, the Court almost always relied on the factual investigation of the Commission. As we saw in the *Greek Case* in Chapter 2, the Commission, not infrequently, took evidence from witnesses and, when necessary, dispatched delegations to the sites of relevant events to hear testimony.[44] In addition to

[40] http://conventions.coe.int/Treaty/Commun/ChercheSig.asp?NT=114&CM=7&DF=30/07/04&CL=ENG.

[41] *See* 'Political Will Required to Abolish Death Penalty—Margelev', Russia and CIS General Newswire, Jan. 10 2007, Lexis-Nexis News-All (English Full Text) Library.

[42] http://conventions.coe.int/Treaty/Commun/ChercheSig.asp?NT=187&CM=7&DF=30/07/04&CL=ENG.

[43] *See*, e.g., *Bader and Others v. Sweden, supra* n. 39, at paras. 39–40, 42.

[44] *See* former Art. 28(1)(g).

the Commission's findings and other written material developed in the Commission's investigation, the Court also sometimes referred to evidence presented in domestic judicial proceedings or to submissions of the parties.[45]

With the elimination of the Commission, the Court adopted a relatively elaborate set of rules for fact-finding in an Annex to the Rules of Court. Those rules give broad authority to a Chamber to take evidence in various forms from a wide assortment of sources. The same powers may be exercised by a delegation appointed by a Chamber 'to conduct an inquiry, carry out an on-site investigation or take evidence in some other manner'. 'The Chamber may, inter alia, invite the parties to produce documentary evidence and decide to hear as a witness or expert or in any other capacity any person whose evidence or statement seems likely to assist it in the carrying out of its tasks'. It may also 'ask any person or institution of its choice to express an opinion or make a written report on any matter considered relevant to the case'.[46]

The new rules also stress the obligation of the parties to assist in the development of evidence. Article 38 of the Convention provides that when the Court deems an investigation necessary, 'the States concerned shall furnish all necessary facilities'. The rules restate this as a general duty to 'assist the Court as needed'.[47] This is supplemented with a number of more specific commitments clearly inspired by frustrations with previous investigations, notably involving Turkey.[48] The party on whose territory an investigation is carried out—almost always the respondent state—is obliged to co-operate, both by providing facilities and by allowing witnesses to travel to the proceedings. That state is also required to see that process is served on witnesses.[49] Significantly, the state must ensure 'that no adverse consequences are suffered' by co-operating witnesses.[50] Concern for the safety of witnesses may also explain the presumption that hearings be conducted *in camera*.[51] And in case witnesses are, nonetheless, prevented from appearing, Rule A3 states that such non-appearance need not by itself justify terminating the proceedings.

The Court has stated that a failure on the part of a respondent state to co-operate in assembling the evidence may justify an adverse inference with respect to the state's assertions on the relevant fact issue.[52] But such non-co-operation may still deprive the Court of evidence that it regards as crucial in finding a violation—especially since (with some exceptions) the standard of proof for finding violations under Articles 2 and 3 has been proof 'beyond a reasonable doubt'. In *Tashin Acar v. Turkey*[53] one of the issues in dispute was whether the applicant's brother had or had not been taken away by the police. Three family members claimed to have seen the applicant in custody

---

[45] *See*, e.g., *Ribitisch v. Austria*, 4 Dec. 1995, 21 E.H.R.R. 573, paras. 30–4.
[46] Rules of Court, Rule A1(1)–(3).
[47] *Id*. Rule A2(1).
[48] *See*, e.g., *Timurtas v. Turkey*, 13 June 2000, 33 E.H.R.R. 6.
[49] *Id*. Rule A5(4).
[50] *Id*. Rule A2(2).
[51] *Id*. Rule A1(5).
[52] E.g. *Tepe v. Turkey*, 9 May 2003, 39 E.H.R.R. 29, para. 128.
[53] [G.C.], 8 April 2004, 38 E.H.R.R. 2.

on a television broadcast. Despite numerous requests from the Court the respondent state never produced the video recording of the broadcast. Therefore, the Court found that it could not be established that the person seen on television was the applicant's brother.[54] (It did, however, find a violation of Article 2 in connection with the authorities' inadequate investigation.[55]) In such cases, the Court has taken to issuing a separate holding that the state has failed to comply with Article 38.[56]

In a separate opinion in *Tashin Acar* Judge Bonello decried the Court's failure to find a substantive violation of Article 2 in light of the state's failure to co-operate in the investigation:

I ask who ought to be penalized for this dearth of evidence and for the two ascertained failings by the Government? Is it the applicant, who was short-changed of any effective means to substantiate his assertions as all the evidence was safely entombed in the State's coffers? Or the Government, bound by the Convention to conduct a proper investigation but did not, and obliged to provide the Court with what evidence it had, but equally did not—at least not with the required diligence?...I consider it incongruous that, as a consequence of violating two Convention duties, the culprit State should reap rewards... In my view the Court ought to have declared boldly and defiantly that, when a State defaults on its duties to investigate and to hand over evidence it has under its control, the burden of proof shifts. It is then for the Government to disprove the applicants allegations. Failure to draw these inferences will only embolden rogue States in their efforts to rig sham investigations, and encourage the suppression of incriminating evidence.[57]

The European Court does not undertake to hear live testimony on the spot or elsewhere in every case involving disputed issues of fact. Indeed, some sharply contested factual matters have been decided based solely on written materials. In the *Tashin Acar* case just discussed, the Court relied solely on written submissions of the parties and on the records of domestic courts and other agencies that dealt with the same questions. These materials were surveyed in one hundred paragraphs of the judgment.[58] There is no clear formula indicating what circumstances call for what kinds of evidence. There is some suggestion that the elimination of the Commission has made the Court more receptive to accepting facts developed in domestic proceedings. In one case the Court said:

It would be inappropriate and contrary to [the Court's] subsidiary role under the Convention to attempt to establish the facts of this case by embarking on a fact-finding exercise on its own by summoning witnesses. Such exercise would duplicate the proceedings before the civil courts which are better placed and equipped as fact-finding tribunals.[59]

This decision was, however, qualified by the assumption that 'there are no concrete factors which could deprive civil courts of their ability to establish the facts'. In the

---

[54] *Id.* at para. 217.
[55] *Id.* at paras. 220–34.
[56] E.g. *id.* at paras. 250–6.
[57] *Id.* Concurring Opinion of Judge Bonello, paras. 7, 9, 12.
[58] *Id.* paras. 85–185.
[59] *McKerr v. United Kingdom*, 4 May 2001, 34 E.H.R.R. 20, para. 117.

same case the Court declined to make findings on critical disputed issues in light of continuing civil proceedings dealing with the same matters. It also refused to consider written submissions of fact by the parties because the assertions in them had not been 'tested in examination and cross-examination'. In the event, the Court simply abstained from deciding whether the death of the decedent violated Article 2 although it did find a breach of the state's 'procedural' obligation to investigate the death.[60]

The policy of deferring to domestic fact-finding has certain logical limits. The Court has stressed that its investigations differ in significant ways from those that might be undertaken in national courts. More particularly, a finding of innocence as a matter of domestic criminal law cannot preclude a judgment in Strasbourg as to the presence or absence of a violation of the Convention.[61] Moreover, the Court, while acknowledging 'that in the normal course of events a criminal trial, with an adversarial procedure before an independent and impartial judge must be regarded as furnishing the strongest safeguards of an effective procedure for the finding of facts and the attribution of criminal responsibility', has repeatedly stressed that 'defects in an investigation may fundamentally undermine the ability of a court to determine responsibility for a death'.[62] Presumably, in those cases the Court will give little weight to findings of fact developed in these flawed procedures.

The Court has held that the proper standard of proof for showing a violation of the Convention is 'beyond a reasonable doubt'. But it has added that 'such proof may follow from the coexistence of sufficient strong, clear and concordant inferences or of similar unrebutted presumptions of fact'.[63] In *Gündem v. Turkey*, in which the Court considered allegations that security forces had burned down the applicants' homes, the Court deferred to a Commission determination that the events described by applicants had not been established beyond a reasonable doubt. The only eyewitness who testified before the Commission's delegates had been unclear about the reasons for the security forces' actions. The applicant himself had not appeared and other witnesses had contradicted his account.[64] On the other hand, the Court has often upheld Commission findings of violations even when based on inconsistent and divided evidence. In one such case a dissenting judge described the manner in which the Commission established the facts as 'so superficial and insufficient and the analysis of these facts so clearly unsatisfactory that, in my view, neither provides a sufficiently sound basis for finding a violation'.[65]

---

[60] *Id.* at paras. 117–21. There is, it will be noted, a possible tension between its decision to remit critical fact-finding to the domestic authorities and the finding of a failure of an adequate investigation. The Court noted that since the civil judicial proceedings had to be initiated by the applicant and did not require identification or punishment of the perpetrator, they could not be taken into account in evaluating the state's fulfillment of its procedural obligation.

[61] *Avşar v. Turkey*, 10 July 2001, 37 E.H.R.R. 53, para. 284.

[62] E.g. *Ağdaş v. Turkey*, 27 July 2004, para. 102

[63] *Ireland v. United Kingdom*, 18 Jan. 1978, 2 E.H.R.R. 25.

[64] 25 May 1998, 32 E.H.R.R. 17, paras 27–9, 66. *See also Ergi v. Turkey*, 28 July 1998, 32 E.H.R.R. 18; *Tanrikulu v. Turkey* [G.C.], 8 July 1999, 30 E.H.R.R. 950.

[65] *Kurt v. Turkey*, 25 May 1998, 26 E.H.R.R. 373 (partly dissenting opinion of Judge Matscher).

Notwithstanding the formal requirement of proof beyond a reasonable doubt, the Court has established a presumption for one situation which not infrequently arises in cases brought under Articles 2 and 3. When someone, previously of good health, is injured while in custody the Court has held that, notwithstanding the usual burden of proof, it is up to the state to provide an explanation.[66] And when someone dies while in custody, the obligation to account for his or her treatment is 'particularly stringent'.[67] The Court has reasoned that in such cases, the state has a peculiar advantage in understanding what happened. Consequently, 'strong presumptions of fact will arise in respect of injuries and death occurring during such detention. Indeed, the burden of proof may be regarded as resting on the authorities to provide a satisfactory and convincing explanation'.[68] The explanation offered by the state must show a certain level of plausibility. In one case the government argued that the victim had died of cardiac arrest. This suggestion conflicted with the presence of bruises on the decedent's foot, ankle and chest. The claim that a broken sternum was caused by an attempt to apply cardiac massage was contradicted by other scientific evidence.[69]

The presumption that the state is responsible for the death of a person in custody has also been applied in cases involving 'disappearances'. If the Court can be persuaded that a person was taken into official custody before the disappearance it may also decide that the person may be presumed to be dead. This has been applied in cases in Turkey where a person involved had engaged in political activities inimical to the government. Given the history of violence and maltreatment of detainees in southeastern Turkey, the Court has been willing to take the disappearance as an indication of death. At that point, the presumption of responsibility for a person in custody is engaged and, absent some reasonable explanation, a violation of Article 2 can be found.[70] Even when the Court has been unwilling to conclude that disappearances could be presumed to involve deaths for which the state was responsible, the extended absence of a person who disappeared in 'life-threatening circumstances' has been held to trigger a state's 'procedural' obligation to conduct ineffective investigation.[71]

In dealing with disappearances under the right to life the European Court has followed the practice of the Inter-American Court of Human Rights in its 1988 judgment in *Velasquez-Rodríguez v. Honduras*.[72] That Court has referred to disappearances as involving 'multiple and continuing violations of many rights' including, besides the right to life, rights of liberty, integrity of the person and against inhuman and degrading treatment.[73]

---

[66] *Tomasi v. France*, 27 Aug. 1992, 15 E.H.R.R. 1.
[67] *Salman v. Turkey*, 27 June 2000, 34 E.H.R.R. 17, para. 99.
[68] *Id.* at para. 100
[69] *Id.* at para. 102.
[70] *See Akdeniz and Others v. Turkey*, 31 May 2005.
[71] *Cyprus v. Turkey*, 10 May 2001, 35 E.H.R.R. 30, paras. 123–36, and *see* Chapter 11(A).
[72] 4 Inter-Am. Ct. H.R. (Ser. C) No. 4 (1988).
[73] *Id.* at paras. 155–8.

5

TORTURE; INHUMAN OR DEGRADING TREATMENT OR PUNISHMENT; AND SLAVERY

ARTICLE 3

No one shall be subjected to torture or to inhuman or degrading treatment or punishment.

ARTICLE 4

1. No one shall be held in slavery or servitude.

2. No one shall be required to perform forced or compulsory labour.

3. For the purpose of this article the term 'forced or compulsory labour' shall not include:

   (a) any work required to be done in the ordinary course of detention imposed according to the provisions of Article 5 of this Convention or during conditional release from such detention;

   (b) any service of a military character or, in case of conscientious objectors in countries where they are recognised, service exacted instead of compulsory military service;

   (c) any service exacted in case of an emergency or calamity threatening the life or well-being of the community;

   (d) any work or service which forms part of normal civic obligations.

The idea that government can abuse its power by the unwarranted infliction of pain is, naturally, an ancient one. A statement that 'excessive bail ought not to be required nor excessive fines imposed nor cruel and unusual punishments inflicted' was included in Article 10 of the English Bill of Rights of 1689. As part of a more general concern with a perceived corrupt judiciary in the reigns of the later Stuarts, the English Parliament was anxious to limit the imposition of arbitrary and excessive punishments. They may have had one celebrated case particularly in mind. That was the punishment given the cleric, Titus Oates, in 1686 for his part in concocting the 'Popish Plot'. Oates was sentenced to a fine, whipping, defrocking, life imprisonment and pillorying four times a year for the rest of his life.[1]

Practically identical language to that of the English Bill of Rights was included in many of the early state constitutions in the United States, and a similar provision was attached to the United States Constitution as the Eighth Amendment when the Bill of Rights, proposed in 1789, was ratified in 1791. In the first Congress, one opponent of that clause complained about its potential scope, arguing that 'it is sometimes necessary to hang a man, villains often deserve whipping, and perhaps having their ears cut off; but are we in future to be prevented from inflicting those punishments because they are cruel?'[2] In Canada's 1960 statutory Bill of Rights a right to be free of 'cruel and unusual treatment and punishment' was expressed. Identical language was adopted in the constitutional Canadian Charter of Rights and Freedoms of 1982.

The drafters of Article 3 of the European Convention in 1949–50 had before them a number of models besides the British and American Bills of Rights. Most notable was Article 5 of the recently adopted Universal Declaration of Human Rights which forbade 'torture or…cruel, inhuman or degrading treatment or punishment'. Initial drafts of the Convention merely declared an all-purpose right to 'security of the person in accordance with Articles 3, 5 and 8 of the Declaration of the United Nations'.[3]

When the drafters adopted their own language for Article 3 they reproduced the words of the Universal Declaration of Rights but, for reasons that are unclear, omitted the adjective, 'cruel'. At one stage in the drafting process a Committee of Experts had prepared two drafts. Draft A set forth broad, general standards of human rights, while Draft B attempted to set out more precise guidelines. With respect to the prohibition in question, however, there was little difference in the degree of generality between the two drafts. Draft A copied the Universal Declaration verbatim, referring to torture, and cruel, inhuman and degrading treatment or punishment, while Draft B listed only torture and inhuman treatment or punishment. The language finally adopted first appeared in a draft compiled by a Conference of Senior Officials in June 1950.[4] No reasons for the precise selection of terms is evident in the history of the drafting process.

Certainly the central idea that the drafters had in mind was suggested by the atrocities of the Nazi regime. In an early debate in the Consultative Assembly a British delegate, Seymour Cocks, referred to 'the terrible wave of barbarism and bestialism which was broken over our world during the last 30 years' and described in detail some of the horrors of that period.[5] Later, however, in the debate on a resolution condemning these practices, some of the difficulties inherent in a broad prohibition became apparent. The last sentence of that resolution would have expressed the Assembly's

---

[1] See L. Schwoerer, The Declaration of Rights, 1689, pp. 92–4, 202 (Baltimore, 1981) Johns Hopkins Press.

[2] Quoted in Furman v. Georgia, 408 U.S. 238, 244 (1972) (Douglas J, concurring).

[3] 1 Travaux Préparatoires 206.

[4] 4 Travaux Préparatoires 52, 58; 4 Travaux Préparatoires 274.

[5] 2 Travaux Préparatoires 38.

'abhorrence of the subjection of any person to any form of mutilation, sterilization or beating'. On the request of a Danish delegate the reference to sterilization was withdrawn in light of legislation in Scandinavian countries calling for the sterilization of some sex offenders. Then an English delegate suggested the deletion of the reference to 'beating' since, in England, corporal punishment was still thought an acceptable punishment for robbery and violence. At this point, on the suggestion of the President, the resolution was committed for redrafting.[6]

This minor debate illustrates the difficulties masked by the general language of Article 3. It is obvious that in order to maintain social order governments must, and usually ought to be, in the business of inflicting unwanted treatment on their citizens. While it may be readily agreed that the use of 'torture, inhuman and degrading treatment or punishment' for this purpose is unacceptable, once a particular practice is at issue, especially in light of its use in connection with a particular social problem, serious differences are bound to emerge. Like many domestic courts with similar constitutional provisions, the European Court of Human Rights has struggled to define the boundary between tolerable and intolerable punishment and treatment. As the materials in this chapter illustrate, the Court's efforts have focused, notwithstanding their unexplained selection, on each of the three different categories specified in the language of Article 3.

A. DEFINING THE TERMS

1. IRELAND V. UNITED KINGDOM

Judgment of 18 January 1978
2 E.H.R.R. 25

11. The tragic and lasting crisis in Northern Ireland lies at the root of the present case. In order to combat what the respondent Government describe as 'the longest and most violent terrorist campaign witnessed in either part of the island of Ireland', the authorities in Northern Ireland exercised from August 1971 until December 1975 a series of extrajudicial powers of arrest, detention and internment. The proceedings in this case concern the scope and the operation in practice of those measures as well as the alleged ill-treatment of persons thereby deprived of their liberty.

12. Up to March 1975, on the figures cited before the Commission by the respondent Government, over 1,100 people had been killed, over 11,150 injured and more than £140,000,000 worth of property destroyed during the recent troubles in Northern Ireland.

---

[6] 2 *Travaux Préparatoires* 238–44.

This violence found its expression in part in civil disorders, in part in terrorism, that is organized violence for political ends...

36. ... The authorities therefore came to the conclusion that it was necessary to introduce a policy of detention and internment of persons suspected of serious terrorist activities but against whom sufficient evidence could not be laid in court. This policy was regarded as a temporary measure primarily aimed at breaking the influence of the IRA. It was intended that a respite would be provided so as to enable the political and social reforms already undertaken to achieve their full effects. [The policy of internment was introduced in August, 1971. In December, the Government of Ireland lodged its application with the Commission.]...

93. ... The procedure followed for the purposes of ascertaining the facts (Article 28, sub-paragraph (a), of the Convention) was one decided upon by the Commission and accepted by the Parties. The Commission examined in detail with medical reports and oral evidence 16 'illustrative' cases selected at its request by the applicant Government. The Commission considered a further 41 cases (the so-called '41 cases') on which it had received medical reports and invited written comments:...

96. Twelve persons arrested on 9 August 1971 and two persons arrested in October 1971 were singled out and taken to one or more unidentified centres. There, between 11 to 17 August and 11 to 18 October respectively, they were submitted to a form of 'interrogation in depth' which involved the combined application of five particular techniques.

These methods, sometimes termed 'disorientation' or 'sensory deprivation' techniques, were not used in any cases other than the fourteen so indicated above. It emerges from the Commission's establishment of the facts that the techniques consisted of:

(a) *wall-standing*: forcing the detainees to remain for periods of some hours in a 'stress position', described by those who underwent it as being 'spreadeagled against the wall, with their fingers put high above the head against the wall, the legs spread apart and the feet back, causing them to stand on their toes with the weight of the body mainly on the fingers';

(b) *hooding*: putting a black or navy coloured bag over the detainees' heads and, at least initially, keeping it there all the time except during interrogation;

(c) *subjection to noise*: pending their interrogations, holding the detainees in a room where there was a continuous loud and hissing noise;

(d) *deprivation of sleep*: pending their interrogations, depriving the detainees of sleep;

(e) *deprivation of food and drink*: subjecting the detainees to a reduced diet during their stay at the centre and pending interrogations....

98. The two operations of interrogation in depth by means of the five techniques led to the obtaining of a considerable quantity of intelligence information, including the identification of 700 members of both IRA factions and the discovery of individual responsibility for about 85 previously unexplained criminal incidents....

[On 2 March 1972 (after the initial application before the Commission had been lodged, but before it had been declared admissible) the United Kingdom Prime Minister had announced that the Government was discontinuing use of the five techniques. The United Kingdom Attorney-General, at a hearing before the European Court of Human Rights on 8 February

1977, gave the Court an 'unqualified undertaking, that the "five techniques" will not in any circumstances be reintroduced as an aid to interrogation'.]...

The Commission found no physical injury to have resulted from the application of the five techniques as such, but loss of weight by the two case-witnesses and acute psychiatric symptoms developed by them during interrogation were recorded in the medical and other evidence. The Commission, on the material before it, was unable to establish the exact degree of any psychiatric after-effects produced... but on the general level it was satisfied that some psychiatric after-effects in certain of the fourteen persons subjected to the techniques could not be excluded...

[The Court reviewed numerous other allegations of ill-treatment including claimed assaults and beatings.]

152. The United Kingdom Government contest neither the breaches of Article 3 as found by the Commission, nor—a point moreover that is beyond doubt—the Court's jurisdiction to examine such breaches. However, relying *inter alia* on the case-law of the International Court of Justice they argue that the European Court has power to decline to exercise its jurisdiction where the objective of an application has been accomplished or where adjudication on the merits would be devoid of purpose. Such, they claim, is the situation here. They maintain that the findings in question not only are not contested but also have been widely publicized and that they do not give rise to problems of interpretation or application of the Convention sufficiently important to require a decision by the Court. Furthermore, for them the subject-matter of those findings now belongs to past history in view of the abandonment of the five techniques (1972), the solemn and unqualified undertaking not to reintroduce these techniques (8 February 1977) and the other measures taken by the United Kingdom to remedy, impose punishment for, and prevent the recurrence of, the various violations found by the Commission...

154. Nevertheless, the Court considers that the responsibilities assigned to it within the framework of the system under the Convention extended to pronouncing on the noncontested allegations of violation of Article 3. The Court's judgments in fact serve not only to decide those cases brought before the Court but, more generally, to elucidate, safeguard and develop the rules instituted by the Convention, thereby contributing to the observance by the States of the engagements undertaken by them as Contracting Parties....

162. As was emphasized by the Commission, ill-treatment must attain a minimum level of severity if it is to fall within the scope of Article 3. The assessment of this minimum is, in the nature of things, relative; it depends on all the circumstances of the case, such as the duration of the treatment, its physical or mental effects and, in some cases, the sex, age and state of health of the victim, etc.

163. The Convention prohibits in absolute terms torture and inhuman or degrading treatment or punishment, irrespective of the victim's conduct. Unlike most of the substantive clauses of the Convention and of Protocols Nos. 1 and 4, Article 3 makes no provision for exceptions and, under Article 15 (2), there can be no derogation therefrom even in the event of a public emergency threatening the life of the nation.

164. In the instant case, the only relevant concepts are 'torture' and 'inhuman or degrading treatment', to the exclusion of 'inhuman or degrading punishment'....

167. The five techniques were applied in combination, with premeditation and for hours at a stretch; they caused, if not actual bodily injury, at least intense physical and mental suffering to the persons subjected thereto and also led to acute psychiatric disturbances during inter-rogation. They accordingly fell into the category of inhuman treatment within the meaning of Article 3. The techniques were also degrading since they were such as to arouse in their victims feelings of fear, anguish and inferiority capable of humiliating and debasing them and possibly breaking their physical or moral resistance.

On these two points, the Court is of the same view as the Commission.

In order to determine whether the five techniques should also be qualified as torture, the Court must have regard to the distinction, embodied in Article 3, between this notion and that of inhuman or degrading treatment.

In the Court's view, this distinction derives principally from a difference in the intensity of the suffering inflicted.

The Court considers in fact that, whilst there exists on the one hand violence which is to be condemned both on moral grounds and also in most cases under the domestic law of the Contracting States but which does not fall within Article 3 of the Convention, it appears on the other hand that it was the intention that the Convention, with its distinction between 'torture' and 'inhuman or degrading treatment', should by the first of these terms attach a special stigma to deliberate inhuman treatment causing very serious and cruel suffering.

Moreover, this seems to be the thinking lying behind Article 1 *in fine* of Resolution 3452 (XXX) adopted by the General Assembly of the United Nations on 9 December 1975, which declares:

> 'Torture constitutes an *aggravated* and deliberate form of cruel, inhuman or degrading treatment or punishment'.

Although the five techniques, as applied in combination, undoubtedly amounted to inhuman and degrading treatment, although their object was the extraction of confessions, the naming of others and/or information and although they were used systematically, they did not occa-sion suffering of the particular intensity and cruelty implied by the word torture as so understood.

> [The Court held by 16 votes to one that the use of the five techniques constituted inhuman and degrading treatment, in violation of Article 3. It held by 13 votes to four that the use of the five techniques did not constitute torture within the meaning of Article 3.]
>
> [The Court also considered other alleged violations of Article 3 and found some uncon-tested and others not supported by adequate proof.
>
> The Court's discussion of claimed violations of Articles 5 and 6 is omitted.]

Separate opinion of Judge Zekia

... It seems to me permissible, in ascertaining whether torture or inhuman treatment has been committed or not, to apply not only the objective test but also the subjective test.

As an example I can refer to the case of an elderly sick man who is exposed to a harsh treatment—after being given several blows and beaten to the floor, he is dragged and kicked on the floor for several hours. I would say without hesitation that the poor man has been tortured. If such treatment is applied on a wrestler or even a young athlete, I would hesitate a lot to describe it as inhuman treatment and I might regard it as a mere rough handling. Another example: if a mother, for interrogation, is separated from her suckling baby by keeping them apart in adjoining rooms and the baby, on account of hunger, starts yelling for hours within the hearing of the mother and she is not allowed to attend her baby, again I should say both the mother and the baby have been subjected to inhuman treatment, the mother by being agonized and the baby by being deprived of the urgent attention of the mother. Neither the mother nor the child has been assaulted....

I do not share the view that extreme intensity of physical or mental suffering is a requisite for a case of ill-treatment to amount to 'torture' within the purport and object of Article 3 of the Convention. The nature of torture admits gradation in its intensity, in its severity and in the methods adopted. It is, therefore, primarily the duty and responsibility of the authority conducting the enquiries from close quarters, after taking into account all the surrounding circumstances, evidence and material available, to say whether in a particular case inhuman ill-treatment reached the degree of torture. In other words, this is a finding of fact for the competent authority dealing with the case in the first instance and which, for reasons we give hereunder, we should not interfere with.

Separate opinion of Judge O'Donoghue

...One is not bound to regard torture as only present in a mediaeval dungeon where the appliances of rack and thumbscrew or similar devices were employed. Indeed in the present-day world there can be little doubt that torture may be inflicted in the mental sphere. Torture is, of course, a more severe type of inhuman treatment. No amount of careful consideration can alter my opinion that the approach of the Commission...was the correct one. Accordingly, I conclude that the combined use of the five techniques constituted a practice of inhuman treatment and torture in breach of Article 3.

Separate opinion of Judge Fitzmaurice

13. ...[It cannot be said that] everyone knows what torture is, what inhuman treatment is, and what is degrading,—since the present case seems to show conclusively that ideas on these questions can differ very greatly, not only with reference to particular acts, but as to the very factors on which an assessment should be based. Yet it can certainly be said that some kinds of treatment *recognisably* amount to torture or inhuman or degrading treatment; whereas other, though censorable, do not....

22. According to my idea of the correct handling of languages and concepts, to call the treatment involved by the use of the five techniques 'inhuman' is excessive and distorting, unless the term is being employed loosely and merely figuratively (see examples below[7]),—and it is clearly not in any such lax or light-hearted sense that Article 3 intends it. Subjection to the five techniques was certainly harsh treatment, ill-treatment, maltreatment, and other descriptions could be found; but the 'inhuman' involves a totally different order or category of concept to which, in my opinion, the five techniques, even used in combination, do not properly belong. To regard them as doing so is to debase the currency of normal speech, because there is then no way left in which to differentiate or distinguish, or to describe instances of truly

---

[7] To give examples of figurative use within most people's experience:—One hears it said 'I call that inhuman', the reference being to the fact that there is no dining-car on the train. 'It's degrading for the poor man', one hears with reference to an employee who is being given all the unpleasant jobs. 'It's absolute torture to me'—and what the speaker means is having to sit through a boring lecture or sermon. There is a lesson to be learnt here on the potential dangers of hyperbole (footnote by Judge Fitzmaurice).

inhuman treatment. If anything that causes an appreciable amount of aching, strain, discomfort, distress, etc., or of deprivation of sleep or sustenance, is to be regarded as 'inhuman', what words shall be found to characterize the much graver treatment that could without serious question be considered inhuman? To give concrete examples, if standing someone against a wall in a strained position over a considerable period, or keeping him with a hood over his head for a certain time, amounts to 'inhuman' treatment, what language should be used to describe kicking a man in the groin, or placing him in a blacked-out cell in the company of a bevy of starving rats? That would also be merely inhuman treatment presumably?—and I say 'merely' because, although the latter instances would clearly constitute inhuman treatment, they would apparently be rated no differently from, and as no worse than, the former relatively minor ones, if these also are to be characterized as 'inhuman'. If the extreme term is to be used for any infliction of physical or mental harm or stress, no way of marking out or attaching the necessary weight to the genuine case remains,—for to employ such locutions as 'very inhuman' or 'severely inhuman' would obviously be ridiculous....

25. ...The essential phrase [in the Court's finding of inhuman treatment]—reads as follows:

> 'they caused, if not actual bodily injury [which means that they did not do so], at least intense physical and mental suffering to the persons subjected thereto and also led to acute psychiatric disturbances during interrogation'.

Most people feel 'disturbed' during an interrogation that must necessarily be of a rigorous, searching and quasi-hostile character, and it is not surprising that there was medical evidence of it in certain particular cases. But what is the basis of the term 'intense', qualifying 'suffering', physical and mental? Such language is surely excessive and disproportionate and not justified by the evidence. To many people, several of the techniques would not cause 'suffering' properly so called at all, and certainly not 'intense' suffering. Even the wall-standing would give rise to something more in the nature of strain, aches and pains, fatigue, and the like. To speak of 'intense physical...suffering' comes very near to speaking of torture, and the Judgment rejects torture. The sort of epithets that would in my view be justified to describe the treatment involved (treatment that did not cause bodily injury) would be 'unpleasant, harsh, tough, severe' and others of that order, but to call it 'barbarous', 'savage', 'brutal' or 'cruel', which is the least that is necessary if the notion of the inhuman is to be attained, constitutes an abuse of language and, as I have said earlier, amounts to a devaluing of what should be kept for much worse things. It is hardly a convincing exercise...

26. ...For my part, I consider that the concept of 'inhuman' treatment should be confined to the kind of treatment that (taking some account of the circumstances) no member of the human species ought to inflict on another, or could so inflict without doing grave violence to the human, as opposed to the animal, element is his or her make-up. This I believe is the sense in which the notion of 'inhuman' treatment was intended to be understood in Article 3,—as something amounting to an atrocity, or at least a barbarity. Hence it should not be employed as a mere figure of speech to denote what is bad treatment, ill treatment, maltreatment, rather than, properly speaking, inhuman treatment....

27. ...['Degrading treatment' should] denote something seriously humiliating, lowering as to human dignity, or disparaging, like having one's head shaved, being tarred and feathered, smeared with filth, pelted with muck, paraded naked in front of strangers, forced to eat

excreta, deface the portrait of one's sovereign or head of State, or dress up in a way calculated to provoke ridicule or contempt,—although here one may pause to wonder whether Christ was really degraded by being made to don a purple robe and crown of thorns and to carry His own cross. Be that as it may, the examples I have given justify asking where exactly the degradation lies in being deprived of sleep and nourishment for limited periods, in being placed for a time in a room where a continuous noise is going on, or even in being 'hooded'—(after all, it has never been suggested that a man is degraded by being blindfolded before being executed although, admittedly, this is supposed to be for his benefit)....

28. ...[The Court states:]

'The techniques were also degrading since they were such as to arouse in their victims feelings of fear, anguish and inferiority capable of humiliating and debasing them and possibly breaking their physical or moral resistance.'...

(a) Feelings of 'fear, anguish and inferiority' are the common lot of mankind constantly experienced by everyone in the course of ordinary everyday life: that is 'la condition humaine'. Yet no one would consider himself, or regard others, as humiliated and debased because of experiencing such feelings, even though some experience them very easily and others only for greater cause. Thus it is not the subjective feelings aroused in the individual that humiliate or debase but the objective character of the act or treatment that gives rise to those feelings—if it does—and even if it does not,—for it is possible for fanatics at one end of the scale, and saints, martyrs and heroes at the other to undergo the most degrading treatment and feel neither humiliated nor debased, but even uplifted. Yet the treatment itself remains none the less degrading....

(b) Nor does 'possibly breaking their physical or moral resistance' furnish any more satisfactory test. Again it is the character of the treatment that counts, not its results. It is easy to think of ways in which physical and moral resistance can be broken without any resort to ill-treatment, the use of force, or acts of degradation. Alcohol will do it, and often does. More generally, simple persuasion, or consideration and indulgence will do it. As has been well said, 'There is no defence against kindness'. The degradation lies not in what the treatment produces, but in how it does it: it might produce no result at all, but still be degrading because of its intrinsic character....

35. Although I agree with the Court's pronouncements [on the absence of 'torture' in this case], and they are correct as far as they go, and propound the essential test that has to be applied, they nevertheless fail to bring out the real point latent in them, which is that not only must a certain intensity of suffering be caused before the process can be called torture, but also that torture involves a wholly different *order* of suffering from what falls short of it. It amounts not to a mere difference of degree but to a difference of kind. If the five techniques are to be regarded as involving torture, how does one characterize e.g. having one's finger-nails torn out, being slowly impaled on a stake through the rectum, or roasted over an electric grid? That is just torture too, is it? Or might it perhaps amount to 'severe' torture?! Or what words do you find to make the difference between treatment of that kind and the mere aches, pains, strains, stresses and discomforts of the five techniques, which pale into insignificance in comparison with the searing, unimaginable, agony of the other? These are not in the same category at all, and cannot be spoken of in the same breath. Nor is the point academic, as it might be if torture of the order I have mentioned were a thing of the past. But it is not; and in Europe

itself there are countries in which such practices have been prevalent in quite recent periods. So what does the European Commission do when, as it easily might, it finds itself faced with a case of real torture? Just pronounce it to constitute treatment contrary to Article 3 of the Convention? Fortunately for the Court, it, at least, has avoided digging this pit for itself.

36. May I conclude this part of the case by registering my emphatic opining that if a commendable zeal for the observance and implementation of the Convention is allowed to drive out common-sense, the whole system will end by becoming discredited. There can be no surer way of doing this than to water down and adulterate the terms of the Convention by enlarging them so as to include concepts and notions that lie outside their just and normal scope....

Separate opinion of Judge Evrigenis

(i) ... The Court's interpretation in this case seems also to be directed to a conception of torture based on methods of inflicting suffering which have already been overtaken by the ingenuity of modern techniques of oppression. Torture no longer presupposes violence, a notion to which the judgment refers expressly and generically. Torture can be practised—and indeed is practised—by using subtle techniques developed in multidisciplinary laboratories which claim to be scientific. By means of new forms of suffering that have little in common with the physical pain caused by conventional torture it aims to bring about, even if only temporarily, the disintegration of an individual's personality, the shattering of his mental and psychological equilibrium and the crushing of his will. I should very much regret it if the definition of torture which emerges from the judgment could not cover these various forms of technologically sophisticated torture. Such an interpretation would overlook the current situation and the historical prospects in which the European Convention on Human Rights should be implemented.

(ii) I take a stronger position than the majority of the Court as regards the assessment of the combined use of the five techniques from the factual point of view. I am sure that the use of these carefully chosen and measured techniques must have caused those who underwent them extremely intense physical, mental and psychological suffering, inevitably covered by even the strictest definition of torture....

Separate opinion of Judge Matscher

... There is no doubt that one can speak of torture within the meaning of Article 3 only when the treatment inflicted on a person is such as to cause him physical or psychological suffering of a certain severity. However, I consider the element of intensity as complementary to the systematic element: the more sophisticated and refined the method, the less acute will be the pain (in the first place physical pain) which it has to cause to achieve its purpose. The modern methods of torture which in their outward aspects differ markedly from the primitive, brutal methods employed in former times are well known. In this sense torture is in no way a higher degree of inhuman treatment. On the contrary, one can envisage forms of brutality which cause much more acute bodily suffering but are not necessarily on that account comprised within the notion of torture.

... 'The five techniques were applied in combination, with premeditation and for hours at a stretch; they caused, if not actual bodily injury, at least intense physical and mental suffering to the persons subjected thereto and also led to acute psychiatric disturbances during interrogation' (paragraph 167 of the judgment). They thus constitute a typical example of torture within the meaning of Article 3 of the Convention.

2. PEERS V. GREECE

Judgment of 19 April 2001
33 E.H.R.R. 51

...

8. On 19 August 1994 the applicant, who had been treated for heroin addiction in the United Kingdom, was arrested at Athens Airport for drug offences. He was transferred to the central police headquarters of Athens in Alexandras Avenue, where he was detained until 24 August 1994.

[The applicant was detained, pending trial, in Koridallos Prison from 21 August 1994 until his conviction on 28 September 1995. For four months he was confined in one of the prison's segregation units. A delegation of the Commission inspected the prison in June 1998 and collected evidence from the prison officials and the applicant's cell-mate. The Court also relied on findings of an inspection of the prison by delegates of the European Commission for the Prevention of Torture and Inhuman or Degrading Treatment or Punishment. Both inspections revealed problems of overcrowding and inadequate facilities, some of which are mentioned in the excerpts below.]

...

64. The applicant submitted that he never asked to be placed in the segregation unit. The prison administration decided to put him there on his arrival in Koridallos Prison. One week later, he was given the possibility of going to the Delta wing proper but he did not agree because he wanted to keep away from drugs. The applicant alleged that the conditions in the segregation unit had not improved significantly between his detention there and the delegates' visit. He complained in particular that he had to spend a considerable part of each day confined to his bed in a cell with no ventilation and no window. He further complained that the prison administration did not provide inmates with sheets, pillows, toilet paper and toiletries. Although indigent prisoners like the applicant could address themselves to the prison's welfare office, it was admitted that their needs could not always be met. The fact that he could have obtained toiletries and toilet paper from his co-detainees does not absolve the respondent State from responsibility under the Convention. The applicant submitted that he ended up sleeping on a blanket with no sheets or pillow during the hottest period of the year. He also complained that he had to use the toilet in the presence of another inmate and be present while the toilet was being used by his cell-mate. The applicant claimed that he felt humiliated and distressed and that the conditions of his detention had had adverse physical and mental effects on him.

65. The Government first submitted that the applicant asked to be detained in the segregation unit. The prison authorities wanted to satisfy his request. However, because there were

no cells available, he had to share a cell with another inmate. As a result, the problem with the toilet arose. The applicant could have moved to another part of the prison at any time if he so wished. It appears that the applicant never asked for such a transfer because, in the meantime, he had developed a friendly relationship with his cell-mate, Mr Papadimitriou. The special character of their relationship is also shown by the fact that they continued sharing a cell when they were both moved to the Alpha wing two months after the applicant's arrest. . . .

66. Moreover, the Government disputed that the treatment complained of had attained the minimum level of severity required to fall within the scope of Article 3. They stressed that the conditions of detention complained of in no way denoted contempt or lack of respect for the applicant as a person. On the contrary, the prison authorities tried to alleviate the situation by allowing the applicant extra telephone calls. The applicant himself accepted that he was never left dirty while in the segregation unit. He could take a shower and had frequent contact with the prison psychiatrist. According to the Government, there was no evidence that the conditions of his detention had caused the applicant injury or any physical or mental suffering.

67. The Court recalls that, according to its case-law, ill-treatment must attain a minimum level of severity if it is to fall within the scope of Article 3. The assessment of this minimum level of severity is relative; it depends on all the circumstances of the case, such as the duration of the treatment, its physical and mental effects and, in some cases, the sex, age and state of health of the victim (see, among other authorities, *Ireland v. the United Kingdom*).

68. Furthermore, in considering whether a treatment is 'degrading' within the meaning of Article 3, the Court will have regard to whether its object is to humiliate and debase the person concerned and whether, as far as the consequences are concerned, it adversely affected his or her personality in a manner incompatible with Article 3.

69. As regards the present case, the Court notes in the first place that, contrary to what the Government argue, the applicant was not placed in the segregation unit because he had so wanted himself. According to the testimony of Ms Fragathula, this was a measure decided by the prison governor and the chief warden and related to the applicant's medical condition, more specifically to the fact that he had been suffering from withdrawal symptoms. According to the same witness, once the applicant became acquainted with the conditions of detention in the segregation unit, he asked for a transfer. He was then offered the possibility of going to the Delta wing, where drug addicts were being detained. Although Ms Fragathula would not expressly admit that there were drugs in the Delta wing, she stated that the 'wing was problematic for someone who wanted to free himself from drugs'. The Court considers that this implies that there were drugs illegally circulating in the Delta wing, a cause for serious concern. In these circumstances, the Court considers that the applicant cannot be blamed for refusing to be moved from the segregation unit. The Court, therefore, considers that the applicant did not in any way consent to being detained in the segregation unit of the Delta wing.

70. Concerning the conditions of detention in the segregation unit, the Court has had regard to the Commission's delegates' findings and especially their findings concerning the size, lighting and ventilation of the applicant's cell, that is, elements which would not have changed between the time of the applicant's detention there and the delegates' visit. As regards ventilation, the Court notes that the delegates' findings do not correspond fully with those of the [European Commission for the Prevention of Torture and Inhuman or Degrading Treatment or Punishment (CPT)], which visited Koridallos Prison in 1993 and submitted its report in 1994. However, the CPT's inspection took place in March, whereas the delegates went to

Koridallos Prison in June, a period of the year when the climatic conditions are closer to those of the period of which the applicant complains. Furthermore, the Court takes into account the fact that the delegates investigated the applicant's complaints in depth, giving special attention, during their inspection, to the conditions in the very place where the applicant had been detained. In these circumstances, the Court considers that the findings of the Commission's delegates are reliable.

71. The Court notes that the applicant accepts that the cell door was open during the day, when he could circulate freely in the segregation unit. Although the unit and its exercise yard were small, the limited possibility of movement enjoyed by the applicant must have given him some form of relief.

72. Nevertheless, the Court recalls that the applicant had to spend at least part of the evening and the entire night in his cell. Although the cell was designed for one person, the applicant had to share it with another inmate. This is one aspect in which the applicant's situation differed from the situation reviewed by the CPT in its 1994 report. Sharing the cell with another inmate meant that, for the best part of the period when the cell door was locked, the applicant was confined to his bed. Moreover, there was no ventilation in the cell, there being no opening other than a peephole in the door. The Court also notes that, during their visit to Koridallos, the delegates found that the cells in the segregation unit were exceedingly hot, although it was only June, a month when temperatures do not normally reach their peak in Greece. It is true that the delegates' visit took place in the afternoon, when the applicant would not normally be locked up in his cell. However, the Court recalls that the applicant was placed in the segregation unit during a period of the year when temperatures have the tendency to rise considerably in Greece, even in the evening and often at night. This was confirmed by Mr Papadimitriou, an inmate who shared the cell with the applicant and who testified that the latter was significantly physically affected by the heat and the lack of ventilation in the cell.

73. The Court also recalls that in the evening and at night when the cell door was locked the applicant had to use the Asian-type toilet in his cell. The toilet was not separated from the rest of the cell by a screen and the applicant was not the cell's only occupant.

74. In the light of the foregoing, the Court considers that in the present case there is no evidence that there was a positive intention of humiliating or debasing the applicant. However, the Court notes that, although the question whether the purpose of the treatment was to humiliate or debase the victim is a factor to be taken into account, the absence of any such purpose cannot conclusively rule out a finding of violation of Article 3.

75. Indeed, in the present case, the fact remains that the competent authorities took no steps to improve the objectively unacceptable conditions of the applicant's detention. In the Court's view, this omission denotes lack of respect for the applicant. The Court takes into account, in particular, that, for at least two months, the applicant had to spend a considerable part of each 24-hour period practically confined to his bed in a cell with no ventilation and no window, which would at times become unbearably hot. He also had to use the toilet in the presence of another inmate and be present while the toilet was being used by his cell-mate. The Court is not convinced by the Government's allegation that these conditions did not affect the applicant in a manner incompatible with Article 3. On the contrary, the Court is of the opinion that the prison conditions complained of diminished the applicant's human dignity and aroused in him feelings of anguish and inferiority capable of humiliating and debasing him and possibly breaking his physical or moral resistance. In sum, the Court considers that the

conditions of the applicant's detention in the segregation unit of the Delta wing of Koridallos Prison amounted to degrading treatment.

[The Court held unanimously that there has been a violation of Article 3 of the Convention. It also found violations of Article 6(2) and Article 8.]

3. JUDICIAL DISTINCTIONS

The *Irish Case* illustrates the tendency to assume that Article 3 prohibits three distinct categories of conduct—(1) torture, (2) inhuman treatment and (3) degrading treatment. The Court's discussion associates inhuman treatment with the following factors: premeditation; long duration; intense physical and mental suffering; acute psychiatric distress. The Court's description of degrading treatment uses these terms: feelings of fear, anguish and inferiority; humiliating and debasing; breaking physical or moral resistance. Although the ideas necessarily overlap,[8] these terms suggest that a court might focus more on physical pain in considering a punishment's inhuman character, and on emotional or dignitary injury when determining whether it is degrading.Notice the separate treatment of the terms in *Peers* (paras. 67–8). With respect to Article 3 in general, the Court refers to the severity of 'physical and mental effects'. Only in reference to 'degrading', does it mention the presence or absence of an intention 'to humiliate and debase' and the effect on the victim's 'personality'.[9]

Peers is one of a series of cases in which the Court has elaborated the meaning of Article 3 in the context of conditions of detention. The drafters of the Convention seem to have had such conditions in mind when formulating Article 3. One of the specifications suggested but not acted upon in the Consultative Assembly was a clause stating that no person should 'be subjected to imprisonment with such an excess of light, darkness, noise or silence as to cause mental suffering'.[10] The Court has examined challenged conditions for these and analogous conditions. Therefore, these cases, like many of those undertaken under Article 2, dealt with in the last chapter, very prominently feature factual issues. Furthermore, although they typically present systemic problems, the Court has insisted that individual applicants show their own personal mistreatment and the particular ill-effects that they suffered.[11] The same factual emphasis has required fairly extensive use of fact-finding delegations, formerly

---

[8] Fionnuala Ni Aolain, 'The European Convention on Human Rights and Its Prohibition of Torture', in *Torture: A Collection* 213, 214 (S. Levinson ed. 2004).

[9] *See also Iwańczuk v. Poland,* 15 Nov. 2001, 38 E.H.R.R. 8, paras. 57–9, where the Court held the strip search of a prisoner to be degrading, in part, because there did not appear to be a security need for the search and the guards 'verbally abused and derided the applicant'; *Yankov v. Bulgaria,* 11 Dec. 2003, 40 E.H.R.R. 36, paras. 112–17, where the same conclusion was reached with respect to the periodic shaving of a prisoner's head.

[10] 1 *Travaux Préparatoires* 252.

[11] *See Aerts v. Belgium,* 30 July 1998, 29 E.H.R.R. 50, paras. 161–7; *Assenov and Others v. Bulgaria,* 28 Oct. 1998, 28 E.H.R.R. 652, paras. 135–6.

of the Commission and now of the Court. In *Peers* the Court also relied on reports of inspections of the facility by the European Commission for the Prevention of Torture and Inhuman and Degrading Treatment and Punishment. The reports of the CPT have played a critical role in many of the Strasbourg Court's judgments on conditions of confinement. In some cases decisions are based almost exclusively on facts found by that agency.[12]

It also follows from the individualized and fact-based approach of the Court that judgments will depend critically on the particular facilities and treatments involved. No one aspect of the challenged conditions might have amounted to a violation in *Peers*; but the Court examined the cumulative effect of the confinement on the applicant. In *Dougoz v. Greece*,[13] decided shortly before *Peers*, the combination of overcrowded and dirty cells, a lack of bedding, hot water and fresh air, and insufficient time out of the cell amounted to degrading punishment.

The Court has summarized the standards against which such challenges are measured in these terms:

> [T]he State must ensure that a person is detained in conditions which are compatible with respect for her human dignity, that the manner and method of the execution of the measure do not subject her to distress or hardship of an intensity exceeding the unavoidable level of suffering inherent in detention, and that, given the practical demands of imprisonment, her health and well-being are adequately secured...[14]

Although the time that an applicant is confined in particular circumstances is certainly relevant to the determination of a violation of the Convention, it is not necessary that the detention persist for an extended period. In *Fedotov v. Russia* the applicant had been held at a police station for 22 hours without food, drink or access to a toilet. The Court found this amounted to inhuman treatment.[15]

While certainly not an exclusive list, Article 3 complaints about the conditions of detention tend to centre on what a Scottish case referred to as the 'triple vices of overcrowding, inadequate sanitary arrangements and poor régime activities'.[16] (Other factors that have been particularly prominent in the Court's case law are ventilation and inadequate or excessive lighting.[17]) Besides *Peers*, overcrowding has been alleged in several cases. In *Kalashnikov v. Russia*,[18] for example, the applicant was detained in a cell measuring (by the government's estimate) 20.8m² with 11 to 14 other inmates. This amounted to about 1 to 2m² per person. The European Committee for the Prevention

---

[12] E.g. *Kehayov v. Bulgaria*, 18 Jan. 2005. On the CPT *see* J. Murdoch, 'The Impact of the Council of Europe's "Torture Committee" and the Evolution of Standard-Setting in Relation to Places of Detention', [2006] 2 *European Human Rights L. Rev.* 158.

[13] 6 March 2001, 34 E.H.R.R. 61, paras. 45–8.

[14] *McGlinchey and Others v. United Kingdom*, 29 April 2003, 37 E.H.R.R. 41, para. 46.

[15] 25 Oct. 2005, 44 E.H.R.R. 26, paras. 67–8.

[16] *Napier v. The Scottish Ministers*, 2004 S.L.T. 555, para. 54.

[17] *See also* the discussion *infra* concerning Article 3 obligations arising from the medical needs of the applicant.

[18] 15 Oct. 2002, 36 E.H.R.R. 34, paras. 97–102.

of Torture and Inhuman and Degrading Treatment or Punishment had set 7m^2 per person as a desirable allocation.[19] This, by itself, raised an issue under Article 3. When combined with other problems—insufficient bedding, inadequate ventilation, insect infestation, the presence of prisoners with contagious diseases—a violation of the Convention was clear.

Sanitation and personal privacy are important aspects of several judgments evaluating prison conditions. In particular, the Court has heard complaints about toilet facilities or the lack thereof. In *Peers* the Court took note of the absence of a partition for the in-cell Asian-type toilet, requiring inmates to use it in the presence of other inmates.[20] Sanitary facilities were also central in a Scottish judgment finding confinement in Berlinnie Prison in Glasgow in violation of Article 3. The Lord Ordinary noted the cumulative effect of inadequate cell space, ventilation and light and extremely limited opportunities for work, exercise or recreation. Prisoners were kept in cells for an average of 20 hours a day. The court found particularly disturbing the practice of 'slopping out'. Without toilet facilities in the cell, inmates were obliged to use chamber pots and urine containers during the night. Each morning a prisoner from each cell had to dispose of the human waste at a central facility, a process that the Court found to involve 'disgusting conditions [including] the pervasive stench and the pressure and chaos of the whole enterprise'.[21]

Matters of space and sanitation involve physical conditions in the place of detention. A third major issue in Article 3, an impoverished régime of prisoner activity, concerns the administration of prison facilities. For example, in *G.B. v. Bulgaria*[22] the Court examined the applicant's eight-year confinement on 'death row'. The applicant was spared execution by virtue of Bulgaria's ultimate abolition of capital punishment. The death penalty was ended in connection with Bulgaria's accession to the Convention and, after a lengthy delay, to Protocol No. 6. The cells in which condemned prisoners were confined measured 10m^2 and were occupied by 1 or 2 persons. The European Court deemed this 'acceptable' although it was conceded that there was also insufficient light and ventilation. The real problem with the confinement was the extremely strict régime to which the applicant was subjected. He was kept in his cell 23 hours a day. He could converse with other inmates only one hour a day during the daily walk. This practice was maintained for a very long time without any particular security justification. The extended deprivation of human contact was enough to convince the Court to find a violation of Article 3. While solitary confinement is not automatically inconsistent with Article 3, the Court has examined individual instances in their own factual contexts. In that regard it has been interested in alternative ways of dealing

---

[19] *Id.* at para. 97. In a subsequent report the Committee said that the 'minimum' acceptable space per person in a multi-occupancy cell was 4m^2. *Cenbauer v. Croatia*, 9 Mar. 2006, 44 E.H.R.R. 49, para. 46.

[20] *See also Kalashnikov v. Russia, supra* n. 18.

[21] *Napier v. Ministers of Scotland, supra* n. 16, at para. 76.

[22] 11 March 2004, paras. 74–88.

with security problems and in the amount of other human contact available to the prisoner.[23]

Compare these cases with *Valašinas v. Lithuania*.[24] The ordinary cells in which the applicant was held allowed only about 3m² per person but the entire room was large and prisoners were free to move within a whole wing of the facility, including a court-yard, for most of the day. The prison provided some concerts and films and a library and television were available. Temporary absence of partitions between toilets, limited access to showers and the lack of work and educational facilities did not make the confinement so severe as to constitute a violation of Article 3.

The detention cases illustrate the central factor in many Article 3 cases—the requirement, first stated in the *Irish Case* and repeated many times thereafter, that ill-treatment inconsistent with the Convention 'must attain a minimum level of sever-ity'. While this formulation is far from helpful in the abstract it provides the guiding concept against which the individual facts of particular applications are measured. So the maltreatment in the detention cases can be compared to that considered by the Court in *Raninen v. Finland*.[25] In that case the applicant had been handcuffed while being transported by military police after one of a series of arrests for refusing military service. The judgment stated that 'handcuffing does not normally give rise to an issue under Article 3...where the measure does not entail use of force or public exposure exceeding what is reasonably considered necessary in the circumstances'. It was agreed in this case that no action of the applicant made the handcuffs necessary. But the Court found no violation of Article 3. There was no showing that the handcuffs had been intended to debase or humiliate. Public exposure had been minimal. Moreover, there was no convincing evidence that the handcuffing had caused subsequent physi-cal or psychological problems. In these circumstances it was not established 'that the treatment in issue attained the minimum level of severity required by Article 3'.[26]

In contrast, in *Sarban v. Moldova*[27] the applicant was handcuffed and held in a cage during hearings although he was hindered in movement because of a medically prescribed surgical collar. He also needed blood pressure monitoring which required reaching through the bars of the cage. The Court concluded that this amounted to unnecessary humiliation and, especially given the high-profile nature of his case, constituted degrading treatment.[28]

The idea that the constitutionality of a punishment turns on an evaluation of its proportionality to a proper state objective has also featured in the American

---

[23] Compare *Mathew v. The Netherlands*, 29 Sept. 2005, 43 E.H.R.R. 23, paras. 202–4 with *Rohde v. Denmark*, 21 July 2005, 43 E.H.R.R. 17, para. 97.

[24] 24 July 2001.

[25] 16 Dec. 1997, 25 E.H.R.R. 563.

[26] *Id*. paras. 56–9. *See also Lopez Ostra v. Spain*, 9 Dec. 1994, 20 E.H.R.R. 277, paras. 55–60, where the Court summarily dismissed a claim that the suffering, including illness and dislocation, caused by place-ment of a sewage treatment plant near the applicant's home rose to the level of 'inhuman or degrading treatment'.

[27] 4 Oct. 2005.

[28] *Id*. at paras. 88–9.

constitutional jurisprudence on conditions of imprisonment. The cases have dealt with many of the same issues that have occupied the Strasbourg Court. In a recent judgment, the United States Supreme Court dealt with the case of an Alabama inmate who had caused a disturbance. He was handcuffed to a 'hitching post' for seven hours, shirtless, in the hot sun. He was given water only once or twice and not allowed to use the toilet. The majority of the Supreme Court concluded that, on these facts, a violation of the Eighth Amendment was 'obvious'. This finding, however, also depended upon the fact that, at the time he was subjected to the treatment, the inmate had been subdued and restrained. 'Any safety concerns had long since abated ...'.[29] This may be contrasted with a subsequent case upholding restrictions on visits to inmates. Inmates who had committed two substance-abuse violations could only receive visits from attorneys and clergy. The Court depended, in part, on the fact that the limitation bore a 'self-evident connection to the State's interest in maintaining security and preventing future crimes'. The Court did say that a complete bar on visits or their indefinite withdrawal 'would present different considerations'.[30]

While the Supreme Court has decided very few prison condition cases, lower courts, both state and federal, have dealt with hundreds of cases challenging conditions of detention.[31] It is not an exaggeration to say that the courts now play a major role in establishing the standards of confinement in American prisons. These decisions deal with many of the same kinds of issues that the European Court has confronted under Article 3 of the Convention. It is impossible to generalize about these holdings which are varied and, sometimes, in conflict. With respect to the constitutionally minimum amount of living space, courts have divided, for example, on whether 50 square feet (about 4.6m^2) per inmate, is sufficient.[32] Like the Strasbourg Court, some American courts have held that prisons must make allowances for the special needs of prisoners with handicaps or health issues.[33] Similarly, United States courts have held the Constitution to be infringed when prison officials failed to provide close supervision of an inmate known to be suffering from psychiatric illness.[34]

Like the European Court of Human Rights, American courts, in approaching these issues, have evaluated the cumulative effect of various deficiencies. In one cases an appellate federal court held that the prisoner had stated a case under the Eighth Amendment when he complained of the conditions to which he had been subjected during 33 days in 'a strip cell'. He was kept there entirely naked for the first eleven days and thereafter given only a thin pair of underwear. The cell was filthy with slime, dirt and human excrement. It had no furniture other than a toilet and sink. He had no

---

[29] *Hope v. Pelzer*, 536 U.S. 730, 738 (2002).

[30] *Overton v. Bazzetta*, 539 U.S. 126, 133, 137 (2003).

[31] Annotation, 51 A.L.R. 3d 111 (2004) (collecting cases).

[32] Compare *Ruiz v. Estelle*, 503 F. Supp. 1265 (S.D. Tex 1980) with *Watson v. Ray*, 90 F.R.D. 143 (S.D. Iowa, 1981).

[33] *See*, e.g., *Simmons v. Cook*, 154 F. 3d 805 (8th Cir. 1998) (paraplegic inmate); *Reid v. Artus*, 984 F. Supp. 191 (S.D. N.Y. 1997) (asthmatic inmate). Compare *Price v. United Kingdom*, discussed *infra*.

[34] *Ferola v. Moran*, 662 F. Supp 814 (D.R.I. 1985).

soap, towel, toilet paper or toothbrush. Windows in front of the cell were kept open exposing him to subfreezing temperatures. He was not permitted to sleep between 7:30 am and 10:30 pm and, when he could sleep, had only a rough concrete floor. The court held that these facts, if proven, were violations of the Constitution that 'forbids treatment so foul, so inhuman and so violative of basic concepts of decency'.[35]

It is clear from the Strasbourg judgments that maltreatment violating Article 3 may take the form of mental as well as physical suffering. When Turkish security forces burned down the home of the applicants in their presence the Court observed that

Mrs. Selcuk and Mr. Asker were respectively 54 and 60 at the time and had lived in the village of Islamköy all their lives. Their homes and most of their property were destroyed by the security forces, depriving the applicants of their livelihoods and forcing them to leave their village. It would appear that the exercise was pre-meditated and carried out contemptuously and without respect for the feelings of the applicants. They were taken unprepared; they had to stand by and watch the burning of the homes; inadequate precautions were taken to secure the safety of Mr. and Mrs. Asker; Mrs. Selcuk's protests were ignored and no assistance provided to them afterwards.

Bearing in mind, in particular, the manner in which the applicants' homes were destroyed and their personal circumstances, it is clear that they must have caused suffering of sufficient severity for the acts of the security forces to be categorized as inhuman treatment within the meaning of Article 3.[36]

Similarly in *Kurt v. Turkey*[37] the Court held the applicant had been subjected to inhuman and degrading treatment caused by the arrest and unexplained disappearance of her son. 'She had witnessed his detention in the village with her own eyes and his non-appearance since that last sighting made her fear for his safety... As a result she had been left with the anguish of knowing that her son had been detained and that there is a complete absence of official information as to his subsequent fate. This anguish has endured over a prolonged period of time'.[38] On the other hand, in *Çakici v. Turkey*,[39] the Court refused to find a violation based on the distress suffered by the disappearance of the applicant's brother. Unlike in *Kurt*, the Court held that there were

no special factors which give the suffering of the applicant a dimension and character distinct from the emotional distress which may be regarded as inevitably caused to relatives of a victim of a serious human rights violation. Relevant elements will include the proximity of the family tie—in that context, a certain weight will attach to the parent–child bond—,the particular circumstances of the relationship, the extent to which the family member witnessed the events in question, the involvement of the family member in the attempts to obtain information about the disappeared person and the way in which the authorities responded to those inquiries. The Court would further emphasize that the essence of such a violation does not so much lie in the fact of the 'disappearance' of the family member but rather concerns the authorities' reactions

---

[35] *Wright v. McMann*, 387 F.2d 519, 521–2, 526 (2d. Cir. 1967).
[36] *Selcuk and Asker v. Turkey*, 24 Apr. 1998, 26 E.H.R.R. 477.
[37] 25 May 1998, 27 E.H.R.R. 373, and *see* Chapter 12(A).
[38] *Id*. para. 133.
[39] 7 July 1999, 31 E.H.R.R. 5.

and attitudes to the situation when it is brought to their attention. It is especially in respect of the latter that a relative may claim directly to be a victim of the authorities conduct.[40]

In this case the applicant, a brother, had a less intimate bond with the disappeared person and had not, as in *Kurt*, actually seen him detained. The 'brunt' of the work of seeking information, moreover, had not been borne by the applicant but by his father.[41] Judge Thommasen joined by Judges Jungwiert and Fischbach dissented on this point. Noting the deep suffering which a brother can feel at the 'uncertainty of the fate of a sibling' and the applicant's involvement in petitions and inquiries about the disappearance, she concluded that the state had 'left the applicant in uncertainty, doubt and apprehension about his brother for more than five and a half years. In doing so they demonstrated a cruel disregard for his feelings and his efforts to find out about his brother's fate'.[42]

Severe psychological distress has also served as grounds supporting the finding of violations of Article 3 in connection with 'strip searches' of people held in custody. The injury from such searches is more psychological than physical. The critical variable for the European Court appears to be the security need for such searches. While the Court has declared that strip searches need not invariably violate Article 3, it has condemned them on each occasion on which they have been challenged. The fact that prisoners in a high security facility were subjected to strip search and anal inspection weekly, whether or not there was any reason to suspect the possibility of contraband, showed the practice 'was not based on any concrete security need or the applicant's behaviour'.[43] The same result followed from a single strip search imposed on the applicant as a prerequisite to allowing him to vote in a special polling place provided in the prison. The applicant had done nothing to indicate that there was any security risk that would be addressed by such an inspection.[44] Moreover, even a strip search that might be justified by some security need must be carried out 'in an appropriate manner'. So a search of a prisoner following a personal visit in which he had been given some additional food was held degrading. The Court determined that the male prisoner had been forced to strip naked in the presence of a female prison officer, ordered to squat and his genitals had been examined by guards who did not wear gloves.[45] A similar finding of unjustified humiliation underlay the Court's holding that periodic shaving of a prisoner's head without any demonstrated health benefit was inconsistent with the Convention.[46]

The infliction of other kinds of psychological pain for which the state is responsible has given rise to Article 3 cases outside the context of detention. In a much publicized case, *V. v. United Kingdom*, the Court heard a challenge to the conviction of

---

[40] *Id.* at para. 98.

[41] *Id.* at para. 99.

[42] *Id.* (partly dissenting opinion of Judge Thommasen joined by Judges Jungwiert and Fischbach).

[43] *Van der Ven v. The Netherlands*, 4 Feb. 2003, 38 E.H.R.R. 46, para. 58.

[44] *Iwańczuk v. Poland*, 15 Nov. 2001, *supra* n. 9, at paras. 54–9.

[45] *Valašinas v. Lithuania*, *supra* n. 24, at paras. 114–17.

[46] *Yankov v. Bulgaria*, *supra* n. 9, at paras. 112–17.

and sentencing of an eleven-year-old boy for murder by bludgeoning of a child aged two. The crime had been committed when the applicant was ten years old. He had been publicly tried as an adult. Among many claims was an argument that the very subjection of a child of that age to this form of criminal process was inhuman and degrading treatment. While some accommodation had been made at the criminal trial for the applicant's age, the public trial, as a whole, did not fully respect the applicant's privacy as suggested by the United Nations Standard Minimum Rules for the Administration of Juvenile Justice ('the Beijing Rules') adopted in 1985. The Court did not doubt the impact on the applicant but noted that regardless of 'whether such inquiry had been carried out in public or in private, attended by the formality of the Crown Court or informally in the youth court', the applicant would have experienced 'feelings of guilt, distress, anguish and fear.... [T]he Court is not convinced that the particular features of the trial process as applied to him caused, to a significant degree, suffering going beyond that which would inevitably have been engendered by any attempt by the authorities to deal with the applicant...'.[47]

The kinds of suffering for which the state might be thought responsible under Article 3 are limited only by the imagination of the applicant. In *Marckx v. Belgium* the applicants complained of laws which put children born out of wedlock at a disadvantage with respect to legal family relations and, particularly, inheritance rights. The Court found violations of Articles 8 and 14. But the claim that the laws created 'degrading treatment' was unanimously rejected. The Court's reasoning consisted of one sentence: '[W]hile the legal rules at issue probably present aspects which the applicants feel to be humiliating, they do not constitute degrading treatment coming within the ambit of Article 3'. In his separate opinion Judge Fitzmaurice stated: '[I]n my view [the Court] should have gone much further and held that such a provision as Article 3 [of the Convention] was concerned with a wholly different class of subject matter and had no sort of applicability at all to such circumstances as those of the applicants'.[48]

A considerably more serious case of the state causing what was alleged to 'inhuman and degrading treatment' arose in *Pretty v. United Kingdom*.[49] A terminally ill woman suffering from motor neuron disease, claimed, among other things, that the United Kingdom law against assisted suicide had an impact on her sufficiently severe to violate Article 3. She argued that '[s]he suffered from a terrible, irreversible disease in its final stages and she would die in an exceedingly distressing and undignified manner as the muscles which controlled her breathing and swallowing weakened to the extent that she would develop respiratory failure and pneumonia'.[50] The Court noted the state's obligations under Article 3 went beyond merely refraining from intentional acts causing suffering and that the state also was obliged 'to take measures designed to insure that individuals within their jurisdiction are not subjected to torture or inhuman or

---

[47] 16 Dec. 1999, 30 E.H.R.R. 121, para. 79. Compare *Sarban v. Moldova, supra* n. 27, holding that confining the applicant in a cage during judicial hearings was degrading treatment in violation of Article 3.

[48] 13 June 1979, 2 E.H.R.R. 330, para. 66; dissenting opinion of Judge Fitzmaurice, para. 5, fn. 2.

[49] 29 April 2002, 35 E.H.R.R. 1.

[50] *Id.* at para. 44.

degrading treatment or punishment, including such treatment administered by private individuals'.[51] Furthermore, 'suffering flowing from naturally occurring illness, physical or mental, may be covered by Article 3, where it is, or risks being, exacerbated by treatment, whether flowing from conditions of detention or other measures, for which the authorities can be held responsible'.[52] In the instant case, however, the Court found that the United Kingdom was not responsible for any ' "act" or "treatment" ' causing the applicant's distress. As to the applicant's insistence that the government had failed to protect her by refusing to provide assurance that it would not prosecute her husband should he assist in her suicide, the Court regarded this as 'a new and extended ... concept of treatment'. To accept it would have been inconsistent with its previous holding, in the same case, that Article 2 does not oblige the state to provide a way for a person to end his or her own life.[53]

An important feature of the Strasbourg Court's jurisprudence on the nature of 'inhuman and degrading treatment' is its willingness to consider the character of treatment in a subjective rather than objective sense. In a frequently repeated dictum it has stated that the inquiry is 'relative' and depends 'in some cases on the sex, age and state of health of the victim'.[54] Therefore, conditions that would not constitute inhuman and degrading treatment for one person, or for most people, might still violate the Article. The imposition of segregation and an additional 28-day sentence on a prisoner for a disciplinary offence might be unobjectionable in most cases. When, however, it was imposed on a person known to be mentally ill and a suicide risk (who did, in fact, commit suicide) it was held to be 'inhuman and degrading treatment and punishment' in violation of the Convention.[55] The cases, already discussed, on the conditions of detention often refer to particular medical needs of detained applicants. It was a violation of Article 3, for example, to house an asthmatic prisoner in a multi-person cell in which smoking was permitted.[56]

A more salient example may be *Price v. United Kingdom*[57] concerning the applicant's three days in custody pursuant to a citation for contempt of court for refusing to answer questions in the course of civil proceedings. The applicant was missing all four limbs resulting from her mother's use of thalidomide. She was kept for one night in an ordinary prison cell where she had to sleep in a wheelchair because the bed was inappropriate for her disability. She was unable to use the toilet or to reach emergency buttons or light switches. She was then moved to the health care centre in another

---

[51] *Id.* at para. 51. The character of a state's 'positive obligations' under the Convention is considered more extensively in Chapter 8(B), *infra*.

[52] *Pretty, supra* n. 49, at para. 52.

[53] *Id.* at para. 54. *See* Chapter 4(A) *supra*.

[54] *Keenan v. United Kingdom*, 3 April 2001, 33 E.H.R.R. 38, para. 108. *See also Sarban v. Moldova, supra* n. 27, where the applicant suffered from serious medical conditions and was detained without medical supervision. Although no serious complications ensued, the Court held the resulting anxiety amounted to degrading treatment. Paras. 86–7.

[55] *Keenan v. United Kingdom, supra* n. 54, at para. 115.

[56] *Ostrovar v. Moldova*, 13 Sept. 2005, 44 E.H.R.R. 19, para. 85.

[57] 10 July 2001, 34 E.H.R.R. 53.

prison where some of the difficulties were alleviated but she still required assistance getting into and out of bed, bathing and personal hygiene. Before her release (four days early) she required catheterization due to fluid retention arising from her difficulty in using the toilet. Although her condition was monitored periodically by doctors, the Court concluded that the applicant had been placed in facilities that were unsuitable for her special needs. '[T]o detain a severely disabled person in conditions where she is dangerously cold, risks developing sores because her bed is too hard or unreachable and is unable to use the toilet or keep clean without the greatest difficulty constitutes degrading treatment contrary to Article 3 of the Convention'.[58] In *Mousiel v. France* the Court employed more general language to indicate that any incarceration of a seriously ill person in circumstances that did not respond to their special needs violated Article 3.[59]

In contrast, in *Papon v. France (No. 1)*[60] the Court held inadmissible as manifestly ill-founded the application of Maurice Papon, a wartime official under the Vichy regime. Papon was convicted in 1998 of crimes against humanity as a result of his participation in 1942–44 in the capture and deportation of French Jews to German extermination camps. He was sentenced to ten years imprisonment. He claimed the sentence amounted to a violation of Article 3 in light of his advanced age. He was 90 years old at the time of the Court's decision. The Court agreed that 'under certain circumstances, the detention of an elderly person over a lengthy period might give rise an issue under Article 3'. It rejected, however, the applicant's argument 'that any form of imprisonment of a man over 90 constituted in itself and in its essence a breach of Article 3'. In this case the Court observed that the authorities had made special arrangements in light of Papon's age and state of health, including regular medical supervision. Therefore, it found his punishment not to have attained the level of severity necessary to ground a violation.

While it is possible to discern some obscure distinctions between inhuman and degrading treatment, 'torture' appears to lack any independent content. The Court views torture simply to be 'inhuman and degrading treatment which is more intense with respect to the suffering inflicted'. Torture must cause 'very serious and cruel suffering'.[61] In fact, the Court in the *Irish Case* found no torture in the application of the 'five techniques'. The Court found no challenged conduct to be torture until 1996. In *Aksoy v. Turkey*[62] the applicant had been detained on suspicion of participation in terrorist activities on behalf of the PKK, a Kurdish nationalist group.

He was interrogated about whether he knew Metin (the man who had identified him). He claimed to have been told, 'If you don't know him now, you will know him under torture'.

---

[58] *Id.* at paras. 25–30.
[59] 14 November 2002, paras. 38–45.
[60] 7 June 2001, 39 E.H.R.R. 10.
[61] *Ireland v. United Kingdom, supra* at para. 167.
[62] 18 Dec. 1996, 23 E.H.R.R. 553.

According to the applicant, on the second day of his detention he was stripped naked, his hands were tied behind his back and he was strung up by his arms in the form of torture known as 'Palestinian hanging'. While he was hanging, the police connected electrodes to his genitals and threw water over him while they electrocuted him. He was kept blindfolded during this torture, which continued for approximately 35 minutes.

During the next two days, he was allegedly beaten repeatedly at intervals of two hours or half an hour, without being suspended. The torture continued for four days, the first two being very intensive.

He claimed that, as a result of the torture, he lost the movement of his arms and hands. His interrogators ordered him to make movements to restore the control of his hands. He asked to see a doctor, but was refused permission.[63]

Accepting this account, the Court declared it 'of such a serious and cruel nature that it can only be described as torture'.[64] In subsequent cases the Court has found torture present when a seventeen year old applicant was held by Turkish security forces for three days during which time she was raped and beaten[65] and when an applicant arrested by French police was repeatedly beaten and, on one occasion urinated on as well as threatened and verbally abused.[66]

The Court has made clear that it regards inhuman treatment and torture as marking merely different degrees of severity. In declining to find torture in the *Irish Case*, it assumed that 'it was the intention that the Convention, with its distinction between "torture" and "inhuman or degrading treatment" should, by the first of these terms, attach a special stigma to deliberate inhuman treatment causing very serious and cruel suffering'.[67] Moreover, the Court, consistent with its characterization of the Convention as a 'living instrument', has explicitly warned that the boundary between these two categories is not fixed but changes over time:

[C]ertain acts which were classified in the past as 'inhuman and degrading treatment' as opposed to 'torture' could be classified differently in future. It takes the view that the increasingly high standard being required in the area of the protection of human rights and fundamental liberties correspondingly and inevitably requires greater firmness in assessing breaches of the fundamental values of democratic societies.[68]

The recent case of *Elci and Others v. Turkey*[69] illustrates how the Court applies the distinction. In that case sixteen applicants complained of their treatment while held in custody by Turkish police. All of the applicants had been confined to cells that were 'cold, dark and damp, with inadequate bedding, food and sanitary conditions'. In addition, however, four of the applicants had been 'insulted, assaulted, stripped naked

---

[63] *Id.* paras. 13–15.

[64] *Id.* para. 64.

[65] *Aydin v. Turkey*, 25 Sept. 1997, 25 E.H.R.R. 251.

[66] *Selmouni v. France*, 28 July 1999 [G.C.] 29 E.H.R.R. 403.

[67] Para. 167. At least one commentator has suggested that there are three categories of maltreatment with 'degrading' treatment regarded as less severe than 'inhuman treatment'.

[68] *Selmouni, supra* n. 66, para. 101; *Bursuc v. Romania*, 12 Jan. 2005, para. 90.

[69] 24 March 2004, paras. 640–1, 646–7.

and hosed down with freezing cold water'. The conditions of confinement were held to be inhuman and degrading. The group of four who had been physically assaulted, had been subjected to 'severe pain and suffering [that] was particularly serious and cruel... [and] must therefore be regarded as constituting torture...'.

The necessity of assessing the severity of maltreatment runs throughout the Article 3 jurisprudence and not solely with the identification of torture. The court made short work, for example, of an argument that the state violated Article 3 by failing, over many years, to enforce a civil judgment causing the applicant, 'an elderly person', to endure 'severe humiliation by having repeatedly to ask the authorities to execute the judgment'. Such suffering was not 'sufficient to amount to inhuman and degrading treatment'.[70] As noted, in *Marckx v. Belgium*[71] the applicants complained of Belgian laws which put illegitimate children at a disadvantage with respect to legal family relations and, particularly, inheritance rights. The Court found violations of Article 8 and of Article 14 in conjunction with Article 8. The applicants' separate claim of 'degrading treatment' in violation of Article 3 was, however, unanimously rejected. The Court did not elaborate: '[W]hile the legal rules at issue probably present aspects which the applicants feel to be humiliating, they do not constitute degrading treatment coming within the ambit of Article 3'.[72] We have already mentioned the separate opinion of Judge Fitzmaurice which emphasized his view that Article 3 was concerned with a wholly different class of subject matter. That opinion may be seen as another example of the highly restrictive approach that this judge took to the interpretation of Article 3.[73]

4. FACT-FINDING UNDER ARTICLE 3

As noted in the previous chapter,[74] disputed questions of fact play an especially prominent role in cases under Article 3. Moreover, as with the right to life, the European Court has constructed a subsidiary duty of the state to investigate plausible claims of torture or degrading punishment or treatment. In *Assenov and Others v. Bulgaria*,[75] the applicant claimed he had been mistreated while in police custody. Given the inconclusive character of the evidence, the Court did not take the alleged misconduct to have been established. That evidence, however, was enough to raise 'a reasonable suspicion' of such treatment. The Court decided that in such a case Article 3 'requires by implication that there should be an effective official investigation' which 'should be capable of leading to the identification and punishment of those responsible... If this

---

[70] *Popov v. Moldova*, 18 Jan. 2005, paras. 26–7.
[71] 13 June 1979, 2 E.H.R.R. 330.
[72] *Id.* para. 5, fn. 2 (dissenting opinion of Judge Fitzmaurice).
[73] *See* his dissenting opinion in *Ireland v. United Kingdom*, Section A(1) *supra*.
[74] *See* Chapter 4(E) *supra*.
[75] 28 Oct. 1998, 28 E.H.R.R. 652.

were not the case the general legal prohibition of torture and inhuman and degrading treatment and punishment, despite its fundamental importance would be ineffective in practice and it would be possible in some cases for agents of the state to abuse the rights of those within its control with virtual impunity'.[76] The Court concluded that the state's response to the allegation in this case did not constitute an effective investigation and that, therefore, there had been a violation of Article 3.[77]

Also similar to its judgment under Article 2, the Court has established a presumption for cases where a person can show that he or she suffered injuries while in official custody. In such a case the state bears the burden of explaining why it should not be deemed responsible for the infliction of those injuries. In the case of *Tomasi v. France*,[78] the applicant complained of beatings and other mistreatment during 40 hours of police interrogation. The police denied any misconduct and the French courts held that Tomasi had not shown a *prima facie* case justifying proceedings against the police. The European Court noted that medical examinations of the applicant after his interrogation had revealed the presence of injuries which could not have been suffered prior to his arrest and that he had promptly called the investigating judge's attention to marks on his body which he attributed to beatings. This showing was sufficient to justify a conclusion that serious injury had been inflicted by the police and that, therefore, there had been a violation of Article 3.

In contrast, when the facts alleged included a significant period when the applicant was not in custody, during which time the relevant injuries might have been suffered, this presumption has much less force and the Court has refused to find a violation.[79] Similarly, a finding of no violation has resulted where the state has offered an alternative explanation. For example, in *Klaas v. Germany*[80] it was conceded that the applicant had received injuries in the course of her arrest. The applicant insisted they were caused by gratuitous violence on the part of the police, while the state (and the domestic courts) had accepted the police version of events, according to which the injuries were the incidental result of the struggle that ensued when the applicant had forcefully resisted the police. The Strasbourg Court emphasized that 'as a general rule, it is for [the domestic] courts to assess the evidence before them'. In this case it noted that the German Regional Court, which had the 'benefit of seeing the various witnesses…, and of evaluating their credibility', had accepted the police officers' version of the facts. On that basis, it found no violation of Article 3.[81] It distinguished *Tomasi* 'where certain inferences could be made from the fact that Mr Tomasi had sustained unexplained injuries during forty-eight hours spent in police custody'.[82]

---

[76] *Id.* at paras. 101–2.
[77] *Id.* at paras. 103–6; *see also Tanrikulu v. Turkey*, 8 July 1999, 30 E.H.R.R. 950, paras. 101–11.
[78] 27 Aug. 1992, 15 E.H.R.R. 1.
[79] *Erdagöz v. Turkey*, 22 Oct. 1997, 32 E.H.R.R. 19, paras. 41–2.
[80] 22 Sept. 1993, 18 E.H.R.R. 305.
[81] *Id.* paras. 29–30.
[82] *Id.* para. 30.

Three judges dissented, each citing *Tomasi*. Judge Walsh summed up what he took to be the principle established by that case:

Once it has been established that physical injury has been sustained by [a] person, while in police custody, the burden falls on the police or their state to show that such injuries were not caused or brought about by the actions of the police or their want of care.[83]

Since no specific evidence of how the injuries had occurred had been offered by the police and the German Court had merely relied on a presumption in their favour, the dissent asserted that a finding of a violation was proper.[84]

5. COMPARISONS

The case law of the European Court of Human Rights on the meaning of Article 3 makes particularly useful an examination of the interpretation of similar provisions in national constitutions. We have already noted the 'cruel and unusual' punishments provisions of the English Bill of Rights, the Eighth Amendment to the United States Constitution and Section 12 of the Canadian Charter of Rights and Freedoms. Article 10 of the English Bill of Rights prohibiting the infliction of 'cruel and unusual punishments' may serve as a legal restriction on executive acts of the government, including the treatment of detained persons.[85] The English Court of Appeal has held that a prisoner may seek judicial review to determine whether his treatment amounted to 'cruel and unusual punishment' in violation of the Bill of Rights. As an example, the Court noted that:

it is generally held to be unacceptable that persons supposedly of normal mentality should be detained in psychiatric institutions as is said to occur in certain parts of the world. Coming close to the alleged facts of this case, if it were to be established that the applicant as a sane person was, for purely administrative purposes, being subjected in the psychiatric wing to the stress of being exposed to the disturbance caused by the behaviour of mentally ill and disturbed prisoners, this might well be considered as a 'cruel and unusual punishment' and one which was not deserved.[86]

One important difference between the European Convention and the American guarantees is the inclusion in the former of both punishment and treatment. The United

---

[83] *Id.* dissenting opinion of Judge Walsh. *See also* the dissenting opinions of Judges Pettiti and Spielmann.

[84] Compare *Ribitsch v. Austria*, 4 Dec. 1995, 21 E.H.R.R. 573, paras. 32–8, refusing to accept an alternative explanation that had been credited by the domestic appeals court. Three judges dissented objecting to the Court's substitution of its own view of the facts for that of the national courts. *Id.* (joint dissenting opinion of Judges Rysdal, Matscher and Jambrek).

[85] A parallel provision was enacted for Scotland in the Claim of Right of 1689, A.P.S. IX, 38.

[86] *R. v. Secretary of State for the Home Department, ex parte Herbage* [1987] Q.B. 1077, [1987] 1 All E.R. 324 (C.A.).

States Supreme Court has held that the Eighth Amendment was only applicable after an adjudication of guilt and the commencement of punishment.[87]

Notwithstanding the addition of the word 'treatment' in Section 12 of the Charter of Rights and Freedoms, the Canadian Supreme Court had held that not all adverse effects of public action are to be regarded as 'treatment' engaging Section 12. In *Rodriguez v. British Columbia (Attorney-General)*, the Court considered a claim that the criminal prohibition on assisted suicide constituted cruel and unusual treatment of the plaintiff, a terminally ill patient. The Court conceded that the 'degree to which "treatment"... may apply outside the context of penalties to ensure the application and enforcement of the law has not been definitely determined by this Court'. Assuming, however, that non-penal treatment was governed by Section 12, a majority held that 'a mere prohibition by the state on certain action, without more, cannot constitute "treatment"'.

The fact that, because of the personal situation in which [plaintiff] finds herself, a particular prohibition impacts on her in a manner which causes her suffering does not subject her to 'treatment' at the hands of the state. The starving person who is prohibited by threat of criminal sanction from 'stealing a mouthful of bread' is likewise not subjected to 'treatment' within the meaning of s.12 by reason of the theft provisions of the Code...[88]

We have already seen that the Strasbourg Court reached a similar result in *Pretty v. United Kingdom*[89] when it held the state's failure to provide a legal way to end the painful life of a terminally ill person did not violate Article 2 or 3. The English Court of Appeal, however, has held the state may be obliged, under Article 3, to provide support to destitute persons awaiting determination of their asylum claims. It would have to be shown, however, that the non-support left the claimant in a truly desperate rather than a merely difficult situation.[90]

Despite the difference in terminology, the American jurisprudence on cruel and unusual punishment has sometimes emphasized some of the same factors that appear to have influenced the European Court's adjudication under Article 3. One prominent theme has been the maintenance of human dignity, even for those convicted of serious offences. This theme was elaborated in *Trop v. Dulles* in which a soldier was deprived of his United States citizenship by virtue of his wartime desertion. The Court acknowledged that death would be a proper penalty for desertion, but still found denationalization 'cruel and unusual':

The basic concept underlying the Eighth Amendment is nothing less than the dignity of man. While the state has the power to punish, the Amendment stands to assure that this power be

---

[87] *Bell v. Wolfish*, 441 U.S. 520 (1979). *See also Revere v. Massachusetts General Hospital*, 463 U.S. 239 (1983) (Eighth Amendment inapplicable to alleged maltreatment of an arrested person). Mistreatment during other kinds of detention, however, may be scrutinized under the due process clauses of the Fifth and Fourteenth Amendments.

[88] [1993] 3 S.C.R. 519, 611.

[89] 29 April 2002, 35 E.H.R.R. 1.

[90] *T. v. Secretary of State for the Home Dept.* [2003] E.W.C.A. Civ. 1285.

exercised within the limits of civilized standards. Fines, imprisonment and even execution may be imposed depending upon the enormity of the crime but any technique outside the bounds of these traditional penalties is constitutionally suspect...[In denationalization] there may be involved no physical mistreatment, no primitive torture. There is instead the total destruction of the individual's status in organized society. It is a form of punishment more primitive than torture, for it destroys for the individual the political existence that was centuries in develop- ment...In short, the expatriate has lost the right to have rights...The punishment is offensive to cardinal principles for which the Constitution stands. It subjects the individual to a fate of ever-increasing fear and distress. He knows not what proscription may be directed against him, and when and for what cause his existence in his native land may be terminated. He may be subject to banishment, a fate universally decried by civilized people. He is stateless, a condition deplored in the international community of democracies.[91]

The idea that the effects of a punishment on the psychological well-being of the sub-ject—'a fate of ever-increasing fear and distress'—and the idea that some punishments are offensive not so much for the physical pain they cause as for their inconsistency with 'human dignity' have their counterparts in the cases reproduced here under the Convention. The application of this notion, of course, is a matter of great imprecision.

One critical and controversial issue that has pervaded American and Canadian cases on the limits of permissible punishment is that of proportionality—the idea that the punishment should fit the crime. In *Weems v. United States*,[92] decided in 1910, one of the earliest Eighth Amendment cases, the Supreme Court found a violation in the imposition by the Philippine territorial government of the 'cadena' for the offence of embezzlement of 616 pesos. The 'cadena', a remnant of the Spanish colonial govern-ment, was described by the Court as follows:

Its minimum degree is confinement in a penal institution for twelve years and one day, a chain at the ankle and wrist of the offender, hard and painful labor, no assistance from friend or relative, no marital authority or parental rights or rights of property, no participation even in the family council. These parts of his penalty endure for the term of imprisonment. From other parts there is no intermission. His prison bars and chains are removed, it is true, after twelve years, but he goes from them to a perpetual limitation of his liberty. He is forever kept under the shadow of his crime, forever kept within voice and view of the criminal magistrate, not being able to change his domicil without giving notice to the 'authority immediately in charge of his surveillance', and without permission in writing. He may not seek, even in other scenes and among other people, to retrieve his fall from rectitude. Even that hope is taken from him and he is subject to tormenting regulations that, if not so tangible as iron bars and stone walls, oppress as much by their continuity, and deprive of essential liberty. No circumstance of degradation is omitted. It may be that even the cruelty of pain is not omitted. He must bear a chain night and day. He is condemned to painful as well as hard labor. What painful labor may mean we have no exact measure. It must be something more than hard labor. It may be hard labor pressed to the point of pain. Such penalties for such offenses amaze those who have formed their concep-tion of the relation of a state to even its offending citizens from the practice of the American

---

[91] 356 U.S. 86, 100–2 (1958).
[92] 217 U.S. 349 (1910).

commonwealths, and believe that it is a precept of justice that punishment for crime should be graduated and proportioned to offense.

The Court found that other more serious crimes were given less severe punishments and that the excesses of the 'cadena' served no useful state functions.

An interesting application of the proportionality analysis was *Robinson v. California*[93] decided in 1962, in which a 90-day sentence was at issue. While the sentence was hardly repugnant in itself, the Court found it disproportionate to the offence of being 'addicted to the use of narcotics', a status which was presumably beyond the capacity of the defendant to avoid. Under this approach there is nothing inherent in any punishment which makes it 'cruel and unusual'. 'Even one day in prison would be cruel and unusual punishment for the "crime" of having a common cold'.[94]

The Court used the same kind of analysis in finding unconstitutional two death penalty statutes. In one, a death sentence for felony murder in which the defendant had no active part in the taking of life was reversed.[95] In another, the same result obtained with respect to a death penalty for rape.[96] The Court has also examined the constitutionality of long prison sentences when challenged as excessive in relation to the crime involved. In *Solem v. Helm*,[97] it struck down a life sentence imposed under the South Dakota recidivist statute. The defendant had been convicted of passing a bad cheque for $100 after having been previously convicted in the previous ten years of third degree burglary three times, obtaining money under false pretenses, grand larceny and driving while intoxicated. But in *Harmelin v. Michigan*,[98] the Court refused to hold unconstitutional a life sentence for possession of more than 650 grams of cocaine. Three judges in the 5–4 majority held that the apportionment of penalty was appropriately within the discretion of the legislature and that the Eighth Amendment forbids 'only extreme sentences that are grossly disproportionate to the crime'. Only on finding such an apparent gross disproportion would it be proper to compare the sentence with those for the same crime in other jurisdictions. The other two judges in the majority went even farther, arguing that it was improper to consider the disproportionality of penalty to offence.[99]

A similar approach has been used by the Supreme Court of Canada in deciding whether or not certain mandatory prison sentences violated Section 12 of the Canadian Charter of Rights and Freedoms. The proper test according to the Court is whether the punishment is 'grossly disproportionate' considering the 'nature of the offense, the circumstances in which it was committed, the character of the offender

---

[93] 370 U.S. 660 (1962).

[94] 370 U.S. at 669.

[95] *Edmund v. Florida*, 458 U.S. 782 (1982).

[96] *Coker v. Georgia*, 433 U.S. 584 (1997).

[97] 463 U.S. 277 (1983).

[98] 501 U.S. 957 (1991).

[99] *See also Ewing v. California*, 528 U.S. 11 (2003). Proportionality has naturally also been a central concern in the interpretation of that part of the Eighth Amendment proscribing 'excessive fines'. The Supreme Court has held that this provision only reaches exactions that are 'grossly disproprotional to the gravity of the defendant's offense'. *United States v. Bajakajian*, 524 U. S. 321, 331 (1998).

as well as deterrence and other penological objectives that go beyond the case of an individual offender'.[100] Applying that criterion, it held invalid a minimum sentence of seven years for importation of narcotics into the country in any amount.[101] On the other hand, imposition of an indeterminate sentence was upheld under a statute prescribing it for specified 'serious personal injury offenses' all of which involved conduct tending to cause 'severe physical danger or severe psychological injury'. Before imposing such a sentence, the sentencing court had to be convinced that a defendant's action was part of a pattern of behaviour involving violence or a failure to control sexual impulses and that that pattern was very likely to continue, being 'substantially or pathologically intractable'. Even after these conditions were proved, a judge had discretion not to impose the indeterminate sentence. In his reasons for judgment, joined by four other justices, LaForest, J. said the statute involved a 'diligent attempt...to carefully define a very small group of offenders whose personal characteristics and particular circumstances militate strenuously in favor of preventive incarceration' and that 'it would be difficult to imagine a better tailored set of criteria'.[102]

The Canadian Court has recently gone beyond an examination of the statutory penalties for certain kinds of offences and has examined the circumstances of the particular conduct involved in an individual case. Thus, in holding that a seven-day minimum sentence for 'driving while prohibited' was not cruel and unusual, the majority called for an examination of, among other things, the gravity of the offence and the personal characteristics of the offender. If, in light of these factors, the penalty would 'outrage decency', a *prima facie* violation of the Charter would be present. The defendant relied on this interpretation in *R v. Latimer*.[103] He was convicted of second-degree murder of his twelve-year-old daughter. The daughter suffered from a severe case of cerebral palsy. She had limited mental capacity and ability to communicate. She was subject to frequent and painful seizures and required assistance for even the most basic personal tasks. She had undergone numerous difficult operations. When her doctors decided she needed further surgery, the defendant killed her by carbon monoxide poisoning. On conviction, he was sentenced to the mandatory life sentence for murder with ten years' ineligibility for parole. On appeal to the Supreme Court, he argued that, in the circumstances of his case, this sentence was grossly disproportionate and a violation of the Charter. His appeal was dismissed. The Court, in a per curiam opinion, stressed the deference due to parliamentary determinations of proper punishment and the exceptional nature of adjudications invalidating such punishments. In making the 'particularized inquiry' in the case of Latimer, the Court decided that the defendant's character and the circumstances of his crime did not 'displace the serious gravity of

---

[100] *Smith v. R.* [1987] 1 S.C.R. 1045. Applying this test the Court found a criminal sentence imposed on a drug dealer that included a ban on possession of firearms did not violate s. 12. *R v. Wiles* 260 D.L.R. 4th 459 (2005).

[101] *Id.*

[102] *Lyons v. R.* [1987] 2 S.C.R. 309.

[103] [2001] 1. S.C.R. 3.

this offense'. It did, however, take note of the availability of a petition for executive clemency.

Apart from an examination of the actual situation of the defendant and his crime, the Supreme Court also evaluates legislatively defined punishments for proportionality in some reasonable hypothetical circumstances.[104] Conversely, the Court has held that an indeterminate sentence with periodic review for 'criminal sexual psychopaths' was not unconstitutional on its face, but, when the reviewing agency misapplied or disregarded the proper statutory criteria for release, a violation of Section 12 was shown.[105]

The Judicial Committee of the Privy Council flatly rejected the idea of portionality in construing the Constitution of the former Southern Rhodesia insofar as it prohibited 'inhuman or degrading punishment or other treatment'. The Committee rejected a challenge to the constitutionality of an act providing a mandatory death sentence for assisting in an attempt to set fire to a house. Expressly rejecting, in this context, the holding of *Weems v. United States*[106] it asserted that an evaluation of the proportionality of the punishment would be an unjustified intrusion into the domain of the legislature:

It can hardly be for the courts, unless clearly so empowered or directed, to rule as to the necessity or propriety of particular legislation. The provision contained in . . . the Constitution enables the court to adjudicate as to whether some form or type or description of punishment, . . . is inhuman or degrading, but it does not enable the Court to declare an enactment imposing a punishment to be *ultra vires* on the ground that the court considers that the punishment laid down by the enactment is inappropriate or excessive for the particular offence.[107]

In 2002, however, after the enactment of the Human Rights Act, the House of Lords considered the compatibility with Article 3 of the 'mandatory life sentence' for murder. Such sentences are administered in two parts. A 'tariff' period is imposed for the purposes of punishment and deterrence as well as to protect the safety of society. Thereafter, the prisoner may continue to be detained until such time as a Parole Board determines it is safe to release him or her. Even after such a release, the convicted murderer may be imprisoned again if he poses a threat to the community.[108] In the appeal the prisoners attacked the second part of the sentence and the consequent undefined length of actual imprisonment and also their liability to be recalled for the balance of their lives. The application of such an open-ended punishment, without regard to the actual dangerousness of particular defendants, was argued to be 'arbitrary, excessive, and disproportionate' in violation of Articles 3 and 5. The Law Lords unanimously dismissed the appeal. Lord Bingham of Cornhill readily undertook an examination

---

[104] *R. v. Goltz* [1991] 3 S.C.R. 485.

[105] *Steele v. Mountain Institution* [1990] 2 S.C.R. 1385.

[106] *See supra* n. 92.

[107] *Runyowa v. R.* [1967] A.C.26 P.C.

[108] This method of sentencing has also given rise to continuing issues under Articles 5 and 6 of the Convention discussed in Chapters 12 and 13, *infra*.

of the features of the sentences complained of with respect to their proportionality to the offence. He stressed the seriousness of any murder, the reasonable likelihood that non-dangerous offenders would be released at the end of their tariff terms and the unlikelihood of their recall. Lord Hutton argued that the inevitable uncertainty of the period of detention did not itself 'constitute treatment of such severity as to come within the ambit of inhuman punishment'.[109]

A proportionality test appears inconsistent with one aspect of Article 3. Like Article 2 but unlike many other guarantees of the Convention, Article 3 is drafted in absolute terms. It may not be infringed in the interest of public safety, welfare or morality (compare Articles 6, 8, 9, 10 and 11). Moreover, under Article 15, the proscriptions of Article 3, unlike those in most of the other articles, are effective even 'in time of war or other public emergency, threatening the life of the nation'. In fact, the prohibitions of Article 3 are arguably *stricter* than those against taking life in Article 2. As we saw, the right to life has been defined to exclude deaths arising from the use of force in three categories.[110] No such exceptions are carved out from the absolute prohibitions of Article 3. Likewise, under Article 15, the right to life may be put aside, upon a proper derogation, for deaths resulting from a lawful war.[111] That article, however, prohibits any derogation from Article 3 even in wartime or public emergency. Some commentators have seen an anomaly in the consequence that the right to be free of inhuman or degrading treatment is more vigorously protected than the right to life.[112] Nonetheless, the Court has sometimes found it impossible to determine whether treatment is inhuman or degrading without taking into account the reasons for which it was imposed. When an applicant complained that he was subjected to inhuman and degrading treatment when he was handcuffed while under arrest, the Court responded that

handcuffing does not normally give rise to an issue under Article 3 of the Convention where the measure has been imposed in connection with a lawful arrest or detention and does not entail the use of force, or public exposure, exceeding what is reasonably considered necessary in the circumstances. In this regard, it is of importance, for instance, whether there is reason to believe that the person concerned would resist arrest or abscond, cause injury or suppress evidence.[113]

Especially in situations concerning the use of force by security forces, the Court has required the state to show that such action was 'absolutely necessary'. Even then, the amount of force applied must be 'proportionate' to the need.[114] In one case Turkish

---

[109] *R. v. Lichniak* [2003] 1 A.C. 903 (H.L.).

[110] The exceptions are for the use of force in defence of persons threatened with unlawful violence, to effect an arrest or to prevent escape of a person lawfully detained, and to quell an insurrection or riot.

[111] In *Gentle and Another v. Prime Minister* [2006] E.W.C.A. Civ. 1690 the Court of Appeal rejected an argument that the reference to 'lawful war' in Article 15 meant that Article 2 applied to deaths arising from a war that the government had no reasonable grounds to think was lawful under international law.

[112] For a discussion of this issue see Henry Shue, 'Torture', in *Torture: A Collection* 47 (S. Levinson, ed., 2004).

[113] *Raninen v. Finland*, 16 Dec. 1997, 26 E.H.R.R. 563.

[114] E.g. *Günaydin v. Turkey*, 13 Oct. 2005, para. 30.

security forces raided a village and, while they searched the buildings, required almost all adult and adolescent male residents to lie face down in the mud and slush of the village square where they were occasionally beaten or kicked in the presence of wives, mothers and young children. The Court found this treatment unjustified in the absence of any resistance from the civilian population. Therefore, the Court inferred, it was intended to 'intimidate, humiliate and debase' to a degree beyond that inherent in any arrest and detention and, therefore, a breach of the Convention.[115]

This approach has led the Court to evaluate, on a case-by-case basis, whether certain measures were necessary in the circumstances involved. In contrast to the restraint found permissible in the handcuffing case, shackling a prisoner to his bed in a hospital where he had been taken for an operation was found excessive in light of the prisoner's condition, history and the possible use of other security measures.[116] Similarly, it was a violation to restrain a seriously ill prisoner in an iron cage during judicial hearings.[117]

On this basis, the Court has determined that it is permissible under Article 3 to force certain medical treatments on detainees. In one case, it held that restraining, sedating and force-feeding an applicant who had been involuntarily committed to a psychiatric hospital was found to be a 'therapeutic necessity [and could not] be regarded as inhuman or degrading'.[118] The same conclusion was reached by the Court of Appeal with respect to the isolation of an involuntary psychiatric patient that did not inflict serious harm.[119] The Court of Appeal contrasted an earlier judgment of the Strasbourg Court that non-therapeutic segregation of a mentally ill prisoner as a punishment for misbehaviour when the authorities ought to have known that such segregation was extremely dangerous given the prisoner's mental state, did amount to inhuman and degrading treatment.[120] The United States Supreme Court has also held that the forced administration of anti-psychotic drugs to a prisoner was permissible under the Due Process clause if the inmate was a danger to himself or others.[121] Forced medication has also been found permissible for the purpose of making a pre-trial detainee competent to stand trial but only if such treatment is unlikely to have side-effects that could interfere with the trial and if other less intrusive alternatives are unavailable.[122]

Notwithstanding the apparent acceptance of a proportionality analysis by the Strasbourg Court, Lord Hope of Craighead has argued that government action that reaches the level contemplated by Article 3 may not be justified by demonstration of

---

[115] *Ahmet Özkan v. Turkey*, 6 April 2004, paras. 341–3. *See also Dalan v. Turkey*, 7 June 2005, para. 27 (violent force inflicted by eight police officers to restrain three women was excessive).

[116] *Hénaf v. France*, 27 November, 40 E.H.R.R. 44. *See also Yankov v. Bugaria, supra* n. 27, finding that periodic shaving of prisoners' heads had not been shown to be necessary for hygiene.

[117] *Sarban v. Moldova, supra* n. 27, para. 89.

[118] *Herczegfalvy v. Austria*, 24 Sept. 1992, 15 E.H.R.R. 437. See also the discussion of the relevance of state interests to Art. 3 determinations related to expulsions or extraditions, *infra*, Section (C).

[119] *R. (Munjaz) v. Mersey Care, NHS Trust and Others* [2003] E.W.C.A. Civ. 1036, [2004] Q.B. 395, paras. 53–60.

[120] *Id.* at para. 54 citing *Keenan v. United Kingdom, supra* n. 54.

[121] *Washington v. Harper*, 494 U.S. 210 (1990).

[122] *Sell v. United States*, 539 U.S. 166 (2003).

important reasons of state policy since to do so would be inconsistent with the absolute character of the prohibition.[123]

6. THE UNITED NATIONS CONVENTION AND THE USE OF TORTURE IN INTERROGATION

The special qualities that make some state action torture or inhuman or degrading have been given a somewhat more extended consideration in the definitions provided in the United Nations Convention Against Torture and Other Cruel Inhuman or Degrading Treatment or Punishment.[124]

Article 1

1. For the purposes of this Convention, torture means any act by which severe pain or suffering, whether physical or mental, is intentionally inflicted on a person for such purposes as obtaining from him or a third person information or a confession, punishing him for an act he or a third person committed or is suspected of having committed, or intimidating or coercing him or a third person, or for any reason based on discrimination of any kind, when such pain or suffering is inflicted by or at the instigation of or with the consent or acquiescence of a public official or other person acting in an official capacity. It does not include pain or suffering arising from, inherent in or incidental to lawful sanctions.

2. This Article is without prejudice to any international instrument or national legislation which does or may contain provisions of wider application....

Article 2

1. Each State Party shall take effective legislative, administrative, judicial or other measures to prevent acts of torture in any territory under its jurisdiction.

2. No exceptional circumstances whatsoever, whether a state of war or a threat of war, internal political instability or any other public emergency, may be invoked as a justification of torture.

3. An order from a superior officer or a public authority may not be invoked as a justification of torture....

Article 3

1. No State Party shall expel, return ('refouler') or extradite a person to another State where there are substantial grounds for believing that he would be in danger of being subjected to torture.

---

[123] *R. (Limbuela) v. Secretary of State for the Home Department* [2005] U.K.H.L. 66, [2006] 1 A.C. 396, para. 55.

[124] Adopted Dec. 1984. Entered into force 26 June 1987. On the operation of the Convention *see* generally T. Buergenthal, *International Human Rights* 72–6 (2nd edn. 1998).

2. For the purposes of determining whether there are such grounds the competent authorities shall take into account all relevant considerations including, where applicable, the existence in the State concerned of a consistent pattern of gross, flagrant or mass violations of human rights.

. . .

Article 16

1. Each State Party shall undertake to prevent in any territory under its jurisdiction other acts of cruel, inhuman or degrading treatment or punishment which do not amount to torture as defined in Article 1, when such acts are committed by or at the instigation of or with the consent or acquiescence of a public official or other person acting in an official capacity. In particular, the obligations contained in Articles 10, 11, 12 and 13 shall apply with the substitution for references to torture of references to other forms of cruel, inhuman or degrading treatment or punishment.

2. The provisions of this Convention are without prejudice to the provisions of any other international instrument or national law which prohibits cruel, inhuman or degrading treatment or punishment or which relate to extradition or expulsion....

. . .

The United Nations Convention has sometimes been cited by the Strasbourg Court in developing its own definitions.[125] Note particularly the requirement in the United Nations Convention's definition (Article 1) that torture be 'intentionally inflicted'. This element has also been held to be essential to a finding of torture under Article 3 of the European Convention. In *Aksoy v. Turkey*,[126] in which the Court concluded that the applicant had suffered torture by being suspended from his arms and subjected to electric shocks and beatings, the Court stated that 'to allow the special stigma of "torture" requires a showing of "deliberate inhuman treatment causing very serious and cruel suffering"'.[127] In that case the applicant's treatment 'could only have been deliberately inflicted; indeed a certain amount of preparation and exertion would have been required to carry it out. It would appear to have been administered with the aim of obtaining admissions or information from the applicant'.[128]

The Court's and the United Nations Convention's mention of 'such purpose as obtaining from him or a third person information or a confession' has also resonated in other European cases finding torture. In one case the Court noted that the applicant's detention appeared designed to elicit information.[129] In another it concluded that the 'pain and suffering were inflicted on the applicant intentionally for the purpose of, *inter alia*, making

---

[125] E.g. *Hatton and Others v. United Kingdom*, 8 July 2003, 37 E.H.R.R. 28.
[126] 18 Dec. 1996, 23 E.H.R.R. 553.
[127] *Id.* para. 63 (citing *Ireland v. United Kingdom, supra*).
[128] *Id.* para. 64.
[129] *Aydin v. Turkey*, 25 Sept. 1997, 25 E.H.R.R. 251, para. 85.

him confess to the offense which he was suspected of having committed'.[130] In no case, however, has the Court stated that maltreatment must be motivated by any particular purpose in order to be torture.

The United States has ratified the Torture Convention but with the following reservation:

The United States understands that, in order to constitute torture, an act must be *specifically intended* to inflict severe physical or mental pain or suffering and that mental pain or suffering refers to prolonged mental pain caused by or resulting from (1) the intentional infliction or threatened infliction of severe physical pain or suffering; (2) administration or application, or threatened administration or application, of mind altering substances or other procedures calculated to disrupt profoundly the senses or the personality; (3) the threat of imminent death; or (4) the threat that another person will imminently be subjected to death, severe physical pain or suffering, or the administration or application of mind-altering substances or other procedures calculated to disrupt profoundly the senses or personality.[131]

The character of American obligations under the Convention became the subject of considerable attention in connection with the interrogation of persons detained as a result of military actions in Afghanistan and Iraq following the terrorist assault in New York on September 11, 2001.[132] In 2002, officials of the United States Department of Justice concluded that the United State would violate its international obligations only by committing acts inflicted with a 'specific intention' to cause 'severe physical or mental pain or suffering'. Mental pain of this kind required that the action must result in 'significant psychological harm of significant duration, e.g. lasting for months or even years' and that it must be caused by one of the acts listed in the reservation, 'threats of imminent death; threats of infliction of the kind of pain that would amount to physical torture; infliction of such physical pain as a means of psychological torture; use of drugs or other procedures designed to deeply disrupt the senses, or fundamentally alter an individuals' personality; or threatening to do any of these things to a third party'. The requisite severe physical pain was something 'equivalent in intensity to the pain accompanying serious physical injury such as organ failure, impairment of bodily function or even death'.[133]

---

[130] *Selmouni v. France, supra* n. 66.

[131] The United States has also entered a reservation to Article 16 of the Convention obliging states to take measures to prevent 'cruel, inhuman or degrading treatment or punishment'. The reservation limits the conduct at issue to 'the cruel, unusual and inhumane treatment or punishment prohibited by the Fifth, Eighth, and-or Fourteenth Amendments to the Constitution of the United States'. A similar reservation has been entered in connection with Article 7 of the International Covenant on Civil and Political Rights, which, like the European Convention, prohibits 'torture ... or cruel, inhuman or degrading treatment or punishment'. 1057 U.N.T.S. 407; 138 Cong. Rec. S4781-01, S4783 (daily ed. 12 April 1992).

[132] *See* generally the essays in *Torture: A Collection* (S. Levinson ed. 2004).

[133] Memorandum for Alberto Gonzales, Counsel to the President from Jay S. Bybee, Assistant Attorney-General, August 1, 2002 reproduced at http://news.findlaw.com/wp/docs/doj/bybee80102mem.pdf (accessed February 9, 2005). The language of the reservation had been codified in 18 U.S.C. 2340A defining the crime of torture.

In November 2002, the United States Secretary of Defense approved the following techniques for detainees held at the United States base at Guantanamo Bay, Cuba. Compare them to those condemned in the *Irish Case*:

a. Category I techniques. During the initial category of interrogation the detainee should be provided a chair and the environment should be generally comfortable. The format of the interrogation is the direct approach. The use of rewards like cookies or cigarettes may be helpful. If the detainee is determined by the interrogator to be uncooperative, the interrogator may use the following techniques....

b. Category II techniques. With the permission of the OIC [Officer in Charge], Interrogation Section, the interrogator may use the following techniques.

(1)   The use of stress positions (like standing), for a maximum of four hours.

(2)   The use of falsified documents of reports.

(3)   Use of the isolation facility for up to 30 days....

(4)   Interrogating the detainee in an environment other than the standard interrogation booth.

(5)   Deprivation of light and auditory stimuli.

(6)   The detainee may also have a hood placed over his head during transportation and questioning. The hood should not restrict breathing in any way and the detainee should be under direct observation when hooded.

(7)   The use of 20 hour interrogations.

(8)   Removal of all comfort items (including religious items).

(9)   Switching the detainee from hot rations to [military ready to eat meals].

(10) Removal of clothing.

(11) Forced grooming (shaving of facial hair, etc).

(12) Using detainees individual phobias (such as fear of dogs) to induce stress.

c. Category III techniques. Techniques in this category may be used only by submitting a request through the Director, JIG, for approval by the Commanding General with appropriate legal review and information to Commander, [United States Southern Command]. These techniques are required for a very small percentage of the most uncooperative detainees (less than 3%). The following techniques and other aversive techniques, such as those used in U.S. military interrogation resistance training or by other U.S. government agencies, may be utilized in a carefully coordinated manner to help interrogate exceptionally resistant detainees. Any of these techniques that require more than light grabbing, poking, or pushing, will be administered only by individuals specifically trained in their safe application.

(1) The use of scenarios designed to convince the detainee that death or severely painful consequences are imminent for him and/or his family.

(2) Exposure to cold weather or water (with appropriate medical monitoring).

(3) Use of a wet towel and dripping water to induce the misperception of suffocation.

(4) Use of mild, non-injurious physical course such as grabbing, poking in the chest with the finger, and light pushing.

At the same time these guidelines were made public, the government disclosed that detainees had, indeed, been subjected to some of these techniques including forced grooming, 20-hour interrogations and light deprivation. After this disclosure, in a new opinion, the Defense Department officially rescinded these guidelines. In April 2003 a considerably more protective set of guidelines was promulgated. It emphasized that detainees were to be treated humanely, although it still provided for 'altering the environment to create moderate discomfort' and 'reversing sleep cycles'.[134]

B. CORPORAL PUNISHMENT

1. TYRER V. UNITED KINGDOM

Judgment of 25 April 1978
(No. 26), 2 E.H.R.R. 1

...

9. Mr. Anthony M. Tyrer, a citizen of the United Kingdom born on 21 September 1956, is a resident in Castletown, Isle of Man. On 7 March 1972, being then aged 15 and of previous good character, he pleaded guilty before the local juvenile court to unlawful assault occasioning actual bodily harm to a senior pupil at his school. The assault, committed by the applicant in company with three other boys, was apparently motivated by the fact that the victim had reported the boys for taking beer into the school, as a result of which they had been caned. The applicant was sentenced on the same day to three strokes of the birch in accordance with the relevant legislation.

10. After waiting in a police station for a considerable time for a doctor to arrive, Mr. Tyrer was birched late in the afternoon of the same day. His father and a doctor were present. The applicant was made to take down his trousers and underpants and bend over a table; he was held by two policemen whilst a third administered the punishment, pieces of the birch breaking at the first stroke. The applicant's father lost his self-control and after the third stroke 'went for' one of the policemen and had to be restrained.

The birching raised, but did not cut, the applicant's skin and he was sore for about a week and a half afterwards.

[The punishment was inflicted under a Manx Statute prescribing caning for males 11 to 16 years old found guilty of assault or beating. The Statute described the cane or rod to be used and the number of strokes. It also called for the caning to take place in private and in the

---

[134] All of the documents mentioned are available at http://www.washingtonpost.com/wp-dyn/articles/A62516–2004Jun22.html (accessed February 8, 2005).

presence of a parent or guardian. Regulations required a medical report prior to imposing the punishment and the presence of a doctor at the caning]...

14. Judicial corporal punishment of adults and juveniles was abolished in England, Wales and Scotland in 1948 and in Northern Ireland in 1968.

15. The punishment remained in existence in the Isle of Man. When Tynwald [the local Parliament] examined the question in 1963 and 1965, it decided to retain judicial corporal punishment, which was considered a deterrent to hooligans visiting the Island as tourists and, more generally, a means of preserving law and order...

29. The Court shares the Commission's view that Mr. Tyrer's punishment did not amount to 'torture' within the meaning of Article 3. The Court does not consider that the facts of this particular case reveal that the applicant underwent suffering of the level inherent in this notion as it was interpreted and applied by the Court in its judgment of 18 January 1978 (*Ireland v. the United Kingdom*).

[Nor does the Court] consider on the facts of the case that that level was attained and it therefore concurs with the Commission that the penalty imposed on Mr. Tyrer was not 'inhuman punishment' within the meaning of Article 3. Accordingly, the only question for decision is whether he was subjected to a 'degrading punishment' contrary to that Article. ...

31. The Attorney-General for the Isle of Man argued that the judicial corporal punishment at issue in this case was not in breach of the Convention since it did not outrage public opinion on the Island. However, even assuming that local public opinion can have an incidence on the interpretation of the concept of 'degrading punishment' appearing in Article 3, the Court does not regard it as established that judicial corporal punishment is not considered degrading by those members of the Manx population who favour its retention: it might well be that one of the reasons why they view the penalty as an effective deterrent is precisely the element of degradation which it involves. As regards their belief that judicial corporal punishment deters criminals, it must be pointed out that a punishment does not lose its degrading character just because it is believed to be, or actually is, an effective deterrent or aid to crime control. Above all, as the Court must emphasise, it is never permissible to have recourse to punishments which are contrary to Article 3, whatever their deterrent effect may be.

The Court must also recall that the Convention is a living instrument which, as the Commission rightly stressed, must be interpreted in the light of presentday conditions. In the case now before it the Court cannot but be influenced by the developments and commonly accepted standards in the penal policy of the member States of the Council of Europe in this field. Indeed, the Attorney-General for the Isle of Man mentioned that, for many years, the provisions of Manx legislation concerning judicial corporal punishment had been under review.

32. As regards the manner and method of execution of the birching inflicted on Mr. Tyrer, the Attorney-General for the Isle of Man drew particular attention to the fact that the punishment was carried out in private and without publication of the name of the offender.

Publicity may be a relevant factor in assessing whether a punishment is 'degrading' within the meaning of Article 3, but the Court does not consider that absence of publicity will necessarily prevent a given punishment from falling into that category: it may well suffice that the victim is humiliated in his own eyes, even if not in the eyes of others.

The Court notes that the relevant Isle of Man legislation, as well as giving the offender a right of appeal against sentence, provides for certain safeguards. Thus, there is a prior medical examination; the number of strokes and dimensions of the birch are regulated in detail; a doctor is present and may order the punishment to be stopped; in the case of a child or young person, the parent may attend if he so desires; the birching is carried out by a police constable in the presence of a more senior colleague.

33. Nevertheless, the Court must consider whether the other circumstances of the applicant's punishment were such as to make it 'degrading' within the meaning of Article 3.

The very nature of judicial corporal punishment is that it involves one human being inflicting physical violence on another human being. Furthermore, it is institutionalised violence, that is in the present case violence permitted by the law, ordered by the judicial authorities of the State and carried out by the police authorities of the State. Thus, although the applicant did not suffer any severe or long-lasting physical effects, his punishment—whereby he was treated as an object in the power of the authorities—constituted an assault on precisely that which it is one of the main purposes of Article 3 to protect, namely a person's dignity and physical integrity. Neither can it be excluded that the punishment may have had adverse psychological effects.

The institutionalised character of this violence is further compounded by the whole aura of official procedure attending the punishment and by the fact that those inflicting it were total strangers to the offender.

Admittedly, the relevant legislation provides that in any event birching shall not take place later than six months after the passing of sentence. However, this does not alter the fact that there had been an interval of several weeks since the applicant's conviction by the juvenile court and a considerable delay in the police station where the punishment was carried out. Accordingly, in addition to the physical pain he experienced, Mr. Tyrer was subjected to the mental anguish of anticipating the violence he was to have inflicted on him.

34. In the present case, the Court does not consider it relevant that the sentence of judicial corporal punishment was imposed on the applicant for an offence of violence. Neither does it consider it relevant that, for Mr. Tyrer, birching was an alternative to a period of detention: the fact that one penalty may be preferable to, or have less adverse effects or be less serious than, another penalty does not of itself mean that the first penalty is not 'degrading' within the meaning of Article 3.

35. Accordingly, viewing these circumstances as a whole, the Court finds that the applicant was subjected to a punishment in which the element of humiliation attained the level inherent in the notion of 'degrading punishment' as explained at paragraph 30 above. The indignity of having the punishment administered over the bare posterior aggravated to some extent the degrading character of the applicant's punishment but it was not the only or determining factor.

The Court therefore concludes that the judicial corporal punishment inflicted on the applicant amounted to degrading punishment within the meaning of Article 3 of the Convention.

[The Court held by six votes to one that the judicial corporal punishment inflicted on the applicant was degrading punishment in breach of Article 3.]

Separate opinion of Judge Fitzmaurice

...[A]ssuming that corporal punishment does involve some degree of degradation, it has never been seen as doing so for a juvenile to anything approaching the same manner or extent for an adult. Put in terms of the Convention and of the Court's criterion, therefore, such punishment does not, in the case of a juvenile, attain the level of degradation needed to constitute it a breach of Article 3, unless of course seriously aggravating circumstances are present over and above the simple fact of the corporal character of the punishment. This is why I could have understood it if the Court had regarded the infliction of the blows on the bare posterior as bringing matters up to the required level of degradation. I would not necessarily have agreed with that view, but it would have been tenable. However, the Court held that this was not a determining element: the punishment was in any event degrading....

12. I have to admit that my own view may be coloured by the fact I was brought up and educated under a system according to which the corporal punishment of schoolboys (some-times at the hands of the senior ones—prefects or monitors—sometimes by masters) was regarded as the normal sanction for serious misbehaviour, and even sometimes for what was much less serious. Generally speaking, and subject to circumstances, it was often considered by the boy himself as preferable to probably alternative punishments such as being kept in on a fine summer's evening to copy out 500 lines or learn several pages of Shakespeare or Virgil by heart, or be denied leave of absence on a holiday occasion. Moreover, these beatings were carried out without any of the safeguards attendant on Mr. Tyrer's: no parents, nurses or doc-tors were ever present. They also not infrequently took place under conditions of far greater intrinsic humiliation than in his case. Yet I cannot remember that any boy felt degraded or debased. Such an idea would have been thought rather ridiculous. The system was the same for all until they attained a certain seniority. If a boy minded, and resolved not to repeat the offence that had resulted in a beating, this was simply because it had hurt, not because he felt degraded by it or was so regarded by his fellows: indeed, such is the natural perversity of the young of the human species that these occasions were often seen as matters of pride and congratulation,—not unlike the way in which members of the student corps in the old German universities regarded their duelling scars as honourable—(though of course that was, in other respects, quite a different case)....

14. Finally, I would like to advert to the remarks I made in paragraphs 15 and 16 of my Separate Opinion in the *Irish Case* which, *mutatis mutandis*, are equally applicable to the question of degrading treatment or punishment. The fact that a certain practice is felt to be distasteful, undesirable, or morally wrong and such as ought not to be allowed to continue, is not a sufficient ground in itself for holding it to be contrary to Article 3. Still less is the fact that the Article fails to provide against types of treatment or punishment which, though they may legitimately be disapproved of, cannot, considered objectively and in relation to all the circumstances involved, reasonably be regarded without exaggeration as amounting, *in the particular case*, to any of the specific forms of treatment or punishment which the Article does provide against. Any other view would mean using the Article as a vehicle of indirect penal reform, for which it was not intended.

2. DEGRADING TREATMENT

Note the factors which the Court in *Tyrer* found do *not* save a punishment from violat-ing Article 3. A punishment may be 'degrading' even though (1) it does not outrage public opinion; (2) it is an effective deterrent; (3) it is administered in private; (4) it inflicts no lasting injury; and (5) it is imposed for crimes of violence. The critical language of the judgment seems to be this:

[H]is punishment—whereby he was treated as an object in the power of the authorities—constituted an assault on precisely that which it is one of the main purposes of Article 3 to protect, namely a person's dignity and physical integrity.

Presumably, mere imprisonment does not violate this test. Why not?[135]

In 1982, in *Campbell and Cosans v. United Kingdom*,[136] the Court considered the use of the 'tawse', a leather strap applied to the palm of the hand to discipline students in Scottish schools. In each case the applicants were the parents of students, neither of whom had actually been punished (although in one case the student had been suspended by reason of his and his parents' refusal to accept corporal punishment).

The Court agreed that 'provided it is sufficiently real and immediate, a mere threat of conduct prohibited in Article 3 might be in conflict with that provision'. But in these cases, given the fact that 'corporal chastisement is traditional in Scottish schools and, indeed, appears to be favoured by a large majority of parents':

...it is not established that pupils at a school where such punishment is used are, solely by reason of the risk of being subjected thereto, humiliated or debased in the eyes of others to the requisite degree or at all.

30. As to whether the applicants' sons were humiliated or debased in their own eyes, the Court observes first that a threat directed to an exceptionally insensitive person may have no significant effect on him but nevertheless be incontrovertibly degrading; and conversely, an exceptionally sensitive person might be deeply affected by a threat that could be described as degrading only by a distortion of the ordinary and usual meaning of the word. In any event, in the case of these two children, the Court, like the Commission, notes that it has not been shown by means of medical certificates or otherwise that they suffered any adverse psychological or other effects.[137]

In *Costello-Roberts v. United Kingdom*[138] the applicant was a seven year old student at an independent boarding school. As a punishment for a series of petty disciplinary breaches, he was subjected to 'three "whacks" on the bottom through his shorts with

---

[135]   Although, as has been noted, infringement of Article 3 rights may not be justified by a public interest, the European Court has held that the intentions with which an action is undertaken may be relevant to the presence or absence of a violation. In holding that the routine handcuffing of an arrested person was not incompatible with Article 3 the Court considered significant the fact that the action was not 'aimed at humiliating or debasing him'. *Raninen v. Finland, supra* n. 25.

[136]   25 Feb. 1982, 4 E.H.R.R. 293.

[137]   The Court did, however, hold that the practice of corporal punishment was inconsistent with Article 2 of Protocol 1 which guarantees respect for parents' religious and philosophical convictions in the education of their children. *See* Chapter 11(D) *infra*.

The *Tyrer* and *Campbell and Cosans* cases present good illustrations of the distinction between 'punishment' and 'treatment'. In *Tyrer* a punishment for a past act was inflicted. The use of the 'tawse' in *Campbell and Cosans* would have been punishment, but it was never administered to the applicants. The apprehensions generated by its potential use was considered 'treatment'.

[138]   25 Mar. 1993, 19 E.H.R.R. 112.

a rubber-soled gym shoe'. The United Kingdom conceded that it was liable under the Convention, if the violation of a person's rights were the result of a failure of the state to secure them against the actions of third parties, such as the school.[139] The Court held, however, that on the facts of this case there was no violation. It distinguished *Tyrer*:

Mr. Costello-Roberts was a young boy punished in accordance with the disciplinary rules in force within the school in which he was a boarder. This amounted to being slippered three times on his buttocks through his shorts with a rubbersoled gym shoe by the headmaster in private. Mr. Tyrer, on the other hand, was a young man sentenced in the local juvenile court to three strokes of the birch on the bare posterior. His punishment was administered three weeks later in a police station where he was held by two policemen whilst a third administered the punishment, pieces of the birch breaking at the first stroke... While the Court has certain misgivings about the automatic nature of the punishment and the three-day wait before its imposition, it considers [the] minimum level of severity not to have been attained in this case.[140]

Four judges dissented, finding that, where the headmaster 'whacked' a lonely and insecure 7-year-old-boy not spontaneously, but in a formal and official manner, after a three-day wait, this punishment was degrading.[141] In 1998 corporal punishment in all British schools, independent as well as state, was prohibited by law.[142]

The reach of Article 3's prohibitions was held to be even broader in *A. v. United Kingdom*.[143] The applicant was a 9-year-old boy who was beaten by his stepfather with a garden cane. The stepfather was acquitted on a charge of assault causing bodily harm after the jury was instructed that the crime did not include 'reasonable' correction by a parent. Although the government conceded the existence of a violation, the Court briefly discussed the issue. It concluded that the treatment of the child applicant—repeated beating with a garden cane applied with 'considerable force'—'reached the level of severity prohibited by Article 3'. It went on to hold that, although the immediate agent of the treatment was a private person, the Convention 'require[d] states to take measures to ensure that individuals within their jurisdiction are not subject to degrading treatment or punishment including such ill-treatment administered by private individuals'.[144]

---

[139] *Id.* paras. 26–8: The relation of the Convention's 'positive obligations' and the action of private persons is discussed in Chapter 8(B).

[140] *Id.* at paras. 31–2.

[141] *Id.* Joint dissenting opinion of Judges Ryssdal, Thor Vilhjálmson, Matscher and Wildhaber.

[142] School Standards and Framework Act 1998, chap. 31, s. 131. That law was, in turn, challenged by parents as contrary to their rights to manifest their religion (Article 9) and to secure an education for their children in conformity with their religious and philosophical beliefs (Protocol 1, Article 2). These claims, under the Human Rights Act, were rejected in *R. (Williamson) and Others v. Secretary of State for Education and Employment* [2005] U.K.H.L. 15, [2005] 2 A.C. 266.

[143] 23 Sept. 1998, 27 E.H.R.R. 611.

[144] *Id.* paras. 21–2. *See also Z and Others v. United Kingdom*, 10 May 2001, 34 E.H.R.R. 3 para. 74 holding that a violation of Article 3 was made out when the state failed to take reasonable measures to protect children from the neglect and psychological abuse of parents.

In *Ingraham v. Wright*,[145] the United States Supreme Court held that students did not have a constitutional protection against corporal punishment for school infractions. In discussing the claim that this practice violated the Eighth Amendment, the Court majority noted the widespread acceptance of the practice in many states. Comparing the situation of students subject to such discipline and that of prisoners who enjoyed the protection of the Eighth Amendment, the Court said:

The prisoner and the schoolchild stand in wholly different circumstances, separated by the harsh facts of criminal conviction and incarceration....The schoolchild has little need for the protection of the Eighth Amendment. Though attendance may not always be voluntary, the public school remains an open institution. Except perhaps when very young, the child is not physically restrained from leaving school during school hours; and at the end of the school day, the child is invariably free to return home. Even while at school, the child brings with him the support of family and friends and is rarely apart from teachers and other pupils who may witness and protest any instances of mistreatment.

The openness of the public school and its supervision by the community afford significant safeguards against the kinds of abuses from which the Eighth Amendment protects the prisoner. In virtually every community where corporal punishment is permitted in the schools, these safeguards are reinforced by the legal constraints of the common law. Public school teachers and administrators are privileged at common law to inflict only such corporal punishment as is reasonably necessary for the proper education and discipline of the child; any punishment going beyond the privilege may result in both civil and criminal liability.

In *Canadian Foundation for Children v. Canada (Attorney-General)*, the Supreme Court of Canada rejected a constitutional challenge to section 43 of the Criminal Code. That provision created a defence to a prosecution for 'intentional, non-consensual application of force to another'. Under section 43 it was permissible for a 'school-teacher or parent' to use such force as 'reasonable under the circumstances' for the purpose of 'correction'. The reasons of Chief Justice McLachlin, writing for a majority of the Court, responded to a claim that the statute was excessively vague by positing a narrow construction inferred from Canada's treaty obligations, judicial decisions and a 'contemporary social consensus'. Taken together these sources indicated that the exemption was only for

minor corrective force of a transitory and trifling nature....[I]t does not apply to corporal punishment of children under two or teenagers. Degrading, inhuman or harmful conduct is not protected. Discipline by the use of objects or blows or slaps to the head is unreasonable. Teachers may reasonably apply force to remove a child from a classroom or secure compliance with instructions but not merely as corporal punishment .... [T]he conduct must be corrective which rules out conduct stemming from the caregiver's frustration, loss of temper or abusive personality ...

The court also rejected a claim that section 43 conflicted with section 12 of the Charter of Rights and Freedoms, infringing the right to be free from 'cruel and unusual treatment

---

[145]   430 U.S. 651 (1977).

or punishment'. As to parents, the Court relied on precedent establishing that section 12 only prohibited treatment by the state. (Contrast this with the approach of the Strasbourg Court discussed above.) While it conceded that the prohibition might apply to some school teachers, it decided the case on the ground that the conduct protected by the statute as interpreted by the Court could not be considered 'cruel and unusual'. 'Conduct cannot be at once reasonable and an outrage to standards of decency'.[146]

3. PUBLIC OPINION

In *Tyrer*, the Court asserted that the absence of public outrage does not immunize a punishment from violating Article 3. But, in the same judgment, it states that it 'cannot but be influenced by the developments and commonly accepted standards in the penal policy of the member states of the Council of Europe'. Judge Fitzmaurice also observed that, in the context of juvenile offenders, infliction of blows has never been regarded as degrading. Similarly, in *Campbell and Cosans*, the wide acceptance of corporal punishment in the schools was cited by the Court in support of its conclusion that the mere risk of its infliction could not be thought to be sufficiently degrading as to violate the Convention.

General attitudes toward, and practices generally used in, punishment of crime have played a role in constitutional decisions interpreting the Eighth Amendment's prohibition of cruel and unusual punishments. In *Solem v. Helm*,[147] in which the Supreme Court found imposition of a life sentence to violate the amendment when imposed for the crime of issuing a bad cheque under South Dakota's recidivist statute, the Court employed, as part of its analysis, an investigation of 'the sentences imposed for commission of the same crime in other jurisdictions'. In declaring that the death penalty may be validly imposed under some circumstances, notwithstanding its apparently contrary opinion in *Furman v. Georgia*,[148] the plurality in *Gregg v. Georgia*[149] relied, in part, on the fact that, in the years after the *Furman* decision, numerous state legislatures had re-enacted death penalty statutes:

The petitioners in the capital cases before the Court today renew the 'standards of decency' argument, but developments during the four years since *Furman* have undercut substantially the assumptions upon which their argument rested. Despite the continuing debate, dating back to the 19th century, over the morality and utility of capital punishment, it is now evident that a large proportion of American society continues to regard it as an appropriate and necessary criminal sanction.

[146] [2004] S.C.C. 4, paras. 40, 49.
[147] 463 U.S. 277 (1983).
[148] 408 U.S. 238 (1972).
[149] 428 U.S. 153 (1976).

The most marked indication of society's endorsement of the death penalty for murder is the legislative response to *Furman*. The legislatures of at least 35 states have enacted new statutes that provide for the death penalty for at least some crimes that result in the death of another person. And the Congress of the United States, in 1974, enacted a statute providing the death penalty for aircraft piracy that results in death...

In the only statewide referendum occurring since *Furman* and brought to our attention, the people of California adopted a constitutional amendment that authorized capital punishment, in effect negating a prior ruling by the Supreme Court of California...

In a dissenting opinion, Justice Marshall commented on the relevance of public opinion to the constitutionality of the death penalty:

Since the decision in *Furman*, the legislatures of 35 States have enacted new statutes authorizing the imposition of the death sentence for certain crimes, and Congress has enacted a law providing the death penalty for air piracy resulting in death. I would be less than candid if I did not acknowledge that these developments have a significant bearing on a realistic assessment of the moral acceptability of the death penalty to the American people. But if the constitutionality of the death penalty turns, as I have urged, on the opinion of an *informed* citizenry, then even the enactment of new death statutes cannot be viewed as conclusive. In *Furman*, I observed that the American people are largely unaware of the information critical to a judgment on the morality of the death penalty, and concluded that if they were better informed they would consider it shocking, unjust, and unacceptable. A recent study, conducted after the enactment of the post-*Furman* statutes, has confirmed that the American people know little about the death penalty and that the opinions of an informed public would differ significantly from those of a public unaware of the consequences and effects of the death penalty.

The relevance of public opinion in determining the reach of constitutional bars on cruel, inhuman or degrading treatment or punishment has been doubted by some courts. Consider, for example, the reasons of the Constitutional Court of South Africa:

If public opinion were to be decisive there would be no need for constitutional adjudication. The protection of rights could then be left to Parliament, which has a mandate from the public and is answerable to the public for the way its mandate is exercised. But this would be a return to parliamentary sovereignty and a retreat from the new legal order established by the 1993 Constitution. By the same token, the issue of the constitutionality of capital punishment cannot be referred to a referendum in which a majority view would prevail over the wishes of any minority. The very reason for establishing the new legal order, and for vesting the power of judicial review of all legislation, in the courts, was to protect the rights of minorities and others who cannot protect their rights adequately through the democratic process... This Court cannot allow itself to be diverted from its duty to act as an independent arbiter of the Constitution by making choices on the basis that they will find favour with the public.[150]

Notwithstanding the 1978 judgment in *Tyrer*, subsequent attempts to repeal the Manx statute authorizing birching did not succeed until 2001. In 1993 a government proposal to that effect was withdrawn in the face of strong public opposition. No actual birchings were carried out after 1975. One Manx member of parliament who opposed repeal was

---

[150] *S. v. Makwanyane*, 1995 (3) S.A. 391 (C.C.), paras. 88–9.

quoted as saying: 'By keeping birching on the statute book we are sending out a clear message to the world that we believe in law and order. It is true that it cannot actually be implemented. But I think it still has a psychological importance'.[151]

C. EXTRADITION, EXPULSION OR DEPORTATION

1. THE RESPONSIBILITY OF THE DEPORTING STATE

An increasingly important and difficult question for the European human rights system concerns attempts by a contracting state to deport an applicant to a *non-contracting* state where, the applicant claims, he or she will be subject to torture, or inhuman or degrading treatment. The Court first considered this issue in *Soering v. United Kingdom*[152] in which the United Kingdom sought, pursuant to treaty, to extradite Soering to Virginia in the United States to stand trial for murder. The Virginia authorities planned to seek the death penalty. Soering claimed that the circumstances surrounding the administration of death sentences in Virginia, particularly the typical delay of six to eight years between imposition and execution of a death sentence, constituted inhuman treatment or punishment. Therefore, he argued, the action of the United Kingdom in exposing him to the risk of such treatment violated Article 3. The United Kingdom, on the other hand, argued that an extraditing state should not be held responsible, under the Convention, for inhuman or degrading treatment or punishment that might be inflicted outside that state's jurisdiction.

The Court held that the extraditing state did have some responsibility under the Convention for the potential maltreatment of extradited individuals. For a state 'knowingly to surrender a fugitive to another state where there were substantial grounds for believing that he would be in danger of being subjected to torture [or inhuman or degrading treatment] however heinous the crime', would 'plainly be contrary to the spirit and intendment of [Article 3'].

89. What amounts to 'inhuman or degrading treatment or punishment' depends on all the circumstances of the case. Furthermore, inherent in the whole of the Convention is a search for a fair balance between the demands of the general interest of the community and the requirements of the protection of the individual's fundamental rights. As movement about the world becomes easier and crime takes on a larger international dimension, it is increasingly in the interest of all nations that suspected offenders who flee abroad should be brought to justice.

---

[151] 'Outcry Halts Isle of Man Proposal to Scrap Birch', *The Daily Telegraph* (London), 24 April 1993, 4. For the abolition of whipping, *see* the Criminal Justice Act 2001 (Isle of Man), s. 61.

[152] 7 July 1989, 11 E.H.R.R. 439.

Conversely, the establishment of safe havens for fugitives would not only result in danger for the State obliged to harbour the protected person but also tend to undermine the foundations of extradition. These considerations must also be included among the factors to be taken into account in the interpretation and application of the notions of inhuman and degrading treatment or punishment in extradition cases.

90. It is not normally for the Convention institutions to pronounce on the existence or otherwise of potential violations of the Convention. However, where an applicant claims that a decision to extradite him would, if implemented, be contrary to Article 3 by reason of its foreseeable consequences in the requesting country, a departure from this principle is necessary, in view of the serious and irreparable nature of the alleged suffering risked, in order to ensure the effectiveness of the safeguard provided by that Article.

91. In sum, the decision by a Contracting State to extradite a fugitive may give rise to an issue under Article 3, and hence engage the responsibility of that State under the Convention, where substantial grounds have been shown for believing that the person concerned, if extradited, faces a real risk of being subjected to torture or to inhuman or degrading treatment or punishment in the requesting country. The establishment of such responsibility inevitably involves an assessment of conditions in the requesting country against the standards of Article 3 of the Convention. Nonetheless, there is no question of adjudicating on or establishing the responsibility of the receiving country, whether under general international law, under the Convention or otherwise. In so far as any liability under the Convention is or may be incurred, it is liability incurred by the extraditing Contracting State by reason of its having taken action which has as a direct consequence the exposure of an individual to proscribed ill-treatment.

In the case at hand, the court found Soering ran a 'real risk' of being convicted, sentenced to death, and being subjected to a long pre-execution delay. Since the Court also found that such delay would itself violate Article 3, the extradition, would, in these circumstances, also be a violation.[153]

The Court cited, among other authorities, Article 3 of the United Nations Convention Against Torture and other Cruel Inhuman or Degrading Treatment or Punishment (reproduced above) that explicitly bars expulsion or extradition where there are 'substantial grounds' for believing a deportee would be subjected to *torture*. The Torture Convention's rules pointedly do not prohibit returning a person to face 'cruel, inhuman or degrading treatment'. The Article 3 violation that the court found to be threatened in *Soering*, the extended wait before execution, was condemned only as inhuman and degrading.

The Supreme Court of Canada has formulated a similar way of dealing with extraditions or expulsion to jurisdictions where unacceptable treatment of the person involved is feared. The Court has consistently held that the prohibition in the Charter of Rights and Freedoms on cruel and unusual punishment is not applicable to decisions to remove. It has reasoned that the link between Canadian official action and the resulting injury is too speculative to find a violation. Such decisions are reviewable, however, under Section 7 of the Charter forbidding deprivations of 'life, liberty or

[153] *Id.* paras. 106–11. On the death penalty *see* Section D *infra*.

security of the person' except in accordance with 'principles of fundamental justice'.[154] On these grounds the Court has held that, barring extraordinary circumstances, a deportation to face torture would be unconstitutional.[155]

In dealing with claims that extraditions to the United States in capital cases might violate Section 7, the Canadian Court has employed the same kind of approach. While there is no constitutional textual bar on capital punishment in Canada, there have been no executions since 1962 and the last statutory remnants of the death penalty were repealed in 1998.[156] Initially, the Supreme Court held that, given the complexity of the issues associated with extradition, a decision by the Minister of Justice to return a fugitive for trial did not sufficiently 'shock[] the Canadian conscience' and therefore met the requirements of Section 7.[157] Ten years later, however, in *United States v. Burns*, the Court declared that 'in the absence of exceptional circumstances, which we refrain from trying to anticipate, assurances [from the destination state that the person extradited will not be executed] in death penalty cases are always constitutionally required'.[158] The Court avoided using the term 'shock the conscience' which it worried might 'obscure the ultimate assessment... whether or not the extradition is in accordance with principles of fundamental justice'. It acted on the assumption that those principles might have changed since its earlier decision. In that regard, it relied on Canadian domestic law as well as on the experience of other democracies and what it saw as a growing international consensus disfavouring capital punishment. It also emphasized an increasing recognition of the fallibility of guilty verdicts in capital cases.

The Constitutional Court of South Africa came to a similar decision, citing the *Burns* case as well as *Soering* and several other Strasbourg cases. In *Mohamed v. President of the Republic of South Africa*,[159] the applicant, a Tanzanian national, was sought by the United States in connection with the Al Qaeda bombing of the American embassies in Nairobi and Dar es Salaam killing more than 200 people and injuring more than 4,500. He had entered South Africa illegally and the local authorities, co-operating with the United States, had arrested him and turned him over to United States agents who returned him to New York. His trial was in progress when the Constitutional Court rendered its decision. It held that surrendering Mohamed to American authorities without securing assurances that he would not be subject to the death penalty violated sections 10, 11 and 12(1)(d) of the South African Constitution, expressing the rights to human dignity, to life and not to be treated or punished in a cruel, inhuman or degrading way. The South African Court's decision was, in some ways, easier than that facing

---

[154] *United States v. Burns* [2001] 1 S.C.R. 283, paras. 50–4.

[155] *Suresh v. Canada* (Minister of Citizenship and Immigration) [2002] 1 S.C.R. 3, paras. 76–9. In the particular case, since the refugee had made a prima facie showing of the risk of torture, the Minister could not deport him without offering a fair procedure for determining whether or not there were substantial grounds to believe that the refugee might be tortured or subjected to other cruel and unusual treatment. Paras. 122–30.

[156] *United States v. Burns, supra* n. 154, para. 76.

[157] *Kindler v. Canada* [1991] S.C.R. 779.

[158] *United States v. Burns, supra* n. 154, para. 65, 68.

[159] 2001 (3) SA 893 (C.C.).

the Canadian and European courts. That is because that court had already determined that capital punishment itself was unconstitutional.[160] Since the unlawful deportation had already been effected, the Court ordered that its judgment be communicated to the United States court where Mohamed was being tried. In the event, he was convicted but, as a result of jury deadlock, was sentenced to life in prison without the possibility of parole.[161]

Compare the Court's reasoning in *Soering* to its subsequent decision in *Banković and Others v. Belgium and Others*.[162] In that case, the Court found inadmissible as outside its jurisdiction, the complaints of residents of Yugoslavia who had been injured, or whose relatives had been injured or killed, in the bombing of Belgrade by the forces of the North Atlantic Treaty Organization (NATO) in connection with the conflict in the province of Kosovo. The Court decided that the applications did not allege a violation of the rights of persons within the jurisdiction of the respondent states as required by Article 1. The applicants cited, inter alia, *Soering* for the proposition that states were held answerable for violations of the Convention even if the relevant acts occurred outside their territorial jurisdiction. The Court insisted that the jurisdiction referred to in Article 1 is 'primarily territorial'. The extradition cases involved action by a state affecting 'a person while he or she is on its territory'. It also distinguished *Loizidou v. Turkey*,[163] and *Cyprus v. Turkey*,[164] in which Turkey was found to have violated the Convention in connection with its military operations in Cyprus. In those cases, the Court noted, the challenged actions occurred in a territory over which Turkey had 'effective control'.

The 'substantial grounds' analysis was further clarified in *Vilvarajah v. United Kingdom*[165] involving five Tamils who entered the United Kingdom illegally and were expelled to Sri Lanka despite their claims that they would be subject to maltreatment there. After their removal to Sri Lanka, a British administrative adjudicator upheld their appeals, finding that each applicant 'had a well-founded fear of persecution'. In the case of three applicants, moreover, it was shown before the Commission and Court that they had, indeed, been beaten and tortured after their return to Sri Lanka. In deciding there was no violation of Article 3, the Court emphasized that 'since the nature of the Contracting States' responsibility ... lies in the act of exposing an individual to the risk of ill-treatment, the existence of the risk must be assessed primarily

---

[160] *S. v. Makwanyane*, 1995 (3) SA 39 (C.C.) discussed *supra*. The Canadian Supreme Court in *Burns* stated that it had no occasion to decide whether or not a hypothetical death penalty enacted by Parliament would violate section 12's bar on cruel or unusual punishment, para. 78, although the logic of its opinion seems clearly to favour such a result. On the ambiguous position of the Strasbourg Court on the relationship of the death penalty to Articles 2 and 3, *see* Section (D) *infra*.

[161] http://www.cbsnews.com/htdocs/embassy_bombings/whois_mohamed.html accessed February 21, 2005.

[162] [G.C.] 12 Dec. 2001, 44 E.H.R.R. SE5 (admissibility decision) reproduced in part in Chapter 2(B) *supra*.

[163] 23 March 1995 (preliminary objections), 20 E.H.R.R. 99 and 18 December 1996 (merits), 23 E.H.R.R. 53.

[164] 10 May 2001, 35 E.H.R.R. 30.

[165] 30 Oct. 1991, 14 E.H.R.R. 248.

with reference to those facts which were known or ought to have been known to the Contracting State at the time of the expulsion'. Subsequent facts coming to light may be useful, however, in confirming or refuting the state's judgments or the applicant's claims. In this case this obliged the Court to concentrate on 'the foreseeable consequences of the removal of the applicant to Sri Lanka in light of the general situation there in February 1988'. The Court decided that, given the improvement in the political and military situation in Sri Lanka at the time of the United Kingdom's decision, the voluntary repatriation of Tamil refugees going on at that time, and the particular circumstances of the applicants, there had been no breach of the Convention. Even with respect to those applicants who ultimately had been abused on their return, 'there existed no special distinguishing feature in their cases that could or ought to have enabled the Secretary of State to foresee that they would be treated in this way'.

The time at which the compatibility with the Convention of a state's decision to deport should be assessed was raised again in *Chahal v. United Kingdom*.[166] In that case, the government sought to expel to India a Sikh political activist on the grounds that his activities constituted a threat to national security. Unlike the applicants in *Vilvarajah*, however, Chahal had been allowed to remain in Britain while the case was adjudicated in Strasbourg. It was argued that between the time of the decision to deport and the decision of the European Court the danger to the applicant had diminished. The Court accepted the government's argument that the later time could be controlling:

[T]he crucial question is whether it has been substantiated that there is a real risk that Mr. Chahal, if expelled, would be subjected to treatment prohibited by that Article [3]. Since he has not yet been deported, the material point in time must be that of the [European] Court's consideration of the case. It follows that, although, the historical position is of interest in so far as it may shed light on the current situation and its likely evolution, it is the present conditions which are decisive.[167]

By the same token, however, an unexecuted extradition decision must be reviewed by the state to be sure that changed conditions have not, in effect, put the accused at risk.[168]

The Court in *Chahal* also considered another question important to the application of Article 3 to cases of extradition and deportation. The United Kingdom argued that the Court was obliged to consider the state's interest in expelling the applicant. In the instant case, this interest, the protection of national security, was presumptively weighty. The Court, noting the fact that, unlike most Convention rights, those in Article 3 were not subject to limitation in order to serve important public interests, and, indeed, were not even defeasible in time of war and public emergency[169] rejected

---

[166] 15 Nov. 1996, 23 E.H.R.R. 413, and *see* Chapter 12(E)4.
[167] *Id.* para. 80.
[168] *Shamayev and Others v. Georgia and Russia*, 12 April 2005, paras. 358–68.
[169] *See* the introduction to this chapter.

this approach. '[T]he activities of the individual in question, however undesirable or dangerous, cannot be a material consideration'.[170]

2. D. V. UNITED KINGDOM

Judgment of 2 May 1997

24 E.H.R.R. 423

[The applicant a native of St. Kitts moved to the United States. In 1991, he was convicted of possession of cocaine. After serving one year of a prison sentence he was deported to St. Kitts. Shortly thereafter he travelled to the United Kingdom. On his arrival at Gatwick Airport in January 1993, he was discovered to be in possession of cocaine valued at about £120,000. He was refused permission to enter the country. Before being deported, however, he was convicted of importing controlled drugs and sentenced, in May 1993, to a prison term of six years. In August 1994, while serving his prison sentence, the applicant was diagnosed as suffering from AIDS. In January 1996, he was released on licence at which time steps were taken to deport him. Various requests to British authorities to allow the applicant to remain on compassionate grounds were refused.]

13. Since August 1995, the applicant's CD4 cell count has been below 10. He has been in the advanced stages of the illness, suffering from recurrent anaemia, bacterial chest infections, malaise, skin rashes, weight loss and periods of extreme fatigue.

14. By letter dated 15 January 1996, Dr Evans, a consultant doctor, stated:

'His current treatment is AZT 250 mgs. b.d. and monthly nebulised pentamidine, he occasionally takes my statin pastilles and skin emollients.

In view of the fact that [the applicant] has now had AIDS for over 18 months and because this is a relentlessly progressive disease his prognosis is extremely poor.

In my professional opinion [the applicant's] life expectancy would be substantially shortened if he were to return to St. Kitts where there is no medication; it is important that he receives pentamidine treatment against PCP and that he receives prompt anti-microbial therapy for any further infections which he is likely to develop....

15. In a medical report provided on 13 June 1996, Professor Pinching, a professor of immunology at a London hospital, stated that the applicant had suffered severe and irreparable damage to his immune system and was extremely vulnerable to a wide range of specific infections and to the development of tumours. The applicant was reaching the end of the average durability of effectiveness of the drug therapy which he was receiving. It was stated that the applicant's prognosis was very poor and limited to 8–12 months on present therapy. It was estimated that withdrawal of the proven effective therapies and of proper medical care would reduce that prognosis to less than half of what would be otherwise expected.

16. By letter dated 20 April 1995, the High Commission for the Eastern Caribbean States informed the doctor treating the applicant in prison that the medical facilities in St. Kitts did not have the capacity to provide the medical treatment that he would require. This was in

---

[170] *Chahal, supra* n. 166, para. 80. *See also Ahmed v. Austria*, 17 Dec. 1996, 24 E.H.R.R. 278.

response to a faxed enquiry of the same date by Dr Hewitt, the managing medical officer of H.M. Prison Wayland. By letter of 24 October 1995, Dr Hewitt informed the Home Office of the contents of the letter from the High Commission, which had also been sent to the Parole Unit on 1 May 1995. He stated that the necessary treatment was not available in St. Kitts but was widely and freely available in the United Kingdom and requested due consideration be given to lifting the deportation order in respect of the applicant. By letter dated 1 August 1996, the High Commission for the Eastern Caribbean States confirmed that the position in St. Kitts had not changed: ...

19. When granted bail on 31 October 1996 ... the applicant was released to reside in special sheltered accommodation for AIDS patients provided by a charitable organisation working with homeless persons. Accommodation, food and services are provided free of charge to the applicant. He also has the emotional support and assistance of a trained volunteer provided by the Terrence Higgins Trust, the leading Charity in the United Kingdom providing practical support, help, counselling and legal and other advice for persons concerned about or having AIDS or HIV infection.

20. In a medical report dated 9 December 1996 Dr J.M. Parkin, a consultant in clinical immunology treating the applicant at a London Hospital, noted that he was at an advanced stage of HIV infection and was severely immunosuppressed. His prognosis was poor. The applicant was being given antiretroviral therapy with D4T and 3TC to reduce the risk of opportunistic infection and was continuing to be prescribed Pentamidine nebulisers to prevent a recurrence of PCP. Preventative treatment for other opportunistic infections was also foreseen. Dr Parkin noted that the lack of treatment with anti-HIV therapy and preventative measures for opportunistic disease would hasten his death if he were to be returned to St. Kitts.

21. The applicant was transferred to an AIDS hospice around the middle of January 1997 for a period of respite care. At the beginning of February there was a sudden deterioration in his condition and he had to be admitted to a hospital on 7 February for examination. At the hearing before the Court on 20 February 1997, it was stated that the applicant's condition was causing concern and that the prognosis was uncertain. According to his counsel, it would appear that the applicant's life was drawing to a close much as the experts had predicted ...

40. The applicant maintained that his removal to St. Kitts would condemn him to spend his remaining days in pain and suffering in conditions of isolation, squalor and destitution. He had no close relatives or friends in St. Kitts to attend to him as he approached death. He had no accommodation, no financial resources and no access to any means of social support. It was an established fact that the withdrawal of his current medical treatment would hasten his death on account of the unavailability of similar treatment in St. Kitts. His already weakened immune system would not be able to resist the many opportunistic infections to which he would be exposed on account of his homelessness, lack of proper diet and the poor sanitation on the island. The hospital facilities were extremely limited and certainly not capable of arresting the development of infections provoked by the harsh physical environment in which he would be obliged to fend for himself. His death would thus not only be further accelerated, it would also come about in conditions which would be inhuman and degrading.

41. In June 1996, his life expectancy was stated to be in the region of eight to twelve months even if he continued to receive treatment in the United Kingdom. His health had declined since

then. As he was now clearly weak and close to death, his removal by the respondent State at this late stage would certainly exacerbate his fate.

42. The Government requested the Court to find that the applicant had no valid claim under Article 3 in the circumstances of the case since he would not be exposed in the receiving country to any form of treatment which breached the standards of Article 3. His hardship and reduced life expectancy would stem from his terminal and incurable illness coupled with the deficiencies in the health and social welfare system of a poor, developing country. He would find himself in the same situation as other AIDS victims in St. Kitts. In fact he would have been returned in January 1993 to St. Kitts, where he had spent most of his life, had it not been for his prosecution and conviction.

43. The Government also disputed the applicant's claim that he would be left alone and without access to treatment for his condition. They maintained that he had at least one cousin living in St. Kitts and that there were hospitals caring for AIDS patients, including those suffering from opportunistic infections. Even if the treatment and medication fell short of that currently administered to the applicant in the United Kingdom, this in itself did not amount to a breach of Article 3 standards.

44. Before the Court the Government observed that it was their policy not to remove a person who was unfit to travel. They gave an undertaking to the Court not to remove the applicant unless, in the light of an assessment of his medical condition after the Court gives judgment, he is fit to travel. . . .

46. The Court recalls at the outset that Contracting States have the right, as a matter of well-established international law and subject to their treaty obligations including the Convention, to control the entry, residence and expulsion of aliens. It also notes the gravity of the offence which was committed by the applicant and is acutely aware of the problems confronting Contracting States in their efforts to combat the harm caused to their societies through the supply of drugs from abroad. The administration of severe sanctions to persons involved in drug trafficking, including expulsion of alien drug couriers like the applicant, is a justified response to this scourge.

47. However in exercising their right to expel such aliens Contracting States must have regard to Article 3 of the Convention which enshrines one of the fundamental values of democratic societies. It is precisely for this reason that the Court has repeatedly stressed in its line of authorities involving extradition, expulsion or deportation of individuals to third countries that Article 3 prohibits in absolute terms torture or inhuman or degrading treatment or punishment and that its guarantees apply irrespective of the reprehensible nature of the conduct of the person in question. . . .

48. The Court observes that the above principle is applicable to the applicant's removal under the Immigration Act 1971. Regardless of whether or not he ever entered the United Kingdom in the technical sense it is to be noted that he has been physically present there and thus within the jurisdiction of the respondent State within the meaning of Article 1 of the Convention since 21 January 1993. It is for the respondent State therefore to secure to the applicant the rights guaranteed under Article 3 irrespective of the gravity of the offence which he committed.

49. It is true that this principle has so far been applied by the Court in contexts in which the risk to the individual of being subjected to any of the proscribed forms of treatment emanates

from intentionally inflicted acts of the public authorities in the receiving country or from those of non-State bodies in that country when the authorities there are unable to afford him appropriate protection.

Aside from these situations and given the fundamental importance of Article 3 in the Convention system, the Court must reserve to itself sufficient flexibility to address the application of that Article in other contexts which might arise. It is not therefore prevented from scrutinizing an applicant's claim under Article 3 where the source of the risk of proscribed treatment in the receiving country stems from factors which cannot engage either directly or indirectly the responsibility of the public authorities of that country, or which, taken alone, do not in themselves infringe the standards of that Article. To limit the application of Article 3 in this manner would be to undermine the absolute character of its protection. In any such contexts, however, the Court must subject all the circumstances surrounding the case to a rigorous scrutiny, especially the applicant's personal situation in the expelling State....

51. The Court notes that the applicant is in the advanced stages of a terminal and incurable illness. At the date of the hearing, it was observed that there had been a marked decline in his condition and he had to be transferred to a hospital. His condition was giving rise to concern. The limited quality of life he now enjoys results from the availability of sophisticated treatment and medication in the United Kingdom and the care and kindness administered by a charitable organization. He has been counselled on how to approach death and has formed bonds with his carers.

52. The abrupt withdrawal of these facilities will entail the most dramatic consequences for him. It is not disputed that his removal will hasten his death. There is a serious danger that the conditions of adversity which await him in St. Kitts will further reduce his already limited life expectancy and subject him to acute mental and physical suffering. Any medical treatment which he might hope to receive there could not contend with the infections which he may possibly contract on account of his lack of shelter and of a proper diet as well as exposure to the health and sanitation problems which beset the population of St. Kitts. While he may have a cousin in St. Kitts no evidence has been adduced to show whether this person would be willing to or capable of attending to the needs of a terminally ill man. There is no evidence of any other form of moral or social support. Nor has it been shown whether the applicant would be guaranteed a bed in either of the hospitals on the island which, according to the Government, care for AIDS patients.

53. In view of these exceptional circumstances and bearing in mind the critical stage now reached in the applicant's fatal illness, the implementation of the decision to remove him to St. Kitts would amount to inhuman treatment by the respondent State in violation of Article 3.

The Court also notes in this respect that the respondent State has assumed responsibility for treating the applicant's condition since August 1994. He has become reliant on the medical and palliative care which he is at present receiving and is no doubt psychologically prepared for death in an environment which is both familiar and compassionate. Although it cannot be said that the conditions which would confront him in the receiving country are themselves a breach of the standards of Article 3, his removal would expose him to a real risk of dying under most distressing circumstances and would thus amount to inhuman treatment.

Without calling into question the good faith of the undertaking given to the Court by the Government, it is to be noted that the above considerations must be seen as wider in scope than the question whether or not the applicant is fit to travel back to St. Kitts.

54. Against this background the Court emphasises that aliens who have served their prison sentences and are subject to expulsion cannot in principle claim any entitlement to remain on the territory of a Contracting State in order to continue to benefit from medical, social or other forms of assistance provided by the expelling State during their stay in prison.

However, in the very exceptional circumstances of this case and given the compelling humanitarian considerations at stake, it must be concluded that the implementation of the decision to remove the applicant would be a violation of Article 3.

[The court held unanimously that there had been a violation of Article 3.]

. . .

D. v. United Kingdom holds that a violation of Article 3 may result in connection with an expulsion even when the danger to the applicant arises from a source other than the public authority of the receiving state. This conclusion makes more sense when we recall that the only violation of human rights over which the Court has jurisdiction is the act of the state party in effecting the deportation. The question must be whether that action amounts to subjecting the applicant to 'torture or to inhuman or degrading treatment or punishment'. This inquiry raises familiar legal questions of foreseeability and causation.

The holding in *D* was foreshadowed in the *Chahal* case mentioned above. In that case the applicant had expressed fear of ill-treatment by the state police of Punjab. The British government responded that Chahal could be deported to other parts of India. The European Court held that such a possibility did not sufficiently reduce the risk to the applicant since the Punjab police had a record of reprisals against Sikh nationalists in other Indian states, and that such police misconduct had not been brought under control by the concededly good faith efforts of the Indian government.[171] Given the lawless character of the incidents under consideration, this holding effectively included unofficial as well as official mistreatment among the threats that had to be considered by the expelling state. Similarly, in *Ahmed v. Austria*,[172] an expulsion to Somalia was held to entail a violation of Article 3. The applicant faced a serious risk of torture or inhuman or degrading treatment inflicted by factions in the continuing civil war in that country. That risk was sufficient to support a holding that expulsion would involve a violation of the Convention, despite, indeed largely because of, 'the current lack of state authority in Somalia'.[173] This understanding was made explicit in *H. L. R. v. France*.[174] There, the applicant was being deported to Colombia because of his involvement in drug trafficking. He claimed he was at risk of retaliation from criminal organizations because he had co-operated with the French police. Although the majority of the Court held there was insufficient evidence of danger to support finding a violation, it stated:

[171] *Chahal, supra* n. 166, paras. 103–5.
[172] 17 Dec. 1996, 24 E.H.R.R. 278.
[173] *Id.* paras. 44–7.
[174] 29 Apr. 1997, 26 E.H.R.R. 29.

Owing to the absolute character of the right guaranteed, the Court does not rule out the possibility that Article 3 of the Convention may also apply where the danger does not emanate
from persons or groups of persons who are not public officials. However, it must be shown that
the risk is real and that the authorities of the receiving state are not able to obviate the risk by
providing appropriate protection.[175]

The House of Lords has held that an expulsion cannot violate the Convention by
virtue of a risk of harm from private actors unless it can be shown that the receiving
state does not provide a reasonable level of protection against such harm.[176]

The holding in *D. v. United Kingdom* that the state is responsible for the suffering
to be expected at the destination of the deportee, even when that suffering is caused,
in the first instance, not by deliberate human action, but by disease and poverty, is in
tension with the holding in *Pretty v. United Kingdom*,[177] where the Court said a state's
treaty obligation was engaged by such suffering only when the state did some affirmative act to exacerbate the condition. In *D* that was the act of expulsion. In *Pretty*, on
the other hand, there was no state 'treatment' that contributed to the applicant's illness
and it was under no positive obligation to allow the applicant a legal licence to alleviate
her situation by securing assistance in suicide. The upshot of the two cases, however,
seems to be that a state party is barred from acting to send a person into a situation
elsewhere that it was entirely free to tolerate in its own country. In *S.C.C. v. Sweden*,
the Court held inadmissible an application from an HIV infected woman who had not
yet contracted AIDS.[178]

In *N. v. Secretary of State for the Home Department*,[179] the House of Lords refused
to apply the holding in *D* to overrule the Secretary's refusal to allow a Ugandan to
remain in residence, although she was suffering from AIDS and had presented medical opinion that her prognosis at home was poor. Lord Hope of Craighead understood
D to be limited to individuals in the direst physical situation, people in the 'final stages
of an incurable disease'. Although he found questionable the European Court's focus
on the relatively healthy condition of an applicant at the time of the adjudication, as
opposed to that which might be expected once beneficial treatment was terminated,
he found the appellant ineligible to make an Article 3 claim since she was not yet in
critical condition.[180]

In the same opinion, Lord Hope referred to the judgment in *D* as 'extending the
application of Article 3 beyond the extension which had been previously recognized'.[181]
To go further 'would have the effect of offering all those in appellant's condition a right
of asylum in the country until such time as the standard of medical facilities available

[175] *Id.* para. 40. *See also N v. Finland*, 30 Nov. 2005, 43 E.H.R.R. 12.
[176] *R. (Bagdanavicius) v. Secretary of State for the Home Dept.* [2005] U.K.H.L. 38, [2005] A.C. 668.
[177] 29 April 2002, 35 E.H.R.R. 1, para. 52. *Pretty* is discussed in the previous chapter in connection with
the claimed violation of Article 2.
[178] 15 Feb. 2000.
[179] [2005] U.K.H.L. 31, [2005] 2 A.C. 296.
[180] *Id.* paras. 51–3.
[181] *Id.* para. 30.

in their home countries for the treatment of HIV/AIDS has reached that which is available in Europe'.[182]

The Strasbourg Court has extended the principle of the *D* case to situations where the applicant was suffering from a mental illness and where removal from the respondent state would seriously increase the risk of suicide,[183] although it has not yet found a violation of Article 3 in such circumstances. The English Court of Appeal, in reviewing suicide cases in this context, has focused on the state of facilities for treatment in the receiving state.[184]

3. THE U.N. REFUGEE CONVENTION

Many of the cases concerning deportation or expulsion dealt with under Article 3 also raise questions under the 1951 Geneva Convention and 1967 Protocol Relating to the Status of Refugees.[185] That Convention defines refugees as those who have left their country because of a 'well-founded fear of persecution'. Article 33 prohibits a state from expelling refugees if it would entail a return to their country of origin where their 'life or freedom would be threatened' on account of their 'race, religion, nationality, membership of a particular social group or political opinion'. These requirements plainly overlap with a European state's obligations under Article 3 of the European Convention, as interpreted by the European Court. The European Convention, however, may be somewhat narrower in its protection. A reasonable threat of execution or imprisonment on prohibited grounds, triggers a right of asylum under the Geneva Convention and Protocol. But neither imprisonment nor capital punishment alone have been held to constitute 'torture, inhuman or degrading' treatment or punishment under Article 3. Therefore, a person who had a proper claim under the Convention on Refugees might not be able to pursue that claim through the Strasbourg institutions. Of course, the threat of imprisonment for the specified reasons might give rise to a claim of violation of Article 14 on the right to equal treatment, in conjunction with Article 3.

On the other hand, in some circumstances, a claim may be cognizable under Article 3 which would fail under the Convention on Refugees. Article 33(2) of that Convention denies its benefits to a 'refugee whom there are reasonable grounds for regarding as a danger to the security of the country in which he is, or who, having been convicted by a final judgment of a particularly serious crime, constitutes a danger to

---

[182] *Id.* at para. 53.

[183] *Bensaid v. United Kingdom*, 6 Feb. 2001, 33 E.H.R.R. 10.

[184] Compare *Tozlukaya v. Secretary of State for the Home Dept.* [2006] EWCA Civ. 379 (deportation to Germany) with *A.J. (Liberia) v. Secretary of State for the Home Dept.* [2006] EWCA Civ. 1736 (deportation to Liberia).

[185] 189 U.N.T.S. 2545; 606 U.N.T.S. 8791. The Convention and Protocol are extensively discussed in J. C. Hathaway, *The Rights of Refugees Under International Law* (2005).

the community of that country'. As noted, the protection of Article 3 being absolute, it has been held to attach without regard to the public safety interests of the deporting state. Violations have been found even where a state has asserted risks to national security[186] and where the applicant has been convicted of serious crimes.[187]

D. THE DEATH PENALTY

As discussed in Section C of the previous chapter, the death penalty has more or less disappeared from the legal systems that are party to the European Convention as a result of Protocols 6 and 13 as well as the independent decisions of the parties. Concomitant with, and partly because of, these developments, the Strasbourg Court has suggested, but not held, that the imposition of the death penalty violates Article 3's prohibition on 'inhuman and degrading treatment'.[188] On this view the language of Article 2, expressly recognizing the permissibility of capital punishment 'in the execution of a sentence of a court following... conviction of a crime', had been 'abrogate[d], or at the very least modif[ied]' by the agreement on these subsequent protocols.[189]

Prior to these developments, the Court had considered the compatibility with Article 3 not of the death penalty itself but of the 'death row phenomenon', the long wait, largely caused by appeals and other legal proceedings, which typically attends the execution of death sentences. That doctrine will continue to have relevance in cases like *Soering*, where the claimed violation involved extradition or expulsion to a state where the applicant may be exposed to such treatment. In the *Soering* case, discussed above, the Court agreed with the applicant's contention that the expected wait on death row, estimated to be 6 to 8 years in Virginia, exposed the condemned person to extended and severe fear, stress and anguish and, therefore, amounted to a violation of Article 3.

The rationale of *Soering* calls for an examination of the question of whether the circumstances surrounding an extradition or expulsion indicated a 'real risk' of torture or inhuman or degrading treatment or punishment in the destination state. The Court has held that the applicant must present specific evidence of the risk to him or her and may not rely solely on generalized reports of human rights violations.[190] So, when a state gives credible assurances that the death penalty will not be imposed, no case for a 'Soering' type violation, premised on a risk of execution, can be made out.[191] The Court has also held that a nine-year detention of a condemned prisoner did not implicate the death row phenomenon since the state (Bulgaria) had established a moratorium on executions that continued in force until the death penalty was abolished nine years

---

[186] *Chahal, supra* n. 166, at para. 80.
[187] *Ahmed, supra* n. 172, at para. 41.
[188] *Öcalan v. Turkey*, 12 March 2003, 37 E.H.R.R. 10, discussed at Chapter 4(D) *supra*.
[189] *Id.* at para. 203.
[190] *Mamatkulov & Askanov v. Turkey*, 4 Feb. 2005, 41 E.H.R.R. 25, paras. 72–5.
[191] *Shamayev & Others v. Georgia and Russia, supra* n. 168, at paras. 343–5.

later. While it acknowledged that the applicant might have experienced 'uncertainty, fear and anxiety', these must have diminished as the moratorium continued.[192] The Court has never extensively addressed the argument that an applicant could not complain of a delay caused by his own legal efforts to escape execution.[193]

That issue was addressed extensively in a 1993 judgment of the Judicial Committee of the Privy Council. The appellants in *Pratt v. Attorney-General for Jamaica*[194] had endured a delay of 12 years after the pronouncing of a sentence of death. The Privy Council, citing the *Soering* case, held this amounted to the infliction of 'inhuman or degrading punishment or other treatment' in contravention of Section 17 of the Jamaican Constitution. The Committee noted the 'instinctive revulsion' against hanging a person after such a long period. It agreed that, to the extent the extended time was due 'entirely to the fault of the accused, such as an escape from custody or frivolous and time wasting resort to legal procedures which amount to an abuse of process, the accused cannot be allowed to take advantage of the delay'.[195] But the same was not true where the accused merely exploited legitimate procedures for review of his conviction and sentence. In such a case:

a state that wishes to retain capital punishment must accept the responsibility of ensuring that execution follows as swiftly as practicable after sentence, allowing a reasonable time for appeal and consideration of reprieve. It is part of the human condition that a condemned man will take every opportunity to save his life through the use of the appellate procedure. If the appellate procedure enables the prisoner to prolong the appellate hearings over a period of years, the fault is to be attributed to the appellate system that permits such delay and not to the prisoner who takes advantages of it.[196]

The Judicial Committee noted that, given the normal time for appellate review of death sentences, any delay beyond five years might be presumed to be inordinate.[197] In a later case, the Committee held that the relevant period ought not to include time spent in custody before trial 'since the state of mind of the person in question during this earlier period is not the agony of a man facing execution'.[198] This conclusion was

---

[192] *G.B. v. Bulgaria*, supra n. 22, paras. 77–80.

[193] For a comparative survey of judicial approaches to the 'death row phenomenon' *see* Patrick Hudson, 'Does the Death Row Phenomenon Violate a Prisoner's Human Rights Under International Law?', 11 *Eur. J. Int'l Law* 833 (2000).

[194] [1993] 4 All E.R. 769. P.C.

[195] *Id.* at 783.

[196] *Id.* at 786.

[197] In a subsequent case arising in the Bahamas (which has an identical constitutional provision) the Privy Council held that this period should be only three and one half years since no account had to be taken of a possible resort to the United Nations Human Rights Committee, the Bahamas not being party to the International Convention on Civil and Political Rights, *Henfield v. Attorney-General* [1997] A.C. 413, 428. When, later, it was pointed out that a parallel petition to the Inter-American Commission on Human Rights was available in the Bahamas, the Board reinstituted the 5-year presumption. *Fisher v. Minister of Public Safety* [1998] A.C. 673.

[198] For commentary on these cases *see* S. C. R. McIntosh, *Caribbean Constitutional Reform: Rethinking the West Indian Polity* (2002); Sir Louis Blom-Cooper & C. Gelber, 'The Privy Council and the Death Penalty in the Caribbean', [1998] *Europ. Hum. Rts. L. Rev.* 386.

disputed by Lord Steyn in dissenting for reasons relying extensively on the Article 3 jurisprudence of the European Court of Human Rights:

It is true that in contrast [to the condemned person] the man still awaiting trial on a charge of murder is assailed by other uncertainties; he hopes to be acquitted. For him the spectre of the macabre meeting with the hangman is somewhat more distant. ... But from the time of his arrest and charge, or at least from the time of his judicial committal for trial on a charge of murder, he is in real jeopardy of being sentenced to death and hanged. And in cases like the present he will be held in prison conditions where he will be exposed to the terror of execution from time to time. Like a distinguished author in this field who argues that presentence delay is relevant, I too would say that 'it is here that the horror of contemplating the sentence would normally begin'.[199]

Apart from the 'death row phenomenon', the Privy Council has recently held that a mandatory death penalty for certain categories of murder was 'inhuman or degrading punishment' in violation of three Caribbean constitutions. The Judicial Committee opined that these constitutional guarantees incorporated the idea of proportionality of culpability and punishment. That requirement could only be satisfied if some provision were made for taking account of mitigating factors in individual cases.[200] The results in these cases have been understood as reinforcing the movement for the abolition of the Privy Council appeal in the Caribbean and its replacement with a Caribbean Court of Appeal.[201]

The United States has ratified the International Covenant on Civil and Political Rights which prohibits 'torture or...cruel, inhuman or degrading treatment or punishment'.[202] It has, however, entered a reservation, partly motivated by the 'death row phenomenon' cases, to the effect that it understands the provision only to prevent actions amounting to ' "cruel and unusual punishment" prohibited by the Fifth, Eighth and/or Fourteenth Amendment to the Constitution of the United States'.[203] A U.S. Senate report on the Covenant recommending the reservation explicitly referred to interpretations of the European Court of Human Rights and the United Nations Human Rights Committee to the effect that 'prolonged judicial proceedings in cases involving capital punishment could in certain circumstances constitute such treatment'.[204]

The United States reservation to the Torture Convention discussed above was more explicit, insisting that the treaty did not restrict executions 'including any constitutional period of confinement prior to the imposition of the death penalty'.[205]

[199] [1998] A.C. 673, 691.
[200] *Reyes v. R* [2002] 2 A.C. 235 (P.C.) (Belize); *R. v. Hughes* [2002] 2 A.C. 259 (P.C.) 1088 (St. Lucia); *Fox v. R.* [2002] 2 A.C. 284 (P.C.) (St. Kitts and Nevis). Compare the American death penalty cases to the same effect discussed in the previous chapter.
[201] Simeon C. R. Mcintosh, *Caribbean Constitutional Reform: Rethinking the West Indian Polity* (2002); Simeon C. R. Mcintosh, *Fundamental Rights and Democratic Governance* (2004).
[202] 1057 U.N.T.S. 407, Art. 7.
[203] 138 Cong. Rec. S4781-01, S4783 (daily ed. 12 Apr. 1992).
[204] S. Exec. Rpt. No. 102–23 at 12 (1992).
[205] 136 Cong. Rec. 36192–36199 (Oct. 27, 1990).

United States courts have consistently rejected claims that long delays in executing death sentences violate the Eighth Amendment's bar on 'cruel and unusual punishment'. The typical judicial reaction to this claim is captured in the opinion of a
Federal Court of Appeals that a defendant who has 'benefitted from this careful and
meticulous process [of appellate and collateral review]...cannot now complain that
the expensive and laborous process...which exists to protect him has violated other of
his rights'.[206] At least three condemned prisoners have attempted to raise the issue in
the United States Supreme Court but the Court has refused to take the cases for review.
In all these cases, however, at least some of the Justices have dissented, expressing
the view that the 'death row phenomenon' presents a serious constitutional issue. The
most extended discussion is in the dissenting and concurring decisions in *Knight v.
Florida*,[207] concerning the execution of two prisoners who had spent 19 and 25 years
respectively on death row. Justice Breyer, dissenting from the denial of petitions for
certiorari review, cited a study showing that 35 per cent of inmates on death row
attempted suicide. He also relied on a number of foreign holdings, including *Soering*,
Pratt and cases from India and Zimbabwe in which the courts 'considered roughly
comparable questions under roughly comparable legal standards'. To the extent the
delays were caused by the petitioners' own action, moreover, a substantial part of that
period was the time necessary to consider their successful challenge to what were, at
the time, unconstitutional procedures.[208] Justice Thomas, on the other hand derided
the proposition 'that a defendant can avail himself of the panoply of appellate and
collateral procedures and then complain when his execution is delayed.... Ironically,
the neoteric Eighth Amendment claim proposed by Justice Breyer would further prolong collateral review by giving virtually every capital prisoner yet another ground on
which to challenge and delay his execution'.[209]

E. ARTICLE 4: SLAVERY AND FORCED
LABOUR

Article 4 prohibits two categories of practices. Paragraph (1) deals with 'slavery or
servitude'. The prohibition is absolute. Like Article 3, it provides for no possible
justifications of infringements of the right. Also like Articles 2 and 3, it may not be
suspended or limited under Article 15(1) even for cases of emergency threatening the

---

[206] *White v. Johnson*, 79 F. 3d 432, 439 (5th Cir. 1996).
[207] 528 U.S. 990 (1999). *See Lackey v. Texas*, 514 U.S. 1045 (1995) (Stevens J joined in part by Breyer J);
Gomez v. Ruiz, 519 U.S. 919 (1996) (Stevens J joined by Breyer J, dissenting). *See also Ceja v. Stewart*, 134 F.
3d 1368 (9th Cir. 1998). In the *Ceja* case, in which the petitioner had been on death row for 23 years, Judge
Fletcher entered a dissent relying in part on the *Soering* case.
[208] *Id*. at 993–8.
[209] *Id*. at 990–3.

life of the nation. Paragraph (2) concerns the performance of 'forced or compulsory labour'. This prohibition is narrowed in paragraph (3) by the exclusion of four categories of obligatory service.[210] Unlike slavery or servitude, forced labour is not excluded from Article 15. That possibility, however, is made superfluous since Article 4(3)(c) itself allows for work required 'in case of an emergency or calamity threatening the life or well being of the community'.[211]

The European Court has issued very few judgments concerning Article 4. There has been, therefore, little elaboration of the nature of the practices specified. It has been suggested that while 'forced or compulsory labour' refers to particular activities, 'slavery and servitude' refer to personal status.[212] As to 'slavery and servitude', the Court has only stated that it does not refer to treatment imposed pursuant to deprivation of liberty that is proper under Article 5 so long as it is not 'a "particularly serious" form of "denial of freedom"'.[213] From this caveat we can infer that some kinds of punishments for crime, even if procedurally perfect, might still be slavery and servitude. While we can only speculate as to what those conditions might amount to, we may suppose that the denial of freedom must at least be more onerous than requiring 'work in the ordinary course of detention' which, in Art. 4(2)(a), is defined out of the less protected category of forced labour.

Beyond this, there is only slightly more elaboration of the concept of 'forced labour' and its exclusions. Mainly, the Court has dealt with the non-obvious question of what kinds of coercion to labour make it 'forced'. More particularly, it has considered whether or not Article 4(2) is engaged when the government requires work as the price of some benefit. It has said, for example, that making release from prison conditional on saving a certain sum of money paid for work done 'is not far away from an obligation in the strict sense of the term'.[214]

A fuller discussion of this issue was provided in *Van der Mussele v. Belgium*,[215] involving the obligation of pupil advocates to provide representation for indigent clients without compensation. The Court adopted the definition of 'forced or compulsory labour' in Convention No. 29 of the International Labour Organization: 'all work or service which is exacted from any person under the menace of any penalty and for which the said person has not offered himself voluntarily'.[216] As to the presence or absence of

---

[210] Although Art. 4(3)(a) refers to work done in detention 'imposed according to the provisions of Article 5', the Court has not read this as requiring that the detention in which the work was exacted must be in perfect compliance with Article 5. Rather it has held that the exception might apply so long as the detention was initiated in compliance with Art. 5(1). The fact that a detainee could not obtain periodic review of the legality of detention as required by Art. 5(4) did not prevent the state from relying on this exception. *DeWilde, Ooms and Versyp v. Belgium (Vagrancy Cases)*, 18 June 1971, 1 E.H.R.R. 373, para. 89.

[211] Emergency derogation in Article 15 is available when 'war or other public emergency threaten[s] the life of the nation'. It also imposes a continuing duty of notification on the derogating party.

[212] J. E. S. Fawcett, *The Application of the European Convention on Human Rights* 55 (1987).

[213] *Van Droogenbroeck v. Belgium*, 24 June 1982, 4 E.H.R.R. 443, para. 58 quoting the Commission Report on the same application, 9 July 1980, paras. 79–80.

[214] *Id.* para. 59. The Court found it unnecessary to resolve this question since, even if required, the work qualified under Art. 4(2)(a).

[215] 23 November 1983, 6 E.H.R.R. 163.

[216] *Id.* para. 32.

a 'menace of penalty', the Court concluded that the threat of being denied registration as an advocate qualified as a sufficiently serious consequence of non-compliance.
Likewise it decided that the fact that the prospective advocate entered the course of
qualification with notice of these requirements was not itself sufficient to establish
the voluntary character of the work. '[H]e had to accept this requirement, whether he
wanted to or not, in order to become an avocat and his consent was determined by the
normal conditions of exercise of the profession at the relevant time. Nor should it be
overlooked that what he gave was an acceptance of a legal regime of a general character'.
The Court announced a test requiring first, that the work be performed against the
person's will. Beyond that, it noted (unhelpfully) that the 'court will have regard to all
the circumstances of the case in the light of the underlying objectives of Article 4'.

In the *Van der Mussele* case, the Court acknowledged that services rendered in
order to obtain professional qualification would not be voluntary if they imposed a
burden that was 'excessive or disproportionate to the advantages attached to the future
exercise of that profession.... [T]his could apply, for example, in the case of a service
unconnected with the profession in question'. This definition, it will be noted, was
appropriate for determining what was 'forced or compulsory'. It was not an application of the exclusions in Article 4(3). Since, however, those exclusions purported to
clarify rather than limit the meaning of 'forced or compulsory labour', the Court held
it proper to refer to them in interpreting the meaning of that term. It inferred that all
of the exclusions were 'grounded on the governing ideas of the general interest, social
solidarity and what is in the normal or ordinary course of affairs'. Given the limited
burden imposed on the applicant, the advantages accruing to him from rendering
those services, their contribution to social solidarity and their similarity to 'normal
civic obligations', the obligations did not constitute compulsory or forced labour. The
Court noted, however, that it had no occasion to rule on the claim 'that the almost
routine allocation of pro-Deo cases to pupil avocats might not be fully consonant with
the need to provide effective legal aid to impecunious litigants'.[217]

Slavery and involuntary servitude were abolished in the United States by the adoption of the Thirteenth Amendment in 1865 at the close of the Civil War. The text of the
amendment excepts 'punishment for crime'. Unlike most constitutional provisions,
the Thirteenth Amendment has been held to apply directly to private relationships.[218]
Judicial interpretation has led to the application of the amendment to 'peonage' systems
as well as to an explicit legal establishment of slavery. 'Peonage' refers to a complex
of laws—such as ones imposing criminal penalties for breach of labour contracts or
obliging convicted criminal defendants to work off their fines in the employ of a private person—that had the effect of requiring long term forced service. They were used
in many southern states after the Civil War to re-impose an effective slavery regime on
the recently liberated African-Americans.[219]

---

[217] Paras. 36–40.
[218] The doctrine of 'positive obligation' under the European Convention, discussed in Chapter 8(B) *infra*,
also would extend the reach of Article 4 to include private slavery and forced labour.
[219] *Bailey v. Alabama*, 219 U.S.219 (1911); *United States v. Reynolds*, 235 U.S. 133 (1914).

Other than the mention of criminal convictions, the Thirteenth Amendment, unlike Article 4 of the Convention, does not carve out permitted categories of forced service. Nevertheless, the Supreme Court has interpreted the amendment as not reaching the same kind of activities. It has held that military conscription, prison labour and even obligatory work on public road maintenance are not reached by the amendment.[220] The most significant impact of the Thirteenth Amendment may be in the power it grants Congress to enforce it by 'appropriate legislation'. The Supreme Court has held that this allows Congress to eliminate the 'badges and incidents of slavery'. In light of the historically racial character of American slavery, this has been interpreted as authorizing statutes eliminating racial discrimination by private persons in contract and property transactions.[221]

[220] *Arver v. United States*, 245 U.S. 366 (1918); *United States v. Reynolds*, 235 U.S. 133, 149–50 (1914); *Butler v. Perry*, 240 U.S. 328 (1916).

[221] *Jones v. Alfred H. Mayer Co.*, 392 U.S. 409 (1968); *Sullivan v. Little Hunting Park. Inc.*, 396 U.S. 229 (1969).

6

FREEDOM OF EXPRESSION; ASSOCIATION

ARTICLE 10

1. Everyone has the right to freedom of expression. This right shall include freedom to hold opinions and to receive and impart information and ideas without interference by public authority and regardless of frontiers. This article shall not prevent States from requiring the licensing of broadcasting, television or cinema enterprises.

2. The exercise of these freedoms, since it carries with it duties and responsibilities, may be subject to such formalities, conditions, restrictions or penalties as are prescribed by law and are necessary in a democratic society, in the interests of national security, territorial integrity or public safety, for the prevention of disorder or crime, for the protection of health or morals, for the protection of the reputation or rights of others, for preventing the disclosure of information received in confidence, or for maintaining the authority and impartiality of the judiciary.

ARTICLE 11

1. Everyone has the right to freedom of peaceful assembly and to freedom of association with others, including the right to form and to join trade unions for the protection of his interests.

2. No restrictions shall be placed on the exercise of these rights other than such as are prescribed by law and are necessary in a democratic society in the interests of national security or public safety, for the prevention of disorder or crime, for the protection of health or morals or for the protection of the rights and freedoms of others. This Article shall not prevent the imposition of lawful restrictions on the exercise of these rights by members of the armed forces, of the police or of the administration of the State.

A. INTRODUCTION

The freedom to express one's opinion must be the most universally recognized 'human right'. A 1978 survey of 142 world constitutions found that 124, or 87.3 per cent, contained a free expression guarantee. (In contrast, only 66, or 46.5 per cent, prohibited torture or cruel, inhuman or degrading treatment.)[1] Versions of this right were found in the earliest modern constitutions including a number of the eighteenth-century constitutions of the American states, Article 11 of the French Declaration of the Rights of Man and Citizen, and the First Amendment to the United States Constitution.[2] Article 10 of the European Convention for the Protection of Human Rights took as a model Article 19 of the Universal Declaration of Human Rights[3] from which it departs in only minor respects.

The justifications for special protection of expression have sometimes been placed in two categories. In the first, speech is recognized as valuable, because public debate is a useful instrument for achieving other social objectives. In the second category, personal expression is seen as a human good in itself.

In so far as freedom of speech is valued instrumentally, it has been associated with two related objectives. Most broadly, it has been justified as the best way of assuring the discovery of truth. The uninhibited clash and consequent testing of opinions and ideas is claimed to comprise the best way to increase knowledge. This belief is well summarized in a much quoted passage from Milton's *Aeropagitica*, itself a banned work:

[T]hough all the winds of doctrine were let loose to play upon the earth, so truth be in the field, we do injuriously, by licensing and prohibiting, to misdoubt her strength. Let her and falsehood grapple; whoever knew truth put to the worse in a free and open encounter?[4]

Much the same idea was elaborated by John Stuart Mill in the nineteenth century[5] and captured by Justice Oliver Wendell Holmes' metaphor of the 'marketplace of ideas'.[6]

A narrower version of the instrumental view of free expression focuses on its utility in the functioning of a representative democracy. The framers of the First Amendment, said Justice Brandeis, believed 'in the power of reason as applied through public discussion [so] they eschewed silence coerced by law'.[7] Democratic self-government depends upon the ability of electors to choose representatives who best reflect their own convictions and interests and on the ability of the representatives to understand the concerns

---

[1] H. van Maarseveen & Ger van der Tang, *Written Constitutions: A Computerized Comparative Study* 105, 110 (1978). About the same number of constitutions protected some combination of the related freedoms of assembly, association, opinion, thought, conscience or religion. *Id.* at 109–11.

[2] *See* Chapter 1(B), *supra*.

[3] *Id.*

[4] John Milton, *Aeropagitica: A Speech for the Liberty of Unlicensed Printing to the Parliament of England* (1644).

[5] John Stuart Mill, *On Liberty* (1859).

[6] *Abrams v. United States*, 250 U.S. 616, 630 (1919) (Holmes J dissenting).

[7] *Whitney v. California*, 274 U.S. 357, 375–6 (1927) (concurring opinion).

of their constituents. Neither the character of the issues at stake nor the effectiveness of representation is possible without a thorough airing of facts and arguments.[8]

The second category of justification for free expression turns on the idea that the free communications of feelings, opinions and ideas is essential to the full development of human personality in society. The desires to persuade, to impress, to assert or to inspire have always been powerful in every social situation, and their suppression has often been thought to stunt some of the most admirable aspects of human nature. Likewise, the chance to be challenged, provoked or encouraged by the ideas of others may be critical to the formation of personal beliefs and are at the core of our capacity for self-definition.[9]

These two kinds of justifications for freedom of expression, which might be called the instrumental and the intrinsic, are evidenced in judicial opinions applying the relevant constitutional guarantees. Thus, Justice Brandeis, in his separate opinion in the United States Supreme Court judgment in *Whitney v. California*[10] spoke of the American founders' appreciation of 'liberty both as an end and as a means'.[11] An early judgment of the German Constitutional Court referred to free expression as 'the most immediate manifestation of the human personality' as well as indispensable for 'the contest of opinions that forms the lifeblood of [a democratic] order'.[12] The Supreme Court of Canada summarized the values underlying the protection of free expression in the following way:

(1) seeking and attaining the truth is an inherently good activity; (2) participation in social and political decision-making is to be fostered and encouraged; and (3) the diversity in forms of individual self-fulfillment and human flourishing ought to be cultivated in an essentially tolerant, indeed welcoming, environment not only for the sake of those who convey a meaning, but also for the sake of those to whom it is conveyed.[13]

B. JUSTIFYING LIMITS ON EXPRESSION

The nature of the 'expression' protected by Article 10 is not always self-evident. In particular, problems may be expected to arise in distinguishing expression from action (intentionally symbolic or otherwise), which is associated with communication

---

[8] *See* Alexander Meiklejohn, *Free Speech and Its Relation to Self-Government* (1948).

[9] *See* T. Scanlon, 'A Theory of Freedom of Expression', 1 *Phil. & Pub. Aff.* 204 (1972); M. Redish, 'The Value of Free Speech', 130 *U. Pa. L. Rev.* 591 (1982).

[10] 274 U.S. 357 (1927).

[11] *Id.* at 375.

[12] *Lüth* Judgment 7 BverfGe 198, 208 (1958) quoted in and translated by D. Currie, *The Constitution of the Federal Republic of Germany* 175 (1999).

[13] *Irwin Toy Ltd. v. Attorney-General (Quebec)* [1989] 1 S.C.R. 927, 976.

of a viewpoint.[14] Unlike its decisions on Article 3,[15] however, the European Court's interpretation of Article 10 has not focused on questions of definition. Rather, as the materials in this chapter illustrate, the Court has more intensively engaged the question of when an admitted public interference with expression may be permissible under Article 10. We have already seen one example of this kind of analysis in *Sunday Times v. United Kingdom*[16] in which the Court rejected a claim that a finding of contempt of court against a newspaper for publishing material related to pending litigation was necessary for 'maintaining the authority and impartiality of the judiciary'.

This presupposes that expression cannot be protected absolutely. It is uncontestable that the utterance of some kinds of language in some situations may impose grave social harms. Thus, to take an example from American constitutional law, no one would question the right of a government to prohibit the wartime 'publication of the sailing dates of transports or the number and location of troops'.[17] More controversial cases are presented by judgments of the Canadian Supreme Court upholding legislation criminalizing speech that promotes hatred and denigration of ethnic or racial groups[18] or pornography that depicts violent sexual activity.[19] The Convention explicitly provides that limitations on the right of free expression do not violate the Convention, if they are for one of the purposes and meet the other criteria listed in Article 10(2). In very large measure, the law of free expression under the Convention is the law of Article 10(2).

1. HANDYSIDE V. UNITED KINGDOM

Judgment of 7 December, 1976
1 E.H.R.R. 737

. . .

[The applicant published *The Little Red Schoolbook*.]

11. ...The book had first been published in Denmark in 1969 and subsequently, after translation and with certain adaptations, in Belgium, Finland, France, the Federal Republic of Germany, Greece, Iceland, Italy, the Netherlands, Norway, Sweden and Switzerland as well as several non-European countries. Furthermore it circulated freely in Austria and Luxembourg.

---

[14] This has been a persistent issue in American constitutional cases. *See*, e.g., *United States v. O'Brien*, 391 U.S. 367 (1968) (draft card burning not protected); John H. Ely, 'Flag Desecration: A Case Study in the Roles of Categorization and Balancing in First Amendment Analysis', 88 *Harv. L. Rev.* 1482 (1975).

[15] *See* Chapter 5, *supra*.

[16] 26 Apr. 1979, 2 E.H.R.R. 245 reproduced in part in Chapter 3(B) *supra*.

[17] *Near v. Minnesota*, 236 U.S. 697, 716 (1931) (dicta).

[18] *R. v. Keegstra* [1990] 3 S.C.R. 697.

[19] *R. v. Butler* [1992] 1 S.C.R. 452.

12. After having arranged for the translation of the book into English the applicant prepared an edition for the United Kingdom with the help of a group of children and teachers. He had previously consulted a variety of people about the value of the book and intended publication in the United Kingdom on 1 April 1971 ...

[The applicant was convicted of violating the Obscene Publication Act. He was fined and the books in his possession were ordered destroyed.] ...

20. The original English language edition of the book, priced at thirty pence a copy, had altogether 208 pages. It contained an introduction headed 'All grown-ups are paper tigers', an 'Introduction to the British edition', and chapters on the following subjects: Education, Learning, Teachers, Pupils and The System. The chapter on Pupils contained a twenty-six page section concerning 'Sex' which included the following sub-sections: Masturbation, Orgasm, Intercourse and petting, Contraceptives, Wet dreams, Menstruation, Child-molesters or 'dirty old men', Pornography, Impotence, Homosexuality, Normal and abnormal, Find out more, Venereal diseases, Abortion, Legal and illegal abortion, Remember, Methods of abortion, Addresses for help and advice on sexual matters. The Introduction stated: 'This book is meant to be a reference book. The idea is not to read it straight through, but to use the list of contents to find and read about the things you're interested in or want to know more about. Even if you're at a particularly progressive school you should find a lot of ideas in the book for improving things'.

21. The applicant had planned the distribution of the book through the ordinary bookselling channels although it was said at the appeal hearing to have been accepted that the work was intended for, and intended to be made available to, school-children of the age of twelve and upwards ...

[The Obscene Publications Acts (the '1959/1964 Acts') defined an item as obscene if its effect,

'if taken as a whole, [was] such as to tend to deprave and corrupt persons who are likely, having regard to all relevant circumstances, to read, see or hear the matter contained or embodied in it'.

A conviction could be avoided if the work involved was

'justified as being for the public good on the ground that it is in the interests of science, literature, art or learning, or of other objects of general concern'.

The defence could be established by evidence of the opinion of 'artistic, literary or scientific' experts.] ...

30. Concerning the Schoolbook itself, the [British] court first stressed that it was intended for children passing through a highly critical stage of their development. At such a time a very high degree of responsibility ought to be exercised by the courts. In the present case, they had before them, as something said to be a perfectly responsible adult opinion, a work of an extreme kind, unrelieved by any indication that there were any alternative views; this was something which detracted from the opportunity for children to form a balanced view on some of the very strong advice given therein.

31. The court then briefly examined the background. For example, looking at the book as a whole, marriage was very largely ignored. Mixing a very one-sided opinion with fact and

purporting to be a book of reference, it would tend to undermine, for a very considerable portion of children, many of the influences, such as those of parents, the Churches and youth organisations, which might otherwise provide the restraint and sense of responsibility for one-self which found inadequate expression in the book....

32. ...As indications of what it considered to result in a tendency to deprave and corrupt, the court quoted or referred to the following:

A. The passage headed 'Be yourself':

'Maybe you smoke pot or go to bed with your boyfriend or girlfriend—and don't tell your parents or teachers, either because you don't dare to or just because you want to keep it secret.
   Don't feel ashamed or guilty about doing things you really want to do and think are right just because your parents or teachers might disapprove. A lot of these things will be more important to you later in life than the things that are "approved of".'

The objectionable point was that there was no reference there to the illegality of smoking pot which was only to be found many pages further on in an entirely different part of the book. Similarly there was no specific mention at all in the book of the illegality of sexual intercourse by a boy who has attained the age of fourteen and a girl who has not yet attained sixteen. It had to be remembered that the Schoolbook was indicated as a work of reference and that one looked up the part which one wanted rather than read it as a whole book....

33. The court concluded 'in the light of the whole of the book, that this book or this article on sex or this section or chapter on pupils, whichever one chooses as an article, looked at as a whole does tend to deprave and corrupt a significant number, significant proportion, of the children likely to read it'. Such children would, it was satisfied, include a very substantial number aged under sixteen....

The court asked itself whether, granted the degree of indecency which it found, the good likely to result from the Schoolbook was such that it ought, nevertheless, to be published in the public interest; it regretfully came to the conclusion that the burden on the appellant to show that 'publication of the article in question is justified as being for the public good' had not been discharged....

43. The various measures challenged—the applicant's criminal conviction, the seizure and subsequent forfeiture and destruction of the matrix and of hundreds of copies of the schoolbook—were without any doubt, and the Government did not deny it, 'interferences by public authority' in the exercise of his freedom of expression which is guaranteed by paragraph 1 of the text cited above. Such interferences entail a 'violation' of Article 10 if they do not fall within one of the exceptions provided for in paragraph 2, which is accordingly of decisive importance in this case ...

46. Sharing the view of the Government and the unanimous opinion of the Commission, the Court first finds that the 1959/1964 Acts have an aim that is legitimate under Article 10 § 2, namely, the protection of morals in a democratic society. Only this latter purpose is relevant in this case since the object of the said Acts—to wage war on 'obscene' publications, defined by their tendency to 'deprave and corrupt'—is linked far more closely to the protection of morals than to any of the further purposes permitted by Article 10 § 2 ...

47. ...The Commission's report and the subsequent hearings before the Court in June 1976 brought to light clear-cut differences of opinion on a crucial problem, namely, how to

determine whether the actual 'restrictions' and 'penalties' complained of by the applicant were 'necessary in a democratic society' 'for the protection of morals'. According to the Government and the majority of the Commission, the Court has only to ensure that the English courts acted reasonably, in good faith and within the limits of the margin of appreciation left to the Contracting States by Article 10 § 2. On the other hand, the minority of the Commission sees the Court's task as being not to review the Inner London Quarter Sessions judgment but to examine the Schoolbook directly in the light of the Convention and of nothing but the Convention.

48. The Court points out that the machinery of protection established by the Convention is subsidiary to the national systems safeguarding human rights. The Convention leaves to each Contracting State, in the first place, the task of securing the rights and freedoms it enshrines. The institutions created by it make their own contribution to this task but they become involved only through contentious proceedings and once all domestic remedies have been exhausted.

These observations apply, notably, to Article 10 § 2. In particular, it is not possible to find in the domestic law of the various Contracting States a uniform European conception of morals. The view taken by their respective laws of the requirements of morals varies from time to time and from place to place, especially in our era which is characterized by a rapid and far-reaching evolution of opinions on the subject. By reason of their direct and continuous contact with the vital forces of their countries, State authorities are in principle in a better position than the international judge to give an opinion on the exact content of these requirements as well as on the 'necessity' of a 'restriction' or 'penalty' intended to meet them. The Court notes at this juncture that, whilst the adjective 'necessary', within the meaning of Article 10 § 2, is not synonymous with 'indispensable' (cf., in Article 2 § 2 and 6 § 1, the words 'absolutely necessary' and 'strictly necessary' and, in Article 15 § 1, the phrase 'to the extent strictly required by the exigencies of the situation'), neither has it the flexibility of such expressions as 'admissible', 'ordinary' (cf. Article 4 § 3), 'useful' (cf. the French text of the first paragraph of Article 1 of Protocol No. 1), 'reasonable' (cf. Articles 5 § 3 and 6 § 1) or 'desirable'. Nevertheless, it is for the national authorities to make the initial assessment of the reality of the pressing social need implied by the notion of 'necessity' in this context.

Consequently, Article 10 § 2 leaves to the Contracting States a margin of appreciation. This margin is given both to the domestic legislator ('prescribed by law') and to the bodies, judicial amongst others, that are called upon to interpret and apply the laws in force.

49. Nevertheless, Article 10 § 2 does not give the Contracting States an unlimited power of appreciation. The Court, which, with the Commission, is responsible for ensuring the observance of those States' engagements (Article 19), is empowered to give the final ruling on whether a 'restriction' or 'penalty' is reconcilable with freedom of expression as protected by Article 10. The domestic margin of appreciation thus goes hand in hand with a European supervision. Such supervision concerns both the aim of the measure challenged and its 'necessity'; it covers not only the basic legislation but also the decision applying it, even one given by an independent court....

The Court's supervisory functions oblige it to pay the utmost attention to the principles characterising a 'democratic society'. Freedom of expression constitutes one of the essential foundations of such a society, one of the basic conditions for its progress and for the development of every man. Subject to paragraph 2 of Article 10, it is applicable not only to 'information' or 'ideas' that are favourably received or regarded as inoffensive or as a matter of indifference, but also to those that offend, shock or disturb the State or any sector of the population. Such are the demands of that pluralism, tolerance and broadmindedness without which there is no 'democratic society'. This means, amongst other things, that every 'formality', 'condition', 'restriction' or 'penalty' imposed in this sphere must be proportionate to the legitimate aim pursued.

50. It follows from this that it is in no way the Court's task to take the place of the competent national courts but rather to review under Article 10 the decisions they delivered in the exercise of their power of appreciation....

52. The Court attaches particular importance to a factor to which the judgment of 29 October 1971 did not fail to draw attention, that is, the intended readership of the Schoolbook. It was aimed above all at children and adolescents aged from twelve to eighteen. Being direct, factual and reduced to essentials in style, it was easily within the comprehension of even the youngest of such readers. The applicant had made it clear that he planned a wide-spread circulation. He had sent the book, with a press release, to numerous daily papers and periodicals for review or for advertising purposes. What is more, he had set a modest sale price (thirty pence), arranged for a reprint of 50,000 copies shortly after the first impression of 20,000 and chosen a [title] suggesting that the work was some kind of handbook for use in schools.

Basically the book contained purely factual information that was generally correct and often useful, as the Quarter Sessions recognised. However, it also included, ...sentences or paragraphs that young people at a critical stage of their development could have interpreted as an encouragement to indulge in precocious activities harmful for them or even to commit certain criminal offences. In these circumstances, despite the variety and the constant evolution in the United Kingdom of views on ethics and education, the competent English judges were entitled, in the exercise of their discretion, to think at the relevant time that the Schoolbook would have pernicious effects on the morals of many of the children and adolescents who would read it....

57. The applicant and the minority of the Commission laid stress on the further point that, in addition to the original Danish edition, translations of the 'Little Book' appeared and circulated freely in the majority of the member states of the Council of Europe.

Here again, the national margin of appreciation and the optional nature of the 'restrictions' and 'penalties' referred to in Article 10 § 2 prevent the Court from accepting the argument. The Contracting States have each fashioned their approach in the light of the situation obtaining in their respective territories; they have had regard, *inter alia*, to the different views prevailing there about the demands of the protection of morals in a democratic society. The fact that most of them decided to allow the work to be distributed does not mean that the contrary decision of the Inner London Quarter Sessions was a breach of Article 10. Besides, some of the editions published outside the United Kingdom do not include the passages, or at least not all the passages, cited in the judgment of 29 October 1971 as striking examples of a tendency to 'deprave and corrupt' ...

...

[The Court held by 13 to 1 that there had been no violation of Article 10.]

[The separate opinions of Judges Mosler and Zekia are omitted.]

2. THE JUSTIFICATION OF INTERFERENCES WITH CONVENTION RIGHTS

A. PROPORTIONALITY AND THE MARGIN OF APPRECIATION

Central to the Court's judgment in the *Handyside Case* is the concept of the 'margin of appreciation' used to decide whether or not a state's interference with a protected right is 'necessary in a democratic society' to achieve certain interests.[20] Such justification is made possible in connection with several rights in the Convention. (See Articles 8(2), 9(2), 11(2), Protocol No. 4, Article 2(3).) How the Court determines the presence or absence of such 'necessity' defines the extent of the protection actually provided.

Underlying the doctrine of the margin of appreciation are two assumptions: First, what is necessary to achieve the stated interests may vary from state to state even in 'democratic societies'; and second, governments presumably in touch with the 'vital forces' of their countries are in a better position to assess that necessity than an international court.[21]

One limit on such deference is the Convention's use of the word 'necessary'. Note the Court's discussion in paragraph 48 of *Handyside*, comparing its use in Article 10(2) with other expressions in the Convention such as Article 2(2).[22] This provision declares that no violation of the right to life occurs when a death results from the use of such force as is 'absolutely necessary for specified purposes'. The Court has interpreted this phrase as denoting 'a stricter and more compelling test of necessity than that normally applicable when determing whether state action is "necessary in a democratic society" under paragraphs 2 of Articles 8 to 11 …'.[23] Also telling is the comparison with Protocol No. 1, Article 1 which protects an individual against deprivation of his 'possessions', but which also recognizes 'the right of a state to enforce such laws as it *deems necessary* to control the use of property in accordance with the general interest'.[24]

In 1988, relying on a number of its precedents, the European Court summarized the test for necessity in a democratic society as follows:

According to the Court's established case-law, the notion of necessity implies that the interference corresponds to a pressing social need and, in particular, that it is proportionate to the

---

[20] *Frette v. France*, 26 Feb. 2002, 38 E.H.R.R. 21.

[21] The state interests eligible for consideration as justification under the Convention cover just about any objective a state is likely to pursue. The Court rarely pauses to evaluate the propriety of any purpose asserted. For an interesting complication of the issue see R. Gordon, 'Legitimate Aim: A Dimly Lit Road', [2002] *Eur. Human Rights L. Rev.* 421.

[22] Note, however, that the term 'strictly required' in Article 15, dealing with derogations in time of national emergency, has been construed with reference to a state's margin of appreciation. *See Ireland v. United Kingdom*, 18 Jan. 1978, 2 E.H.R.R. 25, paras. 207, 243.

[23] *McCann & Others v. United Kingdom*, 27 Sept. 1995, 21 E.H.R.R. 97, para. 149.

[24] The requirement of 'necessity' may be contrasted with the more lenient requirement of 'rationality' established under the British law of judicial review. *See* M. Elliott, 'The Human Rights Act 1998 and the Standard of Substantive Review', 60 *Cambridge L. Rev.* 301 (2001). *See* Chapter 14(D) *infra*.

legitimate aim pursued; in determining whether an interference is 'necessary in a democratic society', the Court will take into account that a margin of appreciation is left to the Contracting States....

... In the first place, [the Court's] review is not limited to ascertaining whether a respondent State exercised its discretion reasonably, carefully and in good faith ... In the second place, in exercising its supervisory jurisdiction, the Court cannot confine itself to considering the impugned decisions in isolation, but must look at them in the light of the case as a whole; it must determine whether the reasons adduced to justify the interferences at issue are 'relevant and sufficient' ....[25]

Related to the margin of appreciation is the requirement that any acceptable interference be 'proportional' to the interest served. This involves an examination of the severity of the interference with Convention rights in comparison with the public injury which might follow from *not completely protecting* the interest cited.[26] It calls for weighing of the relative injuries to the individual and the state which would follow one or another decision.

Note the Court's discussion in paragraph 57 of the practice of other European states in dealing with this publication. Such comparison has become a staple of the Court's margin of appreciation jurisprudence. In *Handyside*, the Court was not impressed with the more tolerant attitude exhibited elsewhere in light of the necessary variation in moral attitudes in different societies. Generally, however, the showing of a consistent policy of regulation or abstention from regulation in other European states will influence the Court's determination of the breadth of the margin of appreciation.[27] Such attention is reasonable when it is recalled that the underlying question is whether or not certain restrictions are 'necessary in a democratic society'. The general resort to such restrictions among members of the Council of Europe is some indication that it is necessary. Its absence is some evidence that it is not.[28]

The European Court's consideration of the justification of interferences with Convention rights turns on the relative effectiveness of different state measures and is, necessarily, an intensely practical one. This is illustrated by its decision in *Observer & Guardian v. United Kingdom*.[29] In that case it evaluated the propriety of an injunction against the publication in the applicants' newspapers of excerpts from *Spycatcher*, a book of memoirs by a former officer of the British Security Service (MI–5) recounting numerous illegal activities by the Service. The restraint had been upheld by the House of Lords and was in effect until October, 1988. At the time the domestic proceedings

---

[25] *Olsson v. Sweden*, 24 Mar. 1988, 11 E.H.R.R. 259.

[26] *See Dudgeon v. United Kingdom*, 22 Oct. 1981, 4 E.H.R.R. 149, para. 60.

[27] *See*, e.g., *Dudgeon v. United Kingdom*, *supra* n. 26; D. J. Harris, M. O'Boyle and C. Warbrick, *Law of the European Convention on Human Rights* 9–11 (1995).

[28] *See also Frette v. France*, *supra* n. 20, paras. 40–1. For critical discussion of the Court's use of comparative material *see* H. C. Yourow, *The Margin of Appreciation Doctrine in the Dynamics of European Human Rights Jurisprudence* 193–6 (1996); P. G. Carozza, 'Uses and Misuses of Comparative Law in International Human Rights: Some Reflection on the Jurisprudence of the European Court of Human Rights', (1998) 73 *Notre Dame L. Rev.* 1217.

[29] 26 Nov. 1991, 14 E.H.R.R. 153.

were begun some of this information had already appeared in other books or television broadcasts. During the pendency of the action, much more of it came to light in articles published in the United Kingdom, the United States and Australia. The entire book was published in the United States and numerous copies had been brought into the United Kingdom. The Strasbourg judgment held the restriction on publication had been justified before 30 July 1987 but not thereafter. By that time a great amount of information in the book was already public and the Court concluded that any attempt at maintaining confidentiality was more or less futile.

Some of the dissenting opinions doubted whether there was a significant difference between the two periods distinguished by the majority. Partly, this was based on an estimate of the information that had already become known when the orders were issued, and on the likelihood that the applicants would have access to new and different information. (See, for example, the separate opinion of Judge Walsh.) In addition, some of the dissenting judges emphasized the inevitability, apparent even in the earlier period, of the disclosure of the material the government wished to keep secret. As Judge Pettiti stated, given modern technology, 'it is impossible to partition territorially thought and its expression'.[30]

Both the Court's judgment and the dissents which have been noted, therefore, depend on an assessment of the *effectiveness* of the attempted suppression of information. The prohibition of publication was not necessary to prevent injury to national security, on this view, because the information would almost certainly become public and the injury would arise notwithstanding the restriction. A futile measure cannot be a necessary one.

B. COMPARISONS

The Strasbourg Court's explanation of the margin of appreciation turns peculiarly on its status as an international court. As such it does not transfer easily to the adjudication of Convention rights by domestic tribunals. Nevertheless, United Kingdom courts, when applying the 1998 Human Rights Act, have held it proper to accord some degree of deference to the decisions made by other government actors with respect to the need for a particular measure. Two different kinds of reasons have been cited in justification. The first is a judgment that 'the judiciary [ought to] defer, on democratic grounds to the considered opinion of the elected body or person whose act or decision is said to

---

[30] Partly dissenting opinion of Judge Pettiti. Paras. 61–4. *See also Vereniging Weekblad Bluf! v. The Netherlands*, 9 Feb. 1995, 20 E.H.R.R. 189 in which the Court reviewed an order requiring the withdrawal from publication of a journal containing a confidential security service report. This action was held incompatible with Art. 10 in part because 2,500 copies had already been distributed. (*See id.* paras. 43–6.) *See also Fressoz & Roire v. France*, 21 Jan. 1999 para. 53 finding a violation of Art. 10 in connection with the applicant's criminal conviction for the publication of income information that was already available to the public and might already have been known to a large number of people; *Sürek v. Turkey*, (No. 2), 8 July 1999, finding a violation in punishing the identification of police officers accused of misconduct claimed to be justified by the risk of terrorist reprisals. The information was not in a form inciting to violence and the same material had already been published in other newspapers.

be incompatible with the Convention'.[31] The second category of reasons relates to relative expertise in certain kinds of decisions. The judges will defer to political decision more readily in matters of economic and social policy.[32] In contrast, the courts will be more confident in reviewing matter more strictly legal or constitutional.[33]

Lord Hoffman in his judgment in *R. (ProLife Alliance) v. British Broadcasting Corporation* objected to use of the term 'deference' in this context with 'its overtones of servility, or perhaps gracious concession....Independence makes the courts more suited to deciding some kinds of questions and being elected makes the legislature or executive more suited to deciding others ... [W]hen a court decides that a decision is within the proper competence of the legislature or executive, it is not showing deference. It is deciding the law'.[34]

The Strasbourg Court has held that, when Convention rights are in issue, United Kingdom courts are obliged under Article 13 to make a more searching review of public actions than the mere 'rationality' required in British administrative law.[35]

The recognition that rights may be violated for important enough reasons entails a recognition that, as a practical matter, few restrictions on state behaviour can be absolute. (Article 3, the right to be free of torture or inhuman or degrading treatment, Article 2, the right to life, and Article 4 the prohibition on slavery, are also phrased in absolute terms, but some kinds of conduct are defined out of the prohibition.) Most national constitutions also provide, either expressly or as a result of judicial interpretation, for expansion or contraction of their rules for sufficient reason. If these reservations are not to swallow the rules, however, some permissible reasons for deviation must be developed. Equally important, some method must be employed to assure that a particular measure is sufficiently related to the privileged objective—whether, in the words of the Convention, the governmental action is 'necessary'. Consider the following definition of 'necessary' from American constitutional law. It refers to Congress' power to make all laws 'necessary and proper' for exercising the powers granted to it. How does it compare with that of the European Court?

The word 'necessary' is considered as ... limiting the right to pass laws for the execution of the granted powers, to such as are indispensable, and without which the power would be nugatory. That it excludes the choice of means, and leaves to Congress, in each case, that only which is most direct and simple.

[31] *R. v. Director of Public Prosecutions, ex parte Kebilene* [2000] 2 A.C. 326 (H.L.) (Lord Hope); *see also* Brown v. Stott [2003] 1 A.C. 681 (P.C.) (Lord Bingham of Cornhill).

[32] *R. v. Director of Public Prosecutions, ex parte Kebilene, supra* n. 31 (Lord Hope); *R. (Kehoe) v. Secretary of State* [2005] U.K.H.L. 48, [2006] 1 A.C. 42, para. 75 (Baroness Hale of Richmond).

[33] *A. & Others v Secretary of State for the Home Department* [2005] U.K.H.L. 71, [2005] 2 A.C. 68, paras. 42–3 (Lord Bingham of Cornhill), para. 108 (Lord Hope).

[34] [2003] U.K.H.L. 23, [2004] A.C. 185, paras. 75–6.

[35] *Smith & Grady v. United Kingdom*, 27 Sept. 1999, 29 E.H.R.R. 493, para. 38. *See also R. (ProLife Alliance) v. British Broadcasting Corporation, supra* n. 34, at paras. 131–5 (Lord Walker of Gestingthorpe); *R. (Begum) v. Head Teacher and Governors of Denbeigh High School* [2006] U.K.H.L. 15, [2006] 2 All E.R. 487; Mark Elliott, 'The Human Rights Act 1998 and the Standard of Substantive Review', [2001] *Cambridge L.J.* 301.

Is it true, that this is the sense in which the word 'necessary' is always used? Does it always import an absolute physical necessity, so strong that one thing, to which another may be termed necessary, cannot exist without that other? We think it does not. If reference be had to its use, in the common affairs of the world, or in approved authors, we find that it frequently imports no more than that one thing is convenient, or useful, or essential to another. To employ the means necessary to an end, is generally understood as employing any means calculated to produce the end, and not as being confined to those single means, without which the end would be entirely unattainable....[36]

Justifications for infringement of constitutional rights are provided for explicitly in the 1982 Canadian Charter of Rights and Freedoms, Section 1 allowing for such 'reasonable limits [on rights] prescribed by law as can be demonstrably justified in a free and democratic society'.

The 1980 draft Charter prepared by the Federal government made the rights subject 'only to such reasonable limits as are generally accepted in a free and democratic society with a parliamentary system of government'. The revised language was generally understood to have narrowed the permissible grounds of justification.

In a series of cases, beginning with *Regina v. Oakes*[37] the Supreme Court of Canada has developed a test for deciding whether a particular limitation of a right was 'demonstrably justified' under Section 1.

The onus of proving that a limit on a right or freedom guaranteed by the Charter is reasonable and demonstrably justified in a free and democratic society rests upon the party seeking to uphold the limitation ...

The standard of proof under s. 1 is the civil standard, namely, proof by a preponderance of probability....

... Where evidence is required in order to prove the constituent elements of a s. 1 inquiry, and this will generally be the case, it should be cogent and persuasive and make clear to the court the consequences of imposing or not imposing the limit: A court will also need to know what alternative measures for implementing the objective were available to the legislators when they made their decisions. I should add, however, that there may be cases where certain elements of the s. 1 analysis are obvious or self-evident.

To establish that a limit is reasonable and demonstrably justified in a free and democratic society, two central criteria must be satisfied. First, the objective, which the measures responsible for a limit on a Charter right or freedom are designed to serve, must be 'of sufficient importance to warrant overriding a constitutionally protected right or freedom': The standard must be high in order to ensure that objectives which are trivial or discordant with the principles integral to a free and democratic society do not gain s. 1 protection. It is necessary, at a minimum, that an objective relate to concerns which are pressing and substantial in a free and democratic society before it can be characterized as sufficiently important.

Second, once a sufficiently significant objective is recognized, then the party invoking s. 1 must show that the means chosen are reasonable and demonstrably justified. This involves 'a form of proportionality test': ... There are, in my view, three important components of a

---

[36] *McCulloch v. Maryland*, 17 U.S. (4 Wheat.) 316, 413–14 (1819).
[37] [1986] 1 S.C.R. 103.

proportionality test. First, the measures adopted must be carefully designed to achieve the objective in question. They must not be arbitrary, unfair or based on irrational considerations. In short, they must be rationally connected to the objective. Secondly, the means, even if rationally connected to the objective in this first sense, should impair 'as little as possible' the right or freedom in question ... Third, there must be a proportionality between the *effects* of the measures which are responsible for limiting the Charter right or freedom, and the objective which has been identified as of 'sufficient importance'.

... Some limits on rights and freedoms protected by the Charter will be more serious than others in terms of the nature of the right or freedom violated, the extent of the violation and the degree to which the measures which impose the limit trench upon the integral principles of a free and democratic society. Even if an objective is of sufficient importance, and the first two elements of that proportionality test are satisfied, it is still possible that, because of the severity of the deleterious effects of a measure on individuals or groups, the measure will not be justified by the purposes it is intended to serve. The more severe the deleterious effects of a measure, the more important the objective must be if the measure is to be reasonable and demonstrably justified in a free and democratic society.

The *Oakes* test, particularly its requirements that the means chosen should impair the right as little as possible and should be proportionate to the severity of the infringement of the right in question, poses, on its face, extremely rigorous requirements for the validity of any action limiting a Charter right. As one astute commentator has observed 'a strict application of the least drastic means requirement would allow only one legislative response to an objective that involved the limiting of a Charter right'.[38] For reasons similar to those underlying the 'margin of appreciation' in European human rights law, the Supreme Court soon found it necessary to restate the test. In *Irwin Toy Ltd. v. Attorney-General (Quebec)*,[39] the Court upheld a sweeping statutory limitation of broadcast advertising aimed at children. The Court found the measure was demonstrably justified in a free and democratic society:

When striking a balance between the claims of competing groups, the choice of means, like the choice of ends, frequently will require an assessment of conflicting scientific evidence and differing justified demands on scarce resources. Democratic institutions are meant to let us all share in the responsibility of these difficult choices. Thus as courts review the results of the legislature's deliberations, particularly with respect to the protection of vulnerable groups, they must be mindful of the legislature's representative function....

... The question is whether the government had a reasonable basis, on the evidence tendered, for concluding that the ban on all advertising directed at children impaired freedom of expression as little as possible given the government's pressing and substantial objective....[40]

While evidence exists that other less intrusive options reflecting more modest objectives were available to the government, there is evidence establishing the necessity of a ban to meet the objectives the government had reasonably set. The Court will not in the name of minimal

38 P. Hogg, *Constitutional Law of Canada*, s. 35 11(b) (3rd edn. 1992).
39 [1989] 1 S.C.R. 927.
40 *Id*. at 993–4.

impairment take a restrictive approach to social science evidence and require the legislature to choose the least ambitious means to protect vulnerable groups....[41]

The application of the *Oakes* test has continued to stir debate in the Court with respect to the degree of deference to be accorded legislative judgments in different circumstances. In *RJR-MacDonald v. Canada (Attorney-General)*,[42] the Court found that a sweeping ban on advertisement of cigarettes violated section 2(b) of the Charter guaranteeing freedom of expression. The justices agreed unanimously that the regulation infringed that right. They divided five to four, however, in deciding that the measure was not justified under section 1. The Court had been presented with massive amounts of conflicting evidence on the relationship between advertising and tobacco consumption. In dissenting, Justice LaForest relied on the reasoning of the *Irwin Toy* case just quoted. He concluded that when the legislature was adjusting the competing claims of different social interests, courts were incompetent to overrule its necessarily uncertain policy choices. He argued that it was wrong in such cases 'to apply rigorously the criterion of civil proof on the balance of probabilities'. To do so would make it 'impossible to govern' and to confer on the judiciary 'a supervisory role over a state itself essentially inactive'.[43] For the majority, however, this approach was an abdication of the Court's duty to see that the standards of section 1 were met in cases where a Charter infringement was present. Justice MacLachlan insisted on the civil standard of proof. This standard, she said, 'does not require scientific demonstration; the balance of probabilities may be established by the application of common sense to what is known'. A more deferential attitude by the courts 'to the point of accepting Parliament's view simply on the basis that the problem is serious and the solution difficult, would be ... to weaken the structure of rights upon which our constitution and our nation is [sic] founded'.[44]

The Supreme Court of Canada has also held that this kind of evaluation is appropriate when courts review administrative decisions that are claimed to infringe rights under the Charter. In so doing it rejected an argument by two dissenting justices that such a test should be reserved for review of 'laws' as such. The *Oakes* test 'was developed to assess legislative policies'.[45]

In reviewing government action for compatibility with the Convention the House of Lords has abandoned the traditional inquiry into whether the decision in question was 'rational'. It has instead employed a three part test very similar to that developed in *Oakes*. It asks

Whether (i) the legislative objective is sufficiently important to justify limiting a fundamental right; (ii) the measures designed to meet the legislative objective are rationally connected to it; and (iii) the means used to impair the right or freedom are no more than is necessary to accomplish the objective.[46]

---

[41] *Id.* at 999.   [42] [1995] 3 S.C.R. 199.

[43] *Id.* at para. 67.

[44] *Id.* at paras. 136–7. *See also id.* at paras. 182–8 (reasons of Iacobucci J).

[45] *Multani v. Commision Scolaire* [2006] 1 S.C.R. 256 , paras. 16–23, para. 122.

[46] *R. (Daly) v. Home Secretary* [2001] U.K.H.L. 26, [2001] 2 A.C. 532, 537.

C. LEVELS OF JUSTIFICATION

The jurisprudence of the European Court of Human Rights on whether or not infringements of protected rights are justified under provisions like Article 10(2) tends to vary the strictness with which such justification will be demanded depending on the circumstances of the particular case. These differences turn sometimes on the particular public aim that the challenged measure seeks to achieve and sometimes on the character of the violation of the right that is complained of. 'The scope of the margin of appreciation will vary according to the circumstances, the subject matter and the background'.[47]

One aspect of the factors influencing the Court's definition of the margin of appreciation is illustrated by the way the Court has dealt with two of the objectives listed in Article 10(2), the protection of morals and the maintenance of the authority and impartiality of the judiciary.

D. THE PROTECTION OF MORALS AND THE RELATIVITY OF VALUE

In *Handyside*, the Court stressed that, given the great variation in different countries on the requirements of morality, it was particularly appropriate for the court to defer to domestic legislative judgments as to what measures were necessary to protect morals. The court applied the same reasoning in *Müller and Others v. Switzerland*.[48] The cantonal authorities in that case had prosecuted an artist and the promoters of an art show for display of obscene materials. The Criminal Cassation Division of the Federal Court of Switzerland summarized the paintings at issue as showing 'an orgy of unnatural sexual practices (sodomy, bestiality, petting), which is crudely depicted in large format'. The applicants were fined and the paintings were ordered held by a museum for inspection only by 'specialists'. The paintings were returned to the owner on his motion eight years later. The European Court found no violation of Article 10:

35. ... The view taken of the requirements of morals varies from time to time and from place to place, especially in our era, characterised as it is by a far-reaching evolution of opinions on the subject. By reason of their direct and continuous contact with the vital forces of their countries, State authorities are in principle in a better position than the international judge to give an opinion on the exact content of these requirements as well as on the 'necessity' of a 'restriction' or 'penalty' intended to meet them.

36. ... The Court recognises, as did the Swiss courts, that conceptions of sexual morality have changed in recent years. Nevertheless, having inspected the original paintings, the Court does not find unreasonable the view taken by the Swiss courts that those paintings, with their emphasis on sexuality in some of its crudest forms, were 'liable grossly to offend the sense of sexual propriety of persons of ordinary sensitivity' ... In the circumstances, having regard to the margin of appreciation left to them under Article 10 §2, the Swiss courts were entitled

---

[47] *Frette v. France, supra* n. 20.
[48] 24 May 1988, 13 E.H.R.R. 212.

to consider it 'necessary' for the protection of morals to impose a fine on the applicants for publishing obscene material.

Judge Spielman, dissenting, argued that states should have greater regard to the relativity of values in the expression of ideas. He also noted that the Court's approach to the state's superior ability to judge the protection of morals could make it 'impossible for an international court to find any violation of Article 10 as the second paragraph of that Article would always apply'.[49]

Judicial review of the sufficiency of moral justifications for limitations of expression raises acute questions of definition. The House of Lords, in construing the English obscenity statute's requirement that the article in question must tend to 'deprave or corrupt', has held that such an effect may be found even when the individuals exposed to it have exhibited no objectionable behaviour manifesting such depravity. Rather the evil in the materials is their 'effect ... on the mind, including the emotions' so as to induce 'thoughts of a most impure and libidinous character'.[50]

United States constitutional law denies protection to 'obscene' matters that, *inter alia*, 'the average person applying contemporary community standards' would find 'appeals, as a whole, to the prurient interest'.[51] This standard allows a state to judge obscenity, at least in part, on the basis of local standards, although there are apparently limits to the extent that idiosyncratically intolerant local standards may apply.[52] Likewise, the English statute on obscenity specifically refers to material that tends 'to deprave and corrupt persons who are likely, having regard to all relevant circumstances, to read, see or hear the matter'.[53] This has been interpreted as adopting 'a relative conception of obscenity. An article cannot be considered obscene in itself; it can only be so in relation to its likely readers'. In particular, a court ought to apply 'different tests to teenagers, members of men's clubs or men in various occupations or localities'.[54]

The judicial application of Canadian statutes for the control of indecency and obscenity has been notable for its studious avoidance of a strictly moral understanding of such laws. The Supreme Court of Canada has, on the contrary, emphasized the 'social harms' associated with such expression and particularly the 'degradation

---

[49] For the same reason the European Court has also applied a deferential standard to matters touching on the relationship between the state and religion. *Layla Sahin v. Turkey*, 29 June 2000, 41 E.H.R.R. 8 para. 108. *See* Chapter 7(C) *infra*.

[50] *Director of Public Prosecutions v. Whyte* [1972] A.C. 849, 864, [1972] 3 All E.R. 12, 21 (Lord Pearson) (quoting *R. v. Hicklin* (1868) L.R. 3 Q.B. 360). It should be noted that English law also still allows criminal prosecution for the common law crime of 'outraging public decency'. In such a case there is no need for the court to show that anyone is at risk of 'depravity' or 'corruption'. Nor is there any defence that the publication serves some literary, scientific or artistic public good. *See R. v. Gibson* [1990] 2 Q.B. 619, [1991] All E.R. 439. Indecency 'includes anything which an ordinary decent man or woman would find to be shocking, disquieting and revolting'. *Knuller (Publishing, Printing and Promotions) Ltd. v. Director of Public Prosecutions* [1973] A.C. 435, 458, [1972] All E.R. 818, 905 (Lord Reid).

[51] *Miller v. California*, 413 U.S. 15, 24 (1973).

[52] *Jenkins v. Georgia*, 418 U.S. 153 (1974).

[53] Obscene Publications Act 1959.

[54] *D.P.P. v. Whyte, supra* n. 50, at 836. The Obscene Publications Act 1959 was held compatible with Article 10 in *R. v. Perrin* [2002] E.W.C.A. 747.

and objectification of women'.[55] It upheld a statue criminalizing possession of child pornography, even if held in private and even if no actual children were used creating it. It found that Parliament was justified in believing that such possession alone contributed to the sexual exploitation of children. It increased the market for, and consequently the production of, such material. It could be used to seduce and train child victims. Such material might also be reasonably believed to 'fuel fantasies' and distort the attitudes of its users '[b]analizing the awful and numbing the conscience', thus making abuse of children more likely.[56] Three judges concurred in finding the statute valid but identified a broader kind of harm, a harm shading into a 'tendency to deprave', caused by possession of such material. They stressed the resulting 'attitudinal harm'. '[A]ll members of society suffer when harmful attitudes are reinforced'. Whether the pornography is produced with real children or imagined ones it still 'fosters and communicates the same harmful and degrading message'. They affirmed, as well, that 'Parliament has the right to make moral judgments in criminalizing certain forms of conduct'.[57]

The United States Supreme Court faced many of the same issues the following year in *Ashcroft v. Free Speech Coalition*.[58] The Court had previously upheld a law against possessing or distributing non-obscene material depicting children performing explicitly sexual acts. The Court had justified the law as a means of protecting children who might be engaged in its production.[59] When Congress extended the law to cover depictions of child sexual conduct whether or not actual children were involved ('virtual child pornography') the law was held unconstitutional. None of the harms identified by the Supreme Court of Canada convinced the American court. Unlike sanctions on pornography that used real children, the creation and publication of this material was not 'intrinsically related' to the exploitation and abuse of children.[60] It did not stimulate the market for pornography in which the production led directly to child abuse. While some of the material might be used to entice children into such activity, the statutory prohibition swept much more broadly. Prior cases had established that protection of children could not justify banning a whole category of expression to which adults otherwise were entitled. Finally the Court refused to uphold the statute on the grounds that it could 'whet the appetite' of child predators. Impermissible conduct could not be discouraged by measures aimed to 'control thought'. 'The government may not prohibit speech because it increases the chance an unlawful act will be committed "at some future time"'.[61]

55 *R. v. Mara* [1997] 2 S.C.R. 630, 647.
56 *R. v. Sharpe* [2001] S.C.C. 2 paras. 83–94.
57 *Id.* at paras. 163, 168 191 (judgment of L'Heureux-Dube, Gonthier & Bastarche JJ)
58 535 U.S. 234 (2002).
59 *New York v. Ferber* 458 U.S. 747 (1982).
60 535 U.S. at 249.
61 *Id.* at 252–4.

E. MAINTAINING THE AUTHORITY AND IMPARTIALITY OF THE JUDICIARY

In contrast to its treatment of the public goal of protecting morals, the European Court has shown less deference to national judgments as to what is needed 'for maintaining the authority and impartiality of the judiciary'. Consider the following from *Sunday Times v. United Kingdom*[62] contrasting the variation in views of morals to:

the far more objective notion of the 'authority' of the judiciary. The domestic law and practice of the Contracting States reveal a fairly substantial measure of common ground in this area. This is reflected in a number of provisions of the Convention, including Article 6, which have no equivalent as far as 'morals' are concerned. Accordingly, here a more extensive European supervision corresponds to a less discretionary power of appreciation.[63]

Judge Zekia in his concurring opinion stated:

Whenever it considers it reasonable and feasible, this Court should work out a uniform international European standard for the enjoyment of the rights and freedoms included in the Convention. This could be done gradually when the occasion arises and after giving the appropriate full consideration to national legal systems....

In the legal systems of those continental States which are the original signatories of the Convention there is, as far as my information and knowledge go, nothing similar to the branch of the common law of contempt of court—with its summary procedure—touching publications which refer to pending civil proceedings. Notwithstanding this fact these countries manage to maintain the authority and impartiality of their judiciary. Am I to accept any submission to the effect that conditions in England are different and that they have to keep alive unaltered the common law of contempt of court under discussion, which is over two centuries old, in order to safeguard the authority and impartiality of the judiciary? My knowledge and experience gained from long years of association with English judges and courts prompt me to say unreservedly that the standard of the judiciary in England is too high to be influenced by any publication in the press ...

In *Worm v. Austria*,[64] the Court found that Article 10 had not been violated when a journalist was convicted of 'influencing the outcome' of judicial proceedings based on an article describing the trial of a high profile political figure for tax evasion. The Court repeated its dictum from *Sunday Times* that the margin of appreciation might be narrower when a state is attempting to maintain the 'authority and impartiality of the judiciary' in light of its 'objective character'. It went on, however, to say that the applicant's conviction could not be held 'contrary to Article 10 of the Convention simply because it might not have been obtained under a different legal system'.[65]

---

[62] 26 Apr. 1979, 2 E.H.R.R. 245, reproduced in part in Chapter 2, *supra*.

[63] *Id.* at para. 59. *See also Weber v. Switzerland*, 22 May 1990, 12 E.H.R.R. 508 where the Court states that a justification based on 'maintaining the authority and impartiality of the judiciary has to be "convincingly established"'. *Id.* at para. 47.

[64] 29 Aug. 1997, 25 E.H.R.R. 454.

[65] *Id.* at para. 49.

F. THE NATURE OF THE VIOLATION

Another category of variations in the level of justification involves the kind (or extent) of violation of the protected right at issue. With respect to the right to respect for one's 'home' in Article 8, the Court has stated that '[t]he importance of such a right to the individual must be taken into account in determining the scope of the margin of appreciation allowed to the government'.[66] The Court has often noted that freedom of expression is 'one of the foundations of a democratic society', and that, consequently, the exceptions in Article 10(2) 'must be narrowly interpreted and the necessity for any restrictions must be convincingly established'.[67]

Another indication that the limitation of certain rights may be harder to justify than others may be found in a comparison of *Handyside* and *Müller* with *Dudgeon v. United Kingdom*.[68] In the latter case, the Court refused to find the protection of morals an adequate justification for criminal laws directed at homosexual activity. It distinguished its more liberal attitude toward state judgments on morals in *Handyside* by noting that the margin of appreciation depends not only on the state interest being advanced, but also on the nature of the particular interference. In *Dudgeon*, the law in question concerned 'a most intimate aspect of private life'. Therefore, a particularly pressing justification was required. Notwithstanding the different results in *Handyside* and *Dudgeon*, the Court subsequently denied that it used different standards in cases involving Article 8 and Article 10.[69]

3. COMPARISONS

Unlike the European Convention, the United States Constitution declares most of its individual rights in absolute terms. Nevertheless, by judicial interpretation these rights have usually been redefined to assure that serious governmental interests may be pursued notwithstanding their impact on otherwise protected activities. And, as has been the case with the European Court, the strength of the justification demanded has varied with the importance of the interest pursued and the right being limited. Thus, like the Court in *Handyside*, the United States Supreme Court has been particularly sensitive to the propriety of regulation to provide protection of the morals of children. In *Ginsberg v. New York*,[70] the Supreme Court upheld a statute prohibiting the sale of sexually oriented literature to minors under 17. The Court agreed that since the material was not obscene, its sales to adults could not be forbidden. The state's interest in preventing the distribution of the same material to children, however, was

---

[66] *Gillow v. United Kingdom*, 24 Nov. 1986, 11 E.H.R.R. 335, para. 55.
[67] *Observer and Guardian v. United Kingdom*, 26 Nov. 1991, 14 E.H.R.R. 153, para. 59.
[68] 23 Sept. 1981, 4 E.H.R.R. 149, reproduced in Chapter 8(C) *infra*.
[69] *Norris v. Ireland*, 26 Oct. 1988, 13 E.H.R.R. 186, discussed in Chapter 8(C) *infra*.
[70] 390 U.S. 629 (1968).

sufficient to support the law in question. This case was distinguished from *Butler v. Michigan*,[71] where the United States Supreme Court held unconstitutional a statute prohibiting generally the sale of material unsuitable for children.[72] 'Surely', the Court had stated in that case, 'this is to burn the house to roast the pig ... [The] incidence of this enactment is to reduce the adult population of Michigan to reading only what is fit for children'. Similarly, in *Reno v. American Civil Liberties Union*,[73] the Court found that the Communications Decency Act of 1996, in its attempt to protect children from inappropriate material on the Internet, inhibited too much protected speech intended for adults. The Act prohibited transmission of any 'obscene or indecent' material if a recipient was known to be under 18 years of age. The effect of the law was to 'suppress [...] a large amount of speech that adults have a constitutional right to receive and address to one another'.[74]

In this connection, it should be noted that while *Handyside* justified the interference with expression by the special need to protect children, the Court did not appear to regard the government's action, and the statute under which it acted, as restricted to communication with children. The government's action was not limited to such particularly objectionable distribution. In that sense, its decision to review the state's action leniently is less persuasive.

In fact, as noted above, English law has been interpreted to require courts to ascertain, as a matter of fact, the likely readers of material and to adjust its holdings on obscenity to the relative vulnerability of such readers to 'depravity and corruption' by the material in question.[75] The reference in the obscenity statute to the likely readership was inserted exactly to prevent an application to all challenged material of 'literary standards [on] the level of something suitable for the decently brought up female aged 14'.[76] Under the relevant statute '[t]he age and kind of person to whom indecent photographs or books are shown or sold is of the greatest importance'.[77]

The United States Supreme Court has tended to demand different levels of justification for constitutional infringements depending on the exact character of the right infringed. This has been a prominent aspect of its decisions applying the equal protection clause of the Fourteenth Amendment. In recognition of the omnipresent need for government to treat people unequally, it will usually hold a classification invalid only if 'the varying treatment of different groups or persons is so unrelated to the achievement of any combination of legitimate purposes that [it] can only conclude that the legislature's actions were irrational'.[78] If, however, the classification turns on

---

[71] 352 U.S. 380 (1962).

[72] *See also Sable Communications v. F.C.C.*, 492 U.S. 115 (1989) (holding protection of children insufficient to justify a blanket ban on 'dial-a-porn' telephone services).

[73] 521 U.S. 844 (1997). *See also Ashcroft v. American Civil Liberties Union* 542 U.S. 656 (2004).

[74] 521 U.S. at 874.

[75] *See Director of Public Prosecutions v. Whyte, supra* n. 50; A. W. Bradley & K. D. Ewing, *Constitutional and Administrative Law* 555–9 (14th edn. 2007).

[76] *R. v. Secker Warburg Ltd.* [1954] 2 All E.R. 683, 686 (Stable J).

[77] *Director of Public Prosecutions v. Whyte, supra* n. 50, at 875 (Lord Salmon).

[78] *Vance v. Bradley*, 440 U.S. 93, 97 (1979).

a factor that, for historical or political reasons, the Court has deemed 'suspect' (racial classifications are the paradigm), or impinges on the exercise of a fundamental right (for example, the right to vote) a more stringent test of justification is applied. In such cases, the government must show 'that such laws are *necessary* to promote a *compelling* governmental interest'. The word necessary is used in a strict way so that 'if there are other, reasonable ways to achieve these goals with a lesser burden on constitutionally protected activity, a State may not choose the way of greater interference'. If it acts at all, it must choose 'less drastic means'.[79]

A similar variation has developed in Canadian constitutional law through inter-pretation of the *Oakes* test for justifying limitations of rights under Section 1 of the Canadian Charter of Rights and Freedoms. It will be recalled that satisfaction of this test required that a sufficient justification must serve a pressing social need and must demonstrate that the measures taken were proportional to the violation of protected rights they involved. The third 'prong' of this proportionality test called for some balance between the advancement of the legislative goal and the interference with Charter rights. The Supreme Court of Canada has held that this inquiry will some-times turn on the specific exercise of the right that is claimed to be infringed. Thus, when the state takes action inhibiting free expression, the Court has found it proper to ask what the nature and content of the disfavoured expression is. The Court held that the Canadian Parliament could, under Section 1, make criminal the publication of pornography, defined as sexually explicit material involving violence or degrading or dehumanizing to women. The Court decided that the legislative response to this expression was appropriately proportional since the material involved 'lies far from the core of the guarantee of freedom of expression. It appeals only to the most base aspect of individual fulfillment, and it is primarily economically motivated'.[80]

. . .

As the cases in this chapter illustrate, the idea of a margin of appreciation, while clear and sensible in concept, has proven highly malleable in application. The numerous fac-tors surveyed which have the capacity to widen or narrow the margin of appreciation may appear in multiple combinations with unpredictable results. One example from the jurisprudence of Article 8(2) arose when a challenge was brought to the policy of the United Kingdom excluding homosexuals from the armed forces. In that case, the Court recognized that in pursuing the aim of national security a state was entitled to a broader margin. But it reiterated that when a state infringes 'a most intimate aspect of an individual's private life, particularly serious reasons by way of justification [are]

---

[79] *Dunn v. Blumstein*, 405 U.S. 330 (1972). Certain classifications, most prominently those based on gen-der, have been held to call for a third, intermediate level of scrutiny. In these cases the Court will uphold such laws if they 'serve important governmental objectives and [are] substantially related to the achievement of those objectives'. *Craig v. Boren*, 429 U.S. 190, 197 (1976).

[80] *R. v. Butler* [1992] 1 S.C.R. 452.

required'.[81] The Court, however, did little more than state these two opposite influences and then proceeded to make an *ad hoc* evaluation of the strength of each of the state's claimed justifications.[82] The variability of the margin of appreciation has sometimes provoked strong reactions from judges frustrated by its imprecision. In one case Judge De Meyer expressed his dissatisfaction in a dissenting opinion:

[W]here human rights are concerned, there is no room for a margin of appreciation which would enable the States to decide what is acceptable and what is not.

On that subject the boundary not to be overstepped must be as clear and precise as possible. It is for the Court, not each state individually, to decide that issue, and the Court's views must apply to everyone within the jurisdiction of each state.

The empty phrases concerning a State's margin of appreciation—repeated in the Court's judgments for too long already—are unnecessary circumlocutions, serving only to indicate abstrusely that the States may do anything the Court does not consider incompatible with human rights.

Such terminology, as wrong in principle as it is pointless in practice, should be abandoned without delay.[83]

The kind of categorization of expression according to the worth of its content for the purpose of determining the extent of constitutional protection afforded, is also common in the constitutional law of the United States,[84] and, as the next section will illustrate, appears to be a prominent feature of adjudication under Article 10 of the European Convention.

C. CATEGORIES OF EXPRESSION

1. POLITICAL EXPRESSION

A. LINGENS V. AUSTRIA

Judgment of 8 July 1986
8 E.H.R.R. 40

8. Mr. Lingens, an Austrian journalist born in 1931 resides in Vienna and is editor of the magazine *Profil*.

[Shortly after the Austrian general elections of 1975 Simon Wiesenthal, President of the Jewish Documentation Centre, accused Friedrick Peter, head of the Austrian Liberal

---

[81] *Smith & Grady v. United Kingdom, supra* n. 35, at para. 90.
[82] *See id.* at paras. 91–110.
[83] *Z v. Finland*, 25 Feb. 1997, 25 E.H.R.R. 371 (partly dissenting opinion of Judge De Meyer).
[84] *See* L. Tribe, *American Constitutional Law* 928–44 (2nd edn. 1988).

Party of having served in an SS brigade during the Second World War. Bruno Kreisky, the Chancellor and head of the Austrian Socialist Party vigorously defended Peter in a televised interview and accused Wiesenthal of 'mafia methods'.]

11. At this juncture, the applicant published two articles in the Vienna magazine *Profil*.

12. The first was published on 14 October 1975 under the heading 'The Peter Case'. It related the above events and in particular the activities of the first SS infantry brigade; it also drew attention to Mr. Peter's role in criminal proceedings instituted in Graz (and later abandoned) against persons who had fought in that brigade. It drew the conclusion that although Mr. Peter was admittedly entitled to the benefit of the presumption of innocence, his past nevertheless rendered him unacceptable as a politician in Austria. The application went on to criticise the attitude of Mr. Kreisky whom he accused of protecting Mr. Peter and other former members of the SS for political reasons. With regard to Mr. Kreisky's criticisms of Mr. Wiesenthal, he wrote 'had they been made by someone else this would probably have been described as the basest opportunism', but added that in the circumstances the position was more complex because Mr. Kreisky believed what he was saying....

13. The second article, published on 21 October 1975, was entitled 'Reconciliation with the Nazis, but how?'....

14. ...With regard to the then Chancellor, he added: 'In truth Mr. Kreisky's behaviour cannot be criticised on rational grounds but only on irrational grounds: it is immoral, undignified'. It was, moreover, unnecessary because Austrians could reconcile themselves with the past without seeking the favours of the former Nazis, minimising the problem of concentration camps or maligning Mr. Wiesenthal by exploiting anti-Semitism.

Finally, Mr. Lingens criticised the lack of tact with which Mr. Kreisky treated the victims of the Nazis.

16. ...After a long disquisition on various types of responsibility, [Lingens] stressed that at the time it had in fact been possible to choose between good and evil and gave examples of persons who had refused to collaborate. He concluded that 'if Bruno Kreisky had used his personal reputation, in the way he used it to protect Mr. Peter, to reveal this other and better Austria, he would have given this country—thirty years afterwards—what it most needed to come to terms with its past: a greater confidence in itself'....

18. ...[In the article Lingens declared that the] 'monstrosity' was not, in his opinion, the fact that Mr. Wiesenthal had raised the matter, but that Mr. Kreisky wished to hush it up.

19. The article ended with a section criticizing the political parties in general owing to the presence of former Nazis among their leaders. The applicant considered that Mr. Peter ought to resign, not to admit his guilt but to prove that he possessed a quality unknown to Mr. Kreisky, namely tact....

20. On 29 October and 12 November 1975, the then Chancellor brought two private prosecutions against Mr. Lingens. He considered that certain passages in the articles summarized above were defamatory and relied on Article III of the Austrian Criminal Code, which reads:

1. Anyone who in such a way that it may be perceived by a third person accuses another of possessing a contemptible character or attitude or of behaviour contrary to honour or morality and of such a nature as to make him contemptible or otherwise lower him in public esteem shall be liable to imprisonment not exceeding six months or a fine.

2. Anyone who commits this offence in a printed document, by broadcasting or otherwise in such a way as to make the defamation accessible to a broad section of the public shall be liable to imprisonment not exceeding one year or a fine.

3. The person making the statement shall not be punished if it is proved to be true. As regards the offence defined in paragraph I, he shall also not be liable if circumstances are established which gave him sufficient reason to assume that the statement was true.

37. In their respective submissions the Commission the Government and the applicant concentrated on the question whether the interference was 'necessary in a democratic society' for achieving the above mentioned aim.

. . .

39. The adjective 'necessary', within the meaning of Article 10(2), implies the existence of a 'pressing social need'. The Contracting States have a certain margin of appreciation in assessing whether such a need exists, but it goes hand in hand with a European supervision, embracing both the legislation and the decisions applying it, even those given by an independent court . . .

40. In exercising its supervisory jurisdiction, the Court cannot confine itself to considering the impugned court decisions in isolation; it must look at them in the light of the case as a whole, including the articles held against the applicant and the context in which they were written. The Court must determine whether the interference at issue was 'proportionate to the legitimate aim pursued' and whether the reasons adduced by the Austrian courts to justify it are 'relevant and sufficient'.

41. In this connection, the Court has to recall that freedom of expression, as secured in paragraph 1 of Article 10, constitutes one of the essential foundations of a democratic society and one of the basic conditions for its progress and for each individual's self-fulfillment. Subject to paragraph 2, it is applicable not only to 'information' or 'ideas' that are favourably received or regarded as inoffensive or as a matter of indifference, but also to those that offend, shock or disturb. Such are the demands of that pluralism, tolerance and broadmindedness without which there is no 'democratic society'.

These principles are of particular importance as far as the press is concerned. Whilst the press must not overstep the bounds set, *inter alia*, for the 'protection of the reputation of others', it is nevertheless incumbent on it to impart information and ideas on political issues just as on those in other areas of public interest. Not only does the press have the task of imparting such information and ideas: the public also has a right to receive them. In this connection, the Court cannot accept the opinion, expressed in the judgment of the Vienna Court of Appeal, to the effect that the task of the press was to impart information, the interpretation of which had to be left primarily to the reader.

42. Freedom of the press furthermore affords the public one of the best means of discovering and forming an opinion of the ideas and attitudes of political leaders. More generally, freedom of political debate is at the very core of the concept of a democratic society which prevails throughout the Convention.

The limits of acceptable criticism are accordingly wider as regards a politician as such than as regards a private individual. Unlike the latter, the former inevitably and knowingly lays himself open to close scrutiny of his every word and deed by both journalists and the public at large, and he must consequently display a greater degree of tolerance. No doubt Article 10(2) enables the reputation of others—that is to say, of all individuals—to be protected, and this protection extends to politicians too, even when they are not acting in their private capacity; but in such cases the requirements of such protection have to be weighed in relation to the interests of open discussion of political issues.

43. The applicant was convicted because he had used certain expressions ('basest opportunism', 'immoral' and 'undignified') apropos of Mr. Kreisky, who was Federal Chancellor at the time, in two articles published in the Viennese magazine *Profil* on 14 and 21 October 1975. The articles dealt with political issues of public interest in Austria which had given rise to many heated discussions concerning the attitude of Austrians in general—and the Chancellor in particular—to National Socialism and to the participation of former Nazis in the governance of the country. The content and tone of the articles were on the whole fairly balanced but the use of the aforementioned expressions in particular appeared likely to harm Mr. Kreisky's reputation.

However, since the case concerned Mr. Kreisky in his capacity as a politician, regard must be had to the background against which these articles were written. They had appeared shortly after the general election of October 1975. Many Austrians had thought beforehand that Mr. Kreisky's party would lose its absolute majority and, in order to be able to govern, would have to form a coalition with Mr. Peter's party. When, after the elections, Mr. Wiesenthal made a number of revelations about Mr. Peter's Nazi past, the Chancellor defended Mr. Peter and attacked his detractor, whose activities he described as 'mafia methods'; hence Mr. Lingens' sharp reaction.

The impugned expressions are therefore to be seen against the background of a post-election political controversy; as the Vienna Regional Court noted in its judgment of 26 March 1979, in this struggle each used the weapons at his disposal; and these were in no way unusual in the hard-fought tussles of politics.

44. On final appeal the Vienna Court of Appeal sentenced Mr. Lingens to a fine; it also ordered confiscation of the relevant issues of *Profil* and publication of the judgment.

As the Government pointed out, the disputed articles had at the time already been widely disseminated, so that although the penalty imposed on the author did not strictly speaking prevent him from expressing himself, it nonetheless amounted to a kind of censure, which would be likely to discourage him from making criticisms of that kind again in the future; the Delegate of the Commission rightly pointed this out. In the context of political debate such a sentence would be likely to deter journalists from contributing to public discussion of issues affecting the life of the community. By the same token, a sanction such as this is liable to hamper the press in performing its task as purveyor of information and public watchdog ...

46. ...[The Austrian Courts] held in substance that there were different ways of assessing Mr. Kreisky's behaviour and that it could not logically be proved that one interpretation was right to the exclusion of all others; they consequently found the applicant guilty of defamation.

In the Court's view, a careful distinction needs to be made between facts and value judgments. The existence of facts can be demonstrated, whereas the truth of value judgments is not susceptible of proof. The Court notes in this connection that the facts on which Mr. Lingens founded his value judgments were undisputed, as was also his good faith.

Under paragraph 3 of Article III of the Criminal Code, read in conjunction with paragraph 2, journalists in a case such as this cannot escape conviction for the matters specified in paragraph 1 unless they can prove the truth of their statements.

As regards value judgments this requirement is impossible of fulfillment and it infringes freedom of opinion itself, which is a fundamental part of the right secured by Article 10 of the Convention ...

47. From the various foregoing considerations it appears that the interference with Mr. Lingens' exercise of the freedom of expression was not 'necessary in a democratic society ... for the protection of the reputation ... of others'; it was disproportionate to the legitimate aim pursued ...

[The Court held unanimously that there had been a violation of Article 10.]

B. BARFOD V. DENMARK

Judgment of 22 February 1989
13 E.H.R.R. 493

[The applicant wrote an article for the magazine *Gronland Dansk* criticizing a judgment of the High Court of Greenland upholding a tax on Danish citizens working on American bases. That Court was composed of a professional judge and two 'lay judges', part time judges who happened to be employed by the Greenland local government. The article clearly implied that the lay judges' votes were influenced by their employment by the government. On a complaint initiated by the professional judge the applicant was prosecuted for defamation, convicted and fined.]

25. As was not disputed, the applicant's conviction clearly amounted to an interference by a public authority with his right to freedom of expression as enshrined in Article 10. Such interferences will not however contravene the Convention provided the conditions laid down in the Article's second paragraph are fulfilled.

26. The applicant did not contest either that the interference was 'prescribed by law' or that its aims were those invoked by the Government, namely the protection of the reputation of others and, indirectly, the maintenance of the authority of the judiciary. Like the Commission, the Court has no cause to doubt that the interference satisfied the requirements of Article 10 §2 in these respects.

27. The sole issue debated before the Court was whether the interference was 'necessary in a democratic society' for achieving the above-mentioned aims.

28. The Court has consistently held that the Contracting States have a certain margin of appreciation in assessing the existence and extent of such a necessity, but this margin is subject to a European supervision, embracing both the legislation and the decisions applying it, even those given by an independent court....

30. The applicant's article contained two elements: firstly, a criticism of the composition of the High Court in the 1981 tax case and, secondly, the statement that the two lay judges 'did their duty', which in this context could only mean that they cast their votes as employees of the Local Government rather than as independent and impartial judges.

31. The interference with the applicant's freedom of expression was prompted by the second element alone. However, in the opinion of the Commission this statement concerned matters of public interest involving the functioning of the public administration, including the judiciary. According to the Commission, the test of necessity had to be particularly strict in such matters: thus, even if the article could be interpreted as an attack on the two lay judges, the general interest in allowing public debate about the functioning of the judiciary weighed more heavily than the interest of the two lay judges in being protected against criticism of the kind expressed in the applicant's article....

... The Government ... disagreed with the Commission's interpretation of the test of necessity: they laid great stress on the national authorities' margin of appreciation. According to the Government, the applicant's accusations were defamatory, unsupported by any evidence and in fact false; furthermore, regardless of whether or not the lay judges were effectively disqualified in the 1981 tax case, the accusations did not constitute a contribution to the formation of public opinion worthy of safeguarding in a democratic society.

32. The basis of the Greenland High Court's judgment was its finding, made in the proper exercise of its jurisdiction, that 'the words of the article to the effect that the two ... lay judges did their duty—namely their duty as employees of the Local Government to rule in its favour—represent a serious accusation which is likely to lower them in public esteem'. Having regard to this and to the other circumstances of the applicant's conviction, the Court is satisfied that the interference with his freedom of expression did not aim at restricting his right under the Convention to criticise publicly the composition of the High Court in the 1981 tax case. Indeed, his right to voice his opinion on this issue was expressly recognised by the High Court in its judgment of 3 July 1984.

33. Furthermore, the applicant's conviction cannot be considered even to have had the result of effectively limiting this right.

It was quite possible to question the composition of the High Court without at the same time attacking the two lay judges personally. In addition, no evidence has been submitted to the effect that the applicant was justified in believing that the two elements of criticism raised by him were so closely connected as to make the statement relating to the two lay judges legitimate. The High Court's finding that there was no proof of the accusations against the lay judges remains unchallenged; the applicant must accordingly be considered to have based his accusations on the mere fact that the lay judges were employed by the Local Government, the defendant in the 1981 tax case. Although this fact may give rise to a difference of opinion as to whether the court was properly composed, it was certainly not proof of actual bias and the applicant cannot reasonably have been unaware of that.

34. The State's legitimate interest in protecting the reputation of the two lay judges was accordingly not in conflict with the applicant's interest in being able to participate in free public debate on the question of the structural impartiality of the High Court ...

35. The applicant alleged that, having regard to the political background to the 1981 tax case, his accusations against the lay judges should be seen as part of political debate, with its wider limits for legitimate criticism.

The court cannot accept this argument. The lay judges exercised judicial functions. The impugned statement was not a criticism of the reasoning in the judgment of 28 January 1981, but rather, as found by the High Court in its judgment of 3 July 1984, a defamatory accusation against the lay judges personally, which was likely to lower them in public esteem and was put forward without any supporting evidence. In view of these considerations, the political context in which the tax case was fought cannot be regarded as relevant for the question of proportionality ...

[The Court held by six votes to one that there had been no violation of Article 10.]

Dissenting opinion of Judge Gölcüklü

3. ... It is in my opinion not possible to extract an *a contrario* argument from the *Lingens* case in which the Court held that 'politicians' must be ready to accept more criticism than non-politicians ... The Court did not of course mean by this that public criticism in political matters could be directed solely against politicians or that the assessment of State institutions and the position of those who, although not politicians in the strict sense, nevertheless take part in public affairs should be excluded from the arena of free discussion and democratic debate.

4. Democracy is an open system of government in which the freedom of expression plays a fundamental role, as the Court stated in its judgment in the *Handyside case* ... I am in full agreement with the opinion of the European Commission of Human Rights when it states: '... For the citizen to keep a critical control of the exercise of public power it is essential that particularly strict limits be imposed on interferences with the publication of opinions which refer to activities of public authorities, including the judiciary'; and '... even if the article in question could be interpreted as an attack on the integrity or reputation of the two lay judges, the general interest in allowing a public debate about the functioning of the judiciary weights more heavily than the interest of the two judges in being protected against criticism of the kind expressed in the applicant's article' ....

C. THE SPECIAL PROTECTION OF POLITICAL EXPRESSION AND THE PRESS

Article 10 refers to 'freedom of expression' generally without specifying particular kinds of expression as more or less deserving of protection. Nevertheless, as we have seen, judicial application of Article 10 has varied depending on the specific kind of expression involved. As *Lingens* illustrates, the Court has argued that speech involving political issues and political figures serves a central role in the functioning of democratic societies. Therefore, arguments that a restriction of such discussion is necessary in such a society will be harder to maintain. Consequently, the Strasbourg Court has been particularly suspicious of penalties imposed for criticism of elected public officials.[85] Likewise, statements made in the course of or about elections have received exacting protection. Thus a British prohibition on expenditures over £25 by non-candidates to influence parliamentary elections was held incompatible with the Convention.[86] Damages of one franc for the applicant's publication of an accusation of electoral fraud in a national legislative election by the applicant's opponent—the incumbent and mayor of Paris, also violated Article 10.[87]

[85] In addition to the principal case *see Feldek v. Slovakia*, 12 July 2001 (Article 10 was violated by a conviction for defamation of a government minister by accusing him of having a fascist past).

[86] *Bowman v. United Kingdom*, 19 Feb. 1998, 26 E.H.R.R. 1.

[87] *Brasilier v. France*, 11 April 2006.

This preference for political speech has its counterparts in other systems of law. In the United States, such expression is at the 'core' of the constitutional guarantee of the First Amendment. Communication on matters of public interest is of a kind 'entitled to the most exacting degree of First Amendment protection'.[88] In a dissenting opinion, Justice McLachlin (as she then was) of the Supreme Court of Canada captured the reasons for this focus in terms that seem equally applicable to the judgments of the European Court of Human Rights:

The right to fully and openly express one's views on social and political issues is fundamental to our democracy and hence to all the other rights and freedoms guaranteed by the Charter. Without free expression, the vigorous debate on policies and values that underlies participatory government is lacking. Without free expression, rights may be trammelled with no recourse in the court of public opinion. Some restrictions on free expression may be necessary and justified and entirely compatible with a free and democratic society. But restrictions which touch the critical core of social and political debate require particularly close consideration because of the dangers inherent in state censorship of such debate. This is of particular importance under §1 of the Charter which expressly requires the court to have regard to whether the limits are reasonable and justified in a free and democratic society.[89]

Of course, it is not always obvious whether or not a particular instance of conduct amounts to political expression. In *Thorgeir Thorgeirsan v. Iceland*,[90] the Strasbourg Court held that a conviction for defamation based on a publication charging unspecified police officers with acts of brutality violated Article 10. The Court rejected the government's argument that the strict rule of *Lingens* should be limited to matters that concerned 'direct or indirect participation of citizens in the decision making process'.[91]

In *Janowski v. Poland*,[92] on the other hand, the Court found that prosecution for 'insult[ing] a civil servant ... during and in connection with carrying out of his official duties' did not violate Article 10. It distinguished civil servants from politicians, noting they must enjoy public confidence in conditions free of undue perturbation if they are to be successful in performing their tasks and it may therefore prove necessary to protect them from offensive and abusive verbal attacks when on duty'.[93]

To the extent this language indicated that states had some greater leeway in dealing with defamation of public servants, that freedom was narrowed, at least with respect to employees dealing with matters of general public interest, in *Busuioc v. Moldova*. In that case, the Court singled out the special need to protect law enforcement officers and prosecutors but declared that this '*Janowski* principle' should not apply to 'all persons who are employed by the State or by State-owned companies'.[94] The Court has also

---

[88] *FCC v. League of Women Voters*, 468 U.S. 364, 375–6 (1984).

[89] *R. v. Keegstra* [1990] 3 S.C.R. 697, 849–50.

[90] 25 June 1992, 14 E.H.R.R. 843.

[91] *Id.* at paras. 61, 64. *See also Pedersen and Baadsgaard v. Denmark*, 17 Dec. 2004, 42 E.H.R.R. 24.

[92] 21 Jan. 1999.

[93] *Id.* at para. 33.

[94] 21 December 2004, 42 E.H.R.R. 14.

stated that journalists may, in some cases, be treated like politicians in that they are public figures and they have at their disposal ready means of protecting themselves.[95]

The scrutiny that the Court brings to the imposition of sanctions for defamatory expression varies not just with the person claiming injury but also with the subject matter of the expression. The reasoning that calls for strict controls on defamation actions brought by politicians supports the same treatment for complaints by private individuals when they are associated with matters of public interest.[96]

D. FREE EXPRESSION AND THE JUDICIAL PROCESS

As the *Barfod* case indicates, the special role and characteristics of the judiciary may raise special concerns when judicial proceedings and institutions are the subject of public comment. This difference is highlighted by Article 10(2)'s specification of 'maintaining the authority and impartiality of the judiciary' as one of the public aims for which speech may be properly limited. That concern is reinforced by the fact that Article 6 declares the important right of dispute settlement by a fair and impartial tribunal.

This issue arises most obviously in expression that may interfere with the proper determination of an ongoing judicial process. We have already observed in the *Sunday Times Case*[97] the European Court's particular caution in dealing with publications that may bias the outcome of civil actions. In *Worms v. Austria*,[98] the Court held that the state was entitled to fine the applicant for writing an article suggesting the guilt of a well known defendant in a tax evasion prosecution. The applicant had been charged with attempting to influence the outcome of a criminal proceeding. Such penalties, moreover, were held permissible even without showing that the publication had, in fact, had some influence on the result.[99] A prohibition on reporting information concerning an ongoing criminal investigation has also been held compatible with Article 10. The Court stressed the state's interest in protecting a defendant's presumption of innocence.[100]

On the other hand, the European Court has found some limitations on speech connected with active proceedings to be unjustifiable. It has, in this regard, noted that the kind of justice guaranteed by the Convention in Article 6 includes hearings that should themselves ordinarily be public.[101] A complete ban on the publication of any photographs of a criminal defendant was thus held disproportionate to any articulated need to protect the fairness of the trial and incompatible with the Convention.[102]

---

[95] *Urbino Rodrigues v. Portugal*, 29 Nov. 2005.
[96] *Bergens Tidende v. Norway*, 2 May 2000, 31 E.H.R.R. 16.
[97] 26 April 1979, 2 E.H.R.R. 245.
[98] 29 August 1997, 25 E.H.R.R. 464.
[99] *Id*. at para. 54.
[100] *Tourancheau v. France*, 24 November 2005.
[101] *News Verlags GmbH & Co. KG v. Austria*, 11 Jan. 2000, 31 E.H.R.R. 8.
[102] *Id*. at paras. 57–8.

An absolute statutory prohibition on the report of any information arising from an ongoing criminal prosecution initiated by private parties was also a violation of Article 10.[103]

Apart from expression dealing with unresolved litigation, the Court, as the *Barfod* case illustrates, has also dealt with limitation of speech more generally critical of judicial decisions or personnel after a case has concluded or unconnected to any particular case. In addition to injuring the reputation of the judges attacked, such speech has implications for the state's right to maintain the 'authority and impartiality of the judiciary'. In *Sunday Times*, the European Court of Human Rights expressed the risk such criticism posed to public respect for and confidence in courts as proper forums for the resolution of disputes. (The more hospitable attitude of the Court toward restrictions on criticism of judges does not extend to criticism of the behaviour of prosecutors.[104]) On the other hand, the Court also recognized that, as with other public agencies, the operation of the judiciary was a matter of legitimate public interest and that the media had a responsibility to report and comment on it.[105] The result has been a case-by-case balancing of these sometimes conflicting factors. The Court agreed it was proper to penalize journalists who published a particularly vitriolic attack on certain named judges and was without any reliable factual basis.[106] But it found a violation in the award of defamation damages for a published accusation of judicial bias in an article broadly treating a controversial child custody judgment that, on the whole, appeared to be carefully researched.[107] The outcome has also turned on how strident and how direct the insult to the courts is. When the President of the Moldovan Bar Association was fined for giving an interview in which he roundly criticized a Constitutional Court decision, the Strasbourg Court decided his remarks were not 'grave or ... insulting' to the judges and did not justify the penalty.[108] In principle, however, a sufficiently insulting statement may be punished even if only expressed in a letter to the judges and not published generally.[109] On the other hand, the Court has expressed its strong reluctance to permit any kind of restriction on statements of counsel in the course of a judicial proceeding.[110]

---

[103] *DuRoy & Malaurie v. France*, 3 Oct. 2000.

[104] *Nikula v. Finland*, 21 March 2002, 38 E.H.R.R. 45.

[105] 26 April 1979, 2 E.H.R.R. 245, paras. 63–5.

[106] *Präger & Oberschlick v. Austria*, 26 Apr. 1995, 21 E.H.R.R. 1. Note Judge Maartens' dissent doubting whether confidence in the judiciary can be maintained by criminal proceedings to punish its critics. Dissenting Opinion of Judge Maartens joined by Judges Pekkanen and Makarczyk, para. 3.

[107] *De Haas & Gijsels v. Belgium*, 24 Feb. 1997, 25 E.H.R.R. 1.

[108] *Amihalachioaie v. Moldova*, 20 April 2004, 40 E.H.R.R. 45. *See also Hrico v. Slovakia*, 20 July 2004, 41 E.H.R.R. 18. Compare *Pasalaris & Press Foundation v. Greece*, 4 July 2002 (application concerning a conviction for accusing a judge of corruption inadmissible) with *Rizos & Daskas v. Greece*, 27 May 2004 (conviction based on publication of an article merely suggesting possible judicial corruption was a violation of Article 10).

[109] *Skalka v. Poland*, 27 May 2003, 38 E.H.R.R 1, para. 41. In this case a violation was found but only because the punishment imposed was deemed excessive.

[110] *Hrico v. Slovakia, supra* n. 108, at para. 55.

The central place of political discussion in freedom of expression has naturally led to a special emphasis on the need to protect the press from regulation and censorship. The press is separately mentioned in the First Amendment to the United States Constitution, although that clause has not been interpreted to provide any preferred status for the press over other speakers.[111] The European Court has frequently stressed the importance of the press in realizing the values Article 10 was intended to safeguard. The discussion in paragraphs 41 and 42 of the *Lingens* case is illustrative. In the *Spycatcher Case*, discussed above, the Court referred to the press's 'vital role of "public watchdog"'.[112]

The importance of an independent press suggests the possibility that Article 10 may prohibit more than direct regulation of the actual publication of material. It might also bar actions which interfere with the ordinary information-gathering and disseminating function of newspapers and other media. The Strasbourg Court dealt with such a case in *Goodwin v. United Kingdom*.[113] In that case, a reporter had received confidential information about the financial condition of a company. The company obtained an injunction preventing the publication of the information and an order requiring the reporter to reveal his source. The Court emphasized that freedom of the press depended on more than a right to publish:

Protection of journalistic sources is one of the basic conditions for press freedom, as is reflected in the laws and the professional codes of conduct in a number of Contracting States ... Without such protection, sources may be deterred from assisting the press in informing the public on matters of public interest. As a result the vital public watchdog role of the press may be undermined and the ability of the press to provide accurate and reliable information may be adversely affected.... Such a measure cannot be compatible with Article 10 of the Convention unless it is justified by an overriding requirement of public interest.[114]

In the case at hand, the Court agreed that preventing economic injury to the company and its employees was a legitimate public interest. But, given the injunction against publication, identifying the source would only deal with the 'residual threat of damage through dissemination of the confidential information otherwise than by the press', and provide aid 'in obtaining compensation and in unmasking a disloyal employee or collaborator ... [E]ven if considered cumulatively [these interests were not] sufficient to outweigh the vital public interest in the protection of the applicant journalist's source'.[115]

When police searched a journalist's office for evidence of his sources in a corruption investigation, the Strasbourg Court found it an even more serious violation of Article 10 than the order to disclose at issue in *Goodwin*. In such a case, authorities

---

[111] *See First National Bank v. Bellotti*, 435 U.S. 765, 795–802 (1978) (Burger CJ concurring).

[112] *Observer & Guardian v. United Kingdom*, 26 Nov. 1991, 14 E.H.R.R. 153, para. 59(b).

[113] 27 Mar. 1996, 22 E.H.R.R. 123.

[114] *Id.* at para. 39.

[115] *Id.* at para. 45. *See also Camelot Group P.L.C. v. Centaur Communications Ltd.* [1998] 1 All E.R. 251 (C.A.).

'have very wide investigative powers as, by definition, they have access to all the documentation held by the journalist'. This conclusion was not changed by the fact that no confidential information was discovered.[116] In contrast, officials were entitled under the Convention to demand outtakes from a television documentary on pedophilia. In that case, the people whose identity might be disclosed were not sources who had cooperated with the journalists on an assurance of anonymity.[117]

English courts deal with the question of the confidentiality of journalistic sources under Section 10 of the Contempt of Court Act 1981. Under that provision, courts may not order journalists to reveal their sources unless 'necessary in the interests of justice or national security or for the prevention of disorder or crime'. The House of Lords has treated this standard as calling for the same kind of balancing of interests undertaken by the European Court under Article 10 of the Convention.[118]

The case-by-case approach to this question employed in both the European Court and the English courts may be contrasted with that adopted by Judge Walsh in his dissenting judgment in *Goodwin*. In contrast to another dissenting opinion joined by seven judges, which accepted the Court's conclusion that it was necessary to assess the competing interests, Judge Walsh questioned whether any Article 10 right could be asserted in these circumstances:

[I]t appears to me that the Court in its decision has decided in effect that under the Convention a journalist is by virtue of his profession to be afforded a privilege not available to other persons. Should not the ordinary citizen writing a letter to the paper for publication be afforded an equal privilege even though he is not by profession a journalist? …

In the present case the applicant did not suffer any denial of expressing himself. Rather he has refused to speak. In consequence a litigant seeking the protection of the law for his interests which were wrongfully injured is left without the remedy the courts had decided he was entitled to.[119]

A plurality of the United States Supreme Court came to a similar conclusion in deciding that the First Amendment to the United States Constitution does not shield a journalist from the obligation to answer questions concerning his or her sources from a grand jury. The Court noted that no issue arose as to any inhibition on publication nor on the use of any investigative method. Like Judge Walsh, it also noted that ordinary citizens had no right to withhold confidential information from a grand jury.[120]

The Supreme Court of Canada has also concluded that media offices cannot be categorically immune to an otherwise proper search warrant. Such premises are, however, 'entitled to special consideration because of the importance of their role in a democratic society'.[121]

---

[116] *Roemen & Schmit v. Luxembourg*, 25 Feb. 2003.

[117] *Nordisk Film and TV A/S v. Denmark*, 8 Dec. 2005.

[118] *Ashworth Security Hospital v. MGN Ltd* [2002] U.K.H.L. 29, [2002] 4 All E.R. 193.

[119] *Goodwin, supra* n. 113 (separate dissenting opinion of Judge Walsh, paras. 1–2).

[120] *Branzburg v. Hayes*, 408 U.S. 665, 681–2 (1972).

[121] *Société Radio-Canada v. Lessord* [1991] 3 S.C.R. 421 para. 14. *See Zurcher v. Stanford Daily*, 436 U.S. 347 (1970).

3. FREEDOM OF EXPRESSION AND PROTECTION
AGAINST DEFAMATION

A. DEFAMATION AND MATTERS OF PUBLIC INTEREST

Article 12 of the Universal Declaration of Human Rights, upon which Article 8 of the European Convention is patterned, declares that 'no one shall be subjected ... to attack upon his honour and reputation'.[122] No such language appears in the Convention but Article 10(2) in setting out the grounds justifying some interference with freedom of expression includes 'protection of the reputation or rights of others'.

Almost every legal system provides redress for individuals whose reputations have been injured by the speech of other people. Many of the Strasbourg cases interpreting Article 10 arise out of civil defamation actions seeking damages or criminal defamation prosecutions instituted by the injured party. But, as per the judgment in *Lingens,* this interest is less compelling when the injured party is a public figure. This is because of the critical social interest in discussing the behaviour and character of such persons. Moreover there is less need to protect the reputations of public figures than those of private persons. Public figures might be thought to have invited such comment by assuming a public role, thus, in a sense, 'waiving' the full measure of 'protection' contemplated in Article 10(2).[123] A public figure may have superior means to respond to unfair criticism. Thus, a private citizen would be more injured by the defamatory expression. Exactly this distinction has shaped the American constitutional doctrine which limits actions of defamation against publications that have published allegedly libellous statements about public officials and other 'public figures'. To succeed in such an action the plaintiff must prove that the statements were made with 'actual malice', that is with knowledge of their falsity or with a reckless disregard of whether they were true or false.[124] But the constitutionally minimum fault necessary to support a defamation action by 'private' plaintiffs is much lower. They need only show some fault.[125]

The European Court has observed the same distinction as indicated by its reference in the *Lingens* case to the special situation of public figures. These figures are less protected even in cases where the defamatory expression is unconnected to a politician's public activities.[126] Even private persons, moreover, may be subject to this standard when they enter into a public debate.[127] A similar approach has been followed when private persons are involved in matters of legitimate public concern. In *Bladet Tromsø*

---

[122] U.N.G.A. Resolution 217A (III), U.N. Doc. A/810, at 71 (1948).

[123] *See* para. 42 of *Lingens v. Austria, supra.*

[124] *See New York Times v. Sullivan,* 376 U.S. 254 (1964); *Curtis Publishing Co. v. Butts,* 388 U.S. 130 (1967).

[125] *Gertz v. Robert Welch Inc.,* 418 U.S. 323 (1974).

[126] *Karhuvaara & Iltalehti v. Finland,* 16 Nov. 2004, 41 E.H.R.R. 51.

[127] *Jerusalem v. Austria,* 27 Feb. 2001, 37 E.H.R.R. 25.

and Stensaas v. Norway,[128] the Court found a violation in the imposition of liability on a newspaper for publishing what turned out to be inaccurate and defamatory statements about the practices of certain seal hunters. It noted that methods of seal hunting were a matter of public debate in Norway. A dissenting opinion emphasized that the individuals whose reputations had been injured were 'private persons *par excellence*'.[129]

In *Steel & Morris v. United Kingdom*,[130] the McDonald's Corporation won a libel judgment against the applicants for distributing a pamphlet accusing the restaurant chain of a long list of anti-social acts. In Strasbourg, the Court found a violation of Article 10. In formulating its approach, however, it concluded that there was a special margin of appreciation to be accorded to a state's procedures for adjudicating such cases. It agreed with the applicants that large public corporations, like public figures, inevitably and knowingly, lay themselves open to public scrutiny of their acts. On the other hand, such companies had a competing interest in 'protecting [their] commercial success and viability'.[131]

In the United Kingdom, the common law developed a number of doctrines which are sensitive to the importance of open debate on public questions in the functioning of a democratic system of government. Thus, an absolute defence of privilege is available for statements made in parliamentary proceedings.[132] Other statements have the benefit of a 'qualified privilege', which serves as a defence to a libel action unless the plaintiff can show that the statement was made with 'express malice'. Included in this category are a variety of reports of official proceedings. Statements are qualifiedly privileged if made pursuant to any legal, social or moral duty. Thus, the House of Lords has held that false defamatory statements made at a meeting of a local council are privileged. It is important that on such occasions the members 'should be able to speak freely and frankly, boldly and bluntly on any matter which affects the interests or welfare of the inhabitants'.[133] When qualified privilege does exist, proof of express malice requires evidence that the speaker knew the statement was false, recklessly ignored its truth or falsity or misused the privilege out of personal spite.[134] Since it is confined to communication made by persons with some kind of duty to report and made to persons with a particular interest in receiving the information, it has been restricted to 'information arising in the conduct of quite intimate professional and personal relationships'. Consequently, it has been hard to invoke qualified privilege in actions directed at communications made to the public at large. In *Reynolds v.*

---

[128] 25 May 1999, 29 E.H.R.R. 125. *See also Prud'homme v. Prud'homme* [2002] 4 S.C.R. 663.

[129] *Id*. paras. 62–3; Joint dissenting opinion of Judges Palm, Fuhrmann and Baka.

[130] 15 Feb. 2005, 41 E.H.R.R. 22.

[131] *Id*. at para. 94.

[132] *See* A. W. Bradley & K. D. Ewing, *Constitutional and Administrative Law* 224–6 (14th edn. 2007).

[133] *See Horrocks v. Lowe* [1975] A.C. 135, 152 [1974] 1 All E.R. 662, 671 H.L. (Lord Diplock). The European Court has recognized a similar interest under Article 10. *See Jerusalem v. Austria, supra* n. 127, at para. 31.

[134] *Horrocks v. Lowe, supra* n. 133, at 150 (Lord Diplock).

Times Newspapers Ltd.,[135] the House of Lords broadened the occasions for invoking the privilege. In a decision upholding a libel award made to the former Taoiseach (Prime Minister) of Ireland for a misleading report of his statements in parliamentary debates, the House rejected an argument that political expression, as a category, ought to enjoy a qualified privilege. It did agree, however, that defendants could claim the privilege for reports which, in the circumstances of a particular case, was found to be of sufficient 'value to the public'. Such value was to be measured by both the subject matter and the 'quality' of the publication. The latter characteristic was to be measured case by case. The speech of Lord Nicholls of Birkenhead listed 10 factors that would be relevant, many of which concerned the care that had been taken in confirming a story's accuracy.[136] It is notable that the Lords regarded this as a threshold inquiry for the court to make before allowing the privilege to be invoked, and not, as might have been expected, as an aspect of the 'malice' that could overcome the privilege.

The decision in *Reynolds* may be compared to an earlier judgment of the High Court of Australia similarly widening the defence of qualified privilege. The Court acted under what it saw as an implicit constitutional requirement that expression on 'political or government matters which enables the people to exercise a free and informed choice as electors' be permitted.[137] Communication within this category could claim the protection of privilege but, in light of the fact that the defamatory aspects of such speech might now reach thousands of people, the Court added to the conditions for claiming the privilege a showing that the publisher had acted 'reasonably'. This requires evidence that the publisher had 'reasonable grounds for believing the imputation was true, took proper steps ... to verify the accuracy of the material and did not believe the imputation to be untrue'. Moreover, the defendant's conduct will not be reasonable unless the defendant (when practicable) has sought a response from the person defamed and published the response.[138] The increasing relevance, in qualified privilege cases, of the defendant's efforts to verify and to present fairly the defamatory material has been paralleled in the European Court's Article 10 jurisprudence. The Court has reduced this concern to a formula requiring that media invoking this right act 'in good faith in order to provide accurate and reliable information in accordance with the ethics of journalism'.[139] It has also indicated that the more serious the defamation, the more caution is expected from the press.[140]

A potentially broader defence to defamation actions which has developed in light of the interest in free political speech is that of 'fair comment'. Under this doctrine, it is an adequate defence to an action for defamation that the statement complained of was the expression of an honestly held opinion on a matter of public interest and

---

[135] [1999] U.K.H.L. 45, [2001] 2 A.C. 127.   [136] Ibid. at 201–5.

[137] *Lange v. Australia Broadcasting Corp.* (1997) 145 A.L.R. 96.

[138] *Id.* The *Lange* case is discussed in I. Loveland, 'The Constitutionalisation of Private Libels in English Common Law?', [1998] *Public Law* 633.

[139] *Selistö v. Finland*, 16 Nov. 2004, 42 E.H.R.R 8, para. 54.

[140] *Radio France & Others v. France*, 30 March 2004, 40 E.H.R.R. 29, para. 39; *Chauvy & Others v. France*, 29 June 2004, 41 E.H.R.R. 29.

particularly on the conduct of public officials.[141] The connection of this defence to freedom of expression values has been made explicit. Lord Justice Scott in the Court of Appeal noted that the defence promoted the 'public interest to have free discussion of matters of public interest', and that this right was 'one of the fundamental rights of free speech and writing which are so dear to the British nation, and it is of vital importance to the rule of law upon which we depend for our personal freedom...'.[142]

More recently, the House of Lords has further emphasized the value of free expression in matters of public concern in holding that governmental institutions had no right to maintain an action for defamation. The House cited both American constitutional cases and judgments of the European Court of Human Rights, although it expressly declined to base its decision on the Convention. Lord Keith held:

It is of the highest public importance that a democratically elected governmental body, or indeed any governmental body, should be open to uninhibited public criticism. The threat of a civil action for defamation must inevitably have an inhibiting effect on freedom of speech.[143]

And, in keeping with the rationale for limiting defamation actions by public figures elaborated in the cases discussed above, Lord Keith noted that '[t]he normal means by which the Crown protects itself against attacks upon its management of the country's affairs is political action and not litigation...'.[144] The House, however, did not take this reasoning as far as the American cases. Individuals who felt defamed for criticism of their performance as public officials could still seek legal redress.[145]

B. FREE EXPRESSION AND THE PROTECTION OF PRIVACY

Many jurisdictions recognize that individuals are entitled not only to protection of their reputations but also to keep certain aspects of their lives hidden from public view. As will be seen, such protection has been recognized as a component of Article 8 of the European Convention. So, when media publish information about the private lives of individuals, the right to free expression may collide with the privacy rights of the people affected. In such cases the Strasbourg Court has balanced the particular interests on both sides to decide which set of values predominate.

A claim of privacy is less likely to defeat an assertion of rights under Article 10 when the individual involved is a politician or other public official about whom the public may have a legitimate reason to be informed. A publisher successfully invoked Article 10 when it was enjoined, on the application of the surviving family, from

---

[141] A. W. Bradley & K. D. Ewing, *Constitutional and Administrative Law* 565 (14th edn. 2007), J. Murphy, *Street on Torts* 562–8 (12th edn. 2007).

[142] *Lyon v. Daily Telegraph Ltd.* [1943] K.B. 746, 752–3.

[143] *Derbyshire County Council v. Times Newspapers Ltd.* [1993] A.C. 534.

[144] *Id.* at 549 (quoting Schreiner JA in *Die Spoorbond v. South African Railways* [1946] A.D. 999, 1012–13).

[145] *Id.* at 549–50. This rule was expanded to ban libel action by political parties in *Goldsmith v. Bhoyrul* [1997] 4 All. E.R. 268 (Q.B.). For a criticism of the limited character of these holdings *see* Loveland, *supra.* n. 138.

distributing a book detailing the medical treatment of the late President Mitterand of France. The book had been written by Mitterand's physician who had breached a duty of confidentiality. The Court considered that the book had been published 'in the context of a wide-ranging debate in France on a matter of public interest, in particular the public's right to be informed about any serious illnesses suffered by the head of state'. It also concluded that the book contributed to the 'public interest in discussion of the history of President Mitterand's two terms of office'.[146]

The vulnerability of the private lives of public officials was even more pronounced in a case where a newspaper was convicted of invasion of privacy for publication of an article about the husband of a member of the Finnish Parliament. The article detailed the prosecution of the husband for drunken and disorderly behaviour and assault on a police officer. It emphasized the marital connection and included a picture of the legislator's spouse. The European Court was persuaded that this information 'could affect people's voting decisions ... [and was] at least to some degree a matter of public interest'.[147] It found a violation of Article 10.

These cases should be contrasted with *Von Hannover v. Germany*.[148] Princess Caroline of Monaco had failed to convince the German courts to protect her privacy from constant intrusions by 'papparazzi'. She and her family were frequently photographed, without their consent, while engaging in the ordinary activities of their lives. These photographs were then published in mass circulation media. The local courts had reasoned that Caroline was a 'public figure, par excellence' and had forfeited her right to privacy in most public places. The European Court found a violation of Germany's positive obligation under Article 8. It stressed that, although the princess represented Monaco's ruling family 'at certain cultural or charitable events ... she [did] not exercise any function within or on behalf of the state'.

The Court considers that a fundamental distinction needs to be made between reporting facts—even controversial ones—capable of contributing to a debate in a democratic society relating to politicians in the exercise of their functions, for example, and reporting details of the private life of an individual who, moreover, as in this case, does not exercise official functions ...

[T]he Court considers that the publication of the photos and articles in question, the sole purpose of which was to satisfy the curiosity of a particular readership regarding the details of the applicant's private life, cannot be deemed to contribute to any debate of general interest to a society despite the applicant being known to the public ...

In these conditions freedom of expression calls for a narrower interpretation ...[149]

Some of the same considerations featured in the House of Lords' judgment in *Campbell v. MGN Limited*.[150] The well known model, Naomi Campbell, had brought a 'breach

---

[146] *Editions Plon v. France*, 18 May 2004, 42 E.H.R.R. 36, paras. 44, 53.

[147] *Karhuvaara & Iltalehti v. Finland*, 16 Nov. 2004, 41 E.H.R.R. 51, para. 45.

[148] 24 June 2004, 40 E.H.R.R. 1.

[149] *Id.* paras. 63–6. For a critical appraisal of the *Von Hannover* judgment *see* M. A. Sanderson, 'Is Von Hannover v. Germany a Step Backward for the Substantive Analysis of Speech and Privacy Interest?', [2004] *European Human Rights L. Rev.* 631.

[150] [2004] U.K.H.L. 22, [2004] 2 A.C. 457.

of confidence' action against the publisher of the Mirror after it published several articles concerning her efforts to overcome a drug addiction and, in particular, her attendance at meetings of Narcotics Anonymous. The articles had been accompanied by a photograph of Campbell in front of a building where such a meeting was held. All of the Law Lords agreed that a breach of confidence action could extend to cases where a defendant published private information without the consent of the plaintiff. They also agreed that the controlling factors in determining liability were the relative weight of the interests in privacy and in free expression protected by Articles 8 and 10 respectively. In a subsequent case, Lord Steyn, speaking for a unanimous court, stated four propositions that he thought had been established in the *Campbell* case:

First, neither article [8 or 10 of the Convention] has *as such* precedence over the other. Secondly, where the values under the two articles are in conflict, an intense focus on the comparative importance of the specific right being claimed in the individual case is necessary. Thirdly, the justifications for interfering with or restricting each right must be taken into account. Finally, the proportionality test must be applied to each. For convenience I will call this the ultimate balancing test.[151]

In *Campbell*, a majority of the Lords decided that the plaintiff's privacy interests prevailed. Partly, this was the consequence of the fact that admittedly permissible disclosure of the plaintiff's addiction and treatment (which were in contradiction to her previous public statements) had adequately served whatever legitimate public interest there was in the story. 'The political and social life of the community and the intellectual, artistic or personal development of individuals are not obviously assisted by pouring over the intimate details of a fashion model's private life'.[152] In contrast, in the second case, quoted above, the Lords held there was insufficient justification for an injunction against publishing the name of a defendant who was accused of murdering her nine year old son. The order had been made by the Family Court to protect the defendant's younger son who, it was feared, would suffer serious psychiatric damage if his connection with the case became known. The single judgment of Lord Steyn noted that the boy's privacy interest was only indirectly implicated since he himself was not a party to the prosecution. More importantly, it stressed the important public value of keeping the administration of justice public.[153]

In *Time, Inc. v. Hill*,[154] the United States Supreme Court held that the First Amendment limited tort actions for disclosing private information or placing the plaintiff in a 'false light'. If a publication touched on a matter of public concern recovery could only be had if the publication were knowingly false or published with reckless disregard as to its truth or falsity. However, in *Zacchini v. Scripps-Howard Broadcasting Co*,[155] the Court

---

[151] *In re S (FC) (a child)* [2004] U.K.H.L. 47, para. 17.
[152] [2004] U.K.H.L. 22, para. 149 (Baroness Hale of Richmond). On the Campbell case *see* N. A. Moreham, 'Privacy in the Common Law: A Doctrinal Analysis', (2005) 121 *L.Q.R.* 628.
[153] [2004] U.K.H.L. 47, paras. 27–30.
[154] 385 U.S. 374, 380–91 (1987).
[155] 433 U.S. 562, 569–79 (1977).

held constitutional a damages judgment against a television station for broadcasting, in its entirety, an entertainer's 'human cannonball' act. The action in this case was based on a state law tort of 'appropriation' or 'right of publicity'. The Court stressed that the economic value of the plaintiff's performance was similar to that accorded protection by copyright and patent laws.

The Supreme Court of Canada discussed the reconciliation of privacy and freedom of expression in *Aubry v. Editions Vice-Versa Inc*,[156] in which the plaintiff sought damages for the publication of her photograph in a magazine article about contemporary urban life. The Court noted that everyone has a presumptive right not to have his or her image published without consent as an aspect of the right to private life. That right, however, must yield in some circumstances to the public right to information and the concomitant right of free expression. No liability for violation of a privacy right should arise, for example, if the plaintiff were 'engaged in a public activity or has acquired a certain notoriety'. This is true, in particular, of artists and politicians but also, more generally, of all those whose professional success depends on 'public opinion'. This would also be the case when an otherwise unknown person became involved, wittingly or unwittingly, with important matters of public interest.[157]

C. FALSEHOODS AND STATEMENTS OF OPINION

Legal remedies for injuries to reputation usually turn critically on the truth or falsity of the statement. Logically, the truth of a statement might be irrelevant if the sole value at stake were the harm to the good name of the complainant. Indeed, the English common law once held that truth could not be a defence, and, in prosecutions for criminal libel, the rule was 'the greater the truth the greater the libel'.[158] The rule is now, almost everywhere, to the contrary. Therefore, in considering the extent of constitutional protection for arguably libellous speech, we ordinarily are dealing only with statements that are false. Falsity alone does not deprive expression of constitutional protection. The United States Supreme Court has stressed that 'erroneous statement is inevitable in free debate and it must be protected if the freedoms of expression are to have the "breathing space" that they "need … to survive"'.[159] Whether such false statements should be privileged has turned on the degree of fault attributable to the speaker in making the incorrect statement. The 'actual malice' standard, cited above, allows a sanction for such speech about a public figure, only when the falsehood was intentional or the result of 'reckless' judgment.[160] The same standard, as noted, must be met before

---

[156] [1998] 1 S.C.R. 591.

[157] *Id.* at paras. 53–9.

[158] W. Prosser, *Handbook of the Law of Torts* 797 (4th edn. 1971).

[159] *New York Times v. Sullivan*, 376 U.S. 254, 271–2 (1964) (quoting *N.A.A.C.P. v. Button*, 371 U.S. 415 (1963)).

[160] *Id.* at 279–80. The Supreme Court of Canada has held that even intentionally false statements may be protected constitutionally. The Court noted the difficulty of identifying 'the essence of [a] communication and determin[ing] that it is false' since a 'given expression may offer many meanings, some which seem false, others of a metaphysical or allegorical nature, which may possess some validity'. Moreover, even a plainly

a defamation judgement is allowed based on a statement accorded 'qualified privilege' under English law. And in American constitutional law, even statements about private persons concerning matters of public interest are redressable only on proof that the speaker had acted, at least, negligently.

Recall that, in *Lingens v. Austria*, the supposed defamatory statements were expressions of opinion, not assertions of fact that might be proven true or false. For the Austrian courts this was grounds for denying Lingens the possibility of defending by showing the truth of his article. For the European Court, however, the impossibility of establishing the truth of 'value judgments' meant the applicant had been convicted for the mere dissemination of his opinions, a restriction which could not be necessary, at least in the absence of a showing of bad faith.[161] It is not always easy, of course, to distinguish between statements expressing opinions or 'value judgments' and statements asserting facts. The European Court has been willing to treat polemical statements in political controversies as value judgments even when couched in the language of fact. Examples include statements that a public official has a 'fascist past',[162] that municipal councillors who appointed themselves to certain posts were 'concerned, above all, about their own interest and that of their families',[163] and that a candidate for office had 'broken your ballot boxes'.[164]

Even value judgments may, consistently with the Convention, be punishable if not made in good faith. The Court has not fully explained what, in these circumstances, good faith entails, but its opinions suggest that it requires some minimum effort on the part of the writer or publisher to inform himself about the facts on which such an opinion ought to be based.[165] This reasoning suggests that there is no easy distinction between fact and opinion. The United States Supreme Court has also rejected an argument that there should be an absolute constitutional defence to any defamation action based on a published statement of opinion.[166] Since certain statements of opinion (for example, 'In my opinion John Jones is a liar') imply knowledge of false and defamatory facts, they may cause as much damage to reputation as ordinary falsehoods. The Court held a libel action could be maintained if the plaintiff could prove a 'false factual connotation' and show the defendant acted with the degree of fault necessary under the particular circumstances. On the other hand, where a statement 'cannot "reasonably

---

deliberate exaggeration or falsehood may further a social interest by stimulating useful social action or discussion. *R. v. Zundel* [1992] 2 S.C.R. 731, 756.

[161] *See also Oberschlik v. Austria*, 23 May 1991, 19 E.H.R.R. 389, para. 63; *Schwabe v. Austria*, 28 Aug. 1992, para. 34; *Ukrainian Media Group v. Ukraine*, 29 March 2005, 43 E.H.R.R. 25, paras. 59–60.

[162] *Feldek v. Slovakia, supra* n. 85.

[163] *Sokolowski v. Poland*, 29 March 2005, at paras. 45–6.

[164] *Brasilier v. France, supra* n. 87, at paras. 14, 37.

[165] *See De Haes & Gijsels v. Belgium*, 27 Feb. 1997, 25 E.H.R.R. 1, para. 47; *Oberschlick v. Austria (No. 2)*, 1 July 1997, 25 E.H.R.R. 357, para. 33; *Bladet Tromsø & Stensaas v. Norway*, 20 May 1999, 29 E.H.R.R. 125, paras. 67–71. In none of these cases did the Court find that the opinions were so unsupported as to permit prosecution consistent with Art. 10. However, this reasoning does appear to support, in part, the refusal to find a violation in an earlier case. *See Prager & Oberschlick v. Austria*, 26 Apr. 1995, 21 E.H.R.R. 1, para. 37, on the relevance of the publisher's care in verifying information.

[166] *Milkovich v. Lorain Journal Co.*, 497 U.S. 1 (1990).

[be] interpreted as stating actual facts" about an individual' no action could lie.[167] The English courts have reached a similar conclusion when dealing with the libel defence of 'fair comment', discussed above. More particularly, that defence is applicable only to expressions of opinion. To the extent that an ostensible statement of opinion may reasonably be read as implying defamatory facts, the defence is unavailable and liability may be imposed. In *Telnikoff v. Matusevitch*,[168] the House of Lords held that, in deciding whether or not a statement should be understood as containing defamatory statements of fact rather than mere comment, it was appropriate to look only at the alleged libel itself without regard to the context in which it was published since possible readers might not have the benefit of that context in interpreting it. 'The writer of a letter to a newspaper', wrote Lord Keith, 'has a duty to take reasonable care to make clear that he is writing comment, and not making misrepresentations about the subject upon which he is commenting'.[169] In a dissenting judgment, Lord Ackner differed with this approach, arguing that it would unduly restrict the right of fair comment and thus impair the public interest in free and open discussion.[170]

D. SANCTIONS FOR DEFAMATION

The Strasbourg Court's jurisprudence on defamation and Article 10 extends to a review of the kind and amount of damages awarded to the defamed person. In *Tolstoy Miloslavsky v. United Kingdom*,[171] a libel plaintiff's award of £1,500,000, more than three times the highest amount previously allowed, was held a violation of Article 10. The European Court held an award for defamation 'must bear a reasonable relationship of proportionality to the injury to reputation suffered'. The Court was especially concerned about the English practice (subsequently modified) of leaving damage calculations to fairly unconstrained jury discretion and providing no effective appellate review of such judgments.[172] The same concern applies a fortiori where a criminal libel prosecution results in a jail sentence. In *Cumpănă and Mazăre v. Romania*, the Court found that the state was justified in imposing non-pecuniary damages in such a case but that seven months imprisonment and deprivation of certain freedoms was a disproportionate response to the social need to protect reputation. The Court emphasized the potential chilling effect of such a sanction on investigative journalists. '[T]he imposition of a prison sentence for a press offence will be compatible with journalists' freedom of expression as guaranteed by Article 10 of the Convention only in exceptional circumstances, notably where other fundamental rights have been seriously impaired, as for example, in the case of hate speech or incitement to violence.'[173]

---

[167] *Id.* at 17 (quoting *Hustler Magazine, Inc. v. Falwell*, 485 U.S. 46, 50 (1988)).
[168] [1992] 2 A.C. 343 (H.L.).
[169] *Id.* at 353.
[170] *Id.* at 361.
[171] 13 July 1995, 20 E.H.R.R. 44.
[172] *Id.* at paras. 49–50.
[173] 17 Dec. 2004, 41 E.H.R.R. 14, paras. 111–19 (quoted language is from para. 115).

The European Court's focus on jury discretion may be compared with the view of the Supreme Court of Canada in *Hill v. Church of Scientology*.[174] In that case, a libel judgment of $1,600,000 was made to a Crown Attorney who had been accused of professional misconduct by the defendants. Appellate review of such judgments in Canada was determined by 'whether the verdict is so exorbitant or so grossly out of proportion to the libel as to shock the Court's conscience and sense of justice'.[175] The jury in this case had requested guidelines on the range of proper awards but had been refused. The Supreme Court emphasized that jury discretion in the calculation of libel damages was particularly appropriate. Noting that a 'defamatory statement can seep into the crevasses of the subconscious and lurk there ever ready to spring forth and spread its cancerous evil', it concluded that it 'is members of the community in which the defamed person lives who will be best able to assess the damages'.[176] The Court also declined to impose a cap on non-pecuniary damages as it had done in personal injury cases. 'If it were known in advance what amount the defamer would be required to pay ... a defendant might look upon that sum as the maximum cost of a license to defame.'[177]

It will be recalled that United States Supreme Court decisions have held that public officials and 'public figures' may only recover for libels published with 'actual malice', that is with knowledge of their falsity or with reckless disregard of their truth or falsity. Private plaintiffs, on the other hand, need only show some 'fault' to recover. In establishing the latter proposition, however, the Supreme Court held that the state's interest in permitting recovery in this kind of case 'extends no further than compensation for actual injury'.[178] Consequently it limited the damages in such cases unless the plaintiff proved actual malice. First, it held unconstitutional the longstanding rule that injury was to be presumed from the mere fact of publication. Any recovery would have to be based on proof of actual injury, although the Court recognized that such injury may include much more than pecuniary loss, mentioning 'impairment of reputation and standing in the community, personal humiliation and mental anguish and suffering'.[179] Furthermore (absent proof of actual malice), punitive damages were impermissible since, as the Court noted, they were 'wholly irrelevant to the state interest that justifies a negligence standard for private defamation actions'.[180] With respect to both presumed and punitive damages the Court's concerns were the same. Each doctrine allowed the jury a more or less uncontrollable discretion, 'invit[ing] juries to punish unpopular opinion rather than to compensate individuals for injury sustained by the publication of a false fact'. This practice would 'unnecessarily compound

---

[174] [1995] 2 S.C.R. 1130.
[175] *Id.* at para. 159.
[176] *Id.* at para. 166.
[177] *Id.* at para. 170.
[178] *Gertz v. Robert Welch, Inc., supra* n. 125, at 356.
[179] *Id.* at 350.
[180] *Id.*

[...] the potential of any system of liability...to inhibit the vigorous exercise of First Amendment freedoms'.[181]

4. FREEDOM OF EXPRESSION AND NATIONAL SECURITY

Necessarily, states feel a particular need to restrict expression in situations affecting military, diplomatic or intelligence matters. When such restrictions have been challenged under the Convention, the European Court has considered them under Article 10(2) which permits limitations on expression 'necessary in a democratic society in the interests of public safety [and] for the prevention of disorder or crime'. In *Observer & Guardian v. United Kingdom*,[182] the Spycatcher Case discussed above,[183] the Court dealt with an injunction against publication of the memoirs of a British intelligence officer. It held this action to be justified before the book had become widely available in other countries and unjustified thereafter.

One might expect any court to be reluctant to overturn national determinations on matters so central to state interests. The United States Supreme Court has stated that even prior restraint of expression might be proper to 'prevent actual obstruction to [the government's] recruiting service or the publication of the sailing dates of transports or the number and location of troops'.[184] Nevertheless, that Court has continued to scrutinize limitations on expression imposed on members of the military insisting that, while the extent of permissible restrictions may differ in that context, citizens do not lose their First Amendment rights on entry into military service.[185]

The European Court of Human Rights has adopted the same approach. In *Grigoriades v. Greece*,[186] an officer was convicted of 'insulting the armed forces' when he sent a letter to his commanding officer sharply critical of the army. The Court stated that Article 10 'does not stop at the gates of army barracks'. It acknowledged, however, that restrictions on expression might be allowed when there is 'a real threat to military discipline, as the proper functioning of an army is hardly imaginable without legal rules designed to prevent servicemen from undermining it'.[187] But this kind of justification has been examined critically. In *Vereinigung Demokratischer Soldaten*

---

[181] *Id.* at 349. The Court made no reference to the proper quantum of damages in actions brought by public officials and public figures who must prove actual malice for any recovery. One commentator has argued that the logic of *Gertz* indicates that such plaintiffs may not recover presumed or punitive damages under any circumstances. J. E. Nowak & R. D. Rotunda, *Constitutional Law* 1095–6 (5th edn. 1995).

[182] 26 Nov. 1991, 14 E.H.R.R. 153.

[183] *See* Section B *supra*.

[184] *Near v. Minnesota*, 283 U.S. 697, 716 (1931); but *see New York Times Co. v. United States*, 403 U.S. 713 (1971) (holding unconstitutional an injunction against publication of a government report on the Vietnam War over a claim that such publication would be contrary to the interests of national security).

[185] *Parker v. Levy*, 417 U.S. 733 (1974).

[186] 25 Nov. 1997, 27 E.H.R.R. 464.

[187] *Id.* at para. 45.

Osterreichs & Gubi v. Austria,[188] it held there was a breach of Article 10 when the Austrian military refused to distribute on a military base a magazine critical of the army. The Court did not accept the state's assertion that the publication presented a threat to discipline:

None of the issues of [the magazine] submitted in evidence recommend disobedience or violence, or even question the usefulness of the army... [D]espite their often polemical tenor, it does not appear they overstepped the bounds of what is permissible in the context of a mere discussion of ideas, which must be tolerated in the army of a democratic State just as it must be in the society that such an army serves.[189]

While acknowledging the primary duty of the government to evaluate and respond to the threat of terrorism, the House of Lords has refused to hold that it cannot review a declaration under Article 15 of the Convention allowing derogation from the Convention in time of emergency.[190]

The armed conflict between Kurdish nationalists and the Turkish state has presented the Court with opportunities to illuminate the limits of free expression in a period of serious threat to the established government. Its response has been to evaluate the degree of danger presented by the expression in each instance and to measure it against the standards justifying limits on expression developed under Article 10(2). So, the Court has held Turkey in violation of the Convention when it interfered with and punished the distribution of a leaflet in Izmir charging the authorities with discrimination against Kurds.[191] But it exhibited a far more deferential attitude to the national authorities when they punished a speaker whose words could be interpreted as supporting the Kurdish insurgents.[192] The applicant was prosecuted for a statement made to a journalist in which he said: 'I support the PKK [Kurdish] national liberation movement; on the other hand, I am not in favour of massacres. Anyone can make mistakes, and the PKK kills women and children by mistake'. The Court noted that, at the time the statement was made, the PKK had carried out a number of 'murderous attacks' in the region. The applicant was a former mayor of Diyarbakir, the most important city in southeast Turkey. He had made the statement to a major national newspaper. In these circumstances, the treatment of the applicant was proportionate to the important social need for maintaining peace and order and was thus justified under Article 10(2).[193]

---

[188] 19 Dec. 1994, 20 E.H.R.R. 56.

[189] *Id.* at para. 38. *See also Vereniging Bluf! v. The Netherlands,* 9 Feb. 1995, 20 E.H.R.R. 189; *Smith & Grady v. United Kingdom, supra* n. 35, and *Lustig-Prean and Beckett v. United Kingdom,* 27 Sept. 1999, 29 E.H.R.R. 548 holding that the wide margin of appreciation granted states with respect to matters of national security and military discipline did not extend to justifying the exclusion of homosexuals from military service. *See* Chapter 8(C) *infra.*

[190] *A and Others v. Secretary of State for the Home Department, supra* n. 33. On review of the state of emergency *see* Chapter 12(H) *infra.*

[191] *Incal v. Turkey,* 9 June 1998, 29 E.H.R.R. 449.

[192] *Zana v. Turkey,* 25 Nov. 1997, 27 E.H.R.R. 667.

[193] *Id.* at paras. 56–62.

This approach has played out in numerous subsequent Turkish cases. These cases deal with written, spoken or broadcast language critical of the Turkish government's Kurdish policies and actions. The material included academic treatises, histories, poetry, interviews, published letters and editorials. In many of the cases the speakers employed highly charged language. But, as long as the Court did not find the communications to contain 'incitements to violence', it has generally held the state restrictions incompatible with Article 10.[194] On the other hand, it declined to find a violation where the government punished the publication of an article about the 'national liberation struggle' of the Kurds and the 'active front of armed violence'. The article described the situation as a 'war directed against the forces of the Republic of Turkey' and concluded 'we want to wage a total liberation struggle'.[195] In another case, the Court agreed that the state could punish the publication of letters accusing the Turkish authorities of massacres and torture even though they did not exhort the readers to violent action.[196] The Court characterized the article in the first case as an 'incitement to violence'[197] and the letters in the second as 'hate speech and the glorification of violence'.[198]

The Court's interpretation of Article 10 in these cases—permitting the suppression of speech when it contains incitement to violence—has a parallel in the constitutional history of the United States. The great American jurist, Learned Hand, in a case dealing with regulation of expression attacking national policies during World War I, interpreted the controlling statute to reach only the advocacy of illegal action.

[W]ords are not only the keys of persuasion but the triggers of action and those which have no purpose but to counsel the violation of law cannot by any latitude of interpretation be a part of that public opinion which is the final source of government in a democratic state... Yet to assimilate agitation, legitimate as such, with direct incitement to violent resistance is to disregard that tolerance of all methods of political agitation which in normal times is a safeguard of the government.[199]

Since none of the texts at issue directly counselled violation of the law, their prohibition was held to be outside the statute.[200]

Hand's approach has a strong resemblance to that of the Strasbourg Court under Article 10. It may be contrasted with the view expounded in the same period in the United States Supreme Court in separate opinions of Justices Holmes and Brandeis and, ultimately adopted by a majority of the Court.[201] This is the well-known 'clear and present danger' test, according to which expression is within the protection of the First

---

[194] See, e.g., Arsian v. Turkey, 8 July 1999 (no violation).
[195] Sürek v. Turkey (No. 1), 8 July 1999; Sürek v. Turkey (No. 3), 8 July 1999.
[196] Sürek v. Turkey (No. 1), supra n. 195, para. 62; Sürek v. Turkey (No. 2), 8 July 1999, para 40.
[197] Sürek v. Turkey (No. 3), para. 40.
[198] Sürek v. Turkey (No. 1), supra n. 195, para. 62. The Turkish cases continue to arise with some frequency. For recent examples see Koy & Tombas v. Turkey, 21 March 2006 (violation); Hacaoguillari v. Turkey, 7 March 2006 (no violation).
[199] Masses Publishing v. Patten, 244 F. 535, 540 (S.D.N.Y. 1917).
[200] Id. at 541–2.
[201] Brandenburg v. Ohio, 395 U.S. 444 (1969).

Amendment unless its utterance could be said to create a risk of serious illegal behaviour that was both highly probable and immediate. It differs from the 'incitement' inquiry in that it demands consideration of more than the content of the communication. Even exhortations to violence are protected if, in the circumstances, they are not likely to produce imminent harm. So, Holmes dissented from the affirmance of a conviction based on the publication of leaflets encouraging workers to frustrate military production. He doubted that 'enough can be squeezed from these poor and puny anonymities to turn the color of litmus paper'.[202] He went on, in much quoted language, to state that 'we should be eternally vigilant against the attempts to check the expression of opinions that we loathe and believe to be fraught with death unless they so imminently interfere with the lawful and pressing purposes of law that an immediate check is required to save the country'.[203]

In several dissenting and concurring opinions in the European Court's Turkish judgments, members of the Court urged an approach similar to the 'clear and present danger' test. Judge Palm urged the Court to go beyond the 'admittedly harsh and vitriolic language' to focus on the 'general context in which the words were used and their likely impact'.[204] Judge Bonello explicitly advocated adoption of the American approach. Thus 'when the invitation to the use of force is intellectualized, abstract and removed in time and space from the facts of actual or impending violence, then the fundamental right to freedom of expression should generally prevail'.[205]

It should be noted, however, that in practice the European Court's decisions have not ignored the context in which regulated expression has arisen. In the Turkish judgments, the opinions of the Court routinely recited that the evaluation of justifications for the government actions had to take into account the dangerous circumstances in southeast Turkey.[206] In one of these decisions it took account of the fact that the message in question had only been read out at a commemorative ceremony 'which considerably restricted its potential impact'.[207] In *Grigoriades v. Greece*,[208] the applicant had been punished because of a letter he had written containing a vitriolic attack on the armed forces, declaring them to be 'a criminal and terrorist apparatus'.[209] Since the letter had merely been delivered to an officer and not published generally, the Court regarded its possible effect on military discipline to be 'insignificant'.[210]

---

[202] *Abrams v. United States*, 250 U.S. 616–29 (1919) (Holmes J, dissenting).

[203] *Id.* at 630 (Holmes J, dissenting).

[204] *Sürek v. Turkey (No 1)*, *supra* n. 195 (partly dissenting opinion of Judge Palm).

[205] *See id.* (partly dissenting opinion of Judge Bonello). Judge Bonello went on to quote from the separate opinions of Justices Holmes and Brandeis noted in the text. An analysis of Article 10 jurisprudence in terms of the 'clear and present danger' test is provided in A. Masson, 'De la Possible Influence de W. O. Holmes sur la Liberté d'Expression dans la Convention Europééne des Droits de l'Homme', (2006) *Revue de Droit Internationale & Comparé* 232–48.

[206] *See, e.g., Baskeya & Okçguoglu v. Turkey*, 8 July 1999, para. 65.

[207] *Gerger v. Turkey*, 8 Jully 1999, para. 50.

[208] 25 Nov. 1997, 27 E.H.R.R. 667.

[209] *Id.* at para. 14.

[210] *Id.* at para. 47.

5. HATE SPEECH AND BLASPHEMY

A. WITZSCH V. GERMANY

Decision of 13 December, 2005 (Admissibility Decision)

In an article published in a German weekly review on 30 September 1999 a well-known historian, Professor Wolffson (thereafter 'W.') made *inter alia* the following statements:

'(…) Hitler wanted the murder of the Jews. He ordered it and certainly knew about it.
Although he had not given a written order, there is evidence that he had given oral orders
on several occasions. The murder of the Jews was wanted and organised from above and by
NS-activists from the bottom (…).'

In a letter of 3 December 1999 the applicant wrote to Professor Wolffson in reply to this
article:

'(…) Your statements which are false and historically unsustainable shall not stand
unanswered (…).

It is actually established that there is no indication in party programs of the National
Socialist German Workers' Party, the NSDAP (*Nationalsozialistische Deutsche
Arbeiterpartei*), that the NSDAP and Hitler intended to murder the Jews. Anybody who—
with all the means at his disposal—fostered the emigration of the Jewish minority until late
after the beginning of the Second World War can hardly be said to have prepared the murder
of the Jews. A long time ago, the historian Irving has publicly proposed to pay a thousand
pounds to any person who could prove that Hitler had ordered, for racial reasons, the murder
of one single Jew. So far, nobody has produced evidence. After the war, tens of thousands of
totally immaculate officials of the NSDAP have attested on oath not to have known until the
end of the war about the murder of Jews. None of the dignitaries of the German Government
accused in Nuremberg admitted to have known about the mass murder of Jews. Not even in
their closing words under the gallows! (…)

The normalisation of the relation between Germans and Jews depends on the will to historical truth and requires not only that one party is blamed for the responsibility it admits
but also that the other party refrains from suppressing its negative contribution to history
(…). Last but not least, the normalisation requires the Jews' clear distancing from the
war and post-war atrocity propaganda (*Kriegs- und Nachkriegsgreuelpropaganda*) against
Germany, directly or indirectly concerning the Jews.

You, Professor Wolffsohn, would highly contribute to this if you would abandon the false
or questionable statements against Germany and seriously endeavour to become acquainted
with the actual academic discourse of contemporary history.'

On 15 December 1999 W. submitted this letter to the police. On 6 April 2000 he explicitly
refused to lodge an application for prosecution.

On 21 June 2000 a police officer informed H.—whose grandparents had died in a concentration camp—about the letter and its content. On the same day, the latter lodged an application
for prosecution.

On 27 July 2001 the Fürth District Court (*Amtsgericht*) convicted the applicant of disparaging the dignity of the deceased pursuant to Section 189 of the German Criminal Code and

sentenced him to three months' imprisonment. With reference to the case-law of the Federal Constitutional Court (*Bundesverfassungsgericht*), it recalled that it was historically proven that the mass killing of Jews in concentration camps was planned and organised by Hitler and the NSDAP. Accordingly, no evidence in this respect had to be adduced, as requested by the applicant. Although the applicant had not denied the Holocaust as such, his denial of Hitler's and the NSDAP's responsibility in this respect was tantamount to a negative value judgment (*negatives Werturteil*). He had thereby denied the victims' extremely cruel and unique fate and accordingly disparaged the dignity of the deceased. Furthermore, as the pertinent passages of the applicant's letter did not express an opinion but had to be categorised as allegations of facts which had been proven untrue, they did not fall within the ambit of Article 5 § 1 of the German Basic Law which protects the freedom of opinion. Given their polemic nature, they neither fell within the ambit of Article 5 § 3 of the German Basic Law which protects the freedom of research. In fixing the sentence, the court took into account that the applicant had been convicted in 1995 and 1996 respectively of disparaging the dignity of the deceased for denying the existence of gas chambers and that the letter at issue had been written during the probationary period.

[The applicant's appeals were dismissed.]

[The applicant's claims under Articles 6, 7 and 14 were held inadmissible as 'manifestly ill-founded.'] ...

The applicant also complained under Articles 9 and 10 of the Convention of an infringement of his right to freedom of expression, in particular because the German courts had not taken into account that the statements at issue had been made in a private letter. ...

The Court notes that, according to the findings of the German courts, the applicant had denied an established historical fact relating to the responsibility of Hitler and the NSDAP as regards the Holocaust and thereby disparaged the dignity of the deceased. In this connection, the Court has regard to Article 17 of the Convention, according to which:

'Nothing in [the] Convention may be interpreted as implying for any State, group or person any right to engage in any activity or perform any act aimed at the destruction of any of the rights and freedoms set forth herein or at their limitation to a greater extent than is provided for in the Convention.'

The Court observes that the general purpose of Article 17 is to make it impossible for individuals to take advantage of a right with the aim of promoting ideas contrary to the text and the spirit of the Convention. The Court, and previously, the European Commission of Human Rights, have found that the freedom of expression guaranteed under Article 10 of the Convention may not be invoked in conflict with Article 17, in particular in cases concerning Holocaust denial and related issues [The Court cited nine Commission decisions and four admissibility decisions of the Court.] Abuse of freedom of expression is incompatible with democracy and human rights and infringes the rights of others.

As regards the circumstances of the present case, the Court notes that the applicant denied neither the Holocaust as such nor the existence of gas chambers. However, he denied an equally significant and established circumstance of the Holocaust considering it false and historically unsustainable that Hitler and the NSDAP had planned, initiated and organised the mass killing of Jews. The applicant's statement that the opinion expressed by W. was part of the war propaganda and after-war atrocity propaganda combined with the denial of Hitler's and the national Socialists' responsibility in the extermination of the Jews showed the applicant's disdain towards the victims of the Holocaust. The Court finds that the views expressed by the applicant ran counter to the text and the spirit of the Convention. Consequently, he cannot, in accordance with Article 17 of the Convention, rely on the provisions of Article 10 as regards his statements at issue. The fact that they were made in a private letter and not before a larger audience is irrelevant.... The applicant's allegation that he did not intend to have a public debate on his views is in any event questionable in the particular circumstances of the instant case.

It follows that this part of the application is incompatible *ratione materiae* with the provisions of the Convention within the meaning of Article 35 § 3 and must be rejected pursuant to Article 35 § 4.

[The Court unanimously held the application inadmissible.]

B. GINIEWSKI V. FRANCE

Judgment of 31 January 2006
45 E.H.R.R. 23

[The applicant wrote an article, 'The Obscurity of Error', published in *Le quotidien de Paris* concerning the papal encyclical 'The Splendour of Truth', which had been published at the end of 1993. Included were the following passages:

'The Catholic Church sets itself up as the sole keeper of divine truth... It proclaims clearly the fulfilment of the Old Covenant in the New, and the superiority of the latter...
... Many Christians have acknowledged that anti-Judaism and the doctrine of the "fulfilment" [in French, "*l'accomplissement*"] of the Old Covenant in the New lead to anti-Semitism and prepared the ground in which the idea and implementation [in French, "*l'accomplissement*"] of Auschwitz took seed'.

A Catholic association initiated a prosecution and civil action for defaming a group on account of religion. The judgment including damages of 1 franc and an order to publish the fact of the judgment, was upheld on appeal.] ...

24. The applicant's statements contribute to a recurrent debate of ideas between historians, theologians and religious authorities. The two most recent Popes, John-Paul II and Benedict XVI, as well as the hierarchy of the Catholic Church, have discussed the possibility that the manner in which the Jews are presented in the New Testament contributed to creating hostility against them. In particular, reference is made to the 'Declaration of Repentance of the Church of France' of 30 September 1997, which emphasises the Church of France's historical responsibility towards the Jewish people; the speech given on 31 October 1997 by John-Paul II during a colloquy on the 'Roots of Anti-Judaism in the Christian Environment'; or, more recently, the book 'The Jewish People and their Sacred Scriptures in the Christian Bible', published in 2001 by the Pontifical Biblical Commission under the direction of Cardinal Joseph Ratzinger; in its preface, the latter writes with regard to the Shoah that 'in the light of what has happened, what ought to emerge now is a new respect for the Jewish interpretation of the Old Testament'. ...

[The Court concluded that there was an interference with Article 10 rights and that the interference had been 'prescribed by law' and had been intended to protect 'the reputation or rights of others'.]

43. As the Court has stated on many occasions, freedom of expression constitutes one of the essential foundations of a democratic society and one of the basic conditions for its progress

and for each individual's self-fulfilment. Subject to paragraph 2 of Article 10, it is applicable not only to 'information' or 'ideas' that are favourably received or regarded as inoffensive or as a matter of indifference, but also to those that offend, shock or disturb. As paragraph 2 of Article 10 recognises, however, the exercise of that freedom carries with it duties and responsibilities. Amongst them—in the context of religious opinions and beliefs—may legitimately be included an obligation to avoid as far as possible expressions that are gratuitously offensive to others and thus an infringement of their rights, and which therefore do not contribute to any form of public debate capable of furthering progress in human affairs.

44. In examining whether restrictions on the rights and freedoms guaranteed by the Convention can be considered 'necessary in a democratic society', the Court has consistently held that the Contracting States enjoy a certain but not unlimited margin of appreciation. The absence of a uniform European conception of the requirements of the protection of the rights of others in relation to attacks on their religious convictions broadens the Contracting States' margin of appreciation when regulating freedom of expression in relation to matters liable to offend intimate personal convictions within the sphere of morals or religion...

45. In the instant case, the Court notes...that the applicant's article essentially accuses the encyclical 'The Splendour of the Truth' of enshrining among theological principles the so-called doctrine of the 'fulfilment' of the Old Covenant in the New, and the superiority of the latter. According to the impugned article, this doctrine contains the seeds of the anti-Semitism which fostered the idea and implementation of the Holocaust.

46. According to the domestic courts...this amounts to accusing 'Catholics and, more generally, Christians of being responsible for the Nazi massacres'. It followed, again according to the court of appeal, that Christians were therefore victims of the offence of defamation on account of their religious beliefs.

47. The Court cannot accept these arguments....

50. The Court considers, in particular, that the applicant sought primarily to develop an argument about the scope of a specific doctrine and its possible links with the origins of the Holocaust. In so doing he had made a contribution, which by definition was open to discussion, to a wide-ranging and ongoing debate without sparking off any controversy that was gratuitous or detached from the reality of contemporary thought.

51. By considering the detrimental effects of a particular doctrine, the article in question contributed to discussion of the various possible reasons behind the extermination of the Jews in Europe, a question of indisputable public interest in a democratic society. In such matters, restrictions on freedom of expression were to be strictly construed. Although the issue raised in the present case concerns a doctrine upheld by the Catholic Church, and hence a religious matter, an analysis of the article in question shows that it does not contain attacks on religious beliefs as such, but a view which the applicant wishes to express as a journalist and historian. In that connection, the Court considers it essential in a democratic society that a debate on the causes of acts of particular gravity amounting to crimes against humanity should be able to take place freely. Furthermore, it has already had occasion to note that 'it is an integral part of freedom of expression to seek historical truth', and that 'it is not its role to arbitrate' the underlying historical issues.

52. While the published text, as the applicant himself acknowledges, contains conclusions and phrases which may offend, shock or disturb some people, the Court has reiterated that such views do not in themselves preclude the enjoyment of freedom of expression. Moreover, the

article in question was not 'gratuitously offensive,' and does not incite to disrespect or hatred. Nor does it cast doubt in any way on clearly established historical facts.

53. In those circumstances, the reasons given by the French courts in support of the applicant's conviction cannot be regarded as sufficient to convince the Court that the interference in the exercise of the applicant's right to freedom of expression was 'necessary in a democratic society'; in particular, his conviction on a charge of public defamation towards the Christian community did not meet a 'pressing social need'.

54. As to the proportionality of the interference in issue to the legitimate aim pursued, the Court reiterates that the nature and severity of the penalties imposed are also factors to be taken into account. The Court must also exercise caution when the measures taken or penalties imposed by the national authority are such as to dissuade the press from taking part in the discussion of matters of legitimate public interest.

55. In the instant case, the applicant was acquitted in the criminal proceedings. In the civil action, he was ordered to pay FRF 1 in damages to the complainant association and, in particular, to publish a notice of the ruling in a national newspaper at his own expense. While the publication of such a notice does not in principle appear to constitute an excessive restriction on freedom of expression in the instant case the fact that it mentioned the criminal offence of defamation undoubtedly had a deterrent effect and the sanction thus imposed appears disproportionate in view of the importance and interest of the debate in which the applicant legitimately sought to take part.

[The court held unanimously that there had been a violation of Article 10.]

As the *Witzsch* decision makes clear, the European Court has been especially deferential to strong public responses to expression inciting religious or ethnic hatred.[211] It is notable that, unlike most admissibility decisions, the Court did not rely in *Witzch* on a finding that the application was 'manifestly ill-founded'. Rather it concluded that the application was inadmissible *ratione materiae*, that is it alleged a subject-matter not within the jurisdiction of the court and therefore 'incompatible with the provisions of the Convention' under Article 35(3). This conclusion apparently proceeds from a finding that, in light of Article 17, Article 10 could not be said to have been triggered by the applicant's conviction.[212]

Nevertheless, as the *Giniewski* case shows, the European Court has sometimes found a violation of Article 10 in connection with sanctions against speech that suggested racial or religious hatred. Context is important. The Court has twice found limitations of expression related to hate speech incompatible with the Convention when the language was uttered by individuals in the course of broadcasts on matters of general interest.[213] It also has held that Article 10 protected the publication of an advertisement defending the action of Phillipe Petain, the head of the Vichy government during World War II. In that case the Court emphasized the passing of time that

---

[211] The Court has also held inadmissible applications involving the refusal to allow the establishment of an anti-Semitic association, *W.P. v. Poland*, 2 Sept. 2004, and challenging a conviction for displaying an anti-Islamic poster, *Norwood v. United Kingdom*, 16 Nov. 2004, 40 E.H.R.R. SE 111.

[212] *See also Garaudy v. France*, 24 June 2003 (admissibility decision).

[213] *Jersild v. Denmark*, 23 Sept. 1994, 19 E.H.R.R. 1, paras. 30–5; *Gündüz v. Turkey*, 4 Dec. 2003, 41 E.H.R.R. 5.

had reduced the inflammatory nature of such arguments and the token fine that had been imposed.[214]

The European experience with racist regimes in the twentieth century has resulted in an acute sensitivity to the dangers of expression denigrating ethnic or religious groups. International law has been developed to regulate such matters. The International Convention on the Elimination of All Forms of Racial Discrimination (1965)[215] has been ratified by more than 150 countries. Article 4 of that Convention obliges states to make punishable 'all dissemination of ideas based on racial superiority or hatred' and to prohibit organizations 'which promote and incite racial discrimination'.[216] The Convention also states that these duties are to be carried out 'with due regard to the principles embodied in the Universal Declaration of Human Rights'. Several contracting states entered declarations and reservations to Article 4 limiting their obligations to actions compatible with freedom of expression.[217]

The Supreme Court of Canada has upheld criminal laws prohibiting the promotion of hatred against ethnic, racial or religious groups.[218] It held that although such laws restricted the freedom of expression protected by section 2(b) of the Charter of Rights and Freedom, they were 'demonstrably justified in a free and democratic society'. Like the Strasbourg Court, the Supreme Court relied, in part, on Canada's obligation under the International Convention in calculating the importance of the law's objective.[219] It also agreed that the goals of suppressing the harmful individual and social effects of hate propaganda should not be left to the ordinary process of public debate:

> While holding that, over the long run, the human mind is repelled by blatant falsehood and seeks the good, it is too often true, in the short run, that emotion displaces reason and individuals perversely reject the demonstrations of truth put before them and foresake the good they know. The successes of modern advertising, the triumphs of impudent propaganda such as Hitler's, have qualified sharply our belief in the rationality of man. We know that under strain and pressure in times of irritation and frustration the individual is swayed and even swept away by hysterical, emotional appeals. We act irresponsibly if we ignore the way in which emotion can drive reason from the field.[220]

The United States Supreme Court has upheld against a First Amendment challenge a state 'group libel' law prohibiting any publication of material adversely depicting any 'class of citizens of any race, color, creed or religion'. The Court analogized such expression to defamatory speech.[221] In 1992, however, the Court held unconstitutional

---

214 *Lehideux & Isorni v. France*, 23 Sept. 1998, 30 E.H.R.R. 665.

215 5 I.L.M. 352 (1966).

216 *Id*. at 355.

217 A complete listing of parties and the character of their ratification may be found at http://www.unher. ch/tbs/doc.nsf.

218 *R. v. Keegstra* [1990] 3 S.C.R. 697.

219 *Id*. at 747–55. The Court also cited a number of reports of the European Commission on Human Rights to the effect that the regulation of such speech was justified under Art. 10(2). *Id*. at 753–4.

220 *Id*. at 747.

221 *Beauharnais v. Illinois*, 343 U.S. 250 (1952).

a municipal ordinance making criminal the burning of crosses, the display of Nazi swastikas or other expressions or acts which could cause 'anger, alarm or resentment in others on the basis of race, color, creed, religion or gender'. The state court had characterized the law as limited to acts which created a risk of imminent violence, a category of expressions unprotected by the First Amendment. The Supreme Court held, however, that the ordinance impermissibly distinguished between different categories of incitements to violence based on the content of the expression.[222] 'In fact the only interest distinctively served by the content limitation is that of displaying the city council's special hostility towards the particular biases thus singled out. That is precisely what the First Amendment forbids'.[223]

Subsequently the Court upheld another statute that made criminal any cross-burning with intent to intimidate. In this case the statute did not specify that the action had to be undertaken because of certain characteristics of the victim. Rather the Court held that the state had the right to single out cross-burning because it was a particularly 'virulent form of intimidation... in light of [its] long and pernicious history as a signal of impending violence'.[224]

Compare the reasoning of the Strasbourg cases with that of the Hungarian Constitutional Court finding a proposed hate speech statute unconstitutional.[225] Acknowledging the propriety of some regulation of extremist expression, the Court stressed the exceptional character of such limitations and the need to 'employ the most moderate means suitable for reaching the specified purpose'.[226] It stated that one goal of freedom of expression was to develop individuals who 'have a stronger character and become intellectually independent persons who can manage their lives in an autonomous way'. Regulation of hate speech was justifiable not because of the 'contents of the opinion but [because of] the direct and foreseeable consequences of its communication'.[227] Only that speech which carried a serious risk of leading to acts of violence could be proscribed. Consequently mere 'disparagement' or 'humiliation' on the basis of national, ethnic or religious affiliation could not be made criminal. Likewise the law could not extend punishment from 'incitement to hatred' to 'provoking hatred'. '[P]rovoking addresses one's mind, while incitement manipulates one's instincts and emotions and mobilises the addressees.' Therefore, incitement is the 'graver act'.[228]

A related category of expression has also received markedly less protection under Article 10. That is blasphemous speech involving statements deprecating a particular religion by insulting its doctrine or its deities. As with hate speech, the European

---

[222]   R.A.V. v. City of Saint Paul, 505 U.S. 377 (1992).
[223]   Id. at 393, 396.
[224]   Virginia v. Black et al, 538 U.S. 343, 362–3 (2003). On the American cross-burning cases see E. Eberle, 'Cross-Burning, Hate Speech and Free Speech in America', 36 Ariz. State L. J. 953 (2004).
[225]   Decision 18/2004 (V. 25) AB.
[226]   Id. at II-1.2.
[227]   Id. at III-2.1.
[228]   Id. at V-2.2, III-3.2.

Court has been sympathetic to states' attempt to control such expression. It has upheld measures directed against films depicting Jesus Christ in sexual activities.[229] The Court agreed that suppression of such expression could be judged necessary to protect the rights of others, namely the 'right not to be insulted in their religious feelings'.[230] Subsequently it reached the same result with respect to the criminal conviction of the publisher of an anti-Islamic novel harshly criticizing Muslim beliefs and including the statement that 'God's messenger broke his fast through sexual intercourse, after dinner and before prayer. Muhammed did not forbid sexual relations with a dead person or a live animal'.[231] Three dissenting judges suggested that the Court should 'revisit' the blasphemy case-law 'which in our view seems to place too much emphasis on uniformity of thought and to reflect an overcautious and timid conception of freedom of the press'.[232] The Court has declined to reconsider its precedents but it refused to apply them in a case concerning a book that challenged the validity of Islamic beliefs and provided unflattering explanations for those beliefs. In this case, however, the opinions were put forward in calmer and more measured prose.[233]

One frequently repeated *dictum* in Article 10 cases is that 'Article 10 protects not only the substance of the ideas and information expressed but also the form in which they are conveyed'.[234] In fact, however, the Strasbourg Court has often found regulation justified on the ground that the speech at issue has been expressed in gratuitously offensive terms.[235] A fuller statement of the latter view was given in the judgment of the United States Supreme Court in *Cohen v. California* in which the profane expression of a political view was held protected by the First Amendment:

We cannot overlook the fact...that much linguistic expression serves a dual communicative function: it conveys not only ideas capable of relatively precise, detached explication, but otherwise inexpressible emotions as well. In fact, words are often chosen as much for their emotive as their cognitive force. We cannot sanction the view that the Constitution, while solicitous of the cognitive content of individual speech, has little or no regard for that emotive function which, practically speaking, may often be the more important element of the overall message sought to be communicated.[236]

---

[229] *Otto Preminger-Institut v. Austria*, 20 Sept. 1994, 19 E.H.R.R. 34; *Wingrove v. United Kingdom*, 25 Nov. 1996, 24 E.H.R.R. 1. The blasphemy cases are considered in connection with Article 9 in Chapter 7 *infra*.

[230] *Otto Preminger-Institut, supra* n. 229, at para. 48.

[231] *İ. A. v. Turkey*, 13 Sept. 2005, 45 E.H.R.R. 30, para. 13.

[232] *Id.* Joint dissenting opinion of Judges Costa, Cabral-Barreto and Jungwiert, para. 8.

[233] *Aydin Tatlav v. Turkey*, 1 Feb. 2000, 42 E.H.R.R. 44.

[234] *Oberschlick v. Austria*, 23 May 1991, 19 E.H.R.R. 389.

[235] E.g *Constantinescu v. Romania*, 27 June 2000, 33 E.H.R.R. 33; *Wabl v. Austria*, 21 March 2001, 31 E.H.R.R. 51.

[236] 403 U.S. 15, 25–6 (1971).

6. COMMERCIAL SPEECH

A. MARKT INTERN AND BEERMANN V. GERMANY

Judgment of 20 November 1989
12 E.H.R.R. 161

8. The first applicant, Markt Intern, is a publishing firm, whose registered office is at Dusseldorf. The second applicant, Mr. Klaus Beermann, is its editor-in-chief.

9. Markt Intern, which was founded and is run by journalists, seeks to defend the interests of small and medium-sized retail businesses against competition from large-scale distribution companies, such as supermarkets and mail-order firms. It provides the less powerful members of the retail trade with financial assistance in test cases, lobbies public authorities, political parties and trade associations on their behalf and has, on occasion, made proposals for legislation to the legislature.

However, its principal activity in their support is the publication of a number of bulletins aimed at specialised commercial sectors such as that of chemists and beauty product retailers. These are weekly news-sheets which provide information on developments in the market and in particular on the commercial practices of large-scale firms and their suppliers. They are printed by offset and are sold by open subscription. They do not contain any advertising or any articles commissioned by the groups whose cause they espouse.

. . .

11. On 20 November 1975 an article by Mr. Klaus Beermann appeared in the information bulletin for chemists and beauty product retailers. It described an incident involving an English mail-order firm, Cosmetic Club International ('the Club'), in the following terms:

'"I ordered the April beauty set...from Cosmetic Club International and paid for it, but returned it a few days later because I was not satisfied. Although the order form clearly and expressly stated that I was entitled to return the set if I was dissatisfied, and that I would be reimbursed, I have not yet seen a pfennig. There was also no reaction to my reminder of 18 June, in which I gave them until 26 June to reply." This is the angry report of Maria Lachau, a chemist at Celle, concerning the commercial practices of this English Cosmetic Club.

On 4 November we telexed the manager of the Club, Doreen Miller, as follows: "Is this an isolated incident, or is this part of your official policy?" In its swift answer of the following day, the Club claimed to have no knowledge of the set returned by Mrs. Lachau or of her reminder of June. It promised however to carry out a prompt investigation of the case and to clarify the matter by contacting the chemist in Celle.

Notwithstanding this provisional answer from Ettlingen, we would like to put the following question to all our colleagues in the chemist and beauty product trade; Have you had similar experiences to that of Mrs. Lachau with the Cosmetic Club? Do you know of similar cases? The question whether or not this incident is an isolated case or one of many is crucial for assessing the Club's policy.' . . .

15. ...[The Club began proceedings against Markt Intern under several statutes, claiming the publication unfairly injured it. The Hamburg Regional Court gave judgment for the Club.]

The Court concluded that the applicants' conduct was punishable. Markt Intern ought not to have generalised from the case of Mrs. Lachau, the circumstances of which had not yet been clarified, and used it to formulate criticism of the Club. This method of proceeding could not be reconciled with the obligations incumbent on journalists. The defendants ought to have begun by taking their enquiries further, but not in the form of their request for information from the retailers....

16. On 31 March 1977 the Hanseatic Court of Appeal found for the applicants and quashed the Regional Court's judgment....

17. The Club appealed to the Federal Court of Justice which on 16 January 1980 set aside the Hanseatic Court of Appeal's judgment and, varying the Hamburg Regional Court's judgment, ordered the applicants to refrain from publishing in their information bulletin the statements disseminated by Markt Intern on 20 November 1975 in the form referred to by the Club in its heads of claim at first instance.

For each contravention, the applicants were liable to a fine or detention to be fixed by the court, but not exceeding 500,000 DM or six months, respectively.

18. The Federal Court of Justice based its judgment on section 1 of the [Unfair Competition Act of 1909], according to which:

'Any person who in the course of business commits, for purposes of competition, acts contrary to honest practices may be enjoined from further engaging in those acts and held liable in damages.'...

... Notwithstanding the lack of a competitive relationship between Markt Intern and the Club, the 1909 Act was said to apply because it was sufficient in this respect that the conduct in question was objectively advantageous to an undertaking, to the detriment of a competitor. That was exactly the aim pursued in this instance...

... Having regard in particular to the previous reports on the Club published by Markt Intern, the Court of Appeal ought to have found that the applicants had not merely provided information as an organ of the press, but had embraced the interests of the specialised chemists trade and, in order to promote those interests, had attacked the Club's commercial practices. The Court of Appeal ought consequently to have concluded that Markt Intern intended to act in favour of the specialized trade and to the detriment of the Club....

[In part of its judgment the Federal Court of Justice stated:] 'By their publication of the article complained of ..., the respondents acted in a way contrary to honest practices within the meaning of section 1 of the 1909 Act. It is immaterial in this connection whether the statements regarding the witness Lachau (first head of claim) were true. The mere fact that a commercially damaging statement is true does not necessarily constitute a defence against a charge of acting in breach of the principles of fair competition. According to the rules of competition, such statements are acceptable only if they are based on sufficient grounds and if the manner and extent of the criticism in question remains within the limits of what is required by the situation because it is contrary to honest practices to engage in competition by making disparaging statements about competitors. In this case, at the time of the publication there was not sufficient cause to report this incident. The exact circumstances had not yet been clarified. The appellant in its reply had agreed to undertake an immediate investigation and to contact Mrs. Lachau in order to clarify the position. The respondents were aware that criticism of the appellant could not be fully justified before further clarification had been sought, as they themselves had described the appellant's reply as a provisional answer. Accordingly, they should have taken into consideration that any such premature publication of this incident was bound to have adverse effects on the appellant's business, because it gave the specialised retailers an effective argument which was capable of being used against the appellant with their mutual customers, and one which could be used even if the incident should turn out to be an isolated mishap from which no conclusion could be drawn as to the appellant's business policy. In these circumstances, at all events at the time of the publication, there were not sufficient grounds for reporting this isolated incident. Such conduct is, moreover, very unusual in business competition.'...

19. The applicants then appealed to the Federal Constitutional Court, claiming a violation of the freedom of the press. (Article 5(1) of the Constitution.)

Sitting as a committee of three judges, the Constitutional Court decided, on 9 February 1983, not to entertain the appeal....

20. Mrs. Lachau was not the only customer to complain about the Club. Two others informed the applicants that they had encountered similar difficulties; the first approached them before the publication of the bulletin of 20 November 1975 and the second after it.

According to its own statements, the Club sold 157,929 beauty sets between 1 December 1974 and 30 November 1975. In 1975, 11,870 identifiable persons returned the sets and were reimbursed....

22. The Commission declared the application admissible on 21 January 1986. In its report of 18 December 1987, it expressed the opinion, by twelve votes to one, that there had been a violation of Article 10....

25. The Government primarily disputed the applicability of Article 10. Before the Court it argued that if the case were examined under that provision, it would fall, by reason of the contents of the publication of 20 November 1975 and the nature of Markt Intern's activities, at the extreme limit of Article 10's field of application. The wording and the aims of the information bulletin in question showed that it was not intended to influence or mobilize public opinion, but to promote the economic interests of a given group of undertakings. In the Government's view, such action fell within the scope of the freedom to conduct business and engage in competition, which is not protected by the Convention.

The applicants did not deny that they defended the interests of the specialised retail trade. However, they asserted that Markt Intern did not intervene directly in the process of supply and demand. The undertaking depended exclusively on its subscribers and made every effort, as was proper, to satisfy the requirements of its readers, whose preoccupation the mainstream press neglected. To restrict the freedom of expression to news items of a political or cultural nature would result in depriving a large proportion of the press of any protection....

26. ... It is clear that the article in question was addressed to a limited circle of trades people and did not directly concern the public as a whole; however, it conveyed information of a commercial nature. Such information cannot be excluded from the scope of Article 10(1) which does not apply solely to certain types of information or ideas or forms of expression....

31. ... According to the actual wording of the judgment of 16 January 1980, the article in question was liable to raise unjustified suspicions concerning the commercial policy of the Club and thus damage its business. The Court finds that the interference was intended to protect the reputation and the rights of others, legitimate aims under Article 10(2)....

32. The applicants argued that the injunction in question could not be regarded as 'necessary in a democratic society'. The Commission agreed with this view.

The Government, however, disputed it. In its view, the article published on 20 November 1975 did not contribute to a debate of interest to the general public, but was part of an unlawful competitive strategy aimed at ridding the beauty products market of an awkward competitor for specialist retailers. The writer of the article had sought, by adopting aggressive tactics and acting in a way contrary to usual practice, to promote the competitiveness of those retailers. The Federal Court of Justice and the Federal Constitutional Court had ruled in accordance with well established case law, having first weighed all the interests at stake.

In addition, in the field of competition, States enjoyed a wide discretion in order to take account of the specific situation in the national market and, in this case, the national notion of good faith in business. The statements made 'for purposes of competition' fell outside the basic nucleus protected by freedom of expression and received a lower level of protection than other 'ideas' or 'information'.

33. The Court has consistently held that the Contracting States have a certain margin of appreciation in assessing the existence and extent of the necessity of an interference, but this margin is subject to a European supervision as regards both the legislation and the decisions applying it, even those given by an independent court. Such a margin of appreciation is essential in commercial matters and, in particular, in an area as complex and fluctuating as that of unfair competition. Otherwise, the European Court of Human Rights would have to undertake a re-examination of the facts and all the circumstances of each case. The Court must confine its review to the question whether the measures taken on the national level are justifiable in principle and proportionate....

34. ... The national courts did weigh the competing interests at stake. In their judgments of 2 July 1976 and 31 March 1977, the Hamburg Regional Court and the Hanseatic Court of Appeal explicitly referred to the right to freedom of expression and of the press, as guaranteed by Article 5 of the Constitution and the Federal Constitutional Court, in its decision of 9 February 1983, considered the case under that provision. The Federal Court of Justice based its judgment of 16 January 1980 on the premature nature of the publication in question and on the lack of sufficient grounds for publicising in the information bulletin an isolated incident and in doing so took into consideration the rights and legal interests meriting protection.

35. In a market economy an undertaking which seeks to set up a business inevitably exposes itself to close scrutiny of its practices by its competitors. Its commercial strategy and the manner in which it honours its commitments may give rise to criticism on the part of consumers and the specialised press. In order to carry out this task, the specialised press must be able to disclose facts which could be of interest to its readers and thereby contribute to the openness of business activities.

However, even the publication of items which are true and describe real events may under certain circumstances be prohibited: the obligation to respect the privacy of others or the duty to respect the confidentiality of certain commercial information are examples. In addition, a correct statement can be and often is qualified by additional remarks, by value judgments, by suppositions or even insinuations. It must also be recognised that an isolated incident can give the false impression that the incident is evidence of a general practice. All these factors can legitimately contribute to the assessment of statements made in a commercial context, and it is primarily for the national courts to decide which statements are permissible and which are not.

36. In the present case, the article was written in a commercial context; Markt Intern was not itself a competitor in relation to the Club but it intended—legitimately—to protect the interests of chemists and beauty product retailers. The article itself undoubtedly contained some true statements, but it also expressed doubts about the reliability of the Club, and it asked the readers to report 'similar experiences' at a moment when the Club had promised to carry out a prompt investigation of the one reported case.

According to the Federal Court of Justice, there was not sufficient cause to report the incident at the time of the publication. The Club had agreed to undertake an immediate investigation in order to clarify the position. Furthermore, the applicants had been aware that criticisms of the Club could not be fully justified before further clarification had been sought, as they themselves had described the reply of the Club as a provisional answer. In the opinion of the Federal Court they should therefore have taken it into consideration that any such premature publication of the incident was bound to have adverse effects on the Club's business because it gave the specialized retailers an effective argument capable of being used against the Club and their customers, and one which could be used even if the incident should turn out to be an isolated mishap from which no conclusion could be drawn as to the Club's business policy.

37. In the light of these findings and having regard to the duties and responsibilities attaching to the freedoms guaranteed by Article 10, it cannot be said that the final decision of the Federal Court of Justice—confirmed from the constitutional point of view by the Federal Constitutional Court—went beyond the margin of appreciation left to the national authorities. It is obvious that opinions may differ as to whether the Federal Court's reaction was appropriate or whether the statements made in the specific case by Markt Intern should be permitted or tolerated. However, the European Court of Human Rights should not substitute its own evaluation for that of the national courts in the instant case, where those courts, on reasonable grounds, had considered the restrictions to be necessary...

[The Court held by nine votes to nine with the casting vote of the President, that there had been no violation of Article 10.]

Joint Dissenting Opinion of Judges Gölcüklü, Pettiti, Russo, Spielmann, De Meyer, Carrillo, Salcedo and Valticos:...

It is just as important to guarantee the freedom of expression in relation to the practices of a commercial undertaking as it is in relation to the conduct of a head of government, which was at issue in the *Lingens Case*.[237] Similarly the right thereto must be able to be exercised as much in the interests of the purchasers of beauty products as in those of the owners of sick animals, the interests at stake in the *Barthold Case*.[238] In fact, freedom of expression serves, above all, the general interest.

The fact that a person defends a given interest, whether it is an economic interest or any other interest, does not, moreover, deprive him of the benefit of freedom of expression.

In order to ensure the openness of business activities, it must be possible to disseminate freely information and ideas concerning the products and services proposed to consumers. Consumers, who are exposed to highly effective distribution techniques and to advertising

[237] Reproduced in Section C (1) *supra* (footnote by editors).
[238] Discussed in the notes following (footnote by editors).

which is frequently less than objective, deserve, for their part too, to be protected, as indeed do retailers....

We find the reasoning set out therein with regard to the 'margin of appreciation' of States a cause for serious concern. As is shown by the result to which it leads in this case, it has the effect in practice of considerably restricting the freedom of expression in commercial matters...

· [The individual dissenting opinions of Judges Pettiti and DeMeyer are omitted.]

Dissenting Opinion of Judge Martens, approved by Judge Macdonald:...

4. The law on unfair competition governs the relationships between competitors on the market. It is based on the assumption that in engaging in competition the competitors seek only to serve their own interests, while attempting to harm those of others. This is why (as the Federal Court notes in its judgment) the German law on unfair competition prohibits persons from engaging in competition by making denigrating statements about their competitors. It is permissible for a competitor to criticise another publicly only if he has sufficient reasons for so doing and if the nature and scope of his criticism remain within the limits required by the situation. In this field, the prohibition on publishing criticism is therefore the norm and it falls to the person who takes the risk of publishing such criticism to show that there were sufficient grounds for his criticism and that it remains within the strictest limits. In considering whether this proof has been furnished, the court weights up only the interests of the two competitors.

In the field of freedom of expression the converse is true. In this field the basic assumption is that this right is used to serve the general interest, in particular as far as the press is concerned, and that is why in this context the freedom to criticise is the norm. Thus in this field it falls to the person who alleges that the criticism is not acceptable to prove that his claim is well-founded. In determining whether he has done so, the court must weight up the general interest, on the one hand, and the individual interests of the party who claims to have been injured, on the other.

5. It follows that to classify under the law on unfair competition the question whether an article published by an organ of the press is acceptable is to place that organ of the press in a legal position which is fundamentally different from that to which it is entitled under Article 10 of the Convention and one which is clearly unfavourable to it. That is why, in my view, for that organ of the press, such a classification constitutes a considerable restriction on the exercise of the freedoms guaranteed to it under Article 10. It should therefore be asked whether it can be necessary in a democratic society to restrict the rights and fundamental freedoms of an organ of the press in this way solely because that organ has espoused the cause of specific economic interests, namely those of a particular sector of a specialised trade. I am in no doubt that this question must be answered in the negative. This is clear from the fact that, as far as I know, such a rule extending the scope of the law on unfair competition to the detriment of freedom of the press is unknown in the other member states of the Council of Europe, and rightly so because, in certain respects, all newspapers may be regarded as partisan, having espoused the cause of certain specific interests.

6. In my view, it follows from the foregoing that the Court ought to have considered that in this instance it had to examine a case in which the assessment of the national authorities suffered from a fundamental defect and that, accordingly, it ought itself to have determined whether the interference was necessary in a democratic society. Indeed, in such circumstances the margin of appreciation plays no role because this margin cannot justify assessments incompatible with the freedoms guaranteed under the Convention. I emphasize this point because,

for my part, I do not deny that in the field of freedom of expression the European Court can limit the scope of its review by leaving the States a certain margin of appreciation.

B. COMPARISONS

There are at least two reasons why expressions directed at commercial or economic interests ought to receive less protection than speech involving political decision-making. First, as a matter of social policy, it might be argued that regulation of such speech poses less of a danger to a central value of the constitutional guarantee, its relation to the democratic process. Second, there is a pervasive and well-established practice of economic regulation which necessarily includes restriction of speech related to economic transactions. In *Markt Intern*, the Court accommodated these concerns by espousing a particularly deferential version of the margin of appreciation, noting that, at least with respect to matters of unfair competition, the Court is in a poor position to evaluate decisions in such a 'complex and fluctuating' area. Its general description of the margin of appreciation is consistent with that put forth in other cases. But the judgment insists that, in these circumstances, the European Court of Human Rights 'should not substitute its own evaluation for that of the national Courts... when those courts on reasonable grounds had considered the restriction to be necessary'.

In a subsequent case, *Casado Coca v. Spain*,[239] the Strasbourg Court relied on *Markt Intern* in holding that an almost total ban on lawyer advertising did not violate Article 10. In its formulation of the proper standards, however, it adopted language somewhat less deferential to the regulating state. It reiterated that a wide margin of appreciation was appropriate in the 'complex and fluctuating area of unfair competition', and that advertising may sometimes properly be restricted to prevent unfair competition. It went on, however, to state that '[a]ny such restrictions must... be closely scrutinized by the court which must weigh the requirements of those particular features against the advertising in question'. The Court must be persuaded that the restriction is 'justifiable and proportionate'.[240] In the case at hand, the Court noted the special status and responsibility of the legal profession and the fact that the regulation of lawyer advertising varied greatly in the various states of the members of the Council of Europe. Only in light of its independent evaluation of these factors did the Court conclude that 'the Bar authorities and the country's courts are in a better position than an international court to determine how at a given time the right balance can be struck between the various interests involved'.[241] Applying the 'justifiable in principle and proportionate' standard, the Court held incompatible with the Convention a pro-

---

[239] 24 Feb. 1994, 18 E.H.R.R. 1.

[240] *Id.* at paras. 50–1.

[241] *Id.* at paras. 50–1. The Court also failed to cite the highly deferential language from *Markt Intern* in its judgment in *Jacubowski v. Germany*, 23 June 1994, 19 E.H.R.R. 64, in which it held there was no violation of Article 10 when the applicant was ordered to desist from circulating material critical of his former employer. The applicant who was hoping to start a new business had distributed the information to potential clients. The Court confined itself to the question of 'whether the measures taken at the national level [were] justifiable in principle and proportionate'.

hibition on a newspaper publishing a comparison of its subscription prices to those of its competitors. The Court was not convinced that this comparison was misleading unless it were accompanied by explanation of differences in editorial quality and news coverage.[242]

In American constitutional law, 'commercial speech', that is speech merely proposing a commercial transaction, was once held to be wholly outside the scope of the First Amendment.[243] Beginning in the 1970s, however, it has been held to enjoy a measure of constitutional protection. In *Virginia State Board of Pharmacy v. Virginia Citizens Consumer Council*,[244] in which a statute prohibiting the advertisement of prices of prescription drugs was held unconstitutional, the Supreme Court noted:

As to the particular consumer's interest in the free flow of commercial information, that interest may be as keen, if not keener by far, than his interest in the day's most urgent political debate. Appellees' case in this respect is a convincing one. Those whom the suppression of prescription drug price information hits the hardest are the poor, the sick, and particularly the aged. A disproportionate amount of their income tends to be spent on prescription drugs; yet they are the least able to learn, by shopping from pharmacist to pharmacist, where their scarce dollars are best spent. When drug prices vary as strikingly as they do, information as to who is charging what becomes more than a convenience. It could mean the alleviation of physical pain or the enjoyment of basic necessities....

... Advertising, however tasteless and excessive it sometimes may seem, is nonetheless dissemination of information as to who is producing and selling what product, for what reason, and at what price. So long as we preserve a predominantly free enterprise economy, the allocation of our resources in large measure will be made through numerous private economic decisions. It is a matter of public interest that those discussions, in the aggregate, be intelligent and well informed. To this end, the free flow of commercial information is indispensable...And, if it is indispensable to the proper allocation of resources in a free enterprise system, it is also indispensable to the formation of intelligent opinions as to how that system ought to be regulated or altered. Therefore, even if the First Amendment were thought to be primarily an instrument to enlighten public decision making in a democracy, we could not say that the free flow of information does not serve that goal.

Still, the Supreme Court, like the European Court, has recognized the public interest in regulation of commercial advertising, and has formulated a somewhat more relaxed test for its validity. This was summed up in a 'four-part' examination expounded in *Central Hudson Gas and Electric Corp. v. Public Service Commission*:[245]

At the outset we must determine whether the expression is protected by the First Amendment. For commercial speech to come within that provision, it at least must concern lawful activity and not be misleading. Next we ask whether the asserted governmental interest is substantial.

---

[242] *Krone Verlag Gmbh v. Austria (No. 3)*, 11 Dec. 2003, 42 E.H.R.R. 28.
[243] *Valentine v. Chrestensen*, 316 U.S. 52 (1942).
[244] 425 U.S. 748, 763–5 (1976).
[245] 447 U. S. 557, 566 (1980). *See Thompson v. Western State Medical Center*, 535 U.S. 357 (2002) (applying the *Central Hudson* test to find unconstitutional a ban on advertising the compounding of 'made to order' prescription drugs).

If both inquiries yield positive answers, we must determine whether the regulation directly advances the governmental interest asserted, and whether it is not more extensive than is necessary to serve that interest.

The United States Supreme Court has also held that the First Amendment limits the extent to which states may restrict the advertising of attorneys.[246] In this regard it has prohibited restriction of non-fraudulent, non-coercive advertising. While states have been held to have authority to limit in-person solicitation at least in certain circumstances,[247] solicitation by letter has been held constitutionally protected.[248] The American doctrine on this question should be compared to the European Court's holding in *Casado Coca*, discussed above, in which a sweeping ban on almost all law-yer advertising was held to be compatible with Article 10.

In *Ford v. Quebec (Attorney General)*,[249] the Supreme Court of Canada held invalid a law prohibiting the use of languages other than French on commercial signs. It rejected an argument that commercial expression was not included in the protection of Section 2(b) of the Canadian Charter of Rights and Freedoms. It noted the 'significant role' such expression plays in 'enabling individuals to make informed economic choices, an important aspect of individual self-fulfillment and personal autonomy'. The next year, in *Irwin Toy Ltd. v. Quebec (Attorney-General)*,[250] however, it upheld, under Section 1, a sweeping ban on advertising directed at children, holding it was justifiable under the *Oakes* test, discussed above. In contrast, in a subsequent five to four decision, the Court held invalid a near total ban on tobacco advertising. In explaining the reasons for her judgment, Justice Mclachlin disagreed with the claim that advertising was only entitled to a reduced degree of protection because it was motivated by a desire for profit: '[B]ook sellers, newspaper owners, toy sellers—all are linked by their shareholders' desire to profit from the corporation's business activity, whether the expression sought to be protected is closely linked to the core values of freedom of expression or not'.[251]

The English Court of Appeal has upheld a ban on advertising by medical practition-ers. It held that the rules formulated by the General Medical Council were a proper exercise of the power conferred on it by statute to provide advice and guidance on ques-tions of ethical professional conduct. The litigant in that case had been refused permis-sion to publish factual, non-promotional information about his practice in the general press. The Court held that the restriction was a reasonable regulation in light of the

---

[246] *Bates v. State Bar*, 433 U. S. 350 (1977).

[247] *Ohralik v. Ohio State Bar*, 436 U. S. 477 (1978). But *see Edenfield v. Fane*, 507 U.S. 761 (1993) (holding unconstitutional a ban on in-person solicitation by certified public accountants).

[248] *Shapero v. Kentucky Bar Assoc.*, 486 U.S. 466 (1988). But *see Florida Bar v. Went For It Inc.*, 515 U.S. 618 (1995) (upholding a prohibition on mail solicitation by lawyers targeted specifically at accident victims within 30 days after an accident).   [249] [1988] 2 S.C.R. 712.

[250] [1989] 1 S.C.R. 927.

[251] *RJR-MacDonald Inc. v. Canada (Attorney-General)* [1995] 3 S.C.R. 199, para. 171. Maclachlan J was responding to these remarks in the dissenting reasons of LaForest J:

It must be kept in mind that tobacco advertising serves no political, scientific or artistic ends; nor does it promote participation in the political process. Rather, its sole purpose is to inform consumers about, and promote the use of, a product that is harmful, and often fatal, to the consumers who use it. The main, if not sole, motivation for this advertising is, of course, profit.

policy to discourage commercial competition among doctors, since such competition might impair the ability of patients to choose physicians on sensible grounds. The Court rejected an argument that it should interpret the governing statute to allow only such restrictions as are consistent with Article 10 of the European Convention.[252]

It is often not at all clear when a statement should be designated as 'commercial' rather than 'political'. In *Barthold v. Germany*,[253] the applicant, a veterinarian, was subject to professional discipline for making statements, quoted in a newspaper article, about the lack of night service by veterinarians in Hamburg. The German court held that the applicant had violated established standards against professional advertising. Since the restriction imposed on the applicant prevented him from expressing opinions and imparting information on 'a topic of general interest', the European Court of Human Rights held that Article 10 applied without 'needing to inquire...whether or not advertising as such comes within [its] scope'. Since, the Court found, the commercial and professional aspects to the applicant's statements were 'altogether secondary, having regard to the principal content of the article and to the nature of the issue being put to the public at large', the German court did not 'achieve a fair balance between the two interests at stake'. The judgment of the national courts, the Court felt, risked 'discouraging members of the liberal professions from contributing to debate on topics affecting the life of the community if ever there is the slightest likelihood of these utterances being treated as entailing, to some degree, an advertising effect'.[254] Even the regulation of matters as far removed from issues of public policy as a highly eccentric commentary on the safety of microwave ovens has been held properly examinable on a stricter standard than that applied to commercial speech. In *Hertel v. Switzerland*,[255] the Court held that such expression was not 'purely "commercial" statements' but was participation in a debate affecting the general interest, for example, over public health.[256] 'It matters little that [the] opinion is a minority one and may appear to be devoid of merit since, in a sphere in which it is unlikely that any certainty exists, it would be particularly unreasonable to restrict freedom of expression only to generally accepted ideas'.[257]

---

[252] *R. v. General Medical Council, ex parte Colman* [1990] 1 All E.R. 489 (C.A.).

[253] 25 Mar. 1985, 7 E.H.R.R. 383, reproduced in part at Chapter 3(C) *supra*.

[254] *Id*. at para 58, para. 37. The problem of characterizing speech also arose in *Jacubowski v. Germany*, *supra* n. 241, in which the Court found no violation where the applicant was ordered to stop circulating information critical of his former employer. Although the applicant's action was in response to public statements of the employer commenting adversely on the applicant's competence as a manager, the Court treated the case mainly as one where the applicant was seeking a competitive advantage in connection with the initiation of his own business. *Id*. at para. 28. Three dissenting judges, on the other hand, emphasized that the applicant 'had an obvious and pressing interest in trying to protect his impugned reputation without delay' and that '[t]here was a parallel public interest to learn whether the applicant would defend himself against his former employer'. *Id*. (dissenting opinion of Judges Walsh, McDonald and Wildhaber).

[255] 25 Aug. 1998, 28 E.H.R.R. 534.

[256] *Id*. at para. 47.

[257] *Id*. at para. 50.

In the United States, the extension of First Amendment protection to commercial speech was prompted, in part, by a recognition that the categories of commercial and political speech could not be confidently distinguished. In *Bigelow v. Virginia*[258] the U.S. Supreme Court considered a state statute prohibiting the publication of an advertisement for a 'profit-making' abortion clinic:

The advertisement published in appellant's newspaper did more than simply propose a commercial transaction. It contained factual material of clear 'public interest'. Portions of its message, most prominently the lines, 'Abortions are now legal in New York. There are no residency requirements', involve the exercise of the freedom of communicating information and disseminating opinion.

Viewed in its entirety, the advertisement conveyed information of potential interest and value to a diverse audience—not only to readers possibly in need of the services offered, but also to those with a general curiosity about, or genuine interest in, the subject matter or the law of another State and its development, and to readers seeking reform in Virginia. The mere existence of the Women's Pavilion in New York City, with the possibility of its being typical of other organizations there, and the availability of the services offered, were not unnewsworthy. Also, the activity advertised pertained to constitutional interests. *See Roe v. Wade*, 410 U.S. 113 (1973), and *Doe v. Bolton*, 410 U.S. 179 (1973). Thus, in this case, appellant's First Amendment interests coincided with the constitutional interests of the general public....

7. ARTISTIC EXPRESSION

While questions of freedom of expression are usually associated with restrictions on political speech, they may also arise in connection with attempts to suppress what the state views as offensive artistic or literary works. 'Beauty has constitutional status too, [and] the life of the imagination is as important to the human adult as the life of the intellect'.[259] As the *Handyside* and *Markt Intern* cases indicate, the European Court has readily applied Article 10 to speech which is not 'political' in any obvious sense. Indeed, it has explicitly held that the protection of Article 10 extends to 'artistic expression':

Admittedly, Article 10 does not specify that freedom of artistic expression ... comes within its ambit; but neither, on the other hand, does it distinguish between the various forms of expression. As those appearing before the Court all acknowledged, it includes freedom of artistic expression—notably within freedom to receive and impart information and ideas—which affords the opportunity to take part in the public exchange of cultural, political and social information and ideas of all kinds. Confirmation, if any were needed, that this interpretation is correct, is provided by the second sentence of paragraph 1 of Article 10, which refers to 'broadcasting, television or cinema enterprises', media whose activities extend to the field of art. Confirmation that the concept of freedom of expression is such as to include artistic expression

[258] 421 U.S. 809 (1977).
[259] Kalven, 'The Metaphysics of the Law of Obscenity', (1960) *Sup. Ct. Rev.* 1 15–16. *See also* Nahmod, 'Artistic Expression and Aesthetic Theory: The Beautiful, The Sublime and the First Amendment', [1987] *Wisc. L. Rev.* 221.

is also to be found in Article 19 §2 of the International Covenant on Civil and Political Rights, which specifically includes within the right of freedom of expression information and ideas 'in the form of art'.[260]

Notwithstanding suggestions by some commentators that the First Amendment ought to be restricted in its coverage to political speech,[261] the Supreme Court of the United States has regularly reviewed restrictions on artistic expression under the First Amendment. In *Miller v. California*, discussed above,[262] the Court stated explicitly that the Constitution 'protects words which, taken as a whole, have serious literary, artistic or political value'. Similarly, in *R. v. Butler*,[263] the Canadian Supreme Court held that the guarantee of Section 2(b) of the Canadian Charter of Rights and Freedoms applies not only to written words but to films, even films portraying solely physical activity, since 'the creation of the film is attempting to convey some meaning'.

The actual character of the protection extended to artistic expression, however, may be different from that accorded political speech. Public regulation of such work typically stems from a desire to suppress material that offends social standards of decency, often standards relating to the proper scope of public discussion or depiction of sexual activity. As has already been discussed, American constitutional law deals with the issue by removing a category of 'obscene' speech from the ambit of First Amendment protection. The case law of the European Convention and the Canadian Charter accords such expression *prima facie* protection, but acknowledges the possibility of regulation justified by other pressing social needs. As we have already seen, the justification invoked may well alter the strictness with which the challenged material is reviewed.[264]

8. BROADCASTING

Article 10 makes special reference to the right of states to license 'broadcasting television or cinema enterprises'. Significantly, this caveat is contained in paragraph 1, rather than being included, or merely left by implication, in paragraph 2, which specifies the various justifications for limitation of the right. This placement implies that broadcast licensing should not be considered an infringement of the right of expression at all.[265]

The Court has, however, held to the contrary. In *Groppera Radio AG and Others v. Switzerland*,[266] the Court held that no violation of Article 10 occurred when Swiss

---

[260] *Müller and Others v. Switzerland*, 24 May 1988, 13 E.H.R.R. 212, para. 27.

[261] *See* Bork, 'Neutral Principles and Some First Amendment Problems', (1971) 47 *Ind. L.J.* 1.

[262] 413 U.S. 15, 24 discussed in Section B *supra*.

[263] [1992] 1 S.C.R. 452.

[264] *See* Section B *supra*.

[265] *See* P. van Dijk & G. J. H. van Hoof, *Theory and Practice of the European Convention on Human Rights* 419 (1990).

[266] 28 Mar. 1990, 12 E.H.R.R. 321.

authorities prohibited the re-transmission by Swiss cable transmission companies of the signal from a radio station broadcasting from Italy but aimed exclusively at a Swiss audience. The direct broadcasts of the station were in violation of the International Telecommunications Convention to which Switzerland and Italy were both parties.

Although the Court found no violation, it did not rely solely on the third sentence of Article 10(1). Rather, it held that the exception to freedom of expression in that sentence was 'of limited scope'. It was directed at licensing systems dealing with 'the way in which broadcasting is organized in [the individual states'] territories, particularly in its technical aspects. It does not, however, provide that licensing measures shall not otherwise be subject to the requirements of paragraph 2, for that would lead to a result contrary to the object and purpose of Article 10 taken as a whole'. Therefore, although the Court found the measure in question was part of a proper licensing scheme, it proceeded to examine it under paragraph 2. The Court concluded that the prohibition was necessary for the 'prevention of disorder', which might follow from the unregulated use of the broadcasting spectrum, and for the 'protection of others' in allowing for the fair allocation of the limited number of broadcast frequencies, both nationally and internationally.

In a concurring opinion, Judge Pinheiro Farinha argued that the Court's approach made the third sentence of paragraph 1 redundant. Under that approach, every licensing measure, like any other restriction on speech, will have to satisfy the criteria of paragraph 2. He would have made the holding 'solely on the basis of the third sentence'. Indeed, in *Autronic AG v. Switzerland*,[267] the Court found that Switzerland's prohibition of a company's reception of Russian satellite transmissions intended for the general public, could not be justified under paragraph 2 and, therefore, violated the Convention. The Court found that international radio agreements did not preclude such reception and, since the signal was intended for the general public in Russia, no issue of privacy was involved. The Court gave no indication that the third sentence of paragraph 1 called for a more generous view of the national regulation. On the contrary, it cited its established case law in non-broadcasting contexts establishing that when the rights of Article 10 were involved, the Court's supervision of a state's margin of appreciation 'must be strict' and the 'necessity for restricting [those rights] must be convincingly established'.

Subsequently, in *Informationsverein Lentia v. Austria*,[268] the Court further clarified its view of the relationship between the third sentence of paragraph (1) and paragraph (2). The authorization of broadcast licensing by a state might be:

made conditional on [technical or] other considerations including such matters as the nature and objectives of a proposed station, its potential audience at national, regional or local level, the rights and needs of a specific audience and the obligations deriving from international legal instruments... This may lead to interferences whose aims will be legitimate under the

---

[267] 22 May 1990, 12 E.H.R.R. 485.
[268] 24 Nov. 1993, 17 E.H.R.R. 93.

third sentence of paragraph 1, even though they do not correspond to any of the aims set out in paragraph 2.[269]

Thus, the licensing provision in paragraph (1) was held to expand the purposes for which broadcasting could be regulated through the licence procedure beyond those of paragraph 2. Any regulatory scheme, however, would still have to satisfy the other requirements of paragraph 2, namely that the restriction be 'prescribed by law' and be 'necessary in a democratic society'.[270]

Using this model, the Court then determined that Article 10 was violated when Austria legislated a public monopoly on broadcasting. The critical question for the Court was whether such a monopoly was necessary for one of the permissible object-ives of a licensing scheme. The Court concluded that it was not necessary to guarantee impartiality, balance and diversity in broadcasting. The Court noted that most other European countries achieved this objective not by restricting licences but through the grant of numerous competitive broadcasting licences subject to specified criteria.[271] As a practical matter, all broadcast communication requires some public regulation to limit signal interference that could frustrate all such activity. Beyond this, however, there is a widely shared understanding that radio and television programming have an especially powerful influence on public opinion and culture and that some social control of the content of the material broadcast is appropriate. In the United Kingdom, the British Broadcasting Corporation held a broadcasting monopoly until 1954, when commercial broadcasting was permitted under a licensing system that has extended its scope to cover many radio and television channels. Both the B.B.C. and the inde-pendent broadcasters, however, are subject to an elaborate scheme of regulation. It aims to maintain standards of public service and decency, while preserving editorial independence. The British courts have been reluctant to second-guess the various agencies charged with balancing these concerns.[272]

The House of Lords has upheld a refusal by the B.B.C. to air a political party's adver-tisement that included a graphic depiction of an abortion and of aborted foetuses. Lord Hoffmann, noting that the advertising was offered as part of the free broadcast time allowed to political parties, emphasized that '[t]here is no human right to use a television channel'. Nonetheless, the Human Rights Act did provide a right that access to broadcast media not be denied on 'discriminatory, arbitrary or unreasonable grounds'. In this case the decision, based on a policy against broadcasting matters offensive to 'taste and decency', was reasonable.[273]

The European Court upheld the refusal of Swiss authorities to grant a licence to a television channel devoted exclusively to matter concerning automobiles. The gov-

---

[269] *Id.* at para. 32.

[270] *Id.*

[271] *Id.* at para. 39. The Court's holding was made notwithstanding the conceded fact that government monopoly of broadcasting was common among the signatory states at the time of the drafting of the Convention. *Id.* at para. 36.

[272] *See* D. Feldman, *Civil Liberties and Human Rights in England and Wales* 825 (2nd edn. 2002).

[273] R. *(ProLife Alliance) v. British Broadcasting Corpn., supra* n. 35, at paras. 56–73.

ernment insisted that, given the special federal nature of Switzerland, it was justified
in requiring all programming to contribute to the development of a 'pluralist' culture. The Court, noting also the essentially commercial character of the proposed
channel, held this decision to be within the state's margin of appreciation.[274] On
the other hand, it has also held that the application of a Swiss law prohibiting the
broadcasting of paid 'political' advertising to a message produced by an animal rights
group was a violation of Article 10. The Court's judgment, however, was cautious
in the extreme. It noted that government had not cited any particularly disturbing
aspect of the message and that no other broadcast outlets were available.[275] It also
declared that it could not 'exclude that prohibition of "political advertising" may be
compatible with ... Article 10 ... in certain situations' but gave no hint of what those
situations might be.[276]

Consistent with this approach, the First Amendment to the United States
Constitution has not been applied to regulation of broadcast expression with the
same rigour with which it has been invoked on behalf of print media. Although
its factual premise may have been undermined by technical developments,[277] the
Supreme Court has reasoned that the scarcity of broadcast frequencies justifies more
active public interference with content decisions by radio and television stations.[278]
Thus, the Court has upheld regulation requiring the presentation of both sides of
controversial issues,[279] the sale of advertising time to political candidates[280] and
prohibiting sexually explicit material at certain times of day.[281] On the other hand,
there are constitutional limits to broadcast regulation. The Supreme Court held that
Congress acted unconstitutionally in prohibiting publicly funded television stations
from broadcasting editorial opinions. The Court stated that the regulation of broadcasts must be related to a narrowly defined and substantial public interest.[282] In 1994,
the Court held unconstitutional a federal regulation whereby cable television opera-
tors were required to carry local broadcasting channels on their service. The Court
concluded that it was permissible to promote over the air broadcasting but, in this
case, there was no showing that local broadcasting was in real jeopardy. Therefore,
the requirement was not shown to be sufficiently related to the stated objective to be
justified under the First Amendment.[283]

---

[274] *DeMuth v. Switzerland*, 5 Nov. 2002, 38 E.H.R.R. 20. Later the Court, without citing its broadcasting
cases, upheld an Irish statute prohibiting the the the broadcast of paid religious advertising. *Murphy v. Ireland*,
10 July 2003, 38 E.H.R.R. 13.

[275] *Vgt Verein Genen Tierfabriken v. Switzerland*, 28 June 2001, 34 E.H.R.R. 4, paras. 76–7.

[276] *Id.* at para. 75.

[277] *See* Lucas A. Powe, *American Broadcasting and the First Amendment* (1987).

[278] *Red Lion Broadcasting Co. v. Federal Communications Commission*, 395 U.S. 367 (1969).

[279] *Id.*

[280] *CBS v. Federal Communications Commission*, 453 U.S. 367 (1981). On the Strasbourg Court's approach
to limitations of election expenditures *see Bowman v. United Kingdom*, 19 Feb. 1998, 26 E.H.R.R. 1 discussed
in Section C(1) *supra*.

[281] *Federal Communications Commission v. Pacifica Foundation*, 438 U.S. 726 (1978).

[282] *Federal Communications Commission v. League of Women Voters*, 468 U.S. 364 (1984).

[283] *Turner Broadcasting System, Inc. v. Federal Communications Commission*, 512 U.S. 622 (1994).

It is worth noting that the Supreme Court has recently declined to extend its some-what relaxed approach to broadcast regulation to regulation of the Internet. It struck down the federal Communications Decency Act of 1991 which prohibited Internet transmission of obscene, indecent or patently offensive material which would be avail-able to persons under 18 years of age. In rejecting the government's argument that it should follow its broadcast jurisprudence, the Court listed some of the relevant differ-ences between the two media:

Neither before nor after the enactment of the CDA have the vast democratic fora of the Internet been subject to the type of government supervision and regulation that has attended the broad-cast industry. Moreover...communications over the Internet do not 'invade' an individual's home or appear on one's computer screen unbidden. Users seldom encounter content 'by acci-dent'...Finally,...the Internet can hardly be considered a 'scarce' expressive commodity. It provides relatively unlimited, low cost capacity for communication of all kinds...Through the use of chat rooms, any person with a phone line can become a town crier with a voice that reso-nates farther than it could from any soapbox. Through the use of web pages, mail exploders, and news groups the same individual can become a pamphleteer.[284]

In *Cable and Wireless Dominica v. Marpin Telecom*,[285] the Privy Council consid-ered the monopoly Dominica had granted to Cable and Wireless over all national and international telecommunications service, including telephone and Internet. The Judicial Committee held that the monopoly implicated the Dominican Constitution's right of free expression including a right to 'receive ideas and information without interference'. The Committee remanded the case on the question of whether or not the monopoly might be justified as a protection of expression by facilitating cross-subsidization in order to serve remote areas.

D. EXPRESSION AND PUBLIC EMPLOYMENT

In a well-known remark, Justice Oliver Wendell Holmes (then on the Massachusetts Supreme Judicial Court) said: 'Petitioner may have a constitutional right to talk polit-ics but he has no constitutional right to be a policeman'.[286] The United States Supreme Court has, however, now moved toward a significantly more expansive, though some-what ill-defined, view of the free speech rights of public employees. A fairly good sum-mary is found in *Pickering v. Board of Education*:[287]

To the extent that the Illinois Supreme Court's opinion may be read to suggest that teachers may constitutionally be compelled to relinquish the First Amendment rights they would otherwise

---

[284] *Reno v. American Civil Liberties Union*, 521 U.S. 844, 868–70 (1997) (internal citations and quotation marks omitted).   [285] [2001] 1 W.L.R. 1123.
[286] *McAuliffe v. New Bedford*, 155 Mass. 216, 220 (1892).
[287] 391 U.S. 563, 568 (1968).

enjoy as citizens to comment on matters of public interest in connection with the operations of the public schools in which they work, it proceeds on a premise that has been unequivocally rejected in numerous prior decisions of this Court... At the same time it cannot be gain-said that the State has interests as an employer in regulating the speech of its employees that differ significantly from those it possesses in connection with regulation of the speech of the citizenry in general. The problem in any case is to arrive at a balance between the interests of the teacher, as a citizen, in commenting upon matters of public concern and the interest of the State, as an employer, in promoting the efficiency of the public services it performs through its employees....

While criminal sanctions and damage awards have a somewhat different impact on the exercise of the right to freedom of speech from dismissal from employment, it is apparent that the threat of dismissal from public employment is nonetheless a potent means of inhibiting speech. We have already noted our disinclination to make an across-the-board equation of dismissal from public employment for remarks critical of superiors with awarding damages in a libel suit by a public official for similar criticism. However, in a case such as the present one, in which the fact of employment is only tangentially and insubstantially involved in the subject matter of the public communication made by a teacher, we conclude that it is necessary to regard the teacher as the member of the general public he seeks to be.

In sum, we hold, in a case such as this, absent proof of false statements knowingly or recklessly made by him, a teacher's exercise of his right to speak on issues of public importance may not furnish the basis for his dismissal from public employment.[288]

When a public employee speaks or writes in his or her official capacity, however, managerial discipline for improper speech is permissible.[289]

When this issue first arose in the European Court of Human Rights it took a very different view. In two judgments delivered in 1986, the Court reviewed the refusal to renew the appointments of two teachers, one in a university and one in a secondary school. Neither applicant had yet earned permanent tenure. The actions were motivated by the teachers' associations with right- or left-wing political parties. The Court held there was no interference with Article 10 rights. Rather these matters fell 'within the sphere of rights of access to the civil service, a right not secured in the Convention'.[290] But in 1995 when a similar case came to the Court in *Vogt v. Germany*, the Court found a violation when another teacher was dismissed because of her active membership in the Communist Party. The state maintained that such membership was a breach of the teacher's duty of political loyalty to the constitutional order, a duty imposed on all civil servants. In contrast to the 1986 cases, this applicant had already achieved the status of a permanent member of the civil service. The Court reaffirmed that:

the refusal to appoint a person as a civil servant cannot as such provide the basis for a complaint under the Convention. This does not mean however, that a person who has been appointed as a

---

[288] *Id.* at 568. *See also Connick v. Meyers*, 461 U.S. 138 (1983). The Court has held that the same considerations govern the legality of public decisions to terminate at-will contracts in response to statements on political issues by the contractors. *Board of County Comm'rs. Wabaunsee County Kansas v. Umbehr*, 518 U.S. 668 (1996).

[289] *Garcetti v. Ceballos*, 126 S. Ct. 1951 (2006).

[290] *Kosiek v. Germany*, 28 Aug. 1986, 9 E.H.R.R. 328, para. 36; *Glasenapp v. Germany*, 28 Aug. 1986, 9 E.H.R.R. 25.

civil servant cannot complain on being dismissed if that dismissal violates his or her rights under the Convention.[291]

The Court went on to hold that the dismissal of a civil servant for the kind of activity at issue in that case was not 'necessary in a democratic society' for the protection of the rights of others, preventing disorder or preserving national security:

The Court proceeds on the basis that a democratic State is entitled to require civil servants to be loyal to the constitutional principles on which it is founded. In this connection it takes into account Germany's experience under the Weimar Republic and during the bitter period that followed the collapse of that regime up to the adoption of the Basic Law in 1949. Germany wished to avoid a repetition of those experiences by founding its new State on the idea that it should be a 'democracy capable of defending itself'. Nor should Germany's position in the political context of the time be forgotten. These circumstances understandably lent extra weight to this underlying notion and to the corresponding duty of political loyalty imposed on civil servants.

Even so, the absolute nature of that duty as construed by the German courts is striking. It is owed equally by every civil servant, regardless of his or her function and rank. It implies that every civil servant, whatever his or her own opinion on the matter, must unambiguously renounce all groups and movements which the competent authorities hold to be inimical to the Constitution. It does not allow for distinctions between service and private life; the duty is always owed, in every context....

[T]here are several reasons for considering dismissal of a secondary-school teacher by way of disciplinary sanction for breach of duty to be a very severe measure. This is firstly because of the effect that such a measure has on the reputation of the person concerned and secondly because secondary-school teachers dismissed in this way lose their livelihood, at least in principle, as the disciplinary court may allow them to keep part of their salary. Finally, secondary-school teachers in this situation may find it well nigh impossible to find another job as a teacher, since in Germany teaching posts outside the civil service are scarce. Consequently, they will almost certainly be deprived of the opportunity to exercise the sole profession for which they have a calling, for which they have been trained and in which they have acquired skills and experience.

A second aspect that should be noted is that Mrs. Vogt was a teacher of German and French in a secondary school, a post which did not intrinsically involve any security risks.

The risk lay in the possibility that, contrary to the special duties and responsibilities incumbent on teachers, she would take advantage of her position to indoctrinate or exert improper influence in another way on her pupils during lessons. Yet no criticism was leveled at her on this point. On the contrary, the applicant's work at school had been considered wholly satisfactory by her superiors and she was held in high regard by her pupils and their parents and also by her colleagues; the disciplinary courts recognised that she had always carried out her duties in a way that was beyond reproach. Indeed the authorities only suspended the applicant more than four years after instituting disciplinary proceedings, thereby showing that they did not consider the need to remove the pupils from her influence to be a very pressing one.

Since teachers are figures of authority to their pupils, their special duties and responsibilities to a certain extent also apply to their activities outside school. However, there is no evidence

---

[291] 26 Sept. 1995, 21 E.H.R.R. 205, para. 43.

that Mrs. Vogt herself, even outside her work at school, actually made anti-constitutional statements or personally adopted an anti-constitutional stance.[292]

The special interest that a state may have even in the non-classroom statements of public
school teachers was explored by the Supreme Court of Canada in *Ross v. New Brunswick
School District No. 15*.[293] In that case, the Court held that it was allowable under the
Charter of Rights and Freedoms for a school board to remove from teaching duties a
high school teacher who had frequently expressed anti-Semitic opinions both in speech
and in published writing. It agreed the board's action infringed freedom of expression
but found it was a permissible limitation of that right under section 1 of the Charter:

Young children are especially vulnerable to the messages conveyed by their teachers. They are
less likely to make an intellectual distinction between comments a teacher makes in the school
and those the teacher makes outside the school. They are, therefore, more likely to feel threatened and isolated by a teacher who makes comments that denigrate personal characteristics of
a group to which they belong. Furthermore, they are unlikely to distinguish between falsehoods
and truth and more likely to accept derogatory views espoused by a teacher...
    The Board held that the fact that the respondent publicly made anti-Semitic statements
contributed to the 'poisoned environment' in the school system and that it was reasonable to
anticipate that his statements and writings had influenced the anti-Semitic sentiment in the
schools... It is thus necessary to remove the respondent from his teaching position to ensure
that no influence of this kind is exerted by him upon his students and to ensure that the educational services are discrimination-free.[294]

The Court held, however, that the Charter prohibited outright termination of employment on account of off-duty statements made by the teacher. His retention in a non-
teaching position would not compromise the ability of the school board to maintain
the appropriate environment in the schools.[295]
    The context-specific character of the European Court's judgment in *Vogt* was clarified
by its decision in *Ahmed and Others v. United Kingdom*.[296] In that case, it upheld by 6–3
a prohibition on partisan political activity by senior civil servants in local government.
The Court found the limitation justified by the government's interest in maintaining a
politically neutral civil service which could act loyally and impartially on behalf of the
democratically chosen authority. The Court noted that the prohibition was limited to
those officers whose duties demanded strict non-partisanship and that these amounted
at most to 2 per cent of 2,300,000 such officers and even for these an exemption process was available.[297] The affected persons, moreover, were not compelled to be silent
on all political matters, but merely actions that could reasonably be judged as 'espousing or opposing a party political view'.[298] Given the state's margin of appreciation, the

---

[292] *Id.* at paras. 59–60.
[293] [1996] 1 S.C.R. 825.
[294] *Id.* at paras. 82–4, 101.
[295] *Id.* at paras. 106–7.
[296] 2 Sept. 1998, 29 E.H.R.R. 1.
[297] *Id.* at paras. 50–3, 59.
[298] *Id.* at para 63.

restrictions were found not disproportionate to the aim pursued. Similarly in *Rekvényi v. Hungary*,[299] it found a limit on political activities by the police to be compatible with Article 10. The Court noted particularly that Hungary was in a period of transition from totalitarianism to democracy and that the prior regime had employed the political co-optation of the police to maintain control. Moreover, as in *Ahmed*, the limits actually imposed left open substantial opportunities for political expression.[300]

These cases may be compared to *Sidabras & Dziantas v. Lithuania*. The applicants, former employes of the KGB, had been dismissed from civil service jobs under a measure disqualifying such persons from public employment. The law was intended to ensure loyalty of the civil service to the Lithuanian state. The European Court held that Article 10 was not applicable since the applicants had not been penalized for engaging in political activities or expressing political views.[301]

E. INTERFERENCES 'PRESCRIBED BY LAW'

Under Article 10(2) and other parallel provisions, a valid interference with a Convention right must not only be necessary to a specified public interest, but it must also be 'prescribed by law'. The value protected by this requirement is often summarized as the value of the 'rule of law'. For similar reasons, in the United States, otherwise properly punishable behaviour may not, consistent with due process of law, be dealt with by an unduly vague statute. The reasons for this doctrine were summed up in *Grayned v. Rockford*:[302]

It is a basic principle of due process that an enactment is void for vagueness if its prohibitions are not clearly defined. Vague laws offend several important values. First, because we assume that man is free to steer between lawful and unlawful conduct, we insist that laws give the person of ordinary intelligence a reasonable opportunity to know what is prohibited, so that he may act accordingly. Vague laws may trap the innocent by not providing fair warning. Second, if arbitrary and discriminatory enforcement is to be prevented, laws must provide explicit standards for those who apply them. A vague law impermissibly delegates basic policy matters to policemen, judges, and juries for resolution on an *ad hoc* and subjective basis, with the attendant dangers of arbitrary and discriminatory application. Third, but related, where a vague statute 'abut[s] upon sensitive areas of basic First Amendment freedoms', it 'operates to inhibit the exercise of [those] freedoms'. Uncertain meanings inevitably lead citizens to 'steer far wider of the unlawful zone'...than if the boundaries of the forbidden areas were clearly marked.

---

[299] 20 May 1999, 30 E.H.R.R. 519.

[300] *Id.* at paras. 44–9. The United States Supreme Court has also upheld limits on the political activities of civil servants as consistent with the First Amendment. *United States Civil Service Comm'n v. National Association of Letter Carriers*, 413 U.S. 548 (1973).

[301] 27 July 2004, 42 E.H.R.R. 6, paras. 67–71. The Court did find a violation of Article 14 in connection with Article 8.

[302] 408 U.S. 104, 108 (1972).

The European Court addressed the requirements imposed by this term in *Sunday Times v. United Kingdom*,[303] in which it considered whether judicial citations for contempt of court, developed in common law decisions, could be justified as interferences 'prescribed by law...for maintaining the authority and impartiality of the judiciary':

46. The applicants argue, *inter alia*, that the law of contempt of court, both before and after the decision of the House of Lords, was so vague and uncertain and the principles enunciated by that decision so novel that the restraint imposed cannot be regarded as 'prescribed by law'. The Government maintain that it suffices, in this context, that the restraint was in accordance with the law; they plead, in the alternative, that on the facts of the case the restraint was at least 'roughly foreseeable'.

47. The Court observes that the word 'law' in the expression 'prescribed by law' covers not only statute but also unwritten law. Accordingly, the Court does not attach importance here to the fact that contempt of court is a creature of the common law and not of legislation. It would clearly be contrary to the intention of the drafters of the Convention to hold that a restriction imposed by virtue of the common law is not 'prescribed by law' on the sole ground that it is not enunciated in legislation: this would deprive a common-law State which is Party to the Convention of the protection of Article 10 §2 and strike at the very roots of that State's legal system....

49. In the Court's opinion, the following are two of the requirements that flow from the expression 'prescribed by law'. First, the law must be adequately accessible: the citizen must be able to have an indication that is adequate in the circumstances of the legal rules applicable to a given case. Secondly, a norm cannot be regarded as a 'law' unless it is formulated with sufficient precision to enable the citizen to regulate his conduct: he must be able—if need be with appropriate advice—to foresee, to a degree that is reasonable in the circumstances, the consequences which a given action may entail. Those consequences need not be foreseeable with absolute certainty: experience shows this to be unattainable. Again, whilst certainty is highly desirable, it may bring in its train excessive rigidity and the law must be able to keep pace with changing circumstances. Accordingly, many laws are inevitably couched in terms which, to a greater or lesser extent, are vague and whose interpretation and application are questions of practice.

The Court found that the rules of contempt of court had been developed with sufficient certainty that a finding of contempt could be considered 'prescribed by law'. Prior cases gave a clear enough indication to enable the applicants to foresee a risk that publication might result in contempt.

This conclusion may be compared with the Court's judgment in *Kruslin v. France*,[304] dealing with a complaint that wiretapping by French authorities was in violation of Article 8. In interpreting the language of Article 8(2) stating that limitations on the rights to privacy and family life must be 'in accordance with law', the Court had previously held that any such law must, as in the case of Article 10(2), be accessible and its

---

[303] *See* Chapter 3(B) *supra*.
[304] 24 Apr. 1990, 12 E.H.R.R. 547. *See also Huvig v. France*, 24 Apr. 1990, 12 E.H.R.R. 528.

application foreseeable.[305] In *Kruslin*, the Court held that, even in a civil law system, interception of telephone conversations was not prevented from being 'in accordance with the law', merely because the governing legal rule had been developed in judicial decisions. Notwithstanding the greater emphasis on enacted law in such systems, 'case-law has traditionally played a major role in Continental countries'. But, in the case at issue, many of the rules governing telephone tapping, including some of the limitations on the investigative authorities, had been 'laid down piecemeal in judgments given over the years, the great majority of them after the interception complained of by Mr. Kruslin... Some have not yet been expressly laid down in case-law at all... [but are said to be inferable] from general enactments or principles or else from an analogical interpretation of legislative provisions—or Court decisions—concerning investigative measures different from telephone tapping'. Moreover, many questions about the scope of authorized wiretapping remained unanswered. Since French law 'written and unwritten, [did] not indicate with reasonable clarity the scope and manner of exercise of the relevant discretion conferred on the public authorities', the interference with his privacy was not 'in accordance with law'.

The Court has also indicated that an interference may or may not be 'prescribed by law' depending on the capacity of the particular applicant to discover the relevant legal authority and rules. Most clearly, the Court has stated that where restrictions on prisoners' correspondence were governed by prison 'orders and instructions', which were not available to prisoners, such interferences could not be 'in accordance with law' in the sense required by Article 8(2).[306] On the other hand, in *Groppera Radio and Others v. Switzerland*[307] the Court held that a Swiss decision to limit the retransmission of broadcasts that was based on administrative regulations promulgated under the International Telecommunications Convention was 'prescribed by law'. This was so even though the regulations had not been published by the Swiss authorities and were 'highly technical and complex'. The Court reasoned that broadcasters who might be affected by the decision should be expected to inform themselves about the relevant rules, which, although not published, had been made available for inspection.

Apart from the quality of the promulgated law, the European Court has found restrictions not to be prescribed by law when courts have relied on enacted law that did not, on its face, appear to extend to the situation in issue. The Court held that when a statute required advance registration of an association's 'leaflets, written statements or similar publications', a conviction for failing to register a written version of remarks made at a press conference had not been prescribed by law.[308]

---

[305] Article 8(2) uses the English term 'in accordance with law' instead of 'prescribed by law' which is found in articles 9(2), 10(2) and 11(2). The French usage, 'prévues par la loi' is identical in all four articles and the Court has held that they should be given an 'identical interpretation'. *Silver v. United Kingdom*, 25 Mar. 1983, 5 E.H.R.R. 347, para. 85.

[306] *Id.* at para. 89.

[307] 28 Mar. 1990, 12 E.H.R.R. 321.

[308] *Karademirci and Others v. Turkey*, 25 Jan. 2005, 44 E.H.R.R. 44; *see also Gaweda v. Poland*, 14 March 2002, 39 E.H.R.R. 4.

Section 1 of the Canadian Charter of Rights and Freedoms states that the rights and freedoms specified in the Charter are 'subject only to such reasonable limits prescribed by law as can be demonstrably justified in a free and democratic society'. The phrase 'prescribed by law' was absent from the original draft of the Charter prepared by the Canadian government but was inserted during parliamentary consideration. The French version of the Charter uses the phrase 'par un règle de droit'. This should be compared with the French version of Article 10(2) of the Convention, which uses the term 'prévues par la loi'. It has been suggested that the Canadian usage more clearly encompasses a wider field including, in addition to statutes, regulations and common law decisions.[309]

The Supreme Court of Canada has not yet had the occasion to examine a common law rule under Section 1, but has expressed the view that a common law limitation could be one 'prescribed by law'.[310]

The Canadian Court did find that a different type of restriction was *not* prescribed by law where an accused was stopped for speeding and required to submit to a 'breath-alyzer' test without having been informed of his right to counsel in violation of Section 10(b) of the Charter. The procedure on stopping the driver was neither prescribed by statute nor in common law. A majority of the Justices appeared to agree that, in such circumstances, a justification under Section 1 of the Charter could not be shown. The limit on the respondent's right to consult counsel was imposed by the conduct of the police officers and not by a rule of law.[311]

The Canadian Supreme Court has held that interference with a Charter right under a broadly drawn statute does not, by itself, mean that interference is not 'prescribed by law'. In *Irwin Toy v. Quebec (Attorney-General)*,[312] it found the criteria of Section 1 met when a regulation provided that an advertisement came within a statutory pro-hibition if it were aimed at children. The regulation also set forth three general and non-conclusive guidelines for making that determination:

Absolute precision in the law exists rarely, if at all. The question is whether the legislature has provided an intelligible standard according to which the judiciary must do its work. The task of interpreting how that standard applies in particular instances might always be characterized as having a discretionary element, because the standard can never specify all the instances in which it applies. On the other hand, where there is no intelligible standard and where the legis-lature has given a plenary discretion to do whatever seems best in a wide set of circumstances, there is no 'limit prescribed by law'.

The Court elaborated its reasons for assuming that the creation of discretionary authority did not prevent its exercise from being 'prescribed by law' in *Osborne v. Canada (Treasury Board)*.[313] It noted that the vagueness of a statute was relevant to

---

[309] See P. Hogg, *Constitutional Law of Canada* 684 (2nd edn. 1986).
[310] *R. v. Thomsen* [1988] 1 S.C.R. 640, 650–1.
[311] *R. v. Therens* [1985] 1 S.C.R. 613, 621.
[312] [1989] 1 S.C.R. 927.
[313] [1991] 2 S.C.R. 69.

the Section 1 inquiry not only with respect to this 'threshold' requirement, but also in connection with the question of whether the interference was a reasonable limitation 'demonstrably justified', since imprecision 'may fail to confine the invasion of a Charter right within reasonable limits'.

... Much of the activity of government is carried on under the aegis of laws which, of necessity, leave a broad discretion to government officials. Since it may very well be reasonable in the circumstances to confer a wide discretion, it is preferable in the vast majority of cases to deal with vagueness in the context of a §1 analysis rather than disqualifying the law *in limine*.

A question may also arise as to whether a limitation of a right is 'prescribed by law' when the *sanction* for the exercise of a right is uncertain. The English Court of Appeal, in *Rantzen v. Mirror Group Newspapers, Ltd.*,[314] reversed an award of £250,000 in damages in a civil action for libel against a newspaper that had been found to have defamed a well known television presenter and child welfare activist. The Court held that appellate courts should carefully scrutinize such awards, noting that the prior practice, where juries were free to award damages, without clear instructions, could, in such case, amount to a limitation of freedom of expression protected by Article 10 of the Convention, and such a limitation was not sufficiently certain to be 'prescribed by law'. '[U]nder the present practice no one, and certainly not a newspaper, had any means whereby, even with appropriate advice, he could foresee the consequences of the exercise by him of his right to freedom of expression'.[315]

F. PRIOR RESTRAINTS

The kinds of interferences with freedom of expression surveyed in this chapter may be divided into two classes. The first involves some kind of sanction imposed as a reaction to speech violating some pre-existing restriction. These cases include those in which someone is required to pay damages for injuring a reputation or is subjected to fines or imprisonment. The second category consists of cases where the state takes action to prevent the publication or dissemination of objectionable expression. In these cases a newspaper may be enjoined from publishing or, as in the *Handyside* case, books are actually seized and destroyed.

Historically, the second category has been thought to pose the greater threat to freedom of expression. This has been a consistent theme in American constitutional law. The text of the First Amendment of the United States Constitution does not refer to the distinction but many state constitutions do so explicitly. Thus, Article First,

---

[314] [1993] 4 All E.R. 975 (C.A.).

[315] *Id.* at 990. In reaching this conclusion, Neill LJ cited the case law of the Court at Strasbourg as well as that of the United States Supreme Court, notably *New York Times v. Sullivan*, 376 U.S. 254 (1964) and *Gertz v. Robert Welch, Inc.*, 418 U.S. 323 (1974).

Section 3 of the Connecticut Constitution provides that '[e]very citizen may freely speak, write and publish his sentiments on all subjects, being responsible for the abuse of that liberty'. The United States Supreme Court has been especially rigorous in examining prior restraints on expression. It has emphasized that, whereas after the fact penalties may discourage speech, prior restraint, without the opportunity of judicial testing, immediately removes the offensive ideas from public discourse. 'If it can be said that a threat of criminal or civil sanctions after publication "chills" speech, prior restraint "freezes" it at least for the time'.[316] Moreover, a system of pre-publication censorship, by its very existence, has been thought to instill a particularly chilling caution in potential speakers.[317] Finally, prior restraint imposes a particular injury on news media who are prevented from reporting information of current interest. 'The suppressed information grows older. Other events crowd upon it. To this extent, any First Amendment infringement that occurs with each passing day is irreparable'.[318]

Some of the same considerations have led the European Court of Human Rights to a similar position. In *The Observer and The Guardian v. United Kingdom*,[319] the Court mentioned that a presumption against prior restraint was particularly pronounced in the case of reporting by the press 'for news is a perishable commodity and to delay its publication even for a short period may well deprive it of all its value and interest'.[320] In a separate opinion in the same case, Judge deMeyer, joined by four other judges, would have gone further, arguing that prior restraint could never be compatible with Article 10 unless permitted under a state of emergency meeting the requirements of Article 15.[321] The Court has now established at least the possibility of justifying prior restraint. It has pointed out that Article 10(2) contemplates the possibility of 'conditions' to, 'restrictions' on and the 'prevention' of the exercise of Article 10 rights. Nevertheless, such restraints 'call for the most careful scrutiny'.[322]

G. ARTICLE 11: FREEDOM OF ASSOCIATION

Closely related to the right of expression is freedom of association provided in Article 11. Association is often recognized as an essential means to effect expression. The United States Supreme Court has identified a right of association in the United

---

[316] *Nebraska Press Ass'n v. Stuart*, 427 U.S. 539, 559 (1976).

[317] *Pittsburgh Press Co. v. Pittsburgh Commission on Human Relations*, 413 U.S. 376, 390 (1973).

[318] *New York Times Co. et al. v. Jascalevich*, 439 U.S. 1317, 1321 (1978).

[319] 26 November 1991, 14 E.H.H.R 153 (1992) discussed in Section B *supra*.

[320] *Id.* at para. 60.

[321] *Id.* (separate opinion).

[322] *Alinak v. Turkey*, 29 March 2005, para. 37. *See also Gawęda v. Poland*, 14 March 2002, 39 E.H.R.R. 4, para. 40. For a case re-affirming, after enactment of the Human Rights Act, the English common-law rule prohibiting orders against publication of allegedly defamatory material unless it 'is clear [the] alleged libel is untrue' *see Green v. Associated Newspapers Ltd* [2004] E.W.C.A. 1462.

States Constitution even though there is no explicit mention of the right in the text. It has found it to be a logical corollary of the First Amendment right of free speech.[323] It has noted that individual expression 'could not be vigorously protected from interference by the State unless a correlative freedom to engage in group effort toward these [desired] ends were not also guaranteed'.[324] The European Court of Human Rights, while dealing with an express right, has also mentioned its affinity with the right of expression, referring to Article 11 as *lex specialis* in relation to the *lex generalis* of Article 10.[325] It has, consequently, invoked the general principles associated with the latter article in dealing with claims under the former.[326]

The most obvious application of this understanding of the right of association is in connection with political parties. When the Constitutional Court of Turkey ordered the dissolution of the United Communist Party, the European Court examined the action with particular intensity, noting that 'political parties are a form of association essential to the proper functioning of democracy'.[327] Given that critical role,

the exceptions set out in Article 11 are, where political parties are concerned, to be construed strictly; only convincing and compelling reasons can justify restrictions on such parties' freedom of association. In determining whether a necessity within the meaning of Article 11(2) exists, the Contracting States possess only a limited margin of appreciation, which goes hand in hand with rigorous European supervision embracing both the law and the decisions applying it, including those given by independent courts.[328]

In the *United Communist Party* case, the Court found no adequate justifications for the dissolution adequate under this standard. There was no evidence that the party in question, whatever its name, was going to engage in activities 'that represented a real threat to Turkish society or the Turkish State'.[329] Since the party programme called for rectifying the grievances of the Kurdish minority in Turkey, the Turkish Constitutional Court inferred that the party was a threat to the unity of the Turkish state. The European Court noted that the party programme did not endorse any special treatment for, much less secession of, the Kurds and that it coupled its position with an insistence on peaceful and democratic means to deal with Kurdish aspirations:

Democracy thrives on freedom of expression. From that point of view there can be no justification for hindering a political group solely because it seeks to debate in public the situation of part of the State's population and to take part in the nation's political life in order to find, according to democratic rules, solutions capable of satisfying everyone considered.[330]

---

[323] *NAACP v. Alabama ex rel Patterson*, 357 U.S. 449 (1958).
[324] *Roberts v. United States Jaycees*, 468 U.S. 609, 622 (1984).
[325] *Ezelin v. France*, 26 Apr. 1991, 14 E.H.R.R. 362, para. 62.
[326] *United Communist Party of Turkey v. Turkey*, 30 Jan. 1998, 26 E.H.R.R. 121, para. 42. The affinity between Articles 10 and 11 is especially obvious in the latter's reference to a 'right of peaceable assembly'. *See Christian Democratic People's Party v. Moldova*, 14 Feb. 2006, 45 E.H.R.R. 13; *Euneri v. Turkey*, 12 July 2005.
[327] *Id.* at para. 25.
[328] *Id.* at para. 46.
[329] *Id.* at para. 54.
[330] *Id.* at para. 57.

The Court has subsequently formulated the factors which would justify dissolution of a political party because of its threat to society:

[A] political party may campaign for a change in the law or the legal and constitutional structures of the State on two conditions: firstly the means used to that end must in every respect be legal and democratic, and secondly, the change proposed must itself be compatible with fundamental democratic principles. It necessarily follows that a political party whose leaders incite to violence or put forward a policy which does not comply with one or more of the rules of democracy and the flouting of the rights and freedoms recognised in a democracy cannot lay claim to the Convention's protections against penalties imposed on these grounds.[331]

The second of these conditions, that the changes advocated by the party be incompatible with 'fundamental democratic principles', clearly presents significant definitional challenges. The Court found that Turkey was justified in dissolving an Islamist party on this test in *Refah Partisi (The Welfare Party) v. Turkey*.[332] Among the features of the party's programme that the Court emphasized was its plans to introduce Islamic law, Sharia, into the Turkish legal system. It found Sharia 'incompatible with the fundamental principles of democracy, as set forth in the Convention' noting particularly 'its criminal law and criminal procedure, its rules on the legal status of women and the way it intervenes in all spheres of public and private life in accordance with religious precepts'.[333] In deciding that forestalling the programme of the party was a 'pressing social need', the Court relied on evidence that its leaders had made statements suggesting that it did not exclude the use of force in effecting its goals. It also noted that the party had won considerable support in recent elections creating 'the real potential to seize power without being restricted by the compromise inherent in a coalition'. '[I]t is not at all improbable that totalitarian movements, organized in the form of political parties, might do away with democracy, after prospering under the democratic regime, there being examples of this in modern European history'.[334]

The Court's strict approach to limitation on political parties was extended to other kinds of associations in *Sidiropoulos v. Greece*.[335] The European Court found that the refusal to register an organization named 'Home of Macedonian Civilisation' was a violation of Article 11. The Greek court dealing with the case had gone outside the judicial record and relied on secondary accounts to conclude that the association aimed to promote a separate Macedonian state. It therefore meant to undermine the territorial integrity of Greece. The European Court noted that the organization had not yet begun functioning and, therefore, these conclusions were based on 'mere suspicion'. The refusal to register it on these grounds was an excessive response to whatever threat the group might pose. It did not, however, 'rule out that, once founded, the association might, under cover of the aims mentioned in its memorandum of association,

[331] *Yazar v. Turkey*, 9 April 2002, 36 E.H.R.R. 6, para. 49.

[332] [G.C.] 13 Feb. 2003, 37 E.H.R.R. 1, excerpted *infra* at Chapter 7(C).

[333] *Id.* at para. 123 quoting Chamber Judgment.

[334] *Id.* at paras. 132, 107–8, 99. On the *Refah* case *see* Paul Harvey, 'Militant Democracy and the European Convention on Human Rights', 29 *Eur. L. Rev.* 407 (2004).

[335] 10 July 1998, 27 E.H.R.R. 633.

have engaged in activities incompatible with those aims'. In such a case the authorities 'would not have been powerless' to deal with it.[336]

Article 11 mentions one form of association expressly—trade unions. Several cases deal with claims that Article 11 requires governments to deal with unions and to refrain from actions that may penalize membership in a union or participation in union activities. The European Court has been reluctant to adopt a broad interpretation of the right. In *National Union of Belgian Police v. Belgium*,[337] the applicant, a police union not recognized by the government, asserted that Article 11 included an implicit right of a union to be recognized by the government. The Court found that while Article 11 does contain a right to join and form trade unions, there is no inherent right to particular treatment by the government. In *Schmit and Dahlström v. Sweden*,[338] the government refused to deal with or recognize a union independently of a larger federation of unions. The individual union subsequently called a strike and the government a lockout in connection with a contract dispute with the union federation. When a contract with the federation was agreed upon, it denied retroactive benefits to members of this striking union, even members like the applicants, who did not take part in the strike. The Court found no violation of applicants' freedom to join trade unions. There was no intent on the part of the government to discourage membership in the applicant union. Even non-striking members of the union by their status lent financial and moral support to the illegal strike.

The Strasbourg Court declined to hold that the right 'to form and join trade unions for the protection of his interests' includes a right to strike. In response to such a claim in *Schmidt and Dahlström*, the Court only noted that, when such a right exists under national law, it may be limited without infringing Article 11. The Court held that the right to form and join unions includes a right to be 'enabled, in conditions not at variance with Article 11, to strive, through the medium of their organizations, for the protection of their occupational interests'. A right to strike, the Court noted, is one means to this end but not the only one.

While the United States Supreme Court has stated that the right of association merited protection whenever it advanced beliefs that 'pertain to political, economic or religious matters',[339] it has been quite tolerant of legislative restrictions on associations for mere economic purposes, such as labour unions. Thus, the Court has upheld a federal law requiring union officials to attest that they were not members or supporters of the Communist Party, since Congress' concerns were found to be with protecting the economy and not with direct regulation of expression or belief.[340]

---

[336] *Id.* at paras. 44–6. Compare *Gorzelik v. Poland*, 14 Feb. 2004, 40 E.H.R.R. 4 where the Court held it was permissible to withhold recognition from a group dedicated to the promotion of Silesian nationality as a means of forestalling subsequent use of that recognition to secure the favourable treatment accorded 'national' minorities in elections.   [337] 27 Oct. 1975, 1 E.H.R.R. 578.

[338] 6 Feb. 1976, 1 E.H.R.R. 632.

[339] *Id.* at 461.

[340] *American Communications Association v. Douds*, 339 U.S. 382 (1950). But *see United States Dept of Agriculture v. United Foods*, 533 U.S. 405 (2001) (grower could not be compelled to contribute to an advertising campaign with which it disagreed).

The European Court elaborated the right to 'strive through the medium of their organizations, for the protection of their occupational interests' in *Wilson, National Union of Journalists and Others v. United Kingdom*.[341] It held that the state had violated Article 11 by allowing employers to discontinue collective bargaining and then, by means of pay incentives, to pressure employees to waive their right to collective representation by signing individual employment agreements.[342] The Court affirmed that states need not make collective bargaining compulsory but declared that it must provide ways in which employees could use the union to 'make representations to their employer or to take action in support of their interests'. Without this capacity, the right to belong to a trade union would be 'illusory'. The ability of employers to use differential pay to discourage such use could substantially frustrate this essential feature of unions and the state was obliged to prevent it.[343]

The Canadian Supreme Court has also considered claims that the right to strike is encompassed in the right of association. The Canadian Charter of Rights and Freedoms, like the European Convention, contains an explicit protection of 'freedom of association' (Section 2(d)) but provides no definition of that freedom. It makes no mention of trade unions. In *Reference Re Public Service Employee Relations Act (Alta.)*,[344] the Supreme Court of Canada considered the nature of the right in connection with challenged provincial statutes which required that certain terms of employment for public service employees, firefighters, and police be settled by compulsory arbitration and which prohibited strikes by such employees. The unions contended that these provisions infringed the right of association. The Court held, by four to two, that the statutes were valid. Three members of the majority held that a union's right to associate does not include a right to bargain collectively or to strike. Justice McIntyre agreed that the statute was constitutional, holding only that the right of association did not include a right to strike. His judgment, part of which follows, contains an illuminating discussion of the right of association:

Various theories have been advanced to define freedom of association guaranteed by the Constitution. They range from the very restrictive to the virtually unlimited. To begin with, it has been said that freedom of association is limited to a right to associate with others in common pursuits or for certain purposes. Neither the objects nor the actions of the group are protected by freedom of association. . . .

A second approach provides that freedom of association guarantees the collective exercise of constitutional rights or, in other words, the freedom to engage collectively in those activities which are constitutionally protected for each individual. This theory has been

---

[341] 2 July 2002, 35 E.H.R.R. 20.

[342] The state was responsible for the acts of the employers under Article 11's 'positive obligation' to make the right effective. The positive obligation is discussed in Chapter 8(B) *infra*.

[343] *Wilson, supra* n. 341, at paras. 46–8.

[344] [1987] 1 S.C.R. 313. In 1999 the Supreme Court held that s. 2(d) did not require the Federal government to extend the same rights of collective bargaining to employee associations of the Royal Canadian Mounted Police that is provided for other federal employees. *Delisle v. Canada (Attorney General)* [1999] 2 S.C.R. 989.

adopted in the United States to define the scope of freedom of association under the American Constitution....

A third approach postulates that freedom of association stands for the principle that an individual is entitled to do in concert with others that which he may lawfully do alone and, conversely, that individuals and organizations have no right to do in concert what is unlawful when done individually....

A fourth approach would constitutionally protect collective activities which may be said to be fundamental to our culture and traditions and which by common assent are deserving of protection...

A fifth approach rests on the proposition that freedom of association, under s. 2(d) of the Charter, extends constitutional protection to all activities which are essential to the lawful goals of an association. This approach was advanced in *Re Service Employees' Int'l Union, Loc. 204 and Broadway Manor Nursing Home* (1983), 4 D.L.R. (4th) 231, 44 O.R. (2d) 392, 10 C.R.R. 37, by the Ontario Divisional Court. The court held that freedom of association included the freedom to bargain collectively and to strike, since, in its view, these activities were essential to the objects of a trade union and without them the association would be emasculated...

The fifth approach was unacceptable to Justice McIntyre because it gave greater constitutional rights to members of a group than to individuals. An activity could not become constitutionally protected simply because it is performed by a group. Rather, the basic purpose of freedom of association is to ensure that an activity, protected if done by an individual, is also protected if done collectively.

Of the remaining approaches, it must surely be accepted that the concept of freedom of association includes at least the right to join with others in lawful, common pursuits and to establish and maintain organizations and associations as set out in the first approach...It is, I believe, equally clear that, in accordance with the second approach, freedom of association should guarantee the collective exercise of constitutional rights. Individual rights protected by the Constitution do not lose that protection when exercised in common with others. People must be free to engage collectively in those activities which are constitutionally protected for each individual....

...Conversely, individuals and organizations have no constitutional right to do in concert what is unlawful when done alone. This approach is broader than the second, since constitutional protection attaches to all group acts which can be lawfully performed by an individual, whether or not the individual has a constitutional right to perform them. It is true, of course, that in this approach the range of Charter-protected activity could be reduced by legislation, because the legislature has the power to declare what is and what is not lawful activity for the individual. The legislature, however, would not be able to attack directly the associational character of the activity, since it would be constitutionally bound to treat groups and individuals alike. A simple example illustrates this point: golf is a lawful but not constitutionally protected activity. Under the third approach, the legislature could prohibit golf entirely. However, the legislature could not constitutionally provide that golf could be played in pairs but in no greater number, for this would infringe the Charter guarantee of freedom of association....

When this definition of freedom of association is applied, it is clear that it does not guarantee the right to strike....

[T]here is no analogy whatever between the cessation of work by a single employee and a strike conducted in accordance with modern labour legislation. The individual has, by reason of the cessation of work, either breached or terminated his contract of employment. It is true that the law will not compel the specific performance of the contract by ordering him back to work ... But, this is markedly different from a lawful strike. An employee who ceases work does not contemplate a return to work. In recognition of this fact, the law does not regard a strike as either a breach of contract or a termination of employment....

The Canadian Supreme Court, like the Strasbourg Court, has found that the government is obliged to maintain a legal framework that makes unionization possible. Consequently, it has ruled that the exclusion of agricultural workers from a provincial labour relations scheme effectively deprived farm workers of the right to associate and violated section 52 of the Charter.[345]

Much of the law under Article 11 and national constitutional rights of association does not concern obstacles to creating and acting through voluntary associations but rather complaints by individuals that they have been compelled to participate in associations against their wills. In *Chassagnou and Others v. France*,[346] landowners complained about a legislative scheme putting the regulation of hunting rights on their property in the hands of a statutorily created 'hunters association'. All affected landowners were made members of this association, thereby giving them some influence over its policies. The applicants were philosophically opposed to hunting. The European Court decided the law violated Article 1 of Protocol 1 as a disproportionate interference with the right to peaceful enjoyment of property. It also held the compulsory membership of the hunters association violated Article 11 even though that membership was essentially formal. It required no payment of dues nor any other participation in the affairs of the organization. Without further explanation, the Court declared that this 'takes nothing away from the compulsory nature of their membership'. It characterized the law in question as one requiring 'an association...fundamentally contrary to [the applicant's] own convictions'.[347] On the other hand, when an applicant could avoid joining an employers association by concluding a substitute collective bargaining agreement, the Court held there was no violation of Article 11 rights.[348]

In *Young, James, and Webster v. United Kingdom*,[349] a British law permitted closed shop agreements, requiring all British rail workers to be members of a union. The Court held the law violated Article 11 and was not justified under Article 11(2). The benefits of keeping down confusion in bargaining and in aiding the formation of trade unions were not sufficiently advanced by the restriction. For similar reasons, the Court held that requiring membership in a private association, as a condition to obtaining and holding a taxi licence, was not 'necessary' for the efficient regulation of

---

[345] *Dunsmore v. Ontario (Attorney General)* [2001] 3 S.C.R. 1016.

[346] 29 Apr. 1999, 29 E.H.R.R. 615.

[347] *Id.* at paras. 115–17.

[348] *Gustafsson v. Sweden*, 25 Apr. 1996, 22 E.H.R.R. 409, at para. 52.

[349] 13 Aug. 1981, 4 E.H.R.R. 38. *See also Sigudur A. Sigurjónsson v. Iceland*, 30 June 1993, 16 E.H.R.R. 462.

taxi cabs. In contrast, in *Gustafsson v. Sweden*,[350] the Court considered a trade union boycott against an employer who had refused either to join the employers association or to conclude a substitute collective bargaining agreement with his employees. Since the applicant could have avoided this result by concluding a substitute agreement, it held that any burden on the right was not disproportionate to the boycotting union's interest in promoting the collective bargaining system.[351]

The existence of a right not to associate depends on the characterization of the organization in which membership is compelled. In *LeCompte, VanLeuven and Demeyere v. Belgium*,[352] the state required that all doctors be members of the Ordre des Médicins. The Court found no violation of Article 11 because the Order performed important public regulatory functions and was, thus, 'not an association within the meaning of Article 11'. Moreover, the applicants were not prevented from joining other societies. On the other hand, in *Sigudur A. Sigurjónnson v. Iceland*,[353] the Court held that a privately organized and operated association of taxi cab drivers was not a 'public-law association' but a private association and thus within Article 11. Although the organization did perform certain public functions, the primary responsibility for public regulation of taxi cabs was in another public agency.[354]

The United States Supreme Court, like the European Court, has also found that the right of association entails some right to refuse to associate with groups with which one disagrees. The Court has held that a state may not require a public employee to contribute funds to a union to support its political activities, although compulsory contributions may be proper to support its collective bargaining activities.[355]

When an employee complained about compulsory due payments to a union that expended funds for political causes with which the employee disagreed, the Supreme Court of Canada was unanimous in upholding the compulsory payments. Three justices so held on the ground that Section 2(d) of the Charter did not include a right to refrain from compulsory association. Three judges held there was such a right since both free association and non-association were essential to an individual's potential for 'self-actualization'. They found, however, that the compelled association in this case was demonstrably necessary for the proper end of allowing unions to participate in political and economic debate and, therefore, there was no violation under Section 1. A seventh judge did not decide if Section 2(d) encompassed a right not to associate since she concluded that, if there were such a right, the interference would be permissible under Section 1.[356]

---

[350] *Supra* n. 348.

[351] *Id.* at paras. 51–5.

[352] 23 June 1981, 4 E.H.R.R. 1.

[353] 30 June 1993, 16 E.H.R.R. 462.

[354] *See also Chassagnou v France, supra* n. 346.

[355] *Abood v. Board of Education*, 431 U.S. 209 (1977). But *see Glickman v. Wileman Bros. & Elliot Inc.*, 521 U.S. 457 (1996) (holding that requiring producers to contribute to an advertising programme does not violate the First Amendment where the producers did not object to the message financed on political or ideological grounds).

[356] *Lavigne v. Ontario Public Service Employees' Union* [1991] 2 S.C.R. 211.

In an important decision which settled a number of contested questions of British constitutional law, the House of Lords upheld a decision by the competent minister to prohibit the civilian employees of the Government Communications Headquarters, an agency concerned with national security and intelligence, from being members of independent trade unions. The House, however, did not address any arguments directly based on a claim of freedom of association.[357] A subsequent application to the European Commission of Human Rights did raise a claim of violation of Article 11, but the Commission found the issue governed by the last sentence of Article 11(2), allowing lawful restrictions on the exercise of these rights 'by…members of the…administration of the states'. In light of the wide leeway granted to a state in dealing with matters of national security,[358] the Commission found the application 'manifestly ill-founded' and, therefore, inadmissible.[359] In 2000, Parliament enacted a statute which made it an offence simply to be a member of certain terrorist organizations.[360]

[357] *Council of Civil Service Unions v. Minister for Civil Service* [1985] 1 A.C. 374, [1984] 3 All E.R. 935 (H.L.).

[358] *See* Section C *supra*.

[359] *Council of Civil Service Unions v. United Kingdom*, 20 Jan. 1987, 10 E.H.R.R. 269 (Commission Decision). On the criteria of admissibility *see* Chapter 2(B) *supra*. In *Rekvényi v. Hungary*, 20 May 1999, 30 E.H.R.R. 519, the Court upheld a ban on police joining a political party citing, *inter alia* the last sentence of Art. 11(2). *Id.* paras. 58–62.

[360] *See* A. W. Bradley & K. D. Ewing, *Constitutional and Administrative Law* 574 (14th edn. 2007).

7

FREEDOM OF THOUGHT, CONSCIENCE AND RELIGION

ARTICLE 9

1. Everyone has the right to freedom of thought, conscience and religion; this right includes freedom to change his religion or belief and freedom, either alone or in community with others and in public or private, to manifest his religion or belief, in worship, teaching, practice and observance.

2. Freedom to manifest one's religion or beliefs shall be subject only to such limitations as are prescribed by law and are necessary in a democratic society in the interests of public safety, for the protection of public order, health or morals, or for the protection of the rights and freedoms of others.

A. THE LANDMARK JUDGMENT

The sensitivity of religious issues long chilled any ardour that the European Court of Human Rights might have had to address cases involving Article 9. Only in 1993 did the Strasbourg Court finally find a government in violation of the Convention provision protecting religious freedom.

1. KOKKINAKIS V. GREECE

Judgment of 23 May 1993
17 E.H.R.R. 397

6. Mr. Minos Kokkinakis, a retired businessman of Greek nationality, was born into an Orthodox family at Sitia (Crete) in 1919. After becoming a Jehovah's Witness in 1936, he was arrested more than sixty times for proselytism. He was also interned and imprisoned on several occasions.

The periods of internment, which were ordered by the administrative authorities on the grounds of his activities in religious matters, were spent on various islands in the Aegean (thirteen months in Amorgos in 1938, six in Milos in 1940 and twelve in Makronisos in 1949).

The periods of imprisonment, to which he was sentenced by the courts, were for acts of proselytism (three sentences of two and a half months in 1939—he was the first Jehovah's Witness to be convicted under the Laws of the Metaxas Government, four and a half months in 1949 and two months in 1962), conscientious objection (eighteen and a half months in 1941) and holding a religious meeting in a private house (six months in 1952).

Between 1960 and 1970 the applicant was arrested four times and prosecuted but not convicted.

7. On 2 March 1986 he and his wife called at the home of Mrs. Kyriakaki in Sitia and engaged in a discussion with her. Mrs. Kyriakaki's husband, who was the cantor at a local Orthodox church, informed the police, who arrested Mr. and Mrs. Kokkinakis and took them to the local police station, where they spent the night of 2–3 March 1986.

8. The applicant and his wife were prosecuted under section 4 of Law no. 1363/1938 making proselytism an offence and were committed for trial at the Lasithi Criminal Court (*trimeles plimmeliodikio*), which heard the case on 20 March 1986.

9. [T]he Criminal Court heard evidence from Mr. and Mrs. Kyriakaki, a defence witness and the two defendants and gave judgment on the same day:

[The defendants], who belong to the Jehovah's Witnesses sect, attempted to proselytise and, directly or indirectly, to intrude on the religious beliefs of Orthodox Christians, with the intention of undermining their beliefs, by taking advantage of their inexperience, their low intellect and their naivety. In particular, they went to the home of [Mrs. Kyriakaki]...and told her that they brought good news; by insisting in a pressing manner, they gained admittance to the house and began to read from a book on the Scriptures which they interpreted with reference to a king of heaven, to events which had not yet occurred but would occur, etc., encouraging her by means of their judicious, skilful explanations...to change her Orthodox Christian beliefs.

The court found Mr. and Mrs. Kokkinakis guilty of proselytism and sentenced each of them to four months' imprisonment, convertible into a pecuniary penalty of 400 drachmas per day's imprisonment, and a fine of 10,000 drachmas. [I]t also ordered the confiscation and destruction of four booklets which they had been hoping to sell to Mrs. Kyriakaki.

10. Mr. and Mrs. Kokkinakis appealed against this judgment to the Crete Court of Appeal (*Efetio*). The Court of Appeal quashed Mrs. Kokkinakis's conviction and upheld her husband's but reduced his prison sentence to three months and converted it into a pecuniary penalty of 400 drachmas per day.

...

According to the record of the hearing of 17 March 1987, Mrs. Kyriakaki had given the following evidence:

They immediately talked to me about Olof Palme, whether he was a pacifist or not, and other subjects that I can't remember. They talked to me about things I did not understand very well. It was not a discussion but a constant monologue by them.... If they had told me they were Jehovah's Witnesses, I would not have let them in. I don't recall whether they spoke to me about the Kingdom of Heaven. They stayed in the house about ten minutes or a quarter of an hour. What they told me was religious in nature, but I don't know why they told it to me. I could not know at the outset what the purpose of their visit was. They may have said something to me at the time with a view to undermining my religious beliefs...[However,] the discussion did not influence my beliefs...

C. The proceedings in the Court of Cassation

11. Mr. Kokkinakis appealed on points of law. He maintained, inter alia, that the provisions of Law no. 1363/1938 contravened Article 13 of the Constitution.

12. The Court of Cassation (*Arios Pagos*) dismissed the appeal on 22 April 1988. It rejected the plea of unconstitutionality for the following reasons:

> Section 4 of Law no. 1363/1938,...not only does not contravene Article 13 of the 1975 Constitution but is fully compatible with the Constitution, which recognizes the inviolability of freedom of conscience in religious matters and provides for freedom to practice any known religion, subject to a formal provision in the same Constitution prohibiting proselytism in that proselytism is forbidden in general whatever the religion against which it is directed, including therefore the dominant religion in Greece, in accordance with Article 3 of the 1975 Constitution, namely the Christian Eastern Orthodox Church.

...

In the opinion of a dissenting member, the Court of Cassation should have quashed the judgment of the court below for having wrongly applied section 4 of Law no. 1363/1938 in that it had made no mention of the promises whereby the defendant had allegedly attempted to intrude on Mrs. Kyriakaki's religious beliefs and had given no particulars of Mrs. Kyriakaki's inexperience and low intellect.

13. The relevant Articles of the 1975 Constitution read as follows:

Article 3

> 1. The dominant religion in Greece is that of the Christian Eastern Orthodox Church. The Greek Orthodox Church which recognises as its head Our Lord Jesus Christ, is indissolubly united, doctrinally, with the Great Church of Constantinople and with any other Christian Church in communion with it (*omodoxi*), immutably observing, like the other Churches, the holy apostolic and synodical canons and the holy traditions. It is autocephalous and is administered by the Holy Synod, composed of all the bishops in office, and by the standing Holy Synod[.]
>
> 3. The text of the Holy Scriptures is unalterable. No official translation into any other form of language may be made without the prior consent of the autocephalous Greek Church and the Great Christian Church at Constantinople.

Article 13

> 1. Freedom of conscience in religious matters is inviolable. The enjoyment of personal and political rights shall not depend on an individual's religious beliefs.
>
> 2. There shall be freedom to practice any known religion; individuals shall be free to perform their rites of worship without hindrance and under the protection of the law. The performance of rites of worship must not prejudice public order or public morals. Proselytism is prohibited.

...

14. The Christian Eastern Orthodox Church, which during nearly four centuries of foreign occupation symbolized the maintenance of Greek culture and the Greek language, took an active part in the Greek people's struggle for emancipation, to such an extent that Hellenism is to some extent identified with the Orthodox faith.

A royal decree of 23 July 1833 entitled 'Proclamation of the Independence of the Greek Church' described the Orthodox Church as 'autocephalous'. Greece's successive Constitutions have referred to the church as being 'dominant'. The overwhelming majority of the population are members of it, and, according to Greek conceptions, it represents de jure and de facto the religion of the State itself, a good number of whose administrative and educational functions (marriage, and family law, compulsory religious instruction, oaths sworn by members of the Government, etc.) it moreover carries out. Its role in public life is reflected by, among other things, the presence of the Minister of Education and Religious Affairs at the sessions of the Church hierarchy at which the Archbishop of Athens is elected and by the participation of the Church authorities in all official State events; the President of the Republic takes his oath of office according to Orthodox ritual; and the official calendar follows that of the Christian Eastern Orthodox Church.

15. Under the reign of Otto I (1832–62), the Orthodox Church, which had long complained of a Bible society's propaganda directed at young Orthodox schoolchildren on behalf of the Evangelical Church, managed to get a clause added to the first Constitution (1844) forbidding 'proselytism and any other action against the dominant religion'. The Constitutions of 1864, 1911 and 1952 reproduced the same clause. The 1975 Constitution prohibits proselytism in general (Article 13 para. 2): the ban covers all 'known religions', meaning those whose doctrines are not apocryphal and in which no secret initiation is required of neophytes.

16. During the dictatorship of Metaxas (1936–1940) proselytism was made a criminal offense for the first time by section 4 of Law (*anagastikos nomos*) no. 1363/1938.

...

17. In [1953] a full court of the Supreme Administrative Court (*Symvoulio tis Epikratias*) gave the following definition of proselytism:

> Article 1 of the Constitution, which establishes the freedom to practice any known religion and to perform rites of worship without hindrance and prohibits proselytism and all other activities directed against the dominant religion, that of the Christian Eastern Orthodox Church, means that purely spiritual teaching does not amount to proselytism, even if it demonstrates the errors of other religions and entices possible disciples away from them, who abandon their original religions of their own free will; this is because spiritual teaching is in the nature of a rite of worship performed freely and without hindrance. Outside such spiritual teaching, which may be freely given, any determined, importunate attempt to entice disciples away from the dominant religion by means that are unlawful or morally reprehensible constitutes proselytism as prohibited by the aforementioned provision of the Constitution.

18. The Greek courts have held that persons were guilty of proselytism who had: likened the saints to 'figures adorning the wall', St. Gerasimos to 'a body stuffed with cotton' and the Church to 'a theatre, a market, a cinema'; preached, while displaying a painting showing a crowd of wretched people in rags, that 'such are all those who do not embrace my faith'; promised Orthodox refugees housing on specially favourable terms if they adhered to the Uniate faith; offered a scholarship for study abroad; sent Orthodox priests booklets with the

recommendation that they should study them and apply their content; distributed 'so-called religious' books and booklets free to 'illiterate peasants' or to 'young schoolchildren'; or promised a young seamstress an improvement in her position if she left the Orthodox Church, whose priests were alleged to be 'exploiters of society'.

...

20. More recently courts have convicted Jehovah's Witnesses for professing the sect's doctrine 'importunately' and accusing the Orthodox Church of being a 'source of suffering for the world'; for entering other people's homes in the guise of Christians wishing to spread the New Testament; and for attempting to give books and booklets to an Orthodox priest at the wheel of his car after stopping him.

[On] the other hand, the Court of Cassation quashed a judgment of the Athens Court of Appeal as having no basis in law because, when convicting a Jehovah's Witness, the Court of Appeal had merely reiterated the words of the indictment and thus not explained how 'the importunate teaching of the doctrines of the Jehovah's Witnesses sect' of 'distribution of the sect's booklets at a minimal price' had amounted to an attempt to intrude on the complainants' religious beliefs, or shown how the defendant had taken advantage of their 'inexperience' and 'low intellect'. The Court of Cassation remitted the case to a differently constituted bench of the Court of Appeal, which acquitted the defendant.

Similarly, it has been held in several court decisions that the offence of proselytism was not made out where there had merely been a discussion about the beliefs of the Jehovah's Witnesses, where booklets had been distributed from door to door, or in the street, or where the tenets of the sect had been explained without any deception to an Orthodox Christian. Lastly, it has been held that being an 'illiterate peasant' is not sufficient to establish the 'naivety', referred to in section 4, of the person whom the alleged proselytizer is addressing.

21. After the revision of the Constitution in 1975, the Jehovah's Witnesses brought legal proceedings to challenge the constitutionality of section 4 of Law no. 1363/1938. They complained that the description of the offence was vague, but above all they objected to the actual title of the Law, which indicated that the Law was designed to preserve Articles 1 and 2 of the Constitution in force at the time, which prohibited proselytism directed against the dominant religion. In the current Constitution this prohibition is extended to all religions and furthermore is no longer included in the chapter concerning religion but in the one dealing with civil and social rights, and more particularly in Article 13, which guarantees freedom of conscience in religious matters.

The courts have always dismissed such objections of unconstitutionality, although they have been widely supported in legal literature.

22. The Jehovah's Witnesses movement appeared in Greece at the beginning of the twentieth century. Estimates of its membership today vary between 25,000 and 70,000. Members belong to one of 338 congregations, the first of which was formed in Athens in 1922.

23. Since the revision of the Constitution in 1975 the Supreme Administrative Court has held on several occasions that the Jehovah's Witnesses come within the definition of a 'known religion'. Some first-instance courts, however, continue to rule to the contrary. In 1986 the Supreme Administrative Court held that a ministerial decision refusing the appointment of a Jehovah's Witness as a literature teacher was contrary to freedom of conscience in religious matters and hence to the Greek Constitution.

24. According to statistics provided by the applicant, 4,400 Jehovah's Witnesses were arrested between 1975 (when democracy was restored) and 1992, and 1,233 of these were committed for trial and 208 convicted.

...

28. The applicant's complaints mainly concerned a restriction on the exercise of his freedom of religion. The Court will accordingly begin by looking at the issues relating to Article 9, which provides:

1. Everyone has the right to freedom of thought, conscience and religion; this right includes freedom to change his religion or belief and freedom, either alone or in community with others and in public or private, to manifest his religion or belief, in worship, teaching, practice and observance.

2. Freedom to manifest one's religion or beliefs shall be subject only to such limitations as are prescribed by law and are necessary in a democratic society in the interests of public safety, for the protection of public order, health or morals, or for the protection of the rights and freedoms of others.

29. The applicant did not only challenge what he claimed to be the wrongful application to him of section 4 of Law no. 1363/1938. His submission concentrated on the broader problem of whether that enactment was compatible with the right enshrined in Article 9 of the Convention, which, he argued, having been part of Greek law since 1953, took precedence under the Constitution over any contrary statute. He pointed to the logical and legal difficulty of drawing any even remotely clear dividing-line between proselytism and freedom to change one's religion or belief and, either alone or in community with others, in public and in private, to manifest it, which encompassed all forms of teaching, publication and preaching between people.

...

31. As enshrined in Article 9, freedom of thought, conscience and religion is one of the foundations of a 'democratic society' within the meaning of the Convention. It is, in its religious dimension, one of the most vital elements that go to make up the identity of believers and their conception of life, but it is also a precious asset for atheists, agnostics, sceptics and the unconcerned. The pluralism indissociable from a democratic society, which has been dearly won over the centuries, depends on it.

While religious freedom is primarily a matter of individual conscience, it also implies, inter alia, freedom to 'manifest [one's] religion'. Bearing witness in words and deeds is bound up with the existence of religious convictions.

According to Article 9, freedom to manifest one's religion is not only exercisable in community with others, 'in public' and within the circle of those whose faith one shares, but can also be asserted 'alone' and 'in private'; furthermore, it includes in principle the right to try to convince one's neighbour, for example through 'teaching', failing which, moreover, 'freedom to change [one's] religion or belief', enshrined in Article 9, would be likely to remain a dead letter.

32. The requirements of Article 9 are reflected in the Greek Constitution in so far as Article 13 of the latter declares that freedom of conscience in religious matters is inviolable and

that there shall be freedom to practice any known religion. Jehovah's Witnesses accordingly enjoy both the status of a 'known religion' and the advantages flowing from that as regards observance.

33. The fundamental nature of the rights guaranteed in Article 9 Para. 1 is also reflected in the wording of the paragraph providing for limitations on them. Unlike the second paragraphs of Articles 8, 10 and 11 which cover all the rights mentioned in the first paragraphs of those Articles, that of Article 9 refers only to 'freedom to manifest one's religion or belief'. In so doing, it recognizes that in democratic societies, in which several religions coexist within one and the same population, it may be necessary to place restrictions on this freedom in order to reconcile the interests of the various groups and ensure that everyone's beliefs are respected.

...

36. The sentence passed by the Lasithi Criminal Court and subsequently reduced by the Crete Court of Appeal amounts to an interference with the exercise of Mr. Kokkinakis's right to 'freedom to manifest [his] religion or belief'. Such an interference is contrary to Article 9 unless it is 'prescribed by law', directed at one or more of the legitimate aims in paragraph 2 and 'necessary in a democratic society' for achieving them.

1. 'Prescribed by law'

...

40. ...[T]he wording of many statutes is not absolutely precise. The need to avoid excessive rigidity and to keep pace with changing circumstances means that many laws are inevitably couched in terms which, to a greater or lesser extent, are vague. Criminal-law provisions on proselytism fall within this category. The interpretation and application of such enactments depend on practice.

In this instance there existed a body of settled national case-law. This case-law, which had been published and was accessible, supplemented the letter of section 4 and was such as to enable Mr. Kokkinakis to regulate his conduct in the matter.

As to the constitutionality of section 4 of Law no. 1363/1938, the Court reiterates that it is, in the first instance, for the national authorities, and in particular the courts, to interpret and apply domestic law. And the Greek courts that have had to deal with the issue have ruled that there is no incompatibility.

41. The measure complained of was therefore 'prescribed by law' within the meaning of Article 9 para. 2 of the Convention.

2. Legitimate aim

42. The Government contended that a democratic State had to ensure the peaceful enjoyment of the personal freedoms of all those living on its territory. If, in particular, it was not vigilant to protect a person's religious beliefs and dignity from attempts to influence them by immoral and deceitful means, Article 9 para. 2 would in practice be rendered wholly nugatory.

43. In the applicant's submission, religion was part of the 'constantly renewable flow of human thought' and it was impossible to conceive of its being excluded from public debate. A fair balance of personal rights made it necessary to accept that others' thought should be

subject to a minimum of influence, otherwise the result would be a 'strange society of silent animals that [would] think but ... not express themselves, that [would] talk but ... not communicate, and that [would] exist but ... not coexist'.

44. Having regard to the circumstances of the case and the actual terms of the relevant court's decisions, the Court considers that the impugned measure was in pursuit of a legitimate aim under Article 9 para. 2, namely the protection of the rights and freedoms of others, relied on by the Government.

3. 'Necessary in a democratic society'

45. Mr. Kokkinakis did not consider it necessary in a democratic society to prohibit a fellow citizen's right to speak when he came to discuss religion with his neighbour. He was curious to know how a discourse delivered with conviction and based on holy books common to all Christians could infringe the rights of others. Mrs. Kyriakaki was an experienced adult woman with intellectual abilities; it was not possible, without flouting fundamental human rights, to make it a criminal offence for a Jehovah's Witness to have a conversation with a cantor's wife. Moreover, the Crete Court of Appeal, although the facts before it were precise and absolutely clear, had not managed to determine the direct or indirect nature of the applicant's attempt to intrude on the complainant's religious beliefs. Its reasoning showed that it had convicted the applicant 'not for something he had done but for what he was'.

The Commission accepted this argument in substance.

46. The Government maintained, on the contrary, that the Greek courts had based themselves on plain facts which amounted to the offence of proselytism: Mr. Kokkinakis's insistence on entering Mrs. Kyriakaki's home on a false pretext; the way in which he had approached her in order to gain her trust; and his 'skilful' analysis of the Holy Scriptures calculated to 'delude' the complainant, who did not possess any 'adequate grounding in doctrine'. They pointed out that if the State remained indifferent to attacks on freedom of religious belief, major unrest would be caused that would probably disturb the social peace.

47. The Court has consistently held that a certain margin of appreciation is to be left to the Contracting States in assessing the existence and extent of the necessity of an interference, but this margin is subject to European supervision, embracing both the legislation and the decisions applying it, even those given by an independent court. The Court's task is to determine whether the measures taken at national level were justified in principle and proportionate.

In order to rule on this latter point, the Court must weigh the requirements of the protection of the rights and liberties of others against the conduct of which the applicant stood accused. In exercising its supervisory jurisdiction, the Court must look at the impugned judicial decisions against the background of the case as a whole (see, inter alia and mutatis mutandis, the *Barfod v. Denmark* judgment of 22 February 1989, para. 28).

48. First of all, a distinction has to be made between bearing Christian witness and improper proselytism. The former corresponds to true evangelism, which a report drawn up in 1956 under the auspices of the World Council of Churches describes as an essential mission and a responsibility of every Christian and every Church. The latter represents a corruption or deformation of it. It may, according to the same report, take the form of activities offering material or social advantages with a view to gaining new members for a Church or exerting improper pressure on people in distress or in need; it may even entail the use of violence or brainwashing; more generally, it is not compatible with respect for the freedom of thought, conscience and religion of others.

Scrutiny of section 4 of Law no. 1363/1938 shows that the relevant criteria adopted by the Greek legislature are reconcilable with the foregoing if and in so far as they are designed only to punish improper proselytism, which the Court does not have to define in the abstract in the present case.

49. The Court notes, however, that in their reasoning the Greek courts established the applicant's liability by merely reproducing the wording of section 4 and did not sufficiently specify in what way the accused had attempted to convince his neighbour by improper means. None of the facts they set out warrants that finding.

That being so, it has not been shown that the applicant's conviction was justified in the circumstances of the case by a pressing social need. The contested measure therefore does not appear to have been proportionate to the legitimate aim pursued or, consequently, 'necessary in a democratic society ... for the protection of the rights and freedoms of others'.

50. In conclusion, there has been a breach of Article 9 of the Convention.

[The Court held there was no breach of Article 7 and that it was unnecessary, given the finding of a violation of Article 9, to examine the complaints about Articles 10 and 14.]

...

For these reasons, the court

1. Holds by six votes to three that there has been a breach of Article 9;

2. Holds by eight votes to one that there has been no breach of Article 7;

3. Holds unanimously that it is unnecessary to examine the case under Article 10 or under Article 14 taken together with Article 9;

4. Holds unanimously that the respondent State is to pay the applicant, within three months, 400,000 drachmas in respect of non-pecuniary damage and 2,789,500 drachmas in respect of costs and expenses.

...

PARTLY CONCURRING OPINION OF JUDGE PETTITI

I was in the majority which voted that there had been a breach of Article 9 but I considered that the reasoning given in the judgment could usefully have been expanded.

Furthermore, I parted company with the majority in that I also took the view that the current criminal legislation in Greece on proselytism was in itself contrary to Article 9.

The Kokkinakis case is of particular importance. It is the first real case concerning freedom of religion to have come before the European Court since it was set up and it has come up for decision at a time when the United Nations and Unesco are preparing a World Year for Tolerance, which is to give further effect to the 1981 United Nations Declaration against all forms of intolerance, which was adopted after twenty years of negotiations.

...

Proselytism is linked to freedom of religion; a believer must be able to communicate his faith and his beliefs in the religious sphere as in the philosophical sphere. Freedom of religion and conscience is a fundamental right and this freedom must be able to be exercised for the benefit of all religions and not for the benefit of a single Church, even if this has traditionally been the established Church or 'dominant religion'.

Freedom of religion and conscience certainly entails accepting proselytism, even where it is 'not respectable'. Believers and agnostic philosophers have a right to expound their beliefs, to try to get other people to share them and even to try to convert those whom they are addressing.

The only limits on the exercise of this right are those dictated by respect for the rights of others where there is an attempt to coerce the person into consenting or to use manipulative techniques.

The other types of unacceptable behaviour—such as brainwashing, breaches of labour law, endangering of public health and incitement to immorality, which are found in the practices of certain pseudo-religious groups—must be punished in positive law as ordinary criminal offences. Proselytism cannot be forbidden under cover of punishing such activities.

Certainly proselytism must not be carried on by coercion or by unfair means that take advantage of minors or persons legally incapacitated under civil law, but such lapses can be alleviated by the ordinary civil and criminal law.

...

Spiritual, religious and philosophical convictions belong to the private sphere of beliefs and call into play the right to express and manifest them. Setting up a system of criminal prosecution and punishment without safeguards is a perilous undertaking, and the authoritarian regimes which, while proclaiming freedom of religion in their Constitutions, have restricted it by means of criminal offences of parasitism, subversion or proselytism have given rise to abuses with which we are all too familiar.

The wording adopted by the majority of the Court in finding a breach, namely that the applicant's conviction was not justified in the circumstances of the case, leaves too much room for a repressive interpretation by the Greek courts in the future, whereas public prosecution must likewise be monitored. In my view, it would have been possible to define impropriety, coercion and duress more clearly and to describe more satisfactorily, in the abstract, the full scope of religious freedom and bearing witness.

The forms of words used by the World Council of Churches, the Second Vatican Council, philosophers and sociologists when referring to coercion, abuse of one's own rights which infringes the rights of others and the manipulation of people by methods which lead to a violation of conscience, all make it possible to define any permissible limits of proselytism. They can provide the member States with positive material for giving effect to the Court's judgment in future and fully implementing the principle and standards of religious freedom under Article 9 of the European Convention.

...

JOINT DISSENTING OPINION OF JUDGES FOIGHEL AND LOIZOU

We regret that we are unable to agree with the opinion of the majority of the Court as we take a different approach to the issues raised in this case. Article 9 para. 1 guarantees to everyone the right to freedom of thought, conscience and religion; this right includes freedom to change one's religion or belief and freedom, either alone or in community with others and in public or private, to manifest one's religion or belief, in worship, teaching, practice and observance. We are concerned here with the freedom one has to teach one's own religion.

The relevant Greek law making proselytism a criminal offence reads as follows:

> By 'proselytism' is meant, in particular, any direct or indirect attempt to intrude on the religious beliefs of a person of a different religious persuasion, with the aim of undermining those beliefs, either by any kind of inducement, or promise of an inducement, or moral support or material assistance, or by fraudulent means or by taking advantage of his inexperience, trust, need, low intellect or naivety.

This definition of the offence of 'proselytism' cannot, in our view, be considered to constitute a violation of Article 9 para. 1. It is only when it takes this kind of intrusive form as opposed to genuine, open and straightforward teaching of a religion that it is a criminal offence.

The term 'teach' entails openness and uprightness and the avoidance of the use of devious or improper means or false pretexts as in this case in order to gain access to a person's home and, once there, by abusing the courtesy and hospitality extended, take advantage of the ignorance or inexperience in theological doctrine of someone who has no specialist training and try to get that person to change his or her religion.

This is all the more so as the term 'teach' has to be read in the context of the whole Article and in conjunction with the limitations prescribed by paragraph 2, in particular that of the protection of the rights and freedoms of others, which no doubt includes a duty imposed on those who are engaged in teaching their religion to respect that of others. Religious tolerance implies respect for the religious beliefs of others.

One cannot be deemed to show respect for the rights and freedoms of others if one employs means that are intended to entrap someone and dominate his mind in order to convert him. This is impermissible in the civilized societies of the Contracting States. The persistent efforts of some fanatics to convert others to their own beliefs by using unacceptable psychological techniques on people, which amount in effect to coercion, cannot in our view come within the ambit of the natural meaning of the term 'teach' to be found in paragraph 1 of this Article.

For the above reasons we find in the circumstances of this case that there has been no breach of Article 9.

2. WAITING FOR ARTICLE 9

Why did it take so long for the Strasbourg Court to apply Article 9? In 1991, two years before *Kokkinakis*, one commentator gently suggested that the Court's failure up to then to find a breach of Article 9 was in part 'because the rights to freedom of thought, conscience and religion are largely exercised inside an individual's heart and mind'.[1] It may also be that many of the judges on the European Court of Human Rights shared an unease with religious questions prevalent among 20th century international lawyers:

The connection between religion and international law is close but nowadays surprisingly little studied or analyzed. This lack of attention has, I think, two causes. First is the effort made in

---

[1] D. Gomien, *Short Guide to the European Convention on Human Rights* 69 (1991).

the 19th and 20th centuries to turn international law into a 'science'. Those who do this often feel that doing law 'scientifically' means keeping religion entirely out of the discipline. Second is the addition in recent decades of more than a hundred new mostly non-Western states to the international political community. Conscious that Western values are not necessarily shared with other cultures, many international lawyers are unwilling to discuss religion, ethics and morals for fear of excluding those whose beliefs may be very different from their own.[2]

How prevalent are such dismissive or defensive views today? Is there an increasing acceptance among international lawyers that religious problems, no matter how difficult, need to be addressed by international law and international courts?

Even after *Kokkinakis*, the Court has not been overly eager to deal with Article 9 and to address the ticklish problems of religion. One judge, Ireland's John Hedigan, has admitted: 'In matters pertaining to religion, it is perhaps better not to stray too far from home'.[3] A review of the 718 cases decided by the Strasbourg Court in 2004 reveals that only seven concerned an Article 9 claim, just about one percent of the Strasbourg caseload.

Greece is not alone amongst the member states of the Council of Europe in establishing a church. Although the exact relationship may differ, at least a dozen states, including Greece, establish churches: Andorra—the Roman Catholic Church (Art. 11 of the Constitution), Armenia—the Armenian Apostolic Church (the 1991 law on Freedom of Conscience and on Religious Organization), Denmark—the Danish Lutheran Church (sect. 4 of the Kingdom's Constitutional Act), United Kingdom—the Church of England (Toleration Act 1689, 1 William & Mary, c. 13) and the Church of Scotland (Church of Scotland Act, 1921, 11 & 12 Geo 5, c. 29), Finland—the Evangelical Lutheran Church of Finland and the Finnish Orthodox Church (Art. 76 of the Constitution), Georgia—the Georgian Orthodox Church (Art. 9 of the Constitution), Iceland—Icelandic Lutheran Church (Art. 62 of the Constitution), Liechtenstein—the Roman Catholic Church (Art. 37 of the Constitution), Malta—the Roman Catholic Church (sect. 2 of the Constitution), Monaco—the Roman Catholic Church (Art. 9 of the Constitution), and Norway—Norwegian Lutheran Church (Art. 2 of the Constitution). Does an established church per se violate Article 9?

In the United States, where established churches are illegal pursuant to the First and Fourteenth Amendments to the U.S. Constitution, some government regulation of proselytism is permitted. For example, the Supreme Court has upheld state police power to require permits for parades or processions, even those conducted for religious purposes. States have been permitted to prohibit demonstrations near schools to 'protect the integrity of the educational mission'.[4]

---

[2] M. W. Janis, 'Introduction', *Religion and International Law* xiii (M. W. Janis & C. Evans eds. 2004).

[3] J. Hedigan, 'Religious Advertising and the European Convention on Human Rights, Congrès des Droits de l'Homme, Istanbul, 16–19 May, 2006', European Court of Human Rights, Document No. 1000421 (hereinafter cited as 'Hedigan').

[4] H. O. Hunter & P. J. Price, 'Regulation of Religious Proselytism in the United States', 2001 *Brigham Young University Law Review* 537, 538–46.

B. THE DEFINITION OF 'RELIGION'

There are a handful of cases where the Court, following *Kokkinakis*, has had little difficulty finding that a government has infringed the Convention's right to religious freedom. *Buscarini*, the first excerpt below, is a good straightforward example. At other times, struggling with the definition of 'religion', the Court has found that a claim was not sufficiently 'religious' to qualify under Article 9. *Pretty*, which follows *Buscarini*, is just such a case. How ought the Court to define 'religion' for the purposes of Article 9? It is not an easy question.

1. BUSCARINI V. SAN MARINO

Judgment of 18 February 1999
30 E.H.R.R. 208

7. The applicants were elected to the General Grand Council (the parliament of the Republic of San Marino) in elections held on 30 May 1993.

8. Shortly afterwards, they requested permission from the Captains-Regent, who act as the heads of government in San Marino, to take the oath required by section 55 of the Elections Act (Law no. 36 of 1958) without making reference to any religious text. The Act in question referred to a decree of 27 June 1909, which laid down the wording of the oath to be taken by members of the Republic's parliament as follows:

I, . . ., swear on the Holy Gospels ever to be faithful to and obey the Constitution of the Republic, to uphold and defend freedom with all my might, ever to observe the Laws and Decrees, whether ancient, modern or yet to be enacted or issued and to nominate and vote for as candidates to the Judiciary and other Public Office only those whom I consider apt, loyal and fit to serve the Republic, without allowing myself to be swayed by any feelings of hatred or love or by any other consideration.

9. In support of their request the applicants referred to Article 4 of the Declaration of Rights of 1974, which guarantees the right to freedom of religion, and Article 9 of the Convention.

10. At the General Grand Council session of 18 June 1993 the applicants took the oath in writing, in the form of words laid down in the decree of 27 June 1909 save for the reference to the Gospels, which they omitted. At the same time, the first applicant drew attention to the obligations undertaken by the Republic of San Marino when it became a party to the European Convention on Human Rights.

11. On 12 July 1993 the Secretariat of the General Grand Council gave an opinion, at the request of the Captains-Regent, on the form of the oath sworn by the applicants, to the effect that it was invalid, and referred the matter to the Council.

12. At its session of 26 July 1993 the General Grand Council adopted a resolution proposed by the Captains-Regent ordering the applicants to retake the oath, this time on the Gospels, on the pain of forfeiting their parliamentary seats.

13. The applicants complied with the Council's order and took the oath on the Gospels, albeit complaining that their right to freedom of religion and conscience had been infringed.

14. Subsequently—before ever the applicants applied to the Commission—Law. no. 115 of 29 October 1993 ('Law no. 115/1993') introduced a choice for newly elected members of the General Grand Council between the traditional oath and one in which the reference to the Gospels, was replaced by the words 'on my honour'. The traditional wording is still mandatory for other offices, such as that of Captain-Regent or of a member of the government.

...

34. The Court reiterates that: 'As enshrined in Article 9, freedom of thought, conscience and religion is one of the foundations of a "democratic society" within the meaning of the Convention. It is, in its religious dimension, one of the most vital elements that go to make up the identity of believers and their conception of life, but it is also a precious asset for atheists, agnostics, sceptics and the unconcerned. The pluralism indissociable from a democratic society, which has been dearly won over the centuries, depends on it' (see *Kokkinakis v. Greece*). That freedom entails, *inter alia*, freedom to hold or not to hold religious beliefs and to practise or not to practise a religion.

In the instant case, requiring Mr. Buscarini and Mr. Della Balda to take an oath on the Gospels did indeed constitute a limitation within the meaning of the second paragraph of Article 9, since it required them to swear allegiance to a particular religion on pain of forfeiting their parliamentary seats. Such interference will be contrary to Article 9 unless it is 'prescribed by law', pursues one or more of the legitimate aims set out in paragraph 2 and is 'necessary in a democratic society'.

1. 'Prescribed by law'

35. As the Commission noted in its report, the 'interference in question was based on section 55 of the Elections Act, Law no. 36 of 1958, which referred to the decree of 27 June 1909 laying down the wording of the oath to be sworn by members of parliament... Therefore, it was "prescribed by law" within the meaning of the second paragraph of Article 9 of the Convention'. That point was not disputed.

2. Legitimate aim and whether 'necessary in a democratic society'

36. The Government emphasised the importance, in any democracy, of the oath taken by elected representatives of the people, which, in their view, was a pledge of loyalty to republican values. Regard being had to the special character of San Marino, deriving from its history, traditions and social fabric, the reaffirmation of traditional values represented by the taking of the oath was necessary in order to maintain public order.

The history and traditions of San Marino were linked to Christianity, since the State had been founded by a saint; today, however, the oath's religious significance had been replaced by the need to preserve public order, in the form of social cohesion and the citizens' trust in their traditional institutions.

It would therefore be inappropriate for the Court to criticise the margin of appreciation which San Marino had to have in this matter.

In any event, the Government maintained, the applicants had had no legal interest in pursuing the Strasbourg proceedings since the entry into force of Law no. 115 of 29 October 1993, which did not require persons elected to the General Grand Council to take the oath on the Gospels.

37. According to Mr. Buscarini and Mr. Della Balda, the resolution requiring them to take the oath in issue was in the nature of a 'premeditated act of coercion' directed at their freedom of conscience and religion. It aimed to humiliate them as persons who, immediately after being elected, had requested that the wording of the oath should be altered so as to conform with, *inter alia*, Article 9 of the Convention.

38. The Court considers it unnecessary in the present case to determine whether the aims referred to by the Government were legitimate within the meaning of the second paragraph of Article 9, since the limitation in question is in any event incompatible with that provision in other respects.

39. The Court notes that at the hearing on 10 December 1998 the Government sought to demonstrate that the Republic of San Marino guaranteed freedom of religion; in support of that submission they cited its founding Statutes of 1600, its Declaration of Rights of 1974, its ratification of the European Convention in 1989 and a whole array of provisions of criminal law, family law, employment law and education law which prohibited any discrimination on the grounds of religion. In the instant case, however, requiring the applicants to take the oath on the Gospels was tantamount to requiring two elected representatives of the people to swear allegiance to a particular religion, a requirement which is not compatible with Article 9 of the Convention.

As the Commission rightly stated in its report, it would be contradictory to make the exercise of a mandate intended to represent different views of society within Parliament subject to a prior declaration of commitment to a particular set of beliefs.

40. The limitation complained of accordingly cannot be regarded as 'necessary in a democratic society'. As to the Government's argument that the application ceased to have any purpose when Law no. 115/1993 was enacted, the Court notes that the oath in issue was taken before the passing of that legislation.

41. In the light of the foregoing [the Court unanimously holds] there has been a violation of Article 9 of the Convention.

2. PRETTY V. UNITED KINGDOM

Judgment of 29 April 2002

35 E.H.R.R. 1

7. The applicant is a 43-year-old woman. She resides with her husband of twenty-five years, their daughter and granddaughter. The applicant suffers from motor neurone disease (MND). This disease is associated with progressive muscle weakness affecting the voluntary muscles of the body. As a result of the progression of the disease, severe weakness of the arms and legs and the muscles involved in the control of breathing are affected. Death usually occurs as a result of weakness of the breathing muscles, in association with weakness of the muscles controlling speaking and swallowing, leading to respiratory failure and pneumonia. No treatment can prevent the progression of the disease.

8. The applicant's condition has deteriorated rapidly since MND was diagnosed in November 1999. The disease is now at an advanced stage. She is essentially paralysed from the neck down, has virtually no decipherable speech and is fed through a tube. Her life expectancy is

very poor, measurable only in weeks or months. However, her intellect and capacity to make decisions are unimpaired. The final stages of the disease are exceedingly distressing and undignified. As she is frightened and distressed at the suffering and indignity that she will endure if the disease runs its course, she very strongly wishes to be able to control how and when she dies and thereby be spared that suffering and indignity.

9. Although it is not a crime to commit suicide under English law, the applicant is prevented by her disease from taking such a step without assistance. It is however a crime to assist another to commit suicide (section 2(1) of the Suicide Act 1961).

10. Intending that she might commit suicide with the assistance of her husband, the applicant's solicitor asked the Director of Public Prosecutions (DPP), in a letter dated 27 July 2001 written on her behalf, to give an undertaking not to prosecute the applicant's husband should he assist her to commit suicide in accordance with her wishes.

11. In a letter dated 8 August 2001, the DPP refused to give the undertaking:

'Successive Directors—and Attorneys General—have explained that they will not grant immunities that condone, require, or purport to authorise or permit the future commission of any criminal offence, no matter how exceptional the circumstances...'.

12. On 20 August 2001 the applicant applied for judicial review of the DPP's decision[.]

13. On 17 October 2001 the Divisional Court refused the application, holding that the DPP did not have the power to give the undertaking not to prosecute and that section 2(1) of the Suicide Act 1961 was not incompatible with the Convention.

14. The applicant appealed to the House of Lords. They dismissed her appeal on 29 November 2001 and upheld the judgment of the Divisional Court.

[The Court finds no violation of Articles 2, 3, and 8 of the Convention.]

82. The Court does not doubt the firmness of the applicant's views concerning assisted suicide but would observe that not all opinions or convictions constitute beliefs in the sense protected by Article 9 para. 1 of the Convention. Her claims do not involve a form of manifestation of a religion or belief, through worship, teaching, practice or observance as described in the second sentence of the first paragraph. As found by the Commission, the term 'practice' as employed in Article 9 para. 1 does not cover each act which is motivated or influenced by a religion or belief (see *Arrowsmith v. the United Kingdom*, no. 7050/77, Commission's report of 12 October 1978, DR 19, p. 19, para. 71). To the extent that the applicant's views reflect her commitment to the principle of personal autonomy, her claim is a restatement of the complaint raised under Article 8 of the Convention.

83. The Court concludes that there has been no violation of Article 9 of the Convention.

[The Court also finds no violation of Article 14 of the Convention.]

3. THE FAILURE TO DEFINE

Is it satisfactory that the Court gives only four sentences to dismiss Mrs. Pretty's Article 9 claim as not involving 'a form of manifestation of a religion or belief'? Is it really that easy to decide that her claims were not made pursuant to 'freedom of thought, conscience and religion'? Why was *Buscarini* so plainly a 'religious' case if *Pretty* was not? How does one decide what is and is not 'religious'?

There was little discussion of Article 9(1) when it was drafted. We know it was modelled on the terms of the 1948 Universal Declaration on Human Rights. Article 9(2) was equally uncontroversial except for opposition from the Turkish delegation that sought, unsuccessfully, to toughen 9(2) to better protect against Islamic fundamentalists who might use religion to undermine secularism. As Professor Carolyn Evans observes, 'when the European Court and Commission of Human Rights came to deal with the problems that have arisen under Article 9 they have not been able to take much guidance from the *travaux préparatoires*'.[5] Professor Evans concludes that the Strasbourg institutions have not gotten much further than did the drafters in defining religion. Indeed, they 'have made their definition almost meaningless'.[6]

Admitting that '[d]efining religion is not so easy', Professor James Nafziger hazards a try. After a careful and sympathetic survey of other definitional efforts, he ventures thus:

Accordingly, the term 'religion', for present purposes, may be described as a practice of ultimate concern about our nature and obligations as human beings, inspired by experience and typically expressed by members of a group or community sharing myths and doctrines whose authority transcends both individual conscience and the state. Such a definition of religion would be consistent with some of the main currents of twentieth century theology hinted at above, as well as that proposed by the special rapporteur for the Sub-Commission on Prevention of Discrimination and Protection of Minorities. Of course, any definition of religion, including the proposed one, is apt to be inadequate and culturally biased, but analysis of the role of 'religion' in the international legal systems requires *some* basis for distinguishing it from other belief systems, especially ideologies. In a preliminary analysis such as this, the alternative to adopting a working definition of religion would be to join Humpty Dumpty on the fence of semantic anarchy or autocracy.[7]

How would Professor Nafziger's definition apply to the facts in *Buscarini* and *Pretty*? If Professor Nafziger can venture a definition of 'religion' for all of international law, why can not the European Court of Human Rights hazard a definition just for the purposes of Article 9 of the European Human Rights Convention?

---

[5] C. Evans, 'Religious Freedom in European Human Rights Law: The Search for a Guiding Conception', in *Religion and International Law* 385, 388–9 (M. W. Janis & C. Evans eds. 2004).

[6] *Id.* at 392.

[7] J. A. R. Nafziger, 'The Functions of Religion in the International Legal System', in *Religion and International Law* 155, 158 (M. W. Janis & C. Evans eds. 2004).

C. THE FREEDOM TO MANIFEST ONE'S RELIGION

The most controversial Article 9 cases to reach the Court have had to do with the right to manifest one's religious beliefs. These, of course, are subject to the limitations of Section 2. How far may a manifestation of religious belief go, for example, before it may be limited to protect the religious convictions of others? *Otto-Preminger*, the first case below, shows the Court at work trying to draw a line between legally permissible and impermissible manifestations of belief. How successful is its effort? Note that the Court, only one year after *Kokkinakis*, treats the case as an Article 10 freedom of expression dispute rather than as an Article 9 freedom of religion problem. Moreover, it uses Article 9, Section 2, as a means for interpreting Article 10. Is this, on the facts or on the law, a sensible approach?

1. OTTO-PREMINGER-INSTITUT V. AUSTRIA

Judgment of 20 September 1994
19 E.H.R.R. 34

9. The applicant, *Otto-Preminger-Institut Für audiovisuelle Mediengestaltung* (OPI), a private association under Austrian law established in Innsbruck[,]...announced a series of six showings, which would be accessible to the general public, of the film '*Das Liebeskonzil*' (Council in Heaven) by Werner Schroeter. The first of these showings was scheduled for 13 May 1985. All were to take place at 10:00 p.m. except for one matinee performance on 19 May at 4 p.m.

This announcement was made in an information bulletin distributed by OPI to its 2,700 members and in various display windows in Innsbruck including that of the Cinematograph itself. It was worded as follows:

'Oskar Panizza's satirical tragedy set in Heaven was filmed by Schroeter from a performance by the *Teatro Belli* in Rome and set in the context of a reconstruction of the writer's trial and conviction in 1895 for blasphemy. Panizza starts from the assumption that syphilis was God's punishment for man's fornication and sinfulness at the time of the Renaissance, especially at the court of the Borgia Pope Alexander VI. In Schroeter's film, God's representatives on Earth carrying the insignia of worldly power resemble the heavenly protagonists.

Trivial imagery and absurdities of the Christian creed are targeted in a caricatural mode and the relationship between religious beliefs and worldly mechanisms of oppression is investigated.'

In addition, the information bulletin carried a statement to the effect that, in accordance with the Tyrolean Cinemas Act (*Tiroler Lichtspielgesetz*), persons under 17 years of age were prohibited from seeing the film.

A regional newspaper also announced the title of the film and the date and place of the showing without giving any particulars as to its contents.

11. At the request of the Innsbruck diocese of the Roman Catholic Church, the Public Prosecutor instituted criminal proceedings against OPI's manager, Mr. Dietmar Zingl, on 10 May 1985. The charge was 'disparaging religious doctrines' (*Herabwurdigung religioser Lehren*), an act prohibited by section 188 of the Penal Code.

12. On 12 May 1985, after the film had been shown at a private session in the presence of a duty judge (*Journalrichter*), the Public Prosecutor made an application for its seizure under section 36 of the Media Act. This application was granted by the Innsbruck Regional Court (*Landesgericht*) the same day. As a result, the public showings announced by OPI, the first of which had been scheduled for the next day, could not take place.

Those who attended at the time set for the first showing were treated to a reading of the script and a discussion instead.

As Mr. Zingl had returned the film to the distributor, the 'Czerny' company in Vienna, it was in fact seized at the latter's premises on 11 June 1985.

13. An appeal by Mr. Zingl against the seizure order, filed with the Innsbruck Court of Appeal (*Oberlandesgericht*), was dismissed on 30 July 1985. The Court of Appeal considered that artistic freedom was necessarily limited by the rights of others to freedom of religion and by the duty of the State to safeguard a society based on order and tolerance. It further held that indignation was 'justified' for the purposes of section 188 of the Penal Code only if its object was such as to offend the religious feelings of an average person with normal religious sensitivity. That condition was fulfilled in the instant case and forfeiture of the film could be ordered in principle, at least in 'objective proceedings'. The wholesale derision of religious feeling outweighed any interest the general public might have in information or the financial interests of persons wishing to show the film.

14. On 24 October 1985 the criminal prosecution against Mr. Zingl was discontinued and the case was pursued in the form of 'objective proceedings' under section 33(2) of the Media Act aimed at suppression of the film.

15. On 10 October 1986 a trial took place before the Innsbruck Regional Court. The film was again shown in closed session; its contents were described in detail in the official records of the hearing.

Mr. Zingl appears in the official records of the hearing as a witness. He stated that he had sent the film back to the distributor following the seizure order because he wanted nothing more to do with the matter.

It appears from the judgment—which was delivered the same day—that Mr. Zingl was considered to be a potentially liable interested party (*Haftungsbeteiligter*).

The Regional Court found it to be established that the distributor of the film had waived its right to be heard and had agreed to the destruction of its copy of the film.

16. In its judgment of the same day, 10 October 1986, the Regional Court ordered the forfeiture of the film. It held:

The public projection scheduled for 13 May 1985 of the film '*Das Liebeskonzil*', in which God the Father is presented both in image and in text as a senile, impotent idiot, Christ as a cretin and Mary Mother of God as a wanton lady with a corresponding manner of expression and in which the Eucharist is ridiculed, came within the definition of the criminal offense of disparaging religious precepts as laid down in section 188 of the Penal Code.

...

Artistic freedom cannot be unlimited. The limitations on artistic freedom are to be found, firstly, in other basic rights and freedoms guaranteed by the Constitution (such as the freedom of religion and conscience), secondly, in the need for an ordered form of human coexistence based on tolerance, and finally in flagrant and extreme violations of other interests protected by law (*Verletzung anderer rechtlich geschützter Güter*), the specific circumstances having to be weighed up against each other in each case, taking due account of all relevant considerations.

...

20. The play on which the film is based was written by Oskar Panizza and published in 1894. In 1895 Panizza was found guilty by the Munich Assize Court (*Schwurgericht*) of 'crimes against religion' and sentenced to a term of imprisonment. The play was banned in Germany although it continued in print elsewhere.

21. The play portrays God the Father as old, infirm and ineffective, Jesus Christ as a 'mummy's boy' of low intelligence and the Virgin Mary, who is obviously in charge, as an unprincipled wanton. Together they decide that mankind must be punished for its immorality. They reject the possibility of outright destruction in favour of a form of punishment which will leave it both 'in need of salvation' and 'capable of redemption'. Being unable to think of such a punishment by themselves, they decide to call on the Devil for help.

The Devil suggests the idea of a sexually transmitted affliction, so that men and women will infect one another without realising it; he procreates with Salome to produce a daughter who will spread it among mankind. The symptoms as described by the Devil are those of syphilis.

As his reward, the Devil claims freedom of thought; Mary says that she will 'think about it'. The Devil then dispatches his daughter to do her work, first among those who represent worldly power, then to the court of the Pope, to the bishops, to the convents and monasteries and finally to the common people.

22. The film, directed by Werner Schroeter, was released in 1981. It begins and ends with scenes purporting to be taken from the trial of Panizza in 1895. In between, it shows a performance of the play by the *Teatro Belli* in Rome. The film portrays the God of the Jewish religion, the Christian religion and the Islamic religion as an apparently senile old man prostrating himself before the devil with whom he exchanges a deep kiss and calling the devil his friend. He is also portrayed as swearing by the devil. Other scenes show the Virgin Mary permitting an obscene story to be read to her and the manifestation of a degree of erotic tension between the Virgin Mary and the devil. The adult Jesus Christ is portrayed as a low grade mental defective and in one scene is shown lasciviously attempting to fondle and kiss his mother's breasts, which she is shown as permitting. God, the Virgin Mary and Christ are shown in the film applauding the devil.

23. Religious freedom is guaranteed by Article 14 of the Basic Law, which reads:

(1) Complete freedom of beliefs and conscience is guaranteed to everyone.

(2) Enjoyment of civil and political rights shall be independent of religious confessions; however, a religious confession may not stand in the way of civic duties.

(3) No one shall be compelled to take any church-related action or to participate in any church-related celebration, except in pursuance of a power conferred by law on another person to whose authority he is subject.

24. Artistic freedom is guaranteed by Article 17a of the Basic Law, which provides:

There shall be freedom of artistic creation and of the publication and teaching of Art.

25. Section 188 of the Penal Code reads as follows:

Whoever, in circumstances where his behavior is likely to arouse justified indignation, disparages or insults a person who, or an object which, is an object of veneration of a church or religious community established within the country, or a dogma, a lawful custom or a lawful institution of such a church or religious community, shall be liable to a prison sentence of up to six months or a fine of up to 360 daily rates.

...

42. The applicant association submitted that the seizure and subsequent forfeiture of the film *Das Liebeskonzil* gave rise to violations of its right to freedom of expression as guaranteed by Article 10 of the Convention, which provides:

1. Everyone has the right to freedom of expression. This right shall include freedom to hold opinions and to receive and impart information and ideas without interference by public authority and regardless of frontiers. This Article shall not prevent States from requiring the licensing of broadcasting, television or cinema enterprises.

2. The exercise of these freedoms, since it carries with it duties and responsibilities, may be subject to such formalities, conditions, restrictions or penalties as are prescribed by law and are necessary in a democratic society, in the interests of national security, territorial integrity or public safety, for the prevention of disorder or crime, for the protection of health or morals, for the protection of the reputation or rights of others, for preventing the disclosure of information received in confidence, or for maintaining the authority and impartiality of the judiciary.

[The Court finds that there has been an interference with the Institute's freedom of expression and that the interference was prescribed by law.]

C. Whether the interferences had a 'legitimate aim'

46. The Government maintained that the seizure and forfeiture of the film were aimed at 'the protection of the rights of others', particularly the right to respect for one's religious feelings, and at 'the prevention of disorder'.

47. As the Court pointed out in its judgment in the case of *Kokkinakis v. Greece* of 25 May 1993, freedom of thought, conscience and religion, which is safeguarded under Article 9 of the Convention, is one of the foundations of a 'democratic society' within the meaning of the Convention. It is, in its religious dimension, one of the most vital elements that go to make up the identity of believers and their conception of life.

Those who choose to exercise the freedom to manifest their religion, irrespective of whether they do so as members of a religious majority or a minority, cannot reasonably expect to be exempt from all criticism. They must tolerate and accept the denial by others of their religious beliefs and even the propagation by others of doctrines hostile to their faith. However, the manner in which religious beliefs and doctrines are opposed or denied is a matter which may engage the responsibility of the State, notably its responsibility to ensure the peaceful enjoyment of the right guaranteed under Article 9 to the holders of those beliefs and doctrines.

Indeed, in extreme cases the effect of particular methods of opposing or denying religious beliefs can be such as to inhibit those who hold such beliefs from exercising their freedom to hold and express them.

In the Kokkinakis judgment the Court held, in the context of Article 9, that a State may legitimately consider it necessary to take measures aimed at repressing certain forms of conduct, including the imparting of information and ideas, judged incompatible with the respect for the freedom of thought, conscience and religion of others. The respect for the religious feelings of believers as guaranteed in Article 9 can legitimately thought to have been violated by provocative portrayals of objects of religious veneration; and such portrayals can be regarded as malicious violation of the spirit of tolerance, which must also be a feature of democratic society. The Convention is to be read as a whole and therefore the interpretation and application of Article 10 in the present case must be in harmony with the logic of the Convention.

48. The measures complained of were based on section 188 of the Austrian Penal Code, which is intended to suppress behaviour directed against objects of religious veneration that is likely to cause 'justified indignation'. It follows that their purpose was to protect the right of citizens not to be insulted in their religious feelings by the public expression of views of other persons. Considering also the terms in which the decisions of the Austrian Courts were phrased, the Court accepts that the impugned measures pursued a legitimate aim under Article 10(2), namely the 'protection of the rights of others'.

D. Whether the seizure and the forfeiture were 'necessary in a democratic society'

49. As the Court has consistently held, freedom of expression constitutes one of the essential foundations of a democratic society, one of the basic conditions for its progress and for the development of everyone. Subject to paragraph 2 of Article 10, it is applicable not only to 'information' or 'ideas' that are favourably received or regarded as inoffensive or as a matter of indifference, but also to those that shock, offend or disturb the State or any sector of the population. Such are the demands of that pluralism, tolerance and broadmindedness without which there is no 'democratic society'.

However, as is borne out by the wording itself of Article 10(2), whoever exercises the rights and freedoms enshrined in the first paragraph of that Article undertakes 'duties and responsibilities'. Amongst them—in the context of religious opinions and beliefs—may legitimately be included an obligation to avoid as far as possible expressions that are gratuitously offensive to others and thus an infringement of their rights, and which therefore do not contribute to any form of public debate capable of furthering progress in human affairs.

This being so, as a matter of principle it may be considered necessary in certain democratic societies to sanction or even prevent improper attacks on objects of religious veneration, provided always that any 'formality', 'condition', 'restriction' or 'penalty' imposed be proportionate to the legitimate aim pursued.

50. As in the case of 'morals'—a concept linked to 'the rights of others'—it is not possible to discern throughout Europe a uniform conception of the significance of religion in society; even within a single country such conceptions may vary. For that reason it is not possible to arrive at a comprehensive definition of what constitutes a permissible interference with the exercise of the right to freedom of expression where such expression is directed against the religious feelings of others. A certain margin of appreciation is therefore to be left to the national authorities in assessing the existence and extent of the necessity of such interference.

The authorities' margin of appreciation, however, is not unlimited. It goes hand in hand with Convention supervision the scope of which will vary according to the circumstances. In cases such as the present one, where there has been an interference with the exercise of the freedoms guaranteed in paragraph 1 of Article 10, the supervision must be strict because of the importance of the freedoms in question. The necessity for any restriction must be convincingly established.

...

55. The issue before the Court involves weighing up the conflicting interests of the exercise of two fundamental freedoms guaranteed under the Convention, namely the right of the applicant association to impart to the public controversial views and, by implication, the right of interested persons to take cognisance of such views, on the one hand, and the right of other persons to proper respect for their freedom of thought, conscience and religion, on the other hand. In so doing, regard must be had to the margin of appreciation left to the national authorities, whose duty it is in a democratic society also to consider, within the limits of their jurisdiction, the interests of society as a whole.

56. The Austrian courts, ordering the seizure and subsequently the forfeiture of the film, held it to be an abusive attack on the Roman Catholic religion according to the conception of the Tyrolean public. Their judgments show that they had due regard to the freedom of artistic expression, which is guaranteed under Article 10 of the Convention and for which Article 17a of the Austrian Basic Law provides specific protection. They did not consider that its merit as a work of art or as a contribution to public debate in Austrian society outweighed those features which made it essentially offensive to the general public within their jurisdiction. The trial courts, after viewing the film, noted the provocative portrayal of God the Father, the Virgin Mary and Jesus Christ. The content of the film cannot be said to be incapable of grounding the conclusions arrived at by the Austrian courts.

The Court cannot disregard the fact that the Roman Catholic religion is the religion of the overwhelming majority of Tyroleans. In seizing the film, the Austrian authorities acted to ensure religious peace in that region and to prevent that some people should feel the object of attacks on their religious beliefs in an unwarranted and offensive manner. It is in the first place for the national authorities, who are better placed than the international judge, to assess the need for such a measure in the light of the situation obtaining locally at a given time. In all the circumstances of the present case, the Court does not consider that the Austrian authorities can be regarded as having overstepped their margin of appreciation in this respect.

No violation of Article 10 can therefore be found as far as the seizure is concerned.

57. The foregoing reasoning also applies to the forfeiture, which determined the ultimate legality of the seizure and under Austrian law was the normal sequel thereto.

Article 10 cannot be interpreted as prohibiting the forfeiture in the public interest of items whose use has lawfully been adjudged illicit. Although the forfeiture made it permanently impossible to show the film anywhere in Austria, the Court considers that the means employed were not disproportionate to the legitimate aim pursued and that therefore the national authorities did not exceed their margin of appreciation in this respect.

There has accordingly been no violation of Article 10 as regards the forfeiture either.

For these reasons, THE COURT

...

3. *Holds*, by six votes to three, that there has been no violation of Article 10 of the Convention as regards either the seizure or the forfeiture of the film.

JOINT DISSENTING OPINION OF JUDGES PALM, PEKKANEN AND MAKARCZYK

1. We regret that we are unable to agree with the majority that there has been no violation of Article 10.

2. The Court is here faced with the necessity of balancing two apparently conflicting Convention rights against each other. In the instant case, of course, the rights to be weighed up against each other are the right to freedom of religion (Article 9), relied on by the Government, and the right to freedom of expression (Article 10), relied on by the applicant association. Since the case concerns restrictions on the latter right, our discussion will centre on whether these were 'necessary in a democratic society' and therefore permitted by the second paragraph of Article 10.

3. As the majority correctly state, echoing the famous passage in the *Handyside* judgment, freedom of expression is a fundamental feature of a 'democratic society'; it is applicable not only to 'information' or 'ideas' that are favourably received or regarded as inoffensive or as a matter of indifference, but *particularly* to those that shock, offend or disturb the State or any sector of the population. There is no point in guaranteeing this freedom only as long as it is used in accordance with accepted opinion.

. . .

6. The Convention does not, in terms, guarantee a right to protection of religious feelings. More particularly, such a right cannot be derived from the right to freedom of religion, which in effect includes a right to express views critical of the religious opinions of others.

Nevertheless, it must be accepted that it may be 'legitimate' for the purpose of Article 10 to protect the religious feelings of certain members of society against criticism and abuse to some extent; tolerance works both ways and the democratic character of a society will be affected if violent and abusive attacks on the reputation of a religious group are allowed. Consequently, it must also be accepted that it may be 'necessary in a democratic society' to set limits to the public expression of such criticism or abuse. To this extent, but no further, we can agree with the majority.

7. The duty and the responsibility of a person seeking to avail himself of his freedom of expression should be to limit, as far as he can reasonably be expected to, the offence that his statement may cause to others. Only if he fails to take necessary action, or if such action is shown to be insufficient, may the State step in.

. . .

9. [T]he film was to have been shown to a paying audience in an 'art cinema' which catered for a relatively small public with a taste for experimental films. It is therefore unlikely that the audience would have included persons not specifically interested in the film.

This audience, moreover, had sufficient opportunity of being warned beforehand about the nature of the film. Unlike the majority, we consider that the announcement put out by the applicant association was intended to provide information about the critical way in which the film dealt with the Roman Catholic religion; in fact, it did so sufficiently clearly to enable the religiously sensitive to make an informed decision to stay away.

It thus appears that there was little likelihood in the instant case of anyone being confronted with objectionable material unwittingly.

We therefore conclude that the applicant association acted responsibly in such a way as to limit, as far as it could reasonably have been expected to do, the possible harmful effects of showing the film.

10. Finally, as was stated by the applicant association and not denied by the Government, it was illegal under Tyrolean law for the film to be seen by persons under 17 years of age and the announcement put out by the applicant association carried a notice to that effect.

Under these circumstances, the danger of the film being seen by persons for whom it was not suitable by reason of their age can be discounted.

The Austrian authorities thus had available to them, and actually made use of, a possibility less restrictive than the seizure of the film to prevent any unwarranted offence.

11. We do not deny that the showing of the film might have offended the religious feelings of certain segments of the population in Tyrol. However, taking into account the measures actually taken by the applicant association in order to protect those who might be offended and the protection offered by Austrian legislation to those under 17 years of age, we are, on balance, of the opinion that the seizure and forfeiture of the film in question were not proportionate to the legitimate aim pursued.

2. ARTICLE 10 OR ARTICLE 9?

Is *Otto-Preminger* really an Article 10 case? Does the dissent properly recognize that the facts demand a legal balancing between the plaintiff's Article 9 rights and the government's Article 10 defence? Note how even the majority rely heavily on *Kokkinakis* to test the government's 'legitimate aim' and then conclude that the film was an 'abusive attack on the Roman Catholic religion'. Ought Article 9 be employed to protect a dominant religion like Roman Catholicism in Austria, rather than a minority religion, like Jehovah's Witnesses in *Kokkinakis*?

One commentator has defended the holding in *Otto-Preminger*, arguing that 'it was the manner in which the message was delivered, and not the content of the message, that implicated a restriction on the freedom to deliver it'.[8] A more critical observer submits that the *Otto-Preminger* court 'overlook[ed] a violation of the right to freedom of speech'. He argues that 'the Court failed to give due weight to the notion that freedom of speech must be interpreted in a way that protects shocking, offensive, and provocative speech—a notion to which the Court itself subscribes—including

---

[8] T. Stahnke, 'Proselytism and the Freedom to Change Religion in International Human Rights Law', 1999 *Brigham Young University Law Review* 251, 297.

those that promote discourse critical of religion, even (and especially) the dominant religion'.[9]

Does the Court conclude that Article 9 guarantees a right for a religion to be free of criticism? Is not Article 9 intended to limit governmental abuses of religious freedom? Is the 'unsatisfactory' result of *Otto-Preminger* to hold that Article 9 imposes 'a positive obligation to ensure the peaceful enjoyment' of religion?[10]

Should *Otto-Preminger* be over-ruled or distinguished by narrowing it to apply only to its special factual context? One Strasbourg judge, Willi Fuhrmann, seems to suggest the latter:

The Otto-Preminger case seems to indicate that freedom of expression will give way to the freedom of majority religious beliefs. This appears to be at odds with the emphasis that the Court has placed on the pluralism in a democratic society of religious belief encompassing skepticism and agnosticism, which was demonstrated, for example, in the Kokkinakis case. Thus, Otto-Preminger should perhaps be seen in the light of its particular facts and the wide margin of appreciation accorded in consequence of those facts.[11]

The following case, *Refah Partisi*, brought as an Article 11 freedom of association case, is also treated as an Article 10 case. Ask again whether it is not more sensible to treat it also as an Article 9 dispute.

3. REFAH PARTISI (WELFARE PARTY) V. TURKEY

Judgment of 31 July 2001
35 E.H.R.R. 3

10. Refah was founded on 19 July 1983. It took part in a number of general and local elections, ultimately obtaining approximately 22 per cent of the votes in the general election of 1995 and about 35 per cent of the votes in the local elections of 3 November 1996.

The results of the 1995 general election made Refah the largest political party in the Turkish parliament with a total of 158 seats in the Grand National Assembly (out of 450 altogether). On 28 June 1996 Refah came to power forming a coalition government with the centre-right True Path Party, led by Mrs Tansu Ciller.

11. On 21 May 1997 Principal State Counsel at the Court of Cassation applied to the Turkish Constitutional Court to have Refah dissolved on the grounds that it was a 'centre' of activities contrary to the principles of secularism. [Refah was dissolved.]

...

[9] J. E. M. Machado, 'Freedom of Religion: A View from Europe', 10 *Roger Williams University Law Review* 451, 505–6 (2005).

[10] R. Clayton & H. Tomlinson, 1 *The Law of Human Rights* 976 (2000).

[11] W. Fuhrmann, 'Perspectives on Religious Freedom from the Vantage Point of the European Court of Human Rights', 2000 *Brigham Young University Law Review* 829, 837.

34. The applicants alleged that Refah's dissolution and the prohibition barring its leaders— including Mr Erbakan, Mr Yilmaz and Mr Tekdal—from holding similar office in any other political party had infringed their right to freedom of association, guaranteed by Article 11 of the Convention, the relevant parts of which provide:

1. Everyone has the right to freedom of peaceful assembly and to freedom of association...

2. No restrictions shall be placed on the exercise of these rights other than such as are prescribed by law and are necessary in a democratic society in the interests of national security or public safety, for the prevention of disorder or crime...or for the protection of the rights and freedoms of others...

[The Court concludes that there was an interference with the applicant's right to freedom of association and that the interference was prescribed by law.]

2. Legitimate aim

40. The Government submitted that the interference complained of pursued several legitimate aims, namely protection of public safety, national security and the rights and freedoms of others and the prevention of crime.

41. The applicants accepted in principle that protection of public safety and the rights and freedoms of others and the prevention of crime might depend on safeguarding the principle of secularism. They observed that in the present case the Constitutional Court had based its judgment on the statements of politicians who had been legitimately elected in democratic elections and whose views had been expressed mainly at a time when they had parliamentary privilege.

42. Taking into account the importance of the principle of secularism for the democratic system in Turkey, the Court considers that Refah's dissolution pursued a number of the legitimate aims listed in Article 11, namely protection of national security and public safety, prevention of disorder or crime and protection of the rights and freedoms of others.

3. Necessary in a democratic society

43. The European Convention on Human Rights must be understood and interpreted as a whole. Human rights form an integrated system for the protection of human dignity; in that connection, democracy and the rule of law have a key role to play.

Democracy requires that the people should be given a role. Only institutions created by and for the people may be vested with the powers and authority of the State; statute law must be interpreted and applied by an independent judicial power. There can be no democracy where the people of a State, even by a majority decision, waive their legislation and judicial powers in favour of an entity which is not responsible to the people it governs, whether it is secular or religious.

The rule of law means that all human beings are equal before the law, in their rights as in their duties. However, legislation must take account of differences, provided that distinctions between people and situations have an objective and reasonable justification, pursue a legitimate aim and are proportionate and consistent with the principles normally upheld by democratic societies. But the rule of law cannot be said to govern a secular society when groups of persons are discriminated against solely on the ground that they are of a different sex or have different political or religious beliefs. Nor is the rule of law upheld where entirely different legal systems are created for such groups.

There is a very close link between the rule of law and democracy. As it is the function of written law to establish distinctions on the basis of relevant differences, the rule of law cannot be sustained over a long period if persons governed by the same laws do not have the last word on the subject of their content and implementation.

...

47. The Court takes the view that a political party may campaign for a change in the law or the legal and constitutional basis of the State on two conditions: (1) the means used to that end must in every respect be legal and democratic; (2) the change proposed must itself be compatible with fundamental democratic principles. It necessarily follows that a political party whose leaders incite recourse to violence, or propose a policy which does not comply with one or more of the rules of democracy or is aimed at the destruction of democracy and infringement of the rights and freedoms afforded under democracy cannot lay claim to the protection of the Convention against penalties imposed for those reasons.

48. Nor can it be ruled out that the programme of a political party or the statements of its leaders may conceal objectives and intentions different from those they proclaim. To verify that it does not, the content of the programme or statements must be compared with the actions of the party and its leaders and the positions they defend taken as a whole.

49. Moreover, the Court reiterates that, as enshrined in Article 9, freedom of thought, conscience and religion is one of the foundations of a 'democratic society' within the meaning of the Convention. It is, in its religious dimension, one of the most vital elements that go to make up the identity of believers and their conception of life, but it is also a precious asset for atheists, agnostics, sceptics and the unconcerned. The pluralism indissociable from a democratic society, which has been dearly won over the centuries, depends on it. That freedom entails, *inter alia*, freedom to hold or not to hold religious beliefs and to practise or not to practise a religion. [See *Kokkinakis v. Greece* (1994) 17 E.H.R.R. 397, para. 31; and *Buscarini and Others v. San Marino* (2000) 30 E.H.R.R. 208.]

50. The Court has pointed out that in democratic societies, in which several religions coexist within one and the same population, it may be necessary to place restrictions on this freedom in order to reconcile the interests of the various groups and ensure that everyone's beliefs are respected. [*Kokkinakis v. Greece, loc. cit.*, para. 33.]

...

52. The Convention institutions have also taken the view that the principle of secularism in Turkey is undoubtedly one of the fundamental principles of the State, which are in harmony with the rule of law and respect for human rights. Any conduct which fails to respect that principle cannot be accepted as being part of the freedom to manifest one's religion and is not protected by Article 9 of the Convention.

...

64. In the present case, the Court's task is to assess whether Refah's dissolution and the accessory penalties imposed on the other applicants met a 'pressing social need' and whether they were 'proportionate to the legitimate aims pursued'.

...

66. The point at issue between the parties before the Court mainly concerns the question whether Refah had become a 'centre of anti-secular activities' and a political group aiming at the installation of a theocratic regime.

67. The Court observes in that connection that Refah was dissolved on account of the declarations and policy statements made by its chairman and its members. Its constitution and programme did not have any part to play in the decision. Like the national authorities, the Court will therefore base its assessment of the necessity of the interference complained of on those declarations and policy statements.

68. The Court considers on this point that, among the grounds for dissolution put forward by Principal State Counsel at the Court of Cassation, those cited by the Constitutional Court as grounds for its finding that Refah had infringed the principle of secularism can be classified in three main categories: (i) those which tended to show that Refah intended to set up a plurality of legal systems, introducing discrimination on the grounds of belief; (ii) those which tended to show that Refah wanted to apply sharia to the Muslim community; and (iii) those based on references made by Refah members to jihad (holy war) as a political method. The Court can therefore limit its examination to these three groups of arguments which were upheld by the Constitutional Court.

69. In support of the first group of grounds for dissolution, concerning the proposed plurality of legal systems, the Constitutional Court cited various statements made by the applicant N Erbakan, Refah's chairman, who had said in his speech of 23 March 1993: 'There must be several legal systems. ... Moreover, that has always been the case throughout our history...there have been various religious movements. Everyone lived according to the legal rules of his own organisation, and so everyone lived in peace...', 'We shall free the administration from centralism. The State which you have installed is a repressive State... You do not follow the freedom to choose one's code of law'. The Constitutional Court found that Refah's intention had been to set up in Turkey a plurality of legal systems under which society would have to be divided into several religious movements; each individual would have to choose the movement to which he wished to belong and would thus be subjected to the rights and obligations prescribed by the religion of his community. The Constitutional Court pointed out that such a system, whose origins lay in the history of Islam as a political regime, was inimical to the consciousness of allegiance to a nation having legislative and judicial unity. It would naturally impair judicial unity since each religious movement would set up its own courts and the ordinary courts would be obliged to apply the law according to the religion of those appearing before them, thus obliging the latter to reveal their beliefs. It would also undermine legislative unity, given that each religious movement would be empowered to decree what legal rules should be applicable to its members.

70. Like the Government, the Court considers that Refah's proposal that there should be a plurality of legal systems would introduce into all legal relationships a distinction between individuals grounded on religion, would categorise everyone according to his religious beliefs and would allow him rights and freedoms not as an individual but according to his allegiance to a religious movement.

The Court takes the view that such a societal model cannot be considered compatible with the Convention system, for two reasons.

First, it would do away with the State's role as the guarantor of individual rights and freedoms and the impartial organiser of the practice of the various beliefs and religions in a democratic society, since it would oblige individuals to obey, not rules laid down by the State in the exercise of its above-mentioned functions, but static rules of law imposed by the religion concerned. But the State has a positive obligation to ensure that everyone within its jurisdiction enjoys in full, and without being able to waive them, the rights and freedoms guaranteed by the Convention.

Secondly, such a system would undeniably infringe the principle of non-discrimination between individuals as regards their enjoyment of public freedoms, which is one of the fundamental principles of democracy. A difference in treatment between individuals in all fields of public and private law according to their religion or beliefs manifestly cannot be justified under the Convention, and more particularly Article 14 thereof, which prohibits discrimination. Such a difference in treatment cannot maintain a fair balance between, on the one hand, the claims of certain religious groups who wish to be governed by their own rules and on the other the interest of society as a whole, which must be based on peace and on tolerance between the various religions and beliefs.

71. With regard to the second group of grounds for dissolution, the Constitutional Court found that Refah intended to introduce sharia (Islamic law) as the ordinary law and as the law applicable to the Muslim community. It held that sharia was the antithesis of democracy in that it was based on dogmatic values and was the opposite of the supremacy of reason and of the concepts of freedom, independence and the ideal of humanity developed in the light of science. A number of public speeches made by those members of Refah mentioned by the Constitutional Court had referred sometimes in explicit terms, to the objective of a regime based on sharia. The Court takes note in particular of the following remarks by Refah members, which explictly reveal the intention of setting up a regime inspired by sharia:

— In a television interview broadcast on 24 November 1996 Hasan Hüseyin Ceylan, MP for the province of Ankara, said that sharia was the solution for the country;

— On 8 May 1997 Ibrahim Halil Çelik, a Refah MP, said: 'I will fight to the end to introduce sharia'.

— In April 1994 Sevki Yilmaz MP said: 'The question Allah will ask you is this: "Why, in the time of the blasphemous regime, did you not work for the construction of an Islamic State?" Erbakan and his friends want to bring Islam to this country in the form of a political party. The prosecutor understood that clearly. If we could understand that as he did, the problem would be solved'.

The Court further notes the following remarks, which implicitly reflect the intention of those who made them to set up a regime based on sharia:

— On 13 April 1994 Necmettin Erbakan said: 'Refah will come to power and a just order will be established', and in a speech on 7 May 1996 he praised 'those who contribute, with conviction, to the supremacy of Allah';

— In April 1994 Sevki Yilmaz, MP for the province of Rize, proposed that the faithful should 'call to account those who turn their backs on the precepts of the Koran and those who deprive Allah's messenger of his jurisdiction in their country' and asserted: 'Only 39 per cent of the rules in the Koran are applied in this country. Six thousand five hundred verses have been quietly forgotten...'. He went on to say: 'The condition to be met before prayer is the islamisation of power. Allah says that, before mosques, it is the path of power which must be Muslim ...';

— While on pilgrimage in 1993 Ahmet Tekdal said: 'If the people...do not work hard enough to bring about the advent of *hak nizami* [a just order or God's order],...they will be tyrannised by [renegades] and will eventually disappear...they will not be able to give a satisfactory account of themselves to Allah, as they will not have worked to establish *haz nizami*'.

72. Like the Constitutional Court, the Court considers that sharia, which faithfully reflects the dogmas and divine rules laid down by religion, is stable and invariable. Principles such as pluralism in the political sphere or the constant evolution of public freedoms have no place in it. The Court notes that, when read together, the offending statements, which contain explicit references to the introduction of sharia, are difficult to reconcile with the fundamental principles of democracy, as conceived in the Convention taken as a whole. It is difficult to declare one's respect for democracy and human rights while at the same time supporting a regime based on sharia, which clearly diverges from Convention values, particularly with regard to its criminal law and criminal procedure, its rules on the legal status of women and the way it intervenes in all spheres of private and public life in accordance with religious precepts. In addition, the statements concerning the desire to found a 'just order' or the 'order of justice' or 'God's order', when read in their context, and even though they lend themselves to various interpretations, have as their common denominator the fact that they refer to religious or divine rules in order to define the political regime advocated by the speakers. They reveal ambiguity about those speakers' attachment to any order not based on religious rules. In the Court's view, a political party whose actions seem to be aimed at introducing sharia in a State party to the Convention can hardly be regarded as an association complying with the democratic ideal that underlies the whole of the Convention.

73. The Court also considers that, taken separately, the policy statements made by Refah's leaders, particularly on the question of Islamic headscarves or organising working hours in the public sector to accommodate prayers, and some of their acts, such as the visit of Mr Kazan, then Minister of Justice, to a member of his party charged with inciting hatred on the ground of religious discrimination, or the reception given by Mr Erbakan to the leaders of the various Islamic movements, did not constitute an imminent threat to the secular regime in Turkey. However, the Court finds persuasive the Government's argument that these acts and policy statements were consistent with Refah's unavowed aim of setting up a political regime based on sharia.

74. The third category of the grounds for dissolution cited by the Constitutional Court is that of the references by certain Refah members to the concept of jihad, whose primary meaning is a holy war, to be waged until the total domination of Islam in society is secured. The Court observes that there is likewise ambiguity in the terminology used by some speakers—Refah members—with regard to the method to be used to gain political power. Although it was not disputed before the Court that so far Refah had pursued its political ends by legitimate means, in the offending speeches its leaders alluded to the possibility of recourse to force in order to overcome various obstacles in the political route envisaged by Refah for gaining and retaining power.

The Court takes note of the remarks made by:

— Necmettin Erbakan, on 13 April 1994, on the question whether power would be gained by violence or by peaceful means (whether the change would involve bloodshed or not);

— Sevki Yilmaz, in April 1994, concerning his interpretation of jihad and the possibility for Muslims of arming themselves after coming to power;

— Hasan Hüseyin Ceylan, on 14 March 1992, who insulted and threatened the supporters of a regime on the Western model;

— Sükrü Karatepe, who, in his speech on 10 December 1996, advised believers to keep alive the rancour and hatred they felt in their hearts; and

— Ibrahim Halil Çelik, on 8 May 1997, who said he wanted blood to flow to prevent the closure of the theological colleges.

While it is true that Refah's leaders did not, in government documents, call for the use of force and violence as a political weapon, they did not take prompt practical steps to distance them-selves from those members of Refah who had publicly referred with approval to the possibility of using force against politicians who opposed them. Consequently, Refah's leaders did not dispel the ambiguity of these statements about the possibility of having recourse to violent methods in order to gain power and retain it.

75. The Court also notes that the remarks made by Hasan Hüseyin Ceylan, MP for the prov-ince of Ankara, in his speech on 14 March 1993, videotapes of which were shown in Refah's local branches, revealed deep hatred for those he considered to be opponents of an Islamist regime. The Court considers in that connection that where the offending conduct reaches a high level of insult and comes close to a negation of the freedom of religion of others it loses the right to society's tolerance. [See, *mutatis mutandis, Otto Preminger Institute v. Austria* (1995) 19 E.H.R.R. 34, para. 47.]

76. The Court cannot accept the applicants' argument that the remarks cited as grounds for Refah's dissolution were taken completely out of context and were inconsistent with each other. In fact, the political statements in question, taken as a whole, suggest that Refah advo-cated setting up a plurality of legal systems, introducing discrimination between individuals on the ground of their religious beliefs and functioning according to different religious rules for each religious community, in which sharia would be the applicable law for the Muslim majority of the country and/or the ordinary law. In addition, they give the impression that Refah did not exclude the possibility of recourse to force in certain circumstances in order to oppose certain political programmes, or to gain power and retain it. The Court considers that such a vision of society is based on the Islamic theocratic regime which has already been imposed in the history of Turkish law. It accordingly concludes that the offending remarks and policy statements made by Refah's leaders form a whole and give a fairly clear picture of a model of State and society organised according to religious rules, which was conceived and proposed by Refah.

77. The Court further considers that Refah's political aims were neither theoretical nor illusory, but achievable, for two reasons. The first of these relates to its influence as a political party and its chances of gaining power, the only possibility for a political party to keep its promises. At the time of its dissolution Refah, with its 157 MPs, had nearly a third of the seats in the Turkish Grand National Assembly. The speeches and policy statements cited by the Constitutional Court as grounds for Refah's dissolution date from the period (1993–1997) during which the party had obtained significant results in the general and local elections and was close to the spheres of power. The second reason lies in the fact that in the past political movements based on religious fundamentalism have been able to seize political power and have had the opportunity to set up the societal model which they advocated. The Court therefore

considers that the real chance Refah had to implement its political plans undeniably made the danger of those plans for public order more tangible and more immediate.

...

83. Accordingly, and having regard to the albeit narrow margin of appreciation left to the national authorities in such a case, the Court considers that the interference complained of was not disproportionate to the legitimate aims pursued, in the light of the fact that they answered a 'pressing social need' and that the grounds cited by the Constitutional Court to justify Refah's dissolution and the temporary forfeiture of certain political rights by the other applicants were 'relevant and sufficient'.

84. Consequently, there has been no violation of Article 11 of the Convention in this case.

...

For these reasons, THE COURT

1. *Holds* by four votes to three that there has been no violation of Article 11 of the Convention;

...

JOINT DISSENTING OPINION OF JUDGES FUHRMANN, LOUCAIDES AND SIR NICOLAS BRATZA

1. We regret we are unable to share the view of the majority of the Court that there has been no violation of the applicants' rights under Article 11 of the Convention in the present case. In our view the order of the Constitutional Court dissolving Refah, depriving the individual applicants of their membership of the National Assembly and prohibiting them for a period of five years from becoming a founder member, administrator or auditor of any other political party, amounted to a disproportionate restriction on their freedom of association as guaranteed by that Article.

...

13. On the crucial question of the necessity of the measures taken by the Constitutional Court, we would begin by making a number of preliminary remarks.

14. In the first place, we can readily accept the Government's argument as to the vital importance of secularism in Turkish society. As the Government points out, the State went through a long and painful struggle to establish a democratic and secular society and remains the only State with a substantially Islamic population which adheres to the principles of a liberal democracy. The example provided by States governed by fundamentalist Islamic regimes underlines the risk to democracy posed by a departure from the secular ideal.

15. Secondly, not only was Refah democratically elected in 1995 as the party with the largest number of seats in the Assembly but, as we have noted above, it is common ground that the party was organised on democratic lines and that there was nothing in its statute or programme to demonstrate or even suggest any departure from the principle of secularism

or any encouragement to the use of violent or undemocratic means to replace the existing constitutional structure of the Turkish society.

...

45. The question which the Constitutional Court was required to determine was whether, having regard to the acts and statements of the leaders of Refah and of its members, the party had become a centre of anti-secular activity for the purposes of the Law on Political Parties. Having decided that it had, the dissolution of the party was mandated by the Law and Constitution.

46. The question before our Court is a different one, namely whether the extreme measure of dissolution (a measure which was alternatively described by the Court in its earlier judgments as 'radical' and 'drastic') could be considered as responding to a pressing social need and as a measure which was proportionate to the legitimate aims served.

47. In answering this question in the affirmative, the majority of the Court have found that the national authorities were entitled to act to prevent the realisation of the political aims which were incompatible with Convention norms before those aims could be put into effect in a manner which compromised civil peace and the democratic system within the country.

48. We regret that we are unpersuaded by this reasoning. What is in our view lacking is any compelling or convincing evidence to suggest that the party, whether before or after entering Government, took any steps to realise political aims which were incompatible with Convention norms, to destroy or undermine the secular society, to engage in or to encourage acts of violence or religious hatred, or otherwise to pose a threat to the legal and democratic order in Turkey.

49. In the absence of such evidence, we find that the dissolution of Refah and the confiscation of its property, as well as the ancillary orders made against the individual applicants were in violation of Article 11 of the Convention.

4. MURPHY V. IRELAND

Judgment of 10 July 2003
38 E.H.R.R. 13

7. The applicant was born in 1949 and lives in Dublin. He is a pastor attached to the Irish Faith Centre, a bible based Christian ministry in Dublin.

8. In early 1995 the Irish Faith Centre submitted an advertisement to an independent, local and commercial radio station for transmission. The text of the advertisement read as follows:

'What think ye of Christ? Would you, like Peter, only say that he is the son of the living God? Have you ever exposed yourself to the historical facts about Christ? The Irish Faith Centre are presenting for Easter week an hour-long video by Dr Jean Scott PhD on the evidence of the resurrection from Monday 10–Saturday 15, April every night at 8.30 and Easter Sunday at 11.30am and also live by satellite at 7.30pm'.

9. The radio station was prepared to broadcast the advertisement. However, in March 1995 the Independent Radio and Television Commission ('IRTC') stopped the broadcast pursuant to s. 10(3) of the Radio and Television Act 1988 ('the 1988 Act'). This ruling did not affect the later transmission of the video by satellite.

10. The applicant applied for leave to take judicial review proceedings. He cited the IRTC and the Attorney-General as respondents and submitted that the IRTC had wrongly construed s. 10(3) and, alternatively and mainly, that if the IRTC had correctly applied s. 10(3) of the 1988 Act, that provision was unconstitutional.

11. By judgment delivered on April 25, 1997, the High Court found that the IRTC had not infringed s. 10(3) of the 1988 Act. It further considered that the unspecified right to communicate guaranteed by Art. 40(3) (1) of the Constitution was at issue since the advertisement had, as its principal purpose, the communication of information. However, it found that s. 10(3) was a reasonable limitation on the right to communicate and that there were good reasons in the public interest for the ban.

[On May 28, 1998, the Irish Supreme Court rejected the appeal of the applicant who then applied to Strasbourg.]

1. Interference

60. The Court notes that the applicant maintained that the application of s. 10(3) of the 1988 Act in his case interfered with his rights guaranteed by Arts 9 and 10 of the Convention. While arguing that there had been no interference with his rights under either Article, the Government's submissions to the Court were, for the most part, expressed in terms of Art. 10 of the Convention.

61. The Court considers that the matter essentially at issue in the present case is the applicant's exclusion from broadcasting an advertisement, an issue concerning primarily the regulation of his means of expression and not his profession or manifestation of his religion. It recalls that Art. 10 protects not only the content and substance of information but also the means of dissemination since any restriction on the means necessarily interferes with the right to receive and impart information. Accordingly, the Court is of the view that the applicant's complaint about the prohibition contained in s. 10(3) of the 1988 Act falls to be examined under Art. 10 of the Convention.

...

[T]he Court reiterates that even expression which could be considered offensive, shocking or disturbing to the religious sensitivities of others falls within the scope of the protection of Art. 10, the question for the Court being whether any restriction imposed on that expression complies with the provisions of that Article.

In addition, having regard to the fact that the applicant was prevented from broadcasting the advertisement as a result of the application of s. 10(3) of the 1988 Act, there clearly has been an interference with his right to freedom of expression.

2. 'Prescribed by law'

62. The parties did not dispute, and the Court considers it clear, that the prohibition applied to the applicant was set out in a clear and accessible manner in s. 10(3) of the 1988 Act.

3. Legitimate aim

63. The Government maintained that the prohibition sought to ensure respect for the religious doctrines and beliefs of others so that the aims of the impugned provision were public order and safety together with the protection of the rights and freedoms of others.

While disputing the necessity of the statutory provision, the applicant did not directly contest that these aims had been pursued by the enactment of s. 10(3) of the 1988 Act.

64. The Court does not see any reason to doubt that these were indeed the aims of the impugned legislation and considers that they constituted legitimate aims for the purposes of Art. 10(2) of the Convention. [*Otto-Preminger-Institut v. Austria.*]

4. 'Necessary in a democratic society'

65. The Court recalls that freedom of expression constitutes one of the essential foundations of a democratic society. As para. 2 of Art. 10 expressly recognises, however, the exercise of that freedom carries with it duties and responsibilities. Amongst them, in the context of religious beliefs, is the general requirement to ensure the peaceful enjoyment of the rights guaranteed under Art. 9 to the holders of such beliefs including a duty to avoid as far as possible an expression that is, in regard to objects of veneration, gratuitously offensive to others and profane.

66. No restriction on freedom of expression, whether in the context of religious beliefs or in any other, can be compatible with Art. 10 unless it satisfies, *inter alia*, the test of necessity as required by the second paragraph of that Article. In examining whether restrictions to the rights and freedoms guaranteed by the Convention can be considered 'necessary in a democratic society' the Court has, however, consistently held that the Contracting States enjoy a certain but not unlimited margin of appreciation.

67. In this latter respect, there is little scope under Art. 10(2) of the Convention for restrictions on political speech or on debate of questions of public interest. However, a wider margin of appreciation is generally available to the Contracting States when regulating freedom of expression in relation to matters liable to offend intimate personal convictions within the sphere of morals or, especially, religion. Moreover, as in the field of morals, and perhaps to an even greater degree, there is no uniform European conception of the requirements of 'the protection of the rights of others' in relation to attacks on their religious convictions. What is likely to cause substantial offence to persons of a particular religious persuasion will vary significantly from time to time and from place to place, especially in an era characterised by an ever-growing array of faiths and denominations. By reason of their direct and continuous contact with the vital forces of their countries, State authorities are in principle in a better position than the international judge to give an opinion on the exact content of these requirements with regard to the rights of others as well as on the 'necessity' of a 'restriction' intended to protect from such material those whose deepest feelings and convictions would be seriously offended.

. . .

68. It is for the European Court to give a final ruling on the restriction's compatibility with the Convention and it will do so by assessing in the circumstances of a particular case, *inter alia*, whether the interference corresponded to a 'pressing social need' and whether it was

'proportionate to the legitimate aim pursued'. Indeed, such supervision can be considered to be all the more necessary given the rather open-ended notion of respect for the religious beliefs of others and the risks of excessive interferences with freedom of expression under the guise of action taken against allegedly offensive material. In this regard, the scope of the restriction in the legislation is especially important. The Court's task in this case is therefore to determine whether the reasons relied on by the national authorities to justify the measures interfering with the applicant's freedom of expression are 'relevant and sufficient' for the purposes of Art. 10(2) of the Convention.

69. Moreover, it is recalled that the potential impact of the medium of expression concerned is an important factor in the consideration of the proportionality of an interference. The Court has acknowledged that account must be taken of the fact that the audio-visual media have a more immediate and powerful effect than the print media.

70. The Court notes at the outset that the nature and purpose of the expression contained in the relevant advertisement accords with it being treated as religious, as opposed to commercial, expression even if the applicant purchased the relevant broadcasting time.

71. The main factor which the Government considered justified the impugned prohibition was the particular religious sensitivities in Irish society which they submitted were such that the broadcasting of any religious advertising could be considered offensive. The applicant agreed that Art. 10 permitted restrictions of religious expression which would offend others' religious sensitivities but submitted that the Convention did not protect an individual from being exposed to a religious view simply because it did not accord with his or her own, noting that his advertisement was innocuous and completely inoffensive. In any event, he disputed the Government's assessment of contemporary religious sensitivities in Ireland.

72. The Court agrees that the concepts of pluralism, tolerance and broadmindedness on which any democratic society is based mean that Art. 10 does not, as such, envisage that an individual is to be protected from exposure to a religious view simply because it is not his or her own. However, the Court observes that it is not to be excluded that an expression, which is not on its face offensive, could have an offensive impact in certain circumstances. The question before the Court is therefore whether a prohibition of a certain type (advertising) of expression (religious) through a particular means (the broadcast media) can be justifiably prohibited in the particular circumstances of the case.

73. Turning therefore to the country-specific religious sensitivities relied on by the Government, the Court has noted that the Minister identified, during the debate on the introduction of s. 20(4) of the 1960 Act, the potential impact on religious sensitivities as justifying prudence in the context of the broadcasting of religious advertising and he drew a distinction between advertising time which was purchased and programming. Section 20(4) was then applied to independent broadcasters through s. 10(3) of the 1988 Act, the provision at issue in the present case. The Court has noted that, during the detailed debate on a proposed dilution of s. 10(3) in April 1999, the Minister emphasised at some length the extreme sensitivity of the question of broadcasting of religious advertising in Ireland and the consequent necessity to proceed towards any proposed amendment of s. 10(3) with care and on the basis of a full consideration of the issues and options.

Moreover, the domestic courts found that the Government was entitled to be prudent in this context. In particular, the High Court considered relevant the fact that religion had been a divisive issue in Northern Ireland. It further considered that Irish people with religious beliefs tended to belong to a particular church so that religious advertising from a different church might be considered offensive and open to the interpretation of proselytism. Indeed, the High Court pointed out that it was the very fact that an advertisement was directed towards a religious end which might have been potentially offensive to the public. The Supreme Court also emphasised that the three subjects highlighted by s. 10(3) of the 1988 Act concerned subjects which had proven 'extremely divisive in Irish society in the past' and it also agreed that the Government had been entitled to take the view that Irish citizens would resent having advertisements touching on these topics broadcast into their homes and that such advertisements could lead to unrest.

74. The Court has also observed that the impugned provision was designed to correspond, and was indeed limited, to these particular concerns and that the bounds of the prohibition are an important consideration in the assessment of its proportionality.

The prohibition concerned only the audio-visual media. The State was, in the Court's view, entitled to be particularly wary of the potential for offence in the broadcasting context, such media being accepted by this Court and acknowledged by the applicant, as having a more immediate, invasive and powerful impact including, as the Government and the High Court noted, on the passive recipient. He was consequently free to advertise the same matter in any of the print media (including local and national newspapers) and during public meetings and other assemblies.

Moreover, the prohibition related only to advertising. This Court considers that this limitation reflects a reasonable distinction made by the State between, on the one hand, purchasing broadcasting time to advertise and, on the other, coverage of religious matters through programming (including documentaries, debates, films, discussions and live coverage of religious events and occasions). Programming is not broadcast because a party has purchased airtime and, as outlined by the Government, must be impartial, neutral and balanced, the objective value of which obligation the parties did not dispute. The applicant retained the same right as any other citizen to participate in programmes on religious matters and to have services of his church broadcast in the audio-visual media. Advertising, however, tends to have a distinctly partial objective: it cannot be, and is not, therefore subject to the above outlined principle of impartiality and the fact that advertising time is purchased would lean in favour of unbalanced usage by religious groups with larger resources and advertising.

Consequently, other than advertisements in the broadcast media, the applicant's religious expression was not otherwise restricted.

75. Such considerations provide, in the Court's view, highly 'relevant reasons' justifying the Irish State's prohibition of the broadcasting of religious advertisements.

76. The applicant, however, also maintained that these reasons were not 'sufficient' and, in particular, that the State could have achieved its aims by a more limited prohibition and, indeed, that it should have gone further than the limited dilution of the prohibition contained in s. 65 of the 2001 Act. However, the Court considers persuasive the Government's argument that a complete or partial relaxation of the impugned prohibition would sit uneasily with the nature and level of the religious sensitivities outlined above and with the principle of neutrality in the broadcast media.

77. In the first place, the Court would accept that a provision allowing one religion, and not another, to advertise would be difficult to justify and that a provision which allowed the filtering by the State or any organ designated by it, on a case by case basis, of unacceptable

or excessive religious advertising would be difficult to apply fairly, objectively and coherently. There is, in this context, some force in the Government's argument that the exclusion of all religious groupings from broadcasting advertisements generates less discomfort than any filtering of the amount and content of such expression by such groupings.

The applicant suggested that such a filtering process is already applied through the application of the principle of neutrality to programmes and programming. However, and as the Court has noted above, the distinct nature of advertising and programming means that the regulatory tools employed for programming are not directly applicable to advertising. The applicant also referred to the fact that advertisements (other than those prohibited by the impugned provision) are already subjected to advertising standards control. The Court does not, however, consider that the same public sensitivities and issues of neutrality arise in the case of religious advertisements and those concerning, for example, commercial services, goods or products.

78. Secondly, the Court considers it reasonable for the State to consider it likely that even a limited freedom to advertise would benefit a dominant religion more than those religions with significantly less adherents and resources. Such a result would jar with the objective of promoting neutrality in broadcasting and, in particular, of ensuring a 'level playing field' for all religions in the medium considered to have the most powerful impact.

79. Thirdly, the applicant did not dispute the Government's concern that allowing limited religious advertising would result in unequal consequences for the national and independent broadcasters.

80. Fourthly, while the State has, subsequent to the facts of the present case, diluted s. 10(3) of the 1988 Act, the Minister's comments in April 1999 together with the limited nature of the 2001 amendment do not undermine, and indeed are consistent with, the State's view of the religious sensitivities in Ireland in 1988 and its understanding of the consequent necessity for full reflection and prudence when considering any evolution including a relaxation of the provisions of s. 10(3) of the 1988 Act. In addition, the nature of the assessment required by s. 65 of the 2001 Act (whether or not the advertisement amounted only to an announcement of the fact that a religious publication is for sale or that a religious event will take place) has been clearly chosen for its relatively objective and, consequently, uncontroversial nature.

81. Finally, and as to the parties' submissions concerning the existence of similar prohibitions on the broadcasting of religious advertising in other countries, the Court observes that there appears to be no clear consensus between the Contracting States as to the manner in which to legislate for the broadcasting of religious advertisements. Certain States have similar prohibitions (for example, Greece, Switzerland and Portugal), certain prohibit religious advertisements considered offensive (for example, Spain and see also Council Directive 89/552) and certain have no legislative restriction (the Netherlands). There appears to be no 'uniform conception of the requirements of the protection of the rights of others' in the context of the legislative regulation of the broadcasting of religious advertising.

82. In the circumstances, and given the margin of appreciation accorded to the State in such matters, the Court considers that the State has demonstrated that there were 'relevant and sufficient' reasons justifying the interference with the applicant's freedom of expression within the meaning of Art. 10 of the Convention.

In consequence, it concludes that there has been no violation of the Convention.

Order

For these reasons, THE COURT unanimously

Holds that there has been no violation of Art. 10 of the Convention, under which Article the Court found the complaint was most appropriately considered.

5. SAHIN V. TURKEY

Judgment of 10 November 2005 (Grand Chamber)
41 E.H.R.R. 8

14. The applicant was born in 1973 and has lived in Vienna since 1999, when she left Istanbul to pursue her medical studies at the Faculty of Medicine at Vienna University. She comes from a traditional family of practising Muslims and considers it her religious duty to wear the Islamic headscarf.

15. On 26 August 1997 the applicant, then in her fifth year at the Faculty of Medicine at Bursa University, enrolled at the Cerrahpasa Faculty of Medicine at Istanbul University. She says that she wore the Islamic headscarf during the four years she spent studying medicine at the University of Bursa and continued to do so until February 1998.

16. On 23 February 1998 the Vice Chancellor of Istanbul University issued a circular, the relevant part of which provides:

'By virtue of the Constitution, the law and regulations, and in accordance with the case-law of the Supreme Administrative Court and the European Commission of Human Rights and the resolutions adopted by the university administrative boards, students whose "heads are covered" (who wear the Islamic headscarf) and students (including overseas students) with beards must not be admitted to lectures, courses or tutorials. Consequently, the name and number of any student with a beard or wearing the Islamic headscarf must not be added to the lists of registered students. However, students who insist on attending tutorials and entering lecture theatres although their names and numbers are not on the lists must be advised of the position and, should they refuse to leave, their names and numbers must be taken and they must be informed that they are not entitled to attend lectures. If they refuse to leave the lecture theatre, the teacher shall record the incident in a report explaining why it was not possible to give the lecture and shall bring the incident to the attention of the university authorities as a matter of urgency so that disciplinary measures can be taken'.

[The applicant was denied access to examinations and was disciplined by the University for wearing the Islamic headscarf, decisions upheld on 27 May 1999, by the Turkish Constitutional Court.]

55. For more than twenty years the place of the Islamic headscarf in State education has been the subject of debate across Europe. In most European countries, the debate has focused mainly on primary and secondary schools. However, in Turkey, Azerbaijan and Albania it has concerned not just the question of individual liberty, but also the political meaning of the Islamic headscarf. These are the only member States to have introduced regulations on wearing the Islamic headscarf in universities.

56. In France, where secularism is regarded as one of the cornerstones of republican values, legislation was passed on 15 March 2004 regulating, in accordance with the principle of secularism, the wearing of signs or dress manifesting a religious affiliation in State primary and secondary schools. The legislation inserted a new Article L. 141-5-1 in the Education Code which provides: 'In State primary and secondary schools, the wearing of signs or dress by which pupils overtly manifest a religious affiliation is prohibited. The school rules shall state that the institution of disciplinary proceedings shall be preceded by dialogue with the pupil'.

The Act applies to all State schools and educational institutions, including post-baccalaureate courses (preparatory classes for entrance to the grandes écoles and vocational training courses). It does not apply to State universities. In addition, as the circular of 18 May 2004 makes clear, it only concerns '...signs..., such as the Islamic headscarf, however named, the kippa or a cross that is manifestly oversized, which make the wearer's religious affiliation immediately identifiable'.

57. In Belgium there is no general ban on wearing religious signs at school. In the French Community a decree of 13 March 1994 stipulates that education shall be neutral within the Community. Pupils are in principle allowed to wear religious signs. However, they may do so only if human rights, the reputation of others, national security, public order, and public health and morals are protected and internal rules complied with. Further, teachers must not permit religious or philosophical proselytism under their authority or the organisation of political militancy by or on behalf of pupils. The decree stipulates that restrictions may be imposed by school rules. On 19 May 2004 the French Community issued a decree intended to institute equality of treatment. In the Flemish Community, there is no uniform policy among schools on whether to allow religious or philosophical signs to be worn. Some do, others do not. When pupils are permitted to wear such signs, restrictions may be imposed on grounds of hygiene or safety.

58. In other countries (Austria, Germany, the Netherlands, Spain, Sweden, Switzerland and the United Kingdom), in some cases following a protracted legal debate, the State education authorities permit Muslim pupils and students to wear the Islamic headscarf.

59. In Germany, where the debate focused on whether teachers should be allowed to wear the Islamic headscarf, the Constitutional Court stated on 24 September 2003 in a case between a teacher and the Land of Baden-Württemberg that the lack of any express statutory prohibition meant that teachers were entitled to wear the headscarf. Consequently, it imposed a duty on the Länder to lay down rules on dress if they wished to prohibit the wearing of the Islamic headscarf in State schools.

60. In Austria there is no special legislation governing the wearing of the headscarf, turban or kippa. In general, it is considered that a ban on wearing the headscarf will only be justified if it poses a health or safety hazard for pupils.

61. In the United Kingdom a tolerant attitude is shown to pupils who wear religious signs. Difficulties with respect to the Islamic headscarf are rare. The issue has also been debated in the context of the elimination of racial discrimination in schools in order to preserve their multicultural character (see, in particular, *Mandla v. Dowell Lee* [1983] 2 A.C. 548). 'The Law Reports' 1983, 548–570). The Commission for Racial Equality, whose opinions have recommendation status only, also considered the issue of the Islamic headscarf in 1988 in the Altrincham Grammar School case, which ended in a compromise between a private school and members of the family of two sisters who wished to be allowed to wear the Islamic headscarf

at the school. The school agreed to allow them to wear the headscarf provided it was navy blue (the colour of the school uniform), kept fastened at the neck and not decorated.

In the case of *R (On the application of Begum) v. Headteacher and Governors of Denbigh High School* [2004], the High Court had to decide a dispute between the school and a Muslim pupil wishing to wear the jilbab (a full-length gown). The school required pupils to wear a uniform, one of the possible options being the headscarf and a shalwar kameeze (long traditional garments from the Indian subcontinent). In June 2004 the High Court dismissed the pupil's application, holding that there had been no violation of her freedom of religion. However, that judgment was reversed in March 2005 by the Court of Appeal, which accepted that there had been interference with the pupil's freedom of religion, as a minority of Muslims in the United Kingdom considered that a religious duty to wear the jilbab from the age of puberty existed and the pupil was genuinely of that opinion. No justification for the interference had been provided by the school authorities, as the decision-making process was not compatible with freedom of religion.

[Editorial Note: The Court of Appeal decision here cited by the Court was itself later reversed by the House of Lords. See *R. (Begum) v. Head Teacher and Governors of Denbigh High School* [2006] U.K.H.L. 15, [2006] 2 All E.R. 487, where the judgments included consideration of the decision that is now being excerpted.]

62. In Spain, there is no express statutory prohibition on pupils' wearing religious head coverings in State schools. By virtue of two royal Decrees of 26 January 1996, which are applicable in primary and secondary schools unless the competent authority—the autonomous community—has introduced specific measures, the school governors have power to issue school rules which may include provisions on dress. Generally speaking, State schools allow the headscarf to be worn.

63. In Finland and Sweden the veil can be worn at school. However, a distinction is made between the burka (the term used to describe the full veil covering the whole of the body and the face) and the niqab (a veil covering all the upper body with the exception of the eyes). In Sweden mandatory directives were issued in 2003 by the National Education Agency. These allow schools to prohibit the burka and niqab, provided they do so in a spirit of dialogue on the common values of equality of the sexes and respect for the democratic principle on which the education system is based.

64. In the Netherlands, where the question of the Islamic headscarf is considered from the standpoint of discrimination rather than of freedom of religion, it is generally tolerated. In 2003 a non-binding directive was issued. Schools may require pupils to wear a uniform provided that the rules are not discriminatory and are included in the school prospectus and that the punishment for transgressions is not disproportionate. A ban on the burka is regarded as justified by the need to be able to identify and communicate with pupils. In addition, the Equal Treatment Commission ruled in 1997 that a ban on wearing the veil during general lessons for safety reasons was not discriminatory.

65. In a number of other countries (the Czech Republic, Greece, Hungary, Poland or Slovakia), the issue of the Islamic headscarf does not yet appear to have given rise to any detailed legal debate.

...

70. The applicant submitted that the ban on wearing the Islamic headscarf in institutions of higher education constituted an unjustified interference with her right to freedom of religion, in particular, her right to manifest her religion.

She relied on Article 9 of the Convention, which provides:

1. Everyone has the right to freedom of thought, conscience and religion; this right includes freedom to change his religion or belief and freedom, either alone or in community with others and in public or private, to manifest his religion or belief, in worship, teaching, practice and observance.

2. Freedom to manifest one's religion or beliefs shall be subject only to such limitations as are prescribed by law and are necessary in a democratic society in the interests of public safety, for the protection of public order, health or morals, or for the protection of the rights and freedoms of others.

71. The Chamber found that the Istanbul University regulations restricting the right to wear the Islamic headscarf and the measures taken thereunder had interfered with the applicant's right to manifest her religion. It went on to find that the interference was prescribed by law and pursued one of the legitimate aims set out in the second paragraph of Article 9 of the Convention. It was justified in principle and proportionate to the aims pursued and could therefore be regarded as having been 'necessary in a democratic society'.

...

104. The Court reiterates that as enshrined in Article 9, freedom of thought, conscience and religion is one of the foundations of a 'democratic society' within the meaning of the Convention. This freedom is, in its religious dimension, one of the most vital elements that go to make up the identity of believers and their conception of life, but it is also a precious asset for atheists, agnostics, sceptics and the unconcerned. The pluralism indissociable from a democratic society, which has been dearly won over the centuries, depends on it. That freedom entails, *inter alia*, freedom to hold or not to hold religious beliefs and to practise or not to practise a religion (see, among other authorities, *Kokkinakis v. Greece*, 25 May 1993, Series A no. 260-A; and *Buscarini and Others v. San Marino* [GC], no. 24645/94, para. 34, ECHR 1999-I).

105. While religious freedom is primarily a matter of individual conscience, it also implies, inter alia, freedom to manifest one's religion, alone and in private, or in community with others, in public and within the circle of those whose faith one shares. Article 9 lists the various forms which manifestation of one's religion or belief may take, namely worship, teaching, practice and observance.

...

106. In democratic societies, in which several religions coexist within one and the same population, it may be necessary to place restrictions on freedom to manifest one's religion or belief in order to reconcile the interests of the various groups and ensure that everyone's beliefs are respected (*Kokkinakis*, cited above, p. 18, para. 33). This follows both from paragraph 2 of Article 9 and the State's positive obligation under Article 1 of the Convention to secure to everyone within its jurisdiction the rights and freedoms defined in the Convention.

107. The Court has frequently emphasised the State's role as the neutral and impartial organiser of the exercise of various religions, faiths and beliefs, and stated that this role is conducive to public order, religious harmony and tolerance in a democratic society.... Accordingly, the role of the authorities in such circumstances is not to remove the cause of tension by eliminating pluralism, but to ensure that the competing groups tolerate each other.

108. Pluralism, tolerance and broadmindedness are hallmarks of a 'democratic society'. Although individual interests must on occasion be subordinated to those of a group, democracy

does not simply mean that the views of a majority must always prevail: a balance must be achieved which ensures the fair and proper treatment of people from minorities and avoids any abuse of a dominant position. Pluralism and democracy must also be based on dialogue and a spirit of compromise necessarily entailing various concessions on the part of individuals or groups of individuals which are justified in order to maintain and promote the ideals and values of a democratic society. Where these 'rights and freedoms' are themselves among those guaranteed by the Convention or its Protocols, it must be accepted that the need to protect them may lead States to restrict other rights or freedoms likewise set forth in the Convention. It is precisely this constant search for a balance between the fundamental rights of each individual which constitutes the foundation of a 'democratic society'.

109. Where questions concerning the relationship between State and religions are at stake, on which opinion in a democratic society may reasonably differ widely, the role of the national decision-making body must be given special importance. This will notably be the case when it comes to regulating the wearing of religious symbols in educational institutions, especially (as the comparative-law materials illustrate) in view of the diversity of the approaches taken by national authorities on the issue. It is not possible to discern throughout Europe a uniform conception of the significance of religion in society (*Otto-Preminger-Institut v. Austria*, judgment of 20 September 1994, Series A no. 295-A, p. 19, para. 50).... Accordingly, the choice of the extent and form such regulations should take must inevitably be left up to a point to the State concerned, as it will depend on the domestic context concerned (see, *mutatis mutandis*, ... *Murphy v. Ireland*, no. 44179/98, para. 73, ECHR 2003-IX (extracts)).

110. This margin of appreciation goes hand in hand with a European supervision embracing both the law and the decisions applying it. The Court's task is to determine whether the measures taken at national level were justified in principle and proportionate. In delimiting the extent of the margin of appreciation in the present case the Court must have regard to what is at stake, namely the need to protect the rights and freedoms of others, to preserve public order and to secure civil peace and true religious pluralism, which is vital to the survival of a democratic society.

...

112. The interference in issue caused by the circular of 23 February 1998 imposing restrictions as to place and manner on the rights of students such as Ms Sahin to wear the Islamic headscarf on university premises was, according to the Turkish courts, based in particular on the two principles of secularism and equality.

113. In its judgment of 7 March 1989, the Constitutional Court stated that secularism, as the guarantor of democratic values, was the meeting point of liberty and equality. The principle prevented the State from manifesting a preference for a particular religion or belief; it thereby guided the State in its role of impartial arbiter, and necessarily entailed freedom of religion and conscience. It also served to protect the individual not only against arbitrary interference by the State but from external pressure from extremist movements. The Constitutional Court added that freedom to manifest one's religion could be restricted in order to defend those values and principles.

114. As the Chamber rightly stated, the Court considers this notion of secularism to be consistent with the values underpinning the Convention. It finds that upholding that principle, which is undoubtedly one of the fundamental principles of the Turkish State which are in harmony

with the rule of law and respect for human rights, may be considered necessary to protect the democratic system in Turkey. An attitude which fails to respect that principle will not necessarily be accepted as being covered by the freedom to manifest one's religion and will not enjoy the protection of Article 9 of the Convention (see *Refah Partisi and Others*, para. 93).

115. After examining the parties' arguments, the Grand Chamber sees no good reason to depart from the approach taken by the Chamber as follows:

> ... The Court... notes the emphasis placed in the Turkish constitutional system on the protection of the rights of women... Gender equality—recognised by the European Court as one of the key principles underlying the Convention and a goal to be achieved by member States of the Council of Europe . . .—was also found by the Turkish Constitutional Court to be a principle implicit in the values underlying the Constitution...
>
> ... In addition, like the Constitutional Court..., the Court considers that, when examining the question of the Islamic headscarf in the Turkish context, there must be borne in mind the impact which wearing such a symbol, which is presented or perceived as a compulsory religious duty, may have on those who choose not to wear it. As has already been noted (see *Refah Partisi and Others*, cited above, para. 95), the issues at stake include the protection of the 'rights and freedoms of others' and the 'maintenance of public order' in a country in which the majority of the population, while professing a strong attachment to the rights of women and a secular way of life, adhere to the Islamic faith. Imposing limitations on freedom in this sphere may, therefore, be regarded as meeting a pressing social need by seeking to achieve those two legitimate aims, especially since, as the Turkish courts stated..., this religious symbol has taken on political significance in Turkey in recent years.
>
> ... The Court does not lose sight of the fact that there are extremist political movements in Turkey which seek to impose on society as a whole their religious symbols and conception of a society founded on religious precepts... It has previously said that each Contracting State may, in accordance with the Convention provisions, take a stance against such political movements, based on its historical experience (*Refah Partisi and Others*, para. 124). The regulations concerned have to be viewed in that context and constitute a measure intended to achieve the legitimate aims referred to above and thereby to preserve pluralism in the university.

116. Having regard to the above background, it is the principle of secularism, as elucidated by the Constitutional Court, which is the paramount consideration underlying the ban on the wearing of religious symbols in universities. In such a context, where the values of pluralism, respect for the rights of others and, in particular, equality before the law of men and women are being taught and applied in practice, it is understandable that the relevant authorities should wish to preserve the secular nature of the institution concerned and so consider it contrary to such values to allow religious attire, including, as in the present case, the Islamic headscarf, to be worn.

117. The Court must now determine whether in the instant case there was a reasonable relationship of proportionality between the means employed and the legitimate objectives pursued by the interference.

118. Like the Chamber, the Grand Chamber notes at the outset that it is common ground that practising Muslim students in Turkish universities are free, within the limits imposed by educational organisational constraints, to manifest their religion in accordance with habitual forms of Muslim observance. In addition, the resolution adopted by Istanbul University

on 9 July 1998 shows that various other forms of religious attire are also forbidden on the university premises.

119. It should also be noted that when the issue of whether students should be allowed to wear the Islamic headscarf surfaced at Istanbul University in 1994 in relation to the medical courses, the Vice Chancellor reminded them of the reasons for the rules on dress. Arguing that calls for permission to wear the Islamic headscarf in all parts of the university premises were misconceived and pointing to the public-order constraints applicable to medical courses, he asked the students to abide by the rules, which were consistent with both the legislation and the case-law of the higher courts.

120. Furthermore, the process whereby the regulations that led to the decision of 9 July 1998 were implemented took several years and was accompanied by a wide debate within Turkish society and the teaching profession. The two highest courts, the Supreme Administrative Court and the Constitutional Court, have managed to establish settled case-law on this issue. It is quite clear that throughout that decision-making process the university authorities sought to adapt to the evolving situation in a way that would not bar access to the university to students wearing the veil, through continued dialogue with those concerned, while at the same time ensuring that order was maintained and in particular that the requirements imposed by the nature of the course in question were complied with.

121. In that connection, the Court does not accept the applicant's submission that the fact that there were no disciplinary penalties for failing to comply with the dress code effectively meant that no rules existed. As to how compliance with the internal rules should have been secured, it is not for the Court to substitute its view for that of the university authorities. By reason of their direct and continuous contact with the education community, the university authorities are in principle better placed than an international court to evaluate local needs and conditions or the requirements of a particular course. Besides, having found that the regulations pursued a legitimate aim, it is not open to the Court to apply the criterion of proportionality in a way that would make the notion of an institution's 'internal rules' devoid of purpose. Article 9 does not always guarantee the right to behave in a manner governed by a religious belief (*Pichon and Sajous v. France* (dec.), no. 49853/99, ECHR 2001-X) and does not confer on people who do so the right to disregard rules that have proved to be justified.

122. In the light of the foregoing and having regard to the Contracting States' margin of appreciation in this sphere, the Court finds that the interference in issue was justified in principle and proportionate to the aim pursued.

123. Consequently, [by sixteen votes to one], there has been no breach of Article 9 of the Convention.

[The Court also held, by sixteen votes to one, that there had been no breach of Article 2, Protocol 1: 'No person shall be denied the right to education', see Chapter 11(F); and, unanimously, that there was no violation of Articles 8, 10, or 14.]

6. RELIGIOUS PREFERENCES?

Is the Strasbourg Court open to the charge that it is readier to protect some religions more than others? After all both *Otto-Preminger* and *Murphy* protected Catholic sensibilities, but *Refah Party* and *Sahin* did not protect those of Muslims. Krassimir Kanev, the Director of the Bulgarian Helsinki Committee, complains that the Court in both *Refah Party* and *Sahin* had little justification for upholding government action against Islamic religious principles. Noting that the Court in *Sahin* rested its judgment in part on the value of promoting the equality of men and women, Mr. Kanev writes that 'it would be interesting to see how the [Court] would apply the above principles in the case of the Catholic Church's refusal to ordain women'.[12]

Note that all seven judges in *Refah* agree that in some circumstances a political party devoted to the promotion of religious values may be legally excluded from the political process. Does either the judgment or the dissenting opinion adequately explain how such a result can be reconciled with Article 9? The 4–3 judgment seems to divide solely on the facts. The majority feel there is sufficient evidence to establish that Refah, if in office, would endanger secularism; the minority feel that the evidence is insufficient. What are the reasons for acting to ban Refah before it takes office?

In *Maestri v. Italy*,[13] the Court found that punishing a judge for being a Freemason violated Article 11's right to freedom of assembly and association. The applicant also complained about violations of his rights under Articles 9 and 10. The Court simply said that it 'considers the applicant's complaints fall most naturally within the scope of Article 11 of the Convention. Accordingly, it will consider them under that provision only'. Is this cursory treatment adequate? Is it due to judicial efficiency or to a reluctance, again, to engage Article 9?

Does *Murphy* repudiate *Kokkinakis*? Why permit Jehovah's Witnesses to go door to door offending the dominant Orthodox majority in Greece but not allow Protestants to go on the air offending the dominant Catholic majority in Ireland? As Professor Johan van der Vyver points out 'controversies centered upon the right to spread one's faith and the right to convert others remain a stumbling block in efforts to establish universal respect for, and adherence to, the vital components of religious freedom as contemplated by the founders of the United Nations'.[14] Proselytism remains a stumbling block for the Strasbourg Court, too. Why is this?

Does the Court adequately pay attention to Article 9 rights in *Murphy*? Take, for example, this passage:

> [T]here is little scope under Art. 10(2) of the Convention for restrictions on political speech or on debate of questions of public interest. However, a wider margin of appreciation is generally available to the Contracting States when regulating matters liable to offend intimate personal convictions within the sphere of morals or, especially, religion.

Note the Court here does not even attempt to balance Article 9 and Article 10 freedoms; it simply disregards Article 9 rights altogether. Does it seem that the *Murphy* judgment views manifesting one's religion more as a problem of freedom of possibly offensive expression than as a right of freedom of religion?

---

[12] K. Kanev, 'Muslim Religious Freedom in the OSCE Area after September 11', 11 *Helsinki Monitor* 233, 238–42 (2004).

[13] 17 February 2004, 39 E.H.R.R. 38.

[14] J. D. van der Vyver, 'Limitations of Freedom of Religion or Belief: International Perspectives', 19 *Emory International Law Review* 499, 502 (2005).

Interestingly, the Irish judge then in Strasbourg, John Hedigan, employed *Murphy* as his principal example when exploring Article 9 at a conference. He explained, 'the reason I have chosen this case is because although decided under Article 10 and the right to communicate, to receive and impart information, the rationale of the decision relates in great part to matters arising under Article 9 and how Governments deal with conflicting interests thereunder'.[15]

The Court, despite *Kokkinakis*, still seems reluctant to take an active role in interpreting Article 9. *Murphy*, saying 'there is no uniform European conception of the requirements of the protection of the rights of others in relation to attacks on their religious convictions', argues that it is up to the states, not Strasbourg, to decide the proper limits on manifestations of religion. But is not the role of the Court to help mould common European standards of human rights? Note that a common strand in *Otto-Preminger*, *Refah Party* and *Murphy* is that the Court employs the margin of appreciation to give the defendant state—Austria, Turkey and Ireland—the discretion to limit manifestations of religion according to national rather than European conceptions. Does this deference by Strasbourg, perhaps, underlie the Court's decision to treat all three as non-Article 9 cases, focusing instead on Article 10 or Article 11? Indeed, is not Article 9 used by the Court, counter-textually, as a limit on individual rights, when it was, like the other rights in the Convention, really meant to limit governments?

In *Cha'are Shalom Ve Tsedak v. France*,[16] the Strasbourg Court rejected an Article 9 complaint from an ultra-orthodox Jewish association that had been prohibited from slaughtering animals without first stunning beasts as required by French law:

76. In the first place, the Court notes that by establishing an exception to the principle that animals must be stunned before slaughter, French law gave practical effect to a positive undertaking on the State's part intended to ensure effective respect for freedom of religion. The 1980 decree, far from restricting exercise of that freedom, is on the contrary calculated to make provision for and organise its free exercise.

77. The Court further considers that the fact that the exceptional rules designed to regulate the practice of ritual slaughter permit only ritual slaughterers authorised by approved religious bodies to engage in it does not in itself lead to the conclusion that there has been an interference with the freedom to manifest one's religion. The Court considers, like the Government, that it is in the general interest to avoid unregulated slaughter, carried out in conditions of doubtful hygiene, and that it is therefore preferable, if there is to be ritual slaughter, for it to be performed in slaughterhouses supervised by the public authorities. Accordingly, when in 1982 the State granted approval to the ACIP, an offshoot of the Central Consistory, which is the body most representative of the Jewish communities of France, it did not in any way infringe the freedom to manifest one's religion.

78. However, when another religious body professing the same religion later lodges an application for approval in order to be able to perform ritual slaughter, it must be ascertained whether or not the method of slaughter it seeks to employ constitutes exercise of the freedom to manifest one's religion guaranteed by Article 9 of the Convention.

79. The Court notes that the method of slaughter employed by the ritual slaughterers of the applicant association is exactly the same as that employed by the ACIP's ritual slaughterers,

---

[15] Hedigan, *supra* n. 3.   [16] 27 June 2000.

and that the only difference lies in the thoroughness of the examination of the slaughtered animal's lungs after death. It is essential for the applicant association to be able to certify meat not only as kosher but also as 'glatt' in order to comply with its interpretation of the dietary laws, whereas the great majority of practising Jews accept the kosher certification made under the aegis of the ACIP.

80. In the Court's opinion, there would be interference with the freedom to manifest one's religion only if the illegality of performing ritual slaughter made it impossible for ultra-orthodox Jews to eat meat from animals slaughtered in accordance with the religious prescriptions they considered applicable.

81. But that is not the case. It is not contested that the applicant association can easily obtain supplies of 'glatt' meat in Belgium. Furthermore, it is apparent from the written depositions and bailiffs' official reports produced by the interveners that a number of butcher's shops operating under the control of the ACIP make meat certified 'glatt' by the Beth Din available to Jews.

82. It emerges from the case file as a whole, and from the oral submissions at the hearing, that Jews who belong to the applicant association can thus obtain 'glatt' meat. In particular, the Government referred, without being contradicted on this point, to negotiations between the applicant association and the ACIP with a view to reaching an agreement whereby the applicant association could perform ritual slaughter itself under cover of the approval granted to the ACIP, an agreement which was not reached, for financial reasons. Admittedly, the applicant association argued that it did not trust the ritual slaughterers authorised by the ACIP as regards the thoroughness of the examination of the lungs of slaughtered animals after death. But the Court takes the view that the right to freedom of religion guaranteed by Article 9 of the Convention cannot extend to the right to take part in person in the performance of ritual slaughter and the subsequent certification process, given that, as pointed out above, the applicant association and its members are not in practice deprived of the possibility of obtaining and eating meat considered by them to be more compatible with religious prescriptions.

83. Since it has not been established that Jews belonging to the applicant association cannot obtain 'glatt' meat, or that the applicant association could not supply them with it by reaching an agreement with the ACIP, in order to be able to engage in ritual slaughter under cover of the approval granted to the ACIP, the Court considers that the refusal of approval complained of did not constitute an interference with the applicant association's right to the freedom to manifest its religion.

Is this an adequate protection of religious liberties? Once again, is the Strasbourg Court less sensitive to protecting religious sensibilities when they are not Catholic sensibilities?

7. AN AMERICAN COMPARISON

The Strasbourg Court uses a great deal of comparative law in *Sahin*. Is it time to ask how universal are rights to religious freedom? Professor Smolin argues:

Whatever may be the virtues and vices of America's no-establishment experiment, there are many nations that have maintained official religious establishments. Nations with religious establishments are religiously and geographically diverse. Christian establishments within Europe include Lutheran state churches in Norway and Denmark, Anglicanism in the United Kingdom, the Greek Orthodox Church in Greece, and Roman Catholicism in Malta and San Marino. Islam is the officially established religion in a number of nations in Africa, Asia, and the Middle East, including Iran, Oman, Jordan, Algeria, Malaysia, and Saudi Arabia. Judaism has a special status in Israel. Hinduism is the established religion in Nepal, and Buddhism is the established religion of Cambodia, Bhutan, and Sri Lanka.

While Americans tend to conflate the no-establishment and religious liberty principles, international human rights principles necessarily separate them, as the mere existence of a state church or officially-sanctioned or favored religion does not of itself violate any norm of international law. Democracy, human rights, and the rule of law have frequently co-existed with state churches and established religions. It would require an extraordinary hubris for the United States to attempt to force the rest of the world to dis-establish in the name of religious liberty when much of the rest of the world considers religious liberty and establishment to be compatible and even complementary principles. Thus, any United States desire to 'export the First Amendment' should not include the Establishment Clause.[17]

Throughout his article, written in the light of the International Religious Freedom Act,[18] Professor Smolin cautions Americans to promote universal values of religious freedom rather than values that are idiosyncratic to the United States. For example, he compares U.S. constitutional protection of hate speech to the mandate of Article 20(2) of the International Covenant on Civil and Political Rights—'Any advocacy of national, racial or religious hatred that constitutes incitement to discrimination, hostility or violence shall be prohibited by law'—and concludes that, more often than in other countries, American human rights law gives greater weight to the value of freedom of speech than it does to the values of 'tolerance and civil peace'.[19]

Looking at the protection of religious freedom in European Human Rights Law and in the United States, would you agree with this conclusion of Professor Sedler based on a comparison of U.S. and Canadian constitutional law:

I would also submit that we would expect to see a similarity of result with *any* free and democratic society, sharing the same legal tradition, in which these individual rights have been given constitutional protection. That is, we would expect to see substantial agreement among the courts of those societies as to what infringements on freedom of religion, expression, and association constitute a 'demonstrably justifiable reasonable limit'.[20]

[17] D. M. Smolin, 'Exporting the First Amendment?: Evangelism, Proselytism, and the International Religious Freedom Act', 31 *Cumberland Law Review* 685, 686–90 (2000–2001) (hereinafter cited as 'Smolin').

[18] 22 U.S.C.A. sect. 6401–81.

[19] Smolin, *supra* n. 17, at 685–94.

[20] R. A. Sedler, 'The Constitutional Protection of Religion, Expression, and Association in Canada and the United States', 20 *Case Western Reserve Journal of International Law* 577, 620 (1988).

8

RESPECT FOR PRIVATE AND
FAMILY LIFE; MARRIAGE

ARTICLE 8

1. Everyone has the right to respect for his private and family life, his home and his correspondence.

2. There shall be no interference by a public authority with the exercise of this right except such as is in accordance with the law and is necessary in a democratic society in the interests of national security, public safety or the economic well-being of the country, for the prevention of disorder or crime, for the protection of health or morals, or for the protection of the rights and freedoms of others.

ARTICLE 12

Men and women of marriageable age have the right to marry and to found a family, according to the national laws governing the exercise of that right.

A. THE SCOPE OF FAMILY
AND PRIVATE LIFE

Like so much of the Convention, the protection of private and family life in Article 8 reflects Europe's terrifying experience with fascism in the 1930s and 40s. The debates of the Consultative Assembly refer to the intrusion of the fascist state into the family, including the racially restrictive Nazi laws on marriage and the policy of totalitarian governments to alienate children from their parents for the purpose of political indoctrination.[1]

[1] *See* 2 *Travaux Préparatoires* 90, 96, 100, 114.

Article 8's phrasing is unique in the Convention. Whereas Article 10 declares 'the right to freedom of expression' and Article 11, the 'right to freedom of peaceful assembly', Article 8 refers directly to no particular protected action. Rather it speaks of a right to 'respect for...private and family life'. Respect, as J. E. S. Fawcett pungently observed, 'belongs to the world of manners rather than the law'.[2] This choice of expression strongly suggests an intention to leave the contracting states considerable leeway in the regulation of private and family relations. That inference is reinforced by the drafting history of Article 8. The first draft put before the Consultative Assembly merely incorporated Article 12 of the Universal Declaration of Human Rights which stated that 'no one should be subject to arbitrary and unlawful interference with his privacy, family, home or correspondence'.[3] A subsequent draft altered this formulation to a declaration that a right to 'privacy in respect of family, home and correspondence, shall be recognized'.[4] This provision was further attenuated into the version finally adopted. These changes indicate that there may, for example, be interferences with the family which do not infringe the right to respect for family life.

The complex of interests described in the text of Article 8 might plausibly be read to concern only the unjustified exposure to public view of matters properly confined to the knowledge of an individual or family group. Section E below surveys the ways that Article 8 limits official collection of private information. More broadly, however, respect for 'private life' has been held to require non-interference with an individual's decisions on ways to live his or her own life. The European Court of Human Rights has understood the right to include the freedom to make particularly personal life choices, notably those involving sexual conduct, without regard to any public disclosure of information.[5]

The transformation of Article 8 into a general charter of individual autonomy is clearly fraught with difficulties. Any restraint on individual choice may be assailed as raising a possible violation of this right. Such an omnibus right is in marked contrast

---

[2] J. E. S. Fawcett, *The Application of the European Convention on Human Rights* 211 (2nd edn. 1987). *See also* Art. 2 of Protocol 1 to the Convention requiring the State to 'respect the right of parents to ensure...education and teaching in conformity with their own religious and philosophical convictions'.

[3] *See* Chapter 1(B) *supra*.

[4] *Travaux Préparatoires*, vol. IV, p. 278.

[5] *See* Section C *infra*. As an extension of this idea the Court has stated that assaults upon or restraints on an individual's person may, since they affect his or her 'personal integrity', give rise to issues under Art. 8. *See X and Y v. The Netherlands*, 26 Mar. 1985 (No. 91), 8 E.H.R.R. 235 (reproduced in part in Section B *infra*) para. 22; *Costello-Roberts v. United Kingdom*, 25 Mar. 1993, 19 E.H.R.R. 112, para. 36. This understanding creates a significant overlap between Art. 8 and other articles of the Convention. In *Raninen v. Finland*, 16 Dec. 1997, 26 E.H.R.R. 563, discussed in Chapter 5(A) *supra*, the applicant complained of being handcuffed during an arrest. He alleged violations of Arts. 3, 5 and 8. In discussing the claim under Art. 8 the Court 'recognize[d] that...aspects of the concept [of private life] extend to situations of deprivation of liberty. Moreover, it does not exclude the possibility that there might be circumstances in which Article 8 could be regarded as affording a protection in relation to conditions during detention which do not attain the level of severity recognized by Article 3'. *Id.* at para. 63. In that case, however, the Court found the handcuffing did not have 'such adverse effects on his physical or moral integrity as to constitute an interference with the applicant's right to respect for private life'. *Id.* at para. 64.

to the apparently modest ambitions for this provision implied by the drafting process. The Convention, itself, may be seen as an enumeration of *particular* ways in which free choice and action are protected, and the supplementing of that specification with such a broad presumption of liberty threatens to make the other rights redundant. One of the most vexing problems confronting the Court is finding ways (short of justification under Article 8(2)), of elaborating some special, narrowing characteristics of the right to respect for private life.[6] As the materials in this chapter illustrate, claims under Article 8 present particularly acute questions of interpretation and definition.

B. FAMILY LIFE

1. JOHNSTON V. IRELAND

Judgment of 18 December 1986
9 E.H.R.R. 203

...

10. The first applicant is Roy H. W. Johnston, who was born in 1930 and is a scientific research and development manager. He resides at Rathmines, Dublin, with the second applicant, Janice Williams-Johnston, who was born in 1938; she is a school-teacher by profession and used to work as director of a play-group in Dublin, but has been unemployed since 1985. The third applicant is their daughter Nessa Doreen Williams-Johnston, who was born in 1978.

11. The first applicant married a Miss M. in 1952 in a Church of Ireland ceremony. Three children were born of this marriage, in 1956, 1959 and 1965.

In 1965, it became clear to both parties that the marriage had irretrievably broken down and they decided to live separately at different levels in the family house. Several years later both of them, with the other's knowledge and consent, formed relationships and began to live with third parties. By mutual agreement, the two couples resided in self-contained flats in the house until 1976, when Roy Johnston's wife moved elsewhere.

In 1978, the second applicant, with whom Roy Johnston had been living since 1971, gave birth to Nessa. He consented to his name being included in the Register of Births as the father....

---

[6] Defining private life is even more problematic when taking into account the Court's doctrine that Art. 8 also imposes 'positive obligations on the state to facilitate the development of family and private life'. *See* Section B *infra*. In response to the potentially limitless reach of such positive obligations the Court has held that they do not require fostering 'interpersonal relations of such broad and indeterminate scope that there can be no conceivable direct link between the measure the State was urged to take...and the applicants' private life'. *Botta v. Italy*, 24 Feb. 1998, 26 E.H.R.R. 24, para. 35.

[The Court cited various provisions of the Irish Constitution including s. 41.3.2, ('No law shall be enacted providing for the grant of a dissolution of marriage') and s. 41.3.3 prohibiting remarriage by Irish residents who were single by virtue of a foreign divorce. It also noted provisions of Irish law allowing legal separation on proof of adultery, cruelty or unnatural offences. Under Irish law Williams-Johnston had no right to maintenance from Johnston. While each could make testamentary dispositions to the other, such bequests were subject to certain statutory rights of the spouse or any legitimate children. Unmarried couples also could not take advantage of certain statutory benefits and public services and could not adopt a child.]

[Under Irish law the child was deemed illegitimate. The Court canvassed the legal situation of illegitimate children and their parents. The mother of an illegitimate child was given full guardianship, but the father's rights were limited to matters of custody and access. An illegitimate child had no rights of intestate succession from the estate of the father and had such rights with respect to the estate of the mother only if she had left no legitimate issue. Taxes on inheritance were more favourable to legitimate than to illegitimate children.]

52. The Court agrees with the Commission that the ordinary meaning of the words 'right to marry' [in Article 12] is clear, in the sense that they cover the formation of marital relationships but not their dissolution. Furthermore, these words are found in a context that includes an express reference to 'national laws'; even if, as the applicants would have it, the prohibition on divorce is to be seen as a restriction on capacity to marry, the Court does not consider that, in a society adhering to the principle of monogamy, such a restriction can be regarded as injuring the substance of the right guaranteed by Article 12.

Moreover, the foregoing interpretation of Article 12 is consistent with its object and purpose as revealed by the *travaux préparatoires*. The text of Article 12 was based on that of Article 16 of the Universal Declaration of Human Rights, paragraph 1 of which reads:

> Men and women of full age, without any limitation due to race, nationality or religion, have the right to marry and to found a family. They are entitled to equal rights as to marriage, during marriage and at its dissolution.

In explaining to the Consultative Assembly why the draft of the future Article 12 did not include the words found in the last sentence of the above-cited paragraph, Mr. Teitgen, Rapporteur of the Committee on Legal and Administrative Questions, said:

> In mentioning the particular Article [of the Universal Declaration], we have used only that part of the paragraph of the Article which affirms the right to marry and to found a family, but not the subsequent provisions of the Article concerning equal rights after marriage, since we only guarantee the right to marry.

In the Court's view, the *travaux préparatoires* disclose no intention to include in Article 12 any guarantee of a right to have the ties of marriage dissolved by divorce....

54. The Court thus concludes that the applicants cannot derive a right to divorce from Article 12. That provision is therefore inapplicable in the present case, either on its own or in conjunction with Article 14.

55. The principles which emerge from the Court's case law on Article 8 include the following:

(a) By guaranteeing the right to respect for family life, Article 8 presupposes the existence of a family.

(b) Article 8 applies to the 'family life' of the 'illegitimate' family as well as to that of the 'legitimate' family.

(c) Although the essential object of Article 8 is to protect the individual against arbitrary interference by the public authorities, there may in addition be positive obligations inherent in an effective 'respect' for family life....

56. In the present case, it is clear that the applicants, the first and second of whom have lived together for some fifteen years, constitute a 'family' for the purposes of Article 8. They are thus entitled to its protection, notwithstanding the fact that their relationship exists outside marriage.

The question that arises, as regards this part of the case, is whether an effective 'respect' for the applicants' family life imposes on Ireland a positive obligation to introduce measures that would permit divorce.

57. It is true that, on this question, Article 8, with its reference to the somewhat vague notion of 'respect' for family life, might appear to lend itself more readily to an evolutive interpretation than does Article 12. Nevertheless, the Convention must be read as a whole and the Court does not consider that a right to divorce, which it has found to be excluded from Article 12, can, with consistency, be derived from Article 8, a provision of more general purpose and scope. The Court is not oblivious to the plight of the first and second applicants. However, it is of the opinion that, although the protection of private or family life may sometimes necessitate means whereby spouses can be relieved from the duty to live together[7] the engagements undertaken by Ireland under Article 8 cannot be regarded as extending to an obligation on its part to introduce measures permitting the divorce and the remarriage which the applicants seek....

[The Court found no violations of Article 14 taken in conjunction with Article 8 or of Article 9.]

64. The Court thus concludes that the complaints related to the inability to divorce and re-marry are not well-founded.

65. The first and second applicants further alleged that, in violation of Article 8, there had been an interference with, or lack of respect for, their family life [in connection with matters other than the ability to divorce and remarry] on account of their status under Irish law ...

66. In the Court's view, there has been no interference by the public authorities with the family life of the first and second applicants: Ireland has done nothing to impede or prevent them from living together and continuing to do so and, indeed, they have been able to take a number of steps to regularise their situation as best they could. Accordingly, the sole question that arises for decision is whether an effective 'respect' for their family life imposes on Ireland a positive obligation to improve their status.

68. It is true that certain legislative provisions designed to support family life are not available to the first and second applicants. However, like the Commission, the Court does not

---

[7] *See Airey v. Ireland*, 9 Oct. 1979, 2 E.H.R.R. 305.

consider that it is possible to derive from Article 8 an obligation on the part of Ireland to establish for unmarried couples a status analogous to that of married couples...

71. Roy Johnston and Janice Williams-Johnston have been able to take a number of steps to integrate their daughter in the family. However, the question arises whether an effective 'respect' for family life imposes on Ireland a positive obligation to improve her legal situation.

72. Of particular relevance to this part of the case, in addition to the principles recalled above, are the following passages from the Court's case law:

> ... when the State determines in its domestic legal system the regime applicable to certain family ties such as those between an unmarried mother and her child, it must act in a manner calculated to allow those concerned to lead a normal family life. As envisaged by Article 8, respect for family life implies in particular, in the Court's view, the existence in domestic law of legal safeguards that render possible as from the moment of birth the child's integration in his family. In this connection, the State has a choice of various means, but a law that fails to satisfy this requirement violates paragraph 1 of Article 8 without there being any call to examine it under paragraph 2.[8]

> In determining whether or not a positive obligation exists, regard must be had to the fair balance that has to be struck between the general interest of the community and the interests of the individual, the search for which balance is inherent in the whole of the Convention... In striking this balance the aims mentioned in the second paragraph of Article 8 may be of a certain relevance, although this provision refers in terms only to interferences with the right protected by the first paragraph—in other words is concerned with the negative obligations flowing therefrom...[9]

74. As is recorded in the Preamble to the European Convention of 15 October 1975 on the Legal Status of Children born out of Wedlock, 'in a great number of member States [of the Council of Europe] efforts have been, or are being, made to improve the legal status of children born out of wedlock by reducing the differences between their legal status and that of children born in wedlock which are to the legal or social disadvantage of the former'. Furthermore, in Ireland itself this trend is reflected in the Status of Children Bill recently laid before Parliament.

In its consideration of this part of the present case, the Court cannot but be influenced by these developments. As it observed in its above mentioned *Marckx* judgment, 'respect' for family life, understood as including the ties between near relatives, implies an obligation for the State to act in a manner calculated to allow these ties to develop normally. And in the present case the normal development of the natural family ties between the first and second applicants and their daughter requires, in the Court's opinion, that she should be placed, legally and socially, in a position akin to that of a legitimate child.

75. Examination of the third applicant's present legal situation, seen as a whole, reveals, however, that it differs considerably from that of a legitimate child; in addition, it has not been shown that there are any means available to her or her parents to eliminate or reduce the differences. Having regard to the particular circumstances of this case and notwithstanding the wide margin of appreciation enjoyed by Ireland in this area, the absence of an appropriate

---

[8] *See Marckx v. Belgium* (discussed in Section B *infra*).
[9] *See Rees v. United Kingdom* (discussed in Section D *infra*).

legal regime reflecting the third applicant's natural family ties amounts to a failure to respect her family life.

Moreover, the close and intimate relationship between the third applicant and her parents is such that there is of necessity also a resultant failure to respect the family life of each of the latter. Contrary to the Government's suggestion, this finding does not amount, in an indirect way, to a conclusion that the first applicant should be entitled to divorce and re-marry; this is demonstrated by the fact that in Ireland itself it is proposed to improve the legal situation of illegitimate children, whilst maintaining the constitutional prohibition on divorce....

[The Court held, 16 to one, that the unavailability of divorce did not violate Article 8. It held unanimously that the other aspects of Irish law affecting the adult applicants did not violate Article 8. It held unanimously that the legal disabilities of the child-applicant violated Article 8.]

Declaration by Judge Pinheiro Farinha ...

Separate Opinion, Partly Dissenting and Partly Concurring, of Judge de Meyer ...

5. We are thus faced with a situation in which, by mutual consent and a considerable time ago, two spouses separated, regulated their own and their children's rights in an apparently satisfactory fashion and embarked on a new life, each with a new partner.

In my view, the absence of any possibility of seeking, in such circumstances, the civil dissolution of the marriage constitutes, first and of itself, a violation, as regards each of the spouses, of the rights guaranteed in Article 8, 9 and 12 of the Convention. Secondly, in that it perforce means that neither spouse can re-marry in a civil ceremony so long as his wife or husband is alive, it constitutes a violation of the same rights as regards each of the spouses and each of the new partners....

On more than one occasion, the Court has pointed out that there can be no such society without pluralism, tolerance and broadmindedness: these are hallmarks of a democratic society.

In a society grounded on principles of this kind, it seems to me excessive to impose, in an inflexible and absolute manner, a rule that marriage is indissoluble, without even allowing consideration to be given to the possibility of exceptions in cases of the present kind.

For so draconian a system to be legitimate, it does not suffice that it corresponds to the desire or will of a substantial majority of the population: the Court has also stated that 'although individual interests must on occasion be subordinated to those of a group, democracy does not simply mean that the views of a majority must always prevail: a balance must be achieved which ensures the fair and proper treatment of minorities and avoids any abuse of a dominant position'....

6. The foregoing considerations do not imply recognition of a right to divorce or that such a right, to the extent that it exists, can be classified as a fundamental right.

They simply mean that the complete exclusion of any possibility of seeking the civil dissolution of a marriage is not compatible with the right to respect for private and family life, with the right to freedom of conscience and religion and with the right to marry and to found a family....

However, it seems to me that it is not sufficient to say that the third applicant should be placed 'in a position akin to that of a legitimate child': in my view, we ought to have stated more clearly and more simply that the legal situation of a child born out of wedlock must be identical to that of a child of a married couple and that, by the same token, there cannot be, as regards relations with or concerning a child, any difference between the legal situation of his

parents and of their families that depends on whether he was the child of a married couple or
a child born out of wedlock....

2. THE DEFINITION OF THE FAMILY

In *Johnston,* the Court held that the three applicants together constituted a family and
were thus entitled to respect for their family life under Article 8. It did so notwithstanding that the adult applicants were not married and they had no Article 12 right to
be married. (Note that as a consequence of the latter holding the Court also found that
the adult applicants could not establish Article 8 family life *inter se.*[10]) In rejecting the
idea that a lawful marriage was an essential prerequisite to a family deserving recognition under Article 8, the Court necessarily held that Article 8 protects 'families' that
lack any kind of positive law sanction. It rejects, that is, the idea that the family itself
is a creature of rules of law.[11]

The Supreme Court of Ireland, in contrast, has limited the term 'family' in the Irish
Constitution to those relationships conforming to positive rules of law. The Court
has held that provisions providing that the state must guarantee the protection of the
family and affirming the rights of parents to control the education of their children, do
not extend to parents becoming such outside of wedlock. Both references, the Court
held, refer to:

the family which is founded on the institution of marriage and, in [this] context...marriage
means valid marriage under the law for the time being in force in the State. While it is true that
unmarried persons cohabitating together and the children of their union may often be referred
to as family and have many, if not all, of the outward appearances of a family, and may indeed
for the purpose of a particular law be regarded as such. Nevertheless, so far as [these constitutional provisions are] concerned the guarantees therein contained are confined to families
based upon marriage.[12]

The European Court in this, as in other instances, has decided that the term family must be given an 'autonomous interpretation'. In *Johnston* this was based on the
presence of a mother, father and child living together in the way families based on
marriage typically do. It is not necessary, however, for this extra-legal family to mimic
that model in every respect. In *Marckx v. Belgium*[13] it accorded the same status to an
unmarried mother, her daughter and the child's grandmother.

---

[10] The Article 12 right to marry is discussed further at Section D *infra.*
[11] *See* F. E. Olsen, 'The Myth of State Intervention in the Family', (1985) 8 *Mich. L. Rev.* 835; Note, 'Looking
for a Family Resemblance: The Unity of the Functional Approach to the Legal Definition of Family', (1992)
104 *Harv. L. Rev.* 1640.   [12] *State (Nicolaou) v. An Bord Uchtala* [1966] I.R. 567, 643.
[13] 13 June 1979, 2 E.H.R.R. 330.

Bringing the relationship of unmarried parents and children within the protection of Article 8's family life required the Court to examine the public justifications for less favourable treatment of such families under paragraph (2) of Article 8. In *Marckx*, the Court discussed the interests asserted by the state for such distinctions in connection with a claim under Article 14 of unjustifiable discrimination in the protection of Convention rights:

39. The Government, relying on the difference between the situations of the unmarried and the married mother, advance the following arguments; whilst the married mother and her husband 'mutually undertake...the obligation to feed, keep and educate their children' (Article 203 of the Civil Code), there is no certainty that the unmarried mother will be willing to bear on her own the responsibilities of motherhood; by leaving the unmarried mother the choice between recognising her child or dissociating herself from him, the law is prompted by a concern for protection of the child, for it would be dangerous to entrust him to the custody and authority of someone who has shown no inclination to care for him; many unmarried mothers do not recognise their child.

In the Court's judgment, the fact that some unmarried mothers, unlike Paula Marckx, do not wish to take care of their child cannot justify the rule of Belgian law whereby the establishment of their maternity is conditional on voluntary recognition or a court declaration. In fact, such an attitude is not a general feature of the relationship between unmarried mothers and their children; besides, this is neither claimed by the Government nor proved by the figures which they advance. As the Commission points out, it may happen that also a married mother might not wish to bring up her child, and yet as far as she is concerned, the birth alone will have created the legal bond of affiliation....

40. The Government do not deny that the present law favours the traditional family but they maintain that the law aims at ensuring that family's full development and is thereby founded on objective and reasonable grounds relating to morals and public order (ordre public).

The Court recognises that support and encouragement of the traditional family is in itself legitimate or even praiseworthy. However, in the achievement of this end recourse must not be had to measures whose object or result is, as in the present case, to prejudice the 'illegitimate' family; the members of the 'illegitimate' family enjoy the guarantees of Article 8 on an equal footing with the members of the traditional family....

The Supreme Court of Canada has extended constitutional protection to *de facto* families under section 15 of the Charter of Rights and Freedoms, mandating equal treatment before the law. In *Miron v. Trudel*[14] the Court ruled that a failure to extend statutory insurance benefits to unmarried as well as married couples violated the Charter. The plurality opinion held that discrimination based on the absence of a formal marriage was on a ground 'analogous' to those expressly listed in section 15—race, national or ethnic origin, colour, religion, sex, age or mental or physical disability.

The plurality considered that 'distinguishing between cohabiting couples on the basis of whether they are legally married or not fails to accord with current social values or realities'.[15] The dissenting justices insisted that a distinction, at least in this context,

---

[14] [1995] 2 S.C.R. 418.   [15] *Id.* paras. 152–5.

between married and unmarried couples was an appropriate means of advancing the legislative goal of fostering and protecting the institution of marriage.[16]

In *M v H*[17] the Court held invalid Ontario's distinction between opposite-sex and same-sex couples in creating obligations of spousal support. The Family Law Act included unmarried persons in its definition of 'spouse' but limited it to relationships between a man and a woman. The Supreme Court had already held that sexual orientation was an 'analogous ground' to those traits expressly listed in section 15.[18] Since, *inter alia*, the exclusion of same-sex couples implied 'that they are judged to be incapable of forming intimate relationships of economic interdependence as compared to opposite-sex couples' a *prima facie* violation of section 15 was made out.[19] The majority declined to find the distinction justifiable under section 1 of the Charter. Since the statute had already been extended to unmarried couples, the province could not rely on the special protection of marriage. The Court found unconvincing the argument that the limited scope of the statute was intentionally related to cases when economic dependence was more of a problem or that it was meant to protect children.[20] But it held that, in any event, these objectives were not rationally furthered by excluding same-sex couples.[21]

The European Court is in line with numerous constitutional courts that have invalidated laws discriminating against 'illegitimate' children.[22] In the United States such laws were common well into the twentieth century. In a series of decisions in the 1960s and 1970s, the Supreme Court held many of these statutes unconstitutional as violating the Equal Protection clause of the Fourteenth Amendment. For the most part, the Supreme Court's principal focus (unlike that of the European Court) was not on the injury done to the family. Rather, the emphasis was on the individual right of the illegitimate child and the peculiar legal disadvantages imposed on it. In one of the earliest cases, *Levy v. Louisiana*,[23] the Court held invalid a wrongful death statute which denied to illegitimate children an action based on the wrongful death of their mother:

Legitimacy or illegitimacy of birth has no relation to the nature of the wrong allegedly inflicted on the mother. These children, though illegitimate, were dependent on her, she cared for them and nurtured them; they were indeed hers in the biological and in the spiritual sense; in her death they suffered wrong in the sense that any dependent would.

We conclude that it is invidious to discriminate against them when no action, conduct, or demeanor of theirs is possibly relevant to the harm that was done the mother.

---

[16] *Id*. paras. 40–5.
[17] [1999] 2 S.C.R. 3.
[18] *See Egan v. Canada* [1995] 2 S.C.R. 513.
[19] [1999] 2 S.C.R. 3 at paras. 73–4.
[20] *Id*. at paras. 86–107.
[21] *Id*. at paras. 109–17.
[22] *See*, e.g., *Bhe v. Khayelitsha* (2005) 1 S.A. 580 (C.C.) (South Africa).
[23] 391 U.S. 68 (1968).

The judgments of the American and European Courts should be contrasted with that of the Irish Supreme Court in *O'B v. S*,[24] where the exclusion of illegitimate children from the definition of 'issue' entitled to shares in the estate of a person who died intestate, was challenged as a violation of the provision of the Irish Constitution that 'all citizens shall, as human persons, be held equal before the law'. The Court held that the intestacy provisions, while discriminatory, were justified as a proper means of fulfilling the state's responsibility under another constitutional article to protect 'the Family'. As noted, the Court emphasized that the 'family' referred to in the Constitution was the 'family based upon marriage'. The distinction in the succession law served this purpose by assuring that 'the family patrimony will be kept within the family on intestacy'. 'It can scarcely be doubted that the [challenged provision] was designed to strengthen the family as required by the Constitution and, for that purpose, to place members of a family based on marriage in a more favourable position than other persons…'.

A frequently litigated issue associated with the non-marital family concerns rights of fathers to custody, visitation, or other legal relations with their children. Historically state law has granted greater rights to the mother in such cases. The resulting inequality is of two kinds, between married and unmarried fathers and between unmarried fathers and mothers. The European Court's Grand Chamber considered such a law in *Sahin v. Germany*.[25] Under German law an unmarried mother having custody could refuse the father access to the child unless the father convinced a court such access was in the child's best interests. In contrast, the access of divorced fathers of children born during marriage was presumed proper unless the contrary was shown. The Court declined to find a violation of Article 8 holding that, in the particular case, the domestic judgment that access would be harmful in light of the tensions between the parents was justifiable. It did, however, find a violation of Article 14 in connection with Article 8 insofar as the unmarried father had to shoulder a heavier burden of proof than the divorced father. The Court held, without explanation, that the same strict approach that it used in examining discrimination based on birth out of wedlock should apply to 'a difference in the treatment of the father of a child born of a relationship where the parties were living together out of wedlock as compared with the father of a child born of a marriage relationship'. No reasons explaining the distinction were placed before the Court and there was no evidence that would justify putting a heavier burden on the applicant given the facts of the particular case.

In 1987 the House of Lords held that controlling statutes denied an unmarried father any notice of and, in fact, any right to contest placement and adoption of his children by public authorities.[26] In 2000, however, the Court of Appeal upheld a judge's exercise of discretion to join the child's unmarried father in deciding

24 [1984] I.R. 316.
25 [G.C.], 11 Oct. 2001, 36 E.H.R.R. 43. *See also Sommerfield v. Germany*, 8 July 2003.
26 *In re M & H* [1990] 1 A.C. 686.

an application for adoption that had been approved by the mother. Lord Justice Thorpe thought that the father's Convention rights 'probably [do] not greatly impact on this discretionary balance' but agreed that the judge was 'wise to take account of' them.[27]

The United States Supreme Court has held that the natural father of children born outside of marriage, who had established a parental relationship with them, had a right under the due process clause of the Fourteenth Amendment to notice and hearing before his children could be made wards of the state.[28] However, an unmarried father who had failed to establish such a relationship and had neglected to register himself on a state-maintained 'putative father registry' was not entitled to notice and hearing in connection with adoption proceedings.[29]

The Supreme Court has also held that the child born abroad of an unmarried father who was a United States national could not automatically acquire citizenship by descent, although such citizenship would be conferred if the mother were a citizen. The Court found the distinction justified by the fact that the parent–child relationship was more easily verifiable in the case of the mother and that the very event of birth gives the mother an opportunity to develop ties with the child that cannot be assured in the case of the father. Since the statute at issue bore a substantial relationship to proper government objectives it was irrelevant that, in the case at issue, the father had raised the child in the United States from the age of six.[30]

The Constitutional Court of South Africa held unconstitutional the provision of the Child Care Act which allowed an illegitimate child to be adopted with the sole consent of the mother.[31] The Court found this arrangement inconsistent with the equality provision of the Constitution. It recognized that, at least in early childhood, the 'biological relationship' between mother and child was 'very direct and not comparable to that of a father'. But, it noted, there could be circumstances where the relationship of the child with the father was as strong or stronger.[32] It also found the law to discriminate between married and unmarried fathers, noting that it was impossible to make a universally valid presumption that the latter class was uninterested or unfit.[33] The Court declined, however, to order a remedy which would require the consent of both parents in every adoption. Rather it left Parliament to craft a law which responded to the various rights relevant in different circumstances.[34]

---

[27] *Re S* [2001] 1 F.C.R. 158, [2001] 1 F.L.R. 302. *Cf. West Lothian Council v. M McG* 2002 S.C.L.R. 733 (Inner House, Second Division).

[28] *Stanley v. Illinois*, 406 U.S. 645 (1972).

[29] *Lehr v. Robertson*, 463 U.S. 248 (1983). *See also Michael H. v. Gerald D.*, 491 U.S. 110 (1989) in which the Supreme Court upheld a statute creating presumption that a child born to a married woman was the child of her husband against a claim that the presumption violated the rights of the natural father.

[30] *Nguyen and Boulais v. INS*, 533 U.S. 53 (2001).

[31] *Fraser v. The Children's Court* [1997] 2 S.A.L.R. 261.

[32] *Id.* at para. 25.

[33] *Id.* at para. 26.

[34] *Id.* at paras. 27–30. The transitional South African Constitution s. 98(5) expressly granted the Court authority to order such a remedy. *See also* Constitution of the Republic of South Africa 1996, s. 172(1)(b).

Having abandoned exclusively legal criteria for identifying the family life protected in Article 8, the European Court has substituted an amalgam of legal, social and biological criteria for evaluating the existence of a family relationship. With respect to the social family, the Court has looked for arrangements that sufficiently resemble the traditional family even when missing both legal and biological connections.

In *X, Y and Z v. United Kingdom*[35] the Court held that a family relationship existed between a female-to-male transsexual and the child (conceived by artificial insemination) of the woman with whom he had lived in a stable relationship for more than 10 years. The Court noted that the couple had applied jointly for the fertilization treatment.

If these kinds of social relationships are the core of the Convention's 'family', it is possible to go further and raise doubts about the *sufficiency* of a mere legal connection. Nevertheless, some opinions of the Court suggest that legal relations automatically create the requisite family ties. In one case, speaking of a child who had been born days after the marriage between the applicant and the child's mother had been dissolved, the Court stated that 'a child born of a [lawful] union is *ipso jure* part of that relationship' from the moment of birth.[36] The importance of legal relations was also confirmed when the Court held that discrimination against adopted children in matters of inheritance violated Article 14 in connection with Article 8.[37] In both of these cases, however, the legal qualification was in addition to a demonstrated established personal relationship. In a 2004 judgment, the Court held that Article 8 was engaged in connection with the relationships between couples and children whose adoption had been approved by law, even though there had been no significant contact between the adoptive parents and children. Public officials, the applicants charged, had not done enough to assist in the transfer of custody in light of resistance by the staff at the institution where the children were resident. The applicants in this case 'had always viewed themselves as the girls' parents and behaved as such toward them through the only means open to them …'. In the event, the Court refused to find a violation of Article 8, but this was based only on its evaluation of the interests of the children, interests that had, to some extent been developed as a result of the delay in consummating the adoptions.[38]

In a recent case, the House of Lords interpreted the Human Fertilisation and Embryology Act 1990 to preclude parental rights for an unmarried man who had completed a 'male partner's acknowledgment' form when a woman began the process of in vitro fertilization with sperm from a third person donor. In so doing he stated that the couple were undergoing treatment together and that he intended to become the legal father of any resulting child. By the time a successful fertilization and implantation

---

[35] 22 Apr. 1997, 24 E.H.R.R. 143.

[36] *Berrehab v. The Netherlands*, 21 June 1988, 11 E.H.R.R. 322, para. 21. *See also Abdulaziz, Cabales & Balkandali v. United Kingdom*, 28 May 1985, 7 E.H.R.R. 471 (legal marriage, even without cohabitation, engages Article 8).

[37] *Pla v. Andorra*, 13 July 2004, 42 E.H.R.R. 25.

[38] *Pini v. Romania*, 22 June 2004, 40 E.H.R.R. 13.

had occurred some months later, the relationship between the man and woman had ended. The relevant part of the Act provided that, in the case of an unmarried woman, when 'treatment services were provided for her and a man together...that man shall be treated as the father of the child'. The judgment of Lord Walker of Gestingthorpe interpreted the statute to preclude any construction that would have made parental status turn solely on a formal act. The 'very significant legal relationship of parenthood should not be based on a fiction...'. The male complainant in that case, moreover, had no rights under Article 8 of the Convention. His claim to 'family life with [the child] (when he is neither her social father nor her biological father) really assumes that which has to be established'.[39]

An even more attenuated relationship supported the claim in *Keegan v. Ireland*.[40] The Court held the adoption of an infant without the knowledge or consent of the natural father was a violation of Article 8. The applicant father had seen the baby the day after it was born but had not been allowed to see it thereafter. Article 8 applied even though the parents were not married and the father had established no personal relationship with the child. The European Court noted that de facto as well as marriage-based relationships could be family life under Article 8, citing *Johnston*. It concluded that the parents' relationship before the birth had all the characteristics of a family. Any child born of this non-marital relationship was 'part of the "family" unit from the moment of its birth and by the very fact of it'. The fact that the family relationship had broken down shortly before the birth 'does not alter this conclusion any more than it would for a couple who were lawfully married in a similar situation'.[41]

A mere biological relationship, however, is insufficient to raise an Article 8 issue. A natural father who had not 'seen the child or formed any emotional bond with her' had not alleged a sufficient basis to make admissible his claim for recognition of paternity under Article 8.[42] In *Haas v. The Netherlands*, the applicant had claimed the estate of the man he alleged to be his biological father. The decedent, however, had never lived with the applicant or with the applicant's mother. Their contacts had been only sporadic. The Court decided that the applicant was not seeking to establish his paternity 'in order to provide him with the emotional security of knowing that he was part of a family'. A claim of inheritance rights without more raised no Article 8 issue.[43]

---

[39] *In re R* [2005] U.K.H.L. 33, [2005] 2 A.C. 621, paras. 42, 44.

[40] 26 May 1994, 18 E.H.R.R. 342.

[41] *Id.* para. 45. In a later case the Court avoided the question of whether family life existed between a natural child and a parent who had given the child up for adoption and had no contact for 30 years by dealing with the issue as one involving the child's 'private life'. *Odièvre v. France*, 13 Feb. 2003, 38 E.H.R.R. 43, para. 28. *See also Yousef v. The Netherlands*, 5 Feb. 2002, 36 E.H.R.R. 20 and *Lebbink v. The Netherlands*, 1 June 2004, 40 E.H.R.R. 18. In the latter case the father-applicant had never co-habited with the mother but the child had been born of a 'genuine relationship' of about three years duration. During the child's first seven months the applicant had made irregular visits, had changed the baby's nappy a few times, and had babysat 'once or twice'. The Court found this contact enough to engage Article 8.

[42] *Nylund v. Finland*, 29 June 1999, (admissibility decision). The Chamber stated that these facts distinguished the case from *Keegan* suggesting that the Court attached significance to the single visit between the applicant and infant in the latter case.

[43] 1 Jan. 2004, 39 E.H.R.R. 41, paras. 42–3.

The European Court further developed its understanding of the factors relevant to the creation of family life in *Kroon v. The Netherlands*[44] in which the competing interests associated with recognition of legal, biological and social families were brought into especially sharp focus. The applicants were a biological mother, father and child. The child had been born while the mother was married to another man from whom she was later divorced. The father and mother never lived together although they had three more children. Under Dutch law a child born to a married woman was presumed to be the issue of her husband. The mother was not permitted to rebut that presumption. The applicant mother and father had been refused in their request to alter the birth records to allow the father to recognize the child. The government disputed the claim that the applicants, who lived in separate households, had a 'family life'. The Court held Article 8 applicable.

Although, as a rule, living together may be a requirement for such a relationship, exceptionally other factors may also serve to demonstrate that a relationship has sufficient constancy to create de facto 'family ties': such is the case here, as since 1983, four children have been born [to the applicants].[45]

In dissent Judge Misful Bonnici argued:

In my opinion 'family life' necessarily implies 'living together as a family'. The exception to this refers to circumstances related to necessity, i.e. separation brought about by reasons of work, illness or other necessities of the family itself.... But, equally clearly this does not apply when the separation is completely voluntary. When it is voluntary then, clearly, the member or members of the family who do so have opted against family life, against living together as a family. And since these are the circumstances of the instant case, where the first two applicants have voluntarily opted not to have a 'family life', I cannot understand how they can call upon Netherlands law to respect something which they have wilfully opted against. The artificiality of this approach is in strident contradiction with the natural value of family life which the Convention guarantees.[46]

The Court held that the Netherlands had failed to respect the family life so recognized. It declared that such respect 'requires that biological and social realities prevail over a legal presumption which, as in the present case, flies in the face of both established fact and the wishes of those concerned without actually benefitting anyone'.[47]

The United States Supreme Court has held that the father of a child born to a woman married to another man may be denied parental rights. In *Michael H. v. Gerald D*,[48] it declared constitutional a state statute creating a presumption similar to that in *Kroon*. The Court determined that, although the father had established a continuing parental relationship with the child, his interest in being recognized as a parent did not amount to a 'fundamental right' so as to require strict protection under the Fourteenth

---

44 27 Oct. 1994, 19 E.H.R.R. 263.
45 *Id.* at para. 30.
46 *Id.* (dissenting opinion).
47 *Id.* para. 40.
48 491 U.S. 110 (1989).

Amendment. Justice Scalia noted that, traditionally, the father of the child of a woman married to another man had not been recognized as part of 'a protected family unit under the historic practices of our society'.[49]

The European Court has refused to treat the relationship of same-sex domestic partners to be 'family life'. In *Mato Estevez v. Spain* a Chamber found inadmissible an application based on the denial to same-sex partners of survivors' benefits available to surviving 'spouses'. The Court, following an earlier Commission decision, found this did not raise an issue under Article 14 in connection with Article 8 rights because it was not a matter within the ambit of 'family life'. It took note particularly of the fact that there was no common approach in European states towards legal 'recognition of stable de facto partnerships between homosexuals'.[50] The Court did consider the disadvantages of such couples, however, under the rubrics of 'private life' and protection of the 'home'.[51]

In *Marckx*, the Court also found a violation of Article 8 with respect to the child's grandmother whose legal relations were affected by the child's status as illegitimate. This raises yet another question as to the definition of the 'family' whose life is protected by Article 8. Near relatives, such as a grandmother, the Court stated, 'may play a considerable part in family life'.[52] Subsequently, however, it found Article 8 was not engaged by an expulsion removing a daughter from proximity to her elderly parents, 'adults who did not belong to the core family and who [had] not been shown to be dependent on the applicants' family life'. A dissenting opinion contested the limitation, noting the 'sociological and human aspects of contemporary European families...."Family life" was plainly inconceivable for [the applicants] if they were denied the possibility of looking after these relatives'.[53]

Decisions of the United States Supreme Court have defined a sphere of family autonomy which is protected from interference under the due process clauses of the Fifth and Fourteenth Amendments. It also has determined that the grandparent–grandchild relationship is protected. In *Moore v. East Cleveland*,[54] the Supreme Court held invalid a zoning ordinance which had the effect of preventing a grandchild from sharing a single family dwelling with his grandmother. The plurality noted that the tradition 'of uncles, aunts, cousins, and especially grandparents sharing a household along with parents and children has roots equally venerable and equally deserving of constitutional recognition'.[55] The U.S. Supreme Court has also held, however, that a state statute authorizing 'any person' to petition for visitation rights with a child was an unconstitutional interference with the privacy rights of

---

[49] *Id.* at 124.

[50] 10 May 2001.

[51] *See* Sections B(4) and C *supra*; *Karner v. Austria*, 24 July 2003, 38 E.H.R.R. 24.

[52] *Id.* at para. 55. *See also Bronda v. Italy*, 9 June 1998, 33 E.H.R.R. 4 (right of grandparents to contest public care order).

[53] *Slivenko v. Latvia*, 9 Oct. 2003, 39 E.H.R.R. 24, para. 97 and dissenting opinion of Judge Kovler.

[54] 431 U.S. 494 (1977).

[55] A survey of the European Court's treatment of various family relationships is found in J. Liddy, 'The Concept of Family Life Under the ECHR', [1998] *European Human Rights Law Review* 15.

the custodial parent, even in the case of a petition brought by the child's grandparents. It made clear, however, that it made no judgment on the extent to which a more narrowly drafted statute might be valid.[56] In a 2003 judgment by O'Sullivan J the High Court of Ireland, interpreting an immigration statute, decided that the term 'family' in the statute and in the Constitution did not include grandparents. The judge dismissed the relevance of the Strasbourg Court's judgment in *Marckx* on the ground that the European Convention on Human Rights was not part of domestic law.[57] (The Convention was incorporated into Irish law in the European Convention on Human Rights Act, 2003. See also Chapter 14(C), *infra*.)

3. POSITIVE OBLIGATIONS

A. X AND Y V. THE NETHERLANDS

Judgment of 26 March 1985
8 E.H.R.R. 235

7. Mr. X and his daughter Y were born in 1929 and on 13 December 1961 respectively. The daughter, who is mentally handicapped, had been living since 1970 in a privately-run home for mentally handicapped children.

8. During the night of 14 to 15 December 1977, Miss Y was woken up by a certain Mr. B, the son-in-law of the directress; he lived with his wife on the premises of the institution although he was not employed there. Mr. B forced the girl to follow him to his room, to undress and to have sexual intercourse with him.

This incident, which occurred on the day after Miss Y's sixteenth birthday, had traumatic consequences for her, causing her major mental disturbance.

9. On 16 December 1977, Mr. X went to the local police station to file a complaint and to ask for criminal proceedings to be instituted.

The police officer said that since Mr. X considered his daughter unable to sign the complaint because of her mental condition, he could do so himself....

10. ... The officer subsequently informed the public prosecutor's office that in the light of the father's statement and of his own observations concerning the girl's mental condition, she did not seem to him capable of filing a complaint herself. According to the headmaster of the school she was attending and another teacher there, she was unable to express her wishes concerning the institution of proceedings....

[Mr. X appealed the public prosecutor's decision not to institute criminal proceedings against Mr. B to the Arnhem Court of Appeal.]

12. ...

---

[56] *Troxel v. Granville*, 530 U.S. 57 (2000).
[57] *Calderas v. Minister for Justice* [2003] 74 J.R. (Transcript).

The Court of Appeal dismissed the appeal on 12 July 1979. In fact, it considered it doubtful whether a charge of rape (Art. 242 of Criminal Code) could be proved. As for Article 248ter, [making criminal the inducement of indecent acts from a minor by gift, promise, deceit or abuse of dominant position] it would have been applicable in the instant case, but only if the victim herself had taken action. [Under Art. 64(1) of the Criminal code a legal representative could lodge the complaint only if the victim were under sixteen years old or under legal guardianship. Guardianship, however, was available only for persons of twenty-one or older.] In the Court of Appeal's view, the father's complaint could not be regarded as a substitute for the complaint which the girl, being over the age of sixteen, should have lodged herself, although the police had regarded her as incapable of doing so; since in the instant case no one was legally empowered to file a complaint, there was on this point a gap in the law, but it could not be filled by means of a broad interpretation to the detriment of Mr. B....

17. At the hearings, counsel for the Government informed the Court that the Ministry of Justice had prepared a Bill modifying the provisions of the Criminal Code that related to sexual offences. Under the Bill, it would be an offence to make sexual advances to a mentally handicapped person....

22. There was no dispute as to the applicability of Article 8: the facts underlying the application to the Commission concern a matter of 'private life', a concept which covers the physical and moral integrity of the person, including his or her sexual life.

23. The Court recalls that although the object of Article 8 is essentially that of protecting the individual against arbitrary interference by the public authorities, it does not merely compel the State to abstain from such interference: in addition to this primarily negative undertaking, there may be positive obligations inherent in an effective respect for private or family life, these obligations may involve the adoption of measures designed to secure respect for private life even in the sphere of the relations of individuals between themselves.

24. The applicants argued that for a young girl like Miss Y, the requisite degree of protection against the wrongdoing in question would have been provided only by means of the criminal law. In the Government's view, the Convention left it to each State to decide upon the means to be utilised and did not prevent it from opting for civil-law provisions.

The Court, which on this point agrees in substance with the opinion of the Commission, observes that the choice of the means calculated to secure compliance with Article 8 in the sphere of the relations of individuals between themselves is in principle a matter that falls within the Contracting States' margin of appreciation. In this connection, there are different ways of ensuring 'respect for private life' and the nature of private life that is at issue. Recourse to the criminal law is not necessarily the only answer.

25. The Government cited the difficulty encountered by the legislature in laying down criminal-law provisions calculated to afford the best possible protection of the physical integrity of the mentally handicapped: to go too far in this direction might lead to unacceptable paternalism and occasion an inadmissible interference by the State with the individual's right to respect for his or her sexual life.

The Government stated that under Article 1401 of the Civil Code, taken together with Article 1407, it would have been possible to bring before or file with the Netherlands courts, on behalf of Miss Y:

— an action for damages against Mr. B for pecuniary or non-pecuniary damage;

— an application for an injunction against Mr. B, to prevent repetition of the offence;

— a similar action or application against the directress of the children's home.

The applicants considered that these civil-law remedies were unsuitable. They submitted that, amongst other things, the absence of any criminal investigation made it harder to furnish evidence on the four matters that had to be established under Article 1401, namely a wrongful act, fault, damage and a causal link between the act and the damage. Furthermore, such proceedings were lengthy and involved difficulties of an emotional nature for the victim, since he or she had to play an active part therein...

27. The Court finds that the protection afforded by the civil law in the case of wrongdoing of the kind inflicted on Miss Y is insufficient. This is a case where fundamental values and essential aspects of private life are at stake. *Effective deterrence is indispensable* in this area and it can be achieved only by criminal-law provisions; indeed, it is by such provisions that the matter is normally regulated.

Moreover, as was pointed out by the Commission, this is in fact an area in which the Netherlands has generally opted for a system of protection based on the criminal law. The only gap, so far as the Commission and the Court have been made aware, is as regards persons in the situation of Miss Y; in such cases, this system meets a procedural obstacle which the Dutch legislature had apparently not foreseen....

29. Two provisions of the Criminal Code are relevant to the present case, namely Article 248ter and Article 239(2).

Article 248ter requires a complaint by the actual victim before criminal proceedings can be instituted against someone who has contravened this provision. The Arnhem Court of Appeal held that, in the case of an individual like Miss Y, the legal representative could not act on the victim's behalf for this purpose. The Court of Appeal did not feel able to fill this gap in the law by means of a broad interpretation to the detriment of Mr. B. It is in no way the task of the European Court of Human Rights to take the place of the competent national courts in the interpretation of domestic law, it regards it as established that in the case in question criminal proceedings could not be instituted on the basis of Article 248ter.

As for Article 239(2) [making criminal indecent acts while another person 'is present against his will', and which had been interpreted by Dutch courts to prohibit sexual advances to mentally handicapped persons], this is apparently designed to penalise indecent exposure and not indecent assault and was not clearly applicable to the present case. Indeed, no one, even the public prosecutor's office, seems to have considered utilising this provision at the time, or even referring to it at the outset of the Strasbourg proceedings.

30. Thus, neither Article 248 nor Article 239(2) of the Criminal Code provided Miss Y with practical and effective protection. It must therefore be concluded, taking account of the nature of the wrongdoing in question, that she was the victim of a violation of Article 8 of the Convention.

[The Court held unanimously that there was a violation of Article 8.]

B. THE REACH OF POSITIVE OBLIGATIONS

Notice that the violation of Article 8 in the principal case is not a result of something the state did. It is rather a consequence of what it did not do. Many of the Convention's rights are presented in similar form: The first paragraph declares the right; the second proscribes certain actions that 'interfere' with or restrict that right except in the specified circumstances. The European Court has read the declaratory first paragraphs as imposing 'positive obligations' to provide the minimum preconditions for the exercise of these rights. So, in *Johnston v. Ireland* the Court found that the state was obliged to provide a legal environment that would allow family life to develop normally. The inference of positive obligations has turned out to be of immense significance in defining the influence of Convention rights.

Many of the cases in which the Court has been asked to find that a state violated Article 8 by failing to discharge a positive obligation have, like the principal case, dealt with some claim of a defect in existing law. So, in *X & Y*, the Netherlands' violation consisted of its failure to allow criminal prosecution of people in the situation of Y's attacker.

In a subsequent case the Court examined the adequacy of a criminal rape law in protecting private life. The Bulgarian statute had been consistently interpreted to preclude prosecution unless it could be shown that the victim had offered active physical resistance. The Court surveyed the gradual disappearance of this element in other European jurisdictions. It held that such a requirement 'risks leaving certain types of rapes unpunished thus jeopardising the effective protection of the individual's sexual autonomy'. The positive obligations of Articles 3 and 8 required prosecution of 'any non-consensual sexual act'.[58]

In *X & Y* the availability of civil action by the victim was found to be insufficient to satisfy the positive obligation since the Court concluded that only criminal law provided effective deterrence. In *Cavelli and Ciglio and Another v. Italy*, however, the Court held that the positive obligation under Article 2 did not require a criminal penalty for the negligent but unintentional causing of death by a doctor. In this context, the availability of a civil remedy was adequate.[59]

Apart from the adequacy of the law in place, the European Court has insisted that such law be effectively enforced. It is necessary to have in place 'effective criminal-law provisions to deter the commission of offences against the person backed up by law-enforcement machinery for the prevention, suppression and sanctioning of breaches of such provisions'.[60] It considered the nature of such an extended duty in *Osman v. United Kingdom*.[61] In that case one of the applicants, a 15-year-old, had been wounded and his father had been shot and killed by a former teacher. The applicants claimed that, over a number of months, the police had been given information which should

[58] *MC v. Bulgaria*, 4 Dec. 2003, 40 E.H.R.R. 20, paras. 153–66.

[59] [G.C.], 17 Jan. 2002. *See also Stubbings and Others v. The United Kingdom*, 22 Oct. 1996, 23 E.H.R.R. 213, para. 64 (holding that a statute of limitations allowing six years after a victim's 18th birthday for civil actions based on child abuse did not fail the state's positive obligation in light of the presence of effective criminal prosecution).

[60] *Osman v. United Kingdom*, 28 Oct. 1998, 29 E.H.R.R. 245, para. 115.

[61] *Id.*

have made clear the danger of an assault, but they had not searched the suspect's home nor arrested him. The Court agreed that there was:

in certain well-defined circumstances a positive obligation on the authorities to take preventive operational measures to protect an individual whose life is at risk from the criminal acts of another individual ...

For the Court, and bearing in mind the difficulties involved in policing modern societies, the unpredictability of human conduct and the operational choices which must be made in terms of priorities and resources, such an obligation must be interpreted in a way which does not impose an impossible or disproportionate burden on the authorities. Accordingly, not every claimed risk to life can entail for the authorities a Convention requirement to take operational measures to prevent that risk from materializing. Another relevant consideration is the need to ensure that the police exercise their powers to control and prevent crime in a manner which fully respects the due process and other guarantees which legitimately place restraints on the scope of their action to investigate crime and bring offenders to justice, including the guarantees contained in Articles 5 and 8 of the Convention.

In the opinion of the Court where there is an allegation that the authorities have violated their positive obligation to protect the right to life in the context of their above-mentioned duty to prevent and suppress offences against the person, it must be established to its satisfaction that the authorities knew or ought to have known at the time of the existence of a real and immediate risk to the life of an identified individual or individuals from the criminal acts of a third party and that they failed to take measures within the scope of their powers which, judged reasonably, might have been expected to avoid that risk. The Court does not accept the Government's view that the failure to perceive the risk to life in the circumstances known at the time or to take preventive measures to avoid that risk must be tantamount to gross negligence or wilful disregard of the duty to protect life. Such a rigid standard must be considered to be incompatible with the requirements of Article 1 of the Convention and the obligations of Contracting States under that Article to secure the practical and effective protection of the rights and freedoms laid down therein, including Article 2. For the Court, and having regard to the nature of the right protected by Article 2, a right fundamental in the scheme of the Convention, it is sufficient for an applicant to show that the authorities did not do all that could be reasonably expected of them to avoid a real and immediate risk to life of which they have or ought to have knowledge. This is a question which can only be answered in the light of all the circumstances of any particular case.[62]

In the case at hand, the Court found no breach of the state's positive obligation since, given the information available to the police at the relevant times, the measures they had taken amounted to a reasonable response.[63]

The European Court has twice applied this doctrine in connection with the failure of child protection agencies to intervene in situations where they had reason to know that children were at risk of abuse. In one case, authorities had a family under observation for almost five years during which time the children suffered physical and mental deterioration, a result of inadequate nutrition and grossly unsanitary conditions. In

---

[62] *Id.* at paras. 115–16.
[63] *Id.* at para. 121.

these circumstances the Strasbourg Court found there was 'no doubt as to the failure of the system' and a violation of Article 3 resulted.[64] In a later case, concerning the undetected sexual abuse of children by their mother's companion, the Court declined to find a violation of the positive obligations since the evidence available to the local authority was insufficient to alert it to the risks. It did, however, find a violation of Article 13 insofar as there were inadequate means available to determine if the agency was fulfilling its obligation.[65]

Partly as a result of these decisions, the House of Lords has modified the law whereby health and child welfare agencies were deemed to have an absolute immunity from claims of breach of duty causing injury to children.[66] It has, moreover, continued to refuse to recognize a duty of care on the part of child welfare officials to refrain from acting on mistaken accusations of parental abuse, reasoning that such a duty might inhibit quick action in cases of suspected mistreatment.[67]

The Constitutional Court of South Africa has rejected any categorical common law immunity for law enforcement officials against civil or criminal claims that they failed to take reasonable actions to forestall criminal activity. That court expressly adopted the reasoning of the European Court in the *Osman* judgment.[68] The United States Supreme Court, on the other hand, has held that the Fourteenth Amendment's requirement that states not deprive individuals of 'due process' did not include an obligation to take affirmative measures to prevent abuse of children within a family.[69]

The European Court has occasionally upheld claims that a state has a positive obligation to take actions that go beyond changing its law. It has held that the state's duty to provide opportunities for individuals to develop family and private life and to enjoy their homes, includes an obligation to take action to deal with severe environmental pollution affecting the applicants' homes. It has found a state in breach for its failure to notify affected residents of the risks associated with the operation of a fertilizer plant, emitting toxic substances and inflammable gases.[70] In contrast, in an earlier case, the Court rejected a claim that the United Kingdom was obliged to regulate more strictly the noise level at Heathrow Airport. While the Court agreed, against the argument of the government, that the applicant's Article 8 rights were affected, it found the government's actions sufficient given a state's wide margin of appreciation in such matters.[71]

---

[64] *Z and Others v. United Kingdom* [GC], 10 May 2001, 34 E.H.R.R. 3.

[65] *DP and JC v. United Kingdom*, 10 Oct. 2002, 36 E.H.R.R. 14.

[66] The case law development is traced in the speech of Lord Bingham of Cornhill in *D. v. East Berkshire Community Health NHS Trust and Others* [2005] U.K.H.L. 23, [2005] A.C. 373, paras. 22–30.

[67] *Id.* at paras. 85–90 (speech of Lord Nicholls of Birkenhead). Lord Bingham of Cornhill dissented in a speech drawing heavily on Strasbourg jurisprudence and cases from other jurisdictions.

[68] *Carmichele v. Minister of Safety and Security* (2001) 4 S.A. 98 (C.C.) paras. 45–9.

[69] *DeShaney v. Winnebago County Dept. of Social Services*, 489 U.S. 189 (1989).

[70] *Guerra v. Italy*, 19 Feb. 1998, 26 E.H.R.R. 357.

[71] *Powell & Raynor v. United Kingdom*, 21 Feb. 1990, 12 E.H.R.R. 355. Subsequently, the Grand Chamber reached the same result, overturning a chamber decision finding a violation. *Hatton v. United Kingdom*, [G.C.] 8 July 2003, 37 E.H.R.R. 28.

The inference of positive obligations associated with Convention rights puts the Strasbourg Court in company with an increasing number of national constitutional courts that have recognized constitutionally based 'affirmative rights', rights not *from* state interference with individual activity but *to* state provision of important social and economic support.[72] Some of these courts, like the European Court, have constructed these affirmative duties as corollaries to more traditional negative rights. The Supreme Court of India held that a state obligation to provide adequate shelter followed from a general constitutional 'right to life'.[73] Beyond this, newer constitutions typically list a set of economic and social rights. In a much noted case, *Government v. Grootboom and Others*, the South African Constitutional Court applied section 26 of the Constitution that declared a 'right to have access to adequate housing…The state must take reasonable legislative and other measures, within its available resources, to achieve the progressive realisation of this right'. The Court issued a declaratory order stating that a municipal government was not in compliance with this provision and that the government was obliged to take 'reasonable measures' to provide relief for homeless people. Some of the difficulties inherent in the enforcement of these rights are indicated by the fact that the Constitutional Court's order was substituted for a High Court order that retained jurisdiction and required the authorities to report progress on implementing an adequate programme within three months. The Constitutional Court held that the Constitution did not 'entitle the respondents to claim shelter or housing immediately upon demand'.[74]

In general, the European Court has taken a cautious approach to this kind of claim. It found no violation in a state's failure to require facilities for handicapped people at a private beach resort visited by the applicant: '[t]he right to gain access to the beach and the sea at a place distinct from his normal place of residence during his holidays concerns interpersonal relations of such broad and indeterminate shape that there can be no conceivable direct link between the measures the State was urged to take in order to make good the omissions of the private bathing establishment and the applicant's private life'.[75]

In cases dealing with positive obligations the question of justification arises in another way. That obligation is inferred from the very assertion of the rights in, say, the first paragraphs of Articles 8–11. But it is only in the second paragraphs, dealing with interferences with rights that permissible justifications are laid out.[76]

The court has summed up its approach to the question as follows:

In determining whether or not a positive obligation exists, regard must be had to the fair balance that has to be struck between the general interest of the community and the interests of the individual, the search for which balance is inherent in the whole of the Convention.

---

[72] For a recent discussion *see* M. Tushnet, 'State Action, Social Welfare Rights, and the Judicial Role: Some Comparative Observations', 3 *Chi. J. Int'l L.* 435 (2002).

[73] *M/S Shanistar Builders v. Narayan Khimalal Totame and Others* (1990) 1 S.C.C. 520.

[74] 2001 (1) SA 46, paras. 16, 95–9.

[75] *Botta v. Italy*, 24 Feb. 1998, 26 E.H.R.R. 611, para. 35.

[76] *See* C. Warbrick, 'The Structure of Article 8', *European Human Rights Law Rev.* 32, 35–6 (1998).

In striking this balance the aims mentioned in the second paragraph of Article 8 may be of certain relevance, although this provision refers in terms only to 'interferences' with the right protected by the first paragraph—in other words is concerned with the negative obligations flowing therefrom.[77]

In fact, notwithstanding the absence of an express set of justifications, the Court has held that the discretion accorded to a state in deciding how to meet its positive obligations is especially broad. In *Johnston v. Ireland* the Court concluded:

Although the essential object of Article 8 is to protect the individual against arbitrary interference by the public authorities, there may in addition be positive obligations inherent in an effective 'respect' for family life. However, especially as far as those positive obligations are concerned, the notion of 'respect' is not clear-cut: having regard to the diversity of the practices followed and the situations obtaining in the Contracting States, the notion's requirements will vary considerably from case to case. Accordingly, this is an area in which the Contracting Parties enjoy a wide margin of appreciation in determining the steps to be taken to ensure compliance with the Convention with due regard to the needs and resources of the community and of individuals.[78]

Positive obligations have been recognized in connection with most Convention rights. The Court has presumed them to be inherent in the right of assembly provided in Article 11. In *Platform 'Ärzte für das Leben' v. Austria*,[79] the applicants complained that the authorities had not provided sufficient protection for their anti-abortion demonstration which had been disrupted by other private groups. The Commission had found the Article 11 claim inadmissible because 'manifestly ill-founded', but it had found a violation of Article 13 requiring states to provide an effective remedy for violations of Convention rights. The Court, in reviewing the Article 13 determination, had to decide whether the facts revealed an 'arguable' violation of Article 11. The Court noted:

31. The Court does not have to develop a general theory of the positive obligations which may flow from the Convention, but before ruling on the arguability of the applicant association's claim it has to give an interpretation of Article 11.

32. A demonstration may annoy or give offence to persons opposed to the ideas or claims that it is seeking to promote. The participants must, however, be able to hold the demonstration without having to fear that they will be subject to physical violence by their opponents; such a fear would be liable to deter associations or other groups supporting common ideas or interests from openly expressing their opinions on highly controversial issues affecting the community. In a democracy the right to counter-demonstrate cannot extend to inhibiting the exercise of the right to demonstrate.

---

[77] *Rees v. United Kingdom*, 17 Oct. 1986, 9 E.H.R.R. 56.

[78] 18 Dec. 1986, 9 E.H.R.R. 203, at para. 55.

[79] 21 June 1988, 13 E.H.R.R. 204. In *Delisle v. Canada (Deputy Attorney General)* [1999] 2 S.C.R. 989 paras. 33–7, the Supreme Court of Canada held that s. 2(a) of the Charter of Rights and Freedoms assuring freedom of association did not oblige the state to include a particular association of public employees within its statutory scheme of collective bargaining.

Genuine, effective freedom of peaceful assembly cannot, therefore, be reduced to a mere duty on the part of the State not to interfere: a purely negative conception would not be compatible with the object and purpose of Article 11. Like Article 8, Article 11 sometimes requires positive measures to be taken, even in the sphere of relations between individuals, if need be.

In the case at issue, however, the Court found the authorities had taken 'reasonable and appropriate measures' and therefore, on these facts, they found no arguable violation of Article 11.[80]

In *Gustafsson v. Sweden*[81] a restaurant owner, who refused to enter into a collective bargaining agreement complained of a union 'blockade'. He claimed that these acts were undertaken to force him into an unwanted association, thus engaging Article 11. Although the pressure was not initiated by the state, the European Court held that 'national authorities may, in certain circumstances, be obliged to intervene in the relationships between private individuals by taking reasonable and appropriate measures to secure the effective enjoyment of the negative right to freedom of association'.[82] The Court went on to hold that the state must be accorded a wide margin of appreciation in deciding which measures to that end should be adopted and, in this case, weighing the state's interest in promoting a system of collective bargaining and the economic injuries suffered by the applicant, the state's positive obligation had not been breached.[83]

On the other hand, the Court has refused to find that Article 10's right of expression entailed a positive obligation on the part of the state to collect and disseminate useful information to citizens:

In cases concerning restrictions on freedom of the press [the Court] has on a number of occasions recognized that the public has a right to receive information as a corollary of the specific function of journalists, which is to impart information and ideas on matters of public interest...[But the] freedom to receive information referred to in paragraph 2 of Article 10 of the Convention 'basically prohibits a government from restricting a person from receiving information that others wish or may be willing to impart to him'. That freedom cannot be construed as imposing on a State...positive obligations to collect and disseminate information of its own motion.[84]

In his dissenting opinion in *Nielsen v. Denmark*,[85] Judge Carillo Salcedo suggested that Article 5 created a positive obligation on the state to protect individuals' liberty. In that case, the Court found that psychiatric commitment of a child approved by his

---

[80] *See also Ouranio Toxo and Others v. Greece*, 20 Oct. 2005 where the Court found the state had not taken adequate measures to protect the headquarters of a political party from private attack.

[81] 25 Apr. 1996, 22 E.H.R.R. 409.

[82] *Id.* at para. 45.

[83] *Id.* at paras. 45–53. In *Young, James & Webster v. United Kingdom*, 26 June 1981, 4 E.H.R.R. 38, the Court suggested that Art. 11 was applicable when employees had been dismissed when they failed to join a union because 'the domestic law in force at the relevant time...made lawful the treatment of which the applicants complained'. *Id.* at para. 49. *See also Sibson v. United Kingdom*, 20 Apr. 1993, 17 E.H.R.R. 193.

[84] *Guerra v. Italy, supra* n. 70 para. 53.

[85] 28 Nov. 1988, 11 E.H.R.R. 175.

mother, the custodial parent, did not violate Article 5. Judge Carillo Salcedo argued:

Like Mr. Frowein, in his partly concurring, partly dissenting opinion [in the Commission], I think that Article 5 is constructed in a very clear way. The first sentence of paragraph 1 imposes a positive obligation on States to protect the freedom of persons subject to their jurisdiction by legislation and other action, while the second sentence of paragraph 1, and sub-paragraphs (a) to (f), protect individuals against specific deprivations of liberty resulting from the action of the public authorities....

In my view, the issue is not, as the majority of the Commission thought, a child's right to oppose a decision of a parent with custody, but the absence in Danish law of adequate procedures for judicial review in connection with the committal of a child to a psychiatric hospital by the parent with custody, where, as in this case, the child in question is not mentally ill and there are disagreements concerning custody.[86]

The inference by the European Court of 'positive obligations' raises fundamental questions about the character of Convention rights. Are the substantive rights listed rights against the state only or also against private individuals? Sometimes, of course, the actions of private persons leading to the violation of Convention rights are required by law or are the result of cooperation with public officials, in which cases, the state may readily be seen to be sufficiently responsible to engage its obligations under the Convention.[87]

The recognition of positive obligations, however, raises the question of the reach of the Convention on a more basic level. To the extent the state has a positive obligation under the Convention to prevent, or at least deter and punish, individual rapists, persons attempting to break up demonstrations, or parents dealing unfairly with their children, the Convention effectively creates standards of conduct for these private individuals. There is some support for this view, as a general matter, in the text of the Convention. In Article 1 the contracting parties undertake not merely to refrain from conduct but to 'secure to everyone within their jurisdiction the rights and freedoms defined in Section 1 of this Convention'. Article 13 obliges each state to provide an effective remedy to everyone whose Convention rights have been violated. Such a remedy is to be maintained 'notwithstanding that the violation has been committed by persons acting in an official capacity'. While this latter phrase is, no doubt, meant to counter any official immunity for official violations, it may also suggest that the drafters contemplated both private and public transgressions.

The Court cited the Article 1 obligation of states to secure Convention rights in deciding to hear a case in which the underlying complaint involved the corporal punishment of a seven-year-old boy by the headmaster of his private boarding school, which received no financial support from the state. The Court held that the state responsibility of the United Kingdom was engaged in these circumstances, although it

---

[86] *Id.* (dissenting opinion of Judge Carillo Salcedo). As discussed below the Court has also effectively recognized a positive state obligation to prevent the infliction of inhuman and degrading treatment under Art. 3.

[87] *See,* e.g. *VgT Verein Gegen Tierfabriken v. Switzerland,* 28 June 2001, 34 E.H.R.R. 4, para. 47; *A v. France,* 23 Nov. 1993, 17 E.H.R.R. 462, para. 36.

concluded that no violation had, in fact, occurred.[88] In a separate opinion, four judges emphasized the fact that the United Kingdom made primary education compulsory in either a state or private school. These judges expressed the view that the state could not avoid the responsibility that it clearly would have in state schools, by allowing an alternative system for private schools. 'On the other hand', noted the judges, 'it is granted that the Convention is not applicable as such, in all respects to relations between private persons'.[89]

This reasoning was carried further in a case holding that the state's positive obligations obliged it to prohibit parental mistreatment of their children in ways which contravene the standards of Article 3. The United Kingdom was found in violation of the Convention on the complaint of a child who had been repeatedly beaten by his stepfather with a garden cane. The stepfather had been acquitted in a prosecution for assault after the jury had been instructed that a parent had the right to use 'moderate' measures to discipline a child. In the European Court's view English law did not provide adequate protection against treatment contrary to Article 3.[90] This decision evoked a strong reaction in Britain, in part, because it was seen as wrongly imposing legal standards on distinctly private conduct. The leader of the parliamentary opposition complained at 'court rulings about what people can do to their own children in their own homes on things like this. It's up to parents to decide whether they want to smack their children. They don't need a European judge to tell them whether they're allowed to do that'.[91]

The Strasbourg Court has inferred from the positive obligation associated with Convention rights a duty of domestic courts to vindicate the Convention's values in deciding cases between private litigants. In construing a will, therefore, it held that the national court was obliged to interpret a bequest so as not to discriminate against children by adoption. The Court has also found the Convention to be violated by an interpretation of a private health insurance policy that excluded coverage for gender re-assignment surgery.[92]

The constitutional laws of Canada and the United States have dealt with very similar questions concerning the possible application of constitutional rules to private conduct. In the United States, the state or government action doctrines have been applied to limit the reach of most constitutional provisions to actions that could be attributed to decisions of the state and federal governments. The distinction between constitutionally regulated public conduct and constitutionally unregulated private conduct has been referred to by the United States Supreme Court as resting on an 'essential

[88] *Costello-Roberts v. United Kingdom*, 25 Mar. 1993, 19 E.H.R.R. 112, para. 26.

[89] *Id.* (Joint partly Dissenting Opinion of Judges Ryssdal, Thór Vilhjálmsson, Matscher and Wildhaber).

[90] *A v. United Kingdom*, 23 Sept. 1998, 27 E.H.R.R. 611, paras. 9–10, 24. Neither the applicability of the Convention nor the finding of a violation was contested by the United Kingdom. *Id.* at para. 18.

[91] T. Shaw & C. Randall, 'Government Defends Right of Parents to Smack', *The Daily Telegraph*, 24 Sept. 1998, 1.

[92] *Pla Puncernau v. Andorra*, 13 July 2004, 42 E.H.R.R. 25 (will); *Van Kück v. Germany*, 12 June 2003, 37 E.H.R.R. 51 (insurance policy). On the significance of such cases *see* R. Kay, 'The European Convention on Human Rights and the Control of Private Law', (2005) *European Human Rights Law Review* 466.

dichotomy'.[93] It has been justified as necessary for marking out an area of flexibility and discretion as to the proper extent and character of legislation governing private conduct. A necessary extension of this idea is that there is no constitutional duty on the government to assure that private conduct conforms to a constitutional norm. The purpose of the Constitution, the Court has suggested, was 'to protect people from the state, not to ensure that the state protected them from each other. The Framers were content to leave the extent of governmental obligation in the latter area to the democratic political process'.[94]

Similarly, in Canada, the Supreme Court has affirmed the idea that the Charter of Rights and Freedoms is, in general, a restraint only on governments and legislatures, and not on private individuals. In *RWDSU v. Dolphin Delivery Ltd.*, the Court held that the securing of an injunction by a private employer against secondary picketers on a common law claim of inducing a breach of contract did not implicate the freedom of expression protected by the Charter.[95] The contrary position:

would be tantamount to setting up an alternative tort system. In the area of private discrimination, an entirely new system of civil liability in competition with the dispute mechanisms tested by human rights legislation would result.[96]

The Court emphasized this distinction in *Hill v. Church of Scientology*, in which it held that a defamation action did not trigger the protections of the Charter even when the plaintiff was a Crown Attorney who was reacting to charges of misconduct in the exercise of his public duty.[97]

Section 39(2) of the South African Constitution of 1996 requires 'every court, tribunal or forum', 'when interpreting any legislation, and when developing the common law or customary law', to 'promote the spirit, purport and objects of the Bill of Rights'. On the basis of that provision the Court held that police and prosecutors had to be under some kind of duty to provide protection to potential victims of violent crime, citing constitutional rights to life and security of the person.[98] In elaborating the duty to develop the common law consistently with the values of the Bill of Rights, the Court relied on and adopted a well established doctrine developed by the German Constitutional Court. That Court has held that the Basic Law's specification of rights creates an 'objective ordering of values' that permeates the legal system as a whole. Thus, while the constitutional rules do not directly restrain private behaviour they

---

[93] *Jackson v. Metropolitan Edison Co.*, 419 U.S. 345, 349 (1974).

[94] *DeShaney v. Winnebago County Dept. of Social Services*, 489 U.S. 189, 197 (1989).

[95] [1986] 2 S.C.R. 573.

[96] *Id.* at 597, quoting Anne McLellan and Bruce P. Elman, 'To Whom Does the Charter Apply? Some Recent Cases on s. 32', (1986) 2 *Alta. L. Rev.* 361, 367.

[97] [1995] 2 S.C.R. 1130, paras. 72–9. The Court did hold, however, that the common law of defamation was to be applied with regard to the values of free expression protected in the Charter. *Id.* at para. 95. *See also Dagenais v. Canadian Broadcasting Corp.* [1994] 3 S.C.R. 835, at paras. 67–79 (applying Charter values to the exercise of discretion by judges in issuing publication bans).

[98] *Carmichele v. Minister of Safety and Security* (2001) 4 S.A. 98 (C.C.), paras. 36–44.

have a *drittwirkung*, an indirect influence, on the interpretation and application of private law rules even in cases in which no state agency is a party.[99]

Insofar as the rules of the European Convention have been incorporated into national law, either on a constitutional or subconstitutional level, the courts of the states involved may find the Convention might also have a *drittwirkung* on the resolution of private litigation, and a number of legal systems have done just that.[100] Since the adoption of the Human Rights Act 1998, there has been a vigorous debate in the United Kingdom over the extent of this effect. It is sometimes attributed to section 2's requirement that legislation be interpreted as consistent with Convention rights, although this section is restricted to legislation. Other advocates have pointed to the Act's applicability to any acts of a 'public authority'. Section 6(3)'s definition of this term is pointedly non-exclusive, opening the possibility that certain ostensibly private entities are 'public authorities' for the purpose of the Act. The definition of public authority, moreover, explicitly includes 'courts or tribunals' suggesting to some writers that common law adjudication, even between private parties, must take into account the Convention rights.[101]

In any event, the Convention rights have plainly influenced decisions in British private common law litigation, even though the exact doctrinal basis of that influence remains obscure. Among the explanations suggested in the judgments are; 1) the requirements of section 6 of the 1998 Act; 2) the positive obligations inherent in the Convention rights themselves, as interpreted by the Strasbourg Court; 3) some inherent horizontal effect of the Act, independent of its specific provisions; and 4) the correct interpretation and development of common law rights that happen to coincide with the values associated with the Convention rights.[102]

Insofar as the European Court of Human Rights is concerned, however, the question must have a very different dimension. To the extent applications have been expressly directed at private persons, the Commission has declared them inadmissible *ratione personae*, that is by reason of a lack of personal jurisdiction.[103] But, as has been noted, the enforcement of a positive obligation on the part of the *state* to bring a certain state

---

[99] *See Lüth Case* (1958) 7 BVerfGE 198 translated and edited in Donald P. Kommers, *The Constitutional Jurisprudence of the Federal Republic of Germany* 368 (1989) and Commentary in *id.* at 376. A very valuable discussion is Peter E. Quint, 'Free Speech and Private Law in German Constitutional Theory', (1989) 48 *Md. L. Rev.* 247. On those questions in the context of United Kingdom law, *see* M. Hunt, 'The Horizontal Effect of the Human Rights Act', [1998] *Public Law* 423. And *see* Chapter 14(D).

[100] *See* Andrew Z. Drzemczewski, *European Human Rights Convention in Domestic Law*, 199–218 (1983).

[101] *See* A. Bradley, 'The Human Rights Act and Judicial Review', in *Judicial Review* (M. Supperstone, e.a. eds. 3rd edn. 2006). For an argument in favour of broad applicability of the Act to private relations see D. Beyleveld & S. Pattinson, 'Horizontal Applicability and Horizontal Effect', 118 *Law. Q. Rev.* 623 (2002).

[102] *See,* among recent authorities, *Campbell v MGN Ltd.* [2004] U.K.H.L. 22, [2004] 2 A.C. 457; *Douglas and Others v Hello! Ltd and Others (No. 3)* [2005] E.W.C.A. Civ. 595, [2006] Q.B. 125 (C.A.); *Copsey v. WWB Devon Clays Ltd.* [2005] E.W.C.A. Civ. 932, [2005] I.R.L.R. 811.

[103] *See* Drzemczewski, *supra* n. 100 at 221; P. van Dijk & G. J. H. van Hoof, *Theory and Practice of the European Convention on Human Rights* 76–8 (2nd edn. 1990). *See* generally A. Clapham, *Human Rights in the Private Sphere* (1993).

of affairs among private persons into existence will often come to the same thing, as it will require the state to deter or punish certain private actions (such as those of B in *X and Y*) that might interfere with the exercise of protected rights.

The European Court has also held that a judicial order with respect to the relative rights of contending parents in a custody dispute may represent an 'interference with the...right to respect for family life', and the fact that it came out of 'a dispute between private individuals makes no difference in this respect'.[104] In connection with a similar dispute, the Canadian Supreme Court has held that judicial orders in a custody dispute do *not* engage the limitations of the Canadian Charter of Rights and Freedoms, under the logic of the *Dolphin Delivery Case* discussed above. Such cases are essentially private in nature and there exists no state action to be impugned.[105] It should also be noted that many of the Strasbourg Court's Article 10 decisions arise in the context of libel actions that, at least in some jurisdictions, are private civil causes of action.[106]

As is the case where constitutional norms are applied against private individuals by national courts, the elaboration of the relative right of individuals and states in these circumstances raises some peculiar problems. The standard form of analysis in determining the presence or absence of violations of the Convention includes an inquiry into whether or not the infringement of the right is justified by pertinent state interests. When the effective cause of the violation is a private action, a question arises how these concerns are to be balanced. The promotion of interests such as the protection of order or of morals raises rather different questions when undertaken by individuals. Moreover, since the private actors whose interests are being considered will not normally be parties to the proceedings in Strasbourg, the Court will be faced with special problems in identifying and measuring those interests.[107]

This problem may be especially acute where the individuals whose actions are claimed to require state control, have plausible arguments that restrictions on their behaviour infringe *their* rights under the Convention.[108] When, for example, Princess Caroline of Monaco complained that the state failed to protect her private life by permitting a privately owned newspaper to publish photographs of her, the Court engaged in an elaborate analysis of the competing interests of the applicant under Article 8 and of the newspaper under Article 10.[109] An interpretation of the Convention insisting on a general observance of the values it protects by private person, as well as states,

---

[104] *Hoffmann v. Austria*, 23 June 1993, 17 E.H.R.R. 293. Compare the dissenting opinions of Judges Matscher and Mifsud Bonnici.

[105] *Young v. Young* [1993] 4 S.C.R. 391. On the general question of the existence of constitutional limits to private actions in the United States, *see* R. Kay, 'The State Action Doctrine, the Public–Private Distinction and the Independence of Constitutional Law', 10 *Constitutional Commentary* 329 (1993).

[106] *See* Chapter 6(C) *supra*.

[107] *Gustaffson v. Sweden*, 25 Apr. 1996, 22 E.H.R.R. 409 (dissenting opinion of Judge Jambrek).

[108] *See* E. Alkema, 'The Third-Party Application or 'Drittwirkung' of the European Convention on Human Rights', in *Protecting Human Rights: The European Dimension* 33 (Matscher & Petzold eds. 1985).

[109] *Von Hannover v. Germany*, 24 June 2004, 40 E.H.R.R. 1, paras. 56–80 discussed in Chapter 6(C) *supra*. *See also Douglas v. Hello! Ltd.* [2005] E.W.C.A. Civ. 695.

therefore, has the potential vastly to enlarge the field of conduct subject to an uncertain supervision by the European Court. The implications of such a development for the rule of law are far from clear. So, in examining a claim by an adopted child that she should be entitled, under French law, to learn the identity of her birth mother, the Court noted that the case involved the privacy interests of the child, the birth mother, the natural father, the adoptive parents and siblings. Given the public interest in providing homes for unwanted children, and in discouraging illegal abortions, the Court decided it was appropriate to recognize a wide margin of appreciation and found that the balance of interests struck by the state was consistent with Article 8.[110]

4. ASPECTS OF FAMILY LIFE

A. THE HOME

Article 8 protects 'the home'. It is difficult to separate rights respecting the home in a physical sense from those associated with 'family life'. A protected private space is essential to the activities which constitute family life. The Strasbourg Court has usually measured the effect of injuries to a home in connection with their impact on the life of the family who lives there. It has refused to restrict the terms to a principal residence, extending Article 8's protection to second homes if used regularly by a family.[111]

Most obviously, the intentional destruction of a dwelling house involves a presumptive violation of Article 8 and several cases involving the burning down of houses by Turkish security forces have so held.[112] The denial of access to a home caused by the Turkish occupation of Northern Cyprus was likewise held inconsistent with Article 8,[113] as was an unjustified entry into a house by the police.[114] When the rightful possessors of apartments had to wait for years for the state's judicial process to remove intruders, the Court found a failure of the positive obligations of Article 8.[115]

More difficult issues are presented when the complaint concerns state action or inaction making the use of the home more difficult or dangerous. In *Powell and Raynor v. United Kingdom*[116] the applicants claimed that noise from Heathrow

---

[110] *Odièvre v. France*, 13 Feb. 2003, 38 E.H.R.R. 43, paras. 44–9.

[111] *Demades v. Turkey*, 31 July 2003, paras. 31–4.

[112] *See Selçuk & Asker v. Turkey*, 24 Apr. 1998, 26 E.H.R.R. 595; *Mentes & Others v. Turkey*, 28 Nov. 1997, 26 E.H.R.R. 595; *Akdivar v. Turkey*, 16 Dec. 1996, 23 E.H.R.R. 143.

[113] *Cyprus v. Turkey*, 10 May 2001, 35 E.H.R.R. 30.

[114] *McLeod v. United Kingdom*, 23 Sept. 1998, 27 E.H.R.R. 493. *See also Larkos v. Cyprus*, 18 Feb. 1999, 30 E.H.R.R. 597 finding discrimination violating Article 14 in connection with Article 8 where the applicant's tenancy in a state-owned house was terminated. It was stipulated that no termination would have been allowed under Cyprus law if the property had been privately owned.

[115] *Crijetic v. Croatia*, 26 Feb. 2004; *Pibernik v. Croatia*, 4 March 2004, 40 E.H.R.R. 28.

[116] 21 Feb. 1990, 12 E.H.R.R. 355.

Airport gave rise to a violation of Article 8. The Court agreed that the 'scope for enjoying the amenities of his home have been adversely affected' and that Article 8 is a 'material provision'. It concluded, however, that in light of the public need for the airport and the efforts that had been made to limit noise, no violation of Article 8 had been made out.[117]

In a subsequent case, however, the Court found a violation when an applicant complained about the placement of a waste treatment plant near her home. For several years she and her family had been subjected to smells, noise and fumes. Although no serious health risk had resulted, the Court found the injury to the applicant's 'quality of life' was not justified by the public need for the plant and that the response of the state to the applicant's difficulties was insufficient.[118] Similarly, when Italian authorities failed to take effective measures to prevent flammable and toxic emissions from a chemical plant and also failed to inform affected residents, a violation of Article 8 was found.[119] Even the decision to allow the opening of a noisy discothèque near the applicant's home has been held a violation of Article 8.[120]

The protection of an individual's choice of home has arisen in a series of cases involving the availability of property to accommodate the transient lifestyle of gypsies or 'travellers'. In *Buckley v. United Kingdom*[121] the applicant was a gypsy who maintained a caravan on her property. The local authorities ordered its removal as being contrary to planning regulations intended to preserve the character of the countryside. The Court held Article 8 applicable over the government's objection that 'home' referred to a 'legally established' home only.[122] It went on, however, to hold that the interference was 'necessary' to public safety, economic wellbeing, protection of health and the protection of the rights of others. The environmental goals of the planning regulations had been pursued in a reasonable and balanced fashion, and had taken into account the special residential practices of the gypsy population. 'Article 8 does not reasonably go so far as to allow individuals' preference as to their place of residence to override the general interest'.[123] In light of the broad margin of appreciation properly accorded a state with respect to 'town and country planning schemes', including the exercise of discretionary judgment, the court held (three judges dissenting) that the applicant had been 'afford[ed] due respect under Article 8'.[124] On the other hand, in *Connors v. United Kingdom*, the court found that summary removal of gypsies' homes by a local authority was not justifiable, in part, because the authority was not required to show specific cause for the action.[125] Subsequently, a divided House of

---

[117] *Id.* paras. 40–5. *See also Hatton and Others v. United Kingdom* [G.C.], 8 July 2003, 37 E.H.R.R. 28.

[118] *Lopez Ostra v. Spain*, 9 Sept. 1994, 20 E.H.R.R. 277, paras. 44–58.

[119] *Guerra and Others v. Italy*, 19 Feb. 1998, 26 E.H.R.R. 357.

[120] *Moreno Gómez v. Spain*, 16 Nov. 2004, 41 E.H.R.R. 40.

[121] 25 Sept. 1996, 23 E.H.R.R. 101.

[122] *Id.* para. 54.

[123] *Id.* para. 81.

[124] *Id.* paras. 74–84. This approach was re-affirmed by the Grand Chamber in *Chapman v. United Kingdom* [G.C.], 18 Jan. 2001, 33 E.H.R.R. 18.

[125] 27 May 2004, 40 E.H.R.R. 9.

Lords narrowly interpreted the holding in *Connors*, deciding that, except in extraordinary circumstances, an ejection in conformity with otherwise proper domestic law raised no Article 8 issue for the County Court.[126]

In *Velosa Baretta v. Portugal*,[127] the Court held that the right to respect for family life does not entail a duty on the part of the state 'to enable each family to have a home for themselves alone'.[128] In that case it upheld Portugal's refusal to allow a property owner to evict a tenant in order to use the house for his own family, thus making it necessary for the applicant's family to continue living with his in-laws.

B. LANGUAGE RIGHTS

Article 8 was first construed by the Court in 1968 in the *Belgian Linguistic Case*,[129] in which French-speaking parents challenged the Belgian school system which divided the country into various regions for the purpose of determining the language of instruction. The principal ground of the challenge was incompatibility with Article 2 of the First Protocol to the Convention which guarantees, *inter alia*, respect for the 'right of parents to ensure such education and teaching in conformity with their own religious and philosophical convictions'.[130] A separate claim was made under Article 8. The Court's judgment is long and detailed, discussing the specific rules in effect in each region. It held that in one respect the system was in violation of the Convention insofar as it denied the children of French-speaking families access to French language education solely on the basis of the parents' residency. This holding was based on a discrimination forbidden by Article 14 in conjunction with Article 2 of the First Protocol. Otherwise the laws at issue were found proper. In its discussion of Article 8, the Court (in paragraph 7) stated:

> ... French-speaking children living in this region can now obtain their only education in Dutch, unless their parents have the financial resources to send them to private French-language schools. This clearly has a certain impact upon family life when parents do not have sufficient means to enrol their children in private school....
>
> Harsh though such consequences may be in individual cases, they do not involve any breach of Article 8. This provision in no way guarantees the right to be educated in the language of one's parents by the public authorities or with their aid. Furthermore, in so far as the legislation leads certain parents to separate themselves from their children, such a separation is not imposed by this legislation: it results from the choice of the parents who place their children in schools situated outside the Dutch unilingual region with the sole purpose of avoiding their being taught in Dutch, that is to say in one of Belgium's national languages.

In 1993, the Parliamentary Assembly of the Council of Europe recommended the addition to the Convention of a Protocol on the rights of minorities. Article 8 of the draft

---

[126] *Kay & Others v. London Borough of Lambeth* [2006] U.K.H.L. 10.

[127] 21 Nov. 1995.

[128] *Id.* at para. 24.

[129] 23 July 1968, 1 E.H.R.R. 252.

[130] This aspect of the case is treated at Chapter 11(B) *infra*.

Protocol provides that each member of a national minority 'shall have the right to learn his/her mother tongue at an appropriate number of schools and state educational and training establishments located in accordance with the geographic distribution of the minority'. Commentary to the Protocol made clear that the right to learn the mother language did not automatically include a right that such language be the principal medium of instruction.

Compare the *Belgian Linguistic Case* with the judgment of the United States Supreme Court in *Meyer v. Nebraska*,[131] in which a Nebraska law forbidding instruction in any language other than English, in a school, public or private, was held invalid as a deprivation of liberty without due process of law. The Court held this liberty included a right 'to marry, establish a home and bring up children'. It went on to say:

> That the State may do much, go very far, indeed, in order to improve the quality of its citizens, physically, mentally and morally, is clear, but the individual has certain fundamental rights which must be respected. The protection of the Constitution extends to all, to those who speak other languages as well as to those born with English on the tongue. Perhaps it would be highly advantageous if all had ready understanding of our ordinary speech, but this cannot be coerced by methods which conflict with the Constitution — a desirable end cannot be promoted by prohibited means.
>
> For the welfare of his Ideal Commonwealth, Plato suggested a law which should provide: 'That the wives of our guardians are to be common, and their children are to be common, and no parent is to know his own child; not any child his parent. The proper officers will take the offspring of the good parents to the pen or fold, and there they will deposit them with certain nurses who dwell in a separate quarter, but the offspring of the inferior, or of the better when they chance to be deformed, will be put away in some mysterious unknown place, as they should be'. In order to submerge the individual and develop ideal citizens, Sparta assembled the males at seven into barracks and entrusted their subsequent education and training to official guardians. Although such measures have been deliberately approved by men of great genius, their ideas touching the relation between individual and State were wholly different from those upon which our institutions rest; and it hardly will be affirmed that any legislature could impose such restrictions upon the people of a State without doing violence to both letter and spirit of the Constitution.
>
> The desire of the legislature to foster a homogeneous people with American ideals prepared readily to understand current discussions of civic matters is easy to appreciate. Unfortunate experiences during the late war and aversion toward every characteristic of truculent adversaries were certainly enough to quicken that aspiration. But the means adopted we think exceed the limitations upon the power of the State and conflict with rights assured to plaintiff in error. The interference is plain enough and no adequate reason therefore in time of peace and domestic tranquility has been shown.

Unlike many other judgments of the 'substantive due process' era, *Meyer* has continued to be cited with approval by the Supreme Court. It has taken on particular importance in light of modern cases creating a special constitutional protection for autonomous private decisions regarding matters of sex, procreation and child-rearing.

---

[131] 262 U.S. 390, 401–3 (1923) (citations omitted).

The matter of language rights is especially critical in countries like Belgium with more than one significant language group. Rather than deal with this issue through ordinary legislation or by invoking more general guarantees of equality, privacy, education and so forth, some of these countries have enacted rather specific constitutional rules on the right to use the minority language in defined situations. Since confederation, the Canadian Constitution has provided that either English or French may be used in legislative or judicial proceedings in the federal government and in the province of Quebec.[132] A similar provision was enacted for the province of Manitoba when it was created in 1870,[133] and for New Brunswick in 1982.[134] Furthermore, in the Constitution Act 1982, very specific rules were included governing minority language education rights for qualifying citizens of Canada in any province 'where numbers warrant'.[135] This provision was relied on by the Supreme Court of Canada to strike down parts of the Quebec Charter of the French Language in 1984, insofar as it denied English language education to certain children.[136] In subsequent cases, that Court has held that linguistic minority communities are entitled to some degree of management and control of the minority language instruction, as well as to a 'distinct physical setting' for the instruction. The exact character and extent of these latter rights should be determined on a 'sliding scale' relating to the number of students involved so that the larger the minority population the more independent its educational establishment must be.[137] The Court, therefore, has held that the provincial duty to supply minority language education 'where numbers warrant' could not be satisfied by providing transportation out of the locality. The Court emphasized that the constitutional rule was intended, in part, to promote the cultural development of minority language communities.[138]

C. IMMIGRATION AND DEPORTATION

In a number of cases applicants have relied on Article 8's insistence on respect for family life as the basis for contesting a decision to refuse entry to or to deport aliens, when the excluded person has family connections in the relevant state. These cases parallel those discussed in Chapter 5 concerning limits on the state's power to remove people at risk of torture or inhuman or degrading treatment. One important difference is that, unlike Article 3, infringements of Article 8 rights are permitted when necessary to protect important state interests. In such cases, therefore, a state may rely on a

---

[132] Constitution Act 1867, §133.

[133] Manitoba Act 1870, §33.

[134] Constitution Act 1982, §§16–20.

[135] Constitution Act 1982, §23.

[136] *Attorney-General of Quebec v. Quebec Association of Protestant School Boards* [1984] 2 S.C.R. 66.

[137] *See Reference Re Public Schools Act (Man.)* [1993] 1 S.C.R. 839; *Mahe v. Alberta* [1990] 1 S.C.R. 342. The impact of the European Convention on a number of aspects of language rights is summarized in A. Connelly, 'The European Convention on Human Rights and the Protection of Linguistic Minorities', 2 *Irish Journal of European Law* 277 (1993).

[138] *Arsenault-Cameron v. Gov't of Prince Edward Island* [2001] 1 S.C.R. 3.

sufficient threat to the safety or economic welfare of its citizens. In *Abdulaziz, Cabales and Balkandali v. United Kingdom*[139] the Court rejected a suggestion that the Fourth Protocol to the Convention was an exhaustive statement of the limits put on national decisions on matters concerning movement and immigration.[140] It stated, moreover, that a state's 'positive obligations' were relevant in determining whether it had acted in conformity with the Convention. It warned, however, that a wide margin of appreciation was in order in light, *inter alia*, of the fact that it is 'well-established international law' that a state has the right to control the entry of non-nationals into its territory. The resulting question then is whether, in the factual circumstances of each case, the state had 'struck a fair balance between the relevant interests'.[141] In *Abdulaziz*, the Court held that the refusal of the United Kingdom to allow the husbands of legally settled women to join them did not, itself, violate Article 8[142] but that the disparate treatment for entry of husbands and wives violated Article 14 in conjunction with Article 8.[143]

In reviewing expulsions argued to amount to interferences in an applicant's private life, the European Court has accepted the view that a *prima facie* infringement arises whenever the applicant has a substantial connection with the deporting state. But it has also assumed such actions generally pursue a legitimate interest such as the prevention of disorder or the protection of health or morals. Thus most cases come down to the question whether the interference is 'necessary in a democratic society' to serve the relevant public interest.

These cases naturally evaluate the particular interests in family life that are subject to disruption—the time that the family has been in place, the number and proximity of relatives involved, and the quality of the relationships.[144] In *Nasri v. France*[145] the applicant was deaf-mute and had lived in France almost his entire life. He had been convicted of numerous offences including participation in a gang rape. Notwithstanding the seriousness of his crimes, the Court was persuaded that the impact of deportation on the applicant's family life was so severe as to support the finding of a violation:

Above all it is necessary to take account of Mr. Nasri's handicap. He has been deaf and dumb since birth and this condition has been aggravated by an illiteracy which was the result in particular of largely inadequate schooling, even though this was to a certain extent attributable to the applicant, since on account of his behaviour he was expelled from the establishments he attended... the Court is inclined to the view that, for a person confronted with such obstacles, the family is especially important, not only in terms of providing a home, but also because it can help to prevent him from lapsing into a life of crime, all the more so in this instance inasmuch as Mr. Nasri has received no therapy adapted to his condition....

[139] 28 May 1985, 7 E.H.R.R. 471.
[140] *Id.* at para. 60.
[141] *See*, e.g., *Dalia v. France*, 19 Feb. 1998, 33 E.H.R.R. 26. The Court of Appeal has held that '[e]ssentially the same balance' is required under British immigration law. *N v. Secretary of State for the Home Dept.* [2004] E.W.C.A. Civ. 1094.
[142] *Abdilaziz, supra* n. 139, at para. 68.
[143] *Id.* at paras. 70–85. *See* Chapter 9(A) *infra*.
[144] *See*, e.g., *Beldjoudi v. France*, 26 Mar. 1992, 14 E.H.R.R. 801.
[145] 13 July 1995, 21 E.H.R.R. 458.

In view of this accumulation of special circumstances, notably his situation as a deaf and dumb person, capable of achieving a minimum psychological and social equilibrium only within his family, the majority of whose members are French nationals with no close ties to Algeria, the decision to deport the applicant, if executed, would not be proportionate to the legitimate aim pursued....[146]

In *Abdulaziz*, in deciding that Article 8 alone was not violated by the refusal to admit the spouses of the applicants, the Court took note of the fact that the family life which was claimed to be impeded by the state's policy might have been established in the resident state of the husband or in some third country. If such a possibility existed recognition of a right to remain in a convention state would be equivalent to finding a Convention right to choose the state in which the family might live.[147] Of course, when there existed serious obstacles to uniting the family in any other place, Article 8 might be more directly implicated. On this basis, the Court found a violation in *Berrehab v. The Netherlands*[148] when the Netherlands attempted to deport the father of a small child resident in that country with her mother, and with whom the father had maintained close ties. As a practical matter, the Court noted, the applicant could not be expected to travel frequently between the Netherlands and Morocco.[149] In these cases the Court asks how easy it would be for an applicant to re-establish family relationships in his or her country of origin. A violation is more likely to be found when the applicant was born in the deporting state or has lived there from an early age. The same would be true where the applicant did not speak the language of his formal nationality or where he or she had few relatives still living there.[150]

The Court has weighed the hardships involved in maintaining family life, against the urgency of the state's reasons for exclusion. In *Moustaquim v. Belgium*[151] the applicant, a Moroccan national, was 20 years old when he was ordered to be deported because of a long series of offences committed as a juvenile and as an adult. He had arrived in Belgium at the age of one. His father, mother and seven siblings were in Belgium. The Court, in finding a violation of Article 8, stressed that most of the applicant's difficulties had occurred while he was an adolescent, and the most serious charges had arisen over a fairly short period. The applicant had committed no offence in the 39 months prior to the deportation order (although admittedly he had been in detention for 16 months of that time). On these facts, the deportation constituted a disproportionate interference with the applicant's family life. The Court has recognized that the elimination of certain social evils, notably commerce in illegal drugs, raises an unusually

---

[146] *Id.* at paras. 43, 46.

[147] *Id.* at para. 68. *See also Cruz Varas v. Sweden*, 20 Mar. 1991, 14 E.H.R.R. 1, para. 88. To the same effect see *Mahmood v. Secretary of State for the Home Dept.* [2001] 2 F.C.R. 63 (C.A.).

[148] 21 June 1988, 11 E.H.R.R. 322.

[149] *Id.* at para. 23.

[150] Compare *Beldjoudi v. France*, 26 Nov. 1992, 14 E.H.R.R. 801; *Moustaquim v. Belgium*, 18 Feb. 1991, 13 E.H.R.R. 802; *Nasri v. France*, 13 July 1995, 21 E.H.R.R. 458 (violations) with *C v. Belgium*, 7 Aug. 1996, 32 E.H.R.R. 2; *Boughanemi v. France*, 24 Apr. 1996, 22 E.H.R.R. 228; *Dalia v. France*, *supra* n. 141 (no violations).

[151] 18 Feb. 1991, 13 E.H.R.R. 802.

strong need for action by the state.[152] But even a record of serious offences does not create a *per se* justification for exclusion. In *Beldjoudi v. France*,[153] the applicant's criminal record was, the Court agreed, 'much worse than that of Mr. Moustaquim'. He had been convicted of a large number of very serious crimes as an adult over a 15-year period and, at the time the case was heard in Strasbourg, the applicant was being held on a fresh offence. Although these facts strengthened France's claim that it was necessary to deport Beldjoudi to maintain public order, the Court also noted that the impact of a deportation on the applicant's family life was extreme. He had been born in France (of Algerian parents), had spent his whole life in France and knew no Arabic. 'He [did] not seem to have any links with Algeria apart from that of nationality'.[154] Most important, the Court noted that he had been married for 20 years to a Frenchwoman who, as a practical matter, could not be expected to uproot herself and move to Algeria. Based on all these factors the Court found the deportation decision 'not... proportionate to the legitimate aim pursued'.[155]

In *Baghli v. France*,[156] however, the applicant's expulsion was deemed consistent with Article 8—even though all of his immediate family was in France where he had lived since the age of two. But he had no wife or children; he had retained Algerian nationality, spoke Arabic and had spent time in that country. Given the seriousness of his conviction for dealing in heroin, deportation was not disproportionate to the state's interest in public safety.[157]

Close individualized examination of the applicant's family life in the deporting and destination countries, and of the applicant's record of criminal behaviour, has resulted in a jurisprudence about which few generalizations are possible. This problem is aggravated by the fact that the Court's balance of factors is more often stated than defended. The *ad hoc* quality of these judgments has disturbed some of the judges. In one case Judge Martens expressed his dissatisfaction in a dissenting opinion:

The majority's case-by-case approach is a lottery for national authorities and a source of embarrassment for the Court. A source of embarrassment since it obliges the Court to make well-nigh impossible comparisons between the merits of the case before it and those which it has already decided. It is—to say the least—far from easy to compare the cases of Moustquim, Beldjoudi, Nasri and Boughanemi. Should one just make a comparison based on the number of convictions and the severity of sentences or should it also take into account personal circumstances? The majority has, obviously, opted for the latter approach and has felt able to make the comparison, but—with due respect—I cannot help feeling the outcome is necessarily tainted with arbitrariness.[158]

An extreme example of this difficulty is *Boujlifa v. France*.[159] The Court merely recited the applicant's experience and family connection in France and the nature of his

---

[152] See *C v. Belgium, supra* n. 150; *Dalia v. France, supra* n. 141.
[153] 26 March 1992, 14 E.H.R.R. 801.   [154] *Id.* at para. 77.
[155] *Id.* at para. 79.   [156] 30 Nov. 1999, 33 E.H.R.R. 10.
[157] *Id.* at paras. 47–9.
[158] *Boughanemi v. France, supra* n. 150 (dissenting opinion of Judge Martens, at para. 4).
[159] 21 Oct. 1997, 30 E.H.R.R. 419.

criminal offences and stated without further explanation: '[the Court] considers that in the instant case the requirements of public order outweighed the personal considerations which prompted the application'.[160] A number of judges writing individual opinions have proposed that the Court should adopt a heavy presumption that deportation of any alien who has spent all or almost all of his or her life in a state ('integrated aliens' or 'second generation aliens') would violate Article 8.[161]

D. GÜL V. SWITZERLAND

Judgment of 19 February 1996
22 E.H.R.R. 93

6. Mr. Gül is a Turkish national who was born in January 1947 and now lives with his wife at Pratteln in the canton of Basle Rural, Switzerland.

7. Until 1983 he lived with his wife and their two sons, Tuncay (born on 12 October 1971) and Ersin (born on 20 January 1983), in the town of Gumushane in Turkey. On 25 April 1983 he travelled to Switzerland, where he applied for political asylum as a Kurd and former member of the Turkish Social Democratic Party (the 'CHP'). He worked in a restaurant there until 1990, when he fell ill. Since then he has been in receipt of a partial-invalidity pension.

8. In 1987 the applicant's wife, who had remained in Turkey with their two sons, seriously burned herself during a fit brought on by her epilepsy, from which she had suffered since 1982. In December 1987, having found that it was impossible for her to obtain proper treatment in the area where she was then living, she joined her husband in Switzerland, where she was taken into hospital as an emergency case. Two of the fingers of her left hand were amputated.

9. On 19 September 1988 in Switzerland Mrs. Gül gave birth to her third child, Nursal, a daughter. As she still suffered from epilepsy, she could not take care of the baby, who was placed in a home in Switzerland, where she has remained ever since. In a written declaration dated 31 March 1989, a Pratteln specialist in internal medicine stated that a return to Turkey would be impossible for Mrs. Gül and might even prove fatal to her, given her serious medical condition....

11. [The applicant's application for political asylum was refused but] [i]n view of the length of time Mr. Gül had been living in Switzerland and his wife's precarious state of health, the police considered that the conditions for the issue of such a permit laid down in Article 13(f) of the Federal Council's Order Limiting the Number of Aliens (the 'OLNA') had been satisfied. The final decision to grant a residence permit was given by the Federal Aliens Office on 15 February 1990....

13. On 14 May 1990 Mr. Gül asked the Basle Rural Cantonal Aliens Police for permission to bring to Switzerland his two sons, Tuncay and Ersin, who had remained in Turkey.

---

[160] *Id.* at para. 44.
[161] *Boughanemi v. France, supra* n. 150 (dissenting opinion of Judge Martens); *Boujlifa v. France, supra* n. 159 (dissenting opinions of Judges Baka and Van Dijk). *See also* C. Warbrick, 'The Structure of Article 8', [1998] *European Human Rights Law Rev.* 32.

14. In a decision of 19 September 1990 the Aliens Police rejected Mr. Gül's request, on the ground that the conditions for family reunion had not been satisfied. (Art 39 of the OLNA.) Firstly, the Gül family's flat did not conform to the standards laid down and, secondly, the applicant did not have sufficient means to provide for his family. In any event, Tuncay was already 18 and was therefore ineligible for a residence permit under the rules governing family reunion. [The applicant's appeals of these decisions was rejected by the cantonal government and the Swiss Federal Court.]...

19. Ersin has lived in Turkey since his birth, at first in Gumushane until 1993 (with his mother until 1987), and then in Istanbul.

According to the Government, he is at present living, as is his grandfather, with the family of his elder brother Tuncay, and has been visited several times by his father.

The applicant maintained that Ersin frequently moved from one home to another and spent two or three days staying with various Kurdish families who used to live in the village where he was born, including the family of his elder brother. Owing to his grandfather's limited financial resources and the distance between the homes of some of these families and the school it was not possible for the boy to attend school on a regular basis.

As is evidenced by an article which appeared in the Turkish newspaper Sabah on 25 July 1995, Mr. and Mrs. Gül visited their son in Turkey in July and August 1995....

[The Commission by a vote of fourteen to ten expressed its opinion that there had been a violation of Article 8.]

29. It is first necessary to determine whether there is a 'family life' within the meaning of Article 8.

30. The Government's primary submission was that Article 8 was not applicable, since in the instant case the element of intention inherent in the concept of family life was missing. Mr. Gül had left Turkey when his younger son Ersin was three months old, and had never attempted to develop a family life in his country of origin. In addition, the focus of that son's family life was in Turkey since, even after his mother's departure, the child had been taken in as a member of his elder brother's family. Furthermore, the fact that Mr. and Mrs. Gül's daughter Nursal had been placed in a home in Switzerland showed that they were in any event incapable of assuming their parental responsibilities with regard to the boy.

33. Admittedly, Mr. Gül left Turkey in 1983, when his son Ersin was only three months old; Mrs. Gül left Ersin in 1987 because of her accident.

However, after obtaining a residence permit on humanitarian grounds in Switzerland in 1990, the applicant asked the Swiss authorities for permission to bring the boy, who was then six years old, to Switzerland. Subsequently, he repeatedly asked the Swiss courts to allow his son to join him, before bringing his case before the Convention institutions. Despite the distance, in geographical terms, between them, the applicant has made a number of visits to Turkey, the last of those being in July and August 1995. It cannot therefore be claimed that the bond of 'family life' between them has been broken.

34. Secondly, it is necessary to ascertain whether there was interference by the Swiss authorities with the applicant's right under Article 8.

35. Mr. Gül submitted that the result in practice of the authorities' persistent refusal to allow Ersin to join him in Switzerland had been to separate the family and make it impossible, owing to lack of sufficient financial resources, for the parents to maintain regular contacts

with their son, whereas, according to the Court's case law, contacts between parents and child were of capital importance. In addition, the length of time Mr. Gül had lived in Switzerland, his invalidity and his wife's ill health made family reunion in Turkey an unrealistic prospect, so that the family could only be brought together again in Switzerland.

36. The Government submitted that the applicant could not rely on a right to family reunion in Switzerland, as he had only a humanitarian permit, which was not a true settlement permit but merely a document authorising residence that could be withdrawn from him. In addition, Switzerland had fully discharged the positive obligations arising under Article 8(1), as the invalidity pension the applicant was in receipt of enabled him to make occasional visits to Turkey. In any event, Switzerland was in no way responsible for the situation the Gül family was in. Lastly, the Swiss authorities were not under any obligation to ensure that the applicant led an optimal family life in Switzerland....

The present case concerns not only family life but also immigration, and the extent of a State's obligation to admit to its territory relatives of settled immigrants will vary according to the particular circumstances of the persons involved and the general interest. As a matter of well established international law and subject to its treaty obligations, a State has the right to control the entry of non-nationals into its territory.

Moreover, where immigration is concerned, Article 8 cannot be considered to impose on a State a general obligation to respect the choice by married couples of the country of their matrimonial residence and to authorise family reunion in its territory....

39. In this case, therefore, the Court's task is to determine to what extent it is true that Ersin's move to Switzerland would be the only way for Mr. Gül to develop family life with his son....

41. By leaving Turkey in 1983, Mr. Gül caused the separation from his son, and he was unable to prove to the Swiss authorities—who refused to grant him political refugee status—that he personally had been a victim of persecution in his home country. In any event, whatever the applicant's initial reasons for applying for political asylum, the visits he has made to his son in recent years tend to show that they are no longer valid. His counsel, moreover, expressly confirmed this at the hearing. In addition, according to the government, by virtue of a social security convention concluded on 1 May 1969 between Switzerland and Turkey, the applicant could continue to receive his ordinary invalidity pension and half of the supplementary benefit he receives at present in respect of his wife, his son Ersin and his daughter Nursal if he returned to his home country.

Mrs. Gül's return to Turkey is more problematic, since it was essentially her state of health that led the Swiss authorities to issue a residence permit on humanitarian grounds. However, although her state of health seemed particularly alarming in 1987, when her accident occurred, it has not been proved that she could not later have received appropriate medical treatment in specialist hospitals in Turkey. She was, moreover, able to visit Turkey with her husband in July and August 1995.

Furthermore, although Mr. and Mrs. Gül are lawfully resident in Switzerland, they do not have a permanent right of abode, as they do not have a settlement permit but merely a residence permit on humanitarian grounds, which could be withdrawn, and which under Swiss law does not give them a right to family reunion.

42. In view of the length of time Mr. and Mrs. Gül have lived in Switzerland, it would admittedly not be easy for them to return to Turkey, but there are, strictly speaking, no obstacles preventing them from developing family life in Turkey. That possibility is all the more real

because Ersin has always lived there and has therefore grown up in the cultural and linguistic environment of his country. On that point the situation is not the same as in the *Berrehab Case*,[162] where the daughter of a Moroccan applicant had been born in the Netherlands and spent all her life there.

43. Having regard to all these considerations, and while acknowledging that the Gül family's situation is very difficult from the human point of view, the Court finds that Switzerland has not failed to fulfil the obligations arising under Article 8(1), and there has therefore been no interference in the applicant's family life within the meaning of that Article.

[The Court held by seven votes to two that there had been no breach of Article 8.]

Dissenting Opinion of Judge Martens, approved by Judge Russo

...

6. 'According to the Court's well established case law, "the mutual enjoyment by parent and child of each other's company constitutes a fundamental element of family life"', as the Court pointed out in paragraph 86 of the *McMichael* Judgment.[163] Consequently, decisions of State authorities hindering such enjoyment in principle amount to an infringement of the State's obligation to respect the family life of those concerned. It follows that the refusal of the Swiss authorities to grant the applicant's son Ersin authorization to reside in Switzerland in principle entails their responsibility under Article 8.

Before it is possible to assess whether the refusal was justified, it is—alas—necessary to give some consideration to the question whether or not Switzerland's obligation under Article 8 is a positive or a negative one.

7. The Court's case law distinguishes between positive and negative obligations. Negative obligations require Member States to refrain from action, positive to take action. The Court has repeatedly stressed that the boundaries between the two types 'do not lend themselves to precise definition'. The present case well illustrates the truth of this proposition since the question whether the Swiss decision violated a positive or a negative obligation, if either, seems hardly more than one of semantics: the refusal of the Swiss authorities to let Ersin and his parents be reunited may be considered as an action from which they should have refrained, whereas it could arguably also be viewed as failing to take an action which they were required to take, viz making a reunion possible by granting the authorisation. If one takes the view that if there is a violation at all, it must be of a positive obligation...then one has to put up with the rather awkward systematic inconsistency that exclusion of a person from a state where his family lives does not fall into the same category of breaches as expulsion of a person from a state where his family lives: the former decision may be in breach of a positive obligation under Article 8, whereas the latter may be in breach of a negative obligation.

8. These and other difficulties in distinguishing between cases where positive and cases where negative obligations are at stake would be immaterial if both kinds of obligation were treated alike. There was a time, however, when the Court's case law did treat them differently.

---

[162] 21 June 1988, 11 E.H.R.R. 322.
[163] 24 Feb. 1995, 20 E.H.R.R. 205.

The *Abdulaziz, Cabales and Balkandali* judgment[164] is a striking instance: see paragraph 67 of that judgment. Under the pretext of the vagueness of the notion 'respect' in Article 8 the Court held that its requirements will vary from case to case, thus creating for itself the possibility of taking into account, when establishing whether or not there is a positive obligation, whether or not there is a consensus between Member States and, moreover, a wide margin of appreciation for the State concerned. This approach has been rightly criticized both outside and inside the Court. One of the main objections was that under this doctrine, in the context of positive obligations, the margin of appreciation might already come into play at the stage of determining the existence of the obligation, whilst in the context of negative obligations it only plays a role, if at all, at the stage of determining whether a breach of the obligation is justified.

The Court's doctrine on this point has, however, evolved considerably since the *Abdulaziz* judgment. The aforementioned difference in treatment between positive and negative obligations has gradually dwindled away. The Court now holds that the applicable principles are similar, adding that in both contexts regard must be had to the fair balance that has to be struck between the competing interests of the individual and the community. (See, *inter alia*, *Keegan v. Ireland*,[165] *Hokkanen v. Finland*[166] and *Stjerna v. Finland.*[167])

10. Was it 'necessary in a democratic society' to refuse the applicant's seven year old son Ersin authorisation to come and live in Switzerland with his parents? In other words, did that decision of the Swiss authorities strike a fair balance between the competing interests of the applicant, his wife and their son on the one hand and those of the community as a whole on the other? ...

13. The Government do not argue that these are not weighty interests. But they seek to diminish their relevance by contending that the applicant—on whom, they add, is the burden— has not shown that there are obstacles to re-establishing the family—father, mother and Ersin—in Turkey. It is clear that the Government are thus relying on paragraph 68 of the *Abdulaziz* judgment. However, they choose to ignore the fact that the Court, in the first sentence of that paragraph, explicitly distinguishes 'the present proceedings'—viz the cases of the three wives that were before the Court—from the case of 'immigrants who already had a family which they left behind in another country until they had achieved settled status in the United Kingdom' (= the country of settlement).

That is an important proviso, for it strongly suggests that in a case of 'immigrants who already had a family which they left behind'—such as the present applicant—different norms should be applied.

14. Which norms? The Court does not answer that question, but it is natural to infer that it intended to make it clear that in respect to such cases it might possibly hold that, in the context of the issue of family reunion, the State of settlement should respect the choice of the immigrants who have achieved settled status there and, accordingly, must accept members of their family which they had left behind for settlement....

On the contrary, the *Abdulaziz* judgment supports the proposition that in cases where a father and mother have achieved settled status in a country and want to be reunited with their child which for the time being they have left behind in their country of origin, it is

164 *Abdulaziz v. United Kingdom*, 28 May 1995, 7 E.H.R.R. 471.
165 26 May 1994, 18 E.H.R.R. 342.
166 23 Sept. 1995, 19 E.H.R.R. 139, at para. 55.
167 25 Nov. 1995, 24 E.H.R.R. 195.

per se unreasonable, if not inhumane to give them the choice between giving up the position which they have acquired in the country of settlement or to renounce the mutual enjoyment by parent and child of each other's company which constitutes a fundamental element of family life.

15. It remains, of course, to be considered whether the latter principle applies in the present case, where the applicant has not 'achieved settled status' in Switzerland, in so far as he and his wife have not been granted a 'settlement permit', but have to base their right of residence on a permit which has, in principle, a temporary character and, consequently, a lower legal status than a settlement permit.

It cannot be denied that, from a point of view of State interest—that is from a point of view of immigration and residence—there is a good case for answering this question in the negative. However, the European Court of Human Rights has to ensure, in particular, that State interests do not crush those of an individual, especially in situations where political pressure—such as the growing dislike of immigrants in most Member States—may inspire State authorities to harsh decisions. As we stressed in paragraph 29 of our aforementioned *Berrehab* judgment, the Court must examine cases like this not only from the point of view of immigration and residence, but also with regard to the mutual interests of the applicant, his wife and Ersin.

Whether he came as a refugee or as a job seeker, at the material time the applicant has been living in Switzerland for seven years and his wife for four years. During these years he had been legally employed, apparently by the same employer, until an unspecified date in 1990 when he fell ill. The Swiss authorities have taken this time element into consideration, since their decision to grant a residence permit was partly based on the time the applicant had been living in Switzerland. Rightly so, for generally speaking it may be assumed that after a period of between three and five years immigrants become rooted in the country of settlement. By then they have formed new social ties there and have definitively begun to adapt themselves to their new homeland. In assessing the humaneness of the choice with which the Swiss authorities confronted the applicant and his wife this element, the fact that they have become integrated in their new homeland—an element which, incidentally, is closely connected with their private life—is of far more importance than the formal status of their permit.

There are some further, specific elements to be taken into account.

The first is that for the applicant and his wife the choice in question was not only between renouncing their son or renouncing the position which they had acquired in Switzerland, but also between renouncing their son Ersin or their little daughter Nursal who was being educated in a home in Switzerland and whose interests almost certainly would have required that she should be left behind.

The second is that the applicant's wife is dependent on medical care which she can certainly get in Switzerland, whilst it is in debate to what extent, if at all, she will be able to get it in Turkey.

The third is that the mere fact that the Turkish authorities did not immediately arrest the applicant when he entered the country as a visitor does not imply that he would not get into trouble if he tried to settle there again on a permanent basis.

The fourth is that the applicant and his wife deserve compassion: whilst his wife had been suffering from epilepsy since 1982 and had a terrible accident in 1987, the applicant himself became disabled in 1990.

Under these circumstances it could not reasonably be required of the applicant and his wife that in order to be reunited with Ersin they should leave Switzerland and return to Turkey.

It follows that a proper balance was not achieved between the interests involved, that the refusal of the Swiss authorities is disproportionate and, as such, not necessary in a democratic society. I thus conclude that there was a violation of Article 8.

The Court, in *Ahmut v. The Netherlands*,[168] was again confronted with a claim based on the refusal of a state to admit the family of a resident, in this case, one who had acquired local nationality. The applicant, when he applied for a residence permit for his son, had lived in the Netherlands for four years and had acquired Dutch nationality two months previously. The son, who was 10 years old, had been raised in Morocco by his mother. After the death of the mother he had been cared for by his maternal grandmother. He then moved to the Netherlands and lived with the applicant but, at the time of the Court's hearing, had been expelled and was enrolled in a boarding school in Morocco. A brother and two uncles remained in Morocco. The European Court viewed the case as raising the state's positive obligation to respect the applicant's family life. It cited the *Gül* case as setting forth the controlling principles. Since the son had a strong linguistic and cultural connection to Morocco and still had family there, he was 'not prevented from maintaining the degree of family life which he himself had opted for when moving to the Netherlands in the first place, nor is there any obstacle to his returning to Morocco ... Article 8 does not guarantee a right to choose the most suitable place to develop family life'.[169]

The general principle that states must refrain from expulsions exposing the subject to violations of Article 8 has been extended to cases other than those dealing with family life. So when severe threats to health may be expected in the receiving country a violation of Article 8 (as well as Article 3) may occur. In this case the right involved would be that from intrusion on 'physical and moral integrity' implicit in the right to 'private life'.[170]

E. PARENTAL RIGHTS

Numerous cases before the Strasbourg Court have applied Article 8's right to protection of family life to cases where the child welfare authorities have removed children from the custody of their parents. Although the Court, characteristically, has insisted that each case must be examined on its own facts, a number of broad principles have emerged. The applicability of Article 8 to these decisions is not in doubt. Moreover, the protection of the children is always a legitimate state objective. Cases, therefore, turn on whether or not the particular action at issue was necessary for that protection. That determination will turn on the persuasiveness of the evidence the authorities had before them and on their behaviour after the initial removal. An important component

---

[168] 28 Nov. 1996, 24 E.H.R.R. 62.

[169] *Id.* at paras. 70–1.

[170] *Bensaid v. United Kingdom*, 6 Feb. 2001, 33 E.H.R.R. 10, para. 46. The House of Lords held that the Secretary of State could not dismiss claims based on risks to mental health upon deportation as 'manifestly unfounded'. *R. (Razgar) v. Sec'y of State for the Home Dept* [2004] U.K.H.L. 27, [2004] 2 A.C. 368, [2004] All E.R. (D) 169.

of this examination has been the extent to which the state procedure allowed for the parents to participate in the decisions, thus establishing a procedural component to the Convention's requirements.[171]

In these cases, the Court has been careful to acknowledge that the state is to be accorded a margin of appreciation since 'perceptions as to the appropriateness of intervention by public authorities in the care of children vary from one Contracting State to another, depending on such factors as traditions relating to the role of the family and to State intervention in family affairs and the availability of resources for public measures in this particular area'.[172] The breadth of the margin of appreciation, however, varies according to the stage of the procedures involved. It is at its widest with respect to the initial decision to remove a child from the home when an estimate of the risk to the child may have to be made quickly.[173] In fact, a failure to act promptly to protect a child at risk might itself violate a state's positive obligation to protect the physical and moral integrity of the child under Article 8 or Article 3.[174]

The Supreme Court of Canada has refused to hold that the Charter of Rights and Freedoms requires judicial authorization before an agency could remove a child from the home even in non-emergency situations. The delay necessitated by the need for a warrant, the Court reasoned, could put the child at serious risk in light of the 'evidentiary difficulties and time pressures associated with child protection situations; and the need for preventive as well as protective state intervention...'. Justice L'Heureux-Dube summarized the dilemmas facing social workers in these cases:

I am very conscious of the difficulties confronting social workers and others in obtaining hard evidence, which will stand up when challenged in court, of the maltreatment meted out to children behind closed doors. Cruelty and physical abuse are notoriously difficult to prove. The task of social workers is usually anxious and often thankless. They are criticised for not having taken action in response to warning signs which are obvious enough when seen in the clear light of hindsight. Or they are criticised for making applications based on serious allegations which, in the event, are not established in court. Sometimes, whatever they do, they cannot do right.[175]

These difficulties, however, do not always carry over to agency decisions made *after* the child has been removed. In matters relating to the parents' access to children already taken into care, the European Court of Human Rights has been more demanding. In these cases the safety of the child is no longer in imminent danger. Moreover, allowing an extended period to elapse without parental contact itself exacerbates the problems associated with reuniting the family.[176] In general, a state, in these circumstances is obliged to deal with the children in a way consistent with 'the ultimate aim of reuniting

---

[171] See, e.g., K.A. v. Finland, 14 Jan. 2003, paras. 102–5.
[172] K. & T. v. Finland [G.C.], 27 April 2000, 31 E.H.R.R. 18.
[173] See, e.g., id. at para. 155.
[174] See D.P. & J.C. v. United Kingdom, 10 Oct. 2002, 36 E.H.R.R. 14.
[175] K.L.W. v. Winnipeg Child and Family Services [2000] 2 S.C.R. 519, para. 99.
[176] K. & T. v. Finland, supra at n. 172; Scozzari & Giunta v. Italy [G.C.], 13 July 2000, 35 E.H.R.R. 12.

the natural parents and child'.[177] At every stage, however, the interests of the child are 'paramount'.[178]

The stress on parental rights may be contrasted with the fundamentally different one of English courts with respect to questions of parental right and child custody. In *Re K.D.*[179] the House of Lords affirmed that normally 'the recognized bond and relationship between parent and child gives rise to universally recognized norms which ought not to be gratuitously interfered with; and which, if interfered with at all, ought to be so only if the welfare of the child dictates it'. But, according to the judgment of Lord Oliver, it was unhelpful to treat this fact as giving rise to a 'right' of access in the parent. He rejected an argument that 'the starting point in every case should be that a parent has a right of access which should be given effect to by the court and curtailed and inhibited only if the court is satisfied that the exercise of the right will be positively inimical to the interests of the child'.[180] He quoted approvingly a trial judge's conclusion that:

So far as access to a child is concerned, there are no rights in the sense in which lawyers understand the word. It is a matter to be decided always entirely on the footing of the best interests of the child, either by agreement between the parties, or by the Court if there is no agreement.[181]

The Law Lords considered that there was nothing in their view incompatible with the judgments of the European Court of Human Rights.[182] The Lords subsequently held that parental rights may be terminated even if no decision has been made regarding post-adoption contacts to be allowed to the objecting parents.[183]

It follows, *a fortiori*, from the European cases that a parent must have minimal rights to participation in decisions to sever parental relations permanently. The Court reached this result, however, not under Article 8 but under Article 6 establishing the right to fair procedures in connection with the determination of a 'civil right'.[184] The House of Lords has gone further and held that, under controlling law, even the consent of the parent to an adoption severing all her legal relations with a child, will not suffice without an independent reason for such an action.[185] American constitutional law also requires notice and hearing before terminating parental rights.[186]

The Strasbourg Court has been especially concerned with custody decisions incorporating unjustifiable discrimination against one of the parents. In *Salgueiro da Silva*

---

[177] *Id.* at para. 178.

[178] E.g. *Monory v. Romania & Hungary*, 5 April 2005, 41 E.H.R.R. 37, para. 83.

[179] [1988] 1 All E.R. 577.

[180] *Id.* at 590.   [181] *Id.* at 589 quoting *A. v. C.* [1985] F.L.R. 445, 455.

[182] *Id.* at 588.

[183] *Down Lisburn Health & Social Services Trust v. H and Another* [2006] U.K.H.L. 36.

[184] See *O & H v. United Kingdom*, 8 July 1987, 10 E.H.R.R. 82.

[185] *In re B* [2001] U.K.H.L. 70, [2002] 1 All E.R. 641.

[186] *Santosky v. Kramer*, 455 U.S. 745 (1982). The same result is implicit in Canadian constitutional law. *New Brunswick (Minister of Health) v. G (J)* [1999] 3 S.C.R. 46.

Mouta v. Portugal[187] it dealt with an award of custody to a mother partly based on the sexual orientation of the father. The Portuguese Court of Appeal had declared that the child should live in 'a traditional Portuguese family' and not 'in the shadow of abnormal situations'.[188] The European Court found this to be impermissible discrimination and thus a violation of Article 14 in conjunction with Article 8. In *Hoffman v. Austria*[189] it had made a similar determination where one of the parents was a Jehovah's Witness. The national court had worried that the children might be at risk from the Jehovah's Witnesses' prohibition on the use of blood transfusions and that they could be treated as 'social outcasts'. The European Court held that the Supreme Court's order amounted to a difference in treatment based on the applicant's religion and that this difference was not based on an 'objective and reasonable justification'. The Court agreed that the interests of the child are paramount but, without elaboration, concluded that '[n]otwithstanding any argument to the contrary, a distinction based essentially on a difference in religion alone is not acceptable'.[190] In dissent, Judge Walsh denied that the Austrian court's judgments were properly understood as based on religion. Noting particularly the risk to the children posed by applicant's views on blood transfusions, he insisted that '[t]he fact that the hazard was brought into existence by a religious belief...does not create a situation where removal of the hazard must necessarily, if at all, be regarded as discrimination on the grounds of religious belief'.[191]

Hoffman may be contrasted with decisions of the Supreme Court of Canada on a related question—judicial restrictions on the right of a non-custodial parent to influence his or her child on religious matters. Like the House of Lords in *K.D.* the Canadian Court has de-emphasized the notion of parental 'rights' in the determination of these questions. The sole criterion applied to access orders is the 'best interests of the child', and any resulting limitations on the religious activities of the parent do not infringe his or her right of religious freedom or expression under Section 2 of the Canadian Charter of Rights and Freedoms: '[W]hile parents are free to engage in religious practices themselves, those activities may be curtailed when they interfere with the best interests of the child without thereby infringing the parent's religious freedom'.[192] In applying the best interests test to the question, however, a majority of the Court has concluded that the value of an open and honest relationship with the noncustodial parent may be as important, and more important, than avoiding any discomfort and stress that the introduction of the religious differences of the parents may create. Thus, the Court overturned a decree barring a non-custodial parent from 'discuss[ing] the Jehovah's Witness religion with the children',[193] but upheld an order (issued after a

---

[187] 21 Dec. 1999, 31 E.H.R.R. 47.

[188] *Id.* at para. 34.

[189] 23 June 1993, 17 E.H.R.R. 293; *see also Palau-Martinez v. France*, 16 Dec. 2003, 41 E.H.R.R. 9.

[190] *Id.* at para. 36. The Court also took note of Article 5 of Protocol 7, which entered into force in Austria after the relevant events, which provides for the equality of spouses with respect to parental rights. Para. 35.

[191] *Id.* (partly dissenting opinion of Judge Walsh).

[192] *Young v. Young* [1993] 4 S.C.R. 3, 94.

[193] *Id.* at 112.

finding that the non-custodial parent's 'religious fanaticism was disturbing to such a young girl') providing that he could 'teach the child the Jehovah's Witness religion but does not have the right to indoctrinate her continually with the precepts and religious practices of Jehovah's Witnesses'.[194]

Article 8 has also been applied in parental 'abduction' cases where one parent has removed a child in violation of a custody order. Although the interference with family rights in such cases arises from the actions of an individual, the European Court has interpreted the state's positive obligation to include a duty to take prompt and vigorous measures to secure the return of the child to the parent with lawful custody. As in the case of state supervised child supervision, these measures 'require urgent handling as the passage of time can have irremediable consequences for relations between the children and parent who does not live with them'.[195]

C. PRIVATE LIFE

1. DUDGEON V. UNITED KINGDOM

Judgment of 22 October 1981
4 E.H.R.R. 149

13. Mr. Jeffrey Dudgeon, who is 35 years of age, is a shipping clerk resident in Belfast, Northern Ireland.

Mr. Dudgeon is a homosexual and his complaints are directed primarily against the existence in Northern Ireland of laws which have the effect of making certain homosexual acts between consenting adult males criminal offences....

[A government proposal to liberalize the law by decriminalizing homosexual acts in private between two consenting males over the age of 21 had been withdrawn in 1978 in the face of intense opposition by a number of groups and especially from religious groups including the Roman Catholic and Presbyterian churches.]

32. The applicant has, on his own evidence, been consciously homosexual from the age of 14. For some time he and others have been conducting a campaign aimed at bringing the law in Northern Ireland into line with that in force in England and Wales and, if possible, achieving a minimum age of consent lower than 21 years....

37. The applicant complained that under the law in force in Northern Ireland he is liable to criminal prosecution on account of his homosexual conduct and that he has experienced

---

[194] *D.P. v. C.S.* [1993] 4 S.C.R. 141, 142 (translation of order).
[195] *Ignaccolo-Zenide v. Romania*, 25 Jan. 2000, 31 E.H.R.R. 7. *See also Sylvester v. Austria*, 24 April 2003, 37 E.H.R.R. 17.

fear, suffering and psychological distress directly caused by the very existence of the laws in question—including fear of harassment and blackmail. He further complained that, following the search of his house in January 1976, he was questioned by the police about certain homosexual activities and that personal papers belonging to him were seized during the search and not returned until more than a year later.

He alleged that, in breach of Article 8 of the Convention he has thereby suffered, and continues to suffer, an unjustified interference with his right to respect for his private life....

39. Although it is not homosexuality itself which is prohibited but the particular acts of gross indecency between males and buggery..., there can be no doubt but that male homosexual practices whose prohibition is the subject of the applicant's complaints come within the scope of the offences punishable under the impugned legislation; it is on that basis that the case has been argued by the Government, the applicant and the Commission. Furthermore, the offences are committed whether the act takes place in public or in private, whatever the age or relationship of the participants involved, and whether or not the participants are consenting....

41. The Court sees no reason to differ from the views of the Commission: the maintenance in force of the impugned legislation constitutes a continuing interference with the applicant's right to respect for his private life (which includes his sexual life) within the meaning of Article 8 §1. In the personal circumstances of the applicant, the very existence of this legislation continuously and directly affects his private life (see, mutatis mutandis, the *Marckx* judgment)...either he respects the law and refrains from engaging—even in private with consenting male partners—in prohibited sexual acts to which he is disposed by reason of his homosexual tendencies, or he commits such acts and thereby becomes liable to criminal prosecution....

49. There can be no denial that some degree of regulation of male homosexual conduct, as indeed of other forms of sexual conduct, by means of the criminal law can be justified as 'necessary in a democratic society'. The overall function served by the criminal law in this field is, in the words of the Wolfenden report, 'to preserve public order and decency [and] to protect the citizen from what is offensive or injurious'. Furthermore, this necessity for some degree of control may even extend to consensual acts committed in private, notably where there is call—to quote the Wolfenden report once more—'to provide sufficient safeguards against exploitation and corruption of others, particularly those who are specially vulnerable because they are young, weak in body or mind, inexperienced, or in a state of special physical, official or economic dependence'. In practice there is legislation on the matter in all the member States of the Council of Europe, but what distinguishes the law in Northern Ireland from that existing in the great majority of the member States is that it prohibits generally gross indecency between males and buggery whatever the circumstances....

50. A number of principles relevant to the assessment of the 'necessity', 'in a democratic society', of a measure taken in furtherance of an aim that is legitimate under the Convention have been stated by the Court in previous judgments.

51. Firstly, 'necessary' in this context does not have the flexibility of such expressions as 'useful', 'reasonable', or 'desirable', but implies the existence of a 'pressing social need' for the interference in question (see the ... *Handyside* judgment) ...

52. In the second place, it is for the national authorities to make the initial assessment of the pressing social need in each case; accordingly, a margin of appreciation is left to them (ibid). However, their decision remains subject to review by the Court (ibid) ...

As was illustrated by the *Sunday Times* judgment, the scope of the margin of appreciation is not identical in respect of each of the aims justifying restrictions on a right... The Government inferred from the *Handyside* judgment that the margin of appreciation will be more extensive where the protection of morals is in issue. It is an indisputable fact, as the Court stated in the *Handyside* judgment, that 'the view taken... of the requirements of morals varies from time to time and from place to place, especially in our era', and that 'by reason of their direct and continuous contact with the vital forces of their countries, State authorities are in principle in a better position than the international judge to give an opinion on the exact content of those requirements'....

However, not only the nature of the aim of the restriction but also the nature of the activities involved will affect the scope of the margin of appreciation. The present case concerns a most intimate aspect of private life. Accordingly, there must exist particularly serious reasons before interferences on the part of the public authorities can be legitimate for the purposes of paragraph 2 of Article 8....

54. The Court's task is to determine on the basis of the aforestated principles whether the reasons purporting to justify the 'interference' in question are relevant and sufficient under Article 8 §2 (see the... Handyside judgment,)... The Court is not concerned with making any value-judgment as to the morality of homosexual relations between adult males....

56. In the first place, the Government drew attention to what they described as profound differences of attitude and public opinion between Northern Ireland and Great Britain in relation to questions of morality. Northern Irish society was said to be more conservative and to place greater emphasis on religious factors, as was illustrated by more restrictive laws even in the field of heterosexual conduct.

Although the applicant qualified this account of the facts as grossly exaggerated, the Court acknowledges that such differences do exist to a certain extent and are a relevant factor. As the Government and the Commission both emphasised, in assessing the requirements of the protection of morals in Northern Ireland, the contested measures must be seen in the context of Northern Irish society.

The fact that similar measures are not considered necessary in other parts of the United Kingdom or in other member States of the Council of Europe does not mean that they cannot be necessary in Northern Ireland... Where there are disparate cultural communities residing within the same State, it may well be that different requirements, both moral and social, will face the governing authorities....

60. The Convention right affected by the impugned legislation protects an essentially private manifestation of the human personality.

As compared with the era when that legislation was enacted, there is now a better understanding, and in consequence an increased tolerance, of homosexual behaviour to the extent that in the great majority of the member States of the Council of Europe it is no longer considered to be necessary or appropriate to treat homosexual practices of the kind now in question as in themselves a matter to which the sanctions of the criminal law should be applied; the Court cannot overlook the marked changes which have occurred in this regard in the domestic law of the member States... In Northern Ireland itself, the authorities have refrained in recent years from enforcing the law in respect of private homosexual acts between consenting males over the age of 21 years capable of valid consent. No evidence has been adduced to show that this has been injurious to moral standards in Northern Ireland or that there has been any public demand for stricter enforcement of the law.

It cannot be maintained in these circumstances that there is a 'pressing social need' to make such acts criminal offences, there being no sufficient justification provided by the risk of harm to vulnerable sections of society requiring protection or by the effects on the public. On the issue of proportionality, the Court considers that such justifications as there are for retaining the law in force unamended are outweighed by the detrimental effects which the very existence of the legislative provisions in question can have on the life of a person of homosexual orientation like the applicant. Although members of the public who regard homosexuality as immoral may be shocked, offended or disturbed by the commission by others of private homosexual acts, this cannot on its own warrant the application of penal sanctions when it is consenting adults alone who are involved.

61. Accordingly, the reasons given by the Government, although relevant, are not sufficient to justify the maintenance in force of the impugned legislation in so far as it has the general effect of criminalising private homosexual relations between adult males capable of valid consent. In particular, the moral attitudes towards male homosexuality in Northern Ireland and the concern that any relaxation in the law would tend to erode existing moral standards cannot, without more, warrant interfering with the applicant's private life to such an extent. 'Decriminalisation' does not imply approval, and a fear that some sectors of the population might draw misguided conclusions in this respect from reform of the legislation does not afford a good ground for maintaining it in force with all its unjustifiable features.

To sum up, the restriction imposed on Mr. Dudgeon under Northern Ireland law, by reason of its breadth and absolute character, is, quite apart from the severity of the possible penalties provided for, disproportionate to the aims sought to be achieved.

62. ... The Court has already acknowledged the legitimate necessity in a democratic society for some degree of control over homosexual conduct notably in order to provide safeguards against the exploitation and corruption of those who are specially vulnerable by reason, for example, of their youth. However, it falls in the first instance to the national authorities to decide on the appropriate safeguards of this kind required for the defence of morals in their society and, in particular, to fix the age under which young people should have the protection of the criminal law.

63. Mr. Dudgeon has suffered and continues to suffer an unjustified interference with his right to respect for his private life. There is accordingly a breach of Article 8....

[The Court held, by 15 to four, that there was a violation of Article 8.]

Dissenting opinion of Judge Walsh

9. This raises the age-old philosophical question of what is the purpose of law. Is there a realm of morality which is not the law's business or is the law properly concerned with moral principles? In the context of United Kingdom jurisprudence and the true philosophy of law this debate in modern times has been between Professor H. L. A. Hart and Lord Devlin. Generally speaking the former accepts the philosophy propounded in the last century by John Stuart Mill while the latter contends that morality is properly the concern of the law. Lord Devlin argues that as the law exists for the protection of society it must not only protect the individual from injury, corruption and exploitation but it

'must protect also the institutions and the community of ideas, political and moral, without which people cannot live together, Society cannot ignore the morality of the individual any more than it can his loyalty; it flourishes on both and without either it dies'.

10. It would appear that the United Kingdom claims that in principle it can legislate against immorality. In modern United Kingdom legislation a number of penal statutes appear to be based upon moral principles. Cruelty to animals is illegal because of a moral condemnation of enjoyment derived from the infliction of pain upon sentient creatures. The laws restricting or preventing gambling are concerned with the ethical significance of gambling which is confined to the effect that it may have on the character of the gambler as a member of society. The legislation against racial discrimination has as its object the shaping of people's moral thinking by legal sanctions and the changing of human behaviour by having the authority to punish.

11. The opposing view, traceable in English jurisprudence to John Stuart Mill, is that the law should not intervene in matters of private moral conduct more than necessary to preserve public order and to protect citizens against what is injurious and offensive and that there is a sphere of moral conduct which is best left to the individual conscience just as if it were equatable to liberty of thought or belief....

14. If it is accepted that the State has a valid interest in the prevention of corruption and in the preservation of the moral ethos of its society, then the State has a right to enact such laws as it may reasonably think necessary to achieve these objects. The rule of law itself depends on a moral consensus in the community and in a democracy the law cannot afford to ignore the moral consensus of the community. If the law is out of touch with the moral consensus of the community, whether by being either too far below it or too far above it, the law is brought into contempt. Virtue cannot be legislated into existence but non-virtue can be if the legislation renders excessively difficult the struggle after virtue. Such a situation can have an eroding effect on the moral ethos of the community in question. The ultimate justification of law is that it serves moral ends. It is true that many forms of immorality which can have a corrupting effect are not the subject of prohibitory or penal legislation. However such omissions do not imply a denial of the possibility of corruption or of the erosion of the moral ethos of the community but acknowledge the practical impossibility of legislating effectively for every area of immorality. Where such legislation is enacted it is a reflection of the concern of the 'prudent legislator'....

16. In my view, the Court's reference to the fact that in most countries in the Council of Europe homosexual acts in private between adults are no longer criminal does not really advance the argument. The twenty-one countries making up the Council of Europe extend geographically from Turkey to Iceland and from the Mediterranean to the Arctic Circle and encompass considerable diversities of culture and moral values. The Court states that it cannot overlook the marked changes which have occurred in the laws regarding homosexual behaviour throughout the member States. It would be unfortunate if this should lead to the erroneous inference that a Euro-norm in the law concerning homosexual practices has been or can be evolved....

19. Even if it should be thought, and I do not so think, that the people of Northern Ireland are more 'backward' than the other societies within the Council of Europe because of their attitude towards homosexual practices, that is very much a value judgment which depends

totally upon the initial premise. It is difficult to gauge what would be the effect on society in Northern Ireland if the law were now to permit (even with safeguards for young people and people in need of protection) homosexual practices of the type at present forbidden by law. I venture the view that the Government concerned, having examined the position, is in a better position to evaluate that than this Court, particularly as the Court admits the competence of the State to legislate in this matter but queries the proportionality of the consequences of the legislation in force.

20. The law has a role in influencing moral attitudes and if the respondent Government is of the opinion that the change sought in the legislation would have a damaging effect on moral attitudes then in my view it is entitled to maintain the legislation it has. The judgment of the Court does not constitute a declaration to the effect that the particular homosexual practices which are subject to penalty by the legislation in question virtually amount to fundamental human rights. However, that will not prevent it being hailed as such by those who seek to blur the essential difference between homosexual and heterosexual activities....

23. It is to be noted that Article 8 §1 of the Convention speaks of 'private and family life'. If the *ejusdem generis* rule is to be applied, then the provision should be interpreted as relating to private life in that context as, for example, the right to raise one's children according to one's own philosophical and religious tenets and generally to pursue without interference the activities which are akin to those pursued in the privacy of family life and as such are in the course of ordinary human and fundamental rights. No such claim can be made for homosexual practices.

24. In my opinion there has been no breach of Article 8 of the Convention....

2. THE DEFINITION OF 'PRIVATE LIFE'

The particular circumstances of Jeffrey Dudgeon, the applicant in the principal case, raise an issue as to the meaning of the term, 'private' life. The Court found that '[f]or some time [Dudgeon] and others have been conducting a campaign aimed at bringing the law in Northern Ireland into line with that in force in England and Wales ...'.[196] Thus, the interference with privacy involved here could not consist of activities of the state in disclosing to public view facts which the applicants wished to keep secret. Rather, the Court holds that respect for private life includes respect for the applicant's sexual life by which, of course, the Court must mean a sexual life of the applicant's own choosing. Thus, 'private' must be read to refer not to questions of disclosure or nondisclosure but to the right to choose certain intimate aspects of one's life, free of government regulation.

The Court has explicitly acknowledged that Article 8 protects an area of 'personal autonomy' to 'conduct one's life in a manner of one's own choosing'.[197] Such autonomy goes so far as to include decisions to end one's own life although the Court has held

---

[196] Para. 32.

[197] *Pretty v. United Kingdom*, 29 April 2002, 35 E.H.R.R. 1.

that a state that prohibits assisted suicide does not violate Article 8. Such a prohibition was held a proportionate means to protect 'the weak and vulnerable and especially those who are not in a condition to take informed decisions...'.[198] The scope of activity in which individual autonomy is protected, moreover, is quite broad. Article 8, for example, controls searches not merely of individuals' 'homes', which are specifically mentioned in Article 8, but of business premises as well:

29. The Court does not consider it possible or necessary to attempt an exhaustive definition of the notion of 'private life'. However, it would be too restrictive to limit the notion to an 'inner circle' in which the individual may live his own personal life as he chooses and to exclude therefrom entirely the outside world not encompassed within that circle. Respect for private life must also comprise to a certain degree the right to establish and develop relationships with other human beings.

There appears, furthermore, to be no reason of principle why this understanding of the notion of 'private life' should be taken to exclude activities of a professional or business nature since it is, after all, in the course of their working lives that the majority of people have a signifi- cant, if not the greatest, opportunity of developing relationships with the outside world. This view is supported by the fact that, as was rightly pointed out by the Commission, it is not always possible to distinguish clearly which of an individual's activities form part of his professional or business life and which do not. Thus, especially in the case of a person exercising a liberal profession, his work in that context may form part and parcel of his life to such a degree that it becomes impossible to know in what capacity he is acting at a given moment of time ...

31. More generally, to interpret the words 'private life' and 'home' as including certain professional or business activities or premises would be consonant with the essential objects and purpose of Article 8, namely to protect the individual against arbitrary interference by the public authorities. Such an interpretation would not unduly hamper the Contracting States, for they would retain their entitlement to 'interfere' to the extent permitted by paragraph 2 of article 8: that entitlement might well be more far-reaching where professional or business activities or premises were involved than would otherwise be the case.[199]

Applying this liberal definition, the Court has held that prohibiting someone from taking certain types of employment engaged the right to private life under Article 8. Such a limitation 'affected the applicants' ability to develop relationships with the outside world to a very significant degree...'.[200] The European Court's expansive idea of private life may be compared with the more limited definition formulated by the Supreme Court of Canada in connection with Section 7 of the Charter of Rights and Freedoms. Protected matters are those that 'can properly be characterized as funda- mentally or inherently personal such that, by their very nature, they implicate choices going to the core of what it means to enjoy individual dignity and independence'.[201]

Notwithstanding the understanding that protection of private life includes matters of personal autonomy, the Strasbourg Court's jurisprudence has continued to take

---

198 *Id.* at para. 74.
199 *Niemietz v. Germany*, 16 Dec. 1992, 16 E.H.R.R. 97.
200 *Sidbaris & Žlautas v. Lithuania*, 27 July 2004, 42 E.H.R.R. 6, para. 48.
201 *Godbout v. Longueil (City)* [1997] 3 S.C.R. 844, para. 66.

account of the security of personal information. Thus it has indicated that the number of people involved in an activity and the degree of secrecy attached to it may be relevant in determining whether it involved 'private life'. In considering whether prosecution of group sado-masochistic practices violated Article 8, the Court observed:

[A]considerable number of people were involved in the activities in question which included, *inter alia*, the recruitment of new 'members' the provision of several specially equipped 'chambers' and the shooting of many video-tapes which were distributed among the 'members'. . . . It may thus be open to question whether the sexual activities of the applicants fell entirely within the notion of 'private life' in the particular circumstances of the case.[202]

The English Court of Appeal has held that Article 8 is not engaged by a criminal conviction and subsequent loss of employment, for performing sexual acts in a public lavatory.[203]

3. PRIVATE ACTS AND THE PROTECTION OF MORALS

Article 8(2) contemplates that privacy rights may be infringed, to some extent, for the 'protection of morals'. The *Dudgeon* case indicates, however, that the state's power in this regard may be strictly construed. It is not clear from the judgment what private consensual acts, if any, may be regulated on that basis. Put another way, it is not clear whether there are any instances of private conduct which are proscribable *just* because they are offensive to public morality. The Court affirms the propriety of legislation against homosexual conduct insofar as necessary to protect against exploitation of vulnerable people—those 'young, weak in body or mind, inexperienced, or in a state of physical, official, or economic dependence'.[204] But, such narrower legislation would be supportable under the Article 8(2) exception for legislation necessary for the 'protection of the rights and freedoms of others'.

As illustrated in Judge Walsh's dissent, the invocation of the protection of morals to limit the exercise of individual rights raises a long-standing difference as to the proper subject of legal regulation. On one side is the idea that the law has no place in restricting any conduct that is freely chosen by the actor and that causes no harm to anyone else—self-regarding conduct. This position is expressed in Article 4 of the French Declaration of Rights of Man and Citizen which states that '[l]iberty consists of the power to do whatever is not injurious to others', and has been elaborated by many

---

[202] *Laskey, Jaggard & Brown v. United Kingdom*, 19 Feb. 1997, 24 E.H.R.R. 39, para. 36. In *Halford v. United Kingdom*, 25 June 1997, 24 E.H.R.R. 523, the Court found Art. 8 applicable when a police officer's office telephone, part of a separate police communication system, was tapped by police authorities. The Court pointed out that the phone was one of two in the applicant's office and had been designated for personal use. *Id.* at paras. 44–5.

[203] *X v. Y* [2004] E.W.C.A. 662.

[204] Para. 49 quoting the Wolfenden Report. *See also* para. 61.

'libertarian' political and legal theorists, most notably probably, John Stuart Mill.[205] The Convention, by explicitly including the protection of morals as a proper justification for limiting some rights, appears to adopt the opposite view. If homosexual activity is 'immoral', it is hard to see how legislation prohibiting it can fail to further the protection of morals. It would have been open, of course, for the Court to conclude, as a matter of the law of the Convention, that homosexuality is not immoral but that is something it explicitly refused to do.[206]

The European Court has only rarely relied on a state's power to protect morals to justify an interference with Convention rights. In the *Handyside Case*, reprinted in the previous chapter, the Court noted that given the variation in moral views, a particularly generous margin of appreciation was appropriate. It relied on this rationale in refusing to find a violation in that case, as well as in the case of *Müller and Others*, where it found permissible a decision to prosecute an artist for a display of obscenity.[207]

The Court's reluctance to rely on the justification of protection of morals was particularly evident in *Laskey, Jaggard & Brown v. United Kingdom*, discussed above, involving group sado-masochistic activities.[208] The Court held there was no violation but relied solely on the risk of physical harm. In the judgment of the House of Lords, in contrast, the moral aspects of the prosecution had been prominent. Lord Templeton insisted that '[s]ociety is entitled and bound to protect itself against a cult of violence. Pleasure derived from the infliction of pain is an evil thing. Cruelty is uncivilized'.[209]

In 2002 the United States Supreme Court held that a state law criminalizing homosexual relations was deprivation of liberty without due process of law, in violation of the Fourteenth Amendment to the U.S. Constitution. The majority opinion, which cited several judgments of the European Court of Human Rights, concluded that the prohibition of sexual relations in private between consenting adults furthered 'no legitimate state interest which can justify its intrusion into the personal and private life of the individual'. The fact, moreover, that 'the governing majority in a state has traditionally viewed a particular practice as immoral is not a sufficient reason for upholding a law prohibiting the practice'. The dissenting opinion understood this reasoning to 'effectively decree the end of all morals legislation'.[210]

In holding a sodomy law invalid the Constitutional Court of South Africa was direct in declining to consider moral values present in society: '[t]he enforcement of the private moral views of a portion of the community, which are based to a large extent on nothing more than prejudice, cannot qualify as such a legitimate purpose [as to justify

[205] E.g. J. S. Mill, *On Liberty* (C. Shields ed. 1956). This is also the view defended by H. L. A. Hart cited in the dissenting opinion in *Dudgeon. See*, e.g., H. L. A. Hart, *Law, Liberty and Morality* (1963).
[206] Para. 54.
[207] *See* Chapter 6(B) *supra*.
[208] On the justification based on the protection of morals *see* C. Nowlin, *The Protection of Morals under the European Convention for the Protection of Human Rights and Fundamental Freedoms*, 24 Human Rights Q. 264 (2004).
[209] *R. v. Brown* [1993] 2 All E.R. 75, 84.
[210] *Lawrence v. Texas*, 539 U.S. 558, 577–8 and 599 (Scalia J dissenting).

legislation limiting rights]. There is accordingly nothing in the proportionality enquiry, to weigh against the extent of the limitation and its harmful impact on gays'.[211]

The Supreme Court of Canada has also diminished the importance of public morality as a sufficient ground for justifying regulation that implicates constitutional protections. A law criminalizing the sale and distribution of obscene material was upheld not on the basis of 'moral disapprobation but the avoidance of [the] harm to society' caused by the exploitation of women and children and its interference with the promotion of gender equality.[212] In 2003, however, the Supreme Court of Canada declined to adopt the general rule that restrictions on conduct that did no specific harm to other people was thereby unconstitutional. It found that the 'harm' principle propounded by Mill was not one of the 'principles of fundamental justice' referred to in section 7 of the Charter of Rights and Freedoms. It cited such laws as those relating to cannibalism, bestiality, incest, duelling, and cruelty to animals as resting on 'their offensiveness to deeply held social values'. In the case being decided, it upheld the criminal ban on possession of marijuana, although it also laid great stress on the risk to other people from the impaired behaviour of users.[213] Later, however, when construing the Criminal Code's prohibition of 'bawdy-houses' used for the 'practice of acts of indecency', it held that acts of indecency must involve 'a risk of harm incompatible with the proper functioning of society'. Referring to 'the fundamental values of our Constitution', it named some things that did not amount to sufficient harm: 'Bad taste does not suffice: Moral views even if strongly held, do not suffice'. Public displays of some sexual conduct, however, since they can 'seriously impair the livability of the environment and significantly constrain autonomy' may constitute the kind of harm that may be prohibited. The reference to autonomy was based on the Court's conclusion that such public activity could limit the lifestyles of people who 'seek to avoid confrontation with acts they find offensive and unacceptable'.[214]

4. PRIVATE LIFE AND SEXUAL PREFERENCES

The European Court reaffirmed its holding in *Dudgeon* in *Norris v. Ireland*.[215] There a challenge was posed to the very same statutes insofar as they were continued in Ireland after independence from the United Kingdom. In that case, the government urged the Court to adopt a more deferential approach to a state's determination that challenged measures were necessary for the protection of morals. It argued that '[w]ithin broad parameters the moral fibre of a democratic nation is a matter for its own

---

[211] *National Coalition for Gay and Lesbian Equality and Another v. Minister for Justice and Other* [1999] S.A.L.R. 6, para. 37.

[212] *R. v. Butler* [1992] 1 S.C.R. 452, 466–7.

[213] *R. v. Malmo-Levine; R. v. Caine* [2003] 3 S.C.R. 571, paras. 106–22; 135–6.

[214] *R. v. Labaye* [2005] 3 S.C.R. 728, at paras. 24, 40–1.

[215] 26 Oct. 1988, 13 E.H.R.R. 186.

institutions'. The Court rejected this suggestion, concluding that to accept it would result in the state's 'discretion in the field of morals [being] unfettered'.[216] In 1993 the Court ruled that the criminal prohibition on homosexual activity in Cyprus violated the Convention, notwithstanding the government's argument that no prosecutions had been brought under the law for a long time and there were no plans to do so. The Court noted that there was no assurance that prosecutions might not be brought or police investigations undertaken in the future.[217] It took Cyprus another five years to comply with the judgment by decriminalizing consensual homosexual conduct.[218]

The European Court of Human Rights has extended the holding in *Dudgeon* to find that Article 8 protects group sexual activity. In *A.D.T. v. United Kingdom*[219] the applicant was convicted of gross indecency after the police found videotapes in his house showing sexual acts with up to four other men. While the Court accepted in principle the government's contention that 'at some point sexual activities can be carried out in such a manner' that state interference is justified for the protection of health or morals, it found that this was not the case where the applicant engaged in sexual activities 'with a restricted number of friends' and where no public health risks were identified. Such 'genuinely "private"' conduct was not proscribable. In *Laskey, Jaggard and Brown v. United Kingdom*,[220] on the other hand, the arrests were for a long course of incidents over ten years involving sado-masochistic sex with a total of as many as 44 other men. The acts recorded included wounding resulting in bleeding and scarring. The Court stressed the violence of the applicants' activities in finding the prosecution necessary for the protection of health.

The reasoning of *Dudgeon* subsequently led the European Court to hold that the imposition of a higher age consent for sexual relationships between men was a violation of Article 14 in conjunction with Article 8.[221] The idea that sexual preference is an impermissible ground for discrimination has been extended beyond the criminal law. The progression of those rights was summed up in an article by Baroness Hale of Richmond, a judge in the House of Lords:

The first steps are taken by the criminal law; permitting homosexual acts by male adults, and then removing age and other distinctions between same- and opposite-sex sexual activity. The next steps are taken by the civil law; prohibiting discrimination against homosexuals in employment, and in the provision of goods, education, housing and other services. The final steps are taken by family law, extending laws applicable to unmarried heterosexual couples to homosexual couples, recognizing the parental relationship between homosexual parents and their own,

---

[216] *Id.* at para 45. The extent of a state's 'margin of appreciation'—especially with regard to the protection of morals—is discussed in Chapter 6(B) *supra*.

[217] *Modinos v. Cyprus*, 22 Apr. 1993, 16 E.H.R.R. 485.

[218] 'Cyprus Parliament Approves "Gay Sex" Law', Agence France Press, 21 May 1998 (available in Lexis/ Nexis, News Library).

[219] 31 July 2000, 31 E.H.R.R. 33.

[220] 19 Feb. 1997, 24 E.H.R.R. 39.

[221] *L & V v. Austria*, 9 Jan. 2003; *S.L. v. Austria*, 9 Jan. 2003, 37 E.H.R.R. 39.

their partners' and even other people's children, providing for registered civil partnerships, and finally providing for marriage.[222]

The Court in Strasbourg has, in this connection, held that a differentiation between a homosexual and heterosexual parent with respect to a right to custody was impermissible under Article 14 of the Convention.[223] But it declined to do the same with respect to a decision to withhold authorization to adopt a child on the grounds of the applicant's sexual orientation. In the latter case, it cited the lack of 'common ground' among contracting states on the question indicating the appropriateness of a wide margin of appreciation. It also observed that 'the scientific community—particularly experts on childhood, psychiatrists and psychologists—is divided over the possible consequences of a child being adopted by one or more homosexual parents'.[224]

The Court in *Karner v. Austria* found impermissible discrimination in connection with the right to a 'home' when a surviving same-sex partner was held not to be a 'life companion' with the right to succeed to a tenancy.[225] The House of Lords followed this judgment when it invoked section 3 of the Human Rights Act[226] to construe 'living with the original tenant as his or her wife or husband' in the Rent Act 1977 as including 'living in a close and stable homosexual relationship' for the purpose of defining the right to succession of a statutory tenancy.[227] On the other hand, the Strasbourg Court dismissed as inadmissible an argument that exclusion of a same-sex partner from social insurance benefits raised an issue of discrimination with respect to family life.[228] In 2006 the House of Lords reached a similar conclusion with respect to the applicability of Articles 8 and 14 to the different calculations of support obligations of non-custodial parents depending on whether they were living with a same or opposite sex partner.[229]

In the United Kingdom, many of these issues were rendered moot on 5 December 2005 by the coming into force of the Civil Partnership Act 2004. That Act places cohabiting homosexual and heterosexual couples in the same position with respect to many legal rules governing taxes and social benefits. The Act further offers same-sex couples the opportunity to register their relationship as a civil partnership, which creates for such couples a status in civil law more or less identical to marriage. The rights of same-sex couples to legally recognized marriage is discussed in Section D(2) below.

The Strasbourg Court has further held that the United Kingdom's policy of excluding and discharging homosexuals from the armed forces violates Article 8.[230]

---

[222] B. Hale, 'Homosexual Rights', 16 *Child and Family Law Quarterly* 125 (2004) quoted in *Secretary of State for Work and Pensions v. M.* [2006] UKHL 11, para. 93 (opinion of Lord Walker of Gestingthorpe).

[223] *Salgueiro da Silva Mouta v. Portugal, supra* n. 187.

[224] *Fretté v. France*, 26 Feb. 2002, 38 E.H.R.R. 21, para. 42.

[225] 24 July 2003, 38 E.H.R.R. 24.

[226] *See* Chapter 14(D), *infra.*

[227] *Ghaidan v. Godin-Mendoza* [2004] U.K.H.L. 30. And *see* Chapter 14(D)(5) *infra.*

[228] *Mato Estevez v. Spain, supra* n. 50.

[229] *Secretary of State for Work and Pensions v. M.* [2006] U.K.H.L. 11.

[230] *Smith & Grady v. United Kingdom* and *Lustig-Prean & Beckett v. United Kingdom*, 27 Sept. 1999, 29 E.H.R.R. 493.

The principal argument of the government was that in military service 'cohesion and morale had to withstand the internal rigours of normal and corporate life, close physical and shared living conditions together with external pressures such as grave danger and work'.[231] In such circumstances, the fact of entrenched attitudes of hostility, suspicion or discomfort directed towards homosexuals could compromise the operational effectiveness and 'fighting power' of the forces.[232] The Court held that, to the extent such consequences were a result of negative attitudes, they could not provide a sufficient justification under Article 8(2), 'any more than similar negative attitudes towards those of a different race, origin or colour'.[233] The Court noted that a strict code of conduct, such as that already in place with respect to discrimination or harassment based on race or gender, was an alternative to the exclusionary policy, with a much less severe impact on the private life of homosexuals.[234]

The constitutional law of Canada has dealt with interference with expression of sexual identity under the equality provision of the Charter which prohibits discrimination 'in particular … based on race, national or ethnic origin, colour, religion, sex, age or mental or physical disability'. In *Egan v. Canada*[235] the Supreme Court held that discrimination against homosexuals was discrimination on a ground 'analogous' to those listed and, therefore, required justification under section 1 of the Charter. Some of the justices based this finding on the personal and practically immutable nature of sexual orientation[236] and some on the history of discrimination suffered by homosexuals.[237] The practice challenged in *Egan*, the exclusion of same-sex couples from old age security benefits, was upheld as justifiable under section 1. But in *Vriend v. Alberta*[238] the Court held that the exclusion of sexual orientation as a prohibited ground of private discrimination in the Alberta Individual Rights Protection Act constituted discrimination against homosexuals and was not justified under section 1.

In *M v. H*,[239] the Canadian Court held invalid under section 15 the Ontario Family Law Act which limited spousal support rights and obligations to participants in heterosexual relationships. The Court reasoned that same-sex relationships could involve the same problems of economic dependence which the Court took to be the target of the law. It held that the statutory limitation in no way contributed to the alleviation of this problem.[240] On the other hand, it has also held that heterosexual couples who had chosen not to marry could not invoke the rules of the provincial Matrimonial Property Act when they separated.[241]

---

[231] *Id.* at para. 77.
[232] *Id.* at para. 95.
[233] *Id.* at para. 97.
[234] *Id.* at para. 102.
[235] [1995] 2 S.C.R. 513.
[236] *Id.* at 528 (La Forest J).
[237] *Id.* at 599–603 (Cory J).
[238] [1997] 1 S.C.R. 493.
[239] [1999] 2 S.C.R. 3.
[240] *Id.* at paras. 108–35.
[241] *Nova Scotia (Attorney-General) v. Walsh* [2002] 4 S.C.R. 325.

There is no explicit provision protecting privacy, intimate decisions or family life in the United States Constitution. The courts, however, have found a right to be free of government coercion in these areas to be part of the 'liberty' protected by the Fifth and Fourteenth Amendments of which a person may not be deprived without due process of law.[242] Modern cases have translated this into a doctrine which requires that governmental interference in this sphere of private life is not permissible in the absence of a particularly strong governmental justification. In 2003, in *Lawrence v. Texas*,[243] the United States Supreme Court held homosexual relations to fall into this category and declared unconstitutional a Texas law criminalizing intimate homosexual conduct. It overruled a 1986 precedent to the contrary and cited the *Dudgeon* case as evidence against the assertion that the condemnation of homosexuality was the rule in the history of Western civilization.[244]

In a case brought before the Constitutional Court of the Federal Republic of Germany, in 1957, two male homosexuals claimed that Section 175 of the Penal Code punishing homosexual acts violated Article 2(1) of the Basic Law which states: 'Everyone should have the right to the free development of his personality insofar as he does not infringe the rights of others or offend against the constitutional order or the moral code'. The Court agreed that this constitutional provision provided some protection for personal decisions regarding sexual conduct. It found, however, that the 'moral code' unequivocally condemned homosexual behaviour. It relied upon the attitude of the two dominant Christian denominations and a long history of anti-homosexuality laws which were rooted in public aversion to such acts. It was not dissuaded from this conclusion by the existence of more liberal laws elsewhere in Western Europe, noting that such changes might be for reasons unrelated to moral judgment and that, in any event, German moral disapproval was decisive.[245]

On the other hand, the Constitutional Court of South Africa has held invalid the criminal prohibition of homosexual acts. It invoked section 9, the equality provision, section 9(3) explicitly listing sexual orientation as a prohibited ground of discrimination. The Court went on to hold that the criminal law was also invalid under section 10, stating a right to 'dignity' and under section 14, the right to privacy. In connection with its holding on section 10 it said that the law's

symbolic effect is to state that in the eyes of our legal system all gay men are criminals. The stigma thus attached to a significant proportion of our population is manifest. But the harm imposed by the criminal law is far more than symbolic. As a result of the criminal offence gay men are at risk of arrest, prosecution and conviction of the offence of sodomy simply because they seek to engage in sexual conduct which is part of their experience of being human. Just as apartheid legislation rendered the lives of couples of different racial groups perpetually at risk,

---

[242] *See Meyer v. Nebraska*, discussed at Section B(4) *supra*.

[243] 539 U.S. 558 (2003).

[244] *Id.* at 573.

[245] BVerfGE 389 (1957) reported in part in Murphy & Tanehous, *Comparative Constitutional Law: Cases and Commentaries* 403 (1977). The German law criminalizing consensual homosexual acts was repealed in 1994. StGB §175 repealed as of 31 May 1994, by Art. 1, No. 1, BGBl–I, 1168.

the sodomy offence builds insecurity and vulnerability into the daily lives of gay men...[The law] degrades and devalues gay men in our broader society. As such it is a palpable invasion of their dignity and a breach of section 10 of the Constitution.[246]

The South African Court subsequently held that limiting joint adoption rights to married couples was unconstitutional. The restriction was held to be an improper discrimination on the grounds of sexual orientation. It was also found inconsistent with section 28(2) of the Constitution declaring that a 'child's best interests are of paramount importance in every matter concerning the child'.[247]

5. PRIVACY RIGHTS AND ABORTION

Laws regulating abortion raise two kinds of problems under the Convention. To the extent they limit the performance of abortions, they may be impermissible invasions of the personal autonomy that the European Court has found encompassed in Article 8's right of privacy. To the extent they allow abortions, they may engage a right to life for the foetus creating a problem under Article 2.

The Court has not addressed the first question directly. An early report of the European Commission acknowledged that limiting access to abortion engaged a pregnant woman's Article 8 rights although it held the restriction in that case justified under Article 8(2).[248] Far more common have been claims that abortions allowed under law violated the right to life. While not directly speaking to the point, the Court's pronounced reluctance to treat the foetus as fully entitled to the Convention's right to life demonstrates a willingness to recognize the importance of the woman's right to decide. In *Vo v. France*, excerpted in Chapter 4, the Court went to some pains to state that 'the unborn child is not regarded as a "person" directly protected by Article 2 of the Convention and that if the unborn do have a "right" to "life," it is implicitly limited by the mother's rights and interests'.[249] A panel of the Court had earlier held inadmissible an application of a father who invoked Article 2 in seeking compensation after his wife procured an abortion over his objection.[250]

In *Open Door Counselling and Dublin Well Woman v. Ireland*,[251] the Court held that the issuance of an injunction by an Irish court against communicating information about the availability of abortions in the United Kingdom was an unjustified interference with the right of free expression under Article 10. In that case, however, the Court carefully avoided expressing an opinion as to 'whether a right to abortion is guaranteed

---

[246] *Nation Coalition for Gay & Lesbian Equality and Another v. Minister for Justice and Another* [1999] 1 S.A.C.R. 6 (10 Sept. 1998).

[247] *DuToit & DeVos v. Minister for Welfare and Population Development* (2002) 10 B.C.L.R. 106 (C.C.)

[248] *Bruggeman and Scheuten v. Germany*, 12 July 1977, 3 E.H.R.R. 244 (Commission report).

[249] 8 July 2004, 40 E.H.R.R. 12, para. 80.

[250] *Boso v. Italy*, 5 Sept. 2002.

[251] 29 Oct. 1992, 15 E.H.R.R. 244.

under the Convention.[252] Similarly, it refused to decide whether the protection of the rights of others, mentioned in Article 10, paragraph 2 extended to the unborn. It did hold, however, that the Irish prohibition of abortion pursued a legitimate aim under that provision—'the protection of morals of which the protection, in Ireland, of the right to life of the unborn is one aspect'. This conclusion was based on the 'profound moral values concerning the nature of life which were reflected in the stance of the majority of the Irish people'.[253]

The best known application of the modern American doctrine protecting the right of privacy has involved the right of a woman to procure an abortion. In *Roe v. Wade*[254] the Supreme Court held that a state could not proscribe abortions in the first trimester of pregnancy and that it could regulate abortions in the second trimester only insofar as reasonably related to maternal health.

In a subsequent decision on abortion, the Supreme Court reformulated the critical test for the validity of restrictions on abortions. Three justices, holding the essential votes for any determination, rejected the trimester analysis. The test throughout a pregnancy was to be the same: 'Only where state regulation imposes an undue burden on a woman's ability to make this [abortion] decision does the power of the state reach into the heart of this liberty'.[255] These justices defined 'undue burden' as one having the purpose or effect of 'placing a substantial obstacle in the path of a woman's choice'. The state's interest in protecting health and potential life would be evaluated within this framework. Four justices joined a separate opinion which would have overruled *Roe*. These justices condemned the 'undue burden' test as an 'inherently manipulable, [one which] will prove hopelessly unworkable in practice'.[256] Nevertheless, the majority of the Court applied the 'undue burden' test in two later cases to bans on 'partial birth' abortions. Different majorities found a state law invalid but a federal law valid. In both cases the question was whether the resulting risk to maternal health from prohibiting the procedure unduly hindered the right to terminate a pregnancy.[257]

In 1988 the Supreme Court of Canada declared invalid Section 251 of the Canadian Criminal Code which limited the performance of abortions to those performed in approved hospitals and certified by a hospital committee as necessary to terminate a pregnancy that would be likely to endanger the life or health of the pregnant woman. The Court found that the provision violated Section 7 of the Canadian Charter of Rights and Freedoms which prohibits deprivation of 'life, liberty or security of the person…except in accordance with the principles of fundamental justice'. The Court concluded first that a ban on abortion could constitute a substantial threat to 'security of the person'. It then found that the statute was not in accordance with 'principles of

---

[252] *Id.* at para. 66.

[253] *Id.* at para. 63.

[254] 410 U.S. 113 (1973).

[255] *Planned Parenthood of Southeastern Pennsylvania v. Casey*, 505 U.S. 833 (1992) (joint opinion of O'Connor, Kennedy and Souter JJ).

[256] *Id.* at 986 (Scalia J concurring in the judgment in part and dissenting in part).

[257] Compare *Stenberg v. Carhart*, 530 U.S. 914 (2004) with *Gonzales v. Carhart* (slip op. 18 April 2007).

fundamental justice', because the procedures it provided had the effect of preventing abortions even for those women who, under the standard set out, Parliament had determined had a sufficient reason for the abortion. The majority did not find it necessary to decide whether Parliament's substantive reasons for restricting abortions were in accord with 'fundamental justice'.[258]

D. PRIVATE LIFE AND PERSONAL IDENTITY

1. SEXUAL IDENTITY

A. CHRISTINE GOODWIN V. UNITED KINGDOM

11 July 2002
[G.C.], 35 E.H.R.R. 18

12. The applicant is a United Kingdom citizen born in 1937 and is a post-operative male to female transsexual.

13. The applicant had a tendency to dress as a woman from early childhood and underwent aversion therapy in 1963–64. In the mid-1960s, she was diagnosed as a transsexual. Though she married a woman and they had four children, her conviction was that her 'brain sex' did not fit her body. From that time until 1984 she dressed as a man for work but as a woman in her free time. In January 1985, the applicant began treatment in earnest, attending appointments once every three months at the Gender Identity Clinic at the Charing Cross Hospital, which included regular consultations with a psychiatrist as well as on occasion a psychologist. She was prescribed hormone therapy, began attending grooming classes and voice training. Since this time, she has lived fully as a woman. In October 1986, she underwent surgery to shorten her vocal chords. In August 1987, she was accepted on the waiting list for gender re-assignment surgery. In 1990, she underwent gender re-assignment surgery at a National Health Service hospital. Her treatment and surgery was provided for and paid for by the National Health Service.

...

20. Under English law, a person is entitled to adopt such first names or surname as he or she wishes. Such names are valid for the purposes of identification and may be used in passports, driving licences, medical and insurance cards, etc. The new names are also entered on the electoral roll.

---

[258] *Morgentaler v. R.* [1988] 1 S.C.R. 60.

21. Under English law, marriage is defined as the voluntary union between a man and a woman. In the case of *Corbett v. Corbett* ([1971] Probate Reports 83), Mr Justice Ormrod ruled that sex for that purpose is to be determined by the application of chromosomal, gonadal and genital tests where these are congruent and without regard to any surgical intervention. This use of biological criteria to determine sex was approved by the Court of Appeal in *R. v. Tan* ([1983] Queen's Bench Reports 1053) and given more general application, the court holding that a person born male had been correctly convicted under a statute penalising men who live on the earnings of prostitution, notwithstanding the fact that the accused had undergone gender reassignment therapy.

[The law of the United Kingdom failed to recognize the change of gender in various official records including the applicant's birth certificate. As a result, the applicant suffered a number of disadvantages with respect to entitlement to government benefits, employment and other financial relations.]

15. Liberty [a third-party intervener] updated the written observations submitted in the case of *Sheffield and Horsham* concerning the legal recognition of transsexuals in comparative law (*Sheffield and Horsham v. United Kingdom* judgment of 30 July 1998, *Reports of Judgments and Decisions* 1998-V, p. 2021, § 35). In its 1998 study, it had found that over the previous decade there had been an unmistakable trend in the member States of the Council of Europe towards giving full legal recognition to gender re-assignment. In particular, it noted that out of thirty seven countries analysed only four (including the United Kingdom) did not permit a change to be made to a person's birth certificate in one form or another to reflect the re-assigned sex of that person. In cases where gender re-assignment was legal and publicly funded, only the United Kingdom and Ireland did not give full legal recognition to the new gender identity.

52. In its follow up study submitted on 17 January 2002, Liberty noted that while there had not been a statistical increase in States giving full legal recognition of gender re-assignment within Europe, information from outside Europe showed developments in this direction. For example, there had been statutory recognition of gender re-assignment in Singapore, and a similar pattern of recognition in Canada, South Africa, Israel, Australia, New Zealand and all except two of the States of the United States of America. It cited in particular the cases of *Attorney-General v. Otahuhu Family Court* [1995] 1 NZLR 60 and *Re Kevin* [2001] FamCA 1074 where in New Zealand and Australia transsexual persons' assigned sex was recognised for the purposes of validating their marriages....

53. As regarded the eligibility of post-operative transsexuals to marry a person of sex opposite to their acquired gender, Liberty's survey indicated that 54% of Contracting States permitted such marriage (Annex 6 listed Austria, Belgium, Denmark, Estonia, Finland, France, Germany, Greece, Iceland, Italy, Latvia, Luxembourg, the Netherlands, Norway, Slovakia, Spain, Sweden, Switzerland, Turkey and Ukraine), while 14% did not (Ireland and the United Kingdom did not permit marriage, while no legislation existed in Moldova, Poland, Romania and Russia). The legal position in the remaining 32% was unclear....

71. This case raises the issue whether or not the respondent State has failed to comply with a positive obligation to ensure the right of the applicant, a post-operative male to female transsexual, to respect for her private life, in particular through the lack of legal recognition given to her gender re-assignment....

73. The Court recalls that it has already examined complaints about the position of trans-sexuals in the United Kingdom (see the *Rees v. United Kingdom* judgment of 17 October 1986, Series A no. 106, the *Cossey v. United Kingdom* judgment of 27 September 1990, Series A no. 184; the *X., Y. and Z. v. United Kingdom* judgment of 22 April 1997, *Reports of Judgments and Decisions* 1997–II, and the *Sheffield and Horsham v. United Kingdom* judgment of 30 July 1998, *Reports* 1998–V, p. 2011). In those cases, it held that the refusal of the United Kingdom Government to alter the register of births or to issue birth certificates whose contents and nature differed from those of the original entries concerning the recorded gender of the individual could not be considered as an interference with the right to respect for private life. It also held that there was no positive obligation on the Government to alter their existing system for the registration of births by establishing a new system or type of documentation to provide proof of current civil status. Similarly, there was no duty on the Government to permit annotations to the existing register of births, or to keep any such annotation secret from third parties. It was found in those cases that the authorities had taken steps to minimise intrusive enquiries (for example, by allowing transsexuals to be issued with driving licences, passports and other types of documents in their new name and gender). Nor had it been shown that the failure to accord general legal recognition of the change of gender had given rise in the applicants' own case histories to detriment of sufficient seriousness to override the respondent State's margin of appreciation in this area.

74. While the Court is not formally bound to follow its previous judgments, it is in the interests of legal certainty, foreseeability and equality before the law that it should not depart, without good reason, from precedents laid down in previous cases. However, since the Convention is first and foremost a system for the protection of human rights, the Court must have regard to the changing conditions within the respondent State and within Contracting States generally and respond, for example, to any evolving convergence as to the standards to be achieved. It is of crucial importance that the Convention is interpreted and applied in a manner which renders its rights practical and effective, not theoretical and illusory. A failure by the Court to maintain a dynamic and evolutive approach would indeed risk rendering it a bar to reform or improvement. In the present context the Court has, on several occasions since 1986, signalled its consciousness of the serious problems facing transsexuals and stressed the importance of keeping the need for appropriate legal measures in this area under review.

...

77. It must also be recognised that serious interference with private life can arise where the state of domestic law conflicts with an important aspect of personal identity (see, *mutatis mutandis, Dudgeon v. United Kingdom* judgment of 22 October 1981, Series A no. 45, § 41). The stress and alienation arising from a discordance between the position in society assumed by a post-operative transsexual and the status imposed by law which refuses to recognise the change of gender cannot, in the Court's view, be regarded as a minor inconvenience arising from a formality. A conflict between social reality and law arises which places the transsexual in an anomalous position, in which he or she may experience feelings of vulnerability, humiliation and anxiety.

78. In this case, as in many others, the applicant's gender re-assignment was carried out by the national health service, which recognises the condition of gender dysphoria and provides, *inter alia*, re-assignment by surgery, with a view to achieving as one of its principal purposes as

close an assimilation as possible to the gender in which the transsexual perceives that he or she properly belongs. The Court is struck by the fact that nonetheless the gender re-assignment which is lawfully provided is not met with full recognition in law, which might be regarded as the final and culminating step in the long and difficult process of transformation which the transsexual has undergone. The coherence of the administrative and legal practices within the domestic system must be regarded as an important factor in the assessment carried out under Article 8 of the Convention. Where a State has authorised the treatment and surgery alleviating the condition of a transsexual, financed or assisted in financing the operations and indeed permits the artificial insemination of a woman living with a female-to-male, it appears illogical to refuse to recognise the legal implications of the result to which the treatment leads....

84. It remains the case that there are no conclusive findings as to the cause of transsexualism and, in particular, whether it is wholly psychological or associated with physical differentiation in the brain. The expert evidence in the domestic case of *Bellinger v. Bellinger* [EWCA Civ 1140 [2001]] was found to indicate a growing acceptance of findings of sexual differences in the brain that are determined pre-natally, though scientific proof for the theory was far from complete. The Court considers it more significant however that transsexualism has wide international recognition as a medical condition for which treatment is provided in order to afford relief (for example, the Diagnostic and Statistical Manual fourth edition (DSM-IV) replaced the diagnosis of transsexualism with 'gender identity disorder'; see also the International Classification of Diseases, tenth edition (ICD-10)). The United Kingdom national health service, in common with the vast majority of Contracting States, acknowledges the existence of the condition and provides or permits treatment, including irreversible surgery. The medical and surgical acts which in this case rendered the gender re-assignment possible were indeed carried out under the supervision of the national health authorities. Nor, given the numerous and painful interventions involved in such surgery and the level of commitment and conviction required to achieve a change in social gender role, can it be suggested that there is anything arbitrary or capricious in the decision taken by a person to undergo gender re-assignment. In those circumstances, the ongoing scientific and medical debate as to the exact causes of the condition is of diminished relevance.

82. While it also remains the case that a transsexual cannot acquire all the biological characteristics of the assigned sex, the Court notes that with increasingly sophisticated surgery and types of hormonal treatments, the principal unchanging biological aspect of gender identity is the chromosomal element. It is known however that chromosomal anomalies may arise naturally (for example, in cases of intersex conditions where the biological criteria at birth are not congruent) and in those cases, some persons have to be assigned to one sex or the other as seems most appropriate in the circumstances of the individual case. It is not apparent to the Court that the chromosomal element, amongst all the others, must inevitably take on decisive significance for the purposes of legal attribution of gender identity for transsssexuals.

83. The Court is not persuaded therefore that the state of medical science or scientific knowledge provides any determining argument as regards the legal recognition of transsexuals.

84. Already at the time of the *Sheffield and Horsham* case, there was an emerging consensus within Contracting States in the Council of Europe on providing legal recognition following gender re-assignment. The latest survey submitted by Liberty in the present case shows a continuing international trend towards legal recognition. In Australia and New Zealand, it

appears that the courts are moving away from the biological birth view of sex (as set out in the United Kingdom case of *Corbett v. Corbett* [cite 1971]) and taking the view that sex, in the context of a transsexual wishing to marry, should depend on a multitude of factors to be assessed at the time of the marriage.

85. The Court observes that in the case of *Rees* in 1986 it had noted that little common ground existed between States, some of which did permit change of gender and some of which did not and that generally speaking the law seemed to be in a state of transition. In the later case of *Sheffield and Horsham*, the Court's judgment laid emphasis on the lack of a common European approach as to how to address the repercussions which the legal recognition of a change of sex may entail for other areas of law such as marriage, filiation, privacy or data protection. While this would appear to remain the case, the lack of such a common approach among forty-three Contracting States with widely diverse legal systems and traditions is hardly surprising. In accordance with the principle of subsidiarity, it is indeed primarily for the Contracting States to decide on the measures necessary to secure Convention rights within their jurisdiction and, in resolving within their domestic legal systems the practical problems created by the legal recognition of post-operative gender status, the Contracting States must enjoy a wide margin of appreciation. The Court accordingly attaches less importance to the lack of evidence of a common European approach to the resolution of the legal and practical problems posed, than to the clear and uncontested evidence of a continuing international trend in favour not only of increased social acceptance of transsexuals but of legal recognition of the new sexual identity of post-operative transsexuals.

86. In the *Rees* case, the Court allowed that great importance could be placed by the Government on the historical nature of the birth record system. The argument that allowing exceptions to this system would undermine its function weighed heavily in the assessment.

87. It may be noted however that exceptions are already made to the historic basis of the birth register system, namely, in the case of legitimisation or adoptions, where there is a possibility of issuing updated certificates to reflect a change in status after birth. To make a further exception in the case of transsexuals (a category estimated as including some 2,000–5,000 persons in the United Kingdom according to the Interdepartmental Working Group Report, p. 26) would not, in the Court's view, pose the threat of overturning the entire system. Though previous reference has been made to detriment suffered by third parties who might be unable to obtain access to the original entries and to complications occurring in the field of family and succession law, these assertions are framed in general terms and the Court does not find, on the basis of the material before it at this time, that any real prospect of prejudice has been identified as likely to arise if changes were made to the current system.

88. Furthermore, the Court notes that the Government have recently issued proposals for reform which would allow ongoing amendment to civil status data. It is not convinced therefore that the need to uphold rigidly the integrity of the historic basis of the birth registration system takes on the same importance in the current climate as it did in 1986.

89. The Court has noted above the difficulties and anomalies of the applicant's situation as a post-operative transsexual. It must be acknowledged that the level of daily interference suffered by the applicant in *B. v. France* (judgment of 25 March 1992, Series A no. 232) has not been attained in this case and that on certain points the risk of difficulties or embarrassment faced by the present applicant may be avoided or minimised by the practices adopted by the authorities.

90. Nonetheless, the very essence of the Convention is respect for human dignity and human freedom. Under Article 8 of the Convention in particular, where the notion of personal autonomy is an important principle underlying the interpretation of its guarantees, protection is given to the personal sphere of each individual, including the right to establish details of their identity as individual human beings. In the twenty first century the right of transsexuals to personal development and to physical and moral security in the full sense enjoyed by others in society cannot be regarded as a matter of controversy requiring the lapse of time to cast clearer light on the issues involved. In short, the unsatisfactory situation in which post-operative transsexuals live in an intermediate zone as not quite one gender or the other is no longer sustainable. ...

91. ... No concrete or substantial hardship or detriment to the public interest has indeed been demonstrated as likely to flow from any change to the status of transsexuals and, as regards other possible consequences, the Court considers that society may reasonably be expected to tolerate a certain inconvenience to enable individuals to live in dignity and worth in accordance with the sexual identity chosen by them at great personal cost. ...

93. Having regard to the above considerations, the Court finds that the respondent Government can no longer claim that the matter falls within their margin of appreciation, save as regards the appropriate means of achieving recognition of the right protected under the Convention. Since there are no significant factors of public interest to weigh against the interest of this individual applicant in obtaining legal recognition of her gender re-assignment, it reaches the conclusion that the fair balance that is inherent in the Convention now tilts decisively in favour of the applicant. There has, accordingly, been a failure to respect her right to private life in breach of Article 8 of the Convention.

[The Court held unanimously that there had been a violation of Article 8. Its opinion on the applicant's claim of a violation of Article 12, the right to marry, is reproduced in the next section. It found no breach of Article 13 and that no separate issue arose with regard to Article 14.]

B. PERSONAL IDENTITY AND GENDER RE-ASSIGNMENT

The European Court's engagement with the claims of transsexuals for official recognition of their new gender illustrates clearly the relevance of European practice to the breadth of the margin of appreciation accorded respondent states. In a series of cases (cited in *Goodwin*) over a 15 year period the Court upheld, with increasing reluctance, the United Kingdom policy that used a post-operative transsexual's original gender for a variety of purposes. In each case, it reviewed the changing attitudes toward such practices in the European states, noting in the *Sheffield and Horsham* case in 1998 that, despite its repeated admonitions to keep the subject under review, the United Kingdom had failed to take steps to do so.[259] By the time of the *Goodwin* case the issue had been the subject of a serious reconsideration. As the judgment shows, the results of that study militated against the government's position.

---

[259] 30 July 1998, 27 E.H.R.R. 163, para. 60.

The general availability of gender re-assignment surgery from the United Kingdom National Health Service followed a judgment in the Court of Appeal that a local authority's blanket refusal to fund such procedures was impermissible under the National Health Service Act. That judgment, based on English principles of judicial review and not on the Convention, required, as a starting point for any policy, a recognition that transsexualism was an illness suitable for treatment.[260] Following the decision in *Goodwin*, the Gender Recognition Act 2004[261] came into force. Under it individuals (without reference to whether or not they have undergone gender re-assignment surgery) may apply to a Gender Recognition Panel for a certificate which is to be granted upon a showing that the applicant 'has or has had gender dysphoria [and] has lived in the acquired gender throughout a period of two years' immediately before the application.[262] Such a certificate will result in the applicant being treated as having the acquired gender as matter of law. In particular, it provides a mechanism for the issuance of a new birth certificate with the new gender and to allow marriage as a person of that gender.[263]

A large majority of European countries now allow birth certificates to be altered to indicate the new sex of the registered person. A number of American states have enacted similar provisions.[264] The European Court of Justice has held that discrimination in employment against a transsexual is sex discrimination prohibited by European Communities directives: '[W]here a person is dismissed on the ground that he or she intends to undergo, or has undergone, gender reassignment, he or she is treated unfavourably by comparison with persons of the sex to which he or she was deemed to belong before undergoing gender reassignment'.[265]

2. ARTICLE 12 AND THE RIGHT TO MARRY

A. CHRISTINE GOODWIN V. UNITED KINGDOM

11 July 2002
[G.C.], 35 E.H.R.R. 18

[That part of the judgment holding that the refusal to treat transsexuals according to their new gender for certain purposes violates Article 8 is excerpted in the previous section.]

---

[260] *R v. North West Lancashire Health Authority, Ex p. A* [2000] 1 W.L.R. 977.

[261] 2004 Ch. 7.

[262] S. 2(1)

[263] Ss. 9–17.

[264] *See*, e.g., La. Rev. Stat. art. 40, sec. 62; Mass. Ann. Laws ch. 46, sec. 13. *See also* Revised Statutes of Ontario (1990), Ch. V. 4, S 36.

[265] *P. v. S.* [1996] 2 C.M.L.R. 247, 263.

97. The Court recalls that in the cases of *Rees, Cossey* and *Sheffield and Horsham* the inability of the transsexuals in those cases to marry a person of the sex opposite to their re-assigned gender was not found in breach of Article 12 of the Convention. These findings were based variously on the reasoning that the right to marry referred to traditional marriage between persons of opposite biological sex, the view that continued adoption of biological criteria in domestic law for determining a person's sex for the purpose of marriage was encompassed within the power of Contracting States to regulate by national law the exercise of the right to marry and the conclusion that national laws in that respect could not be regarded as restricting or reducing the right of a transsexual to marry in such a way or to such an extent that the very essence of the right was impaired Reference was also made to the wording of Article 12 as protecting marriage as the basis of the family.

98. Reviewing the situation in 2002, the Court observes that Article 12 secures the fundamental right of a man and woman to marry and to found a family. The second aspect is not however a condition of the first and the inability of any couple to conceive or parent a child cannot be regarded as *per se* removing their right to enjoy the first limb of this provision.

99. The exercise of the right to marry gives rise to social, personal and legal consequences. It is subject to the national laws of the Contracting States but the limitations thereby introduced must not restrict or reduce the right in such a way or to such an extent that the very essence of the right is impaired (see *F. v. Switzerland* judgment of 18 December 1987, Series A no. 128, § 32).

100. It is true that the first sentence refers in express terms to the right of a man and woman to marry. The Court is not persuaded that at the date of this case it can still be assumed that these terms must refer to a determination of gender by purely biological criteria (as held by Ormrod J. in the case of *Corbett v. Corbett*, paragraph 21 above). There have been major social changes in the institution of marriage since the adoption of the Convention as well as dramatic changes brought about by developments in medicine and science in the field of transsexuality. The Court has found above, under Article 8 of the Convention, that a test of congruent biological factors can no longer be decisive in denying legal recognition to the change of gender of a post-operative transsexual. There are other important factors—the acceptance of the condition of gender identity disorder by the medical professions and health authorities within Contracting States, the provision of treatment including surgery to assimilate the individual as closely as possible to the gender in which they perceive that they properly belong and the assumption by the transsexual of the social role of the assigned gender. The Court would also note that Article 9 of the recently adopted Charter of Fundamental Rights of the European Union departs, no doubt deliberately, from the wording of Article 12 of the Convention in removing the reference to men and women.

101. The right under Article 8 to respect for private life does not however subsume all the issues under Article 12, where conditions imposed by national laws are accorded a specific mention. The Court has therefore considered whether the allocation of sex in national law to that registered at birth is a limitation impairing the very essence of the right to marry in this case. In that regard, it finds that it is artificial to assert that post-operative transsexuals have not been deprived of the right to marry as, according to law, they remain able to marry a person of their former opposite sex. The applicant in this case lives as a woman, is in a relationship with a man and would only wish to marry a man. She has no possibility of doing so. In the Court's view, she may therefore claim that the very essence of her right to marry has been infringed.

102. The Court has not identified any other reason which would prevent it from reaching this conclusion. The Government have argued that in this sensitive area eligibility for marriage under national law should be left to the domestic courts within the State's margin of appreciation, adverting to the potential impact on already existing marriages in which a transsexual is a partner. It appears however from the opinions of the majority of the Court of Appeal judgment in *Bellinger v. Bellinger* that the domestic courts tend to the view that the matter is best handled by the legislature, while the Government have no present intention to introduce legislation.

103. It may be noted from the materials submitted by Liberty that though there is widespread acceptance of the marriage of transsexuals, fewer countries permit the marriage of transsexuals in their assigned gender than recognise the change of gender itself. The Court is not persuaded however that this supports an argument for leaving the matter entirely to the Contracting States as being within their margin of appreciation. This would be tantamount to finding that the range of options open to a Contracting State included an effective bar on any exercise of the right to marry. The margin of appreciation cannot extend so far. While it is for the Contracting State to determine *inter alia* the conditions under which a person claiming legal recognition as a transsexual establishes that gender re-assignment has been properly effected or under which past marriages cease to be valid and the formalities applicable to future marriages (including, for example, the information to be furnished to intended spouses), the Court finds no justification for barring the transsexual from enjoying the right to marry under any circumstances.

[The Court held unanimously that there had been a breach of Article 12.]

B. RESTRICTIONS ON MARRIAGE

The text of Article 12 is unique in that it defines the right in question as one exercisable only 'according to the national laws governing the exercise of that right'. It surely cannot be the case that any restriction imposed on marriage by national law is consistent with the Convention, as that would make the right largely meaningless. The text of the Article seems to suppose a distinction between the right itself and the exercise of the right.

In *F. v. Switzerland*,[266] the European Court considered a law requiring a three year ban on remarriage after the applicant's third divorce. In that proceeding he had been found guilty of adultery and of particularly offensive behaviour. The Court held that national law may not 'restrict or reduce the right in such a way or to such an extent that the legitimate essence is impaired'.[267] It noted that regulation of marriage elsewhere in Europe related only to procedures, capacity or consent. In the case at hand the Court found that the measure affected 'the very essence of the right to marry [and] was disproportionate to the very aim pursued'.[268]

---

[266] 18 Dec. 1987, 10 E.H.R.R. 411.

[267] Para. 32 citing *Rees v. United Kingdom*, 17 Oct. 1986, 9 E.H.R.R. 56, para. 50.

[268] Para. 40. The Commission had reached the same conclusion in the case of a prisoner who was prevented from marrying for at least 15 months, the earliest date of parole. *Hamer v. United Kingdom*, 13 Dec. 1979, 4 E.H.R.R.139. This decision is to be distinguished from those involving prisoners' requests for conjugal visits and artificial insemination discussed below.

Although Article 12 has no counterpart to the justification provisions in the second paragraphs of Articles 8–11, in a recent case the Strasbourg Court seemed to assume that the presence or absence of a violation turned on the strength of the reasons for restriction cited by the government. In *B & L v. United Kingdom*, it found the prohibition of marriage between a man and his ex-daughter-in-law to be in conflict with Article 12. It dismissed the state's claim that the limitation was needed to preserve family integrity and to protect children who 'might be affected by the changing relationships around them'. Since there was nothing in the law to prevent establishment of the actual relationship between men and women so situated, the mere bar on legal status was unlikely to advance those aims.[269]

Article 12's right to marry is associated with the right 'to found a family'. In *P. C. & S. v. United Kingdom,* a case dealing with the removal of children by social welfare authorities, the Court rejected an argument that having children was an essential part of the right. 'Article 12 relates to the right to found a family and does not concern, as such, the circumstances in which interferences with family life between parents and an existing child may be justified, where Article 8 may be regarded as the *lex specialis*'.[270] The Court of Appeal considered challenges under both Article 8 and Article 12 to the refusal of prison authorities to facilitate a prisoner's artificial insemination of his wife. The Court, citing a number of decisions of the European Commission on Human Rights, reasoned that a lawful imprisonment necessarily, and quite intentionally, deprives those confined of the opportunity to exercise many Convention rights.[271]

Article 12 explicitly designates the right to marry as one belonging to 'men and women' (as opposed to 'everyone' in other articles). In *Goodwin* the Court's holding that Article 8 of the Convention obliges states to recognize the new gender of post-operative transsexuals brought the applicant within its terms. A greater difficulty is presented, however, for the claims that Article 12 extends a right to marriage to couples of the same sex. Such a claim will inevitably come before the Court in Strasbourg under Article 12, Article 8 or Protocol 12. Currently, such marriages are allowed in Belgium, the Netherlands and Spain. Many more states provide the facility to register a domestic partnership with many or all of the attributes of marriage. Canada legislated for same-sex marriage in 2005, but only after four courts of appeal held the limitation of marriage to men and women unconstitutional under the equality provision of the Charter of Rights and Freedoms.[272] The same result was reached by the Constitutional Court of South Africa under section 9(3) of the Constitution, that explicitly prohibits 'unfair

---

[269] 29 June 2004, 39 E.H.R.R. SE19, paras. 37–8.

[270] 16 July 2002, para. 142.

[271] *R. v. Secretary of State for the Home Department ex parte Mellor* [2001] E.W.C.A. Civ. 472, paras. 22–43.

[272] Civil Marriage Act, 2005; *EGALE Canada Inc. v. Canada (Attorney General)* [2003] 228 D.L.R. (4th) 416; *Halpern v. Canada (Attorney General)* [2003] 225 D.L.R. (4th) 529; *Hendricks v. Canada (Attorney General)* [2004] 238 D.L.R. (4th) 577; *Dunbar v. Yukon Territory* [2004] 122 C.R.R. (2d) 149. The Supreme Court of Canada upheld the power of the federal government to legislate in this area under the federal division of powers in the Constitution Act, 1867 but it declined to answer a referred question as to the compatibility of same-sex marriage with the Charter of Rights and Freedoms. *Reference Re Same-Sex Marriage* [2004] 3 S.C.R. 698.

discrimination' on grounds, *inter alia*, of sexual orientation.[273] In the United States, the Vermont Supreme Court held that same-sex couples were entitled to recognition of a civil status commensurate with marriage.[274] Such civil partnerships, however, were held inadequate to satisfy the equality provision of the Massachusetts Constitution in a case in which the majority of the Supreme Judicial Court held that same sex couples were entitled to the name as well as the substance of marriage.[275]

3. PERSONAL IDENTITY AND CHOICE OF NAME

The European Court has assumed that obstacles to or limitations on a person's right to choose his or her name implicate the Article 8 right to respect for private life. In *Stjerna v. Finland*[276] the authorities denied the applicant's request to change his name to Tawaststjerna. The Court held that, while this did not constitute an interference with private life under Article 8(2), it did raise questions about the state's positive obligations under Article 8(1), noting that a name 'constitutes a means of personal identification and a link to a family'.[277] In striking the appropriate balance in this regard the Court recognized that the state had an interest in restricting the choice of name 'for example in order to ensure accurate population registration or to safeguard the means of personal identification and of linking the bearers of a given name to a family'.[278] The Court, taking into account the diversity of regulation of member states, also decided that the state should be accorded a wide margin of appreciation. In that light it found neither the inconvenience caused to the applicant in requiring him to use his old name, nor his partiality to the chosen new name, substantial enough to conclude there was a lack of respect for his private life.[279] It reached the same result in *Guillot v. France*[280] in which the Registrar of Births, Deaths and Marriages refused the applicants' request to name their new daughter 'Fleur de Marie', the name of the heroine in a novel by Eugene Sue. Under French law parents were generally required to choose from names of saints and historical figures. Conceding that this limitation imposed some burden, the Court found this did not amount to a failure to respect the applicant's family and private life. The Court took note of the fact that the preferred name could still be used for social purposes. Where the legal name was required the applicants were permitted to give the very similar name, Fleur-Marie.[281] The Court,

---

[273] *Minister of Home Affairs v. Fourie & Bonthuys* (2005) 3 S.A. 429 (C.C.).

[274] *Baker v. Vermont*, 170 Vt. 199, 744 A. 2d 864 (1999). *See* discussion of the United Kingdom Civil Partnership Act, Section C *supra*.

[275] *Goodridge v. Department of Health*, 440 Mass. 309, 798 N.E.2d 941 (2003).

[276] 25 Nov. 1994, 4. E.H.R.R. 195.

[277] *Id.* at para. 37.

[278] *Id.* at para. 39.

[279] *Id.* at paras. 39–45.

[280] 24 Oct. 1996.

[281] *Id.* at para. 27.

therefore, did not have to evaluate the reasons given by French authorities for rejecting the applicant's choice—that it was 'excessively whimsical and so eccentric that the child is likely to be the first victim'.[282] In 2005 a new French law went into effect, liberalizing the rules on parental choice of name. Among other things it permitted use of a surname other than that of the father.[283]

While the Court appears to give the state considerable latitude in regulating individual names it has set limits on the extent to which regulations may differ for men and women. In *Ünal Tekeli v. Turkey* the Court held Turkey's law requiring married women to take their husband's surname, either by itself or in hyphenated form, violated Article 14 in connection with Article 8.[284] In *Burghartz v. Switzerland*[285] it reached the same result with respect to the Swiss Civil Code's provisions whereby married couples could use either spouse's surname but allowed hyphenated names only to the wife. The Court held, moreover, that no reasonable justification for the difference had been shown. The Court held that the injury was not mitigated by the fact that the husband could use the name he preferred informally, since only the legal name could be used 'in a person's official papers'.[286]

E. PUBLIC DISCLOSURE OR INVESTIGATION OF PRIVATE INFORMATION

The expansive reading of the term in the European case law apart, privacy, in its most obvious sense, connotes the capacity to keep certain information secret. The state, as a result of the extensive field of regulation entrusted to it, has a constant need to obtain, monitor and evaluate information.[287] The most acute confrontation of these conflicting tendencies occurs in the investigation and prosecution of criminal offences. Article 8, by insisting on respect for private life, home and correspondence, appears to limit the investigative reach of public authorities. The Court has held that the mere storing of information concerning a person's past political activities constitutes an

---

[282] *Id.* at para. 10.

[283] *New York Times*, 20 Jan. 2005.

[284] 16 Nov. 2004, 42 E.H.R.R. 53.

[285] 22 Feb. 1994, 18 E.H.R.R. 101.

[286] *Id.* at paras. 26–8. *See also* Decision of 3 May 2001 (3-4-1-6-01) in which the Constitutional Review Chamber of the Estonian Supreme Court held unconstitutional a statute prohibiting a person with an Estonian name or of Estonian ancestry from taking a non-Estonian surname. The Court found the law to be an infringement of the right to family and private life and not necessary to preserve Estonian national culture. On the European Court's Art. 8 name jurisprudence *see* A. Gross, 'Rights and Normalization; A Critical Study of European Human Rights Case Law on the Choice and Change of Name', 9 *Harv. Hum. Rts. J.* 269 (1996).

[287] *See,* e.g., *M.S. v. Sweden,* 27 Aug. 1997, 28 E.H.R.R. 313 and *Z v. Finland,* 25 Feb. 1997, 25 E.H.R.R. 371, concerning the disclosure of medical records to public officials for various purposes.

interference with private life under Article 8 and must be justified.[288] Even when the maintenance of personal information by the state is proper public officials are under a positive obligation to provide 'safe custody' to prevent unauthorized disclosure. In Section B above we examined one difficult aspect of the 'positive obligation' to maintain personal privacy. That is, the possible collision, between individual privacy and the right of the press to report news.

As with other impingements on Article 8 rights, of course, the disclosure of information may be compatible with the Convention if necessary 'in the interest of national security, public safety or the economic well-being of the country, for the prevention of disorder or crime, for the protection of health, morals, or for the protection of the rights and freedoms of others'. It is apparent that, to some extent, pursuit of all of these goals depends on the collection and communication of information about individuals. An example of this inquiry is provided by *Z v. Finland*.[289] The applicant was the wife of X who was prosecuted for a series of rapes and for attempted manslaughter. The latter charge was based on the claim that X was infected with HIV virus at the time of the rapes. The prosecution theory was that X knew he had contracted the disease from his wife. Z refused to provide information to the prosecutors citing a privilege against giving testimony against one's spouse. The prosecution then had Z's hospital records seized and the City Court ordered Z's doctors to provide information on her condition. The European Court held these actions to be justifiable for the prevention of crime and the protection of others. It noted the serious nature of the crimes charged and the limitations that had been placed on further dissemination of the information gathered. Two other actions, however, were not so justified: the refusal of the Finnish courts to extend the confidentiality of the information beyond 10 years and the identification of the applicant by name in the judgment of the Court of Appeals (a judgment that Court had immediately forwarded to a large national newspaper). Since there were ways of proceeding which would have served the public need for information without imposing so great a burden on the applicant, these actions were a 'disproportionate' interference with her rights under Article 8.[290]

Many of the Court's judgments dealing with this aspect of privacy have been given in connection with objections to official searches carried out as part of an investigation of criminal activity. The principal protection insisted on by the Court is an assurance that searches be controlled by some process of independent prior approval and supervision. In *Funke v. France*,[291] the Court found the law governing searches by customs officials defective in this regard:

Above all, in the absence of any requirement of a judicial warrant the restrictions and conditions provided for in law…appear too lax and full of loopholes for the interferences with the applicant's rights to have been strictly proportionate to the legitimate aim pursued.

---

[288] *Rotaru v. Romania*, 4 May 2000.
[289] *Supra* n. 287.
[290] *Id.* at paras. 43, 102–14.
[291] 25 Feb. 1993, 16 E.H.R.R. 297, para. 57. *See also Miailhe v. France*, 25 Feb. 1993, 16 E.H.R.R. 332, para. 38.

In a subsequent case the Court stated that it 'must be particularly vigilant where... the authorities are empowered under national law to order and effect searches without a judicial warrant'. In such cases 'a legal framework and very strict limits on such power are called for'.[292]

Although Article 8 names only one *place*—the home—the Court has interpreted that term broadly to include a person's business, noting, among other things, that the French text uses the word 'domicile' which has 'a broad connotation'. In any event, a person's business is protected from searches, in light of the Court's generous view of the term 'private life'.[293]

The Fourth Amendment to the United States Constitution affirms the 'right of the people to be secure in their persons, houses, papers and effects against unreasonable searches or seizures'. What constitutes a search depends, under modern judicial interpretations, on whether or not the person aggrieved had a 'reasonable expectation of privacy' in the place searched.[294] Thus merely looking at or listening outside a house is not within the Amendment, while, ordinarily, entry into an occupied dwelling is.[295] Like the European Court, the United States Supreme Court has held, moreover, that a person may have a reasonable expectation of privacy in places outside the home, including commercial premises.[296] Some searches, however, may not engage the expectation sufficiently to trigger the most rigorous protection of the Fourth Amendment. Searches at the national border, of parolees or by school authorities may be allowed without a warrant issued and upon a less demanding factual showing.[297] A search or seizure is not 'unreasonable', under the Amendment, if it is authorized by a warrant after determination by a 'neutral and detached magistrate', that 'probable cause' exists to believe that contraband or evidence of a crime will be found.[298] There are, however, numerous exceptions to the warrant requirement based on the exigencies of the situation. Thus, police may search an automobile, which might otherwise be quickly removed, without a warrant. Even then, however, the officers must have had probable cause for the search. The Supreme Court has held that evidence obtained from an unconstitutional search may not be introduced in a criminal trial,[299] although, again, there are many exceptions. The most important exception holds that evidence from

---

[292] *Camenzind v. Switzerland*, 16 Dec. 1997, 28 E.H.R.R. 458, para. 45.

[293] *See Niemietz v. Germany*, *supra* n. 199, at paras. 29–31; *Miailhe v. France*, *supra* n. 291, at para. 28. The Court's discussion of 'private life' in the *Niemietz* case is reproduced, in part, at Section C *supra*.

[294] *Katz v. United States*, 389 U.S. 147 (1967).

[295] *See See v. City of Seattle*, 387 U.S. 541 (1967).

[296] *Id.*

[297] *U.S. v. Flores-Montano*, 541 U.S. 149 (2004) (border search); *New Jersey v. T.L.O.*, 469 U.S. 375 (1985) (school search); *Samson v. California*, 126 S. Ct. 2193 (2006) (search of parolee).

[298] *See*, e.g., *Coolidge v. New Hampshire*, 403 U.S. 443 (1971); *Sandwich v. City of Tampa*, 407 U.S. 345 (1967).

[299] *Mapp v. Ohio*, 367 U.S. 643 (1961) (state courts); *Weeks v. United States*, 232 U.S. 383 (1914) (federal courts). The fact that evidence is obtained as a result of a search or other action that violates Art. 8 does not by itself make it a violation of the Convention to use that evidence in a subsequent trial. In each case this question is to be examined under Art. 6 and the question is 'whether the trial as a whole [is] fair'. *Schenk v. Switzerland*, 12 July 1988, 13 E.H.R.R. 242, para. 53.

a search undertaken in good faith on the basis of a warrant issued by a competent authority may be used, even if it turns out the approval of the warrant was made without probable cause.[300]

Section 8 of the Canadian Charter of Rights and Freedoms also prohibits unreasonable searches and seizures, and, like the American Court, the Supreme Court of Canada has held that the critical determination in finding an unconstitutional search is the invasion of a person's reasonable expectation of privacy. Thus, something less than probable cause could justify a border search where travellers' expectations of privacy were unlikely to be substantial.[301] For similar reasons the Supreme Court has held that section 8 is not violated by the use of infrared technology to detect sources of heat in a dwelling that might be associated with marijuana cultivation. The technique in question could identify heat escaping from the house but did not directly detect activity or objects in the house. Binnie J in his judgment for the Court said, 'Living as he does in a land of melting snow and spotty home insulation, I do not believe respondent had a serious privacy interest in the heat pattern on the exposed external walls of his home'.[302] The Canadian decision may be contrasted with the contrary holding by the United States Supreme Court. For that Court it was determinative that the police had used a specialized technology to gather information about the interior of the house, without regard to the manner in which it was obtained.[303] The Canadian Court has followed the United States Supreme Court in holding that the principal way to prevent unreasonable searches is to require prior approval by an independent magistrate based on a finding of probable cause.[304] The use of unlawfully obtained evidence in Canada is governed by Section 24(2) of the Charter which stipulates that such evidence is to be excluded only where its admission would 'bring the administration of justice into disrepute'. In making that determination, the Supreme Court has held that courts should consider the character of the evidence itself, the nature of the conduct by which it was obtained and the effect of excluding the evidence. Again echoing the American law, the Canadian courts have held that, in weighing the second factor, the good faith belief of the police that they were acting lawfully should be taken into account.[305]

The European Court of Human Rights has also made it clear that interception of telephone communications may create an interference with private life and correspondence and thus a violation of Article 8. In *Klass and Others v. Germany*,[306] however, the Court found that the German scheme for authorizing such wiretaps, although it did

---

[300]   *United States v. Leon*, 486 U.S. 397 (1984).

[301]   See *R v. Simmons* [1988] 2 S.C.R. 495; *see also R. v. McKinley Transport* [1990] 1 S.C.R. 627 (diminished expectation of privacy in taxpayer's records concerning income).

[302]   *R. v. Tessling* [2004] 3 S.C.R. 432, para. 41.

[303]   *Kyllo v. United States*, 533 U.S. 27 (2001).

[304]   *Hunter v. Southam* [1984] 2 S.C.R. 145. As in the United States, Canadian courts have recognized a number of exceptions to the warrant requirement. *See*, e.g., *R. v. Rao* (1984) O.R. (2d) 80, 109 (Ontario Court of Appeals) (search of an automobile).

[305]   *See R. v. Dewald* [1996] 1 S.C.R. 68.

[306]   6 Sept. 1978, 2 E.H.R.R. 214.

not provide for judicial review, had strict administrative procedures for the approval of such activity and the use to which the information gathered could be put, and was consistent with Article 8. On the other hand, in *Malone v. United Kingdom*,[307] the Court found a violation in the claimed wiretapping of the applicant's telephone conversations. Unlike the situation in Germany, the government of the United Kingdom did not operate under a single comprehensive set of regulations. Various statutes and common law doctrines governed. Indeed, it was not clear to the Court what legal standards were applicable to the alleged wiretapping in the applicant's case. This being so, the Court found that the interference with Article 8 rights could not be justified under Article 8(2) because it was not 'in accordance with law'. The Court reached a similar conclusion with respect to the French law on wiretapping, which was the product of a number of judicial decisions and where there was no comprehensive and explicit scheme regulating the subject.[308] The Court has been especially demanding of national regulations in this regard. In *Valenzuela Contreras v. Spain*,[309] a domestic court had approved a wiretap on the basis of very broad statutory and constitutional provisions but had also attempted to impose safeguards on the activity. This kind of *ad hoc* judicial protection was insufficient to prevent a violation of Article 8:

The requirement that the effects of the 'law' be foreseeable means, in the sphere of monitoring telephone communications, that the guarantees stating the extent of the authorities' discretion and the manner in which it is to be exercised must be set out in detail in domestic law so that it has a binding force which circumscribes the judges' discretion in the application of such measures.[310]

The United Kingdom responded to *Malone* and other Strasbourg judgments by enacting legislation more carefully defining the criteria for permissible wiretapping and procedures for challenging such decisions.[311]

Although it was, for some time, a doubtful question, it is now clear that interceptions of telephone communications in the United States are treated as 'searches' and thus are subject to the Fourth Amendment.[312] In particular, in normal circumstances it is necessary that a wiretap be approved in advance by a neutral and detached magistrate. In *United States v. United States District Court*, the Supreme Court held improper a wiretap approved only by the Attorney-General in a case allegedly involving a threat to

---

[307] 2 Aug. 1984, 4 E.H.R.R. 330. And *see* Chapter 14(D)(1).

[308] *Kruslin v. France*, 24 Apr. 1990, 12 E.H.R.R. 547; *Huvig v. France*, 24 Apr. 1990, 12 E.H.R.R. 528. *See also Kopp v. Switzerland*, 25 Mar. 1998, 27 E.H.R.R. 91 where the wiretapping of a law office was carried out under a fairly detailed set of regulations. These regulations, however, made no explicit provision for excluding lawyer–client communications although the surveillance was carried out with the intention of respecting the confidentiality of this material. Since the relevant definitions and procedures were not spelled out in the rules, the interference was held not 'in accordance with law'.

[309] 30 July 1998, 28 E.H.R.R. 483.

[310] *Id.* at para. 60.

[311] *See*, e.g., Regulation of Investigatory Powers Act 2000. The stated purpose of the Act was to 'ensure that investigatory powers are used in accordance with human rights'. Explanatory Note, H.M.S.O. (2000) para. 3. *See Attorney-General's Reference No. 5 2002* [2004] U.K.H.L. 40, [2005] 1 A.C. 167.

[312] *Katz v. United States*, 389 U.S. 347 (1967).

national security.[313] The government had argued that in such cases the President's constitutional authority supported such a power. The Supreme Court, like the European Court in the cases cited, focussed on the crucial requirement of an independent review of the decision.

We cannot accept the government's argument that internal security matters are too subtle and complex for judicial evaluation. Courts regularly deal with the most difficult issues of our society. There is no reason to believe that federal judges will be insensitive to or uncomprehending of the issues involved in domestic security cases. Certainly courts can recognize that domestic security surveillance involves different considerations from the surveillance of 'ordinary crime'. If the threat is too subtle or complex for our senior law enforcement officers to convey its significance to a court, one may question whether there is probable cause for surveillance.

The Supreme Court made clear that its decision was limited to matters of *domestic* security. Investigations touching foreign relations might involve different considerations.

American constitutional doctrine has distinguished between the risks to privacy involved in wiretaps and that involved in other types of searches and seizures. In *Berger v. New York*,[314] the Supreme Court held invalid a New York statute providing for authorization of wiretaps for certain periods. It found such authorizations similar to general warrants in their broad sweep:

...[A]uthorization of eavesdropping for a two-month period is the equivalent of a series of intrusions, searches, and seizures pursuant to single showing of probable cause.... During such a long and continuous (24 hours a day) period the conversations of any and all persons coming into the area covered by the device will be seized indiscriminately and without regard to their connection with the crime under investigation.... [T]he statute places no termination date on the eavesdrop once the conversation sought is seized. This is left entirely in the discretion of the officer. Finally, the statute's procedure, necessarily because its success depends on secrecy, has no requirement for notice as do conventional warrants, nor does it overcome this defect by requiring some showing of special facts.

The Supreme Court of Canada has followed the American decisions in holding that electronic surveillance is a search or seizure within Section 8 of the Canadian Charter of Rights and Freedoms.[315] The Court has held that the purpose of the prohibitions on unreasonable search and seizure is to protect a reasonable expectation of privacy, and such an expectation is violated when a third party intercepts a telephone conversation without the knowledge or consent of the participants.[316] In contrast to the United States Supreme Court, which has held that surveillance agreed to by a participant

---

[313]   407 U.S. 297 (1972). An exception to the general requirements of a prior warrant is an interception or recording occurring with the consent of a party to the conversation. *See*, e.g., *U.S. v White*, 401 U.S. 745 (1971). Whether consent of one party to a telephonic communication prevents the interception of the conversation from constituting a violation of Article 8, was raised before the European Court but not addressed, in its judgment in *A. v. France*, 23 Nov. 1993, 17 E.H.R.R. 462.

[314]   388 U.S. 41 (1967).

[315]   *R. v. Duarte* [1990] 1 S.C.R. 30.

[316]   *R. v. Thompson* [1990] 2 S.C.R. 1111.

is not a search or seizure within the Fourth Amendment,[317] the Supreme Court of Canada has refused to draw this distinction.[318]

Article 8 makes explicit reference to respect for correspondence. Indeed, the Court has based its wiretap judgments partly on the protection of private life, and partly on its conclusion that telephone communication represents a form of correspondence.[319] As usual, the Court, in these cases, is called on to balance an individual's desire for privacy in his or her correspondence against genuine public need for information that might be found there. So, for example, a Bankruptcy Trustee, may be given authority in certain cases to intercept and review letters to a bankrupt debtor for the purpose of identifying assets and income to benefit the unsatisfied creditors. Such a process, however, must be designed with such safeguards as to minimize the invasion of the bankrupt's privacy. So a regular practice of reading and copying mail clearly sent from a legal adviser violated Article 8.[320]

Most cases invoking the right to privacy in correspondence have arisen with respect to applicants detained by the state. In *DeWilde, Ooms and Versyp v. Belgium*,[321] the Court held that in the case of a person detained for vagrancy, the general right of the authorities to supervise and censor prisoners' mail was justifiable as necessary for the 'prevention of disorder crime, for the protection of health or morals or for the protection of rights of freedom of others' under Article 8(2). In *Golder v. United Kingdom*,[322] however, it found a violation in official refusal to allow a prisoner to contact a solicitor for purpose of initiating a libel action:

In order to show why the interference complained of by Golder was 'necessary', the Government advanced the prevention of disorder or crime and, up to a certain point, the interests of public safety and the protection of the rights and freedoms of others. Even having regard to the power of appreciation left to the contracting States, the Court cannot discern how these considerations, as they are understood 'in a democratic society', could oblige the Home Secretary to prevent Golder from corresponding with a solicitor with a view to suing Laird for libel. The Court again lays stress on the fact that Golder was seeking to exculpate himself of a charge made against him by that prison officer acting in the course of his duties and relating to an incident in prison. In these circumstances, Golder could justifiably wish to write to a solicitor. It was not for the Home Secretary himself to appraise—no more than it is for the Court today—the prospects of the action contemplated; it was for a solicitor to advise the applicant on his rights and then for a court to rule on any action that might be brought.

---

[317] *United States v. White*, 401 U.S. 745 (1971).

[318] *R. v. Duarte* [1990] 1 S.C.R. 30; *R. v. Wiggins* [1990] 1 S.C.R. In these cases the recordings were, in fact, admitted because the police acted in good faith and the evidence was held not to bring the administration of justice into disrepute, thus satisfying Section 24(2) of the Charter. *See also A. v. France*, 23 Nov. 1993, 17 E.H.R.R. 462, in which the issue was presented to the Strasbourg Court but not decided.

[319] *Klass and Others v. Germany*, 6 Sept. 1978, 2 E.H.R.R. 214.

[320] *Foxley v. United Kingdom*, 20 June 2000, 31 E.H.R.R. 25.

[321] 18 June 1971, 1 E.H.R.R. 373.

[322] 21 Feb. 1975, 1 E.H.R.R. 524.

Similarly, in *Schönenberger and Durmaz v. Switzerland*,[323] the Court found a violation of Article 8 where the prosecutor refused to deliver to a prisoner held in detention on remand, a letter in which a lawyer offered his services and advised the prisoner of his right to refuse to answer questions. The Court held that, given the fact that the prisoner undoubtedly had such a right under Swiss law, this interference with correspondence posed no threat to the normal conduct of the prosecution and, therefore, the prosecutor's action was not necessary for 'the prevention of disorder or crime'. The Court reinforced its strict view of any interference with correspondence between prisoners and their legal advisers in *Campbell v. United Kingdom*[324] in which it held that officials may only open a letter from a lawyer to a prisoner when they have reasonable cause to believe it contains an illicit enclosure. Even then, a letter may not be *read* unless 'the authorities have reasonable cause to believe that the privilege is being abused in that the contents of the letter endanger prison security or the safety of others or are otherwise of a criminal nature'. In *R. v. Secretary of State for the Home Department, Ex Parte Daly*[325] the House of Lords reviewed the policy by which prison officials inspected (but did not read) correspondence, including that from legal advisers, found during cell searches. The prisoner was not present during these searches. The House concluded there was a possibility that such a practice could 'chill' a prisoner's readiness to communicate with a lawyer since he could not be sure that the contents might not be read. In this respect it found the practice incompatible with Article 8 of the Convention. Along similar lines the Court of Appeal has observed that since a prisoner's correspondence with a physician concerning his medical condition 'is confidential and ... potentially embarrassing', disclosure is 'capable of undermining candid communication'. Nevertheless it held that the review of this correspondence by the prison medical officer was a proportionate response to both security needs and the need to oversee the health of the prisoners. This was confirmed by the fact that the monitoring was carefully considered and reviewed in each case.[326]

As was the case with surveillance of telephone conversations, the Court has also insisted that restrictions on correspondence must be stated with some clarity in advance. In *Herczegfalvy v. Austria* it held that a restriction on delivery of letters from the applicant who had been committed to a psychiatric institution was invalid under Article 8. While such a limitation could be appropriate to protect the health of the applicant, in this case the decision on which letters to forward was made in the sole discretion of the applicant's 'curator' or legal guardian. Such unguided authority meant the limitation was not 'in accordance with the law'.[327] In *Petra v. Romania*[328] a statute giving prison governors the right to stop any correspondence unsuited to the process of rehabilitating a prisoner and implemented by unpublished regulations was

---

[323]   20 June 1988, 11 E.H.R.R. 202.
[324]   25 Mar. 1992, 15 E.H.R.R. 137, para. 48. *See also Jankauskas v. Lithuania*, 24 Feb. 2005.
[325]   [2001] U.K.H.L. 26, [2001] 2 A.C. 532.
[326]   *R. (Szuluk) v. Governor of HMP Full Sutton* [2004] E.W.C.A. Civ. 1426.
[327]   24 Sept. 1992, 15 E.H.R.R. 437, paras. 87–91. *See also Calogero Diana v. Italy*, 15 Nov. 1996.
[328]   23 Sept. 1998.

held to provide insufficient guidance on its scope and administration and thus to fail 'the requirement of accessibility'.[329]

In the United States it has been held that sealed letters or packages committed to the mails are fully protected under the Fourth Amendment.[330] With respect to prisoners' mail, the Supreme Court has held that official censorship may violate the First Amendment rights of the non-prison addressee.[331]

---

[329] *Id.* paras. 37–8. *See also Narinen v. Finland*, 1 June 2004; *Salapa v. Poland*, 19 Dec. 2002.

[330] *Ex parte Jackson*, 96 U.S. 727, 730 (1877).

[331] *Procunier v. Martinez*, 416 U.S. 396 (1974).

9

THE RIGHT TO FREEDOM FROM DISCRIMINATION

ARTICLE 14

The enjoyment of the rights and freedoms set forth in this Convention shall be secured without discrimination on any ground such as sex, race, colour, language, religion, political or other opinion, national or social origin, association with a national minority, property, birth or other status.

A. THE 'PARASITIC' QUALITY OF ARTICLE 14

As is evident from its text, Article 14 does not provide 'free-standing' protection against discrimination, being concerned instead with discrimination in '[t]he enjoyment of the rights and freedoms set forth in this Convention'. In this it may be contrasted not only with provisions such as Article 26 of the International Covenant on Civil and Political Rights (which prohibits 'discrimination on any ground such as race, colour, sex, language, religion, political or other opinion, national or social origin, property, birth or other status'), but also with Protocol 12 to the Convention, discussed at Section H below.

It is clear from the earliest case law that the requirement that discrimination relate to '[t]he enjoyment of the rights and freedoms set forth in this Convention' does not rob Article 14 of effect. As Stephen Livingstone has remarked:[1]

Article 14 has not been without an impact, notably on aspects of immigration and family law. Moreover, as we shall see, while it is parasitic on other rights, its invocation may often expand their scope and render a greater range of state conduct open to human rights standards than would otherwise be the case.

---

[1] 'Article 14 and the Prevention of Discrimination in the European Convention on Human Rights', [1997] E.H.R.L.R. 25–34, at 26.

In the *Belgian Linguistic Case*,[2] the first decision of the European Court of Human Rights concerning Article 14, the Court stated:

9. While it is true that this guarantee has no independent existence in the sense that under the terms of Article 14 it relates solely to 'rights and freedoms set forth in the Convention', a measure which in itself is in conformity with the requirements of the Article enshrining the right or freedom in question may however infringe this Article when read in conjunction with Article 14 for the reason that it is of a discriminatory nature.

Thus, persons subject to the jurisdiction of a Contracting State cannot draw from Article 2 of the Protocol the right to obtain from the public authorities the creation of a particular kind of educational establishment; nevertheless, a State which had set up such an establishment could not, in laying down entrance requirements, take discriminatory measures within the meaning of Article 14.

To recall a further example, cited in the course of the proceedings, Article 6 of the Convention does not compel States to institute a system of appeal courts. A State which does set up such courts consequently goes beyond its obligations under Article 6. However it would violate that Article, read in conjunction with Article 14, were it to debar certain persons from these remedies without a legitimate reason while making them available to others in respect of the same type of actions.

In such cases there would be a violation of a guaranteed right or freedom as it is proclaimed by the relevant Article read in conjunction with Article 14. It is as though the latter formed an integral part of each of the Articles laying down rights and freedoms. No distinctions should be made in this respect according to the nature of these rights and freedoms and of their correlative obligations, and for instance as to whether the respect due to the right concerned implies positive action or mere abstention. This is, moreover, clearly shown by the very general nature of the terms employed in Article 14: 'the enjoyment of the rights and freedoms set forth in this Convention shall be secured'.

The application of Article 14 is perhaps best illustrated by the following case.

1. ABDULAZIZ V. UNITED KINGDOM

Judgment of 28 May 1985
7 E.H.R.R. 471

[The applicants, who were resident in the UK, challenged immigration rules ('the 1980 rules') which prevented their husbands from joining them to live in the UK. Had the applicants been male and their circumstances otherwise the same, they would have been permitted to have their wives join them to live in the UK.]

58. The applicants claimed to be victims of a practice in violation of their right to respect for family life, guaranteed by Article 8 of the Convention...

---

2 *The Belgian Linguistic Case (No 2)*, 23 July 1968, 1 E.H.R.R. 252. And *see* Chapter 11(B).

62. The Court recalls that, by guaranteeing the right to respect for family life, Article 8 'presupposes the existence of a family'.

66. The applicants contended that respect for family life—which in their cases the United Kingdom had to secure within its own jurisdiction—encompassed the right to establish one's home in the State of one's nationality or lawful residence; subject only to the provisions of para. 2 of Article 8, the dilemma either of moving abroad or of being separated from one's spouse was inconsistent with this principle. Furthermore, hindrance in fact was just as relevant as hindrance in law: for the couples to live in, respectively, Portugal, the Philippines or Turkey would involve or would have involved them in serious difficulties... although there was no legal impediment to their doing so...

68. The Court observes that the present proceedings do not relate to immigrants who already had a family which they left behind in another country until they had achieved settled status in the United Kingdom. It was only after becoming settled in the United Kingdom, as single persons, that the applicants contracted marriage... The duty imposed by Article 8 cannot be considered as extending to a general obligation on the part of a Contracting State to respect the choice by married couples of the country of their matrimonial residence and to accept the non-national spouses for settlement in that country.

In the present case, the applicants have not shown that there were obstacles to establishing family life in their own or their husbands' home countries or that there were special reasons why that could not be expected of them...

69. There was accordingly no 'lack of respect' for family life and, hence, no breach of Article 8 taken alone.

70. The applicants claimed that, as a result of unjustified differences of treatment in securing the right to respect for their family life, based on sex, race and also—in the case of Mrs Balkandali—birth, they had been victims of a violation of Article 14 of the Convention, taken together with Article 8...

71. According to the Court's established case-law, Article 14 complements the other substantive provisions of the Convention and the Protocols. It has no independent existence since it has effect solely in relation to 'the enjoyment of the rights and freedoms' safeguarded by those provisions. Although the application of Article 14 does not necessarily presuppose a breach of those provisions—and to this extent it is autonomous—, there can be no room for its application unless the facts at issue fall within the ambit of one or more of the latter... The Court has found Article 8 to be applicable.... Although the United Kingdom was not obliged to accept Mr Abdulaziz, Mr Cabales and Mr Balkandali for settlement and the Court therefore did not find a violation of Article 8 taken alone... the facts at issue nevertheless fall within the ambit of that Article...

Article 14 also is therefore applicable...

72. For the purposes of Article 14, a difference of treatment is discriminatory if it 'has no objective and reasonable justification', that is, if it does not pursue a 'legitimate aim' or if there is not a: 'reasonable relationship of proportionality between the means employed and the aim sought to be realised'.

The Contracting States enjoy a certain margin of appreciation in assessing whether and to what extent differences in otherwise similar situations justify a different treatment in law... but it is for the Court to give the final ruling in this respect.

73. In the particular circumstances of the case, the Court considers that it must examine in turn the three grounds on which it was alleged that a discriminatory difference of treatment was based.

B. *Alleged Discrimination on the Ground of Sex...*

75. According to the Government, the difference of treatment complained of had the aim of limiting 'primary immigration'...and was justified by the need to protect the domestic labour market at a time of high unemployment. They placed strong reliance on the margin of appreciation enjoyed by the Contracting States in this area and laid particular stress on what they described as a statistical fact: men were more likely to seek work than women, with the result that male immigrants would have a greater impact than female immigrants on the said market. Furthermore, the reduction, attributed by the Government to the 1980 Rules, of approximately 5,700 per annum in the number of husbands accepted for settlement in the United Kingdom...was claimed to be significant. This was said to be so especially when the reduction was viewed in relation to its cumulative effect over the years and to the total number of acceptances for settlement.

This view was contested by the applicants. For them, the Government's plea ignored the modern role of women and the fact that men may be self-employed and also, as was exemplified by the case of Mr Balkandali...create rather than seek jobs. Furthermore, the Government's figure of 5,700 was said to be insignificant and, for a number of reasons, in any event unreliable...

76. The Government further contended that the measures in question were justified by the need to maintain effective immigration control, which benefited settled immigrants as well as the indigenous population. Immigration caused strains on society; the Government's aim was to advance public tranquillity, and a firm and fair control secured good relations between the different communities living in the United Kingdom.

To this, the applicants replied that the racial prejudice of the United Kingdom population could not be advanced as a justification for the measures...

78. The Court accepts that the 1980 Rules had the aim of protecting the domestic labour market. The fact that, as was suggested by the applicants, this aim might have been further advanced by the abolition of the 'United Kingdom ancestry' and the 'working holiday' rules...in no way alters this finding...

Whilst the aforesaid aim was without doubt legitimate, this does not in itself establish the legitimacy of the difference made in the 1980 Rules as to the possibility for male and female immigrants settled in the United Kingdom to obtain permission for, on the one hand, their non-national wives or fiancées and, on the other hand, their non-national husbands or fiancés to enter or remain in the country.

Although the Contracting States enjoy a certain 'margin of appreciation' in assessing whether and to what extent differences in otherwise similar situations justify a different treatment, the scope of this margin will vary according to the circumstances, the subject-matter and its background...

As to the present matter, it can be said that the advancement of the equality of the sexes is today a major goal in the member States of the Council of Europe. This means that very weighty reasons would have to be advanced before a difference of treatment on the ground of sex could be regarded as compatible with the Convention.

79. In the Court's opinion, the Government's arguments summarised in para. 75 above are not convincing.

It may be correct that on average there is a greater percentage of men of working age than of women of working age who are 'economically active' (for Great Britain 90% of the men and 63% of the women) and that comparable figures hold good for immigrants (according to the statistics, 86% for men and 41% for women for immigrants from the Indian sub-continent and 90% for men and 70% for women for immigrants from the West Indies and Guyana)...

Nevertheless, this does not show that similar differences in fact exist—or would but for the effect of the 1980 Rules have existed—as regards the respective impact on the United Kingdom labour market of immigrant wives and of immigrant husbands. In this connection, other factors must also be taken into account. Being 'economically active' does not always mean that one is seeking to be employed by someone else. Moreover, although a greater number of men than of women may be inclined to seek employment, immigrant husbands were already by far outnumbered, before the introduction of the 1980 Rules, by immigrant wives...many of whom were also 'economically active'. Whilst a considerable proportion of those wives, in so far as they were 'economically active', were engaged in part-time work, the impact on the domestic labour market of women immigrants as compared with men ought not to be underestimated.

In any event, the Court is not convinced that the difference that may nevertheless exist between the respective impact of men and of women on the domestic labour market is sufficiently important to justify the difference of treatment, complained of by the applicants, as to the possibility for a person settled in the United Kingdom to be joined by, as the case may be, his wife or her husband.

80. In this context the Government stressed the importance of the effect on the immigration of husbands of the restrictions contained in the 1980 Rules, which had led, according to their estimate, to an annual reduction of 5,700 (rather than 2,000, as mentioned in the Commission's report) in the number of husbands accepted for settlement.

Without expressing a conclusion on the correctness of the figure of 5,700, the Court notes that in point of time the claimed reduction coincided with a significant increase in unemployment in the United Kingdom and that the Government accepted that some part of the reduction was due to economic conditions rather than to the 1980 Rules themselves...

In any event, for the reasons stated in para. 79 above, the reduction achieved does not justify the difference in treatment between men and women.

81. The Court accepts that the 1980 Rules also had, as the Government stated, the aim of advancing public tranquillity. However, it is not persuaded that this aim was served by the distinction drawn in those rules between husbands and wives.

82. There remains a more general argument advanced by the Government, namely that the United Kingdom was not in violation of Article 14 by reason of the fact that it acted more generously in some respects—that is, as regards the admission of non-national wives and fiancées of men settled in the country—than the Convention required.

The Court cannot accept this argument. It would point out that Article 14 is concerned with the avoidance of discrimination in the enjoyment of the Convention rights in so far as the requirements of the Convention as to those rights can be complied with in different ways. The notion of discrimination within the meaning of Article 14 includes in general cases where a person or group is treated, without proper justification, less favourably than another, even though the more favourable treatment is not called for by the Convention.

83. The Court thus concludes that the applicants have been victims of discrimination on the ground of sex, in violation of Article 14 taken together with Article 8.

84. As regards the alleged discrimination on the ground of race, the applicants...referred, inter alia, to the whole history of and background to the United Kingdom immigration legislation...and to the Parliamentary debates on the immigration rules.

In contesting this claim, the Government submitted that the 1980 Rules were not racially motivated, their aim being to limit 'primary immigration'...

A majority of the Commission concluded that there had been no violation of Article 14 under this head. Most immigration policies—restricting, as they do, free entry—differentiated on the basis of people's nationality, and indirectly their race, ethnic origin and possibly their colour. Whilst a Contracting State could not implement 'policies of a purely racist nature', to give preferential treatment to its nationals or to persons from countries with which it had the closest links did not constitute 'racial discrimination'. The effect in practice of the United Kingdom rules did not mean that they were abhorrent on the grounds of racial discrimination, there being no evidence of an actual difference of treatment on grounds of race.

A minority of the Commission, on the other hand, noted that the main effect of the rules was to prevent immigration from the New Commonwealth and Pakistan. This was not coincidental: the legislative history showed that the intention was to 'lower the number of coloured immigrants'. By their effect and purpose, the rules were indirectly racist and there had thus been a violation of Article 14 under this head in the cases of Mrs Abdulaziz and Mrs Cabales.

85. The Court agrees in this respect with the majority of the Commission.

The 1980 Rules, which were applicable in general to all 'non-patrials' wanting to enter and settle in the United Kingdom, did not contain regulations differentiating between persons or groups on the ground of their race or ethnic origin. The rules included in para. 2 a specific instruction to immigration officers to carry out their duties without regard to the race, colour or religion of the intending entrant, and they were applicable across the board to intending immigrants from all parts of the world, irrespective of their race or origin.

As the Court has already accepted, the main and essential purpose of the 1980 Rules was to curtail 'primary immigration' in order to protect the labour market at a time of high unemployment. This means that their reinforcement of the restrictions on immigration was grounded not on objections regarding the origin of the non-nationals wanting to enter the country but on the need to stem the flow of immigrants at the relevant time.

That the mass immigration against which the rules were directed consisted mainly of would-be immigrants from the New Commonwealth and Pakistan, and that as a result they affected at the material time fewer white people than others, is not a sufficient reason to consider them as racist in character: it is an effect which derives not from the content of the 1980 Rules but from the fact that, among those wishing to immigrate, some ethnic groups outnumbered others.

The Court concludes from the foregoing that the 1980 Rules made no distinction on the ground of race and were therefore not discriminatory on that account. This conclusion is not altered by the following two arguments on which the applicants relied.

(a) The requirement that the wife or fiancée of the intending entrant be born or have a parent born in the United Kingdom and also the 'United Kingdom ancestry rule'...were said to favour persons of a particular ethnic origin. However, the Court regards these provisions as being exceptions designed for the benefit of persons having close links with the United Kingdom, which do not affect the general tenor of the rules.

(b) The requirement that the parties to the marriage or intended marriage must have met...was said to operate to the disadvantage of individuals from the Indian sub-continent, where the practice of arranged marriages is customary. In the Court's view, however, such a requirement cannot be taken as an indication of racial discrimination: its main purpose was to prevent evasion of the rules by means of bogus marriages or engagements. It is, besides, a requirement that has nothing to do with the present cases.

86. The Court accordingly holds that the applicants have not been victims of discrimination on the ground of race.

87. Mrs Balkandali claimed that she had also been the victim of discrimination on the ground of birth, in that, as between women citizens of the United Kingdom and Colonies settled in the United Kingdom, only those born or having a parent born in that country could, under the 1980 Rules, have their non-national husband accepted for settlement there...

It was not disputed that the 1980 Rules established a difference of treatment on the ground of birth, argument being centred on the question whether it had an objective and reasonable justification.

In addition to relying on the Commission's report, Mrs Balkandali submitted that the elimination of this distinction from subsequent immigration rules...demonstrated that it was not previously justified.

The Government maintained that the difference in question was justified by the concern to avoid the hardship which women having close ties to the United Kingdom would encounter if, on marriage, they were obliged to move abroad in order to remain with their husbands.

The Commission considered that, notwithstanding the subsequent elimination of this difference, the general interest and the possibly temporary nature of immigration rules required it to express an opinion. It took the view that a difference of treatment based on the mere accident of birth, without regard to the individual's personal circumstances or merits, constituted discrimination in violation of Article 14.

88. The Court is unable to share the Commission's opinion. The aim cited by the Government is unquestionably legitimate, for the purposes of Article 14. It is true that a person who, like Mrs Balkandali, has been settled in a country for several years may also have formed close ties with it, even if he or she was not born there. Nevertheless, there are in general persuasive social reasons for giving special treatment to those whose link with a country stems from birth within it. The difference of treatment must therefore be regarded as having had an objective and reasonable justification and, in particular, its results have not been shown to transgress the principle of proportionality. This conclusion is not altered by the fact that the immigration rules were subsequently amended on this point.

89. The Court thus holds that Mrs Balkandali was not the victim of discrimination on the ground of birth.

Various aspects of the *Abdulaziz* decision are considered below. The decision is one of the relatively unusual cases in which Article 14 added value to the claim, the Court concluding that the provision had been breached (see further below) though

Article 8 had not. In *Marckx v. Belgium*,[3] to which the Court referred, the Court found that the legal treatment of children born outside marriage breached the Article 8 rights of mother and child and went on to find, in addition, breaches of Article 14 read with Article 8.[4] Other examples of such 'added value' include *Sahin v. Germany*[5] in which the Court, having ruled that Article 8 was not breached, in the particular case, by the denial to the applicant of access to his illegitimate child, went on to find a breach of Article 14 because of the difference in treatment accorded to fathers of children born within and outside marriage.[6] It is all the more ironic therefore that, in a striking illustration of the limitations of 'equality', the UK's reaction to the *Abdulaziz* decision was to 'level down' by removing the advantageous treatment accorded to men under the immigration rules, rather than by extending it to women.[7]

Cases in which the Court moves from an express rejection of the claim under the substantive provision alone to acceptance of the claim under Article 14 and the substantive provision are, in fact, relatively rare. But there are many examples of cases in which applicants do not argue breaches of the substantive Convention arguments alone, but rely solely on Article 14 taken together with the relevant provision, where it is relatively clear that the claim would fail absent Article 14. *Gaygusuz* is one such case.

2. GAYGUSUZ V. AUSTRIA

Judgment of 16 September 1996
23 E.H.R.R. 364

[The applicant was a Turkish national resident in Austria who had paid unemployment insurance contributions in Austria but who was denied emergency assistance when he became unemployed on the sole basis that he did not possess Austrian nationality. He complained that his rights under Article 14 read with Article 1 of the First Protocol to the Convention had been breached.]

36. According to the Court's established case law, Article 14 of the Convention complements the other substantive provisions of the Convention and the Protocols. It has no independent existence since it has effect solely in relation to 'the enjoyment of the rights and freedoms'

---

[3] 13 June 1979, 2 E.H.R.R. 330.

[4] *See also Hoffmann v. Austria*, 23 June 1993, 17 E.H.R.R. 293, *Paulik v. Slovakia*, 10 October 2006 (discussed below) and, to the extent that a breach of Article 2's *procedural* requirements was found by the Court, *Nachova v. Bulgaria*, 6 July 2005, 42 E.H.R.R. 43 (also discussed below). In *Thlimmenos v. Greece*, 6 April 2000, 31 E.H.R.R. 411, by contrast, the Court declined to consider whether there had been a breach of the substantive article having ruled that Article 14 had been breached. In other cases such as *Gaygusuz v. Austria*, 21 Dec 1999, 23 E.H.R.R. 364, *Inze v. Austria*, 28 Oct. 1987, 10 E.H.R.R. 394 and *Salgueiro da Silva Mouta v. Portugal*, 21 Dec. 1999, 31 E.H.R.R. 47 the claim was based only on the substantive article taken with Article 14.

[5] 11 Oct. 2001, 36 E.H.R.R. 43. *See also Sommerfeld v Germany*, 8 July 2003, 38 E.H.R.R. 35 (G.C.).

[6] *See also* the very similar *Hoffmann v. Germany*, 11 Oct. 2003.

[7] Similarly in *Orr v. Orr*, 440 U.S. 268 (1979) the US Supreme Court remarked that the state could solve inequality as regards alimony (to which men were not entitled) by removing entitlement to it from everyone.

safeguarded by those provisions. Although the application of Article 14 does not presuppose a breach of those provisions—and to this extent it is autonomous—there can be no room for its application unless the facts at issue fall within the ambit of one or more of them.

37. The applicant and the Turkish Government argued that Article 14 of the Convention was applicable in conjunction with Article 1 of Protocol No. 1. They referred to the reasoning of the Commission, which found that the award of emergency assistance was linked to the payment of contributions to the unemployment insurance fund.

38. The Austrian Government, however, submitted that emergency assistance did not come within the scope of Article 1 of Protocol No. 1. Entitlement thereto did not result automatically from the payment of contributions to the unemployment insurance fund. It was an emergency payment granted by the State to people in need. Consequently, Article 14 of the Convention was not applicable either.

39. The Court notes that at the material time emergency assistance was granted to persons who had exhausted their entitlement to unemployment benefit and satisfied the other statutory conditions laid down in...the...Act. Entitlement to this social benefit is therefore linked to the payment of contributions to the unemployment insurance fund, which is a precondition for the payment of unemployment benefit. It follows that there is no entitlement to emergency assistance where such contributions have not been made.

40. In the instant case it has not been argued that the applicant did not satisfy that condition; the refusal to grant him emergency assistance was based exclusively on the finding that he did not have Austrian nationality and did not fall into any of the categories exempted from that condition.

41. The Court considers that the right to emergency assistance—in so far as provided for in the applicable legislation—is a pecuniary right for the purposes of Article 1 of Protocol No. 1. That provision is therefore applicable without it being necessary to rely solely on the link between entitlement to emergency assistance and the obligation to pay 'taxes or other contributions'. Accordingly, as the applicant was denied emergency assistance on a ground of distinction covered by Article 14, namely his nationality, that provision is also applicable...

46. The Court notes in the first place that Mr Gaygusuz was legally resident in Austria and worked there at certain times...paying contributions to the unemployment insurance fund in the same capacity and on the same basis as Austrian nationals.

47. It observes that the authorities' refusal to grant him emergency assistance was based exclusively on the fact that he did not have Austrian nationality...

50. The Court therefore finds the arguments put forward by the Austrian Government unpersuasive. It considers, like the Commission, that the difference in treatment between Austrians and non-Austrians as regards entitlement to emergency assistance, of which Mr Gaygusuz was a victim, is not based on any 'objective and reasonable justification'.

The applicant in *Gaygusuz* would have failed in a claim brought under Article 1 of the First Protocol alone because he had no right under Austrian law to the payment in question. Similarly, in *Fretté v. France*,[8] which concerned a challenge by a gay man to a refusal, based on his sexual orientation, to authorize him as an adopter, the Court

---

[8]   26 Feb. 2002, 38 E.H.R.R. 21.

declared that Article 8 did not 'guarantee the right to adopt as such' and that 'the right to respect for family life presupposes the existence of a family and does not safeguard the mere desire to found a family', but went on to consider the claim under Article 14 read with Article 8.[9] In *Fretté* and other cases Article 14 claims have failed because, for example, the differential treatment is regarded as justified, but the Court has nevertheless accepted that the treatment fell 'within the scope of' the relevant substantive Article while not breaching that provision (see *Petrovic. v. Austria*[10] and *Van Der Mussele v. Belgium*,[11] discussed below).

The relationship between Article 14 and the substantive Convention provisions was considered by Laws LJ in the English Court of Appeal in the following case.

3. R. (CARSON) V. SECRETARY OF STATE FOR WORK AND PENSIONS

Judgment of 17 June 2003
[2003] EWCA Civ 797, [2003] 3 All E.R. 577

[The case concerned a challenge to differential treatment on grounds of age in access to social security benefits. Having ruled that the treatment complained of did not breach Article 1 of the First Protocol to the Convention ['Art. 1P'], this because that provision does not provide a right to *acquire* possessions, Laws L.J. went on to consider whether the differential treatment at issue could be said to fall 'within the scope' of that provision for the purposes of an Article 14 claim.]

[33] What troubled me at the outset of the argument was that I could not see, on the facts of either appeal, how any exercise of the art 1P right was involved such as might engage art 14. The right guaranteed by art 1P is to peaceful enjoyment of one's possessions, and not to be deprived of one's possessions save on a permitted justification. As it seemed to me, art 14 would come into play only in certain limited sets of circumstances. One such would arise if there were some apparent or potential interference with a substantive convention right which could however be justified if the case were looked at in isolation (so that there would be no violation of art 1P simpliciter), but which would fall to be condemned under art 14 upon its being shown that the justification imposed, on discriminatory grounds of a kind contemplated in the article, a heavier burden on the complainant than was imposed on another person or class of persons in a comparable situation.

---

[9] A breach of a substantive article may be found as well as a breach of Article 14 in conjunction with that Article (as in *Marckx v. Belgium*, *supra* n. 3, *Hoffmann v. Austria*, *supra* n. 4, and *Chassagnou v. France*, 29 Apr. 1999, 29 E.H.R.R. 615). But unless the discrimination at issue is a 'fundamental aspect' of the case (*Airey v. Ireland*, 9 Oct. 1979, 2 E.H.R.R. 305, para. 30) it is unusual for the Court to give detailed consideration to the Article 14 claim after finding in favour of the applicant. In other cases the Court decides the Article 14 claim in the applicant's favour and declines to consider whether there has been a breach of the substantive Convention provision, taken alone.

[10] 27 Mar. 1998, 33 E.H.R.R. 14.

[11] 23 Nov. 1983, 6 E.H.R.R. 163.

[34] Such a state of affairs might most easily be illustrated by reference to what are some-times called the political rights guaranteed by arts 8–11. In each of these, para 2 of the article states considerations upon which the right may be abrogated or qualified, essentially on public interest grounds. Now, one might readily construct an example where (say) free speech in some particular area is proscribed by the state in various instances. Grounds to justify the prohibition are then put forward by the state under art 10, para 2. In the example, let it be said that in each given instance taken alone the proscription is well justified under para 2 on the grounds put forward. However the grounds of justification thus advanced are more, or less, intrusive or onerous between instances and the difference is attributable to a prohibited discriminatory ground. In that case the fact of such differential justifications between classes (or persons) will offend art 14 unless the state can justify the difference or differences.

[35] Another circumstance which would expose a violation of art 14 might arise in relation to the substantive rights guaranteed by art 6 of the convention. Here, the case would not be constituted by the existence of a potential breach of the substantive right which is however justified, where the art 14 complaint must rest in discriminatory justifications. In this instance the art 14 complaint rests in discrimination as regards what counts as breach of the primary right; there are no issues of justification. Article 6 contains no analogue to para 2 as it appears in each of arts 8–11. However, the standard which the law demands for compliance with the requirement that a person's civil rights or obligations (or a criminal charge against him) be determined under art 6 at 'a fair and public hearing within a reasonable time by an independent and impartial tribunal' is not a unitary or singular standard or set of principles. In the broadest terms there will be a spectrum of standards within which the court will not interfere. It may be said that this is so by force of the Strasbourg court's doctrine of 'margin of appreciation'. I prefer to say that in the real world there are inevitably shades and degrees of every one of the variables in art 6: fairness, publicity, delay, independence, impartiality. So it is that in connection with art 6 a complaint under art 14 may arise where it is said that upon any of these variables the state has applied a different standard to one class of persons compared to another, and done so on a prohibited discriminatory ground. A crude instance of arts 6/14 discrimination would thus arise if a legal system adopted a different rule for the admission of confession evidence for members of one class of society (or for members of a particular racial group) compared with the rule adopted for another. In the courts of ancient Athens the evidence of a slave was inadmissible *unless* he had been tortured.

[36] In each of these examples, and one could generate many others, the enjoyment of the substantive convention right is engaged on the facts of the case fair and square. My difficulty was in seeing how that could be so in these present appeals. In neither case was there any interruption of the appellant's peaceful enjoyment of her possessions. Nor is there any ques-tion of either appellant having been deprived—let alone unjustifiably deprived—of any of her possessions. Each appellant has had in full measure what the domestic law entitles her to have. The complaint of each, in contrast, is that the domestic law should have given her more. It is plain that art 1P provides no such entitlement whatever; I have dealt with the argument for a violation of art 1P taken on its own. In those circumstances I was unable to see how on the facts there could be any complaint of art 14 taken with art 1P. Such a complaint might arise if the state offered differential justifications as between persons or classes for measures of deprivation of property. That would be analogous to the first example given above relating to art 10; but nothing of that sort remotely arises in these appeals.

[37] It is, however, plain that the Strasbourg court has not confined the scope of art 14 within limits of the kind I have described [citing *Gaygusuz*]...

The court concluded that there had been a violation of art 14 taken with art 1P. In doing so, as it seems to me, by necessary implication it held that although the conditions of entitlement to a state benefit under a domestic legal scheme (and an applicant's failure to fulfil them)—as opposed to any conditions under which such a benefit might be *withdrawn*—could not in principle give rise to a claim under art 1P taken on its own, yet they could yield a good claim under art 14 taken with art 1P. On this footing the reach of art 14 is longer than it would be if it were confined to instances of the kind I gave in [34], [35], above. However, it is correctly submitted for the appellants that there is a consistent line of Strasbourg authority which favours the longer reach. Reference is made to *Belgian Linguistic Case (No 2)* (1968) 1 EHRR 252 (in particular at 283 (para 9)), *Walden v Liechtenstein* App no 33916/96 (16 March 2000, unreported), *Matthews v UK* App no 40302/98 (28 November 2000, unreported) and *Shackell v UK* App no 45851/99 (27 April 2000, unreported), whose texts with respect I need not cite, as well as *Gaygusuz v Austria*.

[The Court of Appeal's decision in this case was upheld by the House of Lords at [2005] U.K.H.L. 37, [2005] 2 All E.R. 545.]

The following case illustrates the limits imposed by the 'parasitic' quality of Article 14.

4. BOTTA V. ITALY

Judgment of 24 February 1998
26 E.H.R.R. 241

8. Mr Botta, who was born in 1939 and lives in Trezzano sul Naviglio (Milan province), is physically disabled.

9. In August 1990 he went on holiday to the seaside resort of Lido degli Estensi, near to the town of Comacchio (Ferrara province) with a friend, who is also physically disabled. There he discovered that the bathing establishments were not equipped with the facilities needed to enable disabled people to gain access to the beach and the sea (particularly special access ramps and specially equipped lavatories and washrooms), in breach of Italian legislation, which required a clause obliging private beaches to facilitate the access of disabled people to be added to the relevant concession contracts and made provision for compliance to be enforced by the competent local authorities...

10. The applicant asserts that he was for a time able to gain access in his vehicle to certain public beaches without facilities, but was later prevented from doing so because a barrier had been erected across the entrance by order of the Ravenna harbour-master.

11. On 26 March 1991 the applicant sent a letter to the mayor of Comacchio asking him to take the necessary measures to remedy the shortcomings noted the previous year. No reply was received.

12. In August 1991 Mr Botta returned to Lido degli Estensi, where he found that none of the measures requested had been implemented, although they were mandatory. He was therefore obliged to ask the local coastal authority for permission to drive his vehicle onto a

public beach without facilities. He also wrote to various local bodies, receiving the following replies: the president of the cooperative which ran the resort's private beaches informed him that the concession contracts did not stipulate any obligation to install the facilities requested; the local coastal authority replied that it had to receive an official request before it could authorise the construction of special access ramps on the beaches; the mayor asserted that it was the private beaches' responsibility to install the facilities in question, but nevertheless gave the applicant permission to drive onto a public beach in his vehicle.

In an undated memorandum the coastal authority gave him permission to drive onto a public beach without facilities in his vehicle for a limited period expiring on 31 August 1991.

13. On 9 August 1991 the applicant decided to lodge a complaint with the *carabinieri* against the Minister for Merchant Shipping, the Ravenna harbour-master and the mayor and deputy mayor of Comacchio. He alleged that, by failing to take any steps whatsoever to oblige the private beaches to install the facilities for disabled people prescribed by law on pain of cancellation of their licences, these authorities had committed the offence of omitting to perform an official duty (*omissione d'atti d'ufficio*), as defined in Article 328 of the Criminal Code.

On 20 December 1991 he asked the Ferrara public prosecutor's office to inform him where matters stood in the case.

On 5 May 1992 the public prosecutor's office submitted that the proceedings should be discontinued...

15. According to information supplied by the applicant and not contradicted by the Government, although some of the private beaches in Lido degli Estensi have subsequently installed changing cubicles and lavatories for disabled people, in July 1997 none of them had yet built a ramp designed to permit disabled people to gain access to the beach and the sea. On 29 August 1997 Comacchio District Council informed the registry of the Court of the adoption, on 11 August 1997, of the resort's new improvements plan, under which compliance with the law on bathing establishments had to be achieved by 30 April 1999 at the latest...

31. The Court must determine whether the right asserted by Mr Botta falls within the scope of the concept of 'respect' for 'private life' set forth in Article 8 of the Convention.

32. Private life, in the Court's view, includes a person's physical and psychological integrity; the guarantee afforded by Article 8 of the Convention is primarily intended to ensure the development, without outside interference, of the personality of each individual in his relations with other human beings...

33. In the instant case the applicant complained in substance not of action but of a lack of action by the State. While the essential object of Article 8 is to protect the individual against arbitrary interference by the public authorities, it does not merely compel the State to abstain from such interference: in addition to this negative undertaking, there may be positive obligations inherent in effective respect for private or family life. These obligations may involve the adoption of measures designed to secure respect for private life even in the sphere of the relations of individuals between themselves. However, the concept of respect is not precisely defined. In order to determine whether such obligations exist, regard must be had to the fair balance that has to be struck between the general interest and the interests of the individual, while the State has, in any event, a margin of appreciation.

34. The Court has held that a State has obligations of this type where it has found a direct and immediate link between the measures sought by an applicant and the latter's private and/or family life...

35. In the instant case, however, the right asserted by Mr Botta, namely the right to gain access to the beach and the sea at a place distant from his normal place of residence during his holidays, concerns interpersonal relations of such broad and indeterminate scope that there can be no conceivable direct link between the measures the State was urged to take in order to make good the omissions of the private bathing establishments and the applicant's private life.

Accordingly, Article 8 is not applicable.

37. Relying on Article 14 taken in conjunction with Article 8, the applicant asserted that he was the victim of discrimination against him as a disabled person in the exercise of fundamental rights secured to all. If the concept of discrimination covered all cases in which an individual was treated less favourably than another individual, without proper justification, then a disabled person suffered different, or differentiated, treatment, without objective or reasonable justification, in relation to people who were not disabled. Admittedly, there was no longer any such discrimination *de jure*, since Italian legislation not only contained various provisions designed to ensure equality but also laid down 'positive measures' in favour of disabled people. The disparity continued to exist, however, *de facto*, as could be seen in the situation and circumstances which had obtained in the present case. Moreover, it was the Court's practice to consider the particular circumstances of a given case in order to decide whether there had been any discriminatory treatment; it did not assess the impugned domestic rules in the abstract but rather the manner in which they had been applied to the person concerned...

39. According to the Court's case-law:

'Article 14 complements the other substantive provisions of the Convention and its Protocols. It has no independent existence, since it has effect solely in relation to "the enjoyment of the rights and freedoms" safeguarded by those provisions. Although the application of Article 14 does not presuppose a breach of one or more of those provisions—and to this extent it is autonomous—there can be no room for its application unless the facts of the case fall within the ambit of one or more of the latter'....

As the Court has concluded that Article 8 is not applicable, Article 14 cannot apply to the present case.

It is clear from the *Botta* decision that the 'parasitic' quality of Article 14 imposes real limitations on the functioning of the Convention's non-discrimination guarantee. We shall see below that Protocol 12 to the Convention, which entered into force on 1 April 2005, contains a 'free-standing' equality/non-discrimination provision. It has to date, however, been ratified by only a small minority of the Contracting Parties to the Convention.

B. THE PROTECTED GROUNDS

Article 14 refers to 'discrimination on any ground such as sex, race, colour, language, religion, political or other opinion, national or social origin, association with a national minority, property, birth or other status'. The list is an open-ended one. In *Engel v.*

Netherlands[12] the Court accepted that a 'distinction based on rank may run counter to Article 14', the 'list set out in that provision [being] illustrative and not exhaustive'. Among the grounds of discrimination which the European Court has accepted as covered by Article 14 are sexual orientation, disability and marital and professional status.[13]

In *Kjeldsen, Busk Madsen and Pedersen v. Denmark*[14] the Court suggested that 'status' referred to 'a personal characteristic by which persons or groups of persons are distinguishable from each other', there rejecting a claim that the absence of any mechanism for withdrawing children from sex education classes, while provision was made for withdrawal from religious education classes, breached Article 14. In *National Union of Belgian Police v. Belgium*[15] the Court had, however, accepted that discrimination between general and specialist trade unions could breach Article 14. More recently, in *Spadea and Scalebrino v. Italy*,[16] the Court accepted that Article 14 governed discrimination between owners of residential and non-residential housing; in *Stubbings v. UK*[17] that it applied to discrimination between victims of intentional and unintentional torts; and in *Chassagnou v. France*[18] that it applied to discrimination between large and small landowners (this being a form of discrimination on grounds of property).

The jurisprudence of the European Court on the scope of the grounds covered by Article 14 is less than clear, but the House of Lords has given attention to this issue in a couple of cases. In *R. (S) v. Chief Constable of South Yorkshire Police*[19] their Lordships ruled that differential treatment between persons whose DNA and fingerprints were and were not held by the police did not engage Article 14. In the following case Baroness Hale, though not speaking for the majority of the House, gave close consideration to the scope of grounds covered by Article 14.

1. R. (CLIFT AND OTHERS) V. SECRETARY OF STATE FOR THE HOME DEPARTMENT

Judgment of 13 December 2006
[2006] UKHL 54, [2007] 2 W.L.R. 24

[The case concerned challenges under Articles 5 and 14 brought by a number of prisoners to the terms on which they were entitled to parole. Clift himself challenged differential

---

[12] 23 Nov. 1976, 1 E.H.R.R. 647.

[13] Respectively *Dudgeon v. United Kingdom*, 12 Oct. 1981, 4 E.H.R.R. 149, *Salgueiro da Silva Mouta v. Portugal, supra* n. 4, and *SL v. Austria*, 9 Jan. 2003, 37 E.H.R.R. 39 (sexual orientation); *Botta v. Italy*, 24 Feb. 1998, 26 E.H.R.R. 241 (disability); *Sahin v. Germany, supra* n. 5 (marital status) and *Van der Mussele v. Belgium*, 23 Nov. 1983, 6 E.H.R.R. 163 (professional status).

[14] 7 Dec. 1976, 1 E.H.R.R. 711. And *see* Chapter 11(C).

[15] 27 Oct. 1975, 1 E.H.R.R. 578.

[16] 28 Sept. 1995, 21 E.H.R.R. 482.

[17] 22 Oct. 1996, 23 E.H.R.R. 213.

[18] *Supra* n. 9. 29 E.H.R.R. 615.

[19] [2004] 1 W.L.R. 2196.

treatment between prisoners serving determinate sentences of more than and of less than 15 years, the Secretary of State being entitled to reject the recommendations of the Parole Board in relation to the former (that is, shorter-term prisoners), but not the latter. The others challenged discrimination as regards parole between national and non-national prisoners. The House of Lords accepted that the differential treatment complained of by all three fell within the ambit of Article 5 and, in the cases of the second and third appellants, accepted that there was discrimination on grounds of national origin which breached Article 14. But the House of Lords did not accept that the differential treatment of Mr Clift engaged Article 14's 'other status'. Lord Bingham, with whom Lords Brown, Carswell and Hope and Baroness Hale agreed, suggested that he 'would incline to regard a life sentence as an acquired personal characteristic and a lifer as having an "other status", and it is hard to see why the classification of Mr Clift, based on the length of his sentence and not the nature of his offences, should be differently regarded', but thought that 'a domestic court should hesitate to apply the Convention in a manner not, as I understand, explicitly or impliedly authorised by the Strasbourg jurisprudence'. He 'accordingly, not without hesitation, resolve[d] this question in favour of the Secretary of State and against Mr Clift'. Baroness Hale gave the following exposition of that jurisprudence.]

Baroness Hale:

51. The 14th Amendment to the Constitution of the United States of America requires that 'No state shall . . . deny to any person within its jurisdiction the equal protection of the laws'. Yet many laws have to draw distinctions between different groups or classes of people. The US courts have therefore had to construct a hierarchy of grounds of distinction, from those which they will readily hold to be rationally justified to those which they will subject to the strictest of scrutiny. Modern human rights instruments, on the other hand, have tended to contain a list of grounds which are automatically suspect [citing Article 26 of the International Covenant on Civil and Political Rights]...

Article 14 of the European Convention on Human Rights adds 'association with a national minority' to this list. The list is clearly non-exhaustive so that analogous grounds may be recognised as social conditions change. The most obvious example is sexual orientation.

52. ... The French text is even more open-ended [than] the English referring to 'toute autre situation' rather than 'other status'. So, was article 14 intended to be a general prohibition of discrimination in relation to the enjoyment of the Convention rights unless it could objectively be justified, with the specific grounds listed as a warning that discrimination on such grounds would be particularly difficult to justify? Or were the grounds and the reference to 'other status' intended to limit the kinds of classification which might be covered by the article?

53. The classic accounts of article 14 repeated time and time again in the Strasbourg case law do not specifically address this question...

56. Although the issue is not always addressed, when it is addressed it is clear from the Strasbourg case law that not every basis of distinction between different sorts of people is included in the list of prohibited grounds and residual category of 'other status'...

58. In the vast majority of Strasbourg cases where violations of article 14 have been found, the real basis for the distinction was clearly one of the proscribed grounds or something very close: race, sex, religion, marital or birth status, national origin, foreign residence, language,

or sexual orientation. Unusually, in *Pine Valley Developments Ltd v Ireland* (1991) 14 EHRR 319, the court found a violation of article 14 without reference to a prohibited ground, but the point was not argued because the government was denying that the legislation drew the distinction complained of at all.

59. More instructive are the cases in which the basis of the discrimination has been held to fall outside the proscribed grounds. One example is different laws in different jurisdictional regions within the territory of a member state. Thus, it was not a difference in treatment on grounds of personal status for people in Scotland to be subject to the poll tax before people in England (*P v United Kingdom* (Application No 13473/87) (unreported) 11 July 1988) or for juvenile offenders in Scotland not to be entitled to the remission granted to juvenile offenders in England and Wales: *Nelson v United Kingdom* (1986) 49 DR 170.

60. Another example, pertinent to this case, is differences in the treatment of different criminal offences. In *Gerger v Turkey* (Application No 24919/94) (unreported) 8 July 1999, the court deduced from the fact that people convicted of terrorist offences would be treated less favourably with regard to automatic parole 'that the distinction is made not between different groups of people, but between different types of offence, according to the legislature's view of their gravity': para 69. In *Budak v Turkey* (Application No 57345/00) (unreported) 7 September 2004, the court repeated the 'personal characteristic' test from *Kjeldsen* and held that a distinction in procedure and sentences for offences tried before the state security court from those tried before other courts was made, again, not between different groups of people but between different types of offence.

61. All of this is entirely consistent with the view taken by this House in *R (S) v Chief Constable of South Yorkshire Police* [2004] 1 WLR 2196. At para 48, Lord Steyn cited *Kjeldsen* and continued:

> 'the proscribed grounds in article 14 cannot be unlimited, otherwise the wording of article 14 referring to "other status" beyond the well-established proscribed grounds, including things such as sex, race or colour, would be unnecessary. It would then preclude discrimination on any ground. That is plainly not the meaning of article 14.'

In that case it was held that the possession of fingerprints and DNA samples by the police was simply a matter of historical fact rather than the personal status or characteristics of the people who had supplied them.

62. In this case, it is plain, and now accepted by the Secretary of State, that a different parole regime for foreigners who are liable to deportation from that applicable to citizens or others with the right to remain here, falls within the grounds proscribed by article 14 and thus (subject to the ambit issue) requires objective justification. The same would surely apply to a difference in treatment based on race, sex or the colour of one's hair. But a difference in treatment based on the seriousness of the offence would fall outside those grounds. The real reason for the distinction is not a personal characteristic of the offender but what the offender has done.

C. 'DISCRIMINATION': THE ROLE OF COMPARISON

The discrimination alleged in *Abdulaziz* consisted of obviously less favourable treatment of women than of men, such treatment being accorded on the explicit basis of sex. Other cases have foundered because the European Court has not accepted that relevantly different treatment had been established. This has been articulated on occasion as a finding that those to whose treatment applicants have sought to compare their own ('comparators') have not been in a sufficiently similar position to that of the applicant(s).

1. FREDIN V. SWEDEN

Judgment of 18 February 1991
13 E.H.R.R. 784

[The applicants owned a gravel pit which had been leased to 'the Jehanders' in 1960 for fifty years for an annual fee. The Jehanders subsequently acquired several other gravel pits in the vicinity, gaining a quasi-monopoly on gravel production in the region. In 1963, in which year the state prohibited the extraction of gravel without a permit, a permit was issued in respect of the applicants' gravel pit which provided that exploitation had to be carried out in three stages, each of which should not exceed ten years, and that restoration works had to be carried out continuously during each stage and financial security lodged to cover the costs thereof. By 1979 the Jehanders had still not commenced gravel extraction at the pit, which they agreed to return to the applicants who began to exploit the pit in 1980. In the same year the County Administrative Board granted the applicants an exemption from a general prohibition against building near the seashore and allowed them to build a quay with shiploading equipment. The exemption was valid until further notice, but not for longer than the permit to exploit gravel, and the Board stated that the 'decision [did] not imply that any position [had] been taken as to the possibility of a future reconsideration of the gravel exploitation activities on the property'. The applicants built the quay at a cost of 1,000,000 kronor and also invested 1,250,000 kronor in the gravel exploitation business over the period from 1980 to 1983. In 1983 the County Administrative Board, under powers granted by the relevant legislation, notified the applicants that it was contemplating amending their permit so as to provide that exploitation of the gravel pit should cease by 1 June 1984. The permit was eventually withdrawn in 1988 at which stage the applicants had not yet completed the first of the three exploitation stages provided for in the 1963 permit. In 1989 the County Administrative Board requested the public prosecutor to institute criminal proceedings against the applicants for failure to restore the gravel pit as provided for in the permit.]

31. The applicants have...submitted a report by Mr Dick Karlsson, a consultant, according to which, in a large number of revocation cases concerning businesses that had been carried on for several years, the County Administrative Board had not ordered the restoration of the gravel pits at issue. The Board was also said to have given the holders of the permits in question

the opportunity of obtaining new ones, should the supply of gravel on the market decrease. Mr Karlsson noted that in these cases the permits had been held by two companies, including one of the Jehanders. He concluded that the Board's decision concerning the applicants' permit was exceptional, in that it terminated an ongoing profitable business...

[Having rejected the claim that the treatment complained of breached Article 1 of the First Protocol to the Convention]

57. The applicants also maintained that they were victims of discrimination in the enjoyment of their rights under Article 1 of Protocol No. 1...

They claimed that theirs was the only case in Sweden in which the authorities had stopped an ongoing gravel exploitation business and that they had been singled out for special treatment by the County Administrative Board as they were the only independent contractors in the region.

58. In their memorial to the Court, the applicants first recalled the Government's submission before the Commission: whilst admitting that to their knowledge no other ongoing business had been closed by the authorities under the 1973 amendment to the 1964 Act, they had contended that the applicants' case was exceptional in that a considerable time had elapsed between the granting of the permit and the first exploitation of gravel. The applicants pointed out that the authorities had, however, been well aware of the special reasons for the delay and that, moreover, such a long lapse of time was by no means uncommon; in the near vicinity alone, there were at least two pits quite similar in this respect, but this had not led the authorities to interfere with the activities there.

59. The Government agreed with the Commission that, as there was nothing to show that the applicants were in a position similar to that of those companies whose permits were not revoked, no issue of discrimination could arise.

60. The Court recalls that Article 14 affords protection against discrimination, that is treating differently, without an objective and reasonable justification, persons in 'relevantly' similar situations. For a claim of violation of this Article to succeed, it has therefore to be established, inter alia, that the situation of the alleged victim can be considered similar to that of persons who have been better treated.

61. Before the Commission the applicants endeavoured to demonstrate that this condition was satisfied by submitting a report by Mr Karlsson. After assessing this evidence, the Commission held, however, that there was nothing to show that the applicants were in a similar situation to those companies whose permits were not revoked...

In their submissions to the Court the applicants did not try to refute the Commission's assessment, nor did they adduce other evidence. Their main argument was that, since theirs was the only ongoing business to have been stopped... it was for the Government to explain in what respect their case was dissimilar to those of the other enterprises which had been allowed to continue their activities or to give a plausible reason for their exceptional treatment.

The Court cannot subscribe to this argument. It is true that, in the absence of further information from the Government with regard to the implementation of the 1964 Act and, in particular, the 1973 amendment thereto... the Court has to presume that the applicants' pit is the only one to have been closed by virtue of that amendment. However, this is not sufficient to support a finding that the applicants' situation can be considered similar to that of other ongoing businesses which have not been closed.

The Court perceives no reason why it should assess the evidence otherwise than did the Commission and accordingly holds that no issue of discrimination contrary to Article 14 arises.

The Article 14 claim in *Fredin* failed because the applicants were unable to establish that they had suffered less favourable treatment by reference to any ground expressly or implicitly within the scope of Article 14: there can be no discrimination 'on any ground such as…' unless there it is established that (at the minimum) different treatment[20] has been accorded, or would have been accorded, to persons distinguished by reference to a stated ground. Somewhat similar is *Johnston v. Ireland*,[21] in which the European Court dismissed an Article 14 challenge to the fact that the Irish state did not permit divorce while recognizing divorces obtained elsewhere by persons domiciled outside Ireland. The applicants argued that they were discriminated against on the basis of their financial means. The Court's ruling that the applicants could not be regarded as analogously situated to persons divorced outside the jurisdiction can be explained on the basis that recognizing divorces lawfully obtained elsewhere is substantively different from amending a state's legal system so as to provide a legal mechanism for the granting of in-country divorces, so that the comparison upon which the applicants relied did not demonstrate that they had been subject to differential treatment on the ground alleged. Had they been better positioned financially, they might have been able to become domiciled abroad for the purposes of obtaining a divorce which would subsequently be recognized on any return to Ireland under the general Irish rules of private international law. But Irish law provided that, in order to be regarded as domiciled in a foreign state, a person had not only to be resident there but also had to have the intention of remaining there permanently and to have lost the intention to return. So even on the applicants' own case, the ability to remarry in Ireland was related only tangentially to financial status.

In some cases discrimination can be established without explicit discussion of a comparator: where, for example, what is challenged is (as in *Marckx*) an explicit legislative distinction between different categories of person (there children born to married and unmarried mothers), the differential treatment is evident and the only role for a (real or hypothetical) comparator might be to permit consideration of the question whether the treatment complained of was *less favourable*, as distinct from merely *different*. In other cases it may be necessary to point to the differential treatment of another person who is distinguishable from the applicant by reference to that ground (discrimination on the ground of race against a black person being proven by reference to the treatment accorded a white person, discrimination on the ground of sex against a woman being proven by reference to the treatment accorded a man). The more different the applicant and comparator, the easier it may be for the respondent to assert that the differential treatment complained of was not on the asserted ground, but was referable instead to another characteristic distinguishing the applicant and comparator (seniority in an

---

[20] Indirect discrimination is considered below.
[21] 18 Dec. 1986, 9 E.H.R.R. 203. And *see* Chapter 8(B)(1).

employment-related claim, for example, or productivity, or skill). Thus in *Fredin* the differential treatment complained of by the applicants could have been explained by reference to factors other than that the applicants were independent contractors (this being the ground upon which discrimination was alleged).[22] But a different and more problematic use of the comparator occurred in the following case in which it served to block consideration of whether less favourable treatment on a protected ground was, in the circumstances, justifiable.

2. VAN DER MUSSELE V. BELGIUM

Judgment of 23 November 1983
6 E.H.R.R. 163

9. The applicant is a Belgian national born in 1952. He resides in Antwerp where he exercises the profession of *avocat* (lawyer). After being enrolled as a pupil *avocat* on 27 September 1976, he at once opened his own chambers without ever working in the chambers of another *avocat*; his pupil-master, however, entrusted him with a number of cases and gave him some payment for the work done in regard to them.

Mr Van der Mussele terminated his pupillage on 1 October 1979 and has since then been entered on the register of the *Ordre des avocats* (Bar Association)...

13. The applicant stated that during his pupillage he had dealt with approximately 250 cases, including about 50 cases—representing some 750 hours of work—on which he had acted as officially appointed *avocat*. He also said that his net monthly income before tax was only 15,800BF in his first and second years, increasing to 20,800 BF in the third.

31. The applicant maintained that he had had to perform forced or compulsory labour incompatible with Article 4 of the Convention [this labour consisted of legal work for indigent clients]...

The Court would recall that Mr Van der Mussele had voluntarily entered the profession of *avocat* with knowledge of the practice complained of. This being so, a considerable and unreasonable imbalance between the aim pursued—to qualify as an *avocat*—and the obligations undertaken in order to achieve that aim would alone be capable of warranting the conclusion that the services exacted of Mr Van der Mussele in relation to legal aid were compulsory despite his consent...

Having regard, furthermore, to the standards still generally obtaining in Belgium and in other democratic societies, there was thus no compulsory labour for the purposes of Article 4(2) of the Convention...

42. The applicant also invoked Article 14 read in conjunction with Article 4...

45. ...in the applicant's submission, Belgian *avocats* are subject, in respect of the matters under consideration, to less favourable treatment than that of members of a whole series of

---

[22] Similarly *Johnson, ibid.* For a full discussion of this subject, *see* A. McColgan, 'Cracking the Comparator Problem, "Equal" Treatment and the Role of Comparisons', [2006] *European Human Rights Law Review* 650.

other professions. In legal aid cases, the State accords remuneration to judges and registrars, pays the emoluments of interpreters... and, 'in lieu of the legally aided person', advances:

> 'the travel and subsistence expenses of judicial, public or publicly appointed officers, the costs and fees of experts, the allowances of witnesses..., the disbursements and one quarter of the salaries of bailiffs as well as the disbursements of other public or publicly appointed officers.'...

Medical practitioners, veterinary surgeons, pharmacists and dentists, for their part, are not required to provide their services free of charge to indigent persons. According to the applicant, these all represented instances of arbitrary inequality, being devoid of any 'objective and reasonable justification'... they thereby contravened Articles 14 and 4 taken together. The minority of the Commission shared this view, at least to a large extent.

46. Article 14 safeguards individuals, placed in analogous situations, from discrimination. Yet between the Bar and the various professions cited by the applicant, including even the judicial and parajudicial professions, there exist fundamental differences to which the Government and the majority of the Commission rightly drew attention, namely differences as to legal status, conditions for entry to the profession, the nature of the functions involved, the manner of exercise of those functions, etc. The evidence before the Court does not disclose any similarity between the disparate situations in question: each one is characterised by a corpus of rights and obligations of which it would be artificial to isolate one specific aspect. On the basis of the applicant's grievances, the Court accordingly does not find any breach of Articles 14 and 4 taken together.

The difficulty with this decision is that, unlike that in *Fredin*, it allows the very ground on which discrimination was alleged (differences in professional status) to block comparison between the applicant and comparator on the basis that they were insufficiently similar to compare. This is like rejecting a sex discrimination claim on the basis that men and women are too different to allow their treatment to be compared, an approach which has been applied not infrequently where the discrimination has been related to pregnancy.[23] Instead of focusing the attention on the question whether the differences which are said to exist between applicant and comparator are sufficient and of such a nature to justify their differential treatment, the approach adopted in *Van der Mussele* serves to block consideration of the claim at all. The Court indicates in para. 46 that the approach it adopts in *Van der Mussele* is mandated by the *Marckx* judgment. But although the Court there stated that 'Article 14 safeguards individuals, placed in similar situations, from any discrimination in the enjoyment of the rights and freedoms set forth in' the Convention, this formulation was not adopted to exclude a claim on the basis of any lack of similarity, and was more in the nature of a passing observation. It is a significant step to employ this in order to block a claim, as in *Van der Mussele*, without engaging with its merits. A similar approach was, however, adopted in *Stubbings v. United Kingdom*,[24] where discrimination was alleged as between the

---

[23] *See* (in the UK) *Webb v. EMO (Air Cargo) UK Ltd* [1993] I.C.R. 175 and in the US *General Electric v. Gilbert*, 429 U.S. 125 (1976). *Cf.* the decisions of the ECJ in *Webb* (Case C–32/93 [1994] E.C.R. I-03567) and the Canadian Supreme Court in *Janzen v. Platy Enterprises Ltd* [1989] I S.C.R. 1284.

[24] 22 Oct. 1996, 23 E.H.R.R. 213.

victims of intentional and unintentional torts as regards time limits applicable to their legal claims. The applicants, who had suffered psychiatric injuries as a result of intentional torts inflicted upon them years before, claimed that the application to them of time limits which blocked their claims had the effect of treating them less favourably than those who suffered injuries attributable to unintentional wrongs, in respect of which different time limits applied. The Court ruled that:

the victims of intentionally and negligently inflicted harm cannot be said to be in analogous situations for the purposes of Article 14. In any domestic judicial system there may be a number of separate categories of claimant, classified by reference to the type of harm suffered, the legal basis of the claim or other factors, who are subject to varying rules and procedures. In the instant case, different rules have evolved within the English law of limitation in respect of the victims of intentionally and negligently inflicted injury ... Different considerations may apply to each of these groups; for example, it may be more readily apparent to the victims of deliberate wrongdoing that they have a cause of action. It would be artificial to emphasise the similarities between these groups of claimants and to ignore the distinctions between them for the purposes of Article 14.

The Court in *Stubbings* went on to declare that 'even if a comparison could properly be drawn between the two groups of claimants in question, the difference in treatment may be reasonably and objectively justified, again by reference to their distinctive characteristics'. It may be that full consideration of the justification question would have led to the same result. But the difficulty with the *Van der Mussele/Stubbings* approach is that it results, at best, in cursory analysis of the reasons for different treatment of persons or groups defined by reference to Article 14 grounds.

The *Van der Mussele/Stubbings* approach has not frequently been applied by the European Court despite regular attempts by respondent states to rely upon it. Where it has been applied it appears to function as a device to knock out claims where the ground on which discrimination is alleged is not one in respect of which an onerous standard of justification would be imposed (see below), and where that standard might well be justified on the facts. This was dealt with expressly in the *Stubbings* decision though not in *Van der Mussele*. The shortcomings of the approach can, however, be seen in the Commission's decision in *Shackell v United Kingdom*.

In 1986, in *Lindsay v United Kingdom*[25] the European Commission had dismissed as manifestly unfounded a claim that the UK's tax system (which at the relevant time aggregated a married couple's income for taxation purposes in such a way that in certain circumstances such couples were taxed more heavily than unmarried couples) discriminated against married persons contrary to Article 14 read in conjunction with Article 8 and Article 1 of Protocol 1 to the Convention. According to the Commission, married and unmarried couples could not be considered to be in analogous situations: 'Though in some fields, the *de facto* relationship of cohabitees is now recognised, there still exist differences between married and unmarried couples, in particular, differences in legal status and legal effects. Marriage continues to be characterized by

[25] Comm. Dec. 1 Nov. 86, D.R. 49, p. 181.

a corpus of rights and obligations which differentiate it markedly from the situation of a man and woman who cohabit'. *Lindsay* was relied upon some 14 years later by the Commission in *Shackell v. United Kingdom*[26] which concerned a challenge by a woman who was, because she was unmarried, denied widow's benefits when her partner of 17 years died. She claimed under Articles 8 and 14 on her own behalf and on behalf of her three children who, it was said, were discriminated against because their parents were unmarried. The Court cited the extract from *Lindsay* reproduced above and baldly declared that 'there may well now be an increased social acceptance of stable personal relationships outside the traditional notion of marriage. However, marriage remains an institution which is widely accepted as conferring a particular status on those who enter it. The situation of the Applicant is therefore not comparable to that of a widow'.

It is instructive to contrast the approach taken by South Africa's Constitutional Court in *Volks NO v. Ethel Robinson & Others*.[27] South Africa's Constitution prohibits (section 9(3)) 'unfair' discrimination 'on one or more grounds, including race, gender, sex, pregnancy, marital status, ethnic or social origin, colour, sexual orientation, age, disability, religion, conscience, belief, culture, language and birth', section 9(5) providing that 'Discrimination on one or more of the grounds listed in subsection (3) is unfair unless it is established that the discrimination is fair'.[28]

Volks concerned a challenge by a woman for maintenance against the estate of her deceased former partner with whom she had lived, unmarried, for 16 years until his death. The relevant legislation applied only to surviving spouses. A lower court upheld her challenge and ruled that the legislation had to be read so as to accommodate her maintenance claim. The Constitutional Court, by a majority, disagreed. Thirteen of the 16 judges ruled that she had not been unfairly discriminated against. By contrast with the European Commission in *Shackell*, however, they did so having given substantive consideration to the fairness of the differential treatment complained of.

Seven of the majority in *Volks* reasoned that the impugned legislation was designed to extend after death the inevitable obligations attendant upon marriage (including the obligation of maintenance). Such obligations did not apply between unmarried couples and so the differential treatment of unmarried and married bereaved partners could not, in the view of the majority, be characterized as 'unfair' for the purposes of section 9(3). The remaining six in the majority explicitly accepted that the provisions discriminated against the survivors of heterosexual permanent life partnerships, but agreed that the discrimination was not unfair in view of South Africa's constitutional recognition of marriage and the element of choice involved. The minority judges took the view that the distinction drawn between married and unmarried couples by the legislation at issue was unfair. Sachs J suggested that, in cases in which a woman had 'shared her home and life with her deceased partner, borne and raised children with him, cared for him in

---

[26] 27 April 2000, Application No. 45851/99.

[27] 2005 (5) BCLR 446 (CC).

[28] For fuller discussion of the South African approach to equality *see* R. Clayton and H. Tomlinson, *The Law of Human Rights* (Oxford University Press, 2003), Chapter 17. For the effect of the Human Rights Act (United Kingdom) on the interpretation of legislation to include homosexual couples, *see Ghaidan v. Godin-Mendoza*, Chapter 14(D)(5).

health and in sickness, and dedicated her life to support the family they created together', she should not 'be treated as a legal stranger to his estate, with no claim for subsistence because they were never married'. The 'critical question' for him was 'a familial nexus of such proximity and intensity between the survivor and the deceased as to render it manifestly unfair to deny her the right to claim maintenance from the estate on the same basis as she would have had if she and the deceased had been married?'

The remaining dissenters reasoned that, in those cases in which cohabitation played a 'similar social function to marriage', differential regulation of married and unmarried relationships could (but did not inevitably) involve unfair discrimination. Whether such discrimination was in fact made out would turn on '(a) the position of complainants in society and whether they have previously suffered from patterns of disadvantage; (b) the nature of the provision and the purpose sought to be achieved by it; and (c) the extent to which the discrimination has affected the rights or interests of the complainants and whether it has led to an impairment of their fundamental human dignity or has caused them some other harm of a comparably serious nature'.

The practical outcome for the claimant in *Volks* was the same as that in the *Shackell* case. It cannot be denied, however, that the approach taken by South Africa's Constitutional Court was considerably more nuanced. In place of a 5-page bare dismissal of the claim in the latter case, the judgment of the South African Court extended to 140 pages. This is not to say that length is desirable for its own sake. But what is evident in the *Volks* judgment is a genuine attempt to grapple with the legitimacy of pinning particular benefits to married status. The dissenters in *Volks* ruled in favour of the claimant because they recognized her situation as relevantly similar to that of a widow. Critical scrutiny of the justification for rewarding particular social and legal categories, as distinct from the unquestioning application of those categories, is at the heart of a radical approach to equality/non-discrimination.

Volks is consistent with a strictly comparator-driven approach to equality, though it does not fall into the *Shackell* trap. The following case, however, illustrates that some discrimination claims ought not to turn on a comparator at all.

3. LOVING V. VIRGINIA

Judgment of 12 June 1967
388 U.S. 1

[The petitioners had been convicted under state laws criminalizing 'miscegenation' (that is, marriage between white and 'colored' persons). Virginia was one of 16 US states which had such laws in place at the time. According to the trial judge, who sentenced them to a year's imprisonment suspended for twenty-five years on condition that they did not enter Virginia during that time: 'Almighty God created the races white, black, yellow, malay and red, and he placed them on separate continents. And but for the interference with his arrangement there would be no cause for such marriages. The fact that he separated the races shows that he did not intend for the races to mix'. Virginia's Supreme Court upheld the convictions on the basis that the State had a legitimate aim 'to preserve the racial integrity of its citizens' and to prevent 'the corruption of blood', 'a mongrel breed of citizens', and 'the obliteration of racial pride'. The petitioners challenged their convictions under, *inter alia*, the Equal Protection clause of the US Constitution's Fourteenth Amendment.]

Chief Justice Warren (for the Court):

The...State argues that the meaning of the Equal Protection Clause, as illuminated by the statements of the Framers, is only that state penal laws containing an interracial element as part of the definition of the offense must apply equally to whites and Negroes in the sense that members of each race are punished to the same degree. Thus, the State contends that, because its miscegenation statutes punish equally both the white and the Negro participants in an interracial marriage, these statutes, despite their reliance on racial classifications, do not constitute an invidious discrimination based upon race. The second argument advanced by the State assumes the validity of its equal application theory. The argument is that, if the Equal Protection Clause does not outlaw miscegenation statutes because of their reliance on racial classifications, the question of constitutionality would thus become whether there was any rational basis for a State to treat interracial marriages differently from other marriages. On this question, the State argues, the scientific evidence is substantially in doubt and, consequently, this Court should defer to the wisdom of the state legislature in adopting its policy of discouraging interracial marriages.

Because we reject the notion that the mere 'equal application' of a statute containing racial classifications is enough to remove the classifications from the Fourteenth Amendment's proscription of all invidious racial discriminations, we do not accept the State's contention that these statutes should be upheld if there is any possible basis for concluding that they serve a rational purpose. The mere fact of equal application does not mean that our analysis of these statutes should follow the approach we have taken in cases involving no racial discrimination...

The State argues that statements in the Thirty-ninth Congress about the time of the passage of the Fourteenth Amendment indicate that the Framers did not intend the Amendment to make unconstitutional state miscegenation laws. Many of the statements alluded to by the State concern the debates over the Freedmen's Bureau Bill, which President Johnson vetoed, and the Civil Rights Act of 1866, enacted over his veto. While these statements have some relevance to the intention of Congress in submitting the Fourteenth Amendment, it must be understood that they pertained to the passage of specific statutes and not to the broader, organic purpose of a constitutional amendment. As for the various statements directly concerning the Fourteenth Amendment, we have said in connection with a related problem, that although these historical sources 'cast some light' they are not sufficient to resolve the problem; '[at] best, they are inconclusive. The most avid proponents of the post-War Amendments undoubtedly intended them to remove all legal distinctions among 'all persons born or naturalized in the United States'. Their opponents, just as certainly, were antagonistic to both the letter and the spirit of the Amendments and wished them to have the most limited effect.' We have rejected the proposition that the debates in the Thirty-ninth Congress or in the state legislatures which ratified the Fourteenth Amendment supported the theory advanced by the State, that the requirement of equal protection of the laws is satisfied by penal laws defining offenses based on racial classifications so long as white and Negro participants in the offense were similarly punished....

The Equal Protection Clause requires the consideration of whether the classifications drawn by any statute constitute an arbitrary and invidious discrimination. The clear and central purpose of the Fourteenth Amendment was to eliminate all official state sources of invidious racial discrimination in the States.

There can be no question but that Virginia's miscegenation statutes rest solely upon distinctions drawn according to race. The statutes proscribe generally accepted conduct if engaged in by members of different races. Over the years, this Court has consistently repudiated 'distinctions between citizens solely because of their ancestry' as being 'odious to a free people whose institutions are founded upon the doctrine of equality.' At the very least, the Equal Protection Clause demands that racial classifications, especially suspect in criminal statutes, be subjected to the 'most rigid scrutiny,' *Korematsu* v. *United States* (1944), and, if they are ever to be upheld, they must be shown to be necessary to the accomplishment of some permissible state objective, independent of the racial discrimination which it was the object of the Fourteenth Amendment to eliminate. Indeed, two members of this Court have already stated that they 'cannot conceive of a valid legislative purpose . . . which makes the color of a person's skin the test of whether his conduct is a criminal offense.'

There is patently no legitimate overriding purpose independent of invidious racial discrimination which justifies this classification. The fact that Virginia prohibits only interracial marriages involving white persons demonstrates that the racial classifications must stand on their own justification, as measures designed to maintain White Supremacy. We have consistently denied the constitutionality of measures which restrict the rights of citizens on account of race. There can be no doubt that restricting the freedom to marry solely because of racial classifications violates the central meaning of the Equal Protection Clause.

This decision of the U.S. Supreme Court illustrates perhaps better than any other the short-comings of an approach to discrimination based solely upon comparison. It was clear on the facts in *Loving* that the impugned law punished transgressors regardless of race. It was equally clear that that law's rationale was overtly racist. To follow the urgings of the respondent state would have made the U.S. Supreme Court complicit in racism. Precisely similar arguments have failed to persuade the highest British courts, however, that discrimination based on the sex of a complainant's actual or preferred sexual partner (that is, sexual orientation discrimination) also amounted to sex discrimination contrary to domestic anti-discrimination provisions.[29]

The *Shackell* approach to the comparator question has only ever been applied in a handful of cases, apparently as a quick means of disposing of claims that were regarded as lacking merit, although it has proved very influential in the U.K. courts' approach to Article 14 claims.[30] Invitations to the Strasbourg Court to deploy this line of reasoning have had limited success in recent years. Very recently, in *Burden v. United Kingdom*,[31] which involved a challenge to the differential treatment for inheritance tax purposes of married couples and civil partners, on the one hand, and cohabiting siblings, on the other, a section of the European Court cited *Lindsay* and *Shackell* but took the view

---

[29] *MacDonald v. Advocate General for Scotland; Pearce v. Governing Body of Mayfield School* [2003] UKHL 34, [2003] I.C.R. 937.

[30] *See* in particular the decision of the House of Lords in *R. (Carson) v. Secretary of State for Work and Pensions* [2005] UKHL 37, [2006] 1 A.C. 173, discussed by A. McColgan, 'Cracking The Comparator Problem', n. 22 *supra*.

[31] 12 Dec. 2006, 44 E.H.R.R. 51. The Grand Chamber heard the case in September 2007. The decision is awaited at the time of writing.

that it did not have to decide whether 'the applicants can be regarded as being in an analogous position to married and civil partnership couples' because the difference in treatment was in the Court's view justified given the wide margin of appreciation applicable in tax cases and the protection by the Convention of the right to marry and not to be discriminated against on grounds of sexual orientation.

More significant still, because it resulted in a decision that Article 14 had been breached, was *Sidabras v. Lithuania*, which concerned a claim under Articles 8 and 14 by former KGB officers who challenged a ban on the employment of former KGB officers in various private, as well as public, sector spheres. The Court found a breach of Article 14, notwithstanding the strongly dissenting view of Judge Loucaides who protested that, taking into account the fact that the ban was intended to 'protect national security, public safety and the rights of others, by avoiding a repetition of previous experience which could occur if former KGB officers were to engage in activities similar to those of that organisation', the applicants were not analogously situated to those who had not worked for the KGB. According to the Court:

41 ...the applicants were treated differently from other persons in Lithuania who had not worked for the KGB, and who as a result had no restrictions imposed on them in their choice of professional activities. In addition, in view of the Government's argument that the purpose of the Act was to regulate the employment prospects of persons on the ground of their loyalty or lack of loyalty to the State, there has also been a difference of treatment between the applicants and other persons in this respect. For the Court, this is the appropriate comparison in the instant case for the purposes of art 14.[32]

The Court went on to find a breach of Article 14 on the basis that, although the state had 'a legitimate interest in regulating employment conditions in the public service as well as in the private sector' and 'in requiring civil servants to show loyalty to the constitutional principles on which the society was founded', and the asserted 'reason for the imposition of employment restrictions under the Act was not the applicants' KGB history as such, but their lack of loyalty to the State as evidenced by their former employment with the KGB', the employment restrictions imposed on the applicants were disproportionate (see below). A similar approach has been taken in the recent decision in *Paulik*.

4. PAULIK V. SLOVAKIA

Judgment of 10 October 2006

[The applicant challenged the fact that, whereas national law did not allow him to challenge paternity once it had been established by a court,[33] a mother could request the Prosecutor

---

[32] 27 July 2004, 42 E.H.R.R. 6.

[33] By means of a legal presumption arising from his relationship with the child's mother, in circumstances such that at the time when paternity was legally established no DNA testing had been undergone. This

General to challenge paternity on their behalf as could a man whose paternity had been presumed rather than established by a court.]

51. The Court...reiterates that the right under art 14 not to be discriminated against in the enjoyment of the rights guaranteed under the Convention is violated when States treat differently persons in analogous situations without providing an objective and reasonable justification...

52. The Government submitted that the applicant could not be considered to be in an analogous situation for the purposes of art 14 of the Convention to the persons with whom he sought comparison. In their view, the crucial factor was not the legal ground on which the declaration of his paternity was based, but rather the fact that his paternity had been declared by means of a final and binding judicial decision. The other situations relied on by the applicant were different in that the paternity of the husband of the mother, or that of the man who declared jointly with the mother that he was the father, was presumed and could be challenged in a court.

53. The applicant disagreed and reiterated his complaint. In particular, he asserted that there was only one category of fathers. All fathers essentially had the same duties, rights and responsibilities and should be treated equally. There were no effective legal means at all whereby he could challenge the declaration of paternity although he had new and conclusive evidence that he was not the biological father. In contrast, in situations where paternity was presumed, if new evidence excluding the possibility of biological paternity came to light, the presumed father and the mother could request the Prosecutor General to contest the paternity.

54. The Court accepts that there may be differences between, on the one hand, the applicant and, on the other hand, the putative fathers and the mothers in situations where paternity is legally presumed but has not been judicially determined. However, the fact that there are some differences between two or more individuals does not preclude them from being in sufficiently comparable positions and from having sufficiently comparable interests. The Court finds that with regard to their interest in contesting a status relating to paternity, the applicant and the other parties in question were in an analogous situation for the purposes of art 14 of the Convention. The legal system afforded them different treatment in that, unlike the other parties, the applicant could not request the Prosecutor General to challenge the declaration of paternity in the courts in the interests of society. It remains to be ascertained whether this difference had any objective and reasonable justification.

In *Paulik*, as in *Sidabras*, the Court went on to rule in favour of the applicant.

D. INDIRECT DISCRIMINATION

The cases considered above have concerned *direct* discrimination, that is, less favourable treatment on a protected ground. The regulation of such discrimination alone falls far short of providing protection against disadvantage associated with

was later done and it was at this stage that he wished to challenge paternity but was prevented from so doing.

protected grounds, conditioning equal treatment as it does on the ability to emulate characteristics of the advantaged group; in other words, direct sex discrimination can only be challenged by women who are regarded as relevantly 'like' the men whose treatment they aspire to if they are to avoid a finding that the less favourable treatment of which they complain results, not from discrimination on the ground of sex, but from some other difference between them and their comparators.

Indirect discrimination is concerned with apparently neutral treatment whose *effect*, rather than *form* or *aim*, is to disadvantage persons of particular groups defined by reference to a protected ground. Indirect or 'disparate impact'discrimination was recognized by the US Supreme Court in its famous decision in *Griggs v. Duke Power Co*,[34] in which black workers claimed that the employer's practice of requiring a high school diploma or success in an IQ test as a condition of employment in particular jobs discriminated against them on grounds of race, a disproportionate number of blacks being rendered ineligible by the practice. The lower courts had found that the employer's previous practice of race discrimination had ended, and that there was no evidence that the requirements had been adopted in order to discriminate on racial grounds. The Supreme Court found in favour of the plaintiffs. It should be noted that the decision in *Griggs* was reached under Title VII of the Civil Rights Act 1964 and not under the Constitution's Equal Protection Clause, under which it is necessary to establish discriminatory intent.[35] It nevertheless remains the classic formulation of this type of discrimination.

1. GRIGGS V. DUKE POWER CO.

Judgment of 8 March 1971
401 U.S. 424

Chief Justice Burger, for the Court:

The objective of Congress in the enactment of Title VII is plain from the language of the statute. It was to achieve equality of employment opportunities and remove barriers that have operated in the past to favor an identifiable group of white employees over other employees. Under the Act, practices, procedures, or tests neutral on their face, and even neutral in terms of intent, cannot be maintained if they operate to 'freeze' the status quo of prior discriminatory employment practices.

The Court of Appeals' opinion, and the partial dissent, agreed that, on the record in the present case, 'whites register far better on the Company's alternative requirements' than Negroes... This consequence would appear to be directly traceable to race. Basic intelligence must have the means of articulation to manifest itself fairly in a testing process. Because they are Negroes, petitioners have long received inferior education in segregated schools... Congress did

---

[34] 401 U.S. 424 (1971).
[35] *Washington v. Davis*, 426 U.S. 229 (1976).

not intend by Title VII, however, to guarantee a job to every person regardless of qualifications. In short, the Act does not command that any person be hired simply because he was formerly the subject of discrimination, or because he is a member of a minority group. Discriminatory preference for any group, minority or majority, is precisely and only what Congress has proscribed. What is required by Congress is the removal of artificial, arbitrary, and unnecessary barriers to employment when the barriers operate invidiously to discriminate on the basis of racial or other impermissible classification.

Congress has now provided that tests or criteria for employment or promotion may not provide equality of opportunity merely in the sense of the fabled offer of milk to the stork and the fox. On the contrary, Congress has now required that the posture and condition of the job-seeker be taken into account. It has—to resort again to the fable—provided that the vessel in which the milk is proffered be one all seekers can use. The Act proscribes not only overt discrimination but also practices that are fair in form, but discriminatory in operation. The touchstone is business necessity. If an employment practice which operates to exclude Negroes cannot be shown to be related to job performance, the practice is prohibited.

On the record before us, neither the high school completion requirement nor the general intelligence test is shown to bear a demonstrable relationship to successful performance of the jobs for which it was used. Both were adopted, as the Court of Appeals noted, without meaningful study of their relationship to job-performance ability. Rather, a vice president of the Company testified, the requirements were instituted on the Company's judgment that they generally would improve the overall quality of the work force . . . good intent or absence of discriminatory intent does not redeem employment procedures or testing mechanisms that operate as 'built-in headwinds' for minority groups and are unrelated to measuring job capability . . .

From the start, the European Court's Article 14 decisions hinted that the provision was capable of applying to indirect as well as direct discrimination. In the *Belgian Linguistic* case the Court suggested that the subject 'must be assessed in relation to the aim *and effects* of the measure under consideration' (emphasis added), though that decision was concerned with differential treatment, rather than disparate impact. An early attempt to challenge indirect discrimination under Article 14, however, suggested that Article 14 was concerned primarily or exclusively with direct discrimination. The sex discrimination challenge in *Abdulaziz* was considered above. That case also, however, alleged race discrimination in the operation of the U.K.'s immigration rules (see paras 84–86 of the extract in Section A(1)). As we saw above, this claim failed. The difficulty with the approach adopted by the Court in that case, however, was that it applied a *direct* rather than *indirect* discrimination test. The question should not be whether differential treatment by race was intended; rather, whether differential outcomes were produced. Not until 2000, however, did the European Court rule in favour of an applicant on what might be characterized as an indirect discrimination claim.

2. THLIMMENOS V. GREECE

Judgment of 6 April 2000
31 E.H.R.R. 15

7. On 9 December 1983 the Athens Permanent Army Tribunal (Diarkes Stratodikio), composed of one career military judge and four other officers, convicted the applicant, a Jehovah's Witness, of insubordination for having refused to wear the military uniform at a time of general mobilisation...

8. In June 1988 the applicant sat a public examination for the appointment of 12 chartered accountants, a liberal profession in Greece. He came second among 60 candidates. However, on 8 February 1989 the executive board of the Greek Institute of Chartered Accountants (the board) refused to appoint him on the ground that he had been convicted of a felony (kakuryima)...

33. The court notes that the applicant did not complain about his initial conviction for insubordination. The applicant complained that the law excluding persons convicted of a felony from appointment to a chartered accountant's post did not distinguish between persons convicted as a result of their religious beliefs and persons convicted on other grounds. The applicant invoked art 14 of the convention taken in conjunction with art 9...

41. The court notes that the applicant was not appointed a chartered accountant as a result of his past conviction for insubordination consisting in his refusal to wear the military uniform. He was thus treated differently from the other persons who had applied for that post on the ground of his status as a convicted person. The court considers that such difference of treatment does not generally come within the scope of art 14 in so far as it relates to access to a particular profession, the right to freedom of profession not being guaranteed by the convention.

42. However, the applicant does not complain of the distinction that the rules governing access to the profession make between convicted persons and others. His complaint rather concerns the fact that in the application of the relevant law no distinction is made between persons convicted of offences committed exclusively because of their religious beliefs and persons convicted of other offences. In this context the court notes that the applicant is a member of the Jehovah's Witnesses, a religious group committed to pacifism, and that there is nothing in the file to disprove the applicant's claim that he refused to wear the military uniform only because he considered that his religion prevented him from doing so. In essence, the applicant's argument amounts to saying that he is discriminated against in the exercise of his freedom of religion, as guaranteed by art 9 of the Convention, in that he was treated like any other person convicted of a felony although his own conviction resulted from the very exercise of this freedom. Seen in this perspective, the court accepts that the 'set of facts' complained of by the applicant—his being treated as a person convicted of a felony for the purposes of an appointment to a chartered accountant's post despite the fact that the offence for which he had been convicted was prompted by his religious beliefs—'falls within the ambit of a convention provision', namely art 9...

44. The court has so far considered that the right under art 14 not to be discriminated against in the enjoyment of the rights guaranteed under the Convention is violated when states treat differently persons in analogous situations without providing an objective and reasonable

justification... However, the court considers that this is not the only facet of the prohibition of discrimination in art 14. The right not to be discriminated against in the enjoyment of the rights guaranteed under the Convention is also violated when states without an objective and reasonable justification fail to treat differently persons whose situations are significantly different...

The Court in *Thlimmenos* went on to find a breach of Article 14.[36] It did not use the term 'indirect discrimination', and it may be that the demand there for unequal treatment of differently situated individuals is more radical than the classic indirect discrimination test which would permit the maintenance of disparately impacting practices which are justifiable despite that disparate impact. It is arguable, by contrast, that the *Thlimmenos* approach would require the accommodation of difference by means of some form of 'positive discrimination'. This point is returned to below. That case remains, however, the sole example to date in which what might be characterized as indirect discrimination has been found to breach Article 14.

Typical of subsequent unsuccessful claims was *Jordan v. United Kingdom*,[37] in which the Court rejected an argument that the disproportionate killing by the security forces in Northern Ireland of young Catholic/nationalist men[38] amounted to discrimination on grounds of national origin or association with a national minority contrary to Article 14 taken with Article 2 of the Convention. The Court stated (para. 154) that 'Where a general policy or measure has disproportionately prejudicial effects on a particular group, it is not excluded that this may be considered as discriminatory notwithstanding that it is not specifically aimed or directed at that group', but went on to deny that 'statistics can in themselves disclose a practice which could be classified as discriminatory within the meaning of Article 14. There is no evidence before the Court which would entitle it to conclude that any of those killings, save the four which resulted in convictions, involved the unlawful or excessive use of force by members of the security forces'.

E. PROVING DISCRIMINATION

Jordan is perhaps defensible given the lack of evidence before the court that that the disproportionate number of Catholics/nationalists killed did not result from any greater Catholic/nationalist involvement in unlawful violence. But there have been more

---

[36] Note also *Burghartz v. Switzerland*, 22 Feb. 1994, 18 E.H.R.R. 101, *Van Raalte v. Netherlands*, 21 Feb. 1997, 24 E.H.R.R. 503, *Schmidt v. Germany*, 18 July 1994, 18 E.H.R.R. 513.

[37] 4 May 2001, 37 E.H.R.R. 2.

[38] Between 1969 and March 1994, the overwhelming majority of the 357 people killed by the security forces were young Catholic or nationalist men. Only 31 prosecutions had followed, and these had resulted in only 4 convictions at the date of the application.

recent decisions of the European Court which appear to set an extraordinarily high threshold for the evidence required to establish, in particular, race discrimination.

1. DH AND OTHERS V. CZECH REPUBLIC

Judgment of 6 February 2006
43 E.H.R.R. 41

[The Article 14 claim was by Roma children of average or above-average intelligence who had been placed in 'special schools' intended to cater to children with learning disabilities. The European Court cited extensive evidence of education-related discrimination against Roma children. Among this evidence were reports of the European Commission against Racism and Intolerance (ECRI) and of the Czech Republic itself pursuant to art 25 § 1 of the Framework Convention for the Protection of National Minorities. The ECRI reports disclosed significant levels of concern about the practice of sending Roma children to special schools at which their attendance severely and permanently disadvantaged them. The Commission had drawn attention to the fact that the standardized test for assessing a child's mental level were neither mandatory nor the only means by which decisions as to schooling were made; expressed concern about the sometimes misleading information made available to Roma parents as to the consequences of sending their children to special schools; referred to reports of Roma parents being turned away from ordinary schools; and noted the persistent problem of low levels of Roma participation in secondary and tertiary level education. The Czech Republic's 1999 report acknowledged that 'Romany children with average or above-average intellect are often placed in such schools on the basis of results of psychological tests', that the tests 'are conceived for the majority population and do not take Romany specifics into consideration' and that 'In some special schools Romany pupils made up between 80% and 90% of the total number of pupils'.]

9. Between 1996 and 1999 the applicants were placed in special schools in Ostrava, either directly or after a period in an ordinary primary school. Special schools are a category of specialised school and are intended for children with learning disabilities who are unable to attend 'ordinary' or specialised primary schools. By law, the decision to place a child in a special school is taken by the head teacher on the basis of the results of tests to measure the child's intellectual capacity carried out in an educational psychology and child guidance centre and requires the consent of the parent or legal guardian of the child.

10. The material before the Court shows that the applicants' parents had consented to and in some instances expressly requested their children's placement in a special school. A written decision in the appropriate form was issued by the head teachers of the schools concerned and the applicants' parents were notified of it. The decisions contained instructions on the right to appeal, a right which none of those concerned exercised.

11. On 29 June 1999 the applicants received a letter from the school authorities informing them of the possibilities available for transferring from a special school to a primary school. It appears that four of the applicants (nos. 5, 6, 11 and 16) were successful in aptitude tests and now attend ordinary schools...

32. The applicants alleged that they had been discriminated against in the enjoyment of their right to education on account of their race, colour, association with a national minority and their ethnic origin. They relied on art 14 of the Convention, taken together with art 2 of Protocol No 1 ...

45. The Court notes that the applicants' complaint under art 14 of the Convention, taken together with art 2 of Protocol No 1, is based on a number of serious arguments. It also notes that several organisations, including Council of Europe bodies, have expressed concern about the arrangements whereby Roma children living in the Czech Republic are placed in special schools and about the difficulties they have in gaining access to ordinary schools. The Court points out, however, that its role is different from that of the aforementioned bodies and that, like the Czech Constitutional Court, it is not its task to assess the overall social context. Its sole task in the instant case is to examine the individual applications before it and to establish on the basis of the relevant facts whether the reason for the applicants' placement in the special schools was their ethnic or racial origin.

46. In that connection, the Court observes that, if a policy or general measure has dispro- portionately prejudicial effects on a group of people, the possibility of its being considered discriminatory cannot be ruled out even if it is not specifically aimed or directed at that group. However, statistics are not by themselves sufficient to disclose a practice which could be clas- sified as discriminatory ...

48. In the Court's view, the Government have nevertheless succeeded in establishing that the system of special schools in the Czech Republic was not introduced solely to cater for Roma children and that considerable efforts are made in these schools to help certain categories of pupils to acquire a basic education. The Government said that the criterion for selecting the applicants was not their race or ethnic origin but their learning disabilities as revealed in the psychological tests.

49. The Court observes that the rules governing children's placement in special schools do not refer to the pupils' ethnic origin, but pursue the legitimate aim of adapting the education system to the needs and aptitudes or disabilities of the children. Since these are not legal concepts, it is only right that experts in educational psychology should be responsible for identifying them.

As regards the applicants' argument that there are no uniform rules governing the choice of tests used by the experts or the interpretation of the results, the Court notes that the parties did not dispute that the tests in the instant case were administered by qualified professionals, who are expected to follow the rules of their profession and to be able to select suitable methods. It would be difficult for the Court to go beyond this factual finding and to ask the Government to prove that the psychologists who examined the applicants had not adopted a particular sub- jective attitude. Furthermore, the applicants' representatives have not succeeded in refuting the aforementioned experts' findings that the applicants' learning disabilities were such as to prevent them from following the ordinary primary school curriculum ...

50. It should also be borne in mind that, in their capacity as the applicants' lawful representa- tives, the applicants' parents failed to take any action, despite receiving a clear written decision informing them of their children's placement in a special school; indeed, in some instances it was the parents who asked for their children to be placed or to remain in a special school ...

51. As to the applicants' argument that the parental consent was not 'informed' and, in the case of two of the applicants (nos. 12 and 16), appears to have been pre-dated, the Court

notes that it was the parents' responsibility, as part of their natural duty to ensure that their children receive an education, to find out about the educational opportunities offered by the State, to make sure they knew the date they gave their consent to their children's placement in a particular school and, if necessary, to make an appropriate challenge to the decision ordering the placement if it was issued without their consent.

52. Thus, while acknowledging that these statistics disclose figures that are worrying and that the general situation in the Czech Republic concerning the education of Roma children is by no means perfect, the Court cannot in the circumstances find that the measures taken against the applicants were discriminatory. Although the applicants may have lacked information about the national education system or found themselves in a climate of mistrust, the concrete evidence before the Court in the present case does not enable it to conclude that the applicants' placement or, in some instances, continued placement, in special schools was the result of racial prejudice, as they have alleged.

53. It follows that no violation of art 14 of the Convention, taken together with art 2 of Protocol No 1, has been established.

The decision in *DH* is difficult to understand, in particular in the Court's apparent refusal to place any weight on the evidence from the respondent state (in its 1999 National Minorities report) that Roma children of 'average or above-average intellect' were 'often placed in [special] schools on the basis of results of psychological tests...conceived for the majority population [which did] not take Romany specifics into consideration'. The shortcomings in the majority approach were pointed out in a dissenting opinion by Judge Cabral Barreto, who cited the 1999 report and went on:

In my opinion, this constitutes an express acknowledgement by the Czech State of the discriminatory practices complained of by the applicants.

During the period from 1996 to 1999 the applicants were not placed in schools for the mentally disabled because of mental disability; on the contrary, they possessed 'average or above-average intellect'.

3. The judgment raises first and foremost points that warrant detailed examination, namely that the applicants were selected for placement in the schools by tests and that the placements were made with parental consent.

The Government, however, acknowledged in the 1999 report, which is cited in the judgment, that the tests did not take Romany specifics into consideration.

As to parental consent, I would refer to ECRI's Third Report on the Czech Republic, which was made public on 8 June 2004: 'As far as the other element required in order to send a child to a special school—the consent of a parent or legal guardian of the child—parents making such decisions continue to lack information concerning the long-term negative consequences of sending their children to such schools.'...

In practice, pupils educated in a 'special school' saw their prospects of pursuing their studies in a secondary school reduced to nil.

4. I agree with the majority's statement of the position in para 47: '...with regard to the States' margin of appreciation in the education sphere ... the States cannot be prohibited from setting up different types of school for children with difficulties or implementing special educational programmes to respond to special needs'.

I would even add: the State should take into account pupils who, because of their special circumstances, require a specific form of education.

These pupils who, for various reasons—whether cultural, linguistic or other—find it difficult to pursue a normal school education should be entitled to expect the State to take positive measures to compensate for their handicap and to afford them a means of resuming the normal curriculum.

However, such measures should never result in the handicap being increased as a result of the pupil being placed in a school for children with learning disabilities.

5 ... In the applicants' situation, compliance with art 14 of the Convention required measures to be taken to make up for the differences. However, the Czech State's 'different treatment' of the applicants served, in my view, to aggravate the differences between them and the pupils attending the ordinary schools. It seems to me that the measure is made all the more unjust and incomprehensible in terms of cognitive ability by the fact that the majority of these pupils were average or above-average when compared to pupils attending the ordinary schools. The Czech State thereby prevented them from achieving their cognitive and intellectual potential, as they possessed the requisite capacities.

It is not for me to say what type of positive measures the applicants' situation called for, but what is certain is that enrolling them in schools designed and intended for children with learning disabilities does not appear to be an appropriate means of resolving these children's difficulties, which are of an entirely different order from the cognitive problems characteristic of pupils in such schools ...

6. Lastly, the expression 'all different, all equal' should continue to be the guiding principle in the unceasing fight against discrimination in compliance with all the aspects of art 14 of the Convention, a provision which covers both negative discrimination and, as in the present case, positive discrimination.

DH was a decision of the Second Section of the Court. The Grand Chamber heard oral argument in the case in January 2007 but the decision was still awaited in September 2007. That a similar approach might be taken by the Grand Chamber as by the Second Section, notwithstanding the considerable dissent generated by the *DH* decision,[39] is indicated by the following case.

2. NACHOVA AND OTHERS V. BULGARIA

Judgment of 6 July 2005
42 E.H.R.R. 43

[The claim was brought in relation to the use of disproportionate force against two Roma military deserters with fatal results. The men, who had been unarmed, were pursued by four officers armed with guns (in one case a kalashnikov automatic rifle). They were shot with a kalashnikov while running away in circumstances such that they posed no danger to their pursuers or others. There was evidence from one witness that the soldier who killed the

---

[39] For one critique *see* 'Case Comment: Education: Placement of Roma Children in Special Schools', [2006] *E.H.R.L.R.* 340. On 13 Nov. 2007, the Grand Chamber by 13–4 reversed the Section's decision.

men had used racist language towards him (also a Roma) immediately after the shootings. The First Section ([2004] ECHR 90) had found a breach of Article 2 taken alone, and a breach of Article 14. As the Grand Chamber summarized the First Section's judgment:

'126. The Chamber noted that in cases of deprivation of life arts 2 and 14 of the Convention combined imposed a duty on state authorities to conduct an effective investigation irrespective of the victim's racial or ethnic origin. It also considered that the authorities had the additional duty to take all reasonable steps to unmask any racist motive in an incident involving the use of force by law-enforcement agents.

127. In the present case, despite Mr MM's statement about racist verbal abuse and other evidence which should have alerted the authorities to the need to investigate possible racist motives, no such investigation had been undertaken. The authorities had on that account failed in their duty under art 14 of the Convention taken together with art 2.

128. Considering that the particular evidentiary difficulties involved in proving discrimination called for a specific approach to the issue of proof, the Chamber held that in cases where the authorities had not pursued lines of inquiry that had been clearly warranted in their investigation into acts of violence by state agents and had disregarded evidence of possible discrimination, the Court might, when examining complaints under art 14 of the Convention, draw negative inferences or shift the burden of proof to the respondent government.

129. On the facts of the case, the Chamber considered that the conduct of the investigating authorities—which had omitted to refer to a number of disquieting facts such as the excessive nature of the force used by Major G and the evidence that he had uttered a racist slur—warranted a shift of the burden of proof. It thus fell to the respondent government to satisfy the Court, on the basis of additional evidence or a convincing explanation of the facts, that the events complained of had not been shaped by discrimination on the part of state agents.

130. As the government had not offered a convincing explanation, and noting that there had been previous cases in which the Court had found that law enforcement officers in Bulgaria had subjected Roma to violence resulting in death, the Chamber concluded that there had also been a violation of the substantive aspect of art 14 taken together with art 2 of the convention...'

The Grand Chamber agreed with the First Section on the Article 2 issue. It acknowledged the concern expressed by the European Commission against Racism and Intolerance at the Council of Europe (ECRI) about racially motivated police violence against Roma in a number of countries including Bulgaria. The ECRI's second report on Bulgaria (March 2000) referred to 'numerous...cases of police misconduct towards...Roma...use of excessive physical force during detention for the purposes of extorting evidence; unjustified use of firearms...and threats to the personal security of individuals who had complained against the police to the competent authorities' and findings that 'the majority of complaints filed by [the Human Rights Project] on behalf of Roma victims of police violence have not been followed up by the authorities'. The ECRI's third report on Bulgaria (January 2004) expressed continuing concern, in particular, 'about allegations of instances of excessive use of firearms by the police, which have sometimes led to the death of Roma' and the fact that 'the proportion of people of Roma origin who state that they have been subjected to physical violence in police stations is three times higher than the proportion of people of Bulgarian origin'. The Grand Chamber also referred to reports by Human Rights Project and Amnesty International of 'numerous incidents of alleged racial violence against Roma in Bulgaria, including by law enforcement agents'.]

124. The applicants alleged a violation of art 14 of the Convention in that prejudice and hostile attitudes towards persons of Roma origin had played a role in the events leading up to the deaths of Mr Angelov and Mr Petkov. They also argued that the authorities had failed in their duty to investigate possible racist motives in their killing. The government disputed the applicants' allegations...

145. Discrimination is treating differently, without an objective and reasonable justification, persons in relevantly similar situations. Racial violence is a particular affront to human dignity and, in view of its perilous consequences, requires from the authorities special vigilance and a vigorous reaction. It is for this reason that the authorities must use all available means to combat racism and racist violence, thereby reinforcing democracy's vision of a society in which diversity is not perceived as a threat but as a source of its enrichment. The Court will revert to that issue below.

146. Faced with the applicants' complaint of a violation of art 14, as formulated, the Court's task is to establish whether or not racism was a causal factor in the shooting that led to the deaths of Mr Angelov and Mr Petkov so as to give rise to a breach of art 14 of the Convention taken in conjunction with art 2.

147. It notes in this connection that in assessing evidence, the Court has adopted the standard of proof 'beyond reasonable doubt'. However, it has never been its purpose to borrow the approach of the national legal systems that use that standard. Its role is not to rule on criminal guilt or civil liability but on contracting states' responsibility under the Convention. The specificity of its task under art 19 of the Convention—to ensure the observance by the contracting states of their engagement to secure the fundamental rights enshrined in the Convention—conditions its approach to the issues of evidence and proof. In the proceedings before the Court, there are no procedural barriers to the admissibility of evidence or pre-determined formulae for its assessment. It adopts the conclusions that are, in its view, supported by the free evaluation of all evidence, including such inferences as may flow from the facts and the parties' submissions. According to its established case law, proof may follow from the coexistence of sufficiently strong, clear and concordant inferences or of similar unrebutted presumptions of fact. Moreover, the level of persuasion necessary for reaching a particular conclusion and, in this connection, the distribution of the burden of proof are intrinsically linked to the specificity of the facts, the nature of the allegation made and the Convention right at stake. The Court is also attentive to the seriousness that attaches to a ruling that a contracting state has violated fundamental rights...

148. The applicants have referred to several separate facts and they maintain that sufficient inferences of a racist act can be drawn from them.

149. First, the applicants considered revealing the fact that Major G had discharged bursts of automatic fire in a populated area, in disregard of the public's safety. Considering that there was no rational explanation for such behaviour, the applicants were of the view that racist hatred on the part of Major G was the only plausible explanation and that he would not have acted in that manner in a non-Roma neighbourhood.

150. The Court notes, however, that the use of firearms in the circumstances at issue was regrettably not prohibited under the relevant domestic regulations, a flagrant deficiency which it has earlier condemned... The military police officers carried their automatic rifles 'in accordance with the rules' and were instructed to use all necessary means to effect the arrest... The possibility that Major G was simply adhering strictly to the regulations and would have acted as he did in any similar context, regardless of the ethnicity of the fugitives, cannot therefore be excluded. While the relevant regulations were fundamentally flawed and fell well

short of the Convention requirements on the protection of the right to life, there is nothing to suggest that Major G would not have used his weapon in a non-Roma neighbourhood.

151. It is true, as the Court has found above, that Major G's conduct during the arrest operation calls for serious criticism in that he used grossly excessive force... None the less, it cannot be excluded either that his reaction was shaped by the inadequacy of the legal framework governing the use of firearms and by the fact that he was trained to operate within that framework...

152. The applicants also stated that the military police officers' attitude had been strongly influenced by their knowledge of the victims' Roma origin. However, it is not possible to speculate on whether or not Mr Angelov's and Mr Petkov's Roma origin had any bearing on the officers' perception of them. Furthermore, there is evidence that some of the officers knew one or both of the victims personally...

153. The applicants referred to the statement given by Mr MM, a neighbour of one of the victims, who reported that Major G had shouted at him 'You damn Gipsies' immediately after the shooting. While such evidence of a racial slur being uttered in connection with a violent act should have led the authorities in this case to verify Mr MM's statement, that statement is of itself an insufficient basis for concluding that the respondent state is liable for a racist killing.

154. Lastly, the applicants relied on information about numerous incidents involving the use of force against Roma by Bulgarian law enforcement officers that had not resulted in the conviction of those responsible.

155. It is true that a number of organisations, including intergovernmental bodies, have expressed concern about the occurrence of such incidents... However, the Court cannot lose sight of the fact that its sole concern is to ascertain whether in the case at hand the killing of Mr Angelov and Mr Petkov was motivated by racism.

156. In its judgment the Chamber decided to shift the burden of proof to the respondent government on account of the authorities' failure to carry out an effective investigation into the alleged racist motive for the killing. The inability of the government to satisfy the Chamber that the events complained of were not shaped by racism resulted in its finding a substantive violation of art 14 of the Convention, taken together with art 2.

157. The Grand Chamber reiterates that in certain circumstances, where the events lie wholly, or in large part, within the exclusive knowledge of the authorities, as in the case of death of a person within their control in custody, the burden of proof may be regarded as resting on the authorities to provide a satisfactory and convincing explanation of, in particular, the causes of the detained person's death. The Grand Chamber cannot exclude the possibility that in certain cases of alleged discrimination it may require the respondent government to disprove an arguable allegation of discrimination and—if they fail to do so—find a violation of art 14 of the Convention on that basis. However, where it is alleged—as here—that a violent act was motivated by racial prejudice, such an approach would amount to requiring the respondent government to prove the absence of a particular subjective attitude on the part of the person concerned. While in the legal systems of many countries proof of the discriminatory effect of a policy or decision will dispense with the need to prove intent in respect of alleged discrimination in employment or the provision of services, that approach is difficult to transpose to a case where it is alleged that an act of violence was racially motivated. The Grand Chamber, departing from the Chamber's approach, does not consider that the alleged failure

of the authorities to carry out an effective investigation into the alleged racist motive for the killing should shift the burden of proof to the respondent government with regard to the alleged violation of art 14 in conjunction with the substantive aspect of art 2 of the Convention. The question of the authorities' compliance with their procedural obligation is a separate issue, to which the Court will revert below.

158. In sum, having assessed all relevant elements, the Court does not consider that it has been established that racist attitudes played a role in Mr Angelov's and Mr Petkov's deaths.

159. It thus finds that there has been no violation of art 14 of the Convention taken together with art 2 in its substantive aspect.

The Grand Chamber did, however, go on to rule that there was a procedural breach of Articles 2 and 14 taken together because the state had failed to investigate a possible causal link between alleged racist attitudes and the killing of the two men (this in addition to the procedural breach of Article 2 arising from the failure to conduct a meaningful investigation into the deaths). The Court ruled (para. 164) that 'any evidence of racist verbal abuse being uttered by law enforcement agents in connection with an operation involving the use of force against persons from an ethnic or other minority...must be verified and—if confirmed—a thorough examination of all the facts should be undertaken in order to uncover any possible racist motives'.

Difficulties of proof are not confined to cases arising under Article 14. Proof of discrimination does, however, give rise to particular difficulties. In practice, proof of direct discrimination generally relies on inferences drawn from evidence which would, for example, include the documented background of discrimination against Roma in the *DH* and *Nachova* cases and, in indirect discrimination cases, on statistics. It is to be regretted that the European Court was not prepared, at least in the *DH* case (and subject to any change of approach on the part of the Grand Chamber), to shift the burden to the state to disprove discrimination against the particular applicants in view of the strong evidence of endemic discrimination against Roma children in the Czech educational system.

F. THE JUSTIFICATION OF DIFFERENTIAL TREATMENT

1. INTRODUCTION

The *Belgian Linguistic Case (No. 2)*[40] involved a challenge to legislation which denied funding for French speaking schools in what had been designated a unilingual Flemish

---

[40] 23 July 1968, 1 E.H.R.R. 252. And *see* Chapter 11(B).

area of the country. The Court ruled (at para. 10) that:

In spite of the very general wording of the French version ('*sans distinction aucune*'), Article 14 does not forbid every difference in treatment in the exercise of the rights and freedoms recognised. This version must be read in the light of the more restrictive text of the English version ('without discrimination').

In addition, and in particular, one would reach absurd results were one to give Article 14 an interpretation as wide as that which the French version seems to imply. One would, in effect, be led to judge as contrary to the Convention every one of the many legal or administrative provisions which do not secure to everyone complete equality of treatment in the enjoyment of the rights and freedoms recognised. The competent national authorities are frequently confronted with situations and problems which, on account of differences inherent therein, call for different legal solutions; moreover, certain legal inequalities tend only to correct factual inequalities. The extensive interpretation mentioned above cannot consequently be accepted.

It is important, then, to look for the criteria which enable a determination to be made as to whether or not a given difference in treatment, concerning of course the exercise of one of the rights and freedoms set forth, contravenes Article 14. On this question the Court, following the principles which may be extracted from the legal practice of a large number of democratic States, holds that the principle of equality of treatment is violated if the distinction has no objective and reasonable justification. The existence of such a justification must be assessed in relation to the aim and effects of the measure under consideration, regard being had to the principles which normally prevail in democratic societies. A difference of treatment in the exercise of a right laid down in the Convention must not only pursue a legitimate aim: Article 14 is likewise violated when it is clearly established that there is no reasonable relationship of proportionality between the means employed and the aim sought to be realised.

In attempting to find out in a given case, whether or not there has been an arbitrary distinction, the Court cannot disregard those legal and factual features which characterise the life of the society in the State which, as a Contracting Party, has to answer for the measure in dispute. In so doing it cannot assume the rôle of the competent national authorities, for it would thereby lose sight of the subsidiary nature of the international machinery of collective enforcement established by the Convention. The national authorities remain free to choose the measures which they consider appropriate in those matters which are governed by the Convention. Review by the Court concerns only the conformity of these measures with the requirements of the Convention.

The *Belgian Linguistic Case* suggests that differential treatment is easy to justify for the purposes of Article 14: 'Article 14 is ... violated when it is clearly established that there is no reasonable relationship of proportionality between the means employed and the aim sought to be realised'. A similar formulation was adopted in *National Union of Belgian Police v. Belgium*[41] and in *Swedish Engine Drivers' Union v. Sweden*,[42] both of which cases concerned alleged discrimination between trade unions. In neither case was it accepted that Article 14 had been breached, the Court stressing the 'margin of

[41] 27 Oct. 1975, 1 E.H.R.R. 578.
[42] 6 Feb. 1976, 1 E.H.R.R. 617.

appreciation' accorded to the state 'in assessing whether and to what extent differences in otherwise similar situations justify a different treatment in law'.[43]

The U.S. Supreme Court has created an explicit hierarchy of grounds protected under the U.S. Constitution. The Constitutional right to equal treatment is contained in the Equal Protection Clause of the Fourteenth Amendment,[44] section 1 of which states that 'nor shall any State . . . deny to any person within its jurisdiction the equal protection of the laws'. The clause was originally intended solely to apply to African American men, its initial draft containing the first express restriction of US constitutional rights to 'male' persons. The sex-specific wording of the Amendment was altered, but the general view that it applied only to benefit black men was affirmed by the U.S. Supreme Court in the *Slaughterhouse Cases* (1873) in which the Court declared that the provision was 'so clearly a provision for that race and that emergency, that a strong case would be necessary for its application to any other . . . [w]e doubt very much whether any action of a State not directed by way of discrimination against the negroes as a class, or on account of their race, will ever be held to come within [its] purview'.[45]

The Equal Protection Clause began to be interpreted, however, as extending beyond discrimination based on race to regulate, more generally, governmental classifications between people. The Supreme Court applies 'strict scrutiny' classifications based on race which will be unconstitutional unless 'necessary' or 'narrowly tailored' to promote a 'compelling interest' of government (see further *Loving v. Virginia* above and *Grutter v. Bollinger*, extracted below). By contrast, most classifications will be acceptable if they pass a much more relaxed standard of review: that is, if they are not irrational or arbitrary.[46] By 1976 the Supreme Court had established the 'intermediate standard' of review for sex-based classifications in *Craig v. Boren*, in which it ruled that an Oklahoma statute prohibiting the sale of 3.2% beer to males aged less than 21 and females aged less than 18 breached the Fourteenth Amendment.[47] Under the intermediate standard of review, the Court first examines the statutory or administrative scheme under challenge to determine if its purpose or objective is permissible and important. Secondly, it ascertains how well the classification serves the end, and whether a less discriminatory one would serve the same purpose without substantial loss to the government. Where a classification has some basis in fact, intermediate scrutiny requires evidence of the existence of that fact and its close relationship to the condition for which sex is taken as a proxy.

---

[43] *See also Rasmussen v. Denmark*, 28 Nov. 1984, 7 E.H.R.R. 371: sex discrimination in relation to the establishment of paternity (putative fathers could only contest within the first year after birth whereas mothers could contest paternity at any time).

[44] The Amendment applies only to state, rather than to federal action, and was adopted with race as the sole target of its prohibition. The Supreme Court has, however, interpreted the Fifth Amendment's federally binding guarantee of 'due process' to incorporate the same protection from discrimination as is found in the Fourteenth Amendment's Equal Protection Clause.

[45] 83 U.S. 394, 410.

[46] *See* generally S. Goldberg, 'Equality without Tiers', (2003–4) 77 *Southern California Law Review* 481.

[47] 429 U.S. 190 (1976).

Strict scrutiny is now applied in the U.S. to classifications based on race, national origin, religion, alienage[48] (unless based on membership of a recognized 'political community'[49]). Intermediate scrutiny applies to sex and illegitimacy while all other classifications are subject to rational basis scrutiny alone. Where a classification is seen to rest on stereotype, it will not pass even relaxed scrutiny.[50] Strict scrutiny is a very difficult test to pass, and with the exception of *Korematsu v. United States*[51] in which the Supreme Court upheld the internment during the Second World War of people of Japanese ancestry, that Court has never found race discrimination (other than in the form of affirmative action) to be justified. The application of the strict scrutiny test can be seen in the following case.

2. PALMORE V. SIDOTI

Judgment of 25 April 1984
466 U.S. 429

[The petitioner challenged the decision of a Florida court to award custody of her four year old daughter to her former husband (both white). Custody had initially been awarded to the petitioner but the respondent had had the matter re-opened on the basis of a change of circumstances: namely, that she (the petitioner) was living with an African American man whom she later married. The Florida court ruled that the child's best interests would be better served by not living in a racially mixed household: 'The father's evident resentment of the mother's choice of a black partner is not sufficient to wrest custody from the mother. It is of some significance, however, that the mother did see fit to bring a man into her home and carry on a sexual relationship with him without being married to him. Such action tended to place gratification of her own desires ahead of her concern for the child's future welfare. This Court feels that despite the strides that have been made in bettering relations between the races in this country, it is inevitable that Melanie will, if allowed to remain in her present situation and attains school age and thus more vulnerable to peer pressures, suffer from the social stigmatization that is sure to come.']

Burger CJ (for the unanimous Court):

The court correctly stated that the child's welfare was the controlling factor. But that court was entirely candid and made no effort to place its holding on any ground other than race. Taking the court's findings and rationale at face value, it is clear that the outcome would have been different had petitioner married a Caucasian male of similar respectability.

   A core purpose of the Fourteenth Amendment was to do away with all governmentally imposed discrimination based on race. Classifying persons according to their race is more likely to reflect racial prejudice than legitimate public concerns; the race, not the person, dictates the

---

[48] *Graham v. Richardson*, 403 U.S. 365 (1971).

[49] 413 U.S. 634 (1973).

[50] *Stanton v. Stanton*, 421 U.S. 7 (1975) and 429 U.S. 501 (1977) (sex) and *see Romer v. Evans*, 517 U.S. 620 (1996) on sexual orientation.

[51] 323 U.S. 214 (1944).

category. Such classifications are subject to the most exacting scrutiny; to pass constitutional muster, they must be justified by a compelling governmental interest and must be 'necessary . . . to the accomplishment' of their legitimate purpose.

The State, of course, has a duty of the highest order to protect the interests of minor children, particularly those of tender years. In common with most states, Florida law mandates that custody determinations be made in the best interests of the children involved. The goal of granting custody based on the best interests of the child is indisputably a substantial governmental interest for purposes of the Equal Protection Clause.

It would ignore reality to suggest that racial and ethnic prejudices do not exist or that all manifestations of those prejudices have been eliminated. There is a risk that a child living with a stepparent of a different race may be subject to a variety of pressures and stresses not present if the child were living with parents of the same racial or ethnic origin.

The question, however, is whether the reality of private biases and the possible injury they might inflict are permissible considerations for removal of an infant child from the custody of its natural mother. We have little difficulty concluding that they are not. The Constitution cannot control such prejudices but neither can it tolerate them. Private biases may be outside the reach of the law, but the law cannot, directly or indirectly, give them effect. 'Public officials sworn to uphold the Constitution may not avoid a constitutional duty by bowing to the hypothetical effects of private racial prejudice that they assume to be both widely and deeply held.'

This is by no means the first time that acknowledged racial prejudice has been invoked to justify racial classifications. In *Buchanan v. Warley*, 245 US. 60 (1917), for example, this Court invalidated a Kentucky law forbidding Negroes to buy homes in white neighborhoods.

> 'It is urged that this proposed segregation will promote the public peace by preventing race conflicts. Desirable as this is, and important as is the preservation of the public peace, this aim cannot be accomplished by laws or ordinances which deny rights created or protected by the Federal Constitution.'

Whatever problems racially mixed households may pose for children in 1984 can no more support a denial of constitutional rights than could the stresses that residential integration was thought to entail in 1917. The effects of racial prejudice, however real, cannot justify a racial classification removing an infant child from the custody of its natural mother found to be an appropriate person to have such custody.

There is no formal 'tiered' approach to justification under Article 14, but the jurisprudence of the European Court of Human Rights is suggestive of a hierarchy of protected grounds. Whereas differential treatment in connection with some grounds is subject to the relatively easily satisfied test articulated in the *Belgian Linguistic*, *Belgian Police* and *Swedish Engine Drivers'* cases, differential treatment related to other grounds (referred to by some commentators as 'suspect') requires 'very weighty reasons' by way of justification. The approach is not entirely predictable as the point has not been fully reasoned to date in the Court, though it is clear that discrimination on grounds such as sex, sexual orientation and religion is more difficult to justify than discrimination such as that at issue in the *Belgian Police* or *Spadea* claims.

In *Marckx* v *Belgium*, the Court had found a breach of Article 14 in the denial of full legal recognition to an illegitimate child who was both recognized and formally adopted by her birth mother, and did so even on the *Belgian Linguistic* formulation: 'There was no objective and reasonable justification for depriving a child born illegitimately of automatic maternal affiliation. There was therefore a violation of art 14 of the Convention, taken in conjunction with art 8…'. In that case even the low threshold for justification was not met. In *Abdulaziz*, however, the Court articulated a more rigorous test (see paras. 72–83 of the extract at Section 1(A) above). Similar formulations of the standard of justification have been articulated in relation to illegitimacy,[52] nationality,[53] unmarried status as a parent,[54] religion[55] and sexual orientation.[56]

Even where the lower standard applies, differential treatment may well be found to breach Article 14. The challenge in *Sidabras*, considered above, resulted in a finding that Article 14 had been breached. So too did that in *Chassagnou v. France*[57] (discrimination between large and small land-owners), and in *Darby v. Sweden*,[58] which concerned discrimination on the basis of residence.[59] In *Sidabras* the European Court ruled that the prohibition on the applicants, as former KGB members, from working in a variety of private as well as public sector jobs, breached Article 14. It did so without even finding it 'necessary to answer the question whether the applicants were given an opportunity to show their loyalty to the State or whether their lack of loyalty was indeed proven',[60] this because, although 'the requirement of an employee's loyalty to the State is an inherent condition of employment with State authorities responsible for protecting and securing the general interest…such a requirement is not inevitably the case for employment with private companies'.[61] The Court pointed out that private-sector actors 'are not depositaries of the sovereign power vested in the State' and that they 'may legitimately engage in activities, notably financial and economic, which compete with the goals fixed for public authorities or State-run companies'.[62] For these reasons, 'State-imposed restrictions on the possibility for a person to find employment with a private company for reasons of lack of loyalty to the State cannot be justified from the Convention point of view in the same manner as restrictions governing access to their employment in the public service, regardless of the private company's importance to the State's economic, political or security interests'.[63] The Court went on to find, in addition, that there was no attempt to link the private-sector positions covered by the ban with the aims the ban sought to achieve. For these reasons, and because the ban did not come into effect until between 9 and 13 years after the termination of the applicants' KGB involvement (and

---

[52] *Inze v. Austria*, 28 Oct. 1987, 10 E.H.R.R. 394.

[53] *Gaygusuz v. Austria*, 16 Sept. 1996, 23 E.H.R.R. 364.

[54] *Elsholz v. Germany*, 13 July 2000 (G.C.), 34 E.H.R.R. 58.

[55] *Hoffmann v. Austria*, n. 4 *supra*.

[56] *Salgueiro da Silva Mouta v. Portugal*, n. 4 *supra*.

[57] 29 Apr. 1999, 29 E.H.R.R. 615.

[58] 23 Oct. 1990, 13 E.H.R.R. 774.

[59] In *Gillow v. United Kingdom*, 24 Nov. 1986, 11 E.H.R.R. 335 the Court rejected a challenge to preferential treatment based on a residency requirement on the basis that the requirement was justified.

[60] Para. 56.

[61] Para. 57.

[62] *Id.*

[63] Para. 58.

10 years after Lithuania achieved independence), its application to the private sector could not be regarded as proportionate.

It was said by Marshall J in the U.S. Supreme Court that strict scrutiny is 'strict in theory, but fatal in fact'.[64] This was denied by the Supreme Court in *Grutter v. Bollinger*, extracted below, in which the Court ruled that a race-based affirmative action programme was narrowly tailored to meet a compelling need of the educational institution which operated it. But the test is an extremely difficult one to satisfy.[65] By contrast, there are many examples of cases where the European Court has required 'very weighty reasons' but has gone on to find discrimination justified.

3. PETROVIC V. AUSTRIA

Judgment of 27 March 1998
33 E.H.R.R. 14

[A father who wished to stay at home to look after his young child challenged the fact that parental allowance was available exclusively to women under domestic law. The impugned law had been subsequently revised to allow men to claim the allowance but the applicant was bound by the original rules.]

31. In the applicant's submission, the different treatment of mothers and fathers with respect to granting a parental leave allowance was not justified at all. The allowance was not intended to protect mothers as it was not paid until eight weeks after the birth and until the right to receive maternity benefit had been exhausted, but to assist parents—whether mothers or fathers—who wished to take leave to look after their very young children.

32. The Government, on the other hand, submitted that the fact that there was no common European standard in the matter meant that the Austrian legislature's decision to pay a parental leave allowance only to mothers fell within the margin of appreciation left to the Contracting States in respect of welfare policy. Furthermore, the provisions in question reflected the outlook of society at the time, according to which the mothers had the primary role in looking after young children.

33. The Commission considered that the lack of a common standard with regard to particular welfare benefits reflected the substantial diversity of social-security schemes in the member States, but could not absolve those States which had adopted a special scheme of parental leave allowances from granting those benefits without discrimination. No objective and reasonable grounds such as to justify the difference in treatment had been made out. The applicant had accordingly been discriminated against in the exercise of his right to respect for his family life as guaranteed by Article 8 of the Convention.

34. The Court notes that at the material time parental leave allowances were paid only to mothers, not fathers, once a period of eight weeks had elapsed after the birth and the right to a maternity allowance had been exhausted . . .

---

[64] *Fullilove v. Klutznick*, 448 U.S. 448, 519 (1980).
[65] Except perhaps where affirmative action is at issue.

35. It was not disputed that that amounted to a difference in treatment on grounds of sex.

36. Maternity leave and the associated allowances are primarily intended to enable the mother to recover from the fatigue of childbirth and to breastfeed her baby if she so wishes. Parental leave and the parental leave allowance, on the other hand, relate to the period there-after and are intended to enable the beneficiary to stay at home to look after the infant per-sonally. While aware of the differences which may exist between mother and father in their relationship with the child, the Court starts from the premise that so far as taking care of the child during this period is concerned, both parents are 'similarly placed'.

37. It is true that the advancement of the equality of the sexes is today a major goal in the member States of the Council of Europe and very weighty reasons would be needed for such a difference in treatment to be regarded as compatible with the Convention...

38. However, the Contracting States enjoy a certain margin of appreciation in assessing whether and to what extent differences in otherwise similar situations justify a different treat-ment in law. The scope of the margin of appreciation will vary according to the circumstances, the subject matter and its background; in this respect, one of the relevant factors may be the existence or non-existence of common ground between the laws of the Contracting States [citing *Rasmussen v Denmark*].

39. It is clear that at the material time, that is at the end of the 1980s, there was no common standard in this field, as the majority of the Contracting States did not provide for parental leave allowances to be paid to fathers.

40. The idea of the State giving financial assistance to the mother or the father, at the couple's option, so that the parent concerned can stay at home to look after the children is relatively recent. Originally, welfare measures of this sort—such as parental leave—were primarily intended to protect mothers and to enable them to look after very young children. Only gradually, as society has moved towards a more equal sharing between men and women of responsibilities for the bringing up of their children, have the Contracting States introduced measures extending to fathers, like entitlement to parental leave.

41. In this respect Austrian law has evolved in the same way, the Austrian legislature enact-ing legislation in 1989 to provide for parental leave for fathers. In parallel, eligibility for the parental leave allowance was extended to fathers in 1990... It therefore appears difficult to criticise the Austrian legislature for having introduced in a gradual manner, reflecting the evolution of society in that sphere, legislation which is, all things considered, very progressive in Europe.

42. There still remains a very great disparity between the legal systems of the Contracting States in this field. While measures to give fathers an entitlement to parental leave have now been taken by a large number of States, the same is not true of the parental leave allowance, which only a very few States grant to fathers.

43. The Austrian authorities' refusal to grant the applicant a parental leave allowance has not, therefore, exceeded the margin of appreciation allowed to them. Consequently, the differ-ence in treatment complained of was not discriminatory within the meaning of Article 14.

The existence or non-existence of a 'common European standard' or consensus as to the acceptability of differential treatment in any particular context has proven sig-nificant to the Court's approach to the justification of such treatment. Its influence is seen in the following case, which concerned a challenge by a gay man to a refusal, essentially on grounds of his sexual orientation, to permit him to adopt.

4. FRETTÉ V. FRANCE

Judgment of 26 February 2002
38 E.H.R.R. 21

37. The Court observes that it has found that the decision contested by the applicant was based decisively on the latter's avowed homosexuality. Although the relevant authorities also had regard to other circumstances, these appeared to be secondary grounds.

38. In the Court's opinion there is no doubt that the decisions to reject the applicant's application for authorisation pursued a legitimate aim, namely to protect the health and rights of children who could be involved in an adoption procedure, for which the granting of authorisation was, in principle, a prerequisite. It remains to be ascertained whether the second condition, namely the existence of a justification for the difference of treatment, was also satisfied.

39. The right not to be discriminated against in the enjoyment of the rights guaranteed under the Convention is also violated when States without an objective and reasonable justification fail to treat differently persons whose situations are significantly different...

40. However, the Contracting States enjoy a certain margin of appreciation in assessing whether and to what extent differences in otherwise similar situations justify a different treatment in law. The scope of the margin of appreciation will vary according to the circumstances, the subject matter and its background; in this respect, one of the relevant factors may be the existence or non-existence of common ground between the laws of the Contracting States...

41. It is indisputable that there is no common ground on the question. Although most of the Contracting States do not expressly prohibit homosexuals from adopting where single persons may adopt, it is not possible to find in the legal and social orders of the Contracting States uniform principles on these social issues on which opinions within a democratic society may reasonably differ widely. The Court considers it quite natural that the national authorities, whose duty it is in a democratic society also to consider, within the limits of their jurisdiction, the interests of society as a whole, should enjoy a wide margin of appreciation when they are asked to make rulings on such matters. By reason of their direct and continuous contact with the vital forces of their countries, the national authorities are in principle better placed than an international court to evaluate local needs and conditions. Since the delicate issues raised in the case, therefore, touch on areas where there is little common ground amongst the member States of the Council of Europe and, generally speaking, the law appears to be in a transitional stage, a wide margin of appreciation must be left to the authorities of each State...This margin of appreciation should not, however, be interpreted to grant the State arbitrary power, and the authorities' decision remains subject to review by the Court for conformity with the requirements of art 14 of the Convention.

42. As the Government submitted, at issue here are the competing interests of the applicant and children who are legible for adoption. The mere fact that no specific child is identified

when the application for authorisation is made does not necessarily imply that there is no competing interest. Adoption means 'providing a child with a family, not a family with a child', and the State must see to it that the persons chosen to adopt are those who can offer the child the most suitable home in every respect. The Court points out in that connection that it has already found that where a family tie is established between a parent and a child, 'particular importance must be attached to the best interests of the child, which, depending on their nature and seriousness, may override those of the parent'... It must be observed that the scientific community—particularly experts on childhood, psychiatrists and psychologists—is divided over the possible consequences of a child's being adopted by one or more homosexual parents, especially bearing in mind the limited number of scientific studies conducted on the subject to date. In addition, there are wide differences in national and international opinion, not to mention the fact that there are not enough children to adopt to satisfy demand. This being so, the national authorities, and particularly the Conseil d'Etat, which based its decision, inter alia, on the Government Commissioner's measured and detailed submissions, were legitimately and reasonably entitled to consider that the right to be able to adopt on which the applicant relied under art 343–1 of the Civil Code was limited by the interests of children eligible for adoption, notwithstanding the applicant's legitimate aspirations and without calling his personal choices into question. If account is taken of the broad margin of appreciation to be left to States in this area and the need to protect children's best interests to achieve the desired balance, the refusal to authorise adoption did not infringe the principle of proportionality.

43. In short, the justification given by the Government appears objective and reasonable and the difference in treatment complained of is not discriminatory for the purposes of art 14 of the Convention.

More recently again, in *Stec v. United Kingdom*, extracted below, the Court ruled that discrimination against women in the context of reduced earnings allowance was justifiable. What is perhaps most interesting about the decision is the approach it takes to 'positive' discrimination; that is, differential treatment intended to ameliorate disadvantage associated with one or more protected grounds.

G. 'POSITIVE' DISCRIMINATION

By the term 'positive discrimination' we refer to ameliorative action targeted towards combating the effects of past or present discrimination against disadvantaged groups. Such 'discrimination' entails differential treatment of advantaged and disadvantaged groups but, if justified, might properly be regarded as not 'discrimination' at all. It is sometimes referred to as 'positive action' (which tends, however, to refer to 'softer' measures such as encouraging the up-take by members of disadvantaged groups of opportunities open to all, or targeted training). The term used in the United States is 'affirmative action' which is at once more commonplace and also more controversial than is generally the case in the European context.

Affirmative action programmes have been supported by a number of Presidential Executive Orders beginning with that of President Kennedy (Executive Order 10925) in 1961.[66] The early focus of such programmes was on integrating ethnic minority work-ers and on improving the access of ethnic minority students to education, but from 1967 they began to include (non ethnic minority) women also. Voluntary affirmative action programmes became common across the public and private sectors and, where serious discriminatory practices had been proven against particular bodies, by court order. The policy of affirmative action remained popular at federal level until 1980 when the Republican Reagan administration came into office on a platform hostile to 'raceconscious remedies'.

In 1978, in *Regents of the University of California v. Bakke*[67] the Supreme Court reached its first decision on the constitutionality of a race-based affirmative action programme, striking down a quota-based admissions programme operated by the uni-versity's medical faculty. Four of the judges took the view that any racial quota-based system would offend the 'strict scrutiny' approach. Four held that 'racial classifications designed to further remedial purposes' were not subject to strict scrutiny, but would be lawful where they 'serve important governmental objectives and [are] substantially related to achievement of those objectives'. The ninth Supreme Court judge, Justice Powell, agreed that strict scrutiny must be applied to remedial race-based legislation, though he accepted that, where remedial action was directed at past discrimination by the particular body, it could pass muster under this test. This was not the case here. Justice Powell also accepted that universities could have a compelling interest in tak-ing steps to secure a diverse student group, but demanded 'narrow tailoring' of means to this end and drew the line at rigid quotas such as those operated by the University of California to achieve this purpose.

As a result of Justice Powell's willingness to accept some forms of race-based affirmative action programme, most affirmative action programmes survived *Bakke*. A number of Supreme Court decisions which followed were relatively permissive as regards affirmative action.[68] Despite marked differences of opinion in the Supreme Court, affirmative action programmes were generally upheld between 1978 and 1989, for the most part in the face of strong Presidential resistance.[69] The tide began to turn in 1989.[70] In 1995, in *Adarand Constructors v. Pena*[71] the Supreme Court demanded that federal, state and local affirmative action programmes meet strict scrutiny where

---

[66] For a general account *see* A. McColgan, *Women Under the Law: the False Promise of Human Rights* (Pearson, 1999) Chapter 7.

[67] 438 U.S. 265 (1978).

[68] *United Steelworkers of America v. Weber*, 438 U.S. 265 (1978) which concerned the application of the Civil Rights Act (rather than the Constitution) to the private sector, and *Bushey v. New York State Civil Service Commission* in which the Court accepted affirmative action in the public sector under the Civil Rights Act on an apparently broader basis than *Bakke* (which concerned the Constitutional prohibition on discrimination) without dealing with the apparent contradiction between the two; *Fullilove v. Klutznic*, n. 64 *supra*, in which the Court upheld the constitutionality of a 10% 'minority business enterprise' set-aside in a Federal public works programme.

[69] Though *cf. Firefighters Local v. Stotts*, 467 U.S. 561 (1984) and *Wygant v. Jackson Board of Education*, 476 U.S. 267 (1986).

[70] *See Martin v. Wilks*, 490 U.S. 755 (1989), *Croson v. City of Richmond*, 488 U.S. 469 (1989).

[71] 515 U.S. 200 (1995).

they operated on the basis of racial or ethnic classifications. Justice Stevens, for the dissenters, protested that '[t]here is no moral or constitutional equivalence between a policy that is designed to perpetuate a caste system and one that seeks to eradicate racial subordination. Invidious discrimination is an engine of oppression, subjugating a disfavored group to enhance or maintain the power of the majority. Remedial race-based preferences reflect the opposite impulse: a desire to foster equality in society'. In the following case, however, the Supreme Court gave clear approval to affirmative action, albeit of tightly defined nature and in tightly defined circumstances.

1. GRUTTER V. BOLLINGER

Judgment of 23 June 2003
59 U.S. 306 (2003)

[Barbara Grutter, a white woman, complained that she had been the victim of race discrimination when she was refused a place at the University of Michigan Law School: the Law School gave preference to candidates from underrepresented minority ethnic groups. She argued that the university had no compelling interest to justify its use of race. The university (of which the defendant Bollinger was President) argued that its policy was necessary in order to achieve racial diversity in the student body. A District Court ruled against the university but the Sixth Circuit Court of Appeals reversed the decision, relying on *Bakke* to permit the use of race to further the 'compelling interest' of diversity. The Supreme Court rejected the claimant's appeal. Note that all case citations have been omitted from the following judgment.]

O'Connor J:

The hallmark of [the admissions] policy is its focus on academic ability coupled with a flexible assessment of applicants' talents, experiences, and potential 'to contribute to the learning of those around them'. The policy requires admissions officials to evaluate each applicant based on all the information available in the file, including a personal statement, letters of recommendation, and an essay describing the ways in which the applicant will contribute to the life and diversity of the Law School... The policy stresses that 'no applicant should be admitted unless we expect that applicant to do well enough to graduate with no serious academic problems.'

The policy makes clear, however, that even the highest possible score does not guarantee admission to the Law School. Nor does a low score automatically disqualify an applicant. Rather, the policy requires admissions officials to look beyond grades and test scores to other criteria that are important to the Law School's educational objectives. So-called '"soft" variables' such as 'the enthusiasm of recommenders, the quality of the undergraduate institution, the quality of the applicant's essay, and the areas and difficulty of undergraduate course selection' are all brought to bear in assessing an 'applicant's likely contributions to the intellectual and social life of the institution'.

The policy aspires to 'achieve that diversity which has the potential to enrich everyone's education and thus make a law school class stronger than the sum of its parts'. The policy does not restrict the types of diversity contributions eligible for 'substantial weight' in the admissions process, but instead recognizes 'many possible bases for diversity admissions'. The policy does, however, reaffirm the Law School's longstanding commitment to 'one particular type of diversity', that is, 'racial and ethnic diversity with special reference to the inclusion of students from groups which have been historically discriminated against, like African-Americans, Hispanics and Native Americans, who without this commitment might not be represented in our student body in meaningful numbers'. By enrolling a '"critical mass" of [underrepresented] minority students', the Law School seeks to 'ensur[e] their ability to make unique contributions to the character of the Law School'...

During the 15-day bench trial, the parties introduced extensive evidence concerning the Law School's use of race in the admissions process. Dennis Shields, Director of Admissions when petitioner applied to the Law School, testified that he did not direct his staff to admit a particular percentage or number of minority students, but rather to consider an applicant's race along with all other factors. Shields testified that at the height of the admissions season, he would frequently consult the so-called 'daily reports' that kept track of the racial and ethnic composition of the class (along with other information such as residency status and gender). This was done, Shields testified, to ensure that a critical mass of underrepresented minority students would be reached so as to realize the educational benefits of a diverse student body. *Ibid.* Shields stressed, however, that he did not seek to admit any particular number or percentage of underrepresented minority students.

Erica Munzel, who succeeded Shields as Director of Admissions, testified that 'critical mass' means 'meaningful numbers' or 'meaningful representation' which she understood to mean a number that encourages underrepresented minority students to participate in the classroom and not feel isolated...

We have held that all racial classifications imposed by government 'must be analyzed by a reviewing court under strict scrutiny'. This means that such classifications are constitutional only if they are narrowly tailored to further compelling governmental interests. 'Absent searching judicial inquiry into the justification for such race-based measures', we have no way to determine what 'classifications are "benign" or "remedial"' and what classifications are in fact motivated by illegitimate notions of racial inferiority or simple racial politics'...'We apply strict scrutiny to all racial classifications to "smoke out" illegitimate uses of race by assuring that [government] is pursuing a goal important enough to warrant use of a highly suspect tool'.

Strict scrutiny is not 'strict in theory, but fatal in fact'. Although all governmental uses of race are subject to strict scrutiny, not all are invalidated by it. As we have explained, 'whenever the government treats any person unequally because of his or her race, that person has suffered an injury that falls squarely within the language and spirit of the Constitution's guarantee of equal protection'. But that observation 'says nothing about the ultimate validity of any particular law; that determination is the job of the court applying strict scrutiny'. When race-based action is necessary to further a compelling governmental interest, such action does not violate the constitutional guarantee of equal protection so long as the narrow-tailoring requirement is also satisfied.

Context matters when reviewing race-based governmental action under the Equal Protection Clause...strict scrutiny must take 'relevant differences' into account. Indeed...that is its 'fundamental purpose'. Not every decision influenced by race is equally objectionable and strict scrutiny is designed to provide a framework for carefully examining the importance and the sincerity of the reasons advanced by the governmental decisionmaker for the use of race in that particular context.

With these principles in mind, we turn to the question whether the Law School's use of race is justified by a compelling state interest. Before this Court, as they have throughout this litigation, respondents assert only one justification for their use of race in the admissions process: obtaining 'the educational benefits that flow from a diverse student body'... The Law School's educational judgment that such diversity is essential to its educational mission is one to which we defer... In announcing the principle of student body diversity as a compelling state interest [in *Bakke*], Justice Powell invoked our cases recognizing a constitutional dimension, grounded in the First Amendment, of educational autonomy: 'The freedom of a university to make its own judgments as to education includes the selection of its student body'...Our conclusion that the Law School has a compelling interest in a diverse student body is informed by our view that attaining a diverse student body is at the heart of the Law School's proper institutional mission, and that 'good faith' on the part of a university is 'presumed' absent 'a showing to the contrary'.

...the Law School's admissions policy 'promotes cross-racial understanding', helps to break down racial stereotypes, and 'enables [students] to better understand persons of different races'. These benefits are 'important and laudable' because classroom discussion is livelier, more spirited, and simply more enlightening and interesting when the students have 'the greatest possible variety of backgrounds'.

The Law School's claim of a compelling interest is further bolstered by its *amici*, who point to the educational benefits that flow from student body diversity. In addition to the expert studies and reports entered into evidence at trial, numerous studies show that student body diversity promotes learning outcomes, and 'better prepares students for an increasingly diverse workforce and society, and better prepares them as professionals'.

These benefits are not theoretical but real, as major American businesses have made clear that the skills needed in today's increasingly global marketplace can only be developed through exposure to widely diverse people, cultures, ideas, and viewpoints... What is more, high-ranking retired officers and civilian leaders of the United States military assert that, '[b]ased on [their] decades of experience', a 'highly qualified, racially diverse officer corps... is essential to the military's ability to fulfill its principle mission to provide national security'...

The United States, as *amicus curiae*, affirms that '[e]nsuring that public institutions are open and available to all segments of American society, including people of all races and ethnicities, represents a paramount government objective...And '[n]owhere is the importance of such openness more acute than in the context of higher education'. Effective participation by members of all racial and ethnic groups in the civic life of our Nation is essential if the dream of one Nation, indivisible, is to be realized.

Moreover, universities, and in particular, law schools, represent the training ground for a large number of our Nation's leaders...All members of our heterogeneous society must have confidence in the openness and integrity of the educational institutions that provide this training. As we have recognized, law schools 'cannot be effective in isolation from the individuals and institutions with which the law interacts'. Access to legal education (and thus the legal profession) must be inclusive of talented and qualified individuals of every race and ethnicity, so that all members of our heterogeneous society may participate in the educational institutions that provide the training and education necessary to succeed in America.

The Law School does not premise its need for critical mass on any belief that minority students always (or even consistently) express some characteristic minority viewpoint on any issue. To the contrary, diminishing the force of such stereotypes is both a crucial part of the Law School's mission, and one that it cannot accomplish with only token numbers of minority students. Just as growing up in a particular region or having particular professional experiences is likely to affect an individual's views, so too is one's own, unique experience of being a racial minority in a society, like our own, in which race unfortunately still matters. The Law School has determined, based on its experience and expertise, that a 'critical mass' of underrepresented minorities is necessary to further its compelling interest in securing the educational benefits of a diverse student body.

[Justice O'Connor, for the majority, went on to find that the Law School's admissions policy was 'narrowly tailored' to the compelling interest of student diversity, stressing that quotas were not used and that race was 'only...a "plus" in a particular applicant's file', without 'insulat[ing] the individual from comparison with all other candidates for the available seats'. Further: 'The Law School's goal of attaining a critical mass of underrepresented minority students does not transform its program into a quota... "there is of course some relationship between numbers and achieving the benefits to be derived from a diverse student body, and between numbers and providing a reasonable environment for those students admitted"...'[S]ome attention to numbers, without more, does not transform a flexible admissions system into a rigid quota.']

We acknowledge that 'there are serious problems of justice connected with the idea of preference itself'. Narrow tailoring, therefore, requires that a race-conscious admissions program not unduly harm members of any racial group. Even remedial race-based governmental action generally 'remains subject to continuing oversight to assure that it will work the least harm possible to other innocent persons competing for the benefit'. To be narrowly tailored, a race-conscious admissions program must not 'unduly burden individuals who are not members of the favored racial and ethnic groups'.

We are satisfied that the Law School's admissions program does not. Because the Law School considers 'all pertinent elements of diversity,' it can (and does) select nonminority applicants who have greater potential to enhance student body diversity over underrepresented minority applicants. As Justice Powell recognized in *Bakke*, so long as a race-conscious admissions program uses race as a 'plus' factor in the context of individualized consideration, a rejected applicant 'will not have been foreclosed from all consideration for that seat simply because he was not the right color or had the wrong surname... His qualifications would have been weighed fairly and competitively, and he would have no basis to complain of unequal treatment under the Fourteenth Amendment'...

We are mindful, however, that '[a] core purpose of the Fourteenth Amendment was to do away with all governmentally imposed discrimination based on race'. Accordingly, race-conscious admissions policies must be limited in time. This requirement reflects that racial classifications, however compelling their goals, are potentially so dangerous that they may be employed no more broadly than the interest demands. Enshrining a permanent justification for racial preferences would offend this fundamental equal protection principle. We see no reason to exempt raceconscious admissions programs from the requirement that all governmental use of race must have a logical end point. The Law School, too, concedes that all 'race-conscious programs must have reasonable durational limits'. In the context of higher education, the durational requirement can be met by sunset provisions in raceconscious admissions policies and periodic reviews to determine whether racial preferences are still necessary to achieve student body diversity.[72]

The legality of 'affirmative action' has been a central concern of U.S. equality jurisprudence. By contrast, it has received scant attention in the caselaw of the European Convention organs. In *Gudmundsson v. Iceland*, the Commission rejected an Article 14 claim against Iceland's progressive income tax structure on the basis that unequal cases could and should be treated unequally in proportion to their inequality,[73] and ruled that such a system 'is not discriminatory, provided the progressive measure is proportional and consequently results in a fairer distribution of income than would be the case without it'. In this area, as in so many others, a generous 'margin of appreciation' was to be accorded to the Contracting Parties.

Thlimmenos suggests that positive action could on occasion be mandated, rather than simply permitted, under Article 14 (this because of the court's recognition that equality could require different treatment of differently situated persons as well as similar treatment of those similarly situated). In the extract from the dissenting opinion of Judge Cabral Barreto in the *DH* case, above, he remarked that 'pupils who, for various reasons—whether cultural, linguistic or other—find it difficult to pursue a normal school education *should be entitled to expect the State to take positive measures* to compensate for their handicap and to afford them a means of resuming the normal curriculum' [emphasis added]. Judge Barreto's warning that 'such measures should never result in the handicap being increased', however, appeared to go unheeded by the Grand Chamber in the following case.

2. STEC AND OTHERS V. UNITED KINGDOM

Judgment of 12 April 2006
43 E.H.R.R. 47

[The applicants challenged differential treatment between men and women in the termination of entitlement to a social security benefit, which resulted from the linking of eligibility to that benefit to state pensionable ages which differed between men and women. Ms Stec was in receipt of reduced earnings allowance (REA) as a result of an industrial injury which occurred in 1990. In 1993 she lost her entitlement to REA as she reached state pensionable age (60). She complained that, had she been a man, she would have been entitled to go on receiving REA until she reached 65.

The UK government explained that the different state pensionable ages were introduced in 1940 'in response to a campaign by unmarried women, many of whom spent much of

---

[72] In *Gratz v. Bollinger*, 539 U.S. 244, which was decided on the same day, the Supreme Court struck down a practice of awarding African-American, Hispanic and Native American candidates 20 points of 100 required to gain admission on the basis that it was not 'narrowly tailored' to achieve diversity in that it made the factor of race a decisive factor for virtually all candidates from the under-represented racial groups.

[73] Appl. 511/59 (1960) *Yearbook* III 394.

their lives caring for dependent relatives, and also as part of a package to enable married couples, where the wife was usually younger than the husband and financially dependent on him, to receive a pension at the couples' rate when the husband reached 65'. When, in 1993, it was decided that the pensionable age should be equalised at 65 this was phased in gradually (women born prior to 6 April 1950 being unaffected by the change, with transitional arrangements applying to those born between this date and 6 April 1955) in order to give 'women affected by the change and their employers... ample time to adjust their expectations and arrange their financial affairs accordingly'.]

51. Article 14 does not prohibit a member state from treating groups differently in order to correct 'factual inequalities' between them; indeed in certain circumstances a failure to attempt to correct inequality through different treatment may in itself give rise to a breach of the article. A difference of treatment is, however, discriminatory if it has no objective and reasonable justification; in other words, if it does not pursue a legitimate aim or if there is not a reasonable relationship of proportionality between the means employed and the aim sought to be realised. The contracting state enjoys a margin of appreciation in assessing whether and to what extent differences in otherwise similar situations justify a different treatment.

52. The scope of this margin will vary according to the circumstances, the subject matter and the background. As a general rule, very weighty reasons would have to be put forward before the court could regard a difference in treatment based exclusively on the ground of sex as compatible with the Convention. On the other hand, a wide margin is usually allowed to the state under the Convention when it comes to general measures of economic or social strategy. Because of their direct knowledge of their society and its needs, the national authorities are in principle better placed than the international judge to appreciate what is in the public interest on social or economic grounds, and the Court will generally respect the legislature's policy choice unless it is 'manifestly without reasonable foundation'...

54. The Court recalls that REA is an earnings-related benefit designed to compensate employees or former employees for an impairment of earning capacity due to an accident at work or work-related illness. In or around 1986 it was decided, as a matter of policy, that REA should no longer be paid to claimants who had reached an age at which, even if they had not suffered injury or disease, they would no longer be in paid employment... The applicants concede that it was reasonable to aim to stop paying REA to workers after the age when they would, in any event, have retired, and the Court agrees, since the benefit in question is designed to replace or supplement earnings, and is therefore closely connected to employment and working life.

55. The applicants do not accept, however, that in order to achieve this aim it was necessary to adopt as the upper limit the age at which a man or woman becomes entitled to the state retirement pension, since state pensionable age is at present different for men and women. They suggest that a single cut-off age and/or overlapping benefit regulations could have been used instead.

56. The Court observes, though, that a single cut-off age would not have achieved the same level of consistency with the state pension scheme, which is based upon a notional 'end of working life' at 60 for women and 65 for men. The benefits to which the applicants refer as having the same starting age for men and women—winter fuel payment, prescription charges and bus passes... are not inextricably linked to the concept of paid employment or 'working life' in the way that REA is. Overlapping benefit regulations, to ensure that any REA received was

deducted from the state retirement pension would, moreover, have maintained the impugned difference of treatment, since women would still have become entitled to their pensions and liable to start receiving reduced-rate REA five years before men.

57. The government, for their part, have explained that the use of the state pension age as the cut-off point for REA made the scheme easy to understand and administer... The Court considers that such questions of administrative economy and coherence are generally matters falling within the margin of appreciation referred to in para 52, above.

58. Moreover it finds it significant that, in the present applicants' case, the ECJ [European Court of Justice] found [in *Hepple v Adjudication Officer*[74]], that since REA was intended to compensate people of working age for loss of earning capacity due to an accident at work or occupational disease, it was necessary, in order to preserve coherence with the old-age pension scheme, to link the age-limits... While it is true that art 7(1)(a) of the Directive provides an express exception to the general prohibition on discrimination in social security... the ECJ was called upon, in deciding whether the case fell within the art 7 exception, to make a judgment as to whether the discrimination in the REA scheme arising from the link to differential pensionable age was objectively necessary in order to ensure consistency with the pension scheme. In reaching a conclusion on this issue which, while not determinative of the issue under art 14 of the Convention, is none the less of central importance, particular regard should be had to the strong persuasive value of the ECJ's finding on this point.

59. The Court considers, therefore, for the above reasons, that both the policy decision to stop paying REA to persons who would otherwise have retired from paid employment, and the decision to achieve this aim by linking the cut-off age for REA to the notional 'end of working life', or state pensionable age, pursued a legitimate aim and were reasonably and objectively justified.

60. It remains to be examined whether or not the underlying difference in treatment between men and women in the State pension scheme was acceptable under art 14.

61. Differential pensionable ages were first introduced for men and women in the United Kingdom in 1940, well before the Convention had come into existence, although the disparity persists to the present day. It would appear that the difference in treatment was adopted in order to mitigate financial inequality and hardship arising out of the woman's traditional unpaid role of caring for the family in the home rather than earning money in the workplace. At their origin, therefore, the differential pensionable ages were intended to correct 'factual inequalities' between men and women and appear therefore to have been objectively justified under art 14.

62. It follows that the difference in pensionable ages continued to be justified until such time that social conditions had changed so that women were no longer substantially prejudiced because of a shorter working life. This change, must, by its very nature, have been gradual, and it would be difficult or impossible to pinpoint any particular moment when the unfairness to men caused by differential pensionable ages began to outweigh the need to correct the disadvantaged position of women. Certain indications are available to the Court. Thus, in the 1993 White Paper, the Government asserted that the number of women in paid employment had increased significantly, so that whereas in 1967 only 37% of employees were women, the proportion had increased to 50% in 1992. In addition, various reforms to the way in which

---

[74] Case C-196/98 [2000] E.C.R. I-3701.

pension entitlement was assessed had been introduced in 1977 and 1978, to the benefit of women who spent long periods out of paid employment. As of 1986, it was unlawful for an employer to have different retirement ages for men and women.

63. According to the information before the Court, the Government made a first, concrete, move towards establishing the same pensionable age for both sexes with the publication of the Green Paper in December 1991. It would, no doubt, be possible to argue that this step could, or should, have been made earlier. However, as the Court has observed, the development of parity in the working lives of men and women has been a gradual process, and one which the national authorities are better placed to assess. Moreover, it is significant that many of the other Contracting States still maintain a difference in the ages at which men and women become eligible for the State retirement pension. Within the European Union, this position is recognised by the exception contained in the Directive.

64. In the light of the original justification for the measure as correcting financial inequality between the sexes, the slowly evolving nature of the change in women's working lives, and in the absence of a common standard amongst the Contracting States, the Court finds that the United Kingdom cannot be criticised for not having started earlier on the road towards a single pensionable age.

65. Having once begun the move towards equality, moreover, the Court does not consider it unreasonable of the Government to carry out a thorough process of consultation and review, nor can Parliament be condemned for deciding in 1995 to introduce the reform slowly and in stages. Given the extremely far-reaching and serious implications, for women and for the economy in general, these are matters which clearly fall within the State's margin of appreciation.

66. In conclusion, the Court finds that the difference in state pensionable age between men and women in the United Kingdom was originally intended to correct the disadvantaged economic position of women. It continued to be reasonably and objectively justified on this ground until such time that social and economic changes removed the need for special treatment for women. The respondent state's decisions as to the precise timing and means of putting right the inequality were not so manifestly unreasonable as to exceed the wide margin of appreciation allowed it in such a field... Similarly, the decision to link eligibility for REA to the pension system was reasonably and objectively justified, given that this benefit is intended to compensate for reduced earning capacity during a person's working life. There has not, therefore, been a violation of art 14 taken in conjunction with art 1 of the First Protocol in this case...

The acceptance by the European Court of differential pensionable ages (see paras. 61–65 above) was consistent with the dissenting judgment in *DH*, the justification for the unequal treatment concerning the amelioration of existing disadvantage. But what is noteworthy about the decision in *Stec* is the Court's readiness to apply its conclusion on the justifiability of the difference in state pensionable ages (which operated in favour of women as the economically disadvantaged group) to the difference in age qualifications for REA (which operated to women's disadvantage). The applicants had argued that the standard of justification differed between differential state pensionable ages, which had been in place for over 60 years and which were in any event being phased out, and discrimination in relation to industrial injury benefits, which had been payable on equal terms to men and women prior to 1986, by which time the

Sex Discrimination Act 1975 and the Equal Treatment Directive (Directive 76/207) had rendered discrimination in the field of employment unlawful.

H. PROTOCOL 12

The parasitic nature of Article 14 has been considered above. Protocol 12 to the European Convention, which entered into force on 1 April 2005, provides as follows:

The member States of the Council of Europe signatory hereto,

- Having regard to the fundamental principle according to which all persons are equal before the law and are entitled to the equal protection of the law;

- Being resolved to take further steps to promote the equality of all persons through the collective enforcement of a general prohibition of discrimination by means of the Convention for the Protection of Human Rights and Fundamental Freedoms signed at Rome on 4 November 1950 (hereinafter referred to as 'the Convention');

- Reaffirming that the principle of non-discrimination does not prevent States Parties from taking measures in order to promote full and effective equality, provided that there is an objective and reasonable justification for those measures,

Have agreed as follows:

Article 1—General prohibition of discrimination

1. The enjoyment of any right set forth by law shall be secured without discrimination on any ground such as sex, race, colour, language, religion, political or other opinion, national or social origin, association with a national minority, property, birth or other status.

2. No one shall be discriminated against by any public authority on any ground such as those mentioned in paragraph 1...[75]

The significance of Article 1 of Protocol 12 is explained by the accompanying Explanatory Report which states (para. 18) that 'The meaning of the term "discrimination" in Article 1 is intended to be identical to that in Article 14 of the Convention', but that the 'general non-discrimination clause...extends beyond the "enjoyment of the rights and freedoms set forth in [the] Convention" to cover, in particular, cases where a person is discriminated against':

(i)   in the enjoyment of any right specifically granted to an individual under national law;

(ii)   in the enjoyment of a right which may be inferred from a clear obligation of a public authority under national law, that is, where a public authority is under an obligation under national law to behave in a particular manner;

---

[75] *See* G. Moon, 'The Draft Discrimination Protocol To The European Convention On Human Rights: A Progress Report', [2000] E.H.R.L.R. 1 for the development of the Protocol.

   (iii) by a public authority in the exercise of discretionary power (for example, granting certain subsidies);

   (iv) by any other act or omission by a public authority (for example, the behaviour of law enforcement officers when controlling a riot).[76]

The Explanatory Report declines to stipulate which of these types of discrimination is covered by the different paragraphs of Article 1, stating only (para. 23) that the 'paragraphs are complementary and their combined effect is that all four elements are covered by Article 1. It should also be borne in mind that the distinctions between the respective categories i–iv are not clear-cut and that domestic legal systems may have different approaches as to which case comes under which category'.

The 12th Protocol came in for criticism from some quarters because it did not expand the list of explicitly protected grounds (in particular, to include sexual orientation, disability and age). The Explanatory Report to the Protocol defends the failure to add to the list of grounds expressly protected by Article 14 as follows:

This solution was considered preferable over others, such as expressly including certain additional non-discrimination grounds (for example, physical or mental disability, sexual orientation or age), not because of a lack of awareness that such grounds have become particularly important in today's societies as compared with the time of drafting of Article 14 of the Convention, but because such an inclusion was considered unnecessary from a legal point of view since the list of non-discrimination grounds is not exhaustive, and because inclusion of any particular additional ground might give rise to unwarranted *a contrario* interpretations as regards discrimination based on grounds not so included. It is recalled that the European Court of Human Rights has already applied Article 14 in relation to discrimination grounds not explicitly mentioned in that provision [citing, in particular, the decision in *Salgueiro da Silva Mouta v. Portugal* on sexual orientation].

The U.K. Government has articulated the view that the Convention should contain a free-standing discrimination provision but has refused to sign the Protocol on the ground that its wording is too wide, in particular that the words 'rights set forth by law' might extend to rights included in international conventions to which the U.K. is not a party and (somewhat surprisingly in view of the strict limits on positive action in domestic law) on the basis that 'it does not make provision for positive measures'.[77] The third recital of the preamble makes clear, however, that 'measures [taken] in order to promote full and effective equality' are not prohibited by Protocol 12 provided that there is an objective and reasonable justification for them. And according to the Explanatory Report to the Protocol (para. 16): 'The fact that there are certain groups or categories of persons who are disadvantaged, or the existence of de facto inequalities,

---

[76] Paras. 21–2.

[77] HL Debs, Vol. 617, col. WA37, 11 October 2000, response from Lord Bassam, Parliamentary Under-Secretary of State for the Home Office, to Lord Lester. Lord Bassam also made the surprising observation that Protocol 12 'does not follow the case law of the European Court of Human Rights in allowing objective and reasonably justified distinctions'. The availability of justification under Article 14 has, however, been read into the provision rather than being evident on its face.

may constitute justifications for adopting measures providing for specific advantages in order to promote equality, provided that the proportionality principle is respected'. The Report goes on to state, however, that 'the present Protocol does not impose any obligation to adopt such [positive] measures. Such a programmatic obligation would sit ill with the whole nature of the Convention and its control system which are based on the collective guarantee of individual rights which are formulated in terms sufficiently specific to be justiciable'.

It is too early as yet to gauge the impact of the 12th Protocol. The Protocol had been ratified by 14 member states of the Council of Europe by March 2007 and signed by a further 21, but countries including Denmark, France, Sweden and the UK had neither signed nor ratified and the European Court has yet to hear any cases dealing with its provisions.

10

PROPERTY

FIRST PROTOCOL, ARTICLE 1

Every natural or legal person is entitled to the peaceful enjoyment of his possessions. No one shall be deprived of his possessions except in the public interest and subject to the conditions provided for by law and by the general principles of international law.

The preceding provisions shall not, however, in any way impair the right of a state to enforce such laws at it deems necessary to control the use of property in accordance with the general interest or to secure the payment of taxes or other contributions or penalties.

The right to property can involve a general guarantee either of eligibility to hold property[1] or of protection against improper state expropriation. It is in this second sense that Article 1 of Protocol No. 1 of the European Convention on Human Rights protects property rights, for while the text makes provision for the right to the peaceful enjoyment of property, at the same time it recognizes that the public interest may justify deprivation or control over the use of possessions upon satisfaction of prescribed conditions. In any event, property rights have a strong claim to be considered more akin to economic rather than civil rights, and Strasbourg supervision in this area is covered by recognition of a wide margin of appreciation on the part of state authorities.

A guarantee for property rights is now a common feature in modern constitutions. For example, the Fifth Amendment to the United States Constitution prohibits the federal authorities from depriving any person of 'property without due process of law' or from taking 'private property for public use, without just compensation'. The former clause appears verbatim in the Fourteenth Amendment limiting the powers of the states, and the Supreme Court has interpreted that amendment to incorporate a prohibition of taking of property parallel to that of the Fifth. These provisions have often raised issues similar to those that have engaged the Strasbourg Court under Protocol 1, Article 1. However, at the time of drafting of the European Convention on Human Rights, several west European states (and in particular, the United Kingdom) were taking steps to nationalize significant economic activities, and consequently the entrenchment of this right in the Convention was not without controversy. This helps explain why, ultimately, this provision was not initially included in the main

---

[1] *Cf.* Universal Declaration of Human Rights, Art. 17(1): 'Everyone has the right to own property alone as well as in association with others'.

Convention but only in the optional First Protocol. Similar political influences explain the absence of property protection from the Canadian Charter of Rights and Freedoms. At the time of its drafting, the Liberal government deleted such a provision (which had been included in the statutory Bill of Rights of 1960) to secure the support of the socialist New Democratic Party.[2]

The situations in which states have found it necessary to interfere with property rights are often similar: for example, planning determinations may call for the expropriation of land to allow for the construction of infrastructure of benefit to the wider community, licensing restrictions may be deemed appropriate in order to help enforce social policy, and customs officials may seek to seize property to enforce taxation legislation and prevent the importation of goods deemed inappropriate. However, much of the case law under this guarantee also reflects particular political economic situations which have arisen in European states, including situations whose factual and legal backgrounds reflect recent historical turmoil in Europe. Some of this is indeed reflected in the increasing complexity of the legal issues the Court is called upon to adjudicate. Several judgments, for example, directly concern the nationalization of property by communist regimes in the wake of World War II. Thus in *Broniowski v. Poland*, a systemic problem caused by 'a malfunctioning of [domestic] legislation and administrative practice' resulted in the failure to satisfy entitlement to compensatory property in respect of land lost at the time of the 'repatriation' of individuals and the redefinition of the Polish state's boundaries,[3] while *Jahn and Others v. Germany* concerned steps taken in the dying days of the East German state in respect of agricultural land expropriated after the partition of Germany in 1945.[4] The factual backdrop to case-law in this area, then, is often of some complexity, even if the principles derived from the jurisprudence are of general applicability.

Consideration of whether there has been a violation of Article 1 of Protocol No. 1 involves two initial questions: whether there exists a recognized property right; and whether there has been an 'interference' within the meaning of the provision (and if so, the particular nature of the 'interference'). Thereafter, attention turns to whether the interference constitutes a violation of the guarantee by addressing three questions: whether the interference is lawful; whether it can be said to have been in the 'public' or 'general' interest; and whether it meets the test of proportionality (that is, whether a fair balance between individual and collective interests has been achieved, a matter primarily determined by the question whether reasonable compensation has been offered). In each instance, of course, the applicant must qualify as a 'victim' within the meaning of Article 34 of the Convention. In respect of Article 1 of Protocol No. 1, the text makes it clear that an applicant may be a legal person as well as a natural person, and cases such as *Lithgow and Others v. United Kingdom* illustrate that companies may

---

[2] Alvaro, 'Why Property Rights were Excluded from the Canadian Charter of Rights and Freedoms', 24 *Can. J. Pol. Sci.* 309 (1991).

[3] *Broniowski v. Poland* [G.C.], 22 June 2004, 40 E.H.R.R. 21, paras. 189–94 at para. 189 (the potential number of applicants was some 80,000 individuals).

[4] *Jahn and Others v. Germany*, discussed *infra* Section C.

rely upon the provision.[5] However, shareholders—including both natural and legal persons—seeking to challenge state action directed against companies in which they have a financial interest generally may only do so 'in exceptional circumstances, in particular where it is clearly established that it is impossible for the company to apply to the Convention institutions through the organs set up under its articles of incorporation or—in the event of liquidation—through its liquidation'.[6]

A. DETERMINING WHETHER THERE HAS BEEN AN 'INTERFERENCE'

1. THE COURT'S GENERAL APPROACH IN PROPERTY CASES

The leading judgment in the case law of Article 1 of Protocol No. 1 is *Sporrong and Lönnroth v. Sweden* decided in 1982. This case established the Court's approach to interpretation. In particular, the Court first discussed the 'three rules' found in the guarantee, and established the approach to be taken in determining whether a 'fair balance' had been struck between individual rights and the general public interest.

2. SPORRONG AND LÖNNROTH V. SWEDEN

Judgment of 23 September 1982
5 E.H.R.R. 35

[A planning authority imposed expropriation permits allowing future expropriation and prohibitions on the future construction of certain buildings and land in Stockholm. One property was subject to an expropriation permit for a total of 23 years and to a prohibition on construction for 25 years, and another to an expropriation permit for 8 years and to a prohibition on construction for 12 years. No compensation was payable to the owners. These measures made it more difficult for the owners to dispose of their property by sale, but did not render this impossible in theory. The measures were eventually rescinded upon a change of local planning policy. Here, the key question was whether there had been a *de facto* deprivation of property.]

---

[5] *Lithgow and Others v. United Kingdom*, discussed *infra* Section C.
[6] *Agrotexim and Others v. Greece*, 21 Oct. 1995, 21 E.H.R.R. 250, para. 66.

1. The existence of an interference with the applicants' right of property

58. The applicants did not dispute that the expropriation permits and prohibitions on construction in question were lawful in themselves. On the other hand, they complained of the length of the time-limits granted to the City of Stockholm for the institution of the judicial proceedings for the fixing of compensation for expropriation (five years, extended for three, then for five and finally for ten years, in the case of the Sporrong Estate; ten years in the case of Mrs. Lönnroth). They also complained of the fact that the expropriation permits and the prohibitions on construction had been maintained in force for a lengthy period (twenty-three and eight years for the permits; twenty-five and twelve years for the prohibitions). They pointed to the adverse effects on their right of property allegedly occasioned by these measures when they were combined in such a way. They contended that they had lost the possibility of selling their properties at normal market prices. They added that they would have run too great a risk had they incurred expenditure on their properties and that if all the same they had had work carried out after obtaining a building permit, they would have been obliged to undertake not to claim—in the event of expropriation—any indemnity for the resultant capital appreciation. They also alleged that they would have encountered difficulties in obtaining mortgages had they sought them. Finally, they recalled that any 'new construction' on their own land was prohibited.

Though not claiming that they had been formally and definitively deprived of their possessions, the Sporrong Estate and Mrs. Lönnroth alleged that the permits and prohibitions at issue subjected the enjoyment and power to dispose of their properties to limitations that were excessive and did not give rise to any compensation. Their right of property had accordingly, so they contended, been deprived of its substance whilst the measures in question were in force.

59. The Government accepted that market forces might render it more difficult to sell or let a property that was subject to an expropriation permit and that the longer the permit remained in force the more serious this problem would become. They also recognised that prohibitions on construction restricted the normal exercise of the right of property. However, they asserted that such permits and prohibitions were an intrinsic feature of town planning and did not impair the right of owners to 'the peaceful enjoyment of (their) possessions', within the meaning of Article 1 of Protocol No. 1 .

60. The Court is unable to accept this argument. Although the expropriation permits left intact in law the owners' right to use and dispose of their possessions, they nevertheless in practice significantly reduced the possibility of its exercise. They also affected the very substance of ownership in that they recognised before the event that any expropriation would be lawful and authorised the City of Stockholm to expropriate whenever it found it expedient to do so. The applicants' right of property thus became precarious and defeasible. The prohibitions on construction, for their part, undoubtedly restricted the applicants' right to use their possessions. The Court also considers that the permits and prohibitions should in principle be examined together, except to the extent that analysis of the case may require a distinction to be drawn between them. This is because, even though there was not necessarily a legal connection between the measures and even though they had different periods of validity, they were complementary and had the single objective of facilitating the development of the city in accordance with the successive plans prepared for this purpose. There was therefore an interference with the applicants' right of property and, as the Commission rightly pointed out, the consequences of that interference were undoubtedly rendered more serious by the combined use, over a long period of time, of expropriation permits and prohibitions on construction.

2. *The justification for the interference with the applicants' right of property*

61. It remains to be ascertained whether or not the interference found by the Court violated Article 1.

That Article comprises three distinct rules. The first rule, which is of a general nature, enounces the principle of peaceful enjoyment of property; it is set out in the first sentence of the first paragraph. The second rule covers deprivation of possessions and subjects it to certain conditions; it appears in the second sentence of the same paragraph. The third rule recognises that the States are entitled, amongst other things, to control the use of property in accordance with the general interest, by enforcing such laws as they deem necessary for the purpose; it is contained in the second paragraph. The Court must determine, before considering whether the first rule was complied with, whether the last two are applicable.

(a) The applicability of the second sentence of the first paragraph

62. It should be recalled first of all that the Swedish authorities did not proceed to an expropriation of the applicants' properties. The applicants were therefore not formally 'deprived of their possessions' at any time: they were entitled to use, sell, devise, donate or mortgage their properties.

63. In the absence of a formal expropriation, that is to say a transfer of ownership, the Court considers that it must look behind the appearances and investigate the realities of the situation complained of. Since the Convention is intended to guarantee rights that are 'practical and effective', it has to be ascertained whether that situation amounted to a de facto expropriation, as was argued by the applicants. In the Court's opinion, all the effects complained of (see paragraph 58 above) stemmed from the reduction of the possibility of disposing of the properties concerned. Those effects were occasioned by limitations imposed on the right of property, which right had become precarious, and from the consequences of those limitations on the value of the premises. However, although the right in question lost some of its substance, it did not disappear. The effects of the measures involved are not such that they can be assimilated to a deprivation of possessions. The Court observes in this connection that the applicants could continue to utilise their possessions and that, although it became more difficult to sell properties in Stockholm affected by expropriation permits and prohibitions on construction, the possibility of selling subsisted; according to information supplied by the Government, several dozen sales were carried out.... There was therefore no room for the application of the second sentence of the first paragraph in the present case.

(b) The applicability of the second paragraph

64. The prohibitions on construction clearly amounted to a control of 'the use of [the applicants'] property', within the meaning of the second paragraph.

65. On the other hand, the expropriation permits were not intended to limit or control such use. Since they were an initial step in a procedure leading to deprivation of possessions, they did not fall within the ambit of the second paragraph. They must be examined under the first sentence of the first paragraph.

(c) Compliance with the first sentence of the first paragraph as regards the expropriation permits

66. The applicants' complaints concerned in the first place the length of the time-limits granted to the City of Stockholm, which they regarded as contrary to both Swedish law and the Convention. ...

69. The fact that the permits fell within the ambit neither of the second sentence of the first paragraph nor of the second paragraph does not mean that the interference with the said right violated the rule contained in the first sentence of the first paragraph. For the purposes of the latter provision, the Court must determine whether a fair balance was struck between the demands of the general interest of the community and the requirements of the protection of the individual's fundamental rights. The search for this balance is inherent in the whole of the Convention and is also reflected in the structure of Article 1. The Agent of the Government recognised the need for such a balance. At the hearing..., he pointed out that, under the Expropriation Act, an expropriation permit must not be issued if the public purpose in question can be achieved in a different way; when this is being assessed, full weight must be given both to the interests of the individual and to the public interest.

The Court has not overlooked this concern on the part of the legislature. Moreover, it finds it natural that, in an area as complex and difficult as that of the development of large cities, the Contracting States should enjoy a wide margin of appreciation in order to implement their town-planning policy. Nevertheless, the Court cannot fail to exercise its power of review and must determine whether the requisite balance was maintained in a manner consonant with the applicants' right to 'the peaceful enjoyment of [their] possessions', within the meaning of the first sentence of Article 1.

70. A feature of the law in force at the relevant time was its inflexibility. With the exception of the total withdrawal of the expropriation permits, which required the agreement of the municipality, the law provided no means by which the situation of the property owners involved could be modified at a later date. The Court notes in this connection that the permits granted to the City of Stockholm were granted for five years in the case of the Sporrong Estate—with an extension for three, then for five and finally for ten years—and for ten years in the case of Mrs. Lönnroth. In the events that happened, they remained in force for twenty-three years and eight years respectively. During the whole of this period, the applicants were left in complete uncertainty as to the fate of their properties and were not entitled to have any difficulties which they might have encountered taken into account by the Swedish Government. The Commission's report furnishes an example of such difficulties. Mrs. Lönnroth had requested the Government to withdraw the expropriation permit. The City Council replied that the existing plans did not authorise any derogation; the Government, for their part, refused the request on the ground that they could not revoke the permit without the Council's express consent.

The Court has not overlooked the interest of the City of Stockholm in having the option of expropriating properties in order to implement its plans. However, it does not see why the Swedish legislation should have excluded the possibility of re-assessing, at reasonable intervals during the lengthy periods for which each of the permits was granted and maintained in force, the interests of the City and the interests of the owners. In the instant case, the absence of such a possibility was all the less satisfactory in that the town-planning schemes underlying the expropriation permits and, at the same time, the intended use prescribed for the applicants' properties were modified on several occasions.

71. As is shown by the official statement of reasons accompanying the Bill in which the 1972 Act originated, the Swedish Government conceded that 'in certain respects, the existing system is a source of disadvantages for the property owner'.... The 1972 Act takes partial account of these problems. Admittedly, it does not provide for compensation to be granted to property owners who may have been prejudiced by reason of the length of the validity of the permit; however, it does enable them to obtain a reduction of the time-limit for service of the summons to appear before the Real Estate Court if they establish that the fact that the question of expropriation remains pending has caused significantly more serious prejudice. Since the Act was not applicable in the present case, it could not have been of assistance to the applicants in overcoming any difficulties which they might have encountered.

72. The Court also finds that the existence throughout this period of prohibitions on construction accentuated even further the prejudicial effects of the length of the validity of the permits. Full enjoyment of the applicants' right of property was impeded for a total period of twenty-five years in the case of the Sporrong Estate and of twelve years in the case of Mrs. Lönnroth. In this connection, the Court notes that in 1967 the Parliamentary Ombudsman considered that the adverse effects on property owners that could result from extended prohibitions were irreconcilable with the position that should obtain in a State governed by the rule of law...

73. Being combined in this way, the two series of measures created a situation which upset the fair balance which should be struck between the protection of the right of property and the requirements of the general interest: the Sporrong Estate and Mrs. Lönnroth bore an individual and excessive burden which could have been tendered legitimate only if they had had the possibility of seeking a reduction of the time-limits or of claiming compensation. Yet at the relevant time Swedish law excluded these possibilities and it still excludes the second of them. In the Court's view, it is not appropriate at this stage to determine whether the applicants were in fact prejudiced: it was in their legal situation itself that the requisite balance was no longer to be found.

74. The permits in question, whose consequences were aggravated by the prohibitions on construction, therefore violated Article 1, as regards both applicants.

3. THE MEANING OF 'PROPERTY' FOR THE PURPOSES OF THE GUARANTEE

The text of Article 1 of Protocol No. 1 refers to 'possessions' rather than to 'property', but in substance these two terms are synonymous and include a wide and varied range of economic interests and assets. In other words, these terms are autonomous concepts and their meaning is not dependent upon domestic classification. 'Possessions' will cover both moveable and heritable property, and will include a wide range of interests such as ownership of a house,[7] goodwill of a business,[8] entitlement to rent,[9] a security right *in rem*,[10] an award made by a court,[11] or an entitlement to social welfare benefits even without contributions by the beneficiary.[12] It will also cover a non-registered title or a disputed title[13] to heritable property providing the asserted right has some basis in domestic law.[14] However, only existing rights and assets (rather than future claims to property) are covered since the 'possession' must be sufficiently established in its existence. For example, an expectation to inherit property is not a 'possession' for the purposes of the guarantee.[15] In each instance the facts must be assessed with care. In *Öneryıldız v Turkey*, the Grand Chamber accepted that squatters had established that they had property rights within the scope of the Article. The applicant and his family had occupied land belonging to the state for some five years without legal title. On this land he had constructed a slum dwelling in which he and his family had lived and which had contained all of the family's household and personal effects. The Court could not accept that the hope of having the land legally transferred at some point in the future was enough to constitute an enforceable claim sufficient to amount to a 'possession'. But the Court was satisfied that the fact that the authorities had tolerated the construction of the dwelling, even though this had been contrary to planning regulations, could support 'the conclusion that the authorities also acknowledged *de facto* that the applicant and his close relatives had a proprietary interest in their dwelling and movable goods' sufficient to constitute a recognized interest for the purposes of the guarantee.[16]

On the other hand, the Article may be applicable if it can be shown that there is a legitimate expectation of obtaining effective enjoyment of a particular property right. There is, though, a crucial difference between a mere hope (however understandable such a hope may be in the circumstances) and a 'legitimate expectation' of a more concrete nature. In *Kopecký v. Slovakia,* the Grand Chamber confirmed that 'where the proprietary interest is in the nature of a claim it may be regarded as an "asset" only where it has a sufficient basis in national law, for example where there is settled case-law of the domestic courts confirming it'. Here, the applicant's restitution claim for the return of coins had been a conditional one from the outset and in domestic proceedings the courts

---

[7] *The Former King of Greece and Others v. Greece* [G.C.], 23 Nov. 2000, 33 E.H.R.R. 21 paras. 60–6 (estates owned by the applicants as private persons rather than as members of the royal family considered 'possessions').

[8] *Van Marle v. Netherlands*, 26 June 1986, 8 E.H.R.R. 483 at para. 41 (goodwill of business conducted by chartered accountants).

[9] *Mellacher and Others v. Austria*, 19 Dec. 1989, 12 E.H.R.R. 391, paras. 40–1.

[10] *Gasus Dosier- und Födertechnik v. Netherlands*, 23 Feb. 1995, 20 E.H.R.R. 403, para. 53.

[11] *Sciortino v. Italy*, 18 Oct. 2001, para. 31.

[12] *Stec and Others v. United Kingdom* [G.C.], 12 April 2006, 43 E.H.R.R. 47.

[13] *Iatridis v. Greece*, 25 Mar. 1999, 30 E.H.R.R. 97, paras. 54–5.

[14] *S. v. the United Kingdom*, 14 May 1986, (commission report) (surviving partner occupying a house after the death of the tenant had no contractual right in domestic law and thus no 'possession' within the meaning of Protocol 1 Art. 1).

[15] *Marckx v. Belgium*, 13 June 1979, 2 E.H.R.R. 330, para. 50.

[16] [G.C.], 30 Nov. 2004, 41 E.H.R.R. 20, paras 124–9 at para. 127.

had found that he had not complied in any case with the statutory requirements for the return of the property. In consequence, the claim had not been sufficiently established to qualify as an 'asset' to attract the protection of the guarantee.[17] Thus where such a settled basis is lacking (as where there is a dispute as to the correct interpretation and application of domestic law, and an applicant's submissions have been rejected by national courts) no legitimate expectation can be said to arise. In *Anheuser-Busch Inc v. Portugal*, the domestic courts had upheld the cancellation of the American applicant company's 'Budweiser' trade mark following an agreement between Portugal and Czechoslovakia on the ground that the appellation of origin indicated a product from a particular region. The Grand Chamber confirmed that applications for the registration of trade marks could fall within the scope of protection of the Article even where proprietary rights were revocable under certain conditions in light of 'the bundle of financial rights and interests that arise upon an application for the registration of a trade mark'; but it was not prepared to accept in this case that there had been an interference with property rights as there had been no interference with the applicant company's right to the peaceful enjoyment of its possessions. In this instance, the complaint mainly concerned 'the manner in which the national courts interpreted and applied domestic law in proceedings essentially between two rival claimants to the same name, it being contended in particular that the courts wrongly gave retrospective effect to [a bilateral agreement between two states] ... [It was not] about the application of a law which was on its face retrospective to deprive them of their pre-existing possessions'. This was crucial: the Court's jurisdiction is not to deal with errors of fact or law. Its authority 'to verify that domestic law has been correctly interpreted and applied is limited and it is not its function to take the place of the national courts, its role being rather to ensure that the decisions of those courts are not flawed by arbitrariness or otherwise manifestly unreasonable', particularly as in this case the issues involved difficult questions of interpretation of domestic law.[18]

The notion of property in the United States Constitution has also been extended to include public entitlements including welfare benefits and public employment.[19] As in Strasbourg law, the identification of protected property rights has necessitated a close examination of the law of property, especially that of the states, in order to distinguish between genuine legal entitlements and mere expectations or practices. The Court's approach is summarized in the following passage:

To have a property interest in a benefit, a person clearly must have more than an abstract need or desire for it. He must have more than a unilateral expectation of it. He must, instead, have a legitimate claim of entitlement to it. . . . Property interests, of course, are not created by the Constitution. Rather, they are created and their dimensions are defined by existing rules or understandings that stem from an independent source such as state law—rules or understandings that secure certain benefits and that support claims of entitlement to those benefits.[20]

---

[17] [G.C.], 28 Sept. 2004, 41 E.H.R.R. 43 at paras. 35–61.
[18] [G.C.], 11 Oct. 2005, 44 E.H.R.R. 42, paras. 82–3.
[19] E.g. *Goldberg v. Kelly*, 397 U.S. 254 (1970); *Roth v. Board of Regents*, 408 U.S. 564 (1972).
[20] *Roth, supra* n. 19 at 577.

4. INTERFERENCES WITH PROPERTY RIGHTS: THE THREE RULES

The text refers to the peaceful *enjoyment* of possessions, and thus a broad range of state activity which interferes with any of the normal consequences arising out of ownership or possession will be recognized as giving rise to an issue under the guarantee. 'Interferences' with the right to property can include the seizure and destruction of books considered obscene,[21] limitations placed on the right to dispose of possessions after death,[22] *de facto* appropriation of property caused by 'planning blight' or protracted building prohibitions,[23] and forfeiture of smuggled goods.[24] However, temporary restrictions such as the provisional transfer[25] or confiscation of property[26] will not constitute 'interferences' with property rights. It is thus necessary to look carefully at the actual circumstances. A hindrance can amount to an interference with the peaceful enjoyment of possessions just as much as a formal legal impediment.[27]

As the Court discussed in *Sporrong and Lönnroth v. Sweden*, the textual formulation of the Article indicates three distinct but connected rules: first, a rule of general applicability that 'every natural or legal person is entitled to the peaceful enjoyment of property'; second, a rule that 'no one shall be deprived of his possession except in the public interest and subject to the conditions provided for by law and by the general principles of international law'; and, third, explicit recognition that states may seek to control the use of property by providing that a state continues to enjoy the right without impairment 'to enforce such laws as it deems necessary to control the use of property in accordance with the general interest or to secure the payment of taxes or other contributions or penalties'. There is thus a need at the outset to clarify which rule is involved in an actual interference. This is not always straightforward.

A. THE FIRST RULE: PEACEFUL ENJOYMENT OF PROPERTY

This first rule though just declaratory is still of importance, for even if there has been no deprivation or control of use of property, the facts may still amount to an interference with the peaceful enjoyment of property. In consequence, where the applicability of the second or third rule is in doubt, the issue will be considered under this first rule concerning the peaceful enjoyment of possessions.

---

[21] *Handyside v United Kingdom*, 7 Dec. 1979, 1 E.H.R.R. 737, para. 61.
[22] *Marckx v Belgium, supra* n. 15, para. 63.
[23] *Sporrong and Lönnroth v Sweden*, Section A(2) *supra*, at paras. 60–1.
[24] *AGOSI v United Kingdom*, 24 Oct. 1986, 9 E.H.R.R. 1, para. 49.
[25] *Erkner and Hofauer v Austria*, 29 Sept. 1987, 13 E.H.R.R. 413.
[26] *Raimondo v Italy*, 22 Feb. 1994, 18 E.H.R.R. 237, para. 36.
[27] *Loizidou v Turkey*, 18 Dec. 1996, 23 E.H.R.R. 513, paras. 60–4.

B. THE SECOND RULE: DEPRIVATION OF PROPERTY

Deprivation of property is the most radical form of interference with property rights and includes expropriation and other loss of rights which flow from the legal consequences of property. This will clearly include, for example, property taken under compulsory powers.[28] It may also include the retroactive removal of liability for acts of negligence and which has the effect of depriving individuals of legal claims for compensation.[29] However, the deprivation must be definitive and involve an irrevocable expropriation or transfer of property rights.[30] Mere provisional seizure of property[31] is insufficient to give rise to a 'deprivation', nor does the removal of a licence or imposition of planning controls having a detrimental impact on a business.[32] Since the Convention seeks to guarantee rights that are practical and effective, a deprivation of property may also involve a *de facto* expropriation.

C. THE THIRD RULE: CONTROL OVER THE USE OF PROPERTY

The third rule covers controls over the use of property. Examples of such control include the seizure of goods by state authorities,[33] the prohibition on the importation of goods,[34] imposition of rent controls,[35] and the revocation of a licence resulting in an economic impact on the conduct of a business.[36] Again, merely provisional measures which do not have the purpose or consequence of limiting or controlling the use of property will not fall within the scope of the second paragraph.[37]

The text also specifically provides that the first and second rules do not 'in any way impair the right of a state to enforce such laws as it deems necessary to control the use of property in accordance with the general interest or to secure the payment of taxes or other contributions or penalties'. Taxation policy is covered by a wide margin of appreciation, but is still subject to the requirement that interferences with property rights are not manifestly without reasonable foundation such as to amount to a situation of arbitrary confiscation.

---

[28] *Lithgow and Others v. United Kingdom*, 8 July 1986, 8 E.H.R.R. 329, paras. 105–7.

[29] *Pressos Compania Naviera and Others v. Belgium*, 20 Nov. 1995, 21 E.H.R.R. 34, para. 34.

[30] *Raimondo v. Italy, supra* n. 26, at para. 29.

[31] *Handyside v. United Kingdom, supra* n. 21, at para. 62.

[32] *Tre Traktörer v. Sweden*, 7 July 1989, 13 E.H.R.R. 309, para. 55 (licence for the sale of alcohol); *Pine Valley Developments Ltd and Others v. Ireland*, 29 Nov. 1991, 14 E.H.R.R. 319, para. 56 (imposition of planning controls).

[33] E.g. *Handyside v. United Kingdom, supra* n. 21, at para. 62.

[34] *AGOSI v. United Kingdom, supra* n. 24, at para. 51 (forfeiture of smuggled coins formed a constituent element of the procedures for control of use of gold coins, and thus was better considered as involving control of use rather than deprivation of property).

[35] *Mellacher and Others v. Austria, supra* n. 9, at paras. 43–5.

[36] *Tre Traktörer v. Sweden, supra* n. 32, at para. 55.

[37] *Sporrong and Lönroth v. Sweden*, Section A(2) *supra*, at paras. 64–5.

5. PINE VALLEY DEVELOPMENTS LTD AND
OTHERS V. IRELAND

Judgment of 29 November 1991
14 E.H.R.R. 319

[After the applicant company had purchased land relying upon an existing grant of outline planning permission for industrial development, the domestic courts declared the outline planning
permission *ultra vires*. The initial question was whether this amounted to an interference with
the company's rights under Article 1 of Protocol No. 1. The following extract indicates how the
Court disposed of this issue.]

A. Whether there was an interference with a right of the applicants

51. Bearing in mind that...the [Irish] Supreme Court held that the outline planning permission granted to [the seller of the land] was a nullity ab initio, a first question that arises in
this case is whether the applicants ever enjoyed a right to develop the land in question which
could have been the subject of an interference.

Like the Commission, the Court considers that this question must be answered in the affirmative. When Pine Valley purchased the site, it did so in reliance on the permission which had been
duly recorded in a public register kept for the purpose and which it was perfectly entitled to
assume was valid. That permission amounted to a favourable decision as to the principle of the
proposed development, which could not be reopened by the planning authority. In these circumstances it would be unduly formalistic to hold that the Supreme Court's decision did not constitute an interference. Until it was rendered, the applicants had at least a legitimate expectation
of being able to carry out their proposed development and this has to be regarded, for the
purposes of Article 1 of Protocol No. 1 as a component part of the property in question...

· · ·

B. The Article 1 rule applicable to the case

55. The applicants contended that the interference in question, by annulling the outline
planning permission, constituted a 'deprivation' of possessions, within the meaning of the
second sentence of the first paragraph of Article 1 of Protocol No. 1. The Commission, on
the other hand, saw it as a 'control of the use of property', within the meaning of the second
paragraph of that provision.

56. There was no formal expropriation of the property in question, neither, in the Court's
view, can it be said that there was a de facto deprivation. The impugned measure was basically
designed to ensure that the land was used in conformity with the relevant planning laws and
title remained vested in Healy Holdings, whose powers to take decisions concerning the property were unaffected. Again, the land was not left without any meaningful alternative use, for
it could have been farmed or leased. Finally, although the value of the site was substantially
reduced, it was not rendered worthless, as is evidenced by the fact that it was subsequently
sold in the open market.

Accordingly, the interference must be considered as a control of the use of property falling
within the scope of the second paragraph of Article 1.

6. TRE TRAKTÖRER AKTIEBOLAG V. SWEDEN

Judgment of 7 July 1989
13 E.H.R.R. 309

[The applicant company [TTA] assumed the management of a restaurant that held a licence to serve alcohol. Subsequently, this licence was revoked, and the restaurant, in turn, had closed.]

A. Applicability of Article 1 of the Protocol

53. The Government argued that a licence to serve alcoholic beverages could not be considered to be a 'possession' within the meaning of Article 1 of the Protocol. This provision was therefore, in their opinion, not applicable to the case.

Like the Commission, however, the Court takes the view that the economic interests connected with the running of Le Cardinal were 'possessions' for the purposes of Article 1 of the Protocol. Indeed, the Court has already found that the maintenance of the licence was one of the principal conditions for the carrying on of the applicant company's business, and that its withdrawal had adverse effects on the goodwill and value of the restaurant.

Such withdrawal thus constitutes, in the circumstances of the case, an interference with TTA's right to the 'peaceful enjoyment of [its] possessions'.

B. The Article 1 rule applicable to the case

54. Article 1 in substance guarantees the right of property.... It comprises 'three distinct rules': the first rule, set out in the first sentence of the first paragraph, is of a general nature and enunciates the principle of the peaceful enjoyment of property; the second rule, contained in the second sentence of the first paragraph, covers deprivation of possessions and subjects it to certain conditions; the third rule, stated in the second paragraph, recognises that the Contracting States are entitled, amongst other things, to control the use of property by enforcing such laws as they deem necessary in the general interest (see the Sporrong and Lönnroth judgment of 23 September 1982, para. 61). However, the three rules are not 'distinct' in the sense of being unconnected: the second and third rules are concerned with particular instances of interference with the right to peaceful enjoyment of property and should therefore be construed in the light of the general principle enunciated in the first rule.

55. Severe though it may have been, the interference at issue did not fall within the ambit of the second sentence of the first paragraph. The applicant company, although it could no longer operate Le Cardinal as a restaurant business, kept some economic interests represented by the leasing of the premises and the property assets contained therein, which it finally sold in June 1984. There was accordingly no deprivation of property in terms of Article 1 of the Protocol.

The Court finds, however, that the withdrawal of TTA's licence to serve alcoholic beverages in Le Cardinal constituted a measure of control of the use of property, which falls to be considered under the second paragraph of Article 1 of the Protocol.

C. Compliance with the requirements of the second paragraph

1. Lawfulness and purpose of the interference

56. The applicant company did not contest the legitimacy of the aim of the 1977 Act, and agreed with the Government that it was to implement the long-standing Swedish policy of restricting the consumption and abuse of alcohol. However, it criticised the actual measures of implementation taken by the National Board of Health and Welfare and the County Administrative Board. It complained, first, that they were adopted on the basis of section 64(2), as amended with effect from 1 July 1982, and therefore represented a retroactive application of this section to facts which had taken place in 1980–1981; and secondly, that they did not pursue the aforesaid aim, but sought to obtain the payment of taxes, thus constituting an abuse of power (détournement de pouvoir).

57. By subjecting the sale of alcoholic beverages to a system of licences, the Swedish legislature took measures to implement the national policy in this field. This was in line with Swedish social policy generally and the Court does not doubt that the aim so pursued was the control of the use of property in accordance with the general interest.

58. As to the actual measure of withdrawal in question, the Court notes that the National Board of Health and Welfare relied in its decision of 13 July 1983 on section 64(2) of the 1977 Act taken together with sections 40 and 70.

The Court's power to review compliance with domestic law is limited. It is in the first place for the national authorities to interpret and apply that law, and nothing in the above-mentioned decision suggests that it was contrary to Swedish law.

Neither is there anything in the facts to support the applicant company's contention that the revocation of its licence did not seek the same purpose as the 1977 Act. In the said decision, the National Board of Health and Welfare had referred to the 'great social responsibility' involved in the selling of alcoholic beverages, and had concluded, taking into account the explanations given by TTA as to the thefts of such beverages, that 'those who have had a decisive influence on the business have failed to demonstrate sufficient competence regarding both book-keeping and internal control'.

Thus, the withdrawal of TTA's licence was lawful and pursued the general interest.

2. Proportionality of the interference

59. ...[T]he second paragraph of Article 1 of the Protocol has to be construed in the light of the general principle set out in the first sentence of this Article. This sentence has been interpreted by the Court as including the requirement that a measure of interference should strike a 'fair balance' between the demands of the general interest of the community and the requirements of the protection of the individual's fundamental rights. The search for this balance is reflected in the structure of Article 1 as a whole and hence also in the second paragraph. There must be a reasonable relationship of proportionality between the means employed and the aim sought to be realised.

60. The Government submitted that for the purposes of applying Article 1 of the Protocol the competent authorities enjoy a wide margin of appreciation. That margin was particularly wide with regard to Parliament, whose assessment as to the need for legislation, its aims and its effects should be accepted by the Convention institutions unless it was manifestly unreasonable and imposed an 'excessive burden' on the person concerned. However, the applicant

company had not shown that the closing of Le Cardinal was a consequence of the withdrawal of the licence; thus no economic damage flowed therefrom.

61. In respect of this latter point, the Court refers to its statement in paragraph 53 above. It sees no reason to exclude that the restaurant Le Cardinal closed on 19 July 1983 as a result of the County Administrative Board's decision of 18 July to revoke, with immediate effect, the licence to serve alcoholic beverages. Furthermore, no stay of execution having been granted by the National Board of Health and Welfare, the financial repercussions of the revocation were serious. The Court thus agrees with the Commission that this was a severe measure in the circumstances.

It is true that the measure in question could have been foreseen, especially after the County Administrative Board had informed TTA on 4 November 1982 that it was considering taking this course of action. But it must be borne in mind that, after that date, the competent authorities took three positive decisions in respect of the applicant company: on 7 January 1983 the County Administrative Board decided in the same proceedings to issue only an admonition against TTA under section 64, having regard to the considerable time which had elapsed—almost three years—since the discrepancies in the book-keeping of AB Citykällaren had occurred and to the fact that in the meantime there had been no further deficiencies; on 14 January the same Board renewed the applicant company's licence for Le Cardinal, extending the serving hours until 2.00 a.m.; and on 27 May the District Court of Helsingborg acquitted Mrs Flenman of the offence of hindering control by the fiscal authorities.

On the other hand, the discrepancies in the book-keeping of AB Citykällaren concerning the sale of alcoholic beverages were very significant in relation to the total turnover of the company. The fact that, according to TTA's representatives, these discrepancies were due to thefts does not invalidate the conclusion of the National Board of Health and Welfare that this showed inadequate book-keeping and internal control though the District Court had found that the existence of intent or gross negligence had not been established.

62. The 'burden' placed on TTA as a result of the contested decisions, though heavy, must be weighed against the general interest of the community. In this context, the States enjoy a wide margin of appreciation.

Even though the County Administrative Board and the National Board of Health and Welfare could have taken less severe measures under section 64 of the 1977 Act, the Court, having regard to the legitimate aim of Swedish social policy concerning the consumption of alcohol, finds that the respondent State did not fail to strike a 'fair balance' between the economic interests of the applicant company and the general interest of Swedish society.

3. Conclusion

63. The Court thus concludes that there has been no violation of Article 1 of the Protocol.

7. GASUS DOSIER-UND FÖDERTECHNIK V. NETHERLANDS

Judgment of 23 February 1995
20 E.H.R.R. 403

[A German company received an order from a Dutch company for the supply of a concrete-mixer and ancillary equipment. The terms of contract specified that ownership would only pass once payment was received in respect of all sums due 'both present and future, including ancillary claims arising from business with the customer'. After the mixer had been delivered but before full payment had been made, the Dutch company was declared bankrupt. The mixer was seized by the tax authorities in terms of legislative provisions ('the 1845 Act' or 'the bodemrecht'). Legal proceedings by the applicant company to recover the machinery were unsuccessful.]

A. Whether there was an interference with the applicant company's 'peaceful enjoyment of [their] possessions'

51. The applicant company pointed out that they had sold the concrete-mixer to Atlas subject to retention of title until the full price had been paid. Since at the time of the seizure the full price had not been paid, the ownership of the concrete-mixer still remained with Gasus. This, in their contention, meant that the seizure and subsequent selling of that machine by the Netherlands tax authorities had interfered with their right of ownership....

52. The Government argued that retention of title was more in the nature of a security right in rem than of 'true' ownership and that the 'enjoyment' of it was limited to security for payment of the purchase price. 'True' or 'economic' ownership was vested in the purchaser, who stood to lose by damage to or loss of the goods purchased and stood to gain by their use or resale. At the time of the events complained of, the concrete-mixer was thus no longer a 'possession' whose 'peaceful enjoyment' was guaranteed to Gasus by Article 1 of Protocol No. 1.

53. The Court recalls that the notion 'possessions' (in French: biens) in Article 1 of Protocol No. 1 has an autonomous meaning which is certainly not limited to ownership of physical goods: certain other rights and interests constituting assets can also be regarded as 'property rights', and thus as 'possessions', for the purposes of this provision. In the present context it is therefore immaterial whether Gasus's right to the concrete-mixer is to be considered as a right of ownership or as a security right in rem. In any event, the seizure and sale of the concrete-mixer constituted an 'interference' with the applicant company's right 'to the peaceful enjoyment' of a 'possession' within the meaning of Article 1 of Protocol No. 1.

B. The applicable rule

55. As the Court has often held, Article 1 guarantees in substance the right of property. It comprises three distinct rules.... However, the three rules are not 'distinct' in the sense of being unconnected: the second and third rules are concerned with particular instances of interference with the right to peaceful enjoyment of property and should therefore be construed in the light of the general principle enunciated in the first rule.

56. The applicant company based their entire argument on the premise that they had been deprived of their possessions.

57. In the Commission's opinion, sale under retention of title created a 'special legal situation' in which the respective rights of the vendor and the purchaser depended on the domestic legal rules applicable to the transaction. Normally, the vendor and the purchaser would both be holders of a limited property right protected by Article 1 of Protocol No. 1, but the exact scope

of the right enjoyed by each party might be different according to the legal system involved. In particular, it depended on domestic law to what extent retention of title protected the vendor's property against claims by other creditors. If these other creditors were entitled to have the property seized and sold in settlement of their claims, the result was that the vendor was deprived of his property right. This, in the Commission's view, was what had happened to the applicant company in the present case. The applicable rule was therefore the one contained in the second sentence of the first paragraph.

58. The Government denied that the applicant company had been deprived of their possessions. Firstly, what the tax authorities had done was to seize the concrete-mixer, not to confiscate it; the seizure had left Gasus's property rights intact. Secondly, although the concrete-mixer had eventually been sold and although the sale had been made possible by the seizure, it had been effected under a private contract entered into. Thirdly, they argued that the expression 'deprivation' implied that the natural or legal person concerned was left empty-handed; in fact, Gasus had retained their claim against [the purchaser] for payment of the balance of the purchase price, and the Government were not to be blamed if recovery turned out to be impossible as a result of [the company's] subsequent bankruptcy.

59. The Court considers that the interference complained of in this case was in fact the result of the tax authorities' exercise of their powers under section 16(3) of the 1845 Act. The purpose of that Act was to regulate the collection of direct taxes within the Netherlands, and section 16(3) formed part of the provisions concerning the enforcement of unpaid tax debts. Like all other creditors, the tax authorities could recover unpaid tax debts against all the tax debtor's seizable assets; under section 16(3) they were, moreover, empowered to seize and recover against all movable property found on the tax debtor's premises which qualified as 'furnishings', irrespective of whether or not these goods belonged to the tax debtor.... It was in the exercise of this power that the tax authorities seized the concrete-mixer to which Gasus claimed title, in partial enforcement of [the purhaser's] unpaid tax debts.

Against this background, the most natural approach, in the Court's opinion, is to examine Gasus's complaints under the head of 'securing the payment of taxes', which comes under the rule in the second paragraph of Article 1. That paragraph explicitly reserves the right of Contracting States to pass such laws as they may deem necessary to secure the payment of taxes. The importance which the drafters of the Convention attached to this aspect of the second paragraph of Article 1 may be gauged from the fact that at a stage when the proposed text did not contain such explicit reference to taxes, it was already understood to reserve the States' power to pass whatever fiscal laws they considered desirable, provided always that measures in this field did not amount to arbitrary confiscation.

The fact that current tax legislation makes it possible for the tax authorities, on certain conditions, to recover tax debts against a third party's assets does not warrant any different conclusion as to the applicable rule. Neither does it suffice in itself to describe section 16(3) of the 1845 Act as granting powers of arbitrary confiscation.

Conferring upon a particular creditor the power to recover against goods which, although in fact in the debtor's possession, are legally owned by third parties is, in several legal systems, an accepted method of strengthening that creditor's position in enforcement proceedings. Under Netherlands law as it stood at the material time, landlords had a comparable power with respect to unpaid rent, as they did also under French and Belgian law; the Government have also cited several provisions in the tax laws of other member States that give similar powers to the tax authorities in special cases. Consequently, the fact that the Netherlands legislature has seen fit to strengthen the tax authorities' position in enforcement proceedings against tax debtors does not justify the conclusion that the 1845 Act, or section 16(3) of it, is not aimed at 'securing the payment of taxes', or that using the power conferred by that section constitutes a 'confiscation', whether 'arbitrary' or not, rather than a method of recovering a tax debt.

C. Compliance with the conditions laid down in the second paragraph

60. As follows from the previous paragraph, the present case concerns the right of States to enact such laws as they deem necessary for the purpose of 'securing the payment of taxes'. In the present case the Court is not called upon to ascertain whether this right, as the wording of the provision may suggest, is limited to procedural tax laws (that is to say: laws which regulate the formalities of taxation, including the enforcement of tax debts) or whether it also covers substantive tax laws (that is to say: laws which lay down the circumstances under which tax is due and the amounts payable); the 1845 Act, which is at issue in the present case, was plainly a procedural tax law.

In passing such laws the legislature must be allowed a wide margin of appreciation, especially with regard to the question whether—and if so, to what extent—the tax authorities should be put in a better position to enforce tax debts than ordinary creditors are in to enforce commercial debts. The Court will respect the legislature's assessment in such matters unless it is devoid of reasonable foundation.

61. Section 16(3) of the 1845 Act gave the tax authorities the power to recover tax debts against certain goods which, although in fact in the possession of their debtor—since they were on his premises and served as 'furnishings'—were owned, as a matter of law, by a third party. It thus dispensed the tax authorities from having to consider whether these goods were actually the property of the tax debtor. The purpose of the provision was obviously to facilitate the enforcement of tax debts, which in itself is clearly in the general interest.

It is true that the 1961 Guidelines curtailed the tax authorities' powers under section 16(3). As restricted by those guidelines, section 16(3) empowered the tax authorities to recover only certain tax debts—including those such as the ones owed by [the purchaser]—against 'furnishings' owned by third parties where third-party ownership was intended solely to frustrate recovery against the tax debtor or to afford the third party a preferential right of recovery over the goods concerned.... This, however, did not affect the essential aim of section 16(3), which remained, as was stressed by the Government, to secure tax revenue in the general interest.

62. According to the Court's well-established case-law, the second paragraph of Article 1 of Protocol No. 1 must be construed in the light of the principle laid down in the Article's first sentence. Consequently, an interference must achieve a 'fair balance' between the demands of the general interest of the community and the requirements of the protection of the individual's fundamental rights. The concern to achieve this balance is reflected in the structure of Article 1 as a whole, including the second paragraph: there must therefore be a reasonable relationship of proportionality between the means employed and the aim pursued.

63. Gasus stressed that they had been deprived of their property in payment of a tax debt owed by a third party, the Netherlands company. They pointed out that they were in no way

responsible for causing the tax debt. Moreover, they could not possibly have been aware of it, since in the Netherlands the tax authorities were not allowed to give such information to anyone but the actual debtor. Finally, the fact that the fiduciary title—to goods not considered 'furnishings'—of one of [the purchaser's] bankers had been respected, whereas Gasus's retention of title had not, demonstrated that the interference with Gasus's rights had been arbitrary. In their submission, retention of title was closer to 'true' ownership than fiduciary title was. The latter involved transfer of ownership from a borrower, who remained entitled to use and often even to sell the goods, to a lender who had never had any interest of his own in the goods. Retention of title, on the other hand, was the continuation of the ownership of the former owner until the purchaser had fulfilled his obligations.

64. In the opinion of the Commission, the measure in issue had been taken in accordance with specific rules of Netherlands law. Consequently, the applicant company could have taken these rules into account, if need be with appropriate legal advice; they could have decided not to sell the concrete-mixer at all, or they could have limited their risk by negotiating 'specific security' in addition to the retention of their title or by taking out insurance.

65. The Government preferred to view the case as one concerning the conflicting interests of creditors faced with a common debtor whose assets were insufficient to satisfy them all. Although Netherlands law theoretically recognised the principle of paritas creditorum, it had, like other legal systems, created priority rights favouring certain creditors over others and had ranked the rights of the tax authorities very high. According to the report of the Interdepartmental Working Party... which the Government submitted to the Court, both the high rank of the tax authorities' priority right and their extensive rights of seizure were justified by, inter alia, the following differences between the tax authorities and private creditors: the tax authorities did not choose their debtors; they were expected to show greater leniency than other creditors and were enabled by their priority right (which ensured that tax debts would be paid in any case) to be flexible as regards both the timing of assessments and the collection of the amount due; they were obliged to grant credit; and they were not able to make allowance for the risk that the parties they dealt with might prove insolvent. In addition commercial creditors could in many cases obtain a higher preference by entering into agreements like fiduciary transfer of ownership and retention of title, and the right to seize goods nominally belonging to third parties served to correct the imbalance thereby created.... Finally, the Government recalled that Gasus had retained their claim against [the purchaser] for payment of the purchase price. This meant that Gasus had not been left empty-handed. Although [the] bankruptcy had deprived the claim of its value, that was not a state of affairs for which the Government could be held responsible.

66. The Court notes at the outset that the grant to the tax authorities of a power to recover tax debts against goods owned by certain third parties—such as a seller of goods who retains his title—does not in itself prompt the conclusion that a fair balance between the general interest and the protection of the individual's fundamental rights has not been achieved. The power of recovery against goods which are in fact in a debtor's possession although nominally owned by a third party is a not uncommon device to strengthen a creditor's position in enforcement proceedings; it cannot be held incompatible per se with the requirements of Article 1 of Protocol No. 1. Consequently, a legislature may in principle resort to that device to ensure, in the general interest, that taxation yields as much as possible and that tax debts are recovered as expeditiously as possible. Nonetheless, it cannot be overlooked that, quite apart from the

dangers of abuse, the character of legislation by which the State creates such powers for itself is not the same as that of legislation granting similar powers to narrowly defined categories of private creditors. Consequently, further examination of the issue of proportionality is necessary in this case.

67. In this connection, the Court also notes that in assessing the proportionality of the powers under section 16(3) and their use in the present case it is immaterial that Gasus were a limited company with legal personality under German law and had their registered office in Germany. Gasus had sold and delivered their concrete-mixer to a purchaser based in the Netherlands and installed it on his premises. Gasus could therefore not have expected otherwise than that the effectiveness of their retention of title in the face of seizure depended on Netherlands law. It consequently makes no difference whether a seller who retains title and who finds himself a victim of use by the tax authorities of their power under section 16(3) has his domicile or registered office in the Netherlands or elsewhere. In either case the essential question must be whether as a consequence of the tax authorities' actions against the goods to which title has been retained the vendor has had to bear 'an individual and excessive burden'.

68. Whatever the nature of retention of title compared with 'true' or 'ordinary' property rights—a question on which the Court discerns no common ground among the Contracting States—it is apparent that whoever sells goods subject to retention of title is not interested so much in maintaining the link of ownership with the goods themselves as in receiving the purchase price. A State may therefore legitimately, within its margin of appreciation, differentiate between retention of title and other forms of ownership. It matters little whether such differentiation takes the form of substantive limitations of the right of ownership or is expressed in terms of procedural law; ... such a distinction may be no more than a question of legislative technique.

69. It cannot be ignored that in general the cases in which the tax authorities will make use of their high-ranking priority rights and their powers under section 16(3) of the 1845 Act are precisely those where the tax debtor is unable to satisfy all his creditors. This necessarily implies that in these cases commercial creditors will not be fully paid if they receive any payment at all. The Court therefore does not agree with the Government that the fact that the applicant company's claim against [the purchaser] was rendered worthless is not a consequence of the action taken by the tax authorities.

70. It is nonetheless true, as observed by the Commission, that the applicant company were engaged in a commercial venture which, by its very nature, involved an element of risk. The facts of the case show that Gasus were in fact sufficiently aware of their risk to take steps to limit it. Having allowed Atlas to pay the purchase price of the concrete-mixer in instalments, and being aware of the danger that Atlas might default on its payments, Gasus reserved their title to the concrete-mixer until the full price had been paid. This, under Netherlands law, provided them with a considerable degree of security, as their claims to the concrete-mixer thus took priority over those of all other creditors except the tax authorities, who were entitled under section 16(3) of the 1845 Act to seize it and take the proceeds for the State. Like the Commission, the Court considers that Gasus could have eliminated their risk altogether by declining to extend credit to Atlas: they could have stipulated payment of the entire purchase price in advance or else refused to sell the concrete-mixer in the first place. It also accepts that the applicant company might have obtained additional security, for example in the form of insurance or a banker's guarantee, which pass the risk on to another party.

It is therefore unnecessary for the Court to establish whether the applicant company could have ascertained the existence and extent of [the purchaser's] tax debts, this point being in dispute. Nor is it material that the applicant company bore no responsibility for the tax debt. In the present context it is not without relevance that the owners of goods subject to seizure under section 16(3) of the 1845 Act had knowingly allowed them to serve as 'furnishings' of the tax debtor's premises. They might therefore well be held responsible to some extent for enabling the tax debtor to present a semblance of creditworthiness.

71. Furthermore, whether or not the tax authorities are under any legal or other obligation to be more flexible in respect of tax debtors in temporary financial difficulties, they do not have the same means at their disposal as commercial creditors for protecting themselves against the consequences of their debtors' financial problems. Nor have they any other means of protecting themselves against their debtors' attempts to solve such problems by vesting the title to their 'furnishings' in another party as a device for borrowing against a security.

72. The Court accepts the Government's argument that the fact that the concrete-mixer to which Gasus had reserved title was seized while goods subject to NIB's fiduciary ownership rights were spared does not suffice to demonstrate that the seizure of the concrete-mixer was arbitrary. Whereas the concrete-mixer supplied by Gasus qualified as 'furnishings', this was not the case with the goods over which NIB could claim rights. This distinction was based on the law, as elucidated by a long-established body of case-law, and accorded with the stated policy of the Minister of Finance.

73. Finally, in the Court's opinion, it should be taken into account that, as was made clear by the Supreme Court in its judgment in this case, under Netherlands law third parties whose goods are seized under section 16(3) of the 1845 Act may have the use that has been made of the powers conferred by that section adequately reviewed by a tribunal under a procedure which meets the requirements of Article 6 para. 1 (art. 6-1) of the Convention.

74 In view of the above, the Court comes to the conclusion that the requirement of proportionality has been satisfied. Accordingly, there has been no violation of Article 1 of Protocol No. 1.

B. ASSESSING WHETHER AN INTERFERENCE IS JUSTIFIED: LEGAL CERTAINTY AND THE PUBLIC INTEREST

An interference with property rights will constitute a violation of Article 1 of Protocol No. 1 unless three tests can be satisfied, the onus of establishing which lies with the respondent state:

- the interference must meet the test of legal certainty;
- it must be justified by the general or public interest; and

- there must be a reasonable degree of proportionality between the means selected and the ends sought to be achieved to ensure that a fair balance between individual and collective interests has been maintained.

In practice, however, the focus is likely to be upon two questions concerned with the final test concerning a 'fair balance': whether domestic procedures have afforded the applicant a reasonable opportunity of putting his case and taken due consideration of other relevant factors to help protect against arbitrary decision-making; and whether reasonable compensation has been offered.

1. THE REQUIREMENT OF LAWFULNESS

The textual formulation provides expressly that the *deprivation* of property may take place only 'subject to the conditions provided for by law and by the general principles of international law'. The concept of legal certainty is found throughout the Convention. It is thus of little surprise that the Court has determined that the scrutiny of whether an interference with property rights has been lawful applies to all forms of interference with property rights, and not just to those falling within the second rule. Unless there is an interference with the property rights of non-nationals, however, the focus will be upon compatibility with domestic rather than with international law, for in relation to the taking by a state of property belonging to its own nationals, general principles of international law will not be applicable.[38]

The consequence is that an interference which is not authorized by domestic law will result in a violation of the Article. For example, in *Vasilescu v. Romania,* the police had searched the applicant's house without a warrant and had subsequently seized a substantial number of gold coins that had been deposited into a bank; thereafter the coins were retained even though all charges had been dropped. The state's concession that the reasons for removal of the coins had been unlawful allowed the Court to hold that the continuing retention of the items in question had amounted to a de facto confiscation not authorized by law and one that was thus incompatible with the applicant's rights to the peaceful enjoyment of her possessions.[39] However, as with the interpretation given to 'law' or 'lawful' elsewhere in the Convention, this requirement relates not only to the conformity of a measure with the provisions of domestic law but also as to whether the quality of domestic law is compatible with the rule of law. In particular, the legal justification for an interference with property rights must meet the tests of accessibility, precision and foreseeability.[40] In *Belvedere Alberghiera v. Italy,*

---

[38] *James and Others v. United Kingdom,* 21 Feb. 1986, 8 E.H.R.R. 123, paras. 64–6; *Lithgow and Others v United Kingdom, supra* n. 28, para. 112.

[39] 22 May 1998, 22 E.H.R.R. 241, paras. 48–53.

[40] *Jahn and Others v. Germany,* 22 January 2004, para. 73. [Chamber].

the owners of a hotel also owned adjacent land which gave patrons of the hotel direct access to the sea. The local authority had taken possession of the land and had started work upon a new road. It was successfully argued that Italian law on constructive expropriation had evolved in such a way as to lead to the law being applied inconsistently on occasion, and thus that application of the law could result in unforeseeable or arbitrary outcomes, a situation inconsistent with the requirement of lawfulness.[41] On the other hand, in *Spacek v. Czech Republic*, the Court accepted that the implementation of income tax legislation had sufficient legal basis in domestic law and met the requirements of accessibility and foreseeability. While the rules and regulations were not published in any official gazette in the form of a decree or ruling and so could not amount to binding legislation, the Court noted that 'the term "law" is to be understood in its substantive sense and not in its formal one'; and, further, that the Convention did not lay down any 'specific requirements as to the degree of publicity to be given to a particular legal provision'. Here, the applicant company had been aware of the ways in which the Ministry of Finance published its accounting principles, and thus at the least, should have consulted specialists about any transitional problems. Accordingly, no violation of the guarantee was established.[42]

2. DETERMINING THE 'GENERAL' OR 'PUBLIC' INTEREST FOR AN INTERFERENCE WITH PROPERTY RIGHTS

The text of Article 1 of Protocol No. 1 specifies that any deprivation of property must be in the 'public interest', and further that controls over the use of property are to be 'in accordance with the general interest' or otherwise to secure the payment of taxes or other contributions or penalties. Against this background, the recognition of a wide margin of appreciation on the part of domestic determinations is appropriate, since what an applicant is likely to be challenging in effect is the social or economic policy behind a decision affecting his property rights. Policy-making in such matters as the elimination of social injustice or the determination of the communal good is properly a responsibility of the legislature or executive; such determinations are not readily amenable to international judicial scrutiny. In consequence, what is in the 'general' interest is given the widest interpretation and, in practice, the test is restricted to assessment of whether state action can be deemed to be 'manifestly unreasonable'.[43] Thus public policy decisions such as the need for import controls[44] or for measures to

---

[41] 30 May 2000, paras. 56–8.
[42] 9 Nov. 1999, 30 E.H.R.R. 1010, paras. 54–61 at para. 57.
[43] *James and Others v. United Kingdom, supra* n. 38, at para. 49.
[44] *AGOSI v. United Kingdom, supra* n. 24, at para. 52.

deal with tax evasion[45] or the collection of taxes[46] or drug smuggling,[47] or to prevent illegal sales or uncontrolled development of land[48] are invariably respected as being for the 'public' or 'general' interest. Equally, steps taken with a view to complying with European Union law[49] and implementation of planning and other infrastructure decisions in the areas of licensing,[50] town planning,[51] road improvements,[52] or environmental protection will readily be held to be in pursuance of the general interest.[53]

3. JAMES AND OTHERS V. UNITED KINGDOM

Judgment of 21 February 1986
8 E.H.R.R. 123

[The Leasehold Reform Act 1967 conferred upon tenants of houses held on 'long leases' (over, or renewed for periods totalling over, 21 years) the right to purchase compulsorily the freehold of the property on prescribed terms subject to certain prescribed conditions: in essence, tenants were entitled to become full owners of their properties. The applicants were the trustees of the late Duke of Westminster whose family owned some two thousand houses in central London. They complained that the statute had deprived them, as trustees, of their ownership of a number of properties through the exercise by the occupants of rights of acquisition conferred by the statute.]

2. 'In the public interest': private individuals as beneficiaries

39. The applicants' first contention was that the 'public interest' test in the deprivation rule is satisfied only if the property is taken for a public purpose of benefit to the community generally and that, as a corollary, the transfer of property from one person to another for the latter's private benefit alone can never be 'in the public interest'. In their submission, the contested legislation does not satisfy this condition. The Commission and the Government, on the other hand, were agreed in thinking that a compulsory transfer of property from one individual to another may in principle be considered to be 'in the public interest' if the taking is effected in pursuance of legitimate social policies.

[45] *Gasus Dosier und Fördertechnik v. Netherlands, supra* n. 10, at para. 61.
[46] *National and Provincial Building Society v. United Kingdom*, 23 Oct. 1997, 25 E.H.R.R. 127, at para. 79.
[47] *Air Canada v. United Kingdom*, 5 May 1995, 20 E.H.R.R. 150, at paras. 41–2.
[48] *Holy Monasteries v. Greece*, 9 Dec. 1994, 20 E.H.R.R. 1, at para. 69.
[49] In *Bosphorus Hava Yolları Turizm ve Ticaret Anonim Şirketi v. Ireland* [G.C.], 30 June 2005, 42 E.H.R.R. 1, the seizure of an aircraft leased from Yugoslav Airlines pursuant to a European Community Council regulation implementing sanctions agreed to by the United Nations against the former Federal Republic of Yugoslavia was ruled by the Grand Chamber not to have involved a violation of the Article as the interference with the applicant's property right had been effected pursuant to the state's obligation to comply with EU law, in itself a legitimate aim.
[50] *Tre Traktörer v. Sweden, supra* n. 32, at para. 57.
[51] *Allan Jacobbson v. Sweden*, 28 Oct. 1989, 12 E.H.R.R. 56, at para. 57.
[52] *Tsomtsos and Others v. Greece*, 15 Nov. 1996, at para. 36.
[53] *Pine Valley Developments and Others v. Ireland, supra* n. 32, at para. 57.

40. The Court agrees with the applicants that a deprivation of property effected for no reason other than to confer a private benefit on a private party cannot be 'in the public interest'. Nonetheless, the compulsory transfer of property from one individual to another may, depending upon the circumstances, constitute a legitimate means for promoting the public interest. In this connection, even where the texts in force employ expressions like 'for the public use', no common principle can be identified in the constitutions, legislation and case-law of the Contracting States that would warrant understanding the notion of public interest as outlawing compulsory transfer between private parties. The same may be said of certain other democratic countries; thus, the applicants and the Government cited in argument a judgment of the Supreme Court of the United States of America, which concerned State legislation in Hawaii compulsorily transferring title in real property from lessors to lessees in order to reduce the concentration of land ownership (Hawaii Housing Authority v. Midkiff 104 S.Ct. 2321 [1984]).

41. Neither can it be read into the English expression 'in the public interest' that the transferred property should be put into use for the general public or that the community generally, or even a substantial proportion of it, should directly benefit from the taking. The taking of property in pursuance of a policy calculated to enhance social justice within the community can properly be described as being 'in the public interest'. In particular, the fairness of a system of law governing the contractual or property rights of private parties is a matter of public concern and therefore legislative measures intended to bring about such fairness are capable of being 'in the public interest', even if they involve the compulsory transfer of property from one individual to another.

42. The expression 'pour cause d'utilité publique' used in the French text of Article 1 may indeed be read as having the narrow sense argued by the applicants, as is shown by the domestic law of some, but not all, of the Contracting States where the expression or its equivalent is found in the context of expropriation of property. That, however, is not decisive, as many Convention concepts have been recognised in the Court's case-law as having an 'autonomous' meaning. Moreover, the words 'utilité publique' are also capable of bearing a wider meaning, covering expropriation measures taken in implementation of policies calculated to enhance social justice.

The Court, like the Commission, considers that such an interpretation best reconciles the language of the English and French texts, having regard to the object and purpose of Article 1, which is primarily to guard against the arbitrary confiscation of property.

43. The applicants submitted that the use in the same context of different phrases — 'public interest' in the first paragraph of Article 1 and 'general interest' in the second paragraph — should, according to a generally recognised principle of treaty interpretation, be assumed to indicate an intention to refer to different concepts. They construed Article 1 as granting the State more latitude to control the use of someone's property than to take it away from him.

In the Court's opinion, even if there could be differences between the concepts of 'public interest' and 'general interest' in Article 1, on the point under consideration no fundamental distinction of the kind contended for by the applicants can be drawn between them.

44. The applicants accepted that measures designed to ensure equitable distribution of economic advantages, for example by way of taxation, are licensed by Article 1, but, so they argued, solely by the second paragraph and not by the first paragraph. The Court, however,

sees no cogent reason why a State should be prohibited under Article 1 from implementing such a policy by resort to deprivation of property.

45. For these reasons, the Court comes to the same conclusion as the Commission: a taking of property effected in pursuance of legitimate social, economic or other policies may be 'in the public interest', even if the community at large has no direct use or enjoyment of the property taken. The leasehold reform legislation is not therefore ipso facto an infringement of Article 1 on this ground. Accordingly, it is necessary to inquire whether in other respects the legislation satisfied the 'public interest' test and the remaining requirements laid down in the second sentence of Article 1.

3. Whether the leasehold reform legislation complied with the 'public interest' test and the remaining requirements of the deprivation rule

(a) Margin of appreciation

46. Because of their direct knowledge of their society and its needs, the national authorities are in principle better placed than the international judge to appreciate what is 'in the public interest'. Under the system of protection established by the Convention, it is thus for the national authorities to make the initial assessment both of the existence of a problem of public concern warranting measures of deprivation of property and of the remedial action to be taken. Here, as in other fields to which the safeguards of the Convention extend, the national authorities accordingly enjoy a certain margin of appreciation.

Furthermore, the notion of 'public interest' is necessarily extensive. In particular, as the Commission noted, the decision to enact laws expropriating property will commonly involve consideration of political, economic and social issues on which opinions within a democratic society may reasonably differ widely. The Court, finding it natural that the margin of appreciation available to the legislature in implementing social and economic policies should be a wide one, will respect the legislature's judgment as to what is 'in the public interest' unless that judgment be manifestly without reasonable foundation. In other words, although the Court cannot substitute its own assessment for that of the national authorities, it is bound to review the contested measures under Article 1 of Protocol No. 1 and, in so doing, to make an inquiry into the facts with reference to which the national authorities acted.

(b) Whether the aim of the contested legislation was a legitimate one, in principle and on the facts

47. The aim of the 1967 Act, as spelt out in the 1966 White Paper, was to right the injustice which was felt to be caused to occupying tenants by the operation of the long leasehold system of tenure. The Act was designed to reform the existing law, said to be 'inequitable to the leaseholder', and to give effect to what was described as the occupying tenant's 'moral entitlement' to ownership of the house.

Eliminating what are judged to be social injustices is an example of the functions of a democratic legislature. More especially, modern societies consider housing of the population to be a prime social need, the regulation of which cannot entirely be left to the play of market forces. The margin of appreciation is wide enough to cover legislation aimed at securing greater social justice in the sphere of people's homes, even where such legislation interferes with existing contractual relations between private parties and confers no direct benefit on the State or the community at large. In principle, therefore, the aim pursued by the leasehold reform legislation is a legitimate one.

48. The applicants suggested that the 1967 Act was not enacted for purposes of public benefit but was in reality motivated by purely political considerations as a vote-seeking measure by the Labour Government then in office.

The Court notes, however, that leasehold reform in England and Wales had been a matter of public concern for almost a century and that, when the 1967 Act was passed, enfranchisement was accepted as a principle by all the major political parties, although they expressed different views as to how it should be implemented. It was not disputed by the applicants that the main criticisms now made by them of the substantive provisions of the legislation were voiced at the time and fully debated in Parliament before being rejected. The Court does not find that such political considerations as may have influenced the legislative process, socio-economic legislation being bound to reflect political attitudes to a greater or lesser degree, precluded the objective pursued by the 1967 Act from being a legitimate one 'in the public interest'.

Similar reasoning applies to the applicants' claim that the amendment introduced by the Conservative Government in 1974, whereby a small percentage of more valuable dwelling-houses were for the first time brought within the scope of the legislation, 'was born of political expediency alone'.

49. The applicants further disputed the existence of any problem justifying legislation. According to the applicants, the long leasehold system of tenure, certainly as far as premium leases were concerned, did not in fact suffer from any unfairness and it could not be said that the tenant had any 'moral entitlement' to ownership of the house merely by reason of occupying a house built, repaired or improved by previous tenants in accordance with the contractual terms of a lease.

As stated above (at paragraph 46), the Court has jurisdiction to inquire into the factual basis of the justification pleaded by the respondent Government. That review, however, is limited to determining whether the legislature's assessment of the relevant social and economic conditions came within the State's margin of appreciation. The Government conceded that the convictions on which the 1967 Act was based were by no means universally shared; and this is borne out by the 1962 White Paper. As the Commission observed in its report, the justice or injustice of the leasehold system and the respective 'moral entitlements' of tenants and landlords are matters of judgment on which there is clearly room for legitimate conflict of opinions. The applicants' views cannot be qualified as groundless. Nonetheless, there is sufficient evidence to justify the contrary views. In a building lease the original tenant will have built the house, in a premium lease he will have paid an initial capital sum which typically took account of the building cost, and in both kinds of lease the tenant will have been responsible for all running repairs. This means that the long-leasehold tenant and his predecessors will over the years have invested a considerable amount of money in the house which is their home, whereas the landlord will normally have made no contribution towards its maintenance subsequent to the granting of the original lease.

The Court therefore agrees with the Commission's conclusion: the United Kingdom Parliament's belief in the existence of a social injustice was not such as could be characterised as manifestly unreasonable.

Note the Court's citation of the United States Supreme Court judgment in *Hawaii Housing Authority v. Midkiff*[54] in which it held that the state of Hawaii could use its eminent domain power to acquire property for the purpose of reducing the extreme concentration of land ownership. In that case the state had determined that 47% of all real property was in the hands of 72 owners. The Court refused to substitute its judgment for the legislature's in determining what constituted a public use 'unless the use be palpably without reasonable foundation'.[55] This deferential approach was reaffirmed in *Kelo v. City of New London*, a controversial 5-4 decision, upholding the condemnation of private homes for the construction of a private pharmaceutical plant as part of a larger economic development plan.[56]

4. STRAN GREEK REFINERIES AND STRATIS ANDREADIS V. GREECE

Judgment of 9 December 1994
19 E.H.R.R. 293

[During the period of military dictatorship in Greece, the Government entered into a contract with the applicant company (which was wholly owned by the second applicant) for the construction of a crude oil refinery. This contract was ratified by legislative decree. After the reestablishment of democracy, the new Government terminated the contract on the ground that it was contrary to the economic interests of the state. This in turn resulted in significant financial loss to the company. The resultant legal dispute was determined by an arbitration court in favour of the company, a decision upheld upon appeal ('judgment no. 13910/79'). While a further appeal was still pending in the Court of Cassation, the Government secured the enactment of legislation ('Law no. 1701/1987') annulling the arbitration award in the company's favour.]

1. Whether there was a 'possession' within the meaning of Article 1

...

59. In order to determine whether the applicants had a 'possession' for the purposes of Article 1 of Protocol No. 1, the Court must ascertain whether judgment no. 13910/79 of the Athens Court of First Instance and the arbitration award had given rise to a debt in their favour that was sufficiently established to be enforceable.

60. In the nature of things, a preliminary decision prejudges the merits of a dispute by ordering an investigative measure. Although the Athens Court of First Instance would appear to have accepted the principle that the State owed a debt to the applicants—as the Commission likewise noted—, it nevertheless ordered that witnesses be heard before ruling on the existence

---

[54] 467 U.S. 229 (1984).

[55] *Id.* at 241 quoting *United States v. Gettysburg Electric R. Co.*, 160 U.S. 668, 680 (1896).

[56] 545 U.S. 469 (2005).

and extent of the alleged damage. The effect of such a decision was merely to furnish the applicants with the hope that they would secure recognition of the claim put forward. Whether the resulting debt was enforceable would depend on any review by two superior courts.

61. This is not the case with regard to the arbitration award, which clearly recognised the State's liability up to a maximum of specified amounts in three different currencies.

The Court agrees with the Government that it is not its task to approve or disapprove the substance of that award. It is, however, under a duty to take note of the legal position established by that decision in relation to the parties.

According to its wording, the award was final and binding; it did not require any further enforcement measure and no ordinary or special appeal lay against it. Under Greek legislation arbitration awards have the force of final decisions and are deemed to be enforceable. The grounds for appealing against them are exhaustively listed in Article 897 of the Code of Civil Procedure...; no provision is made for an appeal on the merits.

62. At the moment when Law no. 1701/1987 was passed the arbitration award of 27 February 1984 therefore conferred on the applicants a right in the sums awarded. Admittedly, that right was revocable, since the award could still be annulled, but the ordinary courts had by then already twice held—at first instance and on appeal—that there was no ground for such annulment. Accordingly, in the Court's view, that right constituted a 'possession' within the meaning of Article 1 of Protocol No. 1.

2. Whether there was an interference

63. In the applicants' submission, although no property was transferred to the State, [the effect of the legislation] resulted in a de facto deprivation of their possessions because the result was literally to cancel the debt arising out of a final and binding arbitration award.

64. The Commission considered this to be an infringement of the right to the peaceful enjoyment of possessions within the meaning of the first sentence of the first paragraph of Article 1 of Protocol No. 1.

65. The Government accepted neither of these views. They maintained that paragraph 2 of Article 12 [of Law No. 1701/1987] merely described an inevitable consequence of paragraph 1 and had no independent meaning. In this connection they cited their arguments in relation to Article 6 of the Convention, affirming more specifically that paragraph 2 of Article 12 had no autonomous existence because it presupposed judicial examination of the nullity referred to in paragraph 1 and merely set out the evident consequences of such nullity. The Government added that paragraph 3 introduced a measure whose constitutionality had not been assessed by the national courts, before which an action brought by the applicants was still pending, and that a new action was always possible if the applicants' withdrawal from the first one led to its discontinuance. However, in the latter situation the applicants would encounter the problem of failure to exhaust domestic remedies.

66. The Court finds that there was an interference with the applicants' right of property as guaranteed by Article 1 of Protocol No. 1. Paragraph 2 of Article 12 of Law no. 1701/1987 declared the arbitration award void and unenforceable. Paragraph 3 provided that any claim against the State arising from contracts like those concluded by the applicants was statute-barred. Admittedly the Court of Cassation left open the question of the constitutionality of paragraph 3 and the applicants theoretically have the possibility, as the Government argued,

of pursuing their 1978 action or bringing a new one. However, the prospects of success of such a step appear minimal. Indeed the question arises whether a first-instance court would go so far as to hold this paragraph to be unconstitutional on the basis of general and abstract provisions of the Constitution..., in the light in particular of the [decisions of the Court of Cassation which] had the effect of closing the proceedings in issue once and for all, which was the real objective of the legislature in enacting Article 12. This may be seen from the actual wording of paragraph 4, which was intended to bring to a conclusion the sole dispute of this nature pending before the courts at the time, namely that between the applicants and the State, and from the wording of paragraph 3, which was designed to exclude any future action.

67. It follows that it was impossible for the applicants to secure enforcement of an arbitration award having final effect and under which the State was required to pay them specified sums in respect of expenditure that they had incurred in seeking to fulfil their contractual obligations or even for them to take further action to recover the sums in question through the courts.

In conclusion, there was an interference with the applicants' property right.

3. Whether the interference was justified

68. The interference in question was neither an expropriation nor a measure to control the use of property; it falls to be dealt with under the first sentence of the first paragraph of Article 1.

69. The Court must therefore determine whether a fair balance was struck between the demands of the general interest of the community and the requirements of the protection of the individual's fundamental rights.

70. According to the Government, Laws nos. 141/1975 and 1701/1987 pursued a public interest aim which in the specific context was of much broader significance than the mere elimination of the economic consequences of the dictatorship. These laws were part of a body of measures designed to cleanse public life of the disrepute attaching to the military regime and to proclaim the power and the will of the Greek people to defend the democratic institutions. The applicants' complaints derived from a preferential contract, prejudicial to the national economy, which had helped to sustain the regime and to give the impression at national and international level that it had the support of eminent figures from the Greek business world. The period that had elapsed between the restoration of democracy and the enactment of Law no. 1701/1987, the State's decision to opt for arbitration—a step of a purely technical nature—and the fact that Stran's claims related solely to the reimbursement of its expenses were immaterial.

71. The applicants did not contest the Government's assertion that the brutal practices of the military regime weighed more heavily on the scales of public interest than claims based on transactions concluded with that regime. However, the public interest that the Court was called upon to assess in the case before it was a different one. It would be unjust if every legal relationship entered into with a dictatorial regime was regarded as invalid when the regime came to an end. Moreover, the contract in question related to the construction of an oil refinery, which was of benefit to the economic infrastructure of the country.

72. The Court does not doubt that it was necessary for the democratic Greek State to terminate a contract which it considered to be prejudicial to its economic interests. Indeed according to the case-law of international courts and of arbitration tribunals any State has

a sovereign power to amend or even terminate a contract concluded with private individuals, provided it pays compensation. This both reflects recognition that the superior interests of the State take precedence over contractual obligations and takes account of the need to preserve a fair balance in a contractual relationship. However, the unilateral termination of a contract does not take effect in relation to certain essential clauses of the contract, such as the arbitration clause. To alter the machinery set up by enacting an authoritative amendment to such a clause would make it possible for one of the parties to evade jurisdiction in a dispute in respect of which specific provision was made for arbitration.

73. In this connection, the Court notes that the Greek legal system recognises the principle that arbitration clauses are autonomous and that the Athens Court of First Instance, the Athens Court of Appeal and, it would appear, the judge-rapporteur of the Court of Cassation applied this principle in the present case. Moreover the two courts found that the applicants' claims originating before the termination of the contract were not invalidated thereby.

The State was therefore under a duty to pay the applicants the sums awarded against it at the conclusion of the arbitration procedure, a procedure for which it had itself opted and the validity of which had been accepted until the day of the hearing in the Court of Cassation.

74. By choosing to intervene at that stage of the proceedings in the Court of Cassation by a law which invoked the termination of the contract in question in order to declare void the arbitration clause and to annul the arbitration award of 27 February 1984, the legislature upset, to the detriment of the applicants, the balance that must be struck between the protection of the right of property and the requirements of public interest.

75. There has accordingly been a violation of Article 1 of Protocol No. 1 .

5. BEYELER V. ITALY

[G.C.] Judgment of 5 January 2000
33 E.H.R.R. 52

[The applicant had purchased, through an intermediary agent, the painting 'Portrait of a Young Peasant' by Vincent Van Gogh, a painting previously declared by the Government as being a work of cultural significance within the meaning of a 1939 statute. The painting had been in the applicant's possession for several years before the state exercised its right of pre-emption. This had the legal effect of rendering the sale null and void. The Grand Chamber of the Court had to address the question whether the applicant in the circumstances could claim the protection of Article 1 of Protocol No 1.]

99. The Court notes that the parties disagreed as to whether the applicant had a property interest eligible for protection under Article 1 of Protocol No. 1. Accordingly, the Court must determine whether Mr Beyeler's legal position as a result of purchasing the painting was such as to attract the application of Article 1.

100. The Government and the Commission were of the opinion that the applicant had never become the owner of the painting. In that connection the Court points out that the concept of 'possessions' in the first part of Article 1 has an autonomous meaning which is not limited to

ownership of physical goods and is independent from the formal classification in domestic law: certain other rights and interests constituting assets can also be regarded as 'property rights', and thus as 'possessions' for the purposes of this provision. The issue that needs to be examined is whether the circumstances of the case, considered as a whole, conferred on the applicant title to a substantive interest protected by Article 1 of Protocol No. 1. The Court considers that that approach requires it to take account of the following points of law and of fact.

101. Under Article 1706 of the Italian Civil Code the sale of movable property, such as the painting at issue, through an indirect agency arrangement automatically transfers title to the property to the principal, who can then claim it from the agent.... Where the property is considered to be of cultural or artistic interest, those rules are qualified by the authorities' right of pre-emption which has to be exercised within the time-limit laid down by Law no. 1089 of 1939. Section 61 of that statute provides that transfers and other legal transactions effected in breach of the rules laid down by the statute or without complying with the prescribed terms and conditions shall be null and void.

102. The *Consiglio di Stato* [administrative appeal court] held, in its judgment of 19 October 1990, that the Ministry's exercise of its right of pre-emption fell into the category of expropriation measures and that that form of expropriation was made against the 'real owner' of the property. On the facts, it held that the administrative authorities had not erred in serving the pre-emption order on the applicant as the end purchaser. The Court of Cassation, for its part, reiterated in its order of 11 November 1993 and its judgment of 16 November 1995 the *Consiglio di Stato's* finding that the authorities had not exercised their right of pre-emption until they were certain that the painting had been purchased by the applicant....

103. The Court notes that in 1988 the pre-emption order was served on the applicant as the title-holder on the 1977 sale and that the sum paid at that time was paid to him, which contradicts the Government's submission that on the exercise of a right of pre-emption the price is paid to the vendor.

104. Between the purchase of the work and the exercise by the State of its right of pre-emption, that is, during the period in which the applicant was implicitly subject to the pre-emption rules, the applicant was in possession of the painting for several years. Furthermore, on a number of occasions the applicant appears to have been considered *de facto* by the authorities as having a proprietary interest in the painting, and even as its real owner [...]

105. In the Court's view, those factors prove that the applicant had a proprietary interest recognised under Italian law—even if it was revocable in certain circumstances—from the time the work was purchased until the right of pre-emption was exercised and he was paid compensation (a measure classified by the *Consiglio di Stato* as falling into the category of expropriation measures). This interest therefore constituted a 'possession' for the purposes of Article 1 of Protocol No. 1. That provision is therefore applicable to the instant case.

106. Having regard to the foregoing, the Court does not consider it necessary to rule on whether the second sentence of the first paragraph of Article 1 applies in this case. The complexity of the factual and legal position prevents its being classified in a precise category. The Court does not therefore need to give an opinion on the Italian courts' view that under the relevant domestic provisions the 1977 sale should be considered as null and void. Nor does the Court need to rule on the issue whether under Italian law the applicant should be considered the real owner of the painting. Moreover, the situation envisaged in the second sentence of the

first paragraph of Article 1 is only a particular instance of interference with the right to peaceful enjoyment of property as guaranteed by the general rule set forth in the first sentence. The Court therefore considers that it should examine the situation complained of in the light of that general rule. ...

D. Compliance with Article 1 of Protocol No. 1

2. Compliance with the principle of lawfulness

108. The Court reiterates that an essential condition for an interference to be deemed compatible with Article 1 of Protocol No. 1 is that it should be lawful. '[T]he first and most important requirement of Article 1 of Protocol No. 1 is that any interference by a public authority with the peaceful enjoyment of possessions should be lawful'. The Court has limited power, however, to review compliance with domestic law, especially as there is nothing in the instant case from which it can conclude that the Italian authorities applied the legal provisions in question manifestly erroneously or so as to reach arbitrary conclusions. In that connection the Court also observes that the applicant's allegations of non-compliance with the procedure set forth in Article 67 of Royal Decree no. 363 of 1913 do not appear to be relevant, since that provision refers to public-interest declarations made prior to expropriations effected in accordance with a procedure analogous to that provided for in Law no. 2359 of 1865, and not to declarations that a work is of interest for the artistic heritage of the nation, which are dealt with in section 3 of Law no. 1089 of 1939.

109. However, the principle of lawfulness also presupposes that the applicable provisions of domestic law be sufficiently accessible, precise and foreseeable. The Court observes that in certain respects the statute lacks clarity, particularly in that it leaves open the time-limit for the exercise of a right of pre-emption in the event of an incomplete declaration without, however, indicating how such an omission can subsequently be rectified. Indeed, this seems to have been implicitly acknowledged by the Court of Cassation in its judgment of 16 November 1995. That factor alone cannot, however, lead to the conclusion that the interference in question was unforeseeable or arbitrary and therefore incompatible with the principle of lawfulness.

110. The Court is, nonetheless, required to verify that the manner in which domestic law is interpreted and applied—even where the requirements have been complied with—does not entail consequences at variance with the Convention standards. From that stance, the element of uncertainty in the statute and the considerable latitude it affords the authorities are material considerations to be taken into account in determining whether the measure complained of struck a fair balance.

3. The aim of the interference

112. In the instant case the Court considers that the control by the State of the market in works of art is a legitimate aim for the purposes of protecting a country's cultural and artistic heritage. The Court points out in this respect that the national authorities enjoy a certain margin of appreciation in determining what is in the general interest of the community.

113. As regards works of art by foreign artists, the Court observes that the Unesco Convention of 1970 accords priority, in certain circumstances, to the ties between works of art and their country of origin. It notes, however, that the issue in this case does not concern the return of a work of art to its country of origin. That consideration apart, the Court recognises

that, in relation to works of art lawfully on its territory and belonging to the cultural heritage of all nations, it is legitimate for a State to take measures designed to facilitate in the most effective way wide public access to them, in the general interest of universal culture.

4. Whether there was a fair balance

(a) Conduct of the applicant

115. The Court notes that at the time of the 1977 sale the applicant did not disclose to the vendor that the painting had been purchased on his behalf; he was thus able to buy the painting at a lower price than he would in all certainty have had to pay if his identity had been disclosed to the vendor. In the applicant's submission, sales through an agent are common practice in the art market. However, after the sale the applicant failed to declare to the authorities that he was the end purchaser—that is, the real terms on which title to or possession of the property had been transferred—for the purposes of Law no. 1089 of 1939. On 21 November 1977 Mr Pierangeli, who had already been fully reimbursed by the applicant and had confirmed to him that he had purchased the painting on his behalf, requested in his own name a licence to export the painting, without informing the authorities of the identity of the real owner.

116. The applicant then waited six years (from 1977 to 1983) before declaring his purchase, contrary to the relevant provisions of Italian law of which he was deemed to be aware. He did not approach the authorities until December 1983 when he was intending to sell the painting to the Peggy Guggenheim Collection in Venice for 2,100,000 United States dollars. Throughout that entire period the applicant deliberately avoided any risk of a pre-emption order being made by omitting to comply with the requirements of Italian law. The Court therefore considers that the Government's submission that the applicant had not acted openly and honestly carries some weight, especially as there was nothing to prevent him from informing the authorities of the true position before 2 December 1983 in order to comply with the statutory requirements.

(b) Conduct of the authorities

117. The Court does not put in question either the right of pre-emption over works of art in itself or the State's interest in being informed of all the details of a contract, including the identity of the end purchaser on a sale through an agent, so that the authorities can decide in the full knowledge of the facts whether or not to exercise their right of pre-emption. In that connection the Court notes the Italian authorities' submission that the purchaser's nationality was a factor which could be of some importance, regard being had to the nature of the art market and to the interest in keeping certain works of art in the country.

118. If the Government's reasoning is to be followed, the relevant authorities could, as early as 1 December 1983, when the declaration was made, have relied on the applicant's failure to disclose his identity earlier. They could have considered that the two-month time-limit under Law no. 1089 of 1939 had not expired and exercised their right of pre-emption by paying the 600,000,000 Italian lire paid by the applicant. It should be noted that the applicant invited the Ministry as early as 2 December 1983, when Mr Pierangeli and the applicant informed it that the Peggy Guggenheim Collection in Venice was intending to purchase the painting, to indicate whether it wished to exercise its right of pre-emption.

119. However, after receiving in 1983 the information missing from the declaration made in 1977, that is, the identity of the end purchaser, the Italian authorities waited until 1988 before giving serious consideration to the question of ownership of the painting and deciding

to exercise their right of pre-emption. During that time the authorities' attitude towards the applicant oscillated between ambivalence and assent and they often treated him de facto as the legitimate title-holder under the 1977 sale. Furthermore, the considerable latitude left to the authorities under the applicable provisions, as interpreted by the domestic courts, and the above-mentioned lack of clarity in the law made the situation even more uncertain, to the applicant's detriment. That situation allowed the authorities in 1988 to justify exercising the right of pre-emption much later than both the allegedly invalid sale in 1977 and the time (at the end of 1983) when they became aware that the applicant was the true title-holder under the original sale. As the Court of Cassation noted in its order of 11 November 1993, if the authorities could exercise their right of pre-emption at any time the seller's rights would always be restricted, thus creating continual uncertainty as to the legal position with regard to the work.

5. Conclusion

120. The Court considers that the Government have failed to give a convincing explanation as to why the Italian authorities had not acted at the beginning of 1984 in the same manner as they acted in 1988, regard being had in particular to the fact that, under section 61(2) of Law no. 1089 of 1939, they could have intervened at any time from the end of 1983 onwards and in respect of anyone 'in possession' of the property (and thus without needing first to determine who the owner of the painting was). That is, moreover, apparent from the judgment of the Court of Cassation of 16 November 1995. Thus, taking punitive action in 1988 on the ground that the applicant had made an incomplete declaration, a fact of which the authorities had become aware almost five years earlier, hardly seems justified. In that connection it should be stressed that where an issue in the general interest is at stake it is incumbent on the public authorities to act in good time, in an appropriate manner and with utmost consistency.

121. That state of affairs allowed the Ministry of Cultural Heritage to acquire the painting in 1988 at well below its market value. Having regard to the conduct of the authorities between December 1983 and November 1988, the Court considers that they derived an unjust enrichment from the uncertainty that existed during that period and to which they had largely contributed. Irrespective of the applicant's nationality, such enrichment is incompatible with the requirement of a 'fair balance'.

122. Having regard to all the foregoing factors and to the conditions in which the right of pre-emption was exercised in 1988, the Court concludes that the applicant had to bear a disproportionate and excessive burden. There has therefore been a violation of Article 1 of Protocol No. 1.

C. ASSESSING WHETHER AN INTERFERENCE IS JUSTIFIED: PROPORTIONALITY

An interference with property must satisfy the test of proportionality: that is, there must also be 'a reasonable relationship of proportionality between the means employed and the aim sought to be realised'.[57] This allows the European Court of Human Rights

---

[57] *James and Others v. United Kingdom*, *supra* n. 38, at para. 50.

to assess 'whether a fair balance was struck between the demands of the general interest of the community and the requirements of the protection of the individual's fundamental rights'.[58]

Two particular concerns in this regard are of relevance. First, the degree of protection from arbitrary decision-making that is afforded by domestic proceedings is a factor to be taken into account in the assessment of the proportionality of an interference with property rights.[59] In consequence, factors such as whether the authorities had made available information to relevant parties,[60] or the extent to which domestic decision-making processes were able to address due account of the interests of those affected are of relevance.[61] At the very least, domestic law should ensure that an owner should be aware that property interests may be affected.[62] These matters are closely allied to issues arising under Article 6's guarantee of a fair hearing, but can also be of relevance in determining whether defects such as delay in the decision-making process which results in considerable and prolonged uncertainty can support a determination under Article 1 of Protocol No. 1 that there has been a disproportionate burden placed on the applicant.[63]

Second, and more specifically, there is a strong expectation that interferences with property rights will be compensated in financial terms. While the text of the provision does not expressly provide for the payment of compensation, the Court has determined that an interference with property rights should in principle be redressed by a right of compensation.[64] This applies not only to expropriation of property, but also to other interferences with the peaceful enjoyment of possessions including 'securing the payment of taxes' which permits states to enact such fiscal legislation as they consider desirable but always provided that such measures 'do not amount to arbitrary confiscation'.[65]

---

[58] *Sporrong and Lönnroth v. Sweden*, *supra* Section A(2), at para. 69.

[59] *Hentrich v. France*, 22 Sept. 1994, 18 E.H.R.R. 440, at para. 45.

[60] *Pine Valley Developments and Others v. Ireland*, *supra* n. 32, at para 59.

[61] For example, *AGOSI v. United Kingdom*, *supra* n. 24, at paras. 54–5 (no violation established). The Court examined whether British law, which provided for the confiscation of gold coins smuggled into the country, allowed reasonable account to be taken of relevant considerations such as the degree of fault of the legal owners of the coins.

[62] *JA Pye (Oxford) Ltd and JA Pye (Oxford) Land Ltd v. United Kingdom*, 11 Nov. 2005, 43 E.H.R.R. 3, paras. 59–76 concerned loss of ownership of land by virtue of application of the doctrine of adverse possession. Notice to vacate agricultural land owned by the applicants had been served on neighbouring proprietors on the expiry of a grazing agreement, but the neighbouring proprietors had continued to use the land for grazing without permission and eventually obtained title to the land by virtue of adverse possession for the statutory period. The Chamber, by a bare majority, determined that the applicants had been deprived of their possessions, and that the lack of compensation combined with the lack of procedural guarantees—and in particular, the absence of any requirement of notification—had imposed an individual and excessive burden that upset the fair balance between the public interest and the applicants' right to peaceful enjoyment of their possessions. Note, however, that this case was pending before the grand chamber at the time of writing.

[63] *Matos e Silva and Others v. Portugal*, 16 Sept. 1996, 24 E.H.R.R. 573, at paras. 92–3 (no progress in proceedings for some 13 years); *cf. Prötsch v Austria*, 15 Nov. 1996, 32 E.H.R.R. 12, at paras. 46–8 (provisional transfer of property lasted some six years, but this was not regarded as unreasonably long in all the circumstances).

[64] *James and Others v. United Kingdom*, *supra* n. 38, at paras. 54–6.

[65] *Gasus Dosier- und Fördertechnik v Netherlands*, *supra* n. 10, at paras. 59–74 at para. 59 (citing relevant *travaux préparatoires*).

Normally, then, a failure to pay compensation of an amount reasonably related to the value of the property taken or otherwise subject to interference will normally constitute a disproportionate interference with property rights as failing to strike a 'fair balance' between community and individual interests. For example, compensation terms will appear unreasonable where these involve undue delay in payment where the real value of the compensation is significantly diminished on account of inflation.[66] However, a failure to make provision for the payment of compensation may be permissible in 'exceptional cases'. What constitutes such is not always clear.

Much of the American constitutional law of property rights, too, involves interpretation of the Fifth Amendment's bar on taking private property without just compensation. The United States Supreme Court has developed a convoluted and shifting jurisprudence on the question of when a regulation of property so limits its use as to constitute a 'taking' requiring compensation. The current doctrine is thought to be established by the Supreme Court's decision in *Lucas v. South Carolina Coastal Council*,[67] where an environmental regulation depriving a property owner of the right to erect dwellings on his coastal property was held to be a taking. In this case, the state had 'denie[d] all economically beneficial or productive use of property'. While there may have been a sufficient public justification for this restriction, the state was obliged to compensate the property owner at whose expense that end was being served.[68]

1. LITHGOW AND OTHERS V. UNITED KINGDOM

Judgment of 8 July 1986
8 E.H.R.R. 329

[Nationalization of shipbuilding and aircraft concerns was challenged upon the issue of calculation of the compensation which fell to be paid, the applicants arguing that the scheme of compensation involving the valuation of the companies by reference to their value some three years before the date of the nationalization had resulted in inadequate compensation. The Government answered that the aim had been to arrive at a value which discounted the pending nationalization rather than paying additional compensation in respect of the increase in market value resulting from the future transfer. In response, the applicants suggested that the date of transfer should be the relevant date for valuation purposes in international law.]

C. 'General principles of international law'

111. The applicants argued that the reference in the second sentence of Article 1 to 'the general principles of international law' meant that the international law requirement of, so

---

[66] E.g., *Akkus v. Turkey*, 9 July 1997, 30 E.H.R.R. 365, at paras. 42–50 at para. 47.

[67] 505 U.S. 1003 (1992).

[68] *Id.* The Supreme Court has, on the other hand, held that rent control ordinances did not necessarily effect a compensable taking. *Pennell v. San Jose*, 485 U.S. 1 (1988).

they asserted, prompt, adequate and effective compensation for the deprivation of property of foreigners also applied to nationals.

112. The Commission has consistently held that the principles in question are not applicable to a taking by a State of the property of its own nationals. The Government supported this opinion. The Court likewise agrees with it for the reasons which are already set out in its above-mentioned James and Others judgment and are repeated here, mutatis mutandis.

113. In the first place, purely as a matter of general international law, the principles in question apply solely to non-nationals. They were specifically developed for the benefit of non-nationals. As such, these principles did not relate to the treatment accorded by States to their own nationals.

114. In support of their argument, the applicants relied first on the actual text of Article 1. In their submission, since the second sentence opened with the words 'No one', it was impossible to construe that sentence as meaning that whereas everyone was entitled to the safeguards afforded by the phrases 'in the public interest' and 'subject to the conditions provided for by law', only non-nationals were entitled to the safeguards afforded by the phrase 'subject to the conditions provided for by the general principles of international law'. They further pointed out that where the authors of the Convention intended to differentiate between nationals and non-nationals, they did so expressly, as was exemplified by Article 16.

Whilst there is some force in the applicants' argument as a matter of grammatical construction, there are convincing reasons for a different interpretation. Textually the Court finds it more natural to take the reference to the general principles of international law in Article 1 of Protocol No. 1 to mean that those principles are incorporated into that Article, but only as regards those acts to which they are normally applicable, that is to say acts of a State in relation to non-nationals. Moreover, the words of a treaty should be understood to have their ordinary meaning (see Article 31 of the 1969 Vienna Convention on the Law of Treaties), and to interpret the phrase in question as extending the general principles of international law beyond their normal sphere of applicability is less consistent with the ordinary meaning of the terms used, notwithstanding their context.

115. The applicants also referred to arguments to the effect that, on the Commission's interpretation, the reference in Article 1 to the general principles of international law would be redundant since non-nationals already enjoyed the protection thereof.

The Court does not share this view. The inclusion of the reference can be seen to serve at least two purposes. Firstly, it enables non-nationals to resort directly to the machinery of the Convention to enforce their rights on the basis of the relevant principles of international law, whereas otherwise they would have to seek recourse to diplomatic channels or to other available means of dispute settlement to do so. Secondly, the reference ensures that the position of non-nationals is safeguarded, in that it excludes any possible argument that the entry into force of Protocol No. 1 has led to a diminution of their rights. In this connection, it is also noteworthy that Article 1 expressly provides that deprivation of property must be effected 'in the public interest': since such a requirement has always been included amongst the general principles of international law, this express provision would itself have been superfluous if Article 1 had had the effect of rendering those principles applicable to nationals as well as to non-nationals.

116. Finally, the applicants pointed out that to treat the general principles of international law as inapplicable to a taking by a State of the property of its own nationals would permit differentiation on the ground of nationality. This, they said, would be incompatible with two

provisions that are incorporated in Protocol No. 1 by virtue of Article 5 thereof: Article 1 of the Convention which obliges the Contracting States to secure to everyone within their juris- diction the rights and freedoms guaranteed and Article 14 of the Convention which enshrines the principle of non-discrimination.

As to Article 1 of the Convention, it is true that under most provisions of the Convention and its Protocols nationals and non-nationals enjoy the same protection but this does not exclude exceptions as far as this may be indicated in a particular text (see, for example, Articles 5 para. 1(f) and 16 of the Convention, Articles 3 and 4 of Protocol No. 4).

As to Article 14 of the Convention, the Court has consistently held that differences of treat- ment do not constitute discrimination if they have an 'objective and reasonable justification'.

Especially as regards a taking of property effected in the context of a social reform or an economic restructuring, there may well be good grounds for drawing a distinction between nationals and non-nationals as far as compensation is concerned. To begin with, non-nationals are more vulnerable to domestic legislation: unlike nationals, they will generally have played no part in the election or designation of its authors nor have been consulted on its adoption. Secondly, although a taking of property must always be effected in the public interest, different considerations may apply to nationals and non-nationals and there may well be legitimate rea- son for requiring nationals to bear a greater burden in the public interest than non-nationals.

117. Confronted with a text whose interpretation has given rise to such disagreement, the Court considers it proper to have recourse to the travaux préparatoires as a supplementary means of interpretation.

Examination of the travaux préparatoires reveals that the express reference to a right to compensation contained in earlier drafts of Article 1 was excluded, notably in the face of oppos- ition on the part of the United Kingdom and other States. The mention of the general principles of international law was subsequently included and was the subject of several statements to the effect that they protected only foreigners. Thus, when the German Government stated that they could accept the text provided that it was explicitly recognised that those principles involved the obligation to pay compensation in the event of expropriation, the Swedish delegation pointed out that those principles only applied to relations between a State and non-nationals. And it was then agreed, at the request of the German and Belgian delegations, that 'the general principles of international law, in their present connotation, entailed the obligation to pay compensation to non-nationals in cases of expropriation'.

Above all, in their Resolution (52) 1 of 19 March 1952 approving the text of the Protocol and opening it for signature, the Committee of Ministers expressly stated that, 'as regards Article 1, the general principles of international law in their present connotation entail the obligation to pay compensation to non-nationals in cases of expropriation'. Having regard to the negotiating history as a whole, the Court considers that this Resolution must be taken as a clear indication that the reference to the general principles of international law was not intended to extend to nationals.

The travaux préparatoires accordingly do not support the interpretation for which the appli- cants contended.

118. Finally, it has not been demonstrated that, since the entry into force of Protocol No. 1, State practice has developed to the point where it can be said that the parties to that instrument regard the reference therein to the general principles of international law as being applicable to the treatment accorded by them to their own nationals. The evidence adduced points distinctly in the opposite direction.

119. For all these reasons, the Court concludes that the general principles of international law are not applicable to a taking by a State of the property of its own nationals.

D. Entitlement to compensation

120. The question remains whether the availability and amount of compensation are material considerations under the second sentence of the first paragraph of Article 1, the text of the provision being silent on the point. The Commission, with whom both the Government and the applicants agreed, read Article 1 as in general impliedly requiring the payment of compensation as a necessary condition for the taking of property of anyone within the jurisdiction of a Contracting State.

Like the Commission, the Court observes that under the legal systems of the Contracting States, the taking of property in the public interest without payment of compensation is treated as justifiable only in exceptional circumstances not relevant for present purposes. As far as Article 1 is concerned, the protection of the right of property it affords would be largely illusory and ineffective in the absence of any equivalent principle.

In this connection, the Court recalls that not only must a measure depriving a person of his property pursue, on the facts as well as in principle, a legitimate aim 'in the public interest', but there must also be a reasonable relationship of proportionality between the means employed and the aim sought to be realised. This latter requirement was expressed in other terms in the above-mentioned Sporrong and Lönnroth judgment by the notion of the 'fair balance' that must be struck between the demands of the general interest of the community and the requirements of the protection of the individual's fundamental rights. The requisite balance will not be found if the person concerned has had to bear 'an individual and excessive burden'. Although the Court was speaking in that judgment in the context of the general rule of peaceful enjoyment of property enunciated in the first sentence of the first paragraph, it pointed out that 'the search for this balance is reflected in the structure of Article 1' as a whole.

Clearly, compensation terms are material to the assessment whether a fair balance has been struck between the various interests at stake and, notably, whether or not a disproportionate burden has been imposed on the person who has been deprived of his possessions.

E. Standard of compensation

121. The Court further accepts the Commission's conclusion as to the standard of compensation: the taking of property without payment of an amount reasonably related to its value would normally constitute a disproportionate interference which could not be considered justifiable under Article 1. Article 1 does not, however, guarantee a right to full compensation in all circumstances, since legitimate objectives of 'public interest', such as pursued in measures of economic reform or measures designed to achieve greater social justice, may call for less than reimbursement of the full market value.

In this connection, the applicants contended that, as regards the standard of compensation, no distinction could be drawn between nationalisation and other takings of property by the State, such as the compulsory acquisition of land for public purposes.

The Court is unable to agree. Both the nature of the property taken and the circumstances of the taking in these two categories of cases give rise to different considerations which may legitimately be taken into account in determining a fair balance between the public interest and the private interests concerned. The valuation of major industrial enterprises for the purpose of nationalising a whole industry is in itself a far more complex operation than, for instance, the valuation of land compulsorily acquired and normally calls for specific legislation which can be applied across the board to all the undertakings involved. Accordingly, provided always that the aforesaid fair balance is preserved, the standard of compensation required in a nationalisation case may be different from that required in regard to other takings of property.

122. Whilst not disputing that the State enjoyed a margin of appreciation in deciding whether to deprive an owner of his property, the applicants submitted that the Commission had wrongly concluded from this premise that the State also had a wide discretion in laying down the terms and conditions on which property was to be taken.

The Court is unable to accept this submission. A decision to enact nationalisation legislation will commonly involve consideration of various issues on which opinions within a democratic society may reasonably differ widely. Because of their direct knowledge of their society and its needs and resources, the national authorities are in principle better placed than the inter-national judge to appreciate what measures are appropriate in this area and consequently the margin of appreciation available to them should be a wide one. It would, in the Court's view, be artificial in this respect to divorce the decision as to the compensation terms from the actual decision to nationalise, since the factors influencing the latter will of necessity also influence the former. Accordingly, the Court's power of review in the present case is limited to ascertaining whether the decisions regarding compensation fell outside the United Kingdom's wide margin of appreciation; it will respect the legislature's judgment in this connection unless that judg-ment was manifestly without reasonable foundation.

F. Did the compensation awarded to the applicants meet the standard identified by the Court?

1. Issues common to all the applicants

(a) Approach to the case

123. The applicants criticised the Commission for having, in its report, looked solely at the compensation system, as such, established by the 1977 Act; in their view, it should rather have examined the consequences of applying that system, but had failed to do so.

The Government, on the other hand, submitted that if the valuation method laid down by the legislation were a proper one, then it would of necessity have produced compensation that was real and effective. For them, the value of nationalised property could only be determined by the application of a proper valuation method.

124. In proceedings originating in an individual application the Court has to confine itself, as far as possible, to an examination of the concrete case before it. In the present case, the appli-cants' complaint is that the 1977 Act resulted in the payment of compensation which was not reasonably related to the value of their property when it was taken. This raises issues concerning both the terms and conditions of the legislation and its effects. The Court must therefore direct its attention in the first place to the contested legislation itself, and the effects of the legislation must be considered in the context of terms and conditions which Parliament had to determine in advance and which had to be of general application to the nationalised companies.

...

G. Conclusion on Article 1 of Protocol No. 1

175. In the light of the foregoing, the Court concludes that no violation of Article 1 of Protocol No. 1 has been established in the present case.

The Court is unable to accept the applicants' contention that since the Government had recognised that 'the terms of compensation imposed by the 1977 Act were grossly unfair to some of the companies'..., it was no longer open to them to argue that fair compensation had been paid. The statement in question was made as an expression of opinion in a political context and is not conclusive for the Court in making its appreciation of the case.

2. JAHN AND OTHERS V. GERMANY

Judgments of 22 Jan 2004 and [G.C.] 30 June 2005
42 E.H.R.R. 49

[The applicants had become the owners of property as heirs of 'new settled farmers' who had obtained land specifically allocated for agricultural use in 1946 in the then Soviet-occupied zone of Germany. Prior to reunification, the parliament of the GDR (that is, of East Germany) adopted a new land-reform law in 1990 (the 'Modrow Law') which in turn had been incorporated into the legal order of the new German state upon reunification. In essence, this abolished certain restrictions on disposal of land to which these 'new farmers' had been subject by making the farmers the outright owners of land allocated to them irrespective of the use to which the land was being put at this time. Subsequently, in 1992 and after reunification, a new land-reform law resulted in the applicants having to assign their property to the tax authorities without the right to compensation, the law seeking to redress a perceived injustice that individuals who had failed to meet the original condition that land not being used for agriculture had to be returned to the authorities had unfairly benefited by becoming outright owners. The Chamber and Grand Chamber diverged on whether a 'fair balance' had been achieved: the Chamber unanimously held there had been a violation, but the Grand Chamber found (by a majority of eleven to six) that no violation had been established.]

CHAMBER JUDGMENT

B. Justification for the interference with the right of property

3. Proportionality of the interference

83. In the instant case the second Property Rights Amendment Act of 14 July 1992 does not provide for any compensation for the applicants. As it has already been established that the interference in question satisfied the condition of lawfulness and was not arbitrary, the lack of compensation does not of itself and always make the State's taking of the applicants' property unlawful.... Accordingly, it remains to be determined whether, in the context of a lawful deprivation of property, the applicants had to bear a disproportionate and excessive burden.

84. The Government contended that the interference in question had maintained a fair balance between the requirements of the general interest of the community and the requirements of the protection of the fundamental rights of the individual. In the GDR the applicants, as

heirs of the owners of land redistributed under the land reform, had not acquired a property right in the true sense of the term, but merely a right of usufruct (*Nutzungsrecht*). Under the change of possession decrees, their land should have reverted to the pool of state-owned land without compensation if the heirs were not themselves farming the land. The fact that those rules had frequently not been applied did not give the applicants a right to keep their land. Accordingly, even though they had acquired a formal title to the property, their title was uncertain and entirely illegitimate. The applicants could not expect to maintain their legal position (*Fortbestand ihrer Rechtsposition*) because the real purpose of the Modrow Law had been to ensure, as a matter of priority, that the land was used for agricultural purposes and to allow farmers, and not heirs to the land who were not themselves farming it, to become owners in the true sense of the word so that they could be integrated into the free market economy.

85. The applicants submitted that the deprivation of their property, without compensation and for the benefit of the tax authorities, had been manifestly disproportionate. In 1992 the German legislature had wrongly assumed that land acquired under the land reform did not pass to the owner's heirs. Furthermore, objectively speaking, there were no loopholes in the Modrow Law, which had aimed to re-establish the right of property for all owners of the land, including their heirs. The applicants produced declarations from former senior officials of the GDR in support of their submission. The German legislature should have respected the intention of the GDR parliament in that regard. The applicants maintained that they had been the victims of an unprecedented attack on private property and stated that some 50,000 people who had inherited land that had been acquired under the land reform had already been expropriated, without compensation, for the benefit of the tax authorities of the *Länder*.

86. The Court considers that in the instant case it is not its task to analyse the nature of the right of property that the applicants had had in the GDR as the heirs of owners of land acquired under the land reform. Those events had occurred before the Convention entered into force and in a State which was not a party to it. Moreover, it would be a pointless exercise because, whatever the restrictions on the applicants' right of property at the time might have been, they were clearly lifted by the Modrow Law, as the Federal Constitutional Court itself acknowledged in its decision of 6 October 2000.

87. However, the Court does need to examine the applicants' situation after German reunification and consider, in the light of the principles set out in paragraphs 82 and 83 above, the arguments put forward by the Government to justify depriving the applicants of their property without compensation. Those arguments are mainly based on the Federal Constitutional Court's reasoning in its decision of 6 October 2000.

88. One of the Government's central arguments was that the purpose of the second Property Rights Amendment Act of 14 July 1992, inspired by the principles laid down in the GDR by the land reform decrees and the change of possession decrees, was to put the applicants in the position they would have been in if those principles had been correctly applied at the time. The German legislature thus effectively turned the clocks back in order to prevent the applicants from obtaining, by virtue of the brevity and imprecision of the Modrow Law, unjust enrichment on account of the GDR authorities' failure to apply their own rules.

89. The Court reiterates in the first place that it has already had occasion to take account of the exceptional context of German reunification in examining cases brought before it. It is also aware of the enormous task which befell the German legislature in dealing with all the complex issues relating to the right of property at the time of transition from a socialist property regime

to a market economy system. This is particularly true of all the matters connected with liquidating the land reform, a symbol *par excellence* of the collectivist idea of ownership rights.

90. The Court cannot, however, agree with the Government's reasoning in the instant case regarding the concept of 'illegitimate' ownership, which is an eminently political concept. As the Court has already stated above, regardless of the applicants' situation before the entry into force of the Modrow Law, there is no doubt that they legally acquired full ownership of their land when that Law came into force. It was voted by the GDR parliament before the first free elections in 1990 in negotiations between the two German States during the period between the fall of the Berlin wall and the implementation of German reunification. The aim of the law was to open up the GDR to a market economy, as provided for in the State Treaty of 18 May 1990 between the FRG and the GDR on the Creation of an Economic, Currency and Social Union (see paragraph 48 above), by lifting all the restrictions encumbering land acquired under the land reform. Moreover, if one were to reason in terms of legitimacy, account would also have to be taken of the initial injustice suffered—as the Government themselves acknowledged in their pleadings—by the former owners of the land who were expropriated after 1945 as a result of the land reform. This factor may be relevant in assessing the compensation payable to the applicants.

91. In the instant case, if the German legislature's intention was to correct *ex post facto* the—in its opinion unjust—effects of the Modrow Law by passing a new law two years later, this did not pose a problem in itself. The problem was the content of the new law. In the Court's view, in order to comply with the principle of proportionality, the German legislature could not deprive the applicants of their property for the benefit of the State without making provision for them to be adequately compensated. In the present case the applicants evidently did not receive any compensation at all, however.

92. Admittedly, the second Property Rights Amendment Act did not only benefit the State, but also in some cases provided for the redistribution of land for the benefit of farmers and to the detriment of heirs to the land who had not themselves farmed it. However, the Court is required to deal only with the cases actually brought before it. In the present case the applicants, as the heirs of owners of land that had been acquired under the land reform, had had to reassign their land to the tax authorities without any compensation whatsoever.

93. Having regard to all these factors, the Court concludes that even if the circumstances pertaining to German reunification have to be regarded as exceptional, the lack of any compensation for the State's taking of the applicants' property upsets, to the applicants' detriment, the fair balance which has to be struck between the protection of property and the requirements of the general interest.

There has therefore been a violation of Article 1 of Protocol No. 1.

GRAND CHAMBER

B. Justification for the interference with the right of property

3. Proportionality of the interference

a. Recapitulation of the relevant principles

95. In the instant case the second Property Rights Amendment Act of 14 July 1992 does not provide for any form of compensation for the applicants. As it has already been established

that the interference in question satisfied the condition of lawfulness and was not arbitrary, the lack of compensation does not of itself and always make the State's taking of the applicants' property unlawful ... Accordingly, it remains to be determined whether, in the context of a lawful deprivation of property, the applicants had to bear a disproportionate and excessive burden....

c. The parties' submissions

97. The applicants asked the Court to confirm the Chamber's judgment, submitting that the deprivation of property they had suffered was manifestly disproportionate since it had been carried out without compensation, for the benefit of the tax authorities, and had been totally unjustified.

At the time of the GDR, as the heirs of owners of land acquired under the land reform, they had been the lawful owners of that land, regardless of the entries in the land register. Furthermore, objectively speaking, there had been no loopholes in the Modrow Law, which had aimed to re-establish the right of property in the true sense of the term for all owners of land acquired under the land reform, including their heirs, and to repeal once and for all (*Schlussstrichgesetz*) the contrary provisions of the GDR. The applicants produced declarations from former senior officials of the GDR, including that of the former prime minister and author of the Law, Mr Hans Modrow, in support of their submission. Lastly, the creation of a right of property in the GDR such as existed in market economy systems had even been one of the conditions required by the FRG with a view to achieving German reunification. After the first free elections of 18 March 1990 the GDR parliament, under Mr de Maizière's government, had approved the Modrow Law, as had happened after German reunification under Mr Kohl's government. The GDR, for its part, had always stressed the need to preserve the rights of owners of land acquired under the land reform. In 1992 the German legislature, by arbitrarily depriving the applicants of their inheritance, had sought to establish 'equality in injustice' (*Gleichheit im Unrecht*) by applying a policy which went even further than the one implemented at the time by the GDR authorities and was unworthy of a State governed by the rule of law.

The applicants accordingly maintained that they had been the victims of an unprecedented attack on private property, and pointed out that to date the Court had never found that the circumstances had been exceptional to the point of justifying a deprivation of property without compensation....

98. The Government, on the contrary, contested the Chamber's conclusion on this point, arguing that in exceptional circumstances resulting from a change of regime it might be justifiable not to pay compensation when devising a comprehensive solution to property issues. [...] They observed that in the GDR the applicants, as heirs of the owners of land redistributed under the land reform, had not acquired a property right in the true sense of the term, but merely a right of usufruct. Under the change of possession decrees, their land should have reverted to the pool of state-owned land without compensation if the heirs were not themselves farming the land. The fact that the GDR authorities had often failed to ensure that the land returned to the pool and to amend the entries in the land register in accordance with the principles laid down in those decrees did not give the applicants a right to keep their land. Even if they had acquired a formal title to the property, the applicants could not expect to maintain their legal position (*Fortbestand ihrer Rechtsposition*) and could not rely on the principle of 'protection of legitimate confidence' (*schutzwürdiges Vertrauen*) in that regard. The real purpose of the Modrow Law had been to ensure, as a matter of priority, that the land was used for

agricultural purposes and to allow farmers, and not heirs to the land who were not themselves farming it, to become owners in the true sense of the word so that they could be integrated into the free market economy.

The Government referred to the case of *James and Others v. the United Kingdom* and submitted that, for reasons of social justice, the legislature had had to correct the Modrow Law, which had been passed in the particular circumstances of the GDR by a parliament that had not been democratically elected, without making provision for the payment of compensation.

d. The Court's assessment

99. In order to be able to judge, in the light of the principles set out in paragraphs 93–95 above, whether the 'fair balance' between the protection of the right of property and the public interest has been respected, the Court considers it useful to reiterate certain special features of the present case and, in particular, the historical context in which it arose.

(i) The nature of the right of the 'new farmers' and their heirs in the context of the land reform in the GDR

100. The aim of the land reform, which was implemented as of 1945 in the Soviet Occupied Zone of Germany and continued after 1949 in the GDR, was not only to distribute the land to farmers, who were then called 'new farmers', but also to ensure that the land thus distributed was farmed under the State's control. It is true that the certificates of allotment described the land as 'private property capable of passing to the owner's heirs', and that, in its leading judgment of 17 December 1998, the Federal Court of Justice confirmed that it could pass to the owner's heirs.

101. Nevertheless, the right of the new farmers in the GDR cannot be classified as a property right such as existed at the time under democratic, market-economy regimes. Being, as it was, a reflection of the collectivist system of property rights which characterised the former communist countries, land acquired under the land reform was subject to substantial restrictions on disposal under the land reform decrees of 1945 and the change of possession decrees of 1951, 1975 and 1988.

102. The initial aim of the land reform, which was the agricultural use of the land in question, also explains why the heirs to the land could not validly keep it unless they themselves were working the land or were members of an agricultural cooperative. If they were not, the land was either allocated to persons with superior title or had to be returned to a pool of state-owned land.

103. It appears to be established that although in many cases the land was, in practice, returned to the pool of state-owned land, the GDR authorities did sometimes, often out of indifference since the land was in any event generally managed by agricultural cooperatives, omit to effect these transfers and enter them in the land register.

104. The result of this is that if the GDR authorities had consistently applied the rules in force at the time, the applicants, who were not farming the land themselves and were not members of an agricultural cooperative, would not have been in a position to keep it.

(ii) The nature of the applicants' right after the entry into force of the Law of 6 March 1990 on the rights of owners of land redistributed under the land reform

105. During the transitional period and the negotiations between the two German States and the four former occupying powers which began after the fall of the Berlin Wall on

9 November 1989 the GDR parliament enacted the Law of 6 March 1990 on the rights of owners of land redistributed under the land reform: the Modrow Law, which came into force on 16 March 1990, two days before the first free elections of 18 March 1990. That Law lifted all restrictions on the disposal of land that had been acquired under the land reform, thereby transforming the property titles acquired under the reform into 'full ownership [which] as such fell within the scope of the Basic Law, including in those cases where it had passed to the heirs, that is, in cases where the owner originally registered in the land register had died before 16 March 1990'.

106. However, it should be noted that the Modrow Law itself is very succinct: although it states that the restrictions on disposal are lifted and the change of possession decrees repealed, it does not contain any specific provision regarding the position of the heirs to the land concerned and does not contain any transitional provisions regarding the application of that Law. Given the lack of any uniform practice in the GDR in this area, the position of heirs who were not themselves farming the land and were not members of an agricultural cooperative, as was the applicants' case, can accordingly be regarded as having been uncertain. Having regard to those factors, the Federal Constitutional Court's finding that the Modrow Law contained a 'hidden legislative loophole' does not appear to be unjustified.

(iii) The reasons for the second Property Rights Amendment Act of 14 July 1992

107. On 14 July 1992, less than two years after German reunification took effect on 3 October 1990, the German legislature sought to correct the effects of the Modrow Law for reasons of fairness and social justice.

108. The main purpose of the second Property Rights Amendment Act of 14 July 1992, which was based on the principles set out in the GDR by the land reform decrees and the change of possession decrees, was to place all heirs of land acquired under the land reform in the position they would have been in if those principles had been properly applied at the time. This was to prevent heirs who did not fulfil the conditions for allocation of land from obtaining an unfair advantage over those who, at the time, had had to return the land to the pool of state-owned land because they were not themselves farming the land and were not members of an agricultural cooperative.

(iv) Conclusion

109. The Court notes that it has in the past already been required to rule on whether an intervention by the legislature with a view to reforming the economic sector for reasons of social justice, (see *James and Others*, . . . concerning the reform of the British system of long leasehold tenure), or to correct the flaws in an earlier law in the public interest (see *National & Provincial Building Society, Leeds Permanent Building Society and Yorkshire Building Society v. the United Kingdom,* judgment of 23 October 1997, *Reports of Judgments and Decisions* 1997-VII, examined under the second paragraph of Article 1, and concerning retrospective tax legislation) respected the 'fair balance' between the relevant interests in the light of Article 1 of Protocol No. 1.

110. Admittedly, there are certain similarities between the instant case and the aforementioned cases in that in 1992 the German legislature had sought to correct the flaws in the Modrow Law for reasons of social justice. It differs from the case of *James and Others v. the United Kingdom,* in particular, however, as the second Property Rights Amendment Act does not provide for any compensation whatsoever for the applicants.

111. As the Court has stated above (see paragraph 94), a total lack of compensation can be considered justifiable under Article 1 of Protocol No. 1 only in exceptional circumstances.

112. It must therefore examine, in the light of the unique context of German reunification, whether the special circumstances of the case can be regarded as exceptional circumstances justifying the lack of any compensation.

113. In that connection the Court reiterates that the State has a wide margin of appreciation when passing laws in the context of a change of political and economic regime. It has also reiterated this point regarding the enactment of laws in the unique context of German reunification.

114. In its judgment of 22 January 2004 the Chamber found that, in order to comply with the principle of proportionality, the German legislature 'could not deprive the applicants of their property for the benefit of the State without making provision for them to be adequately compensated'. The Chamber concluded that 'even if the circumstances pertaining to German reunification ha[d] to be regarded as exceptional, the lack of any compensation for the State's taking of the applicants' property upset, to the applicants' detriment, the fair balance which ha[d] to be struck between the protection of property and the requirements of the general interest'.

115. The Court does not share the Chamber's opinion on that point however.

116. Three factors seem to it to be decisive in that connection:

(i) firstly, the circumstances of the enactment of the Modrow Law, which was passed by a parliament that had not been democratically elected, during a transitional period between two regimes that was inevitably marked by upheavals and uncertainties. In those conditions, even if the applicants had acquired a formal property title, they could not be sure that their legal position would be maintained, particularly as in the absence of any reference to heirs in the Modrow Law, the position of those among them who were not farming the land themselves and were not members of an agricultural cooperative remained precarious even after that Law had come into force;

(ii) secondly, the fairly short period of time that elapsed between German reunification becoming effective and the enactment of the second Property Rights Amendment Act. Having regard to the huge task facing the German legislature when dealing with, among other things, all the complex issues relating to property rights during the transition to a democratic, market-economy regime, including those relating to the liquidation of the land reform, the German legislature can be deemed to have intervened within a reasonable time to correct the—in its view unjust—effects of the Modrow Law. It cannot be criticised for having failed to realise the full effect of this Law on the very day on which German reunification took effect;

(iii) thirdly, the reasons for the second Property Rights Amendment Act. In that connection the FRG parliament cannot be deemed to have been unreasonable in considering that it had a duty to correct the effects of the Modrow Law for reasons of social justice so that the acquisition of full ownership by the heirs of land acquired under the land reform did not depend on the action or non-action of the GDR authorities at the time. Likewise, the balancing exercise between the relevant interests carried out by the Federal Constitutional Court, particularly in its leading decision of 6 October 2000, in examining the compatibility of that amending Law with the Basic Law, does not appear to have been arbitrary. Given the 'windfall' from which the applicants undeniably benefited as a result of the Modrow Law under the rules applicable in the GDR to the heirs to land acquired under the land reform, the fact that this was done without paying any compensation was not disproportionate.... It should also be noted in that connection that the second Property Rights Amendment Act did not benefit the State only, but in some cases also provided for the redistribution of land to farmers.

117. Having regard to all the foregoing considerations and taking account, in particular, of the uncertainty of the legal position of heirs and the grounds of social justice relied on by the German authorities, the Court concludes that in the unique context of German reunification, the lack of any compensation does not upset the 'fair balance' which has to be struck between the protection of property and the requirements of the general interest.

There has therefore been no violation of Article 1 of Protocol No. 1.

It will be evident from *Lithgow v. United Kingdom* and *Jahn v. Germany* that the test of proportionality, which is a recurring feature in Strasbourg jurisprudence in general, must, in cases concerning Article 1 of the First Protocol, take close account both of the broad range of views as to the right of property that are held in Europe today and also of the specific context within which the national legislature has reacted to historical events. The right to property has some claim to be more of an economic right than a civil right, but it is seen in liberal democracy as a self-evident right worthy of protection against unjustifiable interference by state bodies. However, from the outset, it has been recognized that the needs of the community may 'trump' the right to property whether held by an individual or by a corporate body on the grounds of social policy or economic development. Such is specifically accepted in the text of the Article. Furthermore, the Court has long recognized that judicial competence—and particularly the competence of an international tribunal—is limited in such policy determinations.

On the other hand, the Court has insisted that the State accords basic procedural safeguards to the decision-making process to protect against arbitary decision-making. It has also insisted upon a 'fair balance' between collective and individual interests being struck in the outcomes of this decision-making process and, in particular, upon compensation being available as a matter of principle. *Jahn v. Germany* is an exception—and a case of exceptional circumstances where it was perhaps considered that general fairness to those who had earlier 'played by the rules' should not lead to an unjustifiable benefit for those who had not done so.

Current cases are not without contemporary political interest: many of these reflect the aftermath of the fall of communism (and some go even further back in time to the fall of fascism). Such applications illustrate the complexities and challenges posed to the Court when adjudicating upon the right of property.

11

THE RIGHT TO EDUCATION

FIRST PROTOCOL, ARTICLE 2

No person shall be denied the right to education. In the exercise of any functions which it assumes in relation to education and to teaching, the State shall respect the right of parents to ensure such education and teaching in conformity with their own religious and philosophical convictions.

A. INTRODUCTION[1]

In what was probably its most important decision of the 20th century, the U.S. Supreme Court held in *Brown v. Board of Education of Topeka* (1954) that to provide racially segregated ('separate but equal') education was in breach of the equal protection of the laws; the unanimous Court said:

Today, education is perhaps the most important function of state and local governments. Compulsory school attendance laws and the great expenditures for education both demonstrate our recognition of the importance of education to our democratic society. It is required in the performance of our most basic public responsibilities, even service in the armed forces. It is the very foundation of good. Today it is a principal instrument in awakening the child to cultural values, in preparing him for later professional training, and in helping him to adjust normally to his environment. In these days, it is doubtful that any child may reasonably be expected to succeed in life if he is denied the opportunity of an education. Such an opportunity, where the state has undertaken to provide it, is a right which must be made available to all on equal terms.[2]

The weight of the decision was qualified in 1973, when the Supreme Court by 5–4 rejected a challenge brought by poor families to the unequal funding of state schools in Texas caused by reliance on local property taxation, holding that despite the undoubted importance of education, the Court should not create a substantive

---

[1] The commentary in this chapter includes material drawn from A. W. Bradley, 'Scope for Review: the Convention Right to Education and the Human Rights Act 1998', [1999] *European Human Rights Law Review* 395–410.

[2] 347 U.S. 483 at 493 (1954) (Warren CJ).

constitutional right to education when this was not among the rights given explicit or implicit protection in the U.S. Constitution.[3] Nonetheless, the view that there is a fundamental right relating to education was held by those who framed the First Protocol to the Convention, which was signed on 20 March 1952 and entered into force on 18 May 1954. The Universal Declaration on Human Rights had earlier stated that 'Everyone has the right to education', declaring that education 'shall be directed to the full development of the human personality and to the strengthening of respect for human rights and fundamental freedoms' and that parents 'have a prior right to choose the kind of education that shall be given to their children'.[4] The right to education also appears in the International Covenant on Economic, Social and Cultural Rights: Article 13 amplifies the general right to education with references to primary education ('which shall be compulsory and available free to all'), secondary education ('in its different forms'), higher education (to be made 'equally accessible to all, on the basis of capacity'), and 'fundamental education' (for those who have not received or completed primary education). Article 13(3) requires states to respect the liberty of parents to choose schools for their children 'which conform to such minimum educational standards as may be laid down or approved by the State' and for the right of parents 'to ensure the religious and moral education of their children in conformity with their own convictions'. Article 13(4) seeks to preserve the liberty of 'individuals and bodies to establish and direct educational institutions' which maintain the principles declared in the Covenant and 'conform to minimum standards laid down by the State'.

By comparison with other Articles in the Convention, the right to education is rather terse and is phrased in very general terms. In fact, the framers had found it very difficult to draft, given the defensiveness of many states over features of their own educational system, for example the relationship between the state sector and organized religion: some states wished education to be wholly lay and secular; others wished to see more support given to a religious basis for education. Many states were reluctant to proclaim that everyone has a right to education, not wishing to impose an open-ended duty on the state to provide education, and they instead adopted a negative formulation. It is evident from the *travaux préparatoires* that the strongest single factor that motivated the preparation of a Convention right to education was the desire to enable parents to have their children educated in accordance with their own beliefs and to resist 'the overwhelming intrusion of totalitarian propaganda and family life' by 'agencies or quasi-agencies of the State'.[5]

Even when the text of Article 2 had been agreed, continuing concerns about the right to education caused several states to attach reservations when they ratified the First Protocol.[6] Germany expressed the opinion that the second sentence of Article 2 imposed no obligation to finance or subsidize schools of a religious or philosophical

---

[3] *San Antonio Independent School District v. Rodriguez*, 411 U.S. 1 (1973) (Powell J).

[4] Universal Declaration of Human Rights, 1948, Art. 26.

[5] 6 *Collected Edition of the Travaux Préparatoires* 162.

[6] *See* Council of Europe, *The ECHR, Collected Texts* (1994), pp. 121–31.

nature. The Netherlands declared that 'the State should not only respect the rights of parents in the matters of education but, if need be, ensure the possibility of exercising those rights by appropriate financial measures'. The United Kingdom accepted the principle affirmed in the second sentence of Article 2 'only so far as it is compatible with the provision of efficient instruction and training and the avoidance of unreasonable public expenditure'.[7] Malta made a similar reservation, but added to it the words, 'having regard to the fact that the population of Malta is overwhelmingly Roman Catholic'. It must be remembered that the legal effect of a reservation made when a state ratifies the Convention or a protocol to it is within the jurisdiction of the Strasbourg Court: a reservation is not able to nullify the substance of the obligations imposed by the provision in question.[8]

Despite the universal importance of education, and the great variety of public provision for education that exists within European countries, there have been few decisions by the Strasbourg Court on the scope of the right to education. A question that arises from the decisions considered in this chapter is whether the relative paucity of cases is explained by the general recognition by states of the importance of education or is related to the limited scope of the Convention right to education. Is there an argument to be made that a substantive right to education would be better included in the category of economic, social and cultural rights than within the category of civil and political rights that comprise the bulk of the Convention rights?[9]

B. THE BELGIAN LINGUISTIC CASE (NO. 2)

Judgment of 23 July 1968
1 E.H.R.R. 252

[A group of French-speaking parents claimed that the Belgian educational system did not permit their children to be educated at French-speaking schools except if they went to schools at a long way from their homes. The country had since 1932 been divided for the organisation of education into unilingual regions (respectively Dutch-speaking and French-speaking); there were also some German-speaking communes, and certain bilingual areas in greater Brussels. There were substantial minorities of French-speaking families in the Dutch regions. The legislation of 1932 was amended in 1963, when a stricter system of 'linguistic control' was introduced; subsidies were withdrawn from private schools that did not comply with the linguistic regime applicable to the area where they were located; penalties were imposed on schools that admitted children in breach of the rules, and recognition was withheld from school-leaving certificates issued by non-conforming schools. The applicants

---

[7] The wording derives from a formula used in the Education Act 1944 to limit the respect that education authorities must show to parental wishes. *See* now the Education Act 1996, s. 9.

[8] *See* Art. 57 and *Belilos v. Switzerland*, 29 April 1988, 10 E.H.R.R. 466.

[9] Compare European Social Charter (Revised) 1996, Art. 10 (the right to vocational training).

relied on Article 2, First Protocol, as well as on Articles 8 and 14. Their complaints were summarised by the Court in this way:]

3. Though the six applications differ on a number of points, they are similar in many respects....[In] substance they complain that the Belgian State:

— does not provide any French-language education in the municipalities where the Applicants live...;

— withholds grants from any institutions in the said municipalities which may fail to comply with the linguistic provisions of the legislation for schools;

— refuses to homologate leaving certificates issued by such institutions;

— does not allow the Applicants' children to attend the French classes which exist in certain places;

— thereby obliges the Applicants either to enrol their children in local schools, a solution which they consider contrary to their aspirations, or to send them to school in the 'Greater Brussels district', where the language of instruction is Dutch or French according to the child's mother-tongue or usual language or in the 'French-speaking region' (Walloon area). Such 'scholastic emigration' is said to entail serious risks and hardships.

[Before dealing with the specific complaints, the Court dealt with the general interpretation to be placed on the Convention right to education (references to Article 2 below are to the First Protocol, Article 2). The Court's analysis deals separately with the two sentences that comprise Article 2.]

3. By the terms of the first sentence of this Article, 'no person shall be denied the right to education'.

In spite of its negative formulation, this provision uses the term 'right' and speaks of a 'right to education'. Likewise the preamble to the Protocol specifies that the object of the Protocol lies in the collective enforcement of 'rights and freedoms'. There is therefore no doubt that Article 2 does enshrine a right.

It remains however to determine the content of this right and the scope of the obligation which is thereby placed upon States.

The negative formulation indicates, as is confirmed by the *travaux préparatoires*...that the Contracting Parties do not recognise such a right to education as would require them to establish at their own expense, or to subsidise, education of any particular type or at any particular level. However, it cannot be concluded from this that the State has no positive obligation to ensure respect for such a right as is protected by Article 2. As a 'right' does exist, it is secured, by virtue of Article 1 of the Convention, to everyone within the jurisdiction of a Contracting State.

To determine the scope of the 'right to education', within the meaning of the first sentence of Article 2, the Court must bear in mind the aim of this provision. It notes...that all member States of the Council of Europe possessed, at the time of the opening of the Protocol to their signature, and still do possess, a general and official educational system. There neither was, nor is now, therefore, any question of requiring each State to establish such a system, but merely of guaranteeing to persons subject to the jurisdiction of the Contracting Parties the right, in principle, to avail themselves of the means of instruction existing at a given time.

The Convention lays down no specific obligations concerning the extent of these means and the manner of their organisation or subsidisation. In particular the first sentence of Article 2 does not specify the language in which education must be conducted in order that the right to education should be respected. It does not contain precise provisions similar to those which appear in Articles 5 (2) and 6 (3) (a) and (e). However the right to education would be meaningless if it did not imply in favour of its beneficiaries, the right to be educated in the national language or in one of the national languages, as the case may be.

4. The first sentence of Article 2 consequently guarantees... a right of access to educational institutions existing at a given time, but such access constitutes only a part of the right to education. For the 'right to education' to be effective, it is further necessary that, inter alia, the individual who is the beneficiary should have the possibility of drawing profit from the education received, that is to say, the right to obtain, in conformity with the rules in force in each State, and in one form or another, official recognition of the studies which he has completed....

5. The right to education guaranteed by the first sentence of Article 2 by its very nature calls for regulation by the State, regulation which may vary in time and place according to the needs and resources of the community and of individuals. It goes without saying that such regulation must never injure the substance of the right to education nor conflict with other rights enshrined in the Convention....

6. The second sentence of Article 2 does not guarantee a right to education; this is clearly shown by its wording...

This provision does not require of States that they should, in the sphere of education or teaching, respect parents' linguistic preferences, but only their religious and philosophical convictions. To interpret the terms 'religious' and 'philosophical' as covering linguistic preferences would amount to a distortion of their ordinary and usual meaning and to read into the Convention something which is not there. Moreover the *travaux préparatoires* confirms that the object of the second sentence of Article 2 was in no way to secure respect by the State of a right for parents to have education conducted in a language other than that of the country in question; indeed in June 1951 the Committee of Experts which had the task of drafting the Protocol set aside a proposal put forward in this sense. Several members of the Committee believed that it concerned an aspect of the problem of ethnic minorities and that it consequently fell outside the scope of the Convention... The second sentence of Article 2 is therefore irrelevant to the problems raised in the present case.

[The Court held that Article 8(1) guaranteed neither a right to education nor a personal right of parents relating to the education of their children.[10] As to the effects of Article 14 of the Convention read with Article 2,[11] the Court said]

11. ... Article 14, even when read in conjunction with Article 2 of the Protocol, does not have the effect of guaranteeing to a child or to his parent the right to obtain instruction in a language of his choice. The object of these two Articles, read in conjunction, is more limited: it is to ensure that the right to education shall be secured by each Contracting Party to everyone within its jurisdiction without discrimination on the ground, for instance, of language. This is the natural and ordinary meaning of Article 14 read in conjunction with Article 2.

---

[10] *See* the discussion of Article 8 in this context, in Chapter 8, Section B(4)(b).
[11] For para. 10 of the judgment, *see* Chapter 9(F).

Furthermore, to interpret the two provisions as conferring on everyone within the jurisdiction of a State a right to obtain education in the language of his own choice would lead to absurd results, for it would be open to anyone to claim any language of instruction in any of the territories of the Contracting Parties....

[The first specific question addressed by the Court concerned the legislation which had led to the State's refusal to establish or subsidise, in the Dutch unilingual region, primary school education in which French was employed as the language of instruction.]

Such a refusal is not incompatible with...the first sentence of Article 2....[That sentence] contains in itself no linguistic requirement. It guarantees the right of access to educational establishments existing at a given time and the right to obtain, in conformity with the rules in force in each State and in one form or another, the official recognition of studies which have been completed...In the unilingual regions, both French-speaking and Dutch-speaking children have access to public or subsidised education, that is to say to education conducted in the language of the region.

The legal provisions in issue, moreover, do not violate Article 8.... It is true that one result of the Acts of 1932 and 1963 has been the disappearance in the Dutch unilingual region of the majority of schools providing education in French. Consequently French-speaking children living in this region can now obtain their education only in Dutch, unless their parents have the financial resources to send them to private French-language schools.... Harsh though such consequences may be in individual cases, they do not involve any breach of Article 8.... Furthermore, in so far as the legislation leads certain parents to separate themselves from their children, such a separation is not imposed by this legislation: it results from the choice of the parents who place their children in schools situated outside the Dutch unilingual region with the sole purpose of avoiding their being taught in Dutch, that is to say in one of Belgium's national languages.

[The Court held that it made no difference to read Article 2 of the Protocol and Article 8 in conjunction with Article 14. In the Court's view, a public interest was served by the legislation, which 'cannot be considered arbitrary'. Nor did it violate the rights of the individual. As for the policy of withdrawing all public subsidies from schools that provided some classes that did not comply with the Government's linguistic policies, as well as classes that did comply, the Court held that this was 'a harsh measure' but that it was not arbitrary since its purpose was 'to avoid the possibility of education which the State does not wish to subsidise...benefiting, in some way or another, from subsidies designed for education which is in conformity with the linguistic legislation. This purpose is plausible in itself and it is not for the Court to determine whether it is possible to realise it in another way'.

There was, however, a special situation in six communes in greater Brussels and at Louvain where teaching in French might under certain circumstances be provided to French-speaking families. The Court found by 8–7 that there was inequality in that Dutch-speaking families could attend Dutch-language schemes in those areas wherever they resided, whereas French-speaking children could attend the French schools only when their parents lived within the commune or locality in question.]

Such a measure is not justified in the light of the requirements of the Convention in that it involves elements of discriminatory treatment of certain individuals, founded even more on language than on residence...

The enjoyment of the right to education as the Court conceives it, and more precisely that of the right of access to existing schools, is not therefore on the point under consideration secured to everyone without discrimination on the ground, in particular, of language....

[The Belgian legislation provided for a national board to homologate certificates given at the end of each stage of secondary education, attesting that the holder was suitable for higher education. The board was not permitted to homologate certificates given by schools which had not conformed with the language regime: the students concerned had to take an additional examination set by the board. The Court held that this scheme did not violate the Convention right to education, nor was it in breach of Article 14.]

...[This inequality in treatment in general results from a difference relating to the administrative system of the schools attended....]... Thus, the State treats unequally situations which are themselves unequal. It does not deprive the pupil of the profit to be drawn from his studies.

> [On the one issue on which the Court found for the French-speaking families, the dissenting judges argued that the principles laid down in the main judgment should have caused the Court to uphold the national rules, since it was for the national authorities to assess 'the requirements implied by the factual and legal features in issue' and they must 'remain free to choose the measures which they consider appropriate in those matters which are governed by the Convention.']

The decision in this case may be contrasted with decisions of the U.S. and Canadian Supreme Courts relating to minority language rights in education and the furtherance of minority cultures.[12] In the *Belgian Linguistic* case, the Court was unanimous in holding that the philosophical and religious convictions of the Belgian parents did not extend to requiring the state to observe their linguistic preference, and thus the second sentence of Protocol 2 was irrelevant to the case. By contrast, at the heart of the two following cases was the question of philosophical and religious convictions.

C. KJELDSEN, BUSK MADSEN AND PEDERSEN V. DENMARK

Judgment of 7 December 1976
1 E.H.R.R. 711

[Three married couples from Denmark, with children at school, challenged the manner in which sex education in state primary schools had been integrated into the curriculum and made compulsory by a law of 1970 that amended the State Schools Act. Under the latter Act, the Minister of Education determined the objectives of schooling; local school authorities fixed the contents of the curriculum. There were two exceptions to this rule (a) religious instruction was to be in the Evangelical Lutheran tradition, but children might be exempted from this; (b) schools were required to include in the curriculum certain topics such as road safety, civics and hygiene. The great majority of Danish children attended local

---

[12] *See* Chapter 8, Section B(4)(b).

authority schools, but a minority attended private schools where the fees were subsidised from public funds. Sex education had been introduced in 1960, when human reproduction became a compulsory part of biology lessons, but the consent of parents was needed for children to receive sex education. During the 1960s, amid concern at an increasing number of unwanted pregnancies, a government committee recommended a scheme for integrating sex education in the compulsory subjects. In 1970, Parliament changed the law to provide that, in primary schools, 'road safety, library organisation and sex education shall form an integral part of teaching in the manner specified by the Minister of Education'. In 1971, the Minister issued an executive order, setting out the objective of sex education, together with a Guide for local authorities.]

27. The principle of integration... is explained as follows in the Guide:

'The main purpose of integration is to place sex guidance in a context where human sexuality does not appear as a special phenomenon. Sexuality is not a purely physical matter... nor is it a purely technical matter.... On the other hand it is not of such emotional impact that it cannot be taken up for objective and sober discussion.... The topic should therefore form an integral part of the overall school education...'

28. As for the... manner and scope of sex education, the Guide indicates the matters that may be included in the State school curricula.

In the first to fourth years instruction begins with the concept of the family and then moves on to the difference between the sexes, conception, birth and development of the child, family planning, relations with adults whom the children do not know and puberty.

The list of subjects suggested for the fifth to seventh years includes the sexual organs, puberty, hormones, heredity, sexual activities (masturbation, intercourse, orgasm), fertilisation, methods of contraception, venereal diseases, sexual deviations (in particular homosexuality) and pornography...

29. The Guide advocates an instruction method centred on informal talks between teachers and children on the basis of the latter questions. It emphasises that 'the instruction must be so tactful as not to offend or frighten the child' and that it 'must respect each child's right to adhere to conceptions it has developed itself'. To the extent that the discussion bears on ethical and moral problems of sexual life, the Guide recommends teachers to adopt an objective attitude...

[In 1972, a new Executive Order replaced the Executive Order of 1971. It provided:]

'*Section 1* (1) The objective of the sex education provided in Folkeskolen shall be to impart to the pupils such knowledge of sex life as will enable them to take care of themselves and show consideration for others in that respect.

(2) Schools are therefore required, as a minimum, to provide instruction on the anatomy of the reproductive organs, on conception and contraception and on venereal diseases to such extent that the pupils will not later in life land themselves or others in difficulties solely on account of lack of knowledge...

(3) Sex education shall start not later than in the third school year; it shall form part of the instruction given in the general school subjects, in particular Danish, knowledge of Christianity, biology (hygiene), history (civics) and domestic relations. In addition, a general survey of the main topics covered by sex education may be given in the sixth or seventh and in the ninth school years....

Section 3 (1) Sex education shall be given by the teachers responsible for giving lessons on the subjects with which it is integrated in the relevant class and in accordance with the directives of the principal of the school....

(2) A teacher cannot be compelled against his will to give the special instruction referred to in the second sentence of section 1 para. 3. Nor shall it be incumbent upon the teacher to impart to pupils information about coital techniques or to use photographic pictures representing erotic situations.

Section 4 On application to the principal of the school, parents may have their children exempted from the special instruction referred to in the second sentence of section 1 para. 3...'

33. [In] 1975, the Danish Parliament passed a new State Schools Act... However, it has not amended any of the provisions relevant to the present case...

While the Bill was being examined by Parliament, the Christian People's Party tabled an amendment according to which parents would be allowed to ask that their children be exempted from attending sex education. This amendment was rejected by 103 votes to 24.

34. Although primary education in private schools must in principle cover all the topics obligatory at State schools..., sex education is an exception in this respect. Private schools are free to decide themselves to what extent they wish to align their teaching in this field with the rules applicable to State schools. However, they must include in the biology syllabus a course on the reproduction of man similar to that obligatory in State schools since 1960...

[In 1971, Mr and Mrs Kjeldsen had asked for free education in a private school for their daughter, but this was refused. For a time they withdrew her from the municipal school and taught her at home. Mr and Mrs Busk Madsen had been unsuccessful in asking for their children to be exempted from sex instruction. Mr and Mrs Pedersen sent four of their five children to private schools to avoid them having to follow sex education courses. The parents invoked Article 2 of Protocol 1.]

50. In their main submission before the Commission, the Government maintained that the second sentence of Article 2 does not apply to State schools... but [before the Court]....they conceded that the existence of private schools perhaps does not necessarily imply in all cases that there is no breach of the said sentence. The Government nevertheless emphasised that Denmark does not force parents to entrust their children to the State schools; it allows parents to educate their children, or to have them educated, at home and, above all, to send them to private institutions to which the State pays very substantial subsidies, thereby assuming a 'function in relation to education and to teaching', within the meaning of Article 2.... The Court notes that in Denmark private schools co-exist with a system of public education. The second sentence of Article 2 is binding upon the Contracting States in the exercise of each and every function... that they undertake in the sphere of education and teaching, including... the organisation and financing of public education.

Furthermore, the second sentence of Article 2 must be read together with the first which enshrines the right of everyone to education. It is on to this fundamental right that is grafted the right of parents to respect for their religious and philosophical convictions, and the first sentence does not distinguish, any more than the second, between State and private teaching.

The *travaux préparatoires*...confirm the interpretation appearing from a first reading of Article 2. Whilst they indisputably demonstrate...the importance attached...to freedom of teaching, that is to say, freedom to establish private schools, the *travaux préparatoires* do not...reveal the intention to go no further than a guarantee of that freedom. Unlike some earlier versions, the text finally adopted does not expressly enounce that freedom; and numerous interventions...show that sight was not lost of the need to ensure, in State teaching, respect for parents' religious and philosophical convictions.

The second sentence of Article 2 aims in short at safeguarding the possibility of pluralism in education which possibility is essential for the preservation of the 'democratic society' as conceived by the Convention. In view of the power of the modern State, it is above all through State teaching that this aim must be realised.

The Court thus concludes...that the Danish State schools do not fall outside the province of Protocol No. 1. In its investigation as to whether Article 2 has been violated, the Court cannot forget, however, that the functions assumed by Denmark in relation to education and to teaching include the grant of substantial assistance to private schools. Although recourse to these schools involves parents in sacrifices which were justifiably mentioned by the applicants, the alternative solution it provides constitutes a factor that should not be disregarded...

51. The Government pleaded in the alternative that the second sentence of Article 2...implies solely the right for parents to have their children exempted from classes offering 'religious instruction of a denominational character'.

The Court does not share this view. Article 2...does not permit a distinction to be drawn between religious instruction and other subjects. It enjoins the State to respect parents' convictions, be they religious or philosophical, throughout the entire State education programme.

52. As is shown by its very structure, Article 2 constitutes a whole that is dominated by its first sentence. By binding themselves not to 'deny the right to education', the Contracting States guarantee to anyone within their jurisdiction 'a right of access to educational institutions existing at a given time' and 'the possibility of drawing', by 'official recognition of the studies which he has completed', 'profit from the education received'.[13] The right set out in the second sentence of Article 2 is an adjunct of this fundamental right to education (paragraph 50 above). It is in the discharge of a natural duty towards their children—parents being primarily responsible for the 'education and teaching' of their children—that parents may require the State to respect their religious and philosophical convictions. Their right thus corresponds to a responsibility closely linked to the enjoyment and the exercise of the right to education.

On the other hand, 'the provisions of the Convention and Protocol must be read as a whole'.[14] Accordingly, the two sentences of Article 2 must be read not only in the light of each other but also, in particular, of Articles 8, 9 and 10...which proclaim the right of everyone, including parents and children, 'to respect for his private and family life', to 'freedom of thought, conscience and religion', and to 'freedom...to receive and impart information and ideas'.

53. It follows...that the setting and planning of the curriculum fall in principle within the competence of the Contracting States. This mainly involves questions of expediency...whose solution may legitimately vary according to the country and the era. In particular, the second sentence of Article 2 does not prevent States from imparting through teaching or education information or knowledge of a directly or indirectly religious or philosophical kind. It does not even permit parents to object to the integration of such teaching or education in the school curriculum, for otherwise all institutionalised teaching would run the risk of proving

---

[13] Citing the *Belgian Linguistic* case.
[14] *Id.*

impracticable. In fact, it seems very difficult for many subjects taught at school not to have, to a greater or lesser extent, some philosophical complexion or implications. The same is true of religious affinities if one remembers the existence of religions forming a very broad dogmatic and moral entity which has or may have answers to every question of a philosophical, cosmological or moral nature.

The second sentence of Article 2 implies on the other hand that the State, in fulfilling the functions assumed by it in regard to education and teaching, must take care that information or knowledge included in the curriculum is conveyed in an objective, critical and pluralistic manner. The State is forbidden to pursue an aim of indoctrination that might be considered as not respecting parents' religious and philosophical convictions. That is the limit that must not be exceeded.

Such an interpretation is consistent...with the first sentence of Article 2 of the Protocol, with Articles 8 to 10 and with the general spirit of the Convention...

54. ...The Danish legislator, who did not neglect to obtain beforehand the advice of qualified experts, clearly took as his starting point the known fact that in Denmark children nowadays discover without difficulty and from several quarters the information that interests them on sexual life. The instruction on the subject given in State schools is aimed less at instilling knowledge they do not have or cannot acquire by other means than at giving them such knowledge more correctly, precisely, objectively and scientifically. ...

Even when circumscribed in this way, such instruction clearly cannot exclude on the part of teachers certain assessments capable of encroaching on the religious or philosophical sphere; for what are involved are matters where appraisals of fact easily lead on to value-judgments.... The Executive Orders... and the other material before the Court... plainly show that the Danish State, by providing children in good time with explanations it considers useful, is attempting to warn them against phenomena it views as disturbing, for example, the excessive frequency of births out of wedlock, induced abortions and venereal diseases. The public authorities wish to enable pupils, when the time comes, 'to take care of themselves and show consideration for others in that respect', 'not...[to] land themselves or others in difficulties solely on account of lack of knowledge' (section 1 of the Executive Order of 1972).

These considerations are indeed of a moral order, but they are very general in character and do not entail overstepping the bounds of what a democratic State may regard as the public interest. Examination of the legislation in dispute establishes in fact that it in no way amounts to an attempt at indoctrination aimed at advocating a specific kind of sexual behaviour.... Further, it does not affect the right of parents to enlighten and advise their children, to exercise with regard to their children natural parental functions as educators, or to guide their children on a path in line with the parents' own religious or philosophical convictions.

Certainly, abuses can occur as to the manner in which the provisions in force are applied by a given school or teacher and the competent authorities have a duty to take the utmost care to see to it that parents' religious and philosophical convictions are not disregarded at this level by carelessness, lack of judgment or misplaced proselytism. However,...the Court is not at present seised of a problem of this kind...

The Court [concludes] that the disputed legislation in itself in no way offends the applicants' religious and philosophical convictions to the extent forbidden by the second sentence of Article 2....

Besides, the Danish State preserves an important expedient for parents who, in the name of their creed or opinions, wish to dissociate their children from integrated sex education; it allows parents either to entrust their children to private schools, which are bound by less strict obligations and moreover heavily subsidised by the State..., or to educate them or have them educated at home...

[The Court rejected an argument by the applicants, based on Article 14, that the legislation improperly discriminated in allowing parents to have children exempted from religious instruction but not from integrated sex education. And the Court found no breaches of Articles 8 and 9, which it had taken into account in interpreting Article 2 of Protocol 1.]

Judge Verdross agreed with much of the Court's judgment but dissented from the decision and the reasons for it in paragraphs 53–54 and 56 above. In his judgment, he said:

Since the applicants...consider themselves wronged in relation to their 'Christian convictions', we can leave aside the question of how the term 'philosophical convictions' is to be understood.... The applicants are in fact objecting to the State prematurely giving 'detailed' teaching on sexual matters; they contend that the State's monopoly in the realm of education deprives them of their basic right 'to ensure their children's education in conformity with their own religious convictions'. This makes it quite plain that they are basing their complaints on a well established Christian doctrine whereby anything affecting the development of children's consciences, that is their moral guidance, is the responsibility of parents and, consequently, in this sphere the State may not intervene between parents and their children against the former's wishes.

... The question thus arises whether the [applicants] may...oppose compulsory sex education in a State school even if..., such education does not constitute an attempt at indoctrination.

...[It] seems to me necessary to distinguish between, on the one hand, factual information on human sexuality that comes within the scope of the natural sciences, above all biology, and, on the other hand, information concerning sexual practices, including contraception. This distinction is required, in my view, by the fact that the former is neutral from the standpoint of morality whereas the latter, even if it is communicated to minors in an objective fashion, always affects the development of their consciences. It follows that even objective information on sexual activity when given too early at school can violate the Christian convictions of parents. The latter accordingly have the right to object....

According to the judgment, [the second clause] of Article 2 prohibits solely education given with the object of indoctrination. However, this clause does not contain any indication justifying a restrictive interpretation of such a kind. On the contrary indeed, it requires the States, in an unqualified manner, to respect parents' religious and philosophical convictions.... Since the applicants consider themselves wronged in relation to their 'Christian convictions' as a result of the obligation on their children to take part in 'detailed' teaching on sexual matters, the Court ought to have restricted itself to ascertaining whether, should there have been any doubt, this complaint tallied or not with the beliefs professed by the applicants.

In this respect, the Court's power seems to me to be similar to that possessed by the bodies responsible, in various countries, for verifying the truth of statements made by persons called up for military service who claim that their religion or philosophy prevents them from carrying arms (conscientious objectors). These bodies have to respect the ideology of the persons concerned once such ideology has been clearly made out.

The distinction between information on the knowledge of man's sexuality in general and that concerning sexual practices is recognised under the Danish legislation itself. While private schools are required...to include in their curricula a biology course on the reproduction of man, they are left the choice whether or not to comply with the other rules compulsory for State schools in sexual matters. The legislature itself is thereby conceding that information on sexual activity may be separated from other information on the subject...

The Danish Act on State schools does not in any way exempt the children of parents having religious convictions at variance with those of the legislature from attending the whole range of classes on sex education. The conclusion must therefore be that the [Act]...is not in harmony with the second sentence of Article 2...

This conclusion is not weakened by the entitlement given to parents to send their children to a private school subsidised by the State or to have them taught at home. On the one hand in fact, the parents' right is a strictly individual right, whereas the opening of a private school always presupposes the existence of a certain group of persons sharing certain convictions...Since the State should respect parents' religious convictions even if there existed one couple alone whose convictions as to the development of their children's consciences differ from those of the majority of the country or of a particular school, it can discharge this particular duty only by exempting the children from the classes on sexual practices. Moreover,...education at a private school, even one subsidised by the State, and teaching at home always entail material sacrifices for the parents. Thus, if the applicants were not entitled to have their children exempted from the classes in question, there would exist an unjustified discrimination, contrary to Article 14..., prejudicing them in comparison with parents whose religious and moral convictions correspond to those of the Danish legislature.

A decision of the UN Human Rights Committee under the International Covenant of Civil and Political Rights may be contrasted with this case. In *Leirvag v. Norway*,[15] humanist parents successfully claimed that a new mandatory religious subject in the Norwegian state system breached their rights as parents under Article 18(4) ICCPR, because exemption was permitted only from certain limited segments of the subject, and the scheme did not make for a practicable separation between teaching religious knowledge and religious practice. Compare also the U.S. Supreme Court's decision in *Edwards v. Aguillard*, where the court invalidated a Louisiana law that forbade the teaching of the theory of evolution in public schools unless accompanied by instruction in 'creationism'; the law was held to have no secular purpose and (contrary to the First Amendment prohibition of laws 'respecting an establishment of religion') to advance the religious belief that a supernatural being created mankind.[16]

In the following case, the Court had to consider whether the 'religious and philosophical convictions' of parents were relevant to matters of discipline and educational administration.

---

[15] (2004) 19 B.H.R.C. 635.
[16] 428 U.S 578 (1987). And *see Stone v. Graham*, 449 U.S. 39 (1983) (holding unconstitutional the display of the Ten Commandments in public school classrooms).

D. CAMPBELL AND COSANS
V. UNITED KINGDOM

Judgment of 25 February 1982
4 E.H.R.R. 293

8. Both Mrs. Campbell and Mrs. Cosans live in Scotland. Each of them had one child of compulsory school age at the time when she applied to the Commission. The applicants' complaints concern the use of corporal punishment as a disciplinary measure in the State schools in Scotland.... For both financial and practical reasons, the applicants had no realistic and acceptable alternative to sending their children to State schools.

9. At the time of Mrs. Campbell's application to the Commission (30 March 1976), her son Gordon, who was born on 3 July 1969, was attending St. Matthew's Roman Catholic Primary School...which is situated in the Strathclyde Region...In that school, corporal punishment is used for disciplinary purposes, although it was disputed...whether it is applied to pupils below the age of 8. The Strathclyde Regional Council had refused Mrs. Campbell's requests for a guarantee that Gordon would not be subjected to this measure. He was, in fact, never so punished whilst at that school, where he remained until July 1979.

10. Mrs. Cosans' son Jeffrey, who was born on 31 May 1961, used to attend Beath Senior High School...which is situated in the Fife Region...On 23 September 1976, he was told to report to the Assistant Headmaster on the following day to receive corporal punishment for having tried to take a prohibited short cut through a cemetery on his way home from school. On his father's advice, Jeffrey duly reported, but refused to accept the punishment. On that account, he was immediately suspended from school until such time as he was willing to accept the punishment.

11. On...18 October, [Jeffrey's parents] had an inconclusive meeting with the Senior Assistant Director of Education of the Fife Regional Council...On 14 January 1977,...that official informed Mr. and Mrs. Cosans by letter that he had decided to lift the suspension in view of the fact that their son's long absence from school constituted punishment enough; however, he added the condition that they should accept, inter alia, that 'Jeffrey will obey the rules, regulations or disciplinary requirements of the school'. However, Mr. and Mrs. Cosans stipulated that if their son were to be readmitted..., he should not receive corporal punishment for any incident while he was a pupil. The official replied that this constituted a refusal to accept the aforesaid condition. Accordingly, Jeffrey's suspension was not lifted and his parents were warned that they might be prosecuted for failure to ensure his attendance at school.

In the event, Jeffrey never returned to school...He ceased to be of compulsory school age on 31 May 1977...

12. Under Scottish law, the use of corporal punishment is controlled by the common law, particularly the law of assault. The general principle is that an assault may give rise to a civil claim for damages or to prosecution for a criminal offence. However, teachers in both State and other schools are...invested by the common law with power to administer such punishment in moderation as a disciplinary measure. Excessive, arbitrary or cruel punishment by a teacher or its infliction for an improper motive would constitute an assault. The teacher's power of chastisement, like that of a parent, derives from his relationship with the children under his care and is therefore not in the nature of a power delegated by the State. Thus, the

administration of corporal punishment . . . is, subject to the limitations imposed by the common law as described above and to any conditions incorporated in the teacher's contract with the education authority employing him, left to the discretion of the teacher.

13. In the two schools concerned, corporal chastisement takes the form of striking the palm of the pupil's hand with a leather strap called a 'tawse'. For misconduct in the classroom, punishment is administered there and then . . . ; for misconduct elsewhere and for serious misconduct, it is administered by the Headmaster, or his deputy, in his room.

The Commission noted that, on the facts of the case, it could not be established that the applicants' children had suffered any adverse psychological or other effects which could be imputed to the use of corporal punishment in their schools.

14. At the [material] time . . . , the administration of the Scottish educational system was regulated by the Education (Scotland) Act 1962 . . . Central government formulates general policy, promotes legislation and exercises supervision; . . . regional education authorities . . . are required to secure that 'adequate and efficient provision' of school education is made for their area. Section 29 (1) of the 1962 Act provided that 'in the exercise and performance of their powers and duties under this Act, the Secretary of State and education authorities shall have regard to the general principle that, so far as is compatible with the provision of suitable instruction and training and the avoidance of unreasonable public expenditure, pupils are to be educated in accordance with the wishes of their parents'.

15. . . . There are, in fact, no statutory provisions governing the use of corporal punishment . . .

16. Following agreement in principle that the teaching profession should be encouraged to move towards the gradual elimination of corporal punishment . . . , a consultative body . . . prepared in 1968 a booklet entitled 'Elimination of Corporal Punishment in Schools: Statement of Principles and Code of Practice'. The Code reads as follows:

'Until corporal punishment is eliminated its use should be subject to the following rules:

(i) It should not be administered for failure or poor performance in a task, even if the failure . . . appears to be due not to lack of ability or any other kind of handicap but to inattention, carelessness or laziness . . .

(ii) Corporal punishment should not be used in infant classes. . . .

(iii) In secondary departments, only in exceptional circumstances should any pupil be strapped by a teacher of the opposite sex or girls be strapped at all.

(iv) Corporal punishment should not be inflicted for truancy or lateness unless the head teacher is satisfied that the child and not the parent is at fault . . .

(vi) Where used, corporal punishment should be used only as a last resort, and should be directed to punishment of the wrong-doer and to securing the conditions necessary for order in the school and for work in the classroom.

(viii) Corporal punishment should be given by striking the palm of the pupil's hand with a strap and by no other means whatever.'

17. . . . The Code of Practice . . . has no statutory force; however, the courts might be expected to have regard thereto in civil or criminal proceedings concerning an allegedly unlawful use of corporal punishment, and failure to observe it might be relevant in disciplinary proceedings.

...[Within] the guidelines set by the Code, it is for the teachers in each school to determine the disciplinary measures needed in the school...

18. In 1974, the Secretary of State...appointed an independent committee of inquiry ('the Pack Committee') to investigate indiscipline and truancy in Scottish schools. The Committee, which reported in 1977, was of the opinion 'that corporal punishment should...disappear by a process of gradual elimination rather than by legislation'.

The Government remain committed to a policy aimed at abolishing corporal punishment as a disciplinary measure in Scottish schools, but they take the view that that policy is best implemented by seeking to secure progress in this direction by consensus of all concerned rather than by statute.... However, its continued use by teachers is apparently, according to a recent opinion survey, favoured by a large majority of Scottish parents and, according to the Pack Committee's report, by pupils, who even prefer it to some other forms of punishment.

19. [Under the Education (Scotland) Act,] an education authority may exclude a pupil from school if 'the parent of the pupil refuses or fails to comply, or to allow the pupil to comply, with the rules, regulation or disciplinary requirements of the school'....[If] a child fails 'without reasonable excuse' to attend school regularly, the parent is guilty of an offence...

[The Court rejected the applicants' allegation of 'degrading treatment' under Article 3,[17] and considered the claims made under Article 2 of Protocol 1.]

33. The Government maintained in the first place that functions relating to the internal administration of a school, such as discipline, were ancillary and were not functions in relation to 'education' and to 'teaching', within the meaning of Article 2...

The Court would point out that the education of children is the whole process whereby, in any society, adults endeavour to transmit their beliefs, culture and other values to the young, whereas teaching or instruction refers in particular to the transmission of knowledge and to intellectual development.

It appears to the Court somewhat artificial to attempt to separate off matters relating to internal administration as if all such matters fell outside the scope of Article 2. The use of corporal punishment may, in a sense, be said to belong to the internal administration of a school, but at the same time it is, when used, an integral part of the process whereby a school seeks to achieve the object for which it was established, including the development and moulding of the character and mental powers of its pupils. Moreover, [citing the *Kjeldsen, Busk Madsen and Pedersen* judgment, above, para. 50], the second sentence of Article 2 is binding upon the Contracting States in the exercise of 'each and every' function that they undertake in the sphere of education and teaching...

34. The Government further argued that in Scotland the 'functions' assumed by central or local government in the educational field did not extend to matters of discipline.

It may be true that the day-to-day maintenance of discipline in the schools in question is left to the individual teacher; when he administers corporal punishment he is exercising not a power delegated to him by the State but a power vested in him by the common law by virtue of his status as a teacher, and the law in this respect can be changed only by Act of Parliament... Nevertheless, in regard to education in Scotland, the State has assumed responsibility for formulating general policy...and the schools attended by the applicants' children were State schools. Discipline is an integral, even indispensable, part of any educational system, with the result that the

---

[17] *See* Chapter 5, Section B(2).

functions assumed by the State in Scotland must be taken to extend to question of discipline in general, even if not to its everyday maintenance. Indeed, this is confirmed by the fact that central and local authorities participated in the preparation of the Code of Practice and that the Government themselves are committed to a policy aimed at abolishing corporal punishment...

35. Thirdly, in the submission of the Government, the obligation to respect philosophical convictions arises only in the relation to the content of, and mode of conveying, information and knowledge and not in relation to all aspects of school administration.

As the Government pointed out, the *Kjeldsen, Busk Madsen and Pedersen* judgment states [above, para. 53]:

> 'The second sentence of Article 2 implies...that the State...must take care that information or knowledge included in the curriculum is conveyed in an objective, critical and pluralistic manner. The State is forbidden to pursue an aim of indoctrination that might be considered as not respecting parents' religious and philosophical convictions....'

However, that case concerned the content of instruction, whereas the second sentence of Article 2 has a broader scope, as is shown by the generality of its wording....

36. The Government also contested the conclusion of the majority of the Commission that the applicants' views on the use of corporal punishment amounted to 'philosophical convictions', arguing, inter alia, that the expression did not extend to opinions on internal school administration, such as discipline, and that, if the majority were correct, there was no reason why objections to other methods of discipline, or simply to discipline in general, should not also amount to 'philosophical convictions'.

In its ordinary meaning the word 'convictions', taken on its own, is not synonymous with the words 'opinions' and 'ideas', such as are utilised in Article 10 of the Convention, which guarantees freedom of expression; it is more akin to the term 'beliefs' (in the French text: 'convictions') appearing in Article 9—which guarantees freedom of thought, conscience and religion—and denotes views that attain a certain level of cogency, seriousness, cohesion and importance.

As regards the adjective 'philosophical', it is not capable of exhaustive definition and little assistance as to its precise significance is to be gleaned from the *travaux préparatoires*. The Commission pointed out that the word 'philosophy' bears numerous meanings: it is used to allude to a fully-fledged system of thought or, rather loosely, to views on more or less trivial matters. The Court agrees...that neither of these two extremes can be adopted for the purposes of interpreting Article 2: the former would too narrowly restrict the scope of a right that is guaranteed to all parents and the latter might result in the inclusion of matters of insufficient weight or substance.

Having regard to the Convention as a whole, including Article 17, the expression 'philosophical convictions'...denotes, in the Court's opinion, such convictions as are worthy of respect in a 'democratic society'[18] and are not incompatible with human dignity; in addition, they must not conflict with the fundamental right of the child to education, the whole of Article 2 being dominated by its first sentence...

The applicants' views relate to a weighty and substantial aspect of human life and behaviour, namely the integrity of the person, the propriety or otherwise of the infliction of corporal punishment and the exclusion of the distress which the risk of such punishment entails. They are

---

[18] Citing *Young, James and Webster v. United Kingdom*, 13 August 1981, 4 E.H.R.R. 20, para. 63.

views which satisfy each of the various criteria listed above; it is this that distinguishes them from opinions that might be held on other methods of discipline or on discipline in general.

37. The Government pleaded, in the alternative, that the obligation to respect the applicants' convictions had been satisfied by the adoption of a policy of gradually eliminating corporal chastisement. They added that any other solution would be incompatible with...the reservation to Article 2 made by the United Kingdom at the time of signing the Protocol.[19]

The Court is unable to accept the submissions.

(a) Whilst the adoption of the policy referred to clearly foreshadows a move in the direction of the position taken by the applicants, it does not amount to 'respect' for their convictions. As is confirmed by the fact that, in the course of the drafting of Article 2, the words 'have regard to' were replaced by the word 'respect'...the latter word means more than 'acknowledge' or 'taken into account'; in addition to a primarily negative undertaking, it implies some positive obligation on the part of the State.[20] This being so, the duty to respect parental convictions...cannot be overridden by the alleged necessity of striking a balance between the conflicting views involved, nor is the Government's policy to move gradually towards the abolition of corporal punishment in itself sufficient to comply with this duty.

(b) ...The Court accepts that certain solutions canvassed—such as the establishment of a dual system whereby in each sector there would be separate schools for the children of parents objecting to corporal punishment—would be incompatible...with the avoidance of unreasonable public expenditure. However, the Court does not regard it as established that other means of respecting the applicants' convictions, such as a system of exemption for individual pupils in a particular school, would necessarily be incompatible with 'the provision of efficient instruction and training, and the avoidance of unreasonable public expenditure'.

38. Mrs. Campbell and Mrs. Cosans have accordingly been victims of a violation of the second sentence of Article 2 of Protocol No. 1.

39. Mrs. Cosans alleged that, by reason of his suspension from school..., her son Jeffrey had been denied the right to education contrary to the first sentence of Article 2.

The Commission found it unnecessary to examine the issue...The government, in an alternative plea, accepted this view but their principal submission was that the right of access to educational facilities...may be made subject to reasonable requirements and that, since Jeffrey's suspension was due to his and his parents' refusal to accept such a requirement, there had been no breach.

40. The Court considers that it is necessary to determine this issue. Of course, the existence of corporal punishment as a disciplinary measure...underlay both of Mrs. Cosans' allegations concerning Article 2, but there is a substantial difference between the factual basis of her two claims. In the case of the second sentence, the situation complained of was attendance at a school where recourse was had to a certain practice, whereas, in the case of the first sentence, it was the fact of being forbidden to attend; the consequences of the latter situation are more far-reaching than those of the former...

[19] For this reservation, *see* Section A, *supra*.
[20] Citing *Marckx v. Belgium*, 13 June 1979, 2 E.H.R.R. 330, para. 31. And *see* Chapter 8, Section B(2).

Again, Article 2 constitutes a whole that is dominated by its first sentence, the right set out in the second sentence being an adjunct of the fundamental right to education.

Finally, there is also a substantial difference between the legal basis of the two claims, for one concerns a right of a parent and the other a right of a child....

41. The right to education guaranteed by the first sentence of Article 2 by its very nature calls for regulation by the State, but such regulation must never injure the substance of the right nor conflict with other rights enshrined in the Convention or its Protocols.[21]

The suspension of Jeffrey Cosans—which remained in force for nearly a whole school year— was motivated by his and his parents' refusal to accept that he receive or be liable to corporal chastisement... His return to school could have been secured only if his parents had acted contrary to their convictions... A condition of access to an educational establishment that conflicts in this way with another right enshrined in Protocol No. 1 cannot be described as reasonable and in any event falls outside the State's power of regulation under Article 2.

There has accordingly also been, as regards Jeffrey Cosans, breach of the first sentence of that Article.

The decisions on Article 2 were made by 6–1. The dissenting judge was Sir Vincent Evans who said:

2. In my opinion,...the majority of the Court have given too wide an interpretation to Article 2...

3. ...In the *Belgian Linguistic* case it was held that this provision did not require of States that they should, in the sphere of education and teaching, respect parents' linguistic preferences, but only their religious and philosophical convictions and that to interpret the terms 'religious' and 'philosophical' as covering linguistic preferences would amount to a distortion of their ordinary and usual meaning and read into the Convention something that was not there...

4. In the course of the preparatory work on Article 2 in the Consultative Assembly of the Council of Europe the expression 'philosophical convictions' was criticised as being so vague that it should not be inserted in a legal instrument purporting to protect human rights... Mr. Teitgen made it clear that the intention was to protect the rights of parents against the use of educational institutions by the State for the ideological indoctrination of children.[22] This was precisely the interpretation put upon the text by the Court in the *Kjeldsen, Busk Madsen and Pedersen* case... In the light of this background, my understanding of the second sentence of Article 2 is that it is concerned with the content of information and knowledge imparted to the child through education and teaching and the manner of imparting such information and knowledge and that the views of parents on such matters as the use of corporal punishment are as much outside the intended scope of the provision as are their linguistic preferences. If there had been any intention that it should apply to disciplinary measures and to the use of corporal punishment in particular, it is inconceivable that the implications of this would not have been raised in the course of the lengthy debates that preceded its adoption.

5. An interpretation of the second sentence of Article 2 extending its application beyond its intended scope could give rise to very considerable difficulties in practice. The maintaining

[21] Citing the *Belgian Linguistic* case, Section B, *supra*.
[22] Official Report of the 35th Sitting of the Consultative Assembly, 8 December 1951, 5 Collected edition 1229–30.

of discipline is certainly an integral part of the educational system...So are many other matters relating to the provision of educational facilities and the internal administration of schools...If the sentence in question is interpreted in a sense wide enough to cover the views of parents opposed to corporal punishment, I do not see how it can reasonably be applied so as to exclude from its scope all manner of other strongly held views regarding the way in which schools are organised and administered. There may be very strongly held beliefs on such matters as the segregation of sexes, the streaming of pupils according to ability or the existence of independent schools, which could be claimed to have a religious or philosophical basis...Different religious and philosophical convictions relating to the content of instruction can be duly respected in the teaching process by presenting information in an objective way. But in regard to such matters as the segregation of the sexes, streaming and the abolition of independent schools, there would be insuperable practical difficulties in respecting equally the views of those who are opposed to and those who favour one system or the other...

6. However, even if the wider interpretation of the second sentence of Article 2 adopted by the Court...were correct, it would be my opinion that there has been no violation of this provision in view of the reservation made by the United Kingdom on signature of the Protocol...[23]

In respect of the United Kingdom,...the obligation...to respect the right of parents has been assumed...only so far as this can be done compatibly with the provision of efficient instruction and training and the avoidance of unreasonable public expenditure.

7. ...[The] majority of the Court has held that the Government's policy to move gradually towards the abolition of corporal punishment is not in itself sufficient to comply with their duty to respect parental convictions. It is implicit in the Court's judgment that some more positive means of respecting the applicants' convictions is called for by the sentence in question....[Only] three possible solutions have been canvassed which, apart from the reservation, would sufficiently comply with the State's obligation as interpreted by the Court. These are:

1. that separate schools should be provided within the State educational system for children of parents who object to corporal punishment;
2. that separate classes within the same school should be provided for such children;
3. that a system should be established in which children in the same class should be treated differently according to the views and wishes of their parents.

[The judge rejected each of these solutions, saying of the third possible solution:]...It seems to me essential that any system of discipline in a school should be seen to be fair and capable of being fairly administered, otherwise a sense of injustice will be generated with harmful consequences both for the upbringing of the individual and for harmonious relations within the group. It will also place the teacher in an impractical position to administer discipline fairly if children in the same class have to be treated differently according to the views of their parents. It has been pointed out that, where corporal punishment is used, exceptions are in any event made in respect of girls and children suffering from a disability. I believe that children will readily understand the reasons for this, but I think they are likely to regard it as arbitrary and unjust if Johnny is exempted simply because his Mum or Dad says so.

9. I conclude therefore that there has been no breach of the second sentence of Article 2.

---

[23] For the reservation, *see* Section A, *supra*.

[Sir Vincent Evans also held that there had been no breach of the first sentence of Article 2 in respect of the suspension of Jeffrey Cosans from school. In his view, it was implicit in the *Belgian Linguistic* judgment that the right of access might be made subject to reasonable requirements, including acceptance of the school's rules and disciplinary requirements.]

The Court's decision, together with that in *Costello-Roberts v. United Kingdom*,[24] led to national legislation that first removed corporal punishment from state schools and eventually excluded it from all schools. This last change in the law caused a group of teachers and parents of children at certain Christian independent schools to claim that they believed on religious grounds that teachers should, in the place of parents, be able to administer reasonable physical punishment to indisciplined children; and that the ban on such punishment was a breach of their Convention rights under Article 9, and under Article 2 of the First Protocol. It was held by the United Kingdom court that their Convention rights were engaged, but that the rights were not absolute; the legislation pursued a legitimate aim, was not disproportionate, and had adopted a proportionate and appropriate way of promoting the well-being of children.[25] In contrast, the Supreme Court of Canada upheld as compatible with the Charter of Rights and Freedoms (and not void for vagueness) a provision of the Criminal Code that permits reasonable force to be used by parents and teachers in correcting children.[26]

E. VALSAMIS V. GREECE

Judgment of 18 December 1996
24 E.H.R.R. 294

[The applicants were Jehovah's Witnesses, being the parents of Victoria, born in 1980, and Victoria herself. For Jehovah's Witnesses, pacifism is a fundamental tenet of their religion and forbids any conduct or practice associated with war or violence, even indirectly. For this reason they refuse to carry out military service or to take part in events with military overtones.]

7. On 20 September 1992 Mr and Mrs Valsamis submitted a written declaration in order that their daughter Victoria, who was then 12 . . . , should be exempted from attending school religious-education lessons, Orthodox Mass and any other event that was contrary to her religious beliefs, including national-holiday celebrations and public processions.

8. Victoria was exempted from attendance at religious-education lessons and Orthodox Mass.

In October 1992, however, she, in common with the other pupils at her school, was asked to take part in the celebration of the National Day on 28 October, when the outbreak of war between Greece and Fascist Italy on 28 October 1940 is commemorated with school and military parades.

---

[24] *See* Chapter 5, Section B, where other decisions on corporal punishment are discussed.
[25] *R. (Williamson) v. Secretary of State for Education and Employment* [2005] UKHL 15, [2005] 2 A.C. 246.
[26] *Canadian Foundation for Children v. Canada* [2004] 1 S.C.R. 76 and *see* Chapter 5, Section B(2).

On this occasion school parades take place in nearly all towns and villages. In the capital there is no military parade on 28 October, and in Salonika the school parade is held on a different day from the military parade. The school and military parades are only held simultaneously in a small number of municipalities.

9. Victoria informed the headmaster that her religious beliefs forbade her joining in the commemoration of a war by taking part...in a school parade that would follow an official Mass and would be held on the same day as a military parade...[Her] request to be excused attendance was refused but she nevertheless did not take part in the school's parade.

10. On 29 October 1992 the headmaster of the school punished her for her failure to attend with one day's suspension from school. That decision was taken in accordance with Circular no. C1/1/1 of 2 January 1990 issued by the Ministry of Education and Religious Affairs (see paragraph 13 below).

[The judgment quotes provisions of the Greek constitution dealing with religion, including Article 3 (the 'dominant religion' to be that of the Christian Eastern Orthodox Church) and Article 13 ('Freedom of conscience in religious matters is inviolable')]

13. [By the Circular of 2 January 1990]...

'Schoolchildren who are Jehovah's Witnesses shall be exempted from attending religious-education lessons, school prayers and Mass...

No schoolchild shall be exempted from taking part in other school activities, such as national events.'

[The Court referred to a Presidential Decree of 1979 that dealt with the behaviour of school pupils and provided for disciplinary measures, 'in increasing order of severity': a warning, a reprimand, exclusion from lessons for an hour, suspension from school for up to five days and transfer to another school. Under the Decree, suspended pupils may remain at school during teaching hours and take part in activities 'under the responsibility of the headmaster'.]

21. ...[The] applicants complained of the penalty of one day's suspension from school that was imposed on the pupil Victoria, who had refused to take part in the school parade.... Since, owing to their religious beliefs, Mr and Mrs Valsamis were opposed to any event with military overtones, they had sought an exemption for their daughter, but in vain. They relied on the Commission's opinion in... *Arrowsmith v. United Kingdom*[27] ... according to which pacifism as a philosophy fell within the ambit of the right to freedom of thought and conscience....[under Article 9(1)]. They therefore claimed recognition of their pacifism under the head of religious beliefs...

22. ...The parents did not allege any breach of Victoria's right to education. On the other hand, they considered that [Article 2] prohibited requiring their daughter to take part in events extolling patriotic ideals to which they did not subscribe; pupils' education should be provided through history lessons rather than school parades.

23. The Government contested the parents' submission, arguing that the school parade on 28 October had no military overtones such as to offend pacifist convictions.

They disputed that Mr and Mrs Valsamis's belief could count as a conviction for the purposes of Article 2...They added that the State's educational function, which had to be understood in

27 (1980) 19 D.R. 5.

a broad sense, allowed it to include in pupils' school curriculum the requirement to parade on 28 October.

The National Day commemorated Greece's attachment to the values of democracy, liberty and human rights which had provided the foundation for the post-war legal order. It was not an expression of bellicose feelings, nor did it glorify military conflict. Communal celebration of it retained today an idealistic and pacifist character that was strengthened by the presence of school parades...

25. The Court does not consider that it must rule of its own motion on the question whether the pupil Victoria's right to education was respected.

It reiterates that 'the two sentences of Article 2 must be read not only in the light of each other but also, in particular, of Articles 8, 9 and 10 of the Convention'.[28]

The term 'belief' ('conviction') appears in Article 9 in the context of the right to freedom of thought, conscience and religion. The concept of 'religious and philosophical convictions' appears in Article 2 of Protocol No. 1. When applying that provision, the Court has held that in its ordinary meaning 'convictions', taken on its own, is not synonymous with the words 'opinions' and 'ideas'. It denotes 'views that attain a certain level of cogency, seriousness, cohesion and importance'.[29]

26. As the Court observed in ... *Kokkinakis v. Greece*[30] Jehovah's Witnesses enjoy both the status of a 'known religion' and the advantages flowing from that as regards observance. Mr and Mrs Valsamis were accordingly entitled to rely on the right to respect for their religious convictions within the meaning of this provision...

27. The Court reiterates that Article 2 ... enjoins the State to respect parents' convictions, be they religious or philosophical, throughout the entire State education programme ... That duty is broad in its extent as it applies not only to the content of education and the manner of its provision but also to the performance of all the 'functions' assumed by the State. The verb 'respect' means more than 'acknowledge' or 'take into account'. In addition to a primarily negative undertaking, it implies some positive obligation on the part of the State.[31]

The Court has also held that 'although individual interests must on occasion be subordinated to those of a group, democracy does not simply mean that the views of a majority must always prevail: a balance must be achieved which ensures the fair and proper treatment of minorities and avoids any abuse of a dominant position'.[32]

28. However, 'the setting and planning of the curriculum fall in principle within the competence of the Contracting States. This mainly involves questions of expediency on which it is not for the Court to rule and whose solution may legitimately vary according to the country and the era'.... Given that discretion, the Court has held that the second sentence of Article 2 ... forbids the State 'to pursue an aim of indoctrination that might be regarded as not respecting parents' religious and philosophical convictions. That is the limit that must not be exceeded'...

29. The imposition of disciplinary penalties is an integral part of the process whereby a school seeks to achieve the object for which it was established, including the development and moulding of the character and mental powers of its pupils.[33]

---

[28] Citing *Kjeldsen, Busk Madsen and Pedersen v. Denmark*, Section C, *supra*, para. 52.

[29] Citing *Campbell and Cosans v. United Kingdom*, Section D, *supra*.

[30] 25 May 1993, 17 E.H.R.R, 397, para. 32.

[31] Citing *Campbell and Cosans*, para. 37.

[32] Citing *Young, James and Webster v. United Kingdom*, *supra* n. 18 para. 63.

[33] *See Campbell and Cosans*, para. 33.

31. While it is not for the Court to rule on the Greek State's decisions as regards the setting and planning of the school curriculum, it is surprised that pupils can be required on pain of suspension from school—even if only for a day—to parade outside the school precincts on a holiday.

Nevertheless, it can discern nothing, either in the purpose of the parade or in the arrangements for it, which could offend the applicants' pacifist convictions to an extent prohibited by the second sentence of Article 2.

Such commemorations of national events serve, in their way, both pacifist objectives and the public interest. The presence of military representatives at some of the parades which take place in Greece . . . does not in itself alter the nature of the parades.

Furthermore, the obligation on the pupil does not deprive her parents of their right 'to enlighten and advise their children, to exercise with regard to their children natural parental functions as educators, or to guide their children on a path in line with the parents' own religious or philosophical convictions'.[34]

32. It is not for the Court to rule on the expediency of other educational methods which, in the applicants' view, would be better suited to the aim of perpetuating historical memory among the younger generation. It notes, however, that the penalty of suspension, which cannot be regarded as an exclusively educational measure and may have some psychological impact on the pupil on whom it is imposed, is nevertheless of limited duration and does not require the exclusion of the pupil from the school premises . . .

33. In conclusion, there has not been a breach of Article 2 of Protocol No. 1.

[The Court found no breaches of Articles 3 or 9 of the Convention, but upheld the complaint that, in breach of Article 13, no effective national remedy was available to the applicants. They were entitled to have their complaint against the penalty considered by a court or other body with power to deal with it on its merits.]

It is instructive to compare the *Valsamis* judgment with that of the U.S. Supreme Court in *West Virginia State Board of Education v. Barnette*,[35] in which (in a factual context that is both similar to and different from that in *Valsamis*) the Court upheld a challenge by Jehovah's Witnesses to a regulation requiring school-children to salute the U.S. flag while pledging their allegiance to it; refusal to do so was treated as insubordination. In his judgment for the majority, Jackson J said: '. . . the refusal of these persons to participate in the ceremony does not interfere with or deny rights of others to do so. Nor is there any question in this case that their behavior is peaceable and orderly. The sole conflict is between the authority and rights of the individual. The State asserts power to condition access to public education on making a prescribed sign and profession and at the same time to coerce attendance by punishing both parent and child'.[36] Taken in connection with the pledges, the flag salute was a form of speech; while the Jehovah's Witnesses objected to this on religious grounds, 'many citizens who do not share these religious views hold such a compulsory rite to infringe constitutional liberty of the individual'.[37] Rejecting the argument that to support the right not to conform was 'to

---

[34] Citing *Kjeldsen, Busk Madsen and Pedersen*, para. 54.
[35] 319 U.S. 624 (1943).
[36] *Id.* 630.
[37] *Id.* 634.

choose weak government over strong government', Jackson J said: 'Free public education, if faithful to the ideal of secular instruction and political neutrality, will not be
partisan or enemy of any class, creed, party, or faction. If it is to impose any ideological
discipline, however, each party or denomination must seek to control, or failing that,
to weaken the influence of the educational system. Observance of the limitations of
the Constitution will not weaken government in the field appropriate for its exercise'.[38]
He concluded: 'Neither our domestic tranquillity in peace nor our martial effort in
war depend on compelling little children to participate in a ceremony which ends in
nothing for them but a fear of spiritual condemnation'.[39]

The following case concerns an issue that in one form or another has arisen in several European countries, namely whether to enjoy access to higher education Muslim
women may be required not to wear the veil that they consider necessary on religious
grounds.

F. SAHIN V. TURKEY

Judgment of 10 November 2005
41 E.H.R.R. 8

[The applicant, a practising Muslim, considered it her religious duty to wear the Islamic
headscarf. Having studied medicine for four years at Bursa University, she enrolled to study
at the Faculty of Medicine, Istanbul University. During the year, the Vice-Chancellor issued
a circular forbidding admission to lectures to students who wore the headscarf or who had
a beard. Ms Sarin refused to comply: when disciplinary proceedings were taken against
her, she unsuccessfully challenged the legality of the circular in the Administrative Court.
In the course of those proceedings, she gave up her studies in Turkey and enrolled at Vienna
University.

The Court examined the legal background to the Vice-Chancellor's circular, noting that by
Article 2 of the Constitution, Turkey 'is a democratic, secular and social state' and that by
Article 10 men and women 'have equal rights'. The Court referred to decisions of the Turkish
Constitutional Court in 1989 and 1991 holding that to grant legal recognition to a religious
symbol like the Islamic headscarf was not compatible with the principle that state education
must be neutral, 'as it would be liable to generate conflicts between students with differing
religious convictions or beliefs';[40] it was thus consistent with the emphasis on secularism
made by the Turkish Constitution that headscarves could not be worn in institutions of higher
education. The Court examined the place of the Islamic headscarf in state education in many
European countries.

In dealing with the case under Article 9, the Court held by 16–1 that the ban on the
headscarf, although an interference with Ms Sahin's right to manifest her religion, was

---

[38] Id. 637.
[39] Id. 644.
[40] Judgment, para. 39.

prescribed by law, served a legitimate aim and was not disproportionate.[41] The Court gave separate consideration to the claim that her right to education had been breached. The first issue was whether the first sentence of Article 2 extended to higher education.]

134. ...Although [Article 2] makes no mention of higher education, there is nothing to suggest that it does not apply to all levels of education, including higher education.

136. The Court does not lose sight of the fact that the development of the right to education, whose content varies from one time or place to another, according to economic and social circumstances, mainly depends on the needs and resources of the community. However, it is of crucial importance that the Convention is interpreted and applied in a manner which renders its rights practical and effective, not theoretical and illusory. Moreover, the Convention is a living instrument which must be interpreted in the light of present-day conditions... While the first sentence of Article 2 essentially establishes access to primary and secondary education, there is no watertight division separating higher education from other forms of education. In a number of recently adopted instruments, the Council of Europe has stressed the key role and importance of higher education in the promotion of human rights and fundamental freedoms and the strengthening of democracy...

137. Consequently, it would be hard to imagine that institutions of higher education existing at a given time do not come within the scope of the first sentence of Article 2... Although that Article does not impose a duty on the Contracting States to set up institutions of higher education, any State so doing will be under an obligation to afford an effective right of access to them.

[The Court reviewed decisions made by the Commission, some of which had stated that Article 2 was primarily concerned with elementary education, and others of which assumed (without deciding) that the right protected by Article 2 applied to all levels of education.]

140. For its part, after the *Belgian Linguistic* case the Court declared a series of cases on higher education inadmissible, not because the first sentence of Article 2... was inapplicable, but on other grounds (complaint of a disabled person who did not satisfy a university's entrance requirements, ...; refusal of permission to an applicant in custody to prepare for and sit a final university examination..., interruption of advanced studies by a valid conviction and sentence).[42]

141. In the light of all the foregoing considerations, it is clear that any institutions of higher education existing at a given time come within the scope of the first sentence of Article 2..., since the right of access to such institutions is an inherent part of the right set out in that provision. This is not an extensive interpretation forcing new obligations on the Contracting States: it is based on the very terms of the first sentence of Article 2 read in its context and having regard to the object and purpose of the Convention...

[As to the merits of the applicant's case]

---

[41] Judgment, paras. 75–123. And *see* Chapter 7(C), *supra*.
[42] Citations to these three decisions omitted.

145. The applicant said that despite wearing the headscarf she had been able to enrol at the university and to pursue her studies there without incident for four and a half years. She therefore argued that at the time of her enrolment...and while pursuing her studies, there had been no domestic source of law that would have enabled her to foresee that she would be denied access to the lecture theatres a number of years later.

147. The applicant argued that making the pursuit of her studies conditional on her abandoning the headscarf and refusing her access to educational institutions if she refused to comply with that condition had effectively and wrongfully violated the substance of her right to education... This had been compounded by the fact that she was a young adult with a fully developed personality and social and moral values who was deprived of all possibility of pursuing her studies in Turkey in a manner consistent with her beliefs.

148. For all these reasons, the applicant submitted that the respondent State had overstepped the limits of its margin of appreciation, however wide it might be, and violated her right to education, read in the light of Articles 8, 9 and 10.

150. [In reply, the Government submitted] that the applicant had enrolled at the... Faculty of Medicine at Istanbul University after studying for five years at the Faculty of Medicine of Bursa University, where she had worn the headscarf. The Vice-Chancellor of Istanbul University had issued a circular prohibiting students from wearing the headscarf in the University. The ban was based on judgments of the Constitutional Court and the Supreme Administrative Court...[The] applicant had not encountered any difficulty in enrolling at [Bursa University], which proved that she had enjoyed equality of treatment in the right of access to educational institutions...

151. The Government concluded by...arguing that the regulations in issue did not contravene the Court's case-law, having regard to the margin of appreciation accorded to the Contracting States.

[The decision of the Court:]

152. The right to education, as set out in the first sentence of Article 2, guarantees everyone within the jurisdiction of the Contracting States 'a right of access to educational institutions existing at a given time', but such access constitutes only a part of the right to education. For that right 'to be effective, it is further necessary that...the individual who is the beneficiary should have...the right to obtain, in conformity with the rules in force in each State, and in one form or another, official recognition of the studies which he has completed'.[43] Similarly, implicit in the phrase 'No person shall...' is the principle of equality of treatment of all citizens in the exercise of their right to education.

153. The fundamental right of everyone to education is a right guaranteed equally to pupils in State and independent schools, without distinction...

154. In spite of its importance, this right is not, however, absolute, but may be subject to limitations; these are permitted by implication since the right of access 'by its very nature calls for regulation by the State'.[44] Admittedly, the regulation of educational institutions may vary in time and in place, *inter alia*, according to the needs and resources of the community and the distinctive features of different levels of education. Consequently, [states] enjoy a certain margin of appreciation in this sphere, although the final decision as to the observance of the

---

[43] Citing the *Belgian Linguistic* case and also *Kjeldsen, Busk Madsen & Pedersen v. Denmark*.
[44] Citing the *Belgian Linguistic* case and other cases.

Convention's requirements rests with the Court. In order to ensure that the restrictions that are imposed do not curtail the right in question to such an extent as to impair its very essence..., the Court must satisfy itself that they are foreseeable for those concerned and pursue a legitimate aim. However, unlike the position with respect to Articles 8 to 11..., it is not bound by an exhaustive list of 'legitimate aims' under Article 2 of Protocol No. 1... Furthermore, a limitation will only be compatible with Article 2... if there is a reasonable relationship of proportionality between the means employed and the aim sought to be achieved.

155. ... The provisions of the Convention and its Protocols must be considered as a whole. Accordingly, the first sentence of Article 2 must, where appropriate, be read in the light in particular of Articles 8, 9 and 10 of the Convention.[45]

156. The right to education does not in principle exclude recourse to disciplinary measures, including suspension or expulsion from an educational institution in order to ensure compliance with its internal rules. The imposition of disciplinary penalties is an integral part of the process whereby a school seeks to achieve the object for which it was established, including the development and moulding of the character and mental powers of its pupils...

157. By analogy with its reasoning on the question of the existence of interference under Article 9,... the Court [accepts] that the regulations on the basis of which the applicant was refused access to various lectures and examinations for wearing the Islamic headscarf constituted a restriction on her right to education, notwithstanding the fact that she had had access to the University and been able to read the subject of her choice in accordance with the results she had achieved in the university entrance examination. However, an analysis of the case by reference to the right to education cannot in this instance be divorced from the conclusion reached by the Court with respect to Article 9...

158. In that connection, the Court has already found that the restriction was foreseeable to those concerned and pursued the legitimate aims of protecting the rights and freedoms of others and maintaining public order... The obvious purpose of the restriction was to preserve the secular character of educational institutions.

159. [In relation to Article 9, the Court has also found]... that there was a reasonable relationship of proportionality between the means used and the aim pursued. In so finding, it relied in particular on the following factors... Firstly, the measures in question manifestly did not hinder the students in performing the duties imposed by the habitual forms of religious observance. Secondly, the decision-making process for applying the internal regulations satisfied, so far as was possible, the requirement to weigh up the various interests at stake. The university authorities judiciously sought a means whereby they could avoid having to turn away students wearing the headscarf and at the same time honour their obligation to protect the rights of others and the interests of the education system. Lastly, the process also appears to have been accompanied by safeguards—the rule requiring conformity with statute and judicial review—that were apt to protect the students' interests...

160. It would, furthermore, be unrealistic to imagine that the applicant, a medical student, was unaware of Istanbul University's internal regulations restricting the places where religious dress could be worn... She could reasonably have foreseen that she ran the risk of being refused access to lectures and examinations if, as subsequently happened, she continued to wear the Islamic headscarf after 23 February 1998.

---

[45] Citing *Kjeldsen, Busk Madsen & Pedersen v. Denmark.*

161. Consequently, the restriction in question did not impair the very essence of the applicant's right to education. In addition,...the restriction did not conflict with other rights enshrined in the Convention....

162. In conclusion, there has been no violation of the first sentence of Article 2 of Protocol No. 1.

Two judges (Rozakis and Valic) concurred in the result, but stated that the case should have been decided solely under Article 9, since in their view the complaint based on the right to education did not raise a separate issue. Judge Tulkens agreed that the right to education extended to higher education, but dissented both as regards Article 9 and Article 2 of the First Protocol. He emphasized the principle in Convention jurisprudence that 'pluralism, tolerance and broadmindedness are hallmarks of a democratic society'; where tensions within a state existed, the authorities should not eliminate pluralism but should 'ensure that the competing groups tolerate each other'. He disagreed with the use made by the Court of the margin of appreciation. While there was a diversity of practice between states on the wearing of religious symbols in educational institutions, 'in none of the member states has the ban on wearing religious symbols extended to university education, which is intended for young adults, who are less amenable to pressure'. The Court had failed to apply a European supervision to the margin of appreciation. 'While the principle of secularism requires education to be provided without any manifestation of religion and while it has to be compulsory for teachers and all public servants, as they have voluntarily taken up posts in a neutral environment, the position of pupils and students seems to me to be different' (para. 7). Judge Tulkens disagreed with the majority's finding of proportionality. The applicant 'simply wished to complete her studies in the conditions that had obtained...during the initial years of her university career, when she had been free to wear the headscarf without any problem' (para. 15). In his view, the Grand Chamber had not weighed up the competing interests, 'namely, on the one hand, the damage sustained by the applicant...and, on the other, the benefit to be gained by Turkish society from prohibiting the applicant from wearing the headscarf on the university premises' (para. 17). 'The question also arises whether such an infringement of the right to education does not, ultimately, amount to an implicit acceptance of discrimination against the applicant on grounds of religion' (para. 18).[46]

The principle of secularism is without doubt of particular significance in the history of the Turkish republic. It is less clear that the Court's judgment deals persuasively with all the educational issues that arise from the application of the headscarf ban to Ms Sahin. For this and other reasons it must not be assumed that the decision provides authority to support such a ban anywhere in Europe.[47]

---

[46] The decision in *Sahin v. Turkey* contrasts with the majority opinion of the UN Human Rights Committee in *Hudoyberganova v. Uzbekistan* (18 January 2005), 19 B.H.R.C. 581, holding that a similar ban in a state university was in breach of Art. 18(2) ICCPR ('No one shall be subject to coercion which would impair his freedom to have or adopt a religion or belief of his choice').

[47] *See* for comparison the decision of the Conseil d'Etat in France (C.E., 2 Nov. 1992, *Kherouaa et al*) and of the House of Lords in the United Kingdom (*R. (Begum) v. Head Teacher and Governors of Denbigh High School* [2006] UKHL 15; [2007] 1 A.C. 100).

G. SOME CONSEQUENCES OF THE CONVENTION RIGHT TO EDUCATION

Taken together, these decisions do not suggest that the Court has given a rich and dynamic substance to the Convention right to education: in this context, states have a very broad 'margin of appreciation'. Except as regards corporal punishment in United Kingdom schools, the case-law gives little encouragement to applicants wishing to use the Convention to secure changes in their national system of education or to obtain redress for grievances in the sphere of education. However, if the facts of *Brown v. Board of Education of Topeka* were to be repeated within a European country, so that admission to state schools depended on the students' race or colour, we would expect a remedy to be found through Article 2 of the First Protocol read together with Article 14. Indeed, in *Timishev v. Russia*,[48] where the local authorities excluded the two children of an ethnic Chechen from the primary school that they were attending, because the applicant had no registered residence and could not produce a 'migrant's card', the Court held that this was a denial of the children's right to education.

It is all the more difficult to understand the Court's decision in *DH and Others v. Czech Republic*[49] to reject the claim by Roma families that Roma children of average or above-average intelligence had been placed in 'special schools' intended for children with learning difficulties. That decision is unfortunate both in limiting the scope of rights under Article 14 and for the apparent reluctance of the Court to intervene in educational decisions, even where there was strong evidence of discrimination on ethnic grounds.

The former European Commission on Human Rights dealt with a wider range of educational cases than the Court itself has done, and some of these will be mentioned in this section.

As a consequence of the *Belgian Linguistic* case, parents and children have no right to require the state to establish or subsidize school institutions of any particular type or level. However, since Article 2 (despite its negative formulation) does impose positive obligations upon the state, it would be difficult for a state to argue that it is not obliged to ensure that school places are available for *all* children. At least at the primary level, every European state ensures provision for many children within its jurisdiction; if the provision is not sufficient for all those children, a state could scarcely fall back on a defence that education is primarily for the parents to provide to their children.

An important corollary of the interest of parents in their children's education is that the state must recognize their right to have children privately educated.[50] While the state does not have a monopoly in providing education, the state may make education compulsory up to a specified age and may require parents who wish to educate children

---

[48] Judgment of 13 Dec. 2005.

[49] *See* Chapter 9(E). On 13 Nov. 2007, the decision was reversed by the Grand Chamber.

[50] *Jordebo v. Sweden*, 6 Mar. 1987, 51 D.R. 125. And compare *Pierce v. Society of Sisters of Holy Names*, 268 U.S. 510 (1925) (unconstitutional for state to require all children aged 8 to 16 to attend public schools).

at home to co-operate in assessing the standards reached.[51] Moreover, the state may
require private schools to reach certain standards and must recognize the results of such
education (for example, by recognizing certificates and diplomas that have been duly
awarded).[52] However, the state need not assist with the cost of private education favoured
by the parents,[53] and may refuse to subsidize a private, secular school.[54] Nonetheless, it
does not follow that a state has complete freedom to decide how to organize support for
education without any regard for the possibility of breaches of Article 14.[55]

Given the cautious approach of the Court to the meaning of 'philosophical and
religious convictions', parents of a seven-year old child in Germany were not entitled
to insist on classes in 'elementary mathematics' rather than 'modern mathematics';[56]
nor could parents in England insist on a place in a single-sex grammar school for their
daughter, despite an array of arguments claiming to show that what they regarded as the
'negative ethos' of a mixed, comprehensive school was contrary to their convictions.[57]
But if parents have religious grounds for believing that single-sex education is required
for their children, this may not be altogether ignored by education authorities.[58]

Parents who have a child with special educational needs, by reason of physical or
mental disabilities, are likely to have a strong desire that the best possible provision
should be made for him or her. Opinions often differ, both in general and in particular
cases, as to whether such a child will fare better in a special school or in a mainstream
school with experience of giving any additional support that is needed. Parents in
the United Kingdom who have challenged assessment and placement decisions made
by education authorities, and decisions relating to the special support that should be
given, have had no success at Strasbourg.[59]

One issue that was previously uncertain was whether the right not to be denied
education applied to all levels of education. Any continuing doubt about the position of higher education was resolved in *Sahin v. Turkey* (above). Certainly, the duty
on the state to respect the religious and philosophical convictions of parents falls
away when children become adults. And, as was held in the *Belgian Linguistic* case,
the right of access to educational facilities 'by its very nature calls for regulation

---

[51] *H v. UK*, 6 Mar. 1984, 37 D.R. 105.

[52] *See* the *Belgian Linguistic* case at 281, 334.

[53] *W & L v. Sweden*, 11 Dec. 1985, 45 D.R. 143 (no duty to subsidize Rudolf Steiner school).

[54] *Verein Gemeinsam Lernen v. Austria* (1995) 20 E.H.R.R. C.D. 78; and *X v. United Kingdom*, 2 May 1978,
14 D.R. 179 (refusal to make a 100% grant for a non-denominational school in Northern Ireland).

[55] If the long-established national policy has been to give public funding to schools associated with a
particular faith or Christian denomination, can the members of a different faith or denomination make out
a case under the Convention for similar public funding for schools associated with their religious beliefs?
And could an unjust and unequal scheme for public funding of schools be in breach of the right to education
of the disadvantaged children, read with Article 14? *Cf. San Antonio School District v. Rodriguez*, 411 U.S. 1
(1973), Section A, *supra*.

[56] *X, Y & Z v. Germany*, 15 July 1982, 29 D.R. 224.

[57] *W & DM v. United Kingdom*, 6 Mar. 1984, 37 D.R. 96.

[58] *Cf. R. (K) v. London Borough of Newham* [2002] EWHC 405 (Admin), [2002] E.L.R. 390.

[59] *See PD v. United Kingdom*, 2 Oct. 1989, 62 D.R. 292; *Simpson v. United Kingdom*, 4 Dec. 1989, 64 D.R.
188; *Graeme v. United Kingdom*, 5 Feb. 1990, 64 D.R. 158; *Cohen v. United Kingdom*, 28 Feb. 1996, 21 E.H.R.R.
C.D. 104; *SP v. United Kingdom*, 12 Jan. 1997, 23 E.H.R.R. C.D. 139.

by the State, regulation which may vary in time and place according to the needs and resources of the community and of individuals'. While a child's right of access to primary education is a universal right and applies even to children with severe learning difficulties, the state may regulate access to further and higher education, according to the individual's aptitudes and to available resources. Where a student had failed his first year examinations as well as resit examinations, and for this reason and because of poor attendance had been excluded from the university, it was not difficult for the Commission to hold that his right to education had not been denied.[60] There was a different outcome in *Eren v. Turkey*,[61] where a high-school leaver needed to pass a two-stage entrance examination to attend a university in Turkey. He failed the first stage, studied privately and later passed a resit of the first stage well enough to sit the second stage. Although he obtained extremely high marks in that examination, he was not permitted to register for a university: on the advice of an academic board, his second stage marks had been annulled because, in the light of his earlier results, his excellent achievement at that stage 'could not be explained'. His challenge to that decision failed in the administrative courts. The Strasbourg Court by 6–1 held that there was no legal basis for the discretion that was claimed to annul the results of candidates on the ground of their inability to explain their success. Dealing with candidates who were found to have cheated was not a matter of discretion: in the circumstances, the decision 'lacked a legal and rational basis, resulting in arbitrariness'.[62] Judge Popovic, dissenting, considered that the state had competence to prescribe conditions for university admission and that, unless those rules were challenged, the Court could not rule on the questions of expediency involved in setting standards. He also considered that the Court should not act in a 'fourth instance' role, that is, it should not provide a further appeal on the merits of appellate decisions taken in national courts.

The power of the state to regulate education carries with it the power to determine the disciplinary system for different levels of education. There is no breach of the right to education if pupils or students are suspended or expelled, provided that national regulations do not prevent them enrolling in another institution to pursue their studies.[63] In common with other Convention rights, complaints of a breach of the right to education must first be raised at a national level, and it should be necessary to apply to Strasbourg only if the decision or action complained of has been held to comply with national law.[64] But it does not follow that action by a school that departs from the prescribed disciplinary procedure is necessarily also a breach of the Convention right.[65] In 1989,

---

[60] *X v. United Kingdom*, 9 Dec. 1980, 23 D.R. 228.

[61] 7 February 2006.

[62] *Id.*, para 50.

[63] *Yanasik v. Turkey*, 6 Jan. 1993, 74 D.R. 14.

[64] But *cf. Timishev v. Russia* (n. 48 *supra*).

[65] *Cf. Ali v. Head Teacher and Governors of Lord Grey School* [2006] UKHL 14, [2006] 2 All E.R. 457, where the House of Lords took a significantly narrower view of the impact of the Convention than the Court of Appeal had done.

the Commission held that the right not to be denied education was not a civil right that gave rise to the right to a fair hearing within Article 6(1) of the Convention.[66]

The right to education does not as a general rule affect the system of immigration control at national level. A state is not required by the Convention to allow students to enter its territory for the purpose of receiving education.[67] But a state would be in breach of the Convention if it were to bar access to education for the children of immigrant families or asylum-seekers who are within the jurisdiction.[68] Rules restricting the admission of such children to local schools would run the risk of being held to deny their right to education, or at least of doing so when Article 2 of the First Protocol is read together with Article 14 (prohibition of discrimination). Moreover, if a state insisted on removing a young person from its territory just before she could sit an important public examination for which she had been preparing for several years, a failure to consider the educational impact on the individual of such a harsh decision could be seen as a disproportionate breach of her right not to be denied education.

[66] *Simpson v. UK* n. 59 *supra*; and *see* Chapter 13, Section B.

[67] *15 foreign students v. United Kingdom*, 19 May 1977, 9 D.R. 185. *Cf. R. (Holub) v. Secretary of State for the Home Department* [2001] 1 W.L.R. 1359 (removal of Polish family to Poland under immigration law was not affected by the argument that the education of a 12 year old girl, who had been for three years doing well at a school in England, would be set back by 3 years if she had to return to schooling in Poland).

[68] *See Timishev v. Russia* (n. 48 *supra*).

12

THE RIGHT TO LIBERTY AND SECURITY OF PERSON

ARTICLE 5

1. Everyone has the right to liberty and security of person. No one shall be deprived of his liberty save in the following cases and in accordance with a procedure prescribed by law:

  (a) the lawful detention of a person after conviction by a competent court;

  (b) the lawful arrest or detention of a person for non-compliance with the lawful order of a court or in order to secure the fulfilment of any obligation prescribed by law;

  (c) the lawful arrest or detention of a person effected for the purpose of bringing him before the competent legal authority on reasonable suspicion of having committed an offence or when it is reasonably considered necessary to prevent his committing an offence or fleeing after having done so;

  (d) the detention of a minor by lawful order for the purpose of educational supervision or his lawful detention for the purpose of bringing him before the competent legal authority;

  (e) the lawful detention of persons for the prevention of the spreading of infectious diseases, of persons of unsound mind, alcoholics or drug addicts or vagrants;

  (f) the lawful arrest or detention of a person to prevent his effecting an unauthorised entry into the country or of a person against whom action is being taken with a view to deportation or extradition.

2. Everyone who is arrested shall be informed promptly, in a language which he understands, of the reasons for his arrest and of any charge against him.

3. Everyone arrested or detained in accordance with the provisions of paragraph (1)(c) of this Article shall be brought promptly before a judge or other officer authorized by law to exercise judicial power and shall be entitled to trial within a reasonable time or to release pending trial. Release may be conditioned by guarantees to appear for trial.

4. Everyone who is deprived of his liberty by arrest or detention shall be entitled to take proceedings by which the lawfulness of his detention shall be decided speedily by a court and his release ordered if the detention is not lawful.

5. Everyone who has been the victim of arrest or detention in contravention of the provisions of this Article shall have an enforceable right to compensation.

A. INTRODUCTION

The individual's right to physical liberty and the security of his or her person is such a manifestly desirable right that in secure democracies which proclaim liberal values it is sometimes taken for granted. Yet the right lies at the heart of any governmental system that claims to observe the rule of law. In Magna Carta in 1215, the celebrated Chapter 39 proclaimed: 'No free man shall be taken or imprisoned...except by the lawful judgment of his peers or by the law of the land' (*Nullus liber homo capiatur, vel imprisonetur,...nisi per legale judicium parium suorum vel per legem terrae*). In the Petition of Right of 1628, the English Parliament reversed a decision by the judges that upheld the right of the King by his special command to detain individuals: the Petition recited Chapter 39 of Magna Carta and declared that 'no free man, in any such manner as is before mentioned, [may] be imprisoned or detained'. By Article 7 of the Declaration of Rights of Man and the Citizen dated 26 August 1789, 'No man may be accused, arrested or detained except in the cases determined by the Law, and following the procedure that it has prescribed'. Under the Fifth Amendment to the United States Constitution ratified in 1791, no person 'shall be deprived of life, liberty, or property, without due process of law'. The Basic Law of the Federal Republic of Germany, promulgated in 1949, declared: 'Every person shall have the right to life and physical integrity. Freedom of the person shall be inviolable. These rights may be interfered with only pursuant to a law'. In the Canadian Charter of Rights and Freedoms 1981, by Section 7: 'Everyone has the right to life, liberty and security of the person and the right not to be deprived thereof except in accordance with the principles of fundamental justice'; and by Section 9: 'Everyone has the right not to be arbitrarily detained or imprisoned'.

Such provisions serve to reinforce the fundamental duty of state organs to respect the right of all human beings to their physical security.

1. KURT V. TURKEY

Judgment of 25 May 1998
27 E.H.R.R. 373

[During several days in November 1993, security operations were carried out in Agilli, a village in south-east Turkey, and houses were burnt down, including that of the applicant. On 24 November, the villagers were required to gather in the village school while soldiers and village guards searched for the applicant's son, Üzeyir Kurt. On the next day, the applicant saw Üzeyir surrounded by soldiers and village guards; his face was bruised and swollen, as if he had been beaten. She fetched him a jacket as he complained of feeling cold, but she was not permitted to stay with him. She never saw him again and could discover no evidence that he had been seen elsewhere. Having failed in all the inquiries that she made, she contacted a human rights association who gave her assistance in approaching the Turkish authorities and in making an application to the European Commission of Human Rights at Strasbourg. Subsequently, the applicant asserted that a public prosecutor in Turkey had attempted to get her to withdraw her allegations that her son had been maltreated. She also made two statements before a notary in which (inter alia) she purported to withdraw her application to Strasbourg, although subsequently she complained that the withdrawal had been forced upon her.

In proceedings at Strasbourg, the Turkish government accepted that there had been a security operation in Agilli at the relevant time against those who were suspected of being terrorist members of the PKK (Kurdish Workers' Party). Denying responsibility for Üzeyir's disappearance, the government contended that he had joined or been kidnapped by the PKK, that his mother had been manipulated by the human rights association and that her account of her events had been distorted.]

118. The applicant submitted that the disappearance of her son gave rise to multiple violations of Article 5 of the Convention...

119. The applicant reasoned that the very fact that her son's detention was unacknowledged meant that he was deprived of his liberty in an arbitrary manner contrary to Article 5(1). She contended that the official cover-up of his whereabouts and fate placed her son beyond the reach of the law and he was accordingly denied the protection of the guarantees contained in Article 5(2), (3), (4) and (5).

120. The Government reiterated that the applicant's contention regarding the disappearance of her son was unsubstantiated by the evidence and had been disproved by the investigation which the authorities had conducted. In its submission, no issue could therefore arise under Article 5....

122. The Court notes at the outset the fundamental importance of the guarantees contained in Article 5 for securing the right of individuals in a democracy to be free from arbitrary detention at the hands of the authorities. It is precisely for that reason that the Court has repeatedly stressed in its case law that any deprivation of liberty must not only have been effected in conformity with the substantive and procedural rules of national law but must equally be in keeping with the very purpose of Article 5, namely to protect the individual from arbitrariness.[1] This insistence on the protection of the individual against any abuse of power is illustrated by the fact that Article 5(1) circumscribes the circumstances in which individuals may be lawfully deprived of their liberty, it being stressed that these circumstances must be given a narrow interpretation having regard to the fact that they constitute exceptions to a most basic guarantee of individual freedom.[2]

123. It must also be stressed that the authors of the Convention reinforced the individual's protection against arbitrary deprivation of his or her liberty by guaranteeing a corpus of substantive rights which are intended to minimise the risks of arbitrariness by allowing the act of deprivation of liberty to be amenable to independent judicial scrutiny and by securing the accountability of the authorities for that act. The requirements of Article 5(3) and (4) with their emphasis on promptitude and judicial control assume particular importance in this context. Prompt judicial intervention may lead to the detection and prevention of life-threatening measures or serious ill treatment which violate the fundamental guarantees contained in Articles 2 and 3 of the Convention.[3] What is at stake is both the protection of the physical liberty

---

[1] *See*, among many other authorities, *Chahal v. United Kingdom*, 15 Nov. 1996, 23 E.H.R.R. 413, para. 118 and *see* Section E(4)(c) *infra*.

[2] *See, mutatis mutandis, Quinn v. France*, 22 Mar. 1996, 21 E.H.R.R. 529, para. 42.

[3] *See, mutatis mutandis, Aksoy v. Turkey*, 18 Dec. 1996, 23 E.H.R.R. 553, para. 76; and Section H(4) *infra*.

of individuals as well as their personal security in a context which, in the absence of safeguards, could result in a subversion of the rule of law and place detainees beyond the reach of the most rudimentary forms of legal protection.

124. The Court emphasises in this respect that the unacknowledged detention of an individual is a complete negation of these guarantees and a most grave violation of Article 5. Having assumed control over that individual it is incumbent on the authorities to account for his or her whereabouts. For this reason, Article 5 must be seen as requiring the authorities to take effective measures to safeguard against the risk of disappearance and to conduct a prompt effective investigation into an arguable claim that a person has been taken into custody and has not been seen since.

125. Against that background, the Court recalls that it has accepted the Commission's finding that Üzeyir Kurt was held by soldiers and village guards on the morning of 25 November 1993. His detention at that time was not logged and there exists no official trace of his subsequent whereabouts or fate. That fact in itself must be considered a most serious failing since it enables those responsible for the act of deprivation of liberty to conceal their involvement in a crime, to cover their tracks and to escape accountability for the fate of the detainee. In the view of the Court, the absence of holding data recording such matters as the date, time and location of detention, the name of the detainee as well as the reasons for the detention and the name of the person effecting it must be seen as incompatible with the very purpose of Article 5 of the Convention.

126. Furthermore, the Court considers that having regard to the applicant's insistence that her son was detained in the village the public prosecutor should have been alert to the need to investigate more thoroughly her claim. He had the powers under the Code of Criminal Procedure to do so. However, he did not request her to explain why she was so adamant in her belief that he was in detention. She was neither asked to provide a written statement nor interviewed orally. Had he done so he may have been able to confront the military personnel involved in the operation in the village with her eyewitness account. However, that line of inquiry was never opened and no statements were taken from any of the soldiers or village guards present in the village at the time. The public prosecutor was unwilling to go beyond the gendarmerie's assertion that the custody records showed that Üzeyir Kurt had neither been held in the village nor was in detention. He accepted without question the explanation that Üzeyir Kurt had probably been kidnapped by the PKK during the military operation and this explanation shaped his future attitude to his inquiries and laid the basis of his subsequent non-jurisdiction decision.

127. The Court, like the Commission, also considers that the alleged PKK involvement in the disappearance of the applicant's son lacked any firm and plausible evidentiary basis. As an explanation it was advanced too hastily by the gendarmerie in the absence of any corroborating evidence; nor can it be maintained that the statements given by the three villagers to the gendarme officers on 28 February 1994 lent credence to what was in effect mere supposition as to the fate of Üzeyir Kurt. The questions put to the villagers can only be described as formulated in a way designed to elicit responses which could enhance the credibility of the PKK kidnapping theory. Furthermore, and as noted earlier, the Government's other contention that the applicant's son had left the village to join the PKK also lacks any firm evidentiary basis.

128. Having regard to these considerations, the Court concludes that the authorities have failed to offer any credible and substantiated explanation for the whereabouts and fate of the

applicant's son after he was detained in the village and that no meaningful investigation was conducted into the applicant's insistence that he was in custody and that she was concerned for his life. They have failed to discharge their responsibility to account for him and it must be accepted that he has been held in unacknowledged detention in the complete absence of the safeguards contained in Article 5.

129. The Court, accordingly, like the Commission, finds that there has been a particularly grave violation of the right to liberty and security of person guaranteed under Article 5 raising serious concerns about the welfare of Üzeyir Kurt.

[The Court reached its decision on Article 5 by a majority of 6 to 3.[4] Judge Petiti explained why he disagreed with the majority's reasoning on the application of Article 5:]

The *Kurt* case concerns a presumed disappearance. Under the ordinary criminal law, disappearances may involve cases of running away, false imprisonment or abduction.

Under public international law, a policy of systematic political disappearances may exist, as occurred in Brazil, Chile and Argentina.

In such cases, especially where they have been verified by the European Committee for the Prevention of Torture, it is for one or more Member States of the Council of Europe to lodge an application against the state concerned. It would be cowardly to avoid the problem by leaving the court to decide on the basis of an application by an individual. An application by a state would occasion an international regional inquiry enabling the situation to be assessed objectively and thoroughly. I could have found that there had been a violation if the case had concerned instructions given by the army, gendarmerie or the police, both with regard to the security operations and to the verification of their implementation and follow up....

In the system of the European Convention on Human Rights, the fact that states are liable for the failings of the authorities of which they are composed means that the court must identify the authorities and police or army units responsible. The *Kurt* case was in any event deficient in that there was no investigation of the type performed in cases before the Hague International Criminal Court and one of the main witnesses and the commanding officers of the gendarmerie units did not give evidence at the trial. The Commission itself acknowledged that it had doubts. The majority of the Court speculates on the basis of a hypothesis of continued detention relying on their personal conviction. That to my mind, is 'heresy' in the international sphere, since the instant case could have been decided on the basis of the case law under Article 5 requiring objective evidence and documents that convince the judges beyond all reasonable doubt; but both documents and witnesses were lacking in the present case....

2. CYPRUS V. TURKEY

Judgment of 10 May 2001
35 E.H.R.R. 30

The Grand Chamber of the Court determined an inter-state complaint arising from the invasion of Cyprus by Turkey in 1974 and the continuing Turkish occupation of Northern Cyprus. Cyprus complained of numerous breaches of the Convention. Before the Court gave

---

[4] For the Court's decision on Art. 13, *see* Chapter 14, Section B(1)(c), *infra*.

its judgment, a lengthy investigation into the facts had been made by the former European Commission on Human Rights. The following extracts deal with the right to liberty guaranteed by Article 5.

20. The applicant Government essentially claimed in their application that about 1,491 Greek Cypriots were still missing twenty years after the cessation of hostilities. These persons were last seen alive in Turkish custody and their fate has never been accounted for by the respondent State.

21. The respondent Government maintained in reply that there was no proof that any of the missing persons were still alive or were being kept in custody. In their principal submission, the issues raised by the applicant Government should continue to be pursued within the framework of the United Nations Committee on Missing Persons [hereafter, 'CMP']... rather than under the Convention.

[The Court referred to findings made by the Commission and continued:]

26. The Commission concluded that, notwithstanding evidence of the killing of Greek-Cypriot prisoners and civilians, there was no proof that any of the missing persons were killed in circumstances for which the respondent State could be held responsible; nor did the Commission find any evidence to the effect that any of the persons taken into custody were still being detained or kept in servitude by the respondent State. On the other hand, the Commission found it established that the facts surrounding the fate of the missing persons had not been clarified by the authorities and brought to the notice of the victims' relatives.

27. The Commission further concluded that its examination of the applicant Government's complaints in the instant application was not precluded by the ongoing work of the CMP. It noted in this connection that the scope of the investigation being conducted by the CMP was limited to determining whether or not any of the missing persons on its list were dead or alive; nor was the CMP empowered to make findings either on the cause of death or on the issue of responsibility for any deaths so established...

119. At the hearing before the Court the applicant Government stated that the number of missing persons was currently 1,485 and that the evidence clearly pointed to the fact that the missing persons were either detained by, or were in the custody of or under the actual authority and responsibility of, the Turkish army or its militia and were last seen in areas which were under the effective control of the respondent State. They maintained, in addition, that the Court should proceed on the assumption that the missing persons were still alive, unless there was evidence to the contrary.

120. The Court notes...that the applicant Government have not contested the facts as found by the Commission.... For its part, it does not see any exceptional circumstances which would lead it to depart from the Commission's findings of fact....

121. Furthermore, the Court shares the Commission's concern to limit its inquiry to ascertaining the extent, if any, to which the authorities of the respondent State have clarified the fate or whereabouts of the missing persons. It is not its task to make findings on the evidence on whether any of these persons are alive or dead or have been killed in circumstances which engage the liability of the respondent State. Indeed, the applicant Government have requested the Court to proceed on the assumption that the persons at issue are still alive...

145. The Commission concluded that the respondent State had failed in its obligation to carry out a prompt and effective investigation in respect of an arguable claim that Greek-Cypriot

persons who were detained by Turkish forces or their agents in 1974 disappeared thereafter. For the Commission, a breach of the Article 5 obligation had to be construed as a continuing violation, given that the Commission had already found in its 1983 report...that no information had been provided by the respondent Government on the fate of missing Greek Cypriots who had disappeared in Turkish custody. The Commission stressed that there could be no limitation in time as regards the duty to investigate and inform, especially as it could not be ruled out that the detained persons who had disappeared might have been the victims of the most serious crimes, including war crimes or crimes against humanity.

146. The Commission, on the other hand, found there had been no violation of Article 5 by virtue of actual detention of Greek-Cypriot missing persons. It noted...that there was no evidence to support the assumption that during the period under consideration any missing Greek Cypriots were still detained by the Turkish or Turkish-Cypriot authorities.

147. The Court stresses at the outset that the unacknowledged detention of an individual is a complete negation of the guarantees of liberty and security of the person contained in Article 5...and a most grave violation of that Article. Having assumed control over a given individual, it is incumbent on the authorities to account for his or her whereabouts. It is for this reason that Article 5 must be seen as requiring the authorities to take effective measures to safeguard against the risk of disappearance and to conduct a prompt and effective investigation into an arguable claim that a person has been taken into custody and has not been seen since.[5]

148. The Court refers to the irrefutable evidence that Greek Cypriots were held by Turkish or Turkish-Cypriot forces. There is no indication of any records having been kept of either the identities of those detained or the dates or location of their detention. From a humanitarian point of view, this failing cannot be excused with reference either to the fighting which took place at the relevant time or to the overall confused and tense state of affairs. Seen in terms of Article 5..., the absence of such information has made it impossible to allay the concerns of the relatives of the missing persons about the latter's fate. Notwithstanding the impossibility of naming those who were taken into custody, the respondent State should have made other inquiries with a view to accounting for the disappearances...

150. The Court concludes that, during the period under consideration, there has been a continuing violation of Article 5...by virtue of the failure of the authorities of the respondent State to conduct an effective investigation into the whereabouts and fate of the missing Greek-Cypriot persons in respect of whom there is an arguable claim that they were in custody at the time they disappeared.

151. The Court, on the other hand finds, like the Commission, that it has not been established that during the period under consideration any of the Greek-Cypriot missing persons were actually being detained by the Turkish-Cypriot authorities.

[Another matter complained of by the Cyprus government concerned the plight of some hundreds of Greek Cypriots who continued to live in northern Cyprus under the Turkish occupation, even though the majority of this community had gone to live elsewhere in Cyprus.]

223. The applicant Government maintained that the evidence clearly established that the personal security of the enclaved Greek Cypriots had been violated as a matter of practice. The

[5] Citing *Kurt v. Turkey (supra)*.

applicant Government relied on Article 5..., the relevant part of which reads:

'1. Everyone has the right to liberty and security of person...'

224. In the applicant Government's submission, the Commission was incorrect in its conclusion that this complaint was not borne out by the evidence. The applicant Government
asserted that the written and oral testimony of witnesses clearly demonstrated the vulnerability and fear of the enclaved population and the impunity with which those responsible
for crimes against the person and property could act. As to the latter point, the applicant
Government observed that, although notified of complaints, the police failed to take action and
without identification of assailants and suspects civil action, even if remedies were available,
was impossible...

226. The Court notes that the applicant Government have not claimed that any members
of the enclaved Greek-Cypriot population were actually detained during the period under consideration. Their complaint relates to the vulnerability of what is an aged and dwindling population to the threat of aggression and criminality and its overall sense of insecurity. However,
the Court considers that these are matters which fall outside the scope of Article 5... and are
more appropriately addressed in the context of its overall assessment of the living conditions
of the Karpas Greek Cypriots seen from the angle of the requirements of Article 8...

The effect of Article 5 where individuals have disappeared after being seen in the custody of state forces matches the manner in which in similar circumstances leading to
a presumed death there is a duty on the state under Article 2 to inquire into how death
occurred.[6] A complete failure by state authorities to observe the Convention rights
of detained persons has more than once been held to constitute the gravest possible
breach of Article 5.[7] Although in *Cyprus v. Turkey* no breach of Article 5 was held
to have occurred in relation to the Greek Cypriots who had stayed on in northern
Cyprus, the Court found that other Convention rights of this community had been
violated (for example, their right to respect for family and private life under Article 8).
The Court's finding that their right to liberty had not been breached raises a matter to
which we return in the next section, namely what constitutes a breach of the right to
physical liberty for the purposes of Article 5.

Even such a fundamental right as the right to physical liberty is not absolute. Within
every legal system there exist situations in which one's liberty must, if necessary, give
way in the face of some other vital interest of the community. These situations arise pre-
eminently (but not exclusively) in the system of criminal justice. The exercise of powers
of arrest and detention by state organs is tolerable only if it is governed by the need to
observe due process of law. Article 5 of the Convention has three aims: (a) to proclaim
the right of individual liberty; (b) to define the range of situations in which the right may
be curtailed by exercise of the state's coercive power; and (c) to lay down the essential
conditions which must be observed if that power is to be controlled by law. The power to
ensure that those conditions are observed is primarily a matter for the national courts as
the custodians of liberty under the law. As a secondary safeguard where a state is a party

---

[6] *See* Chapter 4, Section B(4).
[7] *See Taş v. Turkey*, 14 Nov. 2000, 33 E.H.R.R. 15; *Çiçek v. Turkey*, 27 Feb. 2001, 37 E.H.R.R. 20.

to the Convention, the national laws and the manner in which national judges act as custodians of liberty are subject to supervision and review by organs of the Convention.

There is an evident overlap between the emphasis in Article 5 on due process of law in relation to the deprivation of liberty, and the more general protection for procedural due process granted by Article 6 (see Chapter 13). The main overlap is between Article 5(3) (the arrested person's right to be brought promptly before a judge and the right to trial within a reasonable time or to release on bail) and Article 6(1) (an accused person's right to a trial of his or her case within a reasonable time). Many cases of delay in the criminal process raise questions under both Articles 5 and 6. The selection of cases made in this chapter seeks to avoid duplication with Chapter 13(E), but in their application the two Articles complement each other in an important way.

In contrast to the fairly elaborate limitation in Article 5 of the reasons and manner in which liberty may be restricted, the Fifth and Fourteenth amendments to the United States Constitution merely specify that the state may not deprive any person of 'life, liberty, or property without due process of law'. The content of the terms 'life, liberty and property' and 'due process of law' is discussed in Chapter 13 below in connection with the Article 6 right to a fair procedure in civil and criminal proceedings. While the meaning of 'liberty' in this sense has been much contested in American constitutional law, and while the paradigm deprivation of liberty remains incarceration after criminal conviction, that term has been given a far broader meaning than mere freedom of personal movement. As one standard commentary has summarized it:

While the required procedures may differ depending on the type of action, the government can never impose substantial physical restraints on an individual without establishing a procedure to determine the factual basis and legality of such actions.[8]

Thus it is clear that, under American law, the restrictions dealt with in the principal cases could be imposed only after a procedure consistent with due process of law.

We have seen that Section 7 of the Canadian Charter of Rights and Freedoms declares that no person can be deprived of 'life, liberty and the security of the person...except in accordance with the principles of fundamental justice'. As has been the case with 'due process', the meaning of 'fundamental principles of justice' has been controversial. But there is complete agreement that it at least requires a fair and impartial procedure before the state may deprive someone of the protected interests. Unlike the United States courts, the Canadian courts have restricted the term, 'deprivation of liberty', to some form of physical restraint. The nature of that restraint, however, has been widely construed to include, among other things, compelling a person to provide fingerprints or to produce evidence. In calling these impositions deprivations of liberty, the Supreme Court of Canada has emphasized that they involve elements of physical restraint.[9]

---

[8] J. Nowak and R. Rotunda, *Constitutional Law* (4th edn. 2004), 601.
[9] *See Thompson Newspapers v. Canada* [1990] 1 S.C.R. 425 (dissenting reasons of Wilson J at 446, on which point, however, a majority of the judges concurred). *See also* P. W. Hogg, *Constitutional Law of Canada* (5th edn. Supp. 2007), s. 51.4(g).

B. HAS THERE BEEN A DEPRIVATION OF LIBERTY?

The right to liberty under Article 5 is protected by the duty laid on organs of the state to deprive no-one of their liberty except in cases provided for by Article 5(1) and in accordance with a procedure prescribed by law. Thus the first issue to be answered where Article 5 is invoked, is whether there has on the facts been a deprivation of liberty. If so, the second issue for decision is whether the deprivation of liberty is for one of the purposes stated in Article 5(1).

1. GUZZARDI V. ITALY

Judgment of 6 November 1980
3 E.H.R.R. 333

[Under legislation dating from 1956 and 1965, the courts in Italy could order preventive measures to be taken against persons who presented a danger to security and public morality, including idlers, habitual vagrants who were fit for work, those regularly involved in illicit dealings and those suspected of belonging to mafia-type organizations. The measures included power to impose an order to reside in a specified district. In 1975, Guzzardi was ordered by a court in the city of Milan to reside on Asinara, a small island off Sardinia, where the residence area (Cala Reale) measured 2.5 square kilometres. He had a prison record and was in the course of being prosecuted on serious charges for which he was later sentenced to a long period in prison. However, the power to make a residence order was separate from the criminal proceedings. Having found that the conditions of life on Asinara did not constitute inhuman or degrading treatment within Article 3, the Court considered whether Guzzardi had been deprived of his liberty and, if so, whether there had been a breach of Article 5.]

90.   The Commission was of the view that on Asinara the applicant suffered a deprivation of liberty within the meaning of the Article; it attached particular significance to the extremely small size of the area where he was confined, the almost permanent supervision to which he was subject, the all but complete impossibility for him to make social contacts and the length of his enforced stay at Cala Reale.

91.   The Government disputed the correctness of this analysis. It reasoned as follows. The factors listed above were not sufficient to render the situation of persons in compulsory residence on the island comparable to the situation of prisoners as laid down by Italian law; there existed a whole series of fundamental differences that the Commission had wrongly overlooked. The distinguishing characteristic of freedom was less the amount of space available than the manner in which it could be utilised; a good many districts in Italy and elsewhere were less than 2.5 sq km in area. The applicant was able to leave and return to his dwelling as he wished between the hours of 7 a.m. and 10 p.m. His wife and son lived with him for 14 of the some 16 months he spent on Asinara; the inviolability of his home and of the intimacy of his

family life, two rights that the Convention guaranteed solely to free people, were respected. Even as regards his social relations, he was treated much more favourably than someone in penal detention: he was at liberty to meet, within the boundaries of Cala Reale, the members of the small community of free people—about 200 individuals—living on the island, notably at Cala d'Oliva; to go to Sardinia or the mainland if so authorised; to correspond by letter or telegram without any control; to use the telephone, subject to notifying the *carabinieri* of the name and number of his correspondent. The supervision of which he complained constituted the *raison d'être* of the measure ordered in his respect....

92. The Court recalls that in proclaiming the 'right to liberty', paragraph 1 of Article 5 is contemplating the physical liberty of the person; its aim is to ensure that no one should be dispossessed of this liberty in an arbitrary fashion. As was pointed out by those appearing before the Court, the paragraph is not concerned with mere restrictions on liberty of movement; such restrictions are governed by Article 2 of Protocol No. 4 which has not been ratified by Italy. In order to determine whether someone has been 'deprived of his liberty' within the meaning of Article 5, the starting point must be his concrete situation and account must be taken of a whole range of criteria such as the type, duration, effects and manner of implementation of the measure in question.[10]

93. The difference between deprivation of and restriction upon liberty is nonetheless merely one of degree of intensity, and not one of nature or substance. Although the process of classification into one or other of these categories sometimes proves to be no easy task in that some borderline cases are a matter of pure opinion, the Court cannot avoid making the selection upon which the applicability or inapplicability of Article 5 depends.

94. As provided for under the 1956 Act...special supervision accompanied by an order for compulsory residence in a specified district does not of itself come within the scope of Article 5....

It does not follow that 'deprivation of liberty' may never result from the manner of implementation of such a measure, and in the present case the manner of implementation is the sole issue that falls to be considered....

95. The Government's reasoning (see para. 91 above) is not without weight. It demonstrates very clearly the extent of the difference between the applicant's treatment on Asinara and classic detention in prison or strict arrest imposed on a serviceman.[11] Deprivation of liberty may, however, take numerous other forms. Their variety is being increased by developments in legal standards and in attitudes; and the Convention is to be interpreted in the light of the notions currently prevailing in democratic States.[12]

Whilst the area around which the applicant could move far exceeded the dimensions of a cell and was not bounded by any physical barrier, it covered no more than a tiny fraction of an island to which access was difficult and about nine-tenths of which was occupied by a prison. Mr. Guzzardi was housed in part of the hamlet of Cala Reale which consisted mainly of the buildings of a former medical establishment which were in a state of disrepair or even dilapidation, a *carabinieri* station, a school and a chapel. He lived there principally in the company of other persons subjected to the same measure and of policemen. The permanent population of Asinara resided almost entirely at Cala d'Oliva, which Mr. Guzzardi could not visit, and would

---

[10] *See Engel v. The Netherlands*, 8 June 1976, 1 E.H.R.R. 647, paras. 58–9; and *see* Section B(2) *infra*.

[11] *See id.* at para. 63.

[12] *See* notably *Tyrer v. United Kingdom*, 25 Apr. 1978, 2 E.H.R.R. I, and *see* Chapter 5(B)(1) *supra*.

appear to have made hardly any use of its right to go to Cala Reale. Consequently, there were few opportunities for social contacts available to the applicant other than with his near family, his fellow 'residents' and the supervisory staff. Supervision was carried out strictly and on an almost constant basis. Thus, Mr. Guzzardi was not able to leave his dwelling between 10 p.m. and 7 a.m. without giving prior notification to the authorities in due time. He had to report to the authorities twice a day and inform them of the name and number of his correspondent whenever he wished to use the telephone. He needed the consent of the authorities for each of his trips to Sardinia or the mainland, trips which were rare and, understandably, made under the strict supervision of the *carabinieri*. He was liable to punishment by 'arrest' if he failed to comply with any of his obligations. Finally, more than 16 months elapsed before his arrival at Cala Reale and his departure for Force....

It is admittedly not possible to speak of 'deprivation of liberty' on the strength of any one of these factors taken individually, but cumulatively and in combination they certainly raise an issue of categorisation from the viewpoint of Article 5. In certain respects the treatment complained of resembles detention in an 'open prison' or committal to a disciplinary unit.[13]...

The Court considers on balance that the present case is to be regarded as one involving deprivation of liberty.

96. It remains to be determined whether the situation was one of those exhaustively listed in Article 5(1) of the Convention,[14] in which the contracting States reserve the right to arrest or detain individuals.

97. The Government relied, in the alternative, on sub-paragraph (e) of Article 5(1), maintaining that *mafiosi* like the applicant were 'vagrants' and 'something else besides'.... In the Government's opinion, the imposition on a 'vagrant' of preventive measures restricting, or even depriving him of, his liberty was justified, under the Convention and Italian law, not so much by his lack of fixed abode as by the absence of any apparent occupational activity... and, hence, the impossibility of identifying the source of his means of subsistence. The existence of this danger factor, the Government continued, was recognised by the Milan Regional Court in its decision of 30 January 1975...; in addition and above all, that Court took notice of the far more serious risk stemming from the applicant's links with mafia associations which engaged in kidnapping with a view to extracting ransoms. According to the Government, provision could not be made in an international instrument for the typically Italian phenomenon of the mafia, yet it would be an absurd conclusion to regard Article 5(1)(e) as allowing vagrants but not presumed *mafiosi* to be deprived of their liberty.

98. The Court concurs with the Commission's contrary view....

[In a series of reports made on Guzzardi by the Italian police, prosecutor and courts, there had been no reference to the 'vagrancy' provision in the 1956 Act.]

These authorities relied on the 1956 Act solely in combination with the 1965 Act which concerns individuals whom there are strong reasons to suspect of belonging to mafia-type associations... What is more, they in no way described or depicted Mr. Guzzardi as a vagrant. Admittedly, they noted, in passing, that there were serious doubts as to whether he really worked as a mason as he claimed, but they laid much greater stress on his record, his illegal activities, his contacts with habitual criminals and still more his links with the mafia.

---

[13] *See Engel v. The Netherlands*, 8 June 1976, 1 E.H.R.R. 647, para. 64; and *see* Section B(2) *infra*.
[14] *See Winterwerp v. The Netherlands*, 24 Oct. 1979, 2 E.H.R.R. 387, para. 37; and *see* Section D(1) *infra*.

The Government's argument is open to a further objection. In addition to vagrants, sub-paragraph (e) refers to persons of unsound mind, alcoholics and drug addicts. The reason why the Convention allows the latter individuals, all of whom are socially maladjusted, to be deprived of their liberty is not only that they have to be considered as occasionally dangerous for public safety but also that their own interests may necessitate their detention. One cannot therefore deduce from the fact that Article 5 authorises the detention of vagrants that the same or even stronger reasons apply to anyone who may be regarded as still more dangerous.

[The Court examined the matter under the other sub-paragraphs of Article 5(1), and held that the compulsory residence order was 'not a punishment for a specific offence but a preventive measure taken on the strength of indications of a propensity to crime'. The measure thus did not constitute detention 'after conviction by a competent court'.

The Court held by ten votes to eight that Article 5(1) had been breached. Matscher J was one of the dissenting judges:]

2. ...The nature of the Convention system is such that in the first place it is left to the governments of the contracting States to take the measures they deem appropriate for the accomplishment of their tasks. Amongst those tasks, the protection of the fundamental rights of the general public plays a pre-eminent role. At the same time, it is for the Convention institutions to review those measures in order to determine whether or not they are in conformity with the requirements of the Convention. In the course of this review, the provisions of the Convention should not be interpreted in a vacuum; the measures complained of must always be put back in the general setting to which they belong.

The principle that account must be taken of the general context of the case when examining an application concerning the alleged violation of a fundamental right does not in any way mean that—save for the possibility referred to in Article 15 of the Convention—exceptional circumstances allow the contracting States to take measures that are not compatible with the requirements of the Convention. On the other hand, I do deduce from this principle that certain measures which, from the viewpoint of the Convention, might be seen as open to considerable criticism in a so-called normal situation are less open to criticism and can be considered as being in conformity with the Convention when there is a crisis overshadowing public order and notably when rights of others, which are also guaranteed by the Convention, are being threatened by the activities of certain dangerous and anti-social elements. Such a crisis was obtaining in Italy at the time when the present case began....

3. ...It is obvious to me that the concept of 'deprivation of liberty' is not a matter for formal and precise criteria; quite the contrary—it is a concept of some complexity, having a core which cannot be the subject of argument but which is surrounded by a 'grey zone' where it is extremely difficult to draw the line between 'deprivation of liberty' within the meaning of Article 5(1) and mere restrictions on liberty that do not come within the ambit of that provision.

In fact, the Convention system has itself introduced (in Article 2 of Protocol No. 4), alongside the concept of 'deprivation of liberty', the concept of 'restriction on liberty of movement' and, as the Court has rightly observed (see para. 93 of the present judgment) the difference between the two is merely one of degree or intensity, and not one of nature or substance. In addition, the bounds that Article 5 requires the contracting States not to exceed in their judicial, disciplinary and police systems may vary from one situation to another.

Accordingly, only a careful analysis of the various factors which together made up Mr. Guzzardi's situation on Asinara can provide an answer to the question whether or not that situation fell within the concept of 'deprivation of liberty' within the meaning of Article 5(1). Clearly, since this is a matter of opinion, different views are tenable.

Personally, I do not attach quite the same weight as the majority of the Court to these various factors...taken individually and together. In addition, I take the 'general context of the case' into account. The whole leads me to the conclusion that the measure applied to Mr. Guzzardi amounted to a serious restriction on his liberty, which was motivated by perfectly understandable reasons and was also in conformity with Italian law, but that it did not attain the level and intensity that would cause it necessarily to be classified as a deprivation of liberty within the meaning of Article 5(1) of the Convention....

2. ENGEL AND OTHERS V. THE NETHERLANDS

Judgment of 8 June 1976
1 E.H.R.R. 647

[Engel and four others were conscript soldiers serving in the Dutch armed forces. On separate occasions, they were sentenced under military law to be punished for breaches of discipline and had been held under various forms of detention. Having appealed unsuccessfully to the Supreme Military Court, they complained to Strasbourg of various breaches of the Convention, including Articles 5 and 6. The Court held first that the Convention applies in principle to members of the armed forces and not only to civilians.]

54. ...Nevertheless, when interpreting and applying the rules of the Convention in the present case, the court must bear in mind the particular characteristics of military life and its effects on the situation of individual members of the armed forces....

1. The right to liberty in the context of military service

57. During the preparation and subsequent conclusion of the Convention, the great majority of the Contracting States possessed defence forces and, in consequence, a system of military discipline that by its very nature implied the possibility of placing on certain of the rights and freedoms of the members of these forces limitations incapable of being imposed on civilians. The existence of such a system, which those States have retained since then, does not in itself run counter to their obligations.

Military discipline, nonetheless, does not fall outside the scope of Article 5(1). Not only must this provision be read in the light of Article 1 and 15...but the list of deprivations of liberty set out therein is exhaustive, as is shown by the words 'save in the following cases'. A disciplinary penalty or measure may in consequence constitute a breach of Article 5(1). The Government, moreover, acknowledge this.

58. In proclaiming the 'right to liberty', paragraph 1 of Article 5 is contemplating individual liberty in its classic sense, that is to say the physical liberty of the person. Its aim is to ensure that no one should be dispossessed of liberty in an arbitrary fashion. As pointed out by the Government and the Commission, it does not concern mere restrictions upon liberty of movement (Art. 2 of Protocol No. 4)....

59. In order to determine whether someone has been 'deprived of his liberty' within the meaning of Article 5, the starting point must be his concrete situation. Military service, as encountered in the Contracting States, does not on its own in any way constitute a deprivation of liberty under the Convention, since it is expressly sanctioned in Article 4(3)(b). In addition, rather wide limitations upon the freedom of movement of the members of the armed forces are entailed by reason of the specific demands of military service so that the normal restrictions accompanying it do not come within the ambit of Article 5 either.

Each State is competent to organise its own system of military discipline and enjoys in the matter a certain margin of appreciation. The bounds that Article 5 requires the State not to exceed are not identical for servicemen and civilians. A disciplinary penalty or measure which on analysis would unquestionably be deemed a deprivation of liberty were it to be applied to a civilian may not possess this characteristic when imposed upon a serviceman. Nevertheless, such penalty or measure does not escape the terms of Article 5 when it takes the form of restrictions that clearly deviate from the normal conditions of life within the armed forces of the Contracting States. In order to establish whether this is so, account should be taken of a whole range of factors such as the nature, duration, effects and manner of execution of the penalty or measure in question.

2. The existence of deprivations of liberty in the present case

61. No deprivation of liberty resulted from the three and four days' *light arrest* awarded respectively against Mr. Engel... and Mr. van der Wiel... Although confined during off-duty hours to their dwellings or to military buildings or premises, as the case may be, servicemen subjected to such a penalty are not locked up and continue to perform their duties (Art. 8 of the 1903 Act)... They remain, more or less, within the ordinary framework of their army life.

62. *Aggravated arrest* differs from light arrest on one point alone: in off-duty hours, soldiers serve the arrest in a specially designated place which they may not leave in order to visit the canteen, cinema or recreation rooms, but they are not kept under lock and key (Art. 9-B of the 1903 Act...). Consequently, neither does the court consider as a deprivation of liberty the twelve days' aggravated arrest complained of by Mr. de Wit....

63. *Strict arrest*, abolished in 1974, differed from light arrest and aggravated arrest in that non-commissioned officers and ordinary servicemen served it by day and by night locked in a cell and were accordingly excluded from the performance of their normal duties (Art. 10-B of the 1903 Act...). It thus involved deprivation of liberty. It follows that the *provisional arrest* inflicted on Mr. Engel in the form of strict arrest... had the same character despite its short duration (20–22 March 1971).

64. *Committal to a disciplinary unit*, likewise abolished in 1974 but applied in 1971 to Mr. Dona and Mr. Schul, represented the most severe penalty under military disciplinary law in the Netherlands. Privates condemned to this penalty following disciplinary proceedings were not separated from those so sentenced by way of supplementary punishment under the criminal law, and during a month or more they were not entitled to leave the establishment. The committal lasted for a period of three to six months; this was considerably longer than the duration of the other penalties, including strict arrest which could be imposed for one to 14 days. Furthermore it appears that Mr. Dona and Mr. Schul spent the night locked in a cell... For the various reasons, the court considers that in the circumstances deprivation of liberty occurred....

66. The court thus comes to the conclusion that neither the light arrest of Mr. Engel and Mr. van der Wiel, nor the aggravated arrest of Mr. de Wit,...call for a more thorough examination under paragraph 1 of Article 5.

The punishment of two days' strict arrest inflicted on Mr. Engel on 7 April 1971 and confirmed by the Supreme Military Court on 23 June 1971 coincided in practice with an earlier measure: it was deemed to have been served beforehand, that is from 20 to 22 March 1971, by the applicant's period of provisional arrest....

On the other hand, the court is required to determine whether the lastmentioned provisional arrest, as well as the committal of Mr. Dona and Mr. Schul to a disciplinary unit, complied with Article 5(1).

3. The compatibility of the deprivations of liberty found in the present case with Article 5(1)

67. The Government maintained, in the alternative, that the committal of Mr. Dona and Mr. Schul to a disciplinary unit and the provisional arrest of Mr. Engel satisfied, respectively, the requirements of sub-paragraph (a) and of sub-paragraph (b) of Article 5(1)....

68. Sub-paragraph (a) of Article 5(1) permits the 'lawful detention of a person after conviction by a competent court'....

The court, like the Government...notes that this provision makes no distinction based on the legal character of the offence of which a person has been found guilty. It applies to any 'conviction' occasioning deprivation of liberty pronounced by a 'court', whether the conviction be classified as criminal or disciplinary by the internal law of the State in question.

Mr. Dona and Mr. Schul were indeed deprived of their liberty 'after' their conviction by the Supreme Military Court. Article 64 of the 1903 Act conferred a suspensive effect upon their appeals against the decisions of their commanding officer (8 October 1971) and the complaints officer (19 October 1971)...Consequently, their transfer to the disciplinary barracks at Nieuwersluis occurred only by virtue of the final sentences imposed on 17 November 1971....

It remains to be ascertained that the said sentences were passed by a 'competent court' within the meaning of Article 5(1)(a).

The Supreme Military Court, whose jurisdiction was not at all disputed, constitutes a court from the organisational point of view. Doubtless, its four military members are not irremovable in law, but like the two civilian members they enjoy the independence inherent in the Convention's notion of a 'court'.[15]

Furthermore, it does not appear...that Mr. Dona and Mr. Schul failed to receive before the Supreme Military Court the benefit of adequate judicial guarantees under Article 5(1) (a), an autonomous provision whose requirements are not always co-extensive with those of Article 6. The guarantees afforded to the two applicants show themselves to be 'adequate' for the purposes of Article 5(1)(a) if account is taken of 'the particular nature of the circumstances' under which the proceedings took place....

Finally, the penalty inflicted was imposed and then executed 'lawfully' and 'in accordance with a procedure prescribed by law'. In short, it did not contravene Article 5(1).

69. The provisional arrest of Mr. Engel for its part clearly does not come within the ambit of sub-paragraph (a) of Article 5(1).

---

[15] *See De Wilde, Ooms and Versyp v. Belgium (No. 1)*, 18 June 1971, 1 E.H.R.R. 373, para. 78.

The Government have derived argument from sub-paragraph (b) insofar as the latter permits 'lawful arrest or detention' intended to 'secure the fulfilment of any obligation prescribed by law'.

The court considers that the words 'secure the fulfilment of any obligation prescribed by law' concern only cases where the law permits the detention of a person to compel him to fulfil a specific and concrete obligation which he has until then failed to satisfy. A wide interpretation would entail consequences incompatible with the notion of the rule of law from which the whole Convention draws its inspiration.[16] It would justify, for example, administrative internment meant to compel a citizen to discharge, in relation to any point whatever, his general duty of obedience to the law.

In fact, Mr. Engel's provisional arrest was in no way designed to secure the fulfilment in the future of such an obligation. Article 44 of the 1903 Act, applicable when an offer has 'sufficient indication to suppose that a subordinate has committed a serious offence against military discipline', refers to past behaviour. The measure thereby authorised is a preparatory stage of military disciplinary proceedings and is thus situated in a punitive context. Perhaps this measure also has on occasions the incidental object or effect of inducing a member of the armed forces to comply henceforth with his obligations, but only with great contrivance can it be brought under sub-paragraph (b). If the latter were the case, this sub-paragraph could more-over be extended to punishments *stricto sensu* involving deprivation of liberty on the ground of their deterrent qualities. This would deprive such punishments of the fundamental guarantees of sub-paragraph (a).

The said measure really more resembles that spoken of in sub-paragraph (c) of Article 5(1) of the Convention. However in the present case it did not fulfil one of the requirements of that provision since the detention of Mr. Engel from 20 to 22 March 1971 had not been 'effected for the purpose of bringing him before the competent legal authority'....

In conclusion, the applicant's deprivation of liberty from 20 to 22 March 1971 occurred in conditions at variance with this paragraph....

[The differing opinions of the judges on several issues in the case are omitted.]

In *Raninen v. Finland*,[17] compulsory military service led to a specific breach of Article 5 when the applicant, who objected on grounds of conscience to military service, was subject to a series of arrests, detentions on remand, and convictions. In June 1992, after a court had ordered his release, he was returned to a civil prison and was there handcuffed and driven to army barracks where he spent the night in a military hospital. On the next day, he was again arrested. The Government accepted that until that further arrest, his detention overnight had been contrary to Finnish law. The Strasbourg Court held that Article 5(1) had been breached but also that the handcuffing did not consti-tute 'inhuman or degrading treatment' for purposes of Article 3.[18] Like the European Court, American courts have recognized that while persons in military service do not lose their constitutional rights,[19] the expression of those rights may be more limited

---

[16] *See Golder v. U.K.*, 21 Feb. 1975, 1 E.H.R.R. 524, para. 34.

[17] 16 Dec. 1997, 26 E.H.R.R. 563.

[18] *See* Chapter 5(A)(3) *supra*.

[19] *See* in this connection (in Chapter 13(B)(4) *infra*) the discussion of the judicial attempts to differentiate criminal charges and disciplinary proceedings.

in the military context. Thus, in a decision defining the First Amendment rights of military personnel, the United States Supreme Court noted that '[the] fundamental necessity for imposition of discipline may render permissible within the military that which would be constitutionally impermissible outside it'.[20]

We have seen that the question of whether individuals have suffered a deprivation of liberty arose in the case of *Cyprus v. Turkey*[21] concerning the Greek Cypriots who stayed on in northern Cyprus after that territory had been occupied by Turkish forces. It has arisen also in connection with the enforcement of immigration control and the holding of asylum-seekers in the international transit zone of a French airport[22] and with the removal of an elderly woman, whose son was failing to care for her in her home, to a nursing home in Switzerland.

3. H.M. V. SWITZERLAND

Judgment of 26 February 2002
38 E.H.R.R. 17

41. The applicant complained that she had been placed in the nursing home against her will, whereas the Government contested that the applicant had been deprived of her liberty within the meaning of Article 5....

42. In order to determine whether there has been a deprivation of liberty, the starting-point must be the specific situation of the individual concerned and account must be taken of a whole range of factors such as the type, duration, effects and manner of implementation of the measure in question. The distinction between a deprivation of and restriction upon liberty is merely one of degree or intensity, and not one of nature or substance.[23]

43. The Court refers to *Nielsen v. Denmark*, which concerned the placement of a 12-year-old boy, at his mother's request, in the psychiatric ward of a State hospital for five and a half months. In that case, in which no deprivation of liberty within the meaning of Article 5(1)...was found, the Court considered that:

'The applicant was in need of medical treatment for his nervous condition and the treatment administered to him was curative, aiming at securing his recovery from his neurosis ...

The restrictions on the applicant's freedom of movement and contacts with the outside world were not much different from restrictions which might be imposed on a child in an ordinary hospital: it is true that the door of the ward, like all children's wards in the hospital, was locked, but...the applicant was allowed to leave the ward, with permission, to go for instance to the library and he went with other children, accompanied by a member of the staff, to visit playgrounds and museums...; he was also able to visit his mother and father regularly and his

---

[20] *Parker v. Levy*, 417 U.S. 733, 758 (1954).

[21] *See* Section A(2) *supra*.

[22] *See Amuur v. France*, Section E(5)(a) *infra*.

[23] Citing *Ashingdane v. United Kingdom*, 28 May 1985, 7 E.H.R.R. 528, para. 41.

old school friends and, towards the end of his stay in hospital, he started going to school again; in general, conditions in the ward were said to be 'as similar as possible to a real home' ...

The duration of the applicant's treatment was 5½ months. This may appear to be a rather long time for a boy of 12 years of age, but it did not exceed the average period of therapy at the Ward and, in addition, the restrictions imposed were relaxed as treatment progressed ...

Nor did the intervention of the police, which would have been appropriate for the return of any runaway child of that age even to parental custody, throw a different light on the situation.'[24]

44. Turning to the...present case, the Court notes that the applicant had had the possibility of staying at home and being cared for by the Lyss Association for Home Visits to the Sick and Housebound, but she and her son had refused to cooperate with the association. Subsequently, the living conditions of the applicant at home deteriorated to such an extent that the competent authorities of the Canton of Berne decided to take action. On 16 December 1996 the Aarberg District Governor visited the applicant at home...and, finding that she was suffering from serious neglect, decided on 17 December 1996 to place her in the S. Nursing Home. On 16 January 1997, after carefully reviewing the circumstances of the case, the Cantonal Appeals Commission...concluded that the living conditions and standards of hygiene and of medical care at the applicant's home were unsatisfactory, and that the nursing home concerned, which was in an area which the applicant knew, could provide her with the necessary care.

45. Furthermore,...the applicant was not placed in the secure ward of the nursing home...Rather, she had freedom of movement and was able to maintain social contact with the outside world.

46. The Court notes, in addition, the decision of the Cantonal Appeals Commission of 16 January 1997, according to which the applicant was hardly aware of the effects of her stay in the nursing home, which were mainly felt by her son who did not wish to leave his mother. Moreover, the applicant herself was undecided as to which solution she in fact preferred...

47. Finally, the Court notes that, after moving to the nursing home, the applicant agreed to stay there. As a result, the Aarberg District Government Office had lifted the order for the applicant's placement on 14 January 1998.

48. Bearing these elements in mind, in particular the fact that the Cantonal Appeals Commission had ordered the applicant's placement in the nursing home in her own interests in order to provide her with the necessary medical care and satisfactory living conditions and standards of hygiene, and also taking into consideration the comparable circumstances in *Nielsen* (cited above), the Court concludes that...the applicant's placement in the nursing home did not amount to a deprivation of liberty within the meaning of Article 5(1), but was a responsible measure taken by the competent authorities in the applicant's interests....

[Two judges disagreed with this finding. Judge Gaukur Jörundsson held that the applicant had been deprived of her liberty but the deprivation was within Article 5(1)(e) as being a lawful detention of a person of unsound mind. Judge Loucaides agreed that there had been a deprivation of liberty, but also held that HM's placement in the nursing home was not within Article 5(1)(e). On the first of these issues, Loucaides J said]...

---

[24] *Nielsen v. Denmark*, 28 November 1988, 11 E.H.R.R. 175, paras. 70 and 72.

The applicant's placement in the nursing home was against her will. It was implemented by the police under an order explicitly defined by the national law itself and referred to by the national authorities as a measure of deprivation of liberty..., and she was not permitted to leave the nursing home. In these circumstances, I cannot see how her situation could be regarded as anything else than a deprivation of liberty...

   Detainees in prisons and other places of detention, which amount to typical cases of deprivation of liberty for the purposes of Article 5..., may be allowed to move freely within defined areas and have social contact with the outside world through telephone calls, correspondence and visits, for example; some may also be allowed day release. Yet, so long as they...are not permitted to leave the place where they are detained and go anywhere they like and at any time they want they are certainly 'deprived of their liberty'.

   In *De Wilde, Ooms and Versyp v. Belgium*,[25] the Court went as far as to hold that the fact that a person has submitted voluntarily to a particular regime of detention does not exclude the operation of Article 5 when it came to challenging its lawfulness or seeking release. The Court stated:

   '...the right to liberty is too important in a 'democratic society' within the meaning of the Convention for a person to lose the benefit of the protection of the Convention for the single reason that he gives himself up to be taken into detention. Detention might violate Article 5 even although the person concerned might have agreed to it.'...

[In the present case, the] majority appear to have relied heavily on 'the fact that the Cantonal Appeals Commission ordered the applicant's placement in the nursing home *in her own interests* in order to provide her with the necessary medical care and satisfactory living conditions and standards of hygiene' (emphasis added). Relying on that consideration and taking into account the 'comparable circumstances in *Nielsen*', the majority concluded that 'the applicant's placement in the nursing home did not amount to a deprivation of liberty within the meaning of Article 5 § 1, *but was a responsible measure* taken by the competent authorities in *the applicant's interests*' (emphasis added).

   It is my opinion that the question whether a measure amounts to a deprivation of liberty does not depend on whether it is intended to serve or actually serves the interests of the person concerned. This is illustrated by *De Wilde, Ooms and Versyp* (cited above) and the examples of minors and persons of unsound mind requiring educational supervision, whose detention is expressly justified under the provisions of Article 5(1)(d) and (e) on the premise that their case concerns 'deprivation of liberty', even though such detention may be exclusively in the detainees' interests....

   It is true that there are situations not specifically mentioned in Article 5 where deprivation of liberty may be necessary for good reasons. The present case may, possibly, be an example of this. However, these situations could comply with Article 5...if appropriate national legislation brought them within the exception of sub-paragraph 1(b) of Article 5. In this way the safeguards of Article 5 (1)(b) will serve to protect against, for example, the danger of elderly people being deprived of their liberty at the behest of scheming relatives seeking to make personal gain from their compulsory removal to institutions on the general, feeble grounds of 'mental disability' or 'senile dementia'...

---

[25] 18 June 1971, 1 E.H.R.R. 373, para. 65.

The question of whether preventive measures that take the form of restricting the movement of persons suspected of serious crime amount to a deprivation of liberty within Article 5(1) depends on the severity of the measures in question. A requirement to reside at a particular address and to report to the police at regular intervals would not be a deprivation of liberty, but confinement to a person's residence for 24 hours a day ('house arrest') would be such a deprivation, even if this might be more comfortable than detention in prison.[26] The distinction between the two forms of restriction entered into the law of the United Kingdom by the Prevention of Terrorism Act 2005. The Act authorized two forms of 'control order': (a) 'non-derogating control orders': orders that do not involve a deprivation of liberty, and thus may be imposed without the need for the United Kingdom to derogate under Article 15 from Article 5;[27] and (b) 'derogating control orders': orders that involve a deprivation of liberty and thus requiring a derogation from Article 5 if they are not to breach the Convention. In 2006, the Court of Appeal considered control orders that required the individual to remain within his residence (a one-bedroom apartment) for 18 hours each day; he could go out between 10 am and 4 pm, but was restricted to a defined urban area (that included a mosque, hospital, shops and places of entertainment); his visitors had to provide their full details to the Home Office; and the residence could be searched at any time by the police. Applying *Guzzardi v. Italy* (above), the court held that the obligations imposed by the control order were so severe that they amounted to a deprivation of liberty contrary to Article 5 and must thus be treated as 'derogating control orders'.[28]

C. DETENTION AFTER CONVICTION

In the ordinary case where a person is convicted of criminal charges and receives a prison sentence that is lawful in national law, the Convention is not infringed. The prisoner may have rights of appeal by national law against the conviction and/or against sentence. However, if the sentence is for life or for an indeterminate period, further decisions may have to be made as to how long the prisoner must be detained and when he/she can be released. Practice in European countries varies in this respect, some countries providing for further preventive detention for persistent offenders. Often the release of long-term prisoners is regarded more as an executive than a judicial function. Do such decisions involve a breach of Article 5 as an impermissible deprivation of liberty? Or are they consistent with Article 5 since the original custodial sentence will have taken effect 'after' a decision by the criminal court?

---

[26] *Lavents v. Latvia*, 28 November 2002, para. 63.

[27] *See* Section H *infra*.

[28] *Secretary of State for the Home Department v. JJ* [2006] E.W.C.A. Civ 1141; [2006] 3 W.L.R. 866.

1. VAN DROOGENBROECK V. BELGIUM

Judgment of 24 June 1982
4 E.H.R.R. 443

[Acting under Section 23 of the 'Social Protection' Act of 1 July 1964, the Belgian criminal court in 1970 sentenced Mr. van Droogenbroeck to two years' imprisonment for theft. The court also ordered that he be 'placed at the Government's disposal' for ten years, on the basis that he was a recidivist who manifested a persistent tendency to crime. After serving his principal sentence, he was in 1972 placed by the Ministry of Justice in semi-custodial care intended to secure his rehabilitation, but he quickly absconded and was later arrested on further charges of theft. Other attempts at rehabilitation having failed, he was committed by the Ministry, acting under the 1964 Act, to prison in a block reserved for recidivists. After he was once more released, similar events were repeated, and several times he appeared before an executive body known as the Body for Recidivists. He complained to Strasbourg that, *inter alia*, he had for several years been detained by ministerial order and not by order of a court.]

34. As regards paragraph 1(a), there is no dispute as to the 'competence' of the 'court' which ordered the measure complained of, namely the Ghent Court of Appeal by its judgment of 20 October 1970.

The same is true of the question whether any deprivation of liberty occurred. In this connection, it should be recalled that according to Belgian case law the placing of recidivists and habitual offenders at the Government's disposal is to be classified as a penalty involving deprivation of liberty; this is so irrespective of the form which implementation of the order may take in a given case or at a given time, be it detention, semi-custodial care, or remaining at liberty under supervision or on probation. However, the Court will take into account solely the first of such forms, this being the only one of which Mr. van Droogenbroeck complained....[The] Court will confine its examination to the periods of detention which were the subject of Mr. van Droogenbroeck's application...namely those running from 21 January 1976 to 1 June 1977 and from 21 December 1977 to 18 March 1980.

35. The Court has to determine whether those periods of detention occurred 'after conviction' by the Ghent Court of Appeal.

Having regard to the French text, the word 'conviction', for the purposes of Article 5(1)(a), has to be understood as signifying both a 'finding of guilt', after 'it has been established in accordance with the law that there has been an offence'[29] and the imposition of a penalty or other measure involving deprivation of liberty. These conditions are satisfied in the instant case.

The word 'after' does not simply mean that the 'detention' must follow the 'conviction' in point of time: in addition, the 'detention' must result from, 'follow and depend upon' or occur 'by virtue of' the 'conviction.'[30]

---

[29] *See Guzzardi v. Italy*, 6 Nov. 1980, 3 E.H.R.R. 333, para. 100.

[30] *See X v. United Kingdom*, 24 Oct. 1981, 4 E.H.R.R. 188, para. 39 (and *see* Section D(2) *infra*); *Engel v. The Netherlands (No. 1)*, 8 June 1976, 1 E.H.R.R. 647 (and *see* Section B(2) *supra*).

36. According to the applicant, the deprivations of liberty complained of stemmed not from a sentence imposed by a 'competent court' but from decisions taken by the Minister of Justice.

The respondent State, on the other hand, maintained that detention occurred 'by operation of law' following the judicial decision placing a recidivist at the Government's disposal and represented 'the principal method of implementing' such a decision; it was only release that required 'a Ministerial decision'. The 'task entrusted to the Minister...by the Act of 1 July 1964' was said to be confined 'to determining the modalities for the execution of a sentence involving deprivation of liberty', for example 'by suspending', on such conditions as he determined, 'the detention entailed by such a penalty...' Accordingly, so it was argued, 'by not deciding to release, the Minister does not decide to detain'.

37. This is a controversial point in Belgian law....

Even when an offender is not set free after serving his initial sentence—something which did not occur in the instant case and is nowadays exceptional—this is apparently the result of Ministerial instructions to the effect that he should be detained. At any rate, that such is the position emerges from paragraph 6 of a circular of 20 December 1930, which was supplied by the Government.

In any event, the Ministerial decisions of 11 January and 11 September 1975 revoking the conditional release granted to Mr. van Droogenbroeck did order that he be 'detained'.

38. Be that as it may, one must look beyond the appearances and the language used and concentrate on the realities of the situation.

This is a matter in which the Government enjoy a wide measure of discretion... In a judgment of 4 April 1978, the Belgian Court of Cassation observed that 'execution of the penalty' in question 'is to a large extent a matter for the discretion of the Minister of Justice....' In short, to adopt the language used by the Commission's delegate, 'the court decision does not order the detention' of recidivists and habitual offenders: it 'authorises' it.

39. In these circumstances, the Court has to consider whether there was a sufficient connection, for the purposes of Article 5, between the last-mentioned decision and the deprivation of liberty at issue.

This question must receive an affirmative reply since the Minister's discretion is exercised within a framework set both by the Act and by the sentence pronounced by the 'competent court'. In this respect, the Court notes that, according to Belgian case law, a judgment which sentences the person concerned to imprisonment and, by way of a supplementary or accessory penalty, places him at the Government's disposal pursuant to section 22 or section 23 of the 1964 Act constitutes 'an inseparable whole'. There are two components to the judgment: the first is a penalty involving deprivation of liberty which the offender must undergo for a period specified in the court decision, and the second is the placing of the offender at the Government's disposal, the execution of which may take different forms ranging from remaining at liberty under supervision to detention.

The choice between these forms of execution is a matter for the discretion of the Minister of Justice. Nevertheless he does not enjoy an unlimited power in making his decision: within the bounds laid down by the Act, he must assess the degree of danger presented by the individual concerned and the short- or medium-term prospects of reintegrating him into society.

40. In fact, sight must not be lost of what the title and general structure of the 1964 Act, the drafting history and Belgian case law show to be the objectives of this statute that is to say

not only 'to protect society against the danger presented by recidivists and habitual offenders' but also 'to provide [the Government] with the possibility of endeavouring to reform [them]'. Attempting to achieve these objectives requires that account be taken of circumstances that, by their nature, differ from case to case and are susceptible of modification. At the time of its decision, the court can, in the nature of things, do no more than estimate how the individual will develop in the future. The Minister of Justice, for his part, is able, through and with the assistance of his officials, to monitor that development more closely and at frequent intervals but this very fact means that with the passage of time the link between his decisions not to release or to re-detain and the initial judgment gradually becomes less strong. The link might eventually be broken if a position were reached in which those decisions were based on grounds that had no connection with the objectives of the legislature and the court or on an assessment that was unreasonable in terms of those objectives. In those circumstances, a detention that was lawful at the outset would be transformed into a deprivation of liberty that was arbitrary and, hence, incompatible with Article 5.

Such a situation did not obtain in the present case. The Belgian authorities showed patience and trust towards Mr. van Droogenbroeck: notwithstanding his conduct, they gave him several opportunities to mend his ways. The manner in which they exercised their discretion respected the requirements of the Convention, which allows a measure of indeterminacy in sentencing and does not oblige the Contracting States to entrust to the courts the general supervision of the execution of sentences.

[The Court therefore found that there had been no violation of Article 5(1). However, the Court found a violation of Article 5(4), by which someone who is deprived of their liberty is entitled to take proceedings by which the lawfulness of the detention may be decided speedily by a court. Although the original decision to sentence Mr. van Droogenbroeck had been taken by a court, the statutory duty of the Minister of Justice thereafter was to consider whether continued detention was needed on such grounds as a 'persistent tendency to crime' or 'danger to society'. In the Court's opinion, 'the very logic of the Belgian system' required subsequent judicial review, at reasonable intervals, of the justification for the continuing deprivation of liberty.[31] The reason for this was to ensure that detention decisions taken by the Minister of Justice were not arbitrary and that the conditions initially justifying indefinite detention had not ceased to exist.]

2. WEEKS V. UNITED KINGDOM

Judgment of 2 March 1987
10 E.H.R.R. 293

[In 1966, when aged 17, Mr. Weeks pleaded guilty to armed robbery: with the aid of a starting pistol loaded with blank cartridges, he had stolen 35 pence (less than 1 U.S. $) from a small shop. He was sentenced to life imprisonment, the Court of Appeal stating that this might enable him to be released much sooner than if a fixed term of imprisonment had been imposed. He was released on licence in 1976 by the Home Secretary, who under the Criminal Justice Act 1967 acted on the recommendation of an advisory body, the Parole Board.

---

[31] Para. 47.

Thereafter he committed various criminal acts and his licence was revoked more than once, so that he was reimprisoned in 1977 and again in 1985 under the sentence imposed in 1966. He complained that there had been breaches of Article 5(1) and 5(4).]

38. The applicant did not dispute that his original detention following his conviction in 1966 was justified under Article 5(1) of the Convention. He contended, however, that his detention subsequent to the revocation of his licence in June 1977 was not in accordance with this provision...

39. In what it described as its central submission, the Government argued that the applicant's recall to prison in 1977 had not deprived him of his liberty because both his liberty and his right to liberty had been taken away from him for the rest of his life by virtue of the sentence of life imprisonment imposed on him in 1966. The applicant was on this ground alone said to be precluded from claiming a breach of Article 5, whether paragraph 1 or paragraph 4. The Government drew a distinction between liberty, properly understood, and a life prisoner being permitted to live on licence outside prison. In the latter case, the Government explained, the prisoner was still serving his sentence, albeit outside prison as a result of a privilege granted to him by the Home Secretary, but his right to liberty had not been restored to him. In sum, it was one and the same deprivation of liberty in June 1977 as in December 1966, based on his original conviction and sentence, and no new issue arose under Article 5.

40. The Court is not convinced by such reasoning.

It is true that in terms of English law, except in the event of a free pardon or an exercise of the Royal Prerogative commuting the sentence, a person sentenced to life imprisonment never regains his right to liberty, even when released on licence. This is not to say, however, that Mr. Weeks lost his 'right to liberty and security of person', as guaranteed by Article 5 of the Convention, as from the moment he was sentenced to life imprisonment in December 1966. Article 5 applies to 'everyone'. All persons, whether at liberty or in detention, are entitled to the protection of Article 5....

Whether Mr. Weeks regained his 'liberty', for the purposes of Article 5 of the Convention, when released on licence in March 1976 is a question of fact, depending upon the actual circumstances of the régime to which he was subject. ... Admittedly, for persons sentenced to life imprisonment, any release under the 1967 Act is granted as an act of clemency and is always conditional... Nevertheless, the restrictions to which Mr. Weeks' freedom outside prison was subject under the law are not sufficient to prevent its being qualified as a state of 'liberty' for the purposes of Article 5. Hence, when recalling Mr. Weeks to prison in 1977, the Home Secretary was ordering his removal from an actual state of liberty, albeit one enjoyed in law as a privilege and not as of right, to a state of custody....

41. Following his 'conviction by a competent court' in December 1966, Mr. Weeks was sentenced to life imprisonment. The issue in the present case is whether his re-detention on recall to prison some ten years later was 'in accordance with a procedure prescribed by law', 'lawful' and undergone 'after' that conviction.

42. It was not contested that Mr. Weeks' re-detention as from 30 June 1977 was in accordance with a procedure prescribed by English law and otherwise lawful under English law. That, however, is not necessarily decisive. The 'lawfulness' required by the Convention presupposes not only conformity with domestic law but also, as confirmed by Article 18, conformity with

the purposes of the deprivation of liberty permitted by sub-paragraph (a) of Article 5(1).[32] Furthermore, the word 'after' in sub-paragraph (a) does not simply mean that the detention must follow the 'conviction' in point of time: in addition, the 'detention' must result from, 'follow and depend upon' or occur 'by virtue of' the 'conviction'.[33] In short, there must be a sufficient causal connection between the conviction and the deprivation of liberty at issue.[34]

43. The contested decision of the Home Secretary was taken within the legal framework set by the life sentence passed by the 'competent court' in 1966, taken together with the provisions in the 1967 Act governing the release on licence and recall to prison of persons sentenced to life imprisonment. A life sentence can never be terminated, save by pardon or in the event of being commuted, and except in those circumstances any release after sentence will always be conditional. The 1967 Act confers on the Home Secretary the power to order both release on licence and recall, but the discretion granted is not unfettered, as it was under the system in force when the applicant was sentenced. The Home Secretary can only release on the recommendation of the Parole Board and, in the case of a life prisoner, only after consulting the Lord Chief Justice and the trial judge if available. Similarly, he may revoke the licence if recommended to do so by the Parole Board. He also has the power to revoke the licence without consulting the Board 'where it appears to him that it is expedient in the public interest to recall [the] person before such consultation is practicable'. However, a further constraint upon his power of recall is that his decision may be overruled by the Parole Board. The revocation of the licence reactivates the original sentence of life imprisonment by making the recalled prisoner 'liable to be detained in pursuance of his sentence'....

45. In the submission of the Government, the lawfulness of any action taken by the Home Secretary in the present case derived from the immutable fact of Mr. Weeks' conviction and sentence in 1966. This in itself was sufficient to justify, under Article 5(1)(a), his re-detention after a period of conditional release. Whilst recognising that the instability of Mr. Weeks' personality undoubtedly did influence the choice of sentence, the Government maintained that this is not material to the issue under Article 5(1) since, in its view, it is not legitimate to distinguish one life sentence from another....

46. As the Delegate of the Commission pointed out, it may be extremely difficult, if not impossible, to disentangle different elements underlying a particular sentence in a given case and to determine which of those elements was accorded more importance by the sentencing judge; in the present case, however, it was the trial court itself and the Court of Appeal that explained in detail the reasons why Mr. Weeks received a life sentence as opposed to a determinate sentence. The Court agrees with the Commission and the applicant that the clearly stated purpose for which Mr. Weeks' sentence was imposed, taken together with the particular facts pertaining to the offence for which he was convicted, places the sentence in a special category.

Mr. Weeks was convicted of armed robbery and, aged only 17, was sentenced to life imprisonment, the severest sentence known to English law.... Armed with a starting pistol loaded with blank cartridges, he had entered a pet shop and stolen 35 pence, which sum was later found on the shop floor. Later the same day, he had telephoned the police to announce that he would give himself up. It emerged from the evidence that he had committed the robbery because he owed

---

[32] See *Bozano v. France*, 18 Dec. 1986, 9 E.H.R.R. 297, para. 54.

[33] *Id.* at para. 53 and *Van Droogenbroeck v. Belgium*, 24 June 1982, 4 E.H.R.R. 443, para. 35 and *see* Section C(1) *supra*.

[34] *See Van Droogenbroeck, supra* n. 33, para. 39.

his mother £3. What otherwise would appear a 'terrible' sentence in relation to these pathetic circumstances was seen by the trial judge and the Court of Appeal as appropriate in the light of the purpose intended to be achieved.

The intention was to make the applicant, who was qualified both by the trial judge and by the Court of Appeal as a 'dangerous young man', subject to a continuing security measure in the interests of public safety. The sentencing judges recognised that it was not possible for them to forecast how long his instability and personality disorders would endure....[They] accordingly had recourse to an 'indeterminate sentence': this would enable the appropriate authority, namely the Home Secretary, to monitor his progress and release him back into the community when he was no longer judged to represent a danger to society or to himself, and thus hopefully sooner than would have been possible if he had been sentenced to a long term of imprisonment... In substance, Mr. Weeks was being put at the disposal of the State because he needed continued supervision in custody for an unforeseeable length of time and, as a corollary, periodic reassessment in order to ascertain the most appropriate manner of dealing with him.

The grounds expressly relied on by the sentencing courts for ordering this form of deprivation of liberty against Mr. Weeks are by their very nature susceptible of change with the passage of time, whereas the measure will remain in force for the whole of his life. In this, his sentence differs from a life sentence imposed on a person because of the gravity of the offence.

47. In this sense, the measure ordered against Mr. Weeks is thus comparable to the Belgian measure at issue in the *Van Droogenbroeck* case, that is the placing of a recidivist or habitual offender at the disposal of the Government—although in the present case the placement was for a whole lifetime and not for a limited period. The legitimate aim (of social protection and the rehabilitation of offenders) pursued by the measure and its effect on the convicted person are substantially the same in both cases....

49. Applying the principles stated in the *Van Droogenbroeck* judgment, the formal legal connection between Mr. Weeks' conviction in 1966 and his recall to prison some ten years later is not on its own sufficient to justify the contested detention under Article 5(1)(a). The causal link required by sub-paragraph (a) might eventually be broken if a position were reached in which a decision not to release or to re-detain was based on grounds that were inconsistent with the objectives of the sentencing court. 'In those circumstances, a detention that was lawful at the outset would be transformed into a deprivation of liberty that was arbitrary and, hence, incompatible with Article 5'.[35]

50. In the submission of the applicant, the objectives of the courts in 1966 and 1967 as regards the length of his loss of liberty were satisfied on his release in March 1976; the requisite link was broken at that stage, so that his full rights under Article 5 were restored to him and his re-detention fifteen months later was no longer justified under Article 5(1)(e).

The Court does not accept this contention. As a matter of English law, it was inherent in Mr. Weeks' life sentence that, whether he was inside or outside prison, his liberty was at the discretion of the executive for the rest of his life (subject to the controls subsequently introduced by the 1967 Act, notably the Parole Board). This the sentencing judges must be taken to have known and intended. It is not for the Court, within the context of Article 5, to review the appropriateness of the original sentence, a matter which moreover has not been disputed by the applicant in the present proceedings.

---

[35] *Van Droogenbroek v. Belgium, supra* n. 33, para. 40.

It remains to examine the sufficiency of the grounds on which his re-detention in June 1977 and thereafter was based. In this area, as in many others, the national authorities are to be recognized as having a certain discretion since they are better placed than the international judge to evaluate the evidence in a particular case....

The Court reviewed the evidence as to Mr. Weeks' behaviour in 1977, found that it was still 'unstable, disturbed and aggressive' and concluded that his recall to prison in 1977 and subsequent detention were compatible with Article 5(1).

Mr. Weeks also complained of a breach of Article 5(4). The Court again emphasized that his 'indeterminate' sentence was in a special category because it was imposed for the stated purpose of social protection and rehabilitation: 'unlike the case of a person sentenced to life imprisonment because of the gravity of the offence committed, the grounds relied on by the sentencing judge for deciding that the length of the deprivation of Mr. Weeks' liberty should be subject to the discretion of the executive for the rest of his life are by their nature susceptible of change with the passage of time'.[36]

For the purposes of Article 5(4), Weeks was therefore entitled to a decision by a court as to the lawfulness of his detention. The Court reviewed the constitution and powers of the Parole Board which had considered his case. Could the Board be regarded as a judicial body for the purposes of Article 5(4)? The Court held that while the Board's members were independent and impartial, it lacked the power to do more than advise the Home Secretary to release a prisoner; and its procedure did not require the Board to disclose to the prisoner any adverse material which it held about him (which a judicial body would be required to do). The Court further held that the scope of judicial review of the Board's advice and the Home Secretary's decisions was not wide enough to ensure that an individual's detention was 'consistent with and therefore justified by the objectives of the indeterminate sentence imposed on him'.[37] There had thus been a breach of Mr. Weeks' rights under Article 5(4).

While the circumstances of Mr. Weeks' sentence and subsequent history were exceptional, the principles adopted by the Court have been applied in the context of the most serious criminal conduct.[38]

3. THYNNE, WILSON AND GUNNELL V. UNITED KINGDOM

Judgment of 25 October 1990
13 E.H.R.R. 666

[In English law, the maximum sentence that can be imposed for serious offences such as rape is life imprisonment. Each of the three applicants had committed grave sexual offences

---

[36] *Weeks v. United Kingdom*, 2 Mar. 1987, 10 E.H.R.R. 293, para. 58.

[37] *Id.* at para. 69.

[38] *See Hussain v. United Kingdom*, 21 Feb. 1996, 22 E.H.R.R. 1 and *T and V v. United Kingdom*, 16 Dec. 1999, 30 E.H.R.R. 121.

and assaults and was sentenced to life imprisonment. In each case psychiatric evidence indicated that the applicant was suffering from a mental or personality disorder. As in *Weeks v. United Kingdom*, the effect of a life sentence was to give the Home Secretary the power to decide when a prisoner can be released. The European Court had already decided, in *Van Droogenbroeck v. Belgium* and in *Weeks*, that the taking of discretionary decisions as to whether a life prisoner should be released was a matter which, under Article 5(4), must be subject to an adequate level of judicial control. But the British government had not changed the system, so the same issues again came before the Strasbourg Court.]

A. Whether the requisite judicial control was incorporated in the original conviction

65. The applicants claimed that a discretionary life sentence is composed of a punitive element—i.e. a period of imprisonment to satisfy the needs of retribution and deterrence (the 'tariff' period)—and a security element based on the need to protect the public. They maintained that they had received discretionary life sentences because, as in the *Weeks* case,[39] the courts considered them to be mentally unstable and dangerous and that such a sentence would enable the Secretary of State to monitor their progress and decide when it was safe to release them. Since these factors were susceptible to change with the passage of time a right to judicial review at reasonable intervals of the continued lawfulness of their detention was required.

66. The Government argued that the present cases did not fall into the same category as the *Weeks* case. In that case, as perceived by the Court, the facts relating to the offence could not be described as grave and the sole purpose of the sentence as stated by the courts was to detain the offender because he might present a danger to the public for an indeterminate period in the future. The need for punishment was not a factor in the stated purpose of the life sentence in that case. In contrast, the present applicants had committed particularly serious offences and the sentencing courts had emphasised the need for punishment.

The Government contended that in a normal discretionary life sentence no clear dividing line can be drawn by reference to the 'tariff' period between the punitive and security purposes for which the sentence is imposed. In its submission there is no clearly identifiable point after which the sole justification of the sentence is protective detention.

In the first place it stated that the purpose of the tariff has been wrongly understood by both the applicants and the Commission as providing support for such a division. The 'tariff' was a notional period communicated by the judges to the Secretary of State in both mandatory and discretionary life sentences to enable him to fix the first review date by the Local Review Committee. It represented the judges' views as to the minimum period of detention necessary to satisfy the requirements of retribution and deterrence. The judges' recommendation in this respect, however, was relevant only to the fixing of the date for the first review. When considering release, the Secretary of State was not bound by the judicial view on 'tariff', but had to take into account a variety of factors which it was impossible to subject to finite analysis....

In the second place the gravity of the offences was relevant at all times throughout the sentence, especially when the Secretary of State was called on to assess the risk factor when considering release. Gravity also remained the immutable justification in a discretionary life sentence—although not the sole justification—for the continued detention or recall of the life prisoner.

[39] *See* Section C(2) *supra*.

67. In proceedings originating in an individual application, the Court has, without losing sight of the general context, to confine its attention as far as possible to the issues raised by the concrete case before it. Accordingly, it will limit its examination to the application of Article 5(4) to the particular circumstances of the present applicants.

68. It was held in the *De Wilde, Ooms and Versyp* judgment of 18 June 1971 that where a sentence of imprisonment is imposed after 'conviction by a competent court', the supervision required by Article 5(4) is incorporated in the decision of the court.[40] In subsequent cases the Court made it clear that this finding related only to 'the initial decision depriving a person of his liberty' and did not purport 'to deal with an ensuing period of detention in which new issues affecting the lawfulness of the detention might arise'.[41] In this connection the concept of lawfulness under Article 5(4) requires that the detention be in conformity not only with domestic law but also with the text of the Convention, the general principle embodied therein and the aim of the restrictions permitted by Article 5(1).

69. In cases concerning detention of persons of unsound mind under Article 5(1)(e) where the reasons initially warranting detention may cease to exist the Court has held that 'it would be contrary to the object and purpose of Article 5...to interpret paragraph 4...as making this category of confinement immune from subsequent review of lawfulness merely provided that the initial decision issued from a court...'[42] This interpretation of Article 5(4) has also, in certain circumstances, been applied to detention 'after conviction by a competent court' under Article 5(1)(a).[43] What is of importance in this context is the nature and purpose of the detention in question, viewed in the light of the objectives of the sentencing court, and not the category to which it belongs under Article 5(1).[44]

[Citing its earlier decisions in *Weeks* and *Van Droogenbroeck*, the Court summarized the psychiatric evidence relating to the three applicants when they were convicted, and continued:]

Each of the applicants was thus sentenced to life imprisonment because, in addition to the need for punishment, he was considered by the courts to be suffering from a mental or personality disorder and to be dangerous and in need of treatment. Life imprisonment was judged to be the most appropriate sentence in the circumstances since it enabled the Secretary of State to assess their progress and to act accordingly. Thus the courts' sentencing objectives were in that respect similar to those in *Weeks*, but also took into account the much greater gravity of the offences committed.

73. As regards the nature and purpose of the discretionary life sentence under English law, the Government's main submission was that it is impossible to disentangle the punitive and security components of such sentences. The Court is not persuaded by this argument: the discretionary life sentence has clearly developed in English law as a measure to deal with mentally unstable and dangerous offenders; numerous judicial statements have recognized

---

[40] 1 E.H.R.R. 373.

[41] *See, inter alia, Weeks* (Section C(2) *supra*).

[42] *See X v. United Kingdom*, 24 Oct. 1981, 4 E.H.R.R. 188 (Section D(2) *infra*).

[43] *See, inter alia, Van Droogenbroeck v. Belgium*, 24 June 1982, 4 E.H.R.R. 443 (Section C(2) *supra*), *Weeks v. United Kingdom*, 2 Mar. 1987, 10 E.H.R.R. 293 (Section C(2) *supra*) and *E. v. Norway*, 29 Aug. 1990, 17 E.H.R.R. 30, para. 50.

[44] *See Van Droogenbroeck, supra* n. 33.

the protective purpose of this form of life sentence. Although the dividing line may be difficult to draw in particular cases, it seems clear that the principles underlying such sentences, unlike mandatory life sentences, have developed in the sense that they are composed of a punitive element and subsequently of a security element designed to confer on the Secretary of State the responsibility for determining when the public interest permits the prisoner's release. This view is confirmed by the judicial description of the 'tariff' as denoting the period of detention considered necessary to meet the requirements of retribution and deterrence.

74. The Court accepts the Government's submissions that the 'tariff' is also communicated to the Secretary of State in cases of mandatory life imprisonment; that the Secretary of State in considering release may not be bound by the intimation of the 'tariff'; and that in the assessment of the risk factor in deciding on release the Secretary of State will also have regard to the gravity of the offences committed.

However, in the Court's view this does not alter the fact that the objectives of the discretionary life sentence as seen above are distinct from the punitive purposes of the mandatory life sentence and have been so described by the courts in the relevant cases.

75. It is clear from the judgments of the sentencing courts that in their view the three applicants, unlike Mr. Weeks, had committed offences of the utmost gravity meriting lengthy terms of imprisonment. Nevertheless, the Court is satisfied that in each case the punitive period of the discretionary life sentence has expired....

76. Having regard to the foregoing, the Court finds that the detention of the applicants after the expiry of the punitive periods of their sentences is comparable to that at issue in the *Van Droogenbroeck* and *Weeks* cases: the factors of mental instability and dangerousness are susceptible to change over the passage of time and new issues of lawfulness may thus arise in the course of detention. It follows that at this phase in the execution of their sentences, the applicants are entitled under Article 5(4) to take proceedings to have the lawfulness of their continued detention decided by a court at reasonable intervals and to have the lawfulness of any re-detention determined by a court....

B. Whether the available remedies satisfied the requirements of Article 5(4)

79. Article 5(4) does not guarantee a right to judicial control of such scope as to empower the 'court' on all aspects of the case, including questions of expediency, to substitute its own discretion for that of the decision-making authority; the review should, nevertheless, be wide enough to bear on those conditions which, according to the Convention, are essential for the lawful detention of a person subject to the special type of deprivation of liberty ordered against these three applicants.

80. The Court sees no reason to depart from its finding in the *Weeks* judgment that neither the Parole Board nor judicial review proceedings—no other remedy of a judicial character being available to the three applicants—satisfy the requirements of Article 5(4). Indeed, this was not disputed by the Government....

The decision in *Thynne, Wilson and Gunnell v. United Kingdom* concerned 'discretionary life sentences', that is, sentences of life imprisonment imposed by the trial court in exercise of its sentencing powers. Initially, the Strasbourg court accepted that where persons were convicted of murder, for which the law imposed a mandatory sentence of life imprisonment, different considerations might arise (see *Thynne, Wilson and Gunnell,* para. 74). In *Wynne v United Kingdom* in 1994,[45] the distinction between 'discretionary' and 'mandatory' life sentences was confirmed, it being held that in the case of mandatory life sentences the requirements of Article 5(4) were satisfied by the judgment at the trial. How valid was this distinction? The Court returned to the issue in 2002.

4. STAFFORD V. UNITED KINGDOM

Judgment of 28 May 2002
35 E.H.R.R. 1121 [G.C.]

10. In January 1967 the applicant was convicted of murder. He was released on licence in April 1979. His licence required him to cooperate with his probation officer and to remain in the United Kingdom unless his probation officer agreed to his travelling abroad.

11. Soon after release the applicant left the United Kingdom in breach of his licence and went to live in South Africa. In September 1980 his licence was revoked and thereafter he was continuously 'unlawfully at large'.

12. In April 1989 the applicant was arrested in the United Kingdom, having returned from South Africa in possession of a false passport. Possession of a false passport led to a fine. He remained in custody, however, due to the revocation of the life licence....

13. In November 1990 the [Parole] Board recommended the applicant's release subject to a satisfactory release plan.... In March 1991 the applicant was released on life licence.

14. In July 1993 the applicant was arrested and remanded in custody on counterfeiting charges. On 19 July 1994 he was convicted on two counts of conspiracy to forge travellers' cheques and passports and sentenced to six years' imprisonment.

16. In 1996 the Parole Board conducted a formal review of the applicant's case and recommended his release on life licence. It said:

> 'This case is exceptional in that it is a recall one and he has previously made a successful transition from prison to the community without violent reoffending... The Panel took the view after lengthy consideration that nothing further would be gained by a period in open conditions....'

17. By letter of 27 February 1997 to the applicant, the Secretary of State rejected the Board's recommendation...:

> '...[The Secretary of State] notes with concern the circumstances surrounding your two recalls to prison... Both these occasions represent a serious and grave breach of the trust placed in you as a life licensee and demonstrate a lack of regard for the requirements of supervision. Against this background the Secretary of State is not yet satisfied that if released on licence for a third time, you would fully comply with the conditions of your life licence....'

---

[45] 18 July 1994, 19 E.H.R.R. 333.

For these reasons, the Secretary of State considers that you should be transferred to an open prison for a final period of testing and preparation. Your next formal review by the Parole Board will begin 2 years after your arrival there.'

[This decision was the subject of judicial review proceedings brought by the applicant.]

20. The Secretary of State acknowledged in the proceedings that there was not a significant risk that the applicant would commit further violent offences, but asserted that he could lawfully detain a post-tariff mandatory life prisoner solely because there was a risk that he might commit further non-violent imprisonable offences.

[The Secretary of State's assertion was rejected by the High Court]

22. On 26 November 1997 the Court of Appeal allowed the Secretary of State's appeal, holding that...the [Criminal Justice Act 1991] conferred a broad discretion on the Secretary of State to direct the release of mandatory life prisoners and his decision not to release the applicant was in accordance with the previously stated policy whereby the risk of reoffending was taken into account, such risk not having been expressed as being limited to offences of a violent or sexual nature. [In his judgment, Lord Bingham CJ said:] '...The imposition of what is in effect a substantial term of imprisonment by the exercise of executive discretion, without trial, lies uneasily with ordinary concepts of the rule of law. I hope that the Secretary of State may, even now, think it right to give further consideration to the case.'...

[A domestic appeal by Stafford having been dismissed, he applied to the Strasbourg Court. That court summarized the background to the case:]

30. Over the years, the Secretary of State has adopted a 'tariff' policy in exercising his discretion whether to release offenders sentenced to life imprisonment.... In essence, the tariff approach involves breaking down the life sentence into component parts, namely retribution, deterrence and protection of the public. The 'tariff' represents the minimum period which the prisoner will have to serve to satisfy the requirements of retribution and deterrence. The Home Secretary will not refer the case to the Parole Board until three years before the expiry of the tariff period, and will not exercise his discretion to release on licence until after the tariff period has been completed.

31. [Under the Criminal Justice Act 1991], the tariff of a discretionary life prisoner is fixed in open court by the trial judge after conviction. After the tariff has expired, the prisoner may require the Secretary of State to refer his case to the Parole Board, which has the power to order his release if it is satisfied that it is no longer necessary to detain him for the protection of the public.

32. A different regime, however, applied under the 1991 Act to persons serving a mandatory sentence of life imprisonment.... In relation to these prisoners, the Secretary of State decides the length of the tariff. The view of the trial judge is made known to the prisoner after his trial, as is the opinion of the Lord Chief Justice. The prisoner is afforded the opportunity to make representations to the Secretary of State, who then proceeds to fix the tariff and is entitled to depart from the judicial view.

[After reviewing the domestic case-law, the Court made its own assessment.]

62. The question to be determined is whether, after the expiry on 1 July 1997 of the fixed-term sentence imposed on the applicant for fraud, the continued detention of the applicant under the original mandatory life sentence imposed on him for murder in 1967 complied with the requirements of Article 5 (1)....

63. Where the 'lawfulness' of detention is in issue, the Convention refers essentially to national law and lays down the obligation to conform to the substantive and procedural rules of national law. This primarily requires any arrest or detention to have a legal basis in domestic law but also relates to the quality of the law, requiring it to be compatible with the rule of law... In addition, any deprivation of liberty should be in keeping with the purpose of Article 5, namely to protect the individual from arbitrariness...

64. It is not contested that the applicant's detention from 1 July 1997 was in accordance with a procedure prescribed by English law and otherwise lawful under English law.... This is not however conclusive of the matter....

66. Much of the argument from the parties has focused on the nature and purpose of the mandatory life sentence as compared with other forms of life sentence and whether the detention after 1 July 1997 continued to conform with the objectives of that sentence....

67. Of particular importance in this regard is *Wynne*, decided in 1994, in which this Court found that no violation arose under Article 5(4) in relation to the continued detention after release and recall to prison of a mandatory life prisoner convicted of an intervening offence of manslaughter, the tariff element of which had expired. This provides strong support for the Government's case...

68. While the Court is not formally bound to follow any of its previous judgments, it is in the interests of legal certainty, foreseeability and equality before the law that it should not depart, without cogent reason, from precedents laid down in previous cases. Since the Convention is first and foremost a system for the protection of human rights, the Court must however have regard to the changing conditions in Contracting States and respond, for example, to any emerging consensus as to the standards to be achieved.[46] It is of crucial importance that the Convention is interpreted and applied in a manner which renders its rights practical and effective, not theoretical and illusory....

69. Similar considerations apply as regards the changing conditions and any emerging consensus discernible within the domestic legal order of the respondent Contracting State....

70. The mandatory life sentence [in the United Kingdom] is imposed pursuant to statute in all cases of murder. This position has not changed, although there has been increasing criticism of the inflexibility of the statutory regime, which does not reflect the differing types of killing covered by the offence, from so-called mercy killing to brutal psychopathic serial attacks...

71. The inflexibility of this regime was, from a very early stage, mitigated by the approach of the Secretary of State, who in all types of life sentences—mandatory, discretionary and detention during Her Majesty's pleasure—adopted a practice of setting a specific term known as the 'tariff' to represent the element of deterrence and retribution. This was generally the minimum period of detention which would be served before an offender could hope to be

---

[46] *See,* among other authorities, *Cossey v. United Kingdom,* 27 September 1990, 13 E.H.R.R. 622, para. 35, and *Chapman v. United Kingdom* [G.C.], 18 January 2001, 33 E.H.R.R. 18, para. 70.

released. It was never anticipated that prisoners serving mandatory life sentences would in fact stay in prison for life, save in exceptional cases. Similarly, the decision as to the release of all life prisoners also lay generally with the Secretary of State. The tariff-fixing and release procedures applicable to life sentences have however been modified considerably over the past twenty years, to a large extent due to the case-law of this Court....

[Previous decisions were outlined, including *T v United Kingdom* and *V v. United Kingdom*[47] which concerned two juvenile murderers, detained during Her Majesty's pleasure.]

74. ...Although this type of sentence, as with the adult mandatory life sentence, was imposed automatically for the offence of murder, the Court was not persuaded that it could be regarded as a true sentence of punishment to detention for life. Such a term applied to children would have conflicted with United Nations instruments and raised serious problems under Article 3 of the Convention. Considering that it must be regarded in practice as an indeterminate sentence which could only be justified by considerations based on the need to protect the public and therefore linked to assessments of the offender's mental development and maturity, it therefore held that a review by a court of the continued existence of grounds of detention was required for the purposes of Article 5(4).[48]

75. The issues arising from the sentencing process for juvenile murderers at the tariff-fixing stage were then examined both in the domestic courts and in Strasbourg.... This Court found that Article 6(1) applied to the fixing of the tariff, which represented the requirements of retribution and deterrence and was thus a sentencing exercise. The fact that it was decided by the Secretary of State, a member of the executive and therefore not independent, was found to violate this provision.[49]

77. While mandatory life prisoners alone remained under the old regime, the coming into force... of the Human Rights Act 1998 provided the opportunity for the first direct challenges to the mandatory life regime under the provisions of the Convention in the domestic courts.

[The decisions of domestic courts were reviewed.]

78. The above developments demonstrate an evolving analysis, in terms of the right to liberty and its underlying values, of the role of the Secretary of State concerning life sentences. The abolition of the death penalty in 1965 and the conferring on the Secretary of State of the power to release convicted murderers represented, at that time, a major and progressive reform. However, with the wider recognition of the need to develop and apply, in relation to mandatory life prisoners, judicial procedures reflecting standards of independence, fairness and openness, the continuing role of the Secretary of State in fixing the tariff and in deciding on a prisoner's release following its expiry has become increasingly difficult to reconcile with the notion of separation of powers between the executive and the judiciary...

79. [It] may now be regarded as established in domestic law that there is no distinction between mandatory life prisoners, discretionary life prisoners and juvenile murderers as regards the nature of tariff-fixing. It is a sentencing exercise. The mandatory life sentence does not impose imprisonment for life as a punishment. The tariff, which reflects the individual circumstances of the offence and the offender, represents the element of punishment....[The] finding in *Wynne* that the mandatory life sentence constituted punishment for life can no

---

[47] 16 December 1999, 30 E.H.R.R. 121.
[48] *See Hussain v. United Kingdom, supra* n. 38.
[49] *T and V v. United Kingdom, supra* n. 38.

longer be regarded as reflecting the real position in the domestic criminal justice system of the mandatory life prisoner. This conclusion is reinforced by the fact that a whole life tariff may, in exceptional cases, be imposed where justified by the gravity of the particular offence....

80. The Government maintained that the mandatory life sentence was nonetheless an indeterminate sentence which was not based on any individual characteristic of the offender, such as youth and dangerousness, and therefore there was no question of any change in the relevant circumstances of the offender that might raise lawfulness issues concerning the basis for his continued detention. However, the Court is not convinced by this argument. Once the punishment element of the sentence (as reflected in the tariff) has been satisfied, the grounds for the continued detention, as in discretionary life and juvenile murderer cases, must be considerations of risk and dangerousness....

81. In the Court's view, the applicant in the present case must be regarded as having exhausted the punishment element for his offence of murder.... When his sentence for the later fraud offence expired on 1 July 1997, his continued detention under the mandatory life sentence cannot be regarded as justified by his punishment for the original murder. Nor, in contrast to the recall of the applicant in *Weeks*, was the continued detention of the present applicant justified by the Secretary of State on grounds of mental instability and dangerousness to the public from the risk of further violence. The Secretary of State expressly relied on the risk of non-violent offending by the applicant. The Court finds no sufficient causal connection, as required by the notion of lawfulness in Article 5(1)(a)..., between the possible commission of other non-violent offences and the original sentence for murder in 1967.

82. The Government have argued that it would be absurd if a Secretary of State were bound to release a mandatory life prisoner who was likely to commit serious non-violent offences. [However],...the applicant was sentenced for the fraud which he committed while on release and served the sentence found appropriate as punishment by the trial court. There was no power under domestic law to impose indefinite detention on him to prevent future non-violent offending.... The Court cannot accept that a decision-making power by the executive to detain the applicant on the basis of perceived fears of future non-violent criminal conduct unrelated to his original murder conviction accords with the spirit of the Convention, with its emphasis on the rule of law and protection from arbitrariness.

83. The Court concludes that the applicant's detention after 1 July 1997 was not justified in terms of Article 5(1)(a)....

[Had there also been a violation of Article 5(4)?]

87. The Court has found above that the tariff comprises the punishment element of the mandatory life sentence. The Secretary of State's role in fixing the tariff is a sentencing exercise, not the administrative implementation of the sentence of the court as can be seen in cases of early or conditional release from a determinate term of imprisonment. After the expiry of the tariff, continued detention depends on elements of dangerousness and risk associated with the objectives of the original sentence of murder. These elements may change with the course of time, and thus new issues of lawfulness arise requiring determination by a body satisfying the requirements of Article 5(4). It can no longer be maintained that the original trial and appeal proceedings satisfied, once and for all, issues of compatibility of subsequent detention of mandatory life prisoners with the provisions of Article 5(1)....

89. From 1 July 1997 to the date of his release on 22 December 1998, the lawfulness of the applicant's continued detention was not reviewed by a body with the power to release or following a procedure containing the necessary judicial safeguards....

90. There has, accordingly, been a violation of Article 5(4)....

This was a unanimous decision by the Grand Chamber of the Court. Short concurring judgments were delivered by four judges (Rozakis, Costa, Zagrebelsky and Tulkens) who questioned aspects of paragraphs 81 and 82 in the Court's judgment.[50]

The American courts have held that the trial preceding a criminal conviction provides that due process which is constitutionally required to deprive a person of ordinary liberty. Upon conviction, the imprisoned persons may usually be regulated and confined as directed by correctional authorities without providing any particular procedures. Thus, prisoners may be transferred to less favourable conditions of confinement,[51] or subjected to solitary confinement[52] without a prior hearing, on the theory that such changes are all within the ordinary limits of the original sentence. The Supreme Court has also held, however, that even persons properly convicted and confined retain certain liberty interests and certain kinds of treatment which could not reasonably have been contemplated at the time of sentencing may invade those interests. Thus, the state may not transfer a prisoner to a mental hospital or administer anti-psychotic drugs without providing a means in which the legality of those actions could be contested.[53] The Supreme Court has also held that the state may, by its own practices and regulations, create expectations as to the way it will deal with convicted persons so as to give rise to constitutionally protected liberty interests. At one time it determined the existence of such state-created interests by a close analysis of the language of any relevant regulations. More recently, it has held that the proper inquiry is whether or not the changes in the conditions of confinement complained of impose 'atypical and significant hardship on the inmate in relation to the ordinary incidents of prison life'.[54]

---

[50] Issues similar to those in *Stafford v. UK* have been before the Court in other cases from the United Kingdom, including *Benjamin v. UK*, 26 Sept. 2002, 36 E.H.R.R. 1; *Blackstock v. UK*, 21 June 2005, 42 E.H.R.R. 2 (review of detention of long-term prisoner occurred only after excessive delay); and *Waite v. UK*, 10 Dec. 2002, 36 E.H.R.R. 54 (Art. 5(4) breached when Parole Board refused oral hearing and legal representation before deciding to revoke the release on licence of W, who when aged 16 had been convicted of murder and detained 'at Her Majesty's pleasure').

[51] *Meachum v. Fano*, 427 U.S. 215 (1976). *See also Olim v. Wakinekona*, 461 U.S. 238 (1983) (transfer from Hawaii to California).

[52] *Hewitt v. Helms*, 459 U.S. 460 (1983).

[53] *See Vitek v. Jones*, 445 U.S. 480 (1980); *Washington v. Harper*, 494 U.S. 210 (1990).

[54] *Sandin v. Connor*, 515 U.S. 472, 484 (1995). Illustrations of the Court's jurisprudence on the point include *Morrisey v. Brewer*, 408 U.S. 471 (1972) (parole); *Gagnon v. Scarpelli*, 411 U.S. 778 (1973) (probation); *Wolff v. McDonnell*, 418 U.S. 539 (1974) (good time credit); *Young v. Harper*, 520 U.S. 143 (1997) (pre-parole programme). The Court has held that the initial decision to grant parole must also employ a fair procedure where the state has sufficiently precisely defined the factors of eligibility. *See Greenholz v. Inmates*, 442 U.S. 1 (1979). On the other hand, no particular procedure need be associated with a governor's decision to grant or withhold a pardon or commutation of sentence. *Connecticut Board of Pardons v. Dumschat*, 452 U.S. 458 (1981); *Ohio Adult Parole Authority v. Woodward*, 523 U.S. 272 (1998).

The due process clauses have also been interpreted to prohibit the state from continuing the detention of a person properly detained for one purpose when it is conceded that that purpose is no longer served. To the extent the state wishes to justify confinement on some other basis, it is obliged to provide fair procedures for testing the new factual and legal predicates of such an action. Thus, the Supreme Court has stated that a person serving a sentence after conviction may not be detained beyond the time of his sentence on the grounds of mental illness and dangerousness without affording that person the same procedural protections required for civil commitments in general.[55] Along the same lines, in *Foucha v. Louisiana*,[56] a defendant had been committed to a state mental hospital after a verdict of not guilty by reason of insanity. State law provided that he should remain confined, even after he was no longer suffering from a mental illness, until he could show that he was no longer dangerous to himself or others. The Supreme Court held such detention unconstitutional.

It does not follow merely because a person is sentenced to an indeterminate term, that the absence of periodic judicial review violates a right to have the legality of a deprivation of liberty determined. The question, as stated by the European Court in the *Thynne, Wilson and Gunnell* case (and illustrated by the *Foucha* case) is whether, at some point, there occurs 'a period of detention in which new issues affecting [its] lawfulness might arise'.[57] Where, however, the reasons for the indefinite sentence were fully determined at the original trial, the 'requisite judicial control [may have been] incorporated in the original conviction'.[58] Reasoning like this underlay the judgment of the Supreme Court of Canada in upholding indeterminate sentences for 'dangerous offenders' in *R. v. Lyons*.[59] According to the reasons for judgment of Justice LaForest in which a majority joined, the defendant, in such a case:

is clearly being sentenced for the 'serious personal injury offence' he or she may have been found guilty of committing albeit in a different way than ordinarily would be done... Thus the appellant's contention that he is being punished for what he might do rather than for what he has done... must be rejected. The punishment, as I noted, flows from the actual commission of a specific crime, the requisite elements of which have been proved beyond a reasonable doubt.[60]

Moreover, Justice LaForest stated that it was appropriate for the trial court, in deciding the appropriateness of such a sentence in the first instance to consider not only the gravity of the offence but the potential risk to the public in the future.[61] The sentence, therefore, was not arbitrary and violated neither Section 7 nor Section 9 of the Charter.

---

[55] *See Jackson v. Indiana*, 406 U.S. 715, 724–30 (1972) discussing *Baxstrom v. Herald*, 383 U.S. 107 (1966). The standards and procedures for civil commitment under American constitutional law are discussed at Section (D)(3) *infra*.

[56] 504 U.S. 71 (1992).

[57] 25 Oct. 1990, 13 E.H.R.R. 666, para. 68 quoting *DeWilde, Ooms and Versyp v. Belgium*, 18 June 1971, 1 E.H.R.R. 373.

[58] *Id.*

[59] [1987] 2 S.C.R. 309.

[60] *Id.* at 328.

[61] *Id.*

The sufficiency of the original determination was made clear by the Court's decision in *R. v. Milne* decided the same day as *Lyons*. In that case, the defendant had been declared a dangerous offender and given an indeterminate sentence after conviction of a crime which was subsequently deleted from the list of offences in the dangerous offender statute. This later legislative judgment that the offence did not provide a predicate for a finding of dangerousness did not affect the constitutionality of the original sentence.[62]

D. DETENTION OF MENTAL PATIENTS

The principles which were applied in *Van Droogenbroeck, Weeks, Thynne, Wilson and Gunnell* and *Stafford* are also relevant to the treatment of mentally disordered persons, who are vulnerable to the risk of being deprived of their liberty over lengthy periods.

1. WINTERWERP V. THE NETHERLANDS

Judgment of 24 October 1979
2 E.H.R.R. 387

[Article 5(1)(e) permits the lawful detention of persons of unsound mind. Mr. Winterwerp had been compulsorily detained for a considerable period between 1968 and 1978, originally on his wife's application, under the Mentally Ill Persons Act of 1884. The Act regulated in detail the procedures for detention and the periods for which detention could be authorized. Among the arguments advanced by Mr. Winterwerp before the Court were that he was not a person of unsound mind, that he had been confined solely by administrative action, and that his detention from year to year had been renewed by proceedings in which he played no part.]

A. 'The lawful detention of persons of unsound mind'

36. Mr. Winterwerp maintains in the first place that his deprivation of liberty did not meet the requirements embodied in the words 'lawful detention of persons of unsound mind'. Neither the Government nor the Commission agrees with this contention.

37. The Convention does not state what is to be understood by the words 'persons of unsound mind'. This term is...a term whose meaning is continually evolving as research in psychiatry progresses, an increasing flexibility in treatment is developing and society's attitudes to mental illness change, in particular so that a greater understanding of the problems of mental patients is becoming more widespread.

---

[62] [1987] 2 S.C.R. 512. The judgments of the Supreme Court of Canada as to the compatibility of indeterminate sentences with the Charter's prohibition of cruel or unusual punishment are discussed in Chapter 5(A)(5), *supra*.

In any event, sub-paragraph (e) of Article 5(1) obviously cannot be taken as permitting the detention of a person simply because his views or behaviour deviate from the norms prevailing in a particular society. To hold otherwise would not be reconcilable with the text of Article 5(1), which sets out an exhaustive list[63] of exceptions calling for a narrow interpretation.[64] Neither would it be in conformity with the object and purpose of Article 5(1), namely, to ensure that no one should be dispossessed of his liberty in an arbitrary fashion.[65] Moreover, it would disregard the importance of the right to liberty in a democratic society.[66]

> [The Court examined the provisions of the Mentally Ill Persons Act governing detention, found that in practice only a person whose mental disorder was of such a kind or of such gravity as to be an actual danger to himself or to others was liable to be detained, and concluded that the detention of such a person under the Act 'in principle falls within the ambit of Article 5(1)(e)'.]

39. The next issue to be examined is the 'lawfulness' of the detention for the purposes of Article 5(1)(e). Such 'lawfulness' presupposes conformity with the domestic law in the first place and also, as confirmed by Article 18, conformity with the purpose of the restrictions permitted by Article 5(1)(e); it is required in respect of both the ordering and the execution of the measures involving deprivation of liberty....

As regards the conformity with the domestic law, the Court points out that the term 'lawful' covers procedural as well as substantive rules. There thus exists a certain overlapping between this term and the general requirement stated at the beginning of Article 5(1), namely, observance of 'a procedure prescribed by law' (see para. 45 below).

Indeed, these two expressions reflect the importance of the aim underlying Article 5(1) (see para. 37 above): in a democratic society subscribing to the rule of law, no detention that is arbitrary can ever be regarded as 'lawful'.

The Commission likewise stresses that there must be no element of arbitrariness; the conclusion it draws is that no one may be confined as 'a person of unsound mind' in the absence of medical evidence establishing that his mental state is such as to justify his compulsory hospitalization...

The Court fully agrees with this line of reasoning. In the Court's opinion, except in emergency cases, the individual concerned should not be deprived of his liberty unless he has been reliably shown to be of 'unsound mind'. The very nature of what has to be established before the competent national authority—that is, a true mental disorder—calls for objective medical expertise. Further, the mental disorder must be of a kind or degree warranting compulsory confinement. What is more, the validity of continued confinement depends upon the persistence of such a disorder.[67]

40. The Court undoubtedly has the jurisdiction to verify the 'lawfulness' of the detention. Mr. Winterwerp in fact alleges unlawfulness by reason of procedural defects in the making of

---

[63] See Engel v. The Netherlands, 8 June 1976, 1 E.H.R.R. 647, para. 57, Section B(2) supra and Ireland v. United Kingdom, 18 Jan. 1978, 2 E.H.R.R. 25, para. 194.

[64] See, mutatis mutandis, Klass v. Germany, 6 Sept. 1978, 2 E.H.R.R. 214, para. 42 and The Sunday Times v. United Kingdom, 26 Apr. 1979, 2 E.H.R.R. 245, para. 65.

[65] See Lawless v. Ireland (No. 3), 1 July 1961, 1 E.H.R.R. 15, 27–8, Section H(1) infra and Engel v. The Netherlands, supra n. 63, para. 58.

[66] See De Wilde, Ooms and Versyp v. Belgium, 18 June 1971, 1 E.H.R.R. 373, para. 65, and Engel v. The Netherlands, supra n. 63, para. 82.

[67] See, mutatis mutandis, Stögmüller v. Austria, 10 Nov. 1969, 1 E.H.R.R. 155, para. 4, and De Wilde, Ooms and Versyp v. Belgium, supra n. 66, para. 82.

three of the detention orders under consideration. Those allegations are dealt with below in connection with the closely linked issue of compliance with 'a procedure prescribed by law'... In the present context, it suffices to add the following: in deciding whether an individual should be detained as a 'person of unsound mind', the national authorities are to be recognized as having a certain discretion, since it is in the first place for the national authorities to evaluate the evidence adduced before them in a particular case; the Court's task is to review under the Convention the decisions of those authorities.[68]

41. As to the facts of the instant case, the medical evidence submitted to the courts indicated in substance that the applicant showed schizophrenic and paranoiac reactions, that he was unaware of his pathological condition and that, on several occasions, he had committed some fairly serious acts without appreciating their consequences. In addition, various attempts at his gradual rehabilitation into society have failed....

42. Mr. Winterwerp criticises the medical reports as unsatisfactory for the purposes of Article 5(1)(e). In addition, he queries whether the burgomaster's initial direction to detain was founded on psychiatric evidence.

In the Court's view, the events that prompted the burgomaster's direction in May 1968...are of a nature to justify an 'emergency' confinement of the kind provided for at that time under section 14 of the Netherlands Act. While some hesitation may be felt as to the need for such confinement to continue for as long as six weeks, the period is not so excessive as to render the detention 'unlawful'. Despite the applicant's criticisms, the Court has no reason whatso-ever to doubt the objectivity and reliability of the medical evidence on the basis of which the Netherlands courts from June 1968 onwards, have authorised his detention as a person of unsound mind. Neither is there any indication that the contested deprivation of liberty was effected for a wrongful purpose.

43. The Court accordingly concludes that Mr. Winterwerp's confinement, during all the various phases under consideration, constituted 'the lawful detention of [a person] of unsound mind' within the meaning of sub-paragraph (e) of Article 5(1).

B. 'In accordance with a procedure prescribed by law'

44. The applicant maintains that his deprivation of liberty was not carried out 'in accord-ance with a procedure prescribed by law'. For the applicant, this expression implies respect for certain elementary principles of legal procedure, such as informing and hearing the person concerned and affording him some kind of participation and legal assistance in the proceed-ings. In his submission, these principles have not been observed in his case.

The Government reply that the relevant procedure under Netherlands law, in ensuring regu-lar review by an independent judge who bases his decision on medical declarations, undoubt-edly meets such requirements as may be made in this respect by Article 5(1)....

45. The Court for its part considers that the words 'in accordance with a procedure pre-scribed by law' essentially refer back to domestic law; they state the need for compliance with the relevant procedure under that law.

However, the domestic law must itself be in conformity with the Convention, including the general principles expressed or implied therein. The notion underlying the term in question is one of fair and proper procedure, namely, that any measure depriving a person of his liberty

---

[68] *See* notably, *mutatis mutandis, Handyside v. United Kingdom*, 7 Dec. 1976, 1 E.H.R.R. 737, paras. 48 and 50; *Klass v. Germany, supra* n. 64, para. 49 and *The Sunday Times v. United Kingdom, supra* n. 64, para. 59.

should issue from and be executed by an appropriate authority and should not be arbitrary. The Netherlands Mentally Ill Persons Act... satisfies this condition.

46. Whether the procedure prescribed by that Act was in fact respected in the applicant's case is a question that the Court has jurisdiction to examine. Whilst it is not normally the Court's task to review the observance of domestic law by the national authorities, it is otherwise in relation to matters where, as here, the Convention refers directly back to that law; for, in such matters, disregard of the domestic law entails breach of the Convention, with the consequence that the Court can and should exercise a certain power of review.

However, the logic of the system of safeguard established by the Convention sets limits upon the scope of this review. It is in the first place for the national authorities, notably the courts, to interpret and apply the domestic law, even in those fields where the Convention 'incorporates' the rules of that law: the national authorities are, in the nature of things, particularly qualified to settle the issues arising in this connection.

> [The Court then considered and rejected two allegations of procedural defects made by Mr. Winterwerp. Having found that Article 5(1) had not been violated, the Court considered whether the Dutch legislation satisfied the individual's right under Article 5(4) to take proceedings before a court for a speedy decision as to the lawfulness of his detention. The main issue under Article 5(4) was whether the Dutch courts had been obliged to give Mr. Winterwerp a hearing.]

The judicial proceedings referred to in Article 5(4) need not, it is true, always be attended by the same guarantees as those required under Article 6(1) for civil or criminal litigation. Nonetheless, it is essential that the person concerned should have access to a court and the opportunity to be heard either in person or, where necessary, through some form of representation, failing which he will not have been afforded 'the fundamental guarantees of procedure applied in matters of deprivation of liberty'.[69] Mental illness may entail restricting or modifying the manner of exercise of such a right, but it cannot justify impairing the very essence of the right. Indeed, special procedural safeguards may prove called for in order to protect the interests of persons who, on account of their mental disabilities, are not fully capable of acting for themselves.

61. Under... the Mentally Ill Persons Act,... neither the District Court nor the Regional Court was obliged to hear the individual whose detention was being sought....

As to the particular facts, the applicant was never associated, either personally or through a representative, in the proceedings leading to the various detention orders made against him: he was never notified of the proceedings or of their outcome; neither was he heard by the courts or given the opportunity to argue his case.

> [Accordingly Article 5(4) had been breached. The Court further found that Article 6(1) had been breached, since the Dutch court's decision to divest the applicant of the capacity to deal with his property (in which decision neither he nor a representative had any opportunity to take part) was a 'determination of his civil rights and obligations' (see Chapter 13, section B *infra*).]

---

[69] *De Wilde, Ooms and Versyp v. Belgium, supra.* n. 66, para. 76.

2. X V. UNITED KINGDOM

Judgment of 24 October 1981
4 E.H.R.R. 188

[Under English law, certain convicted criminals may be treated as mental patients and kept in custody in a secure hospital rather than be sent to prison. X was in 1968 convicted of wounding with intent to cause grievous bodily harm and because of his mental condition was sent to such a hospital. In 1971 the Home Secretary approved his conditional discharge and X returned to live with his wife at home and got a job. In 1974, his wife complained to a probation officer of X's conduct; he was arrested and taken back to the same hospital. Two years later, he was again released. His claim, similar to those made in *Van Droogenbroeck* and *Weeks*, was that the decision to recall him to hospital was an administrative one and subject to no judicial safeguards.]

40. In its *Winterwerp* judgment, the Court stated three minimum conditions which have to be satisfied in order for there to be 'the lawful detention of a person of unsound mind' within the meaning of Article 5(1)(e): except in emergency cases, the individual concerned must be reliably shown to be of unsound mind, that is to say, a true mental disorder must be established before a competent authority on the basis of objective medical expertise; the mental disorder must be of a kind or degree warranting compulsory confinement; and the validity of continued confinement depends upon the persistence of such a disorder.

41. The applicant's counsel argued that the recall procedures established under section 66 of the [Mental Health Act 1959], since they do not lay down any minimum conditions comparable to those stated in the *Winterwerp* judgment, and in particular the need for objective medical evidence, were incompatible with Article 5(1)(e). The unfettered discretion vested in the Home Secretary meant, so it was submitted, that any recall decision, even one taken in good faith, must by its very nature be arbitrary.

Section 66(3) is, it is true, framed in very wide terms; the Home Secretary may at any time recall to hospital a 'restricted patient' who has been conditionally discharged. Nevertheless, it is apparent from other sections in the Act that the Home Secretary's discretionary power under section 66(3) is not unlimited. Section 147(1) defines a 'patient' as 'a person suffering or appearing to be suffering from mental disorder' and section 4(1) defines 'mental disorder' as 'mental illness, arrested or incomplete development of mind, psychopathic disorder, and any other disorder or disability of mind'. According to the Government, it is implicit in section 66(3) that unless the Home Secretary on the medical evidence available to him decides that the candidate for recall falls within this statutory definition, no power of recall can arise.

Certainly, the domestic law itself must be in conformity with the Convention, including the general principles expressed or implied therein. However, section 66(3), it should not be forgotten, is concerned with the recall, perhaps in circumstances when some danger is apprehended, of patients whose discharge from hospital has been restricted for the protection of the public. The *Winterwerp* judgment expressly identified 'emergency cases' as constituting an exception to the principle that the individual concerned should not be deprived of his liberty 'unless he has been reliably shown to be of "unsound mind" '; neither can it be inferred from the *Winterwerp* judgment that the 'objective medical expertise' must in all conceivable cases be obtained before rather than after confinement of a person on the ground of unsoundness of mind.... A wide discretion must in the nature of things be enjoyed by the national authority empowered to order such emergency confinements....

42. It is not disputed that the applicant's deprivation of liberty was effected 'in accordance with a procedure prescribed by law' and that throughout it was 'lawful' in the sense of being in conformity with the relevant domestic law. However, it was submitted on behalf of the applicant that his deprivation of liberty was arbitrary and unlawful, and thus not justified under Article 5(1)(e), because he had not been 'reliably' shown to be of unsound mind by objective medical evidence existing at the time of his recall.

43. The object and purpose of Article 5(1) is precisely to ensure that no one should be deprived of his liberty in an arbitrary fashion; consequently, quite apart from conformity with domestic law, 'no detention that is arbitrary can ever be regarded as "lawful"'.[70] Three minimum conditions required for 'the lawful detention of a person of unsound mind' are set out above (at para. 40). Whilst the Court undoubtedly has the jurisdiction to verify the fulfilment of these conditions in a given case, the logic of the system of safeguard established by the Convention places limits on the scope of this control; since the national authorities are better placed to evaluate the evidence adduced before them, they are to be recognized as having a certain discretion in the matter and the Court's task is limited to reviewing under the Convention the decisions they have taken.[71]

44. The applicant was a man with a history of psychiatric troubles. He was first committed to Broadmoor Hospital after his conviction for an offence involving a violent attack on a workmate. His discharge was made conditional upon, *inter alia*, his being subject to medical supervision at a psychiatric outpatients' clinic. The consultant psychiatrist who treated him during the period of his conditional discharge considered him to be 'a querulous suspicious person liable to paranoid ideation [who] inevitably presents a risk to the community'; in a letter written in 1971 to the Sheffield probation service, the consultant psychiatrist spoke of the need to 'steer [X] clear of depressed situations which could lead to murder or serious bodily harm to other people'. Lastly, X's wife visited the probation officer and told him that, contrary to what she had stated earlier, her husband remained deluded and threatening.

... On being informed of the wife's complaints, the responsible medical officer at Broadmoor, who had copies of the psychiatric reports prepared concerning the applicant during the period of his conditional release, became alarmed at the possibility of a recurrence of violent behaviour by the applicant, especially if he came to know of his wife's intention to leave him. The responsible medical officer therefore referred the matter to the Home Office and, acting on the doctor's advice, the Home Secretary issued a warrant in pursuance of which the applicant was recalled to hospital the same day, without prior medical examination or verification of the wife's allegations....

45. Regard must also be had to the overall system under the 1959 Act governing the discharge and recall of restricted patients. Under section 65(1), a court may direct that a hospital order against an offender be made subject to restrictions in respect of discharge only where it appears necessary for the protection of the public... When the Home Secretary, pursuant to section 66(2), discharges a patient from hospital while a restriction order is in force...he is thus suspending a measure taken to protect the public. As was stated by one of the Divisional Court judges at the hearing on 21 June 1974 in the habeas corpus proceedings brought by X, very often the only way patients of this kind can be allowed back into the community is by

---

[70] *See Winterwerp v. The Netherlands, supra*, paras. 37, 39.
[71] *See id.*, paras. 40, 46.

releasing them on licence, with very careful supervision and an immediate reaction in the event of a sign of new danger....

In such circumstances, the interests of the protection of the public prevail over the individual's right to liberty to the extent of justifying an emergency confinement in the absence of the usual guarantees implied in Article 5(1)(e)...On the facts of the present case, there was sufficient reason for the Home Secretary to have considered that the applicant's continued liberty constituted a danger to the public, and in particular to his wife.

46. While these considerations were enough to justify X's recall as an emergency measure and for a short duration, his further detention in hospital until February 1976 must, for its part, satisfy the minimum conditions described above (at para. 40). These conditions were satisfied in the case of X....

47. In conclusion, there was no breach of Article 5(1).

[The Court proceeded to consider whether there had been a breach of X's rights under Article 5(4). Having first held, in accordance with precedent, that a person of unsound mind was entitled in principle to take proceedings at reasonable intervals to review the lawfulness of his detention, the Court considered whether this right had been satisfied by habeas corpus proceedings which X had taken—unsuccessfully—in the English High Court. Referring to those proceedings, the Court said:]

56. ... The case was considered by the Divisional Court on the basis of affidavits, including one by the applicant. Such medical evidence as there was before the Divisional Court...was obtained by X's solicitors. The Home Secretary was himself under no obligation to produce material justification for X's detention.

All this, however, followed from the nature of the remedy provided. In habeas corpus proceedings, in examining an administrative decision to detain, the court's task is to enquire whether the detention is in compliance with the requirements stated in the relevant legislation and with the applicable principles of the common law. According to these principles, such a decision (even though technically legal on its face) may be upset, *inter alia*, if the detaining authority misused its powers by acting in bad faith or capriciously or for a wrongful purpose, or if the decision is supported by no sufficient evidence or is one which no reasonable person could have reached in the circumstances. Subject to the foregoing, the court will not be able to review the grounds or merits of a decision taken by an administrative authority to the extent that under the legislation in question these are exclusively a matter for determination by that authority....

In the present case, once it was established that X was a patient who had been conditionally discharged whilst still subject to a restriction order, the statutory requirements for recall by warrant under section 66(3) of the 1959 Act were satisfied... This being so, it was then effectively up to X to show, within the limits permitted by English law, some reason why the apparently legal detention was unlawful. The evidence adduced by X did not disclose any such reason and the Divisional Court had no option but to dismiss the application....

58. Notwithstanding the limited nature of the review possible in relation to decisions taken under section 66(3) of the 1959 Act, the remedy of habeas corpus can on occasions constitute an effective check against arbitrariness in this sphere. It may be regarded as adequate, for the purposes of Article 5(4), for emergency measures for the detention of persons on the ground of unsoundness of mind....

On the other hand, in the Court's opinion, a judicial review as limited as that available in the habeas corpus procedure in the present case is not sufficient for a continuing confinement such as the one undergone by X. Article 5(4), the Government are quite correct to affirm, does not embody a right to judicial control of such scope as to empower the court, on all aspects of the case, to substitute its own discretion for that of the decision-making authority. The review should, however, be wide enough to bear on those conditions which, according to the Convention, are essential for the 'lawful' detention of a person on the ground of unsoundness of mind, especially as the reasons capable of initially justifying such a detention may cease to exist... This means that in the instant case Article 5(4) required an appropriate procedure allowing a court to examine whether the patient's disorder still persisted and whether the Home Secretary was entitled to think that a continuation of the compulsory confinement was necessary in the interests of public safety.

59. The habeas corpus proceedings brought by X in 1974 did not therefore secure him the enjoyment of the right guaranteed by Article 5(4); this would also have been the case had he made any fresh application at a later date....

The Court examined other procedures available to X and decided that certain bodies known as mental health review tribunals, created by the Mental Health Act 1959, were not judicial bodies for the purposes of Article 5(4) since they had advisory functions only. In consequence of the decision in *X's Case*, the British legislation was amended to give to a review tribunal power in such cases to release the detained patient from custody (see now Part V of the Mental Health Act 1983).

3. JOHNSON V. UNITED KINGDOM

Judgment of 24 October 1997
27 E.H.R.R. 296

[The applicant had been charged with a criminal assault in 1984, was found to be suffering from mental illness and was detained in a secure state hospital. In June 1989, a mental health review tribunal found that he was no longer suffering from mental illness. Although this finding was confirmed by three successive tribunals, the applicant was not released from the hospital until January 1993. The reason for the delayed release was that the tribunals took the view that he was not immediately ready to lead an independent life and that his release should be conditional upon residence for the purpose of rehabilitation in an approved hostel under psychiatric and social worker supervision. No place for him at such a hostel could be found.]

51. Johnson in his primary submission maintained that the June 1989 Tribunal should have ordered his immediate and unconditional discharge. Having regard to the strength of the psychiatric evidence before it and to its own assessment of his condition, that Tribunal was satisfied that he was no longer suffering from mental illness... Relying on the Court's *Winterwerp v. The Netherlands* judgment of 24 October 1979[72] he asserted that the authorities could not invoke any margin of appreciation to justify his continued detention beyond 15 June 1989 leaving aside any short period of time which might be needed to implement arrangements

[72] *See* Section D(1) *supra*.

for his discharge.... The Tribunal had not been justified in denying him an immediate and unconditional discharge on account of a possible risk of recurrence of mental illness given that any such risk had been neutralised by reason of the treatment he had received in Rampton Hospital.

52. While acknowledging by way of an alternative submission that the discharge of a person who is found to be no longer of unsound mind may be made subject to conditions, the applicant contended that any such conditions must not hinder immediate or near immediate release and certainly not delay it excessively as occurred in his case. The imposition of the hostel residence condition was not only an onerous, unnecessary and disproportionate requirement which could in itself be considered to be a breach of Article 5(1) of the Convention if implemented, it was also causative of a delay of three years and seven months before he was eventually released....

53. While disputing the lawfulness of the hostel requirement and the benefit which he would have gained from it, the applicant asserted that it was for the authorities to ensure that a placement in a hostel could be guaranteed if not immediately then within a matter of weeks, if they considered such a course of action necessary. In no event could a deferral of discharge for three and a half years pending the finding of a placement be justified....

54. The Government contended that Article 5(1)(e) of the Convention should not be interpreted in a way which requires the authorities in all cases to order the immediate and unconditional release of a patient who is no longer suffering from mental illness. Such an approach in the instant case would have prevented the 1989 Tribunal from assessing whether or not the applicant's own interests and those of the community would be best served by ordering his immediate and unconditional release because of his apparent recovery. The Tribunal needed to have sufficient flexibility or discretion to assess those twin interests having regard to the applicant's previous history of unprovoked and indiscriminate violence and to the unpredictable nature of mental illness especially where, as in the applicant's case, it manifested itself in violent behaviour....

56. The Government maintained that the authorities had made considerable efforts to secure a suitable hostel, ... but the applicant's intransigence and lack of co-operation, especially after October 1990, did not facilitate their task....

In view of the applicant's case history particular care was required in finding him an appropriate hostel. Given that he had still not complied with the hostel requirement, the 1990 and 1991 Tribunals were justified in continuing to defer his discharge....

[The Court examined the detention after 15 July 1989 under Article 5(1)(e) alone, and without regard to Article 5(1)(a), since the applicant was detained on the basis of an order under the Mental Health Act 1989 made without limit in time to undergo psychiatric treatment. It was not contested by the applicant that the continued detention was lawful in domestic law, in view of the tribunal's statutory power to impose conditions on the discharge of patients who are no longer mentally ill and to delay discharge until the conditions are fulfilled.]

60. The Court stresses, however, that the lawfulness of the applicant's continued detention under domestic law is not in itself decisive. It must also be established that his detention after 15 June 1989 was in conformity with the purpose of Article 5(1) of the Convention, which is to prevent persons from being deprived of their liberty in an arbitrary fashion and with the aim of the restriction contained in sub-paragraph (e). In this latter respect the Court recalls that, according to its established case law, an individual cannot be considered to be of 'unsound

mind' and deprived of his liberty unless the following three minimum conditions are satisfied: first, he must reliably be shown to be of unsound mind; secondly, the mental disorder must be of a kind or degree warranting compulsory confinement; thirdly, and of sole relevance to the case at issue, the validity of continued confinement depends upon the persistence of such a disorder.[73]

61. By maintaining that the 1989 Tribunal was satisfied that he was no longer suffering from the mental illness which led to his committal to Rampton Hospital, Johnson is arguing that the abovementioned third condition as to the persistence of mental disorder was not fulfilled and he should as a consequence have been immediately and unconditionally released from detention.

The Court cannot accept that submission. In its view it does not automatically follow from a finding by an expert authority that the mental disorder which justified a patient's compulsory confinement no longer persists, that the latter must be immediately and unconditionally released.

Such a rigid approach to the interpretation of that condition would place an unacceptable degree of constraint on the responsible authority's exercise of judgment to determine in particular cases and on the basis of all the relevant circumstances whether the interests of the patient and the community into which he is to be released would in fact be best served by this course of action. It must also be observed that in the field of mental illness the assessment as to whether the disappearance of the symptoms of the illness is confirmation of complete recovery is not an exact science. Whether or not recovery from an episode of mental illness which justified a patient's confinement is complete and definitive or merely apparent cannot in all cases be measured with absolute certainty. It is the behaviour of the patient in the period spent outside the confines of the psychiatric institution which will be conclusive of this.

62. [The] Court in its *Luberti v. Italy* judgment accepted that the termination of the confinement of an individual who has previously been found by a court to be of unsound mind and to present a danger to society is a matter that concerns, as well as that individual, the community in which he will live if released. Having regard to the pressing nature of the interests at stake, and in particular the very serious nature of the offence committed by Luberti when mentally ill, it was accepted in that case that the responsible authority was entitled to proceed with caution and needed some time to consider whether to terminate his confinement, even if the medical evidence pointed to his recovery.

63. In the view of the Court it must also be acknowledged that a responsible authority is entitled to exercise a similar measure of discretion in deciding whether in the light of all the relevant circumstances and the interests at stake it would in fact be appropriate to order the immediate and absolute discharge of a person who is no longer suffering from the mental disorder which led to his confinement. That authority should be able to retain some measure of supervision over the progress of the person once he is released into the community and to that end make his discharge subject to conditions.... It is however of paramount importance that appropriate safeguards are in place so as to ensure that any deferral of discharge is consonant with the purpose of Article 5(1)...and, in particular, that discharge is not unreasonably delayed.

---

[73] *See Winterwerp v. The Netherlands*, Section D(1) *supra*, para. 40, and *Luberti v. Italy*, 23 Feb. 1984, 6 E.H.R.R. 440, para. 27.

64. Having regard to the above considerations, the Court is of the opinion that the 1989 Tribunal could in the exercise of its judgment properly conclude that it was premature to order Johnson's absolute and immediate discharge from Rampton Hospital. While it was true that the Tribunal was satisfied on the basis of its own assessment and the medical evidence before it that the applicant was no longer suffering from mental illness, it nevertheless considered that a phased conditional discharge was appropriate in the circumstances.... As an expert review body which included a doctor who had interviewed the applicant, the Tribunal could properly have regard to the fact that as recently as 10 February 1988 the applicant was still found to be suffering from mental illness and that his disorder had manifested itself prior to his confinement in acts of spontaneous and unprovoked violence against members of the public.... The Tribunal was also in principle justified in deferring the applicant's release in order to enable the authorities to locate a hostel which best suited his needs and provided him with the most appropriate conditions for his successful rehabilitation.

66. However...the Tribunal lacked the power to guarantee that the applicant would be relocated to a suitable post-discharge hostel within a reasonable period of time. The onus was on the authorities to secure a hostel willing to admit the applicant. It is to be observed that they were expected to proceed with all reasonable expedition in finalising the arrangements for a placement. While the authorities made considerable efforts to this end these efforts were frustrated by the reluctance of certain hostels to accept the applicant as well as by the latter's negative attitude.... Admittedly a suitable hostel may have been located within a reasonable period of time had the applicant adopted a more positive approach to his rehabilitation. However, this cannot refute the conclusion that neither the Tribunal nor the authorities possessed the necessary powers to ensure that the condition could be implemented within a reasonable time. Furthermore, the earliest date on which the applicant could have had his continued detention reviewed was 12 months after the review conducted by the June 1989 Tribunal....

67. In these circumstances it must be concluded that the imposition of the hostel residence condition by the June 1989 Tribunal led to the indefinite deferral of the applicant's release from Rampton Hospital especially since the applicant was unwilling after October 1990 to co-operate further with the authorities in their efforts to secure a hostel.... While the 1990 and 1991 Tribunals considered the applicant's case afresh, they were obliged to order his continued detention since he had not yet fulfilled the terms of the conditional discharge imposed by the June 1989 Tribunal.

Having regard to the situation which resulted from the decision taken by the latter Tribunal and to the lack of adequate safeguards including provision for judicial review to ensure that the applicant's release from detention would not be unreasonably delayed, it must be considered that his continued confinement after 15 June 1989 cannot be justified on the basis of Article 5(1)(e) of the Convention.

[The Court found it unnecessary to deal with issues relating to Article 5(4). The applicant had claimed £100,000 compensation under Article 41 for his detention between June 1989 and January 1993, basing this claim on awards made by English courts in cases where an individual's detention had been unlawful. Ruling that some delay was inevitable while the search was made for a suitable hostel, and noting the applicant's refusal to co-operate in the search, the Court awarded £10,000 as compensation for non-pecuniary damage.]

The judgments in *Winterwerp*, *X* and *Johnson* contain statements of principle that continue to be authoritative. Three later decisions may be mentioned. *Hutchinson Reid v. United Kingdom*[74] concerned the detention of a person suffering a psychopathic disorder that showed itself in abnormally aggressive behaviour, but was not considered to be capable of clinical treatment; the Court held that Article 5(1)(e) does not require the illness or disorder to be of a nature amenable to medical treatment, and that confinement may be justified where necessary to prevent the individual causing harm to himself or to others. As regards a detained person's right under Article 5(4) to have the lawfulness of the detention reviewed by a court, the Court held that it was implicit in its case-law that the burden of proving the lawfulness of the detention lay on the national authorities. In *Brand v. Netherlands*,[75] the applicant suffered from a mental disorder and was dangerous to others; in sentencing him to prison for robbery with violence, the court ordered that he be detained in a custodial clinic after serving the prison sentence, but no place was found in a clinic until he had been held for many months in a remand centre. The Dutch courts awarded him compensation for the time spent in the remand centre in excess of six months. The Strasbourg Court (by 5–2) held that, while the authorities could not be expected to ensure that a place in the custodial clinic was immediately available, a delay of six months was not acceptable. 'To hold otherwise would entail a serious weakening of the fundamental right to liberty to the detriment of the person concerned…'.[76] *HL v. United Kingdom*[77] concerned a man who was autistic, profoundly mentally retarded and incapable of making decisions for himself, but able to live with paid carers; he had been detained in a psychiatric hospital when he became agitated while attending a day centre. The hospital did not follow any statutory procedures in detaining him, treating him as an 'informal patient'. Somewhat surprisingly, the House of Lords held that the detention was justified on the basis of the common law doctrine of necessity.[78] The Strasbourg Court held that he had not been free to leave the hospital and that the hospital's reliance on the common law, with its lack of relevant procedures, failed to protect against arbitrary deprivations of liberty; moreover, no procedure had been available to him that met the requirements of Article 5(4).

Under the Fifth and Fourteenth Amendments to the United States Constitution, a person may be committed involuntarily to a mental hospital only on a showing by 'clear and convincing' evidence that that person suffers from a mental illness and is likely to be dangerous to him or herself or to others. This standard of proof requires that the state show more than a mere preponderance of the evidence, but given the inevitable 'lack of certainty and the fallibility of psychiatric diagnosis', these facts need not be proven beyond a reasonable doubt, the constitutionally required standard of

---

[74] 20 February 2003, 37 E.H.R.R. 211. For domestic proceedings in this case, *see Anderson v. Scottish Ministers* [2001] U.K.P.C. D5; [2003] 2 A.C. 602.

[75] 11 May 2004, 17 B.H.R.C. 398.

[76] *Id.*, para. 66.

[77] 5 October 2004, 17 B.H.R.C. 418.

[78] *See R. v. Bournewood Community and Mental Health Trust, ex p L* [1999] 1 A.C. 458.

proof for criminal conviction.[79] The Supreme Court has never held squarely that persons committed civilly are entitled as a matter of constitutional law to periodic review of the propriety of their confinement.[80] Certain state courts, however, extending the logic of the holdings discussed above on the need for new hearings where the basis of detention has changed, have so held under their state constitutions.[81]

E. OTHER PERMITTED GROUNDS OF DETENTION

1. LAWFUL ARREST OR DETENTION ON REASONABLE SUSPICION OF HAVING COMMITTED AN OFFENCE

In the ordinary course of criminal justice, it frequently occurs that someone suspected of an offence is arrested and detained by the police, only to be released later when it is decided on further inquiry that there are insufficient grounds to justify his or her detention. The right to liberty under Article 5 is not infringed merely because the individual is never prosecuted for the suspected offence, or because he or she is acquitted after a trial. Ordinarily the police and other investigative authorities have

---

[79] *Addington v. Texas*, 441 U.S. 418, 429 (1979). *See also Heller v. Doe*, 509 U.S. 312 (1998) holding constitutional against an equal protection challenge a state law requiring a higher standard of proof for committals based on 'mental illness' than for those based on 'mental retardation'. In *Jones v. United States*, 463 U.S. 354 (1983), however, the Court held that a criminal defendant, acquitted by reason of insanity, could on that basis alone be committed even though his mental condition had been proven by a mere preponderance of the evidence. But *see Foucha v. Louisiana*, 507 U.S. 71 (1992) discussed at section C above, holding that after such a person has been found no longer to suffer from mental illness his or her release may not be conditioned on such a person affirmatively proving that he or she is no longer dangerous. In *R v. Swain* [1991] 1 S.C.R. 933, the Supreme Court of Canada held unconstitutional as improper interference with liberty under s. 7 of the Charter, the Criminal Code provisions requiring every insanity acquittee to be detained without hearing at the pleasure of the Lieutenant Governor. The Court held that the safeguards of the criminal trial alone were not sufficient protection against the post-acquittal detention. In response to this decision, the Canadian Parliament introduced a new verdict of 'not criminally responsible', described by the Supreme Court as neither a conviction nor an acquittal. After such a verdict the court and, periodically, a review board would consider whether the individual should be detained, released on conditions or released absolutely (Canadian Criminal Code, s. 672.54). On each occasion the court or review board is to consider the safety of the public but, in that light, it is also to make the disposition 'least onerous and least restrictive to the accused'. The Supreme Court, taking constitutional principles into account, has interpreted the statute to require an absolute discharge unless there is evidence of a 'significant threat to the safety of the public'. The hearings are not to be adversarial and 'there is never any legal burden on the [not criminally responsible] accused to show that he or she does not pose a significant threat to the safety of the public': *Winko v. British Columbia (Forensic Psychiatric Institute)* [1999] 2 S.C.R. 625, paras. 31–2, 48, 52, 62.

[80] It has suggested as much, however, in dicta. *See Parham v. J.R.*, 442 U.S. 584, 617 (1979).

[81] *See Fasulo v. Arafeh*, 378 A.2d 553 (Conn. 1977); *State v. Fields*, 390 A.2d 574 (N.J. 1978).

a wide discretion in how they use their powers of arrest, subject to limits imposed by national law. But the arrest or detention of an individual may lead to a breach of Article 5, if for instance the arrest is unlawful by national law and no redress is obtainable by recourse to national remedies, or if the arrest although lawful by national law[82] is nonetheless 'arbitrary' according to the jurisprudence of the Strasbourg Court.

The following cases illustrate aspects of that jurisprudence, arising from situations in which the Court has decided whether an arrest or detention was justified under Article 5(1)(c). Thus the individual must be suspected of having committed an offence in national law, and the offence must not itself be such as to impinge unduly on rights or freedoms protected under the Convention. Mere suspicion is not enough; reasonable grounds for suspicion must exist, but the police need not have evidence sufficient to use in a criminal trial to overcome the presumption of innocence under Article 6(2). The requirement of 'reasonable suspicion' must be satisfied at the time of arrest, but if detention continues during a protracted police inquiry the test for detention changes its character, as will be seen in the case of *Jablonski v. Poland* (below).

In such cases, Article 5(3) guarantees both the right to be brought promptly before a judge and the right to trial within a reasonable time or to release pending trial. In respect of release on bail, the Court has long applied the principle that unless the national authorities justify continued detention by reasons that in the opinion of the Court are relevant and sufficient, the detention will be in breach of Article 5(3).[83]

Although the Strasbourg Court repeatedly insists that national courts are better placed than an international court to make detailed assessments of the facts and norms that apply to an individual's detention in relation to criminal justice, the Court will intervene when it considers that a national decision is 'arbitrary' in the sense that there is no reasonable basis for it if the national law is properly understood. One instance of this is given by *Tsirlis and Kouloumpas v. Greece*,[84] where a Greek military court breached Article 5(1)(a) by sending two Jehovah's Witness ministers to prison for refusing to perform military service, having 'blatantly ignored' case law that made it clear that the applicants were ministers of a 'known religion' and thus entitled to be exempted from service in the army. Another example is provided by *Loukanov v. Bulgaria*.

---

[82] *See*, e.g., *Anguelova v. Bulgaria*, 13 June 2002, 38 E.H.R.R. 31: breach of Art. 5(1) where A's son, Z, a Roma, died overnight while held in police custody: the lack of a written order for Z's arrest made it unlawful by national law, coupled with a total failure by police to record the facts of his custody.

[83] *Wemhoff v. Germany*, 27 June 1968, 1 E.H.R.R. 55; and *Letellier v. France*, 26 June 1991, 14 E.H.R.R. 83. On aspects of Art. 5(3), *see* Section F *infra*. *See also SBC v. United Kingdom*, 19 June 2001, 34 E.H.R.R. 21 (breaches of Art. 5 arising from legislation that excluded bail for those accused of certain serious crimes).

[84] 29 May 1997, 25 E.H.R.R. 198.

A. LOUKANOV V. BULGARIA

Judgment of 20 March 1997
24 E.H.R.R. 121

[Mr. Loukanov was a former Prime Minister of Bulgaria who on 9 July 1992 was arrested on suspicion of having misappropriated public funds, in that while in office he had taken part in collective decisions to provide aid by way of grants and loans to various developing countries. He was released from detention on 30 December 1992, some three months after Bulgaria had ratified the European Convention on Human Rights and recognized the compulsory jurisdiction of the Court. While the case was pending before the Court, Mr. Loukanov was shot dead; his widow and children were permitted by the Court to pursue the application on his behalf.]

37. The applicant, with whom the Commission agreed, was of the opinion that the facts which had been invoked against him at the time of his arrest and during his continued detention could not, in the eyes of an objective observer, be construed as misappropriation of funds or as a breach of official duties aimed at facilitating the commission of such an offence. Accordingly, there had been no 'reasonable suspicion of [his] having committed an offence' within the meaning of Article 5(1)(c). Nor could the detention be 'reasonably considered necessary to prevent his committing an offence or fleeing after having done so'...

The applicant, for his part, stressed that the decisions leading to the charges against him and his being detained on remand had been taken collectively by the Government at the time and in a manner which was consistent with the relevant law, including the then Bulgarian Constitution; the allocation of the funds in question had been effected in accordance with the national budget as adopted by the National Assembly and had subsequently been approved by the latter. The measures had been in keeping not only with the policies of the Government at the time but also with relevant United Nations resolutions on development assistance. They had not benefited any members of the Government or any third parties; the funds had been received in their entirety by the addressee countries.

38. The Government maintained before the Commission that the applicant's detention had been effected on the grounds of suspicion of his having committed a crime and had been in conformity with Bulgarian law. Although it was true that the allocation of development aid had not as such constituted a criminal offence, the charges in question had been brought because the transfers of funds had, under the cover of development assistance, involved improper 'deals' causing damage to Bulgaria's economic interests. The Government were, however, not in a position to provide any details of such 'deals' as it would adversely affect the confidentiality of the criminal proceedings instituted against the applicant and eight other former Government members.

Before the Court the Government stated that they were prepared to accept the Commission's opinion that there had been a violation of Article 5(1) of the Convention, whilst at the same time informing the Court of the views of the Prosecutor General, the authority which had ordered the applicant's detention on remand. In this regard the Government pointed out that it was not within its powers to assess the measures taken in this case by the prosecution and the Supreme Court which, under the Constitution, were both independent judicial authorities.

[The Prosecutor-General observed to the Court that in Bulgarian law guilt did not depend on whether the offender had obtained an advantage for himself or for a third party and that because of the complex circumstances, the issue of criminal intent could be determined only during preliminary investigations. The decision to detain the applicant on remand had been taken in view of such factors as who he was, the gravity of the offences, his opportunities of absconding and the fact that he had appealed against the withdrawal of his passport, which according to the Bulgarian Supreme Court had justified the suspicion that he might commit further offences.]

40. The Court observes at the outset that it has jurisdiction to examine the facts and circumstances of the applicant's complaints in so far as they related to the period after 7 September 1992, when Bulgaria ratified the Convention and recognised the Court's compulsory jurisdiction. In doing so, it will take into account the state of the proceedings as of that date,[85] in particular the fact that the grounds for his detention, stated in the detention order of 9 July and the Supreme Court judgment of 13 July upholding the order, remained the same until his release on 30 December 1992....

As to the observations made by the Government concerning the independence of the authorities which had taken the measures giving rise to the applicant's Convention complaints, it should be emphasised that the Governments are answerable under the Convention for the acts of such authorities as they are for those of any other State agency. In all cases before the Court, what is in issue is the international responsibility of the State.

41. ...The Court is of the view that the central issue in the case under consideration is whether the applicant's detention from 7 September to 30 December 1992 was 'lawful' within the meaning of Article 5(1), including whether it was effected 'in accordance with a procedure prescribed by law'. The Court reiterates that the Convention here refers essentially to national law, but it also requires that any measure depriving the individual of his liberty must be compatible with the purpose of Article 5, namely to protect the individual from arbitrariness.

Where the Convention refers directly back to domestic law, as in Article 5, compliance with such law is an integral part of the obligations of the Contracting States and the Court is accordingly competent to satisfy itself of such compliance where relevant; the scope of its task in this connection, however, is subject to limits inherent in the logic of the European system of protection, since it is in the first place for the national authorities, notably the courts, to interpret and apply domestic law.[86]

42. Turning to the particular circumstances of the case,...it is undisputed that the applicant had, as a member of the Bulgarian Government, taken part in the decisions—granting funds in assistance and loans to certain developing countries—which had given rise to the charges against him.

43. However, none of the provisions of the Criminal Code relied on to justify the detention...specified or even implied that anyone could incur criminal liability by taking part in collective decisions of this nature. Moreover, no evidence has been adduced to show that such decisions were unlawful, that is to say contrary to Bulgaria's constitution or legislation, or more specifically that the decisions were taken in excess of powers or were contrary to the law on the national budget.

---

[85] *See*, for instance, *Benham v. United Kingdom*, 10 June 1996, 22 E.H.R.R. 293, para. 40; Section E(2)(a) *infra*.

[86] *See*, *inter alia*, *Bozano v. France*, 18 Dec. 1986, 9 E.H.R.R. 297, para. 58; and *Kemmache v. France (No. 3)*, 24 Nov. 1994, 19 E.H.R.R. 349, para. 42.

In the light of the above, the Court is not persuaded that the conduct for which the applicant was prosecuted constituted a criminal offence under Bulgarian law at the relevant time.

44. What is more, the Public Prosecutor's order of detention of 9 July 1992 and the Supreme Court's decision of 13 July upholding the order, referred to Articles 201 to 203 of the Criminal Code. As appears from the case law supplied to the Court, a constituent element of the offence of misappropriation under Articles 201 to 203 of the Criminal Code was that the offender had sought to obtain for himself or herself or for a third party an advantage....

However, the Court has not been provided with any fact or information capable of showing that the applicant was at the time reasonably suspected of having sought to obtain for himself or a third party an advantage from his participation in the allocation of funds in question.[87] ... Indeed, it was not contended before the Convention institutions that the funds had not been received by the States concerned.

45. In these circumstances, the Court does not find that the deprivation of the applicant's liberty during the period under consideration was 'lawful detention' effected 'on reasonable suspicion of [his] having committed an offence'.

Having reached this conclusion, the Court does not need to examine whether the detention could reasonably be considered necessary to prevent his committing an offence or fleeing after having committed one.

46. Accordingly, there has been a violation of Article 5(1) in the present case.[88]

The facts of *Loukanov* illustrate difficulties that may occur when a country such as Bulgaria moves from an authoritarian system of government in which there is recourse to criminal law as a sanction for political behaviour, to a more democratic system in which rule of law values are applied to criminal justice. But even in mature democracies, there is a risk that the criminal justice system may be used to restrict legitimate expression of opinion.

B. STEEL AND OTHERS V. UNITED KINGDOM

Judgment of 23 September 1998
28 E.H.R.R. 603

[The first applicant, Helen Steel, took part in a protest against a grouse shoot on a Yorkshire moor; despite police warnings, she walked in front of a member of the party as he lifted his shotgun to aim, thus preventing him from enjoying his sport. She was arrested and held in a police station for 44 hours before being brought before a magistrate and released on bail. She was later convicted of an offence against section 5 of the Public Order Act 1986, for which she was fined £70, and found to have committed a breach of the peace, for which she was ordered to be bound over to keep the peace for 12 months in the sum of £100. Refusing to be bound over, she was sent to prison for 28 days. The second applicant, Rebecca Lush, had protested against the extension of a motorway in Wanstead, London; while standing under the bucket of an earth-digging machine, she was arrested and detained for 17 hours before being released on bail. She was convicted of conduct likely to cause a breach of the peace and was ordered to be bound over for 12 months in the sum of £100. Refusing to be

---

[87] *See*, for instance, *Murray v. United Kingdom*, 28 Oct. 1994, 19 E.H.R.R. 193, para. 51.
[88] For somewhat similar facts, *see Pantea v. Romania*, 3 June 2003, 40 E.H.R.R. 627 (initial and continued detention in breach of national law).

bound over, she was sent to prison for seven days. The other applicants (Needham, Polden and Cole) attended a peaceful protest in London outside premises where a conference to promote the sale of military helicopters was being held. Distributing leaflets and holding banners, they were arrested by the police and detained for seven hours before being released on bail. Subsequently no evidence was offered against them.

These applications raised a variety of issues, including issues under Article 10 (right to freedom of expression). Having set out the relevant rules of English law, the Court dealt with the arrests and initial detention of all five applicants.]

47. The Court recalls that each applicant was arrested for acting in a manner which allegedly caused or was likely to cause a breach of the peace and detained until he or she could be brought before a magistrates' court.

48. Breach of the peace is not classed as a criminal offence under English law. However, the Court observes that the duty to keep the peace is in the nature of a public duty; the police have powers to arrest any person who has breached the peace or who they reasonably fear will breach the peace; and the magistrates may commit to prison any person who refuses to be bound over not to breach the peace where there is evidence beyond reasonable doubt that his or her conduct caused or was likely to cause a breach of the peace and that he or she would otherwise cause a breach of the peace in the future.

49. Bearing in mind the nature of the proceedings in question and the penalty at stake, the Court considers that breach of the peace must be regarded as an 'offence' within the meaning of Article 5(1)(c).[89]

50. The court therefore finds that each applicant was arrested and detained with the purpose of bringing him or her before the competent legal authority on suspicion of having committed an 'offence' or because it was considered necessary to prevent the commission of an 'offence'.

[The Court proceeded to consider whether that suspicion was reasonable in connection with the issue of lawfulness.]

52. The applicants contended that their arrests and initial periods of detention had not been 'lawful', since the concept of breach of the peace and the attendant powers of arrest were insufficiently certain under English law.

First, they submitted that if, as appeared from the national case law, an individual committed a breach of the peace when he or she behaved in a manner the natural consequence of which was that others would react violently, it was difficult to judge the extent to which one could engage in protest activity, in the presence of those who might be annoyed, without causing a breach of the peace. Secondly, the power to arrest whenever there were reasonable grounds for apprehending that a breach of the peace was about to take place granted too wide a discretion to the police. Thirdly, there had been conflicting decisions at Court of Appeal level as to the definition of breach of the peace....

53. The Commission found that there had been no violation of Article 5(1) since the arrests and initial detention had not been arbitrary and there had been no suggestion of any lack of conformity with domestic law.

54. The Court recalls that the expressions 'lawful' and 'in accordance with a procedure prescribed by law' in Article 5(1) stipulate not only full compliance with the procedural and

---

[89] See, mutatis mutandis, Benham v. United Kingdom, supra n. 85, para. 56.

substantive rules of national law, but also that any deprivation of liberty be consistent with the purpose of Article 5 and not arbitrary.[90] In addition, given the importance of personal liberty, it is essential that the applicable national law meets the standard of 'lawfulness' set by the Convention, which requires that all law, whether written or unwritten, be sufficiently precise to allow the citizen—if need be, with appropriate advice—to foresee, to a degree that is reasonable in the circumstances, the consequences which a given action may entail.[91]

55. In this connection, the Court observes that the concept of breach of the peace has been clarified by the English courts over the last two decades, to the extent that it is now sufficiently established that a breach of the peace is committed only when an individual causes harm, or appears likely to cause harm, to persons or property or acts in a manner the natural consequence of which would be to provoke others to violence. It is also clear that a person may be arrested for causing a breach of the peace or where it is reasonably apprehended that he or she is likely to cause a breach of the peace.

Accordingly, the Court considers that the relevant legal rules provided sufficient guidance and were formulated with the degree of precision required by the Convention.[92]

56. When considering whether the arrest and detention of each applicant was carried out in accordance with English law, the Court recalls that it is in the first place for the national authorities, notably the courts, to interpret and apply domestic law. However, since failure to comply with domestic law entails a breach of Article 5(1), the Court can and should exercise a certain power of review in this matter.[93]

57. The Court has already noted that under English law there is a power to arrest an individual who causes a breach of the peace or who is reasonably apprehended to be likely to cause a breach of the peace. It will therefore examine the circumstances of each applicant's arrest to determine whether one of these criteria applied.

[In respect of Helen Steel and Rebecca Lush:]

60. The Court notes that the national courts which dealt with these cases were satisfied that each applicant had caused or had been likely to cause a breach of the peace.

The Court, having itself examined the evidence before it, finds no reason to doubt that the police were justified in fearing that these applicants' behaviour, if persisted in, might provoke others to violence. It follows that the arrest and initial detention of the first and second applicants complied with English law. Moreover, there is no evidence to suggest that these deprivations of liberty were arbitrary.

61. In conclusion, there has been no violation of Article 5(1) in respect of the arrests and initial detention of the first and second applicants.

[In respect of Steel and Lush, the Court found that their detention for refusing to be bound over to keep the peace amounted to detention for non-compliance with the order of a court, and was within Article 5(1)(b); further, the detention was lawful since the applicants could reasonably have foreseen that if they acted in a manner the natural consequence of which would be to provoke others to violence, they might be bound over to keep the peace. The

---

[90] *See id.* at para. 40.

[91] *S.W. v. United Kingdom*, 22 Nov. 1995, 21 E.H.R.R. 363, paras. 35–6 and, *mutatis mutandis, The Sunday Times v. United Kingdom*, 26 Apr. 1979, 2 E.H.R.R. 245, para. 49 and *Halford v. United Kingdom*, 25 June 1997, 24 E.H.R.R. 523, para. 49.

[92] *See,* e.g., *Larissis v. Greece*, 24 Feb. 1998, 27 E.H.R.R. 329, para. 34.

[93] *See Benham v. United Kingdom, supra* n. 85, para. 41.

Court reached a different conclusion in respect of the other applicants, Needham, Polden and Cole:]

63. The Court notes that there is no ruling of a national court on the question whether the arrests and detention of these applicants accorded with English law, since the prosecution decided to withdraw the allegations of breach of the peace from the magistrates and since the applicants did not bring any civil claim for false imprisonment against the police. It observes that the government has not raised any preliminary objection in respect of this omission by the applicants, and, in the absence of such a plea, it is not necessary for the Court to consider whether the complaint should have been declared inadmissible for non-exhaustion of domestic remedies.[94]

64. Having itself considered the evidence available to it relating to the arrests of these three applicants, the Court sees no reason to regard their protest as other than entirely peaceful. It does not find any indication that they significantly obstructed or attempted to obstruct those attending the conference, or took any other action likely to provoke these others to violence. Indeed it would not appear that there was anything in their behaviour which could have justi-fied the police in fearing that a breach of the peace was likely to be caused.

For this reason, in the absence of any national decision on the question, the Court is not satisfied that their arrests and subsequent detention for seven hours complied with English law so as to be 'lawful' within the meaning of Article 5(1).

65. It follows that there has been a violation of Article 5(1) in respect of the third, fourth and fifth applicants.

In respect of Article 10, the Court found against Steel (by five to four) and Lush (by seven to two), but upheld unanimously the complaints by Needham, Polden and Cole. In their partly dissenting opinion in respect of Steel, Judges Valticos and Makarczyk said that it was debatable whether the vague power of the magistrates to bind per-sons over to be of good behaviour was compatible with the letter and spirit of the Convention, and continued:

What is not in any event debatable is that to detain for 44 hours and then sentence to 28 days imprisonment a person who, albeit in an extreme manner, jumped up and down in front of a member of the shoot to prevent him from killing a feathered friend is so manifestly extreme, particularly in a country known for its fondness for animals, that it amounted, in our view, to a violation of the Convention.

C. FOX, CAMPBELL AND HARTLEY V. UNITED KINGDOM

Judgment of 30 August 1990
13 E.H.R.R. 157

[Under the same legislation that gave rise to *Brogan v. United Kingdom*,[95] three persons had been detained in Northern Ireland as suspected terrorists for periods ranging between 30 and 48 hours. They complained *inter alia* that they had been detained in breach of Article 5(1)(c), since the police had no 'reasonable suspicion' that they had committed an offence

---

[94] *See Olsson v. Sweden (No. 1)*, 24 Mar. 1988, 11 E.H.R.R. 259, para. 56 and *Open Door Counselling and Dublin Well Woman v. Ireland*, 29 Oct. 1992, 15 E.H.R.R. 244, para. 46.

[95] Section F(2)(a) *infra*.

and had in fact arrested them to gain information about terrorist activities generally without necessarily intending to charge them with criminal offences. In this case, the Court revisited an important matter of interpretation which in *Brogan* it had resolved in favour of the security forces.]

32. The 'reasonableness' of the suspicion on which an arrest must be based forms an essential part of the safeguard against arbitrary arrest and detention which is laid down in Article 5(1)(c). The Court agrees with the Commission and the Government that having a 'reasonable suspicion' presupposes the existence of facts or information which would satisfy an objective observer that the person concerned may have committed the offence. What may be regarded as 'reasonable' will however depend upon all the circumstances.

In this respect, terrorist crime falls into a special category. Because of the attendant risk of loss of life and human suffering, the police are obliged to act with utmost urgency in following up all information, including information from secret sources. Further, the police may frequently have to arrest a suspected terrorist on the basis of information which is reliable but which cannot, without putting in jeopardy the source of the information, be revealed to the suspect or produced in court to support a charge.

As the Government pointed out, in view of the difficulties inherent in the investigation and prosecution of terrorist-type offences in Northern Ireland, the 'reasonableness' of the suspicion justifying such arrests cannot always be judged according to the same standards as are applied in dealing with conventional crime. Nevertheless, the exigencies of dealing with terrorist crime cannot justify stretching the notion of 'reasonableness' to the point where the essence of the safeguard secured by Article 5(1)(c) is impaired.

33. ... The Government argued that it was unable to disclose the acutely sensitive material on which the suspicion against the three applicants was based because of the risk of disclosing the source of the material and thereby placing in danger the lives and safety of others. In support of its contention that there was nevertheless reasonable suspicion, it pointed to the facts that the first two applicants had previous convictions for serious acts of terrorism connected with the Provisional IRA and that all three applicants were questioned during their detention about specific terrorist acts of which they were suspected. In the Government's submission these facts were sufficient to confirm that the arresting officer had a *bona fide* or genuine suspicion and it maintained that there was no difference in substance between a *bona fide* or genuine suspicion and a reasonable suspicion. The Government observed moreover that the applicants themselves did not contest that they were arrested and detained in connection with acts of terrorism.

The Government also stated that, although it could not disclose the information or identify the source of the information which led to the arrest of the applicants, there did exist in the case of the first and second applicants strong grounds for suggesting that at the time of their arrest the applicants were engaged in intelligence gathering and courier work for the Provisional IRA and that in the case of the third applicant there was available to the police material connecting him with the kidnapping attempt about which he was questioned.

34. Certainly Article 5(1)(c) of the Convention should not be applied in such a manner as to put disproportionate difficulties in the way of the police authorities of the Contracting States in taking effective measures to counter organised terrorism. It follows that the Contracting States cannot be asked to establish the reasonableness of the suspicion grounding the arrest of a suspected terrorist by disclosing the confidential sources of supporting information or even facts which would be susceptible of indicating such sources or their identity.

Nevertheless the Court must be enabled to ascertain whether the essence of the safeguard afforded by Article 5(1)(c) has been secured. Consequently the respondent government has to furnish at least some facts or information capable of satisfying the Court that the arrested person was reasonably suspected of having committed the alleged offence. This is all the more necessary where, as in the present case, the domestic law does not require reasonable suspicion, but sets a lower threshold by merely requiring honest suspicion.

35. The Court accepts that the arrest and detention of each of the present applicants was based on a *bona fide* suspicion that he or she was a terrorist, and that each of them, including Mr. Hartley, was questioned during his or her detention about specific terrorist acts of which he or she was suspected.

The fact that Mr. Fox and Ms. Campbell both have previous convictions for acts of terrorism connected with the IRA, although it could reinforce a suspicion linking them to the commission of terrorist-type offences, cannot form the sole basis of a suspicion justifying their arrest in 1986, some seven years later....

The aforementioned elements on their own are insufficient to support the conclusion that there was 'reasonable suspicion.' The Government has not provided any further material on which the suspicion against the applicants was based. Its explanations therefore do not meet the minimum standard set by Article 5(1)(c) for judging the reasonableness of a suspicion for the arrest of an individual.

> [The Court by a majority of four to three held that the British government had not shown that the police had 'reasonable suspicion' within the meaning of Article 5(1)(c). The applicants' rights had thus been breached.]

While the Court's power to intervene in a national system of criminal justice was illustrated in the three preceding cases, the Court will not intervene merely because the national authorities have made what to the persons detained may seem a harsh or unnecessary decision. In *Kemmache v. France (No. 3)*[96] the applicant had been released on bail pending trial on charges concerning counterfeit currency; he surrendered to bail on the eve of the trial, but the trial was adjourned on the request of a co-accused. When Kemmache sought release on bail once again, this was refused by the Assize Court. In deciding by eight to one that there had been no breach of Article 5(1), the Strasbourg Court said:

> In principle, and without prejudice to its power to examine the compatibility of national decisions with the Convention, it is not the Court's role to assess itself the facts which have led a national court to adopt one decision rather than another. If it were otherwise, the Court would be acting as a court of third or fourth instance, which would be to disregard the limits imposed on its action.[97]

In *Kemmache*, the Court found that the decisions of the French courts disclosed neither abuse of authority, bad faith nor arbitrariness. They could not therefore be held unlawful, especially in view of the right to apply for release still open to Kemmache

---

[96] 24 Nov. 1994, 19 E.H.R.R. 349.
[97] *Id.*, at para. 44.

in French law. Judge Walsh, dissenting, considered that the reasons advanced by the French court for refusing to release Kemmache were 'entirely based on a specula- tive and intuitive approach on the part of the national judicial authorities. Such an approach cannot be a substitute for evidence'.[98]

We have seen in *Fox, Campbell and Hartley* that the Court found the available material insufficient to show that there was 'reasonable suspicion' justifying detention of the applicants. In *O'Hara v. United Kingdom*[99] the Court again considered the test laid down in *Fox, Campbell and Hartley* in the context of the 'particular problems' posed by terrorist crime. O'Hara's arrest was said by the government to have been based on information obtained independently from four informers that he had been involved in a specific murder. This information was held to have created 'the required level' of suspicion, and the purpose of the arrest—to confirm or dispel that suspicion— came within Article 5(1).

D. JABLONSKI V. POLAND

Judgment of 21 December 2000
36 E.H.R.R. 27

[In May 1992, the applicant was arrested on suspicion of having caused serious injuries to the victim of a violent theft a month previously. Having been charged with attempted homicide, armed robbery and aggravated theft, he was held on remand for nearly five years until he was tried, convicted and sentenced to 15 years in prison. Of the remand period, 3 years and 10 months occurred after Poland had ratified the Convention. During this time he repeatedly sought release without success, entering on a long hunger strike and injuring himself in various ways. The resulting state of his health caused postponements in dates arranged for his trial. The reasons given for his continued detention were initially stated to be that the offences charged were serious and there was reasonable suspicion that he had committed them.]

79. The Court reiterates that the question of whether or not a period of detention is reason- able cannot be assessed in the abstract. Whether it is reasonable for an accused to remain in detention must be assessed in each case according to its special features. Continued detention can be justified in a given case only if there are specific indications of a genuine requirement

---

[98] *Id.*, dissenting judgment, para. 3. In *K-F v. Germany*, 27 Nov. 1997, 26 E.H.R.R. 390, the Court took a similar approach to that in *Kemmache*, in holding that detention of the applicant overnight on suspicion of fraud was lawful, and that, since the detention exceeded the statutory period of 12 hours, to that extent only had Art. 5(1)(c) been breached. In *Scott v. Spain*, 18 Dec. 1996, 24 E.H.R.R. 39, the facts relating to a detention lasting for four years were complex: there were at various times grounds for detention under both Art. 5(1)(c) and 5(1)(f), since while Scott was detained in respect of an alleged rape in Spain of a foreign tourist, the United Kingdom was seeking his extradition on a charge of mur- der. The Court by 8–1, by reasoning that is unclear, found no breach of Art. 5(1)(c), but unanimously found a breach of Art. 5(3) in respect of delay before Scott was tried for rape. The majority's reasoning on Art. 5(1)(c) was forcefully criticized by Judge Repik, who found that the power to detain in relation to extradition had been used improperly for purposes of the rape charge.

[99] 16 Oct. 2001, 34 E.H.R.R. 32.

of public interest which, notwithstanding the presumption of innocence, outweighs the rule of respect for individual liberty laid down in Article 5....[100]

It falls in the first place to the national judicial authorities to ensure that, in a given case, the pre-trial detention of an accused person does not exceed a reasonable time. To this end they must, paying due regard to the principle of the presumption of innocence, examine all the facts arguing for or against the existence of the above-mentioned demand of public interest justifying a departure from the rule in Article 5 and must set them out in their decisions on the applications for release. It is essentially on the basis of the reasons given in these decisions and of the well-documented facts stated by the applicant in his appeals that the Court is called upon to decide whether or not there has been a violation of Article 5(3).[101]

80. The persistence of reasonable suspicion that the person arrested has committed an offence is a condition *sine qua non* for the lawfulness of the continued detention, but after a certain lapse of time it no longer suffices. The Court must then establish whether the other grounds given by the judicial authorities continued to justify the deprivation of liberty. Where such grounds were 'relevant' and 'sufficient', the Court must also be satisfied that the national authorities displayed 'special diligence' in the conduct of the proceedings.

81. ...[In] the present case the judicial authorities first of all relied on the reasonable suspicion that the applicant had committed the offences with which he had been charged, the serious nature of those offences and the need to ensure the proper conduct of the proceedings. They repeated those grounds in nearly all their decisions made from 1 May 1993 to 28 February 1997...

When the applicant went on hunger-strike and, afterwards, when he repeatedly inflicted various injuries on himself, the courts began to base their decisions on the fact that his poor condition was caused by his deliberate acts of self-harm in prison and for that reason refused to release him on health grounds. They considered that the applicant's behaviour was aimed at forcing them to release him. They also held that the applicant should be kept in custody because, given that he was under medical care in prison, his continued detention did not amount to a danger to his life....

82. The Court accepts that the suspicion against the applicant of having committed the serious offences with which he had been charged may initially have justified his detention. Yet the Court does not accept that it could constitute a 'relevant and sufficient' ground for his being held in custody for the entire relevant period.

The applicant suggested that the courts should have released him because his health was very bad and had constantly been aggravated by his detention. The Court would however point out that Article 5(3) cannot be read as obliging the national authorities to release a detainee on account of his state of health. The question of whether or not the condition of the person in custody is compatible with his continued detention should primarily be determined by the national courts and, as the Court has held in the context of Article 3..., those courts are in general not obliged to release him on health grounds or to place him in a civil hospital to enable him to receive a particular kind of medical treatment.[102]

83. On the other hand, ... under Article 5(3) the authorities, when deciding whether a person should be released or detained, are obliged to consider alternative measures of ensuring

---

[100] Citing *Kudła v. Poland*, 26 Oct. 2000, 35 E.H.R.R. 11, paras. 110 *et seq.*
[101] Citing *Muller v. France*, 17 March 1997, para. 35.
[102] Citing *Kudła v. Poland*, para. 93.

his appearance at trial. Indeed, that Article lays down not only the right to 'trial within a reasonable time or release pending trial' but also provides that 'release may be conditioned by guarantees to appear for trial'.[103]

That provision does not give the judicial authorities a choice between either bringing the accused to trial within a reasonable time or granting him provisional release—even subject to guarantees. Until conviction he must be presumed innocent, and the purpose of Article 5(3) is essentially to require his provisional release once his continuing detention ceases to be reasonable...

84.... [Over] the period of those several years which the applicant spent in pre-trial detention no consideration appears to have been given to the possibility of imposing on him other 'preventive measures'—such as bail or police supervision—expressly foreseen by Polish law to secure the proper conduct of the criminal proceedings....

Repeating that the applicant should be kept in detention in order to ensure the proper conduct of the trial, the relevant courts did not take into account any other guarantees that he would appear for trial. They did not mention why those alternative measures would not have warranted his presence before the court or why, had the applicant been released, his trial would not have followed its proper course. Nor did they point to any factor indicating that there was a risk of his absconding, going into hiding, or otherwise evading justice.

...[No] account was taken of the fact that with the passage of time and given the number and character of the applicant's acts of self-aggression in prison, it became more and more acutely obvious that keeping him in detention no longer served the purpose of bringing him to 'trial within a reasonable time'...

In the circumstances, the Court is of the opinion that the applicant's prolonged detention could not be considered 'necessary' from the point of view of ensuring the due course of the proceedings.

85. The Court accordingly concludes that the reasons relied on by the courts in their decisions were not sufficient to justify the applicant's being held in custody for the period of three years and nearly ten months covered by the Court's jurisdiction *ratione temporis*.

There has therefore been a violation of Article 5(3)....

[The Court also held that a decision by the Polish Supreme Court to prolong the applicant's detention beyond the statutory time-limit had not been decided 'speedily', causing there to have been a violation of his rights under Article 5(4).]

The problem of delays in judicial proceedings has arisen very often in cases coming to the Strasbourg Court, a problem considered below in the context of Article 6(1).[104] Questions of delay have also arisen from the excessive prolongation of pre-trial detention, as in the case of *Jablonski*. In such cases, the Court examines the whole history of the proceedings and reviews the factors relied on as justifying the length of detention. Widespread instances of excessive detention have been found to occur.[105] In contrast,

---

[103] Citing *Neumeister v. Austria*, 27 June 1968, 1 E.H.R.R. 91, para. 3.

[104] *See* Chapter 13(E).

[105] *See*, e.g., *Bati v. Turkey*, 3 June 2004, 42 E.H.R.R. 37, *Pantea v. Romania*, 3 June 2003, 40 E.H.R.R. 26, *Szeloch v. Poland*, 22 Feb. 2001, 37 E.H.R.R. 46, *Kalashnikov v. Russia*, 15 July 2002, 36 E.H.R.R. 34, *Barfuss v. Czech Republic*, 31 July 2000, 34 E.H.R.R. 37, *Cesky v. Czech Republic*, 6 June 2000, 33 E.H.R.R. 8, *Lavents v. Latvia*, 28 November 2002 and *Nevmerzhistsky v. Ukraine*, 5 April 2005, 19 B.H.R.C. 177.

in *Grisez v. Belgium*,[106] the applicant was detained for 2 years and 3 months before his trial for murder, at which he was convicted and sentenced to 30 years in prison. The Court ruled by 4–3 that his pre-trial detention had been justified and the total period of detention was not excessive. The minority held that there had been excessive delay by the prosecution in obtaining three psychiatric reports, delay for which the state must be liable.

Such cases give rise to several questions: (a) if in *Grisez*, the applicant had been acquitted of the charge of murder, would (or should) the Court's conclusion have been the same? (b) if someone receives a long prison sentence on being convicted for a serious crime after excessive pre-trial detention, does he or she have grounds for complaint under Article 5 if the prison sentence is (whether by law or in practice) treated as commencing from the original date of detention, and not the date of conviction? (c) would the prosecuting authorities have a stronger incentive to ensure speedier trials if national legislation provided a maximum time-limit for pre-trial detention, a breach of which would entitle the individual to be released, and the prosecution to be barred?[107]

The difficulties for the Strasbourg Court in assessing the performance of national legal systems are illustrated by *Chraidi v. Germany*.[108] The applicant was a stateless person, extradited from Lebanon to Germany in May 1996 and held in remand on suspicion of being involved with a serious terrorist attack in Berlin in 1986. Chraidi was convicted on numerous counts in November 2001 after a trial, with four other defendants, that had begun in September 1997; the hearings took place over 281 days, the court sitting on an average of two days each week, and 169 witnesses gave evidence. The Court held unanimously that there were throughout sufficient grounds for his detention and that the German court had acted with the necessary 'special diligence' in conducting the protracted trial.[109]

2. ARREST OR DETENTION TO SECURE THE FULFILMENT OF AN OBLIGATION PRESCRIBED BY LAW

A. BENHAM V. UNITED KINGDOM

Judgment of 10 June 1996
22 E.H.R.R. 293

[In 1990, a new form of local tax, known in law as the community charge but popularly called the 'poll tax', was imposed upon all adults in England and Wales, the amount due being a fixed sum that had no regard to the taxpayer's resources. Benham was a young

---

[106] 26 Sept. 2002, 36 E.H.R.R. 48.

[107] *See* for the United Kingdom, Prosecution of Offenders Act 1985, s. 22 (English law) and for Scotland, the Criminal Procedure (Scotland) Act 1995, s. 65.

[108] 26 October 2006.

[109] One judge, Borrego J, concurring, disagreed with the emphasis given in the Court's judgment to the fact that the case arose from an act of 'international terrorism'.

unemployed man who failed to pay the sum of £325 due in 1990–1. The legislation empowered local magistrates to commit a poll-tax debtor to prison for up to three months where
non-payment was due to his 'wilful failure or culpable neglect'. Remarking that Benham
could have made greater efforts to find work, the magistrates sent him to prison for 30 days,
without his having been legally represented before them. Eleven days later, the English High
Court ordered his release on bail; the High Court later held that the magistrates ought not to
have sent him to prison when there was no evidence either that he had the resources to pay
or that there had been 'wilful failure or culpable neglect'. At Strasbourg, Benham claimed
that there had been breaches of Article 5(1) and 5(5) (duty to compensate for unlawful
detention) and of Article 6.]

39. The Court first observes that this case falls to be examined under subparagraph (b) of
Article 5(1), since the purpose of the detention was to secure the fulfilment of B's obligation
to pay the community charge owed by him.

40. The main issue to be determined in the present case is whether the disputed detention was 'lawful', including whether it complied with 'a procedure prescribed by law'. The
Convention here essentially refers back to national law and states the obligation to conform to
the substantive and procedural rules thereof, but it requires in addition that any deprivation of
liberty should be consistent with the purpose of Article 5, namely to protect individuals from
arbitrariness.[110]

41. It is in the first place for the national authorities, notably the courts, to interpret and
apply domestic law. However, since under Article 5(1) failure to comply with domestic law
entails a breach of the Convention, it follows that the Court can and should exercise a certain
power to review whether this law has been complied with.[111]

42. A period of detention will in principle be lawful if it is carried out pursuant to a court
order. A subsequent finding that the court erred under domestic law in making the order
will not necessarily retrospectively affect the validity of the intervening period of detention.
For this reason, the Strasbourg organs have consistently refused to uphold applications from
persons convicted of criminal offences who complain that their convictions or sentences were
found by the appellate courts to have been based on errors of fact or law.[112]

43. It was agreed by those appearing before the Court that the principles of English law
which should be taken into account in this case distinguished between acts of a magistrates'
court which were within its jurisdiction and those which were in excess of jurisdiction. The former were valid and effective unless or until they were overturned by a superior court, whereas
the latter were null and void from the outset.

[The Court reviewed the authorities in national law on the question whether the magistrates
had exceeded their jurisdiction in sending Benham to prison, and examined the reasons given
by the English High Court for deciding that the magistrates had acted wrongly.]

46. Against the above background, it cannot be said with any degree of certainty that the
judgment of the [High] Court was to the effect that the magistrates acted in excess of jurisdiction within the meaning of English law. It follows that the Court does not find it established
that the order for detention was invalid, and thus that the detention which resulted from it was

---

[110] *See Quinn v. France*, 22 Mar. 1995, 21 E.H.R.R. 529, para. 47.
[111] *See Bouamar v. Belgium*, 29 Feb. 1988, 11 E.H.R.R. 1, para. 49.
[112] *See Bozano v. France*, 18 Dec. 1986, 9 E.H.R.R. 297, para. 55.

unlawful under national law. The mere fact that the order was set aside on appeal did not in itself affect the lawfulness of the detention.

47. Nor does the Court find that the detention was arbitrary. It has not been suggested that the magistrates who ordered B's detention acted in bad faith, nor that they neglected to attempt to apply the relevant legislation correctly. It considers the question of the lack of legal aid to be less relevant to the present head of complaint than to that under Article 6.

Accordingly, the Court finds no violation of Article 5(1) of the Convention.

Since there was no breach of Article 5(1), the Court also rejected the applicant's claim under Article 5(5) (right to compensation for unlawful detention). However, the Court held that Benham's rights under Article 6 had been breached.[113]

Another instance of detention within Article 5(1)(b) (power 'to secure the fulfilment of any obligation prescribed by law') is afforded by *Steel v. United Kingdom*[114] where, as we have seen, the Court upheld the power of English magistrates to require persons convicted of public order offences to agree to be bound over to keep the peace, failing which they would be sent to prison.

3. ARREST OR DETENTION FOR THE PREVENTION OF THE SPREADING OF INFECTIOUS DISEASES

A. ENHORN V. SWEDEN

Judgment of 25 January 2005
41 E.H.R.R. 30

[The applicant, who was homosexual, discovered that he was infected with the HIV virus and that he had transmitted the virus to another man. Under the Infectious Diseases Act 1988, a county medical officer in 1994 required the applicant to take certain steps to prevent him from spreading the HIV infection and to attend medical appointments. When Enhorn failed to observe these instructions, a court order was obtained for his compulsory isolation in a hospital for up to three months. The Administrative Court of Appeal rejected his appeal, and the order for his confinement was extended several times. He absconded from hospital on four occasions and lived in the community for varying periods, until in 2002 the medical officer decided that there were no grounds for his continued isolation in hospital. The Strasbourg Court emphasised that, by Article 5(1), any deprivation of liberty must have been 'in accordance with a procedure prescribed by law'.]

---

[113] Although in English law the proceedings before the magistrates were viewed as civil and not criminal, the Court held that Benham had in essence been 'charged with a criminal offence' within Art. 6(1) and (3); as the magistrates could impose a prison sentence of up to three months, the interests of justice required that Benham should have had legal aid before the magistrates. *See* Chapter 13(B)(2).

[114] Section E(1)(b) *supra*.

36. The expressions 'lawful' and 'in accordance with a procedure prescribed by law' in Article 5(1) essentially refer back to national law and state the obligation to conform to the substantive and procedural rules thereof. Where deprivation of liberty is concerned, it is particularly important that the general principle of legal certainty be satisfied....

Moreover, an essential element of the 'lawfulness' of a detention within the meaning of Article 5(1)(e) is the absence of arbitrariness...The detention of an individual is such a serious measure that it is only justified where other, less severe measures have been considered and found to be insufficient to safeguard the individual or the public interest which might require that the person concerned be detained. That means that it does not suffice that the deprivation of liberty is in conformity with national law, it must also be necessary in the circumstances...and in accordance with the principle of proportionality...

37. [The] applicant maintained that the notions 'reasonable cause' and 'manifest risk of the infection being spread' under section 38 of the 1988 Act were too vague; that the preparatory work on the Act did not give any indications in this regard; and that the requirements of clearness and foreseeability had therefore not been fulfilled.

[The Court examined the measures taken against the applicant by the Swedish authorities.]

39. In these circumstances the Court is satisfied that the applicant's detention had a basis in Swedish law.

40. The Court must therefore proceed to examine whether the deprivation of the applicant's liberty amounted to 'the lawful detention of a person in order to prevent the spreading of infectious diseases' within the meaning of Article 5(1)(e)....

41. The Court has only to a very limited extent decided cases where a person has been detained 'for the prevention of the spreading of infectious diseases'. It is therefore called upon to establish which criteria are relevant when assessing whether such a detention is in compliance with the principle of proportionality and the requirement that any detention must be free from arbitrariness.

[The Court looked by way of comparison at the principles established in its case-law on the detention of mentally disordered persons, alcoholics, drug addicts and vagrants.]

44. Taking the above principles into account, the Court finds that the essential criteria when assessing the 'lawfulness' of the detention of a person 'for the prevention of the spreading of infectious diseases' are whether the spreading of the infectious disease is dangerous to public health or safety, and whether detention of the person infected is the last resort in order to prevent the spreading of the disease, because less severe measures have been considered and found to be insufficient to safeguard the public interest....

45. Turning to the instant case, it is undisputed that the first criterion was fulfilled, in that the HIV virus was and is dangerous to public health and safety.

46. It thus remains to be examined whether the applicant's detention could be said to be the last resort in order to prevent the spreading of the virus, because less severe measures had been considered and found to be insufficient to safeguard the public interest.

47. In a judgment of 16 February 1995, the County Administrative Court ordered that the applicant be kept in compulsory isolation for up to three months under section 38 of the 1988

Act. Thereafter, orders to prolong his deprivation of liberty were continuously issued every six months until 12 December 2001 ... Accordingly, the order to deprive the applicant of his liberty was in force for almost seven years.

Admittedly, since the applicant absconded several times, his actual deprivation of liberty lasted [for five separate periods between March 1995 and June 1999] ... —almost one and a half years altogether.

48. The Government submitted that ... voluntary measures had been attempted in vain during the period between September 1994 and February 1995 to ensure that the applicant's behaviour would not contribute to the spread of the HIV infection. Also, they noted the particular circumstances of the case, notably as to the applicant's personality and behaviour, as described by various physicians and psychiatrists; his preference for teenage boys; the fact that he had transmitted the HIV virus to a young man; and the fact that he had absconded several times and refused to cooperate with the staff at the hospital. Thus, the Government found that the involuntary placement of the applicant in hospital had been proportionate to the purpose of the measure, namely to prevent him from spreading the infectious disease.

49. The Court notes that the Government have not provided any examples of less severe measures which might have been considered for the applicant in the period from 16 February 1995 until 12 December 2001, but were apparently found to be insufficient to safeguard the public interest.

50. It is undisputed that the applicant failed to comply with the instruction issued by the county medical officer on 1 September 1994, which stated that he should visit his consulting physician again and keep to appointments set up by the county medical officer. ...

> [The Court summarized other respects in which the applicant failed to comply with instructions from the county medical officer, dealing with such matters as informing doctors of his condition when medical services were required, and avoiding the excessive consumption of alcohol. The Court observed that the instructions did not require the applicant to consult a psychiatrist.]

54. The instructions issued on 1 September 1994 prohibited the applicant from having sexual intercourse without first having informed his partner about his HIV infection. Also, he was to use a condom. The Court notes ... that, despite his being at large for most of the period from 16 February 1995 until 12 December 2001, there is no evidence or indication that during that period the applicant transmitted the HIV virus to anybody, or that he had sexual intercourse without first informing his partner about his HIV infection, or that he did not use a condom, or that he had any sexual relations at all for that matter. It is true that the applicant infected the 19-year-old man with whom he had first had sexual contact in 1990. This was discovered in 1994, when the applicant himself became aware of his infection. However, there is no indication that the applicant transmitted the HIV virus to the young man as a result of intent or gross neglect, which in many of the Contracting States, including Sweden, would have been considered a criminal offence.

55. In these circumstances, the Court finds that the compulsory isolation of the applicant was not a last resort in order to prevent him from spreading the HIV virus because less severe measures had been considered and found to be insufficient to safeguard the public interest. Moreover, the Court considers that by extending over a period of almost seven years the order

for the applicant's compulsory isolation, with the result that he was placed involuntarily in a hospital for almost one and a half years in total, the authorities failed to strike a fair balance between the need to ensure that the HIV virus did not spread and the applicant's right to liberty.

56. There has accordingly been a violation of Article 5(1)....

[The Court's decision was unanimous, but two concurring judgments were delivered. Judge Cabral Barreto issued a warning against it being supposed that Article 5 permitted a state 'a certain margin of appreciation' concerning the review of the proportionality of a measure depriving an individual of liberty. Judge Costa referred to the need to prevent arbitrariness in using lawful powers of the detention and said:]

11. That is where the assessment becomes delicate. On the one hand, allowing a person to infect healthy individuals, thereby exposing them to a serious and usually fatal illness, poses a grave danger to public health and, above all, to the right of individuals to health. A few days ago in France a person was sentenced to six years' imprisonment for deliberately transmitting Aids to uninfected partners. On the other hand, it should again be emphasised that liberty (which gives rise to responsibility) is and should be the rule. Systematic confinement of persons capable of spreading infectious diseases would turn them into outcasts; this would be an unacceptable step backwards in terms of human rights, which are founded on the principle of freedom and responsibility of the human being....

12. Paragraph 54 of the judgment attempts to provide a key to the problem. Repeated orders for the applicant's isolation were made over a total period of seven years. Such orders are the most radical measures available; other, less severe ones could have been taken. In sum, therefore, they were not balanced or proportionate, hence the finding of a violation.

13. I both agree and disagree with this reasoning. On a general level, it is consistent with the case-law, at least with regard to the existence of 'less severe' measures—although the judgment does not identify them....

14. However, I consider above all that the judgment should have drawn attention to two—contradictory—weaknesses in the approach taken by the Swedish authorities in this case. Firstly, for more than three-quarters of the lengthy period in which he was placed in isolation the applicant was at large, having absconded several times, apparently without any great effort being made to find him. If he was so dangerous that his confinement had to be prolonged, why was he de facto left at liberty with the risk of transmitting Aids? Secondly, it appears from the evidence that Mr Enhorn did not actually infect anyone, or indeed have any sexual relations, after 1994...A fortiori, if there was no established risk that the applicant might pass on Aids, why was the order for his continued isolation extended for a further two and a half years?

4. ARREST OR DETENTION TO PREVENT AN UNAUTHORIZED ENTRY INTO THE COUNTRY OR WITH A VIEW TO DEPORTATION OR EXTRADITION

For a state to be able to enforce its immigration laws, whether by refusing entry to illegal entrants or by removing from its territory those subject to deportation or extradition, detention of the individuals concerned may be necessary. The purpose of such detention may be to give time for inquiries to be made, to prevent the detainees absconding and (as with proposed deportation or extradition) to enable the individual to challenge the proposed action in national courts. Lawful authority for a detention must exist and questions may arise as to the conditions of detention, its duration and the extent of judicial protection for the detainee. It may be argued that those who seek without permission to enter the country and are then detained bring the detention upon themselves, since they may at any time go free by deciding to leave the country. The first case in this section indicates how the Strasbourg Court has responded to this argument. While the essential rights of those seeking asylum as refugees derive from the Geneva Convention of 1951 on the Status of Refugees, the second and third cases illustrate how the right to liberty under Article 5 ECHR may assist asylum-seekers.[115]

A. AMUUR V. FRANCE

Judgment of 25 June 1996
22 E.H.R.R. 533

[The applicants (three brothers and a sister) were Somali nationals who arrived at Orly airport, Paris, on a flight from Syria and claimed that they had fled Somalia where their lives were at risk following the overthrow of the President. The French authorities detained them for 20 days at the airport and in a secure section of the Arcade Hotel nearby. The Somalis had no access to legal advice for 15 days, but shortly thereafter challenged their detention in the French courts. They were returned to Syria two days before the French court held that the detention was unlawful. When the Somalis claimed under the Convention that Article 5(1) had been breached, the Commission by 16–10 rejected the claim, the majority stating that the applicants could at any time have left France for Syria, where their lives were not in danger, and the necessary 'deprivation of liberty' was lacking.]

38. The applicants complained of the physical conditions of their 'detention' in the transit zone.... In addition, these conditions had been aggravated by the excessive length of their 'detention'.... They also emphasised that under the relevant international conventions and national legislation they should, as asylum seekers, have enjoyed special protection and more favourable treatment than unlawful immigrants. The detention of asylum seekers could not be justified unless their application for asylum was considered manifestly ill-founded, which was clearly not so in the applicants' case, as the other members of their family were granted refugee status by the French Office for the Protection of Refugees and Stateless Persons.

---

[115] *See also* Chapter 5(C).

39. According to the Government, the applicants' stay in the transit zone was not comparable to detention. They had been lodged in part of the Hôtel Arcade where the 'physical conditions' of the accommodation were described as satisfactory.... The original reason why they were held and for the length of time they were held had been their obstinacy in seeking to enter French territory despite being refused leave to enter. They could not therefore 'validly complain of a situation which they had largely created', as the Court itself had held in the *Kolumpar v. Belgium* judgment of 24 September 1992.[116]

41. The Court notes in the first place that in the fourth paragraph of the Preamble to its Constitution of 27 October 1946 (incorporated into that of 4 October 1958), France enunciated the right to asylum in 'the territories of the Republic' for 'everyone persecuted on account of his action in the cause of freedom'. France is also party to the 1951 Geneva Convention Relating to the Status of Refugees...

The Court also notes that many Member States of the Council of Europe have been confronted for a number of years now with an increasing flow of asylum seekers. It is aware of the difficulties involved in the reception of asylum seekers at most large European airports and in the processing of their applications....

Contracting States have the undeniable sovereign right to control aliens' entry into and residence in their territory. The Court emphasizes, however, that this right must be exercised in accordance with the provisions of the Convention, including Article 5.

42. In proclaiming the right to liberty, Article 5(1) contemplates the physical liberty of the person; its aim is to ensure that no one should be dispossessed of this liberty in an arbitrary fashion. On the other hand, it is not in principle concerned with mere restrictions on the liberty of movement; such restrictions are governed by Article 2 of Protocol No. 4.

[On whether the applicants had been deprived of their liberty, the Court referred to *Guzzardi v Italy*[117] and continued:]

43. Holding aliens in the international zone does indeed involve a restriction upon liberty, but one which is not in every respect comparable to that which obtains in centres for the detention of aliens pending deportation. Such confinement, accompanied by suitable safeguards for the persons concerned, is acceptable only in order to enable States to prevent unlawful immigration while complying with their international obligations, particularly under the 1951 Geneva Convention... States' legitimate concern to foil the increasingly frequent attempts to get round immigration restrictions must not deprive asylum seekers of the protection afforded by these Conventions.

Such holding should not be prolonged excessively, otherwise there would be a risk of it turning a mere restriction on liberty—inevitable with a view to organising the practical details of the alien's repatriation or, where he has requested asylum, while his application for leave to enter the territory for that purpose is considered—into a deprivation of liberty. In that connection account should be taken of the fact that the measure is applicable not to those who have committed criminal offences but to aliens who, often fearing for their lives, have fled from their own country.

Although by the force of circumstances the decision to order holding must necessarily be taken by the administrative or police authorities, its prolongation requires speedy review by the

---

[116] *Kolumpar v. Belgium*, 24 Sept. 1992, 16 E.H.R.R. 197.
[117] *Guzzardi v. Italy*, 6 Nov. 1980, 3 E.H.R.R. 333, para. 92; Section B(1) *supra*.

courts, the traditional guardians of personal liberties. Above all, such confinement must not deprive the asylum seeker of the right to gain effective access to the procedure for determining refugee status...

[The Court summarized the facts relating to the detention of the applicants between 9 and 29 March 1992, found that they were sent back to Syria before being able to make an effective application to the authority with jurisdiction to rule on their refugee status, and continued:]

46. In concluding that there was no deprivation of liberty, the Government and the Commission attached particular weight to the fact that the applicants could at any time have removed themselves from the sphere of application of the measure in issue. More particularly, the Government argued that although the transit zone is 'closed on the French side', it remains 'open to the outside', so that the applicants could have returned of their own accord to Syria, where their safety was guaranteed, in view of the assurances which the Syrian authorities had given the French Government....

47. The applicants maintained that such reasoning would amount to binding the application of Article 5 to that of Article 3 of the Convention, this would be to ignore the specific object of Article 5, and its wording, which had to be strictly construed; it would also deprive Article 5 of any useful effect, particularly with regard to asylum applications.

48. The mere fact that it is possible for asylum seekers to leave voluntarily the country where they wish to take refuge cannot exclude a restriction on liberty, the right to leave any country, including one's own, being guaranteed, moreover, by Protocol No. 4 to the Convention. Furthermore, this possibility becomes theoretical if no other country offering protection comparable to the protection they expect to find in the country where they are seeking asylum is inclined or prepared to take them in.

Sending the applicants back to Syria only became possible, apart from the practical problems of the journey, following negotiations between the French and Syrian authorities. As for the assurances of the latter, these were dependent on the vagaries of diplomatic relations, regard being had to the fact that Syria was not bound by the Geneva Convention relating to the Status of Refugees.

49. The Court concludes that holding the applicants in the transit zone of Paris-Orly Airport was equivalent in practice, in view of the restrictions suffered, to a deprivation of liberty. Article 5(1) is therefore applicable to the case.

50. It remains to be determined whether the deprivation of liberty found to be established in the present case was compatible with paragraph 1 of Article 5. Where the 'lawfulness' of detention is in issue,...the Convention refers essentially to national law and lays down the obligation to conform to the substantive and procedural rules of national law, but it requires in addition that any deprivation of liberty should be in keeping with the purpose of Article 5, namely to protect the individual from arbitrariness....

In order to ascertain whether a deprivation of liberty has complied with the principle of compatibility with domestic law, it therefore falls to the Court to assess not only the legislation in force in the field under consideration, but also the quality of the other legal rules applicable to the persons concerned. Quality in this sense implies that where a national law authorizes deprivation of liberty—especially in respect of a foreign asylum seeker—it must be sufficiently accessible and precise, in order to avoid all risk of arbitrariness. These characteristics are of fundamental importance with regard to asylum seekers at airports, particularly in view of the need to reconcile the protection of fundamental rights with the requirements of States' immigration policies.

51. The applicants asserted that their detention had no legal basis, whether under the French legislation in force at the time or under international law. They had found themselves in a legal vacuum in which they had neither access to a lawyer nor information about exactly where they stood at the time. In support of the above argument, they rely on the reasons for the judgment of the Créteil tribunal de grande instance, ruling on their application for an interim order.

52. The Court notes that even though the applicants were not in France within the meaning of the Ordinance of 2 November 1945, holding them in the international zone of Paris-Orly Airport made them subject to French law....

[The Court examined the executive rules that at the relevant time governed the holding of persons in the transit zone of airports in France.]

53. The Court emphasises that from 9 to 29 March 1992 the applicants were in the situation of asylum seekers whose application had not yet been considered. In that connection, neither the Decree of 27 May 1982 nor the—unpublished—circular of 26 June 1990 (the only text at the material time which specifically dealt with the practice of holding aliens in the transit zone) constituted a 'law' of sufficient 'quality' within the meaning of the Court's case law; there must be adequate legal protection in domestic law against arbitrary interferences by public authorities with the rights safeguarded by the Convention[118]... The above mentioned circular consisted, by its very nature, of instructions given by the Minister of the Interior to Prefects and Chief Constables concerning aliens refused leave to enter at the frontiers. ... At the material time none of these texts allowed the ordinary courts to review the conditions under which aliens were held or, if necessary, to impose a limit on the administrative authorities as regards the length of time for which they were held. They did not provide for legal, humanitarian and social assistance, nor did they lay down procedures and time-limits for access to such assistance so that asylum seekers like the applicants could take the necessary steps.

54. The French legal rules in force at the time, as applied in the present case, did not sufficiently guarantee the applicants' right to liberty.

There has accordingly been a breach of Article 5(1).

B. CONKA V. BELGIUM

Judgment of 5 February 2002
34 E.H.R.R. 54

[In November 1998, a group of Roma from Slovakia went to Belgium where they claimed asylum on the basis of a history of assaults by skinheads with which the Slovakian police had failed to deal. The claims were rejected by the Belgian authorities.]

18. At the end of September 1999 the Ghent police sent a notice to a number of Slovakian Roma families, including the applicants, requiring them to attend the police station on 1 October 1999. The notice was drafted in Dutch and Slovak and stated that their attendance was required to enable the files concerning their applications for asylum to be completed.

---

[118] *Malone v. United Kingdom*, 2 Aug. 1984, 7 E.H.R.R. 14, para. 67.

19. At the police station, where a Slovak-speaking interpreter was also present, the applicants were served with a fresh order to leave the territory dated 29 September 1999, accompanied by a decision for their removal to Slovakia and their detention for that purpose. The documents served, which were all in identical terms, informed the recipients that they could apply to the *Conseil d'Etat* for judicial review of the deportation order and for a stay of execution—provided that they did so within sixty days of service of the decision—and to the committals division (*chambre du conseil*) of the criminal court against the order for their detention. According to the Government, some of the aliens concerned were nevertheless allowed to leave the police station of their own free will on humanitarian grounds or for administrative reasons.

20. A few hours later the applicants and other Roma families, accompanied by an interpreter, were taken to a closed transit centre...near Brussels Airport. It appears that the interpreter only remained at the centre briefly. According to the Government, he could have been recalled to the centre at the applicants' request. The applicants say that they were told that they had no further remedy against the deportation order.

21. ...At 10.30 p.m. on Friday 1 October 1999 the applicants' counsel, Mr van Overloop, was informed by the President of the Roma Rights League that his clients were in custody. Taking the view that he was still instructed by them, Mr van Overloop sent a fax on 4 October 1999 to the Aliens Office.... He requested that no action be taken to deport them, as they had to take care of a member of their family who was in hospital. However, Mr van Overloop did not appeal against the deportation or detention orders made on 29 September 1999.

22. On 5 October 1999 the families concerned were taken to Melsbroek Military Airport, where the seat numbers allocated to them in the aircraft were marked on their hands with a ballpoint pen. The aircraft left Belgium for Slovakia at 5.45 p.m.

23. Shortly afterwards the Minister of the Interior declared in reply to a parliamentary question...:

'Owing to the large concentration of asylum-seekers of Slovakian nationality in Ghent, arrangements have been made for their collective repatriation to Slovakia.... Reports I have received...indicate that the operation was properly prepared, even if the unfortunate wording of the letter sent by the Ghent police to some of the Slovaks may have been misleading. Both the Aliens Office and the Ghent Police Department were surprised by the large number of Slovaks who responded to the notice sent to them. That factual circumstance resulted in their being detained...for deportation a few days later....'

[Before stating its decision, the Court summarized the submissions of the parties.]

36. As regards the merits, the applicants denied that their arrest had been necessary to secure their departure from Belgium. They complained above all of the manner of their arrest, saying that they had been lured into a trap as they had been induced into believing that their attendance at the police station was necessary to complete their asylum applications when, from the outset, the sole intention of the authorities had been to deprive them of their liberty....[A]ccordingly, there had been an abuse of power that amounted to a violation of Article 5(1).

Consequently, no blame could attach to the applicants for their refusal to place any further trust in the authorities and their decision not to lodge an appeal with the Belgian courts. ...

... At no stage between the applicants' arrest and the execution of the deportation order had any direct contact between them and their lawyer been possible... Admittedly, they could have telephoned out, but they were convinced that it was impossible to appeal against their detention....

37. The Government pointed out that the applicants had been served on 3 March and 18 June 1999 with orders to leave the territory, which expressly stated that they were liable to detention with a view to deportation if they failed to comply....

[The] fact that the tenor of the notice was potentially ambiguous could not suffice to give rise to an inference that there had been an abuse of power. That was a serious accusation that could only be made out if the authority had acted solely for unlawful reasons, which was manifestly not the case. Besides, the Minister of the Interior had publicly expressed regret for the 'unfortunate wording' of the notice. However, the fact that other aliens who had attended the police station after receiving the notice were released after their cases had been considered demonstrated that the notices had not been sent with the sole aim of carrying out arrests. Even if they had been, the method used was nonetheless preferable to going to aliens' homes or to their children's schools to arrest them....

38. The Court notes that it is common ground that the applicants were arrested so that they could be deported from Belgium. Article 5(1)(f) of the Convention is thus applicable.... [However, this did not entitle the applicants to contest the necessity of their arrest for that purpose.[119]]

39. Where the 'lawfulness' of detention is in issue, including the question whether 'a procedure prescribed by law' has been followed, the Convention refers essentially to the obligation to conform to the substantive and procedural rules of national law, but it requires in addition that any deprivation of liberty should be in keeping with the purpose of Article 5, namely to protect the individual from arbitrariness.[120]

40. ...[The] applicants received a written notice... inviting them to attend Ghent police station on 1 October to 'enable the file concerning their application for asylum to be completed'. On their arrival at the police station they were served with an order to leave the territory dated 29 September 1999 and a decision for their removal to Slovakia and for their arrest for that purpose. A few hours later they were taken to a closed transit centre....

41. ...[According] to the Government, while the wording of the notice was admittedly unfortunate,... that did not suffice to vitiate the entire arrest procedure, or to warrant its being qualified as an abuse of power.

While the Court has reservations about the compatibility of such practices with Belgian law, particularly as the practice in the instant case was not reviewed by a competent national court, the Convention requires that any measure depriving an individual of his liberty must be compatible with the purpose of Article 5, namely to protect the individual from arbitrariness... Although the Court by no means excludes its being legitimate for the police to use stratagems in order, for instance, to counter criminal activities more effectively, acts whereby the authorities seek to gain the trust of asylum-seekers with a view to arresting and subsequently deporting them may be found to contravene the general principles stated or implicit in the Convention.

---

[119] Citing *Chahal v. United Kingdom* (*infra*), para. 112
[120] Citing *Bozano v. France*, 18 December 1986, 9 E.H.R.R. 297, para. 54, and *Chahal* (*infra*), para. 118.

...[While] the wording of the notice was 'unfortunate', it was not the result of inadvertence; on the contrary, it was chosen deliberately in order to secure the compliance of the largest possible number of recipients. At the hearing, counsel for the Government referred in that connection to a 'little ruse', which the authorities had knowingly used to ensure that the 'collective repatriation'...they had decided to arrange was successful.

42. The Court reiterates that the list of exceptions to the right to liberty secured in Article 5(1) is an exhaustive one and only a narrow interpretation of those exceptions is consistent with the aim of that provision...In the Court's view, that requirement must also be reflected in the reliability of communications such as those sent to the applicants, irrespective of whether the recipients are lawfully present in the country or not. It follows that, even as regards overstayers, a conscious decision by the authorities to facilitate or improve the effectiveness of a planned operation for the expulsion of aliens by misleading them about the purpose of a notice so as to make it easier to deprive them of their liberty is not compatible with Article 5.

[The Court considered the Government's preliminary objection based on the applicants' failure to exhaust national remedies.]

43. ...[The] Court reiterates that by virtue of Article 35(1)...normal recourse should be had by an applicant to remedies which are available and sufficient to afford redress in respect of the breaches alleged. The existence of the remedies in question must be sufficiently certain not only in theory but in practice, failing which they will lack the requisite accessibility and effectiveness....[121]

44. In the instant case, the Court identifies a number of factors which undoubtedly affected the accessibility of the remedy which the Government claim was not exercised. These include the fact that the information on the available remedies handed to the applicants on their arrival at the police station was printed in tiny characters and in a language they did not understand; only one interpreter was available to assist the large number of Roma families who attended the police station...and, although he was present at the police station, he did not stay with them at the closed centre. In those circumstances, the applicants undoubtedly had little prospect of being able to contact a lawyer from the police station with the help of the interpreter and, although they could have contacted a lawyer by telephone from the closed transit centre, they would no longer have been able to call upon the interpreter's services; despite those difficulties, the authorities did not offer any form of legal assistance at either the police station or the centre.

45. Whatever the position—and this factor is decisive in the eyes of the Court—[the applicants' lawyer]...was only informed of the events in issue...at 10.30 p.m. on Friday 1 October 1999, such that any appeal to the committals division would have been pointless because, had he lodged an appeal with the division on 4 October, the case could not have been heard until 6 October, a day after the applicants' expulsion on 5 October....

46. The Convention is intended to guarantee rights that are not theoretical or illusory, but practical and effective...As regards the accessibility of a remedy within the meaning of Article 35 (1)..., the circumstances voluntarily created by the authorities must be such as to afford applicants a realistic possibility of using the remedy. That did not happen in the present case and the preliminary objection must therefore be dismissed.

---

[121] Citing *Akdivar v. Turkey*, 16 September 1996, 23 E.H.R.R. 143, para. 66.

Consequently, there has been a violation of Article 5(1)....

[As to whether the Belgian authorities had informed the applicants promptly of the reasons for their arrest, in a language which they understood, the Court held that the presence of the interpreter at the police station when the applicants were arrested and served with notices of removal was sufficient to satisfy Article 5(2). The Court also held that there had been a breach of Article 5(4): although the applicants were detained for only five days before they were released in Slovakia, they had been prevented from making any meaningful appeal to the committals division of the criminal court under section 71 of the Aliens Act.]

The importance of there being an effective remedy for challenging the legality of detention under Article 5(1)(f) was stressed in a case from Malta, when there was held to be no appropriate national remedy when the extradition of a Moroccan citizen had been sought in connection with alleged drug trafficking,[122] and also when in Greece a Syrian citizen had no opportunity to challenge the lawfulness of his detention pending expulsion.[123]

In *Conka v Belgium*, as we have seen, the Court was critical of the deception that was practised in detaining the applicants. By contrast, in *Öcalan v Turkey*[124] a Turkish citizen was leader of a separatist movement engaged in an armed struggle against Turkish forces and he had fled to Kenya; there he was arrested by Turkish officials on boarding a plane in Nairobi, having been told by the Kenyan authorities that he was free to leave for a destination of his choice. Rejecting his claim under Article 5(1)(f), the Court held that the Convention did not exclude co-operation between states in relation to extradition or deportation, and was not concerned with 'disguised extradition' provided that the requesting state had issued a warrant for the individual's arrest; in the circumstances, no breach of international law had arisen through this extra-territorial exercise of Turkish jurisdiction.[125]

C. CHAHAL V. UNITED KINGDOM

Judgment of 15 November 1996
23 E.H.R.R. 413

[This case has already been considered[126] in relation to issues under Article 3 (degrading and inhuman treatment) that arose when the British government sought to deport to India a Sikh nationalist who was considered to be a threat to national security. By the date of the Court's decision, the applicant had been detained for over six years and his attempts to secure release in the United Kingdom had failed. Having decided that his deportation to India would involve a breach of Article 3, the Court considered whether breaches of Article 5(1) and 5(4) had occurred in respect of his lengthy detention.]

---

[122] *Kadem v. Malta*, 9 Jan. 2003, 37 E.H.R.R. 18.
[123] *Dougoz v. Greece*, 6 March 2001, 34 E.H.R.R. 61. *See also Al-Nashif v. Bulgaria*, 20 June 2002, 36 E.H.R.R. 37.
[124] 12 May 2005, 41 E.H.R.R. 45 (G.C.).
[125] *Id.*, paras. 86–103.
[126] Chapter 5(C)(1) *supra*.

112. The Court recalls that it is not in dispute that Mr. Chahal has been detained 'with a view to deportation' within the meaning of Article 5(1)(f). Article 5(1)(f) does not demand that the detention of a person against whom action is being taken with a view to deportation be reasonably considered necessary, for example to prevent his committing an offence or fleeing; in this respect Article 5(1)(f) provides a different level of protection from Article 5(1)(c).

Indeed, all that is required under this provision is that 'action is being taken with a view to deportation'. It is therefore immaterial, for the purposes of Article 5(1)(f), whether the under-lying decision to expel can be justified under national or Convention law.

113. The Court recalls, however, that any deprivation of liberty under Article 5(1)(f) will be justified only for as long as deportation proceedings are in progress. If such proceed-ings are not prosecuted with due diligence, the detention will cease to be permissible under Article 5(1)(f).[127]

It is thus necessary to determine whether the duration of the deportation proceedings was excessive.

114. The period under consideration commenced on 16 August 1990, when Mr. Chahal was first detained with a view to deportation. It terminated on 3 March 1994, when the domestic proceedings came to an end with the refusal of the House of Lords to allow leave to appeal. Although he has remained in custody until the present day, this latter period must be distinguished because during this time the Government have refrained from deporting him in compliance with the request made by the Commission....

[The Court examined the various stages of the administrative and judicial proceedings taken in the applicant's case in the United Kingdom.]

117. As the Court has observed in the context of Article 3, Mr. Chahal's case involves considerations of an extremely serious and weighty nature. It is neither in the interests of the individual applicant nor in the general public interest in the administration of justice that such decisions be taken hastily, without due regard to all the relevant issues and evidence.

Against this background,...none of the periods complained of can be regarded as exces-sive, taken either individually or in combination. Accordingly, there has been no violation of Article 5(1) of the Convention on account of the diligence, or lack of it, with which the domestic procedures were conducted.

118. It also falls to the Court to examine whether Mr. Chahal's detention was 'lawful' for the purposes of Article 5(1)(f), with particular reference to the safeguards provided by the national system....

119. There is no doubt that Mr. Chahal's detention was lawful under national law and was effected 'in accordance with a procedure prescribed by law'. However, in view of the extremely long period during which Mr. Chahal has been detained, it is also necessary to consider whether there existed sufficient guarantees against arbitrariness.

120. In this context, the Court observes that the applicant has been detained since 16 August 1990 on the ground, essentially, that successive Secretaries of State have main-tained that, in view of the threat to national security represented by him, he could not safely be

---

[127] In *Quinn v. France*, 22 Mar. 1995, 21 E.H.R.R. 529, there had been a breach of Art. 5(1)(f) during a period of almost two years that Quinn was held in France pending extradition to Switzerland. The proceed-ings had not been conducted with due diligence, separate delays of three months and 10 months having occurred during the period.

released. The applicant has, however, consistently denied that he posed any threat whatsoever to national security, and has given reasons in support of this denial.

121. The Court further notes that, since the Secretaries of State asserted that national security was involved, the domestic courts were not in a position effectively to control whether the decisions to keep Mr. Chahal in detention were justified, because the full material on which these decisions were based was not made available to them.

122. However, in the context of Article 5(1) of the Convention, the advisory panel procedure provided an important safeguard against arbitrariness. This panel, which included experienced judicial figures, was able fully to review the evidence relating to the national security threat represented by the applicant. Although its report has never been disclosed, at the hearing before the Court the Government indicated that the panel had agreed with the Home Secretary that Mr. Chahal ought to be deported on national security grounds. The Court considers that this procedure provided an adequate guarantee that there were at least *prima facie* grounds for believing that if Mr. Chahal were at liberty, national security would be put at risk and thus, that the executive had not acted arbitrarily when it ordered him to be kept in detention.

123. In conclusion, the Court recalls that Mr. Chahal has undoubtedly been detained for a length of time which is bound to give rise to serious concern. However, in view of the exceptional circumstances of the case and the facts that the national authorities have acted with due diligence throughout the deportation proceedings against him and that there were sufficient guarantees against the arbitrary deprivation of his liberty, this detention complied with the requirements of Article 5(1)(f).

It follows that there has been no violation of Article 5(1).

[This decision was reached by a majority of 13 votes to six. The Court then considered whether the proceedings that Mr. Chahal had been able to take in the British courts satisfied Article 5(4), by which every detained person is entitled to take proceedings by which the lawfulness of the detention shall be decided speedily by a court. The Court commented generally on Article 5(4) before dealing with the specific circumstances of Mr. Chahal:]

127. The Court...recalls that the notion of 'lawfulness' under paragraph 4 of Article 5 has the same meaning as in paragraph 1, so that the detained person is entitled to a review of his detention in the light not only of the requirements of domestic law but also of the text of the Convention, the general principles embodied therein and the aim of the restrictions permitted by Article 5(1).[128]

The scope of the obligations under Article 5(4) is not identical for every kind of deprivation of liberty;[129] this applies notably to the extent of the judicial review afforded. Nonetheless, it is clear that Article 5(4) does not guarantee a right to judicial review of such breadth as to empower the court, on all aspects of the case including questions of pure expediency, to substitute its own discretion for that of the decision-making authority. The review should, however, be wide enough to bear on those conditions which are essential for the 'lawful' detention of a person according to Article 5(1)....[130]

---

[128] *See E. v. Norway*, 29 Aug. 1990, 17 E.H.R.R. 30, para. 49.

[129] *See, inter alia, Bouamar v. Belgium*, 29 Feb. 1988, 11 E.H.R.R. 1; Section G(2) *infra*.

[130] *See E. v. Norway, supra* n. 128, para. 50.

129. The notion of 'lawfulness' in Article 5(1)(f) does not refer solely to the obligation to conform to the substantive and procedural rules of national law; it requires in addition that any deprivation of liberty should be in keeping with the purpose of Article 5. The question therefore arises whether the available proceedings to challenge the lawfulness of Mr. Chahal's detention and to seek bail provided an adequate control by the domestic courts.

130. The Court recollects that, because national security was involved, the domestic courts were not in a position to review whether the decisions to detain Mr. Chahal and to keep him in detention were justified on national security grounds. Furthermore, although the procedure before the advisory panel undoubtedly provided some degree of control, bearing in mind that Mr. Chahal was not entitled to legal representation before the panel, that he was only given an outline of the grounds for the notice of intention to deport, that the panel had no power of decision and that its advice to the Home Secretary was not binding and was not disclosed, the panel could not be considered as a 'court' within the meaning of Article 5(4).[131]

131. The Court recognises that the use of confidential material may be unavoidable where national security is at stake. This does not mean, however, that the national authorities can be free from effective control by the domestic courts whenever they choose to assert that national security and terrorism are involved....

In the Court's unanimous view, such effective control did not exist and Article 5(4) had been breached, since neither the proceedings in the British courts nor the hearing before the advisory panel satisfied Article 5(4). In regard to Article 5(1), judges in the minority differed sharply from the majority. Judge de Meyer considered that it was 'clearly excessive' for Chahal to have been detained for over six years. Judge Pettiti held that it was clear from past cases (such as *Amuur v. France*)[132] that if proceedings for deportation were not conducted by the state with due diligence or if there had been a misuse of authority, detention might cease to be justifiable; in his view, Chahal had been treated by the British authorities even more severely than a convicted criminal, since his detention amounted to an indefinite sentence and the authorities had 'clearly refused to seek a means of expelling him to a third country'.

The decision in *Chahal* was to assume great significance after the events of 9/11, particularly in the United Kingdom where the Anti-terrorism, Crime and Security Act 2001, Part IV gave additional powers to the government to detain for an indefinite period non-British citizens suspected of involvement in international terrorism who could not be deported to their countries of origin because of the ruling in *Chahal* that to do so could involve breach of their Article 3 rights, but who could not be detained under Article 5(1)(f) because no action was being taken 'with a view to their deportation'. When the new powers were invoked, and an order was made derogating from the United Kingdom's duties under Article 5(1), the order was quashed by the House of Lords and it was declared that provisions in the 2001 Act were incompatible with the Convention.[133]

---

[131] *See, mutatis mutandis, X. v. United Kingdom*, 24 Oct. 1981, 4 E.H.R.R. 188, para. 61.

[132] *See* Section E(4)(a) *supra*.

[133] *A v. Secretary of State for the Home Department* [2004] U.K.H.L. 56; [2005] 2 A.C. 68. And *see* Section H *infra*, and Chapter 14(D)(6).

F. RIGHT TO BE BROUGHT PROMPTLY BEFORE A JUDGE OR OTHER OFFICER AUTHORIZED TO EXERCISE JUDICIAL POWER

Two aspects of this right are examined below. The first concerns the nature of the 'judge or other officer authorized to exercise judicial power' before whom the arrested person has the right to be brought. The second concerns the meaning of 'promptly': what period of time is allowed to the police between arresting a suspect and bringing him or her before a 'judge or other officer authorized to exercise judicial power'?

1. WHO MAY EXERCISE JUDICIAL POWER FOR THE PURPOSES OF ARTICLE 5(3)?

Many European legal systems have commonly provided for the public prosecutor, a salaried lawyer in the public service, to exercise investigatory functions into particular crimes before deciding whether and whom to prosecute and, in the course of the investigation, to have power to release a suspect on bail or to order that he or she be held in custody. In *Schiesser v. Switzerland*,[134] Mr. Schiesser was arrested on charges of theft and was at once brought before the District Attorney for Winterthur, who ordered that he be detained on remand. Schiesser's appeal against detention was later rejected both by the Zurich Public Prosecutor and by the prosecution chamber of the Zurich Court of Appeal. In the Swiss legal system, the District Attorney is both an investigating and a prosecuting authority. When Schiesser alleged a breach of Article 5(3), the Strasbourg Court decided (by five to two) that the District Attorney was 'an officer authorised by law to exercise judicial power'. The Court observed that Article 5(3) left a state a choice between entrusting decisions as to bail to a judge sitting in court or to a category of 'other officers'. This second category was capable of including officials in public prosecutors' departments. Since the purpose of Article 5 was to ensure that no one should be dispossessed arbitrarily of his liberty, the 'officer' referred to in Article 5(3) must 'offer guarantees befitting the "judicial" power conferred on him by law'. Amongst the essential conditions were that the officer must be independent of the executive and of the parties; that the officer must hear the individual; and that the officer must review the substantive grounds relied on that should determine whether or not the detainee could be released. The Court examined in detail the status of the District Attorney in Swiss law and concluded that in practice the District Attorney acted in complete independence of the Public Prosecutor and exercised a personal

---

[134] 4 Dec. 1979, 2 E.H.R.R. 417.

discretion conferred by law. The Court emphasized that in Mr. Schiesser's case:

the District Attorney intervened exclusively in his capacity as an investigating authority, that is, in considering whether Mr. Schiesser should be charged and detained on remand and, subsequently, in conducting enquiries with an obligation to be equally thorough in gathering evidence in his favour and evidence against him... He did not assume the mantle of prosecutor: he neither drew up the indictment nor represented the prosecuting authorities before the trial court... He therefore did not exercise concurrent investigating and prosecuting functions, with the result that the Court is not called upon to determine whether the converse situation would have been in conformity with Article 5(3).[135]

Judges Ryssdal and Evrigenis dissented. In the course of his judgment, Judge Ryssdal stated:

The purpose of Article 5(3) is to establish a system of judicial review and, by that means, to give specific guarantees to persons deprived of their liberty. If a contracting State leaves such judicial power to an 'officer' other than a judge, it is necessary that this 'other officer' should not be dependent on or controlled by the administration and also that he can be regarded as independent and impartial. Depriving a person of his liberty is a very serious measure, and the purpose of Article 5(3) is to give the utmost protection to individual liberty.[136]

In 1990, the decision of the majority in *Schiesser* came up for re-consideration by the Court.

A. HUBER V. SWITZERLAND

Judgment of 23 October 1990

[The applicant, Mrs. Huber, had been taken before the District Attorney in Zurich for questioning as a witness and at the end of his examination the District Attorney ordered that she be held in custody on grave suspicion of having given false evidence. Subsequent proceedings against her led to her being fined 4,000 Swiss francs for attempting to give false evidence. She complained in the Federal Court that, in breach of Article 5(3) of the Convention, the same District Attorney (Mr. J.) had both ordered her detention and drawn up the indictment. The Federal Court applied the judgment of the European Court in *Schiesser*, and held that the Attorney's independence and impartiality 'must be considered exclusively at the time of the arrest and not in the light of the mere possibility that he may play a role later in the proceedings and draw up the indictment'. When Mrs. Huber's complaint of a breach of Article 5(3) reached the European Court, a plenary court of 22 judges was convened and again examined the legal position of the District Attorney in Zurich.]

37. ... Mrs. Huber argued further that in general a prosecutor (*Ankläger*) could never be regarded as an 'officer' within the meaning of Article 5(3). In the present case, of the various functions a District Attorney was called upon to perform, that of prosecution predominated: the duty to establish incriminating and exonerating evidence with equal care made no difference in this respect.

---

[135] *Id.* at para. 34.
[136] *Id.* at para. 4.

38. The Commission took the view that Mr. J. could not be regarded as independent of the parties to the trial because he could be one of them and indeed was.

Its Delegate invited the Court to depart from the *Schiesser* judgment of 4 December 1979.[137] ... In the Delegate's view, the Court's case-law has moved towards the principle that prosecution and judicial functions must be completely separated; such separation was, he considered, necessary at this stage in the development of the protection of human rights in Europe.

In this connection he noted a difference between the *Schiesser* and *Huber* cases. In the former the District Attorney had not assumed the role of prosecuting authority, whereas in the latter he drew up the indictment. The Delegate did not attach decisive importance to this, since circumstances of this nature were determined by the subsequent course of the criminal proceedings and the lawfulness of the Attorney's action in relation to Article 5(3) should, in his opinion, be clear at the outset.

39. The Government contended that the District Attorney was in substance, despite his title, an investigating judge. In this, he could be clearly distinguished from the officers of the prosecuting authority whom the Court had to consider in the cases of *Skoogström v. Sweden* and *Pauwels v. Belgium*.[138] Clearly it fell to him to draw up the indictment, but cantonal law required him to take into account exonerating evidence as well as incriminating evidence, without setting out the grounds of suspicion or any legal considerations...

In the present case he had ordered Mrs. Huber's arrest in complete independence and at that stage he was in no way called upon to express an opinion on her guilt. The mere fact that, fourteen months later, he had submitted the indictment could not compromise his independence retrospectively: the Government fully endorsed the reasoning of the Federal Court in its judgment of 14 March 1989, according to which the position of the District Attorney had to be considered exclusively at the time of the arrest without taking into account the possibility that he might subsequently play a role as prosecuting authority....

Moreover, the applicant had not contested the detention order, or the lawfulness of her detention on remand, under Article 5(4) or challenged the investigative measures. Yet she had not been unaware that Mr. J. could subsequently play another role. Nor had she ever claimed that he was prejudiced against her. In general, it was, in the Government's opinion, hard to see what an accused person might gain from having the indictment drawn up by a different judicial officer from the official responsible for his arrest.

The *Schiesser* judgment had, according to the Government, left open the question of the compatibility with the Convention of the combination of the functions of investigation (*instruction*) and prosecution. Furthermore, the Commission and the Court had based their decision at the time on a number of factors taken together; an isolated circumstance—the drawing up of the indictment—could not justify overruling their case-law. The Swiss authorities were therefore entitled to rely on the above-mentioned judgment in such circumstances, unless there were compelling reasons to the contrary such as a manifest failure on the part of the District Attorney to fulfil his duties or action by him which was *ultra vires*....

40. The Court notes in the first place that the only issue in dispute is the impartiality of the Zürich District Attorney when the detention order was made. Mrs. Huber did not deny that he was independent of the executive, that he heard her himself before placing her in detention on

---

[137] 4 Dec. 1979, 2 E.H.R.R. 417 discussed at Section F(1) *supra*.
[138] Respectively, 2 Oct. 1984, 7 E.H.R.R. 263 and 26 May 1988, 11 E.H.R.R. 238.

remand and that he examined with equal care the circumstances militating for and against such detention.

41. In the present case Mr. J. first intervened at the stage of the investigation. He considered whether it was necessary to charge the applicant and ordered her detention on remand, then conducted the investigation....

Subsequently, fourteen months after the arrest, he acted as prosecuting authority in drawing up the indictment. However, he did not assume the role of prosecuting counsel in the trial court, the Zürich District Court, although he could have done so because the Cantonal Code of Criminal Procedure attributed to him the status of a party in the trial proceedings....

42. In several judgments which post-date the *Schiesser* judgment of 4 December 1979 and which concern Netherlands legislation on the arrest and detention of military personnel,[139] the Court found that the *auditeur-militair*, who had ordered the detention of the applicants, could also be called upon to assume, in the same case, the role of prosecuting authority after referral of the case to the Military Court. It concluded from this that he could not be 'independent of the parties' at that preliminary stage precisely because he was 'liable' to become one of the parties at the next stage in the procedure.

43. The Court sees no grounds for reaching a different conclusion in this case as regards criminal justice under the ordinary law. Clearly the Convention does not rule out the possibility of the judicial officer who orders the detention carrying out other duties, but his impartiality is capable of appearing open to doubt[140] if he is entitled to intervene in the subsequent criminal proceedings as a representative of the prosecuting authority.

Since that was the situation in the present case (...) there has been a breach of Article 5(3).

In *Brincat v. Italy*,[141] the Court was invited by the Italian government to depart from the position laid down in *Huber v. Switzerland* (namely that legitimate doubt is raised about a judicial officer's impartiality if he is entitled to intervene in subsequent proceedings) and to return to *Schiesser v. Switzerland* (no breach of Article 5(3) if the judicial officer had not sought to exercise his prosecutorial functions at the time he decided to detain a suspect in custody). The Court saw no reason for departing from the position which it adopted in *Huber* and in many other cases, such as *De Jong, Baljet and Van Den Brink v. The Netherlands*.[142] In *Hood v. United Kingdom*,[143] which was one of many cases against the United Kingdom finding that the British system of courts martial did not meet the minimum standards for an independent and impartial court

---

[139] *See, e.g., De Jong, Baljet and Van den Brink v. Netherlands*, 22 May 1984, 8 E.H.R.R. 20, discussed at Section G *infra*.

[140] *See Pauwels v. Belgium*, 26 May 1988, 11 E.H.R.R. 238, para. 38 and *mutatis mutandis, Piersack v. Belgium*, 1 Oct. 1982, 5 E.H.R.R. 169, para. 31; *De Cubber v. Belgium*, 26 Oct. 1984, 7 E.H.R.R. 236, para. 30; and *Hauschildt v. Denmark*, 24 May 1989, 12 E.H.R.R. 266, para. 52 *in fine*.

[141] 26 Nov. 1992, 16 E.H.R.R. 591.

[142] *See supra* n. 139.

[143] 18 Feb. 1999, 29 E.H.R.R. 365. *See also Findlay v. United Kingdom*, 27 Feb. 1997, 24 E.H.R.R. 221; *Coyne v. United Kingdom*, 24 Sept. 1997; and *Thompson v. United Kingdom*, 15 June 2004, 40 E.H.R.R. 11. The law relating to courts martial in the United Kingdom was amended by the Armed Forces Act 1996 in response to these challenges.

set by Article 6(1), the Court applied *Huber v. Switzerland* in holding that Article 5(3) had been breached in respect of the applicant's pre-trial detention by decision of his commanding officer.

Despite the position adopted by the Court in *Huber* and *Brincat*, breaches of Article 5(3) have continued to occur, when decisions to authorize continuing detention are made by prosecutors who do not qualify as officers entitled to exercise judicial power.[144]

2. THE MEANING OF 'PROMPTLY' IN ARTICLE 5(3)

The requirement in Article 5(3) that an arrested person be brought promptly before a judge or other officer was interpreted in *McGoff v. Sweden*.[145] Under a warrant of arrest issued in Stockholm, McGoff, an Irish citizen, was extradited from Switzerland to Sweden on charges of smuggling narcotics. He was brought to Stockholm on 24 January 1980 and held in prison, appearing before a court only on 8 February 1980. After his subsequent trial, conviction and imprisonment, the main issue before the European Court was whether he had been brought promptly before a judge. Under the Swedish law at that time, the Swedish court had to be notified immediately when an arrest warrant had been executed and could then order the detained person to be tried within two weeks. If the trial could not be held within two weeks, the court had at least once every two weeks to decide in a public hearing whether detention should be continued. The Court had no difficulty in dealing with the question of delay:

27. The Court, like the Commission, notes that the Stockholm District Court did not hear Mr. McGoff in person when it issued a warrant for his arrest in October 1977 and that his detention began more than two years later. This being so, the arrest warrant did not preclude the subsequent application of the guarantees in Article 5(3). However, fifteen days elapsed between the time when Mr. McGoff was placed in custody in Sweden (24 January 1980) and when he was brought before the District Court (8 February 1980). An interval of this length cannot be regarded as consistent with the required 'promptness'. By way of comparison, reference may be made to the *De Jong, Baljet and Van Den Brink* judgment of 22 May 1984[146] where the Court held that, six days after arrest, the limits laid down by the Convention had already been exceeded.

Accordingly, there has been a breach of Article 5(3).

---

[144] *See Vasilescu v. Romania*, 22 May 1998, 28 E.H.R.R. 241; *Pantea v. Romania*, 3 June 2003, 40 E.H.R.R. 627; and *Nevmerzhitsky v. Ukraine*, 5 April 2005, 19 B.H.R.C. 177, paras. 115–21.

[145] 26 Oct. 1984, 8 E.H.R.R. 246.

[146] *See supra* n. 139.

A. BROGAN V. UNITED KINGDOM

Judgment of 24 November 1988
11 E.H.R.R. 117

[During and after the 1970s, because of the commission of acts of terrorism arising from events in Northern Ireland, the British Parliament conferred on the police special powers for detaining those suspected of IRA membership or other terrorist activities. Under the Prevention of Terrorism (Temporary Provisions) Act 1984, the police could hold those suspected of being concerned in terrorism for up to 48 hours and, with authority from the Secretary of State, for a further five days. By contrast, under the general criminal law, suspects might be detained by the police for 36 hours at most before being brought into court for a decision as to whether they should continue to be detained pending the bringing of charges.

Brogan and three others from Northern Ireland were held by the police under the 1984 Act for periods ranging between four days six hours, and six days 16 hours, authority for their detention beyond 48 hours having been obtained from the Secretary of State. Each was then released without being charged with any offences. At Strasbourg they claimed breaches of paragraphs 1, 3, 4 and 5 of Article 5.]

48. The government has adverted extensively to the existence of particularly difficult circumstances in Northern Ireland, notably the threat posed by organized terrorism.

The Court, having taken notice of the growth of terrorism in modern society, has already recognised the need, inherent in the Convention system, for a proper balance between the defence of the institutions of democracy in the common interest and the protection of individual rights...Examination of the case must proceed on the basis that the Articles of the Convention in respect of which complaints have been made are fully applicable. This does not, however, preclude proper account being taken of the background circumstances of the case. In the context of Article 5, it is for the Court to determine the significance to be attached to those circumstances and to ascertain whether, in the instant case, the balance struck complied with the applicable provisions of that Article in the light of their particular wording and its overall object and purpose.

[In respect of the claimed breach of Article 5(1), the applicants argued that they had been detained on suspicion of involvement in unspecified acts of terrorism, not on suspicion of having committed a specific offence. They argued that they had been subjected to administrative detention exercised for the purpose of gathering information, as was corroborated by the use in practice of the special powers. The Court rejected these arguments by a majority of 16–3, holding that the detention fell within Article 5(1)(c). The Court said that the fact that the applicants were neither charged nor brought before a court did not necessarily mean that the purpose of their detention was inconsistent with Article 5(1)(c). There was no reason to believe that the police investigation was not in good faith or that the detention of the applicants was not intended to further that investigation. On whether there had been a breach of Article 5(3), the Court was also divided.]

55. Under the 1984 Act, a person arrested under section 12 on reasonable suspicion of involvement in acts of terrorism may be detained by police for an initial period of 48 hours, and, on the authorisation of the Secretary of State for Northern Ireland, for a further period or periods of up to five days....

The applicants noted that a person arrested under the ordinary law of Northern Ireland must be brought before a Magistrates' Court within 48 hours and that under the ordinary law in England and Wales (Police and Criminal Evidence Act 1984) the maximum period of detention permitted without charge is four days, judicial approval being required at the 36 hour stage. In their submission, there was no plausible reason why a seven-day detention period was necessary, marking as it did such a radical departure from ordinary law and even from the three-day period permitted under the special powers of detention embodied in the Northern Ireland (Emergency Provisions) Act 1978. Nor was there any justification for not entrusting such decisions to the judiciary of Northern Ireland.

56. The government has argued that in view of the nature and extent of the terrorist threat and the resulting problems in obtaining evidence sufficient to bring charges, the maximum statutory period of detention of seven days was an indispensable part of the effort to combat that threat... In particular, they drew attention to the difficulty faced by the security forces in obtaining evidence which is both admissible and usable in consequence of training in anti-interrogation techniques adopted by those involved in terrorism. Time was also needed to undertake necessary scientific examinations, to correlate information from other detainees and to liaise with other security forces. The government claimed that the need for a power of extension of the period of detention was borne out by statistics. For instance, in 1987 extensions were granted in Northern Ireland in respect of 365 persons. Some 83 were detained in excess of five days and of this number 39 were charged with serious terrorist offences during the extended period.

As regards the suggestion that extensions of detention beyond the initial 48-hour period should be controlled or even authorised by a judge, the government pointed out the difficulty, in view of the acute sensitivity of some of the information on which the suspicion was based, of producing it in court. Not only would the court have to sit *in camera* but neither the detained person nor his legal advisers could be present or told any of the details. This would require a fundamental and undesirable change in the law and procedure of the United Kingdom...

In all the circumstances, the Secretary of State was better placed to take such decisions and to ensure a consistent approach. Moreover, the merits of each request to extend detention were personally scrutinised by the Secretary of State or, if he was unavailable, by another Minister....

58. The fact that a detained person is not charged or brought before a court does not in itself amount to a violation of the first part of Article 5(3). No violation of Article 5(3) can arise if the arrested person is released 'promptly' before any judicial control of his detention would have been feasible. If the arrested person is not released promptly, he is entitled to a prompt appearance before a judge or judicial officer.

The assessment of 'promptness' has to be made in the light of the object and purpose of Article 5. The Court has regard to the importance of this Article in the Convention system: it enshrines a fundamental human right, namely the protection of the individual against arbitrary interferences by the State with his right to liberty....

59. The obligation expressed in English by the word 'promptly' and in French by the word '*aussitôt*' is clearly distinguishable from the less strict requirement in the second part of paragraph 3 ('reasonable time'/'*délai raisonnable*') and even from that in paragraph 4 of Article 5 ('speedily'/'*à bref délai*')....

Whereas promptness is to be assessed in each case according to its special features, the significance to be attached to those features can never be taken to the point of impairing the very essence of the right guaranteed by Article 5(3), that is the point of effectively negativing the State's obligation to ensure a prompt release or a prompt appearance before a judicial authority....

61. The investigation of terrorist offences undoubtedly presents the authorities with special problems.... The Court takes full judicial notice of the factors adverted to by the government in this connection. It is also true that in Northern Ireland the referral of police requests for extended detention to the Secretary of State and the individual scrutiny of each police request by a Minister do provide a form of executive control. In addition, the need for the continuation of the special powers has been constantly monitored by Parliament and their operation regularly reviewed by independent personalities. The Court accepts that, subject to the existence of adequate safeguards, the context of terrorism in Northern Ireland has the effect of prolonging the period during which the authorities may, without violating Article 5(3), keep a person suspected of serious terrorist offences in custody before bringing him before a judge or other judicial officer.

The difficulties, alluded to by the government, of judicial control over decisions to arrest and detain suspected terrorists may affect the manner of implementation of Article 5(3), for example in calling for appropriate procedural precautions in view of the nature of the suspected offences. However, they cannot justify, under Article 5(3), dispensing altogether with 'prompt' judicial control.

62. As indicated above, the scope for flexibility in interpreting and applying the notion of 'promptness' is very limited. In the court's view, even the shortest of the four periods of detention namely the four days and six hours spent in police custody by Mr. McFadden, falls outside the strict constraints as to time permitted by the first part of Article 5(3). To attach such importance to the special features of this case as to justify so lengthy a period of detention without appearance before a judge or other judicial officer would be an unacceptably wide interpretation of the plain meaning of the word 'promptly'. An interpretation to this effect would import into Article 5(3) a serious weakening of a procedural guarantee to the detriment of the individual and would entail consequences impairing the very essence of the right protected by this provision. The Court thus has to conclude that none of the applicants was either brought 'promptly' before a judicial authority or released 'promptly' following his arrest. The undoubted fact that the arrest and detention of the applicants were inspired by the legitimate aim of protecting the community as a whole from terrorism is not on its own sufficient to ensure compliance with the specific requirements of Article 5(3).

There has thus been a breach of Article 5(3) in respect of all four applicants...

This decision that Article 5(3) had been breached was taken by a majority of twelve votes to seven. The Court held unanimously that there had been no breach of Article 5(4), since the remedy of habeas corpus was available to the applicants, although they had not made use of it; and, further, (by thirteen votes to six) that Article 5(5) had been breached, since the violations of Article 5(3) had not given rise to an enforceable right to compensation in the Northern Ireland courts. A short account of the sequel to this important decision will be found in the final section of this Chapter. What was decided in *Brogan* as regards Article (5)(1)(c) was, as we have seen, reconsidered by the Court in *Fox, Campbell and Hartley v. United Kingdom*.[147]

In *Sakik v. Turkey*,[148] six applicants, members of the Democratic Party, were former members of the Turkish National Assembly and of a political party which had been dissolved on account of its unconstitutional activities. In March 1994, they were arrested (two of them while leaving the Parliament building in Ankara on 2 March and the rest on 4 March) and detained on charges of having committed terrorist activities. Their detention was authorised by the prosecutor attached to the Ankara National Security Court until 16 March 1994. Only on 17 March was their continued detention authorized by the court. The applicants complained *inter alia* of breaches of Article 5(3) and 5(4). As regards Article 5(3), the Court said, citing decisions such as *Brogan v. United Kingdom*:

> The Court has already accepted on several occasions that the investigation of terrorist offences undoubtedly presents the authorities with special problems. This does not mean, however, that the investigating authorities have *carte blanche* under Article 5 to arrest suspects for questioning, free from effective control by the domestic courts and, ultimately, by the Convention supervisory institutions, whenever they choose to assert that terrorism is involved.
>
> What is at stake here is the importance of Article 5 in the Convention system: it enshrines a fundamental human right, namely the protection of the individual against arbitrary interferences by the State with his right to liberty...[paragraph 44]
>
> ...Even supposing that the activities of which the applicants stood accused were linked to a terrorist threat, the Court cannot accept that it was necessary to detain them for 12 or 14 days without judicial intervention [paragraph 45].

The Court also held that there had been breaches of Article 5(4) (in the absence of an available remedy to enable a court to rule on the legality of the detention) and of Article 5(5), since the applicants had no realistic prospect in national law of obtaining compensation for detention in breach of their Convention rights. The Turkish government relied unsuccessfully on a derogation filed under Article 15 of the Convention relating to the security situation in south-east Turkey.[149]

Other decisions involving breaches of the obligation to provide a prompt hearing before a judicial officer include *Bati v. Turkey* (11–13 days),[150] *Ocalan v. Turkey* (applying *Brogan v. United Kingdom*, seven days too long, even in respect of someone suspected of terrorist offences)[151] and *Pantea v. Romania* (four months before a hearing before a judicial officer).[152]

---

[147] *See* Section E(1)(c) *supra*.
[148] 26 Nov. 1997, 26 E.H.R.R. 662.
[149] *See* Section H *infra*.
[150] 3 June 2004, 42 E.H.R.R. 37.
[151] N. 124 *supra*.
[152] N. 144 *supra*.

G. THE RIGHT TO A DECISION BY A COURT AS TO THE LEGALITY OF DETENTION

An all-pervasive theme in Article 5 is that an act interfering with individual liberty must not only be for one of the stated grounds but must also be 'lawful'. Article 5 requires at the least that such an act must be authorized in national law, both as to the grounds and as to the procedure involved. Where someone has been deprived of their liberty, he or she is entitled by Article 5(4) to a 'speedy' decision by a national court as to whether the deprivation is lawful and to an order for his or her release if it is not.

It is one thing for a national constitution to contain finely phrased guarantees of individual liberty. It is another thing for a legal system, through the decisions of its courts, to provide a prompt and effective remedy against any official body that has taken away someone's liberty. It is such a remedy which English law has for long sought to provide by means of the writ of habeas corpus. As the nineteenth-century jurist A. V. Dicey wrote:

There is no difficulty, and there is often very little gain, in declaring the existence of a right to personal freedom. The true difficulty is to secure its enforcement. The Habeas Corpus Acts have achieved this end, and have therefore done for the liberty of Englishmen more than could have been achieved by any declaration of rights.[153]

And, even more sweepingly, Dicey proclaimed:

The Habeas Corpus Acts declare no principle and define no rights, but they are for practical purposes worth a hundred constitutional articles guaranteeing individual liberty.

Under the Convention, Article 5(4) is the 'habeas corpus' clause. It recognizes that the deprivation of an individual's liberty may well be disputed, and requires such disputes to be resolved speedily by the national courts.

One distinction drawn in the case-law (as we saw in *Winterwerp v. The Netherlands*, above) is that where the decision depriving the individual of liberty is taken by an administrative body, Article 5(4) requires a state to make available a right of recourse to a court; but if the initial decision is itself taken by a court, the requirements of Article 5(4) may be incorporated in that decision, provided that an adequate procedure, respecting the rights of the individual, has been observed.[154] However, even if judicial procedure appears to have been observed initially, a decision by an inferior court affecting individual liberty ought to be subject to possible review and supervision by a superior court. Such review must itself be made 'speedily', i.e. without excessive delay.[155] Article 5(4) 'does not guarantee a right to judicial control of all aspects

---

[153] A. V. Dicey, *Law and the Constitution* (10th edn., by E. C. S. Wade, 1959), 221.

[154] *See De Wilde, Ooms and Versyp v. Belgium*, 18 June 1971, 1 E.H.R.R. 373, para. 73.

[155] *See*, e.g., *Luberti v. Italy*, 23 Feb. 1984, 6 E.H.R.R. 440, 451–4: undue delay where, in 'an urgent case involving deprivation of liberty', it took the superior courts over 18 months to review the decision of committal; and *E v. Norway*, 29 Aug. 1990, 17 E.H.R.R. 30 discussed at Section G(1) *infra*.

or details of the detention',[156] but does require a review of the essential grounds of a detention. It is somewhat ironic, as we have already seen (in *X v. United Kingdom* and in *Chahal v. United Kingdom*, above), that the habeas corpus procedure in English law does not always meet this requirement. The Court has also laid down the minimum procedural requirements which such hearings must observe.

In *De Jong, Baljet and Van Den Brink v. The Netherlands*,[157] three conscripts to the Dutch army refused to obey orders on grounds of conscientious objection. They were arrested and kept in custody pending trial before a military court. The Court decided that paragraphs 3 and 4 of Article 5 could be applied concurrently, since, in the Court's words, 'the guarantee assured by paragraph 4 is of a different order from, and additional to, that provided by paragraph 3'.[158] With respect to Article 5(4), the Court said:

58. The two remedies relied on by the Government in connection with paragraph 4 of Article 5 were those available under Articles 13 and 34 of the Military Code.

Article 13, which is applicable in the period prior to referral for trial, allows a suspected serviceman who has been in custody on remand for 14 days to petition the Military Court to fix a term within which the commanding general must either decide whether the case is to be referred for trial or else terminate the detention. The fact that this remedy could not be exercised until at least two weeks after the arrest prevented the applicants from being able to obtain a 'speedy' decision, even having regard to the exigencies of military life and military justice.

Following referral and prior to the commencement of the trial, Article 34 permits the detained serviceman to address a request for release to the Military Court. It was not disputed in the present case that the Military Court could be regarded as a 'court' for the purposes of Article 5(4), in the sense of enjoying the necessary independence and offering sufficient procedural safeguards appropriate to the category of deprivation of liberty being dealt with. In addition, Article 34 of the Military Code is capable in practice of leading to a 'speedy' decision, depending upon how rapidly the referral for trial occurs in the particular circumstances. Mr. de Jong was seven days, Mr. Baljet 11 days and Mr. van den Brink six days in custody, before being referred for trial and hence without a remedy. In the Court's view, even having regard to the exigencies of military life and military justice, the length of absence of access to a court was in each case such as to deprive the applicant of his entitlement to bring proceedings to obtain a 'speedy' review of the lawfulness of his detention.

The cases below deal with different aspects of the procedure by which a court performs the function under Article 5(4) of deciding 'speedily' on the lawfulness of a determination. The principles emerging from these cases do not create a precise code for determining the lawfulness of all kinds of detention, but the Court does insist on observance of certain matters that go to the fairness of judicial procedure.

---

[156] *Ashingdane v. United Kingdom*, 28 May 1985, 7 E.H.R.R. 528, para. 52.

[157] 22 May 1984, 8 E.H.R.R. 20.

[158] *Id.* at para. 57. The Court also held that the *'auditeur-militair'*, an officer in the Dutch army with prosecutorial functions, was not an officer 'authorised by law to exercise judicial power for the purposes of Article 5(3)': *id.* paras. 46–50. And *see Huber v. Switzerland*, Section F(1)(A) *supra*, and *Hood v. United Kingdom*, 18 Feb. 1999, discussed at Section F(1)(A) *supra*.

1. SANCHEZ-REISSE V. SWITZERLAND

Judgment of 21 October 1986

9 E.H.R.R. 71

[An Argentinian citizen, Mr. Sanchez-Reisse, was alleged to have been involved in a kidnapping conspiracy in Argentina. He was arrested in Lausanne and held in prison while the Argentine government instituted proceedings for his extradition from Switzerland. Two requests for release made to the Swiss authorities were refused after some delay in each case. He complained both of the nature of the procedure by which his requests for release were considered and of the delays that occurred.]

44. In the first place, he complained of the fact that he had not been able to apply directly to a court. Being obliged, like anyone who was detained with a view to extradition, to turn first of all to an administrative body, he did not have, so he maintained, direct access to the judicial authority competent to hear a request by him for provisional release....

45. As Mr. Sanchez-Reisse had stated that he objected to being extradited, the Federal Court had exclusive jurisdiction to rule on the question of release. Although, legally speaking, the request was addressed solely to the Federal Court, the practice—since enshrined in the 1981 Act—was that the request went first to the [Federal Police] Office, which examined it and gave an opinion thereon.

The Court considers that the intervention of the Office did not impede the applicant's access to the Federal Court or limit the latter's power of review. Moreover, it may meet a legitimate concern: as extradition, by its very nature, involves a State's international relations, it is understandable that the executive should have an opportunity to express its views on a measure likely to have an influence in such a sensitive area.

46. The applicant made a second complaint, concerning the impossibility of conducting one's own defence, due to the fact that the exclusively written nature of the procedure necessitated the assistance of a lawyer. He alleged that a detainee needed to be able to check the action taken by the lawyer, in particular by attending the oral proceedings, especially as the latter might have been appointed by the Office....

47. In the Court's view, the allegation of the applicant—who in fact chose his lawyer himself—does not stand up to examination. It has no basis in the actual text of Article 5(4). What is more, it loses sight of the fact that Swiss law, by requiring the assistance of a lawyer, affords an important guarantee to the person concerned by an extradition procedure. The detainee is, by definition, a foreigner in the country in question and therefore often unfamiliar with its legal system. Furthermore, Mr. Sanchez-Reisse furnished no evidence that his legal knowledge was sufficient to enable him to present his requests effectively in writing.

48. Mr. Sanchez-Reisse also alleged that he should have had an opportunity of replying to the Office's opinion, which was *ex hypothesi* negative since its very existence presupposed a refusal on the part of the administrative authority to grant release.

At the same time he complained of the fact that he had not been able to appear—either as of right or on his application—before a court in order to argue the case for his release. In his view, this was the cause of the worsening of his state of health, which was the main ground of his requests for release. The lack of any contact with a court was, he said, incompatible with the very nature of habeas corpus. It was all the harsher as detention with a view to extradition afforded the detainee fewer points of reference than ordinary pretrial detention: in Switzerland a court hearing extradition cases confined itself to reviewing compliance with the conditions of the treaty and thus did not consider the merits of the charge.

49. The Government maintained that the Office's opinion was the counterpart of the reasons adduced by the detainee in support of his request for release. There was thus equality of arms.

The Government also disputed the existence of any right to appear in person. They advocated a systematic interpretation of Article 5, stressing notably a contrast between paragraphs 3 and 4; they relied in this connection on the Court's case law, in particular the *Winterwerp* judgment of 24 October 1979[159] and the judgment of 5 November 1981 in the case of *X v. United Kingdom*.[160] In the Government's submission, to deprive a person against whom extradition proceedings were being taken of his liberty was a measure of international co-operation, and this made the particular circumstances of the individual of secondary importance....

51. In the Court's opinion, Article 5(4) required in the present case that Mr. Sanchez-Reisse be provided, in some way or another, with the benefit of an adversarial procedure.

Giving him the possibility of submitting written comments on the Office's opinion would have constituted an appropriate means, but there is nothing to show that he was offered such a possibility. Admittedly, he had already indicated in his request the circumstances which, in his view, justified his release, but this of itself did not provide the 'equality of arms' that is indispensable: the opinion could subsequently have referred to new points of fact or of law giving rise, on the detainee's part, to reactions or criticisms or even to questions of which the Federal Court should have been able to take notice before rendering its decision.

The applicant's reply did not, however, necessarily have to be in writing: the result required by Article 5(4) could also have been attained if he had appeared in person before the Federal Court.

The possibility for a detainee 'to be heard either in person or, where necessary, through some form of representation' features in certain instances among the 'fundamental guarantees of procedure applied in matters of deprivation of liberty'.[161] Despite the difference in wording between paragraph 3 (right to be brought before a judge or other officer) and paragraph 4 (right to take proceedings) of Article 5, the Court's previous decisions relating to these two paragraphs have hitherto tended to acknowledge the need for a hearing before the judicial authority. These decisions concerned, however, only matters falling within the ambit of sub-paragraphs (c) and (e) *in fine* of paragraph 1. And, in fact, 'the forms of the procedure required by the Convention need not...necessarily be identical in each of the cases where the intervention of a court is required'.[162]

In the present case, the Federal Court was led to take into consideration the applicant's worsening state of health, a factor which might have militated in favour of his appearing in person, but it had at its disposal the medical certificates appended to the third request for provisional release from custody. There is no reason to believe that the applicant's presence could have convinced the Federal Court that he had to be released.

---

159 *Winterwerp v. The Nethlands*, 24 Oct. 1979, 2 E.H.R.R. 387; Section D(1) *supra*.
160 4 E.H.R.R. 188; Section D(2) *supra*.
161 *De Wilde, Ooms and Versyp v. Belgium*, 18 June 1971, 1 E.H.R.R. 373, para. 76.
162 *See Winterwerp v. The Netherlands*, *supra*, n. 159 and *Schiesser v. Switzerland*, 4 Dec. 1979, 2 E.H.R.R. 417 discussed at Section F(1) *supra*.

Nevertheless, it remains the case that Mr. Sanchez-Reisse did not receive the benefit of a procedure that was really adversarial.

52. To sum up, the procedure followed in the two cases in dispute did not, viewed as a whole, fully comply with the guarantees afforded by Article 5(4).

[Judges Ganshof van der Meersch and Walsh concurred, but differed from the majority judgment on a significant point of principle:]

...In our view, an exclusively written procedure does not satisfy the requirements of Article 5(4) of the Convention, even if the person concerned does have the benefit of the assistance of a lawyer and of the opportunity to challenge the legality of his detention before competent courts.

Despite the silence of the provision in question, it seems to us that only the opportunity for the prisoner to be heard in person provides a complete answer to Article 5(4). This latter is inspired by the institution of habeas corpus which fundamentally consists of appearing in flesh and blood before the court.

Moreover, the same solution is woven into the thread of the Court's case law which has hitherto, as the Court's judgment mentions, tended to acknowledge the necessity of a hearing by a judicial authority. It is true that the case law so far only concerns hypotheses relevant to letters (c) and (e) *in fine* of paragraph 1, but we cannot see any reasons why a person 'against whom action is being taken with a view to deportation of extradition' (letter (f)) should be so deprived.

In brief, the personal appearance of the applicant before the court was necessary.

The Court also considered whether the Swiss authorities had in two instances complied with the requirement in Article 5(4) that the question of whether a detention was lawful must be 'decided speedily'. Delays had occurred both while the Federal Police Office processed the papers (21 and 20 days) and while the matter was before the court (10 and 26 days). The Court held (by six to one) that, in what was a straightforward case, these delays were excessive. For this reason too, there had been a breach of Article 5(4).

The requirement that judicial proceedings reviewing the legality of detention be 'decided speedily' was considered in *E v. Norway*.[163] E, who had repeatedly been convicted of crimes of violence, and was considered to be an untreatable psychopath, was subject to a decision by the Ministry of Justice that for a short but indefinite time he should be held in a secure institution. E sought judicial review of that decision, but it was over eight weeks before the Oslo court upheld the detention. E claimed that Article 5(4) had been infringed, contending *inter alia* that the lawfulness of his detention had not been decided 'speedily'. His detention had been authorized on 21 July 1988, proceedings to challenge the detention were instituted on 3 August, a hearing held on 7 September and judgment was delivered on 27 September. The Strasbourg Court found that one reason for initial delay in Oslo was that the challenge had been instituted during the vacation period, and observed that the Convention

---

[163] 29 Aug. 1990, 17 E.H.R.R. 30.

requires states:

to organise their legal systems so as to enable the courts to comply with its various requirements. It is incumbent on the judicial authorities to make the necessary administrative arrangements, even during a vacation period to ensure that urgent matters are dealt with speedily, and this is particularly necessary when the individual's personal liberty is at stake [paragraph 66].

Even after the hearing, it took the judge three weeks to deliver judgment. The Court concluded that Article 5(4) had been breached, since E had not received the speedy decision to which he was entitled.

In *GB v. Switzerland*, a person suspected of involvement in terrorist crimes was remanded in custody; when he sought his release a month later, this was refused a day later by the Federal Attorney, acting as an administrative authority, but a breach of Article 5(4) occurred when it took 32 days for the appeal to be decided by the Federal Court.[164]

2. BOUAMAR V. BELGIUM

Judgment of 29 February 1988
11 E.H.R.R. 1

[Naim Bouamar, a Moroccan boy living in Belgium, had a disturbed personality owing mainly to family problems. He was suspected of various criminal offences and on no less than nine occasions in 1980, when he was aged 16, he was detained in a remand prison for adults for periods not exceeding 15 days, after which he would return to an open juvenile institution or to his family home. In all, he spent 119 days in prison during 1980. A succession of appeals against the commitments to prison were unsuccessful. The European Court rejected the main submission by the Belgian government that the successive detentions were within Article 5(1)(d) (detention of a minor by lawful order for the purpose of educational supervision) and then considered whether there had been breaches of Article 5(4).]

56. The Government submitted that the review required in Article 5(4) was incorporated in the decision to deprive a person of his liberty where, as in the instant case, it was taken by a judicial body.

57. The Juvenile Court, which is a single-judge section of the Liège *Tribunal de Première Instance*, is undoubtedly a 'court' from the organisational point of view, but the European Court has consistently held that the intervention of a single body of this kind will satisfy Article 5(4) only on condition that 'the procedure followed has a judicial character and gives to the individual concerned guarantees appropriate to the kind of deprivation of liberty in question; in order to determine whether a proceeding provides adequate guarantees, regard must be had to the particular nature of the circumstances in which such proceeding takes place'.

---

[164] 30 November 2000, 34 E.H.R.R. 10. A similar decision was made when someone held for alleged contempt of court in connection with his trial for assaulting a neighbour was held in a psychiatric hospital for observation: *Vondenicarov v. Slovakia*, 21 December 2000, 37 E.H.R.R. 36.

58. That being so, it must be determined whether the applicant enjoyed such guarantees before the Juvenile Court.

The 1965 Act does contain some of them. Section 62 lays down that the provisions relating to proceedings in respect of lesser criminal offences normally apply also to proceedings against juveniles. Furthermore, sections 54 and 55 permit juveniles to be represented by a lawyer, who will be allowed access to all the documents in the file.

59. The applicant, however, complained of the informal nature of these proceedings. The 1965 Act made no provision for any hearing *inter partes* where the Juvenile Court judge had to make an interim custody order in chambers. He was free to take his decision on the basis of what he considered to be adequate information.

The Government contended that the informal nature of the proceedings was justified by the youth of the persons concerned, the urgency of the measures to be taken and the short duration of their effects. ...At all events, the Government maintained, Mr. Bouamar had been given a hearing by a judge before each placement was ordered and his lawyer had had every opportunity to plead his case.

The young man's lawyers stated, however, that as they had never been given notice to attend, they had never been present at the hearings in chambers which had taken place each time before the juvenile was sent to the remand prison, whereas they had sometimes appeared before the juvenile courts in this case on other occasions. In addition, they had not been enabled to comment on the submissions of Crown Counsel—when the latter made an application to the Juvenile Court—or on the welfare reports, to which they had had no access.

60. The Court reiterates that the scope of the obligation under Article 5(4) is not identical in all circumstances or for every kind of deprivation of liberty. Nevertheless, in a case of the present kind, it is essential not only that the individual concerned should have the opportunity to be heard in person but that he should also have the effective assistance of his lawyer. The impugned orders make it clear that the juvenile was given a hearing by the Juvenile Court, except in one instance when he refused to be heard. However, they do not give any indication that one of his lawyers was present; counsel for the applicant moreover denied that one of them was present, and the Government did not dispute their statements. The mere fact that Mr. Bouamar—who was very young at the time—appeared in person before the court did not, in the circumstances of the case, afford him the necessary safeguards.

61. The Court must consequently ascertain whether the remedies available against the aforementioned placement orders satisfied the conditions in Article 5(4), as was argued by the Government but disputed by the applicant. In the first place, an ordinary appeal (*appel*) could be lodged and, in the second place, where appropriate, an appeal lay on points of law (*pourvoi en cassation*). It was also possible both for the Juvenile Court and for the Juvenile Court of Appeal in further interim proceedings to revoke or vary the initial decision, either on an application by Crown Counsel or of their own motion.

62. In the instant case, several of the orders for provisional placement in a remand prison were varied or revoked, expressly or by implication, by further interim orders made either on appeal ... or by the Juvenile Court.

However, most of the further interim proceedings before the Juvenile Court and the Juvenile Court of Appeal suffered from the same defect as the earlier proceedings: they took place in the absence of Mr. Bouamar's lawyers.

63. At the hearings of the applicant's appeals against the orders of 18 January, 4 March, 7 May and 4 July 1980, the juvenile chamber of the Court of Appeal heard one or other of Mr. Bouamar's lawyers. But it did not give its decision until 29 April 1980 on the appeals against the orders of 18 January and 4 March 1980; 30 June 1980 on the appeal against the order of 7 May 1980; and 3 February 1981 on the appeal against the order of 4 July 1980. Such lapses of time are scarcely compatible with the speed required by the terms of Article 5(4) of the Convention.

Furthermore, the appellate court did not really 'decide' the 'lawfulness' of the placement measures which were challenged before it, although it did go into the issue of lawfulness in some of the reasons given in two of its three decisions: following established case law, it held in the operative part of its judgments of 29 April 1980, 30 June 1980 and 3 February 1981, that the appeals were inadmissible because devoid of purpose, since Mr. Bouamar had in the meantime been released pursuant to interim orders.

The Court of Cassation held likewise...

The applicant's ordinary appeals and appeals on points of law thus had no practical effect.

64. In sum, there was a breach of Article 5(4)....

The opportunity to participate in the procedure leading to a judicial decision is fundamental to Article 5(4). Thus in *Toth v. Austria*,[165] the applicant had been arrested on charges of having committed a series of bank frauds and detained on remand for over two years before his trial and conviction. His applications for release on bail had been dealt with in a judicial manner by the court of first instance, but his appeals against refusal of bail had not been accorded due process by the Linz Court of Appeal. That court ruled on his appeals against the refusal of bail without giving either him or his lawyer a hearing, whereas the public prosecutor had been represented before the court. The Strasbourg Court observed that Article 5(4) did not compel a state to provide a second level of jurisdiction to deal with applications for release from detention. But if a state chose to do so, it must afford to detainees the same guarantees on appeal as at first instance. The Court has repeatedly ruled that the question of whether Article 5(4) has been observed must be determined in the light of the circumstances of each case. Thus in *RMD v. Switzerland*,[166] the applicant was detained on suspicion of having committed thefts in seven cantons. Within a period of two months, he was moved from prison to prison in those cantons; attempts by his lawyers to obtain his release were frustrated as by Swiss law an application for release had to be struck out when the detainee was no longer within the canton.

The explanation for that situation lies in the federal structure of the Swiss Confederation, in which each canton has its own code of criminal procedure, and it is not for the Court to express a view on the system as such. Like the Commission, however, the Court considers that those circumstances cannot justify the applicant's being deprived of his rights under Article 5(4). Where...a detained person is continually transferred from one canton to another, it is for the

---

[165] 12 Dec. 1991, 14 E.H.R.R. 551. *See also Kampanis v. Greece*, 13 July 1995, 21 E.H.R.R. 43 (breach of Art. 5(4) where applicant has been denied the opportunity of hearing and replying to the prosecutor's oral submissions to the court).

[166] 26 Sept. 1997, 28 E.H.R.R. 224.

State to organise its judicial system in such a way as to enable its courts to comply with the requirements of that Article [paragraphs 53, 54].

The necessity for legal representation and fair procedure has also been emphasized in cases involving mental illness.

3. MEGYERI V. GERMANY

Judgment of 12 May 1992
15 E.H.R.R. 584

[A Hungarian citizen resident in Germany was found by a German court, at which he was represented by appointed counsel, to have committed criminal offences while suffering from a schizophrenic psychosis with signs of paranoia. He was committed to a psychiatric hospital and his detention was at intervals reviewed by a criminal court, in proceedings for which no counsel were assigned to represent him.]

22. The principles which emerge from the Court's case law on Article 5(4) include the following.

    (a) A person of unsound mind who is compulsorily confined in a psychiatric institution for an indefinite or lengthy period is in principle entitled, at any rate where there is no automatic periodic review of a judicial character, to take proceedings at reasonable intervals before a court to put in issue the 'lawfulness'—within the meaning of the Convention—of his detention.

    (b) Article 5(4) requires that the procedure followed has a judicial character and gives to the individual concerned guarantees appropriate to the kind of deprivation of liberty in question; in order to determine whether a proceeding provides adequate guarantees, regard must be had to the particular nature of the circumstances in which such proceeding takes place.

    (c) The judicial proceedings referred to in Article 5(4) need not always be attended by the same guarantees as those required under Article 6(1) for civil or criminal litigation. Nonetheless, it is essential that the person concerned should have access to a court and the opportunity to be heard either in person or, where necessary, through some form of representation. Special procedural safeguards may prove called for in order to protect the interests of persons who, on account of their mental disabilities, are not fully capable of acting for themselves.

    (d) Article 5(4) does not require that persons committed to care under the head of 'unsound mind' should themselves take the initiative in obtaining legal representation before having recourse to a court.

23. It follows from the foregoing that where a person is confined in a psychiatric institution on the ground of the commission of acts which constituted criminal offences but for which he could not be held responsible on account of mental illness, he should—unless there are special circumstances—receive legal assistance in subsequent proceedings relating to the

continuation, suspension or termination of his detention. The importance of what is at stake for him—personal liberty—taken together with the very nature of his affliction—diminished mental capacity—compels this conclusion.

24. As regards Mr. Megyeri's state of mental health, the Court recalls that the origin of his confinement was the finding by the Cologne Regional Court on 14 March 1983—in criminal proceedings in which he had been represented by officially-appointed counsel—that he could not be held responsible for his acts because he was suffering from a schizophrenic psychosis with signs of paranoia.

In July 1986 the Aachen Regional Court had before it expert evidence to the effect that there had been a further deterioration in his condition, that he was not willing to undergo treatment and that he showed a distinct propensity towards aggressive behaviour and violence. There had, in addition, been previous court judgments which pointed in the same direction: the applicant was incapable of conducting court proceedings and his mental illness was so obvious that no expert's opinion on the point was necessary; his delusions had become more severe and guardianship proceedings should be instituted.

25. One of the issues falling to be determined in the 1986 review was whether, if Mr. Megyeri were released on probation, he would be likely to commit illegal acts similar to those that had occasioned the original confinement order. In this connection, the Aachen Regional Court not only considered a report by three experts but also heard the applicant in person, in order to form its own impression of him. It is doubtful, to say the least, whether Mr. Megyeri, acting on his own, was able to marshal and present adequately points in his favour on this issue, involving as it did matters of medical knowledge and expertise.

Again, it is even more doubtful whether, on his own, he was in a position adequately to address the legal issue arising: would his continued confinement be proportionate to the aim pursued (the protection of the public), in the sense contemplated in the Federal Constitutional Court's leading judgment of 8 October 1985?

26. Finally, the Court notes that by July 1986 the applicant had already spent more than four years in a psychiatric hospital. As required by German law, his confinement was reviewed by courts at yearly intervals and the 1986 proceedings before the Aachen Regional Court formed part of this series. . . .

27. Nothing in the foregoing analysis reveals that this was a case in which legal assistance was unnecessary, even if it is correct that Mr. Megyeri did not specifically ask the Aachen Regional Court or the Cologne Court of Appeal to assign counsel to him in the proceedings in question. . . .

There has therefore been a breach of Article 5(4). . . .

Further instances of application of the principles summarized by the Court in *Megyeri's* case (para. 22, above) are found in more recent decisions. Although the proceedings need not comply with all the requirements of a fair hearing under Article 6(1),[167] they must comply with some essential Article 6(1) standards. Thus they must have an adversarial character:[168] as we have seen, a decision as to the continued detention of a convicted prisoner serving an indefinite sentence for murder breached Article 5(4) when he was denied

[167] *Niedbala v. Poland*, 4 July 2000, 33 E.H.R.R. 48, para. 66 and *see Reinprecht v. Austria (infra).*
[168] *Niedbala v. Poland.*

rights to attend an oral hearing, to have legal representation and to call witnesses.[169] 'Equality of arms' was breached when essential information relating to the police investigation was withheld from lawyers acting for a suspected drug trafficker,[170] and when the individual's lawyer had to leave the court-room while the prosecutor addressed the judges.[171] The Court held by 12–5 that unfairness occurred when a judicial body deciding whether a psychiatric patient should be released included as one of its members a doctor who had previously given an opinion adverse to the patient.[172] The right to legal representation was not satisfied by the assignment to the detainee of a pupil advocate, even if the judge thought that there was no legal issue to be resolved.[173] Above all, the individual has the right to a decision by a court with power to decide the issue of lawfulness;[174] and the fact that an issue of national security is involved is no reason for excluding the right to a court decision.[175] However, in 2005, in *Reinprecht v. Austria*,[176] the Court held that hearings on pre-trial detention need not be in open court: while some aspects of procedural rights under Article 6(1) applied at the pre-trial stage, Articles 5(4) and 6(1) were held to 'pursue different purposes', the former providing for speedy review of the lawfulness of detention, the latter guaranteeing that criminal charges be determined by a 'fair and public hearing'. 'This difference of aims explains why Article 5(4) contains more flexible procedural requirements than Article 6 while being much more stringent as regards speediness.'[177] The Court noted that hearings on the lawfulness of pre-trial detention were often held in remand prisons, but the Court did not exclude the possibility that particular circumstances might require a hearing in public to be held.

The United States Supreme Court has held that the determination of the propriety of detention of a person pending criminal trial is governed by the Fourth Amendment to the Constitution, which declares that no person may be seized without probable cause. Such cause must be based on 'facts and circumstances sufficient to warrant a prudent man in believing that [the suspect] had committed or was committing an offense'.[178] The Court has held that the decision as to probable cause justifying the initial arrest does not require a prior warrant in every case. It may also be made by a law enforcement officer or a prosecutor. In such cases, however, the detained person is entitled to a judicial determination 'promptly after arrest'.[179] The Supreme Court has refused to

---

[169] *Waite v. United Kingdom*, 10 Dec. 2002, 36 E.H.R.R. 54.

[170] *Garcia Alva v. Germany*, 13 Feb. 2001, 37 E.H.R.R. 12.

[171] *Wloch v. Poland*, 19 Oct. 2000, 34 E.H.R.R. 9.

[172] *DN v. Switzerland*, 29 March 2001, 37 E.H.R.R. 21.

[173] *Magalhaes Pereira v. Portugal*, 26 Feb 2002, 36 E.H.R.R. 49.

[174] E.g. *Sabeur Ben Ali v. Malta*, 29 June 2000, 34 E.H.R.R. 26.

[175] *Al-Nashif v. Bulgaria*, 20 June 2002, 36 E.H.R.R. 37.

[176] Judgment of 15 November 2005.

[177] *Id.*, para. 40. In paras. 43–55, the Court considered whether Article 6(1) may apply to decisions as to the lawfulness of pre-trial detention, and held that Article 5(4) contains specific guarantees for deprivation of liberty (*lex specialis*) which are distinct from the general guarantees in Article 6(1), (*cf. Aerts v. Belgium* 30 July 1998, 29 E.H.R.R. 50).

[178] *Gerstein v. Pugh*, 420 U.S. 103, 111 (1974) quoting *Beck v. Ohio*, 379 U.S. 89, 91 (1964) (internal quotation marks omitted).

[179] 420 U.S. 103, 125 (1974).

set an inflexible rule as to what amount of time may pass before such a hearing. It has held, however, that a hearing within 48 hours is generally sufficient. Beyond that time the state bears the burden of showing a pressing reason for the further delay.[180] While the presence or absence of probable cause is, in many states, decided in a full blown adversary hearing, the Court has held that such a procedure is not constitutionally required. It is sufficient if the question is 'decided by a magistrate in a nonadversary proceeding on hearsay and written testimony...'.[181] In particular the Constitution does not require the presence of appointed counsel at this stage in the prosecution.[182]

The Canadian Criminal Code provides that a person who is arrested is to be brought before a justice, where a justice is available within a period of 24 hours after the arrest 'without unreasonable delay and in any event within that period'. Some Canadian courts have held that this provision may be violated even when a person is held for less than 24 hours.[183]

Section 9 of the Charter, moreover, prohibits explicitly arbitrary detentions, and a failure to provide a prompt judicial determination of the propriety of the detention might, on reasoning similar to that of the American law discussed, be thought to make it arbitrary, in violation of that provision. Finally, Section 10(c) of the Charter guarantees a right to have the validity of a detention 'determined by way of habeas corpus and to be released if the detention is not lawful'.[184]

The most common guarantee against unjustified detention of a person accused of crime pending trial is the institution of bail, allowing release upon the posting of sufficient security. The English Bill of Rights of 1689 provided that 'excessive bail ought not to be required',[185] and this provided the model for parallel provisions in the Eighth Amendment to the United States Constitution, which states 'excessive bail shall not be required', and in Section 11 of the Canadian Charter of Rights and Freedoms, which declares that every person charged with an offence has the right 'not to be denied reasonable bail without just cause'. All of these formulations, it will be noted, suggest that the *amount* of bail may differ for different cases so long as it is 'reasonable' or not 'excessive'. What is reasonable in a given case depends on the purpose for which the bail is demanded. The central purpose of this requirement has historically been to provide some assurance that the accused will appear for trial. Consequently, the calculation of reasonableness has turned on the risk, in each case, that the defendant may abscond before trial.[186] The factors to be considered in assessing that risk include the severity of the offence charged and the possible punishment,

---

[180] *County of Riverside v. McLaughlin*, 500 U.S. 44, 56–7 (1991).

[181] *Gerstein v. Pugh*, 420 U.S. 103, 111 (1974) quoting *Beck v. Ohio*, at 120.

[182] *Id.* at 122–3.

[183] R.S.C. 1985, c. C–46, s. 503. *See R v. Koszulap* (1974) 20 C.C.C. (2d) 193 and *R v. Tam* (1995) 100 C.C.C. (3d) 196, paras. 36–57.

[184] *See*, P. Hogg, *Constitutional Law of Canada* (5th edn. supp. 2007), s. 50.5. The U.S. Supreme Court has expressly rejected a 24 hour rule as a constitutional requirement; *County of Riverside v. McLaughlin*, n. 128 *supra*.

[185] 1 W. & M. sess. 2, c. 2.

[186] *See Stack v. Boyle*, 342 U.S. 1 (1951).

the financial circumstances of the defendant, his history, character and connection to the community where he is to appear.[187]

As there is no right to bail, *per se*, merely a right that the amount set be not excessive, it follows that in certain cases no bail may be allowed at all, if, in those circumstances, no amount of money offers sufficient security that the accused will appear for trial. More controversial is the assertion that bail may be denied, not because of doubts about the appearance of the defendant, but because of concerns that his release would create a danger for the community. Statutes of both Canada and the United States provide that such issues are properly considered in deciding whether any bail will be allowed.[188] Although earlier dicta of the Court had indicated that the propriety and amount of bail could, consistent with the presumption of innocence, only be assessed in light of the risk of non-appearance, the United States Supreme Court has held that this procedure does not violate the due process clause of the Fifth Amendment, nor the excessive bail clause of the Eighth Amendment.[189] The Supreme Court of Canada has upheld the constitutionality of provisions authorizing preventive detention for the purpose of protecting public safety. However, it held invalid as impermissibly vague provision for detention when 'in the public interest'.[190]

H. THE CHALLENGE OF TERRORISM AND THE RIGHT OF STATES TO DEROGATE FROM THE CONVENTION

Only some of the duties of states and some individual rights are phrased by the Convention in absolute terms. Thus, while the right not to be tortured is absolute, the rights to respect for private and family life and to freedom of expression (Articles 8 and 10) are subject to qualifications and limitations which are 'prescribed by law and necessary in a democratic society' for stated purposes such as national security or public safety (see Chapters 8 and 6, respectively). Other rights are expressly limited by a test of reasonableness, such as the right of a detained person (under Article 5(3)) to be tried 'within a reasonable time'—the sole right under Article 5 to be qualified in this way. What, then, is the position if a state wishes to impose extraordinary restrictions on individual liberty (for instance, preventive detention for suspected terrorists)

---

[187] *See*, e.g., *id.*; *Truong Dinh Hung v. United States*, 439 U.S. 1326 (Brennan, Circuit Justice 1978). The Supreme Court of Canada has held valid, as consistent with s. 11 of the Charter provisions that place on a detained person the burden of showing that his or her detention is unjustified if the person is charged with an indictable offence committed while on bail for another indictable offence or with having committed an offence under the Narcotics Control Act: *R. v. Pearson* [1992] 3 S.C.R. 665; *B. v. Morales* [1992] 3 S.C.R. 711.

[188] 18 U.S.C. 1342 (g) (1994) (United States); R.S.C. 1985, c. C–46, ss. 515–26.

[189] *United States v. Salerno*, 481 U.S. 739 (1987).

[190] *R v. Pearson, R v. Morales*, both n. 187 *supra*.

which go well beyond ordinary criminal process? Such restrictions are inherently likely to involve breaches of Article 5.

The answer to this question is that a state may secure relief from Article 5 (and certain other duties) by exercising the right to derogate from Convention obligations, which is authorized by Article 15. By this provision, 'in time of war or other emergency threatening the life of the nation', a state may take steps to derogate from those Convention duties which permit derogation.

The very first case to reach the Court at Strasbourg concerned a derogation by Ireland from Article 5 because of the threat from the IRA.

1. LAWLESS V. REPUBLIC OF IRELAND (NO. 3)

Judgment of 1 July 1961
1 E.H.R.R. 15

[The applicant, an Irish citizen, was detained without trial for five months in 1957 because of his active membership of the IRA. The Court held that detention without trial was a restriction of liberty which was not authorized by Article 5. However, before detaining Mr. Lawless, the Irish government had notified the Secretary-General of the Council of Europe of its intention to use special powers to deal with the threat from the IRA. Did such a derogation exclude the jurisdiction of the Strasbourg Court? In giving its answer to this question, the Court read Article 15, and continued:]

22. It follows from these provisions that, without being released from all its undertakings assumed in the Convention, the Government of any High Contracting Party has the right, in case of war or public emergency threatening the life of the nation, to take measures derogating from its obligations under the Convention other than those named in Article 15(2), provided that such measures are strictly limited to what is required by the exigencies of the situation and also that they do not conflict with other obligations under international law. It is for the Court to determine whether the conditions laid down in Article 15 for the exercise of the exceptional right of derogation have been fulfilled in the present case.

23. The Irish Government, by a Proclamation dated 5 July 1957 and published in the *Official Gazette* on 8 July 1957, brought into force the extraordinary powers conferred upon it by Part II of the Offences against the State (Amendment) Act 1940 'to secure the preservation of public peace and order'.

24. By letter dated 20 July 1957 addressed to the Secretary-General of the Council of Europe, the Irish Government expressly stated that 'the detention of persons under the Act is considered necessary to prevent the commission of offences against public peace and order and to prevent the maintaining of military or armed forces other than those authorized by the Constitution'....

28. In the general context of Article 15 of the Convention, the natural and customary meaning of the words 'other public emergency threatening the life of the nation' is sufficiently clear; they refer to an exceptional situation of crisis or emergency which affects the whole

population and constitutes a threat to the organised life of the community of which the State is composed...[The] Court must determine whether the facts and circumstances which led the Irish Government to make their Proclamation of 5 July 1957 come within this conception. The Court, after an examination, finds this to be the case; the existence at the time of a 'public emergency threatening the life of the nation' was reasonably deduced by the Irish Government from a combination of several factors, namely in the first place, the existence in the territory of the Republic of Ireland of a secret army engaged in unconstitutional activities and using violence to attain its purposes; secondly, the fact that this army was also operating outside the territory of the State, thus seriously jeopardising the relations of the Republic of Ireland with its neighbour; thirdly, the steady and alarming increase in terrorist activities from the autumn of 1956 and throughout the first half of 1957.

29. Despite the gravity of the situation, the Government had succeeded, by using means available under ordinary legislation, in keeping public institutions functioning more or less normally, but the homicidal ambush on the night of 3 to 4 July 1957 in the territory of Northern Ireland near the border had brought to light, just before 12 July—a date, which, for historical reasons, is particularly critical for the preservation of public peace and order—the imminent danger to the nation caused by the continuance of unlawful activities in Northern Ireland by the IRA and various associated groups, operating from the territory of the Republic of Ireland.

30. In conclusion, the Irish Government were justified in declaring that there was a public emergency in the Republic of Ireland threatening the life of the nation and were hence entitled, applying the provisions of Article 15 (1) of the Convention for the purposes for which those provisions were made, to take measures derogating from their obligations under the Convention.

31. Article 15(1) provides that a High Contracting Party may derogate from its obligations under the Convention only 'to the extent strictly required by the exigencies of the situation'. It is therefore necessary... to examine whether the bringing into force of Part II of the 1940 Act was a measure strictly required by the emergency existing in 1957.

32. G. R. Lawless contended before the Commission that even if the situation in 1957 was such as to justify derogation from obligations under the Convention, the bringing into operation and the enforcement of Part II of the Offences against the State (Amendment) Act 1940 were disproportionate to the strict requirements of the situation....

36. However, in the judgment of the Court, in 1957 the application of the ordinary law had proved unable to check the growing danger which threatened the Republic of Ireland. The ordinary criminal courts, or even the special criminal court or military courts, could not suffice to restore peace and order; in particular, the amassing of the necessary evidence to convict persons involved in activities of the IRA and its splinter groups was meeting with great difficulties caused by the military, secret and terrorist character of those groups and the fear they created among the population. The fact that these groups operated mainly in Northern Ireland, their activities in the Republic of Ireland being virtually limited to the preparation of armed raids across the border, was an additional impediment to the gathering of sufficient evidence. The sealing of the border would have had extremely serious repercussions on the population as a whole, beyond the extent required by the exigencies of the emergency.

It follows from the foregoing that none of the above-mentioned means would have made it possible to deal with the situation existing in Ireland in 1957. Therefore, the administrative detention...of individuals suspected of intending to take part in terrorist activities, appeared, despite its gravity, to be a measure required by the circumstances.

37. Moreover, the Offences against the State (Amendment) Act of 1940 was subject to a number of safeguards designed to prevent abuses in the operation of the system of administrative detention. The application of the Act was thus subject to constant supervision by Parliament, which not only received precise details of its enforcement at regular intervals but could also at any time, by a resolution, annul the Government's Proclamation which had brought the Act into force. The Offences against the State (Amendment) Act 1940 provided for the establishment of a Detention Commission made up of three members,...the members being an officer of the Defence Forces and two judges. Any person detained under this Act could refer his case to that Commission whose opinion, if favourable to the release of the person concerned, was binding upon the Government; moreover, the ordinary courts could themselves compel the Detention Commission to carry out its functions.

In conclusion, immediately after the Proclamation which brought the power of detention into force, the Government publicly announced that it would release any person detained who gave an undertaking to respect the Constitution and the law and not to engage in any illegal activity...The persons arrested were informed immediately after their arrest that they would be released following the undertaking in question. In a democratic country such as Ireland, the existence of this guarantee of release given publicly by the Government constituted a legal obligation on the Government to release all persons who gave the undertaking.

Therefore, it follows from the foregoing that the detention without trial provided for by the 1940 Act, subject to the above-mentioned safeguards, appears to be a measure strictly required by the exigencies of the situation within the meaning of Article 15 of the Convention....

In the case of *Ireland v. United Kingdom* (Chapter 5(A)) it was the British government's decision to introduce detention without trial which enabled the security forces to adopt the methods of interrogation in depth that gave rise to the complaints of torture and inhuman and degrading treatment. Quite apart from the practice of interrogation, the detentions themselves would necessarily have involved breaches of Article 5. As the Court held in *Ireland v. United Kingdom*:

(a) the power to detain without trial is not within the list of permitted grounds in Article 5(1);

(b) those arrested were not informed promptly of the reasons for their arrest (Article 5(2));

(c) they were not brought promptly before a court or other competent judicial authority (Article 5(3)); and

(d) their rights in national law to seek judicial review of the legality of their detention were not sufficient to satisfy Article 5(4).

However, the Court also held (citing *Lawless v. Ireland (No. 3)*, above) that the United Kingdom had derogated validly from its obligations under Article 5, and the government had stayed within the 'margin of appreciation' available to it under Article 15 when it adopted the policy of detention without trial. As the Court stated:

207. ...It falls in the first place to each Contracting State, with its responsibility for 'the life of [its] nation', to determine whether that life is threatened by a 'public emergency' and, if

so, how far it is necessary to go in attempting to overcome the emergency. By reason of their direct and continuous contact with the pressing needs of the moment, the national authorities are in principle in a better position than the international judge to decide both on the presence of such an emergency and on the nature and scope of derogations necessary to avert it. In this matter, Article 15(1) leaves those authorities a wide margin of appreciation.

Nevertheless, the States do not enjoy an unlimited power in this respect. The Court, which, with the Commission, is responsible for ensuring the observance of the States' engagements...is empowered to rule on whether the States have gone beyond the 'extent strictly required by the exigencies' of the crisis. The domestic margin of appreciation is thus accompanied by a European supervision.

2. THE SEQUEL TO BROGAN V. UNITED KINGDOM

The derogation under Article 15 which was considered in *Ireland v. United Kingdom* was withdrawn by the British government in August 1984, several years after the government had given up the policy of detaining suspected terrorists without trial (although the legislation permitting detention without trial was not repealed). No derogation under Article 15 was in force at the time of the arrests which gave rise to *Brogan v. United Kingdom*.[191] As we have seen, the Court in *Brogan* held that the legislation authorizing detention by authority of the Secretary of State for up to seven days was incompatible with the rights guaranteed by Article 5. In response to the Court's decision, the United Kingdom legislation could have been amended, either by reducing the period of detention for questioning or by requiring a detainee to be brought promptly before a judge or other officer exercising judicial power. In fact, the government insisted that the ability to hold suspects for up to seven days was necessary in the fight against terrorism and that it was not possible to introduce 'a satisfactory procedure for the review of detention of terrorist suspects involving the judiciary'.[192] Being unwilling to change the law, the government lodged a derogation under Article 15 so that it might continue to detain suspects for up to seven days without any judicial authority being obtained. Was this derogation a proper use of Article 15?

3. BRANNIGAN V. UNITED KINGDOM

Judgment of 26 May 1993
17 E.H.R.R. 594

[On facts very similar to those in *Brogan v. United Kingdom* above, the two applicants had been held for questioning for periods of six days 14 hours and four days six hours respectively.

---

[191] 24 Nov. 1988, 11 E.H.R.R. 117; Section F(2)(a) *supra*.
[192] Hansard, HC Deb, 14 Nov. 1989, col. 209, WA.

The main issue for decision was whether the United Kingdom's derogation complied with Article 15. Having held that a public emergency in the United Kingdom existed which threatened the life of the nation, the Court considered whether the measures taken were strictly required by the exigencies of the situation.]

49. For the applicants, the purported derogation was not a necessary response to any new or altered state of affairs but was the Government's reaction to the decision in *Brogan and Others* and was lodged merely to circumvent the consequences of this judgment.

50. The Government and the Commission maintained that, while it was true that this judgment triggered off the derogation, the exigencies of the situation have at all times since 1974 required the powers of extended detention conferred by the Prevention of Terrorism legislation. It was the view of successive governments that these powers were consistent with Article 5(3) and that no derogation was necessary. However, both the measures and the derogation were direct responses to the emergency with which the United Kingdom was and continues to be confronted.

51. The Court first observes that the power of arrest and extended detention has been considered necessary by the Government since 1974 in dealing with the threat of terrorism. Following the *Brogan and Others* judgment the Government were then faced with the option of either introducing judicial control of the decision to detain under section 12 of the 1984 Act or lodging a derogation from their Convention obligations in this respect. The adoption of the view by the Government that judicial control compatible with Article 5(3) was not feasible because of the special difficulties associated with the investigation and prosecution of terrorist crime rendered derogation inevitable. Accordingly, the power of extended detention without such judicial control and the derogation of 23 December 1988 being clearly linked to the persistence of the emergency situation, there is no indication that the derogation was other than a genuine response.

52. The applicants maintained that derogation was an interim measure which Article 15 did not provide for since it appeared from the notice of derogation communicated to the Secretary General of the Council of Europe on 23 December 1988 that the Government had not reached a 'firm or final view' on the need to derogate from Article 5(3) and required a further period of reflection and consultation. Following this period the Secretary of State for the Home Department confirmed the derogation in a statement to Parliament on 14 November 1989. Prior to this concluded view Article 15 did not permit derogation. Furthermore, even at this date the Government had not properly examined whether the obligation in Article 5(3) could be satisfied by an 'officer authorised by law to exercise judicial power.'

53. The Government contended that the validity of the derogation was not affected by its examination of the possibility of judicial control of extended detention since, as the Commission had pointed out, it was consistent with the requirements of Article 15(3) to keep derogation measures under constant review.

54. The Court does not accept the applicants' argument that the derogation was premature.

While it is true that Article 15 does not envisage an interim suspension of Convention guarantees pending consideration of the necessity to derogate, it is clear from the notice of derogation that 'against the background of the terrorist campaign, and the over-riding need to bring terrorists to justice, the Government did not believe that the maximum period of detention should be reduced.' However it remained the Government's wish 'to find a judicial process under which extended detention might be reviewed and, where appropriate, authorized by a judge or other judicial officer.'

The validity of the derogation cannot be called into question for the sole reason that the Government had decided to examine whether in the future a way could be found of ensuring greater conformity with Convention obligations. Indeed, such a process of continued reflection is not only in keeping with Article 15(3) which requires permanent review of the need for emergency measures but is also implicit in the very notion of proportionality.

55. The applicants further considered that there was no basis for the Government's assertion that control of extended detention by a judge or other officer authorised by law to exercise judicial power was not possible or that a period of seven days' detention was necessary. They did not accept that the material required to satisfy a court of the justification for extended detention could be more sensitive than that needed in proceedings for habeas corpus. They and the Standing Advisory Commission on Human Rights also pointed out that the courts in Northern Ireland were frequently called on to deal with submissions based on confidential information—for example, in bail applications—and that there were sufficient procedural and evidential safeguards to protect confidentiality. Procedures also existed where judges were required to act on the basis of material which would not be disclosed either to the legal adviser or to his client. This was the case, for example, with claims by the executive to public interest immunity or application by the police to extend detention under the Police and Criminal Evidence (Northern Ireland) Order 1989.

56. On this point the Government responded that none of the above procedures involved both the non-disclosure of material to the detainee or his legal adviser and an executive act of the court....

It was also emphasised that the Government had reluctantly concluded that, within the framework of the common-law system, it was not feasible to introduce a system which would be compatible with Article 5(3) but would not weaken the effectiveness of the response to the terrorist threat. Decisions to prolong detention were taken on the basis of information the nature and source of which could not be revealed to a suspect or his legal adviser without risk to individuals assisting the police or the prospect of further valuable intelligence being lost. Moreover, involving the judiciary in the process of granting or approving extensions of detention created a real risk of undermining their independence as they would inevitably be seen as part of the investigation and prosecution process.

In addition, the Government did not accept that the comparison with habeas corpus was a valid one since judicial involvement in the grant or approval of extension would require the disclosure of a considerable amount of additional sensitive information which it would not be necessary to produce in habeas corpus proceedings. In particular, a court would have to be provided with details of the nature and extent of police inquiries following the arrest, including details of witnesses interviewed and information obtained from other sources as well as information about the future course of the police investigation....

58. The Court notes the opinions expressed in the various Reports reviewing the operation of the Prevention of Terrorism legislation that the difficulties of investigating and prosecuting terrorist crime give rise to the need for an extended period of detention which would not be subject to judicial control. Moreover, these special difficulties were recognized in its above mentioned *Brogan and Others* judgment.[193]

---

[193] *Supra* n. 191.

It further observes that it remains the view of the respondent Government that it is essential to prevent the disclosure to the detainee and his legal adviser of information on the basis of which decisions on the extension of detention are made and that, in the adversarial system of the common law, the independence of the judiciary would be compromised if judges or other judicial officers were to be involved in the granting or approval of extensions.

The Court also notes that the introduction of a 'judge or other officer authorized by law to exercise judicial power' into the process of extension of periods of detention would not of itself necessarily bring about a situation of compliance with Article 5(3). That provision—like Article 5(4)—must be understood to require the necessity of following a procedure that has a judicial character although that procedure need not necessarily be identical in each of the cases where the intervention of a judge is required.

59. It is not the Court's role to substitute its view as to what measures were most appropriate or expedient at the relevant time in dealing with an emergency situation for that of the Government which has direct responsibility for establishing the balance between the taking of effective measures to combat terrorism on the one hand, and respecting individual rights on the other. In the context of Northern Ireland, where the judiciary is small and vulnerable to terrorist attacks, public confidence in the independence of the judiciary is understandably a matter to which the Government attaches great importance.

60. In the light of these considerations it cannot be said that the Government has exceeded their margin of appreciation in deciding, in the prevailing circumstances, against judicial control.

[The Court then rejected arguments for the applicants which sought to show that there were inadequate safeguards against abuse of the power to detain for questioning and that the government was in breach of its obligations under Article 4 of the International Covenant on Civil and Political Rights. The Court concluded that the derogation lodged by the United Kingdom satisfied the requirements of Article 15, and the complaints of breaches of Article 5(3) were rejected. This decision was reached by a majority of 22 to four. In the course of his dissenting judgment, Judge Walsh said:]

6. One of the suggested remedies for arrested persons in the present case is the ancient writ of habeas corpus. This remedy can only be obtained if there is a proven breach of the national law. A breach of the Convention cannot ground such relief unless it is also a breach of the national law. It is unfortunate that the Court has been allowed to believe otherwise... Yet in the present case the Government suggest that in habeas corpus proceedings the genuineness of the 'reasonable belief' may be tested (though I doubt if the secret sources would be required to be disclosed in any court) although that remedy, which fits into Article 5(4) of the Convention, has not been sought to be excluded by the terms of the derogation. A habeas corpus writ can, in theory, be sought within an hour or so after an arrest; in other words well within the period encompassed in the expression 'promptly' in Article 5(3). That procedure, if it is possible to avail of it, could thus impart the disadvantage to the police secrecy which the respondent Government claims it is entitled to avoid; yet the Government has not sought to explain this inconsistency.

7. It appears to me to be an inescapable inference that the Government does not wish any such arrested person to be brought before a judge at any time unless and until they are in a position to and desire to prefer a charge. The real target might appear to be Article 5(1)(c). The admitted purpose of the arrest is to interrogate the arrested person in the hope or expectation

that he will incriminate himself. Article 5 makes it quite clear that no arrest can be justified under the Convention if the sole justification for it is the desire to interrogate the arrested person. If an arresting officer has a 'reasonable belief' that is coupled to the knowledge or intention that the grounds will never be revealed to a judge, and that the arrested person must be released if no revealable evidence is forthcoming, such arrest ought not to be regarded as an arrest in good faith for the purposes of Article 5(1)(c) of the Convention.

9. Article 5(3) of the Convention is an essential safeguard against arbitrary executive arrest or detention, failure to observe which could easily give rise to complaints under Article 3 of the Convention which cannot be the subject of derogation. Prolonged and sustained interrogation over periods of days, particularly without a judicial intervention, could well fall into the category of inhuman or degrading treatment in particular cases. In the present case, the applicant Brannigan, during 158 hours of detention, was interrogated forty-three times which means he was interrogated on average every two-and-a-half hours over that period, assuming he was allowed the regulation period of eight hours free from interrogation every 24 hours. The applicant McBride on the same basis was interrogated on average every three hours over his period of detention of 96 hours. The object of these interrogations was to gain 'sufficient admissions' to sustain a charge, or charges.

10. The Government's plea that it is motivated by a wish to preserve public confidence in the independence of the judiciary is, in effect, to say that such confidence is to be maintained or achieved by not permitting them to have a role in the protection of the personal liberty of the arrested persons. One would think that such a role was one which the public would expect the judges to have. It is also to be noted that neither Parliament nor the Government appears to have made any serious effort to rearrange the judicial procedure or jurisdiction, in spite of being advised to do so by the persons appointed to review the system, to cater for the requirement of Article 5(3) in cases of the type now under review. It is the function of national authorities so to arrange their affairs as not to clash with the requirements of the Convention. The Convention is not to be remoulded to assume the shape of national procedures.

[Another of the dissenting judges was Judge Makarczyk, who had newly joined the Court:]

I regret that I am unable to share the position of the majority of the Court in the present case. This is for three main reasons: the general consequences of the judgment; the question of a time-limit for the derogation and the reasons for the derogation as put forward by the respondent Government.

1. The principle that a judgment of the Court deals with a specific case and solves a particular problem does not, in my opinion, apply to cases concerning the validity of a derogation made by a State under Article 15 of the Convention. A derogation made by any State affects not only the position of that State, but also the integrity of the Convention system of protection as a whole. It is relevant for other Member States—old and new—and even for States aspiring to become Parties which are in the process of adapting their legal systems to the standards of the Convention. For the new Contracting Parties, the fact of being admitted, often after long periods of preparation and negotiation, means not only the acceptance of Convention obligations, but also recognition by the community of European States of their equal standing as regards the democratic system and the rule of law. In other words, what is considered by the old democracies as a natural state of affairs, is seen as a privilege by the newcomers which is not to be disposed of lightly. A derogation made by a new Contracting Party from Eastern

and Central Europe would call into question this new legitimacy and is, in my opinion, quite improbable. Any decision of the Court concerning Article 15 should encourage and confirm this philosophy. In any event it should not reinforce the views of those in the new Member States for whom European standards clash with interests which they have inherited from the past. I am not convinced that the reasoning adopted by the majority fulfils these requirements. This is especially so as the derogation concerns a provision of the Convention which, for some, should not be the subject of any derogation at all.

2. I fully recognise the difficulties, and even the impossibility, for the Court in setting a precise time-limit for the derogation as a precondition of its validity under Article 15. However, I believe that the judgment should very clearly and unequivocally indicate that the Court accepts the derogation only as a strictly temporary measure. After all, it recognizes the non-observance of Article 5(3) of the Convention, a basic provision of which the applicants cannot avail themselves because of the derogation. The Court also considers the time factor as essential when speaking of its supervisory role in respect of the margin of appreciation. It is true that the Court emphasises the obligation of the derogating State to review the situation on a regular basis. But this obligation clearly results from the third paragraph of Article 15 and the emphasis does not contribute to reassure the international community that the Court is doing all that is legally possible for the full applicability of the Convention to be restored as soon as practicable. On the contrary, the present wording of the judgment tends rather to perpetuate the status quo and opens, for the derogating State, an unlimited possibility of applying extended administrative detention for an uncertain period of time, to the detriment of the integrity of the Convention system and, I firmly believe, of the derogating State itself.

3. This leads me to the third reason for my dissent which I consider to be of vital importance.

The main point that, in my opinion, the United Kingdom Government should attempt to prove before the Court is that extended administrative detention does in fact contribute to eliminate the reasons for which the extraordinary measures needed to be introduced—in other words the prevention and combatting of terrorism. But, as far as I can see, no such attempt has been made either in the Government's Memorial and the attached documents, or in the pleading before the Court. Instead, the Government's main arguments have centred on the alleged detrimental effects on the judiciary, of control by a judge of extended detention without the normal judicial procedure.

I will not enlarge on this last argument, which has been skilfully called into question by dissenters both in the Commission and in the Court. I can only add that any form of judicial control could be beneficial for all concerned. If the Government had been able to provide valid arguments that extended detention without any form of judicial control does in fact contribute both to the punishment and prevention of the crime of terrorism, I would be ready to accept the legality of the derogation, notwithstanding the first two reasons of my dissent....

The main question raised by *Brannigan* is whether the majority's decision to approve the derogation from Article 5(3) goes too far in permitting a state to cut back on its duties under Article 5. For example, should the Court have scrutinized more rigorously the government's claim that the measures derogated from its obligations 'to the extent strictly required by the exigencies of the situation'? There is a potential danger that a state found to have committed breaches of the Convention (apart from obligations from which no derogation is permitted) may decide that the least onerous course of compliance is to lodge a specific derogation with the Council of Europe, of the kind approved in *Brannigan*. For instance, does the approach of the Court in *Brannigan* permit a state to suspend the the judicial protection of liberty under Article 5(4)?[194] The Court was reluctant to give a positive answer to this question in a case arising from unrest and conflict in areas of Turkey.

4. AKSOY V. TURKEY

Judgment of 18 December 1996
23 E.H.R.R. 553

[The applicant had lived in south east Turkey, most of which had been subject to emergency rule since 1987. On a date that he claimed to be 24 November 1992, he was arrested and detained on suspicion of terrorist activities. He was subjected to brutality and torture before being released on 10 December 1992, requiring hospital treatment. He was at a later date shot dead after having been threatened because of his complaint to Strasbourg. The majority of the Court (the Turkish judge dissenting) rejected preliminary objections raised by the Turkish government and held that Aksoy's rights under Article 3 had been violated. In relation to Article 5(3), he had been held for 14 or more days without being brought before a judge. The government relied on the fact that Turkey had on 5 May 1992 derogated from its obligations under Article 5. The Court referred to earlier decisions on Article 15, found that terrorist activity in south east Turkey had created a 'public emergency threatening the life of the nation' and considered whether the government's measures were 'strictly required by the exigencies of the situation'.]

(a) The length of the unsupervised detention

71. The Government asserted that the applicant had been arrested on 26 November 1992 along with 13 others on suspicion of aiding and abetting PKK terrorists... He was held in custody for 14 days, in accordance with Turkish law, which allows a person detained in connection with a collective offence to be held for up to 30 days in the state of emergency region.

72. They explained that the place in which the applicant was arrested and detained fell within the area covered by the Turkish derogation. ... The investigation of terrorist offences presented the authorities with special problems,... because the members of terrorist organizations were expert in withstanding interrogation, had secret support networks and access to substantial resources. A great deal of time and effort was required to secure and verify evidence in a large region confronted with a terrorist organisation that had strategic and technical support from neighbouring countries. These difficulties meant that it was impossible to provide judicial supervision during a suspect's detention in police custody....

74. While [the applicant] did not present detailed arguments against the validity of the Turkish derogation as a whole, he questioned whether the situation in South East Turkey

---

[194] For extended criticism of *Brannigan*, *see* S. Marks, 'Civil Liberties at the Margin: the United Kingdom Derogation and the ECHR', 15 *OJLS* 69 (1995).

necessitated the holding of suspects for 14 days or more without judicial supervision. He submitted that judges in South East Turkey would not be put at risk if they were permitted and required to review the legality of detention at shorter intervals....

[Stressing the importance of Article 5 in the Convention system, the Court continued:].

76. Judicial control of interferences by the executive with the individual's right to liberty is an essential feature of the guarantee embodied in Article 5(3)... Furthermore, prompt judicial intervention may lead to the detection and prevention of serious ill-treatment, which... is prohibited by the Convention in absolute and non-derogable terms.

77. In the *Brannigan and McBride* judgment, the Court held that the United Kingdom Government had not exceeded their margin of appreciation by derogating from their obligations under Article 5 of the Convention to the extent that individuals suspected of terrorist offences were allowed to be held for up to seven days without judicial control.

In the instant case, the applicant was detained for at least 14 days without being brought before a judge or other officer. The Government have sought to justify this measure by reference to the particular demands of police investigations in a geographically vast area faced with a terrorist organization receiving outside support.

78. Although the Court is of the view... that the investigation of terrorist offences undoubtedly presents the authorities with special problems, it cannot accept that it is necessary to hold a suspect for 14 days without judicial intervention. This period is exceptionally long, and left the applicant vulnerable not only to arbitrary interference with his right to liberty but also to torture. Moreover, the Government have not adduced any detailed reasons before the Court as to why the fight against terrorism in South East Turkey rendered judicial intervention impracticable.

(b) Safeguards

79. The Government emphasized that both the derogation and the national legal system provided sufficient safeguards to protect human rights. Thus, the derogation itself was limited to the strict minimum required for the fight against terrorism; the permissible length of detention was prescribed by law and the consent of a Public Prosecutor was necessary if the police wished to remand a suspect in custody beyond these periods. Torture was prohibited by Article 243 of the Criminal Code....

80. The applicant pointed out that long periods of unsupervised detention, together with the lack of safeguards provided for the protection of prisoners, facilitated the practice of torture. Thus, he was tortured with particular intensity on his third and fourth days in detention, and was held thereafter to allow his injuries to heal; throughout this time he was denied access to either a lawyer or a doctor. Moreover, he was kept blindfolded during interrogation, which meant that he could not identify those who mistreated him. The reports of Amnesty International, the European Committee for the Prevention of Torture and the United Nations Committee against Torture, showed that the safeguards contained in the Turkish Criminal Code, which were in any case inadequate, were routinely ignored in the state of emergency region....

82. In its... *Brannigan and McBride* judgment,[195] the Court was satisfied that there were effective safeguards in operation in Northern Ireland which provided an important measure of protection against arbitrary behaviour and incommunicado detention. For example, the

---

[195] *See* Section H(3) *supra*.

remedy of habeas corpus was available to test the lawfulness of the original arrest and detention, there was an absolute and legally enforceable right to consult a solicitor 48 hours after the time of arrest and detainees were entitled to inform a relative or friend about their detention and to have access to a doctor.

83. In contrast, however, the Court considers that in this case insufficient safeguards were available to the applicant, who was detained over a long period of time. In particular, the denial of access to a lawyer, doctor, relative or friend and the absence of any realistic possibility of being brought before a court to test the legality of the detention meant that he was left completely at the mercy of those holding him.

84. The Court has taken account of the unquestionably serious problem of terrorism in South East Turkey and the difficulties faced by the State in taking effective measures against it. However, it is not persuaded that the exigencies of the situation necessitated the holding of the applicant on suspicion of involvement in terrorist offences for 14 days or more in incommunicado detention without access to a judge or other judicial officer....

87. In conclusion, the Court finds that there has been a violation of Article 5(3) of the Convention.

In view of the above decision, the Court did not find it necessary to decide whether the Turkish derogation met the formal requirements of Article 15(3). In *Sakik v. Turkey*,[196] where the applicants were detained in the capital, Ankara, the government relied on the same derogation. However, the area of the emergency referred to in the derogation did not include Ankara. Rejecting the argument that the terrorist threat in south-east Turkey extended to the whole of Turkey, the Court noted that Article 15 authorizes derogations 'only to the extent strictly required by the exigencies of the situation':

> In the present case the Court would be working against the object and purpose of that
> provision if, when assessing the territorial scope of the derogation concerned, it were to
> extend its effects to a part of Turkish territory not explicitly named in the instrument of
> derogation. It follows that the derogation in question is inapplicable *ratione loci* to the facts
> of the case [paragraph 39, 26 E.H.R.R. 662].

In *Demir v. Turkey*,[197] the Turkish government attempted again to rely on the derogation, and sought to distinguish the circumstances in *Aksoy*'s case; it argued that a criminal investigation into allegedly subversive activities was protracted for the reason that it involved 35 persons accused of belonging to an illegal organization (the PKK), that there were adequate safeguards in place to guard against the risks of torture, and that some of the suspects were eventually convicted. These arguments failed, the Court observing that the fact that an investigation had not been completed did not justify departing from Article 5(3), which was 'intended to apply precisely while inquiries or investigations are in progress'.[198] In *Elci v. Turkey*,[199] breaches of

---

[196] 26 Nov. 1997, 26 E.H.R.R. 662.
[197] 23 September 1998.
[198] *Id.*, para. 52.
[199] 13 November 2003. *See also Nuray Sen v. Turkey*, 17 June 2003.

Article 5 were committed when 16 lawyers who had acted for persons associated with PKK were detained and subjected to various abuses while in detention. On the evidence, there was no written authorization for the detentions: the Court held that, even if the derogation from Article 5 and the associated legislative decrees could be considered relevant, the Government had 'not shown how the applicants' detention without adequate authorisation could have been strictly required by the exigencies of the situation envisaged by Article 15(1)'. From these cases, it is evident that even if derogation from Article 5 may be justified, this does not prevent the Court from scrutinizing closely acts taken in reliance on the derogation.

As we have seen above, in *Brannigan* the United Kingdom's derogation from Article 5 was upheld by the Court. When further authority was needed in Britain for the power to hold suspects for up to seven days for questioning, the Terrorism Act 2000 removed the inconsistency with Article 5 by providing that detention beyond the first 36 hours must be authorized by a judge; the existing derogation was accordingly withdrawn. However, in the immediate aftermath of 9/11, the law was once more changed by the Anti-terrorism, Crime and Security Act 2001, Part 4, which empowered the Secretary of State to detain foreign citizens indefinitely who were suspected of being associated with international terrorism, but who could not be deported because they would be at risk of torture if sent to their own countries.[200] Since the unlimited power to detain did not comply with Article 5(1)(f), the UK Government notified Strasbourg of a fresh derogation, this time from Article 5(1)(f). In *A v. Secretary of State for the Home Department*,[201] the British judges, applying the Strasbourg case-law, upheld by 8–1 the Secretary of State's decision that there was a 'public emergency threatening the life of the nation' but held that indefinite detention for foreign citizens was not strictly required within the meaning of Article 15 and was also discriminatory in breach of Article 14. The Prevention of Terrorism Act 2005 was passed thereafter in an attempt to give the control over suspected terrorists that the government hoped could be achieved without a derogation from Article 5.[202]

5. HABEAS CORPUS IN EMERGENCY SITUATIONS

Advisory Opinion OC-8/87, Inter-American Court of Human Rights
11 E.H.R.R. 33

[The American Convention on Human Rights provides in Article 27(1) (Suspension of Guarantees) that in time of war, public danger or other emergency threatening a state's independence or security, the state may take measures derogating from its Convention obligations to the extent strictly required by the exigencies of the situation. By Article 27(2),

---

[200] See Section E(4)(c) *supra*.
[201] [2004] U.K.H.L. 56, [2005] 2 A.C. 68.
[202] See *Secretary of State for the Home Department v. JJ* [2006] E.W.C.A. Civ. 1141, [2006] 3 W.L.R. 866; and Section B(3) *supra*.

such derogation may not authorize suspension of eleven specified articles (including the right to life, the right to humane treatment, and freedom from slavery) nor of 'the judicial guarantees essential for the protection of such rights'. The Inter-American Commission of Human Rights requested an advisory opinion from the Inter-American Court on whether the writ of habeas corpus is one of the 'judicial guarantees' which cannot be suspended in times of national emergency. The Commission stated this reason for its request:

Some States Parties to the American Convention on Human Rights have assumed that one of the rights that may be suspended in emergency situations is the right to judicial protection afforded by the writ of habeas corpus. Some States have even promulgated special laws or have instituted a practice enabling them to hold a detainee *incommunicado* for a prolonged period of time, in some cases for as long as 15 days. During that time, the detainee may be refused all contact with the outside world, thus preventing resort to the writ of habeas corpus.

[The Court's advisory opinion concluded unanimously that judicial remedies such as habeas corpus, which are essential for the protection of rights and freedoms which under the American Convention are non-derogable, may not be suspended even in time of emergency.]

20. It cannot be denied that under certain circumstances the suspension of guarantees may be the only way to deal with emergency situations and, thereby, to preserve the highest values of a democratic society. The Court cannot, however, ignore the fact that abuses may result from the application of emergency measures not objectively justified in the light of the requirements prescribed in Article 27....

21. It is clear that no right guaranteed in the Convention may be suspended unless very strict conditions—those laid down in Article 27(1)—are met. Moreover, even when these conditions are satisfied, Article 27(2) provides that certain categories of rights may not be suspended under any circumstances. Hence, rather than adopting a philosophy that favours the suspension of rights, the Convention establishes the contrary principle, namely, that all rights are to be guaranteed and enforced unless very special circumstances justify the suspension of some, and that some rights may never be suspended, however serious the emergency....

24. The suspension of guarantees also constitutes an emergency situation in which it is lawful for a government to subject rights and freedoms to certain restrictive measures that, under normal circumstances, would be prohibited or more strictly controlled. This does not mean, however, that the suspension of guarantees implies a temporary suspension of the rule of law, nor does it authorize those in power to act in disregard of the principle of legality by which they are bound at all times. When guarantees are suspended, some legal restraints applicable to the acts of public authorities may differ from those in effect under normal conditions. These restraints may not be considered to be non-existent, however, nor can the government be deemed thereby to have acquired absolute powers that go beyond the circumstances justifying the grant of such exceptional legal measures....

27. As the Court has already noted, in serious emergency situations it is lawful temporarily to suspend certain rights and freedoms whose free exercise must, under normal circumstances, be respected and guaranteed by the State. However, since not all of these rights and freedoms may be suspended even temporarily, it is imperative that 'the judicial guarantees essential for (their) protection' remain in force. Article 27(2) does not link these judicial guarantees to any specific provision of the Convention, which indicates that what is important is that

these judicial remedies have the character of being essential to ensure the protection of those rights....

30. The guarantees must be not only essential but also judicial. The expression 'judicial' can only refer to those judicial remedies that are truly capable of protecting these rights. Implicit in this conception is the active involvement of an independent and impartial judicial body having the power to pass on the lawfulness of measures adopted in a state of emergency....

35. In order for habeas corpus to achieve its purpose, which is to obtain a judicial determination of the lawfulness of a detention, it is necessary that the detained person be brought before a competent judge or tribunal with jurisdiction over him. Here habeas corpus performs a vital role in ensuring that a person's life and physical integrity are respected, in preventing his disappearance or the keeping of his whereabouts secret and in protecting him against torture or other cruel, inhumane, or degrading punishment or treatment.

36. This conclusion is buttressed by the realities that have been the experience of some of the peoples of this hemisphere in recent decades, particularly disappearances, torture and murder committed or tolerated by some governments. This experience has demonstrated over and over again that the right to life and to humane treatment are threatened whenever the right to habeas corpus is partially or wholly suspended....

38. If...the suspension of guarantees may not exceed the limits of that strictly required to deal with the emergency, any action on the part of the public authorities that goes beyond those limits, which must be specified with precision in the decree promulgating the state of emergency, would also be unlawful notwithstanding the existence of the emergency situation.

39. The Court should also point out that since it is improper to suspend guarantees without complying with the conditions referred to in the preceding paragraph, it follows that the specific measures applicable to the rights or freedoms that have been suspended may also not violate these general principles. Such violation would occur, for example, if the measures taken infringed the legal régime of the state emergency, if they lasted longer than the time limit specified, if they were manifestly irrational, unnecessary or disproportionate, or if, in adopting them, there was a misuse or abuse of power.

40. If this is so, it follows that in a system governed by the rule of law it is entirely in order for an autonomous and independent judicial order to exercise control over the lawfulness of such measures by verifying, for example, whether a detention based on the suspension of personal freedom complies with the legislation authorized by the state of emergency. In this context, habeas corpus acquires a new dimension of fundamental importance....

The European and American Conventions on Human Rights are not identical in the provision which they make for derogation. Nonetheless, one conclusion which may be drawn from this Opinion of the American Court is that no European state should be permitted to derogate from its duties under Article 5(4) of the European Convention, even though this is not expressly excluded by Article 15(2).

13

THE RIGHT TO A FAIR AND PUBLIC HEARING

ARTICLE 6

1. In the determination of his civil rights and obligations or of any criminal charge against him, everyone is entitled to a fair and public hearing within a reasonable time by an independent and impartial tribunal established by law. Judgment shall be pronounced publicly but the press and public may be excluded from all or part of the trial in the interest of morals, public order or national security in a democratic society, where the interests of juveniles or the protection of the private life of the parties so require, or to the extent strictly necessary in the opinion of the court in special circumstances where publicity would prejudice the interests of justice.

2. Everyone charged with a criminal offence shall be presumed innocent until proved guilty according to law.

3. Everyone charged with a criminal offence has the following minimum rights:

   (a) to be informed promptly, in a language which he understands and in detail, of the nature and cause of the accusation against him;

   (b) to have adequate time and facilities for the preparation of his defence;

   (c) to defend himself in person or through legal assistance of his own choosing or, if he has not sufficient means to pay for legal assistance, to be given it free when the interests of justice so require;

   (d) to examine or have examined witnesses against him and to obtain the attendance and examination of witnesses on his behalf under the same conditions as witnesses against him;

   (e) to have the free assistance of an interpreter if he cannot understand or speak the language used in court.

A. INTRODUCTION

Article 6 of the Convention deals with the rights of people subjected to or threatened with conviction of a crime, some other deprivation of liberty, and in one significant reference, to a modification of their 'civil rights and obligations'. Predominantly, it concerns the manner in which these actions are carried out and the fairness of the procedures accompanying them.

The idea that the abuse of government power may effectively be limited by channelling its exercise through procedures that are regular, impartial and that give affected persons a chance to be heard, is an ancient insight of the law. The Magna Carta in 1215 compelled the King to pledge that '[t]o no one we will sell, to no one will we deny or delay right or justice'; and that '[no] free man shall be taken or imprisoned or disseised … or outlawed or exiled or in any wise destroyed, nor will we go upon him, nor will we send upon him, unless by the lawful judgment of his peers, or by the law of the land'. The common law has developed the concept of fair procedure in the doctrine of 'natural justice' under which courts and other official bodies may act only after notice to the affected parties and after an opportunity for them to respond, and only when the judges themselves are free of any extraneous bias.[1]

Almost everywhere where 'written' constitutions govern, fair procedure has been constitutionalized.[2] In the United States Constitution, governments are barred by the Fifth and Fourteenth Amendments from depriving 'any person of life, liberty or property without due process of law', a requirement which has, first and foremost, been held to involve a fair and impartial procedure.[3] Beyond this general guarantee, the United States Constitution sets out certain specific procedural rights especially for those charged with criminal offences. Similarly, the Canadian Charter of Rights and Freedoms, in Section 7, secures the 'right to life, liberty, and security of the person and the right not to be deprived thereof except in accordance with the principles of fundamental justice'. At the time of enactment the phrase 'fundamental justice' was understood to be a synonym for the common law idea of 'natural justice', which, as noted, is a procedural concept.[4] And, like the United States Constitution, it crystallized this general requirement into certain specific procedural rules applicable to criminal defendants.[5]

The European Convention follows a directly comparable model. In Article 6(1) it mandates that everyone facing criminal conviction or a determination of civil rights is entitled to a 'fair and public hearing within a reasonable time by an independent and impartial tribunal established by law'. Then, in Article 6(2) and 6(3), it particularizes certain aspects of that right for those charged with a criminal offence.

Procedural rights, those provided in Article 6 and those in Article 5, surveyed in the last chapter, have been the rights most commonly invoked before the European Court of Human Rights. Given the volume of jurisprudence, all that can be done here

---

[1] *Dr. Bentley's Case*, 1 Stra. 557 (1723); *Dr. Bonham's Case*, Co. Rep. 1135 (1610); *see* A. W. Bradley and K. D. Ewing, *Constitutional and Administrative Law* 743–53 (14th edn. 2007).

[2] H. van Marrseveen & G. von der Tang, *Written Constitutions: A Computerized Comparative Study* 105–6 (1978).

[3] *See Hurtado v. California*, 110 U.S. 516 (1884); *Joint Anti-Fascist Refugee Committee v. McGrath*, 341 U.S. 123 (1951).

[4] *See* P. Hogg, *Constitutional Law of Canada* 1060–1 (student edn. 2006).

[5] Canadian Charter of Rights and Freedoms, Canada Act, 1982, Sections 8–14.

is to deal with a selection of leading issues that have arisen under Article 6. These materials will focus on three matters that are central to the matrix of issues involved in Article 6 claims. The first is the definition of the situations affecting individuals that trigger the procedural guarantees. The second concerns the essential characteristics of a 'fair hearing' in an 'impartial tribunal'. Finally, we will examine the requirement that adversaries in a judicial procedure should be on an equal footing insofar as they are allowed to present their cases.

It is useful in examining Article 6 to keep in mind the extent to which its requirements may overlap with those of Article 5. There may be occasions on which both Articles will have to be satisfied. Article 5 governs the circumstances and procedures which must be associated with a deprivation of personal liberty. Article 6 concerns the procedures which are required in civil and criminal adjudications. For example, Article 6(3) specifies the particular rights of individuals accused of crimes in the preparation and presentation of their defence. To the extent that conviction might lead to a deprivation of liberty, these may also be seen as safeguards against that eventuality. Similarly Article 5(2)–(4), dealing with rights of arrested persons, might be seen as procedural guarantees associated with the criminal adjudicatory process. Articles 5(3) and 6(1) both deal with the promptness with which an adjudication must proceed against criminal defendants.[6]

B. CRIMINAL CHARGES AND CIVIL RIGHTS

In this section, we consider the main situations in which a right to protection under Article 6(1) may arise. As Article 6(1) states, the right to 'a fair and public hearing within a reasonable time by an independent and impartial tribunal established by law' arises both 'in the determination of his civil rights and obligations' and 'in the determination of any criminal charge'. Article 6 does not amplify this guarantee of due process in respect of 'civil rights and obligations', but paragraphs (2) and (3) specify additional rights that apply when someone faces a criminal charge, including the all-important presumption of innocence.

It will be obvious that the guarantee of due process given by Article 6(1) is breached if a judge hearing a criminal or civil case is corrupt, shows favouritism to one party to litigation, is directed by the government what decision to make, or refuses one party a hearing. When such abuses occur, the individuals affected must endeavour to seek redress in their own country. Unless such redress is available, the integrity of the system of justice in that country is brought into question. Article 6 enables the Strasbourg Court to decide in particular cases whether a legal system has met the minimum standards of justice vital to the existence of the rule of law. In fact, the prolific case-law on Article 6 demonstrates that failures of justice may occur in many

---

[6] These provisions are discussed in Section D *infra*. *See also* Chapter 12(F) *supra*.

ways. Later sections address implications of the guarantees afforded by Article 6. Here, emphasis is placed on identifying the situations in which the guarantees apply. They include forms of decision-making that in many countries fall outside the mainstream business of civil and criminal courts. While the primary thrust of Article 6 is to ensure that the ordinary courts observe due process in deciding the cases that come to them, we will have to consider whether Article 6 is also concerned with extending the use of judicial procedures into areas which are not necessarily entrusted to the courts.

Among the questions to be addressed are:

(a) How are criminal charges identified, and how is criminal jurisdiction distinguished from matters of 'civil right and obligation'?

(b) Are disciplinary proceedings (for instance in the armed forces, in prisons and the professions) subject to Article 6(1)?

(c) Does the concept of 'civil rights and obligations' extend to administrative and executive decision-making?

(d) To what extent does Article 6(1) protect access to justice?

1. ÖZTÜRK V. GERMANY

Judgment of 21 February 1984
6 E.H.R.R. 409

[The applicant, a Turkish citizen resident in Germany since 1964 and a worker in the car industry, was in 1978 involved in a road accident. When the police came to the scene, they gave him a notice in Turkish informing him of his rights; details of the accident were sent to the local administrative authorities. In April 1978 they imposed on him a penalty of 60 DMks for causing a traffic accident by colliding with another vehicle as a result of careless driving. The penalty was imposed under the Regulatory Offences Act of 1968/1975 and under road traffic regulations that authorized financial penalties against those who were guilty of a 'regulatory offence'. Mr Öztürk initially disputed this penalty and exercised his right to a public hearing before a court. The district court heard him, assisted by an interpreter, and three witnesses, and he then withdrew his objection to the penalty. The court ordered him to bear court costs of 184 DMks, that were assessed under the Code of Criminal Procedure and included 64 DMks in respect of the fee paid to the interpreter. Mr Öztürk unsuccessfully claimed in the German courts that the requirement to pay the interpreter's fee was a breach of Article 6(3)(e).]

46. According to the Government, Article 6 § 3 (e) is not applicable in the circumstances since Mr. Öztürk was not 'charged with a criminal offence'. Under the 1968/1975 Act, which 'decriminalised' petty offences, notably in the road traffic sphere, the facts alleged against Mr. Öztürk constituted a mere 'regulatory offence' (*Ordnungswidrigkeit*). Such offences were said to be distinguishable from criminal offences not only by the procedure laid down for their prosecution and punishment but also by their juridical characteristics and consequences.

The applicant disputed the correctness of this analysis....

47. According to the French version of Article 6 § 3(e), the right guaranteed is applicable only to an 'accusé'. The corresponding English expression (person 'charged with a criminal offence') and paragraph 1 of Article 6 ('criminal charge'/'accusation en matière pénale')...make it quite clear that the 'accusation' ('charge') referred to in the French wording of Article 6 § 3 (e) must concern a 'criminal offence'.[7]

Under German law, the misconduct committed by Mr. Öztürk is not treated as a criminal offence (*Straftat*) but as a 'regulatory offence' (*Ordnungswidrigkeit*). The question arises whether this classification is the determining factor in terms of the Convention.

48. The Court was confronted with a similar issue in [*Engel v. The Netherlands*].... The facts of that case admittedly concerned penalties imposed on conscript servicemen and treated as disciplinary according to Netherlands law. In its judgment..., the Court was careful to state that it was confining its attention to the sphere of military service.[8] The Court nevertheless considers that the principles set forth in that judgment...are also relevant, *mutatis mutandis*, in the instant case.

49. The Convention is not opposed to States, in the performance of their task as guardians of the public interest, both creating or maintaining a distinction between different categories of offences for the purposes of their domestic law and drawing the dividing line, but it does not follow that the classification thus made by the States is decisive for the purposes of the Convention.

By removing certain forms of conduct from the category of criminal offences under domestic law, the law-maker may be able to serve the interests of the individual...[9] as well as the needs of the proper administration of justice, in particular in so far as the judicial authorities are thereby relieved of the task of prosecuting and punishing contraventions...of road traffic rules. The Convention is not opposed to the moves towards 'decriminalisation' which are taking place—in extremely varied forms—in the member States of the Council of Europe.... Nevertheless, if...States were able at their discretion, by classifying an offence as 'regulatory' instead of criminal, to exclude the operation of the fundamental clauses of Articles 6 and 7, the application of these provisions would be subordinated to their sovereign will....

50. ...[What] the Court must determine is whether or not the 'regulatory offence' committed by the applicant was a 'criminal' one within the meaning of that Article. For this purpose, the Court will rely on the criteria adopted in [*Engel v. The Netherlands*]. The first matter to be ascertained is whether or not the text defining the offence in issue belongs, according to the legal system of the respondent State, to criminal law; next, the nature of the offence and, finally, the nature and degree of severity of the penalty that the person concerned risked incurring must be examined, having regard to the object and purpose of Article 6, to the ordinary meaning of the terms of that Article and to the laws of the Contracting States.

51. ...The 1968/1975 legislation marks an important step in the process of 'decriminalisation' of petty offences in...Germany. Although legal commentators in Germany do not seem unanimous in considering that the law on 'regulatory offences' no longer belongs in reality to criminal law, the drafting history of the 1968/1975 Act nonetheless makes it clear that the offences in question have been removed from the criminal law sphere by that Act.[10]

---

[7] Citing *Adolf v. Austria*, Section B(3) *infra*, para. 30.
[8] *Engel v. The Netherlands*, 8 June 1976, 1 E.H.R.R. 643.
[9] Citing *Engel v. The Netherlands*, *supra* n. 8, para. 80.
[10] Citing decisions of German courts to this effect.

Whilst the Court thus accepts the Government's arguments on this point, it has nonetheless not lost sight of the fact that no absolute partition separates German criminal law from the law on 'regulatory offences', in particular where there exists a close connection between a criminal offence and a 'regulatory offence'... Nor has the Court overlooked that the provisions of the ordinary law governing criminal procedure apply by analogy to 'regulatory' proceedings..., notably in relation to the judicial stage, if any, of such proceedings.

52. In any event, the indications furnished by the domestic law of the respondent State have only a relative value. The second criterion stated above—the very nature of the offence, considered also in relation to the nature of the corresponding penalty—represents a factor of appreciation of greater weight.

In the opinion of the Commission — with the exception of five of its members — and of Mr. Öztürk, the offence committed by the latter was criminal in character.

For the Government in contrast, the offence in question was beyond doubt one of those contraventions of minor importance—numbering approximately five million each year...—which came within a category of quite a different order from that of criminal offences. The Government's submissions can be summarised as follows. By means of criminal law, society endeavoured to safeguard its very foundations as well as the rights and interests essential for the life of the community. The law on *Ordnungswidrigkeiten*, on the other hand, sought above all to maintain public order. As a general rule... commission of a 'regulatory offence' did not involve a degree of ethical unworthiness such as to merit for its perpetrator the moral value-judgment of reproach (*Unwerturteil*) that characterised penal punishment (*Strafe*)....

[The Court surveyed the ways in which procedure for regulatory offences differed from criminal procedure.]

...[Instead] of a penal fine (*Geldstrafe*) and imprisonment the legislature had substituted a mere 'regulatory' fine (*Geldbusse*....). Imprisonment was not an alternative...to the latter type of fine as it was to the former and no coercive imprisonment...could be ordered unless the person concerned had failed to pay the sum due without having established his inability to pay... Furthermore, a 'regulatory offence' was not entered in the judicial criminal records but solely, in certain circumstances, on the central traffic register...

The reforms accomplished in 1968/1975 thus, so the Government concluded, reflected a concern to 'decriminalise' minor offences to the benefit not only of the individual,..., but also of the effective functioning of the courts...

53. ...The Court recognises that the legislation in question marks an important stage in the history of the reform of German criminal law and that the innovations introduced in 1968/1975 represent more than a simple change of terminology.

Nonetheless,... according to the ordinary meaning of the terms, there generally come within the ambit of the criminal law offences that make their perpetrator liable to penalties intended, *inter alia*, to be deterrent and usually consisting of fines and of measures depriving the person of his liberty.

In addition, misconduct of the kind committed by Mr. Öztürk continues to be classified as part of the criminal law in the vast majority of the Contracting States, as it was in... Germany until the entry into force of the 1968/1975 legislation....

Moreover, the changes resulting from [that] legislation relate essentially to procedural matters and to the range of sanctions, henceforth limited to *Geldbussen*. Whilst the latter penalty appears less burdensome in some respects than *Geldstrafen*, it has nonetheless retained a punitive character, which is the customary distinguishing feature of criminal penalties. The rule of law infringed by the applicant has, for its part, undergone no change of content. It is a rule that is directed, not towards a given group possessing a special status—in the manner, for example, of disciplinary law—, but towards all citizens in their capacity as road-users; it prescribes conduct of a certain kind and makes the resultant requirement subject to a sanction that is punitive. Indeed, the sanction...seeks to punish as well as to deter. It matters little whether the legal provision contravened by Mr. Öztürk is aimed at protecting the rights and interests of others or solely at meeting the demands of road traffic. These two ends are not mutually exclusive. Above all, the general character of the rule and the purpose of the penalty, being both deterrent and punitive, suffice to show that the offence in question was, in terms of Article 6 of the Convention, criminal in nature.

The fact that it was admittedly a minor offence hardly likely to harm the reputation of the offender does not take it outside the ambit of Article 6. There is in fact nothing to suggest that the criminal offence referred to in the Convention necessarily implies a certain degree of seriousness....[It] would be contrary to the object and purpose of Article 6, which guarantees to 'everyone charged with a criminal offence' the right to a court and to a fair trial, if the State were allowed to remove from the scope of this Article a whole category of offences merely on the ground of regarding them as petty....

54. As the contravention committed by Mr. Öztürk was criminal for the purposes of Article 6...there is no need to examine it also in the light of the final criterion stated above (at paragraph 50). The relative lack of seriousness of the penalty at stake...cannot divest an offence of its inherently criminal character.

55. [The Court rejected the Government's further argument that the applicant was not a person 'charged with a criminal offence' because of the language used in the legislation.] On this point, the Court would simply refer back to its well-established case-law holding that 'charge', for the purposes of Article 6, may in general be defined as 'the official notification given to an individual by the competent authority of an allegation that he has committed a criminal offence', although 'it may in some instances take the form of other measures which carry the implication of such an allegation and which likewise substantially affect the situation of the suspect'.[11]...

56. Article 6 §3 (e) was thus applicable in the instant case. It in no wise follows from this, the Court would want to make clear, that the very principle of the system adopted in the matter by the German legislature is being put in question.... Conferring the prosecution and punishment of minor offences on administrative authorities is not inconsistent with the Convention provided that the person concerned is enabled to take any decision thus made against him before a tribunal that does offer the guarantees of Article 6.[12]

[There had thus been a breach of Article 6(3)(e), which, as the Court had previously held, 'entails, for anyone who cannot speak or understand the language used in court, the right to receive the free assistance of an interpreter, without subsequently having claimed back from him the payment of the costs thereby incurred'.][13]

---

[11] Citing *Foti v. Italy*, 10 Dec. 1982, 5 E.H.R.R. 313, para. 52, and *Corigliano v. Italy*, 10 Dec. 1982, para. 34.

[12] Citations omitted.

[13] *Luedicke, Belkacem & Koc v. Germany*, 28 Nov. 1978, 2 E.H.R.R. 149, para. 46.

2. BENHAM V. UNITED KINGDOM

10 June 1996
22 E.H.R.R. 293

[For the facts of this case, see Chapter 12, Section E(2). In addition to his claim under Article 5, Mr Benham claimed under Article 6 that the magistrates' proceedings against him had involved a criminal charge and that he had not been entitled to legal representation before being sent to prison. The following extracts deal with his Article 6 claim.]

51. The applicant contended that the fact that he had no automatic right to legal representation at the hearing before the magistrates meant that he was denied access to a fair hearing for the purposes of Article 6 para. 1...

53. The applicant further complained that his lack of legal representation during the proceedings before the magistrates constituted a violation of Article 6 para. 3(c).

54. The applicant...argued that the proceedings before the magistrates involved the determination of a criminal charge for the purposes of Article 6 para. 3(c).

He referred to the facts that what was in issue was not a dispute between individuals but rather liability to pay a tax to a public authority, and that the proceedings had many 'criminal' features, such as the safeguards available to defendants aged under 21, the severity of the applicable penalty and the requirement of a finding of culpability before a term of imprisonment could be imposed. Furthermore, it was by no means clear that the proceedings were classified as civil rather than criminal under the domestic law.

55. The Government argued that Article 6 para. 3(c) did not apply because the proceedings before the magistrates were civil rather than criminal in nature, as was borne out by the weight of the English case-law. The purpose of the detention was to coerce the applicant into paying the tax owed, rather than to punish him for not having paid it.

56. The case-law of the Court establishes that there are three criteria to be taken into account when deciding whether a person was 'charged with a criminal offence' for the purposes of Article 6. These are the classification of the proceedings under national law, the nature of the proceedings and the nature and degree of severity of the penalty.[14]

As to the first of these criteria, the Court agrees with the Government that the weight of the domestic authority indicates that, under English law, the proceedings in question are regarded as civil rather than criminal in nature. However, this factor is of relative weight and serves only as a starting-point.[15]

The second criterion, the nature of the proceedings, carries more weight....[The] Court notes that the law concerning liability to pay the community charge and the procedure upon non-payment was of general application to all citizens, and that the proceedings in question were brought by a public authority under statutory powers of enforcement. In addition, the proceedings had some punitive elements. For example, the magistrates could only exercise their power of committal to prison on a finding of wilful refusal to pay or of culpable neglect.

---

[14] Citing *Ravnsborg v. Sweden*, 23 March 1994, 18 E.H.R.R. 38. *See also Öztürk v. Germany*, 21 Feb. 1984, 18 E.H.R.R. 38, para. 50, *supra*.

[15] Citing *Weber v. Switzerland*, 22 May 1990, 12 E.H.R.R. 508, para. 31.

Finally, . . . the applicant faced a relatively severe maximum penalty of three months' imprisonment, and was in fact ordered to be detained for thirty days.[16]

Having regard to these factors, the Court concludes that Mr Benham was 'charged with a criminal offence' for the purposes of Article 6 paras. 1 and 3 . . .

[If the national legislation had treated the matter as one of criminal law, Mr Benham would have had a right to legal aid. Since it was regarded as a civil matter, he had no such entitlement.]

60. It was not disputed that Mr Benham lacked sufficient means to pay for legal assistance himself. The only issue before the Court is, therefore, whether the interests of justice required that Mr Benham be provided with free legal representation at the hearing before the magistrates. In answering this question, regard must be had to the severity of the penalty at stake and the complexity of the case.[17]

61. The Court agrees with the Commission that where deprivation of liberty is at stake, the interests of justice in principle call for legal representation . . . In this case, Mr Benham faced a maximum term of three months' imprisonment.

64. In view of the severity of the penalty risked by Mr Benham and the complexity of the applicable law, . . . the interests of justice demanded that, in order to receive a fair hearing, Mr Benham ought to have benefited from free legal representation during the proceedings before the magistrates.

In conclusion, there has been a violation of Article 6 paras. 1 and 3(c) of the Convention taken together.

3. WHEN HAS A CRIMINAL CHARGE BEEN DETERMINED?

It will be evident from both *Öztürk v. Germany* and *Benham v. United Kingdom* that the European Court refuses to be bound by the legal classifications used by respondent states. Rather, the words 'criminal charge' in Article 6 have an 'autonomous meaning'. Thus it is for the Court to decide which instances of official decision-making, in response to what kinds of conduct, entailing what consequences, amount to the determination of a criminal charge. The three-factor test formulated by the Court and applied in *Öztürk* and *Benham* is a recurring feature of such cases. The Court applied this approach in deciding that the finding of 'minor offences' for unruly public behaviour was the determination of a criminal charge even though no imprisonment and only minor fines were employed as sanctions.[18] It was enough that the rules invoked were imposed on all citizens for the protection of public order.[19] In six cases

---

[16] Citing *Bendenoun v. France*, 24 Feb. 1994, 18 E.H.R.R. 54, para. 47.

[17] Citing *Quaranta v. Switzerland*, 24 May 1991, paras. 32–8.

[18] *Kadubec v. Slovakia*, 2 Sept. 1998. *See also Lauko v. Slovakia*, 2 Sept. 1998, 33 E.H.R.R. 40.

[19] *Kadubec v. Slovakia*, *supra* n. 18, para. 52.

decided on the same day, the Court found that the Austrian procedure for dealing with motor vehicle offences came within Article 6. It took note of the acts prohibited, the terminology used in the relevant statutes, and the possible imposition of fines the non-payment of which could result in imprisonment.[20]

The Court has also held that the deduction of 'points' leading to possible suspension of driving privileges after conviction for a traffic offence was a procedure subject to Article 6. Although the procedure was administered separately from the underlying offence, it was found to be a secondary penalty with a punitive or deterrent function.[21]

On the other hand, not every similarity between a nominally administrative procedure and a classic criminal charge suffices to bring it under Article 6. This includes the use of involuntary detention. In an unexplained dictum the Court has stated that such detention in a mental health facility following a violent crime 'did not involve "determination of a criminal charge"'.[22] It did, however, find a violation of Article 6 with respect to the applicant's 'civil rights' and of Article 5(1).[23]

The background to *Adolf v. Austria*[24] lay in an allegation that the applicant, an accountant, had thrown a bunch of keys during a quarrel, hitting a woman and causing her minor bruising. On the advice of the prosecutor, the district court disposed of the case without a trial, acting under a power in the Austrian Penal Code to dispose of proceedings where a criminal trial would not be justified. The court's decision recorded that the guilt of the accountant was slight, that the act had trifling consequences, and that punishment was not necessary to deter him from committing criminal offences. Mr Adolf complained that the court had recorded a finding of guilt against him, without having given him a hearing. In rejecting this complaint, the Austrian Supreme Court held that the district court's decision should not be read as a finding of guilt: in the procedure for disposing of trivial cases without trial, the Penal Code 'simply requires the existence of a suspicion. Even if a court describes the suspect's conduct in terms of findings of fact, any statements to this effect could not be described as judicial findings.... Howsoever the reasons given may be worded, any such decision contains…a negative ruling on the merits of the case and does not at all amount to a declaration, equivalent to a finding of guilt, that the suspect has (unlawfully and with criminal intent) committed a punishable act'.[25] The Supreme Court added that it would have been preferable if the district court had 'stated this explicitly, and without ambiguity in the decision being challenged'.

---

[20] *Schmautzer v. Austria*, 23 Oct. 1995, 21 E.H.R.R. 511, para. 28 (seatbelt violation). *See also Umlauft v. Austria*, 23 Oct. 1995, 22 E.H.R.R. 76. The same reasoning was applied to proceedings against a contractor for violation of planning regulations: *Pramstaller v. Austria*, 23 Oct. 1995.

[21] *Malige v. France*, 23 Sept. 1998, 28 E.H.R.R. 578, paras. 37–9.

[22] *Aerts v. Belgium*, 30 July 1998, 29 E.H.R.R. 50, para. 59.

[23] *Id*. at paras. 59–60, 45–50.

[24] 26 March 1982, 4 E.H.R.R. 313.

[25] *Id*., para. 16, quoting the Supreme Court's judgment.

At Strasbourg, the Court held by 4–3 that at the time the district court dealt with the matter, a criminal charge against Mr Adolf existed and Article 6(1) applied; however, if the district court's decision was read as the Supreme Court had directed it should be read, there had been no finding of guilt against Adolf and the presumption of his innocence was not called into question. The action taken by the district court 'could not terminate with any finding of guilt' and no hearing was necessary. Article 6 had not been breached. The minority judges rejected the approach taken by the Austrian Supreme Court, saying trenchantly: 'what was found by the district court in unambiguous and unmistakable language cannot be made to mean other than what it obviously and unavoidably means. The "fact" of those findings was not erased by mere "hypothetical" whitewashing'.[26]

In *Adolf v. Austria*, the applicant was neither imprisoned nor fined. He complained that the information concerning the proceedings was available to the public. An important aspect of a criminal conviction is the 'stigma' that may attach to the defendant.

In *Paul v. Davis*,[27] the United States Supreme Court dealt with an action brought against the local police, who had distributed to merchants the name and picture of the plaintiff on a list of 'active shoplifters'. The Court found that mere injury to reputation did not amount to a deprivation of liberty triggering the procedural requirements of the Fourteenth Amendment. Justice Brennan dissented. He emphasized the close connection between the kind of injury inflicted on the plaintiff and that associated with criminal conviction:

The Court today holds that police officials [may] on their own initiative and without trial constitutionally condemn innocent individuals as criminals and thereby brand them with one of the most stigmatizing and debilitating labels in our society. If there are no constitutional restraints on such oppressive behavior, the safeguards constitutionally accorded an accused in a criminal trial are rendered a sham, and no individual can feel secure that he will not be arbitrarily singled out for similar ex parte punishment by those primarily charged with fair enforcement of the law.... The logical and disturbing corollary of this holding is that no due process infirmities would inhere in a statute constituting a commission to conduct ex parte trials of individuals, so long as the only official judgment pronounced was limited to the public condemnation and branding of a person as a Communist, a traitor, an 'active murderer', a homosexual or any other mark that 'merely' carries social opprobrium. The potential of today's decision is frightening for a free people.[28]

Is the injury in *Adolf v. Austria* distinguishable?[29]

Several European cases deal with the consequences of a criminal proceeding which is terminated before a verdict is entered. In *Minelli v. Switzerland*,[30] the applicant was the

---

[26] *Id.*, para. 7 of the joint dissenting opinion of Judges Cremona, Liesch and Pettiti.
[27] 424 U.S. 693 (1976).
[28] *Id.* at 714, 721.
[29] For a consideration by the European Court of the relation of Art. 6 to state procedures affecting reputation, *see Fayed v. United Kingdom*, 21 Sept. 1994, 18 E.H.R.R. 393.
[30] 25 Mar. 1983, 5 E.H.R.R. 554.

subject of a criminal defamation action that was discontinued before hearing because of the passage of the limitation period. The Swiss trial court charged the applicant with the bulk of the court costs of the action and part of the costs of the private prosecutors. It made that assessment based on its determination that, had it been possible for the case to go forward, 'he would in all probability have been convicted'. That determination was based on the court's estimate of the evidence that had been submitted and on the outcome of a related case. A subsequent determination on appeal by the federal court added nuances to the prior judgment but 'approved the substance of the decision on the essential points'. The European Court found a violation of Article 6(2), the presumption of innocence. After concluding that Article 6 was applicable to private prosecutions it held:

> [T]he presumption of innocence will be violated if, without the accused's having previously been proved guilty according to law and, notably, without his having had the opportunity of exercising his rights of defence, a judicial decision concerning him reflects an opinion that he is guilty. This may be so even in the absence of any formal finding; it suffices that there is some reasoning suggesting that the court regards the accused as guilty.[31]

The Court reached a different conclusion when the issue was a claim for reimbursement of costs instead of the initial charging of costs after a criminal action had been discontinued. In *Lutz v. Germany*,[32] the applicant had objected to a finding that he was guilty of a traffic violation (a 'regulatory offence'), but the applicable limitation period expired before a court could consider his objection. The domestic courts refused to order reimbursement of his costs finding that, but for the time bar, the applicant 'would most probably have been convicted'. In *Englert v. Germany*,[33] a prosecution for extortion was discontinued because the prosecutor, acting pursuant to the Criminal Code, determined that any sentence expected would be negligible in comparison with that imposed for a subsequent conviction. Again, the domestic courts refused to reimburse the applicant's costs or to compensate him for time held in detention pending trial, stating that 'a conviction is clearly more likely than an acquittal' and that Englert's own actions had given rise to 'the strong suspicion that he had committed an offence'. In both these cases, the European Court found no violation of Article 6. It was conceded by the applicants that the mere imposition of costs in a criminal proceeding did not offend the presumption of innocence. Moreover, in these cases the reasons for refusing to reimburse costs were not actually findings of guilt. They were described as a 'state of suspicion' which justified, on an equitable basis, the withholding of public reimbursement of costs. Article 6 does not require a state 'where a prosecution has been discontinued to indemnify a person "charged with a criminal offence" for any detriment he may have suffered'. Judge Cremona dissented, finding the *Minelli* case controlling. He argued that '[w]hat is decisive is that at the end of the day one is left with the impression that the courts did consider that the applicant was in fact guilty'.

---

[31] *Id.* at para. 37.
[32] 25 Aug. 1987, 10 E.H.R.R. 182.
[33] 25 Aug. 1987, 13 E.H.R.R. 392.

Even in cases where a criminal charge is undeniably lodged there may be a question exactly when the requirements of Article 6—and especially the special rights of the accused under Article 6(3)—attach. Again the Court has refused to be bound by the formal definitions of the local legal system, asking instead whether the applicant had, at the relevant time, in fact become the focus of a criminal investigation.[34] As the cases discussed in the previous paragraph indicate, there may also be a question of when an individual ceases to be under a criminal charge. In addition to cases of discontinued prosecution, the Court has assumed that Article 6 applies to proceedings in appellate courts.[35]

4. DO DISCIPLINARY AND OTHER PUNITIVE PROCEDURES INVOLVE THE DETERMINATION OF CRIMINAL CHARGES?

In considering the scope of Article 6(1), we must not assume that the right to a fair hearing necessarily arises in every area of the legal system. One issue in the early decision in *Engel v. Netherlands*[36] was whether due process rights applied to disciplinary proceedings in the armed forces. The applicants were conscript soldiers on whom penalties had been imposed for breaches of discipline, including various forms of detention, confinement to barracks, and removal to a punishment unit.[37] When charged, and being subject to a range of penalties if the charges were proved, did the soldiers have the right to a fair hearing? The Court said:

All the Contracting States make a distinction of long standing, albeit in different forms and degrees, between disciplinary and criminal proceedings. For the individuals affected, the former usually offer substantial advantages in comparison with the latter, for example as concerns the sentences passed. Disciplinary sentences, in general less severe, do not appear in the person's criminal record and entail more limited consequences. It may nevertheless be otherwise; moreover, criminal proceedings are ordinarily accompanied by fuller guarantees.[38]

The Court examined what was meant by the 'autonomy' of the concept of 'criminal'.

The Convention without any doubt allows the States, in the performance of their functions as guardians of the public interest, to maintain or establish a distinction between criminal law and disciplinary law, and to draw a dividing law, but only subject to certain conditions. The Convention leaves the States free to designate as a criminal offence an act or omission not constituting the normal exercise of one of the rights that it protects. This is made especially

---

[34] *See*, e.g., *Sevres v. France*, 20 Oct. 1997, 28 E.H.R.R. 265.

[35] *See*, e.g., *Hadjianastassiou v. Greece*, 16 Dec. 1992, 16 E.H.R.R. 219.

[36] 8 June 1976, 1 E.H.R.R. 647.

[37] For aspects of this case relating to Article 5, *see* Chapter 12(B) *supra*.

[38] *Engels v. Netherlands*, *supra* n. 36, para. 80.

clear by Article 7. Such a choice, which has the effect of rendering applicable Articles 6 and 7, in principle escapes supervision by the court.

The converse choice...is subject to stricter rules. If the Contracting States were able at their discretion to classify an offence as disciplinary instead of criminal, or to prosecute the author of a 'mixed' offence on the disciplinary rather than on the criminal plane, the operation of the fundamental clauses of Articles 6 and 7 would be subordinated to their sovereign will. A latitude extending thus far might lead to results incompatible with the purpose and object of the Convention. The court therefore has jurisdiction...to satisfy itself that the disciplinary does not improperly encroach upon the criminal.

In short, the 'autonomy' of the concept of 'criminal' operates, as it were, one way only.[39]

The Court reviewed the various military offences and punishments affecting the applicants, looking in particular at the severity of the penalty that the individuals risked incurring. It said: 'In a society subscribing to the rule of law, there belong to the "criminal" sphere deprivations of liberty liable to be imposed as a punishment, except those which by their nature, duration or manner of execution cannot be appreciably detrimental'. Applying this test, the Court held by a majority that three of the applicants should have been afforded the procedural guarantees of Article 6, but that this did not apply to the least serious penalties.

The question of disciplinary proceedings has arisen in several other contexts, including the use of such proceedings in the management of prison sentences being served by convicted offenders.

5. CAMPBELL AND FELLS V. UNITED KINGDOM

Judgment of 28 June 1984
7 E.H.R.R. 165

[The applicants were serving prison sentences of 10 years and 12 years respectively, imposed in 1973, when in 1976 they were involved with other prisoners in a disturbance protesting at the treatment of another prisoner. The prisoners were charged with disciplinary offences. Mr Campbell was charged with mutiny or incitement to mutiny, and with doing gross personal violence to an officer by striking him with a broom-handle. He was found guilty of both the mutiny and violence offences and was sentenced to the loss of 450 days and 120 days remission respectively, together with 56 and 35 days loss of privileges. Both applicants took steps to challenge the procedures that had been followed by the prison governor and by the prison's board of visitors.[40] At that time, the board exercised broad disciplinary powers which were becoming increasingly subject to judicial review by the High Court. At Strasbourg, the applicants claimed that they had in effect been convicted of criminal charges without a hearing as required by Article 6(1).]

[39] *Id.*, para. 81.
[40] On the functions of the visitors *see also* Section C(6) *infra*.

The government submitted that Article 6 was inapplicable to the proceedings. Citing prior case law,[41] the Court set forth the following principles for deciding when a 'criminal charge' was in contest:

70. The first matter to be ascertained is whether or not the text defining the offences in issue belongs, according to the domestic legal system, to criminal law, disciplinary law or both concurrently....

It is clear that, in English law, the offences with which Mr. Campbell was charged belong to disciplinary law: Rule 47 states that conduct of this kind on the part of a prisoner shall be 'an offence against discipline' and the Rules go on to provide how it shall be dealt with under the special prison disciplinary regime....

71. In any event, the indications so afforded by the national law have only a relative value: the very nature of the offence is a factor of greater import.

In this respect, it has to be borne in mind that misconduct by a prisoner may take different forms; certain acts are clearly no more than a question of internal discipline, whereas others cannot be seen in the same light. Firstly, some matters may be more serious than others; in fact, the Rules grade offences, classifying those committed by Mr. Campbell as 'especially grave'. Secondly, the illegality of some acts may not turn on the fact that they were committed in prison: certain conduct which constitutes an offence under the Rules may also amount to an offence under the criminal law. Thus, doing gross personal violence to a prison officer may correspond to the crime of 'assault occasioning actual bodily harm' and, although mutiny and incitement to mutiny are not as such offences under the general criminal law, the underlying facts may found a criminal charge of conspiracy. It also has to be remembered that, theoretically at least, there is nothing to prevent conduct of this kind being the subject of both criminal and disciplinary proceedings.

The Court considers that these factors, whilst not of themselves sufficient to lead to the conclusion that the offences with which the applicant was charged have to be regarded as 'criminal' for Convention purposes, do give them a certain colouring which does not entirely coincide with that of a purely disciplinary matter.

72. It is therefore necessary to turn to the last criterion stated in the above-mentioned *Engel and Others* judgment and in the above-mentioned *Öztürk* judgment, namely the nature and degree of severity of the penalty that Mr. Campbell risked incurring. The maximum penalties which could have been imposed on him included forfeiture of all of the remission of sentence available to him at the time of the Board's award (slightly less than three years), forfeiture of certain privileges for an unlimited time and, for each offence, exclusion from associated work, stoppage of earnings and cellular confinement for a maximum of 56 days; he was in fact awarded a total of 570 days' loss of remission and subjected to the other penalties mentioned for a total of 91 days. ...

In its above-mentioned *Engel and Others* judgment, the Court stated that deprivation of liberty liable to be imposed as a punishment was, in general, a penalty that belonged to the 'criminal' sphere. It is true that in the present case the legal basis for the detention remained, even after the Board's award, the original sentence of imprisonment and that nothing was added thereto. However, the Court is of the opinion that the forfeiture of remission which Mr. Campbell risked incurring and the forfeiture actually awarded involved such serious

---

[41] *Engel v. The Netherlands, supra* n. 36; *Öztürk v. Germany, supra.*

consequences as regards the length of his detention that these penalties have to be regarded, for Convention purposes, as 'criminal'. By causing detention to continue for substantially longer than would otherwise have been the case, the sanction came close to, even if it did not technically constitute, deprivation of liberty and the object and purpose of the Convention require that the imposition of a measure of such gravity should be accompanied by the guarantees of Article 6....[42]

After this decision was made, many legislative changes were made in the United Kingdom that emphasized the judicial nature of the disciplinary system and gave the adjudicating bodies power to order prisoners to serve 'added days' in detention, before they could be released on licence. In *Ezeh v. United Kingdom*,[43] the Grand Chamber considered complaints by two convicted prisoners who were denied the right to be legally represented in disciplinary proceedings, were found guilty and were awarded respectively 40 and 7 'added days'. The government maintained that Article 6 was not applicable since the charges against the applicants were not criminal but disciplinary, and relied on the decision of a national court holding that a punishment that required the applicants to serve 'added days' 'did not have the effect of adding to their sentence'.[44] By 11–6, the Grand Chamber upheld the earlier jurisprudence, citing in

---

[42] The United States Supreme Court has held that certain decisions by prison officials may amount to a deprivation of some 'liberty' retained even by convicted criminals, and therefore that they can only be effected with 'due process of law' entailing minimum procedural safeguards. This reasoning has been applied to revocation of parole, *Morrisey v. Brewer*, 408 U.S. 471 (1972), probation, *Gagnon v. Scarpelli*, 411 U.S. 778 (1973), forfeiture of 'good time credit', *Wolff v. McDonnell*, 418 U.S. 539 (1974), and to involuntary commitment of a prisoner to a mental hospital, *Vitek v. Jones*, 445 U.S. 480 (1980). No liberty interest, however, was found implicated, and no procedural protection required, for transfer of prisoners to different institutions or facilities or for other changes in the conditions of confinement: *Olim v. Wakinekona*, 461 U.S. 238 (1983), or changes in visitation rights, *Kentucky Dept. of Corrections v. Thompson*, 490 U.S. 454 (1989).

In most of these cases the Supreme Court decided the presence of a liberty interest based on an examination of the text of the statute or regulation which appeared to create the entitlement. Thus it held there was a protected interest even in the initial decision to parole where the language seemed to make such release mandatory on the occurrence of certain conditions. *Greenholz v. Inmates*, 472 U.S. 1 (1979) (*see also Hewitt v. Helms*, 459 U.S. 460 (1983) finding a liberty interest against 'administrative segregation' based on 'language of an unmistakably mandatory character'. *Id.* at 471). In *Sandin v. O'Connor*, 515 U.S. 472 (1995), however, the Court rejected a text-based approach holding the imposition of restrictions on prisoners required constitutionally minimum procedural safeguards only when those restrictions 'impos[e] atypical and significant hardship on the inmate in relation to the ordinary incidents of prison life'. *Id.* at 484.

The Supreme Court of Canada has held that under s. 7 of the Canadian Charter of Rights and Freedom, a prisoner's 'liberty' is affected by significant changes in the manner of his confinement and in the possibilities for release. Consequently, such changes may only be effected if not 'contrary to the principles of fundamental justice' in both substance and procedure. *Cunningham v. Canada* [1993] 2 S.C.R. 243.

In the United Kingdom, the House of Lords has held that while the legality of changes in the circumstances of confinement of a convicted prisoner may be challenged in a public law proceeding for judicial review, *Leech v. Deputy Governor, Parkhurst Prison* [1988] A.C. 533, such a prisoner had no private law remedy for damages. The House found that neither the relevant prison rules, nor the authorizing legislation, contemplated such a right of action. Nor were such acts by prison authorities the basis for an action in tort for false imprisonment since the prisoner had already been lawfully confined. Unlike the United States Supreme Court, the House denied that a prisoner had any 'residual liberty' of which he might be deprived. *R. v. Deputy Governor of Parkhurst Prison ex parte Hague* [1992] 1 A.C. 58.

[43] 9 Oct. 2003, 39 E.H.R.R. 1.

[44] *R. (Carroll) v. Secretary of State for the Home Department* [2001] E.W.C.A. Civ. 1224; [2002] 1 W.L.R. 545, para. [44].

particular *Engel v. Netherlands* and *Campbell and Fell v. United Kingdom*. The majority held that 'the nature of the charges together with the nature and severity of the penalties' were such that the applicants had been facing criminal charges and had been entitled to legal representation under Article 6(3)(c). The dissenting judges took the view that the disciplinary charges against the applicants were much less serious than in the case of *Campbell and Fell*, and that the nature of the charges moved the case 'further from the criminal sphere' than in that case.[45]

The Court has attempted to separate disciplinary action from 'criminal charges' in many other cases. In *Weber v. Switzerland*,[46] the Court held that a fine imposed on the complainant in a criminal proceeding for revealing information concerning the case was the result of a criminal charge. The Code of Criminal Procedure in the Swiss Canton of Vaud bound 'parties, their counsel, employees of their counsel and experts and witnesses to maintain the confidentiality of the investigation'. The state argued that this was merely a matter of internal discipline limited to those involved in judicial procedure. The Court found this unconvincing with respect to the restriction imposed on the parties:

As persons who above all others are bound by the confidentiality of an investigation, judges, lawyers and all those closely associated with the functioning of the courts are liable in such an event, independently of any criminal sanctions, to disciplinary measures on account of their profession. The parties, on the other hand, only take part in the proceedings as people subject to the jurisdiction of the courts and they therefore do not come within the disciplinary sphere of the judicial system. As [the relevant provision], however, potentially affects the whole population, the offence it defines, and to which it attaches a punitive sanction is a 'criminal' one....[47]

On the other hand, the levying of fines on a party for 'improper statements' made in written submissions to the court has been held non-criminal, since they were used only in reaction to statements in judicial proceedings and 'not to such statements made in a different context or by a person falling outside the circle of people covered by that provision'. 'Rules enabling a Court to sanction disorderly conduct in proceedings before it are a common feature of legal systems of the Contracting States' and are 'more akin to the exercise of disciplinary powers than to the imposition of a punishment for commission of a criminal offence'. The amount of the fines (three fines of 1,000 Swedish Krona (about U.S.$150 or £75) each) and the fact that the applicant was liable to imprisonment for non-payment did not change the Court's conclusion.[48] The Court reached the same result in a later case involving offensive oral and written statements in which the amount of the fines was considerably higher. In this case the maximum

[45] *Ezeh v. United Kingdom, supra* n. 43, dissenting judgment of Judges Pellonpaa, Wildhaber, Palm and Caflisch.
[46] 22 May 1990, 12 E.H.R.R. 508.
[47] *Id.* at para. 33. For the American constitutional law on the characterization of sanctions for noncompliance with judicial orders *see* the discussion of *United Mine Workers v. Bagwell, infra.*
[48] *Ravnsborg v. Sweden, supra* n. 14, para. 34.

fine was 10,000 Austrian schillings (about U.S.$950 or £475) and the total amount fined was 22,500 schillings.[49] Judge Jungwiert dissented in the second case arguing that the penalties were 'at the level of a criminal punishment'.[50]

The distinction between sanctions directed at a limited number of participants in specified activities and those applied to the public at large was also evident in *Demicoli v. Malta*,[51] where the applicant had been held punishable by the Maltese House of Representatives for a satirical article about the House. In a fairly summary proceeding, that body had found the applicant guilty of a defamatory libel, breaching the privileges of the House. While breach of parliamentary privilege was not formally classified as criminal in Maltese law, the Court noted that, in the proceedings against the applicant, certain members of the House equated its judgment with criminal proceedings and that defamatory libel was also a criminal offence in Maltese law. The Court also stressed that the action against the applicant was distinct from matters relating merely to the 'internal regulation and orderly functioning' of the House. Finally, it noted that the whole population was subject to such actions without regard to where the offending conduct took place.

The assessment of tax surcharges was held to involve the equivalent of a 'criminal charge' in *Bendenoun v. France*.[52] It was not classed as such under domestic law and was vested in administrative, not criminal, courts. Moreover, the amounts involved were calculated on the basis of the tax originally due and, in case of death of the taxpayer, were charged against his estate. Conceding that these factors militated against characterization as criminal, the Court, nonetheless, felt they were outweighed by other aspects of the procedure. As in the *Weber* and *Demicoli* cases, the surcharges were imposed not on a selected group but, potentially, on 'all citizens in their capacity as taxpayers'. They were intended not as compensation for a loss caused, but for their punitive and deterrent effects. Finally, the Court noted that the amounts involved were very large and that, on a nonpayment, a person could be remitted to the criminal courts where he was liable to imprisonment.[53]

The Supreme Court of Canada has addressed the distinction between criminal charges and disciplinary proceedings in the context of actions involving officers of the Royal Canadian Mounted Police. It held that a 'major service offence' amounts to an offence within Section 11 of the Canadian Charter of Rights and Freedoms, and thus must be accompanied by a series of procedural safeguards. It sought to distinguish such offences from other disciplinary and regulatory infractions by identifying two

---

[49] *Putz v. Austria*, 22 Feb. 1996.

[50] *Id.* (Judge Jungwiert dissenting). Compare the holding in *Putz* with that in *Garyfallou AEBE v. Greece*, 24 Sept. 1997, 28 E.H.R.R. 344 in which the Court found that a maximum fine of 15,500 Deutsche Marks for violation of trade regulation, with non-payment resulting in possible seizure of property or detention, should be regarded as involving a criminal charge without regard to the nature of the underlying conduct.

[51] 27 Aug. 1991, 14 E.H.R.R. 47.

[52] 24 Feb. 1994, 18 E.H.R.R. 54.

[53] *Id.* at paras. 45–7. To the same effect *see A.P.M.P. & T.P. v. Switzerland*, 29 Aug. 1997, 26 E.H.R.R. 541; *E.L., R.L. & J.O.L. v. Switzerland*, 29 Aug. 1997.

characteristics, either of which would be sufficient to create a 'criminal or penal matter', that define such an offence. Note the similarity of these factors to those identified
by the Strasbourg Court in addressing the same question under Article 6. First, an
offence is present in a matter of 'public nature, intended to promote public order and
welfare within a public sphere of activity' as distinguished from 'private, domestic
or disciplinary matters which are regulatory, protective or corrective and which are
primarily intended to maintain discipline, professional integrity and professional
standards or to regulate conduct within a limited private sphere of activity'. Second,
any matter is an 'offence' which is accompanied by a 'true penal consequence' defined
as 'imprisonment or a fine which, by its magnitude, would appear to be imposed for
the purpose of redressing the wrong done to society rather than the maintenance of
internal discipline within the limited sphere of activity'. Although, generally, service
offences would not meet the first test, as they were imposed to maintain discipline
within a limited sphere, in the offence at bar, physical abuse of a suspect, the allowable
punishment of one year's imprisonment entailed a 'true penal consequence'.[54]

Canadian courts have long been called on to characterize legislation as criminal or
non-criminal in connection with the distribution of powers under the Constitution
Act, 1867. That Act gives exclusive legislative authority over matters of criminal law to
the federal Parliament.[55] In these federalism cases the Court has stated the criteria for
criminal law somewhat more broadly than in connection with Charter issues. It has
noted two requirements: such laws 'must contain prohibitions backed by penalties; and
they must be directed at a "legitimate public purpose"'.[56] In 1997 the Supreme Court
upheld the Environmental Protection Act against an argument by dissenting justices
that the law prohibited no primary conduct. Rather it merely vested in administrative
officers a power to prescribe the degree and manner of use of various substances.[57]
The majority, noting the special difficulties of environmental regulation, regarded the
Act as one in which Parliament made 'provision for carefully tailoring the prohibited
action to specified substances used or dealt with in specific circumstances'.[58]

The United States Supreme Court has had to grapple with the defining characteristics
of criminal proceedings in several contexts. Many of the rights accorded by the Fifth
and Sixth amendments to the Constitution are available only to the accused in a criminal prosecution. The Court has stated the essence of such a criminal law to be that the
'sanction... [it] impose[s] is punishment'.[59] This is principally a question of legislative
intent. In *Kennedy v. Mendoza-Martin*[60] the Court decided that a statute withdrawing

---

[54] *R. v. Wigglesworth* [1987] 2 S.C.R. 541. *See also R. v. Généreux* [1992] 1 S.C.R. 259, holding that trial in
a court martial of a breach of the Military Code of Service Discipline involved an 'offense' under s. 11. The
Code made a 'service offense' of any violation of the Criminal Code and, in this case, the underlying conduct
alleged was a violation of the Narcotics Control Act.

[55] Constitution Act 1867, s. 91(27). *See generally* P. Hogg, *Constitutional Law of Canada* (student edn.
2006), 485–92.

[56] *R. v. Hydro-Quebec* [1997] 3 S.C.R. 213, para. 35 (Lamer & Iacobucci JJ dissenting).

[57] *Id.* at paras. 45–63 (dissenting opinion).

[58] *Id.* at para. 151.

[59] 372 U.S. 144, 167 (1963).   [60] *Id.*

citizenship from persons leaving the country to avoid the draft was 'criminal' based on an extensive review of the legislative history, which was replete with references to 'punishments' and 'penalties'.[61] The Court also set forth a more general approach to be used in the absence of such a clear legislative record:

Whether the sanction involves an affirmative disability or restraint, whether it has historically been regarded as punishment, whether it comes into play only on a finding of scienter, whether its operation will promote the traditional aims of punishment—retribution and deterrence, whether the behavior to which it applies is already a crime, whether an alternative purpose to which it may rationally be connected is assignable for it, and whether it appears excessive in relation to the alternative purpose assigned, are all relevant to the inquiry, and may often point in differing directions. Absent conclusive evidence of Congressional intent as to the penal nature of a statute, these factors must be considered in relation to the statute on its face.[62]

In *Allen v. Illinois*[63] the Court considered an Illinois procedure for the civil commitment of 'sexually dangerous' persons. It held that the Fifth Amendment's privilege against self-incrimination was not applicable in such proceedings. Under the statute a person could be committed if he was found to suffer from a mental disorder and to possess 'criminal propensities toward acts of sexual assault'. It was a prerequisite to the commitment, which was of indefinite duration, that the person be shown to have committed at least one act or attempt at sexual assault. On commitment he was to be provided with 'care and treatment' and to be released if a court found him to be no longer dangerous. The Supreme Court noted that the legislation expressly declared itself to be 'civil in nature'. It agreed that such labels were not dispositive but required in such cases the 'clearest proof' that 'the statutory scheme [is] so punitive either in purpose or effect as to negate [the state's] intention'.[64] The Court held that such proof had not been produced. The requirement of an earlier act of sexual assault need not be understood as a predicate 'to punish past misdeeds, but primarily to show the accused's mental condition and to predict future behavior'.[65]

The Court reached the same conclusion with respect to a similar scheme in *Kansas v. Hendricks*.[66] In that case, however, the committal, which was to a maximum security institution, was not to be initiated until the subject was ending a prison term for sexual assault and little or no treatment was contemplated after commitment. The Court noted that a state 'may take measures to restrict the freedom of the dangerously mentally ill. This is a legitimate non-punitive governmental objective and has been historically so regarded'.[67] The protection of the public was a sufficient and non-criminal basis for detention even in the absence of treatment.

---

[61] *Id.* at 170–85.
[62] *Id.* at 168–9.
[63] 478 U.S. 364 (1986).
[64] *Id.* at 368–9, quoting *United States v. Ward*, 448. U.S. 242, 248–9 (1972) (quotation marks and brackets in original).
[65] *Id.* at 371.
[66] 521 U.S. 346 (1997).
[67] *Id.* at 363.

The American courts have also been called on to draw a constitutional distinction between civil and criminal proceedings in connection with the appropriate procedure to be employed in adjudicating citations of contempt of court where an individual has failed to follow an order of a court. A characterization of contempt as criminal requires elaborate procedure, including a jury trial. In 1994 the United States Supreme Court (like the European Court in *Bendenoun*) placed considerable emphasis on the punitive, as opposed to compensatory, purpose of an adjudication of contempt. In *United Mine Workers v. Bagwell*,[68] a state court had enjoined a labour union from engaging in certain illegal activities in connection with a strike and associated picketing. It further announced that any violation of its order would result in fines of $20,000 each if the infraction were nonviolent, and $100,000 if it were violent. In a six-month period the court levied fines of more than $64 million. The Supreme Court held that these fines could, consistent with the Fourteenth Amendment to the United States Constitution, be imposed only if preceded by a criminal trial. The fines were conceded to be noncompensatory. The Court distinguished fines of increasing daily amounts, intended to coerce compliance with judicial orders. Rather, these were 'analogous to fixed, determinate, retrospective criminal fines which [the contemnors] had no opportunity to purge once imposed'.[69]

6. CIVIL RIGHTS AND PUBLIC RIGHTS[70]

The previous section considered whether disciplinary and other proceedings involve the determination of criminal charges. We now consider whether disciplinary law of a different kind may be within Article 6(1) as involving the determination of 'civil rights and obligations'. In *Le Compte, Van Leuven and De Meyere v. Belgium*,[71] the applicants were suspended from practising medicine by a disciplinary tribunal of the Belgian *Ordre des médecins* on various charges of professional misconduct; the charges included giving an interview to the press that was incompatible with the reputation of the profession (Le Compte), limiting their fees to the amounts reimbursed by Social Security, and in a magazine making comments judged offensive to colleagues (Van Leuven and De Meyere). The applicants claimed that they had been entitled to the procedural guarantees afforded by Article 6(1). The Belgian government argued that the procedures involved neither the determination of a criminal charge, nor the determination of 'civil rights and obligations'. The Court by 15–5, applying earlier authority

---

68 512 U.S. 821 (1994).

69 *Id.* at 837.

70 *See* P. Craig, 'The Human Rights Act, Article 6 and Procedural Rights', [2003] *Public Law* 753; and J. Herberg, A. Le Sueur and J. Mulcahy, 'Determining Civil Rights and Obligations', in J. Jowell and J. Cooper (eds.), *Understanding Human Rights Principles* (2001), pp. 91–137.

71 23 June 1981, 4 E.H.R.R. 1.

on Article 6(1),[72] held that, while the disciplinary proceedings did not involve criminal charges, they were 'proceedings the result of which is decisive for private rights and obligations', namely the right to practise as a medical practitioner. A tenuous connection between the proceedings and the right to practise would not have been sufficient, but the primary object of the proceedings was to decide whether the applicants could continue to work as doctors. The majority added that

it is by means of private relationships with their clients or patients that medical practitioners in private practice . . . avail themselves of the right to continue to practise; in Belgian law, these relationships are usually contractual or quasi-contractual and, in any event, are directly established between individuals on a personal basis and without any intervention of an essential or determining nature by a public authority. Accordingly, it is a private right that is at issue, notwithstanding the specific character of the medical profession . . . and the duties incumbent on its members.[73]

It was held that the procedural guarantees under Article 6(1) applied to this disciplinary scheme.

The dissenting judges did not agree that Article 6(1) applied, giving a narrower interpretation to the term 'civil rights and obligations'. Judge Pinheiro Farinha considered that the case concerned solely the violation of rules of professional conduct. Judge Sir Vincent Evans observed that the object of the disciplinary proceedings was 'to ensure the observance of rules of professional conduct—and not the determination of private rights'. In his view, the majority were imposing procedural requirements on professional discipline that were inappropriate (for instance, the rule that hearings must be in public), and had never been intended by the framers of the Convention to apply in that context.

The division of opinion in *Le Compte v. Belgium* is only one instance of deep differences of approach to Article 6(1) that exist within the Court. We have seen that when the Convention was framed, the purpose behind the article was to guarantee the integrity of national systems of civil and criminal justice. It is reasonably certain that the framers of the Article did not intend court-like procedures to be observed whenever action is 'taken by administrative bodies exercising disciplinary powers conferred on them by law'.[74] However, the original intention behind Article 6(1) does not govern its interpretation by the Court. The interpretation of the article has not been helped by differences between the English and French texts.[75] Particularly influential

---

[72] In particular *Ringeisen v. Austria*, 16 July 1971, 1 E.H.R.R. 455 and *König v. Germany*, 28 June 1978, 2 E.H.R.R. 170.

[73] *Le Compte, supra* n. 71, para. 49.

[74] *See* the comment by The Danish jurist, Max Sørensen, quoted in the minority judgment in *Feldbrugge v. Netherlands*, Section B(7) below. *See also* C. F. Newman, 'Natural Justice, Due Process and the New International Covenants on Human Rights', [1967] *Public Law* 274.

[75] The first sentence of the French text reads: 'Toute personne a droit à ce que sa cause soit entendue équitablement, publiquement et dans un delai raisonnable, par un tribunal indépendant et impartial, établi par la loi, qui décidera, soit des contestations sur ses droits et obligations de caractère civil, soit du bien-fondé de toute accusation en matière pénale dirigée contre elle'.

has been the phrase in the French text: 'des contestations sur des droits et obligations *de caractère civil*'.[76]

It might appear from the English text that disputes about someone's rights and obligations that do not involve criminal charges necessarily involve civil rights and obligations (on the basis that, as regards rights and obligations, what is not criminal must be civil). But in civil law systems, the term *droits et obligations de caractère civil* is understood to refer to the rights of individuals between themselves, governed by private law (*droit civil*) on property, succession, family relations, contracts and civil wrongs etc. In such systems, there is a fundamental division between private law and public law, the law regulating activities of the state. In many countries, private law disputes go to the civil courts, while public law disputes are decided by a separate structure of administrative courts or tribunals, as in France. Over time the administrative courts developed their own, formidable bodies of law, but the segregation of matters of public administration was premised originally on an implicit assumption that the ordinary courts and civil procedure were unsuited to regulate the exercise of public authority.[77]

Commentators on the English common law, by contrast, have traditionally regarded the distinction between private law and public law as incompatible with the basic assumptions of the common law. Albert Venn Dicey, in his classic account of *The Law of the Constitution*, first published in 1885, drew a sharp contrast between British constitutional law and the French *droit administratif*: 'Any official who exceeds the authority given him by the law', wrote Dicey, 'incurs the common law responsibility for his wrongful act; he is amenable to the authority of the ordinary courts, and the ordinary courts have themselves jurisdiction to determine what is the extent of his legal power, and whether the orders under which he has acted were legal and valid'.[78]

Developments in the 20th century in administrative law, both in civil law and in common law countries, mean that a simple dichotomy between private and public law is seldom possible. There is a universal need for effective means of ensuring that public authorities observe the law, even if the practical implications of this are worked out in ways that differ from country to country. At the heart of Article 6(1) is the guarantee that in certain circumstances the individual has a right to a fair hearing. Quite apart from Article 6(1), the right to a fair hearing is recognized in administrative law in situations where someone is faced with the exercise of official power in a matter that directly affects his or her rights and interests. Often the procedures that involve a fair hearing are expressly authorized in legislation. But the right to a hearing may be implied when it would be unfair for a power to be exercised by the administration without granting the individual a hearing. When controversial public schemes and

---

[76] Literally, 'disputes over rights and obligations of a civil character'.

[77] *See* J. H. Merryman, *The Civil Law Tradition* 87–8, 92–3, 97 (2nd edn. 1985); A. T. von Mehren and J. R. Gordley, *The Civil Law System* 343–4 (1977).

[78] A. V. Dicey, *The Law of the Constitution* 256 (8th edn. 1915) (Liberty Classics Reprint 1987). For a comparative treatment of the public–private law distinction today, *see* J. Allison, *A Continental Distinction in the Common Law: a Historical and Comparative Perspective on English Public Law* (1996).

proposals are in progress, a reviewing court must remember that it is not dealing simply with a dispute between two parties, since a wide range of public and private rights and interests may be in play that go well beyond the rights that are typically protected by private law.[79]

This idea of 'public rights' also has some distinct analogues in North American law, especially in connection with determining the proper forum for resolving disputes. As in the civil law system, it is founded on the idea that there is some inevitable discretion inherent in the operation of government. Some decisions could quite reasonably be taken by officials without any formal procedure. No one acquires a right to a particular decision or process just because the government sets up a more formal judicial-style mechanism. In the United States the concept is employed in identifying the questions which must be committed to federal courts staffed by judges with life tenure and salaries which may not be reduced under Article III of the Constitution. That Article exclusively vests the 'judicial power of the United States' in such courts. The Supreme Court, however, has decided that matters of 'public rights' may be decided by non-Article III tribunals created by the Congress. The permissible jurisdiction of such 'legislative' courts was discussed in *Northern Pipeline Const. Co. v. Marathon Pipeline Co.*:[80]

... The doctrine extends only to matters arising 'between the Government and persons subject to its authority in connection with the performance of the constitutional functions of the executive or legislative departments', *Crowell v. Benson* 285 U.S. 22, 50 (1932), and only to matters that historically could have been determined exclusively by those departments.... The understanding of these cases is that the Framers expected that Congress would be free to commit such matters completely to non-judicial executive determination, and that as a result there can be no constitutional objection to Congress' employing the less drastic expedient of committing their determination to a legislative court or an administrative agency.

The public-rights doctrine is grounded in a historically recognized distinction between matters that could be conclusively determined by the Executive and Legislative Branches and matters that are 'inherently ... judicial'. ...

The distinction between public rights and private rights has not been definitively explained in our precedents. Nor is it necessary to do so in the present case, for it suffices to observe that a matter of public rights must at a minimum arise 'between the government and others'. In contrast, 'the liability of one individual to another under the law as defined', is a matter of private rights. Our precedents clearly establish that *only* controversies in the former category may be removed from Article III courts and delegated to legislative courts or administrative agencies for their determination.... Private-rights disputes on the other hand, lie at the core of the historically recognized judicial power.[81]

---

[79] *See*, in English law, *Bushell v. Secretary of State for the Environment* [1981] A.C. 75; and, for the effect of Article 6(1) rights on town planning procedures, *R. (Alconbury Developments Ltd) v. Secretary of State for the Environment* [2001] U.K.H.L. 23; [2003] 2 A.C. 295.

[80] 458 U.S. 50 (1982).

[81] *Id.* at 67–70.

Similarly, under the Canadian Constitution Act 1867, it has become necessary to decide which matters may be decided by provincially created tribunals and which must be heard in 's. 96' Superior Courts in which the judges are appointed and salaries set by the federal government. The Supreme Court of Canada addressed the question in *Re Residential Tenancies Act*[82] in which it considered a provincial scheme for resolving disputes between residential tenants and landlords. It formulated a three-part test for deciding whether the power of a provincial tribunal conflicted with the exclusive jurisdiction of the Superior Courts. First, a court had to decide if the decision at issue was one within the jurisdiction of superior, district or county courts in 1867, the time of confederation. If so, it would have to be considered whether, in light of the institutional setting of the challenged action, it could still reasonably be regarded as stating a 'judicial question':

> ... The primary issue is the nature of the question which the tribunal is called upon to decide. Where the tribunal is faced with a private dispute between parties, and is called upon to adjudicate through the application of a recognized body of rules in a manner consistent with fairness and impartiality, then, normally, it is acting in a 'judicial capacity'. To borrow the terminology of Professor Ronald Dworkin, the judicial task involves questions of 'principle', that is, consideration of the competing rights of individuals or groups. This can be contrasted with questions of 'policy' involving competing views of the collective good of the community as a whole. (See Dworkin, *Taking Rights Seriously* (Duckworth, 1977) pp. 82–90)....
>
> ... [I]f the power or jurisdiction is exercised in a judicial manner, then it becomes necessary to proceed to the third and final step in the analysis and review the tribunal's function as a whole in order to appraise the impugned function in its entire institutional context.... It will all depend on the context of the exercise of the power. It may be that the impugned 'judicial powers' are merely subsidiary or ancillary to general administrative functions assigned to the tribunal ... or the powers may be necessarily incidental to the achievement of a broader policy goal of the legislature.... In such a situation, the grant of judicial power to provincial appointees is valid. The scheme is only invalid when the adjudicative function is a sole or central function of the tribunal ... so that the tribunal can be said to be operating 'like a s. 96 court'. ...[83]

The Strasbourg Court has often been faced with cases in which claimants have relied on Article 6(1) in relation to the exercise of administrative power. The Court has had to deal with these claims in a way that gives effect to the requirement made by the text of Article 6(1) that claims must relate to 'civil rights and obligations'. The Court has frequently upheld these claims, and in so doing have imposed obligations of due process on many public authorities. However, this is the outcome of the decisions, rather than their rationale, for the distinction between civil law and public law still influences the interpretation of Article 6(1), albeit to a diminishing extent.

In an early decision, *Ringeisen v. Austria (No. 1)*,[84] an Austrian property speculator bought agricultural land and purported to sell off many plots for building new homes, even though legislation provided that a sale of agricultural land for other purposes

---

[82] [1981] 1 S.C.R. 714.
[83] [1981] 1 S.C.R. at 734–6.
[84] *Supra* n. 72.

could take effect only when the Real Property Transactions Commission for the district had approved the transaction in question. Approval for Ringeisen's purchase was refused by the district Commission and, on appeal, the regional Commission. Ringeisen, later the subject of a lengthy prosecution for fraud in relation to his dealings, challenged the proceedings of the two Commissions on the ground that some of their members were biased. His challenge failed in the Austrian Constitutional Court. At Strasbourg he claimed a breach of his Article 6(1) rights. The Government denied that the proceedings before the two Commissions involved the 'determination of civil rights and obligations'. The Court stated:

94. For Article 6(1) to be applicable to a case (*contestation*) it is not necessary that both parties to the proceedings should be private persons, which is the view...of the Government. The wording of Article 6(1) is far wider; the French expression '*contestations sur (des) droits et obligations de caractère civil*' covers all proceedings the result of which is decisive for private rights and obligations. The English text, 'determination of...civil rights and obligations' confirms this interpretation.

The character of the legislation which governs how the matter is to be determined (civil, commercial, administrative law, etc) and that of the authority which is invested with jurisdiction in the matter (ordinary court, administrative body, etc.) are therefore of little consequence.

In the present case, when Ringeisen purchased property from the Roth couple, he had a right to have the contract for sale which they had made with him approved if he fulfilled, as he claimed to do, the conditions laid down in the Act. Although it was applying rules of administrative law, the Regional Commission's decision was to be decisive for the relations in civil law (*de caractère civil*) between Ringeisen and the Roth couple. This is enough to make it necessary for the Court to decide whether or not the proceedings in this case complied with the requirements of Article 6(1)...

The Court held that the Regional Commission, whose membership comprised a judge, civil servants and representatives of interested bodies, was a 'tribunal' within the meaning of Article 6(1), 'as it is independent of the executive and also of the parties, its members are appointed for a term of five years and the proceedings before it offer the necessary guarantees'.[85] The Court rejected allegations that members of the Commission were biased.

The *Ringeisen* decision was significant for holding that there need not be a pre-existing dispute between two parties before the right to a hearing under Article 6(1) can apply; and that the decision-making body was an independent and impartial tribunal. Most crucially, *Ringeisen* held that Article 6(1) applies to 'all proceedings the result of which is decisive for private rights and obligations'. We have seen how this test was applied to disciplinary proceedings in respect of the medical profession.[86] The same test has been applied to decisions with an economic impact on the enjoyment of civil rights, such as

---

[85] *Id.* para 95.
[86] *See Lecompte v. Belgium, supra* n. 71, following the earlier decision in *König v. Germany, supra* n. 72.

control over the right of owners to develop their land,[87] and licensing schemes. For an instance of such schemes, *Benthem v. The Netherlands* concerned the revocation of a licence permitting Benthem to sell liquefied petroleum gas to motorists.[88] The Court held by 11–6 that the grant of the licence was 'closely associated with the right to use one's possessions in conformity with the law's requirements'; the licence had a proprietary character, since it could be transferred to third parties; and there were 'direct links' between the grant of the licence and the applicant's commercial activities. The six dissenting judges held that the granting of the licence depended on whether it was compatible with the interests of the community, 'interests whose protection is a typical function of administrative law': the result of the proceedings was 'no more than indirectly decisive for [Benthem's] civil rights and had only remote consequences as regards such rights'.[89]

The majority view in *Benthem* was applied to a decision by a local authority to revoke a licence to run a taxi service and a twelve-seater bus (granted to the applicant 18 months previously), the reason for revocation being to enable a large bus company to provide a monopoly service.[90] In *Tre Traktörer Aktiebolag v. Sweden*,[91] owners of a restaurant had lost their licence to sell alcohol. The Court held that under national law the owners were entitled to run the restaurant with the alcohol licence, unless they contravened the conditions on which the licence was held. It made no difference that, unlike the situation in *Benthem v. Netherlands*, the alcohol licence was not transferable and that the state in Sweden had a monopoly of the wholesale distribution of alcohol. The sole dissenting judge in *Tre Traktörer*, Judge Pinheiro Farinha, held that Article 6(1) did not apply, for the reason that 'the grounds on which a licence may be revoked fall exclusively within the administrative sphere and relate to the achievement of social policy objectives'.[92]

These cases concerned the power of public authorities to impose restrictions on economic activities that individuals would otherwise be free to undertake. Some of them arose because of inadequate or non-existent national provision for enabling decisions of public authorities to be subject to judicial review.[93] The subject-matter of the next case is different, but it will be seen that the legislation in question provided rights of appeal for individuals who were dissatisfied by decisions made in their cases.

---

[87] *Sporrong and Lönnroth v. Sweden*, 23 Sept. 1982, 5 E.H.R.R. 35; and *see* Chapter 10(A). *See also Bodén v. Sweden*, 27 Oct. 1987, 10 E.H.R.R. 367 (expropriation proceedings).
[88] *Benthem v. Netherlands*, 23 Oct. 1985, 8 E.H.R.R. 1.
[89] *Id.*, p. 13.
[90] *Pudas v. Sweden*, 27 Oct. 1987, 10 E.H.R.R. 380.
[91] 7 July 1989, 13 E.H.R.R. 309.
[92] *Id.*
[93] *See*, e.g., *Benthem, supra* n. 88.

7. FELDBRUGGE V. THE NETHERLANDS

Judgment of 29 May 1986
8 E.H.R.R. 425

11. Mrs. Geziena Hendrika Maria Feldbrugge was born in 1945 and is resident at Anna Paulowna. She is of Dutch nationality.

In or about 1978, although she had been unemployed for some time, Mrs. Feldbrugge ceased to register at the Regional Employment Exchange. This was because she had fallen ill and did not consider herself sufficiently recovered to be fit to work.

On 11 April 1978, the Governing Board of the Occupational Association of the Banking and Insurance Wholesale Trade and Self-Employment Sector in Amsterdam decided that as from 24 March 1978 she was no longer entitled to the sickness allowances she had been receiving until then, as the Association's consulting doctor had judged her fit to resume work on that date.

12. She appealed to the Appeals Board in Haarlem.

The President of the Appeals Board sought the opinion of one of the permanent medical experts attached to the Board, a gynaecologist.... After consulting three other doctors...the expert concluded on 1 June 1978 that, gynaecologically speaking, she had been fit for work since 24 March; however, he felt it necessary also to consult an orthopaedic specialist.

On 18 August 1978, another permanent medical expert, an orthopaedic surgeon, examined the applicant and offered her the opportunity to comment.... In his report of 22 August 1978, he too found that Mrs. Feldbrugge had been fit to resume employment as from 24 March of that year.

On the basis of these two reports, the President of the Appeals Board ruled against the applicant.

[Further appeals by the applicant were unsuccessful.]

15. As far as health insurance is concerned, social security in the Netherlands is managed jointly by the State—which in general confines itself to establishing the legal framework of the scheme and to seeing to co-ordination—by employers and by employees.

The branches of the economy, including the liberal professions, are divided into sectors, each with an occupational association responsible for implementation of the social security legislation....

16. ... In case of unfitness for work through sickness, an employed person receives an allowance of 80 percent of his daily pay. He or she applies directly to the occupational association to which his or her employer belongs.

The entitlement to an allowance flows directly from the Act.

17. The scheme is administered by the occupational associations, and the funding is provided entirely by employers and employees....

18. ... On the lodging of an appeal of this kind, the President of the Appeals Board...may immediately instruct its permanent medical expert to carry out an enquiry into the matter.

Within three days of notification of the appeal, the authority that delivered the decision which is challenged must submit all relevant files on the case.

The permanent medical expert consults the private practitioner of the person concerned and the relevant occupational association doctor, except where the file shows that they share his opinion. He summons and examines the appellant; he may consult another practitioner. Finally, he makes a written report to the President of the Appeals Board.

The President—who is a judge appointed for life—gives a reasoned decision which refers to the conclusions of the medical expert....

26. According to the case law of the Court, 'the notion of "civil rights and obligations" cannot be interpreted solely by reference to the domestic law of the respondent State'...

29. There exists great diversity in the legislation and case law of the member states of the Council of Europe as regards the juridical nature of the entitlement to health insurance benefits under social security schemes... Some States—including the Netherlands—treat it as a public-law right, whereas others, on the contrary, treat it as a private-law right; others still would appear to operate a mixed system. What is more, even within the same legal order differences of approach can be found in the case law. Thus, in some States where the public-law aspect is predominant, some court decisions have nonetheless held Article 6(1) to be applicable to claims similar to the one in issue in the present case. Accordingly, there exists no common standard pointing to a uniform European notion in this regard....

31. A number of factors might tend to suggest that the dispute in question should be considered as one falling within the sphere of public law....

32. The first such factor is the character of the legislation. The legal rules governing social security benefits in the context of health insurance differ in many respects from the rules which apply to insurance in general and which are part of civil law. The Netherlands State has assumed the responsibility of regulating the framework of the health insurance scheme and of overseeing the operation of that scheme. To this end, it specifies the categories of beneficiaries, defines the limits of the protection afforded, lays down the rates of the contributions and the allowances, etc.

In several cases, State intervention by means of a statute or delegated legislation has nonetheless not prevented the Court from finding the right in issue to have a private, and hence civil, character. In the present case likewise, such intervention cannot suffice to bring within the sphere of public law the right asserted by the applicant....

33. A second factor of relevance is the obligation to be insured against illness... In other words, those concerned can neither opt out of the benefits nor avoid having to pay the relevant contributions.

Comparable obligations can be found in other fields. Examples are provided by the rules making insurance cover compulsory for the performance of certain activities—such as driving a motor vehicle—or for householders. Yet the entitlement to benefits to which this kind of insurance contract gives rise cannot be qualified as a public-law right. The Court does not therefore discern why the obligation to belong to a health insurance scheme should change the nature of the corresponding right...

34. One final aspect to be considered is the assumption, by the State or by public or semi-public institutions, of full or partial responsibility for ensuring social protection. This was what happened in the present case by virtue of the health insurance scheme operated by the Occupational Association... in Amsterdam. Whether viewed as the culmination of or a stage in the development of the role of the State, such a factor implies, *prima facie*, an extension of the public-law domain.

On the other hand—and the Court will revert to the point later—the present case concerns a matter having affinities with insurance under the ordinary law, which insurance is traditionally governed by private law. ...

35. In sum, even taken together the three foregoing factors, on analysis, do not suffice to establish that Article 6 is inapplicable....

36. In contrast, various considerations argue in favour of the opposite conclusion....

37. To begin with, Mrs. Feldbrugge was not affected in her relations with the public authorities as such, acting in the exercise of discretionary powers, but in her personal capacity as a private individual. She suffered an interference with her means of subsistence and was claiming a right flowing from specific rules laid down by the legislation in force.

For the individual asserting it, such a right is often of crucial importance; this is especially so in the case of health insurance benefits when the employee who is unable to work by reason of illness enjoys no other source of income. In short, the right in question was a personal, economic and individual right, a factor that brought it close to the civil sphere....

38. Secondly, the position of Mrs. Feldbrugge was closely linked with the fact of her being a member of the working population, having been a salaried employee. The applicant was admittedly unemployed at the relevant time, but the availability of the health benefits was determined by reference to the terms of her former contract of employment and the legislation applicable to that contract.

The legal basis of the work that she had performed was a contract of employment governed by private law. Whilst it is true that the insurance provisions derived directly from statute and not from an express clause in the contract, these provisions were in a way grafted onto the contract. They thus formed one of the constituents of the relationship between employer and employee.

In addition, the sickness allowance claimed by Mrs. Feldbrugge was a substitute for the salary payable under the contract, the civil character of this salary being beyond doubt. This allowance shared the same nature as the contract and hence was also invested with a civil character for the purposes of the Convention....

39. Finally, the Dutch health insurance is similar in several respects to insurance under the ordinary law. Thus, under the Dutch health insurance scheme recourse is had to techniques of risk covering and to management methods which are inspired by those current in the private insurance sphere. In the Netherlands, the occupational associations conduct their dealings, notably with those insured, in the same way as a company providing insurance under the ordinary law ...

There exists a further feature of relevance. Complementary insurance policies, taken out with friendly societies or private insurance companies, allow employees to improve their social protection at the price of an increased or fresh financial outlay; such policies constitute in sum an optional extension of compulsory insurance cover. Proceedings instituted in their connection are incontestably civil proceedings. Yet in both cases the risk insured against (for example, ill-health) is the same. ...

Such differences as may exist between private sector insurance and social security insurance do not affect the essential character of the link between the insured and the insurer.

Finally, the Court would draw attention to the fact that in the Netherlands, as in some other countries, the insured themselves participate in the financing of all or some of the social security schemes. Deductions at source are made from their salaries, which deductions establish a close connection between the contributions called for and the allowances granted. Thus, when Mrs. Feldbrugge was working, her employer withheld from her pay a sum paid over to the Occupational Association. In addition, her employer also bore a portion of the insurance contributions, which were included in the firm's accounts under the head of social insurance expenses. The Netherlands State, for its part, was not involved in the financing of the scheme....

40. Having thus evaluated the relative cogency of the features of public and private law present in the instant case, the Court finds the latter to be predominant. None of these various features of private law is decisive on its own, but taken together and cumulatively they confer on the asserted entitlement the character of a civil right within the meaning of Article 6(1)....

41. The Court must therefore inquire whether the proceedings before the bodies responsible for determining Mrs. Feldbrugge's asserted right satisfied the conditions laid down in Article 6(1)....

42. ... [The applicant] submitted that she had been denied a 'fair hearing' before the President of the Appeals Board. In this connection, she alleged a twofold violation of the principle of equality of arms with the Occupational Association. In the first place, she had not had the opportunity of appearing—either in person or represented by a lawyer—to argue her case. Secondly, the reports of the two permanent medical experts had not been made available to her, with the result that she had not been able either to comment on them or, if thought necessary, to call for further reports; yet in practice these documents provided the President of the Appeals Board with the sole basis for his decision.

43. The Government replied that the President is not able himself to enter into the merits of a medical dispute and is thus bound to confine himself to verifying that the permanent medical expert has observed the procedure prescribed by the Appeals Act, notably the obligation to consult the doctors of both parties and to examine the person concerned....

44. It is not within the province of the Court to review in isolation the Dutch institution of the permanent medical expert. The Court confines itself to noting that the permanent medical expert cannot himself determine a dispute over a civil right. The sole responsibility for taking the decision falls to the President of the Appeals Board...

... [T]he procedure followed before the President of the Appeals Board by virtue of the Dutch legislation was clearly not such as to allow proper participation of the contending parties, at any rate during the final and decisive stage of that procedure. To begin with, the President neither heard the applicant nor asked her to file written pleadings. Secondly, he did not afford her or her representative the opportunity to consult the evidence in the case file, in particular the two reports—which were the basis of the decision—drawn up by the permanent experts, and to formulate her objections thereto. Whilst the experts admittedly examined Mrs. Feldbrugge and gave her the opportunity to formulate any comments she might have had, the resultant failing was not thereby cured. In short, the proceedings conducted before the President of the Appeals Board were not attended, to a sufficient degree, by one of the principal guarantees of a judicial procedure. ...

[The Court held by ten votes to seven that there was a violation of Art. 6(1).]

[A declaration by Judge Pinheiro Farinha is omitted.]

Joint Dissenting Opinion of Judges Ryssdal, Bindschedler-Robert, Lagergren, Matscher, Sir Vincent Evans, Bernhardt and Gersing:

1. We agree with the view of the majority of the Court as to the existence in the present case of a 'contestation' (dispute) over a right claimed by the applicant, Mrs. Feldbrugge. In our opinion, however, the dispute did not involve the determination of her 'civil rights and obligations'....

13. The right to a sickness allowance claimed by Mrs. Feldbrugge was an economic right deriving, not from the private contract between herself and her former employer, but from a collective scheme of protection of the working population set up by the legislature. An allocation of society's resources as generated within the employment context has been decided upon by the domestic legislature; and the applicant, as a member of the section of society concerned, was compelled to participate in that scheme. Such schemes represent performance of society's duty to protect the health and welfare of its members; they are not merely examples of the State taking on or regulating an insurance activity equally capable of being carried on by the private sector....

15. ... The judicialisation of dispute procedures, as guaranteed by Article 6(1), is eminently appropriate in the realm of relations between individuals but not necessarily so in the administrative sphere, where organisational, social and economic considerations may legitimately warrant dispute procedures of a less judicial and formal kind. The present case is concerned with the operation of a collective statutory scheme for the allocation of public welfare. As examples of the special characteristics of such schemes, material to the issue of procedural safeguards, one might cite the large numbers of decisions to be taken, the medical aspects, the lack of resources or expertise of the persons affected, the need to balance the public interest for efficient administration against the private interest. Judicialisation of procedures for allocation of public welfare benefits would in many cases necessitate recourse by claimants to lawyers and medical experts and hence lead to an increase in expense and the length of the proceedings....

16. We have not overlooked the fact that the overall object of the Convention is the humanitarian one of the protection of the individual and that, for the man or woman in the street, entitlement to social security benefits is of extreme importance for his or her daily life. However, ... the economic importance for Mrs. Feldbrugge's livelihood of the allowance claimed is insufficient, on its own, to bring into play the applicability of Article 6(1) and its specific judicial guarantees. Of course, it is equally essential that in the administrative field justice should be done and the individual's claims should be investigated in a responsible and objective manner in accordance with the rules laid down, but that is not to say that all the various requirements of Article 6(1)... are therefore applicable. Indeed, as pointed out above, in the present opinion, there exist underlying considerations justifying special procedures in social welfare cases....

19. The foregoing analysis is corroborated by the fact that the relevant legislation predates the elaboration of the Convention by some decades, and there existed similar legislation predating the Convention in many other of the Contracting States. It is therefore reasonable to assume that the intention of the drafters of Article 6(1) was not to include such statutory schemes of collective social protection within its ambit. On examination, the drafting history confirms this reading of the text.

20. The adjective 'civil' was added to the English version of Article 6(1) in November 1950 on the day before the Convention was opened for signature, when a committee of experts examined the text of the Convention for the last time and 'made a certain number of formal corrections and corrections of translations'. Whilst no specific explanation was given for the last-minute change to Article 6(1), it is a fair inference that the reason was merely to align the English text more closely with the language of the French text: prior to the change, although the French version had spoken, as now, of 'droits et obligations de caractère civil', the English version had read 'rights and obligations in a suit of law'.

These two expressions had first been introduced at a meeting (March 1950) of the Committee of Experts on Human Rights of the Council of Europe and were evidently taken directly from the equivalent Article of the then existing draft of the International Covenant on Civil and Political Rights of the United Nations. It is therefore relevant to trace their history in the *travaux préparatoires* of the International Covenant.

21. The crucial discussion on the draft International Covenant took place on 1 June 1949 during the fifth session of the United Nations Commission on Human Rights. The French and Egyptian delegations had presented an amendment that referred to '*droits et obligations*' 'rights and obligations', without qualification. The reaction of the Danish representative (Mr. Sørensen) to this amendment was reported as follows:

> The representatives of France and Egypt proposed that everyone should have the right to have a tribunal determine his rights and obligations. Mr. Sørensen considered that that provision was much too broad in scope; it would tend to submit to a judicial decision any action taken by administrative organs exercising discretionary power conferred on them by law. He appreciated that the individual should be ensured protection against any abuse of power by administrative organs but the question was extremely delicate and it was doubtful whether the Commission would settle it there and then. The study of the division of power between administrative and judicial organs could be undertaken later.... Mr. Sørensen asked the representatives of France and Egypt whether the scope of the provision in question might be limited to indicate that only cases between individuals and not those between individuals and the State were intended.

The French representative (Mr. Cassin), speaking in French, replied that 'the Danish representative's statement had convinced him that it was very difficult to settle in that Article all questions concerning the exercise of justice in the relationships between individuals and governments'. He was therefore prepared to let the words '*soit de ses droits et obligations*' in the first sentence of the Franco-Egyptian amendment be replaced by the expression '*soit des contestations sur ses droits et obligations de caractère civil*' (rendered in the English version of the summary record as 'or of his rights and obligations in a suit of law'). He agreed that the problem 'had not been fully thrashed out and should be examined more thoroughly'.

Later the same day, a drafting committee produced a text which contained the expression 'in a suit of law' in English and '*de caractère civil*' in French. The formula employed in this text is the one that was ultimately adopted for Article 14 of the International Covenant in 1966.

22. It thus seems reasonably clear that the intended effect of the insertion of the qualifying term '*de caractère civil*' in the French text of the draft International Covenant was to exclude from the scope of the provision certain categories of disputes in the field of administration 'concerning the exercise of justice in the relationships between individuals and governments'....

At the same time as deciding *Feldbrugge*, the Court decided *Deumeland v. Germany*,[94] concerning the German scheme for insuring workers against injuries incurred in course of employment. That scheme had many features in common with sickness insurance in the Netherlands, subject to the difference that it did not require contributions to be paid by employees.[95] The complaint in *Deumeland* was that it had taken

---

[94] 29 May 1988, 8 E.H.R.R. 448.

[95] The difference caused one judge, Pinheiro Farinha, in the majority in *Feldbrugge*, to join the minority in *Deumeland*, but this did not affect the outcome.

nearly eleven years for the authorities to decide whether a fall by the worker on an icy pavement while he was returning from work was covered by the scheme. The majority of the Court applied the same reasoning as in *Feldbrugge*; Article 6(1) applied and had been breached by the excessive delay, only part of which had been explained.

In *Feldbrugge* and *Deumeland*, the Court balanced the 'private law' features of the scheme in question against its 'public law' features. We shall see that in later cases the Court has tended to emphasize the economic or pecuniary effect of the scheme on the individual in deciding the issue of 'civil rights'. In *Salesi v. Italy*[96] the applicant complained of delay associated with her appeal against the refusal of a disability pension. In *Salesi*, the benefits were not associated with a private employment contract and were entirely funded by the state, and the Court found decisive the fact that 'the applicant was claiming an individual economic right flowing from specific rules laid down in a statute ...'.[97] By similar reasoning, the Court found disputes over employers' contributions to social welfare plans to involve 'civil rights and obligations'.[98]

In the *Feldbrugge* case it was not contested that the applicant was entitled by law to the benefits she sought on a showing of certain facts. The only issue was the character of such a right. In some cases, however, a prior question is whether or not the applicant's claim involves a procedure for the determination of something properly called a 'right' at all. Unlike the question whether a right is public or civil, the existence of a right is determined solely by reference to the law of the state involved. It must be shown that the dispute was over 'a "right" which can be said, at least on arguable grounds, to be recognized under domestic law'.[99] This requires a close examination of the municipal law sources with an aim to seeing if they define a set of conditions and procedure which trigger an entitlement to the benefit claimed.[100] In *Masson & Van Zon v. The Netherlands*[101] the applicants complained about the procedure for determining whether they were entitled to compensation for their detention in connection with criminal charges on which they were later acquitted. The Netherlands law on which they relied provided that a court 'may' order such compensation if it was 'of the opinion that [there are] reasons in equity' to do so. The Strasbourg Court held that '[t]he grant to a public authority of such a measure of discretion indicates that no actual right is recognized'.[102] This holding may be compared with *Werner v. Austria*[103] where Austrian procedures for similar compensation claims were considered. In the latter case the Court held that Article 6 was applicable. Compensation under Austrian law was to be awarded if 'the suspicion that he committed the offence has been dispelled'. The Court held that unlike *Masson & Van Zon*, in which the decision 'was left entirely

---

[96] 6 Feb. 1993, 26 E.H.R.R. 187.

[97] *Id*. at para. 19. *See also Schuler-Zgraggen v. Switzerland*, 24 June 1993, 16 E.H.R.R. 405.

[98] *Schouten & Meldrum v. Netherlands*, 9 Dec. 1994, 19 E.H.R.R. 432.

[99] *Masson & Van Zon v. The Netherlands*, 28 Sept. 1995, 22 E.H.R.R. 491, para. 44.

[100] *See*, e.g., *Rolf Gustafson v. Sweden*, 1 July 1997, 25 E.H.R.R. 623, para. 40.

[101] 28 Sept. 1995, 22 E.H.R.R. 491.

[102] *Id*. at para. 51. *See also Andersson v. Sweden*, 27 Aug. 1997, 25 E.H.R.R. 722; *M.S. v. Sweden*, 27 Aug. 1997, 28 E.H.R.R. 313.

[103] 24 Nov. 1997, 26 E.H.R.R. 310.

to the discretion of the Court', in this case there was a 'right to be compensated... provided the statutory requirements were satisfied'.[104]

Compare the Court's approach to deciding whether a 'right' is in issue in these cases with the view of Judge de Meyer in a concurring opinion:

Any right which a citizen (civis) may feel entitled to assert, either under national law or under supranational or international law has indeed to be considered a 'civil' right within the meaning of Article 6, para. 1 of the Convention, which enshrines a right which is so prominent that 'there can be no justification for interpreting [it] restrictively'.[105]

The sources of domestic law which may support rights are extensive. The Court has, for example, held that individuals obtained a right to compensation from an international protocol between France and Morocco establishing a lump sum payment for French-owned property expropriated by Morocco. The protocol stated (without further specification) that the apportionment of this payment was to be the responsibility of the French government.[106]

The Strasbourg Court's formulation of the issue is similar to that developed under the United States Constitution to decide whether a person is complaining of a deprivation of 'liberty' or 'property', so as to bring into play a state's obligation to provide 'due process of law' under the Fourteenth Amendment. The gist of the Supreme Courts's modern jurisprudence on this matter is that such a deprivation occurs whenever someone has lost a benefit to which he is entitled by law, be it the common law of property or contract or a positive enactment by the state. In such cases an individual is entitled to a fair procedure for determining whether the state's action was in accordance with the governing law. This reasoning has been applied to the termination of such state benefits as drivers' licences,[107] public education,[108] and non-probationary government employment.[109] Similarly, public welfare benefits may not be terminated in the absence of a fair hearing, since to do so would be a deprivation of 'property' without due process of law.[110]

A cognizable claim under Article 6 requires more than just showing a dispute over a 'right'. The applicant must also show that the procedure about which he or she is complaining was decisive for the determination of that right. In *Fayed v. United Kingdom*[111] the applicant was the target of an investigation by the Department of Trade and Industry concerning possible fraudulent statements made in connection with his acquisition of a public company. The applicant believed that publication of the report of the investigation injured his reputation. The European Court agreed that under

---

[104] *Id.* at paras. 33–5. *See also Szucs v. Austria*, 24 Nov. 1997, 26 E.H.R.R. 310.

[105] *Rolf Gustafson v. Sweden*, 1 July 1997, 25 E.H.R.R. 623 (concurring opinion) (quoting *Moreira de Azevedo v. Portugal*, 23 Oct. 1990, 13 E.H.R.R. 721, at para. 66).

[106] *Beaumartin v. France*, 24 Nov. 1994, 19 E.H.R.R. 485.

[107] *Bell v. Burson*, 402 U.S. 535 (1971).

[108] *Goss v. Lopez*, 419 U.S. 565 (1975).

[109] *Perry v. Sindermann*, 408 U.S. 593 (1972).

[110] *Goldberg v. Kelly*, 397 U.S. 254 (1970).

[111] 21 Sept. 1994, 18 E.H.R.R. 393.

English law, the applicant had a right against unjustified attacks on his reputation. But the investigation did not, as a matter of law, determine liability in connection with that right:

However, the Court is satisfied that the functions performed by the Inspector were, in practice as well as in theory, essentially investigative (see the similar analysis by the Supreme Court of the United States of America of the functions of the Federal Civil Rights Commission in the case of Hannah v. Larche (363 U.S. 420 (1960))). The inspectors did not adjudicate, either in form or in substance. They themselves said in their report that their findings would not be dispositive of anything. They did not make a legal determination as to criminal or civil liability concerning the Fayed brothers, and in particular concerning the latter's civil right to honour and reputation. The purpose of their inquiry was to ascertain and record facts which might subsequently be used as the basis for action by other competent authorities—prosecuting, regulatory, disciplinary or even legislative.[112]

The Court has also held that parties objecting to the licensing procedure for nuclear plants in Switzerland stated no Article 6 claim because they had not established that the operation of the plant posed a risk to their physical health. Since they were relying on a right to physical integrity conceded to be part of Swiss law, this lack of proof was fatal to any conclusion that the procedure complained of was decisive for the determination of that right.[113] On the other hand, the European Court has held that, not withstanding their special character, Constitutional Courts are subject to Article 6 where their decisions have a decisive effect on the outcome of litigation in which civil rights are at stake in ordinary courts.[114]

The case-law of the Court on Article 6(1) retains a degree of complexity that some commentators regard as unnecessary and undesirable.[115] The Court has come to emphasize the economic significance of what is in dispute between the individual and the public authority: this is seen both in the decisions on social welfare and in the decisions on professional regulation and licensing that we have already considered. In the licensing cases, for instance *Tre Traktören Aktiebolag v. Sweden*,[116] it was emphasized that in the absence of the regulatory scheme, the individual would have been entitled to carry on the activity in question, and that possessing a licence enabled him to make contracts with his customers. The effect of such cases may have been to redirect the legal inquiry from the particular character of the right claimed to the presence of a substantial injury to an individual caused by an action of the state argued to be in violation of state law.

In a potentially substantial extension of the range of proceedings governed by Article 6, the Court held it applicable to complaints of individuals who claim an

---

[112] *Id.* at para. 61. *See also Canada (Attorney-General) v. Canada (Commission of Inquiry on the Blood System)* [1997] 3 S.C.R. 440.

[113] *Balmer-Schafroth & Others v. Switzerland*, 26 Aug. 1997, 25 E.H.R.R. 598, para. 40.

[114] *See*, e.g., *Sussman v. Germany*, 16 Sept. 1996, 25 E.H.R.R. 64, para. 40.

[115] *See*, e.g., P. van Dijk, 'Access to Court', in R. St J Macdonald, F. Matscher and H. Petzold (eds.), *The European System for the Protection of Human Rights* (1993), 345.

[116] *Supra* n. 91.

interest in disputes between the state and third parties. For example, it has held that Article 6 covered a claim by adjacent landowners that a permit to dispose of hazardous waste should not have been granted to a third party without more stringent conditions protecting the water supply on their property. The Court held that since the applicant had the right under national law to request that the issuing board impose the conditions, as well as a right to appeal the decisions to the government, they had an arguable entitlement in municipal law to the requested protection. Since, moreover, their claim concerned the ability to use the well on their property for drinking purposes, it was essentially based on a property right which was a 'civil right' under Article 6.[117] Likewise Article 6 was applied to the procedure for dealing with a neighbouring landowner's objection to a development plan for the construction of housing. The government had argued that the issues turned on legal provisions implementing public environmental policy. The Court, however, was more impressed with the fact that the applicant 'wished to avoid any infringement of her pecuniary rights because she considered that the works on the land adjoining her property would jeopardise her enjoyment of it and would reduce its market value'.[118]

The Court's judgments in these cases seem to embody a general rule that any legal issue, the determination of which entails financial consequences for a person, involves his or her 'civil rights and obligations'. In an often repeated formula the Court has stated that Article 6(1) 'applies where the subject matter of an action is "pecuniary" in nature and is founded on an alleged infringement of rights which are likewise pecuniary'.[119] Thus a claim under anti-discrimination law has been held to be a civil right and not a public right because the decision might result in a financial benefit to the applicant.[120] The right to initiate a criminal prosecution as a civil party complainant was held to come under Article 6 because of the prospect of possible compensation.[121] In a subsequent case, however, the Court declined to find that the state's refusal to initiate criminal proceedings which the applicant might have joined as a civil party raised Article 6 issues. It noted that it was open to the applicant to seek compensation in a civil action.[122] The Court has not, therefore, made the presence of a financial interest sufficient to a make out a claim of a civil right. In *Schouten & Meldrum v. The Netherlands*[123] it held that Article 6 did apply to a dispute concerning the obligation of an employer to contribute to social insurance plans, but it voiced this caution:

Nor is it in itself sufficient to show that a dispute is 'pecuniary' in nature. There may exist 'pecuniary' obligations *vis-à-vis* the State or its subordinate authorities which, for the purpose of Article 6 §1, are to be considered as belonging exclusively to the realm of public law and are accordingly not covered by the notion of 'civil rights and obligations'. Apart from fines imposed

---

[117] *Zander v. Sweden*, 25 Nov. 1993, 18 E.H.R.R. 175.

[118] *Ortenberg v. Austria*, 25 Nov. 1994, 19 E.H.R.R. 524, para. 28.   [119] *Id.*

[120] *Tinnelly & Sons Ltd. & Others and McElduff & Others v. United Kingdom*, 10 July 1998, 27 E.H.R.R. 249.

[121] *Ait-Mouhous v. France*, 28 Oct. 1998, 30 E.H.R.R. 382.

[122] *Assenov and Others v Bulgaria*, 28 Oct. 1998, 28 E.H.R.R. 652, paras. 107–13.

[123] 9 Dec. 1994, 19 E.H.R.R. 432.

by way of 'criminal sanction', this will be the case, in particular, when an obligation which is pecuniary in nature derives from tax legislation or is otherwise part of normal civic duties in a democratic society.[124]

There continue to be categories of official decisions that are held not to concern 'civil rights and obligations' and thus to be outside Article 6(1), even if they involve economic or pecuniary aspects. Two categories of such decisions relate to immigration and asylum law[125] and disputes over electoral law and other 'political' matters.[126] We now examine a third category, employment in the public sector.

8. EMPLOYMENT IN THE PUBLIC SERVICE

Since the Convention guarantees extend to everyone in the jurisdiction of the contracting states, in principle all public sector employees, whether in central or local government, the police, the armed forces, or other public services such as education, enjoy rights under the Convention. But as regards specific rights and freedoms, the status and duties of a public servant may justify greater restrictions on the freedom than would ordinarily apply.[127] In many countries, the relationship between a state and its employees forms an important branch of public law, and disputes arising from the relationship are entrusted to the administrative courts. Even where this is not the case, many government servants are subject to rules that preserve executive authority; these rules may derive from the constitution, from legislation or (in the United Kingdom) from the prerogative powers of the Crown.[128] The Strasbourg jurisprudence initially reflected the view that disputes arising from the public service do not involve matters of 'civil right or obligation'. The formula applied by the Court was that 'disputes relating to the recruitment, careers and termination of service of public servants' are in general outside Article 6(1). This was qualified by an exception for disputes over the pension rights of former public servants. Thus in *Massa v. Italy*,[129] the Court accepted jurisdiction in the case of a widower who had for years been trying to establish his right to a pension arising from his late wife's position as head-teacher in a state school. In order to clarify a complex body of case-law, a ruling of great importance was made in 1999 by the Grand Chamber in *Pellegrin v. France*.[130] This decision held sway until 2007, when the law was further developed by the Grand Chamber.

---

[124] *Id.* at para. 50.
[125] *Maaouia v. France*, 5 Oct. 2000, 33 E.H.R.R. 42; *see* section B *infra*.
[126] *Pierre-Bloch v. France*, 21 Oct. 1997, 26 E.H.R.R. 202.
[127] On the applicability of the right of free expression to civil servants, *see* Chapter 6(D) *supra*.
[128] *Council of Civil Service Unions v. Minister for the Civil Service* [1985] A.C. 374.
[129] 24 Aug. 1993, 18 E.H.R.R. 266.
[130] 8 Dec. 1999, 31 E.H.R.R. 26.

9. ESKELINEN V. FINLAND

Judgment of 19 April 2007
45 E.H.R.R. 1

[Several serving police officers, together with a civilian assistant employed in the police, were in dispute with the authorities over the loss of an allowance that had previously been paid as a bonus for working in a remote part of the country. In 1990, changes were made in the police districts and the remote-area supplement was abolished. The claimants alleged that the local police command promised that their loss would be compensated. In July 1991, the Ministry of Finance, without giving reasons, refused to authorize any extra payments. The claim went in March 1993 to the Kuopio County Administrative Board. In March 1997, the Board rejected the claim, relying simply on the decision by the Ministry of Finance in 1991 and denying that the local police command had competence to promise compensation. The Board's decision was upheld in June 1998 by the County Administrative Court, and in April 2000 by the Supreme Administrative Court. The two Courts refused an oral hearing to the claimants regarding the alleged promise made to them, since such a promise had 'no legal relevance' to the case. The applicants claimed at Strasbourg that the decision had not been made in a reasonable time, and that they had been denied a hearing.]

39. The Government have contested the applicability of Article 6 on two grounds, namely whether there was a 'right' and whether it was 'civil' in nature.

40. First, the Court will examine whether there existed a 'right' in the present case. According to the principles enunciated in its case-law,[131] the dispute over a 'right', which can be said at least on arguable grounds to be recognised under domestic law, must be genuine and serious; it may relate not only to the actual existence of a right but also to its scope and the manner of its exercise; and, finally, the result of the proceedings must be directly decisive for the right in question.

41. The Court notes that it has not been disputed that the Provincial Police Command had promised the applicants compensation. The case file also discloses that individual wage supplements were granted in situations which were not entirely dissimilar from that of the applicants.... While it is true that their claims were rejected, the Administrative Courts may be regarded as having examined the merits of the application and in so doing they determined the dispute over their rights. The Court considers that against such a background the applicants could claim to have a right on arguable grounds.[132]

42. Secondly, the Court has examined the Government's argument, relying on *Pellegrin v. France*...that Article 6 is not applicable since disputes raised by servants of the State such as police officers over their conditions of service are excluded from its ambit.... In order to determine this question the Court must recall the background to and the *ratio* of the *Pellegrin* judgment and how this has been applied in practice in subsequent cases.

---

[131] Citing *Pudas v. Sweden*, 27 Oct. 1987, 10 E.H.R.R. 380, para. 31.
[132] Citing *Neves e Silva v. Portugal*, 27 Apr. 1989, para. 37.

1. Summary of the case-law

43. Before the *Pellegrin* judgment the Court had held that disputes relating to the recruitment, careers and termination of service of civil servants were as a general rule outside the scope of Article 6 § 1. That general principle of exclusion had however been limited and clarified in a number of judgments. For example, in the cases of *Francesco Lombardo v. Italy*[133] and *Massa v. Italy*[134] the Court had considered that the applicants' complaints related neither to the 'recruitment' nor to the 'careers' of civil servants and only indirectly to 'termination of service' as they consisted in claims for purely pecuniary rights arising in law after termination of service. In those circumstances and in view of the fact that the Italian State was not using 'discretionary powers' in performing its obligation to pay the pensions in issue and could be compared to an employer who was a party to a contract of employment governed by private law, the Court had held that the applicants' claims were 'civil' in nature within the meaning of Article 6 § 1.

44. On the other hand, in the case of *Neigel v. France*[135] the decision contested by the applicant, namely the refusal to reinstate her to a permanent post in the civil service, had been held by the Court to concern 'her "recruitment", her "career" and the "termination of [her] service"'. Nor did the applicant's claim for payment of the salary she would have received if she had been reinstated render Article 6 § 1 applicable as an award of such compensation by the administrative court was 'directly dependent on a prior finding that the refusal to reinstate [had been] unlawful'. The Court had accordingly decided that the dispute did not concern a 'civil' right within the meaning of Article 6 § 1.

45. According to other judgments, Article 6 § 1 had applied where the claim in issue related to a 'purely economic' right—such as payment of salary....—or an 'essentially economic' one...and did not mainly call in question 'the authorities' discretionary powers'...[136]

46. When the Court came to review the situation in the case of *Pellegrin* (§ 60) it considered that the above case-law contained a degree of uncertainty for Contracting States as to the scope of their obligations under Article 6 § 1 in disputes raised by employees in the public sector over their conditions of service. The Court sought to put an end to that uncertainty by establishing an autonomous interpretation of the term 'civil service' which would make it possible to afford equal treatment to public servants performing equivalent or similar duties in the States Parties to the Convention, irrespective of the...nature of the legal relation between the official and the administrative authority.

47. To that end the Court introduced a functional criterion based on the nature of the employee's duties and responsibilities. The holders of posts involving responsibilities in the general interest or participation in the exercise of powers conferred by public law wielded a portion of the State's sovereign power. The State therefore had a legitimate interest in requiring of these officials a special bond of trust and loyalty. On the other hand, in respect of other posts which did not have this 'public administration' aspect, there was no such interest... The Court therefore ruled that the only disputes excluded from the scope of Article 6 § 1 were those which were raised by public servants whose duties typified the specific activities of the public

---

[133] 26 Nov. 1992, 18 E.H.R.R. 266, para. 17.
[134] 24 August 1993, 18 E.H.R.R. 266, para. 26.
[135] 17 March 1997, 30 E.H.R.R. 310, para. 44.
[136] Citations in this paragraph omitted.

service in so far as the latter was acting as the depositary of public authority responsible for protecting the general interests of the State or other public authorities. A manifest example of such activities was provided by the armed forces and the police ... It concluded that no disputes between administrative authorities and employees who occupied posts involving participation in the exercise of powers conferred by public law attracted the application of Article 6 § 1 ...

48. The Court observes that *Pellegrin* was categorical in its wording; where the post belonged to the said category, all disputes were excluded from Article 6 irrespective of their nature. It allowed only one exception: disputes concerning pensions all came within the ambit of Article 6 § 1 because, on retirement, the special bond between the employees and the authorities was broken; the employees then found themselves in a situation exactly comparable to that of employees under private law in that the special relationship of trust and loyalty binding them to the State had ceased to exist and the employee could no longer wield a portion of the State's sovereign power (see the judgment in *Pellegrin*, § 67).

49. It is important to note that the Court emphasised that in applying a functional criterion it must adopt a restrictive interpretation ... of the exceptions to the safeguards afforded by Article 6 §1 .... This was to limit the cases in which public servants could be denied the practical and effective protection afforded to them ...

2. Whether there is a need for a development of the case-law

50. The *Pellegrin* judgment ... was intended to provide a workable concept by which it was to be ascertained, on a case-by-case basis, whether the applicant's post entailed—in the light of the nature of the duties and responsibilities appertaining to it—direct or indirect participation in the exercise of powers conferred by public law and duties designed to safeguard the general interests of the State or of other public authorities. It then had to be determined whether the applicant, in the framework of one of these categories of posts, did indeed exercise functions which could be characterised as falling within the exercise of public power, that is, whether the applicant's position within the State hierarchy was sufficiently important or elevated to speak of a participation in wielding State power.

51. The present case, however, highlights that the application of the functional criterion may itself lead to anomalous results. At the material time the applicants were employed by the Ministry of the Interior. Five of them were employed as police officers, which typifies the specific activities of the public service as defined above. This entailed participating directly in the exercise of powers conferred by public law and the performance of duties designed to safeguard the general interests of the State. The functions of the office assistant applicant were purely administrative, without any decision-making competence or other exercise directly or indirectly of public power.... On a strict application of the *Pellegrin* approach it would appear that the office assistant applicant ... would enjoy the guarantees of Article 6 § 1, whereas there is no doubt that the police officer applicants would not. This would be so irrespective of the fact that the dispute was identical for all the applicants.

52. Further, an examination of the cases decided since *Pellegrin* shows that ascertaining the nature and status of the applicant's functions has not been an easy task; nor has the category of public service in which the applicant works always been clearly distinguishable on the basis of his or her actual role....

For example, in *Kępka v. Poland*[137] the Court found that, although the applicant, unfit for fire-fighting duties, worked throughout his career in the national fire service as a lecturer, his duties, which involved research and access to information of a sensitive nature, had to be regarded as falling within the sphere of national defence, in which the State exercised sovereign power, and as having entailed, at least indirectly, participation in the performance of duties designed to safeguard the general interests of the State...Accordingly, Article 6 was inapplicable. [In] *Kanayev v. Russia*,[138] where the applicant was an active officer of the Russian navy, a third-rank captain, and thus in that capacity 'wielded a portion of the State's sovereign power', Article 6 § 1 was held not to apply, even though the dispute related to non-enforcement of a court judgment in his favour which related to disputed travel expenses....

53. Furthermore,...taken literally, the 'functional approach' requires that Article 6 be excluded from application to disputes where the position of the applicant as a State official does not differ from the position of any other litigant, or, in other words, where the dispute between the employee and the employer is not especially marked by a 'special bond of trust and loyalty'.

54. That it was the applicant's position and not the nature of the dispute which was decisive was, however, confirmed in the case of *Martinie v. France*[139] where the Grand Chamber concluded that Article 6 § 1 was applicable, as the Chamber had done...but on the basis of different reasoning. It had regard to the fact that the applicant was a civil servant who worked as an accountant for a school, without any participation in the exercise of public powers, whereas the Chamber had mainly had regard to the nature of the dispute between the applicant and the State, namely his liability to repay unauthorised payments, in reaching the conclusion that the obligations of the applicant were 'civil' ones within the meaning of Article 6 § 1....

55. The Court can only conclude that the functional criterion, as applied in practice, has not simplified the analysis of the applicability of Article 6 in proceedings to which a civil servant is a party...

56. It is against this background and for these reasons that the Court finds that the functional criterion adopted in the case of *Pellegrin* must be further developed. While it is in the interests of legal certainty, foreseeability and equality before the law that the Court should not depart, without good reason, from precedents laid down in previous cases, a failure by the Court to maintain a dynamic and evolutive approach would risk rendering it a bar to reform or improvement.[140]

57. *Pellegrin* should be understood...as constituting a first step away from the previous principle of inapplicability of Article 6 to the civil service, towards partial applicability. It reflected the basic premise that certain civil servants, because of their functions, are bound by a special bond of trust and loyalty towards their employer. However,...in very many Contracting States access to a court is accorded to civil servants, allowing them to bring claims for salary and allowances, even dismissal or recruitment, on a similar basis to employees in the private sector. The domestic system, in such circumstances, perceives no conflict between the vital interests of the State and the right of the individual to protection. Indeed, while neither the

---

[137] 11 July 2000 (admissibility decision).
[138] 27 July 2006, para. 18.
[139] [G.C.], 12 Apr. 2006, 42 E.H.R.R. 15, para. 30.
[140] Citing *Mamatkulov and Askarov v. Turkey* [G.C.], 41 E.H.R.R. 25, para. 121.

Convention nor its Protocols guarantee a right of recruitment to the civil service, it does not follow that in other respects civil servants fall outside the scope of the Convention.[141]

59. ... In the present case, where the applicants, police officers and administrative assistant alike, had, according to the national legislation, the right to have their claims for allowances examined by a tribunal, no ground related to the effective functioning of the State or any other public necessity has been advanced which might require the removal of Convention protection against unfair or lengthy proceedings.

60. Looking to European law generally, ... the Court notes that *Pellegrin* sought support in the categories of activities and posts listed by the European Commission and by the Court of Justice of the European Communities in connection with the exception to the freedom of movement ... However, ... the Luxembourg Court itself applies a wider approach in favour of judicial control, as shown by its landmark judgment in the case of *Marguerite Johnston v. Chief Constable of the Royal Ulster Constabulary*[142] brought by a female police officer on the basis of the Directive on non-discrimination....

This and other case-law ... indicate that the scope of applicability of judicial control in EU law is wide. If an individual can rely on a material right guaranteed by Community law, his or her status as a holder of public power does not render the requirements of judicial control inapplicable....

61. The Court recognises the State's interest in controlling access to a court when it comes to certain categories of staff. However, it is primarily for the Contracting States, in particular the competent national legislature, not the Court, to identify expressly those areas of public service involving the exercise of the discretionary powers intrinsic to State sovereignty where the interests of the individual must give way. The Court exerts its supervisory role subject to the principle of subsidiarity.[143] If a domestic system bars access to a court, the Court will verify that the dispute is indeed such as to justify the application of the exception to the guarantees of Article 6. If it does not, then there is no issue and Article 6 § 1 will apply.

It should be emphasised, however, that this situation is distinct from other cases, which due to the claims being made are regarded as falling outside the civil and criminal heads of Article 6 § 1 of the Convention (see, *inter alia*, for the assessment of tax;[144] for matters of asylum, nationality and residence in a country;[145] and for the adjudication of election disputes in respect of members of Parliament[146]). The reasoning in this case is therefore limited to the situation of civil servants.

62. To recapitulate, in order for the respondent State to be able to rely before the Court on the applicant's status as a civil servant in excluding the protection embodied in Article 6, two conditions must be fulfilled. Firstly, the State in its national law must have expressly excluded access to a court for the post or category of staff in question. Secondly, the exclusion must be justified on objective grounds in the State's interest.... In order for the exclusion to be justified, it is not enough for the State to establish that the civil servant in question participates in the exercise of public power or that there exists ... a 'special bond of trust and loyalty' between

---

[141] Citing, *inter alia*, *Glasenapp v. Germany*, 28 Aug. 1986, 9 E.H.R.R. 25, para. 49.

[142] Case 222/84, [1986] E.C.R. 1651, para. 18.

[143] Citing *Z and Others v. United Kingdom* [G.C.], 34 E.H.R.R. 3, para. 103.

[144] Citing *Ferrazzini v. Italy* [G.C.], 34 E.H.R.R. 45.

[145] Citing *Maaouia v. France, supra* n. 125.

[146] Citing *Pierre-Bloch v. France, supra* n. 126.

the civil servant and the State, as employer. It is also for the State to show that the subject matter of the dispute in issue is related to the exercise of State power or that it has called into question the special bond. Thus, there can in principle be no justification for the exclusion... of ordinary labour disputes, such as those relating to salaries, allowances or similar entitlements, on the basis of the special nature of relationship between the particular civil servant and the State in question. There will, in effect, be a presumption that Article 6 applies. It will be for the respondent Government to demonstrate, first, that a civil-servant applicant does not have a right of access to a court under national law and, second, that the exclusion of the rights under Article 6 for the civil servant is justified.

63. In the present case it is common ground that the applicants all had access to a court under national law. Accordingly, Article 6 § 1 is applicable.

[Dealing with the guarantees under Article 6(1) that were relied on by the applicants, the Court decided on the evidence that (a) the Government had given no sufficient explanation as to why the County Administrative Board had taken four years to decide a case that was not complex, but (b) the applicants had had ample opportunity to put forward their case in writing and there had been a good reason for denying them an oral hearing.]

In the course of its judgment, the Court referred to Article 47 of the Charter of Fundamental Rights of the European Union, which on the right to an effective remedy and a fair trial provides *inter alia*: 'Everyone is entitled to a fair and public hearing within a reasonable time by an independent and impartial tribunal previously established by law'. The Court observed that in EU law the right to a fair hearing is not confined to disputes relating to civil law rights and obligations.

The five dissenting judges (Costa, Wildhaber, Türmen, Borrego Borrego and Jociene) wished to uphold the approach in *Pellegrin v. France*. They said:

4. Through this... well-known judgment, the Court had sought to 'put an end to the uncertainty which surrounds application of the guarantees of Article 6 § 1 to disputes between States and their servants' (§ 61). To this end, it had abandoned criteria such as that relating to the economic nature of the dispute, which '[left] scope for a degree of arbitrariness' (§ 60), in favour of 'a functional criterion based on the nature of the employee's duties and responsibilities' (§ 64). While adopting a restrictive interpretation of the exceptions to the safeguards afforded by Article 6 § 1, the Court decided that 'the only disputes excluded from the scope of Article 6 § 1 of the Convention are those which are raised by public servants whose duties typify the specific activities of the public service in so far as the latter is acting as the depositary of public authority responsible for protecting the general interests of the State or other public authorities. *A manifest example of such activities is provided by the armed forces and the police*' (our emphasis) (§ 66).

5. It is well-known that, in defining this functional criterion, the Court relied on the... case-law of the Court of Justice of the European Communities, reviewed in *Pellegrin* in §§ 37 to 41. In this respect, we disagree with the majority when, in the instant judgment, it refers, in paragraph 60, to a 'landmark judgment' of the Court of Justice, namely that delivered in [the case of *Marguerite Johnston*]. Admittedly, that was indeed a landmark judgment, ... which held that judicial control reflects a general principle of law... However, its scope differs from that which is presumed in the instant judgment. The issue was not one of determining whether every dispute between the State and its agents fell within the scope of Article 6 of the Convention, but

merely of confirming that, by virtue of a general principle of law, every act by a public authority must, in principle, be open to supervision of its lawfulness (such as the *recours pour excès de pouvoir* in French law).

6. In any event, we fail to see what theoretical or practical necessity required the Court to abandon the *Pellegrin* case-law.... It has been applied by the Court for seven years without any real problem and... it has extended rather than restricted the application of the guarantees secured under Article 6 § 1. The categories of agents excluded from these guarantees, such as the police service in its entirety, are limited when compared with public service employees as a whole... Legal certainty has certainly improved if we compare the situation with that which obtained prior to the *Pellegrin* judgment. As to the argument based on the existence of access to a domestic court, we are not convinced by it. As Article 53 of the Convention rightly points out, nothing prevents a High Contracting Party from recognising in its law freedoms or guarantees which go further than those set forth in the Convention; in addition, as legal systems vary from one State to another, the reasoning in the instant judgment is likely to have the effect of making the applicability of Article 6 § 1 to disputes between the State and its agents dependent on there existing access to a court with jurisdiction to decide them within the domestic legal system. To sum up, instead of the 'autonomous interpretation' (by the Court) that the latter considered it important to establish for the purposes of Article 6 § 1 (see the *Pellegrin* judgment, § 63), the instant judgment encourages a dependent and variable, not to say uncertain, interpretation, in other words an arbitrary one. In our opinion, this is an inappropriate step back.

7. In conclusion, the Court has overturned its well-established case-law. Admittedly, it is entitled to do so (even if the case-law in question is relatively recent). In general, however, the Court takes this step where there are new developments and where a new need arises. This is not the case here. Abandoning a solid precedent in such conditions creates legal uncertainty and, in our opinion, will make it difficult for the States to identify the extent of their obligations.

The effect of *Eskelinen v. Finland* is likely to be that, where national law provides protection for public servants against unfair or unlawful treatment, whether in administrative law (as in France) or in employment law (as in the United Kingdom), the access of public servants to Strasbourg will become easier. Where national law denies public servants the right to a remedy in a court or tribunal, their hope in coming to Strasbourg will be to persuade the Court that exclusion of their rights under Article 6 is not justified (see the judgment in *Eskelinen*, para. 62).

10. FURTHER ASPECTS OF THE SCOPE OF ARTICLE 6(1)

In light of the broader meaning given in *Eskelinen* to Article 6(1), it may be asked whether the Court is still justified in restricting the scope of the article by reference to the fact that a dispute concerns a public right or obligation and not a civil right or obligation. It will be seen from the *Eskelinen* judgment (para. 61) that there are at least three categories of public law claims that are denied the protection of the Convention guarantee of due process. Each of these categories is debatable.

(1) In *Ferrazzini v. Italy*, a complaint of delay in the making of tax assessments was held by the Court by 11–6 to be outside Article 6(1); the majority stated that 'tax matters still form part of the hard core of public-authority prerogatives, with the public nature of the relationship between the taxpayer and the tax authority remaining predominant'.[147] The minority took a very different view: while accepting that 'civil rights' did not mean any rights that were not criminal, they emphasized that any imposition of tax directly affects the individual's financial position[148] and that tax law is not based on the exercise of discretionary powers by the administration.

(2) The second category comprises disputes over the exercise of political rights, such as the right to stand for election or incurring campaign expenditure, even if matters of pecuniary interest are affected,[149] and even though the First Protocol, Article 3, protects the right to free elections. The exclusion from Article 6(1) of political questions extends beyond election disputes into such matters as examination of the legality of a political party's aims and methods.[150]

(3) Thirdly, excluded from Article 6(1) are disputes involving the entry, residence and deportation of foreign citizens, including claims for asylum.[151] Such disputes may well involve matters to which the individual's Convention rights are relevant.[152] Executive decisions of this kind ought not to be assigned to a residual area in which a state's arbitrary power may be exercised, immune from control on grounds of due process.

One issue that has some jurisdictional sensitivity is whether Article 6(1) guarantees apply to questions decided by a constitutional court. In some countries, litigation between private parties over their civil rights may go into suspense while constitutional aspects of the case are referred to the Constitutional Court. Does Article 6(1) require such a court to decide the issues within a reasonable time and to observe the procedural rights of the parties? The Court gave an affirmative answer to this question in *Ruiz-Mateos v. Spain*;[153] but rights under Article 6(1) do not extend to constitutional procedures that do not directly involve an individual's rights.

In the previous section, an issue that was emphasized in the minority judgment in *Feldbrugge v. Netherlands*, continues to be of great practical significance.[154] If Article 6(1) properly interpreted applies to many decisions made by public authorities, to what

---

[147] *Supra* n. 144, para. 29. *See also* the important qualification made in the concurring judgment of Judge Ress.

[148] Citing *Editions Périscope v. France*, 26 Mar. 1992, 14 E.H.R.R. 597.

[149] *Pierre-Bloch v. France, supra* n. 126. And *see Valentin Gorizdra v. Moldova* 2 July 2002.

[150] *Yazar, Karatas and Aksoy v. Turkey*, 9 April 2002, 36 E.H.R.R. 6.

[151] *Maaouia v. France, supra* n. 125.

[152] Consider e.g. *Soering v. United Kingdom*, 7 July 1989, 11 E.H.R.R. 439; and *Abudulaziz, Cabales and Balkandali v. United Kingdom*, 28 May 1985, 7 E.H.R.R. 471.

[153] 23 June 1993, 16 E.H.R.R. 505. In *Deumeland v. Germany, supra* n. 94, the Court had held that proceedings in the German Constitutional Court must be completed within a reasonable time. *See also Becker v. Germany*, 26 Sept. 2002 and *Voggenreiter v. Germany*, 8 Jan. 2004, 42 E.H.R.R. 22.

[154] The following account draws on a fuller discussion of this topic, referring to the United Kingdom, in M. Supperstone, J. Goudie and P. Walker, *Judicial Review* (3rd edn. 2005), sections 4.19–4.23 (by A. W. Bradley).

extent, if at all, should all public authorities be required to adopt decision-making procedures modelled on those of the courts? A senior United Kingdom judge, Lord Hoffmann, commented on the Article 6(1) case-law:

> The [Strasbourg Court] has not simply said . . . that one can have a 'civil right' to a lawful decision by an administrator. Instead, the court has accepted that 'civil rights' mean only rights in private law and has applied Article 6(1) to administrative decisions on the ground that they can determine or affect rights in private law.[155]

The official bodies that make these decisions at first instance are unlikely themselves to meet the criteria required for them to have the status of an 'independent and impartial court or tribunal'. In fact, their decisions are often subject to appeal or review. If the initial administrative decision is not made by an independent and impartial tribunal (as will often be the case), when will review or appeal proceedings be sufficient to meet the requirements of Article 6(1)? In *Albert and Le Compte v. Belgium*, the Court laid down the principle that:

> the Convention calls at least for one of the two following systems: either the jurisdictional organs themselves comply with . . . Article 6(1), or they do not so comply but are subject to subsequent control *by a judicial body that has full jurisdiction* and does provide the guarantees of Article 6(1).[156]

In deciding the impact of Article 6(1) on administrative decisions, the Court may thus take into account both the initial decision-making procedure and any subsequent rights of access to a court or tribunal by way of appeal or review. Article 6(1) guarantees may be satisfied at the appellate or review level. This approach underlines the need for an effective system of judicial review.[157] The passage quoted above from *Albert and Le Compte* refers to the need for subsequent control by a judicial body 'that has full jurisdiction'. Does this require the reviewing court to have full power to decide all questions of law, fact, merits and discretion? If so, this would require of the national system of judicial review more than it can provide in many European countries. In 1993, the Strasbourg Court referred to the 'respect which must be afforded to decisions taken by administrative authorities on grounds of expediency'; the Court held that, on a compulsory purchase of land in Austria, it was not necessary for the Administrative Court to be able to review the merits of a policy decision.[158]

Observations on this position have been made by two judges in the United Kingdom. Lord Hoffman said of the term 'full jurisdiction' that it 'does not mean full decision-making powers. It means full jurisdiction *to deal with the case as the nature of the decision requires*'.[159] And in a case concerning a claim for housing by a homeless person, Lord Bingham drew attention to the inter-relation within Article 6(1) between

---

[155] *R. (Alconbury Developments Ltd) v. Secretary of State for the Environment* [2003] 2 A.C. 295, para. 79.
[156] *Supra* n. 71, at para. 29, emphasis supplied.
[157] *See*, e.g., *Zander v. Sweden*, 25 Nov. 1993, 18 E.H.R.R. 175.
[158] *Zumtobel v. Austria*, 2 Sept. 1993, 17 E.H.R.R. 116, at para. 32.
[159] In the *Alconbury Developments Ltd* case, *supra* n. 155, para. 87 (emphasis supplied).

the concept of 'civil rights' and the requirement of an 'independent and impartial tribunal':

> The narrower the interpretation given to 'civil rights', the greater the need to insist on review by a judicial tribunal exercising full powers. Conversely, the more elastic the interpretation given to 'civil rights', the more flexible must be the approach to the requirement of independent and impartial review if the emasculation (by over-judicialisation) of administrative welfare schemes is to be avoided.[160]

These perceptive observations give guidance on a complex body of case-law and should help to prevent Article 6(1) becoming a straitjacket that requires inappropriate procedures to be observed by public authorities.

One other important aspect of Article 6(1) must be mentioned briefly.

Article 6 provides the right to certain procedures 'in the determination of ... civil rights and obligations'. On its face this provision might be understood to apply only to situations where a person finds him- or herself facing a formal legal procedure in which his or her rights have been placed in jeopardy. That is, it might be read as a 'defendant's' right. In *Golder v. United Kingdom*,[161] an important early case, the European Court held that Article 6 also includes a right to invoke legal procedures consistent with the article when a person faces a loss of rights or an imposition of obligations. That is, it recognized a 'plaintiff's' right as well. The Court reached this conclusion partly by a close examination of the French and English texts but also for the more general reason that 'one can scarcely conceive of the rule of law without there being a possibility of having access to the courts'.[162]

> It would be inconceivable, in the opinion of the Court, that Article 6§1 should describe in detail the procedural guarantees afforded to parties in a pending lawsuit and should not first protect that which alone makes it in fact possible to benefit from such guarantees, that is, access to a Court.[163]

The right of access to a court has been construed as including the right to effective enforcement of judgments. In a decision in which it held that Article 6(1) was violated when an eviction order went unenforced for 13 years, the Strasbourg Court repeated dicta it had applied in prior cases:

> the right to a court would be illusory if a Contracting State's domestic legal system allowed a final, binding judicial decision to remain inoperative to the detriment of one party. It would be inconceivable that Article 6 §1 should describe in detail procedural guarantees afforded to the litigants—proceedings that are fair, public and expeditious—without protecting the implementation of judicial decisions; to construe Article 6 as being concerned exclusively with access to a court and the conduct of proceedings would be likely to lead to situations incompatible with the principle of the rule of law which the Contracting State undertook to respect when they ratified

---

[160] *Runa Begum v. Tower Hamlets LBC* [2003] U.K.H.L. 5; [2003] 2 A.C. 430, para. 5.
[161] 7 May 1974, 1 E.H.R.R. 524.
[162] *Id.* at para. 34.
[163] *Id.* at para. 35.

the Convention. Execution of a judgment given by any Court must therefore be regarded as an integral part of the 'trial' for the purposes of Article 6.[164]

C. AN INDEPENDENT AND IMPARTIAL TRIBUNAL

What does Article 6 (1) mean when it requires a fair trial 'by an independent and impartial tribunal established by law'? Our answer below proceeds in six parts. First and second, we look at the *Piersack Case* and see how the Court decides whether judges ought to be excluded from legal proceedings because of doubts about their impartiality due to prior involvement in a case. Third and fourth, we read the *Sigurdsson Case* and examine the need for so-called 'objective impartiality'. Fifth, we explore the Court's jurisprudence about independent tribunals. Sixth and finally, we look at how these rules apply to administrative agencies and disciplinary bodies.

1. PIERSACK V. BELGIUM

Judgment of 1 October 1982
5 E.H.R.R. 169

7. The applicant, a Belgian national born in 1948, is a gunsmith. He is in the process of serving in Mons prison a sentence of 18 years hard labour imposed on him on 10 November 1978 by the Brabant Assize Court for murder.

8. During the night of 22–23 April 1976, two Frenchmen, Mr. Gilles Gros and Mr. Michel Dulon, were killed by revolver shots in Brussels whilst they were in a motor-car with Mr. Piersack, Mr. Constantions Kavadias (against whom proceedings were subsequently discontinued) and a Portuguese national, Mr. Joao Tadeo Santos de Sousa Gravo....

9. On 9 July 1976, Mr. Preuveneers, an investigating judge at the Brussels Court of First Instance, issued a warrant for the arrest of the applicant, who was suspected of having caused both deaths. He was in France at the time, but was arrested by the French authorities who, after agreeing to grant his extradition, handed him over to the Belgian police on 13 January 1977. The Coutrai *procureur du Roi* (public prosecutor) so informed his colleague in Brussels by a letter of the same date. Mr. Pierre Van de Walle, a senior deputy *procureur*, initialled the letter and forwarded it to the official in the public prosecutor's department who was dealing with the case, Mrs. del Carril. She transmitted it to Mr. Preuveneers with a covering note dated 17 January.

---

[164] *Immobiliare Saffi v. Italy*, 26 July 1999, 30 E.H.R.R. 756, para. 63 citing *Hornsby v. Greece*, 19 Mar. 1997, 24 E.H.R.R. 250, para. 40.

10. On 4 February 1977, the investigating judge wrote to the Brussels *procureur du Roi* to enquire whether, as regards the co-accused Santos de Sousa, the public prosecutor's department intended to report the facts to the Portuguese authorities, those authorities apparently being no longer willing to grant his extradition. On his covering note, the judge added in manuscript, between brackets, the words 'for the attention of Mr. P. Van de Walle'. Mrs. del Carril replied to Mr. Preuveneers on 9 February 1977.

11. On 20 June, the *procureur général* (State prosecutor) attached to the Brussels Court of Appeal sent to the *procureur du Roi* the results of letters rogatory executed in Portugal concerning Mr. Santos de Sousa. After initialling the covering note, Mr. Van de Walle forwarded it to Mr. De Nauw, the deputy who had taken over from Mrs. del Carril in dealing with the case; Mr. De Nauw transmitted the note to the investigating judge on 22 June.

12. On 13 December 1977, Mr. Van de Walle took his oath as a judge of the Brussels Court of Appeal, to which office he had been appointed on 18 November. Most of the investigations had been completed by that time, although some further formal steps were taken at a later date....

14. The trial took place from 6 to 10 November 1978 before the Assize Court which was presided over by Mr. Van de Walle. After the Court had heard, amongst others, numerous prosecution and defence witnesses, the 12 members of the jury withdrew to consider their verdict. Mr. Piersack had maintained throughout that he was innocent. On the third question put to them, concerning the 'principal count', they arrived at a verdict of guilty, but only by seven votes to five. After deliberating on that question in private, the President and the two other judges declared that they agreed with the majority.

In the final event, the Assize Court convicted the applicant of the murder of Mr. Dulon and acquitted him as regards the other charges; it accepted that there were mitigating circumstances and sentenced him on 10 November 1978 to 18 years' hard labour. It also recorded that on account of his nationality it had not been possible to obtain the extradition to Belgium of Mr. Santos de Sousa, who had been arrested in Portugal.

15. The applicant then appealed on points of law to the Court of Cassation. His sixth ground of appeal, the only ground that is relevant in the present case, was that there had been a violation of Article 127 of the Judicial Code, which provides that 'proceedings before an assize court shall be null and void if they have been presided over by a judicial officer who has acted in the case as public prosecutor...'. [The Court of Cassation dismissed the appeal.]...

29. ... According to the Government, at the relevant time it was the *procureur du Roi* himself, and not the senior deputy, Mr. Van de Walle, who handled cases involving an indictable offence; they maintained that each of the deputies—on this occasion, Mrs. del Carril and then Mr. De Nauw—reported to the *procureur* on such cases directly and not through Mr. Van de Walle, the latter's role being principally an administrative one that was unconnected with the conduct of the prosecution and consisted, *inter alia*, of initialling numerous documents, such as the covering notes of 13 January and 20 June 1977. As regards the covering note of 4 February 1977, the investigating judge, Mr. Preuveneers, was said to have written thereon the words 'for the attention of Mr. P. Van de Walle' solely because he knew that Mrs. del Carril was frequently on sick-leave. In addition, so the Government stated, there was no evidence to show that Mr. Van de Walle had received that note and, in any event, it was not he but Mrs. del Carril who had replied to Mr. Preuveneers.

30. Whilst impartiality normally denotes absence of prejudice or bias, its existence or otherwise can, notably under Article 6(1) of the Convention, be tested in various ways. A distinction can be drawn in this context between a subjective approach, that is endeavouring to ascertain the personal conviction of a given judge in a given case, and an objective approach, that is determining whether he offered guarantees sufficient to exclude any legitimate doubt in this respect.

(a) As regards the first approach, the Court notes that the applicant is pleased to pay tribute to Mr. Van de Walle's personal impartiality; it does not itself have any cause for doubt on this score and indeed personal impartiality is to be presumed until there is proof to the contrary.

However, it is not possible to confine oneself to a purely subjective test. In this area, even appearances may be of a certain importance. As the Belgian Court of Cassation observed in its judgment of 21 February 1979, any judge in respect of whom there is a legitimate reason to fear a lack of impartiality must withdraw. What is at stake is the confidence which the courts must inspire in the public in a democratic society.

(b) It would be going too far to the opposite extreme to maintain that former judicial officers in the public prosecutor's department were unable to sit on the bench in every case that had been examined initially by that department, even though they had never had to deal with the case themselves. So radical a solution, based on an inflexible and formalistic conception of the unity and indivisibility of the public prosecutor's department, would erect a virtually impenetrable barrier between that department and the bench. It would lead to an upheaval in the judicial system of several Contracting States where transfers from one of those offices to the other are a frequent occurrence. Above all, the mere fact that a judge was once a member of the public prosecutor's department is not a reason for fearing that he lacks impartiality; the Court concurs with the Government on this point.

(c) The Belgian Court of Cassation, which took Article 6(1) into consideration of its own motion, adopted in this case a criterion based on the functions exercised, namely whether the judge had previously intervened 'in the case in or on the occasion of the exercise of...functions as a judicial officer in the public prosecutor's department'. It dismissed Mr. Piersack's appeal on points of law because the documents before it did not, in its view, show that there had been any such intervention on the part of Mr. Van de Walle in the capacity of senior deputy to the Brussels *procureur du Roi*, even in some form other than the adoption of a personal standpoint or the taking of a specific step in the process of prosecution or investigation.

(d) Even when clarified in the manner just mentioned, a criterion of this kind does not fully meet the requirements of Article 6(1). In order that the courts may inspire in the public the confidence which is indispensable, account must also be taken of questions of internal organisation. If an individual, after holding in the public prosecutor's department an office whose nature is such that he may have to deal with a given matter in the course of his duties, subsequently sits in the same case as a judge, the public are entitled to fear that he does not offer sufficient guarantees of impartiality.

31. This was what occurred in the present case. In November 1978, Mr. Van de Walle presided over the Brabant Assize Court before which the Indictments Chamber of the Brussels

Court of Appeal had remitted the applicant for trial. In that capacity, he enjoyed during the hearings and the deliberations extensive powers to which, moreover, he was led to have recourse, for example the discretionary power of deciding, with the other judges, on the guilt of the accused should the jury arrive at a verdict of guilty by no more than a simple majority.

Yet previously and until November 1977, Mr. Van de Walle had been the head of section B of the Brussels public prosecutor's department, which was responsible for the prosecution instituted against Mr. Piersack. As the hierarchical superior of the deputies in charge of the file, Mrs. del Carril and then Mr. De Nauw, he had been entitled to revise any written submissions by them to the courts, to discuss with them the approach to be adopted in the case and to give them advice on points of law. Besides, the information obtained by the Commission and the Court tends to confirm that Mr. Van de Walle did in fact play a certain part in the proceedings.

Whether or not Mr. Piersack was, as the Government believe, unaware of all these facts at the relevant time is of little moment. Neither is it necessary to endeavour to gauge the precise extent of the role played by Mr. Van de Walle, by undertaking further enquiries in order to ascertain, for example, whether or not he received the covering note of 4 February 1977 himself and whether or not he discussed this particular case with Mrs. del Carril and Mr. De Nauw. It is sufficient to find that the impartiality of the 'tribunal' which had to determine the merits (in the French text: 'bien-fondé') of the charge was capable of appearing open to doubt.

[The Court held unanimously that there had been a violation of Article 6(1).]

2. THE PROBLEM OF PRIOR INVOLVEMENT

The idea that a fair tribunal must exclude persons who have had a previous part in the legal proceedings is based on an assumption that human beings are predisposed to maintain positions they have formed, even if in a different role. In that sense they will be evaluating themselves in the relevant case, violating the principle expressed in the common law axiom that no person may be a judge in his own case.[165] The European Court has, for example, ruled that the Luxembourg Council of State which reviewed the legality of administrative decisions was not acting consistently with Article 6 since four of its five members had sat on a panel that had previously given an advisory opinion concerning the matter in question. In such a case the applicant 'had legitimate grounds for fearing that the members of the Judicial Committee [of the Council] had felt bound by the opinion previously given'.[166]

In judgments subsequent to *Piersack* the European Court has considered how much prior involvement of a judge is consistent with the maintenance of impartiality under Article 6(1). In each case, the Court reviewed the precise actions of the judge in the earlier stages of the proceeding to determine whether or not such involvement could

---

[165] *Dr. Bonham's Case* (1610) 8 Co. Rep. 114a.
[166] *Procola v. Luxembourg*, 28 Sept. 1995, 22 E.H.R.R. 193, para. 45.

reasonably be perceived as creating a likelihood that the judge had formed an adverse opinion as to the guilt of the applicant.

In *DeCubber v. Belgium*,[167] one of three judges at the applicant's trial for forgery had previously served as an 'investigating judge' in the case and, as such, had been in charge of the preliminary investigation. The investigating judge was authorized by Belgian law to 'summon the accused to appear or issue a warrant for his detention, production before a court or arrest; question the accused, hear witnesses, confront witnesses with each other, visit the scene of the crime, visit and search premises, take possession of evidence, and so on ...'. The government argued that these functions did not impair the objectivity of the judge:

> They pointed out that in Belgium an investigating judge is fully independent in the performance of his duties; that unlike the judicial officers in the public prosecutor's department, whose submissions are not binding on him, he does not have the status of party to criminal proceedings and is not 'an instrument of the prosecution'; that 'the object of his activity' is not, despite Mr. DeCubber's allegations, 'to establish the guilt of the person he believes to be guilty', but to 'assemble in an impartial manner evidence in favour of as well as against the accused', whilst maintaining, 'a just balance between prosecution and defence', since he 'never ceases to be a judge'; ...[168]

The European Court, however, held these factors not to be decisive. The Court noted that an investigating judge had many of the same duties as a prosecutor and was, at least formally, under the supervision of the *procureur général*. In this case, the measures taken by the challenged judge in conducting the investigation were likely to have been extensive. They were, moreover, conducted in secret. In light of the fact that the judge would become quite familiar with the details of the case, an accused might well fear that the judge had already formed an opinion on guilt or innocence, as well as that he would have inordinate influence in the decisions of the trial court, including possibly a review of his own decisions as investigating judge. On this basis, the Court found that the applicant had been denied his right to trial before an independent and impartial tribunal.

The holding in *DeCubber* raised problems for judicial systems with limited personnel where it is not uncommon for a judge to deal with the same matter at different stages and in different capacities. The rule of the case was later applied to a situation where an appeal court had decided adversely to a criminal defendant on a preliminary question whether an essential element of the crime had been alleged. The European Court held that some judges on the court could not, consistently with Article 6, hear the appeal against the subsequent conviction.[169] In *Thomann v. Switzerland*,[170]

---

[167] 26 Oct. 1984, 7 E.H.R.R. 236.

[168] *Id.* at para. 28.

[169] *Oberschlick v. Austria*, 23 May 1991, 19 E.H.R.R. 389. *See also De Haan v. The Netherlands*, 26 Aug. 1997, 26 E.H.R.R. 417, finding a violation of Art. 6 where the presiding judge on an employment benefits appeals tribunal sat in the Chamber considering the applicant's objection to his prior decision. *See* text at n. 181 *infra*.

[170] 10 June 1996, 24 E.H.R.R. 553.

however, no violation was found where the same panel of judges who had convicted an applicant in absentia sat on the later trial in his presence. The Court observed 'that the instant case does not concern the successive exercise of different judicial functions, but judges who sat twice in the same capacity'.[171]

In later cases, the Court further developed a framework for dealing with these questions. In *Hauschildt v. Denmark*[172] it held that the mere fact that a Danish judge had made preliminary decisions in a criminal case, including decisions on the custody of the accused, did not, under Article 6, prevent such a judge from presiding at the trial. In Denmark, unlike Belgium, there is no investigating judge. Investigation and prosecution are conducted entirely by police and prosecutors. The pre-trial judge merely decides if sufficient evidence has been produced to justify detention. Ordinarily this would not give rise to the same apprehension as those held by the applicant in *DeCubber*. Under the actual facts of *Hauschildt*, however, the challenged judge had made repeated rulings under a particular section of the Administration of Justice Act which required proof of a 'particularly confirmed suspicion'. The Court held that the difference between this finding and the one a judge would have to make at trial was 'tenuous' and, in these circumstances, there was a violation of Article 6. The same result was reached when a judge in the court convicting the applicants had presided over another trial in which the other participants in the same criminal incident had been convicted. In that case the Court noted that the judge in question had made repeated reference to the applicants as 'co-perpetrators'.[173]

In other cases the Court has evaluated critically claims that the judge was disqualified by virtue of some prior involvement. 'The mere fact that [a judge] made pre-trial decisions...cannot be taken as in itself justifying fears as to his impartiality; what matters is the scope and nature of these decisions'.[174] Thus, it has found no violation where, at earlier hearings, the trial judge had been entitled to act for an absent prosecutor. On the actual facts of the case, the Court found that the judge had taken no actions of any significance.[175] Nor, in another case, did the fact that two of three trial judges had participated previously in review of a decision refusing to release the applicant from detention pending trial, lead to the finding of a violation. The previous decision had been 'confined to making a brief assessment of the available facts in order to establish whether, *prima facie*, the police suspicions had some substance and gave grounds for fearing that there was a risk of the accused's absconding'. Given this limited action, any fears of bias were not 'objectively justified'.[176] In *Fey v. Austria*,[177] the trial judge in the Austrian District Court had interviewed a witness and had written to parties with

---

[171] *Id.* at para. 32.

[172] 24 May 1989, 12 E.H.R.R. 226.

[173] *Ferrantelli & Santangelo v. Italy*, 7 Aug. 1996, 23 E.H.R.R. 288, paras. 54–60. *See also Castillo Algar v. Spain*, 28 Oct. 1998, 30 E.H.R.R. 287.

[174] *Nortier v. The Netherlands*, 24 Aug. 1993, 17 E.H.R.R. 273.

[175] *Thorgeir Thorgeirson v. Iceland*, 25 June 1992, 14 E.H.R.R. 843.

[176] *Sainte-Marie v. France*, 16 Dec. 1992, 16 E.H.R.R. 116. To the same effect *see Nortier v. The Netherlands*, *supra* n. 174; *Saravia de Carvahlo v. Portugal*, 22 April 1994, 18 E.H.R.R. 543.

[177] 24 Feb. 1993, 16 E.H.R.R. 387.

relevant information. She had also made the decision to set the case down for trial. Under Austrian law a District Court judge could carry out 'preliminary inquiries' and in so doing was bound to observe the same rules as those that were applicable to an investigating judge of the regional court. The European Court found the case distinguishable from *DeCubber* in that the measures taken were limited and formal, whereas in *DeCubber* the judge had 'carried out extensive investigations in the case, including numerous interrogations of the accused'.[178] The fact that a member of the Court had previously questioned two witnesses was similarly held not to taint the impartiality of the tribunal in *Bulut v. Austria*.[179] The judge's prior actions 'did not entail any assessment of the evidence by him nor did it require him to reach any kind of conclusion as to the applicant's involvement'.[180]

The idea that a judge cannot be considered impartial from an objective point of view when he or she has previously taken actions of substance in a case was challenged by Judge van Dijk's dissent in *De Haan v. The Netherlands*,[181] in which the Court found a violation of Article 6 in the Dutch procedure for dealing with disputes over entitlement to sick pay. The Court held that a judge who had issued a preliminary ruling on the applicant's claim could not, consistently with the Convention, sit on the panel reviewing the applicant's objection to that ruling. Judge van Dijk pointed out that in this case, unlike others in which a violation had been found, 'the judge... sat twice in the same capacity at the same instance'.[182] But his objection went much further, questioning the psychological premise on which much of the Court's jurisprudence rests. Since, to use the language of the Belgian government in *DeCubber*, a judge 'never ceases to be a judge', on what grounds can we conclude that he or she will be unable to take a fresh and unbiased view of a case in which he or she had previously participated? 'Of course', he wrote, 'Judge S had formed an opinion about the case before the hearing and made it known to the applicant. This does not imply that he no longer offered sufficient guarantees that in participating in the Chamber, he based his opinion solely on the law and the facts; foreknowledge is not the same as bias'.[183] He went on to quote the Court's judgment in an earlier case that judges' 'professional training and experience' ensure that a subsequent action would not be 'predetermined' by a previous decision.[184]

In *Delcourt v. Belgium*,[185] decided in 1970, the applicant complained about the participation of the *avocat général*, a member of the department of the *Procureur Général*,

---

[178] *Id.* at para. 35. *See also Padovani v. Italy*, 26 Feb. 1993.

[179] 22 Feb. 1996, 24 E.H.R.R. 84.

[180] *Id.* at para. 34. Compare *2747–3174 Quebec Inc. v. Quebec (Régie des Permis d'Alcohol)* [1996] 3 S.C.R. 919, in which the Supreme Court of Canada found that there could be a reasonable apprehension of bias in an administrative agency in which the same person who decides to initiate a proceeding and convene a hearing participated in the decision. *Id.* at paras. 59–60.

[181] 26 Aug. 1997, 26 E.H.R.R. 417.

[182] *Id.* (dissenting opinion of Judge van Dijk joined by Judge Matscher). For American law on this point *see infra*.

[183] *Id.*

[184] *Id.* quoting *Thomann v. Switzerland*, 10 June 1996, 24 E.H.R.R. 553, para. 71.

[185] 17 Jan. 1970, 1 E.H.R.R. 355.

in the decision of appeals in criminal cases to the Belgian Court of Cassation. The *avocat général* submitted his views of the case to the Court after the parties had been heard and participated in the court's deliberations. The European Court found that such an arrangement did not render the Court of Cassation less than independent and impartial. The section of the *Procureur Général*'s department attached to the court was found to be independent of that part of the department that had been involved in the prosecution of the applicant. As such, it served as an impartial adviser to the court. In 1991, however, the same Belgian procedure was challenged successfully before the European Court in *Borgers v. Belgium*.[186] The Court had been invited by the report of the Commission to reconsider its decision in *Delcourt*, but it held instead that the prior case's findings on the Court of Cassation's independence and impartiality 'remain entirely valid'. But it went on to question whether the participation of the *avocat général*, nonetheless, violated Article 6's requirements, as interpreted in case law following *Delcourt*, that criminal defendants be given a fair opportunity to present their defence and be accorded an 'equality of arms' with the prosecution.[187] The Court found that these principles were infringed in the Belgian appellate procedure in that the applicant had no right to respond to the *avocat général*'s submission and was put at a further disadvantage by that officer's participation in the deliberations. As to the observation that the *avocat général* could not be considered a party to the proceedings, the judgment stated:

No one questions the objectivity with which the *procureur général*'s department at the Court of Cassation discharges its functions.... Nevertheless the opinion of the *procureur général*'s department cannot be regarded as neutral from the point of view of the parties to the cassation proceedings. By recommending that an accused's appeal be allowed or dismissed, the official of the *procureur général*'s department becomes objectively speaking his ally or opponent. In the latter event, Article 6(1) requires that the rights of defence and the principle of equality of arms be respected.[188]

A number of the separate opinions in *Borgers* proceeded on the assumption that the judgment had overruled *Delcourt*.[189] The holding in *Borgers* was extended to civil cases in *Lobo Machado v. Portugal*.[190] In that case a Deputy Attorney-General made a

---

[186] 30 Oct. 1991, 15 E.H.R.R. 92.

[187] *Id.* at para. 24. On the concepts of rights of defence and equality of arms *see* generally Stephanos Stavros, *The Guarantees for Accused Persons Under Article 6 of the European Convention on Human Rights* 52–4, 175–86 (1993).

[188] *Borgers, supra* n. 186.

[189] *See also* cases on the impartiality of British court-martial tribunals discussed at Section C(5) *infra*, and *Bulut v. Austria*, 22 Feb. 1996, 24 E.H.R.R. 84. The Court has applied a similar analysis to that employed under Article 6(1) in deciding whether a detained person has been 'brought promptly before a judge or other officer authorized by law to exercise judicial power' as required by Article 5(4). It has held that such an officer must be 'independent of the parties'. Therefore it is, in principle, impermissible for the detention decision to be made by a prosecutor who might at a later point take part in the criminal prosecution since the 'impartiality' of such a person is 'capable of appearing open to doubt'. *See*, e.g., *Huber v. Switzerland*, 23 Oct. 1990, overruling *Schiesser v. Switzerland*, 4 Dec. 1979, 2 E.H.R.R. 417; *Brincat v. Italy*, 26 Nov. 1992, 16 E.H.R.R. 591. See Chapter 12(F) *supra*.

[190] 20 Feb. 1996, 23 E.H.R.R. 79.

preliminary recommendation on an appeal to the Supreme Court and was present during the Court's deliberations. The case was an employment complaint brought against a state controlled company. The European Court received a submission from the government of Belgium as amicus curiae in support of the Portuguese procedure which was also that followed in Belgian civil appeals.[191]

The problem exemplified by *Piersack*, given common career patterns, is a necessarily frequent occurrence. In the United States, the various jurisdictions differ with respect to the standards which have been developed to deal with this problem. But, as in the European cases, U.S. courts tend to examine the particular involvement which a judge had in previous aspects of a pending case. The code of Judicial Conduct, promulgated by the American Bar Association and widely adopted by state judiciaries, specifies in Canon 3.c(1)(b) that a judge should disqualify himself when 'he served as lawyer in the matter in controversy, or a lawyer with whom he previously practised law served during such association as a lawyer concerning the matter'. The Commentary to the section states that '[a] lawyer in a governmental agency does not necessarily have an association with other lawyers employed by that agency within the meaning of this subsection; a judge formerly employed by a governmental agency, however, should disqualify himself in a proceeding if his impartiality might reasonably be questioned because of such association'.

Federal statutes governing disqualification of federal judges are not much more specific, insisting judges recuse themselves when they have been of counsel in a case before them.[192] Case law has generally developed an approach in which the more personal responsibility and specific work a prosecutor had in a case, the more likely he is to be disqualified from sitting on it as a judge. Thus, the mere fact that a judge had once held a position as a prosecutor has been held insufficient grounds for recusal in criminal cases. It is necessary to show that the judge was actually involved enough in the particular case at issue as to have developed a substantial interest.[193] Conducting the particular prosecution clearly meets this test and participating in the investigation of a case has been held to require the same conclusion.[194] Other courts have held that prosecuting attorneys involved in drafting pleadings or who received a conviction or guilty plea are also disqualified. But merely drafting an indictment has been held insufficient involvement to call for recusal.[195]

In contrast to some of the European judgments,[196] the federal law in the United States on judicial disqualification has been interpreted quite strictly with respect to claims of bias based on previous statements or actions by the judge in his or her

---

[191] *Id.* at para. 27.

[192] 28 U.S.C.A. §455.

[193] *See Edelstein v. Wilentz*, 812 F. 2d 128, 131 (3rd Cir. 1987); *United States v. Wilson*, 426 F.2d 268, 269 (6th Cir. 1970).

[194] *See Barry v. United States*, 528 F.2d 1094 (7th Cir. 1976) *cert. denied* 429 U.S. 820 (1977); *Adams v. United States*, 302 F.2d 307 (5th Cir. 1962).

[195] Compare *United States v. Vasilick*, 160 F.2d 631, 632 (3rd Cir. 1947) with *General Tire and Rubber Co. v. Watkins*, 363 F.2d 87, 89 (4th Cir. 1966) *cert. denied* 385 U.S. 899 (1966).

[196] *See*, e.g., *De Haan v. The Netherlands, supra* n. 169.

judicial capacity. The Supreme Court has held that 'judicial rulings alone almost never constitute valid basis for a bias or partiality motion'. Moreover:

opinions formed by the judge on the basis of facts introduced or events occurring in the course of the current proceedings, or of prior proceedings, do not constitute a basis for a bias or partiality motion unless they display a deep-seated favoritism or antagonism that would make fair judgment impossible. Thus, judicial remarks, during the course of a trial that are critical or disapproving of, or even hostile to counsel, the parties, or their cases ordinarily do not support a bias or partiality challenge.[197]

A distinction between a judge's conduct 'as judge' in the course of litigation and his or her conduct outside that role may not always be simple to draw. For example, the Supreme Court of Canada held that a judge had engaged in unacceptable behaviour when, during a trial, he contacted a high official in the Attorney-General's office to complain about the way a crown attorney was behaving, asking that the attorney be removed, and suggesting that he (the judge) would 'secure that end' if no action were taken. The Supreme Court had little difficulty concluding that the action gave rise to a 'reasonable apprehension of bias'.[198] The English Court of Appeal in *National Bank v. Hague*,[199] also considered the extent to which the involvement of a judge at a prior stage of civil proceedings might disqualify him from serving on a panel hearing an appeal in the same case. The judge in question had made provisional *ex parte* orders extending the time in which a writ could be served and allowing substitute service. After full argument a second judge had refused to discharge those orders, and it was the second decision which was the subject of the appeal on which the first judge (now a judge of the Court of Appeal) was to sit. The Court held that the judge could hear this appeal without violating a statute barring judges from hearing appeals of judgments or orders 'made in any case by himself'. Nor was there any impropriety merely because the judge had some involvement with the question on appeal. In her judgment, Butler-Sloss LJ said 'it stands out a mile...that Evans J's part has been throughout peripheral'. Indeed, the judge in question might well have reversed his own decision after full hearing:

He has formed no concluded view about the rightness of the order which he made *ex parte*. He is equally able to think he might have been wrong as he might have thought had he heard the evidence that Creswell, J. heard...

[197] *Liteky v. United States*, 510 U.S. 540 (1994).

[198] *R. v. Curragh* [1997] 1 S.C.R. 537, at para. 3. Two judges dissented arguing, *inter alia*, that the telephone call did not demonstrate bias towards the defendant. One might conclude, they said, that the trial judge was partial to the Crown 'since he seemed concerned that the Crown case be conducted effectively'. *Id.* at para. 104 (McLachlin and Major JJ dissenting).

[199] [1994] [Transcript: John Larking, 21 Jan., 1994 in LEXIS, Enggen Library, Cases File].

3. SIGURDSSON V. ICELAND

Judgment of 10 April 2003

40 E.H.R.R. 15

8. The applicant is an Icelandic national, born in 1954. He is a practising lawyer and lives in Reykjavik, Iceland.

9. The applicant instituted proceedings against the National Bank of Iceland, claiming compensation under the law of torts, on the grounds that one of the Bank's legally trained employees had made an incorrect declaration in 1992 which was instrumental in the Supreme Court's finding that a certain claim was no longer enforceable. As the District Court found for the defendant bank, the applicant, by a summons of 31 May 1996, instituted appeal proceedings before the Supreme Court. . . .

11. By a judgment of 25 April 1997, the Supreme Court, by three votes to two, rejected the applicant's claim. The minority found that the applicant's claim should be upheld and that the National Bank was liable to pay him 8,746,319 Icelandic krónur (ISK) in compensation, plus default interest from 30 August 1993.

12. One of the three judges forming the majority was Mrs Justice Guðrún Erlendsdóttir. The applicant submitted that after the delivery of the Supreme Court's judgment, it came to light that Mrs Justice Guðrún Erlendsdóttir and her husband, a Supreme Court lawyer, had a financial relationship with the National Bank of such a nature as to disqualify her from sitting in the applicant's case.

13. In the spring of 1996 Mr Örn Clausen, husband of Mrs Justice Guðrún Erlendsdóttir, had sought a solution to certain financial problems arising from the inability of a debtor, Mr Edvard Lövdal, to pay certain debts with respect to which Mr Örn Clausen was one of the guarantors, and the inability of other guarantors to honour the guarantee. In early May 1996 twenty-one creditors, one of which was the National Bank, possessed claims under the guarantees amounting to approximately ISK 50,000,000. This included a claim of approximately ISK 16,000,000 by the National Bank. Another large creditor was the Savings Banks' Hedge Fund which, on behalf of the S-Þingeyinga Savings Bank ('the Savings Bank'), held a claim of approximately ISK 17,500,000.

14. In order to solve these problems Mr Örn Clausen attempted to reach a settlement with each of the creditors. An economic consultant company, Ráð, agreed to examine his financial situation and to look into the possibilities of obtaining full settlement against partial payment, starting with the two largest creditors and thereafter opening negotiations with the smaller ones, to be completed within six months.

A settlement request made by the company to the National Bank's lawyer on 15 April 1996, included the following observations:

'. . . Mr Örn Clausen has informed us that he had, for the sake of friendship, provided guarantees with respect to Mr Lövdahl's debts, as they have been friends for decades. He also informs us that he owns no property, and that he will foreseeably have to answer for guarantees on account of Mr Lövdahl in an amount of approximately ISK 49,550,000. His other liabilities amount to approximately ISK 10,000,000 around ISK 8,000,000 of which are taxes. Mr Örn Clausen's wife owns [two] real properties. . . [These] are owned by her separately under their marriage agreement dating from 1967. She has declared her readiness to use their net value by mortgage or sale for settling the debts, provided that Mr Örn Clausen is released from his personal guarantees and that his bankruptcy is avoided.

We consequently ask you to recommend to your client, the National Bank, acceptance of 25% in final settlement of the total debt to which Mr Örn Clausen must answer as surety. This would release him from his surety liability. The payment would be made simultaneously with the signature of an agreement to this effect'.

15. On 30 May 1996, in order to obtain funds to pay the creditors, the judge's husband Mr Örn Clausen issued four debt certificates to Landsbréf hf, Verðbréfamarkaður Landsbankans (Landsbréf, the Securities Market of the National Bank, a financial institution owned by the National Bank), totalling approximately ISK 13,600,000. The debts were secured on two properties owned by Mrs Justice Guðrún Erlendsdóttir, namely the couple's main residence and one apartment in which her husband had his law office.

16. On 4 June 1996 Landsbréf sold the above four debt certificates to Eignarhaldsfélag Alþýðubankans (People's Bank Holding Company—'the EFA'), a company specialising in high-risk investments. Ever since, the four debt certificates have been in that company's ownership.

17. On 4 June 1996, in accordance with a settlement agreement of the same date between the National Bank and Mr Örn Clausen, he paid approximately ISK 4,370,000, of which ISK 3,677,195 were towards his debts to the National Bank and the remainder covering his lawyer's fees. Moreover, under the terms of the settlement agreement with the bank, he was released from ISK 11,031,584 of debts originating in his guarantees for Mr Edvard Lövdal's debts, which amounted to ISK 14,708,779. The above settlement was in conformity with a decision taken on 3 June 1996 by the National Bank's Governing Board.

18. As regards the state of Mr Örn Clausen's debts vis-à-vis the National Bank, the Government relied on the following information provided on 4 March 2002 by the head of the bank's legal department:

'The National Bank of Iceland hereby confirms that a settlement agreement was concluded with Mr Örn Clausen on 6 June 1996 concerning his undertakings to guarantee the payment of debts to the National Bank, by which the Bank cancelled 75% of its claims against Mr Örn Clausen against a final payment of 25%. We confirm that the Bank did not extend a new credit to Mr Örn Clausen for the said 25%.

On 4 June 1996 Mr Örn Clausen's total debts to the Bank amounted to ISK 17,298,940; his debts that did not come under the settlement agreement were a note issued 12 September 1991 in the amount of ISK 2,090,161.10, and a suretyship obligation for payment of a loan originally in the amount of ISK 500,000, which was not in arrears (remaining amount as at 31 December 1996: ISK 195,656).

Mr Örn Clausen's total debts on 25 April 1997 were a note issued 12 September 1991, in the amount of ISK 2,394,028.60, and a suretyship obligation for payment of a loan originally in the amount of ISK 500,000, which was not in arrears (remaining amount as at 31 December 1997 ISK 27,777)'.

19. Under an agreement concluded on 6 June 1996 the Savings Bank too decided to cancel 75% of its claim against a final payment of 25% by Mr Örn Clausen.

20. The fact that the two largest creditors had accepted the settlement arrangements described above was of significant help in Mr Örn Clausen's efforts to obtain settlement agreements with other creditors, all or most of whom accepted debt cancellation against partial payment.

21. The applicant submitted that there was evidence that on 4 June 1996 the debts of the husband of Mrs Justice Guðrún Erlendsdóttir towards the National Bank amounted to more than ISK 31,000,000. Moreover, in April 1997, at the time when the Supreme Court gave its judgment, the debts in question apparently amounted to approximately ISK 29,000,000.

22. The applicant lodged two petitions to the Supreme Court requesting the reopening of the proceedings in his case against the National Bank on the ground of Mrs Justice Guðrún Erlendsdóttir's alleged lack of impartiality.

23. The first petition was submitted to the Supreme Court on 9 June 1997. The Supreme Court, sitting as a full court, unanimously rejected it on 10 July 1997. Its decision reads:

In support of his assertion relating to the disqualification of Supreme Court Judge Guðrún Erlendsdóttir, the petitioner refers to four debt certificates issued to the name of Landsbréf, which are secured by mortgage upon two real estates owned by the judge. By reason of the National Bank's ownership of Landsbréf, the petitioner considers that this situation disqualified the judge from adjudicating the case. The secured debts in question amount to a total of ISK 13,600,000 which, as stated in the certificates, corresponds to approximately 55% of the total assessed sale price of the properties. The certificates were issued in May 1996 for a period of twenty-five years. The petitioner does not maintain that the certificates are in arrears.

It is shown from the information provided by the lawyer for the National Bank that the debt certificates are not, and were not at the time when the case was being considered by the Supreme Court, in the ownership of Landsbréf, the National Bank or any [other] company linked to the Bank. Mortgages on the said properties referred to in the petition, which now have been struck out of the records, and secure debts due to other parties are deemed irrelevant here.

Although the above-mentioned letter of [the applicant] does not refer to the particular statutory provisions authorising the reopening of proceedings, it is to be assumed that the petition is based on section 169 of the Civil Procedure Act, Law no. 91/1991. The petitioner has not referred to any new fact or adduced any new evidence having a bearing on the merits of the case, cf. section 169(1), sub-paragraphs (a) and (b) of Law no. 91/1991.

In the light of the above consideration concerning the said mortgages, none of the conditions which provide the petitioner with a reason to believe that the said judge was not impartial and therefore disqualified from adjudicating the case have been fulfilled, cf. section 6, subsections (1) and (9), of the Supreme Court Act, Law no. 75/1973; section 5, subsection (g) of Law no. 91/1991, Article 70 of the Constitution of the Republic of Iceland (no. 33/1944), cf. section 8 of Constitutional Act no. 97/1995, and Article 6 of the European Convention on Human Rights, cf. Law no. 62/1994. Accordingly, since the legal conditions for granting the petitioner's request for reopening of the proceedings have not been fulfilled, the request is rejected.

24. The applicant submitted that, after the Supreme Court had given its decision of 10 July 1997 in the first revision case, he realised that Mrs Justice Guðrún Erlendsdóttir's husband

had additional financial ties with the National Bank. During the period from 1988 to 1991 he had assumed large-scale financial obligations vis-à-vis the bank and for years his debts to the bank had been seriously in arrears. According to the applicant, although this could not be affirmed with certainty, it was possible that the National Bank had released Mrs Justice Guðrún Erlendsdóttir's husband from a debt of over ISK 11,000,000.

25. On 23 October 1997 the applicant filed a new petition with the Supreme Court, asking for the reopening of his compensation case. The Supreme Court rejected the petition on 20 November 1997 on the ground that, under the relevant provisions of the Civil Procedure Act, a party may apply only once for re-examination of a case....

28. The applicant complained that, because of the close financial relationship between, on the one hand, Mrs Justice Guðrún Erlendsdóttir of the Supreme Court sitting in his case and her husband and, on the other hand, the National Bank of Iceland, his case brought against the bank had not been heard by an independent and impartial tribunal as required by Article 6 § 1 of the Convention....

37. The Court considers that it is essentially the requirement of 'impartiality' that is in issue in the present case. The existence of impartiality for the purposes of Article 6 § 1 of the Convention must be determined according to a subjective test, that is on the basis of the personal conviction of a particular judge in a given case, and also according to an objective test, that is, by ascertaining whether the judge offered guarantees sufficient to exclude any legitimate doubt in this respect.

As to the subjective test, the personal impartiality of a judge must be presumed until there is proof to the contrary; the applicant has adduced no evidence to suggest that Mrs Justice Guðrún Erlendsdóttir was personally biased.

Under the objective test, it must be determined whether, quite apart from the judge's personal conduct, there are ascertainable facts which may raise doubts as to his impartiality. In this respect even appearances may be of a certain importance. What is at stake is the confidence which the courts in a democratic society must inspire in the public. Accordingly, any judge in respect of whom there is a legitimate reason to fear a lack of impartiality must withdraw. This implies that in deciding whether in a given case there is a legitimate reason to fear that a particular judge lacks impartiality, the standpoint of the party concerned is important but not decisive. What is decisive is whether this fear can be held to be objectively justified.

38. The Court observes that, apart from the existence under Iceland's law of appropriate safeguards to ensure the impartiality of judges, there is nothing to suggest that the judge's personal interests were at stake in the proceedings between the applicant and the National Bank.

However, shortly before and while the applicant's case was pending before the Supreme Court, the judge's husband had serious financial problems, being unable to honour as a guarantor his obligations amounting to approximately ISK 50,000,000 under a debt agreement concluded by a third party with the bank and twenty other creditors. In the view of the Court, it transpires from the evidence submitted to it that there are three sets of circumstances which could give rise to an issue with regard to the requirements of impartiality under Article 6 § 1 of the Convention, namely the husband's debts to the National Bank when the case was being considered by the Supreme Court in April 1997, the four mortgage certificates which he contracted with Landsbréf on 30 May 1996 and his debt cancellation agreement with the National Bank of 6 June 1996.

39. As regards the first point, the Court notes that on 25 April 1997, when the Supreme Court adjudicated the applicant's case, the Supreme Court judge's husband had certain debts vis-à-vis the National Bank, the opposing party in the applicant's case. The size of those debts is disputed between the Government and the applicant. However, the Court sees no reason to doubt the information provided by the Government to the effect that, as at 25 April 1997, the husband owed approximately ISK 2,500,000 to the bank. In the view of the Court, this could reasonably be considered a moderate amount and there is nothing to suggest that this fact, on its own, could have constituted financial pressure capable of affecting the judge's impartiality.

40. Secondly, the Court observes that ten months earlier, on 30 May 1996, the husband issued four debt certificates, for amounts totalling ISK 13,600,000 to Landsbréf. The certificates were sold a few days later, on 4 June 1996, to an independent financial institution, the EFA, which became the creditor with respect to those amounts. The Court accepts the Government's submission that it was the EFA, not Landsbréf, which was the creditor with respect to these amounts after 4 June 1996. After that date it does not appear that the debt certificates as such established any direct financial link between the husband and the National Bank that could shed negative light on the judge's impartiality.

41. However, the Court considers that neither of the two sets of circumstances mentioned can be dissociated from the third factor, namely the wider context of the debt settlement agreement reached between Mr Örn Clausen and the bank on 6 June 1996.

42. In this connection the Court notes in particular the role played by Mrs Justice Guðrún Erlendsdóttir in facilitating the debt settlement achieved by her husband. It would appear that the security in her properties, which she offered to her husband, enabled him to raise the ISK 13,600,000 (currently corresponding to approximately 160,000 euros (EUR)) under the mortgage certificates of 30 May 1996. These funds, so it seems, were destined to cover his part of the debt settlement agreements reached with the National Bank and other creditors. The amounts involved were by no means negligible and the objects offered in security were nothing less than the couple's main residence. Presumably, without the security provided by Mrs Justice Guðrún Erlendsdóttir, the debt settlements in question would not have materialised. Furthermore, the cancellation of the debt was a condition for the judge to provide the security.

43. The Court appreciates that Mr Örn Clausen's difficulties in May 1996 did not stem directly from his own personal financial situation but from that of an insolvent third party, Mr Edvard Lövdal, for whom he was a guarantor, as well as from the inability of other guarantors to honour their guarantees.

It remains, however, that Mr Örn Clausen had a legal obligation to cover claims from the twenty-one creditors totalling approximately ISK 50,000,000, including ISK 16,000,000 (approximately EUR 190,000) to the National Bank as one of the two major creditors (the other being the Savings Banks' Hedging Fund which had a claim amounting to ISK 17,000,000). The debt cancellation released him from debts amounting to ISK 11,000,000 towards the National Bank, of an even higher sum towards the Savings Banks' Hedge Fund, and of multiple smaller sums owed to other creditors. The stance adopted by the National Bank and the Hedge Fund became a weighty factor in the attempts to make other creditors follow suit. Yet a further consequence was the fact that Mr Örn Clausen's debts to the National Bank had decreased to an ordinary level by April 1997, which state of affairs could not have been unrelated to the settlement with the National Bank in June 1996.

In view of the above, the Court is not persuaded by the Government's argument that the debt settlement agreement between Mr Örn Clausen and the National Bank as well as other creditors, securing the latter recovery of 25% of the debts, was for them an attractive alternative to declaring him bankrupt and one that could not be viewed as a favour towards him personally. On the contrary, even assuming that the solution reached suited creditors, it finds that the cancellation of 75% of such large debts must be considered a favourable treatment of Mr Örn Clausen.

44. It should also be noted that when the four mortgage certificates were brokered by Landsbréf and the debt settlement agreement was concluded with the National Bank, the applicant's case, in which the National Bank was an opposing party, was already pending before the Supreme Court.

45. Against this background, there was at least the appearance of a link between the steps taken by Mrs Justice Guðrún Erlendsdóttir in favour of her husband and the advantages he obtained from the National Bank. The Court will not speculate as to whether she derived any personal benefit from the operation and finds no reason to believe that either she or her husband had any direct interest in the outcome in the case between the applicant and the National Bank. However, the judge's involvement in the debt settlement, the favours received by her husband and his links to the National Bank were of such a nature and amplitude and were so close in time to the Supreme Court's examination of the case that the applicant could entertain reasonable fears that it lacked the requisite impartiality.

46. Accordingly, the Court finds that there has been a violation of Article 6 § 1 of the Convention in the present case.

4. OBJECTIVE IMPARTIALITY

In its various cases examining the impartiality of a tribunal, the Court has not been entirely consistent in its formulation of the proper standard for deciding whether or not a decisionmaker met the required level of 'objective impartiality'. In *DeCubber*, the Court found a violation because the judge 'might in the eyes of the accused' appear to be predisposed against him.[200] In *Borgers*, the neutrality of the *avocat général* was to be regarded from 'the point of view of the parties'.[201] These formulations, it will be observed, are versions of the maxim that not only justice but the appearance of justice is required. But they take the, at least contestable, position that the critical appearance is that perceived *by the accused*. In *Hauschildt v. Denmark*, discussed above, however, the Court offered a somewhat different test that has been repeated verbatim in several later judgments:

---

[200] 26 Oct. 1984, 7 E.H.R.R., para. 29.
[201] *Borgers, supra* n. 186, at para. 26.

[A]ny judge in respect of whom there is a legitimate reason to fear a lack of impartiality must withdraw... This implies that... the standpoint of the accused is important but not decisive. What is decisive is whether the fear can be held objectively justified.[202]

In 2004 in *AB Kurt Kellermann v. Sweden*, the applicant company complained that, in deciding on the legality of an industrial action, the Swedish Labour Court improperly employed a majority of lay assessors nominated by employers' associations and employees' unions (Kellermann did not belong to an employers' association), rather than professional judges. Rejecting Kellermann's complaint, the Court held that 'the decisive issue is whether the balance of interests in the composition of the Labour Court was upset.... This could be so either if the lay assessors had a common interest contrary to those of the applicant or if their interests, although not common, were such that they were nevertheless opposed to those of the applicant'.[203] Because the lay assessors were not ruling on Swedish law, under which the industrial action was admittedly legal, but only on the correct application of Article 11 of the European Convention, the Court felt that the applicant 'could not legitimately fear' facing a partial tribunal.[204]

The European Court's formulation of the standard of objective impartiality has influenced the development of the test for bias in English law. in *R v. Gough*[205] the Law Lords were confronted with two potential tests for situations in which a judge or juror should be disqualified. It rejected that which held disqualification proper whenever 'a reasonable person might reasonably suspect bias'. Rather it held (as stated in the judgment of Lord Goff of Chieveley) the proper test to be:

whether, having regard to [the relevant] circumstances, there was a real danger of bias on the part of the relevant member of the tribunal in question, in the sense that he might unfairly regard (or have unfairly regarded) with favour or disfavour, the case of a party to the issue under consideration before him.[206]

The term 'real danger' was considered preferable to 'real likelihood' because it would better 'ensure that the court is thinking in terms of possibility rather than probability of bias'.[207] This formulation, Lord Goff stated, was fully capable of enforcing the principle 'that justice must manifestly be seen to be done'.[208] However, the test was criticized on several grounds, in part for diverging from the Strasbourg jurisprudence. In *Porter v. Magill* the House of Lords held that, in considering whether the circumstances give rise to a reasonable apprehension that a tribunal was biased, the question is 'whether the fair-minded and informed observer having considered the facts would conclude that there was a real possibility that the tribunal was biased'.[209] This formulation now provides the ruling test in English law.

---

[202] *Supra* n. 172, at para. 48.
[203] *A B Kurt Kellermann v. Sweden*, 26 Oct. 2005, para. 63.
[204] *Id.* at paras. 65–9.
[205] 24 May 1989, 12 E.H.R.R. 266, para. 48.
[206] *Id.* at 670.
[207] *R. v. Gough* [1993] A.C. 646 at 670.
[208] *Id.* at 661.
[209] [2002] 2 A.C. 357 at para. 103 (Lord Hope of Craighill).

The Supreme Court of Canada has stated the test as being 'whether a well-informed and reasonable observer would perceive that judicial independence has been compromised'.[210]

Even if there are no reasonable grounds for inferring a 'real possibility' of bias, an English judge is automatically disqualified if he or she has a personal interest in the outcome of a case. The much noted decision of the House of Lords in *R. v. Bow Street Metropolitan Stipendiary Magistrate ex parte Pinochet Ugarte (No. 2)*[211] made clear that the character of such interests extends beyond the pecuniary or proprietary. In that case, Lord Hoffmann, who had sat on the House's original decision on the extradition of Pinochet to Spain for human rights violations was found to have substantial links to Amnesty International which had intervened in the case. In his speech Lord Browne-Wilkinson noted that if the controversy 'does not relate to money or economic advantage but is concerned with the promotion of the cause, the rationale disqualifying a judge applies just as much if the judge's decision will lead to the promotion of a cause in which the judge is involved together with one of the parties'.[212]

5. INDEPENDENCE

There is no sharp dividing line between Article 6's requirements that a tribunal be 'impartial' and 'independent'. The latter quality, however, seems to point more to the institutional aspects of the decision-making body than to the personal experiences and attitudes of the human beings comprising it. Much of the Court's doctrine on the content of independence has developed in cases dealing with administrative agencies and disciplinary bodies which will be treated in the next section. It has also considered such factors in cases where ordinary judicial duties have been conferred on officers and bodies who might be thought dependent on or too closely associated with the executive department.

In *Belilos v. Switzerland*[213] the European Court decided that adjudication of minor criminal offences by a Police Board, whose findings of fact could not be reviewed, violated Article 6(1). In the Swiss canton involved, such a Board could consist of a single police official. This official was not under police supervision and could not be removed during his or her four-year term. But the Court decided that the fact that such an official might ultimately return to other police functions, might feel subordinate to other police officials and might have a sense of loyalty to his or her colleagues, could undermine the perception of impartiality. Since a defendant could 'legitimately have

---

[210] *Canada (Minister of Citizenship and Immigration) v. Tobiass* [1997] 3 S.C.R. 391, at para. 70.
[211] [2000] 1 A.C. 119.
[212] *Id.* at 135.
[213] 29 Apr. 1988, 10 E.H.R.R. 466.

doubts as to the independence and organizational impartiality of the Police Board',[214] Article 6 (1) had not been satisfied.

In two cases from Slovakia, the Court found a violation of Article 6 in the state's decision to commit the adjudication of 'minor offences' to local and district officials. There was no general definition of such offences. Rather, they were identified in various laws. On conviction a person was subject to reprimand, prohibition of certain activities, or fines or confiscation. If the last two sanctions were of a value of 2,000 Slovakian Koruna (at the time about US$57 or £35) the penalty could be reviewed by a court. The European Court noted that '[i]n order to determine whether a body can be considered to be "independent" of the executive it is necessary to have regard to the manner of its appointment of its members and the duration of their term of office, the existence of guarantees against outside pressures and the question whether the body presents an appearance of independence'. The appointment of these officials was in the hands of the Executive and their status was that of salaried employees. As such there were insufficient 'guarantees against outside pressure' and these bodies could not be judged 'independent' in the absence of further judicial review.[215]

These considerations have also led the Court to examine critically the composition of courts martial which traditionally have been integrated into the military command structure. The Court found that courts martial in the United Kingdom, prior to reforms implemented in 1996, were inconsistent with Article 6's requirements of impartiality and independence. It noted that all members of a court were appointed by a 'convening officer', an officer superior in rank to and often holding direct or indirect command over the appointed members. The convening officer was also a key figure in the prosecution, making the decision to proceed with the trial, holding supervisory authority over decisions of the prosecuting officers, and confirming the judgment of the Court. In these circumstances a defendant might well have objectively justified misgivings about the Court's independence and impartiality.[216]

Notwithstanding the 1996 Act, problems with UK courts martial persisted. In 2002 in *Morris v. United Kingdom*, though the Court concluded that 'a separation has existed since the entering into force of the 1996 Act between the prosecutory and adjudicatory functions at a court martial which was not present in *Findlay*', it held that there was still a violation of Article 6 because 'two relatively junior officers' without legal training sat on a court martial who were at 'risk of outside pressure'.[217] The newspaper, the *Scotsman*, reported that courts martial would be delayed for two months after *Morris* while the 'government amended the Armed Forces Discipline Act—the

---

[214] *Id.* at para. 67.

[215] *Lauko v. Slovakia, supra* n. 18 at paras. 63–4; *Kadubec v. Slovakia*, 2 Sept. 1998, paras. 56–7.

[216] *Findlay v. United Kingdom*, 25 Feb. 1997, 24 E.H.R.R. 221, paras. 74–80. *See also Coyne v United Kingdom*, 24 Sept. 1997; *Hood v. United Kingdom*, 18 Feb. 1999, 29 E.H.R.R. 365; *Moore & Gordon v United Kingdom*, 29 Sept. 1999, 29 E.H.R.R. 728; *Smith & Ford v United Kingdom*, 29 Sept. 1999.

[217] *Morris v. United Kingdom*, 26 Feb. 2002, 34 E.H.R.R. 52, paras. 62–72.

fourth attempt to make courts martial comply with human rights legislation'.[218] The reforms instituted by the 1996 Act as amended seem to have finally alleviated the problem. In 2003 in *Cooper v. United Kingdom*, a Grand Chamber of the European Court concluded 'that the applicant's misgivings about the independence and impartiality of his court martial, convened under the 1996 Act, were not objectively justified and that the courts martial proceedings cannot consequently be said to have been unfair'.[219]

The European Court's doctrine with regard to military judges was taken a step further in *Incal v. Turkey*,[220] in which the Court held that the composition of Turkey's National Security Courts violated Article 6. These courts, provided for in the Turkish Constitution, had jurisdiction to try crimes 'against the Republic—whose constituent qualities are enunciated in the Constitution—against the indivisible unity of the State—meaning both the national territory and its people—or against the free democratic system of government and offences directly affecting the State's internal or external security'. They consisted of two civilian judges and one military judge.[221] The courts were constituted this way, as the government noted in a later case, because of the 'experience of the armed forces in the anti-terrorism campaign. [To] strengthen these courts [they] includ[ed] a military judge in order to provide them with the necessary expertise and knowledge to deal with threats to the security and integrity of the State'.[222] Unlike the United Kingdom, Turkish military judges were not appointed by or under the command of any authorities involved in the prosecution of the case.[223] The Strasbourg Court's objection to their participation was stated in the following terms:

Other aspects of these judges' status make it questionable. Firstly they are servicemen who still belong to the army, which in turn takes its orders from the executive. Secondly, they remain subject to military discipline and assessment reports are compiled on them by the army for that purpose. Decisions pertaining to their appointment are to a great extent taken by the administrative authorities and the army. Lastly, their term of office as National Security Court judges is only four years and can be renewed.... In addition, the Court attaches great importance to the fact that a civilian had to appear before a Court composed, even if only in part, of members of the armed forces.... It follows that the applicant could legitimately fear that because one of the judges of the Izmir National Security Court was a military judge it might allow itself to be unduly influenced by considerations which had nothing to do with the nature of the case.[224]

The Supreme Court of Canada made an extensive review of the attributes of the independence of courts guaranteed by section 11(d) of the Canadian Charter of Rights and Freedoms in a reference concerning various aspects of the terms, appointment and compensation of provincial court judges. Provincial courts comprise the lowest tier of the Canadian judiciary and, unlike in superior courts, the judges are appointed

---

[218] Http://news.scotsman.com/topics.cfm (Last updated 24 Feb. 2005).

[219] *Cooper v. United Kingdom*, 16 Dec. 2003, 39 E.H.R.R. 8, para. 134.

[220] 9 June 1998, 29 E.H.R.R. 449.

[221] *Id.* at para. 28.   [222] *Baskaya v. Turkey*, 8 July 1999, 31 E.H.R.R. 10, para. 55.

[223] *Incal, supra* n. 220, paras. 28–9; *Baskaya, supra* n. 222, para. 55.

[224] *Incal, supra* n. 220, paras. 68, 72.

and paid by the provincial governments. The Supreme Court listed three 'core characteristics' of judicial independence—security of tenure, financial security and administrative independence. Each of these characteristics was important with respect to its impact on both individual judges and on courts as institutions.[225] These factors dictated that any freeze or reduction in judicial salaries be preceded by a non-binding consultation with an independent and apolitical commission. The Court suggested further that any pay reduction singling judges out from other public employees would entail a heavy burden of justification. The Court also stated that it was inconsistent with judicial independence for there to be any judicial negotiation with the executive or legislative authorities over judicial remuneration. Finally, any salary reduction could not take compensation to a level where judges could be perceived as susceptible to political pressure through economic manipulation.[226]

The requirement of an impartial tribunal has been held by the Strasbourg Court to extend to members of juries. In *Holm v. Sweden*[227] it was held that a private prosecutor in a criminal libel case was deprived of an impartial jury. A majority of the jurors were members of a political party that owned the company which had published the alleged libel. The relevant writing, moreover, concerned the political activities of the applicant, partly in opposition to that party.[228] But in *Pullar v. United Kingdom*[229] the Court refused to find a violation where a juror was an employee of one of the main prosecution witnesses in a solicitation of bribery case. The Court noted that the juror in question had not been shown to have had personal knowledge of the events at issue. It also relied on the fact that the juror was one of 15 (the verdict in this Scottish court was by majority vote) and that he had taken an oath to judge the facts dispassionately.[230]

In two cases the Court has dealt with claims that racist attitudes in a jury prevented a court from being impartial. In the first the Court held that Article 6 required a judge to take action, or at least to make further inquiry, when it was alleged that one of the jurors selected in a homicide trial against an Algerian defendant had been overheard declaring himself a racist.[231] But in the second case the Court held that an English judge acted consistently with Article 6 when he responded to an ambiguous note from the jury suggesting some racial aspects to its deliberations by a strongly worded instruction

---

[225] *Re. Remuneration of Judges* [1997] 3 S.C.R. 3, paras. 115–20. Compare these factors to those listed by the European Court in, for example, *Lauko v. Slovakia, supra* n. 215, at para. 56.

[226] [1997] 3 S.C.R. 3, at paras. 133–5. In Scotland an important consequence of the enactment of the Human Rights Act 1998 was that the practice by which the Lord Advocate, as a member of the Scottish Executive, appointed temporary sheriffs to conduct criminal trials was held to be in serious breach of Article 6(1); in the absence of any security of tenure, the temporary sheriffs did not constitute an independent and impartial tribunal. *See Starrs v. Ruxton* [2000], J.C. 208 and *Millar v. Dickinson* [2001] U.K.P.C. D4, [2001] 1 W.L.R. 1615.

[227] 25 Nov. 1993, 18 E.H.R.R. 79.

[228] The House of Lords has also held that the same test of bias is applicable to judges and jurors. *R. v. Gough* [1993] A.C. 646.

[229] 10 June 1996, 22 E.H.R.R. 391.

[230] *Id.* at paras. 39–40.

[231] *Remli v. France*, 23 Apr. 1996, 22 E.H.R.R. 253.

to act solely on the evidence.[232] The judge's responses in this situation were limited by the English rule against any inquiry into the content of a jury's deliberations, a rule the Strasbourg Court accepted as a 'crucial and legitimate feature of English trial law which serves to reinforce the jury's role as the ultimate arbiter of fact and to guarantee open and frank deliberation'.[233]

The Supreme Court of Canada has held that before trial a criminal defendant is entitled to examine potential jurors for possible racial prejudice even in the absence of any *prima facie* indication of such an attitude. The Court in *R. v. Williams*[234] noted that potential jurors in Canada are 'presumed to be indifferent or impartial' and that before they may be questioned to establish the contrary some basis for suspecting bias must be brought forward. This could be supplied by evidence of widespread racial prejudice on either a national or a provincial scale. Once this was shown potential jurors could be examined to determine whether they shared such attitudes and whether they were able, nonetheless, to act impartially.[235] The Court expressed its view that this liberalized approach to jury challenges need not 'evolve into the approach in the United States of routine and sometimes lengthy challenges for cause of every juror in every case with attendant cost, delay and invasion of juror privacy'.[236]

As indicated by this quotation, examination of potential jurors for partiality in the United States is both common and extensive. Such examination, even to discover racial bias, however, has not been held to be constitutionally required in the guilt determination phase of criminal trials absent the presence of some racial element in the crime charged.[237] A majority of the United States Supreme Court has held, however, that such an inquiry *must* be permitted in capital cases arising from interracial crimes. Given the unusual discretion accorded juries in deciding the appropriateness of capital punishment, there is a 'unique opportunity for racial prejudice to operate but remain undetected'.[238]

6. ADMINISTRATIVE AGENCIES AND DISCIPLINARY BODIES

Article 6's requirement of an independent and impartial tribunal has been applied to actions outside the familiar context of judicial proceedings. In *Demicoli v. Malta* the European Court decided that the Maltese House of Representatives was not an impartial tribunal for the purpose of deciding whether an applicant was guilty of breaching

---

[232] *Gregory v. United Kingdom*, 25 Feb. 1997, 25 E.H.R.R. 577.
[233] *Id.* at para. 44.
[234] [1998] 1 S.C.R. 1128.
[235] *Id.* at paras. 30, 33.
[236] *Id.* at paras. 51–7.
[237] *Ristaino v. Ross*, 424 U.S. 589 (1976).
[238] *Turner v. Murray*, 476 U.S. 28, 35 (1986).

the privileges of the House by publishing a satirical article allegedly defaming that body. The Court noted particularly the fact that certain members who had been especially ridiculed in the article participated in the proceedings.[239]

But by far the most important extra-judicial application of Article 6 is with respect to the activities of administrative agencies and other regulatory bodies—as illustrated by the *Feldbrugge* case reported above.[240] The requirement of impartiality in this context has at least two important aspects. First, such agencies tend to become identified with certain policies and interests in the fields they regulate. Second, the agencies often play multiple roles in the legal process of regulation—making rules, overseeing their enforcement and adjudicating disputes concerning them.[241] Naturally, these arrangements raise the concerns which are evident in the principal cases.

The character of the first difficulty noted is also evident in bodies regulating particular professions or trades: The Court dealt with such a situation in *Albert and LeCompte v. Belgium*,[242] where the Court held that the Belgian procedure for discipline of physicians did not violate Article 6(1). First, the Court found that, since the right to practise their profession was in issue, the applicants had presented a case involving the determination of a civil right and not a mere 'public right'.[243] The Court reached this conclusion 'notwithstanding the specific character of the medical profession—a profession which is exercised in the general interest—and the special duties incumbent on its members'.[244]

It then held that the fact that the adjudicatory body was in part staffed with physicians did not prevent it from being an impartial tribunal in the absence of a showing of individual bias. The physician-members sat not as representatives of the profession but in a 'personal capacity'.[245]

In *H v. Belgium*,[246] the Court expressly declined to consider the structural impartiality of the Council of the *Orders des avocats*, in light of its finding that the procedure followed by the Council was otherwise defective in ways that violated Article 6(1). The Council, which decided applications for the re-admission of disbarred attorneys, was composed entirely of lawyers. In separate statements, judges expressed doubts as to the impartiality of such a tribunal.

It has been held that the procedure for investigating and adjudicating charges of professional misconduct against barristers in England did not violate the principle of impartiality merely because members of the tribunal and members of the Professional Conduct Committee charged with investigation and prosecution were drawn from the same governing body. The relevant rules provided that no one who had served on

---

[239] 27 Aug. 1991, 14 E.H.R.R. 47.

[240] *See* Section B(7) *supra*.

[241] *See* A. W. Bradley & K. D. Ewing, *Constitutional and Administrative Law* 657–71 (14th edn. 2006).

[242] 10 Feb. 1983, 5 E.H.R.R. 533. And *see* Section B(6) *supra*.

[243] On 'public rights' *see* Section B(6) *supra*.

[244] *Albert & LeCompte v. Belgium*, *supra* n. 242, para. 28.

[245] *Id*. at para. 32. *See also Debled v. Belgium*, 22 Sept. 1994, 19 E.H.R.R. 506 (Procedure for dealing with challenges to members of physician disciplinary bodies compatible with Article 6(1)).

[246] 30 Nov. 1987, 10 E.H.R.R. 339.

the Committee while the charges were being considered could serve on the tribunal. Nor was the tribunal held to be biased merely because a majority of its members were barristers: '[I]t has always been accepted that professional men are peculiarly well fitted...to determine whether there has been a breach of the code of conduct governing the profession and to judge the gravity of it if it is proven'.[247]

The same type of issue was presented to the United States Supreme Court in *Gibson v. Berryhill*.[248] The appellants challenged the constitutionality of professional discipline proceedings brought against them by the Alabama Optometry Association before the Alabama Board of Optometry. The unprofessional conduct alleged consisted of the appellants' employment by a corporation. This, the Association claimed, facilitated the unlicensed practice of optometry by the corporation. By statute the membership of the Board was restricted to members of the Association and expressly excluded any optometrists employed by another person or entity. The Supreme Court affirmed the District Court's judgment that this arrangement involved sufficient risk of bias to make the proceedings inconsistent with the Fourteenth Amendment's prohibition against deprivations without due process of law. Note that the facts in *Gibson* present a far stronger case for finding potential unfairness than those before the Court in the *Albert and LeCompte* case.

The European Court did, however, find a violation on the grounds of lack of impartiality outside the context of disciplinary bodies in *Lanborger v. Sweden*.[249] The applicant, a tenant in an apartment building, initiated proceedings to delete from his lease a 'rent negotiation clause', whereby he and the landlord were bound by rent agreements negotiated by the National Tenants' Union and the Landlords' Union. Two of the four judges who sat on the Housing and Tenancy Court, which ruled on his request, were 'lay assessors', one nominated by the Tenants' Union, the other by the Landlords' Union. While each assessor acted in a personal capacity, each had a long-standing association with the nominating union. Those unions, the Court noted, each 'had an interest in the negotiation clause. As the applicant sought the deletion from the lease of this clause, he could legitimately fear that the lay assessors had a common interest contrary to his own ...'.[250] In their dissenting opinion, Judges Valticos and Pettiti noted that tribunals in which interested parties were represented were deemed useful in the resolution of industrial and social conflicts. In the case at issue, moreover, no decision could be made without the assent of the two professional judges. To rule these kinds of panels unacceptable, they argued, would place the legitimacy of many specialized courts in doubt.

The Strasbourg Court has also upheld the procedure for challenging land reform orders issued by local authorities in Austria. Affected landowners could bring suit and appeal to a provincial Land Reform Board and from there to a National Supreme Land Reform Board. The majority of those boards were, in each case, composed of civil

---

[247] *In Re S (A Barrister)* [1981] Q.B. 683. This judgment was given by a panel of three High Court judges sitting as visitors to the Inns of Court.

[248] 411 U.S. 564 (1973).

[249] 22 June 1989, 12 E.H.R.R. 416.   [250] *Id.* at para. 35.

servants with expertise in agricultural specialties. This fact alone was held insufficient to bring the Boards' impartiality into question. The expert members, moreover, were practically irremovable during their five year term and did not act pursuant to any instructions from their superiors.[251]

The second issue, the mixing of adjudicatory and administrative and rule making functions, was raised in *Campbell and Fells v. United Kingdom*,[252] involving the determination of breaches of prison disciplinary rules by a Board of Visitors:

32. A Board of Visitors is a body that had to be appointed, by the Home Secretary, for each prison in England and Wales; its members...hold office for three years or such less period as the Home Secretary may appoint. They may be re-appointed.

There are 115 Boards in all and each has between 8 and 24 members, who are unpaid but are reimbursed their expenses...[T]here is no express statutory provision enabling the Home Secretary to dismiss a member and resignation before expiry of a term of office would, according to the Government, be required only in the most exceptional circumstances.

33. A Board's duties include, in addition to inquiring into charges of disciplinary offences, satisfying itself as to the state of the premises, the administration of the prison and the treatment of inmates, hearing a prisoner's complaints or requests, directing the governor's attention to matters calling for his attention and making reports to the Home Secretary...Its members are required to visit the prison frequently, have a right of access to every part of the prison and to prison records and may interview any prisoner out of the sight and hearing of officers. A Board's adjudicatory functions generally account for a small proportion of its overall duties and, of the small percentage of prison disciplinary proceedings which are conducted before Boards, few concern 'especially grave offences'....

81. ... [A] Board is, as the Government pointed out, intended to exercise an independent oversight of the administration of the prison. In the nature of things, supervision must involve a Board in frequent contacts with the prison officials and just as much with the inmates themselves; yet this in no way alters the fact that its function, even when discharging its administrative duties, is to 'hold the ring' between the parties concerned, independently of both of them. The impression which prisoners may have that Boards are closely associated with the executive and the prison administration is a factor of greater weight, particularly bearing in mind the importance in the context of Article 6 of the maxim 'justice must not only be done: it must also be seen to be done'. However, the existence of such sentiments on the part of inmates, which is probably unavoidable in a custodial setting, is not sufficient to establish a lack of 'independence'. This requirement of Article 6 would not be satisfied if prisoners were reasonably entitled, on account of the frequent contacts between a Board and the authorities, to think that the former was dependent on the latter (see, the abovementioned *Piersack* judgment); however, the Court does not consider that the mere fact of these contacts, which exist also with the prisoners themselves, could justify such an impression.

82. In the light of the foregoing, the Court sees no reason to conclude that the Board in question was not 'independent', within the meaning of Article 6.

---

[251] *Ettl v. Austria*, 23 Apr. 1987, 10 E.H.R.R. 255. *See also Ringeisen v. Austria, supra* n. 72.
[252] 28 June 1984, 7 E.H.R.R. 165. *See also* Section B(5) *supra*.

In *Withrow v. Larkin*,[253] the United States Supreme Court considered whether the fact that a professional disciplinary board investigated, presented charges and adjudicated, constituted a violation of the requirement of due process:

The contention that the combination of investigative and adjudicative functions necessarily creates an unconstitutional risk of bias in administrative adjudication has a much more difficult burden of persuasion to carry. It must overcome a presumption of honesty and integrity in those serving as adjudicators; and it must convince that, under a realistic appraisal of psychological tendencies and human weakness, conferring investigative and adjudicative powers on the same individuals poses such a risk of actual bias or prejudgment that the practice must be forbidden if the guarantee of due process is to be adequately implemented.[254]

[The Court quoted from *FTC v. Cement Institute*,[255] in which the fairness of the Federal Trade Commission's adjudication of the legality of a cement pricing method was challenged in light of some of the Commissioners' previous investigation of and public statements about the pricing system.]

'[T]he fact that the Commission had entertained such views as the result of its prior *ex parte* investigations did not necessarily mean that the minds of its members were irrevocably closed on the subject of the respondents' basing point practices. Here, in contrast to the Commission's investigations, members of the cement industry were legally authorized participants in the hearings. They produced evidence—volumes of it. They were free to point out to the Commission by testimony, by cross-examination of witnesses, and by arguments, conditions of the trade practices under attack which they thought kept these practices within the range of legally permissible business activities'. ...

That is not to say that there is nothing to the argument that those who have investigated should not then adjudicate. The issue is substantial, it is not new, and legislators and others concerned with the operations of administrative agencies have given much attention to whether and to what extent distinctive administrative functions should be performed by the same persons. No single answer has been reached. Indeed, the growth, variety, and complexity of the administrative processes have made any one solution highly unlikely. Within the Federal Government itself, Congress has addressed the issue in several different ways, providing for varying degrees of separation from complete separation of functions to virtually none at all ...

That the combination of investigative and adjudicative functions does not, without more, constitute a due process violation, does not preclude a court from determining from the special facts and circumstances present in the case before it that the risk of unfairness is intolerably high.[256] Compare the judgment of the Supreme Court of Canada in *2747–3174 Quebec Inc. v. Quebec (Régie des Permis d'Alcool)*.[257] In that case the Court held that the Quebec procedure for cancellation of liquor permits was inconsistent with section 23 of the Quebec Charter of Human Rights and Freedoms because the Régie did not operate in the context of an 'independent and impartial tribunal'. The Court noted that the governing statute allowed 'employees of the Régie to participate in the investigation, the filing of complaints, the presentation of the case to the directors and the decision'.[258] It agreed that a combination of such functions in the same

[253] 421 U.S. 35 (1975).   [254] *Id*. at 47.   [255] 333 U.S. 683 (1948).
[256] *Id*. at 48, 51–2, 58.   [257] [1996] 3 S.C.R.R. 919.   [258] *Id*. at para. 46.

agency did not, by itself, create a constitutional problem.[259] In this case, however, there was no assurance by rule or statute that a single individual might not exercise several of these functions successively in the same case. 'The possibility that a jurist who has made submissions to the directors might advise them in respect of the same matter is disturbing, especially since some of the directors have no legal training'.[260]

D. EQUALITY OF ARMS

Apart from its requirement that civil rights and criminal charges be determined by an independent and impartial tribunal, Article 6 demands that such determinations be made in a 'fair and public hearing'. The structure and personnel of the tribunal must be fair but so must the manner in which the decision is made. These two aspects of fairness are not always easy to separate. Consider, in this regard, the European Court's judgments in the *DeCubber* and *Borgers* cases, discussed in the previous section, concerning the participation of the *avocat général* in the deliberations of the Belgian Court of Cassation. That is, certain standard procedures favouring the prosecution may be regarded as infecting the impartiality of the tribunal.

Although the phrase is absent from the Convention, fairness in this regard has been held to require an 'equality of arms'. '[E]ach party must be afforded a reasonable opportunity to present his case—including his evidence—under conditions that do not place him at a substantial disadvantage vis-à-vis his opponent'.[261] As this formulation appears to recognize, the nature of legal proceedings preclude a perfect equality between the parties. In every instance of litigation one party must suffer the disadvantage of bearing the burden of proof. Article 6 itself requires that criminal defendants be presumed innocent until proved guilty, guaranteeing that the state, in this respect, is at a significant disadvantage.

More generally, the employment of a presumption of liability from the proof of certain facts does not by itself violate Article 6 although it obviously confers a comparative advantage on one party.[262] The Court has also stated, however, that, at least in criminal cases, where a defendant is entitled to the presumption of innocence, the Court does not 'regard presumptions of fact or law... with indifference. It requires States to confine them within reasonable limits which take into account the importance of what is at stake and maintain the rights of the defence'.[263]

---

[259] *Id.* at para. 47.   [260] *Id.* at para. 54.

[261] *Dombo Beheer B.V. v. The Netherlands*, 27 Oct. 1993, 18 E.H.R.R. 213, para. 33.

[262] *Salabiaku v. France*, 7 Oct. 1988, 13 E.H.R.R. 379, para. 28. *See also R. v. Rose* [1998] 2 S.C.R. 262 holding that the prosecution's rights to give the closing argument when the defence has presented evidence was consistent with the Canadian Charter of Rights and Freedoms.

[263] *Salabiaku, supra* n. 262, para. 28. The Canadian Charter of Rights and Freedoms establishes a presumption of innocence in section 11(d) for those accused of crimes. The Supreme Court has held this prohibits criminal conviction without proof of some fault. *B.C. Motor Vehicle Reference* [1985] 2 S.C.R. 486. Placing the burden of proving absence of fault on the defendant has been held compatible with the Charter

This principle of equality of arms applies to civil proceedings as well as criminal prosecutions. With respect to the latter, however, many provisions of Article 6 detail specific aspects of the right to a fair trial. The European Court frequently deals with both particular and general aspects of complaints about a criminal procedure in a single omnibus discussion.[264]

1. DOMBO BEHEER B.V. V. THE NETHERLANDS

Judgment of 27 Oct. 1993

18 E.H.R.R. 213

7. The applicant (hereinafter 'Dombo') is a limited liability company under Netherlands law.... The shares in Dombo were held by a foundation (stichting) which issued certificates of shares; these were apparently all held by a Mr H.C. van Reijendam. The company's management also included Mr van Reijendam; he was the sole managing director from 1963 until his dismissal, except for a short period between 4 February 1981 and 23 March 1981 during which he was suspended as managing director and temporarily replaced by a Mr C.U. and a Mrs van L.

At the material time, Dombo banked with the Nederlandsche Middenstandsbank N.V. (hereinafter 'the Bank') through its branch office in Nijmegen. The manager of that office was a Mr van W.; under the Bank's company statutes his position was not that of managing director of the Bank itself and his powers to represent the Bank, which included allowing credit up to a certain maximum, were strictly circumscribed.

[Dombo and the Bank disagreed as to the extent of the Bank's authorization of credit. The Bank cut off further advances and Dombo sought damages for losses caused by what it alleged to be the failure of the bank to honour its commitment. The case was heard by the Arnhem Court of Appeal.]

15. Dombo called a number of witnesses, including Mr van Reijendam. Producing the minutes of a shareholders' meeting dated 29 June 1984, it claimed that Mr van Reijendam had been dismissed as managing director for reason of 'lack of funds'. It further produced a document from which it appeared that Mr van Reijendam had been registered as an unemployed person seeking employment on 27 November 1984 and an extract from the commercial register from which it appeared that another person had been appointed managing director of Dombo on 10 December 1984.

with respect to 'regulatory offences' but unconstitutional with respect to 'true crimes' dealing with inherently wrongful conduct. *R. v. Wholesale Travel Group* [1991] 3 S.C.R. 154. The distinction, however, has not always been clear in subsequent cases. *See* P. Hogg, *Constitutional Law of Canada*, 1071–80 (Student edn., 2006). The Due Process clauses of the United States Constitution forbid the use of a presumption that shifts to the defendant in a criminal case the burden of proving the absence of an essential element of the offence. *Mullaney v. Wilbur*, 421 U.S. 684 (1975). The Supreme Court has, however, also held that it is permissible to place on a criminal defendant the burden of proving an affirmative defence such as insanity, either by a preponderance of the evidence or by clear and convincing evidence. *Leland v. Oregon*, 343 U.S. 790 (1952).

[264] E.g. *Van Mechelen v. The Netherlands*, 23 April 1997, 25 E.H.R.R. 647, para. 49.

16. The Bank objected to Mr van Reijendam being heard. It based this objection on the rule that a party to the proceedings could not himself be heard as a witness. It claimed that Mr van Reijendam's dismissal did not reflect the true state of affairs but had been effected only to enable him to testify.

In a judgment of 12 February 1985 Judge Van E. upheld this objection and refused to hear Mr van Reijendam. He had become convinced that both Mr van Reijendam's dismissal as managing director of Dombo and the appointment in his place of another person were shams (schijnhandelingen) which served no other purpose than to enable Mr van Reijendam to testify in the instant proceedings. He pointed out that Mr van Reijendam had been present at the oral pleadings before the Court of Appeal on 30 October 1984 and had not protested when Dombo's lawyer referred to him as Dombo's managing director. He added that in his view the motives alleged for the dismissal were implausible.

The other six witnesses produced by Dombo were heard on 13 and 20 February 1985. ...

17. In the exercise of its right to have its own witnesses heard in reply (contra-enquête), the Bank called two of its employees, one of whom was the manager of its Nijmegen branch office, Mr van W.

Dombo objected to the hearing of Mr van W., stating the view that at all stages of the credit relationship, and also in the instant proceedings, he had been and remained the formal representative of the Bank; to hear him as a witness at this point, when Mr van Reijendam had not been so heard, would upset the fair balance that should exist between parties in civil proceedings.

18. By a decision delivered orally on 13 March 1985 Judge Van E. dismissed Dombo's objection. He considered first and foremost that Mr van W. was a competent witness in the instant case since he was not a party to the proceedings either formally or in fact and went on to state that it could not follow from the fact that Dombo was put at a disadvantage because Mr van Reijendam was not heard as a witness while Mr van W. was so heard that Mr van W. was no longer a competent witness. ...

19. The Court of Appeal delivered its final judgment on 11 March 1986. It first examined the witnesses' statements in detail. ...

The Court of Appeal went on to hold:

'The Court of Appeal is of the opinion that the evidence required from Dombo has not been provided. ... Although the ease with which the [Bank] allowed [Dombo] to exceed consider-ably the credit limit officially in force provides food for thought, it can be explained by the negotiations between the parties, which came to light during the proceedings, concerning the establishment of a substantially higher credit limit, in which—as was also common ground between the parties—the sum of NLG 2,600,000 was mentioned. It is clear from the statement of the witness [Van W.]—and Dombo did not contest this again after the examination of that witness—that at the end of January 1981 the then managing director of Dombo, by misleading the witness, twice succeeded in drawing considerable sums over and above what was already to be regarded as officially a substantial overdraft on Dombo's consolidated accounts. This amount could reasonably provide the [Bank] with grounds for temporarily "shutting off the flow of credit" to Dombo'. ...

[On appeal to the Supreme Court Dombo argued that the refusal to hear van Reijendam's testimony violated Article 6 of the Convention. During the appeal Parliament approved a law allowing parties to give evidence.]

22. The Supreme Court...rejected the complaint based on Article 6 para. 1 of the Convention; this was based, according to the Supreme Court, on the argument that the Court of Appeal had violated the principle that 'the procedural rights of both parties should be equivalent'. This line of argument, in the opinion of the Supreme Court, '...fails to recognise that in assessing the convincingness of the content of witnesses' statements, the judge with competence to determine questions of fact is free to consider the nature and degree of involvement of a witness with a party in proceedings and that he must also judge a witness's statement in the light of what the opposing party has put forward in its written pleadings or when appearing before the court in person'.

The applicant company complained about the refusal by the national courts to allow its former managing director, Mr van Reijendam, to give evidence, whereas the branch manager of the Bank, Mr van W., who had been the only other person present when the oral agreement was entered into, had been able to testify. In its contention, the national courts had thereby failed to observe the principle of 'equality of arms', in breach of its right to a 'fair hearing' as guaranteed by Article 6 para. 1...

31. ...It is not within the province of the Court to substitute its own assessment of the facts for that of the national courts. The Court's task is to ascertain whether the proceedings in their entirety, including the way in which evidence was permitted, were 'fair' within the meaning of Article 6 para. 1.

32. The requirements inherent in the concept of 'fair hearing' are not necessarily the same in cases concerning the determination of civil rights and obligations as they are in cases concerning the determination of a criminal charge. This is borne out by the absence of detailed provisions such as paragraphs 2 and 3 of Article 6 applying to cases of the former category. Thus, although these provisions have a certain relevance outside the strict confines of criminal law the Contracting States have greater latitude when dealing with civil cases concerning civil rights and obligations than they have when dealing with criminal cases.

33. Nevertheless, certain principles concerning the notion of a 'fair hearing' in cases concerning civil rights and obligations emerge from the Court's case-law. Most significantly for the present case, it is clear that the requirement of 'equality of arms', in the sense of a 'fair balance' between the parties, applies in principle to such cases as well as to criminal cases.

The Court agrees with the Commission that as regards litigation involving opposing private interests, 'equality of arms' implies that each party must be afforded a reasonable opportunity to present his case—including his evidence—under conditions that do not place him at a substantial disadvantage vis-à-vis his opponent.

It is left to the national authorities to ensure in each individual case that the requirements of a 'fair hearing' are met.

34. In the instant case, it was incumbent upon the applicant company to prove that there was an oral agreement between it and the Bank to extend certain credit facilities. Only two persons had been present at the meeting at which this agreement had allegedly been reached, namely Mr van Reijendam representing the applicant company and Mr van W. representing the Bank. Yet only one of these two key persons was permitted to be heard, namely the person who had represented the Bank. The applicant company was denied the possibility of calling the person who had represented it, because the Court of Appeal identified him with the applicant company itself.

35. During the relevant negotiations Mr van Reijendam and Mr van W. acted on an equal footing, both being empowered to negotiate on behalf of their respective parties. It is therefore difficult to see why they should not both have been allowed to give evidence...

[The Court held 5–4 that there has been a violation of Article 6.]

Dissenting Opinion of Judge Martens joined by Judge Pettiti

...The Court restricts itself to ascertaining whether the proceedings between Dombo and the Bank 'in their entirety, including the way in which evidence was permitted, were "fair" within the meaning of Article 6 para. 1'. Its decisive argument for answering this question in the negative is that since '[d]uring the relevant negotiations Mr van Reijendam and Mr van W. acted on an equal footing, both being empowered to negotiate on behalf of their respective parties, [i]t is...difficult to see why they should not both have been allowed to give evidence'. However, under a law of evidence such as that in force in the Netherlands at the relevant time it cannot be maintained that Mr van Reijendam and Mr van W. acted 'on an equal footing'. Mr van W. was merely an employee representing his employer, whereas Mr van Reijendam was to be identified with Dombo, being at the material time not only its sole managing director but also—indirectly—its only shareholder. Since the above rule is based on the irrefutable presumption that testimony given by 'a witness in his own case' is not to be trusted, the difference in the roles of Mr van W. and Mr van Reijendam provided a decisive and sufficient explanation 'why they should not both have been allowed to give evidence'.

In other words, in all situations in which a party to civil proceedings has to rely mainly if not exclusively on his own declarations to refute assertions made by his opponent and corroborated by witnesses, the aforementioned rule of the Netherlands law of evidence in civil proceedings necessarily places that party at a disadvantage vis-à-vis his opponent; and it is this consequence which, in the Court's opinion, justifies the conclusion that the principle of equality of arms has been violated. This means that the Court does not condemn the rule's application in concreto but the rule itself.

I very much doubt, however, whether that condemnation is justified. The rule that a person who is a party to civil proceedings cannot be heard as a witness in his own case is evidently based on the view that such testimony is intrinsically untrustworthy. Moreover, it apparently dates from an era when the oath to be sworn by witnesses was seen as having so great a (religious) significance that it was deemed imperative to protect a party to civil litigation from perjury and the other party from the possibility that the judge might feel compelled to give credit to the declarations of his opponent because they were made under oath. For a long time the rule that nemo in propria causa testis esse debet was generally accepted and formed part of the law of evidence in civil procedure in all European States. Since the second half of the last century it has been set aside in a number of countries. Considerations of procedural expediency may no doubt be advanced to justify such a reform, but the rule still applies in a good number of European States—such as Belgium, France, Italy, Switzerland, Spain and Turkey—which apparently prefer to maintain the traditional distrust of allowing a litigant to testify in his own case.

Against this background I think that it is very difficult to condemn the rule as being incompatible with the basic principles of fair procedure. In any event one should not do so without taking into account the other opportunities afforded by the national law of evidence for hearing a party to civil proceedings in person and without any argument other than that it is 'difficult to see why' a party should not be allowed to give evidence on his own behalf....

5. Both parties had ample—and equal—opportunities to present their case in writing and both parties had ample—and equal—opportunities to present their evidence. Both sides submitted documents and called witnesses.

It is true that the Bank was able to bring as a witness its negotiator (Mr van W.), whilst Dombo did not have the opportunity to call its negotiator, Mr van Reijendam. There are, however, good grounds for holding that this did not place Dombo 'at a substantial disadvantage vis-à-vis' the Bank. Firstly, under Netherlands law the courts are completely free in their assessment of the evidence of witnesses. Thus, the domestic courts were free to take into account the fact that Mr van W. was professionally involved with the Bank and therefore had a certain interest in the outcome of the proceedings. Similarly they would have been free to ignore statements made by Mr van Reijendam had he been permitted to testify. Consequently, the mere fact that Mr van W. was able to testify, whilst Mr van Reijendam was not cannot be said to have resulted in a substantial disadvantage for Dombo...

Joint Dissenting Opinion of Judges Berhhardt and Pekkanen

...In our opinion, equality of arms in civil proceedings requires the equality of chances and possibilities to submit the relevant material to the court concerned. In proceedings with a legal person as a party, any individual representing that person may be identified under national procedural law with the legal person and therefore excluded from the formal status of a witness. In our opinion, what is decisive is that the parties enjoy in fact and in law equality of arms before the national court. We are convinced that Dombo Beheer, the applicant in this case, enjoyed this equality of arms. In this respect we refer to paragraph 5 of the dissenting opinion of Judge Martens.

2. ASPECTS OF EQUALITY

The principal case involved the determination of a civil right. In such disputes Article 6 mandates a 'fair hearing' but does not specify particular aspects of the proceedings. In criminal cases, on the other hand, Article 6(3)(d) declares that a defendant has the right 'to obtain the attendance and examination of witnesses on his behalf under the same conditions as witnesses against him'. It is not enough to satisfy this provision to decide a case solely on the basis of the case file without hearing witnesses offered by either side.[265]

Note that in the principal case, the general rule about the testimony of parties applied to both sides although, on the facts of this case, it disadvantaged only the applicant. The Court in Strasbourg has shown itself willing to take into account the difficulties that a challenged procedure imposes arising from the particular situation of the applicant.

---

[265] *Vidal v. Belgium*, 22 April 1992. *See also Popov v. Russia*, 11 Dec. 2006, paras. 183–7. (Under Article 6 a judge may not refuse to hear defence witnesses without considering the importance of their testimony.)

Consequently, a rule restricting access to the case file to lawyers violated Article 6 when it disadvantaged a criminal defendant who was representing himself.[266]

The equality of arms also applies to the 'time and facilities' available to a party to prepare its case before the hearing. Article 6(3)(b) requires 'adequate time and facilities' for criminal defendants. When that requirement is met, literal equality is not required. In *Kremzow v. Austria*,[267] for example, the Court found no violation of Article 6 where a defendant received a copy of the Attorney General's position paper (*croquis*) three weeks before the Supreme Court's hearing on the case even though the Court had received it much earlier and had, indeed, prepared a draft judgment based largely on that paper. The time allowed was held adequate to satisfy Article 6(3)(b) and there was no violation of the equality of arms although 'the applicant may have been to some extent disadvantaged in the preparation of his defence'.[268]

In *Bönisch v. Austria*[269] the applicant was prosecuted twice for violations of the Food Code in connection with his business's process for smoking meat. Both prosecutions were initiated by the Federal Food Control Institute based on its tests of samples of the meat. In each case the court appointed the Director of the Institute as an expert. The applicant was permitted to present another expert as his own witness in the first but not in the second case. The European Court found impermissible inequality in both proceedings. Even when the applicant had been permitted to call his own witness, the appointment of the Director as the court's expert 'formally invested [him] with the function of neutral auxiliary of the court…'. Unlike the defence expert, the Director had been able to participate throughout the proceedings and to question witnesses. Given the fact that it was the Director's report that prompted the bringing of the case in the first place, he was 'more like a witness against the accused'.[270] On the other hand, in another case, the fact that psychiatric experts had given opinions of the applicant's dangerousness in highly inflammatory terms did impair the applicant's presumption of innocence.[271]

The European Court's examination of the presence or absence of equality of arms is not to be directed at a particular feature of procedure in isolation.[272] The Appeal Court of the High Court of Judiciary, therefore, held application of the Scottish Sexual Offences (Procedure and Evidence) Act 2002 compatible with Article 6.[273] That Act sharply restricted the extent to which a defendant in a sexual offence prosecution could examine the complaining witness. The defendant argued that this created a clear inequality since the Crown was not similarly limited in its examination of the defendant and his witnesses. The Lord Justice Clerk held that

---

[266] *Foucher v. France*, 18 Mar. 1997, 25 E.H.R.R. 234, paras. 32–7.
[267] 21 Sept. 1993, 17 E.H.R.R. 322.
[268] *Id.* at paras. 45–50. *See also Klimentyev v. Russia*, 16 Nov. 2006.
[269] 6 May 1985, 19 E.H.R.R. 191.
[270] *Id.* at paras. 32–3.
[271] *Bernard v. France*, 23 April 1998, 30 E.H.R.R. 808.
[272] *See*, e.g., *Edwards v. United Kingdom*, 25 Nov. 1992, 15 E.H.R.R. 417, para. 34.
[273] *M.M. v. Her Majesty's Advocate*, 2004 S.C.C.R. 658.

[e]quality of arms is no more than a figure of speech that refers to the basic principle that both sides should have the opportunity to present their cases without unfair restriction and that neither side should be put at a substantial disadvantage. Equality of arms cannot mean that both prosecution and defence must be subject to identical rules

In a sense there is a built-in inequality of arms in the criminal prosecution system since the Crown must give advance notice of the charge that they make, whereas the accused is not obliged, except where a special defence is necessary, to disclose his line of defence. The Crown, unlike the defence, bears the onus of proof from the outset; must prove all material facts by corroborated evidence, and must prove their case beyond reasonable doubt. In every prosecution the Crown have a duty to intimate to the defence any information in their possession that may assist the defence case or undermine the Crown case. The defence have no such duty. ...

With these considerations in mind, I do not see how the entitlement of the Crown to cross-examine the accused and his witnesses without any restriction [and] without having to give notice to the defence, can be seen to involve any real issue under article 6. During the continual process of reform in criminal law and procedure, the balance of advantage will swing from time to time between prosecution and defence. I cannot see how this legislation so upsets the balance as to compromise the overall fairness of the trial.[274]

3. R. (ROBERTS) V. PAROLE BOARD AND ANOTHER

[2005] U.K.H.L. 45, [2005] 2 A.C. 738

Lord Bingham of Cornhill (dissenting):

1. My Lords, on 12 December 1966 the appellant, Mr Harry Roberts, was convicted on three counts of murder, having pleaded guilty to two counts and been convicted of the third. The victims in each case were police officers, killed in cold blood at Shepherd's Bush in August 1966 when, in the course of their duty, they stopped a car in which the appellant and two accomplices were travelling to commit an armed robbery. The trial judge rightly described these crimes, which aroused widespread public outrage, as heinous and suggested that the case was one in which the appellant might never be released. He formally recommended that the appellant serve a term of at least 30 years, and in due course the Home Secretary of the day fixed 30 years as the appellant's punitive or tariff term. That term expired in 1996, when the appellant was aged 60. The fifth review of his case by the Parole Board, still current, began in September 2001, and this appeal concerns the procedure to be followed in that review. The issue to be determined by the House is agreed to be whether the Parole Board, a statutory tribunal of limited jurisdiction, is able, within the powers granted by the Criminal Justice Act 1991, and compatibly with article 5 of the European Convention on Human Rights (a) to withhold material relevant to the appellant's parole review from the appellant's legal representatives and (b) instead, to disclose that material to a specially appointed advocate, who

---

[274] *Id.* at paras. 47–9. For a Canadian judgment holding that a restrictive rape shield law violated the Charter, *see R. v. Seaboyer* [1991] 2 S.C.R. 577.

would represent the appellant, in the absence of the appellant and his legal representatives, at a closed hearing before the Parole Board.

2. ... On 1 October 2001 a parole dossier was disclosed to the appellant's solicitors containing a number of reports, all favourable to the appellant and recommending his immediate release on life licence. However, on 2 October 2001 the appellant was removed from open to closed conditions, where he has since remained. The appellant has received a general indication of the allegations against him which led to his removal, but these have not been the subject of any criminal or disciplinary charge, they have not been investigated at any adversarial hearing and they have been consistently challenged by the appellant.

3. On 11 February 2002 the Secretary of State for the Home Department, who appears in this appeal as an interested party, disclosed to the appellant further material that had been submitted by him to the Parole Board for purposes of the parole review. The material related to alleged breaches of trust committed by the appellant while held in open conditions. The appellant was notified on 22 April 2002 that further material was to be withheld from both him and his legal representatives, but would be submitted to the Parole Board (henceforward 'the board') for its consideration. It is the treatment of this further material, conveniently described as 'the sensitive material', which gives rise to this appeal. The ground upon which the sensitive material has been withheld is that the safety of the source of the information or evidence would be at risk if the material were to be disclosed. It has not been suggested that there is in this case any threat to national security. ...

5. On 15 November 2002 Scott Baker LJ, as vice-chairman of the board, decided that before a decision was made on the procedure to be adopted in respect of the sensitive material at the substantive hearing before the board, that material should in the first instance be disclosed to a specially appointed advocate agreeable to both parties, who could then make representations on the disclosure issues. The sensitive material was not to be disclosed to the appellant or his legal representatives or anyone else without the consent of the board. Scott Baker LJ proposed that a hearing should then take place to resolve the disclosure issues. He acknowledged that the procedure for appointing special advocates was statutory in other fields but he could see no reason why it should not be used in the present circumstances.

6. With the agreement of the appellant and the Secretary of State, the Attorney General appointed Mr Nicholas Blake QC to act as 'independent counsel', in effect as a special advocate. In an advice written for the board before seeing the sensitive material Mr Blake advised that resort to the special advocate procedure infringed ordinary standards of fairness. After seeing the sensitive material he submitted to the board that it be disclosed to the appellant's solicitor.

7. On 9 May 2003 a hearing took place before Sir Richard Tucker as chairman of the board's mandatory lifer panel. The appellant and the Secretary of State were represented, and Mr Blake attended. The hearing consisted of an open session when the appellant's solicitor made representations on his behalf, and a closed session when submissions were made about the sensitive material by the Secretary of State's counsel and Mr Blake, in the absence of the appellant and his solicitor. A decision was made by Sir Richard the same day, but complaints about the conduct of the hearing led to a further hearing attended by counsel for the appellant and the Secretary of State on 30 May 2003. In a detailed letter dated 13 June 2003 the board communicated its decision, which was that the sensitive material should not be disclosed to the appellant or his legal representatives, but should be disclosed to the specially appointed

advocate. The board directed that there should be a two-stage hearing, one considering the open material and the other the sensitive material, the specially appointed advocate appearing at both stages.

8. The judicial review proceedings giving rise to this appeal were initiated to challenge this decision of 13 June. It was agreed that the judge (Maurice Kay J) should read the sensitive material and hear submissions on it in closed session by counsel for the board and the Secretary of State, and by Mr Blake. There was again a two-stage hearing, one addressed by counsel for the appellant and the other, in the absence of the appellant and his counsel, directed to the sensitive material. The judge delivered two judgments on 19 December 2003. In the first, open, judgment he upheld the lawfulness of the proposed procedure and dismissed the appellant's application [2003] EWHC 3120 (Admin); [2004] 2 All ER 776. The second was a closed judgment, not disclosed to the appellant or his legal representatives, but disclosed to Mr Blake who advised the appellant that there was no basis for challenging the findings in the closed judgment on appeal.

9. The appellant challenged the lawfulness of the proposed procedure in principle on appeal to the Court of Appeal ...

11. ... A life sentence prisoner such as the appellant [who has completed the punitive or 'tariff' part of his sentence] has a right to bring proceedings to challenge the lawfulness of his continued detention and a right to be released, no matter what the enormity of the crime or crimes for which he was imprisoned, if he is judged to present no continuing threat to the safety of the public. ...

16. The ordinary principle governing the conduct of judicial inquiries in this country is not, in my opinion, open to doubt. In *In re K (Infants)* [1963] Ch 381, 405–406, Upjohn LJ expressed it thus:

> It seems to be fundamental to any judicial inquiry that a person or other properly interested party must have the right to see all the information put before the judge, to comment on it, to challenge it and if needs be to combat it, and to try to establish by contrary evidence that it is wrong. It cannot be withheld from him in whole or in part. If it is so withheld and yet the judge takes such information into account in reaching his conclusion without disclosure to those parties who are properly and naturally vitally concerned, the proceedings cannot be described as judicial.

On appeal to the House in the same case [1965] AC 201, Lord Devlin referred, at p. 237, to 'the fundamental principle of justice that the judge should not look at material that the parties before him have not seen', and at p. 238, referring to 'the ordinary principles of a judicial inquiry'. ...

17. The European court has affirmed the importance of this principle in criminal cases governed by article 6(1) of the Convention, holding that as a general rule all evidence must be produced in the presence of the accused at a public hearing with a view to adversarial argument, giving him an adequate and proper opportunity to challenge and question witnesses against him. In non-criminal article 5(4) cases the approach of the court has been similar, generally requiring disclosure of adverse material and an adversarial procedure of a judicial character in which the person affected has the effective assistance of his lawyer and has the opportunity to call and question witnesses ... :

18. It is in my opinion plain that the procedure which the board propose to adopt in resolving the appellant's parole review will infringe the principles discussed in the foregoing paragraphs. The board will receive and be free to act on material adverse to the appellant which will not, even in an anonymised or summarised form, be made available to him or his legal representatives. Both he and his legal representatives will be excluded from the hearing when such evidence is given or adduced, denying him and them the opportunity to participate in the hearing, by questioning any witness or challenging any evidence called or adduced to vouch the sensitive material, or by giving or calling evidence to contradict that material, or by addressing argument. The appellant and his legal representatives are free to instruct the specially appointed advocate (whose integrity and skill are not in question) so long as none of them knows anything of the case made against the appellant on the basis of the sensitive material, but the specially appointed advocate is forbidden to communicate with the appellant or his legal representatives once he knows the nature of the case against the appellant based on the sensitive material. It is only at that stage that meaningful instructions can be given, unless the appellant has successfully predicted the nature of the case in advance, in which case he may well have identified the source and undermined the need for secrecy. The Parole Board assert that the specially appointed advocate may call witnesses, and in the absence of any warrant or authority to adopt the specially appointed advocate procedure that may be so.... But even if a specially appointed advocate is free to call witnesses, it is hard to see how he can know who to call or what to ask if he cannot take instructions from the appellant or divulge any of the sensitive material to the witness.... In the vivid language used by Lord Hewart CJ in a very different context in *Coles v Odhams Press Ltd* [1936] 1 KB 416, 426, the specially-appointed advocate would inevitably be 'taking blind shots at a hidden target'.

19. ... But I would decline the appellant's invitation to rule, at this stage, that the adoption of the proposed procedure is necessarily incompatible with article 5(4). The practice of the European court is to consider the proceedings in question as a whole, including the decisions of appellate courts: *Edwards v. United Kingdom*.[275] Thus its judgment is almost necessarily made in retrospect, when there is evidence of what actually happened. This reflects the acute sensitivity of the court to the facts of a given case. Save where an issue of compatibility turns on a pure question of statutory construction, the House should in my opinion be similarly reluctant to rule without knowing what has actually happened. This seems to me important because there are some outcomes which would not in my opinion offend article 5(4) despite the employment of a specially appointed advocate. It might, for instance, be that the board, having heard the sensitive material tested by the specially appointed advocate, wholly rejected it. Or having heard the material tested in that way the board might decline to continue the review unless the sensitive material, or at least the substance of it, were disclosed at least to the appellant's legal representatives ... If any of these possibilities were to eventuate, I do not think there would be a violation of article 5(4).

20. That conclusion makes it necessary to consider the other major question debated in argument, whether the board has power to adopt this procedure. [Lord Bingham concluded that the Board was without power to create the Special Advocate procedure.]

---

[275] 16 Dec. 1992, 15 E.H.R.R. 417, para. 34.

Lord Woolf CJ:

43. ... Provision has to be made when it is necessary for derogation from the golden rule of full disclosure but the derogation must be the minimum necessary to protect the public interest. When there has to be derogation there can be cases in which the appointment of an SAA is, in the interests of justice, advantageous. The European Court of Human Rights has accepted that some operations 'must be conducted secretly if they are to be conducted effectively'. Finally, there is the fact that the trial judge should not be placed in a straitjacket. Instead the decision sets out principles and indicates those principles should be applied on a case by case basis: 'in the infinitely diverse situations with which trial judges have to deal ... the touchstone is to ascertain what justice requires in the circumstances of the particular case'. These points are all highly relevant to the determination of the issue...

50. While we do not know the contents of the closed evidence in this case, we have to accept that a case could well occur where a witness would be able to satisfy the board that there would be a real danger of a prisoner killing someone if he is released, but the witness who could provide the evidence of this is not prepared to make available the evidence if it may be disclosed to the prisoner or his representatives. In such a situation it appears that there can be no alternative but for the board to weigh up the conflicting interests of the prisoner and society. It would conflict with the board's statutory duty for the board to ignore the evidence unless this is what article 5(4) or domestic law require.

51. The fact that the prisoner has been convicted of the most serious of crimes and been sentenced to life imprisonment makes his position significantly different from that of someone who has not been convicted and who is awaiting trial. In the latter situation, the predicament has, if necessary, to be resolved in the accused's favour. If necessary, the prosecution may have to be discontinued if disclosure is essential for the proper conduct of the prosecution: see *Edwards and Lewis v United Kingdom*.[276] In *Stafford v United Kingdom*,[277] the European Court of Human Rights, while condemning the approach of the executive at that time, was careful to restrict its criticisms to 'perceived fears of future *non-violent* criminal conduct unrelated to his original murder conviction'.[278] This does not however mean that the prisoner has no rights that have to be respected. As I will explain later both under article 5(4) and domestic law his fundamental right to have a hearing that in all the circumstances at least meets the minimum standards that for reasons of fairness have to be respected....

60. The use of an SAA [Special Appointed Advocate] is, however, never a panacea for the grave disadvantages of a person affected not being aware of the case against him. The use of an SAA can be, however, a way of mitigating those disadvantages. For example, the SAA can persuade the tribunal that there could perfectly properly be disclosure subject to no restrictions or less stringent restrictions than the tribunal was minded to impose. The SAA may be able to destroy the credibility of a witness whose evidence is not disclosed. Although the SAA may not be allowed to communicate with the person affected, in appropriate circumstances the SAA can be authorised to communicate with those who do represent the person affected or the SAA may, before he has been instructed, receive useful information. In addition, as this case illustrates, the SAA can ensure that the decision as to non disclosure is challenged on judicial review.

---

[276] 22 July 2003, 40 E.H.R.R. 24.
[277] [G.C.], 28 May 2002, 35 E.H.R.R. 32. *See also* Chapter 12(C) *supra*.
[278] *Id.* at para. 82 (emphasis added).

61. The appellant relies on the fact that there is no statutory authority, whether in primary legislation or rules, that authorises the use of an SAA for hearings before the board. [Lord Woolf, Lord Rodger of Earlsberry and Lord Carswell all held that the Parole Board's authority included the power to employ the special advocacy procedure.]

76. The fact that information is withheld from a prisoner does not mean that there is automatically such a fundamental breach of the prisoner's rights either under article 5(4) or under domestic law. There can be an infinite variety of circumstances as to the degree of information that is withheld completely or partially without any significant unfairness being caused. The responsibility of the panel is to ensure that any unfairness is kept to a minimum while balancing the triumvirate of interests to which I have already referred. There may need initially to be a total withholding of information, but at an early stage of the hearing the prisoner may be able to be informed of the gist of what is relied on against him. Documents can be edited. There has to be detailed management of the hearing to ensure that the prisoner has the widest information possible. In relation to this management the SAA can have a critical role to play on the prisoner's behalf.

77. There are two extreme positions so far as the prisoner is concerned. On the one hand there is full disclosure and on the other hand there is no knowledge of the case against him being made available to the prisoner, so that even with an SAA he cannot defend himself. In between the two there is a grey area and within that grey area is the border which is the parameter between what is acceptable and what is not acceptable. Where that border is situated is fact-specific, depending on all the circumstances that have to be balanced. So far as article 5(4) is concerned the need to examine the facts as a whole, including any appellate process, before coming to a decision is critical as Lord Bingham points out in his speech, at para 19. The same is true in domestic law. To make rulings in advance of the actual hearing would be to introduce a rigidity that would make the task of the board extraordinarily difficult. The position has to be looked at in the round examining the proceedings as a whole with hindsight and taking into account the task of the board. The board's existing statutory framework, including the Rules, do not entitle the board to conduct its hearing in a manner that results in a significant injustice to a prisoner and in view of article 5(4) I do not anticipate that primary legislation can now be introduced that expressly authorises such a result without contravening the Human Rights Act 1998 even if express legislative authority was thought to be desirable....

79. Having had the advantage of reading my noble and learned friend Lord Steyn's speech in draft, I have been acutely concerned that his conclusions about the outcome of this case are so dramatically different from my own. As far as I have been able to ascertain, the explanation for our differences of opinion appears to be due to our adopting different approaches. Lord Steyn considers it right to focus primarily on the position of the prisoner. In his opinion the use of an SAA inevitably involves a significant curtailment of the prisoner's rights and for that reason the issue must be determined now in the appellant's favour. On the other hand I consider that it is essential to focus, in addition, on the problem the board faces in having to protect both the safety of the public and the rights of the prisoner.

80. The members of the public who could be affected by a decision of the board have human rights as well as the appellant. If the board releases a prisoner when it is unsafe to do so, the public's individual rights can be grievously affected. In addition in a situation where the board has to consider whether to withhold evidence from a prisoner, for example to protect an individual whose life could be threatened if his identity were revealed, the board is under a duty to protect

this individual's interests. Not to do so could involve the breach of article 2 or 3 of the European Convention. The board can refuse to pay any attention to the information that the individual could provide. This would mean, however, that the board could be in breach of its express statutory duty. So it is my view that the information should only be disregarded if there is no other way in which the prisoner's fundamental right to be treated fairly can be protected...

Lord Steyn:

88. The Parole Board decided to attenuate Roberts's right to a hearing in a drastic manner by imposing upon him in place of an advocate, who would be able to represent him in the ordinary way, a special advocate. What this entails is described in careful and measured terms by my noble and learned friend, Lord Bingham of Cornhill, in para 18 of his opinion. Under this procedure the prisoner and his legal representatives are not allowed to know anything of the case made against the prisoner. Once the special advocate becomes aware of the case against the prisoner he may not divulge that information to the prisoner. It is not to the point to say that the special advocate procedure is 'better than nothing'. Taken as a whole, the procedure completely lacks the essential characteristics of a fair hearing. It is important not to pussy-foot about such a fundamental matter: the special advocate procedure undermines the very essence of elementary justice. It involves a phantom hearing only. ...

93. The special advocate procedure strikes at the root of the prisoner's fundamental right to a basically fair procedure. If such departures are to be introduced it must be done by Parliament. It would be quite wrong to make an assumption that, if Parliament had been faced with the question whether it should authorise, in this particular field, the special advocate procedure, it would have sanctioned it. After all, in our system the working assumption is that Parliament legislates for a European liberal democracy which respects fundamental rights. Even before the Human Rights Act 1998 came into force, and a fortiori since then, the courts have been entitled to assume that Parliament does not lightly override fundamental rights. ...

95. My noble and learned friend, Lord Carswell, commented that a prisoner against whom unfounded allegations have been made is in a Kafkaesque situation. That was an apposite reference to *The Trial* (1925), the masterpiece of Franz Kafka. A passage in *The Trial* has a striking resonance for the present case. Joseph K was informed

> the legal records of the case, and above all the actual charge-sheets, were inaccessible to the accused and his counsel, consequently one did not know in general, or at least did not know with any precision, what charges to meet in the first plea; accordingly it could be only by pure chance that it contained really relevant matter ... In such circumstances the defence was naturally in a very ticklish and difficult position. Yet that, too, was intentional. For the defence was not actually countenanced by the law, but only tolerated, and there were differences of opinion even on that point, whether the law could be interpreted to admit such tolerance at all. Strictly speaking, therefore, none of the advocates was recognised by the court, all who appeared before the court as advocates being in reality merely in the position of hole-and-corner advocates.

96. In its decision of 13 June 2003 the Parole Board observed:

> ... Ms Kaufmann [the counsel of Roberts] sets out two respects in which she argues that Mr Roberts would be prejudiced by the special advocate procedure being adopted: (a) The board has already found that there can be no disclosure of even a gist to Mr Roberts.

Mr Roberts cannot therefore in any sense whatever answer the case against him. (b) It is fair to assume that the material is being placed before the board because it has an important bearing on Mr Roberts's alleged dangerousness. If the board accepts the source's evidence and does not direct Mr Roberts's release as a result, the prejudice to Mr Roberts will not end there. Just as the board cannot disclose the gist to him now, it will not be in a position to do so when it comes to provide reasons for its decision. Mr Roberts will continue to be detained on the basis of allegations about which he remains completely ignorant. He will not therefore be able to address the concerns underlying his continued detention or take any steps to reduce the risk.

'It is true that it will be the task of the specially appointed advocate to represent the interests of Mr Roberts, but he is in that respect at a serious disadvantage to [Mr Creighton], who have acted for Mr Roberts for a very long period. Mr Eadie on behalf of the Secretary of State pointed out on 30 May that although there would be constraints upon the specially appointed advocate in communicating with Mr Roberts or his representatives, there was no objection to Mr Roberts's representatives supplying information to the specially appointed advocate on the basis of their having acted for him for many years. There is some merit in Mr Eadie's point, but the board accepts that there is very considerable force in Ms Kaufmann's arguments and that if the special advocate procedure is adopted this will result in prejudice to Mr Roberts in the respects identified by Ms Kaufmann'.

My noble and learned friend, Lord Woolf CJ, has observed inter alia that if the board reveals at least the gist of the case against the prisoner then there will be no injustice. But the board affirmatively found in the present case that there can be no disclosure of even a gist to the prisoner. I note that Lord Woolf CJ observes that

> both under article 5(4) and domestic law [the prisoner's] fundamental right to have a hearing that in all the circumstances at least meets the minimum standards that for reasons of fairness have to be respected.

In my view it is a formalistic outcome to describe a phantom hearing involving a special advocate (as directed by the board) as meeting minimum standards of fairness. In truth the special advocate procedure empties the prisoner's fundamental right to an oral hearing of all meaningful content.

97. In my view the outcome of this case is deeply austere. It encroaches on the prerogatives of the legislature in our system of parliamentary democracy. It is contrary to the rule of law. It is not likely to survive scrutiny in Strasbourg....

99. I am in full agreement with the reasons given by my noble and learned friend, Lord Bingham of Cornhill, for his conclusion that the decision of the Parole Board in this case was ultra vires. I would allow the appeal.

Lord Rodger of Earlsferry:

112. So far as the argument based on the European Convention is concerned, substantially for the reasons given by Lord Bingham, I consider that the House cannot decide in advance whether the full hearing, involving the specially appointed advocate, meets the requirements of article 5(4). The same competing interests fall to be considered for the purposes of article 5(4), but the weight to be attached to the various factors may well depend, in part at least, on what happens at the hearing. For example, perhaps in the light of the advocate's

cross-examination based on a study of the solicitor's file, the board may reject the evidence of the source as unreliable or incredible. Or else, the board may accept it in part but none the less order Mr Roberts's release. These and similar possibilities mean that a court will be in a position to determine whether Mr Roberts has had the kind of hearing required by article 5(4) only once the hearing has taken place and the board have reached their decision.

113. For these reasons I would dismiss the appeal.

Lord Carswell:

144. Having balanced these interests, I conclude that the interests which I have outlined of the informant and the public must prevail over those of the appellant, strong though the latter may be. I emphasise, however, that my conclusions relating to the powers of the Parole Board to use the SAA procedure and their compatibility with article 5(4) are a decision in principle, for that was all that was before the House. We were not asked, nor were we in a position to decide, whether it was proper in the instant case of the appellant. I accept that there may well be cases in which it would not be sufficiently fair to be justifiable and each case will require consideration on its own facts. I would agree that the SAA procedure should be used only in rare and exceptional cases and, as Lord Bingham of Cornhill said in *R v H*[279] as a course of last and never first resort. The appellant's case was, however, founded on the proposition that in no case would it lawfully be used, and this I cannot accept.

145. I would therefore dismiss the appeal.

[The House of Lords dismissed the appeal 3–2, holding that it was, in the circumstances, within the power of the Parole Board to adopt the SAA procedure.]

The *Roberts* case, it will be noted, is based not on Article 6 but on Article 5(4)'s right to judicial review of the lawfulness of detention.[280] The European Court in 1986 held that the procedures called for in that article required a 'minimum adversarial element' in which equality of arms was 'indispensable'.[281] It subsequently refused to adopt an argument that the requirements of Article 5(4) review were less rigorous than those of Article 6.[282]

4. THE RIGHT TO CONFRONT WITNESSES

A core element of adversarial proceedings is the presumed capacity of each side to challenge the probative force of evidence produced by the other. The Court has held that 'it is a requirement of fairness under paragraph 1 of Article 6 . . . that the prosecution authorities disclose to the defence all material evidence for or against the accused

---

[279] [2004] 2 A.C. 134, para. 22.

[280] See Chapter 12(G) *supra*.

[281] *Sanchez-Reisse v. Switzerland*, 21 Oct. 1986, 9 E.H.R.R. 71, paras. 50–1. *See also G.K. v. Poland*, 20 Jan. 2004, para. 91. Note Judge Bindschedler-Robert's dissenting opinion in *Sanchez-Reisse* disputing that Article 5(4) proceedings 'are to be equated with the civil or criminal proceedings envisaged in Article 6'.

[282] *Lamy v. Belgium*, 30 March 1989, 11 E.H.R.R. 529, paras. 28–9.

and that the failure to do so [gives] rise to a defect in the trial proceedings'.[283] More particularly Article 6(3)(d) declares the right of criminal defendants to 'examine or have examined witnesses against him'. In fact, it is not uncommon for evidence to be offered in such a form as to eliminate or to limit the effectiveness of such examination. Such evidence may, as in the principal case, actually have been presented to the decision-maker. Alternatively, undisclosed facts never produced at trial might have been helpful to the other side in preparing its case and in securing evidence that it did use in the trial.[284] The latter situation typically arises where police or prosecution is in possession of exculpatory evidence never revealed to the defendant. The House of Lords' judgment in *Roberts* presents an extreme case where a decision was based on evidence and neither the content nor source of that evidence was made known to the accused or his counsel.

As indicated in *Roberts*, the Strasbourg Court has dealt with similar cases. In *Rowe and Davis v. United Kingdom*[285] the police had based its investigation in part on information secured from an informer who had been paid £10,300 and granted immunity. The applicants were convicted of murder. On appeal of the convictions in the Court of Appeal, the Crown submitted material to the Court about the identity of informers which had been withheld from the defendants at trial. The Court of Appeal received the information and agreed that it would continue to be kept from the defence. The Strasbourg Court ruled that the applicants' conviction was inconsistent with Article 6:

[T]he entitlement to the disclosure of relevant evidence is not an absolute right. In any criminal proceedings there may be competing interests, such as national security or the need to protect witnesses at risk of reprisals or keep secret police methods of investigation of crime which must be weighed against the rights of the accused … However, only such measures restricting the rights of the defence which are strictly necessary are permissible under Article 6(1). Moreover, in order to ensure that the accused receives a fair trial, any difficulties caused to the defence by a limitation on its rights must be sufficiently counter balanced by the procedures followed by the judicial authorities.[286]

The Court held that review of the question by the appellate court did not cure the unfairness at the trial. Only the first-instance court was in a position to evaluate the need for non-disclosure as the trial developed. The Court of Appeal 'was obliged to carry out its appraisal *ex post facto* and may even, to a certain extent, have unconsciously been influenced by the jury's verdict into underestimating the significance of the undisclosed evidence'.[287]

In a carefully guarded decision, the United States Supreme Court has held that the procedures of proposed military commissions to try 'enemy combatants' accused

---

[283] *Edwards v. United Kingdom*, 25 Nov. 1992, 15 E.H.R.R. 417, para. 36.

[284] The United States Constitution also guarantees defendants a right to be informed of exculpatory evidence. *Brady v. Maryland*, 373 U.S. 83 (1963).

[285] 16 Feb. 2000, 30 E.H.R.R. 1.

[286] *Id.* para. 61.

[287] *Id.* para. 65. The same result was reached in *Atlan v. United Kingdom*, 19 June 2001, 34 E.H.R.R. 33.

of terrorist acts did not conform to the Uniform Code of Military Justice or to the requirements of relevant international conventions. The holding was based, in part, on the fact that the procedures allowed the presentation of evidence outside the presence of the accused or his or her counsel, the contents of which might never be disclosed to them.[288]

Less drastic restrictions also engage the equality of arms. In some cases the content of evidence is made known to a party but its source is withheld. In *Van Mechelen & Others v. The Netherlands*[289] the applicant's conviction for robbery was supported, in part, by the testimony of unnamed police officers who were examined in a separate room from the defendant and his counsel. The latter were able to listen through a sound link. The 'defence was thus not only unaware of the identity of the police witnesses but were also prevented from observing their demeanour under direct questioning and thus from testing their reliability'. Although the witnesses had said they feared for their safety and that of their family, the European Court found such fears unsupported by the record in the case. Nor was there any explanation of why the 'operational needs' of the police were jeopardized by such identification. The Court noted the less drastic possibilities of 'using make-up or disguise and the prevention of eye contact'.[290]

The Court in *Van Mechelen* distinguished the case of *Doorson v. The Netherlands*[291] where the identity of police informants was withheld in a drug dealing case. In *Doorson* the defendant had been excluded from the anonymous witnesses' examination but his lawyer had been present and had been given the opportunity to cross-examine. The Court also observed that although there had been no threats against the witnesses by the defendant, it was established 'that drug dealers frequently resorted to threats or actual violence against person who gave evidence against them'.[292] An evaluation of the risk to witnesses has figured in other cases as well. A court was entitled to rely on depositions from witnesses residing abroad who had provided information on terrorist organizations. These witnesses ran a real risk of suffering acts of revenge and were outside the possible protection of the government.[293] Even when a persuasive case for anonymity can be made out, however, it is incumbent on the domestic courts to take measures to minimize the defendant's disadvantage. Thus the use of evidence provided by anonymous informants in a case arising out of a prison riot was held incompatible with Article 6 because the trial court had failed 'to question anonymous witnesses and to conduct a scrutiny of the manner and circumstances in which the anonymous statements had been obtained...'.[294]

---

[288] *Hamdan v. Rumsfeld*, 126 S. Ct. 2749 (2006).
[289] *Supra* n. 264.
[290] *Id.* paras. 59–61. *See also Lüdi v. Switzerland*, 15 June 1992, 15 E.H.R.R. 173.
[291] 26 March 1996, 22 E.H.R.R. 330.
[292] *Id.* paras. 71–4.
[293] *Haas v. Germany*, 17 Nov. 2005 (admissibility decision).
[294] *Birutis & Others v. Lithuania*, 28 June 2002.

Article 6 may be violated, moreover, when evidence is taken from known witnesses in circumstances that prevent the opposing party from challenging their testimony by means of face to face confrontation. In one case the complaining witness in a prosecution for forgery and embezzlement failed to appear in open court for medical reasons. The European Court, noting the extent to which the domestic court had relied on the witness's accusation, held that the procedure had been unfair since 'the applicants should have an opportunity to challenge any aspect of the complainant's account during a confrontation, either in public or, if necessary, at his home'.[295] The Court has held, however, that the use of a videotaped interview from the victim in a child sexual abuse prosecution was consistent with Article 6, given the special need for protecting the witness in such cases and the subsequent opportunities given to the defendant to challenge the victim's account.[296] The House of Lords and the United States and Canadian Supreme Courts have reached similar conclusions.[297]

In its most general form, the presumptive right to examine witnesses under Article 6 raises questions with respect to every use of hearsay evidence. Consequently the Convention's criteria must be added to any limitation on such evidence already imposed by domestic law. In the United States, hearsay evidence is presumed to be inadmissible in any procedure but is allowable under a host of exceptions. The Sixth Amendment to the Constitution, however, provides that the accused in all criminal prosecutions has the right 'to be confronted with the witnesses against him'. The United States Supreme Court has refused to read this provision as preempting the use of hearsay exceptions but has struggled to formulate general criteria for identifying hearsay that offends the 'confrontation clause'. After a period in which it called for a re-evaluation of the reliability of the hearsay challenged,[298] it has recently settled on a test especially disfavouring 'testimonial' hearsay, a term not fully defined, but suggesting statements understood to be part of a process of criminal investigation and prosecution.[299]

The English law of evidence allows the use of hearsay if the trial court is 'satisfied that it is in the interests of justice'.[300] The Court of Appeal has held that the admission of evidence against an accused under this standard was not inconsistent with Article 6. The Court noted that a court could still exclude the evidence if it were shown that 'the reasons for excluding the statement substantially outweighed the case for admitting it, taking account of the value of the evidence'[301] and that a court was obliged to exclude it if it determined that its admission violated the Human Rights Act 1998. There was

---

[295] *Bricmont v. Belgium*, 7 July 1989, 12 E.H.R.R. 217.

[296] *S.N. v. Sweden*, 2 July 2002, 39 E.H.R.R. 13, paras. 52–3. Two judges dissented saying that in such cases the videotaped evidence should be corroborated by other evidence. Dissenting Opinions of Judges Türmen and Maruste.

[297] *R. (D.) v. Camberwell Green Youth Court* [2005] U.K.H.L. 4, [2005] 1 All E.R. 999; *Maryland v. Craig*, 497 U.S. 836 (1989); *R. v. L. (D.O.)* [1993] 4 S.C.R. 419.

[298] *Ohio v. Roberts*, 448 U.S. 56 (1980).   [299] *Crawford v. Washington*, 541 U.S. 36 (2004).

[300] Criminal Justice Act 2003, s. 114.

[301] Criminal Justice Act 2003, s. 126[b].

no violation of equality of arms since the rules applied 'equally to prosecution and defence'.[302]

Concerns about the inequality of arms have also been applied to ex parte submissions of written evidence. In responding to an appeal of a zoning decision, a municipality made a submission to the reviewing court providing information that had not appeared in the previous record. These comments were not served on the applicants. The European Court held that the principle of equality of arms had been infringed. Fairness implied 'the right for the parties to have knowledge of and to comment on all evidence adduced or observations filed'.[303] The same result followed when a trial court transmitted its view of a case it had decided to an appellate court.[304] The doctrine also applies to arguments of law to which a party has no chance to reply. In consequence, the observations of the Attorney-General as to how the Austrian Supreme Court should deal with the applicant's appeal violated Article 6 when there was no chance to respond.[305]

Even if it is concluded that a party was deprived of a fair opportunity to present or to challenge witness or written evidence, it does not follow that a violation of Article 6 has occurred. In several cases the Strasbourg Court has gone on to inquire how important the the applicant's examination would have been to the outcome of the case. If the evidence presented ex parte was nonetheless critically examined by the judge or was corroborated by other evidence or if the domestic courts did not rely on the material in arriving at judgment, the Court may find no violation. For example, in *Haas v. Germany* the domestic courts received statements from anonymous informers as well as from a named participant in the crime who was not available for confrontation. The European Court found that even though the German courts had relied on this material, there were independent reasons to find it trustworthy. Moreover, it 'had by far not been the only evidence relied on'. The application was held inadmissible as 'manifestly ill-founded'.[306] The Court frequently inquires as to whether the decision complained of was based 'to a decisive extent' on the flawed evidence.[307]

Another line of cases, however, shuns any evaluation of the practical effect of the unfair procedure on the result of the case. In a series of cases in which written material was submitted to an appellate court without giving the opponents a chance to respond, the Court has held the actual effect of the material to be 'of little consequence'[308] and that 'only the parties could properly decide whether or not the submissions called for

---

[302] *R. v. Xhabri* [2005] E.W.C.A. Crim 3135, [2006] 1 All E.R. 776, paras. 42–4.

[303] *Steck-Risch & Others v. Lichtenstein*, 19 May 2005, 42 E.H.R.R. 18.

[304] *Nideröst-Huber v. Switzerland*, 18 Feb. 1997, 25 E.H.R.R. 709. The Court did not deviate from this holding in a subsequent case in which the opposing party was informed such observations would be submitted but still had no opportunity to respond. *See also Buchberger v. Austria*, 20 Dec. 2001, 37 E.H.R.R. 13; *Moser v. Austria*, 21 Dec. 2006.

[305] *Bulut v. Austria*, 22 Feb. 1996, 24 E.H.R.R. 84.

[306] *Supra* n. 293.

[307] E.g. *Kok v. The Netherlands*, 4 July 2000 (admissibility decision) (citing authorities).

[308] *Ziegler v. Switzerland*, 21 Feb. 2002, para. 38.

their comments'.[309] In *Bulut v. Austria*, where the applicant complained of his inability to respond to a recommendation submitted to the Supreme Court by the Attorney-General, the Court agreed with the Commission that 'the principle of equality of arms does not depend on further, quantifiable unfairness flowing from a procedural inequality'.[310] This position is based on the idea that '[w]hat is particularly at stake is litigants' confidence in the workings of justice, which is based on, *inter alia*, the knowledge that they have had the opportunity to express their views on every document in the file'.[311]

5. THE RIGHT TO COUNSEL

A. GRANGER V. UNITED KINGDOM

Judgment of 28 March 1990
12 E.H.R.R. 469

8. A number of serious incidents between rival groups in Glasgow in the early 1980's culminated in a fire-raising attack on industrial premises, followed by a petrol-bomb attack on an apartment resulting in the death of six members of the same family.

9. Mr Granger, who is a British citizen born in 1960 and resident in Glasgow, was interviewed by the police during their investigations; on 23 and 25 May 1984, in signed statements, he gave details of how the crimes had been committed and named the persons responsible, that is Thomas Lafferty and six others. This evidence was considered by the Crown to be important and was a major basis for the decision to prosecute those persons. Steps were taken to secure the applicant's safety until the trial.

10. The trial of Thomas Lafferty and the six others on charges relating, inter alia, to the fire-raising and the murders took place before the High Court of Justiciary in Glasgow in September 1984. Mr Granger appeared as a principal witness for the Crown. However, once in the witness-box, he denied all knowledge of any matters relevant to the crimes. He also denied that he had given the above-mentioned statements, claiming instead that they had been made up by the police, who had pressurised him into signing them.

11. Shortly afterwards, the applicant was arrested and prosecuted on indictment in the High Court of Justiciary for perjury. ...

12. The applicant received legal aid for the preparation of his defence by his solicitor and for representation at his trial by both senior and junior counsel.

The Crown was represented by the Solicitor General for Scotland, since the gravity of the charges was considered to warrant the presence of a senior prosecutor and since the most senior Advocate Depute, who had appeared for the prosecution at the Lafferty trial, was to be a witness at the applicant's trial.

---

[309] *Loimaseita Oy v. Finland*, 5 July 2005, para. 36.
[310] 22 Feb. 1996, 24 E.H.R.R. 84, para. 49.   [311] *Ziegler v. Switzerland, supra* n. 308, at para. 38.

After a four-week trial before the High Court of Justiciary in Glasgow in February 1985, Mr Granger was found guilty [of three charges.]

13. The applicant's solicitor subsequently lodged an intimation of intention to appeal against conviction. The legal aid granted for the perjury trial covered this work, as well as the solicitor's advising on the prospects of an appeal, obtaining counsel's opinion on the same point, having counsel frame a note of appeal setting out the grounds of appeal, lodging the note of appeal and making an application for legal aid to pay for representation at the hearing of the appeal itself.

14. Such an application was submitted on behalf of Mr Granger, who had insufficient means to pay for legal assistance, to the Supreme Court Legal Aid Committee of the Law Society of Scotland on 6 June 1985. It was accompanied by a memorandum, a copy note of appeal (with a supplementary statement of the grounds) and the judge's summing-up to the jury at the applicant's trial; later a copy of the indictment and a note of previous convictions were also lodged.

15. The Committee considered the material before it to be insufficient and asked the applicant's solicitor to furnish counsel's opinion on the prospects of the appeal. This he did on 4 July 1985.

The solicitor had, in fact, already obtained such an opinion, on 14 May 1985, from the senior and junior counsel who had represented Mr Granger at his trial; the senior counsel, in particular, had considerable experience in presenting appeals before the High Court of Justiciary. The authors of the opinion concluded that they could not advise that the appeal should proceed: in their view, neither of the two possible stateable grounds of appeal was of sufficient substance as to have reasonable prospects of success and, in any event, there was no real prospect of satisfying the court that there had been a miscarriage of justice.

The solicitor also provided the Committee with a copy of his letter of 23 May 1985 to his Edinburgh agents, indicating that he disagreed with counsel's opinion. Although he had obtained on 5 February 1985, for the purposes of the applicant's trial, a psychiatric report which stated that the applicant was of modest intelligence but with a poor command of English and poor comprehension of written material, he did not communicate this to the Committee. Neither did he refer, in any material he placed before it, to any intellectual or linguistic limitations of his client.

16. By decision of 11 July 1985, which was stated to be final, the Committee refused the application, since it was not satisfied that Mr Granger had substantial grounds for his appeal.

17. The applicant nevertheless continued to receive advice and assistance from his solicitor and decided to proceed with the appeal. The grounds were the same as those considered by counsel in the opinion of May 1985. The applicant maintained that there had been a miscarriage of justice [on several grounds including a claim that] the judge had erred in admitting in evidence a statement made by the applicant on 23 May 1984, notwithstanding a defence objection that it was inadmissible as being in the nature of a precognition, that is a statement made by a potential witness at an advanced stage of an investigation outlining the evidence he is likely to give at a forthcoming trial . . .

18. The hearing of the appeal opened before the High Court of Justiciary, sitting in Edinburgh as an appellate court of three judges, on 27 September 1985. The Crown was again represented by the Solicitor General for Scotland, accompanied by junior counsel and a member of the staff of the Crown Office.

Since the refusal of legal aid precluded the instruction of counsel and since solicitors do not have rights of audience in the High Court of Justiciary, Mr Granger presented his appeal himself. He read out a statement, prepared by his solicitor, which elaborated on the written grounds of appeal. The Solicitor General replied, addressing the court for about ninety minutes.

19. The principal point discussed at the hearing was whether the court could determine [the error alleged] without considering a transcript of the relevant parts of the evidence given at the applicant's trial. Notwithstanding the Solicitor General's arguments to the contrary, the court decided that it could not. It therefore ordered that a transcript be prepared and adjourned the hearing to 6 March 1986. The applicant's solicitor subsequently assisted in the preparation of the transcript.

Following this adjournment, Mr Granger did not renew, or request reconsideration of, his legal-aid application, nor did he advise the Legal Aid Committee of the court's order.

20. At the resumed hearing the applicant had again been provided by his solicitor with a written speech, which dealt with all the grounds of appeal. Although the court pointed out that it wished to hear submissions on [the cited] ground only, it allowed the applicant, who was unable to comprehend the legal niceties, to read out the speech in full.

21. The High Court of Justiciary unanimously refused the appeal on all grounds. In his written judgment the Lord Justice-Clerk, who presided, gave full consideration to each of the grounds, but was satisfied that none of them had substance and that there had been no miscarriage of justice. He described the appellant's submissions as 'well prepared and clearly expressed'.

22. Mr Granger was released from prison on 16 July 1988 after serving two-thirds of his sentence, the remainder having been remitted...

42. Mr Granger complained of the refusal to grant him legal aid for his appeal and of the inequality of arms he attributed thereto....

43. Since the guarantees in paragraph 3 of Article 6 are specific aspects of the right to a fair trial in criminal proceedings stated in paragraph 1, the Court considers it appropriate to examine the applicant's complaints from the angle of paragraphs 3(c) and 1 taken together.

44. As regards paragraph 3(c), it was common ground that Mr Granger did not have 'sufficient means to pay for legal assistance'; the sole issue under this paragraph is therefore whether 'the interests of justice' required that he be given such assistance free.

In this connection, the Court recalls that the manner in which paragraph 1, as well as paragraph 3(c), of Article 6 is to be applied in relation to appellate or cassation courts depends upon the special features of the proceedings involved; account must be taken of the entirety of the proceedings conducted in the domestic legal order and of the role of the appellate or cassation court therein...

45. The Government maintained that the Commission's conclusion was not justified by the various factors on which it had relied. In their view, the interests of justice, the evaluation whereof lay in the first place with the domestic authorities, did not require a grant of legal aid for the appeal, which they described as being 'wholly without substance' and having 'no reasonable prospects of success'. They pointed out that Mr Granger had had full legal aid for his trial, extending to the obtaining of counsel's opinion on the prospects of an appeal, which

opinion had been negative. . . ; and that the case had to be seen in the context of the Scottish system in which an active role was played by the appeal court and an impartial role was expected of the Crown and where the automatic right of appeal resulted in the filing of many appeals which were without merit. . . .

47. Mr Granger had been convicted on indictment of perjury and sentenced to five years' imprisonment. There can thus be no question as to the importance of what was at stake in the appeal.

Before the High Court of Justiciary, the Solicitor General, on account of his familiarity with the case, appeared for the Crown and addressed the judges at length. On the other hand, the applicant, as was not contested, was not in a position fully to comprehend the pre-prepared speeches he read out or the opposing arguments submitted to the court. It is also clear that, had the occasion arisen, he would not have been able to make an effective reply to those arguments or to questions from the bench.

The foregoing factors are of particular weight in the present case in view of the complexity of one of the issues involved. Whilst the High Court of Justiciary apparently had little trouble in disposing of four of Mr Granger's grounds of appeal, the same did not apply to the remaining one. After hearing argument, it decided that this ground—which turned on what the Solicitor General himself described at the European Court's hearing as the 'difficult' distinction between 'precognitions' and other statements—deserved more detailed consideration. It adjourned its hearing and called for a transcript of the evidence given at the applicant's trial, so as to be able to examine the matter more thoroughly. It thus became clear that this ground of appeal raised an issue of complexity and importance.

In this situation some means should have been available to the competent authorities, including the High Court of Justiciary in exercise of its overall responsibility for ensuring the fair conduct of the appeal proceedings, to have the refusal of legal aid reconsidered. According to the scheme in operation at the relevant time, however, the Legal Aid Committee's decision of 11 July 1985 was stated to be final. . . . It would appear to the Court that in all the circumstances of the case it would have been in the interests of justice for free legal assistance to be given to the applicant at least at that stage for the ensuing proceedings. . . .

[The Court held unanimously that there had been a violation of paragraph 3(c), taken together with paragraph 1, of Article 6. It declined to examine the applicant's claims under Articles 5, 8 and 13.]

Article 6(3) recognizes a right to free legal representation in criminal prosecutions where the defendant lacks 'sufficient means' to pay for it and where 'the interests of justice so require'. Such legal aid is more or less universal in European countries at some point in the initial criminal adjudication. As the principal case illustrates, the applicability of the right to appellate procedures has been left to determination on a case-by-case basis. In a subsequent case raising a similar issue, the European Court held that free legal assistance on an appeal was required by Article 6 even when the legal issue 'may not have been particularly complex'. Although the applicant, unlike Granger, might have been able to understand the legal claim, its advocacy still 'require[d] a certain legal skill and experience'. The Court was more concerned in that case with the serious penalty of eight years' imprisonment.[312]

[312] *Boner v. United Kingdom*, 28 Oct. 1994, 19 E.H.R.R. 246, para. 41.

Although Article 6's explicit right of legal assistance attaches only to those accused of criminal offences, the Court has held that in some circumstances the inability of a party to afford legal assistance may result in a violation of the Article 6(1) right to a fair hearing. The applicant in *Airey v. Ireland*[313] was unable to afford legal representation in her attempt to petition for a 'decree of judicial separation', then the only way for a separated married person to secure a legal settlement of relations with his or her spouse. Although the applicant might have tried to represent herself, the Court was persuaded that procedure in the High Court, where such decrees had to be sought, was unusually complex. In these circumstances the Court conluded that the applicant was effectively precluded from securing the hearing that Article 6(1) requires. The government argued that such a holding effectively extended the right to free legal representation from criminal cases to all cases dealing with the determination of a 'civil right'. The Court denied that this would necessarily follow, noting that, in simpler cases a pro se appearance might be sufficient. It noted that it was open to Ireland, for example, to simplify the procedure for obtaining a legal separation.[314] The Court has also held that unreasonably high court fees may amount to the deprivation of the right to an Article 6(1) hearing in the determination of civil rights.[315]

E. THE REQUIREMENTS OF PROMPT ADJUDICATION

Delays in the resolution of legal disputes have been the single most litigated issue before the European Court of Human Rights. They are, therefore, a significant cause of the Court's suffocating backlog. The principle of prompt adjudication is almost universal in Western democracies. The European Convention, the Constitution of the United States, and the Canadian Charter of Rights and Freedoms, all make provision for the right to prompt adjudication. However, the manner in which this right is recognized and the scope it is given varies in each of the relevant judicial systems.

Some of the issues relating to the timing of judicial proceedings have already been canvassed in connection with Article 5's protection against restraint of personal liberty. Article 6's concerns are more general. The Article states: 'In the determination of his civil rights and obligations or of any criminal charge . . . everyone is entitled to a . . . hearing within a reasonable time by a . . . tribunal . . .'. The purpose of the Article is, in part, to 'ensure that the accused person does not have to be under a charge too long and that the charge is determined'.[316] It is important to note, however, that the right covers civil as well as criminal litigation.

---

[313] 9 Oct. 1979, 2 E.H.R.R. 305.   [314] *Id*. at paras. 25–6.
[315] *Kreuz v. Poland*, 20 April 1998, 25 E.H.R.R. CD80.
[316] *Wemhoff v. Germany*, 27 June 1968, 1 E.H.R.R. 55, para. 18.

The length of time governed by Article 6(1) has been defined as the time between the 'charge' or 'judicial notification'[317] and the day of judgment, even if reached on appeal.[318] In civil proceedings, the 'reasonable time' referred to in Article 6(1) normally begins to run from the moment the action was instituted before the 'tribunal'.[319] It is deemed to continue, moreover, until the conclusion of enforcement proceedings in which the amount of any damages owing is calculated.[320] In criminal matters, a person may be 'charged' as early as the date of arrest, the date preliminary investigations were opened, or the date he or she was officially notified of the prosecution or allegation that he or she has committed a criminal offence.[321] To determine whether or not proceedings before the state's constitutional court are to be included in the reckoning of the relevant period, '[i]t has to be considered whether the Constitutional Court's decision was capable of affecting the outcome of the case which has been litigated before the ordinary courts'.[322]

In determining what constitutes a 'reasonable time', the European Court has held that the individual circumstances of the case are decisive:

The court has to have regard, inter alia, to the complexity of the factual or legal issues raised by the case, to the conduct of the applicants and the competent authorities and to what was at stake for the former; in addition, only delays attributable to the State may justify a finding of a failure to comply with the 'reasonable time' requirement.[323]

The same factors may not be examined in the same way in every case. Sometimes the circumstances 'call for a global assessment so that the Court does not consider it necessary to consider these questions in detail'.[324]

---

[317] *Corrigliano v. Italy*, 10 Dec. 1982, 5 E.H.R.R. 334, paras. 34–5.

[318] *Wemhoff v. Germany, supra* n. 316, at para. 18.

[319] *Poiss v. Austria*, 23 Apr. 1987, 10 E.H.R.R. 231, para. 50.

[320] *Silva Pontes v. Portugal*, 23 Mar. 1994, 18 E.H.R.R. 156; *Torri v. Italy*, 1 July 1997, para. 19. In *Hornsby v. Greece*, 19 Mar. 1997, 24 E.H.R.R. 250, a violation of Art. 6(1) was found where administrative authorities refrained for over five years from complying with two judgments of the Supreme Administrative Court, refusing to grant applicants authorization to open a language school: 'Where administrative authorities refuse or fail to comply, or even delay doing so, the guarantees under Article 6 enjoyed by a litigant during the judicial phase of the proceedings are rendered devoid of purpose'. *Id.* at para. 41. *See also Estima Jorge v. Portugal*, 21 Apr. 1998, extending the Art. 6(1) period to enforcement proceedings concerning not a judgment, but a notarial deed providing security for a specific debt. Though the proceedings presupposed that the applicant's right had already been established, and hence did not concern a 'dispute', the Court noted that 'the word "contestation" (dispute) should not be construed too technically…and should be given a substantive rather than a formal meaning'. *Id.* at para. 37.

[321] Essentially the time begins to run when the situation of the suspect has been substantially affected. *Eckle v. Germany*, 15 July 1982, 5 E.H.R.R. 1, at para. 73.

[322] *Bock v. Germany*, 29 Mar. 1989, 12 E.H.R.R. 247, para. 37. This is also the test where the proceedings at issue consist only of those in a constitutional court, i.e. they are not an 'extension' of proceedings in the ordinary courts, *Sussmann v. Germany*, 16 Sept. 1996, 25 E.H.R.R. 64, paras. 40–6.

[323] *Zimmerman and Steiner v. Switzerland*, 13 July 1983, 6 E.H.R.R. 17, para. 24.

[324] *Obermeier v. Austria*, 28 June 1990, 13 E.H.R.R. 290, para. 72. *See also Paskhalidis v. Greece*, 19 Mar. 1997, concerning the claims of 93 applicants. In *Vastaberger Taxi Aktiebolag & Valic v. Sweden*, 23 July 2002, the Court determined that the applicants were substantially affected by the proceedings at the time they were informed by the Tax Authority of its intention to impose additional taxes and surcharges. *Id.* para. 104. *See Janosevic v. Sweden*, 23 July 2002, 38 E.H.R.R. 22 to the same effect.

Once the Court has declared a time period to be unreasonable on its face, the state is required to offer justification for the delay. In *König v. Germany*[325] a delay of over ten years offered a clear example of such an unreasonable delay. Delays of slightly over three years at a single jurisdictional level also have been held to be presumptively unreasonable.[326] But longer time periods have not been treated as excessive where the cases dealt with complex legal issues, arose in a sensitive political climate, involved several jurisdictional levels or required many witnesses or sources of information.[327] On the other hand, the Court has stressed the need for more expeditious decisions in certain types of disputes, such as those involving pensions and other employment issues, finding, for instance, a delay of more than nine years in reaching a final decision excessive even when the case was very complex.[328]

The Court is reluctant to find a violation if the delay is attributable mainly to the applicant's conduct. The Court clarified the duty of the applicant in this regard in a case where national law provided that the responsibility for the progress of proceedings rested with the parties. This did not, the Court held:

absolve the courts from ensuring compliance with the requirements of Article 6 concerning reasonable time....[T]he Court considers that the person concerned is required only to show diligence in carrying out the procedural steps relating to him, to refrain from using delaying tactics and to avail himself of the scope afforded by domestic law for shortening the proceedings. He is under no duty to take action which is not apt for the purpose.[329]

However, the Court has held that, in a criminal case, although the applicant was not required to co-operate with the prosecutors, he was responsible for any delays caused by his behaviour.[330] If it is shown in a civil case that 'the applicant did not display the

---

[325] 28 June 1978, 2 E.H.R.R. 170.

[326] *Zimmerman and Steiner v. Switzerland, supra* n. 323, para. 23. But *see Katikaridis v. Greece*, 15 Nov. 1996, 32 E.H.R.R. 6, finding no violation where proceedings lasted over three years in the Court of Cassation as a result of the matter coming before three different benches of that Court. Two Divisions' rulings on a complex matter were in conflict, and needed to be resolved by the full Court. *Id.* at para. 42. And in *Sussmann v. Germany*, n. 322 *supra*, proceedings in the Federal Constitutional Court lasting over three years four months were held not to violate Article 6(1). The Court noted that while the 'obligation [to hear cases within a reasonable time] also applies to a Constitutional Court...[Article 6(1)] cannot be construed in the same way as for an ordinary court. Its role as a guardian of the Constitution makes it particularly necessary for a Constitutional Court sometimes to take into account other considerations than the mere chronological order in which cases are entered on the list, such as the nature of the case and its importance in political and social terms'. *Id.* at para. 56.

[327] *See, e.g., Wemhoff v. Germany, supra* n. 316; *Acquaviva v. France*, 21 Nov. 1995; *Matznetter v. Austria*, 10 Nov. 1969, 1 E.H.R.R. 198; *Buchholz v. Germany*, 5 May 1981, 3 E.H.R.R. 597.

[328] *Obermeier v. Austria, supra* n. 324, para. 72. *See also Steffano v. Italy*, 27 Feb. 1992, paras. 16–17.

[329] *Union Alimentaria Sandars, S.A. v. Spain*, 7 July 1989, 12 E.H.R.R. 24, para. 35, citing *Martins Moreira v. Portugal*, 26 Oct. 1988, 13 E.H.R.R. 517, para. 46; *Guincho v. Portugal*, 28 June 1984, 7 E.H.R.R. 223, para. 34.

[330] *See Buchholz v. Germany, supra* n. 327, para. 63. The principle that a person charged with a criminal offence is not required by Article 6(1) to co-operate actively with the judicial authorities was reiterated in *Corrigliano v. Italy, supra* n. 317, para. 42, and *I.A. v. France*, 23 Sept. 1998, para. 121. Moreover, '[p]eople charged with criminal offences cannot...be criticised for sending to the judicial officers handling the investigation of their case evidence that they consider establishes their innocence or for asking them to investigate particular matters'. *Reinhardt & Slimane-Kaid v. France*, 31 Mar. 1998, 28 E.H.R.R. 59, para. 99.

diligence to be expected of a party to litigation of this kind' and, therefore, 'contributed to prolonging the proceedings', a violation will not be found.[331] Although 'applicants cannot be blamed for making full use of the remedies available to them under domestic law' their 'behaviour... constitutes an objective fact which cannot be attributed to the respondent State and which must be taken into account for the purpose of determining whether or not the reasonable time referred to in Article 6(1) has been exceeded'.[332] Thus, in *Vernillo v. France*,[333] where the civil action began in December 1977 and ended on 5 June 1985, the proceedings were not found to be excessive where only a year of that time was caused by 'abnormal' court delays, while the defendants were responsible for one year and eight and a half months' worth of delays and the plaintiffs were responsible for about two and a half years of delay time.

In contrast, an unreasonable delay will be a violation if it is due mainly to the actions of the state.[334] Sometimes such delays are the result of individual decisions in particular cases.[335] But often such a delay is caused by the backlog of cases in the judicial system.[336] The Court has divided these backlogs into two types. The first type involves an emergency situation, such as a recession,[337] where the state has no prior warning of a massive increase in litigation and, once aware of the problem, takes fast and effective steps to eliminate it:

The Convention places the Contracting States under a duty to organise their legal systems so as to enable the courts to comply with the requirements of Article 6(1), including that of trial within a 'reasonable time'; nonetheless, a temporary backlog of business does not involve liability on the part of the Contracting States provided that they take, with the requisite promptness, remedial action to deal with an exceptional situation of this kind.[338]

The second type of backlog is a structural one, where more cases exist than can be handled by the judicial system. 'Less important' cases are continually put on hold to accommodate more critical ones, or the state has reacted to a critical situation in an ineffective or inefficient manner. In such circumstances, the Court has held violations

---

[331] *Deumeland v. Germany*, 29 May 1986, 8 E.H.R.R. 448, para. 80. *See also Pretto and Others v. Italy*, 8 Dec. 1983, 6 E.H.R.R. 182, paras. 33–4; *H. v. France*, 24 Oct. 1989, 12 E.H.R.R. 74, para. 55.

[332] *Poiss v. Austria*, *supra* n. 319, at para. 57.

[333] 20 Feb. 1991, 13 E.H.R.R. 880. *See also Ciricosta & Viola v. Italy*, 4 Dec. 1995, in which delays in civil proceedings lasting 15 years and still pending were found to be mainly attributable to the applicants, who had requested or acceded to some 23 adjournments.

[334] *See H. v. United Kingdom*, 8 July 1987, 10 E.H.R.R. 958; *H. v. France*, *supra* n. 331, para. 55.

[335] In one case, the domestic courts failed for five years to sever the civil claim from the criminal complaint, substantially delaying satisfaction of the applicants' claims for compensation: *Moldovan and Others v. Romania (No. 2)*, 12 July 2005, 44 E.H.R.R. 16. The same result followed from the failure of the state to separate the applicant's case from that of a co-accused, where the co-accused had to be extradited and the extradition proceedings caused the delay: *Kemmache v. France*, 27 Nov. 1991, 14 E.H.R.R. 520, paras. 68–71; and when a court failed to compel forensic and witness testimony in a timely manner: *Yasar v. Turkey*, 24 Jan. 2006.

[336] The basic principle that contracting states have the obligation to organize their legal systems so as to allow the national courts to comply with Article 6(1) has been repeated again and again by the Court. *See*, e.g., *Massa v. Italy*, 24 Aug. 1993, 18 E.H.R.R. 266, para. 31.

[337] *See Buchholz v. Germany*, *supra* n. 327.

[338] *Milasi v. Italy*, 25 June 1987, 10 E.H.R.R. 333, para. 18.

to occur when the texts of judgments are inordinately late,[339] hearings are delayed,[340] or when judgments are not registered in a timely manner[341] due to the excessive work-load of the judge. The European Court of Human Rights' lack of sympathy for struc-tural delays was particularly evident in *Guincho v. Portugal*.[342] In that case, the Court held that since the flood of litigation resulting from a return to democracy in Portugal was not totally unforeseen, efforts taken by Portugal which proved ineffective were not sufficient to avoid liability.[343] Thus, while the Court is willing to assess a particu-lar case in light of recently instituted structural reforms, they will not necessarily be found to justify the delay.[344]

The Court has held that what is at stake for the applicant has to be taken into account in assessing the reasonableness of the length of proceedings. When certain issues are involved the courts must act even more expeditiously. In cases which have a 'particular quality of irreversibility', the authorities 'are under a duty to exercise exceptional diligence since…there is always the danger that any procedural delay will result in the de facto determination of the issue submitted to the court before it has held its hearing'.[345] This has been found to be true in cases involving family relationships,[346] employment,[347] the contracting of AIDS through contaminated blood supplies,[348] and where the applicant is held in detention pending determination of a criminal charge against him.[349]

---

[339] E.g. *B. v. Austria*, 28 Mar. 1990, 13 E.H.R.R. 20, paras. 53–4.

[340] *Portington v. Greece*, 23 Sept. 1998, at para. 33.

[341] E.g. *Monaco v. Italy*, 26 Feb. 1992, para. 17. A similar result was obtained when the delay was due to the actions of extra-judicial state agencies. See *Martins Moreira v. Portugal*, *supra* n. 329, para. 60 where the state was held responsible for delays by the Lisbon Institute of Forensic Medicine; *Wiesinger v. Austria*, 24 Sept. 1991, 16 E.H.R.R. 258, paras. 62–4 where the state was held responsible for delays caused by a lack of coordin-ation between the municipal and agricultural authorities in carrying out a consolidation and rezoning plan; *Tomasi v. France*, 27 Aug. 1992, 15 E.H.R.R. 1, para. 125, where delays were caused by the public prosecutor. But see *Pafitis v. Greece*, 26 Feb. 1998, 27 E.H.R.R. 566, where the Court refused to impute to the state time which elapsed during a strike by the Athens Bar ('notwithstanding the Bar's legal personality under public law…in calling on its members to withdraw their services it was taking action designed to defend their professional interests, not exercising one of the functions of a public authority'), and during an adjournment called by the Athens District Court to refer a question to the European Court of Justice, which lasted over 2 years 7 months ('to take it into account would adversely affect the system instituted by Article 177 of the EEC treaty and work against the aim pursued in substance in that Article'). *Id.* at paras. 95–6.

[342] *Supra* n. 329.

[343] *Id.* para. 40. *See also* the similar holding relating to the restoration of democracy in Spain, *Case of Union Alimentaria Sandars, S.A.*, *supra* n. 329.

[344] *See Fisanotti v. Italy*, 23 Apr. 1998, para. 22, and *S.R. v. Italy*, 23 Apr. 1998, para. 21, where the Court considered delays in pension litigation exceeding five and seven years, respectively, to be unaffected by reforms designed to speed up the examination of cases in the Court of Audit.

[345] *H. v. United Kingdom*, *supra* n. 334, para. 85.

[346] *Id.* para. 71; *Bock v. Germany*, *supra* n. 322. *Paulsen-Medalen v. Sweden*, 19 Feb. 1998, 26 E.H.R.R. 260. But see *Hokkanen v. Finland*, 23 Sept. 1994, 19 E.H.R.R. 139.

[347] E.g. *Obermeier v. Austria*, *supra* n. 324.

[348] *X. v. France*, 23 Mar. 1991, 14 E.H.R.R. 483. *See also A & Others v. Denmark*, 8 Feb. 1996, 22 E.H.R.R. 458.

[349] *Tomasi v. France*, *supra* n. 341, para. 84; *Herczegfalvy v. Austria*, 24 Sept. 1992, 15 E.H.R.R. 437, paras. 71–2; *Abdoella v. the Netherlands*, 25 Nov. 1992, 20 E.H.R.R. 585, para. 24. *See also Vastaberger Taxi Aktiebolag & Valic v. Sweden*, *supra* n. 324, at paras. 100–2 where the Court found a particular need for expedition in light of the fact that the disputed tax liability had already been assessed against the applicants' property and they had been thereby placed in bankruptcy.

As explained in the previous chapter, Article 5 demands that every arrested person be brought 'promptly' before a judge and that every detained person has a right to challenge 'speedily' the legality of his or her detention. Article 5(3) seems to offer the judicial authorities a choice between conducting the trial 'within a reasonable time' or releasing the suspect until the trial date. 'Reasonable time' as used in Article 5(3) applies only to the length of the detention, not the length of the proceedings. This period runs from the time of detention until the person is released on bond or until the day of judgment: 'Obviously, the "time", the reasonable character of which must be assessed, ceases when the person in question is released if he is released before judgment is given in the first instance'.[350] As the inquiry under Article 5 relates only to the applicant's deprivation of liberty, a proceeding which complies with that Article may still contravene Article 6(1) if the final resolution of the charge is inordinately delayed.[351]

As in the case law under Article 6(1), the Court has declined to set rigid standards for deciding the reasonableness of a period of detention.[352] Rather, the matter 'must be assessed in each case according to its special features'.[353] However, the Court has held that, given the connotation of immediacy in the use of the word *'aussitôt'* in the French text, its flexibility in determining promptness:

is limited even if the attendant circumstances can never be ignored for the purposes of the assessment under [Section 5(3)]. Whereas promptness is to be assessed in each case according to its special features..., the significance to be attached to those features can never be taken to the point of impairing the very essence of the right guaranteed by Article 5 § 3, that is to the point of effectively negativing the State's obligation to ensure a prompt release or a prompt appearance before a judicial authority.[354]

Domestic courts reviewing the lawfulness of detention are obliged to consider all relevant factors.[355]

Among the factors justifying detention, persistence of the reasonable suspicion which led to the arrest, is a *sine qua non*,[356] although such suspicion itself has been held to be

---

[350] *Neumeister v. Austria*, 27 June 1968, 1 E.H.R.R. 91, para. 6. When the amount of security for bail is fixed at a very high sum which requires some time to collect and there is no negligence by the applicant with respect to the deposit of his security, the end of the period of detention is not the date on which the conditional order for bail is made, but that on which the security is paid and the applicant is actually released. *Van der Tang v. Spain*, 13 July 1995, 22 E.H.R.R. 363, para. 59.

[351] *See Wemhoff v. Germany*, supra n. 316, para. 4 (a violation of Article 6(1) may still occur although the applicant has been released). *See also Abdoella v. the Netherlands*, supra n. 349, para. 24 (the time a person is kept in detention pending the determination of criminal charges can be a factor in assessing whether the requirement of Article 6(1) that there be a decision on the merits in a reasonable time has been met). *Cf. I.A. v. France*, supra n. 330, at paras. 112, 122, finding a violation of Art. 5(3) but not Art. 6(1).

[352] *See*, for instance, *W. v. Switzerland*, 26 Jan. 1993, 17 E.H.R.R. 60, para. 30: ('The Commission's opinion was based on the idea that Article 5 §3 implies a maximum length of pre-trial detention: The Court cannot subscribe to this opinion, which moreover finds no support in its case-law'.)

[353] *Wemhoff v. Germany*, supra n. 316, para. 10.

[354] *Koster v. the Netherlands*, 28 Nov. 1991, 14 E.H.R.R. 396, para. 24. *See also Brogan and Others v. United Kingdom*, 29 Nov. 1988, 11 E.H.R.R. 117, paras. 59, 62 and dissents.

[355] *See Ilijkov v. Bulgaria*, 26 July 2004, para. 86.

[356] *I.A. v. France*, supra n. 330, para. 103.

insufficient after the lapse of some period of time.[357] The Court also accepts that certain offences, because of their gravity and public reaction to them, may give rise to social disturbance capable of justifying pretrial detention. 'However, this ground can be regarded as relevant and sufficient only provided that it is based on facts capable of showing that the accused's release would actually disturb public order. In addition, detention will continue to be legitimate only if public order remains actually threatened'.[358]

Other reasons for detention include: the complexity of the investigation,[359] the safety of the accused,[360] fear that the accused will suppress evidence, fear that the accused will repeat the offence, and the danger the accused will abscond.[361] The possibility that the accused may flee, however, is not sufficient to justify detention if it is possible to obtain 'guarantees' of his appearance for trial.[362] Furthermore, the Court has held:

> ... the danger of an accused absconding does not result just because it is possible or easy for him to cross the frontier; there must be a whole set of circumstances, particularly, the heavy sentence to be expected or the accused's particular distaste for detention, or the lack of well established ties in the country, which give reason to suppose that the consequences and hazards of flight will seem to him to be the lesser evil than continued imprisonment.[363]

Moreover, in making the assessment whether or not the accused may flee, 'regard must be had in particular to the character of the person involved, his morals, his assets, his links with the State in which he is being prosecuted and his international contacts'.[364] While risk of flight might sometimes justify continuing detention, other characteristics of the accused might indicate the propriety of release. These include the inability to commit further offences of a similar kind, lack of a criminal record, poor health, youth or strong family relations.[365]

While the Court accepts that the investigation of terrorist offences presents the authorities with special problems, 'this does not mean ... that the investigating authorities have carte blanche under Article 5 to arrest suspects for questioning, free from effective control by the domestic courts ... whenever they choose to assert that terrorism is involved'.[366] Perhaps in reaction to the apparent intractability of the problem of

---

[357] Id.   [358] Id.

[359] Van der Tang, supra n. 350, at para. 55.

[360] I.A. v. France, supra n. 330, at para. 108. ('However, this can be so only in exceptional circumstances having to do with the nature of the offences concerned, the conditions in which they were committed and the context in which they took place'.) Id.

[361] See id. paras. 13, 14–15; Stögmüller v. Austria, 10 Nov. 1969, 1 E.H.R.R. 155, paras. 14–15; Ringeisen v. Austria, 16 July 1971, 1 E.H.R.R. 455, paras. 106–8.

[362] Wemhoff v. Germany, supra n. 316, para. 15.

[363] Stögmüller v. Austria, supra n. 361, para. 33. However, 'the danger of an accused's absconding cannot be gauged solely on the basis of the severity of the sentence risked'. Mansur v. Turkey, 8 June 1995, 20 E.H.R.R. 535, at para. 55.

[364] W. v. Switzerland, supra n. 352 para. 33. See also Quinn v. France, 22 Mar. 1995, 21 E.H.R.R. 529, where a one year detention of an applicant charged in an international fraudulent investment scheme was found justified in light of the danger of his absconding, where he was a foreign national who had been arrested in possession of false passports, had several residences outside France, and a large number of accomplices.

[365] Id. at para. 16; Matznetter v. Austria, supra n. 327, para. 76; Khudobin v. Russia, 26 Oct. 2006.

[366] Sakik v. Turkey, 26 Nov. 1997, 27 E.H.R.R. 662, at para. 44. The applicants' detention in police custody of 12 to 14 days without judicial intervention was held to violate Art. 5(3), even supposing that the activities

excessive pre-trial detention, the Court has admonished domestic courts to examine petitions for release with attention to the specific factors present in each case. It has condemned the unexplained recitation of 'stereotyped terms' such as 'the nature of the offence, the state of the evidence and the control of the file'.[367]

In the United States, a speedy trial is a 'fundamental right' guaranteed to an accused by the Sixth Amendment to the Constitution[368] and imposed on the states by the due process clause of the Fourteenth Amendment. 'The speedy trial guarantee is designed to minimize the possibility of lengthy incarceration prior to trial, to reduce the lesser, but nevertheless substantial, impairment of liberty imposed on an accused while released on bail, and to shorten the disruption of life caused by arrest and the presence of unresolved criminal charges'.[369] The Sixth Amendment right to speedy trial combines characteristics of both Articles 5 and 6 of the European Convention. Limiting pre-trial incarceration is an element of Article 5, while seeking to minimize the time a person is under a charge is found in Article 6. The Sixth Amendment (like Article 5) applies only in criminal prosecutions not in civil cases, that are covered by Article 6(1).

The scope of the American right to a speedy trial differs from the 'reasonable time' requirements of the European Convention. Article 6 mandates that a judicial *determination* be made within a reasonable time, while the Sixth Amendment guarantees only that the accused be brought to trial speedily. While most American courts have based their decisions on the assumption that the Sixth Amendment right extends through the initial sentencing, the Supreme Court has never explicitly so held.[370] The European Court also considers the time spent on interlocutory appeals, which the American courts generally exclude.[371]

The time period prescribed by the Sixth Amendment is not expressly defined. It has been held that 'a violation of the right to a speedy trial [does not exist] unless the circumstances of the case are such that further delay would endanger the values the right protects'.[372] Like the European Court, the Supreme Court has held that the reasonable time for trial under the Sixth Amendment depends on the particular circumstances of the case.

In *Barker v. Wingo* in 1972, the Supreme Court identified four factors to be used in determining if the accused has been deprived of his right to a speedy trial: 'length of delay, the reason for delay, the defendant's assertion of his right, and prejudice to the defendant'.[373]

---

of which they stood accused were linked to a terrorist threat. *Id.* at paras. 45–6. A violation may still be found where the state attempts to derogate from its Art. 5 obligations under Art. 15. *Demir v. Turkey*, 23 Sept. 1998, 33 E.H.R.R. 43, at paras. 52–8. *See also Ikincisoy v. Turkey*, 27 July 2004, para. 105. And Chapter 12(H) *supra*.

[367] *Yasar v. Turkey, supra*, n. 335, paras. 52–3.

[368] The Sixth Amendment reads in pertinent part: 'In all criminal prosecutions, the accused shall enjoy the right to a speedy... trial, by an impartial jury of the State and district wherein the crime shall have been committed'.

[369] *United States v. MacDonald*, 456 U.S. 1, 8 (1982).

[370] *See Tinghitella v. California*, 718 F.2d 308, 312 (9th Cir. 1983).

[371] *See United States v. Loud Hawk*, 474 U.S. 302 (1986).

[372] *Barker v. Wingo*, 407 U.S. 514, 522 (1972).

[373] *Id.* at 530.

The length of delay must be prejudicial on its face to compel examination of the other factors. What makes a delay 'presumptively prejudicial' is dependent on the circumstances of the case. Both the European Court and the Supreme Court consider the complexity of the case in evaluating whether or not a violation has occurred. The Supreme Court has noted that 'the delay that can be tolerated for an ordinary street crime is considerably less than for a serious, complex conspiracy charge'.[374]

Once a delay is deemed 'presumptively prejudicial', the courts will examine the reasons for delay. Different weights are attributed to different reasons and the culpability of the state for any delay is considered. *Barker v. Wingo* offered examples of the weighing system:

— A deliberate attempt to delay the trial in order to hamper the defense should be weighed heavily against the government.

— A more neutral reason such as negligence or overcrowded courts, should be weighed less heavily but nevertheless should be considered since the ultimate responsibility for such circumstances must rest with the government rather than the defendant.

— Finally, a valid reason, such as a missing witness, should serve to justify appropriate delay.[375]

The American system of weighing differently the reasons for delay has no counterpart in the European Court. The European Court weighs all delays attributable to the domestic state identically and no concessions are made for those which are 'neutral' or merely negligent in nature. The practical effect of this is that a delay due to ordinary judicial backlog in the courts may be excused to a certain extent, under the American system, but not under the European Convention, unless substantial and effective steps have been taken to remedy the situation.[376]

Prejudice due to delay is not assumed automatically under the Speedy Trial Clause of the Sixth Amendment. 'Prejudice... should be assessed in light of the interests of defendants which the speedy trial was designed to protect: (i) to prevent oppressive pre-trial incarcerations; (ii) to minimize anxiety and concerns of the accused; and (iii) to limit the possibility that the defense will be impaired'.[377] The courts, therefore, review the damage that delay may have done to the defendant's case. If no damage is found or it appears that the delay was to the defendant's advantage, it is likely that no prejudice will be found.[378] However, a plurality of the Court has held that:

consideration of prejudice is not limited to the specifically demonstrable.... And though time can tilt the case against either side... one cannot generally be sure which of them it has prejudiced more severely. Thus, we generally have to recognize that excessive delay presumptively

---

[374] *Id.* at 531.   [375] *Id.*

[376] Compare *Strunk v. United States*, 412 U.S. 434, 435 (1973) with *Guincho v. Portugal, supra* n. 329, paras. 37–40.

[377] *Barker v. Wingo, supra* n. 372, at 537 (1972).

[378] *Id.* at 534.

compromises the reliability of a trial in ways that neither party can prove or, for that matter, identify.[379]

The Canadian Charter of Rights and Freedoms also contains provisions concerning the right to prompt adjudication. Section 11(b) states: 'Any person charged with an offence has the right…to be tried within a reasonable time…'. Like the Sixth Amendment and Article 5 of the Convention, but unlike Article 6, this right is limited to criminal defendants.

The time period under consideration in determining a 'reasonable time' is 'the period between the laying of the charge and the conclusion of the trial'.[380] The Canadian courts have expressly held that pre-charge (i.e., before an information is sworn or an indictment preferred) delays are not to be counted in determining the length of the delay. Likewise Section 11(b) does not apply to delay in respect to an appeal from conviction by the accused nor from an acquittal by the Crown.[381] The Art. 11(b) right does, however, extend through the post-conviction sentencing phase.[382] The time period considered, thus, is most similar to that which has been explicitly recognized by the United States courts as covered by the Sixth Amendment and by Article 5(3) of the European Convention.[383]

The Canadian right more closely resembles the American version than that of the European Convention insofar as it covers impairments of liberty incurred by restrictions while released on bail. Furthermore, both the Canadian and the United States Supreme Courts have explicitly recognized that the interests protected by the right to a speedy trial are both individual and societal.[384] Thus, in *R. v. Morin*[385] Sopinka J writing for the majority of the Court stated:

The individual rights which the section seeks to protect are: (1) the right to security of the person, (2) the right to liberty, and (3) the right to a fair trial…. The secondary societal interest is most obvious when it parallels that of the accused. Society as a whole has an interest in seeing that the least fortunate of its citizens who are accused of crimes are treated humanely and fairly. In this respect trials held promptly enjoy the confidence of the public…. In some cases, however, the accused has no interest in an early trial and society's interest will not parallel that of the accused.[386]

---

[379] *Doggett v. United States*, 505 U.S. 647, 655 (1992) (opinion of Souter J). In this case, the criminal defendant had been indicted eight and a half years before his arrest for conspiracy to import cocaine. It was found that he did not know of his indictment before his arrest and that the government was negligent in not tracking him down during the six years he was living openly under his own name.

[380] *R. v. Kalanj* [1989] 1 S.C.R. 1594.

[381] *R. v. Potvin* [1993] 2 S.C.R. 880.

[382] *R. v. MacDougall* [1998] 3 S.C.R. 45, paras. 9–39. The Court noted that the values that Art. 11(b) were intended to protect are directly implicated during sentencing, though they should have a more limited scope at this stage. *Id.* at para. 32.

[383] *See R. v. Potvin, supra* n. 381 (discussing the distinction between the language in Section 11(b) of the Charter and Articles 5(3) and 6(1) of the Convention, as discussed in the *Wemhoff Case, supra* n. 316, and American jurisprudence on the Sixth Amendment's Speedy Trial Clause).

[384] *See R. v. Askov* [1990] 2 S.C.R. 1199, 1208–9, 1219–20; *Barker v. Wingo, supra* n. 372, at 520–1.

[385] [1992] 1 S.C.R. 771.

[386] *Id.* at 786.

Like the Supreme Court of the United States, the Canadian Court adopted an explicit list of factors to determine violations. In deciding whether a delay is too long, the Court considers the following factors:

1. the length of the delay;

2. waiver of time periods;

3. the reasons for the delay, including

    (a) inherent time requirements of the case,

    (b) actions of the accused,

    (c) actions of the Crown,

    (d) limits on institutional resources, and

    (e) other reasons for delay; and

4. prejudice to the accused.[387]

Unlike the United States Court, however, particular weights have not been given to different reasons for delay. Nor is the burden of proof on the state once it has been determined that there has been an unreasonable delay, as in the European Court.[388] The preferred method of determining when there has been a violation of Section 11(b) of the Canadian Charter is 'balancing' all of these factors insofar as they are relevant in a given case.[389] In the United Kingdom, contrasting decisions have been made regarding the effect of an undue delay between criminal charge and trial. In *H. M. Advocate v. R*[390] the Privy Council held, 3–2, that, in Scotland, after an unconscionable delay, no prosecution could be brought. But in 2003, the House of Lords held that, in English law, even if there had been a breach of the reasonable time rule of Article 6(1), proceedings should not be stayed unless there could no longer be a fair trial or it was otherwise unfair to try the defendant.[391]

---

[387] *Id.* at 787–8. These factors were discussed in the earlier cases, *R. v. Smith* [1989] 2 S.C.R. 1120 at 1131 and *R. v. Askov, supra* n. 384, at 1231–2. This test replaces the balancing articulated in *R v. Mills* [1986] 1 S.C.R. 863, para. 219 of the 'growing impairment of the interests of the accused by the passage of time' against: 'the waiver of time periods; the time requirements inherent in the nature of the case; and the limited nature of institutional resources'.

[388] *R. v. Smith, supra* n. 387.

[389] *See R. v. Morin* [1992] 1 S.C.R. 771, 788. 'The analysis must not proceed in a mechanical manner. The factors and framework set out in *Askov* and *Morin* are not immutable or inflexible.... [T]he list of factors can never be exhaustive. Nor is an unyielding focus on only certain periods of the delay appropriate. In every case it must be borne in mind that the ultimate question for determination is the reasonableness of the overall delay'. *R. v. MacDougall, supra* n. 382, at para. 41.

[390] [2002] U.K.P.C. D3, [2004] A.C. 462.

[391] *Attorney-General's Reference (No. 2 of 2001)* [2003] U.K.H.L. 68, [2004] 2 A.C. 72.

PART III

THE IMPACT OF THE STRASBOURG SYSTEM

14

THE EFFECT IN NATIONAL LAW OF THE EUROPEAN CONVENTION ON HUMAN RIGHTS

A. THE DIVERSE LEGAL SYSTEMS IN EUROPE

We have seen in earlier chapters how the Convention enables the European Court of Human Rights to exercise a form of supervision over the exercise of state power on human rights grounds that in some ways resembles the supervision over such power that can be exercised by a constitutional court, or supreme court, where the constitution includes protection for fundamental rights. An important difference is that while a national court often has power to set aside an offending decision and grant a remedy to the claimant that has immediate effect in national law, the Strasbourg Court, as an international tribunal, does not have the same power to provide such a remedy. Nonetheless, the Court's powers may be exercised whether the action complained of results directly from primary legislation, from judicial decisions made by the courts, or from executive measures taken by government departments or other public authorities.

Each of the 47 states which are party to the Convention has its own constitutional and political history and legal system.[1] Wide variations exist between these different constitutions and legal systems. Some constitutions are well over 100 years old. Others have been created in recent years, as central and eastern Europe has shaken off the effects of Communism. In nearly all states, the national constitution provides in some measure for the liberties and rights of the individual. But the constitutions differ widely—both in how they define the rights and freedoms which are protected

---

[1] In this chapter, any reference to a state or to a European state will, unless the context dictates a different meaning, refer to a state that is a party to the Convention.

(the 'catalogue' of rights), and also in the procedure provided for enforcing those rights.[2]

In Germany, for instance, the Federal Constitutional Court is the ultimate guardian of the very full catalogue of fundamental rights contained in Part I of the Basic Law: the Court exercises the function of constitutional review over federal legislation or executive action which infringes those rights. There are also administrative courts whose primary function is to control the acts of public authorities on grounds of legality. Another form of review is found in the Constitution of the Fifth French Republic, by which the conformity to the Constitution of a proposed law may be considered by the Conseil Constitutionnel. But the ordinary courts in France have no power to review the constitutionality of enacted laws. The Conseil d'Etat and the *tribunaux administratifs* exercise a controlling jurisdiction over the acts and decisions of the government and public authorities. This jurisdiction extends to disputes over the contractual and non-contractual liability of public authorities, disputes which in most other European legal systems are entrusted to the ordinary civil courts. By contrast with both France and Germany, the position of the United Kingdom has been notable for the lack of both a written constitution and of a catalogue of fundamental rights; the doctrine of the legislative supremacy, or sovereignty, of Parliament has prevented the courts from having power to review the contents of legislation enacted by Parliament. However, the ordinary courts have long exercised an important function of review and supervision, on grounds of legality, over the acts of government departments and other authorities; this control extends to such matters as secondary legislation, departmental policies and guidelines, and decisions made in the exercise of statutory and common law powers. The evolution of this public law jurisdiction moved into an important new phase with the enactment at Westminster of the Human Rights Act 1998, which made far-reaching changes in the British system for protecting rights under the European Convention.[3]

Each state that adheres to the Convention has its own constitution and legal system, and its own history of dealing with claims of human rights. In the many former socialist states that have acquired new constitutions since the fall of the Berlin wall in 1989, their constitutions are likely to reflect contemporary attitudes in favour of an effective system of protecting human rights. Since 1989, the Council of Europe has been able to influence these states in adopting constitutions that, at least on paper, come up to the level of protection set by the European Convention on Human Rights. Nonetheless, the decision to adopt a particular constitution is made within the state concerned; and it is on the diverse national legal systems that the primary burden of protecting the individual's rights and freedoms must fall. The role of the Convention is to complement those systems, and provide redress at an international level where shortcomings in them exist.

---

[2] For a valuable collection of current constitutions, in English translation, *see Constitutions of Europe: Texts collected by the Council of Europe Venice Commission* (2004).

[3] *See* Section D *infra*.

B. THE DUTY OF STATES TO GIVE EFFECT TO THE CONVENTION IN NATIONAL LAW

Even though the Strasbourg Court subjects the rules of national legal systems to close scrutiny, and in some countries its decisions may have a quasi-constitutional effect, the formal status of the Convention remains that of a treaty at international law. The existence, content, interpretation and binding effect of a treaty as between the parties to it are matters governed by international law. By contrast, the question whether a treaty has any effect within national law is a matter governed essentially by the constitutional law of the state in question.[4] If a treaty *requires* effect to be given to it in national law (as did the treaties which set up the European Communities), such an obligation prevails in international law over any supposed obstacles that exist in national law (and see Section E below). The reason for this is that at international law, the national law of a state (which includes its constitutional law) may not be relied on by that state as a justification for failure to perform its obligations under a treaty (and see the Vienna Convention on Treaties, Article 27).

Against this background, several related questions arise:

1. does the Convention *require* states (a) to give direct effect in national law to the substantive rights protected by the Convention? and (b) to provide a procedure in national law for enabling individuals to remedy breaches of their Convention rights? and

2. is it the *duty* of a state to comply with remedial measures required following a breach of the Convention?

While the answers to these questions depend on interpretation of the Convention, and the extent of the obligations imposed on states is a matter of international law, provisions of the Convention may in some states have direct effect in national law, whether as a result of constitutional provisions or specific legislation; moreover, a state may well give greater protection to human rights in its own legal system than is required by the Convention, a possibility that is safeguarded by Article 53 of the Convention.

1. DOES THE CONVENTION REQUIRE STATES (A) TO GIVE DIRECT EFFECT IN NATIONAL LAW TO THE SUBSTANTIVE RIGHTS PROTECTED BY THE CONVENTION? AND (B) TO PROVIDE A PROCEDURE IN NATIONAL LAW FOR ENABLING INDIVIDUALS TO REMEDY BREACHES OF THOSE CONVENTION RIGHTS?

Article 1 imposes on each state the fundamental duty of securing to everyone within their jurisdiction the rights and freedoms defined in the Convention. By Article 13,

---

[4] *See* generally F. G. Jacobs and S. Roberts (eds.), *The Effect of Treaties in Domestic Law* (1987).

everyone whose rights and freedoms so defined are violated:

shall have an effective remedy before a national authority notwithstanding that the violation has been committed by persons acting in an official capacity.

In *Swedish Engine Drivers' Union v. Sweden*[5] a trade union, representing a minority of employees of the Swedish state railways, complained of a breach of their rights under Article 11 (freedom of association). The complaint was that the union was excluded from taking part in the collective bargaining procedures for the railways, which were confined to the union representing the majority of railway employees. The Court held that Article 11 did not extend to giving any union the right to take part in collective bargaining. The union also complained of a breach of Article 13 in that, under Swedish law, it had no effective remedy for redressing its grievance, other than complaining to the Swedish Labour Court. On this aspect of the case, the Court said:

50. The Court notes that Swedish legislation offered the applicant union a remedy of which, moreover, the union had availed itself, namely the institution of proceedings before the Labour Court. The claim of the applicant union was no doubt rejected, but this fact alone cannot establish that the remedy was ineffective. On the contrary, a reading of the judgment of 18 February 1972 reveals that the Labour Court carefully examined the complaints brought before it in the light of the legislation in force and...taking into account Sweden's international undertakings. In addition, neither Article 13 nor the Convention in general lays down for the Contracting States any given manner for ensuring within their internal law the effective implementation of any of the provisions of the Convention.

The Court thus reaches a conclusion in line with the secondary argument advanced by the Government on the issue under consideration. In these circumstances, the Court is not called upon to rule whether, as the Government contended in its main submission and the Commission affirmed at paragraph 98 of its report, Article 13 is applicable only when a right guaranteed by another Article of the Convention has been violated.

In *Republic of Ireland v. United Kingdom*[6] the Irish government claimed that Article 1 of the Convention had been breached because the law in Northern Ireland did not expressly prohibit infringement of the relevant Convention rights:

236. The Irish Government's submission is as follows: the laws in force in [Northern Ireland] did not in terms prohibit violations of the rights and freedoms protected by Articles 3, 5, 6 and 14; several of those laws, as well as certain administrative practices, even authorized or permitted such violations; the United Kingdom was thereby in breach, in respect of each of those Articles, of an inter-State obligation separate from its obligations towards individuals and arising from Article 1, which provides:

The High Contracting Parties shall secure to everyone within their jurisdiction the rights and freedoms defined in Section 1 of [the] Convention.

Neither the British Government nor the Commission in its report concur with this argument. They consider, briefly, that Article 1 cannot be the subject of a separate breach since it grants no rights in addition to those mentioned in Section I....

---

[5] 6 Feb. 1976, 1 E.H.R.R. 617.
[6] 18 Jan. 1978, 2 E.H.R.R. 25, and *see* Chapter 5 (A)(1) *supra*.

238. Article 1, together with Articles 14, 2 to 13 and [56], demarcates the scope of the Convention *ratione personae, materiae* and *loci;* it is also one of the many Articles that attest the binding character of the Convention. Article 1 is drafted by reference to the provisions contained in Section I and thus comes into operation only when taken in conjunction with them; a violation of Article 1 follows automatically from, but adds nothing to, a breach of those provisions; hitherto, when the Court has found such a breach, it has never held that Article 1 has been violated.

239. However, the Irish Government's argument prompts the Court to clarify the nature of the engagements placed under its supervision. Unlike international treaties of the classic kind, the Convention comprises more than mere reciprocal engagements between contracting States. It creates, over and above a network of mutual, bilateral undertakings, objective obligations which, in the words of the Preamble, benefit from a 'collective enforcement'. By virtue of Article [33], the Convention allows Contracting States to require the observance of those obligations without having to justify an interest deriving, for example, from the fact that a measure they complain of has prejudiced one of their own nationals. By substituting the words 'shall secure' for the words 'undertake to secure' in the text of Article 1, the drafters of the Convention also intended to make it clear that the rights and freedoms set out in Section I would be directly secured to anyone within the jurisdiction of the Contracting States.[7] That intention finds a particularly faithful reflection in those instances where the Convention has been incorporated into domestic law.[8]

The Convention does not merely oblige the higher authorities of the Contracting States to respect for their own part the rights and freedoms it embodies; as is shown by Article 14 and the English text of Article 1 ('shall secure'), the Convention also has the consequence that, in order to secure the enjoyment of those rights and freedoms, those authorities must prevent or remedy any breach at subordinate levels.

240. The problem in the present case is essentially whether a Contracting State is entitled to challenge under the Convention a law *in abstracto.*

The answer to this problem is to be found much less in Article 1 than in Article [33]. Whereas, in order to be able to lodge a valid petition, a 'person, non-governmental organization or group of individuals' must, under Article [34], claim 'to be the victim of a violation...of the rights set forth', Article [33] enables each Contracting State to refer to the Commission 'any alleged breach of [any of] the provisions of the Convention by another [State]'.

Such a 'breach' results from the mere existence of a law which introduces, directs or authorizes measures incompatible with the rights and freedoms safeguarded; this is confirmed unequivocally by the *travaux préparatoires.*[9]

Nevertheless, the institutions established by the Convention may find a breach of this kind only if the law challenged pursuant to Article [33] is couched in terms sufficiently clear and precise to make the breach immediately apparent; otherwise, the decision of the Convention institutions must be arrived at by reference to the manner in which the respondent State interprets and applies *in concreto* the impugned text or texts.

---

[7] Document H (61) 4, pp. 664, 703 and 927.

[8] *De Wilde, Ooms and Versyp v. Belgium*, 18 June 1971, 1 E.H.R.R. 438, para. 82; and *Swedish Engine Drivers' Union v. Sweden, supra* n. 5, para. 50.

[9] Document H (61) 4, pp. 384, 502, 703 and 706.

The absence of a law expressly prohibiting this or that violation does not suffice to establish a breach since such a prohibition does not represent the sole method of securing the enjoyment of the rights and freedoms guaranteed.

241. In the present case, the Court has found two practices in breach of Article 3 ... Those practices automatically infringed Article 1 as well, but this is a finding which adds nothing to the previous finding and which there is no reason to include in the operative provisions of this judgment.

Examination *in abstracto* of the legislation in force at the relevant time in Northern Ireland reveals that it never introduced, directed or authorized recourse to torture or to inhuman or degrading treatment. On the contrary, it forbade any such ill-treatment in increasingly clear terms.... More generally, as from the end of August 1971, the higher authorities in the United Kingdom took a number of appropriate steps to prevent or remedy the individual violations of Article 3 ...

The Court considered other aspects of the legislation authorizing detention without trial in Northern Ireland, outlined the pattern of events, and held that in the public emergency threatening the life of the nation, the British government enjoyed a margin of appreciation which had not been exceeded.

The Court has consistently held that a state is not obliged to adopt a particular method of ensuring the observance of rights guaranteed by the Convention—in particular, that a state is not required to incorporate the terms of the Convention in national law. What matters is that the substance of the guaranteed rights should in fact be enjoyed by the individuals affected by state action.

This approach has influenced the Court's interpretation of Article 13. Many applicants have argued (often without success) that Article 13 requires there to be an effective remedy in national law for apparent breaches of the Convention. In 1984, two judges (Matscher and Pinheiro Farina) said in a dissenting opinion:

We recognize that Article 13 constitutes one of the most obscure clauses in the Convention and that its application raises extremely difficult and complicated problems of interpretation. This is probably the reason why, for approximately two decades, the Convention institutions avoided analysing this provision, for the most part advancing barely convincing reasons.[10]

They also commented that, in several recent decisions, in particular *Klass v. Germany* and *Silver v. United Kingdom*, the Court had laid the foundation for a coherent meaning to be given to Article 13.

(A) KLASS V. GERMANY

Judgment of 6 September 1978
2 E.H.R.R. 214

[Five German lawyers claimed that their Convention rights (under Articles 6, 8 and 13) had been infringed by a federal law of 1968 (called for convenience 'the G10') which

---

[10] *Malone v. United Kingdom*, 2 Aug. 1984, 7 E.H.R.R. 14, para. 48. The Court in *Malone* had held (by 16–2) that because of its finding that a breach of Art. 8 had occurred, it was not necessary to consider the alleged breach of Art. 13.

authorized the opening of letters and the tapping of telephones. The applicants relied, *inter alia*, on the fact that their rights might be infringed by secret surveillance. The Court examined the purposes, conditions and procedural safeguards stated in law for the exercise of these powers and found that Articles 6 and 8 had not been breached.]

62. In the applicants' view, the Contracting States are obliged under Article 13 to provide an effective remedy for any *alleged* breach of the Convention; any other interpretation of this provision would render it meaningless. On the other hand, both the Government and the Commission consider that there is no basis for the application of Article 13 unless a right guaranteed by another Article of the Convention has been violated.

63. In *Swedish Engine Drivers' Union v. Sweden*[11] the Court, having found there to be in fact an effective remedy before a national authority, considered that it was not called upon to rule whether Article 13 was applicable only when a right guaranteed by another Article of the Convention has been violated. The Court proposes in the present case to decide on the applicability of Article 13, before examining, if necessary, the effectiveness of any relevant remedy under German law.

64. Article 13 states that any individual whose Convention rights and freedoms 'are violated' is to have an effective remedy before a national authority even where 'the violation has been committed' by persons in an official capacity. This provision, read literally, seems to say that a person is entitled to a national remedy only if a 'violation' has occurred. However, a person cannot establish a 'violation' before a national authority unless he is first able to lodge with such an authority a complaint to that effect. Consequently, ... it cannot be a prerequisite for the application of Article 13 that the Convention be in fact violated. In the Court's view, Article 13 requires that where an individual considers himself to have been prejudiced by a measure allegedly in breach of the Convention, he should have a remedy before a national authority in order both to have his claim decided and, if appropriate, to obtain redress. Thus, Article 13 must be interpreted as guaranteeing an 'effective remedy before a national authority' to everyone who *claims* that his rights and freedoms under the Convention have been violated.

65. Accordingly, although the Court has found no breach of the right guaranteed to the applicants by Article 8, it falls to be ascertained whether German law afforded the applicants 'an effective remedy before a national authority' within the meaning of Article 13.

The applicants are not claiming that, in relation to particular surveillance measures actually applied to them, they lacked an effective remedy for alleged violation of their rights under the Convention. Rather, their complaint is directed against what they consider to be a shortcoming in the content of the contested legislation. While conceding that some forms of recourse exist in certain circumstances, they contend that the legislation itself, since it prevents them from even knowing whether their rights under the Convention have been interfered with by a concrete measure of surveillance, thereby denies them in principle an effective remedy under national law. Neither the Commission nor the Government agree with this contention. Consequently, although the applicants are challenging the terms of the legislation itself, the Court must examine, *inter alia*, what remedies are in fact available under German law and whether these remedies are effective in the circumstances.

66. The Court observes firstly that the applicants themselves enjoyed 'an effective remedy', within the meaning of Article 13, in so far as they challenged before the Federal Constitutional

---

[11] *Supra* n. 5. *See also De Wilde, Ooms and Versyp v. Belgium, supra* n. 8.

Court the conformity of the relevant legislation with their right to respect for correspondence and with their right of access to the courts. Admittedly, that Court examined the applicants' complaints with reference not to the Convention but solely to the Basic Law. It should be noted, however, that the rights invoked by the applicants before the Constitutional Court are substantially the same as those whose violation was alleged before the Convention institutions,[12] reading of the judgment of 15 December 1970 reveals that the Constitutional Court carefully examined the complaints brought before it in the light, *inter alia*, of the fundamental principles and democratic values embodied in the Basic Law.

67. As regards the issue whether there is 'an effective remedy' in relation to the implementation of concrete surveillance measures under the G10, the applicants argued in the first place that to qualify as a 'national authority', within the meaning of Article 13, a body should at least be composed of members who are impartial and who enjoy the safeguards of judicial independence. The Government in reply submitted that, in contrast to Article 6, Article 13 does not require a legal remedy through the courts.

In the Court's opinion, the authority referred to in Article 13 may not necessarily in all instances be a judicial authority in the strict sense.[13] Nevertheless, the powers and procedural guarantees an authority possesses are relevant in determining whether the remedy before it is effective.

68. The concept of an 'effective remedy', in the applicants' submission, presupposes that the person concerned should be placed in a position, by means of subsequent information, to defend himself against any inadmissible encroachment upon his guaranteed rights. Both the Government and the Commission were agreed that no unrestricted right to notification of surveillance measures can be deduced from Article 13 once the contested legislation, including the lack of information, has been held to be 'necessary in a democratic society' for any one of the purposes mentioned in Article 8.

The Court has already pointed out that it is the secrecy of the measures which renders it difficult, if not impossible, for the person concerned to seek any remedy of his own accord, particularly while surveillance is in progress... Secret surveillance and its implications are facts that the Court, albeit to its regret, has held to be necessary, in modern-day conditions in a democratic society, in the interests of national security and for the prevention of disorder or crime... The Convention is to be read as a whole and therefore, as the Commission indicated in its report, any interpretation of Article 13 must be in harmony with the logic of the Convention. The Court cannot interpret or apply Article 13 so as to arrive at a result tantamount in fact to nullifying its conclusion that the absence of notification to the persons concerned is compatible with Article 8 in order to ensure the efficacy of surveillance measures... Consequently, the Court, consistently with its conclusions concerning Article 8, holds that the lack of notification does not, in the circumstances of the case, entail a breach of Article 13.

69. For the purposes of the present proceedings, an 'effective remedy' under Article 13 must mean a remedy that is as effective as can be having regard to the restricted scope for recourse inherent in any system of secret surveillance. It therefore remains to examine the various remedies available to the applicants under German law in order to see whether they are 'effective' in this limited sense.

---

[12] *Cf., mutatis mutandis, Swedish Engine Drivers' Union v. Sweden, supra* n. 5.
[13] *See Golder v. United Kingdom*, 21 Feb. 1975, 1 E.H.R.R. 524.

70. Although, according to the G10, there can be no recourse to the courts in respect of the ordering and implementation of restrictive measures, certain other remedies are nevertheless open to the individual believing himself to be under surveillance: he has the opportunity of complaining to the G10 Commission and to the Constitutional Court....Admittedly, the effectiveness of these remedies is limited and they will in principle apply only in exceptional cases. However, in the circumstances of the present proceedings, it is hard to conceive of more effective remedies being possible.

71. On the other hand, in pursuance of the Federal Constitutional Court's judgment of 15 December 1970, the competent authority is bound to inform the person concerned as soon as the surveillance measures are discontinued and notification can be made without jeopardizing the purpose of the restriction...From the moment of such notification, various legal remedies—before the courts—become available to the individual. According to the information supplied by the Government, the individual may have reviewed by an administrative court, in an action for a declaration, the lawfulness of the application to him of the G10 and the conformity with the law of the surveillance measures ordered; bring an action for damages in a civil court if he has been prejudiced; bring an action for the destruction or, if appropriate, restitution of documents; finally, if none of these remedies is successful, apply to the Federal Constitutional Court for a ruling as to whether there has been a breach of the Basic Law....

72. Accordingly, the Court considers that, in the particular circumstances of this case, the aggregate of remedies provided for under German law satisfies the requirements of Article 13...

(B) SILVER V. UNITED KINGDOM

Judgment of 25 March 1983
5 E.H.R.R. 347

[Here the Court had reviewed in detail the manner in which prison authorities censored the correspondence of convicted prisoners and held that both Articles 6(1) and 8 had been breached. In relation to the breach of Article 6(1), the Court held it to be unnecessary to examine the complaint under Article 13 since the requirements of Article 6(1) had 'absorbed' the requirements of Article 13. The Court examined the alleged breach of Article 13 taken together with Article 8.]

113. The principles that emerge from the Court's *jurisprudence* on the interpretation of Article 13 include the following:

(a) where an individual has an arguable claim to be the victim of a violation of the rights set forth in the Convention, he should have a remedy before a national authority in order both to have his claim decided and, if appropriate, to obtain redress;

(b) the authority referred to in Article 13 may not necessarily be a judicial authority but, if it is not, its powers and the guarantees which it affords are relevant in determining whether the remedy before it is effective;

(c) although no single remedy may itself entirely satisfy the requirements of Article 13, the aggregate of remedies provided for under domestic law may do so;

(d) neither Article 13 nor the Convention in general lays down for the Contracting States any given manner for ensuring within their internal law the effective implementation of any of the provisions of the Convention—for example, by incorporating the Convention into domestic law.

It follows from the last-mentioned principle that the application of Article 13 in a given case will depend upon the manner in which the Contracting State concerned has chosen to discharge its obligation under Article 1 directly to secure to anyone within its jurisdiction the rights and freedoms set out in section 1.[14]

114. In the present case, it was not suggested that any remedies were available to the applicants other than the four channels of complaint examined by the Commission, namely an application to the Board of Visitors, an application to the Parliamentary [Ombudsman], a petition to the Home Secretary and the institution of proceedings before the English courts.

115. As regards the first two channels, the Court, like the Commission, considers that they do not constitute an 'effective remedy' for the present purposes.

The Board of Visitors cannot enforce its conclusions...nor can it entertain applications from individuals like Mrs. Colne who are not in prison.

As regards the Parliamentary [Ombudsman], it suffices to note that he has himself no power to render a binding decision granting redress....

116. As for the Home Secretary, if there were a complaint to him as to the validity of an Order or Instruction under which a measure of control over correspondence had been carried out, he could not be considered to have a sufficiently independent standpoint to satisfy the requirements of Article 13 [since] as the author of the directives in question, he would in reality be judge in his own cause. The position, however, would be otherwise if the complainant alleged that a measure of control resulted from a misapplication of one of those directives. The Court is satisfied that in such cases a petition to the Home Secretary would in general be effective to secure compliance with the directive, if the complaint was well-founded. The Court notes, however, that even in these cases..., the conditions for the submission of such petitions imposed limitations on the availability of this remedy in some circumstances....

117. The English courts, for their part, are endowed with a certain supervisory jurisdiction over the exercise of the powers conferred on the Home Secretary and the prison authorities by the Prison Act and the Rules... However, their jurisdiction is limited to determining whether or not those powers have been exercised arbitrarily, in bad faith, for an improper motive or in an *ultra vires* manner....

118. The applicants made no allegation that the interferences with their correspondence were contrary to English law... Like the Commission, the Court has found that the majority of the measures complained of in the present proceedings were incompatible with the Convention... In most of the cases, the Government did not contest the Commission's findings. Neither did they maintain that the English courts could have found the measures to have been taken arbitrarily, in bad faith, for an improper motive or in an *ultra vires* manner.

In the Court's view, to the extent that the applicable norms, whether contained in the Rules or in the relevant Orders of Instructions, were incompatible with the Convention there could be no effective remedy as required by Article 13 and consequently there has been a violation of that Article.

---

[14] *See Ireland v. United Kingdom, supra* n. 6, at para. 239.

To the extent, however, that the said norms were compatible with Article 8, the aggregate of the remedies available satisfied the requirements of Article 13, at least in those cases in which it was possible for a petition to be submitted to the Home Secretary (see paragraph 116 above): a petition to the Home Secretary was available to secure compliance with the directives issued by him and as regards compliance with the Rules, the English courts had the supervisory jurisdiction described in paragraph 117 above.

119. To sum up, in those instances where the norms in question were incompatible with the Convention and where the Court has found a violation of Article 8 to have occurred there was no effective remedy and Article 13 has therefore also been violated. In the remaining cases, there is no reason to assume that the applicants' complaints could not have been duly examined by the Home Secretary and/or the English courts and Article 13 has therefore not been violated; ...

In *Lithgow v. United Kingdom*[15] the owners of a shipbuilding company which had been nationalized by Act of Parliament challenged the basis of the compensation laid down in the legislation, arguing that it fell below the level guaranteed by Article 1 of the First Protocol to the Convention and alleging as regards Article 13 that no 'effective remedy' was available to them in the British courts. Rejecting this complaint, the Court said:

206. The Convention is not part of the domestic law of the United Kingdom, nor does there exist any constitutional procedure permitting the validity of laws to be challenged for non-observance of fundamental rights. There thus was, and could be, no domestic remedy in respect of a complaint by Sir William Lithgow that the nationalization legislation itself did not measure up to the standards of the Convention and Protocol No. 1. The Court, however, concurs with the Commission that Article 13 does not go so far as to guarantee a remedy allowing a Contracting State's laws as such to be challenged before a national authority on the ground of being contrary to the Convention or to equivalent domestic legal norms.[16] The Court is therefore unable to uphold the applicant's allegation in so far as it may relate to the 1977 Act as such.

207. In so far as the allegation relates to the application of the legislation, the Court notes that it was open to the Stockholders' representative in any case to refer the question of compensation to the Arbitration Tribunal or to test in the ordinary courts whether the Secretary of State had erred in law by misinterpreting or misapplying the 1977 Act. Even if these remedies were not directly available to Sir William Lithgow himself, he did have the benefit of the collective system established by the Act. The Court has found this system not to be in breach of the requirements of Article 6(1), an Article whose requirements are stricter than those of Article 13. In addition, the applicant would have had a remedy in the domestic courts against the Kincaid Stockholders' Representative for failure to comply with his obligations under the 1977 Act or with his common law obligations as agent.

In these circumstances, the Court concludes that the aggregate of remedies available to Sir William Lithgow did constitute domestic machinery whereby he could, to a sufficient degree, secure compliance with the relevant legislation.

By a majority of 15 to three, the Court held that there had been no breach of Article 13.

---

[15] 8 July 1986, 8 E.H.R.R. 329.
[16] This interpretation of Art. 13 has also been applied in cases such as *James v. United Kingdom*, 21 Feb. 1986, 8 E.H.R.R. 123, para. 85 and *Leander v. Sweden*, 25 Mar. 1987, 9 E.H.R.R. 443, para. 77.

In *Boyle and Rice v. United Kingdom*,[17] convicted prisoners in Scotland complained of interferences with their correspondence and family life, and of discriminatory prison regimes; they also complained of the lack of effective remedies in respect of these matters. The European Court said:

52. The stopping of one of Mr. Boyle's letters has been found by the Court to constitute a breach of Article 8. All the remaining claims of violation forming the basis of the applicants' complaints under Article 13 were rejected by the Commission at the admissibility stage on the ground of being manifestly ill-founded....

Notwithstanding the terms of Article 13 read literally, the existence of an actual breach of another provision of the Convention (a 'substantive' provision) is not a prerequisite for the application of the Article.[18] Article 13 guarantees the availability of a remedy at national level to enforce—and hence to allege non-compliance with—the substance of the Convention rights and freedoms in whatever form they may happen to be secured in the domestic legal order.[19]

However, Article 13 cannot reasonably be interpreted so as to require a remedy in domestic law in respect of any supposed grievance under the Convention that an individual may have, no matter how unmeritorious his complaint may be: the grievance must be an arguable one in terms of the Convention.[20]

53. The Government maintained that a claim of violation of one of the substantive Articles of the Convention which has been declared by the Commission to be 'manifestly ill-founded' cannot be regarded as 'arguable' for the purposes of Article 13.

The Commission did not agree with this contention. According to the Delegate, in deciding whether a complaint is 'manifestly ill-founded' under Article [35(3)] the Commission applied a spectrum of standards that encompassed but ranged beyond absence of arguability. In his submission, to be arguable a claim 'only needs to raise a Convention issue which merits further examination', whereas a conclusion that a complaint is manifestly ill-founded may be reached after considerable written and oral argument.

54. As the Court pointed out in its *Airey* judgment of 9 October 1979, rejection of a complaint as 'manifestly ill-founded' amounts to a decision that 'there is not even a *prima facie* case against the respondent state'.[21] On the ordinary meaning of the words, it is difficult to conceive how a claim that is 'manifestly ill-founded' can nevertheless be 'arguable', and *vice versa*.

This does not mean, however, that the Court must hold a claim to be excluded from the operation of Article 13 if the Commission has previously declared it manifestly ill-founded under the substantive Article. The Commission's decision declaring an application admissible determines the scope of the case brought before the Court.[22] The Court is precluded from reviewing on their merits under the relevant Article the complaints rejected as manifestly ill-founded, but empowered to entertain those complaints which the Commission had declared admissible and which have been duly referred to it. The Court is thus competent to take cognizance of all

---

[17] 27 April 1988, 10 E.H.R.R. 425.
[18] *See Klass v. Germany*, para. 64; Section B(1)(a) *supra*.
[19] *See Lithgow v. United Kingdom*, 8 July 1986, 8 E.H.R.R., para. 205 and the authorities cited there.
[20] *See Leander v. Sweden*, 26 Mar. 1987, 9 E.H.R.R. 443, para. 79(a).
[21] *Airey v. Ireland*, 9 Oct. 1979, 2 E.H.R.R. 305, para. 18.
[22] *See Ireland v. United Kingdom, supra* n. 6, at para 157.

questions of fact and of law arising in the context of the complaints before it under Article 13, including the arguability or not of the claims of violation of the substantive provisions. In this connection, the Commission's decision on the admissibility of the underlying claims and the reasoning therein, whilst not being decisive, provide significant pointers as to the arguable character of the claims for the purposes of Article 13.

55. The Court does not think that it should give an abstract definition of the notion of arguability. Rather it must be determined, in the light of the particular facts and the nature of the legal issue or issues raised, whether each individual claim of violation forming the basis of a complaint under Article 13 was arguable and, if so, whether the requirements of Article 13 were met in relation thereto.

Having examined the complaints of the applicants in detail, the Court found that in most of the complaints there was no arguable claim of violation of the Convention and thus no breach of Article 13. In the case of some complaints, the Court found that there might have been an arguable breach of a Convention right, but that there was a sufficient remedy available to the applicants in the form of a petition to the Secretary of State for Scotland, backed up by a possible application for judicial review should an adverse decision on the petition be made by the Secretary of State.

As *Lithgow* and *Boyle and Rice* demonstrate, while the Convention's status in the United Kingdom was that of an unincorporated treaty, it was difficult to know whether the remedy of judicial review was sufficiently effective to satisfy Article 13. In *Vilvarajah v. United Kingdom*,[23] five Tamils from Sri Lanka, whose request for political asylum had been refused by the Home Secretary, were unsuccessful in seeking judicial review of that decision. At Strasbourg, they argued that the scope of the remedy available in English administrative law was too narrow in view of what was at stake when they were facing a forced return to conditions of persecution. The Court held (by seven to two) that the procedure of judicial review provided 'an effective degree of control over the decisions of the administrative authorities in asylum cases' and was sufficient to satisfy Article 13.

Judges Walsh and Russo, dissenting, pointed to the limitations in English law of the remedy of judicial review, which was not equipped to deal with the disputes of fact which arose in the case. They considered that the power of the English courts to set aside an executive decision as 'unreasonable' in the *Wednesbury* sense[24] did not enable the courts to decide whether or not the facts disclosed a breach of the Convention. The Strasbourg Court considered these questions again in the following case.

---

[23] 30 Oct. 1991, 14 E.H.R.R. 248.

[24] In *Associated Provincial Picture Houses Ltd v. Wednesbury Corporation* [1948] 1 K.B. 223, the English Court of Appeal held that the courts could review a decision taken by the competent authority if it was 'so unreasonable that no reasonable authority could ever have come to it'.

(C) CHAHAL V. UNITED KINGDOM

Judgment of 15 November 1996

23 E.H.R.R. 413

[In this case, Article 3 and 5 were held to have been breached.[25] Had there also been a breach of Article 13 in relation to Article 3? The applicants sought to distinguish *Vilvarajah*, arguing that the remedy of judicial review did not provide an evaluation of considerations relating to Article 3, but could determine only whether the proposed deportation of Mr Chahal was reasonable as a matter of English administrative law.]

148. The Court recalls that in its *Vilvarajah* judgment, it found judicial review proceedings to be an effective remedy in relation to the applicants' complaints under Article 3. It was satisfied that the English courts could review a decision by the Secretary of State to refuse asylum and could rule it unlawful on the grounds that it was tainted with illegality, irrationality or procedural impropriety. In particular, it was accepted that a court would have jurisdiction to quash a challenged decision to send a fugitive to a country where it was established that there was a serious risk of inhuman or degrading treatment, on the ground that in all the circumstances of the case the decision was one that no reasonable Secretary of State could take.

149. The Court further recalls that in assessing whether there exists a real risk of treatment in breach of Article 3 in expulsion cases such as the present, the fact that the person is perceived as a danger to the national security of the respondent State is not a material consideration.

150. It is true, as the Government have pointed out, that in the cases of *Klass and Others v. Germany* and *Leander v. Sweden*[26] the Court held that Article 13 only required a remedy that was 'as effective as can be' in circumstances where national security considerations did not permit the divulging of certain sensitive information. However, it must be borne in mind that these cases concerned complaints under Articles 8 and 10 of the Convention and that their examination required the Court to have regard to the national security claims which had been advanced by the Government. The requirement of a remedy which is 'as effective as can be' is not appropriate in respect of a complaint that a person's deportation will expose him or her to a real risk of treatment in breach of Article 3, where the issues concerning national security are immaterial.

151. In such cases, given the irreversible nature of the harm that might occur if the risk of ill-treatment materialized and the importance the Court attaches to Article 3, the notion of an effective remedy under Article 13 requires independent scrutiny of the claim that there exist substantial grounds for fearing a real risk of treatment contrary to Article 3. This scrutiny must be carried out without regard to what the person may have done to warrant expulsion or to any perceived threat to the national security of the expelling State.

152. Such scrutiny need not be provided by a judicial authority but, if it is not, the powers and guarantees which it affords are relevant in determining whether the remedy before it is effective.

153. In the present case, neither the advisory panel nor the courts could review the decision of the Home Secretary to deport Mr Chahal to India with reference solely to the question of

---

[25] *See* Chapter 5, Section C(1) and Chapter 12, Section E(5)(c).

[26] *See Klass v. Germany*, Section B(1)(a) *supra* and *Leander v. Sweden, supra* n. 20.

risk, leaving aside national security considerations. On the contrary, the courts' approach was one of satisfying themselves that the Home Secretary had balanced the risk to Mr Chahal against the danger to national security. It follows from the above considerations that these cannot be considered effective remedies in respect of Mr Chahal's Article 3 complaint for the purposes of Article 13 of the Convention.

154. Moreover, the Court notes that in the proceedings before the advisory panel the applicant was not entitled, *inter alia*, to legal representation, that he was only given an outline of the grounds for the notice of intention to deport, that the panel had no power of decision and that its advice to the Home Secretary was not binding and was not disclosed. In these circumstances, the advisory panel could not be considered to offer sufficient procedural safeguards for the purposes of Article 13.

155. Having regard to the extent of the deficiencies of both judicial review proceedings and the advisory panel, the Court cannot consider that the remedies taken together satisfy the requirements of Article 13 in conjunction with Article 3.

Accordingly, there has been a violation of Article 13.

In *D v. United Kingdom*[27] the Court held, following *Vilvarajah*, that there was no breach of Article 13 where the national court in judicial review proceedings had expressly considered, but rejected, the submissions of an applicant who was seriously ill with AIDS against removal to a small Caribbean island with inferior medical facilities.

These decisions concerning the United Kingdom all arose before the substantive provisions of the Convention had been given direct effect in that country. Now that the Human Rights Act 1998 (see Section D below) requires all courts and tribunals in the United Kingdom to give effect to the Convention rights wherever possible, it will be very difficult for claimants at Strasbourg to argue that the scope of judicial review in the United Kingdom is too limited to comply with Article 13. Nonetheless, Article 13 requires that national remedies must be effective, not theoretical. In many cases involving serious breaches of human rights, the Turkish legal system has failed to provide an effective remedy even though the action of the authorities may have been unlawful in national law. In *Aksoy v. Turkey*,[28] allegations were made that the applicant had been tortured while in police custody; the Court took judicial notice of the fact that such allegations are extremely difficult for the victim to substantiate if he is held in isolation, without access to doctors, lawyers, family or friends.

98. The nature of the right safeguarded under Article 3 of the Convention has implications for Article 13. Given the fundamental importance of the prohibition of torture and the especially vulnerable position of torture victims, Article 13 imposes, without prejudice to any other remedy available under the domestic system, an obligation on States to carry out a thorough and effective investigation of incidents of torture.

Accordingly, as regards Article 13, where an individual has an arguable claim that he has been tortured by agents of the State, the notion of an 'effective remedy' entails, in addition to the payment of compensation where appropriate, a thorough and effective investigation

---

[27] 2 May 1997, 24 E.H.R.R. 423; Chapter 5, Section C(2).
[28] 18 Dec. 1996, 23 E.H.R.R. 553 discussed at Chapter 5, Section A(3) *supra*.

capable of leading to the identification and punishment of those responsible and including effective access for the complainant to the investigatory procedure. It is true that no express provision exists in the Convention such as can be found in Article 12 of the 1984 United Nations Convention against Torture and Other Cruel, Inhuman or Degrading Treatment or Punishment, which imposes a duty to proceed to a 'prompt and impartial' investigation whenever there is a reasonable ground to believe that an act of torture has been committed. However, in the Court's view, such a requirement is implicit in the notion of an 'effective remedy' under Article 13.

99. Indeed, under Turkish law the Prosecutor was under a duty to carry out an investigation. However, and whether or not Mr Aksoy made an explicit complaint to him, he ignored the visible evidence before him that the latter had been tortured and no investigation took place. No evidence has been adduced before the Court to show that any other action was taken, despite the Prosecutor's awareness of the applicant's injuries.

Moreover, in the Court's view, in the circumstances of Mr Aksoy's case, such an attitude from a State official under a duty to investigate criminal offences was tantamount to undermining the effectiveness of any other remedies that may have existed.

100. Accordingly, in view in particular of the lack of any investigation, the Court finds that the applicant was denied an effective remedy in respect of his allegation of torture.

Similarly, in *Aydin v. Turkey*,[29] where a female detainee alleged that she had been tortured, raped and denied access to a court, she and her family had made specific complaints to the public prosecutor. Although he was required by Turkish law to investigate the allegations, the prosecutor made an incomplete inquiry, failing to visit the scene of events and failing to question officers who were implicated.

His failure to look for corroborating evidence at the headquarters and his deferential attitude to the members of the security forces must be considered to be a particularly serious shortcoming in the investigation [paragraph 106].

He had ordered three medical examinations to be made of the applicant with the aim of discovering whether she had lost her virginity, rather than whether she had been a rape victim.

107. ... The Court notes that the requirement of a thorough and effective investigation into an allegation of rape in custody at the hands of a state official also implies that the victim be examined, with all appropriate sensitivity, by medical professionals with particular competence in this area and whose independence is not circumscribed by instructions given by the prosecuting authority as to the scope of the examination ...

The Court by 16 votes to five found that no effective investigation had been made into the allegations and that this failure undermined the effectiveness of other remedies which may have existed in Turkish law. The minority of five judges viewed the facts differently, finding that the conduct of the applicant and her representatives in relation to her complaint made it impossible to find a violation of her rights under Articles 6(1) and 13. Breaches of Article 13 also occurred when the applicant's son had disappeared,

---

[29] 25 Sept. 1997, 25 E.H.R.R. 251.

last seen in custody of Turkish security forces[30] and when those forces were alleged to have deliberately destroyed applicants' homes and possessions.[31] The nature and gravity of such complaints have implications for Article 13, which requires thorough investigation to be made, capable of leading to the identification and punishment of those responsible.

Article 13 was breached in a different setting when the owner of a house that was searched unlawfully in Switzerland was denied a remedy in national law for the reason that the search had been completed;[32] and when a prisoner had no redress against a judge's decision that correspondence with his lawyer should be censored.[33] But there was no breach of Article 13 where a civil remedy for assault existed relating to the corporal punishment of a schoolboy by his head-teacher, even if it was uncertain whether such proceedings would have succeeded.[34]

Where other Convention provisions (particularly Articles 5(4) and 6(1)) confer on an individual the right to a judicial decision on a matter, the Court will not consider the Article 13 claim, since duties under Article 13 are absorbed by the stricter requirements of Article 5(4) or 6(1).[35]

As well as emphasizing that the state must not connive at the breach of an individual's rights by officials, Article 13 encourages states to deal with complaints by domestic procedure, thus reducing the need for recourse to Strasbourg. It reinforces the rule under Article 35(1) that for an application to be admissible, an applicant to Strasbourg must first have exhausted the domestic remedies available.[36]

2. IS IT THE DUTY OF A STATE TO COMPLY WITH REMEDIAL MEASURES REQUIRED FOLLOWING A BREACH OF THE CONVENTION?

When the Court has held that Convention rights have been breached in a particular case, the Court must also consider whether, under Article 41, if national law allows only partial reparation to be made, it is necessary for 'just satisfaction' to be afforded

---

[30] *Kurt v. Turkey*, 25 May 1998, 27 E.H.R.R. 373; *see* Chapter 12, Section A(1).

[31] *Mentes v. Turkey*, 28 Nov. 1997, 26 E.H.R.R. 595. *See also Yasa v. Turkey* (allegations of murder and attempted murder), 2 Sept. 1998, 28 E.H.R.R. 408.

[32] *Camenzind v. Switzerland*, 16 Dec. 1997, 28 E.H.R.R. 458.

[33] *Domenichini v. Italy*, 15 Nov. 1996, 32 E.H.R.R. 68. And *see Halford v. United Kingdom*, 25 June 1997, 24 E.H.R.R. 523 (no remedy where senior police officer's personal calls intercepted by other police).

[34] *Costello-Roberts v. United Kingdom*, 25 Mar. 1993, 19 E.H.R.R. 112.

[35] *Hentrich v. France*, 22 Sept. 1994, 18 E.H.R.R. 440, *Murray v. United Kingdom*, 28 Oct. 1994, 19 E.H.R.R. 193, *Balmer-Schafroth v. Switzerland*, 26 Aug. 1997, 25 E.H.R.R. 398 and *Vasilescu v. Romania*, 22 May 1998, 28 E.H.R.R. 241.

[36] *See*, e.g., *Beis v. Greece*, 20 Mar. 1997, 25 E.H.R.R. 335.

to the injured party.[37] Under Article 46(1), states 'undertake to abide by the final judgment of the Court in any case to which they are parties'. By Article 46(2), the final judgment of the Court is sent to the Committee of Ministers of the Council of Europe, which body 'shall supervise its execution'.[38] The Strasbourg Court has no power to take on this supervisory role, but it has held:

[A] judgment in which the Court finds a breach of the Convention imposes on the respondent state a legal obligation to put an end to the breach and make reparation for its consequences in such a way as to restore as far as possible the situation existing before the breach.[39]

The duty to comply with Court decisions is an essential part of the Convention scheme. If a state paid no regard to them and allowed rights to be abused on a wide scale, its place in the Council of Europe could be at risk, since membership is open only to a state that 'accepts the principles of the rule of law and of the enjoyment by all persons within its jurisdiction of human rights and fundamental freedoms'. If a state were to be in serious breach of this obligation, it could be suspended from membership or forced to withdraw from the Council.[40]

In practice, narrower questions of compliance often arise. If, for instance, the Court decides that a breach of a Convention right was caused by national legislation, similar breaches will occur unless the legislation is amended or unless a way is found of applying the legislation differently. A failure to amend the legislation might come before the Committee of Ministers under Article 46(2) as a failure in execution of the judgment. If further violations of rights occur because the same legislation is still applied, the victims may make their own applications to the Court. One question that has arisen is whether, if the law must be changed, a state has a reasonable time for the legislative process to operate, even though further violations may occur until the new legislation takes effect—or must the decision of the Court be given effect without delay?

(A) VERMEIRE V. BELGIUM

Judgment of 29 November 1991
15 E.H.R.R. 488

[This decision is a sequel to the Court's decision in *Marckx v. Belgium*[41] which held that Belgian legislation on family succession was in breach of the Convention because of its failure to make provision for children born outside marriage.]

19. The applicant complained of having been excluded from inheritance rights in her paternal grandparents' estates. She relied on Article 8 in conjunction with Article 14 of the Convention....

---

[37] *See* Chapter 3, Section C(2).   [38] *See* Chapter 2.

[39] *Papamichalopoulos v. Greece*, 31 Oct. 1995, 16 E.H.R.R. 440, para. 34.

[40] Arts. 3 and 8, Statute of the Council of Europe. For comparable procedure in relation to the European Union, see Art. 6 TEU (old F. 1) and Art. 309 (old Art. 236) of TEC.

[41] 13 June 1979, 2 E.H.R.R. 330 discussed at Chapter 8 (B)(2) *supra*.

She pointed out that in the *Marckx* judgment of 13 June 1979 the European Court had held that the total lack of inheritance rights on intestacy by reason solely of the 'illegitimate' nature of the affiliation between one of the applicants and her near relatives on her mother's side was discriminatory and hence incompatible with these Articles. Mrs. Vermeire maintained that the domestic courts should have applied Article 8 and 14, so interpreted, directly to the estates in which she was interested; at the very least the Belgian legislature should have given the Act of 31 March 1987, amending the legislation complained of, retrospective effect as from the date of that judgment.

20. The Court stated in the *Marckx* case that the principle of legal certainty absolved the Belgian State from reopening legal acts or situations that antedated the delivery of the judgment.

The present case concerns the estates of a grandmother who died before and a grandfather who died after that date.

A. The grandmother's estate

21. The applicant maintained that the succession to her grandmother's estate could not be regarded as having taken place before 13 June 1979. The date of death was indeed 16 January 1975, but the distribution, which alone determined the nature and extent of the heirs' claims, had not been carried out until after that judgment, jointly with that of the grandfather's estate.

22. The succession to Irma Vermeire née Van den Berghe took place on her death and the estate devolved on her 'legitimate' heirs as of that date.

The estate was undoubtedly not wound up until after 13 June 1979, but by reason of its declaratory nature the distribution had effect as from the date of death, that is to say, 16 January 1975.

What is at issue here is therefore a legal situation antedating the delivery of the *Marckx* judgment. There is no reason to reopen it.

B. The grandfather's estate

23. With reference to her grandfather's estate, the applicant alleged that it was for the Belgian authorities to ensure that it was distributed in a manner consistent with Articles 8 and 14 as interpreted by the European Court in the *Marckx* judgment. In her opinion they could have performed their obligation either by direct application of those Articles or by amending the legislation, retrospectively if need be.

24. The Government stated that it did not dispute the principles which followed from the *Marckx* judgment; it considered, however, that these principles compelled the Belgian State to carry out a thorough revision of the legal status of children born out of wedlock. Responsibility for this fell exclusively on the legislative power as the only body in a position to make full use of the freedom left to the State to choose the means to be utilised in its domestic legal system for fulfilling its undertaking under Article [46(1)]. Articles 8 and 14 were not sufficiently precise and comprehensive on the points at issue in this case, and were thus not suitable for direct application by the domestic courts.

The Government further maintained that the legislature could not be criticised for any want of diligence. A first draft reform had been introduced on 15 February 1978. That it had taken over nine years to complete the task could be explained both by the acknowledged complexity of the issue and by Parliament's foresight. Rather than partial, fragmentary alterations, Parliament had preferred an overall and systematic revision, extending, *inter alia*, to the delicate question of the status of children born in adultery. It had also pondered long over the temporal extent to be given to the new provisions; in the end concern for the legal certainty to be preserved in the interests of families, third parties and the state, together with the fear that a large number of lawsuits would follow, had induced it not to give the Act of 31 March 1987 any retrospective effect.

25. The *Marckx* judgment held that the total lack of inheritance rights on intestacy, based only on the 'illegitimate' nature of the affiliation, was discriminatory.

This finding related to facts which were so close to those of the instant case that it applies equally to the succession in issue, which took place after its delivery.

It cannot be seen what could have prevented the Brussels Court of Appeal and the Court of Cassation from complying with the findings of the *Marckx* judgment, as the Court of First Instance had done. There was nothing imprecise or incomplete about the rule which prohibited discrimination against Astrid Vermeire compared with her cousins Francine and Michel, on the grounds of the 'illegitimate' nature of the kinship between her and the deceased.

26. An overall revision of the legislation, with the aim of carrying out a thoroughgoing and consistent amendment of the whole of the law on affiliation and inheritance on intestacy, was not necessary at all as an essential preliminary to compliance with the Convention as interpreted by the Court in the *Marckx* case.

The freedom of choice allowed to a State as to the means of fulfilling its obligation under Article [46(1)] cannot allow it to suspend the application of the Convention while waiting for such a reform to be completed, to the extent of compelling the Court to reject in 1991, with respect to a succession which took effect on 22 July 1980, complaints identical to those which it upheld on 13 June 1979.

27. In a case similar to the present one, from the point of view of Articles 6 and 6*bis* of the Belgian Constitution according to which all Belgians are equal before the law and must be able to enjoy their rights and freedoms without discrimination, the Belgian Court of Arbitration, relying in particular on the *Marckx* judgment, held that 'the old Article 756 of the Civil Code, preserved in force by virtue of section 107 of the Act of 31 March 1987, breach[ed] Articles 6 and 6*bis* [aforesaid] in so far as it appli[ed] to successions taking place from 13 June 1979 on'.[42]

28. Similarly, it should be found that the applicant's exclusion from the estate of her grandfather Camiel Vermeire violated Article 14 in conjunction with Article 8 of the Convention....

It will be evident from *Vermeire* that, in general, no retrospective remedial action is required, but a state which has been found by the Court to have breached its Convention obligations as a result of national legislation is at risk of committing similar breaches of the Convention until remedial legislation has been enacted. As can be seen from the next section, this risk is reduced in states in which direct effect is given to the Convention rights, since the national courts may then be able to provide adequate protection for those rights.

---

[42] 18/91 of 4 July 1991, *Verryt v. Van Calster* [1991] M.B. 18144, 18149 and 18153.

Nonetheless, there are innumerable instances in which a decision by the Court that a breach of rights has occurred leads directly to remedial action being taken, often in the form of legislation to change the law so that a similar breach does not recur. To give but one example, the Court's decision in *Benthem v. The Netherlands*[43] that the Dutch system of administrative appeals to the Crown was in breach of Article 6(1) led to significant structural changes in the system. Similarly, decisions of the Court have been the cause of very many legislative changes in the United Kingdom.[44] Although a state has a duty to comply with a decision of the Court, and is at risk of again being held in breach when it does not bring national law or practice into line with such a decision, if there is a strong reason for disagreeing with a ruling by the Court a state may take an opportunity presented by a later case at Strasbourg of trying to persuade the Court to think again. Such a course of action was successfully followed by the United Kingdom in *Z v. United Kingdom*: the Court was persuaded that, in the earlier case of *Osman v. United Kingdom* where a breach of Article 6(1) had been found, it had not fully understood the procedure in English litigation by which the court may strike out an action as disclosing no arguable case after assuming that all the facts were as alleged by the claimant.[45]

C. INCORPORATION OF THE CONVENTION— THE PRACTICE OF STATES

As we have seen from decisions such as *Ireland v. United Kingdom*,[46] the Court does not require states to give direct effect to the Convention within national law: it is not a breach of the Convention that national courts may not directly enforce the Convention rights. In fact, in some states the Convention may, as a treaty that has been concluded in accordance with national law, be capable of having domestic effect and may be applied by national courts. In other states, the Convention may have no direct effect in

---

[43] 23 Oct. 1985, 8 E.H.R.R. 1. *See* note by N. Verheij, [1990] *Public Law* 23. *Benthem* was 'one of the most disturbing decisions of the European Court for the Dutch legal order': Y. Klerk and E. J. de Jonge, 'The Netherlands', C. Gearty (ed.), *European Civil Liberties and the ECHR* (1997), 105, 131. For a later Strasbourg decision concerning the system of administrative justice in the Netherlands, *see Kleyn v. Netherlands*, 6 May 2003 (holding by 12–5 that the Council of State procedure did not breach the requirements of Article 6(1)).

[44] *See* R. R. Churchill and J. R. Young, 'Compliance with Judgments of the European Court of Human Rights and Decisions of the Committee of Ministers: the Experience of the United Kingdom 1975–1987', [1991] B.Y.I.L. 283, and Gearty, n. 45 *infra*.

[45] *See Osman v. United Kingdom*, 28 Oct. 1998, 29 E.H.R.R. 245 and *Z v. United Kingdom*, 21 May 2001, 34 E.H.R.R. 3. In the latter case, the Court stated: 'There is no reason to consider the striking out procedure which rules on the existence of sustainable causes of action as *per se* offending the principle of access to court' (para. 97); however, the Court found that there had in the circumstances been a breach of Z's right under Article 13 to an effective remedy. On these issues, *see* articles by C. A. Gearty in (2001) 64 *Modern Law Review* 159 and (2002) 65 *Modern Law Review* 87.

[46] *See supra* n. 6.

national law in the absence of legislation that expressly 'incorporates' it in the national legal system.

In this respect, the Convention is in a weaker position than the European Community treaties, which require the courts in *all* member states to be able uniformly to protect the individual's Community rights, even if this means overriding or disapplying provisions of national law.[47]

Because the Convention does not call for a particular solution to this question, there is wide variation in the extent to which states have given effect to the Convention within national law.[48] This variation largely reflects different provisions and traditions in national law relating to the power of the executive to enter into treaties and to the relationship between international and national law. In some countries, the legal tradition is inclined towards 'monism', which seeks to minimize the divergence between international and national law. In others, the tradition favours 'dualism', which maintains a strict distinction between national and international law. It is not necessary to summarize those different traditions here,[49] but some examples of differing national practice may be given.

In considering these illustrations, we must remember that in the early decades of the Convention's existence, at least until 1980, the impact of the Convention in many countries was barely felt: it was only after 1980 as the Court began to deliver more decisions that many questions as to the status of the Convention in national law arose.

Austria is among the states that have gone furthest in incorporating the Convention. In 1964, the Austrian Constitution was amended[50] to confirm that the Convention (ratified in 1958) had the status of constitutional law and was directly applicable. Having the same status as the constitutional bill of rights, the Convention is binding on national authorities that exercise legislative, judicial and administrative power. If there is inconsistency between the Convention and the national bill of rights, the Constitutional Court may adopt the interpretation that is more favourable to the individual. That Court has often exercised its jurisdiction to quash laws and administrative decisions that infringe Convention rights and freedoms.

---

[47] *See*, e.g., *R. v. Secretary of State for Transport, ex parte Factortame Ltd. (No. 2)* Case C-213/89, [1991] 1 A.C. 603.

[48] For full discussion of the effect of the Convention in the legal systems of 32 states, *see* R. Blackburn and J. Polakiewicz (eds.), *Fundamental Rights in Europe: The ECHR and its Member States, 1950–2000* (2001). Much of the material in this section is drawn from this source. For earlier accounts, *see* A. Drzemczewski, *European Human Rights Convention in Domestic Law* (1983); G. Ress, 'The Effects of Judgments and Decisions in Domestic Law', in R. St. J. Macdonald, F. Matscher and H. Petzold (eds.), *The European System for the Protection of Human Rights* (1993), pp. 801–51. For the constitutions themselves, *see Constitutions of Europe* (n. 2 *supra*).

[49] *See* F. G. Jacobs and S. Roberts (eds.), *The Effect of Treaties in Domestic Law* (1987) examining the position in (*inter alia*) Belgium, Denmark, France, Germany, Italy, the Netherlands and the United Kingdom. Jacobs emphasizes (p. xxiv) that the reality is always more complex than a simple contrast between the extreme models of monism and dualism.

[50] *See* Article II No. 7 of the Federal Constitutional Law, BGBl 59/1964 (reference supplied by Professor Manfred Stelzer). *See also* H. Tretter, 'Austria', Chap. 5, in *Fundamental Rights in Europe* (n. 48 *supra*). Since the Constitutional Court has no power to review decisions by other courts, the Supreme Court, as the final appellate court, determines the effects of the Convention in criminal and civil law cases.

In *Belgium*, *France*, *The Netherlands* and *Switzerland*, the directly applicable provisions of the Convention (without being incorporated in the national constitution) have direct effect in national law and may prevail over inconsistent provisions in national legislation of whatever date. To this extent, the Convention has a greater effect than ordinary legislation since the general rule is that in the event of conflict between two provisions of the same rank in the hierarchy of norms, the later in time prevails (*lex posteriori derogat lege priori*).

In *Belgium*, the Convention benefited from an influential decision of the Cour de Cassation in 1971 holding, in a case involving European Community law, that the directly applicable provisions of *all* treaties prevail over conflicting provisions of national legislation, regardless of whether that legislation was enacted before or after the ratification of the treaty.[51] To be regarded as directly applicable, the treaty provision must be a clear and 'legally complete' rule which imposes a duty on the state to act or to refrain from acting, and which may be invoked as a source of rights by those within the state. This test is satisfied by most substantive provisions of the Convention.[52] The Court of Arbitration, which is the constitutional court for Belgium, has since its creation in 1984 always enforced the Convention. In *France*, decisions of similar significance to those in Belgium were made by the Cour de Cassation in 1975 and by the Conseil d'Etat in 1989,[53] applying Article 55 of the French Constitution of 1958 whereby treaties that have signed, ratified and published take precedence over French legislation of whatever date. However, when the Conseil Constitutionnel is examining the constitutionality of new legislation, it does not take treaties (including the Convention) into account, although it does if necessary take into account the Convention when it is determining electoral disputes.

In *The Netherlands*, although judicial review of legislation on constitutional grounds is excluded, treaties that are binding by virtue of their content and have been published are binding on all persons; and statutory regulations must be disapplied if they conflict with treaty obligations.[54] The Dutch courts were initially restrictive in using these provisions, but over time they have come to apply them more frequently. In *Switzerland*, where the position was affected by the federal constitution and the state's traditional neutrality in its foreign relations, the Convention (which in 1974 was approved by a federal law, not by referendum) has been held to have the status of a federal law, and also to contain rules of 'constitutional rank' for purposes of judicial enforcement. The Swiss courts, including the Federal Supreme Court, have decided many questions relating to the protection of Convention rights.

---

[51] *SA fromagerie franco-suisse 'Le Ski'*, Pas. Bel. (27 May 1971) 1.886; in English translation at [1972] C.M.L.R. 330.

[52] *See* S. & P. Marcus-Helmons, 'Belgium', Chap. 6, in *Fundamental Rights in Europe* (n. 48 *supra*).

[53] *See* respectively *Administration des Douanes c. Société J. Vabre* (24 May 1975) D. 1975 497, concl. Touffait; and *Nicolo* (20 Oct. 1989), Rec., p. 190. *See also* C. Dupré, 'France', Chap. 13, in *Fundamental Rights in Europe* (n. 48 *supra*).

[54] Constitution of 1983, Articles 93, 94.

In *Germany*, the directly applicable provisions of the Convention have the status of federal legislation, that is, they prevail over all laws of the *Länder* (regions) and over legislation enacted before the Convention came into effect in German law. The Convention does not prevail over later federal legislation and its status is not equal to that of the German Basic Law. However, the courts attribute greater weight to the Convention than the formal position would suggest.[55] Almost all the substantive guarantees in the Convention have been held to be directly applicable, and individuals can rely on these provisions when dealing with public authorities. Although a complaint to the Constitutional Court cannot be based directly on a violation of the Convention, such a complaint may be based on a violation of the 'general rules of international law' which, under Article 25 of the Basic Law, are an 'integral part' of federal law. As in other countries, the Convention has been increasingly cited in national courts since 1980. In *Italy*, the Convention was ratified by parliament in 1955 and the directly applicable provisions of the Convention thereby have the force of ordinary legislation. They reinforce the human rights guaranteed by the Constitution; in principle every individual may apply to a national court if his or her Convention rights are infringed. The Convention has a significant influence in the interpretation of all legislation, whenever enacted: it has been held to have what is termed a 'special legal force' (*forza di resistenza*) that enables it to prevail by process of interpretation over both earlier and later statutes that are inconsistent with it.

In *Ireland* and the *United Kingdom*, which share a common law background that favours a dualist approach to treaties, the Convention has direct effect only so far as this has been brought about by legislation. In the next section, we examine the United Kingdom's Human Rights Act 1998. In *Ireland*, the Constitution of 1937 provided for judicial protection of fundamental rights. Ireland ratified the Convention in 1953 but, in the absence of incorporating legislation, for many years the courts could do no more than consider Strasbourg decisions for their persuasive effect alongside Irish legislation and case law.[56] In 2003, an Act was passed to enable domestic effect to be given, subject to the Constitution, to the substantive provisions of the Convention. The Act is to an extent based on the United Kingdom's Human Rights Act. In interpreting or applying any rule of law, including the common law, the Irish courts must, so far as possible and subject to legal rules of interpretation, do so in a manner compatible with Ireland's obligations under the Convention (s. 2). Every organ of the state (apart from the President and the Oireachtas (parliament)) must perform its functions in a manner compatible with the Convention (s. 3(1)). A remedy in damages is provided for breach of this obligation (s. 3(2)). The superior courts may make a declaration of incompatibility where no other legal remedy is adequate and available, and in this event *ex gratia* compensation may be paid to an individual (s. 5).

---

[55] In 1987 the Federal Constitutional Court in Germany held that in principle the Convention prevails over later legislation unless the contrary will of the legislature is clearly established; and that the Basic Law is to be interpreted in the light of the Convention: Ress, n. 48 *supra*, 831–6. *See also* A. Zimmermann, 'Germany', Chap. 14, in *Fundamental Rights in Europe* (n. 48 *supra*), 339.

[56] *See* D. O'Connell, 'Ireland', Chap. 18, in *Fundamental Rights in Europe* (n. 48 *supra*).

It was formerly the position in the Scandinavian countries that the Convention did not have effect in national law, but incorporating legislation has been enacted in *Denmark* (taking effect on 1 July 1992), *Iceland* (30 May 1994), *Sweden* (1 January 1995) and *Norway* (21 May 1999).[57] In *Finland*, which ratified the Convention only in May 1990, this was authorized by an Act that provided for the Convention to be part of Finnish law; the Act was approved by a two-thirds majority in Parliament because of the perceived impact of the Convention on the sovereignty of Finland. The Act ranks as ordinary legislation and it could, as a matter of law, be amended or even repealed by later legislation passed by a simple majority. However, in interpreting that legislation the courts would presume that Parliament had not wished to depart from the Convention, 'one of the cornerstones of Finland's international commitments', unless that intention had been made clear.[58]

The newer democracies in central and eastern Europe have been required by the Council of Europe both to adhere to the Convention and to make acceptable provision in their constitutions for observance of international law and protecting human rights. For instance, by the Constitution of the *Slovak Republic*, that took effect in 1993, international agreements on human rights and fundamental liberties that have been ratified and published in accordance with the law take precedence over the laws (Art. 7(5)). Part 2 of the Constitution deals in detail with fundamental rights and freedoms: many of these provisions are closely comparable with the Convention rights, although some protected rights go beyond the scope of the Convention, for instance in respect of economic, social and cultural matters. Under Part 7 of the Constitution, there is a Constitutional Court, with power *inter alia* to decide whether laws, decrees and regulations comply with international agreements that are binding on the Republic. For countries without an established tradition of judicial protection for individual rights, there are overwhelming practical advantages in ensuring that the national text setting out fundamental rights is closely comparable with the Convention, as it is in the Slovak Republic.

The effect of a dualist approach is that, until incorporation of the Convention takes place, a national court may reject an individual claim against a public authority as unfounded, even though Convention rights may well have been breached. When that occurs, the individual will have a strong incentive to apply to Strasbourg, since this will be necessary if he or she is to be able to rely fully on the Convention arguments. The awkwardness of this position was formerly acute in the United Kingdom, where the unwritten constitution gave no formal protection for fundamental rights, and did not permit judicial review of primary legislation.

---

[57] *See* respectively (in *Fundamental Rights in Europe*, n. 48 *supra*) P. Germer, 'Denmark', Chap. 10; G. Gauksdöttir, 'Iceland', Chap. 17; I. Cameron, 'Sweden', Chap. 32; and E. Mose, 'Norway', Chap. 24.
[58] A. Rosas, Chap. 12, 'Finland', in *Fundamental Rights in Europe* (n. 48 *supra*) at 296.

D. THE EFFECT OF THE CONVENTION IN THE LAW OF THE UNITED KINGDOM

The United Kingdom government has full power under the royal prerogative to enter into international treaties and exercised this power in ratifying the Convention. However, without the authority of an Act of Parliament, a treaty may not alter the law of the United Kingdom. Except to the extent that a treaty is incorporated into national law by statute, the courts have no power to enforce treaty rights and obligations.[59] Although the United Kingdom was the first state to ratify the Convention in 1951, it was the policy of successive governments until 1997 that it was unnecessary to incorporate the Convention into national law. This policy was based on two assumptions: (a) that although the United Kingdom lacked formal machinery for protecting human rights, in substance the Convention rights were observed in national law and practice; (b) that if the Strasbourg Court should hold that Convention rights had been violated in the United Kingdom, the government would comply with the judgment and, if necessary, ensure that legislation was enacted to achieve specific compliance.

Although national courts did not give direct effect to the Convention, they could in some circumstances take it into account. Thus the courts observed a principle of interpretation that, if legislation was ambiguous, the court should adopt the meaning that was consistent with the Convention, rather than a meaning that was not. This principle, at its strongest where the legislation had been enacted to give effect to a Convention obligation, was summarized in these words:

it is a principle of construction of United Kingdom statutes, now too well established to call for citation of authority, that the words of a statute passed after the treaty has been signed and dealing with the subject matter of the international obligation of the United Kingdom, are to be construed, if they are reasonably capable of bearing such a meaning, as intended to carry out the obligation and not to be inconsistent with it.[60]

Further, if a point of the common law was not settled, the courts could take the Convention into account as an aid to the process of developing the law and resolving uncertainties.[61] Although it was argued that all officials ought to be aware of the state's international obligations in taking discretionary decisions which affected individuals, the courts did not accept that this was the case in the absence of legislation to give domestic effect to the Convention; nor that an executive power was limited by the need to ensure that Convention rights were not breached.[62] However, at a time when

---

[59] *Rayner (Mincing Lane) Ltd v. Department of Trade* [1990] 2 A.C. 418, 577.

[60] *Garland v. British Rail Engineering Ltd.* [1983] A.C. 751, 771 (Lord Diplock). In various forms, this approach is found in other legal systems—*see* Jacobs and Roberts, *supra* n. 49, at 33 (Denmark), 60 (France), 69 (Germany), 100 (Italy) and 160 (U.S.A.).

[61] For analysis of the circumstances in which English courts could apply the Convention before it was incorporated into national law, *see* M. Hunt, *Using Human Rights Law in English Courts* (1997).

[62] On both these points, *see R. v. Secretary of State for the Home Department, ex parte Brind*, Section D(2) *infra.*

principles of administrative law were being rapidly developed by the courts, the influence of the Convention was one factor that caused the courts to accept that where an
executive power directly affected a person's fundamental rights, such as the right to
life or the right not to be tortured, the court must take that into account in deciding
whether a challenge to a discretionary decision should succeed. The new position was
summarized in this way:

The court may not interfere with the exercise of an administrative discretion on substantive
grounds save where the court is satisfied that the decision is unreasonable in the sense that it is
beyond the range of responses open to a reasonable decision-maker. But in judging whether the
decision-maker has exceeded this margin of appreciation the human rights context is important. The more substantial the interference with human rights, the more the court will require
by way of justification before it is satisfied that the decision is reasonable in the sense outlined
above.[63]

In this section, two cases, *Malone* and *ex parte Brind*, illustrate the position before
the Convention had effect within United Kingdom law. There follows material outlining the government's reasons for its decision in 1997 to introduce legislation giving
effect to the Convention in national law, and the section concludes with comment
on the Human Rights Act 1998[64] and with two of the most significant cases that have
arisen under the Act.

1. MALONE V. METROPOLITAN POLICE COMMISSIONER

[1979] Ch. 344

[In 1978 a London antique dealer, Malone, who had been tried and acquitted on charges of
dishonesty, sought a declaration from the High Court that the police had no lawful authority to tap his phone. As part of his case, Malone relied on the decision of the European
Court in *Klass v. Germany*.[65] He claimed that in the absence of legislation to authorize
and control the tapping of telephones, tapping his phone had infringed his right to privacy
under Article 8 of the Convention. The judge (Megarry V-C) gave a full account of the
decision in *Klass v. Germany*, emphasizing the safeguards in the system of surveillance
then operating in Germany:]

I have devoted some space to setting out a summary of the *Klass* decision because counsel for
the plaintiff placed so much weight on it, and because of the background that it provides for
the present case. The main thrust of his argument . . . was that although a treaty forms no part
of the law of this country, it might nevertheless have some effect in English law. In this case,
he said, the Convention, as construed in the *Klass* case, could and should have a significant
effect in determining what the law was on a point which, like this, was devoid of any direct
authority.

[63] This was approved in *R. v. Ministry of Defence, ex parte Smith* [1996] Q.B. 517.
[64] For which, *see* Appendix C.   [65] *See* Section B(1)(a) *supra*.

[Rejecting this argument, the judge cited Article 1 of the Convention and said that the obligation which this created was not justiciable in British courts: the Convention 'does not, as a matter of English law, confer any direct rights on the plaintiff that he can enforce in the English courts'.[66] He compared the position in England where telephone tapping was unregulated by law with the Court's decision in *Klass v. Germany* and concluded that 'adequate and effective safeguards against abuse' were lacking.]

I therefore find it impossible to see how English law could be said to satisfy the requirements of the Convention, as interpreted in the *Klass* case, unless that law not only prohibited all telephone tapping save in suitably limited classes of case, but also laid down detailed restrictions on the exercise of the power in those limited classes. It may perhaps be that the common law is sufficiently fertile to achieve what is required by the first limb of this; possible ways of expressing such a rule may be seen in what I have already said. But I see the greatest difficulty in the common law framing the safeguards required by the second limb. Various institutions or offices would have to be brought into being to exercise various defined functions. The more complex and indefinite the subject-matter, the greater the difficulty in the court doing what it is really appropriate, and only appropriate, for the legislature to do....

Any regulation of so complex a matter as telephone tapping is essentially a matter for Parliament, not the courts; and neither the Convention nor the *Klass* case can, I think, play any proper part in deciding the issue before me....

I would only add that, even if it was not clear before, this case seems to me to make it plain that telephone tapping is a subject which cries out for legislation....

Notwithstanding this decision, the British government refused to introduce legislation on telephone-tapping. Malone took the matter to Strasbourg and the Court upheld Malone's claim that his rights under Article 8 had been breached.[67] It was only after this that the Interception of Communications Act 1985 gave telephone-tapping a firm basis in United Kingdom law and laid down certain restrictions and remedies in respect of allegations of unlawful tapping.

2. R. V. SECRETARY OF STATE FOR THE HOME DEPARTMENT, *EX PARTE* BRIND

[1991] 1 A.C. 696

[The Home Secretary, responsible for regulating broadcasting, issued directives to the broadcasting authorities in Britain under the Broadcasting Act 1981 imposing a ban on the direct transmission of the spoken words of representatives or supporters of proscribed terrorist organizations in Northern Ireland. A news reporter challenged the ban, claiming, *inter alia*, that the directives violated Article 10 of the Convention and that the Home Secretary's powers under the 1981 Act were limited by his duty to observe Article 10:]

---

[66] [1979] Ch. 344, 378.
[67] *Malone v. United Kingdom*, 2 Aug. 1984, 7 E.H.R.R. 14.

LORD BRIDGE OF HARWICH My Lords, this appeal has been argued primarily on the basis that the power of the Secretary of State...to impose restrictions on the matters which the Independent Broadcasting Authority (the IBA) and the BBC respectively may broadcast may only be lawfully exercised in accordance with Art. 10 of the European Convention on Human Rights. Any exercise by the Secretary of State of the power in question necessarily imposes some restriction on freedom of expression. The obligations of the United Kingdom, as a party to the Convention, are to secure to every one within its jurisdiction the rights which the Convention defines, including both the right to freedom of expression under art. 10 and the right under art. 13 to 'an effective remedy before a national authority' for any violation of the other rights secured by the Convention. It is accepted, of course, by the appellants that, like any other treaty obligations which have not been embodied in the law by statute, the Convention is not part of the domestic law, that the courts accordingly have no power to enforce Convention rights directly and that, if domestic legislation conflicts with the Convention, the courts must nevertheless enforce it. But it is already well settled that, in construing any provision in domestic legislation which is ambiguous in the sense that it is capable of a meaning which either conforms to or conflicts with the Convention, the courts will presume that Parliament intended to legislate in conformity with the Convention, not in conflict with it. Hence, it is submitted, when a statute confers upon an administrative authority a discretion capable of being exercised in a way which infringes any basic human right protected by the Convention, it may similarly be presumed that the legislative intention was that the discretion should be exercised within the limitations which the Convention imposes. I confess that I found considerable persuasive force in this submission. But in the end I have been convinced that the logic of it is flawed. When confronted with a simple choice between two possible interpretations of some specific statutory provision, the presumption whereby the courts prefer that which avoids conflict between our domestic legislation and our international treaty obligations is a mere canon of construction which involves no importation of international law into the domestic field. But where Parliament has conferred on the executive an administrative discretion without indicating the precise limits within which it must be exercised, to presume that it must be exercised within Convention limits would be to go far beyond the resolution of an ambiguity. It would be to impute to Parliament an intention not only that the executive should exercise the discretion in conformity with the Convention, but also that the domestic courts should enforce that conformity by the importation into domestic administrative law of the text of the Convention and the jurisprudence of the European Court of Human Rights in the interpretation and application of it. If such a presumption is to apply to the statutory discretion...in the instant case, it must also apply to any other statutory discretion exercised by the executive which is capable of involving an infringement of Convention rights. When Parliament has been content for so long to leave those who complain that their Convention rights have been infringed to seek their remedy in Strasbourg, it would be surprising suddenly to find that the judiciary had, without Parliament's aid, the means to incorporate the Convention into such an important area of domestic law and I cannot escape the conclusion that this would be a judicial usurpation of the legislative function.

But I do not accept that this conclusion means that the courts are powerless to prevent the exercise by the executive of administrative discretions, even when conferred, as in the instant case, in terms which are on their face unlimited, in a way which infringes fundamental human rights. Most of the rights spelled out in terms in the Convention, including the right to freedom of expression, are less than absolute and must in some cases yield to the claims of competing public interests.

[In deciding whether the Secretary of State, in the exercise of his discretion, could reasonably impose the restriction he has imposed on the broadcasting organizations, the judges are entitled]

... to start from the premise that any restriction of the right to freedom of expression requires to be justified and that nothing less than an important competing public interest will be sufficient to justify it. The primary judgment as to whether the particular competing public interest justifies the particular restriction imposed falls to be made by the Secretary of State to whom Parliament has entrusted the discretion. But we are entitled to exercise a secondary judgment by asking whether a reasonable Secretary of State, on the material before him, could reasonably make that primary judgment.

Applying these principles to the circumstances of the case, ... I find it impossible to say that the Secretary of State exceeded the limits of his discretion. In any civilized and law-abiding society the defeat of the terrorist is a public interest of the first importance.... The Secretary of State, for the reasons he made so clear in Parliament, decided that it was necessary to deny to the terrorist and his supporters the opportunity to speak directly to the public through the most influential of all the media of communication and that this justified some interference with editorial freedom. I do not see how this judgment can be categorized as unreasonable....

LORD ACKNER [Referring to the argument advanced for Brind that the Secretary of State should have had regard to Article 10 when deciding how to exercise his statutory discretion] The fallacy of this submission is however plain. If the Secretary of State was obliged to have proper regard to the Convention, i.e. to conform with art. 10, this inevitably would result in incorporating the Convention into English domestic law by the back door. It would oblige the courts to police the operation of the Convention and to ask itself in each case, where there was a challenge, whether the restrictions were 'necessary in a democratic society...' applying the principles enunciated in the decisions of the European Court of Human Rights. The treaty, not having been incorporated in English law, cannot be a source of rights and obligations and the question—did the Secretary of State act in breach of art. 10?—does not therefore arise....

Lords Roskill, Templeman and Lowry gave concurring judgments. This decision rejected the claimant's argument that, in reviewing the legality of executive decisions, the court must take into account and if necessary apply rules and principles (such as that of proportionality) derived from the Convention; it thus reinforced the then existing position by which persons in the United Kingdom could enforce their Convention rights only by applying to the European Court. In the instant case, Brind's subsequent challenge at Strasbourg to the restriction on live broadcasting by terrorist representatives was rejected.[68] But in many other cases, the Strasbourg Court gave protection to Convention rights that at that time lay outside the power of courts in the United Kingdom. One prominent example concerned the government ban on homosexual men and women serving in the armed forces. A judicial review of this ban failed in the United Kingdom, but the challenge succeeded at Strasbourg, where it was held that the policy and its enforcement infringed the applicants' right to private life under Article 8.[69] Instances such as these showed that the lack of direct effect in national

---

[68] *Brind v. United Kingdom*, 9 May 1994, 77–A D.R. 42.

[69] *R v. Ministry of Defence ex parte Smith* [1996] Q.B. 517; *Lustig-Prean v. United Kingdom*, 27 Sept. 1999, 29 E.H.R.R. 548.

law for Convention rights imposed a serious restriction on judicial decision-making. Indeed, the view that it should be possible to rely on Convention rights in United Kingdom courts was supported by senior judges.[70]

The legislative sovereignty of the British Parliament was considered by some to present a serious obstacle to incorporation of the Convention,[71] at least in the sense of 'entrenching' the Convention as a text that would bind future Parliaments. During the 1980s and early 1990s, several private members' Bills sought to give effect to the Convention in domestic law but failed to pass through Parliament.[72] However, at the general election in May 1997, the joint constitutional programme of the Labour and Liberal Democrat parties included a commitment to incorporating the Convention. In October 1997, the new government published a white paper, outlining reasons for giving domestic effect to the Convention and explaining the proposed legislation.

3. GIVING EFFECT TO THE CONVENTION IN UNITED KINGDOM LAW

A. RIGHTS BROUGHT HOME: THE HUMAN RIGHTS BILL

(Cm 3782, 1997)

The case for incorporation

1.14 The effect of non-incorporation on the British people is a very practical one. The rights, originally developed with major help from the United Kingdom Government, are no longer actually seen as British rights. And enforcing them takes too long and costs too much. It takes on average five years to get an action into the European Court of Human Rights once all domestic remedies have been exhausted; and it costs an average of £30,000. Bringing these rights home will mean that the British people will be able to argue for their rights in the British courts—without this inordinate delay and cost. It will also mean that the rights will be brought much more fully into the jurisprudence of the courts throughout the United Kingdom, and their interpretation will thus be far more subtly and powerfully woven into our law. And there will be another distinct benefit. British judges will be enabled to make a distinctively British contribution to the development of the jurisprudence of human rights in Europe.

---

[70] See Lord Browne-Wilkinson, 'The Infiltration of a Bill of Rights', [1992] *Public Law* 397; Sir John Laws, 'Is the High Court the Guardian of Fundamental Constitutional Rights?', [1993] *Public Law* 59; Sir Thomas Bingham, 'The ECHR: Time to Incorporate', (1993) 109 *Law Quarterly Review* 390; Sir Stephen Sedley, 'Human Rights: a 21st Century Agenda', [1995] *Public Law* 386.

[71] See Report of a Committee of the House of Lords on a Bill of Rights (HL 176, 1977–78). *Cf.* A. W. Bradley, 'The Sovereignty of Parliament—Form or Substance?', in J. Jowell and D. Oliver (eds.), *The Changing Constitution* (6th edn. 2007), Chap. 2.

[72] On the last of this line of Bills, see Lord Lester, 'The Mouse that Roared: the Human Rights Bill 1995', [1995] *Public Law* 198.

1.15 Moreover, in the Government's view, the approach which the United Kingdom has so far adopted towards the Convention does not sufficiently reflect its importance and has not stood the test of time.

1.16 The most obvious proof of this lies in the number of cases in which the European Commission and Court have found that there have been violations of the Convention rights in the United Kingdom. The causes vary. The Government recognizes that interpretations of the rights guaranteed under the Convention have developed over the years, reflecting changes in society and attitudes. Sometimes United Kingdom laws have proved to be inherently at odds with the Convention rights. On other occasions, although the law has been satisfactory, something has been done which our courts have held to be lawful by United Kingdom standards but which breaches the Convention. In other cases again, there has simply been no framework within which the compatibility with the Convention rights of an executive act or decision can be tested in the British courts: ... It is plainly unsatisfactory that someone should be the victim of a breach of the Convention standards by the State yet cannot bring any case at all in the British courts, simply because British law does not recognise the right in the same terms as one contained in the Convention.

Bringing rights home

1.18 We therefore believe that the time has come to enable people to enforce their Convention rights against the State in the British courts, rather than having to incur the delays and expense which are involved in taking a case to the European Human Rights Commission and Court in Strasbourg and which may altogether deter some people from pursuing their rights. Enabling courts in the United Kingdom to rule on the application of the Convention will also help to influence the development of case law on the Convention by the European Court of Human Rights on the basis of familiarity with our laws and customs and of sensitivity to practices and procedures in the United Kingdom.... Enabling the Convention rights to be judged by British courts will also lead to closer scrutiny of the human rights implications of new legislation and new policies. If legislation is enacted which is incompatible with the Convention, a ruling by the domestic courts to that effect will be much more direct and immediate than a ruling from the European Court of Human Rights. The Government of the day, and Parliament, will want to minimise the risk of that happening.

1.19 Our aim is a straightforward one. It is to make more directly accessible the rights which the British people already enjoy under the Convention. In other words, to bring those rights home.

[The document explains the choices made by the government in structuring the Bill.]

A new requirement on public authorities

2.2 Although the United Kingdom has an international obligation to comply with the Convention, there at present is no requirement in our domestic law on central and local government, or others exercising similar executive powers, to exercise those powers in a way which is compatible with the Convention. This Bill will change that by making it unlawful for public authorities to act in a way which is incompatible with the Convention rights. The definition of what constitutes a public authority is in wide terms. Examples of persons or organizations whose acts or omissions it is intended should be able to be challenged include central government (including executive agencies); local government; the police; immigration officers; prisons; courts and tribunals themselves; and, to the extent that they are exercising public functions, companies responsible for areas of activity which were previously within the public sector, such as the privatized utilities. The actions of Parliament, however, are excluded.

2.3 A person who is aggrieved by an act or omission on the part of a public authority which is incompatible with the Convention rights will be able to challenge the act or omission in the courts. The effects will be wide-ranging. They will extend both to legal actions which a public authority pursues against individuals (for example, where a criminal prosecution is brought or where an administrative decision is being enforced through legal proceedings) and to cases which individuals pursue against a public authority (for example, for judicial review of an executive decision). Convention points will normally be taken in the context of proceedings instituted against individuals or already open to them, but, if none is available, it will be possible for people to bring cases on Convention grounds alone. Individuals or organizations seeking judicial review of decisions by public authorities on Convention grounds will need to show that they have been directly affected, as they must if they take a case to Strasbourg.

2.4 It is our intention that people or organisations should be able to argue that their Convention rights have been infringed by a public authority in our courts at any level. This will enable the Convention rights to be applied from the outset against the facts and background of a particular case, and the people concerned to obtain their remedy at the earliest possible moment.... In considering Convention points, our courts will be required to take account of relevant decisions of the European Commission and Court of Human Rights (although these will not be binding).

2.5 The Convention is often described as a 'living instrument' because it is interpreted by the European Court in the light of present day conditions and therefore reflects changing social attitudes and the changes in the circumstances of society. In future our judges will be able to contribute to this dynamic and evolving interpretation of the Convention....

Remedies for a failure to comply with the Convention

2.6 A public authority which is found to have acted unlawfully by failing to comply with the Convention will not be exposed to criminal penalties. But the court or tribunal will be able to grant the injured person any remedy which is within its normal powers to grant and which it considers appropriate and just in the circumstances.... In some cases, the right course may be for the decision of the public authority in the particular case to be quashed. In other cases, the only appropriate remedy may be an award of damages. The Bill provides that, in considering an award of damages on Convention grounds, the courts are to take into account the principles applied by the European Court of Human Rights in awarding compensation....

Interpretation of legislation

2.7 The Bill provides for legislation—both Acts of Parliament and secondary legislation—to be interpreted so far as possible so as to be compatible with the Convention. This goes far beyond the present rule which enables the courts to take the Convention into account in resolving any ambiguity in a legislative provision. The courts will be required to interpret legislation so as to uphold the Convention rights unless the legislation itself is so clearly incompatible with the Convention that it is impossible to do so.

2.8 This 'rule of construction' is to apply to past as well as to future legislation. To the extent that it affects the meaning of a legislative provision, the courts will not be bound by previous interpretations. They will be able to build a new body of case law, taking into account the Convention rights.

A declaration of incompatibility with the convention rights

2.9 If the courts decide in any case that it is impossible to interpret an Act of Parliament in a way which is compatible with the Convention, the Bill enables a formal declaration to be made that its provisions are incompatible with the Convention. A declaration of incompatibility will be an important statement to make, and the power to make it will be reserved to the higher courts.... The Government will have the right to intervene in any proceedings where such a declaration is a possible outcome. A decision by the High Court or Court of Appeal, determining whether or not such a declaration should be made, will itself be appealable.

Effect of court decisions on legislation

2.10 A declaration that legislation is incompatible with the Convention rights will not of itself have the effect of changing the law, which will continue to apply. But it will almost certainly prompt the Government and Parliament to change the law.

2.11 The Government has considered very carefully whether it would be right for the Bill to go further, and give to courts in the United Kingdom the power to set aside an Act of Parliament which they believe is incompatible with the Convention rights. In considering this question, we have looked at a number of models. The Canadian Charter of Rights and Freedoms 1982 enables the courts to strike down any legislation which is inconsistent with the Charter, unless the legislation contains an explicit statement that it is to apply 'notwithstanding' the provisions of the Charter. But legislation which has been struck down may be re-enacted with a 'notwithstanding' clause. In New Zealand, on the other hand...[the] New Zealand Bill of Rights Act 1990 is an 'interpretative' statute which requires past and future legislation to be interpreted consistently with the rights contained in the Act as far as possible but provides that legislation stands if that is impossible. In Hong Kong, a middle course was adopted. The Hong Kong Bill of Rights Ordinance 1991 distinguishes between legislation enacted before and after the Ordinance took effect: previous legislation is subordinated to the provisions of the Ordinance, but subsequent legislation takes precedence over it....

2.13 The Government has reached the conclusion that courts should not have the power to set aside primary legislation, past or future, on the ground of incompatibility with the Convention. This conclusion arises from the importance which the Government attaches to Parliamentary sovereignty. In this context, Parliamentary sovereignty means that Parliament is competent to make any law on any matter of its choosing and no court may question the validity of any Act that it passes. In enacting legislation, Parliament is making decisions about important matters of public policy. The authority to make those decisions derives from a democratic mandate. Members of Parliament in the House of Commons possess such a mandate because they are elected, accountable and representative. To make provision in the Bill for the courts to set aside Acts of Parliament would confer on the judiciary a general power over the decisions of Parliament which under our present constitutional arrangements they do not possess, and would be likely on occasions to draw the judiciary into serious conflict with Parliament. There is no evidence to suggest that they desire this power, nor that the public wish them to have it. Certainly, this Government has no mandate for any such change.

2.14 It has been suggested that the courts should be able to uphold the rights in the Human Rights Bill in preference to any provisions of earlier legislation which are incompatible with those rights. This is on the basis that a later Act of Parliament takes precedence over an earlier Act if there is a conflict. But the Human Rights Bill is intended to provide a new basis for judicial interpretation of all legislation, not a basis for striking down any part of it.

2.15 The courts will, however, be able to strike down or set aside secondary legislation which is incompatible with the Convention, unless the terms of the parent statute make this impossible. The courts can already strike down or set aside secondary legislation when they consider it to be outside the powers conferred by the statute under which it is made, and it is right that they should be able to do so when it is incompatible with the Convention rights and could have been framed differently.

Entrenchment

2.16 On one view, human rights legislation is so important that it should be given added protection from subsequent amendment or repeal.... But an arrangement of this kind could not be reconciled with our own constitutional traditions, which allow any Act of Parliament to be amended or repealed by a subsequent Act of Parliament. We do not believe that it is necessary or would be desirable to attempt to devise such a special arrangement for this Bill.

Amending legislation

2.17 Although the Bill does not allow the courts to set aside Acts of Parliament, it will nevertheless have a profound impact on the way that legislation is interpreted and applied, and it will have the effect of putting the issues squarely to the Government and Parliament for further consideration. It is important to ensure that the Government and Parliament, for their part, can respond quickly ...

2.18 The Bill provides for a fast-track procedure for changing legislation in response either to a declaration of incompatibility by our own higher courts or to a finding of a violation of the Convention in Strasbourg. The appropriate Government Minister will be able to amend the legislation by Order so as to make it compatible with the Convention. The Order will be subject to approval by both Houses of Parliament before taking effect, except where the need to amend the legislation is particularly urgent, when the Order will take effect immediately but will expire after a short period if not approved by Parliament....

Scotland

2.20 In Scotland, the position with regard to Acts of the Westminster Parliament will be the same as in England and Wales. All courts will be required to interpret the legislation in a way which is compatible with the Convention so far as possible. If a provision is found to be incompatible with the Convention, the Court of Session or the High Court will be able to make a declarator to that effect, but this will not affect the validity or continuing operation of the provision.

2.21 The position will be different, however, in relation to Acts of the Scottish Parliament when it is established. The Government has decided that the Scottish Parliament will have no power to legislate in a way which is incompatible with the Convention; and similarly that the Scottish Executive will have no power to make subordinate legislation or to take executive action which is incompatible with the Convention. It will accordingly be possible to challenge such legislation and actions in the Scottish courts on the ground that the Scottish Parliament or Executive has incorrectly applied its powers. If the challenge is successful then the legislation or action would be held to be unlawful....

4. THE HUMAN RIGHTS ACT 1998

The Human Rights Act, which is based very closely indeed on the reasoning set out above, came into force on 2 October 2000. The operative provisions of the Act are in Appendix C. The Act contains only two sections that were not in the published Bill. Section 12 requires a court to 'have particular regard' to the importance of freedom of expression before the court grants any relief that might affect that freedom (for instance, an order to ban a newspaper from publishing confidential material). Section 13 requires a court to 'have particular regard' to the importance of the freedom of thought, conscience and religion, in making any determination that might affect the exercise by a religious organization (or its members) of that freedom. These sections were included in response to fear in sections of the media that the Act would limit freedom of expression, and to the fear of some religious bodies that their freedom would be prejudiced; in each case, the concern was that the courts would unduly favour the Convention rights of private persons (for instance, the right to respect for private life, or the right not to be discriminated against) that came into conflict with, respectively, press freedom or religious freedom.

As we have seen in Section C, states exercise a wide discretion in deciding how the Convention should have effect in national law and there is no prescribed method of 'incorporation'. Set out in a schedule to the Act, the substantive Convention rights, together with the rights in certain Protocols, are declared 'to have effect for the purposes of this Act' (section 1(2)), not that they are to have full effect in national law.[73] The Act sets out the purposes for which Convention rights have effect, how they must be protected by courts, tribunals and public authorities, and the means by which those who claim to be victims of a breach of their rights can have the issue decided.

Some aspects of the scheme have been criticized,[74] but the criticisms are of minor significance compared with the main features established by the Act.[75] In brief, these are: (a) a broad new interpretative duty that applies not only to courts and tribunals but to all bodies entrusted with public powers, namely the duty, 'so far as it is possible

---

[73] Thus the Human Rights Act does not go so far as the European Communities Act 1972 did in giving direct effect to rights under European Community law.

[74] *See*, e.g., (1) the rule in s 7(3) that only those who may at Strasbourg claim to be victims of a breach of Convention rights can rely on Convention rights in applying for judicial review; (2) the omission of Arts. 1 and 13 from the Convention rights directly protected by the Act; and (3) the limited retrospective provision made by the Act.

[75] For a detailed account of the Act, including its background, *see* R. Blackburn, 'The United Kingdom', Chap. 36, in *Fundamental Rights in Europe* (n. 48 *supra*).

to do so', to 'read and give effect' to all national legislation, primary and secondary, whenever it has been enacted, in a way that is compatible with the Convention rights (section 3); (b) the duty of all courts and tribunals to take account of Strasbourg jurisprudence when this is relevant to issues raised before them (section 2); (c) the power of courts and tribunals to set aside delegated legislation, administrative policies and individual decisions for non-compliance with the Convention (implied by sections 3, 4 and 6), except only when the action in question was mandated by primary legislation; (d) the power of superior courts to declare provisions of primary legislation to be incompatible with the Convention, when it has not been 'possible' to interpret them in a way that is so compatible; (e) the power of the government, where a declaration of incompatibility is made under (d), to amend the legislation so as to remove the incompatibility by the use of broad delegated powers, subject to parliamentary oversight (section 10); and (f) the provision of appropriate remedies, including compensation in accordance with the Strasbourg approach to 'just satisfaction', when Convention rights have been infringed (sections 7–9).

From a comparative viewpoint, a very positive feature of the Act is that by scheduling the English text of all the Convention and Protocol rights that the United Kingdom has ratified,[76] national courts and tribunals can take full account of the Strasbourg case-law without needing to consider any questions of conflict or discrepancy between the Convention rights and the contents of a national bill of rights. Since all courts and tribunals have the duty to take Convention rights into account when these are relevant to pending proceedings, not only those who adjudicate in these bodies but also all who appear before them must be alert to the potential significance of the Convention. As we have seen, the policy underlying the Act stresses the need to maintain the 'sovereignty' of Parliament, and courts and tribunals have no power to quash or set aside primary legislation. Nevertheless, the superior courts may issue a declaration of incompatibility when a conflict between primary legislation and the Convention cannot be resolved by recourse to interpretation. This means that Acts of Parliament are fully subject to review by the superior courts on Convention grounds, except for the limitation that the courts may not quash or set aside an Act. As we shall see below in the case of *Ghaidan v. Godin-Mendoza,* the manner in which the higher courts exercise their duty to interpret legislation if possible in conformity with the Convention will impact directly upon their need to consider issuing a declaration of incompatibility.

It is not possible here to attempt anything approaching a summary of the immense impact that the Human Rights Act has had on the law of the United Kingdom.[77] The numerous decisions made by the House of Lords since 2000 include cases dealing with the extent to which the acts of British troops in Iraq are subject to the Human

---

[76] Apart from Articles 1 and 13.

[77] The very extensive literature includes A. Lester & D. Pannick (eds.), *Human Rights Law and Practice* (2nd edn. 2004); R. Clayton & H. Tomlinson, *The Law of Human Rights* (2000). For the impact on administrative law, *see* A. W. Bradley, 'The Human Rights Act and Judicial Review', in M. Supperstone, J. Goudie & P. Walker, *Judicial Review* (3rd edn. 2005), Chap. 4.

Rights Act;[78] the extent to which executive decision-making procedures are subject to Article 6(1);[79] the meaning of 'public authority' as the term is used in the Act to define the application of Convention rights;[80] the principles to be followed by national courts in awarding compensation where Convention rights have been infringed;[81] and the extent to which Convention rights have a 'horizontal' effect upon disputes between private persons as to their rights and duties.[82] Extracts follow from two decisions that give striking illustrations of the powers conferred on the courts by the Human Rights Act. It will be seen that, at the price of creating some new constitutional questions, the Act has resolved the main difficulties that arose during the unduly long period in which applicants from the United Kingdom could protect their Convention rights only by crossing the Channel to Strasbourg.

5. THE DUTY TO INTERPRET LEGISLATION IN ACCORDANCE WITH THE CONVENTION

(A) GHAIDAN V. GODIN-MENDOZA

[2004] UKHL 30, [2004] 2 A.C. 557

[When the tenancy of a dwelling-house in England and Wales is protected by the Rent Act 1977, and the protected tenant dies, his or her surviving spouse becomes a statutory ten-ant by succession. But marriage is not essential for this purpose: the Act provides that a person living with the original tenant 'as his or her wife or husband' is to be treated as the spouse of the tenant.[83] In an earlier decision by the House of Lords, *Fitzpatrick v. Sterling Housing Association Ltd*,[84] it had been held that this provision did not include persons in a same-sex relationship, and that the survivor of a same-sex couple was under the Act a member of the original tenant's family, and had merely a lesser right of succession. The issue in the present case was whether, when the original tenant died after the Human Rights Act came into effect, the Rent Act could be interpreted as treating the survivor of a same-sex couple as if he or she were the 'wife or husband' of the deceased tenant. Here, the surviving member of the couple, Mr Ghodin-Mendoza, claimed that any other result would be discriminatory, in breach of Article 14 ECHR, read with Article 8. The Law Lords

---

[78] *R. (Al Skeini) v. Secretary of State for Defence* [2007] UKHL 26, [2007] 3 All E.R. 685, considering *inter alia Bancovic v. Belgium*, 12 Dec. 2001; and *see* Chapter 2(B)(6).

[79] *R. (Alconbury Developments Ltd) v. Secretary of State for the Environment* [2003] 2 A.C. 295; and *Runa Begum v. Tower Hamlets LBC* [2003] UKHL 5, [2003] 2 A.C. 430; and *see* Chapter 13(B)(10).

[80] *Aston Cantlow PCC v. Wallbank* [2003] UKHL 37, [2004] 1 A.C. 546 and *Johnson v Havering LBC* [2007] UKHL 27 (by 3–2, upholding *R. (Heather) v. Leonard Cheshire Foundation* [2002] EWCA Civ 366, [2002] 2 All E.R. 936).

[81] *R. (Greenfield) v. Secretary of State for the Home Dept* [2005] UKHL 14, [2005] 2 All E.R. 240 and *Ali v. Head Teacher and Governors of Lord Grey School* [2006] UKHL 14, [2006] 2 All E.R. 467. *Cf.* the award of just satisfaction by the Strasbourg Court, Chapter 3(C)(2).

[82] *Campbell v. MGN Ltd* [2004] UKHL 22, [2004] 2 A.C. 457.

[83] Rent Act 1977, Sched. 1, para. 2(2).   [84] [2001] 1 A.C. 27.

agreed with this view. But did the Human Rights Act enable or require the national courts to provide relief against the discriminatory effect of the Rent Act?]

LORD NICHOLLS

26. Section 3 is a key section in the Human Rights Act 1998.... Parliament has decreed that all legislation, existing and future,... must be read and given effect to in a way which is compatible with the Convention rights 'so far as it is possible to do so'. This is the intention of Parliament, expressed in section 3, and the courts must give effect to this intention.

27. Unfortunately, in making this provision for the interpretation of legislation, section 3 itself is not free from ambiguity.... The difficulty lies in the word 'possible'. Section 3(1), read in conjunction with section 3(2) and section 4, makes one matter clear: Parliament expressly envisaged that not all legislation would be capable of being made Convention-compliant by application of section 3. Sometimes it would be possible, sometimes not. What is not clear is the test to be applied in separating the sheep from the goats. What is the standard, or the criterion, by which 'possibility' is to be judged? A comprehensive answer to this question is proving elusive....

28.   One tenable interpretation of the word 'possible' would be that section 3 is confined to requiring courts to resolve ambiguities. Where the words under consideration fairly admit of more than one meaning the Convention-compliant meaning is to prevail. Words should be given the meaning which best accords with the Convention rights.

29. This interpretation of section 3 would give the section a comparatively narrow scope. This is not the view which has prevailed. It is now generally accepted that the application of section 3 does not depend upon the presence of ambiguity in the legislation being interpreted. Even if, construed according to the ordinary principles of interpretation, the meaning of the legislation admits of no doubt, section 3 may none the less require the legislation to be given a different meaning. The decision... in R v. A (No. 2)[85] is an instance of this. [This] House read words into section 41 of the Youth Justice and Criminal Evidence Act 1999 so as to make that section compliant with an accused's right to a fair trial under article 6. The House did so even though the statutory language was not ambiguous.

30. From this it follows that the interpretative obligation decreed by section 3 is of an unusual and far-reaching character.... In the ordinary course the interpretation of legislation involves seeking the intention reasonably to be attributed to Parliament in using the language in question. Section 3 may require the court to depart from this legislative intention, that is, depart from the intention of the Parliament which enacted the legislation. The question of difficulty is how far, and in what circumstances, section 3 requires a court to depart from the intention of the enacting Parliament. The answer to this question depends upon the intention reasonably to be attributed to Parliament in enacting section 3.

31. On this the first point to be considered is how far, when enacting section 3, Parliament intended that the actual language of a statute, as distinct from the concept expressed in that language, should be determinative. Since section 3 relates to the 'interpretation' of legislation, it is natural to focus attention initially on the language used in the legislative provision being considered. But once it is accepted that section 3 may require legislation to bear a meaning which departs from the unambiguous meaning the legislation would otherwise bear, it becomes impossible to suppose Parliament intended that the operation of section 3 should

---

[85]   [2001] U.K.H.L. 25, [2002] 1 A.C. 45. And see Chapter 13(D).

depend critically upon the particular form of words adopted by the parliamentary draftsman in the statutory provision under consideration. That would make the application of section 3 something of a semantic lottery....

32. From this the conclusion which seems inescapable is that the mere fact the language under consideration is inconsistent with a Convention-compliant meaning does not of itself make a Convention-compliant interpretation under section 3 impossible. Section 3 enables language to be interpreted restrictively or expansively. But section 3 goes further than this. It is also apt to require a court to read in words which change the meaning of the enacted legislation, so as to make it Convention-compliant. In other words, the intention of Parliament in enacting section 3 was that, to an extent bounded only by what is 'possible', a court can modify the meaning, and hence the effect, of primary and secondary legislation.

33. Parliament, however, cannot have intended that in the discharge of this extended interpretative function the courts should adopt a meaning inconsistent with a fundamental feature of legislation. That would be to cross the constitutional boundary section 3 seeks to demarcate and preserve. Parliament has retained the right to enact legislation in terms which are not Convention-compliant. The meaning imported by application of section 3 must be compatible with the underlying thrust of the legislation being construed. Words implied must, in the phrase of... Lord Rodger of Earlsferry, 'go with the grain of the legislation'. Nor can Parliament have intended that section 3 should require courts to make decisions for which they are not equipped. There may be several ways of making a provision Convention-compliant, and the choice may involve issues calling for legislative deliberation.

34. ...[Three earlier decisions of the House of Lords are cited by way of illustration].[86]

35. In some cases difficult problems may arise. No difficulty arises in the present case. Paragraph 2 of Schedule 1 to the Rent Act 1977 is unambiguous. But the social policy underlying the...extension of security of tenure under para 2 to the survivor of couples living together as husband and wife is equally applicable to the survivor of homosexual couples living together in a close and stable relationship. In this circumstance I see no reason to doubt that application of section 3 to para 2 has the effect that para 2 should be read and given effect to as though the survivor of such a homosexual couple were the surviving spouse of the original tenant. Reading para 2 in this way would have the result that cohabiting heterosexual couples and cohabiting homosexual couples would be treated alike for the purposes of succession as a statutory tenant. This would eliminate the discriminatory effect of para 2 and would do so consistently with the social policy underlying para 2. The precise form of words read in for this purpose is of no significance. It is their substantive effect which matters....

Agreeing with Lord Nicholls, Lord Steyn concentrated on the factors that should influence the courts in deciding how they should react when they are confronted by legislation that does not comply with the Convention. In Lord Steyn's view, 'What is necessary... is to emphasise that interpretation under s 3(1) is the prime remedial remedy and that resort to s 4 [to make a declaration of incompatibility] must always be an

---

86 *In re S (Minors) (Care Order: Implementation of Care Plan)* [2002] U.K.H.L. 10, [2002] 2 A.C. 291; *R. (Anderson) v. Secretary of State for the Home Department* [2002] U.K.H.L. 46, [2003] 1 A.C. 837; *Bellinger v. Bellinger (Lord Chancellor intervening)* [2001] U.K.H.L. 21, [2003] 2 A.C. 467.

exceptional course'.[87] Drawing an analogy with the way in which national legislation had been given an effect consistent with European Community law,[88] Lord Rodger said that the court could

supply by implication words that are appropriate to ensure that legislation is read in a way which is compatible with Convention rights. When the court spells out the words that are to be implied, it may look as if it is 'amending' the legislation, but that is not the case. If the court implies words that are consistent with the scheme of the legislation but necessary to make it compatible with Convention rights, it is simply performing the duty which Parliament has imposed on it and on others. It is reading the legislation in a way that draws out the full implications of its terms and of the Convention rights. And, by its very nature, an implication will go with the grain of the legislation. By contrast, using a Convention right to read in words that are inconsistent with the scheme of the legislation or with its essential principles as disclosed by its provisions does not involve any form of interpretation, by implication or otherwise. It falls on the wrong side of the boundary between interpretation and amendment of the statute.

Baroness Hale gave a concurring judgment. Lord Millett (dissenting on the effect of section 3 of the 1998 Act) held that the section 'does not entitle the court to supply words which are inconsistent with a fundamental feature of the legislative scheme; nor to repeal, delete or contradict the language of the offending statute... Persons cannot be or be treated as married to each other or live together as husband and wife unless they are of the opposite sex'.[89] In his view, questions that arose from the conflict between the Rent Act and the Convention right not to suffer discrimination were 'essentially questions of social policy that should be left to Parliament'.[90]

6. JUDICIAL REVIEW OF LEGISLATION THAT IS INCONSISTENT WITH THE CONVENTION

(A) A V. SECRETARY OF STATE FOR THE HOME DEPARTMENT

[2004] UKHL 56, [2005] 2 AC 68

[The Anti-terrorism, Crime and Security Act 2001 was enacted by Parliament after 9/11. Part 4 of the Act gave the Home Secretary a power of indefinite detention without trial that applied to foreigners (but not to British citizens) who were suspected of involvement in international terrorism, against whom sufficient evidence for a prosecution was not available, and who could not be deported because to do so would expose them to the risk of torture contrary to Article 3, ECHR.[91] In December 2001, a dozen foreigners were detained

---

[87] *Ghaidan v. Godin-Mendoza*, [50]. Lord Steyn's opinion includes a valuable appendix showing the incidence of declarations of incompatibility and of interpretative outcomes under the 1998 Act.

[88] In particular, *Pickstone v. Freemans plc* [1989] A.C. 66 and *Litster v. Forth Dry Dock and Engineering Co Ltd* [1990] 1 A.C. 546.   [89] *Ghaidan v. Godin-Mendoza*, [68], [82]

[90] *Id.*, [101].

[91] *See Chahal v. United Kingdom* (1996) 23 E.H.R.R. 413; and Section B(1)(c), *supra*.

in prison in London as suspected terrorists, although they were free to leave the country if they could find another country to admit them. The British government notified the Council of Europe of its derogation from Article 5, on the ground that there was a 'public emergency threatening the life of the nation' (Article 15).[92] Three years later, the detentions were continuing.

Under the 2001 Act, the detainees appealed to a tribunal called the Special Immigration Appeals Commission, but neither the detainees nor their legal representatives were allowed to see material available to the security services that had led to them being detained. The Commission held that the scheme for detention was discriminatory and breached Article 14, since the power of detention did not apply to British citizens. On appeal to the House of Lords, nine judges formed the court.[93] (1) It was held by 8–1 that the Government's decision that there was a public emergency threatening the life of the nation such as to justify a derogation from Article 5 was one that could, on the basis of the disclosed evidence, properly be made. On this matter, great weight should be given to the views of the government and Parliament, as a pre-eminently political judgment had to be made. (2) Seven judges held that measures to restrain the liberty of the detainees must under the Convention be limited to what was strictly required to afford effective protection. On this basis, the scheme of detention was disproportionate, since it applied only to foreigners suspected of terrorist involvement and not to British citizens who were so suspected; and it permitted foreigners to leave the country and carry on terrorist activities abroad. In all, the scheme breached Article 14 since it discriminated against foreigners, treating them differently because of their immigration status. (3) Accordingly, the judges by 8–1 quashed the derogation order issued by the Government and declared that detention under the Act of 2001 was incompatible with Articles 5 and 14.]

LORD BINGHAM examined the Strasbourg jurisprudence, and said:

42. It follows from this analysis that the appellants are in my opinion entitled to invite the courts to review, on proportionality grounds, the Derogation Order and the compatibility with the Convention of section 23 and the courts are not effectively precluded by any doctrine of deference from scrutinising the issues raised. It also follows that I do not accept the full breadth of the Attorney General's submissions [for the Secretary of State]. I do not in particular accept the distinction which he drew between democratic institutions and the courts. It is of course true that the judges in this country are not elected and are not answerable to Parliament. It is also of course true...that Parliament, the executive and the courts have different functions. But the function of independent judges charged to interpret and apply the law is universally recognised as a cardinal feature of the modern democratic state, a cornerstone of the rule of law itself. The Attorney General is fully entitled to insist on the proper limits of judicial authority, but he is wrong to stigmatise judicial decision-making as in some way undemocratic. It is particularly inappropriate in a case such as the present in which Parliament has expressly legislated in section 6 of the 1998 Act to render unlawful any act of a public authority, including a court, incompatible with a Convention right, has required courts (in section 2) to take account of relevant Strasbourg jurisprudence, has (in section

---

92 And see Chapter 12, Section H.

93 On the Act of 2001, see A. Tomkins, 'Legislating against Terror', [2002] *Public Law* 205; and see also (same author), 'Readings of *A v. Secretary of State for the Home Dept*', [2005] *Public Law* 259.

3) required courts, so far as possible, to give effect to Convention rights and has conferred a right of appeal on derogation issues. The effect is not, of course, to override the sovereign legislative authority of the Queen in Parliament, since if primary legislation is declared to be incompatible the validity of the legislation is unaffected (section 4(6)) and the remedy lies with the appropriate minister (section 10), who is answerable to Parliament. The 1998 Act gives the courts a very specific, wholly democratic, mandate. As Professor Jowell has put it: 'The courts are charged by Parliament with delineating the boundaries of a rights-based democracy'.[94]

43. The appellants' proportionality challenge to the Order and section 23 is, in my opinion, sound, for all the reasons they gave and also for those given by the European Commissioner for Human Rights.... The Attorney General could give no persuasive answer.

LORD NICHOLLS: 74. Indefinite imprisonment without charge or trial is anathema in any country which observes the rule of law. It deprives the detained person of the protection a criminal trial is intended to afford. Wholly exceptional circumstances must exist before this extreme step can be justified.

75. The government contends that these post-9/11 days are wholly exceptional. The circumstances require and justify the indefinite detention of non-nationals suspected of being international terrorists.

76. The principal weakness in the government's case lies in the different treatment accorded to nationals and non-nationals. The extended power of detention conferred by Part 4 of the [Act of 2001] applies only to persons who are not British citizens. It is difficult to see how the extreme circumstances, which alone would justify such detention, can exist when lesser protective steps apparently suffice in the case of British citizens suspected of being international terrorists.

77. Three years have now elapsed since the terrorist attacks of 11 September 2001. A significant number of persons suspected of terrorist involvement in this country are British citizens. In the case of these nationals the government has, apparently, felt able to counter the threat they pose by other means. Although they too present a threat to national security, in their case the government has not found it necessary to resort to the extreme step of seeking an extended power of detention comparable to that contained in the 2001 Act.

78. No satisfactory explanation has been forthcoming on this point. The government has vouchsafed no persuasive explanation of why national security calls for a power of indefinite detention in one case but not the other. Non-nationals may comprise the predominant and more immediate source of the threat to national security, but they are not the only source.

79. All courts are very much aware of the heavy burden, resting on the elected government and not the judiciary, to protect the security of this country and all who live here. All courts are acutely conscious that the government alone is able to evaluate and decide what counter-terrorism steps are needed and what steps will suffice. Courts are not equipped to make such decisions, nor are they charged with that responsibility.

---

[94] 'Judicial Deference: servility, civility or institutional capacity?', [2003] *Public Law* 592, 597. *See also* R. Clayton, 'Judicial deference and "democratic dialogue": the legitimacy of judicial intervention under the Human Rights Act 1998', [2004] *Public Law* 33.

80. But Parliament has charged the courts with a particular responsibility. It is a responsibility as much applicable to the 2001 Act and the [Designated Derogation Order 2001] as it is to all other legislation and ministers' decisions. The duty of the courts is to check that legislation and ministerial decisions do not overlook the human rights of persons adversely affected. In enacting legislation and reaching decisions Parliament and ministers must give due weight to fundamental rights and freedoms. For their part, when carrying out their assigned task the courts will accord to Parliament and ministers, as the primary decision-makers, an appropriate degree of latitude. The latitude will vary according to the subject matter under consideration, the importance of the human right in question, and the extent of the encroachment upon that right. The courts will intervene only when it is apparent that, in balancing the various considerations involved, the primary decision-maker must have given insufficient weight to the human rights factor.

81. In the present case I see no escape from the conclusion that Parliament must be regarded as having attached insufficient weight to the human rights of non-nationals. The subject matter of the legislation is the needs of national security. This subject matter dictates that, in the ordinary course, substantial latitude should be accorded to the legislature. But the human right in question, the right to individual liberty, is one of the most fundamental of human rights. Indefinite detention without trial wholly negates that right for an indefinite period.

LORD HOFFMANN dissented from the majority, holding that the government had not established that there was an emergency situation 'threatening the life of the nation' and that the fabric of life in the United Kingdom was not put at risk by threats of violence. Arguing that 'nothing could be more antithetical to the instincts and traditions of the people of the United Kingdom' than indefinite detention without trial, [86] he said: 'The real threat to the life of the nation, in the sense of a people living in accordance with its traditional laws and political values, comes not from terrorism but from laws such as these. That is the true measure of what terrorism may achieve. It is for Parliament to decide whether to give the terrorists such a victory'. [97]

LORD SCOTT 155. ... [Having outlined the 2001 Act procedure] The individual may then be detained in prison indefinitely. True it is that he can leave the United Kingdom if he elects to do so but the reality in many cases will be that the only country to which he is entitled to go will be a country where he is likely to undergo torture if he does go there. He can challenge before the [Special Commission] the reasonableness of the Secretary of State's suspicion that he is a terrorist but has no right to know the grounds on which the Secretary of State has formed that suspicion. The grounds can be made known to a special advocate appointed to represent him but the special advocate may not inform him of the grounds and, therefore, cannot take instructions from him in refutation of the allegations made against him. Indefinite imprisonment in consequence of a denunciation on grounds that are not disclosed and made by a person whose identity cannot be disclosed is the stuff of nightmares, associated whether accurately or inaccurately with France before and during the Revolution, with Soviet Russia in the Stalinist era and now associated, as a result of section 23 of the 2001 Act, with the United Kingdom....

[Lords Carswell, Hope and Rodger, and Baroness Hale gave judgments concurring in the result. Lord Walker dissented, *inter alia* for the reason that when 'the country is faced, as it is, with imminent threats from enemies who make use of secrecy, deception and

surprise, the need for anti-terrorist measures to be "strictly necessary" must be interpreted in accordance with the precautionary principle recognised by the Strasbourg Court
in *Ireland v. UK* (1978) 2 EHRR 25'. [209]. In his view, the scheme of detention under the
2001 Act showed a 'genuine determination' that 'the Act should not be used to encroach
on human rights any more than is strictly necessary' [218].]

The declaration of incompatibility made by the House of Lords in this case went to the
essence of the power to detain. Although the Human Rights Act states that legislation
that is declared incompatible remains in effect as a matter of law, the government
promptly obtained new powers from Parliament to impose 'control orders' restricting
the freedom of movement of both foreigners and British citizens suspected of terrorist involvement. It will be evident that the Human Rights Act caused the judges
to make assessments of the efficacy and proportionality of the scheme authorized by
Parliament that would have been wholly impossible apart from the Act. The United
Kingdom still lacks a written constitution, and it has no constitutional court in the
usual sense of the term. But the jurisdiction now exercised by the Law Lords under the
1998 Act[95] is comparable with the process of constitutional adjudication that exists in
many other European countries.[96]

E. THE RELATION BETWEEN THE
CONVENTION AND COMMUNITY LAW

In this book, we have examined the significance of the Convention in international
law, how the Convention is applied by the Strasbourg Court, how the Convention has
developed as legal process since it came into effect in 1953, and also the relationship
between the Convention and national legal systems in Europe. Over the same period
of time, the countries of western Europe have co-operated in the scheme for economic
integration that was initiated in 1957 when the European Economic Community with
six members was created by the Treaty of Rome. Its subsequent development, expansion into other spheres and geographical enlargement have led to the present European
Union of 27 states. This complex structure is founded on a system of law interpreted
and applied by courts sitting in Luxembourg (the European Court of Justice and the
Court of First Instance), that are quite separate from the European Court of Human
Rights at Strasbourg.

---

[95] Under the Constitutional Reform Act 2005, the senior judges in the House of Lords will become justices
in a Supreme Court for the United Kingdom, when that court begins to operate. The present jurisdiction of
the House of Lords will go to the new court, without any change in the limits of that jurisdiction.

[96] For an expert view of the operation of the Act, *see* Joint Committee on Human Rights, *The Human
Rights Act: the Department of Constitutional Affairs and Home Office Reviews*, 32nd report, 2005–06 (HL
Paper 278, HC 1716). Also D. Nicol, 'Law and Politics after the Human Rights Act', [2006] *Public Law* 722.

Although it derives from a series of treaties, Community law depends for its efficacy on the fundamental rule that it has direct effect within the national laws of the member states. As the European Court of Justice has repeatedly held:

every national court must, in a case within its jurisdiction, apply Community law in its entirety and protect rights which the latter confers on individuals and must accordingly set aside any provision of national law which may conflict with it, whether prior or subsequent to the Community rule.[97]

Although the Treaty of Rome of 1957 sought to establish specific freedoms of an economic nature, such as the free movement of workers, no general reference to human or fundamental rights of the individual was made in the Treaty. It was formerly a matter of controversy whether such rights could be taken into account by the European Court of Justice in developing the general principles of Community law, or by national courts when they were applying Community law. One difficulty was that, as we have seen, the definition of fundamental rights in national constitutions differs from state to state; the primacy of Community law excluded the possibility of a differential application of Community rules according to national constitutions. Nor could the European Court of Justice choose one or two national constitutions as the model for a Community scheme of fundamental rights. There was, therefore, an advantage in taking the definition of human rights for Community purposes from a common, international source. And by 1974, the European Convention on Human Rights had been ratified by all Community states.

One factor that helped to propel growth within Community law of protection for fundamental rights was the opposition to development of Community law that came from states such as Germany and Italy in which such rights received a high degree of formal constitutional protection. Unless a way could be found of assuring protection for fundamental rights in Community law, the legitimacy of the exercise of powers by Community organs at Brussels was called into question, since the transfer of functions from national governments to the Community would mean that the exercise of those powers would no longer be limited by the need to protect fundamental rights.[98]

After initial hesitation, the European Court of Justice declared in 1969 that it would ensure respect for fundamental human rights in the context of the European Community.[99] Thereafter, in an important series of decisions, the Court went progressively further by declaring that in considering the fundamental rights to be protected, it would have regard not merely to common principles that emerged from the constitutional traditions of member states but also to human rights treaties, in

---

[97] Case 106/77, *Amministrazione delle Finanze dello Stato v. Simmenthal* [1978] E.C.R. 629.

[98] The German Constitutional Court at first refused to accept that Community law should prevail over national protection for human rights (the *Internationale Handelsgesellschaft Case* [1974] 2 C.M.L.R. 540), changing its position only when it had become clear that the European Court of Justice would protect human rights in ensuring the observance of general principles of law in interpretation and application of the European Treaties (the *Wilnsche Handelsgesellschaft Case* [1987] 3 C.M.L.R. 225).

[99] Case 29/69. *Stauder v. City of Ulm* [1969] E.C.R. 419.

particular the European Convention.[100] Without giving up the primacy and autonomy of Community law, the Court is now prepared if necessary to take into account
the extent to which national constitutions protect particular rights and the effect of
the Convention itself.[101] The duty to respect fundamental rights has been declared to
apply not only to measures adopted by organs of the Community,[102] but also to action
taken by national authorities whether in implementing Community law[103] or in derogating from freedoms protected by Community law.[104] But the Luxembourg Court has
refused to intervene to protect fundamental rights in the case of national legislation
that lies outside the scope of Community law.[105]

The European Court of Justice has thus created an unwritten charter of rights for
the Community, by means of a series of judicial decisions and without waiting for a
written charter of rights to emerge from the political process. The Court has been
criticized for expanding its jurisdiction into areas that should be reserved for national
courts. One risk that this dimension of Community law creates is the possibility of
divergent decisions being made by the Luxembourg and Strasbourg Courts. The danger is not merely that the two Courts take a different view of the same fundamental
rights, although this has occurred,[106] but also that conflicts may develop between the
two jurisdictions. In fact, so far as the acts of Community organs are concerned, an
actual conflict is unlikely for the reason that the Community and its organs are not
parties to the Convention and are thus outside Strasbourg's jurisdiction.[107] The position is different in respect of action by national authorities that may fall within the
province of Community law, since action by those authorities is in principle subject to

---

[100] The cases are reviewed in T. C. Hartley, *The Foundations of European Community Law* (5th edn. 2003),
chap. 5; and P. Craig and G. de Burca, *EU Law: Text, Cases and Materials* (3rd edn. 2002), chap. 7. *See also*
M. Hunt, *Using Human Rights Law in English Courts* (1997), chap. 7; N. Grief, 'The Domestic Impact of the
E.C.H.R. as mediated through Community Law', [1991] *Public Law* 555; and Ress, *supra* n. 48, at 849–51.

[101] Case 44/79, *Hauer v. Land Rheinland-Pfalz* [1979] E.C.R. 3727 (review of restrictions on right of property under the Convention, First Protocol, Art. 1 and the German, Italian and Irish constitutions).

[102] As in the *Stauder, Internationale Handelsgesellschaft* and *Hauer* cases *supra. See*, e.g., Case C–331/88,
R. v. Ministry of Agriculture, ex parte Fédération Europénne de la Santé Animale [1991] 1 C.M.L.R. 507; Council
Dir. 88/146/EEC could not authorize retrospective criminal proceedings in breach of Art. 7, E.C.H.R.

[103] *See*, e.g., *Johnston v. Chief Constable, Royal Constabulary* Case No. 222/84, [1986] E.C.R. 1651; para.
18 of the judgment notes that Arts. 6 and 13 E.C.H.R. embody a requirement of judicial control which is a
'general principle of law which underlies the constitutional traditions common to the member states'. *See
also* Case 63/83, *R. v. Kent Kirk* [1984] E.C.R. 2689 and Case 5/88, *Wachauf v. Germany* [1989] E.C.R. 2609.

[104] Case C–260/89, *ERT case* [1991] E.C.R. 1–2925.

[105] *See*, e.g., Case 12/86, *Demirel v. Stadt Schwäbisch Gmünd* [1987] E.C.R. 3719 (Turkish woman ordered
to leave Germany).

[106] Thus in 1989 the E.C.J. held that Art. 8 E.C.H.R. did not protect business premises against an intrusive
search in enforcement of competition law: Cases 46/87 & 227/88, *Hoechst v. Commission* [1989] E.C.R. 2859.
The Strasbourg Court has held that Art. 8 is capable of protecting business premises: *Niemietz v. Germany*,
16 Dec. 1992 (No. 251B), 16 E.H.R.R. 97. For different approaches to the right not to incriminate oneself,
see Case 374/87, *Orkem v. Commission* [1989] E.C.R. 3283 and *Funke v. France*, 25 Feb. 1993 (No. 256A), 16
E.H.R.R. 297.

[107] On 28 Mar. 1996, the European Court of Justice in *Opinion 2/94* [1996] E.C.R. I–1759 held that the
Treaty of Rome would need to be amended by the member states to enable the Community to accede to the
Convention.

the Convention. Thus a national decision may be challenged for breach of fundamental rights before the Luxembourg Court and for breach of Convention rights before the Strasbourg Court, and may succeed in one and not in the other.[108] No way yet exists of preventing such conflicts, which scarcely make for legal certainty.

The development of this evolving relationship has not been solely the work of the European Court of Justice. On 5 April 1977, the European Parliament, Council and Commission adopted a joint declaration which stressed the importance that they attached to the protection of fundamental rights, derived in particular from national constitutions and the Convention. In 1989, the European Parliament issued a more elaborate Declaration of Fundamental Rights and Freedoms, although this lacked the force of law.[109]

In 1992, by Article F(2) of the Treaty of Maastricht, which created the European Union, the 12 Community states resolved that the Union would respect fundamental rights, guaranteed by the Convention and by constitutional traditions common to the member states, as general principles of Community law. The Community's commitment to protecting fundamental rights was taken further by the Amsterdam Treaty of 1 October 1997, which confirmed the Maastricht provision by declaring that the European Union:

is founded on the principles of liberty, democracy, respect for human rights and fundamental freedoms, and the rule of law, principles which are common to the Member States.

Respect for human rights was stated to be a precondition for accession to the Community. The 1997 Treaty also extended the power of the European Court of Justice to supervise co-operative measures in the fields of justice and home affairs, and authorized the imposition of sanctions upon states that seriously and persistently violate fundamental rights. These new provisions did not, however, settle comprehensively the position of fundamental rights within the European Union. In June 1999, the meeting of the European Council at Cologne initiated a process designed to lead to the adoption of a European Union Charter to consolidate fundamental rights at the level of the Union. This Charter was to contain a statement of fundamental rights and freedoms as well as the rights guaranteed by the European Convention on Human Rights and derived from the constitutional traditions common to Member States and already enjoyed as general principles of Community law.

In October 1999, the European Council authorized the appointment of a 'Convention' of 62 persons to prepare such a Charter, working within a time limit of nine months. The final text prepared by this body was on 7 December 2000 at Nice 'solemnly proclaimed' by the presidents of the European Parliament, the Council of Ministers and the European Commission to be the European Union Charter of Fundamental Rights. Although so proclaimed, the need for the Charter and its contents were not universally

---

[108] *See*, e.g., Case C–159/90, *Society for Protection of Unborn Children (Ireland) Ltd v. Grogan* [1991] E.C.R. I–4685 (E.C.J.) and *Open Door Counselling and Dublin Woman v. Ireland*, 29 Oct. 1992, 15 E.H.R.R. 244.
[109] [1989] OJ C120/51; EC Bull. 4/1989.

agreed (being opposed in particular by the United Kingdom) and the Charter was not legally enforceable. The Charter is a much longer document than the European Convention on Human Rights. The 50 rights that it declares derive from many existing European and international texts; they include economic and social rights as well as civil and political rights, and deal with current issues such as the protection of personal data and issues as to bioethics. The Charter is addressed to the institutions of the Union and to the member states only when they are implementing Union law. Where it includes rights found also in the ECHR, those rights are to have the same 'meaning and scope' as those contained in the ECHR.

The EU Charter of Fundamental Rights was thereafter incorporated in the proposed draft Constitution for Europe, issued in 2003. Adoption of the draft Constitution was subject to ratification by all EU member states, and in 2005, the electorate in France and the Netherlands voted against the proposed Constitution. There the matter rested until the meeting of the European Council in Brussels in June 2007, when the Council issued a mandate for the preparation of a treaty to reform the existing EU treaties, with the intention that the Reform Treaty would be in force in June 2009 and would include the Charter of Fundamental Rights. Sustained opposition from the United Kingdom to the Charter led to the European Council agreeing to an additional protocol, stating that 'the Charter does not extend the ability of the Court of Justice, or any court or tribunal of the United Kingdom, to find that the laws, regulations or administrative provisions...of the United Kingdom are inconsistent with the fundamental rights, freedoms and principles' affirmed in the Charter. Further, in case there should be any doubt on the matter, the Council also agreed that 'nothing in the Charter creates justiciable rights applicable to the United Kingdom except in so far as the United Kingdom has provided for such rights in its national law'.

At the time of writing, it remains to be seen whether the time-table for giving legal effect to the EU Charter of Fundamental Rights will be observed; and, if so, what the effects of the Charter will be on the legal systems of Europe, and whether the United Kingdom will be able to maintain its insular position in respect of the Charter. These are not merely questions as to technicalities, involving as they do far-reaching issues about the future integration of European law and government.[110]

---

[110] The vast literature on the place of human rights in European law includes P. Alston (ed.), *The EU and Human Rights* (1999). For a perceptive survey of the issues discussed in this section, *see* S. Douglas-Scott, *Constitutional Law of the European Union* (2002). Also R. Blackburn, in *Fundamental Rights in Europe* (n. 48 *supra*), pp. 89–100.

15

PROBLEMS AND PROSPECTS

What are the prospects for European human rights law? In many ways, it is already a remarkable triumph. Sitting at the apex of the most successful international legal regime for the protection of human rights, the European Court of Human Rights has generated, as we have seen, a remarkable jurisprudence, having rendered hundreds of judgments about a wide range of specific substantive human rights. Moreover, the Strasbourg system has made an enormous impact on the legal and administrative processes of most, if not all, of its 47 member states, a quarter of all countries in the world.

However, Strasbourg's very success has created its own problems, four of which we examine here. First is the problem of case load. Now that European human rights law is perceived as so important, individuals and their lawyers are flooding Strasbourg with applications, more than 40,000 each year. The Court generates about 800 judgments a year, a number simultaneously too small and too large. On the one hand, 800 judgments are too few because they leave 98 per cent of all applications unadjudicated. On the other hand, 800 is too many because they swamp the Court with too much work and the Court has to struggle to generate measured and thoughtful judgments. This, then, is Strasbourg's second problem: intellectual coherence.

The third problem is coverage. Despite the many protections of the Convention, there remain important human rights unprotected by the Strasbourg system. The fourth problem is compliance. Although, European human rights law has an efficacy second to none among international human rights regimes, there are still too many troubling instances of non-compliance. We turn now to readings and commentary about these problems—case load, coherence, coverage and compliance—and ask about Strasbourg's prospects.

A. WHAT TO DO ABOUT CASE LOAD AND COHERENCE?

Almost every participant in and observer of European human rights law agrees that the principal and foremost challenge facing Strasbourg is its case load. There are simply more applications coming in than can be reasonably and coherently handled. It is also generally agreed that neither Protocol No. 11, which came into force in 1998, nor Protocol No. 14, which, as of September 2007 still awaited a single remaining state ratification, Russia's, to permit implementation, have adequately addressed these problems. Following are three accounts of the case load and coherence problems and a short commentary.

1. THE FLOOD OF APPLICATIONS

L. Wildhaber
'Changing Ideas About the Tasks of the European Court of Human Rights'
The European Court of Human Rights 1998–2006:
History, Achievements, Reform 136, 141–145, 148–149 (2006)

After the disappearance of the iron curtain in 1989, the Convention mechanism spread to the 'new democracies' of central and eastern Europe. These were allowed to join the Council of Europe relatively quickly, raising the number of member States to 45, compared to 22 at the beginning of 1989. The new members were all required to ratify the Convention within a year of joining. Until the entry into force of Protocol No. 11 in 1998, the effect of the eastward expansion on case numbers was slow initially, but it became increasingly marked as time went by. After 1998, the shift in the balance towards the new member States certainly became very much more obvious.

Discussion about reform had already begun in 1985, at the Swiss government's instigation, so it predated the post-1989 eastward expansion. By 1985, it was already obvious that part-time institutions would no longer be able to cope with the increase in applications from the 21 member States of the time, so it was decided to merge the Commission and the Court into a single, full-time institution. In retrospect it can be seen that the rapid pace of change surpassed the ability to foresee and anticipate future trends. This is surely the explanation for the lamentable failure to design the new Court as a fully-fledged, independent authority and for its treatment as if it were still a group of part-time experts.

Protocol No. 11 'judicialised' the whole Convention system. The right of individual petition and the jurisdiction of the Court, which had been optional, now became compulsory. The non-binding, somewhat more political aspects of the system (namely the power of the Committee of Ministers to approve reports by the Commission) were abolished. However, the extent of this 'judicialisation' should not be overestimated either, for the Committee of Ministers still takes decisions on the Court's budget and the execution of judgments, and the Convention system is still just as reliant on co-operation in good faith by the national authorities.

On the whole the Convention system seemed in 1998 to be tending more towards the idea of a comprehensive right of individual petition, although it was still highly uncertain how many of the participants realised just what kind of journey they had embarked upon. The initial focus on fundamental questions of democracy and the rule of law was still evident mainly in the few leading judgments in which the Convention was described as 'a constitutional instrument of European public order'. The period around 1998 seemed to bring a hopeful change in the Convention system. Signs of the impending overload were ignored, and instead the scales seemed to be tipping in favour of a comprehensive right of individual petition and a role for the Court as a Europe-wide, quasi-constitutional court.

When Protocol No. 11 came into force in 1998, the Court became a full-time body. A consequence of the accession of the new member States and the comprehensive judicialisation of the Convention system was that, from 1998 onwards, the number of applications increased year on year by an average of 15%. In 2004, there were 44,100 applications. As a result of continuous rationalisation, the Court managed to increase its productivity substantially. Between 1998 and 2004, its budget was raised by 54% while the number of settled cases increased by 470%.

Protocol No. 14, which was opened for signature on 13 May 2004, is an attempt to respond to some extent to the flood of applications. The Court's idea of introducing a separate filter system and a new pilot-judgment procedure came to nought. Instead, it was decided to replace the three-judge committee which decided on the admissibility of applications by a single judge supported by rapporteurs. Instead of the seven-judge chambers, a mere three judges would now rule on manifestly well-founded applications. The Council of Europe Commissioner for Human Rights could issue written opinions and take part in public hearings. Lastly, Article 35 of the Convention was amended by Protocol No. 14 to provide that applications from persons who had 'not suffered a significant disadvantage' could be declared inadmissible, provided that the domestic courts had duly assessed such applications in the light of Convention standards and the nature of the application did not necessitate an examination.

What Protocol No. 14 will achieve in detail depends largely on the way in which it is applied by the Court and on whether national courts, governments and parliaments are prepared to transpose the Convention and its case-law effectively into their own national legislation. Protocol No. 14 is quite clearly a compromise. Most states wanted to reduce the number of applications in such a way that the right of individual application would be seen to be undermined as little as possible. Only the principle 'de minimis non curat praetor' (higher authorities shall not deal with trivial matters) was to apply. Monitoring was to be reinforced by bringing in the Human Rights Commissioner. A minority of states, together with the non-governmental organisations, a number of academic commentators and some judges, argued that the right of individual petition should not be touched at all. The fact that this right loses real substance when the processing of applications becomes ever more delayed was basically never refuted. Bafflingly, this aspect was generally simply ignored.

The Warsaw Council of Europe Summit in May 2005 called unanimously for Protocol No. 14 to come into force in 2006.

In the run-up to the Council of Europe Summit in Warsaw in May 2005, two audit reports commissioned by the Secretary General for the period up to the end of 2004 confirmed that the Court would need at least twice the number of staff to be able to deal in a reasonable time with the flood of new cases coming in. Put simply, the audit reports recommended that by the end of 2007, some 500 (or, according to the latest estimates, 660) new posts would have to be created to process all the applications. In order to deal with the 80,000 or so cases pending at the beginning of 2005 (of which some 6,000 fell within the definition of a 'backlog' because they could not be dealt with within the three-year deadline set by the Court itself), just over 1,000 additional posts would have to be created on a temporary basis. This would mean a 75% increase in the Court's budget, which came to some €42 million in 2005, by 2007. A further 25% would have to be contributed to the Council of Europe's overall administration costs.

...

It is important to make the Convention system more effective and credible again and refocus it on its priorities. The point of the individual petition mechanism must be to bring serious human rights violations to Strasbourg, even against the will of the relevant governments. For most of the manifestly ill-founded applications the Court's examination should perhaps be reduced to a kind of ombudsperson's function. And the thousands or perhaps tens of thousands of manifestly well-founded applications on grounds of excessively lengthy proceedings or failure to enforce final judgments ought to be repatriated to domestic legal systems... provided that the Court settles these issues by means of pilot judgments and can subsequently keep them under regular supervision.

The solution will probably come from a mixed package of measures. Whatever happens, it seems to me indisputable that the current system of an unrestricted right of individual petition is no longer capable of attaining the right goals and priorities, that, as a result of the system, too many important applications go unsettled for too long, and that the Convention system needs a new direction if it is not to be submerged by the flood of applications or lose all credibility.

2. A VICTIM OF ITS OWN SUCCESS?

P. L. McKaskle
'The European Court of Human Rights:
What It Is, How It Works, and Its Future'
40 *University of San Francisco Law Review* 1, 58–63 (2005)

The Strasbourg Court has become a victim of its own success. It has received an increasing flood of applications seeking relief and is finding it increasingly difficult to keep up with the caseload. Almost from the beginning it has taken a long time between the triggering event and a final decision by the Court. When it was a two-tier process, with proceedings in a Commission before an appeal could be made to the Court, it sometimes took the better part of a decade between the triggering event and the Court's final decision, and by then, in some cases, no truly effective relief was available. In other words, as the cliché goes, justice delayed is justice denied.

The Strasbourg Court and its parent organization, the Council of Europe, have been well aware of the huge problem of increasing numbers of cases with which the Court must deal. During the Court's early years, it had only a small number of cases to decide, but today it considers many thousands of cases and issues hundreds of judgments. Part of the increase is due to the expansion in the number of countries that are member states of the Convention, and part of the increase is due to increased awareness of citizens of member states of the opportunity to seek relief from the Court. In addition, expansive interpretations of the scope of the Convention very likely add to the volume of cases.

...

In sum, the Court has been and will continue to be confronted with a serious problem because of the growing volume of cases it must decide, and the problem will, almost undoubtedly get worse. In 2000, a three-person Evaluation Group (including the President of the Court) was set up by the Council of Europe, and it filed a fairly comprehensive report on the problem making a number of suggestions. Many of the suggestions sounded similar to methods used by courts of last resort in the United States. The Evaluation Group suggested at least some discretionary authority on the part of the Court to reject cases (or at least treat them in summary fashion) if they 'raise an issue that is, in the view of the Court, of ... minor or secondary importance'. It also suggested creating a mechanism to remit (or remand) cases back to national authorities for reconsideration; that 'senior officials' of the Registrar's office be given power to decide procedural issues or that independent persons be appointed with 'judicial status' to carry out many of the duties currently undertaken by a judge-rapporteur or by the three judges who make up the various committees of the Court.

The Committee of Ministers of the Council of Europe then set up internal review committees to consider the Evaluation Group report and recommendations. After two and a half years of internal review and reports, in 2004, the Committee of Ministers adopted Protocol 14 and circulated it for member state approval. Protocol 14 incorporated only some of the Evaluation Group's recommendations. It provides that a single judge initially screen cases for admissibility instead of a three-judge committee; it allows a three-judge committee (instead of a seven-judge Chamber) to render a judgment on the merits of a case 'if the underlying question in the case, concerning the interpretation or the application of the Convention ... is already the subject of well established case-law of the Court'; and it permits the Court to declare an application inadmissible where 'the applicant has not suffered a significant disadvantage,' unless the issue has not been duly considered by a tribunal of the defendant member state. Protocol 14 also provides that judges will serve a nine year nonrenewable term.

The provisions authorizing use of a single judge to reject applications lacking merit and three-judge committees to decide repetitive cases will help somewhat in dealing with the burgeoning caseload. Unfortunately, it appears likely to improve things only marginally. Granted, this reduces the collective amount of time judges spend on admission decisions and repetitive case decisions, thereby allowing judges more time to deal with more important matters. But as to admission decisions, it may be little more than regularizing what might go on under the present system. It may well be that the great bulk of the current admissibility decisions are made almost entirely on the basis of the recommendations of the deputy registrar assigned to the case, and by the position taken by the judge 'rapporteur' who initially handles the case. If so, not a great deal of time is saved. Somewhat similarly, as to repetitive cases, even if they make up as much as sixty percent of the current caseload, the amount of time deciding them (if the case law is truly clear and there are no unusual factors) should be a far smaller percentage of judge time.

In sum, though the proposals appear laudable, they do not seem to provide a real answer to the problem facing the Court. The original Evaluation Group suggestions were somewhat more far-reaching. They envisioned that the Court would have the power to simply remand cases to member state courts and to decline to hear cases that raise relatively minor issues—at least until it appeared that some guidance was required from the Court. The peculiar relation of the Court to the member states may make it impossible to establish an effective method of remand, and there is a real political reluctance to restrict access to the Court. As such, perhaps the changes incorporated in Protocol 14 are all that are politically possible at this time. More far-reaching reforms, politically impossible at this time, may have to wait until the Court has sunk deeper in the morass of cases pending but unheard.

3. PILOT JUDGMENTS

Report of the Group of Wise Persons to the Committee of Ministers
Council of Europe, Committee of Ministers, CM (2006) 2003, 15 November 2006
www.coe.int (accessed on 26 February, 2007)

Among the many different initiatives taken by the Court to speed up the processing of the cases brought before it, the Group focused particular attention on the measures to facilitate increased use of the 'pilot judgment' procedure.

In its judgment of 22 June 2004 in the *Broniowski v. Poland* case, which concerned the compatibility with the Convention of legislative provisions affecting a large number of people (approximately 80,000), the Court for the first time found a systemic violation, which it defined as a situation where 'the facts of the case disclose the existence, within the [domestic] legal order, of a shortcoming as a consequence of which a whole class of individuals have been or are still denied the peaceful enjoyment of [a right safeguarded by the Convention]' and where 'the deficiencies in national law and practice identified in the applicant's individual case may give rise to numerous subsequent well-founded applications'. The Court also found in this case that the violation originated in a 'widespread problem which resulted from a malfunctioning of Polish legislation and administrative practice and which has affected and remains capable of affecting a large number of persons'.

In that connection, the Court directed that 'the respondent State must, through appropriate legal measures and administrative practice, secure the implementation of the property right in question in respect of the remaining . . . claimants or provide them with equivalent redress in lieu, in accordance with the principles of protection of property rights under Article 1 of Protocol No. 1.'

The object in the Court's designating a case for a 'pilot-judgment procedure' is to facilitate the most speedy and effective resolution of a dysfunction affecting the protection of the Convention right in question in the national legal order. One of the relevant factors considered by the Court in devising and applying that procedure has been the growing threat to the Convention system resulting from large numbers of repetitive cases that derive from, among other things, the same structural or systemic problem (see judgment of 19 June 2006 in the case of *Hutten-Czapska v. Poland*, para 234).

In its Rules for the supervision of the execution of judgments of 10 May 2006 [CM(2006)90], the Committee of Ministers said that it will give priority to supervision of judgments in which the Court has identified a systemic problem (Rule 4, paragraph 1). In addition, Resolution (2004)3 of the Committee of Ministers on judgments revealing an underlying systemic problem invited the Court to identify in these judgments what it considered to be the underlying systemic problem and the source of this problem and to notify such judgments to, among others, the states concerned and the Committee of Ministers.

The Group supports these developments. In the light of practical experience, consideration would need to be given in future to the question of whether the existing judicial machinery, including the Court's rules of procedure, will suffice for this model to be able to produce the desired results or whether a reform of the Convention should be contemplated in this connection. In any event, the Group encourages the Court to use the 'pilot judgment' procedure as far as possible in future. To ensure that victims who have already applied to the Court do not have to wait indefinitely for just satisfaction, time-limits subject to supervision by the Court should be laid down.

4. COPING WITH THE CASE LOAD AND COHERENCE

The problem of the flood of applications is well set out in the first reading from Luzius Wildhaber, the Swiss judge on the Court from 1991 to 2006. Judge Wildhaber, who served as President of the Court from 1998 to 2006, points out that the case load problem was identified well before the expansion of the system to central and eastern Europe in the 1990s. Both Protocol No. 11, in force in 1998, and Protocol No. 14, which might be in force in 2008, aim to simplify the Court's procedures and permit Strasbourg to deal with more cases.

The next reading, from an American observer is critical of the reforms so far. Professor McKaskle argues that the Court needs to be given even more discretion to easily dismiss most applications, so as to focus on the most important cases. The third reading is an excerpt from the Report of the Group of Wise Persons, an *ad hoc* body tasked by the Council of Europe's Committee of Ministers to suggest improvements *beyond* those provided for in Protocol No. 14. We read about one of their suggestions, perhaps the most important: pilot-judgments, which might diminish some of the repeated applications reaching the Court about a single sort of violation against a member state.

Central to all the readings above is the tension between two laudable goals of the Strasbourg system. On the one hand, there is a wish that, in the words of eight nongovernmental human rights organizations, 'the Court continues to recognize that the process of filtering out such claims remains a judicial one and consequently falls clearly within the Court's responsibility'.[1] On the other hand, as we can see from the excerpts above, there is a desire that the Court escape from much of its admissibility work so that it can prepare carefully-wrought judgments setting out significant models or precedents. This second goal, giving the Court more opportunity to address meaningful cases, seems to be preferred by the member states, the Council of Europe, and the Court itself. It is, however, opposed, not only by the NGOs, but by some critics, who complain that stream-lining the system has as 'its most unfortunate development...the apparent intention to go through and close "undeserving" cases quickly, whatever the implications'.[2]

Other than Protocols No. 11 and No. 14 and the suggestions above, how might this tension between paying careful attention to all applications and producing a

---

[1] *NGO Comments on the Group of Wise Persons—Interim Report* 3, Amnesty International (August 2006).

[2] M.-B. Dembour, ' "Finishing Off" Cases: The Radical Solution to the Problem of the Expanding ECHR Caseload', 5 *European Human Rights Law Review* 604, 622 (2002).

meaningful jurisprudence be relieved? One possibility would be simply to increase the number of judges sitting on the Court. However, governments are reluctant to spend even more than they already do on the Strasbourg system. Moreover, there could be new difficulties in achieving a consistent and meaningful body of case law. As the then Registrar of the Court, Paul Mahoney, argued in 2002, '[g]enuine collegiality capable of producing a consistent coherent case law would be impossible in a Court comprising 90 judges'.[3] A compromise might be a new two-tiered system, the lower level reminiscent of the now-departed Commission, with new Strasbourg trial judges deciding at first instance, and then a smaller high court, reminiscent of the old pre-1998 Court, that would decide only the more important or precedent-setting cases.

B. WHAT TO DO ABOUT COVERAGE AND COMPLIANCE?

1. EXTENDING THE RIGHTS PROTECTED

Jacobs & White, The European Convention on Human Rights 512–513
(C. Overy & R.C.A. White 4th edn. 2006)

The rights protected in the Convention and its Protocols are traditional civil and political rights. Yet even this restricted range of rights has not found universal acceptance even among the existing Contracting Parties. There are significant gaps in the ratifications to Protocol 1 on rights of property, education, and to free elections, to Protocol 4 on freedom of movement and related rights, and to Protocol 7 on certain rights connected with the criminal process and equality in marriage. Protocol 12 adds a general right to equality of treatment; it has entered into force, but awaits ratification by most States in western Europe, and has not even been signed by some States. Around a quarter of the Contracting States have yet to ratify Protocol 13.

In the past, there have been calls for a protocol dealing with the rights of persons deprived of their liberty, where such current protection as exists arises from the interaction of a number of provisions of the Convention.

...

Within the Council of Europe, there is certain to be a debate concerning the content of the Convention, which very much reflects the agenda of civil and political rights in 1950. Already, there is evidence of specialist arrangements providing for more detailed treatment of particular areas. The range of rights protected under the developing case law under Article 8 of the

---

[3] P. Mahoney, 'New Challenges for the European Court of Human Rights Resulting from the Expanding Case Load and Membership', 21 *Penn State International Law Review* 101, 106 (2002).

Convention suggests that there is a place for more detailed rules on the protection of privacy, and on environmental rights. There are also important rights, which are not touched upon by the Convention. One example is women's rights to equal pay and equal treatment, though there is extensive coverage of these rights in European Community law.

The development of specifically European standards may at some stage produce conflict with other international agreements. The majority of the Contracting Parties to the European Convention are also party to international conventions on human rights protection having a global character. The conflict has so far been avoided because generally the European standards have been more explicitly and better developed than any global counterpart. It is also true that where other international bodies have been called upon to determine the content of rights protected, they have made reference to the deliberations of the European Court of Human Rights on similar issues. The result has been that, to date, the other international regimes have provided a base line of protection which the European Convention system has further developed as the minimum guarantee of protection in each of the Contracting States. These, in turn, have been able in many cases to provide a higher level of protection than the minimum level required by the European Convention throughout the jurisdictions of all the Contracting States.

2. ADDING THE EUROPEAN UNION

H. C. Krüger
'Reflections Concerning Accession of the European Communities
to the European Convention on Human Rights'
21 *Penn State International Law Review* 89, 92–96 (2002)

The best means of achieving the necessary coherence between the European Convention on Human Rights and Community law is for the European Communities or the European Union to accede to the former. This has repeatedly been advocated by not only the Council of Europe's Secretary General and Parliamentary Assembly, but also by the European Commission and the European Parliament. In a resolution adopted on March 16, 2000, the European Parliament once again called on the Intergovernmental Conference 'to enable the Union to become a party to the European Convention on Human Rights so as to establish close co-operation with the Council of Europe, whilst ensuring that appropriate action is taken to avoid possible conflicts or overlapping between the Court of Justice of the European Communities and the European Court of Human Rights.'

Accession and the European Union Charter should be seen not as in the alternative, but, rather, complementary. At the drafting Convention's very first sitting on December 17, 1999, European Union Commissioner António Vitorino said that the adoption of a Charter of Fundamental Rights would neither prevent accession to the European Convention on Human Rights nor make it unnecessary. In view of the progress of integration within the European Union, it seems appropriate for the European Union to have a written bill of rights, not unlike most of its member States. Article 53 of the European Convention on Human Rights makes it clear that the Convention does not aim to restrict or prejudice in any way more extensive national or international guarantees of fundamental rights. For reasons of legal clarity and legal certainty, accession to the European Convention on Human Rights would be a logical and sensible addition to the Charter.

The arguments used in the past to support accession have gained added weight through the extension of the European Union's powers by the Treaties of Amsterdam and Nice. Accession would improve the protection of citizens' fundamental rights and lead to a coherent system for human rights protection in Europe. Achieving this coherence is not simply a legal, but also a highly political matter. Just over 10 years after the fall of the Berlin Wall, it makes no sense to create a new division in Europe and to undermine the effectiveness of the most successful system ever devised for the protection of human rights. As far back as 1979, the European Commission declared that 'the European Convention on Human Rights and the protection of fundamental rights ensured by the Court of Justice of the European Communities essentially have the same aim, namely the protection of a heritage of fundamental rights considered inalienable by those European States organized on a democratic basis. The protection of this Western European heritage should ultimately be uniform and accordingly assigned, as regards the Community also, to those bodies set up specifically for this purpose.'

The credibility of the European Union's human rights policy is at stake, too. There is a growing contradiction between the human rights commitments demanded from non-European Union States, for instance in connection with development aid and association agreements, and the lack of any external scrutiny whatsoever of the Union's own actions. Does it really make sense to make ratification of the European Convention on Human Rights a condition for European Union membership, when the European Union itself, and its legislation, are wholly exempt from supervision by the Convention bodies?

Since the European Communities are not Parties to the European Convention on Human Rights, Europeans have, at present, no possibility of bringing complaints against the European Union institutions directly before the European Court of Human Rights. Following the adoption of a European Union Charter of Fundamental Rights, it seems increasingly anachronistic that the European Union should be the only 'legal space' left in Europe which is not subject to external scrutiny by the Strasbourg Court. While all national laws, regulations, court judgments, and other measures fall within that court's jurisdiction, European Union legal acts do not.

There have been two major objections to accession. These objections relate to the autonomy of the European Union's legal system and the problem of subordination of the European Court of Justice to the European Court of Human Rights. The following remarks are an attempt to answer these objections.

Any scheme for integration of the European Union into the European Convention on Human Rights system must allow for the autonomy of the Community legal system and the special status of the European Court of Justice. Under Article 220 of the European Community Treaty (ex Article 164), the Court of Justice of the European Communities is the ultimate authority on the interpretation of all Community law. But is it appropriate to talk of autonomy when the protection of fundamental and human rights is the issue? These rights are not merely another area into which Community competence will extend. The idea of human rights is based on universal values and, in Europe, that idea has found expression in the European Convention on Human Rights and in the establishment of the European Court of Human Rights as an independent international supervisory body. When it comes to the protection of fundamental and human rights, the European Convention on Human Rights and Community law is based on the same values and principles. In other words, accession in no way means that the European

Union must be incorporated into a legal order foreign to its nature. Instead, it would simply be recognizing the international monitoring system, which applies to all its member States. All of these member States have accepted supervision by the European Court of Human Rights, and the European Union itself should now do the same. No one can claim, for instance, that the German Constitutional Court or the Finnish Supreme Court neglect fundamental rights in their rulings. Like the Court of Justice of the European Communities, they have an excellent reputation. Nevertheless, the existence of a European monitoring system, operating outside the national systems whose legal measures it examines, gives the public a guarantee that their rights will be protected—and dispensing with the monitoring system is unthinkable.

In the debate on European Union accession to the European Convention on Human Rights, it has been suggested that establishing a sequence of courts from the Court of Justice of the European Communities to the European Court of Human Rights would leave the Court of Justice subordinate to a Council of Europe body. This overlooks the fact that the European Court of Human Rights would by no means review all the European Court of Justice's judgments. The jurisdiction of the Court of Human Rights would be limited to cases raising issues involving the protection of fundamental and human rights under the European Convention on Human Rights. These constitute a small percentage of the cases brought before the Court of Justice. Moreover, the subsidiarity principle, which governs the Strasbourg system's relationship with national authorities—and which the Strasbourg Court has repeated emphasized—would also apply. Even after accession, the European Union institutions, including the Court of Justice and the Court of First Instance, would primarily be responsible for ensuring that the rights enshrined in the Convention were respected. Supervision by the European Court of Human Rights is subsidiary in character, a fact reflected, in particular, in the recognition of national margins of appreciation. The issue here is not subordination or primacy of courts, but, rather, the submission of final decisions on alleged violations of fundamental rights to a uniform, specialized, pan-European body, with power merely to verify whether Community law and Community measures are compatible with fundamental rights. The Strasbourg Court is in no sense a higher court than the Supreme Courts or the Constitutional Courts of other countries. It is simply a 'more specialized' court, responsible under the European Convention on Human Rights for '[ensuring] the observance of the engagements undertaken by the High Contracting Parties in the Convention and the Protocols thereto'.

If the European Union acceded to the European Convention on Human Rights, the tasks of the Luxembourg and Strasbourg Courts would be complementary. The Court of Justice of the European Communities would continue to review the final decisions on all questions of Community law. If the Strasbourg Court found incompatibilities between the Convention and European Community or European Union law, the relevant European Union institutions would then be responsible for taking the action needed to bring the corresponding regulations, or their application in specific cases, into line with the Conventions's requirements. Like other Parties, the European Union institutions would, under Article 46, paragraph 1, of the European Convention on Human Rights, have a measure of discretion in executing the Strasbourg Court's judgments. In other words, external scrutiny in the field of fundamental and human rights in no way conflicts with the Court of Justice's role as the court of last instance for the interpretation of Community law.

3. IMPLEMENTING JUDGMENTS

Parliamentary Assembly, Council of Europe
'Implementation of Judgments of the European Court of Human Rights'
Doc. 11020 (18 September 2006), at 1, 11–12, 14–18

The Parliamentary Assembly stresses that the authority of the European Court of Human Rights depends on the effective execution of its judgments by member states. Although by virtue of Article 46 of the European Convention on Human Rights, the supervision of judgments is the responsibility of the Committee of Ministers, this report confirms that the Assembly and parliaments of member states can, and increasingly do, contribute substantially to the speedy and effective implementation of the Court's judgments.

The Assembly's Committee of Legal Affairs and Human Rights has now taken a more proactive approach by giving priority to the examination of cases which concern major structural problems and in which unacceptable delays of implementation have arisen, especially in five states: Italy, the Russian Federation, Turkey, Ukraine and the United Kingdom. Special *in situ* visits were paid by the Committee's rapporteur to these states to examine, with national decision-makers and parliaments, the urgent need to solve outstanding problems. Reasons for non-compliance and difficulties in execution of the Strasbourg Court's judgments in eight other states (Bulgaria, France, Germany, Greece, Latvia, Moldova, Poland and Romania) were also analysed on the basis of written replies received from parliamentary delegations of these states.

Although recognising positive developments in several states, including special domestic mechanisms put into place in Italy, Ukraine and the United Kingdom, the Committee is gravely concerned with the continuing existence of a number of major structural deficiencies and/or a lack of effective domestic mechanisms in several countries. The need to provide effective domestic mechanisms must, in specific instances, be co-ordinated at the highest political level.

There is an imperative need for member states to accelerate and fully execute judgments of the Strasbourg Court, and the Committee proposes that it continues to monitor the situation closely, especially in states in which major problems have been identified.

...

Italy

a. General situation: important problems of non-compliance

30. In November 2004, the Assembly adopted Recommendation 1684 (2004) and Resolution 1411 (2004) focusing on the implementation problems and called for appropriate action to be taken by Italy and by the Committee of Ministers so as to ensure rapid compliance with the Court's judgments.

31. It appears from the present exercise that the problem of Italy's compliance with the Court's judgments remains a serious concern, both as regards the number of cases pending for a long time before the Committee of Ministers (more than a half of all cases are Italian cases) and the number and the extent of structural problems that remain to be solved to comply with the judgments (some 12% of the structural problems concern Italy).

32. The Committee of Ministers has adopted a number of Interim Resolutions, repeatedly calling for Italy's compliance and suggesting specific measures. However, in spite of these efforts, real, effective progress by Italy has remained insufficient.

33. A number of problematic cases/issues have been selected for this report. It is encouraging that some of them have been solved (e.g. case of *Grand Oriente v. Italy*, where the Region of Marches has amended its legislation impugned by the Court as restricting the freedom of association). Progress in some other areas has been made as showed by the recent public information provided by the Committee of Ministers. However, the three following problems remain of major concern:

— Structural deficiencies of the judicial system resulting in excessively lengthy proceedings, especially in civil cases, which also leads to ineffective protection of a wide range of other substantial rights; this causes large numbers of repetitive violations of the ECHR and represents a serious danger to the Rule of Law and efficient government in Italy;

— Italian law still does not allow reopening of domestic criminal proceedings impugned by the Court; Italy has thus not complied up to this day with its obligations in the *Dorigo case*, where the applicant still suffers from serious consequences of unfair criminal proceedings, more than 6 years after the finding of the violation;

— The systemic problem of 'indirect expropriation', an abusive practice conducted by local authorities to the detriment of the applicants' property rights under the ECHR.

b. Recent measures to improve Italy's capacity to implement the Court's judgments

34. In order to respond to the Assembly's concerns, the Italian Parliament adopted in January 2006 a Bill submitted by the then Chairman of the Italian Delegation to the Assembly, Mr. Azzolini. This Law creates a legislative basis for a special procedure for supervision of the implementation of judgments by the Government and Parliament. In addition the Presidents of the Senate and of the Chamber issued circulars insisting on the importance of systematic verification of the compatibility of draft laws with the Convention with a view to anticipating and more effectively preventing violations.

35. Moreover, a draft Law on reopening of domestic proceedings impugned by the Court, would appear to have recently been transmitted to the newly elected Parliament, although the Rapporteur received conflicting information as to this matter. In parallel, Italian courts appear to be developing a case law ensuring that sanctions imposed in violation of the ECHR cannot be executed. Awaiting the entry into force of the legislative reform, this development has to be strongly supported.

c. Rapporteur's visit to Italy

36. During his visit to Italy on 5–7 July 2006, the Rapporteur welcomed the new constructive attitude of the Italian authorities, not least of the PACE Delegation Chairman, and their understanding that Italy's record of compliance with judgments should be urgently improved. The Rapporteur also noted the positive approaches demonstrated by the Head of Legal and Legislative Affairs Department of the Council of Ministers, the officials of the Ministry of Justice and the members of the Supreme Council of the Judiciary.

37. The Rapporteur notes with interest that the new Government has held a first meeting of a monitoring/co-ordinating group designated to ensure appropriate implementation of the

Azzolini law and strongly encourages its speedy implementation of this law which may play a decisive role in resolving unacceptable systemic problems in Italy.

38. The Rapporteur encourages the Ministry of Justice to complete its work aimed at the improvement of the Pinto law and to permit reopening of judicial proceedings subsequent to an adverse finding by the Strasbourg Court.

39. On a more general level, it is encouraging to hear, from a number of sources within the state apparatus, declarations that the resolution of the problem of the excessive length of the proceedings has at long last been given the top priority. It would appear important to start an in-depth analysis of the root causes of this deeply disturbing phenomenon in Italy, including of the attitudes of the key actors (judges, lawyers, citizens). In this respect, the Rapporteur noted with interest the Supreme Council of the Judiciary's awareness of the need to improve judges—and prosecutors—managerial and administrative skills, to change the professional culture and the attitude to their responsibilities.

40. The Rapporteur stresses that the complexity of the underlying problems is such as to require enhanced and concerted efforts of all actors of the Italian legal system. Thorough reform strategies in this respect still remain to be established. The Rapporteur counts on very close involvement of Parliament in this process.

...

Russian Federation

a. General situation: important systemic problems revealed

55. After the prompt reactions to the first European Court's judgments, the execution process has slowed down in the adoption of further legislative and other reforms to solve important structural problems revealed in Strasbourg.

56. The Russian Federation is presently confronted with an increasing number of complex issues raised in recent judgments of the Court, including some important systemic problems. These problems have already been described in the Supplementary Introductory Memorandum and will only be briefly recalled below:

— the deficient judicial review over pretrial detention, which results in its excessive length and overcrowding of detention facilities (see CM Interim Resolution DH(2003)123);

— chronic non-enforcement of domestic judicial decisions delivered against the State (CM/Inf(2006)19);

— violations of the requirement of legal certainty by extensive quashing of binding judicial decisions through the *nadzor* procedure (CM Interim Resolution DH(2006)1);

— violations found by the Court on account of abuses by the security forces in the Chechen Republic or elsewhere disclose other problems requiring comprehensive measures, including those relating to disappearances (see recent Court judgment of 27/07/2006 in *Bazorkina v. Russia*).

57. The solution to these problems should be sought urgently because they affect a very large number of people in the Russian Federation. The influx of numerous clone cases in the Court is also likely to undermine the effectiveness of the ECHR mechanism.

b. Rapporteur's visit to the Russian Federation

58. The Rapporteur welcomes the frank and open position of most of the Russian officials and institutions he met in Moscow as well as their clear understanding that the above problems put at stake the effectiveness of the Russian judicial system, and indeed, of the State as a whole. It is perhaps indicative that especially the presidents of the Constitutional Court and of the Supreme Court showed a very constructive attitude, as both of them recognized the problems and encouraged the Rapporteur in his endeavours to help find a solution for them.

59. The authorities provided assurances that the most important problems would be addressed as a matter of priority and that appropriate steps would be taken to ensure rapid adoption of reforms required by the European Court's judgments.

60. The Russian officials' clear willingness to come to grips with the aforementioned important problems is most welcome. The Rapporteur stresses that the complexity of these issues is such as to require enhanced and concerted efforts of all actors within the Russian legal system.

61. Thorough reform strategies in this respect, however, still remain to be established. In view of the present problems raised in the judgments and others still to come, the Rapporteur has strongly recommended to the authorities to set up a special mechanism of interagency cooperation in the implementation of Strasbourg Court judgments. Constant involvement of Parliament and the Russian delegation to the Assembly in the implementation process is also necessary. The Rapporteur is convinced that his Russian parliamentary colleagues will seriously consider his recommendation to set up a specific mechanism and procedure for parliamentary oversight to implement Strasbourg Court judgments, as well as other relevant proposals made in the draft resolution. The Rapporteur also trusts that the members of the Russian delegation to the Assembly will promote and follow-up the adoption of the specific measures required by certain judgments.

...

Turkey

a. The general situation

68. It is recalled that the main problems of compliance that have warranted the Rapporteur's special attention with respect to Turkey are as follows:

— The reopening of domestic proceedings in the *Hulki Guneş* case, in which the applicant continues to serve his prison sentence on the basis of the conviction imposed with serious violations of the right to a fair trial;

— Further progress to be made in implementation of the *Cyprus v. Turkey* judgment following the Committee of Ministers—recent Interim Resolution ResDH(2005)44, notably to ensure effective investigations into the fate of Greek Cypriot missing persons;

— Strict implementation of the new legal framework aiming at the respect of the ECHR by the security forces in line with the recent Interim Resolution ResDH(2005)43;

— Application of the current provisions governing freedom of expression and the activity of political parties in accordance with the Convention and the Court's judgments, as prescribes new Article 90 of the Constitution;

— *Doğgan v. Turkey* judgment of 29/06/2004 concerning the problem of compensation to internally displaced persons and of their return to villages in the south-east.

b. Rapporteur's visit to Turkey

69. During his visit to Turkey, on 5–7 April 2006, the Rapporteur discussed the above issues with Foreign Minister Abdullah Gül, decision-makers of the Turkish parliament, government administration and the highest judicial bodies. He welcomes the assurances received from the Turkish authorities that all implementation issues were being addressed 'as a matter of priority'.

70. He noted in particular, with satisfaction, the positive response to the *Doğgan* judgment, following which Turkey adopted and implemented a new Compensation Law, thus providing to internally displaced persons an effective domestic remedy to obtain compensation for property destroyed. The effectiveness of this remedy has been confirmed by the Court in its recent decision in the case of *Ilçyer*. It was noted, however, that the findings of the Court in the case of *Ilçyer* did not address the problem of whether the applicant(s), or persons in the same situation, can, in fact, return to their villages.

71. As regards judgments concerning the freedom of expression, despite the comprehensive reforms adopted, doubts still remain as to whether the authorities interpret the new provisions in conformity with the ECHR. Similar concerns exist in the field of the implementation of the existing rules governing the activities of the security forces.

72. Of great concern is the lack of any progress in the implementation of the *Hulki Guneş* judgment either through the reopening of impugned proceedings or other *ad hoc* measures granting redress to the applicant.

73. The implementation of judgments concerning the Cyprus issue should no doubt call for the special attention of the Assembly and more generally of the Council of Europe. While important progress has been achieved, more remain to be done, not least on the issue of missing persons. The successful implementation of all judgments concerning Cyprus may constitute a valuable and tangible contribution of the Council of Europe to a comprehensive solution of the Cyprus issue. The Rapporteur tried to convey this message to the Turkish authorities and trusts they will enhance their constructive efforts to fully comply with these judgments.

74. He welcomes the assurances received from the Turkish authorities that all implementation issues were being addressed 'as a matter of priority' and looks forward to receiving information about the results so achieved.

United Kingdom

a. General situation

75. The United Kingdom has a relatively big number of old judgments of the Court that have not yet been fully implemented, due principally to delays in adoption of legislation. The Committee of Ministers has been awaiting for years some important legislative or other reforms to be adopted in order, for example, to prohibit the physical punishment of children amounting to ill-treatment, to introduce adequate legal safeguards during detention in mental hospitals, to ensure clarity and precision of 'binding-over' orders and to ensure that no negative conclusion could be drawn from the accused person's silence during interrogation without legal counsel.

76. Of particular importance are the measures required by the Court's judgments finding violations of the ECHR by the security forces in the Northern Ireland. While significant progress was made to prevent new similar violations, issues still remain with regard to the UK's

continuing obligation to conduct effective investigations into the applicants' death so as to remedy the procedural shortcomings highlighted by the Court. In this respect, the domestic courts' failure to order the reexamination of old decisions not to prosecute and the apparent shortcomings related thereto, from the ECHR's viewpoint, of the new Inquiries Act are of particular concern.

b. Progress Report in Parliament on the implementation of judgments

77. On 8 March 2006, the Joint Parliamentary Committee on Human Rights issued its first Progress Report concerning the implementation of the Court's judgments. The Report takes stock of the outstanding implementation problems and of the recent action taken by the authorities to remedy them. The Report also analyses certain general issues, such as the remaining obstacles to the reopening of domestic proceedings, the non-retroactivity of the Human Rights Act, and makes various recommendations in order to improve compliance with judgments.

c. Rapporteur's visit to the United Kingdom

78. During his visit to the United Kingdom on 8–10 March 2006, the Rapporteur hailed the first progress report of the Parliamentary Joint Committee on Human Rights as 'a model to be followed by other parliamentary bodies'. He is grateful to his British colleagues for having positively responded to his previous recommendations to pose parliamentary questions to their Government in relation to the outstanding implementation issues.

79. In his meetings with the competent authorities, the Rapporteur also raised a number of these issues and discussed prospects for their solution. He noted with satisfaction that in most of the cases selected for his report, the United Kingdom swiftly responded to the Court's judgments by adopting interim measures in practice and announced a legal reform to ensure full coherence between the new practice and the legal texts.

80. The Rapporteur has the feeling that the problems of non-implementation in the UK find their basis in the traditional British way of tackling general problems by taking practical measures to solve them. In this case by preventing repetition of the government action which violated the Convention, without at the same time changing formally the legislation or the policy which led to the impugned action in the first place.

81. When legal reforms are announced by a respondent state, the Committee of Ministers tends to wait until their formal (legislative) adoption, considering that the implementation process is not complete until this is done. The authorities are thus encouraged to complete the reforms announced to the Committee of Ministers, unless they conclude that the measures adopted in practice are sufficient so as to obviate the need for further reforms. In so doing, misunderstandings as to why cases remain on the Committee of Ministers agenda for many years—even though in practice the problem has been solved—would be dissipated.

82. The Rapporteur also discussed with the authorities the problematic issue of non-retroactive effect of the Human Rights Act and its consequences for the United Kingdom's capacity to honour its obligation to abide by the Strasbourg Court's judgments, in particular as far as individual measures are concerned. The possibility of using Section 10 (remedial measures) of the Human Rights Act was discussed in this context.

4. ADDRESSING SYSTEMIC VIOLATIONS
OF THE CONVENTION

S. Greer
'Improving Compliance'
The European Convention on Human Rights:
Achievements, Problems and Prospects 278–281 (2006)

As things currently stand—apart from persuasion, suspension of voting rights on the Committee of Ministers, and expulsion—the Council of Europe lacks any direct means of inducing states to improve their Convention violation records. In many countries... systemic violations stem from problems which are simply too intractable to be dealt with by executive or legislative fiat, while in others the national and international legal and political costs of violation rank lower than those associated with making the necessary changes. Among other things... these difficulties could be ameliorated by further development of the Court's currently cautious policy of identifying what needs to be done at the national level to correct the source of violations, and by refinements to the method of adjudication at Strasbourg. However, of themselves these are unlikely to be sufficient. The key question, therefore, is what more the Council of Europe can do to increase domestic compliance pressures. A key element concerns the effective delivery of information from member states to Strasbourg and vice versa. While improving the role of existing national and European institutions may provide part of the answer, ... a case can also be made for the creation of a European Fair Trials Commission.

...

National legal systems are already a key site for the exertion of domestic pressure upon states to improve Convention compliance because, with the possible exception of Russia and some of the Caucasian republics..., the rule of law is now sufficiently well established throughout Europe to ensure that a refusal, by a non-judicial public body, to abide by the clear decision of a national court will rapidly induce a national constitutional crisis which most governments will want to avoid in all but the most exceptional circumstances. However, several problems limit the domestic legal impact which the judgments of the European Court of Human Rights might otherwise have. First, there is 'no obligation arising out of the Convention to make judgments of the ECHR executable within the domestic legal system'... many national courts do not accept that judgments of the European Court of Human Rights are binding on them, even when made against their own state. In 2002, for example, twenty-one European constitutional courts declared themselves not bound by rulings of the European Court of Human Rights, although a larger majority said they were influenced by them.

Second, the orthodox view of Article 46(1)—which provides that the 'High Contracting Parties undertake to abide by the final judgment of the Court in any case to which they are parties'—is that any state is obliged to observe *only* those judgments made directly against it.

...

It is of course open to states to incorporate not only the Convention in national law, but the entire case law of the Strasbourg institutions as binding authority as well. However, most seem to regard the Strasbourg case law as of only 'persuasive' authority, probably in order to avoid limiting the scope of national courts to interpret the Convention to meet national requirements.

While it is difficult to see how Convention compliance can be improved unless all member states regard the entire Convention case law as binding on their national courts, even full erga omnes effect, comprehensively acknowledged, has its limitations. For one thing, there is the enormous challenge of translating the entire Convention acquis into every official European language. Furthermore, even if this were universally achieved it is difficult if not impossible to identify concrete legal norms from the thinly reasoned Strasbourg jurisprudence. It is also very unlikely that the facts upon which any previous decision or judgment of the Strasbourg institutions is based will be repeated in all particulars in another state. As a result, there will virtually always be ample scope for lawyers to persuade national courts to refuse to follow a putatively relevant Strasbourg judgment on the grounds that, although binding authority, it does not cover the facts of the dispute at issue.

The third problem limiting the impact of the Court's judgments on domestic legal systems is that, in spite of the requirement in Article 13 of the Convention to provide effective remedies, and notwithstanding the fact that all member states have either incorporated the Convention into their domestic law—or have substantially the same standards in domestic constitutional bills of rights—not all states have equally effective means by which violations of Convention standards can be litigated in domestic courts. A case can, therefore, be made for Article 13 to be revised to require effective *judicial* remedies to be made available to all member states. This would involve granting jurisdiction to all domestic courts in each member state to consider complaints about the violation of Convention standards when adjudicating complaints against public authorities, and the provision of individual constitutional complaints processes to all national constitutional courts or their equivalents.

5. IMPROVING COVERAGE AND COMPLIANCE

Acknowledging that Strasbourg already has problems handling case load and rendering coherent judgments, should it take on even more work by adding to the rights it is charged to protect? The excerpt from Jacobs & White outlines some of the gaps that still remain in the fabric of European human rights law. The second reading is from Hans-Christian Krüger, a long-time member of the Commission Secretariat and later the Deputy Secretary General of the Council of Europe. He raises what by now is a long-standing and often-frustrated proposal that the European Union institutions based in Brussels be made subject to the Convention and to the supervision of the Strasbourg Court. Is it simply too ambitious, given the present difficulties of case load and coherence, for Strasbourg to take on more work? Or is it more important that Strasbourg's protections be extended? Beyond addressing new rights and adding the EU, should the Strasbourg system be made available to states outside of geographical Europe? When does the system become spread too thin?

Our final problem is compliance. The Report of the Parliamentary Assembly of the Council of Europe documents some of the on-going problems in implementing the judgments of the European Court of Human Rights. The given excerpt focuses only on a few countries identified as having major structural issues. There are of course also difficulties in some states with specific cases. As the Report shows, some countries like Italy, Russia and Turkey generate a disproportionate share of Strasbourg's case load. Looking at Russia, a newspaper article notes that '[m]ore cases against Russia are pending in Strasbourg than against any other country—13,945 at the end of 2005'; Russian complaints in 2005 were a sixth of all those received in Strasbourg.[4] This seems to be due to the failures of the Russian legal system: '[f]rustrated Russians treat Strasbourg as a kind of general court of appeal'.[5]

The final reading, by Professor Greer, looks to improvement in national legal systems as the key to solving the compliance problems. He urges the Court and domestic legal systems to be bolder in treating all Strasbourg judgments as generally legally binding, both on the state and on national judicial proceedings. Would this make the European Court of Human Rights the 'supreme' constitutional court of Europe? Would the member states be willing to cede this much authority to the Strasbourg system?

---

[4] G. Chazan, 'In Russia, Grim Case Spotlights Distress of Justice Denied', *Wall Street Journal*, April 26, 2006, at 1.

[5] *Id.*

APPENDIX A

CONVENTION FOR THE PROTECTION OF HUMAN RIGHTS AND FUNDAMENTAL FREEDOMS AS AMENDED BY PROTOCOL NO. 11 WITH PROTOCOL NOS. 1, 4, 6, 7, 12 AND 13

Registry of the European Court of Human Rights
(accessed 5 June 2007, www.coe.int)

The text of the Convention had been amended according to the provisions of Protocol No. 3 (ETS No. 45), which entered into force on 21 September 1970, of Protocol No. 5 (ETS No. 55), which entered into force on 20 December 1971 and of Protocol No. 8 (ETS No. 118), which entered into force on 1 January 1990, and comprised also the text of Protocol No. 2 (ETS No. 44) which, in accordance with Article 5, paragraph 3 thereof, had been an integral part of the Convention since its entry into force on 21 September 1970. All provisions which had been amended or added by these Protocols are replaced by Protocol No. 11 (ETS No. 155), as from the date of its entry into force on 1 November 1998. As from that date, Protocol No. 9 (ETS No. 140), which entered into force on 1 October 1994, is repealed.

Convention for the protection of Human Rights and Fundamental Freedoms

Rome, 4.XI.1950

The governments signatory hereto, being members of the Council of Europe,

Considering the Universal Declaration of Human Rights proclaimed by the General Assembly of the United Nations on 10th December 1948;

Considering that this Declaration aims at securing the universal and effective recognition and observance of the Rights therein declared;

Considering that the aim of the Council of Europe is the achievement of greater unity between its members and that one of the methods by which that aim is to be pursued is the maintenance and further realization of human rights and fundamental freedoms;

Reaffirming their profound belief in those fundamental freedoms which are the foundation of justice and peace in the world and are best maintained on the one hand by an effective political democracy and on the other by a common understanding and observance of the human rights upon which they depend;

Being resolved, as the governments of European countries which are like-minded and have a common heritage of political traditions, ideals, freedom and the rule of law, to take the first steps for the collective enforcement of certain of the rights stated in the Universal Declaration,

Have agreed as follows:

Article 1—Obligation to respect human rights

The High Contracting Parties shall secure to everyone within their jurisdiction the rights and freedoms defined in Section I of this Convention.

Section I—Rights and freedoms

Article 2—Right to life

1. Everyone's right to life shall be protected by law. No one shall be deprived of his life intentionally save in the execution of a sentence of a court following his conviction of a crime for which this penalty is provided by law.

2. Deprivation of life shall not be regarded as inflicted in contravention of this article when it results from the use of force which is no more than absolutely necessary:

    (a) in defence of any person from unlawful violence;
    (b) in order to effect a lawful arrest or to prevent the escape of a person lawfully detained;
    (c) in action lawfully taken for the purpose of quelling a riot or insurrection.

Article 3—Prohibition of torture

No one shall be subjected to torture or to inhuman or degrading treatment or punishment.

Article 4—Prohibition of slavery and forced labour

1. No one shall be held in slavery or servitude.

2. No one shall be required to perform forced or compulsory labour.

3. For the purpose of this article the term 'forced or compulsory labour' shall not include:

    (a) any work required to be done in the ordinary course of detention imposed according to the provisions of Article 5 of this Convention or during conditional release from such detention;

(b) any service of a military character or, in case of conscientious objectors in countries where they are recognized, service exacted instead of compulsory military service;

(c) any service exacted in case of an emergency or calamity threatening the life or well-being of the community;

(d) any work or service which forms part of normal civic obligations.

Article 5—Right to liberty and security

1. Everyone has the right to liberty and security of person. No one shall be deprived of his liberty save in the following cases and in accordance with a procedure prescribed by law:

   (a) the lawful detention of a person after conviction by a competent court;

   (b) the lawful arrest or detention of a person for non-compliance with the lawful order of a court or in order to secure the fulfilment of any obligation prescribed by law;

   (c) the lawful arrest or detention of a person effected for the purpose of bringing him before the competent legal authority on reasonable suspicion of having committed an offence or when it is reasonably considered necessary to prevent his committing an offence or fleeing after having done so;

   (d) the detention of a minor by lawful order for the purpose of educational supervision or his lawful detention for the purpose of bringing him before the competent legal authority;

   (e) the lawful detention of persons for the prevention of the spreading of infectious diseases, of persons of unsound mind, alcoholics or drug addicts or vagrants;

   (f) the lawful arrest or detention of a person to prevent his effecting an unauthorized entry into the country or of a person against whom action is being taken with a view to deportation or extradition.

2. Everyone who is arrested shall be informed promptly, in a language which he understands, of the reasons for his arrest and of any charge against him.

3. Everyone arrested or detained in accordance with the provisions of paragraph 1.c of this article shall be brought promptly before a judge or other officer authorized by law to exercise judicial power and shall be entitled to trial within a reasonable time or to release pending trial. Release may be conditioned by guarantees to appear for trial.

4. Everyone who is deprived of his liberty by arrest or detention shall be entitled to take proceedings by which the lawfulness of his detention shall be decided speedily by a court and his release ordered if the detention is not lawful.

5. Everyone who has been the victim of arrest or detention in contravention of the provisions of this article shall have an enforceable right to compensation.

Article 6—Right to a fair trial

1. In the determination of his civil rights and obligations or of any criminal charge against him, everyone is entitled to a fair and public hearing within a reasonable time by an independent and impartial tribunal established by law. Judgment shall be pronounced publicly but the press and public may be excluded from all or part of the trial in the interests of morals, public order or national security in a democratic society, where the interests of juveniles or the protection of the private life of the parties so require, or to the extent strictly necessary in the opinion of the court in special circumstances where publicity would prejudice the interests of justice.

2. Everyone charged with a criminal offence shall be presumed innocent until proved guilty according to law.

3. Everyone charged with a criminal offence has the following minimum rights:

    (a) to be informed promptly, in a language which he understands and in detail, of the nature and cause of the accusation against him;
    (b) to have adequate time and facilities for the preparation of his defence;
    (c) to defend himself in person or through legal assistance of his own choosing or, if he has not sufficient means to pay for legal assistance, to be given it free when the interests of justice so require;
    (d) to examine or have examined witnesses against him and to obtain the attendance and examination of witnesses on his behalf under the same conditions as witnesses against him;
    (e) to have the free assistance of an interpreter if he cannot understand or speak the language used in court.

Article 7—No punishment without law

1. No one shall be held guilty of any criminal offence on account of any act or omission which did not constitute a criminal offence under national or international law at the time when it was committed. Nor shall a heavier penalty be imposed than the one that was applicable at the time the criminal offence was committed.

2. This article shall not prejudice the trial and punishment of any person for any act or omission which, at the time when it was committed, was criminal according to the general principles of law recognized by civilized nations.

Article 8—Right to respect for private and family life

1. Everyone has the right to respect for his private and family life, his home and his correspondence.

2. There shall be no interference by a public authority with the exercise of this right except such as is in accordance with the law and is necessary in a democratic society in the interests of national security, public safety or the economic well-being of

the country, for the prevention of disorder or crime, for the protection of health or morals, or for the protection of the rights and freedoms of others.

Article 9—Freedom of thought, conscience and religion

1. Everyone has the right to freedom of thought, conscience and religion; this right includes freedom to change his religion or belief and freedom, either alone or in community with others and in public or private, to manifest his religion or belief, in worship, teaching, practice and observance.

2. Freedom to manifest one's religion or beliefs shall be subject only to such limitations as are prescribed by law and are necessary in a democratic society in the interests of public safety, for the protection of public order, health or morals, or for the protection of the rights and freedoms of others.

Article 10—Freedom of expression

1. Everyone has the right to freedom of expression. This right shall include freedom to hold opinions and to receive and impart information and ideas without interference by public authority and regardless of frontiers. This article shall not prevent States from requiring the licensing of broadcasting, television or cinema enterprises.

2. The exercise of these freedoms, since it carries with it duties and responsibilities, may be subject to such formalities, conditions, restrictions or penalties as are prescribed by law and are necessary in a democratic society, in the interests of national security, territorial integrity or public safety, for the prevention of disorder or crime, for the protection of health or morals, for the protection of the reputation or rights of others, for preventing the disclosure of information received in confidence, or for maintaining the authority and impartiality of the judiciary.

Article 11—Freedom of assembly and association

1. Everyone has the right to freedom of peaceful assembly and to freedom of association with others, including the right to form and to join trade unions for the protection of his interests.

2. No restrictions shall be placed on the exercise of these rights other than such as are prescribed by law and are necessary in a democratic society in the interests of national security or public safety, for the prevention of disorder or crime, for the protection of health or morals or for the protection of the rights and freedoms of others. This article shall not prevent the imposition of lawful restrictions on the exercise of these rights by members of the armed forces, of the police or of the administration of the State.

Article 12—Right to marry

Men and women of marriageable age have the right to marry and to found a family, according to the national laws governing the exercise of this right.

Article 13—Right to an effective remedy

Everyone whose rights and freedoms as set forth in this Convention are violated shall have an effective remedy before a national authority notwithstanding that the violation has been committed by persons acting in an official capacity.

Article 14—Prohibition of discrimination

The enjoyment of the rights and freedoms set forth in this Convention shall be secured without discrimination on any ground such as sex, race, colour, language, religion, political or other opinion, national or social origin, association with a national minority, property, birth or other status.

Article 15—Derogation in time of emergency

1. In time of war or other public emergency threatening the life of the nation any High Contracting Party may take measures derogating from its obligations under this Convention to the extent strictly required by the exigencies of the situation, provided that such measures are not inconsistent with its other obligations under international law.

2. No derogation from Article 2, except in respect of deaths resulting from lawful acts of war, or from Articles 3, 4 (paragraph 1) and 7 shall be made under this provision.

3. Any High Contracting Party availing itself of this right of derogation shall keep the Secretary General of the Council of Europe fully informed of the measures which it has taken and the reasons therefor. It shall also inform the Secretary General of the Council of Europe when such measures have ceased to operate and the provisions of the Convention are again being fully executed.

Article 16—Restrictions on political activity of aliens

Nothing in Articles 10, 11 and 14 shall be regarded as preventing the High Contracting Parties from imposing restrictions on the political activity of aliens.

Article 17—Prohibition of abuse of rights

Nothing in this Convention may be interpreted as implying for any State, group or person any right to engage in any activity or perform any act aimed at the destruction of any of the rights and freedoms set forth herein or at their limitation to a greater extent than is provided for in the Convention.

Article 18—Limitation on use of restrictions on rights

The restrictions permitted under this Convention to the said rights and freedoms shall not be applied for any purpose other than those for which they have been prescribed.

Section II—European Court of Human Rights

Article 19—Establishment of the Court

To ensure the observance of the engagements undertaken by the High Contracting Parties in the Convention and the Protocols thereto, there shall be set up a European Court of Human Rights, hereinafter referred to as 'the Court'. It shall function on a permanent basis.

Article 20—Number of judges

The Court shall consist of a number of judges equal to that of the High Contracting Parties.

Article 21—Criteria for office

1. The judges shall be of high moral character and must either possess the qualifications required for appointment to high judicial office or be jurisconsults of recognized competence.

2. The judges shall sit on the Court in their individual capacity.

3. During their term of office the judges shall not engage in any activity which is incompatible with their independence, impartiality or with the demands of a full-time office; all questions arising from the application of this paragraph shall be decided by the Court.

Article 22—Election of judges

1. The judges shall be elected by the Parliamentary Assembly with respect to each High Contracting Party by a majority of votes cast from a list of three candidates nominated by the High Contracting Party.

2. The same procedure shall be followed to complete the Court in the event of the accession of new High Contracting Parties and in filling casual vacancies.

Article 23—Terms of office

1. The judges shall be elected for a period of six years. They may be re-elected. However, the terms of office of one-half of the judges elected at the first election shall expire at the end of three years.

2. The judges whose terms of office are to expire at the end of the initial period of three years shall be chosen by lot by the Secretary General of the Council of Europe immediately after their election.

3. In order to ensure that, as far as possible, the terms of office of one-half of the judges are renewed every three years, the Parliamentary Assembly may decide, before proceeding to any subsequent election, that the term or terms of office of one or more

judges to be elected shall be for a period other than six years but not more than nine and not less than three years.

4. In cases where more than one term of office is involved and where the Parliamentary Assembly applies the preceding paragraph, the allocation of the terms of office shall be effected by a drawing of lots by the Secretary General of the Council of Europe immediately after the election.

5. A judge elected to replace a judge whose term of office has not expired shall hold office for the remainder of his predecessor's term.

6. The terms of office of judges shall expire when they reach the age of 70.

7. The judges shall hold office until replaced. They shall, however, continue to deal with such cases as they already have under consideration.

Article 24—Dismissal
No judge may be dismissed from his office unless the other judges decide by a majority of two-thirds that he has ceased to fulfil the required conditions.

Article 25—Registry and legal secretaries
The Court shall have a registry, the functions and organization of which shall be laid down in the rules of the Court. The Court shall be assisted by legal secretaries.

Article 26—Plenary Court
The plenary Court shall

   (a) elect its President and one or two Vice-Presidents for a period of three years; they may be re-elected;
   (b) set up Chambers, constituted for a fixed period of time;
   (c) elect the Presidents of the Chambers of the Court; they may be re-elected;
   (d) adopt the rules of the Court, and
   (e) elect the Registrar and one or more Deputy Registrars.

Article 27—Committees, Chambers and Grand Chamber
1. To consider cases brought before it, the Court shall sit in committees of three judges, in Chambers of seven judges and in a Grand Chamber of seventeen judges. The Court's Chambers shall set up committees for a fixed period of time.

2. There shall sit as an *ex officio* member of the Chamber and the Grand Chamber the judge elected in respect of the State Party concerned or, if there is none or if he is unable to sit, a person of its choice who shall sit in the capacity of judge.

3. The Grand Chamber shall also include the President of the Court, the Vice-Presidents, the Presidents of the Chambers and other judges chosen in accordance with the rules of the Court. When a case is referred to the Grand Chamber under

Article 43, no judge from the Chamber which rendered the judgment shall sit in the Grand Chamber, with the exception of the President of the Chamber and the judge who sat in respect of the State Party concerned.

Article 28—Declarations of inadmissibility by committees

A committee may, by a unanimous vote, declare inadmissible or strike out of its list of cases an application submitted under Article 34 where such a decision can be taken without further examination. The decision shall be final.

Article 29—Decisions by Chambers on admissibility and merits

1. If no decision is taken under Article 28, a Chamber shall decide on the admissibility and merits of individual applications submitted under Article 34.

2. A Chamber shall decide on the admissibility and merits of inter-State applications submitted under Article 33.

3. The decision on admissibility shall be taken separately unless the Court, in exceptional cases, decides otherwise.

Article 30—Relinquishment of jurisdiction to the Grand Chamber

Where a case pending before a Chamber raises a serious question affecting the interpretation of the Convention or the protocols thereto, or where the resolution of a question before the Chamber might have a result inconsistent with a judgment previously delivered by the Court, the Chamber may, at any time before it has rendered its judgment, relinquish jurisdiction in favour of the Grand Chamber, unless one of the parties to the case objects.

Article 31—Powers of the Grand Chamber

The Grand Chamber shall

(a) determine applications submitted either under Article 33 or Article 34 when a Chamber has relinquished jurisdiction under Article 30 or when the case has been referred to it under Article 43; and

(b) consider requests for advisory opinions submitted under Article 47.

Article 32—Jurisdiction of the Court

1. The jurisdiction of the Court shall extend to all matters concerning the interpretation and application of the Convention and the protocols thereto which are referred to it as provided in Articles 33, 34 and 47.

2. In the event of dispute as to whether the Court has jurisdiction, the Court shall decide.

Article 33—Inter-State cases

Any High Contracting Party may refer to the Court any alleged breach of the provisions of the Convention and the protocols thereto by another High Contracting Party.

Article 34—Individual applications

The Court may receive applications from any person, non-governmental organization or group of individuals claiming to be the victim of a violation by one of the High Contracting Parties of the rights set forth in the Convention or the protocols thereto. The High Contracting Parties undertake not to hinder in any way the effective exercise of this right.

Article 35—Admissibility criteria

1. The Court may only deal with the matter after all domestic remedies have been exhausted, according to the generally recognized rules of international law, and within a period of six months from the date on which the final decision was taken.

2. The Court shall not deal with any application submitted under Article 34 that

   (a) is anonymous; or
   (b) is substantially the same as a matter that has already been examined by the Court or has already been submitted to another procedure of international investigation or settlement and contains no relevant new information.

3. The Court shall declare inadmissible any individual application submitted under Article 34 which it considers incompatible with the provisions of the Convention or the protocols thereto, manifestly ill-founded, or an abuse of the right of application.

4. The Court shall reject any application which it considers inadmissible under this Article. It may do so at any stage of the proceedings.

Article 36—Third party intervention

1. In all cases before a Chamber of the Grand Chamber, a High Contracting Party one of whose nationals is an applicant shall have the right to submit written comments and to take part in hearings.

2. The President of the Court may, in the interest of the proper administration of justice, invite any High Contracting Party which is not a party to the proceedings or any person concerned who is not the applicant to submit written comments or take part in hearings.

Article 37—Striking out applications

1. The Court may at any stage of the proceedings decide to strike an application out of its list of cases where the circumstances lead to the conclusion that

   (a) the applicant does not intend to pursue his application; or

(b) the matter has been resolved; or

(c) for any other reason established by the Court, it is no longer justified to continue the examination of the application.

However, the Court shall continue the examination of the application if respect for human rights as defined in the Convention and the protocols thereto so requires.

2. The Court may decide to restore an application to its list of cases if it considers that the circumstances justify such a course.

Article 38—Examination of the case and friendly settlement proceedings

1. If the Court declares the application admissible, it shall

(a) pursue the examination of the case, together with the representatives of the parties, and if need be, undertake an investigation, for the effective conduct of which the States concerned shall furnish all necessary facilities;

(b) place itself at the disposal of the parties concerned with a view to securing a friendly settlement of the matter on the basis of respect for human rights as defined in the Convention and the protocols thereto.

2. Proceedings conducted under paragraph 1.b shall be confidential.

Article 39—Finding of a friendly settlement

If a friendly settlement is effected, the Court shall strike the case out of its list by means of a decision which shall be confined to a brief statement of the facts and of the solution reached.

Article 40—Public hearings and access to documents

1. Hearings shall be in public unless the Court in exceptional circumstances decides otherwise.

2. Documents deposited with the Registrar shall be accessible to the public unless the President of the Court decides otherwise.

Article 41—Just satisfaction

If the Court finds that there has been a violation of the Convention or the protocols thereto, and if the internal law of the High Contracting Party concerned allows only partial reparation to be made, the Court shall, if necessary, afford just satisfaction to the injured party.

Article 42—Judgments of Chambers

Judgments of Chambers shall become final in accordance with the provisions of Article 44, paragraph 2.

Article 43—Referral to the Grand Chamber
1. Within a period of three months from the date of the judgment of the Chamber, any party to the case may, in exceptional cases, request that the case be referred to the Grand Chamber.

2. A panel of five judges of the Grand Chamber shall accept the request if the case raises a serious question affecting the interpretation or application of the Convention or the protocols thereto, or a serious issue of general importance.

3. If the panel accepts the request, the Grand Chamber shall decide the case by means of a judgment.

Article 44—Final judgments
1. The judgment of the Grand Chamber shall be final.

2. The judgment of a Chamber shall become final

   (a) when the parties declare that they will not request that the case be referred to the Grand Chamber; or
   (b) three months after the date of the judgment, if reference of the case to the Grand Chamber has not been requested; or
   (c) when the panel of the Grand Chamber rejects the request to refer under Article 43.

3. The final judgment shall be published.

Article 45—Reasons for judgments and decisions
1. Reasons shall be given for judgments as well as for decisions declaring applications admissible or inadmissible.

2. If a judgment does not represent, in whole or in part, the unanimous opinion of the judges, any judge shall be entitled to deliver a separate opinion.

Article 46—Binding force and execution of judgments
1. The High Contracting Parties undertake to abide by the final judgment of the Court in any case to which they are parties.

2. The final judgment of the Court shall be transmitted to the Committee of Ministers, which shall supervise its execution.

Article 47—Advisory opinions
1. The Court may, at the request of the Committee of Ministers, give advisory opinions on legal questions concerning the interpretation of the Convention and the protocols thereto.

2. Such opinions shall not deal with any question relating to the content or scope of the rights or freedoms defined in Section I of the Convention and the protocols thereto,

or with any other question which the Court or the Committee of Ministers might have to consider in consequence of any such proceedings as could be instituted in accordance with the Convention.

3. Decisions of the Committee of Ministers to request an advisory opinion of the Court shall require a majority vote of the representatives entitled to sit on the Committee.

Article 48—Advisory jurisdiction of the Court

The Court shall decide whether a request for an advisory opinion submitted by the Committee of Ministers is within its competence as defined in Article 47.

Article 49—Reasons for advisory opinions

1. Reasons shall be given for advisory opinions of the Court.

2. If the advisory opinion does not represent, in whole or in part, the unanimous opinion of the judges, any judge shall be entitled to deliver a separate opinion.

3. Advisory opinions of the Court shall be communicated to the Committee of Ministers.

Article 50—Expenditure on the Court

The expenditure on the Court shall be borne by the Council of Europe.

Article 51—Privileges and immunities of judges

The judges shall be entitled, during the exercise of their functions, to the privileges and immunities provided for in Article 40 of the Statute of the Council of Europe and in the agreements made thereunder.

Section III—Miscellaneous provisions

Article 52—Inquiries by the Secretary General

On receipt of a request from the Secretary General of the Council of Europe any High Contracting Party shall furnish an explanation of the manner in which its internal law ensures the effective implementation of any of the provisions of the Convention.

Article 53—Safeguard for existing human rights

Nothing in this Convention shall be construed as limiting or derogating from any of the human rights and fundamental freedoms which may be ensured under the laws of any High Contracting Party or under any other agreement to which it is a Party.

Article 54—Powers of the Committee of Ministers

Nothing in this Convention shall prejudice the powers conferred on the Committee of Ministers by the Statute of the Council of Europe.

Article 55—Exclusion of other means of dispute settlement

The High Contracting Parties agree that, except by special agreement, they will not avail themselves of treaties, conventions or declarations in force between them for the purpose of submitting, by way of petition, a dispute arising out of the interpretation or application of this Convention to a means of settlement other than those provided for in this Convention.

Article 56—Territorial application

1. Any State may at the time of its ratification or at any time thereafter declare by notification addressed to the Secretary General of the Council of Europe that the present Convention shall, subject to paragraph 4 of this Article, extend to all or any of the territories for whose international relations it is responsible.

2. The Convention shall extend to the territory or territories named in the notification as from the thirtieth day after the receipt of this notification by the Secretary General of the Council of Europe.

3. The provisions of this Convention shall be applied in such territories with due regard, however, to local requirements.

4. Any State which has made a declaration in accordance with paragraph 1 of this article may at any time thereafter declare on behalf of one or more of the territories to which the declaration relates that it accepts the competence of the Court to receive applications from individuals, non-governmental organizations or groups of individuals as provided by Article 34 of the Convention.

Article 57—Reservations

1. Any State may, when signing this Convention or when depositing its instrument of ratification, make a reservation in respect of any particular provision of the Convention to the extent that any law then in force in its territory is not in conformity with the provision. Reservations of a general character shall not be permitted under this article.

2. Any reservation made under this article shall contain a brief statement of the law concerned.

Article 58—Denunciation

1. A High Contracting Party may denounce the present Convention only after the expiry of five years from the date on which it became a party to it and after six months' notice contained in a notification addressed to the Secretary General of the Council of Europe, who shall inform the other High Contracting Parties.

2. Such a denunciation shall not have the effect of releasing the High Contracting Party concerned from its obligations under this Convention in respect of any act which, being capable of constituting a violation of such obligations, may have been performed by it before the date at which the denunciation became effective.

3. Any High Contracting Party which shall cease to be a member of the Council of Europe shall cease to be a Party to this Convention under the same conditions.

4. The Convention may be denounced in accordance with the provisions of the preceding paragraphs in respect of any territory to which it has been declared to extend under the terms of Article 56.

Article 59—Signature and ratification

1. This Convention shall be open to the signature of the members of the Council of Europe. It shall be ratified. Ratifications shall be deposited with the Secretary General of the Council of Europe.

2. The present Convention shall come into force after the deposit of ten instruments of ratification.

3. As regards any signatory ratifying subsequently, the Convention shall come into force at the date of the deposit of its instrument of ratification.

4. The Secretary General of the Council of Europe shall notify all the members of the Council of Europe of the entry into force of the Convention, the names of the High Contracting Parties who have ratified it, and the deposit of all instruments of ratification which may be effected subsequently.

Done at Rome this 4th day of November 1950, in English and French, both texts being equally authentic, in a single copy which shall remain deposited in the archives of the Council of Europe. The Secretary General shall transmit certified copies to each of the signatories.

Protocol No. 1 to the Convention for the Protection of Human Rights and Fundamental Freedoms

Paris, 20.III.1952

The governments signatory hereto, being members of the Council of Europe,

Being resolved to take steps to ensure the collective enforcement of certain rights and freedoms other than those already included in Section I of the Convention for the Protection of Human Rights and Fundamental Freedoms signed at Rome on 4 November 1950 (hereinafter referred to as 'the Convention'),

Have agreed as follows:

Article 1—Protection of property

Every natural or legal person is entitled to the peaceful enjoyment of his possessions. No one shall be deprived of his possessions except in the public interest and subject to the conditions provided for by law and by the general principles of international law.

The preceding provisions shall not, however, in any way impair the right of a State to enforce such laws as it deems necessary to control the use of property in accordance with the general interest or to secure the payment of taxes or other contributions or penalties.

Article 2—Right to education

No person shall be denied the right to education. In the exercise of any functions which it assumes in relation to education and to teaching, the State shall respect the right of parents to ensure such education and teaching in conformity with their own religious and philosophical convictions.

Article 3—Right to free elections

The High Contracting Parties undertake to hold free elections at reasonable intervals by secret ballot, under conditions which will ensure the free expression of the opinion of the people in the choice of the legislature.

Article 4—Territorial application

Any High Contracting Party may at the time of signature or ratification or at any time thereafter communicate to the Secretary General of the Council of Europe a declaration stating the extent to which it undertakes that the provisions of the present Protocol shall apply to such of the territories for the international relations of which it is responsible as are named therein.

Any High Contracting Party which has communicated a declaration in virtue of the preceding paragraph may from time to time communicate a further declaration modifying the terms of any former declaration or terminating the application of the provisions of this Protocol in respect of any territory.

A declaration made in accordance with this article shall be deemed to have been made in accordance with paragraph 1 of Article 56 of the Convention.

Article 5—Relationship to the Convention

As between the High Contracting Parties the provisions of Articles 1, 2, 3 and 4 of this Protocol shall be regarded as additional articles to the Convention and all the provisions of the Convention shall apply accordingly.

Article 6—Signature and ratification

This Protocol shall be open for signature by the members of the Council of Europe, who are the signatories of the Convention; it shall be ratified at the same time as or after the ratification of the Convention. It shall enter into force after the deposit of ten instruments of ratification. As regards any signatory ratifying subsequently, the Protocol shall enter into force at the date of the deposit of its instrument of ratification.

The instruments of ratification shall be deposited with the Secretary General of the Council of Europe, who will notify all members of the names of those who have ratified.

Done at Paris on the 20th day of March 1952, in English and French, both texts being equally authentic, in a single copy which shall remain deposited in the archives of the Council of Europe. The Secretary General shall transmit certified copies to each of the signatory governments.

Protocol No. 4 to the Convention for the Protection of Human Rights and Fundamental Freedoms securing certain rights and freedoms other than those already included in the Convention and in the first Protocol thereto

Strasbourg, 16.IX.1963

The governments signatory hereto, being members of the Council of Europe,

Being resolved to take steps to ensure the collective enforcement of certain rights and freedoms other than those already included in Section 1 of the Convention for the Protection of Human Rights and Fundamental Freedoms signed at Rome on 4th November 1950 (hereinafter referred to as the 'Convention') and in Articles 1 to 3 of the First Protocol to the Convention, signed at Paris on 20th March 1952,

Have agreed as follows:

Article 1—Prohibition of imprisonment for debt
No one shall be deprived of his liberty merely on the ground of inability to fulfil a contractual obligation.

Article 2—Freedom of movement
1. Everyone lawfully within the territory of a State shall, within that territory, have the right to liberty of movement and freedom to choose his residence.

2. Everyone shall be free to leave any country, including his own.

3. No restrictions shall be placed on the exercise of these rights other than such as are in accordance with law and are necessary in a democratic society in the interests of national security or public safety, for the maintenance of *ordre public*, for the prevention of crime, for the protection of health or morals, or for the protection of the rights and freedoms of others.

4. The rights set forth in paragraph 1 may also be subject, in particular areas, to restrictions imposed in accordance with law and justified by the public interest in a democratic society.

Article 3—Prohibition of expulsion of nationals

1. No one shall be expelled, by means either of an individual or of a collective measure, from the territory of the State of which he is a national.

2. No one shall be deprived of the right to enter the territory of the state of which he is a national.

Article 4—Prohibition of collective expulsion of aliens

Collective expulsion of aliens is prohibited.

Article 5—Territorial application

1. Any High Contracting Party may, at the time of signature or ratification of this Protocol, or at any time thereafter, communicate to the Secretary General of the Council of Europe a declaration stating the extent to which it undertakes that the provisions of this Protocol shall apply to such of the territories for the international relations of which it is responsible as are named therein.

2. Any High Contracting Party which has communicated a declaration in virtue of the preceding paragraph may, from time to time, communicate a further declaration modifying the terms of any former declaration or terminating the application of the provisions of this Protocol in respect of any territory.

3. A declaration made in accordance with this article shall be deemed to have been made in accordance with paragraph 1 of Article 56 of the Convention.

4. The territory of any State to which this Protocol applies by virtue of ratification or acceptance by that State, and each territory to which this Protocol is applied by virtue of a declaration by that State under this article, shall be treated as separate territories for the purpose of the references in Articles 2 and 3 to the territory of a State.

5. Any State which has made a declaration in accordance with paragraph 1 or 2 of this Article may at any time thereafter declare on behalf of one or more of the territories to which the declaration relates that it accepts the competence of the Court to receive applications from individuals, non-governmental organizations or groups of individuals as provided in Article 34 of the Convention in respect of all or any of Articles 1 to 4 of this Protocol.

Article 6—Relationship to the Convention

As between the High Contracting Parties the provisions of Articles 1 to 5 of this Protocol shall be regarded as additional Articles to the Convention, and all the provisions of the Convention shall apply accordingly.

Article 7—Signature and ratification

1. This Protocol shall be open for signature by the members of the Council of Europe who are the signatories of the Convention; it shall be ratified at the same time as or

after the ratification of the Convention. It shall enter into force after the deposit of five instruments of ratification. As regards any signatory ratifying subsequently, the Protocol shall enter into force at the date of the deposit of its instrument of ratification.

2. The instruments of ratification shall be deposited with the Secretary General of the Council of Europe, who will notify all members of the names of those who have ratified.

In witness whereof the undersigned, being duly authorized thereto, have signed this Protocol.

Done at Strasbourg, this 16th day of September 1963, in English and in French, both texts being equally authoritative, in a single copy which shall remain deposited in the archives of the Council of Europe. The Secretary General shall transmit certified copies to each of the signatory states.

Protocol No. 6 to the Convention for the Protection of Human Rights and Fundamental Freedoms concerning the abolition of the death penalty

Strasbourg, 28.IV.1983

The member States of the Council of Europe, signatory to this Protocol to the Convention for the Protection of Human Rights and Fundamental Freedoms, signed at Rome on 4 November 1950 (hereinafter referred to as 'the Convention'),

Considering that the evolution that has occurred in several member States of the Council of Europe expresses a general tendency in favour of abolition of the death penalty;

Have agreed as follows:

Article 1—Abolition of the death penalty
The death penalty shall be abolished. No-one shall be condemned to such penalty or executed.

Article 2—Death penalty in time of war
A State may make provision in its law for the death penalty in respect of acts committed in time of war or of imminent threat of war; such penalty shall be applied only in the instances laid down in the law and in accordance with its provisions. The State shall communicate to the Secretary General of the Council of Europe the relevant provisions of that law.

Article 3—Prohibition of derogations

No derogation from the provisions of this Protocol shall be made under Article 15 of the Convention.

Article 4—Prohibition of reservations

No reservation may be made under Article 57 of the Convention in respect of the provisions of this Protocol.

Article 5—Territorial application

1. Any State may at the time of signature or when depositing its instrument of ratification, acceptance or approval, specify the territory or territories to which this Protocol shall apply.

2. Any State may at any later date, by a declaration addressed to the Secretary General of the Council of Europe, extend the application of this Protocol to any other territory specified in the declaration. In respect of such territory the Protocol shall enter into force on the first day of the month following the date of receipt of such declaration by the Secretary General.

3. Any declaration made under the two preceding paragraphs may, in respect of any territory specified in such declaration, be withdrawn by a notification addressed to the Secretary General. The withdrawal shall become effective on the first day of the month following the date of receipt of such notification by the Secretary General.

Article 6—Relationship to the Convention

As between the States Parties the provisions of Articles 1 to 5 of this Protocol shall be regarded as additional articles to the Convention and all the provisions of the Convention shall apply accordingly.

Article 7—Signature and ratification

The Protocol shall be open for signature by the member States of the Council of Europe, signatories to the Convention. It shall be subject to ratification, acceptance or approval. A member State of the Council of Europe may not ratify, accept or approve this Protocol unless it has, simultaneously or previously, ratified the Convention. Instruments of ratification, acceptance or approval shall be deposited with the Secretary General of the Council of Europe.

Article 8—Entry into force

1. This Protocol shall enter into force on the first day of the month following the date on which five member States of the Council of Europe have expressed their consent to be bound by the Protocol in accordance with the provisions of Article 7.

2. In respect of any member State which subsequently expresses its consent to be bound by it, the Protocol shall enter into force on the first day of the month following the date of the deposit of the instrument of ratification, acceptance or approval.

Article 9—Depositary functions

The Secretary General of the Council of Europe shall notify the member States of the Council of:

   (a) any signature;
   (b) the deposit of any instrument of ratification, acceptance or approval;
   (c) any date of entry into force of this Protocol in accordance with Articles 5 and 8;
   (d) any other act, notification or communication relating to this Protocol.

In witness whereof the undersigned, being duly authorized thereto, have signed this Protocol.

Done at Strasbourg, this 28th day of April 1983, in English and in French, both texts being equally authentic, in a single copy which shall be deposited in the archives of the Council of Europe. The Secretary General of the Council of Europe shall transmit certified copies to each member State of the Council of Europe.

Protocol No. 7 to the Convention for the Protection of Human Rights and Fundamental Freedoms

Strasbourg, 22.XI.1984

The member States of the Council of Europe signatory hereto,

Being resolved to take further steps to ensure the collective enforcement of certain rights and freedoms by means of the Convention for the Protection of Human Rights and Fundamental Freedoms signed at Rome on 4 November 1950 (hereinafter referred to as 'the Convention'),

Have agreed as follows:

Article 1—Procedural safeguards relating to expulsion of aliens

1. An alien lawfully resident in the territory of a State shall not be expelled therefrom except in pursuance of a decision reached in accordance with law and shall be allowed:

   (a) to submit reasons against his expulsion,
   (b) to have his case reviewed, and
   (c) to be represented for these purposes before the competent authority or a person or persons designated by that authority.

2. An alien may be expelled before the exercise of his rights under paragraph 1.a, b and c of this Article, when such expulsion is necessary in the interests of public order or is grounded on reasons of national security.

Article 2—Right of appeal in criminal matters

1. Everyone convicted of a criminal offence by a tribunal shall have the right to have his conviction or sentence reviewed by a higher tribunal. The exercise of this right, including the grounds on which it may be exercised, shall be governed by law.

2. This right may be subject to exceptions in regard to offences of a minor character, as prescribed by law, or in cases in which the person concerned was tried in the first instance by the highest tribunal or was convicted following an appeal against acquittal.

Article 3—Compensation for wrongful conviction

When a person has by a final decision been convicted of a criminal offence and when subsequently his conviction has been reversed, or he has been pardoned, on the ground that a new or newly discovered fact shows conclusively that there has been a miscarriage of justice, the person who has suffered punishment as a result of such conviction shall be compensated according to the law or the practice of the State concerned, unless it is proved that the non-disclosure of the unknown fact in time is wholly or partly attributable to him.

Article 4—Right not to be tried or punished twice

1. No one shall be liable to be tried or punished again in criminal proceedings under the jurisdiction of the same State for an offence for which he has already been finally acquitted or convicted in accordance with the law and penal procedure of that State.

2. The provisions of the preceding paragraph shall not prevent the reopening of the case in accordance with the law and penal procedure of the State concerned, if there is evidence of new or newly discovered facts, or if there has been a fundamental defect in the previous proceedings, which could affect the outcome of the case.

3. No derogation from this Article shall be made under Article 15 of the Convention.

Article 5—Equality between spouses

Spouses shall enjoy equality of rights and responsibilities of a private law character between them, and in their relations with their children, as to marriage, during marriage and in the event of its dissolution. This Article shall not prevent States from taking such measures as are necessary in the interests of the children.

Article 6—Territorial application

1. Any State may at the time of signature or when depositing its instrument of ratification, acceptance or approval, specify the territory or territories to which the

Protocol shall apply and state the extent to which it undertakes that the provisions of this Protocol shall apply to such territory or territories.

2. Any State may at any later date, by a declaration addressed to the Secretary General of the Council of Europe, extend the application of this Protocol to any other territory specified in the declaration. In respect of such territory the Protocol shall enter into force on the first day of the month following the expiration of a period of two months after the date of receipt by the Secretary General of such declaration.

3. Any declaration made under the two preceding paragraphs may, in respect of any territory specified in such declaration, be withdrawn or modified by a notification addressed to the Secretary General. The withdrawal or modification shall become effective on the first day of the month following the expiration of a period of two months after the date of receipt of such notification by the Secretary General.

4. A declaration made in accordance with this Article shall be deemed to have been made in accordance with paragraph 1 of Article 56 of the Convention.

5. The territory of any State to which this Protocol applies by virtue of ratification, acceptance or approval by that State, and each territory to which this Protocol is applied by virtue of a declaration by that State under this Article, may be treated as separate territories for the purpose of the reference in Article 1 to the territory of a State.

6. Any State which has made a declaration in accordance with paragraph 1 or 2 of this Article may at any time thereafter declare on behalf of one or more of the territories to which the declaration relates that it accepts the competence of the Court to receive applications from individuals, non-governmental organizations or groups of individuals as provided in Article 34 of the Convention in respect of Articles 1 to 5 of this Protocol.

Article 7—Relationship to the Convention
As between the States Parties, the provisions of Article 1 to 6 of this Protocol shall be regarded as additional Articles to the Convention, and all the provisions of the Convention shall apply accordingly.

Article 8—Signature and ratification
This Protocol shall be open for signature by member States of the Council of Europe which have signed the Convention. It is subject to ratification, acceptance or approval. A member State of the Council of Europe may not ratify, accept or approve this Protocol without previously or simultaneously ratifying the Convention. Instruments of ratification, acceptance or approval shall be deposited with the Secretary General of the Council of Europe.

Article 9—Entry into force
1. This Protocol shall enter into force on the first day of the month following the expiration of a period of two months after the date on which seven member States of the

Council of Europe have expressed their consent to be bound by the Protocol in accordance with the provisions of Article 8.

2. In respect of any member State which subsequently expresses its consent to be bound by it, the Protocol shall enter into force on the first day of the month following the expiration of a period of two months after the date of the deposit of the instrument of ratification, acceptance or approval.

Article 10—Depositary functions

The Secretary General of the Council of Europe shall notify all the member States of the Council of Europe of:

(a) any signature;
(b) the deposit of any instrument of ratification, acceptance or approval;
(c) any date of entry into force of this Protocol in accordance with Articles 6 and 9;
(d) any other act, notification or declaration relating to this Protocol.

In witness whereof, the undersigned, being duly authorized thereto, have signed this Protocol.

Done at Strasbourg, this 22nd day of November 1984, in English and French, both texts being equally authentic, in a single copy which shall be deposited in the archives of the Council of Europe. The Secretary General of the Council of Europe shall transmit certified copies to each member State of the Council of Europe.

Protocol No. 12 to the Convention for the Protection of Human Rights and Fundamental Freedoms

Rome, 4.XI.2000

The member States of the Council of Europe signatory hereto,

Having regard to the fundamental principle according to which all persons are equal before the law and are entitled to the equal protection of the law;

Being resolved to take further steps to promote the equality of all persons through the collective enforcement of a general prohibtion of discrimination by means of the Convention for the Protection of Human Rights and Fundamental Freedoms signed at Rome on 4 November 1950 (hereinafter referred to as 'the Convention');

Reaffirming that the principle of non-discrimination does not prevent States Parties from taking measures in order to promote full and effective equality, provided that there is an objective and reasonable justification for those measures,

Have agreed as follows:

Article 1—General prohibition of discrimination

1. The enjoyment of any right set forth by law shall be secured without discrimination on any ground such as sex, race, colour, language, religion, political or other opinion, national or social origin, association with a national minority, property, birth or other status.

2. No one shall be discriminated against by any public authority on any ground such as those mentioned in paragraph 1.

Article 2—Territorial application

1. Any State may, at the time of signature or when depositing its instrument of ratification, acceptance or approval, specify the territory or territories to which this Protocol shall apply.

2. Any State may at any later date, by a declaration addressed to the Secretary General of the Council of Europe, extend the application of this Protocol to any other territory specified in the declaration. In respect of such territory the Protocol shall enter into force on the first day of the month following the expiration of a period of three months after the date of receipt by the Secretary General of such declaration.

3. Any declaration made under the two preceding paragraphs may, in respect of any territory specified in such declaration, be withdrawn or modified by a notification addressed to the Secretary General of the Council of Europe. The withdrawal or modification shall become effective on the first day of the month following the expiration of a period of three months after the date of receipt of such notification by the Secretary General.

4. A declaration made in accordance with this article shall be deemed to have been made in accordance with paragraph 1 of Article 56 of the Convention.

5. Any State which has made a declaration in accordance with paragraph 1 or 2 of this article may at any time thereafter declare on behalf of one or more of the territories to which the declaration relates that it accepts the competence of the Court to receive applications from individuals, non-governmental organizations or groups of individuals as provided by Article 34 of the Convention in respect of Article 1 of this Protocol.

Article 3—Relationship to the Convention

As between the States Parties, the provisions of Articles 1 and 2 of this Protocol shall be regarded as additional articles to the Convention, and all the provisions of the Convention shall apply accordingly.

Article 4— Signature and ratification

This Protocol shall be open for signature by member States of the Council of Europe which have signed the Convention. It is subject to ratification, acceptance or approval.

A member State of the Council of Europe may not ratify, accept or approve this Protocol without previously or simultaneously ratifying the Convention. Instruments of ratification, acceptance or approval shall be deposited with the Secretary General of the Council of Europe.

Article 5—Entry into force

1. This Protocol shall enter into force on the first day of the month following the expiration of a period of three months after the date on which ten member States of the Council of Europe have expressed their consent to be bound by the Protocol in accordance with the provisions of Article 4.

2. In respect of any member State which subsequently expresses its consent to be bound by it, the Protocol shall enter into force on the first day of the month following the expiration of a period of three months after the date of the deposit of the instrument of ratification, acceptance or approval.

Article 6—Depositary functions

The Secretary General of the Council of Europe shall notify all the member States of the Council of Europe of:

  (a) any signature;
  (b) the deposit of any instrument of ratification, acceptance or approval;
  (c) any date of entry into force of this Protocol in accordance with Articles 2 and 5;
  (d) any other act, notification or communication relating to this Protocol.

In witness whereof the undersigned, being duly authorized thereto, have signed this Protocol.

Done at Rome, this 4th day of November 2000, in English and in French, both texts being equally authentic, in a single copy which shall be deposited in the archives of the Council of Europe. The Secretary General of the Council of Europe shall transmit certified copies to each member State of the Council of Europe.

Protocol No. 13 to the Convention for the Protection of
Human Rights and Fundamental Freedoms
Concerning the abolition of the death
penalty in all circumstances

Vilnius, 3.V.2002

The member States of the Council of Europe signatory hereto,

Convinced that everyone's right to life is a basic value in a democratic society and that the abolition of the death penalty is essential for the protection of this right and for the full recognition of the inherent dignity of all human beings;

Wishing to strengthen the protection of the right to life guaranteed by the Convention for the Protection of Human Rights and Fundamental Freedoms signed at Rome on 4 November 1950 (hereinafter referred to as 'the Convention');

Noting that Protocol No. 6 to the Convention, concerning the Abolition of the Death Penalty, signed at Strasbourg on 28 April 1983, does not exclude the death penalty in respect of acts committed in time of war or of imminent threat of war;

Being resolved to take the final step in order to abolish the death penalty in all circumstances,

Have agreed as follows:

Article 1—Abolition of the death penalty
The death penalty shall be abolished. No one shall be condemned to such penalty or executed.

Article 2—Prohibitions of derogations
No derogation from the provisions of this Protocol shall be made under Article 15 of the Convention.

Article 3—Prohibitions of reservations
No reservation may be made under Article 57 of the Convention in respect of the provisions of this Protocol.

Article 4—Territorial application
1. Any state may, at the time of signature or when depositing its instrument of ratification, acceptance or approval, specify the territory or territories to which this Protocol shall apply.

2. Any state may at any later date, by a declaration addressed to the Secretary General of the Council of Europe, extend the application of this Protocol to any other territory specified in the declaration. In respect of such territory the Protocol shall enter into force on the first day of the month following the expiration of a period of three months after the date of receipt by the Secretary General of such declaration.

3. Any declaration made under the two preceding paragraphs may, in respect of any territory specified in such declaration, be withdrawn or modified by a notification addressed to the Secretary General. The withdrawal or modification shall become effective on the first day of the month following the expiration of a period of three months after the date of receipt of such notification by the Secretary General.

Article 5—Relationship to the Convention

As between the states Parties the provisions of Articles 1 to 4 of this Protocol shall be regarded as additional articles to the Convention, and all the provisions of the Convention shall apply accordingly.

Article 6—Signature and ratification

This Protocol shall be open for signature by member states of the Council of Europe which have signed the Convention. It is subject to ratification, acceptance or approval. A member state of the Council of Europe may not ratify, accept or approve this Protocol without previously or simultaneously ratifying the Convention. Instruments of ratification, acceptance or approval shall be deposited with the Secretary General of the Council of Europe.

Article 7—Entry into force

1. This Protocol shall enter into force on the first day of the month following the expiration of a period of three months after the date on which ten member states of the Council of Europe have expressed their consent to be bound by the Protocol in accordance with the provisions of Article 6.

2. In respect of any member state which subsequently expresses its consent to be bound by it, the Protocol shall enter into force on the first day of the month following the expiration of a period of three months after the date of the deposit of the instrument of ratification, acceptance or approval.

Article 8—Depositary functions

The Secretary General of the Council of Europe shall notify all the member states of the Council of Europe of:

(a) any signature;

(b) the deposit of any instrument of ratification, acceptance or approval;

(c) any date of entry into force of this Protocol in accordance with Articles 4 and 7;

(d) any other act, notification or communication relating to this Protocol;

In witness whereof the undersigned, being duly authorized thereto, have signed this Protocol.

Done at Vilnius, this 3rd day of May 2002, in English and in French, both texts being equally authentic, in a single copy which shall be deposited in the archives of the Council of Europe. The Secretary General of the Council of Europe shall transmit certified copies to each member state of the Council of Europe.

APPENDIX B

PROPOSED PROTOCOL 14 TO THE CONVENTION

Protocol 14 was opened for signature on 13 May 2004. It has been signed by every member of the Council of Europe. As of June 2007 it has also been ratified by every member with the exception of Russia where the State Duma has refused to approve it.

PROTOCOL 14, 13 MAY 2004

Preamble

The member States of the Council of Europe, signatories to this Protocol to the Convention for the Protection of Human Rights and Fundamental Freedoms, signed at Rome on 4 November 1950 (hereinafter referred to as 'the Convention'),

Having regard to Resolution No. 1 and the Declaration adopted at the European Ministerial Conference on Human Rights, held in Rome on 3 and 4 November 2000;

Having regard to the Declarations adopted by the Committee of Ministers on 8 November 2001, 7 November 2002 and 15 May 2003, at their 109th, 111th and 112th Sessions, respectively;

Having regard to Opinion No. 251 (2004) adopted by the Parliamentary Assembly of the Council of Europe on 28 April 2004;

Considering the urgent need to amend certain provisions of the Convention in order to maintain and improve the efficiency of the control system for the long term, mainly in the light of the continuing increase in the workload of the European Court of Human Rights and the Committee of Ministers of the Council of Europe;

Considering, in particular, the need to ensure that the Court can continue to play its pre-eminent role in protecting human rights in Europe,

Have agreed as follows:

Article 1
Paragraph 2 of Article 22 of the Convention shall be deleted.

Article 2
Article 23 of the Convention shall be amended to read as follows:
   'Article 23—Terms of office and dismissal

1. The judges shall be elected for a period of nine years. They may not be re-elected.

2. The terms of office of judges shall expire when they reach the age of 70.

3. The judges shall hold office until replaced. They shall, however, continue to deal with such cases as they already have under consideration.

4. No judge may be dismissed from office unless the other judges decide by a majority of two-thirds that that judge has ceased to fulfil the required conditions.'

Article 3
Article 24 of the Convention shall be deleted.

Article 4
Article 25 of the Convention shall become Article 24 and its text shall be amended to read as follows:
   'Article 24—Registry and rapporteurs

1. The Court shall have a registry, the functions and organization of which shall be laid down in the rules of the Court.

2. When sitting in a single-judge formation, the Court shall be assisted by rapporteurs who shall function under the authority of the President of the Court. They shall form part of the Court's registry.'

Article 5
Article 26 of the Convention shall become Article 25 ('Plenary Court') and its text shall be amended as follows:

1. At the end of paragraph d, the comma shall be replaced by a semi-colon and the word 'and' shall be deleted.

2. At the end of paragraph e, the full stop shall be replaced by a semi-colon.

3. A new paragraph f shall be added which shall read as follows:
   'f make any request under Article 26, paragraph 2.'

Article 6
Article 27 of the Convention shall become Article 26 and its text shall be amended to read as follows:
   'Article 26—Single-judge formation, committees, Chambers and Grand Chamber

1. To consider cases brought before it, the Court shall sit in a single-judge formation, in committees of three judges, in Chambers of seven judges and in a Grand

Chamber of seventeen judges. The Court's Chambers shall set up committees for a fixed period of time.

2. At the request of the plenary Court, the Committee of Ministers may, by a unanimous decision and for a fixed period, reduce to five the number of judges of the Chambers.

3. When sitting as a single judge, a judge shall not examine any application against the High Contracting Party in respect of which that judge has been elected.

4. There shall sit as an *ex officio* member of the Chamber and the Grand Chamber the judge elected in respect of the High Contracting Party concerned. If there is none or if that judge is unable to sit, a person chosen by the President of the Court from a list submitted in advance by that Party shall sit in the capacity of judge.

5. The Grand Chamber shall also include the President of the Court, the Vice-Presidents, the Presidents of the Chambers and other judges chosen in accordance with the rules of the Court. When a case is referred to the Grand Chamber under Article 43, no judge from the Chamber which rendered the judgment shall sit in the Grand Chamber, with the exception of the President of the Chamber and the judge who sat in respect of the High Contracting Party concerned.'

Article 7
After the new Article 26, a new Article 27 shall be inserted into the Convention, which shall read as follows:
'**Article 27—Competence of single judges**

1. A single judge may declare inadmissible or strike out of the Court's list of cases an application submitted under Article 34, where such a decision can be taken without further examination.

2. The decision shall be final.

3. If the single judge does not declare an application inadmissible or strike it out, that judge shall forward it to a committee or to a Chamber for further examination.'

Article 8
Article 28 of the Convention shall be amended to read as follows:
'**Article 28—Competence of committees**

1. In respect of an application submitted under Article 34, a committee may, by a unanimous vote,

    (a) declare it inadmissible or strike it out of its list of cases, where such decision can be taken without further examination; or
    (b) declare it admissible and render at the same time a judgment on the merits, if the underlying question in the case, concerning the interpretation or the application of the Convention or the Protocols thereto, is already the subject of well-established case-law of the Court.

2. Decisions and judgments under paragraph 1 shall be final.

3. If the judge elected in respect of the High Contracting Party concerned is not a member of the committee, the committee may at any stage of the proceedings invite that judge to take the place of one of the members of the committee, having regard to all relevant factors, including whether that Party has contested the application of the procedure under paragraph 1.b.'

Article 9
Article 29 of the Convention shall be amended as follows:

1. Paragraph 1 shall be amended to read as follows: 'If no decision is taken under Article 27 or 28, or no judgment rendered under Article 28, a Chamber shall decide on the admissibility and merits of individual applications submitted under Article 34. The decision on admissibility may be taken separately.'

2. At the end of paragraph 2 a new sentence shall be added which shall read as follows: 'The decision on admissibility shall be taken separately unless the Court, in exceptional cases, decides otherwise.'

3. Paragraph 3 shall be deleted.

Article 10
Article 31 of the Convention shall be amended as follows:

1. At the end of paragraph a, the word 'and' shall be deleted.

2. Paragraph b shall become paragraph c and a new paragraph b shall be inserted and shall read as follows:
   'b decide on issues referred to the Court by the Committee of Ministers in accordance with Article 46, paragraph 4; and'.

Article 11
Article 32 of the Convention shall be amended as follows:
   At the end of paragraph 1, a comma and the number 46 shall be inserted after the number 34.

Article 12
Paragraph 3 of Article 35 of the Convention shall be amended to read as follows:
   '3 The Court shall declare inadmissible any individual application submitted under Article 34 if it considers that:

   (a) the application is incompatible with the provisions of the Convention or the Protocols thereto, manifestly ill-founded, or an abuse of the right of individual application; or

(b) the applicant has not suffered a significant disadvantage, unless respect for human rights as defined in the Convention and the Protocols thereto requires an examination of the application on the merits and provided that no case may be rejected on this ground which has not been duly considered by a domestic tribunal.'

Article 13

A new paragraph 3 shall be added at the end of Article 36 of the Convention, which shall read as follows:

'3 In all cases before a Chamber or the Grand Chamber, the Council of Europe Commissioner for Human Rights may submit written comments and take part in hearings.'

Article 14

Article 38 of the Convention shall be amended to read as follows:

'Article 38—Examination of the case

The Court shall examine the case together with the representatives of the parties and, if need be, undertake an investigation, for the effective conduct of which the High Contracting Parties concerned shall furnish all necessary facilities.'

Article 15

Article 39 of the Convention shall be amended to read as follows:

'Article 39—Friendly settlements

1. At any stage of the proceedings, the Court may place itself at the disposal of the parties concerned with a view to securing a friendly settlement of the matter on the basis of respect for human rights as defined in the Convention and the Protocols thereto.

2. Proceedings conducted under paragraph 1 shall be confidential.

3. If a friendly settlement is effected, the Court shall strike the case out of its list by means of a decision which shall be confined to a brief statement of the facts and of the solution reached.

4. This decision shall be transmitted to the Committee of Ministers, which shall supervise the execution of the terms of the friendly settlement as set out in the decision.'

Article 16

Article 46 of the Convention shall be amended to read as follows:

'Article 46—Binding force and execution of judgments

1. The High Contracting Parties undertake to abide by the final judgment of the Court in any case to which they are parties.

2. The final judgment of the Court shall be transmitted to the Committee of Ministers, which shall supervise its execution.

3. If the Committee of Ministers considers that the supervision of the execution of a final judgment is hindered by a problem of interpretation of the judgment, it may refer the matter to the Court for a ruling on the question of interpretation. A referral decision shall require a majority vote of two thirds of the representatives entitled to sit on the Committee.

4. If the Committee of Ministers considers that a High Contracting Party refuses to abide by a final judgment in a case to which it is a party, it may, after serving formal notice on that Party and by decision adopted by a majority vote of two thirds of the representatives entitled to sit on the Committee, refer to the Court the question whether that Party has failed to fulfil its obligation under paragraph 1.

5. If the Court finds a violation of paragraph 1, it shall refer the case to the Committee of Ministers for consideration of the measures to be taken. If the Court finds no violation of paragraph 1, it shall refer the case to the Committee of Ministers, which shall close its examination of the case.'

Article 17
Article 59 of the Convention shall be amended as follows:

1. A new paragraph 2 shall be inserted which shall read as follows:
   '2 The European Union may accede to this Convention.'

2. Paragraphs 2, 3 and 4 shall become paragraphs 3, 4 and 5 respectively.

   Final and transitional provisions

Article 18
1. This Protocol shall be open for signature by member States of the Council of Europe signatories to the Convention, which may express their consent to be bound by

   (a) signature without reservation as to ratification, acceptance or approval; or
   (b) signature subject to ratification, acceptance or approval, followed by ratification, acceptance or approval.

2. The instruments of ratification, acceptance or approval shall be deposited with the Secretary General of the Council of Europe.

Article 19
This Protocol shall enter into force on the first day of the month following the expiration of a period of three months after the date on which all Parties to the Convention have expressed their consent to be bound by the Protocol, in accordance with the provisions of Article 18.

Article 20

1. From the date of the entry into force of this Protocol, its provisions shall apply to all applications pending before the Court as well as to all judgments whose execution is under supervision by the Committee of Ministers.

2. The new admissibility criterion inserted by Article 12 of this Protocol in Article 35, paragraph 3.b of the Convention, shall not apply to applications declared admissible before the entry into force of the Protocol. In the two years following the entry into force of this Protocol, the new admissibility criterion may only be applied by Chambers and the Grand Chamber of the Court.

Article 21

The term of office of judges serving their first term of office on the date of entry into force of this Protocol shall be extended *ipso jure* so as to amount to a total period of nine years. The other judges shall complete their term of office, which shall be extended *ipso jure* by two years.

Article 22

The Secretary General of the Council of Europe shall notify the member States of the Council of Europe of:

(a) any signature;
(b) the deposit of any instrument of ratification, acceptance or approval;
(c) the date of entry into force of this Protocol in accordance with Article 19; and
(d) any other act, notification or communication relating to this Protocol.

In witness whereof, the undersigned, being duly authorized thereto, have signed this Protocol.

Done at Strasbourg, this 13th day of May 2004, in English and in French, both texts being equally authentic, in a single copy which shall be deposited in the archives of the Council of Europe. The Secretary General of the Council of Europe shall transmit certified copies to each member State of the Council of Europe.

APPENDIX C

THE HUMAN RIGHTS ACT 1998 (UNITED KINGDOM)

The effect of the European Convention on Human Rights in the law of the United Kingdom was examined in Chapter 14. The Human Rights Act 1998 was enacted on 9 November 1998, but it came fully into effect only on 2 October 2000. The following text omits Schedule 1, which sets out Articles 2–12, 14 and 16–18 of the Convention, together with Articles 1–3 of the First Protocol to the Convention and Articles 1 and 2 of the Sixth Protocol. These Articles are all found in Appendices A and B above. Also omitted from this Appendix are (1) Section 18, subsections (4) to (7) (provisions consequential upon the appointment to the Strasbourg Court of a person who holds judicial office in the United Kingdom); (2) Schedule 3 (which sets out in full (a) the United Kingdom derogation under Article 15(1) of the Convention, relating to the detention of suspected terrorists under legislation, as to which see *Brogan v United Kingdom* (Chapter 12(F)(2)) and *Brannigan v United Kingdom* (Chapter 12(H)(3)); and (b) the United Kingdom reservation made in ratifying the First Protocol, Article 2 (right to education)); and (3) Schedule 4 (judical pensions).

HUMAN RIGHTS ACT 1998

1998 chapter 42

An Act to give further effect to rights and freedoms guaranteed under the European Convention on Human Rights; to make provision with respect to holders of certain judicial offices who become judges of the European Court of Human Rights; and for connected purposes.

[9th November 1998]

Introduction

1. The Convention Rights

(1) In this Act 'the Convention rights' means the rights and fundamental freedoms set out in—

    (a) Articles 2 to 12 and 14 of the Convention,

    (b) Articles 1 to 3 of the First Protocol, and

    (c) Articles 1 and 2 of the Sixth Protocol,

as read with Articles 16 to 18 of the Convention.

(2) Those Articles are to have effect for the purposes of this Act subject to any designated derogation or reservation (as to which see sections 14 and 15).

(3) The Articles are set out in Schedule 1.

(4) The Secretary of State may by order make such amendments to this Act as he considers appropriate to reflect the effect, in relation to the United Kingdom, of a protocol.

(5) In subsection (4) 'protocol' means a protocol to the Convention—

    (a) which the United Kingdom has ratified; or

    (b) which the United Kingdom has signed with a view to ratification.

(6) No amendment may be made by an order under subsection (4) so as to come into force before the protocol concerned is in force in relation to the United Kingdom.

2. Interpretation of Convention rights

(1) A court of tribunal determining a question which has arisen in connection with a Convention right must take into account any—

    (a) judgment, decision, declaration or advisory opinion of the European Court of Human Rights,

    (b) opinion of the Commission given in a report adopted under Article 31 of the Convention,

    (c) decision of the Commission in connection with Article 26 or 27(2) of the Convention, or

    (d) decision of the Committee of Ministers taken under Article 46 of the Convention,

whenever made or given, so far as, in the opinion of the court or tribunal, it is relevant to the proceedings in which that question has arisen.

(2) Evidence of any judgment, decision, declaration or opinion of which account may have to be taken under this section is to be given in proceedings before any court or tribunal in such manner as may be provided by rules.

(3) In this section 'rules' means rules of court or, in the case of proceedings before a tribunal, rules made for the purposes of this section—

    (a) by the Lord Chancellor or the Secretary of State, in relation to any proceedings outside Scotland;

    (b) by the Secretary of State, in relation to proceedings in Scotland; or

    (c) by a Northern Ireland department, in relation to proceedings before a tribunal in Northern Ireland—

        (i) which deals with transferred matters; and

        (ii) for which no rules made under paragraph (a) are in force.

Legislation

3. Interpretation of legislation

(1) So far as it is possible to do so, primary legislation and subordinate legislation must be read and given effect in a way which is compatible with the Convention rights.

(2) This section—

    (a) applies to primary legislation and subordinate legislation whenever enacted;

    (b) does not affect the validity, continuing operation or enforcement of any incompatible primary legislation; and

    (c) does not affect the validity, continuing operation or enforcement of any incompatible subordinate legislation if (disregarding any possibility of revocation) primary legislation prevents removal of the incompatibility.

4. Declaration of incompatibility

(1) Subsection (2) applies in any proceedings in which a court determines whether a provision of primary legislation is compatible with a Convention right.

(2) If the court is satisfied that the provision is incompatible with a Convention right, it may make a declaration of that incompatibility.

(3) Subsection (4) applies in any proceedings in which a court determines whether a provision of subordinate legislation, made in the exercise of a power conferred by primary legislation, is compatible with a Convention right.

(4) If the court is satisfied—

    (a) that the provision is incompatible with a Convention right, and

    (b) that (disregarding any possibility of revocation) the primary legislation concerned prevents removal of that incompatibility, it may make a declaration of that incompatibility.

(5) In this section 'court' means—

    (a) the House of Lords;

    (b) the Judicial Committee of the Privy Council;

    (c) the Courts-Martial Appeal Court;

    (d) in Scotland, the High Court of Justiciary sitting otherwise than as a trial court or the Court of Session;

    (e) in England and Wales or Northern Ireland, the High Court or the Court of Appeal.

(6) A declaration under this section ('a declaration of incompatibility')—

    (a) does not affect the validity, continuing operation or enforcement of the provision in respect of which it is given; and

    (b) is not binding on the parties to the proceedings in which it is made.

5. Right of Crown to intervene

(1) Where a court is considering whether to make a declaration of incompatibility, the Crown is entitled to notice in accordance with rules of court.

(2) In any case to which subsection (1) applies—

    (a) a Minister of the Crown (or a person nominated by him),

    (b) a member of the Scottish Executive,

    (c) a Northern Ireland Minister,

    (d) a Northern Ireland department,

is entitled, on giving notice in accordance with rules of court, to be joined as a party to the proceedings.

(3) Notice under subsection (2) may be given at any time during the proceedings.

(4) A person who has been made a party to criminal proceedings (other than in Scotland) as the result of a notice under subsection (2) may, with leave, appeal to the House of Lords against any declaration of incompatibility made in the proceedings.

(5) In subsection (4)—

'criminal proceedings' includes all proceedings before the Courts-Martial Appeal Court; and

'leave' means leave granted by the court making the declaration of incompatibility or by the House of Lords.

Public authorities

6. Acts of public authorities

(1) It is unlawful for a public authority to act in a way which is incompatible with a Convention right.

(2) Subsection (1) does not apply to an act if—

    (a) as the result of one or more provisions of primary legislation, the authority could not have acted differently; or

    (b) in the case of one or more provisions of, or made under, primary legislation which cannot be read or given effect in a way which is compatible with the Convention rights, the authority was acting so as to give effect to or enforce those provisions.

(3) In this section 'public authority' includes—

    (a) a court or tribunal, and

    (b) any person certain of whose functions are functions of a public nature,

    but does not include either House of Parliament or a person exercising functions in connection with proceedings in Parliament.

(4) In subsection (3) 'Parliament' does not include the House of Lords in its judicial capacity.

(5) In relation to a particular act, a person is not a public authority by virtue only of subsection (3)(b) if the nature of the act is private.

(6) 'An act' includes a failure to act but does not include a failure to—

(a) introduce in, or lay before, Parliament a proposal for legislation; or

(b) make any primary legislation or remedial order.

7. Proceedings

(1) A person who claims that a public authority has acted (or proposes to act) in a way which is made unlawful by section 6(1) may—

(a) bring proceedings against the authority under this Act in the appropriate court or tribunal, or

(b) rely on the Convention right or rights concerned in any legal proceedings,

but only if he is (or would be) a victim of the unlawful act.

(2) In subsection (1)(a) 'appropriate court or tribunal' means such court or tribunal as may be determined in accordance with rules; and proceedings against an authority include a counterclaim or similar proceeding.

(3) If the proceedings are brought on an application for judicial review, the applicant is to be taken to have a sufficient interest in relation to the unlawful act only if he is, or would be, a victim of that act.

(4) If the proceedings are made by way of a petition for judicial review in Scotland, the applicant shall be taken to have title and interest to sue in relation to the unlawful act only if he is, or would be, a victim of that act.

(5) Proceedings under subsection (1)(a) must be brought before the end of—

(a) the period of one year beginning with the date on which the act complained of took place; or

(b) such longer period as the court or tribunal considers equitable having regard to all the circumstances,

but that is subject to any rule imposing a stricter time limit in relation to the procedure in question.

(6) In subsection (1)(b) 'legal proceedings' includes—

(a) proceedings brought by or at the instigation of a public authority; and

(b) an appeal against the decision of a court or tribunal.

(7) For the purposes of this section, a person is a victim of an unlawful act only if he would be a victim for the purposes of Article 34 of the Convention if proceedings were brought in the European Court of Human Rights in respect of that act.

(8) Nothing in this Act creates a criminal offence.

(9) In this section 'rules' means—

(a) in relation to proceedings before a court or tribunal outside Scotland, rules made by the Lord Chancellor or the Secretary of State for the purposes of this section or rules of court,

(b) in relation to proceedings before a court or tribunal in Scotland, rules made by the Secretary of State for those purposes,

(c) in relation to proceedings before a tribunal in Northern Ireland—

(i) which deals with transferred matters; and

(ii) for which no rules made under paragraph (a) are in force,

rules made by a Northern Ireland department for those purposes, and includes provision made by order under section 1 of the Courts and Legal Services Act 1990.

(10) In making rules, regard must be had to section 9.

(11) The Minister who has power to make rules in relation to a particular tribunal may, to the extent he considers it necessary to ensure that the tribunal can provide an appropriate remedy in relation to an act (or proposed act) of a public authority which is (or would be) unlawful as a result of section 6(1), by order add to—

(a) the relief or remedies which the tribunal may grant; or

(b) the grounds on which it may grant any of them.

(12) An order made under subsection (11) may contain such incidental, supplemental, consequential or transitional provision as the Minister making it considers appropriate.

(13) 'The Minister' includes the Northern Ireland department concerned.

8. Judicial remedies

(1) In relation to any act (or proposed act) of a public authority which the court finds is (or would be) unlawful, it may grant such relief or remedy, or make such order, within its powers as it considers just and appropriate.

(2) But damages may be awarded only by a court which has power to award damages, or to order the payment of compensation, in civil proceedings.

(3) No award of damages is to be made unless, taking account of all the circumstances of the case, including—

(a) any other relief or remedy granted, or order made, in relation to the act in question (by that or any other court), and

(b) the consequences of any decision (of that or any other court) in respect of that act,

the court is satisfied that the award is necessary to afford just satisfaction to the person in whose favour it is made.

(4) In determining—

(a) whether to award damages, or

(b) the amount of an award,

the court must take into account the principles applied by the European Court of Human Rights in relation to the award of compensation under Article 41 of the Convention.

(5) A public authority against which damages are awarded is to be treated—

(a) in Scotland, for the purposes of section 3 of the Law Reform (Miscellaneous Provisions) (Scotland) Act 1940 as if the award were made in an action of damages in which the authority has been found liable in respect of loss or damage to the person to whom the award is made;

(b) for the purposes of the Civil Liability (Contribution) Act 1978 as liable in respect of damage suffered by the person to whom the award is made.

(6) In this section—

'court' includes a tribunal;

'damages' means damages for an unlawful act of a public authority; and 'unlawful' means unlawful under section 6(1).

9. Judicial acts

(1) Proceedings under section 7(1)(a) in respect of a judicial act may be brought only—

(a) by exercising a right of appeal;

(b) on an application (in Scotland a petition) for judicial review; or

(c) in such other forum as may be prescribed by rules.

(2) That does not affect any rule of law which prevents a court from being the subject of judicial review.

(3) In proceedings under this Act in respect of a judicial act done in good faith, damages may not be awarded otherwise than to compensate a person to the extent required by Article 5(5) of the Convention.

(4) An award of damages permitted by subsection (3) is to be made against the Crown; but no award may be made unless the appropriate person, if not a party to the proceedings, is joined.

(5) In this section—

'appropriate person' means the Minister responsible for the court concerned, or a person or government department nominated by him;

'court' includes a tribunal;

'judge' includes a member of a tribunal, a justice of the peace and a clerk or other officer entitled to exercise the jurisdiction of a court;

'judicial act' means a judicial act of a court and includes an act done on the instructions, or on behalf, of a judge; and

'rules' has the same meaning as in section 7(9).

Remedial action

10. Power to take remedial action

(1) This section applies if—

(a) a provision of legislation has been declared under section 4 to be incompatible with a Convention right and, if an appeal lies—

(i)   all persons who may appeal have stated in writing that they do not intend to do so;

(ii) the time for bringing an appeal has expired and no appeal has been brought within that time; or

(iii) an appeal brought within that time has been determined or abandoned; or

(b) it appears to a Minister of the Crown or Her Majesty in Council that, having regard to a finding of the European Court of Human Rights made after the coming into force of this section in proceedings against the United

Kingdom, a provision of legislation is incompatible with an obligation of the United Kingdom arising from the Convention.

(2) If a Minister of the Crown considers that there are compelling reasons for proceeding under this section, he may by order make such amendments to the legislation as he considers necessary to remove the incompatibility.

(3) If, in the case of subordinate legislation, a Minister of the Crown considers—

(a) that it is necessary to amend the primary legislation under which the subordinate legislation in question was made, in order to enable the incompatibility to be removed, and

(b) that there are compelling reasons for proceeding under this section, he may by order make such amendments to the primary legislation as he considers necessary.

(4) This section also applies where the provision in question is in subordinate legislation and has been quashed, or declared invalid, by reason of incompatibility with a Convention right and the Minister proposes to proceed under paragraph 2(b) of Schedule 2.

(5) If the legislation is an Order in Council, the power conferred by subsection (2) or (3) is exercisable by Her Majesty in Council.

(6) In this section 'legislation' does not include a Measure of the Church Assembly or of the General Synod of the Church of England.

(7) Schedule 2 makes further provision about remedial orders.

Other rights and proceedings

11. Safeguard for existing human rights

A person's reliance on a Convention right does not restrict—

(a) any other right or freedom conferred on him by or under any law having effect in any part of the United Kingdom; or

(b) his right to make any claim or bring any proceedings which he could make or bring apart from sections 7 to 9.

12. Freedom of expression

(1) This section applies if a court is considering whether to grant any relief which, if granted, might affect the exercise of the Convention right to freedom of expression.

(2) If the person against whom the application for relief is made ('the respondent') is neither present nor represented, no such relief is to be granted unless the court is satisfied—

(a) that the applicant has taken all practicable steps to notify the respondent; or

(b) that there are compelling reasons why the respondent should not be notified.

(3) No such relief is to be granted so as to restrain publication before trial unless the court is satisfied that the applicant is likely to establish that publication should not be allowed.

(4) The court must have particular regard to the importance of the Convention right to freedom of expression and, where the proceedings relate to material which the respondent claims, or which appears to the court, to be journalistic, literary or artistic material (or to conduct connected with such material), to—

(a) the extent to which—

    (i) the material has, or is about to, become available to the public; or

    (ii) it is, or would be, in the public interest for the material to be published;

(b) any relevant privacy code.

(5) In this section—

'court' includes a tribunal; and

'relief' includes any remedy or order (other than in criminal proceedings).

13. Freedom of thought, conscience and religion

(1) If a court's determination of any question arising under this Act might affect the exercise by a religious organization (itself or its members collectively) of the Convention right to freedom of thought, conscience and religion, it must have particular regard to the importance of that right.

(2) In this section 'court' includes a tribunal.

Derogations and reservations

14. Derogations

(1) In this Act 'designated derogation' means—

(a) the United Kingdom's derogation from Article 5(3) of the Convention; and

(b) any derogation by the United Kingdom from an Article of the Convention, or of any protocol to the Convention, which is designated for the purposes of this Act in an order made by the Secretary of State.

(2) The derogation referred to in subsection (1)(a) is set out in Part I of Schedule 3. [*Not reproduced*]

(3) If a designated derogation is amended or replaced it ceases to be a designated derogation.

(4) But subsection (3) does not prevent the Secretary of State from exercising his power under subsection (1)(b) to make a fresh designation order in respect of the Article concerned.

(5) The Secretary of State must by order make such amendments to Schedule 3 as he considers appropriate to reflect—

(a) any designation order; or

(b) the effect of subsection (3).

(6) A designation order may be made in anticipation of the making by the United Kingdom of a proposed derogation.

15. Reservations

(1) In this Act 'designated reservation' means—

    (a) the United Kingdom's reservation to Article 2 of the First Protocol to the Convention; and

    (b) any other reservation by the United Kingdom to an Article of the Convention, or of any protocol to the Convention, which is designated for the purposes of this Act in an order made by the Secretary of State.

(2) The text of the reservation referred to in subsection (1)(a) is set out in Part II of Schedule 3. [*Not reproduced*]

(3) If a designated reservation is withdrawn wholly or in part it ceases to be a designated reservation.

(4) But subsection (3) does not prevent the Secretary of State from exercising his power under subsection (1)(b) to make a fresh designation order in respect of the Article concerned.

(5) The Secretary of State must by order make such amendments to this Act as he considers appropriate to reflect—

    (a) any designation order; or

    (b) the effect of subsection (3).

16. Period for which designated derogations have effect

(1) If it has not already been withdrawn by the United Kingdom, a designated derogation ceases to have effect for the purposes of this Act—

    (a) in the case of the derogation referred to in section 14(1)(a), at the end of the period of five years beginning with the date on which section 1(2) came into force;

    (b) in the case of any other derogation, at the end of the period of five years beginning with the date on which the order designating it was made.

(2) At any time before the period—

    (a) fixed by subsection (1)(a) or (b), or

    (b) extended by an order under this subsection,

comes to an end, the Secretary of State may by order extend it by a further period of five years.

(3) An order under section 14(1)(b) ceases to have effect at the end of the period for consideration, unless a resolution has been passed by each House approving the order.

(4) Subsection (3) does not affect—

    (a) anything done in reliance on the order; or

    (b) the power to make a fresh order under section 14(1)(b).

(5) In subsection (3) 'period for consideration' means the period of forty days beginning with the day on which the order was made.

(6) In calculating the period for consideration, no account is to be taken of any time during which—

    (a) Parliament is dissolved or prorogued; or

(b) both Houses are adjourned for more than four days.

(7) If a designated derogation is withdrawn by the United Kingdom, the Secretary of State must by order make such amendments to this Act as he considers are required to reflect that withdrawal.

17. Periodic review of designated reservations

(1) The appropriate Minister must review the designated reservation referred to in section 15(1)(a)—

    (a) before the end of the period of five years beginning with the date on which section 1(2) came into force; and

    (b) if that designation is still in force, before the end of the period of five years beginning with the date on which the last report relating to it was laid under subsection (3).

(2) The appropriate Minister must review each of the other designated reservations (if any)—

    (a) before the end of the period of five years beginning with the date on which the order designating the reservation first came into force; and

    (b) if the designation is still in force, before the end of the period of five years beginning with the date on which the last report relating to it was laid under subsection (3).

(3) The Minister conducting a review under this section must prepare a report on the result of the review and lay a copy of it before each House of Parliament.

Judges of the European Court of Human Rights

18. Appointment to European Court of Human Rights

(1) In this section 'judicial office' means the office of—

    (a) Lord Justice of Appeal, Justice of the High Court or Circuit judge, in England and Wales;

    (b) judge of the Court of Session or sheriff, in Scotland;

    (c) Lord Justice of Appeal, judge of the High Court or county court judge, in Northern Ireland.

(2) The holder of a judicial office may become a judge of the European Court of Human Rights ('the Court') without being required to relinquish his office.

(3) But he is not required to perform the duties of his judicial office while he is a judge of the Court.

[Subsections (4)–(7) not reproduced]

Parliamentary procedure

19. Statements of compatibility

(1) A Minister of the Crown in charge of a Bill in either House of Parliament must, before Second Reading of the Bill—

    (a) make a statement to the effect that in his view the provisions of the Bill are compatible with the Convention rights ('a statement of compatibility'); or

(b) make a statement to the effect that although he is unable to make a statement of compatibility the government nevertheless wishes the House to proceed with the Bill.

(2) The statement must be in writing and be published in such manner as the Minister making it considers appropriate.

Supplemental

20. Orders etc. under this Act

(1) Any power of a Minister of the Crown to make an order under this Act is exercisable by statutory instrument.

(2) The power of the Lord Chancellor or the Secretary of State to make rules (other than rules of court) under section 2(3) or 7(9) is exercisable by statutory instrument.

(3) Any statutory instrument made under section 14, 15 or 16(7) must be laid before Parliament.

(4) No order may be made by the Lord Chancellor or the Secretary of State under section 1(4), 7(11) or 16(2) unless a draft of the order has been laid before, and approved by, each House of Parliament.

(5) Any statutory instrument made under section 18(7) or Schedule 4, or to which subsection (2) applies, shall be subject to annulment in pursuance of a resolution of either House of Parliament.

(6) The power of a Northern Ireland department to make—

(a) rules under section 2(3)(c) or 7(9)(c), or

(b) an order under section 7(11),

is exercisable by statutory rule for the purposes of the Statutory Rules (Northern Ireland) Order 1979.

(7) Any rules made under section 2(3)(c) or 7(9)(c) shall be subject to negative resolution; and section 41(6) of the Interpretation Act (Northern Ireland) 1954 (meaning of 'subject to negative resolution') shall apply as if the power to make the rules were conferred by an Act of the Northern Ireland Assembly.

(8) No order may be made by a Northern Ireland department under section 7(11) unless a draft of the order has been laid before, and approved by, the Northern Ireland Assembly.

21. Interpretation etc.

(1) In this Act—

'amend' includes repeal and apply (with or without modifications);

'the appropriate Minister' means the Minister of the Crown having charge of the appropriate authorized government department (within the meaning of the Crown Proceedings Act 1947);

'the Commission' means the European Commission of Human Rights;

'the Convention' means the Convention for the Protection of Human Rights and Fundamental Freedoms, agreed by the Council of Europe at Rome on 4th November 1950 as it has effect for the time being in relation to the United Kingdom;

'declaration of incompatibility' means a declaration under section 4;

'Minister of the Crown' has the same meaning as in the Ministers of the Crown Act 1975;

'Northern Ireland Minister' includes the First Minister and the deputy First Minister in Northern Ireland;

'primary legislation' means any—

    (a) public general Act;

    (b) local and personal Act;

    (c) private Act;

    (d) Measure of the Church Assembly;

    (e) Measure of the General Synod of the Church of England;

    (f) Order in Council—

        (i)   made in exercise of Her Majesty's Royal Prerogative;

        (ii)   made under section 38(1)(a) of the Northern Ireland Constitution Act 1973 or the corresponding provision of the Northern Ireland Act 1998; or

        (iii) amending an Act of a kind mentioned in paragraph (a), (b) or (c);

and includes an order or other instrument made under primary legislation (otherwise than by the National Assembly for Wales, a member of the Scottish Executive, a Northern Ireland Minister or a Northern Ireland department) to the extent to which it operates to bring one or more provisions of that legislation into force or amends any primary legislation;

'the First Protocol' means the protocol to the Convention agreed at Paris on 20th March 1952;

'the Sixth Protocol' means the protocol to the Convention agreed at Strasbourg on 28th April 1983;

'the Eleventh Protocol' means the protocol to the Convention (restructuring the control machinery established by the Convention) agreed at Strasbourg on 11th May 1994;

'remedial order' means an order under section 10;

'subordinate legislation' means any—

    (a) Order in Council other than one—

        (i)   made in exercise of Her Majesty's Royal Prerogative;

        (ii)   made under section 38(1)(a) of the Northern Ireland Constitution Act 1973 or the corresponding provision of the Northern Ireland Act 1998; or

        (iii) amending an Act of a kind mentioned in the definition of primary legislation;

    (b) Act of the Scottish Parliament;

    (c) Act of the Parliament of Northern Ireland;

(d) Measure of the Assembly established under section 1 of the Northern Ireland Assembly Act 1973;

(e) Act of the Northern Ireland Assembly;

(f) order, rules, regulations, scheme, warrant, byelaw or other instrument made under primary legislation (except to the extent to which it operates to bring one or more provisions of that legislation into force or amends any primary legislation);

(g) order, rules, regulations, scheme, warrant, byelaw or other instrument made under legislation mentioned in paragraph (b), (c), (d) or (e) or made under an Order in Council applying only to Northern Ireland;

(h) order, rules, regulations, scheme, warrant, byelaw or other instrument made by a member of the Scottish Executive, a Northern Ireland Minister or a Northern Ireland department in exercise of prerogative or other executive functions of Her Majesty which are exercisable by such a person on behalf of Her Majesty;

'transferred matters' has the same meaning as in the Northern Ireland Act 1998; and

'tribunal' means any tribunal in which legal proceedings may be brought.

(2) The references in paragraphs (b) and (c) of section 2(1) to Articles are to Articles of the Convention as they had effect immediately before the coming into force of the Eleventh Protocol.

(3) The reference in paragraph (d) of section 2(1) to Article 46 includes a reference to Articles 32 and 54 of the Convention as they had effect immediately before the coming into force of the Eleventh Protocol.

(4) The references in section 2(1) to a report or decision of the Commission or a decision of the Committee of Ministers include references to a report or decision made as provided by paragraphs 3, 4 and 6 of Article 5 of the Eleventh Protocol (transitional provisions).

(5) Any liability under the Army Act 1955, the Air Force Act 1955 or the Naval Discipline Act 1957 to suffer death for an offence is replaced by a liability to imprisonment for life or any less punishment authorized by those Acts; and those Acts shall accordingly have effect with the necessary modifications.

22. Short title, commencement, application and extent

(1) This Act may be cited as the Human Rights Act 1998.

(2) Sections 18, 20 and 21(5) and this section come into force on the passing of this Act.

(3) The other provisions of this Act come into force on such day as the Secretary of State may by order appoint; and different days may be appointed for different purposes.

(4) Paragraph (b) of subsection (1) of section 7 applies to proceedings brought by or at the instigation of a public authority whenever the act in question took place; but

otherwise that subsection does not apply to an act taking place before the coming into force of that section.

(5) This Act binds the Crown.

(6) This Act extends to Northern Ireland.

(7) Section 21(5), so far as it relates to any provision contained in the Army Act 1955, the Air Force Act 1955 or the Naval Discipline Act 1957, extends to any place to which that provision extends.

[SCHEDULE 1 NOT REPRODUCED]

Schedule 2

REMEDIAL ORDERS

Orders

1.—(1) A remedial order may—
   (a) contain such incidental, supplemental, consequential or transitional provision as the person making it considers appropriate;
   (b) be made so as to have effect from a date earlier than that on which it is made;
   (c) make provision for the delegation of specific functions;
   (d) make different provision for different cases.

(2) The power conferred by sub-paragraph (1)(a) includes—
   (a) power to amend primary legislation (including primary legislation other than that which contains the incompatible provision); and
   (b) power to amend or revoke subordinate legislation (including subordinate legislation other than that which contains the incompatible provision).

(3) A remedial order may be made so as to have the same extent as the legislation which it affects.

(4) No person is to be guilty of an offence solely as a result of the retrospective effect of a remedial order.

Procedure

2. No remedial order may be made unless—
   (a) a draft of the order has been approved by a resolution of each House of Parliament made after the end of the period of 60 days beginning with the day on which the draft was laid; or
   (b) it is declared in the order that it appears to the person making it that, because of the urgency of the matter, it is necessary to make the order without a draft being so approved.

Orders laid in draft

3.—(1) No draft may be laid under paragraph 2(a) unless—

(a) the person proposing to make the order has laid before Parliament a document which contains a draft of the proposed order and the required information; and

(b) the period of 60 days, beginning with the day on which the document required by this sub-paragraph was laid, has ended.

(2) If representations have been made during that period, the draft laid under paragraph 2(a) must be accompanied by a statement containing—

(a) a summary of the representations; and

(b) if, as a result of the representations, the proposed order has been changed, details of the changes.

Urgent cases

4.—(1) If a remedial order ('the original order') is made without being approved in draft, the person making it must lay it before Parliament, accompanied by the required information, after it is made.

(2) If representations have been made during the period of 60 days beginning with the day on which the original order was made, the person making it must (after the end of that period) lay before Parliament a statement containing—

(a) a summary of the representations; and

(b) if, as a result of the representations, he considers it appropriate to make changes to the original order, details of the changes.

(3) If sub-paragraph (2)(b) applies, the person making the statement must—

(a) make a further remedial order replacing the original order; and

(b) lay the replacement order before Parliament.

(4) If, at the end of the period of 120 days beginning with the day on which the original order was made, a resolution has not been passed by each House approving the original or replacement order, the order ceases to have effect (but without that affecting anything previously done under either order or the power to make a fresh remedial order).

Definitions

5. In this Schedule—

'representations' means representations about a remedial order (or proposed remedial order) made to the person making (or proposing to make) it and includes any relevant Parliamentary report or resolution; and

'required information' means—

(a) an explanation of the incompatibility which the order (or proposed order) seeks to remove, including particulars of the relevant declaration, finding or order; and

(b) a statement of the reasons for proceeding under section 10 and for making an order in those terms.

Calculating periods

6. In calculating any period for the purposes of this Schedule, no account is to be taken of any time during which—

(a) Parliament is dissolved or prorogued; or

(b) both Houses are adjourned for more than four days.

[SCHEDULE 3 (DEROGATION AND RESERVATION) AND
SCHEDULE 4 (JUDICAL PENSIONS) NOT REPRODUCED]

INDEX